MEDIEVAL HISTORY AND CIVILIZATION

Medieval
HISTORY & CIVILIZATION

BY
DANIEL D. McGARRY
Professor of History, Curriculum of Medieval Studies in History
Saint Louis University

MACMILLAN PUBLISHING CO., INC.
NEW YORK
Collier Macmillan Publishers
LONDON

Copyright © 1976, Daniel D. McGarry

PRINTED IN THE UNITED STATES OF AMERICA

All rights reserved. No part of this book may be reproduced or transmitted in any form or by any means, electronic or mechanical, including photocopying, recording, or any information storage and retrieval system, without permission in writing from the Publisher.

Macmillan Publishing Co., Inc.
866 Third Avenue, New York, New York 10022
Collier Macmillan Canada, Ltd.

Library of Congress Cataloging in Publication Data

McGarry, Daniel D
  Medieval history and civilization.

  Includes bibliographies and index.
  1. Middle Ages—History. 2. Europe—History—476–1492. 3. Civilization, Medieval. I. Title.
D117.M23   909.07   75-9631
ISBN 0-02-379100-4

Printing: 1 2 3 4 5 6 7 8   Year: 6 7 8 9 0 1 2 3

THIS WORK IS DEDICATED
TO ALL WHO HAVE MADE IT POSSIBLE
AND TO ALL WHO WILL USE IT

PREFACE

THE present work introduces the student to leading facets of medieval history and civilization and provides select bibliographies for further reading. It concentrates on Europe during the Middle Ages, but includes Byzantium and Islam. Its extensive coverage will reduce the amount of detailed information that must be added by the professor, as well as provide a comprehensive survey and useful reference. Its increased size, will, it is hoped, be compensated for by the fuller information it makes readily available and the valuable time it saves.

This study is based on the labors and insights of numerous distinguished historical scholars, to whom we are, to use a medieval expression, "as pygmies perched on the shoulders of giants." It is dedicated both to all who have made it possible and to all who will use it. Included are colleagues, teachers, students, administrators, the publisher, and especially the author's patient family. As a result of its mode of division, the text is easily adaptable to various types of courses in medieval history and civilization. Although there are many ways of subdividing its subject, the present work prefers the simple one of "Foundations," "Early Middle Ages," "High Middle Ages," and "Later Middle Ages."

D. D. McG.

CONTENTS

INTRODUCTION: The Middle Ages in History   2

PART I. FOUNDATIONS OF THE MIDDLE AGES IN THE WEST   4
    References for Part I · 4

CHAPTER 1. Geographical Milieu and Roman Heritage of Medieval Western Civilization   4
  § 1 The Geographical Setting · 5
  § 2 The Roman Legacy · 9
  § 3 Roman Decline Followed by Incomplete Recovery (180–395) · 20
    References for Chapter 1 · 27

CHAPTER 2. The Christian Foundation of the Middle Ages   29
  § 4 Christianity Triumphs in the Roman World · 29
  § 5 The Early Church · 34
  § 6 Early Christian Doctrines · 43
    References for Chapter 2 · 50

CHAPTER 3. The Barbarian Background   53
  § 7 The European Barbarians · 53
  § 8 The Early Germans · 59
  § 9 Early Germanic Culture and Progress · 66
    References for Chapter 3 · 72

CHAPTER 4. The Barbarians and the Empire in the Age of the Invasions   74
  § 10 The Barbarian Invasions Begin (ca. 378–455) · 74
  § 11 The Western Empire Succumbs (395–493) · 80
  § 12 The Barbarian Invasions Run Their Course (455ff.) · 86
    References for Chapter 4 · 92

PART II. THE EARLY MIDDLE AGES (ca. 400–1050)   94
    References for Part II · 94

CHAPTER 5. The "New West": The Early Germanic Kingdoms (ca. 400–700)   95
  § 13 The Early Germanic Kingdoms on Roman Soil · 95
  § 14 Rise and Ascendance of the Franks · 102
  § 15 Civilization in the Early Germanic Kingdoms · 107
    References for Chapter 5 · 114

Contents

Chapter 6. Byzantine History and Civilization — 116
§ 16 Origins and First Golden Age of the Byzantine Empire (284–610) · 116
§ 17 Byzantine Crises and Recovery (610–1057) · 123
§ 18 Byzantine Civilization · 129
  References for Chapter 6 · 138

Chapter 7. The Moslem Challenge: Rise and Civilization of Islam — 140
§ 19 The Rise of Islam (to 632) · 140
§ 20 The Caliphate (632ff.) · 145
§ 21 Islamic Civilization · 154
  References for Chapter 7 · 163

Chapter 8. The Carolingian Empire and Renaissance — 165
§ 22 From Mayors to Monarchs: The Carolingians to 768 · 165
§ 23 Charlemagne Establishes an Empire · 172
§ 24 Carolingian Civilization and Renaissance · 178
  References for Chapter 8 · 187

Chapter 9. Disintegration of Frankland and the Advent of Feudalism — 188
§ 25 Factors for Disintegration · 188
§ 26 The Northmen or Vikings · 193
§ 27 Collapse of the Carolingian Empire (814–888) · 198
  References for Chapter 9 · 205

Chapter 10. Feudalism: The Medieval Compromise — 206
§ 28 Origins and Nature of the Feudal "System" · 207
§ 29 The Feudal State · 214
§ 30 Feudal Life · 219
  References for Chapter 10 · 229

Chapter 11. Economic Recession and Rural Society During the Early Middle Ages — 231
§ 31 The Decline of Commerce and Industry · 231
§ 32 Early Medieval Agriculture and the Manorial System · 235
§ 33 Early Medieval Society Other Than the Aristocracy · 243
  References for Chapter 11 · 251

Chapter 12. Western Europe in the Early Feudal Period — 253
§ 34 Feudal France (888–1106) · 253
§ 35 The Iberian Peninsula During Moslem Dominance (711–1086) · 259
§ 36 Anglo-Saxon England (ca. 800–1066) · 265
  References for Chapter 12 · 272

Contents

Chapter 13. The Western Empire and the Slavs in the Early Middle Ages   274
§ 37 The Rise of the Medieval German Empire (888–973) · 274
§ 38 The Western Empire Attains an Early Apogee (973–1056) · 282
§ 39 The Slavs and Their States in the Early Middle Ages · 287
    References for Chapter 13 · 295

Chapter 14. The Church in the Early Middle Ages   297
§ 40 Papal Leadership · 297
§ 41 Monasticism to the Eleventh Century · 303
§ 42 Christian Life in the Early Middle Ages · 309
    References for Chapter 14 · 317

Chapter 15. Early Medieval Culture in the West   319
§ 43 Early Medieval Education and Learning · 319
§ 44 Early Medieval Literature and Historiography · 326
§ 45 Early Medieval Architecture, Arts, and Music · 332
    References for Chapter 15 · 338

PART III. THE HIGH MIDDLE AGES (ca. 1050–1300)   340
    References for Part III · 340

Chapter 16. The Commercial Revolution: Economic and Social Progress in the High Middle Ages   341
§ 46 The "Commercial Revolution" and Industrial Development · 341
§ 47 Money and Finance, Town and Country · 348
§ 48 Social Advances and Other Progress · 354
    References for Chapter 16 · 361

Chapter 17. Expansion and Crusades in the High Middle Ages   363
§ 49 Territorial Expansion of Christian Western Europe · 363
§ 50 The First Crusade and the Latin Kingdom of Jerusalem · 367
§ 51 Decline and Fall of the Crusader States · 376
    References for Chapter 17 · 382

Chapter 18. The Western Empire in the High Middle Ages (1056–1273)   384
§ 52 The Later Franconians and the Investiture Struggle (1056–1125) · 384
§ 53 First Phase of the Guelph Versus Hohenstaufen Contest (1125–1197) and Partial Imperial Success · 392
§ 54 Final Phase of the Guelph Versus Hohenstaufen Contest (1187–1273) and Failure of the Empire · 400
    References for Chapter 18 · 405

Contents

CHAPTER 19. The Making of England and Foundations of the English Constitution (1066–1307) — 406

§ 55 Strengthening the English Monarchy (1066–1199) · 407
§ 56 Limiting the English Monarchy (1199–1272) · 416
§ 57 The "Edwardian Compromise" (1272–1307) · 422
References for Chapter 19 · 427

CHAPTER 20. The Rise of France to Hegemony in Europe — 429

§ 58 Growing Power of the Capetian Monarchy (1108–1223) · 429
§ 59 Further Progress of French Monarchical Power (1223–1314) · 434
§ 60 Evolution of French Governmental Institutions · 441
References for Chapter 20 · 448

CHAPTER 21. Other European States in the High Middle Ages — 449

§ 61 Mediterranean Europe: The Iberian and Balkan Peninsulas · 449
§ 62 States of East Central and Northern Europe · 457
§ 63 Eastern Europe (Russia) and the Mongols in the Middle Ages · 462
References for Chapter 21 · 468

CHAPTER 22. Apogee of the Church During the High Middle Ages — 471

§ 64 Ascendance of the Papacy and Relations of Church and State · 471
§ 65 The Multiplication of Religious Orders · 479
§ 66 Christian Teachings and Life in the High Middle Ages · 485
References for Chapter 22 · 492

CHAPTER 23. High Tide of Medieval Culture: The Rise of Universities and Scholastic Learning — 494

§ 67 High Medieval Education and the Rise of Universities · 495
§ 68 The Rise of Scholastic Philosophy and Theology · 503
§ 69 Social and Natural Sciences in the High Middle Ages · 509
References for Chapter 23 · 518

CHAPTER 24. High Medieval Expression: Literature, the Arts, and Music — 520

§ 70 Latin Literature in the High Middle Ages · 521
§ 71 Vernacular Literatures in the High Middle Ages · 525
§ 72 The Arts and Music in the High Middle Ages · 536
References for Chapter 24 · 545

PART IV. THE LATER MIDDLE AGES (ca. 1300–1500): TRANSITION OR "RENAISSANCE"? — 548

References for Part IV · 549

Contents

CHAPTER 25. Recession and Recovery: Late Medieval Economic and Social Conditions   550
§ 73 The Ebb and Flow of Commerce and Industry · 550
§ 74 Growth of Capitalism and Governmental Involvement · 557
§ 75 Social and Other Concomitants of Economic Changes · 562
   References for Chapter 25 · 570

CHAPTER 26. England and France in the Later Middle Ages   572
§ 76 The Hundred Years' War (1337–1453) · 572
§ 77 England in the Later Middle Ages · 581
§ 78 France in the Later Middle Ages · 587
   References for Chapter 26 · 595

CHAPTER 27. Central and Eastern Europe in the Later Middle Ages   596
§ 79 The German Empire in the Later Middle Ages · 596
§ 80 East Central and Northern Europe in the Latter Middle Ages · 603
§ 81 Russia in the Later Middle Ages · 610
   References for Chapter 27 · 616

CHAPTER 28. The Rise of Southern Europe in the Later Middle Ages   618
§ 82 The States of Italy in the Later Middle Ages · 618
§ 83 Spain and Portugal in the Later Middle Ages · 626
§ 84 The Balkans and the Ottoman Turks · 633
   References for Chapter 28 · 639

CHAPTER 29. Decline of the Church in the Later Middle Ages   642
§ 85 Era of French Ascendance in the Church (1294–1378) · 642
§ 86 The Great Western Schism, Conciliarism, and the Renaissance Popes (1378–1500) · 649
§ 87 Trends, Theories, and Life in the Late Medieval Church · 657
   References for Chapter 29 · 664

CHAPTER 30. Renaissance and Late Gothic Culture   666
§ 88 Italian Renaissance Learning and Literature · 666
§ 89 Transalpine Learning and Literature in the Later Middle Ages · 673
§ 90 Renaissance and Late Gothic Arts and Music · 679
   References for Chapter 30 · 687

EPILOGUE   690

Contents

APPENDIX. *Medieval Popes and Rulers of Major States*   692
  I. Medieval Popes · 692
 II. Rulers of Frankland · 694
III. Western Kings and Emperors of Germany · 695
IV. Rulers of England · 695
 V. Kings of France · 696
VI. Byzantine Emperors · 697

Index   698

MAPS

The Roman Empire About A.D. 117	10–11
Europe and the Middle East About 800	152–153
Carolingian Empire About 814	179
Europe and the Crusader States About 1140	372–373
Europe About 1360	578–579

CHARTS

The Carolingians	169
The English Monarchy, 1216–1519	420
The French Monarchy, 1270–1515	590

[Opposite: The printer's device of Nicolas Jenson, Venice, 1470]

([MEDIEVAL HISTORY AND CIVILIZATION.

❰ INTRODUCTION. THE MIDDLE AGES IN HISTORY.

HE DESIGNATION "Middle Ages" originally suggested an unproductive interval between classical antiquity and modern times. The way for this terminology was made plain by Renaissance humanists, who regarded their own age as one of rebirth and awakening, and by early Protestants, who hailed the Reformation as a return to the original purity of primitive Christianity. In the second half of the seventeenth century, a Dutch historian, Christopher Keller, published a series of three texbooks which he entitled *Ancient History, History of the Middle Ages . . .* , and *Modern History.* An unfavorable estimate of the Middle Ages was supported by eighteenth-century philosophers, enamored of their "Age of Reason," and critical of authority and faith.

Although the name endures, its connotation is no longer derogatory. The romanticism of the early nineteenth century brought a certain idealization of the Middle Ages. The succeeding Age of Science (from the mid-nineteenth century on) insisted upon intensive historical research as a basis for generalizations and led to a much more favorable evaluation of the era. With each succeeding generation of researchers, our appreciation of the Middle Ages has increased.

Despite disagreement as to the exact beginning and end of the Middle Ages, there is general recognition that the period is bounded by Classical Antiquity on the one hand and the Protestant Reformation on the other. Efforts to establish an exact date—such as 378, 395, or 476 for the beginning, and 1453, 1492, or 1517 for the end of the Middle Ages—are doomed to failure. Round numbers such as 400 and 1500 admit an absence of precision. If these dates are used, the initial century was transitional from antiquity, while the final two centuries were transitional to modern times.

The Middle Ages were a formative "youth time" of Western European civilization. If people of the period frequently displayed the exuberance and naïveté of youth, they also exhibited its idealism and energy. Even as "the boy is father of the man," so the essential lineaments of our civilization took shape during the Middle Ages. Among political features of Western civilization that emerged were national states, representative parliaments, limited government, explicit charters of human rights, Christianization of law, and trial by jury. Among economic and social features was the Commercial Revolution: the growth of capitalism and credit, recognition of the nobility of manual work, emancipation of labor, and the rise of the middle class. Among religious developments were the spread of Christianity throughout Europe, maturization of the Christian Church and its doctrines, separation of the Western and Eastern churches, formation of religious orders, and extensive ecclesiastical reform. Among cultural contributions were full-time boarding schools, self-governing uni-

Introduction

versities for higher learning, Scholastic conciliation of faith and reason, systematic theology, renewed philosophical and scientific interests, the emergence of modern vernacular literatures, and Romanesque, Gothic, and Renaissance architecture, arts, and music.

❡ PART I. FOUNDATIONS OF THE MIDDLE AGES IN THE WEST.

THE CIVILIZATION of the Middle Ages grew in the favorable geographical environment of Europe from three main sources: Roman, Christian, and barbarian. Roman civilization provided highly developed political, social, and economic institutions, together with a rich culture. Christianity contributed inspiring religious ideals and invigorating morality, as well as an institutional Church, which rendered many important services. Indo-European barbarians, at first mainly Germanic, brought healthy bodies, alert minds, aspirations for freedom and equality, fresh vigor and youthful enthusiasm.

References for Part I[a]

[a] Recommended general readings are listed at the beginning of each of the four Parts of this book as an aid to the interested student.

AMONG good general works surveying ancient Foundations of the Middle Ages are ALBERT A. TREVER, *A History of Ancient Civilization*, 2 vols. (New York: Harcourt, 1939); JOSEPH W. SWAIN, *The Ancient World*, 2 vols. (New York: Harper, 1950); CLIFTON E. VAN SICKLE, *Political and Cultural History of the Ancient World*, 2 vols. (Boston: Houghton, 1947–1948); and MIKHAIL I. ROSTOVTZEFF, ed., *History of the Ancient World*, tr. J. D. DUFF, 2 vols. (Oxford: Clarendon, 1936–1938). Good one-volume accounts include CHARLES A. ROBINSON, *Ancient History . . .* , 2nd ed. (New York: Macmillan, 1967); CHARLES E. SMITH and PAUL G. MOORHEAD, *A Short History of the Ancient World* (New York: Appleton, 1939); JAMES HENRY BREASTED, *The Conquest of Civilization*, ed. E. E. WARE (rev., New York: Harper, 1938); and ARTHUR B. BRODEUR, *The Pageant of Civilization* (New York: McBride, 1931). Contributions of the ancient world are highlighted in WILLIAM G. DE BURGH, *The Legacy of the Ancient World* (New York: Macmillan, 1924); JULES F. TOUTAIN, *The Economic Life of the Ancient World*, tr. M. R. DOBIE (New York: Knopf, 1930); CHARLES A. SINGER, *A History of Technology*, vol. I (Oxford: Clarendon, 1955); and HENRY O. TAYLOR, *Ancient Ideals. . .* , 2 vols. (New York: Macmillan, 1930).

❡ GEOGRAPHICAL MILIEU AND ROMAN HERITAGE OF MEDIEVAL WESTERN CIVILIZATION.   Chapter 1.

AMONG initial advantages of medieval Western civilization were its fortunate geography and rich Roman heritage. Favorably located in the temperate zone, in the vicinity of man's earliest homeland, adjacent to principal seas, Europe both enjoyed an equable maritime climate and was generously endowed with natural resources. Medieval Europeans were heirs to a complex advanced civilization derived directly from the Romans and indirectly from the ancient Near East and the Greeks. In its later days the Roman Empire suffered various maladies, but its legacy was not thereby notably diminished.

Geographical Milieu and Roman Heritage

THE GEOGRAPHICAL SETTING.
Section 1.

> Europe has within itself resources both for war and peace. . . . Its whole extent is diversified by plains and mountains. . . . It is distinguished for producing in perfection all the fruits of the earth necessary for life and all the useful metals. [STRABO, *Geography* (first century of the Christian era).]

EUROPE'S name, even as its civilization, derived from the ancient Near East, where people referred to the West as *Erib* or "[land of] the setting sun" and the East as *Asu* or "[land of] the rising sun." Europe contains only about one fifteenth of the world's land surface, but its historical importance has far surpassed its size. In over-all aspect, Europe is a triangular peninsula, with numerous indentations, encompassed by seas, and pointing towards the Americas, with its base in the Urals and its apex in the Iberian peninsula. Its dominant feature is its maritime nature, which further moderates the invigorating climate of a continent already in the temperate zone. Abundant moisture providing adequate rainfall is wafted from adjacent waters by prevailing westerlies and offshore winds. Surrounding seas invite Europeans to maritime trade and travel; stimulate fruitful contacts and a cosmopolitan outlook; and encourage a spirit of adventure, commercial enterprise, and colonial expansion.

Europe possesses fertile lowlands for agriculture, grassy plateaus and hillsides for pasturage, thick forests of coniferous and deciduous trees, and generous mineral and carboniferous deposits. It also has numerous inland rivers which empty into adjacent seas well stocked with fish. Its resources are diversified and promote internal as well as external exchange of goods. Its compartmentalized nature, emphasized by mountains and rivers, as well as by maritime intrusions and peninsular projections, has led to the development of several separate independent states, whose competition has stimulated progress.

Mountains and uplands

The mountains and uplands of Europe not only serve as barriers and boundaries but also act as watersheds and river sources and provide useful minerals and coal, building stones and timber, as well as scenic beauty and recreational opportunities. While the mountain systems of Europe are divided into "old" and "young," both types usually have an east-to-west orientation which allows for deeper penetration of moderating, moisture-bearing winds from the sea.

The "old" mountain systems of Europe, which have been worn down by weathering processes long at work, are generally rich in mineral and carboniferous deposits, well forested, and intersected by fertile valleys, as well as comparatively easy to traverse. The oldest mountains of Europe, known as the Atlantic Shield, are low crystalline uplifts of marine sedimentation, which run through Norway and Sweden, the highlands of Scotland, and northern and western Ireland. Since they were largely formed prior to the Carboniferous period, they lack coal. They are also limited in mineral resources, although often rich in building materials such as granite, marble, and timber. Most of the rest of Europe's old mountains, which were formed during later Paleozoic times, are rich in both coal and mineral deposits, as well as stone and timber. The majority belong to the so-called Hercynian system (named from the Harz Mountains of Germany), which complex includes old mountains and plateaus of southern Russia, southern Poland, Czechoslovakia, and southern Germany. It also branches southwestward through the Massif Central of south central France and the Meseta of the Iberian Peninsula, and northwestward through Brittany, western England, Wales, and southern Ireland; and it seems to crop up in the uplands of eastern Hungary, the eastern Balkans, and in the interior of Asia Minor. Among other old mountains are the Urals, which run from north to south between Russia and Siberia. As a result of their age, such mountains are generally irregular in shape, warped, and broken by plateaus and valleys.

The young mountains of Europe, all located in the southern part of the continent, are generally high and rugged, and rather poor in mineral resources and coal. Except for occasional passes, they are deterrents to overland travel and transportation. They give rise, however, to important rivers and streams which can provide water power; and they are sources of timber and some valuable deposits. The so-called Alpides include the Caucasus, Crimean, Balkan, and Carpathian Mountains in the east, and the Alps and Pyrenees in the west. The Alpides are paralleled to the south by the so-called Dinarides, which include most of the mountains of the Balkan Peninsula, the Apennines in Italy, mountainous islands of the western Mediterranean, and the Sierra Madres and Sierra Nevadas in Spain.

Gateways Mountain passes have provided historically important gateways between mountain ranges. Through the Ural-Caspian gate between the Ural Mountains and the Caspian Sea, many Asian invaders have entered Europe. The Iron Gate between the Balkan Mountains and the Transylvanian Alps leads from the lower to the middle Danubian valley. The Moravian Gate between the northwestern Carpathians and the Sudetes Mountains opens a way from the upper Oder to the middle Danube via the Moravian River valley. Several Alpine passes provide routes between Italy on the one hand, and France, Switzerland, Germany, Austria, and Yugoslavia on the other. A few passes are to be found in the Pyrenees between France and Spain. The Poitevan Gateway (Gate of Poitou) in the vicinity of Poitiers and Orléans, which leads from southwestern to northern France, has been the scene of many famous battles. The upper Saône Valley in southeastern France connects with northwestern France through the Côte-d'Or, and with Germany through the Burgundian Gate. Several gates, such as those of Nancy, Toul, Vitry, and Épernay, lead from northern France to Germany, but the widest, easiest route is through the Low Countries, where many decisive conflicts have occurred. The Great Plain of Europe begins to the south of the North Sea and widens as it progresses eastward, providing ready access between Germany, Poland, the East Baltic states, and Russia: a condition which has made its western part a frequent battleground of the races.

Geographical Milieu and Roman Heritage

Over half the continent of Europe is made up of plains and lowlands, while a considerable part of the remainder consists of plateaus. The most extensive lowland is the Great Plain, which fans out from northern Germany, across Poland, and over Russia, where its vast expanse is broken only by scattered highlands. In general, the most fertile plains are those whose topsoil has been formed by erosion and alluvial deposition, as in river valleys. Extensive alluvial plains occur in the southwestern and northwestern parts of the Iberian Peninsula, northern Italy, southeastern, southwestern, and northern France, the Rhineland, the Old Valley Zone of the interior of northern Germany, central Poland, Hungary, and southern Russia. Less fertile, although susceptible to cultivation, are the recently glaciated plains of far northern Germany and Poland, Denmark, southern Sweden, and the Baltic area in general. Where glaciation has recently occurred, the soil is sandy, gravelly, poorly drained, and acidic as a result of glacial drifts. Semiplanular plateaus, which are really parts of old mountain systems, include the Meseta in the interior of the Iberian Peninsula, the Massif Central and Armorican Plateau of France, the highlands of central and southern Germany, and most of Czechoslovakia, eastern Hungary, and northern Bulgaria. Such plateaus are usually most adaptable to stockraising, but they are also used for agriculture.

Plains, lowlands, and plateaus

Europe abounds in rivers providing easy means of communication, sources of fish, water and water power, ready access to seas, natural boundaries, and scenic beauty. Their most important contribution has been their long work of erosion, alluvial deposition, and drainage, which has built up excellent soil in their valleys. Most of the great cities of Europe have grown up on the banks or at the mouths of rivers.

Rivers, valleys, peninsulas and islands

Most of the rivers of Europe flow either westward and northward or eastward and southward. Among leading westward and northward flowing rivers are the Guadalquivir, Guadiana, Tagus, and Douro in Spain and Portugal; the Garonne, Dordogne, Loire, and Seine in France; the Meuse, Rhine, Weser, Elbe, and Oder in the Low Countries and Germany; the Vistula in Poland; and the Niemen, Narva, and South (or West) Dvina and North Dvina in Russia. Among important eastward and southward flowing rivers are the Ebro, from which the Iberian Peninsula gets its name; the Po, whose valley is the most extensive agricultural and industrial part of Italy; the famous Danube, which flows from the Alpine highlands to the Black Sea and has four national capitals along its way; and the Russian Dniester, Bug, Dnieper, Donetz, and Don Rivers, which empty into the Black Sea, and the Volga and Ural Rivers which debouch into the Caspian.

Increasing the maritime nature of Europe are several peninsulas, notably the Scandinavian Peninsula, Denmark, Brittany, the Iberian Peninsula, Italy, the Balkans, and the Crimea. Europe also has numerous offshore islands, of which the British Isles in the Atlantic Ocean and Sardinia, Sicily, and Crete in the Mediterranean Sea are the largest.

Europe is located in the temperate zone, and its climate is further moderated by air currents from the Atlantic Ocean and adjacent areas. Although the bulk of Europe is in the same latitudes as Siberia and

The climate of Europe

Canada, its climate is more comparable to that of the United States. Most of Europe is in the zone of prevailing westerly winds which blow from southwest to northeast. As the moisture-laden air from the seas moves inland from warmer to cooler latitudes and upward to higher altitudes, its saturation point declines and excess moisture is deposited in the form of rain. Other moisture-bearing air masses moving in various directions have the same result.

Mediterranean Europe

The first part of Europe to come into historical prominence was Mediterranean or southern Europe. The characteristic Mediterranean climate is mild and much like that of southern California, with two main seasons: winter and summer. Rainfall is largely limited to the winter months, when westerly winds blow to more northern, cooler latitudes from the southwest, and hence tend to precipitate their moisture. In the summer months trade winds blowing overland from the northeast prevail because of the seasonal shift in the earth's axis, and dryness results. The Mediterranean landscape is small-scale and segmented; the prevalence of mountains encouraged the development of numerous small, independent city-states in this area prior to the rise of the Roman Empire. The fertile lowlands of the Mediterranean area have been utilized for agriculture, and the hillsides and plateaus for grazing since early times, while Mediterranean peoples have regularly engaged in fishing, seafaring, and commerce. Construction and sculpture in stone have been encouraged by the presence of many excellent limestones and marbles.

Western Europe

Western Europe, which includes France, the British Isles, the Low Countries, Denmark, and Norway, has a marine type of climate, equable and moist, as a result of winds from the sea. Comparatively warm waters from the tropical central Atlantic and the Gulf of Mexico move northward along the coast of Western Europe. Throughout the year, abundant rainfall is borne inland and northward by westerly winds from the Atlantic. Its landscape is on a larger scale than that of the Mediterranean area, but smaller than that of central Europe. The area includes numerous fertile river valleys admirably suited to agriculture and grassy uplands well adapted to stockraising. Its old mountains cradle valuable industrial resources such as coal and iron. Its strategic position and ready access to the Atlantic, as well as its highly favorable climate and natural resources help to account for its historical importance in medieval and modern times.

Central Europe

Central Europe proper includes Germany, Austria, Switzerland, Czechoslovakia, Poland, and Hungary. In an extended sense, central Europe also includes the Baltic lands of Sweden, Finland, Estonia, Latvia, and Lithuania, and the northern and central Balkan states of Yugoslavia, Bulgaria, and Rumania. Central Europe's winters are colder and its summers hotter than those of Western Europe, but not as extreme or continental as those of Eastern Europe. Although central Europe's rainfall is not as abundant as that of Western Europe, it is still adequate. Its landscape is more extended than that of Western Europe, but considerably less so than that of Eastern Europe. Far northern Germany and Poland, as well as Denmark and the Baltic states are handicapped by sandy, acidic poorly drained soils produced by comparatively recent glacial drifts. South of this area, in north central Germany and central Poland, a loess, a fine clay type of soil borne by winds from glacial areas, has been cut and drained by rivers which have also added fertile alluvial deposits. Extensive alluvial soils are also found in Hungary and eastern Rumania. Across the middle of Europe lies the heartland of the sprawling Hercynian mountain system, rich in minerals, coal, and forest cover.

Eastern Europe is practically coterminous with present-day Soviet Russia. Although varying from north to south and west to east, Russia's climate is more continental than that of the rest of Europe, so that its winters are very cold and its summers very hot. Much of its climate comes from Siberia. Although rainfall in Eastern Europe is generally sufficient, it is less abundant than in Central Europe. The landscape of Eastern Europe is on a much larger scale than that of the rest of Europe, since Russia is mostly a plain, whose soils and natural vegetation are divided into successive belts. The tundra region in the far north is a sort of polar desert, whose undrained earth is perpetually frozen beneath the surface and covered with low, scrubby, matted vegetation. South of the tundra is the so-called Boreal (Northern) Forest Region which composes about one fourth of Russia. Here the natural vegetation consists of coniferous forests and soil that is poor and not well drained. Next comes the Mixed or Open Forest Region, over one fourth of Russia, with better soil, where the natural vegetation consists of mixed coniferous and deciduous forests. Moscow is located in this region. To the south are the cultivated steppes, whose soil is a rich dark chernozem and whose natural vegetation is thick grasses. This area, which includes the Ukraine, is the best agricultural region of Russia. In the far southeast to the north and northwest of the Caspian Sea, where rainfall is very limited, are the salty steppes, more suitable for the grazing of livestock.

Eastern Europe

Strewn over the Russian plain in scattered fashion are worn-down old mountain regions, or highlands, often rich in minerals and coal or oil. Among such are the Northern Lake Region, the Valdai Hills, the Central Russian Highlands, the Donets Heights, the Volga Heights, and (to the east) the Ural Mountains. Russia is also favored by a radial system of rivers which flow to the Baltic, Black, and Caspian Seas. Since the Ural-Caspian Gate is located in its southeastern corner, Russia has known many invasions of Asians.

THE ROMAN LEGACY.
Section 2.

But thine, oh Roman, remember, to rule over every race: This is thy art, thy glory: the ways of peace to proclaim, Mercy to show to the fallen, the proud in battle to tame! [VERGIL, concerning the Roman genius in the *Aeneid* (first century B.C.).]

MUCH of medieval progress consisted in a gradual reappropriation of the rich Roman legacy. Although at the close of antiquity the Roman world was in decline, most of the elements of its civilization sur-

Geographical Milieu and Roman Heritage

Foundations of the Middle Ages

vived in some form or other in various areas. Survival was especially considerable in parts of Italy, Gaul, and Spain, and in the Byzantine Empire, particularly manuscripts and works of sculpture and architecture. A medieval history properly begins with a picture of this legacy in its fullness, when Roman civilization was at its height.

The Roman Empire

The Roman Empire enclosed the Mediterranean, and extended from the Scottish highlands to the Sahara, and from the Atlantic Ocean to the upper Tigris-Euphrates valley, thus including parts of three continents. The Rhine and Danube constituted its regular European boundaries, although at times it extended beyond them. The Empire was notable not only for its extent, but also for its longevity.

The Roman Empire had evolved gradually from a cluster of Latin villages located on hills overlooking a much-used ford of the Tiber River in central western Italy. According to Roman tradition, these villages were united into a city about 753 B.C., apparently by the more advanced Etruscans, from whom the Romans learned much. About 509 B.C. the Romans overthrew their Etruscan king and established a Republic. The aristocratic and plutocratic Roman Senate dominated this Republic throughout most of the latter's five centuries of existence, although the ordinary citizens or plebs managed to obtain considerable rights during the first century and a half (ca. 509–367 B.C.).

Because of its exposed and envied position, Rome was obliged from the start to defend itself in order to survive, and eventually subjected its neighbors for its own security. It controlled the external relations of its subordinate allies, but allowed them to manage their own internal affairs. In general, Roman rule was beneficial. As Rome expanded, it encountered new neighbors and enemies, and thus the process continued. Rome gradually subjected its neighbors in Italy (367–264 B.C.); and then, by defeating Carthage in a series of wars, obtained control of the western Mediterranean world (264–146 B.C.). Thereafter, its attention was increasingly drawn to the eastern Mediterranean, where it subjected the Balkans, Asia Minor, and Syria-Palestine. It finally rounded out its conquests by taking Gaul and Britain in the west and Egypt in the east.

Problems multiplied with the growth of Rome's Empire and resulted in civil wars and dictatorships. Following the assassination of Julius Caesar in 44 B.C. and further civil war, a continuing imperial form of government was established by Octavian, who came to be known as Augustus and who united all the chief offices of the state in himself in an hereditary manner. In the Golden Era of the two centuries beginning with Augustus (31 B.C.ff.) and culminating with the Adoptive or Good Emperors (A.D. 96–180), the power of the Emperors steadily increased at the expense of that of the Senate. This was the period of the famous *Pax Romana* or universal Roman Peace, when the Empire was at its height.

The Roman genius: government

The Romans excelled in practical and social fields, such as government and law, architecture and engineering. At the same time the Romans assimilated and passed on to the Middle Ages most of the better features of the civilizations and cultures with which they came in contact, as exemplified by their adoption of Greek culture and Christianity.

Geographical Milieu and Roman Heritage

To some extent the Romans had social competence and political greatness thrust upon them. Because of their exposed position, as has been noted, the Romans were faced with the alternatives of conquering or being conquered. Their successful struggle to remain free resulted not only in their acquisition of extensive territories, but also in the development of habits of patriotism and courage, common sense and prudence, toleration and practical "social engineering."

Roman government evolved gradually, with the Romans generally retaining old forms while giving them new meanings. Supported by a well-organized, efficient bureaucracy and by the army, the power of the Emperor grew steadily at the expense of that of the composite Senate. The Roman central government became more and more monarchical and bureaucratic. The early medieval Germanic monarchs attempted to assume many of the powers and prerogatives of the Roman emperors, whom they at first claimed to represent.

Most administrative subdivisions of the Roman Empire survived, and local government institutions frequently continued or were revived in the Middle Ages. The Roman conquest and organization of various parts of Europe brought the first real political unification of these areas, becoming the precedent for later nation-states such as Italy, Spain, France, and England. Subdivisions within these areas, known as the *civitates*, which were the forerunners of later counties, consisted of a town and the surrounding countryside as far as the boundaries of adjacent municipalities. It was chiefly on this municipal level that Roman government came into direct contact with most of its citizens and carried on most of its essential processes, such as the administration of justice and collection of taxes. The government of these municipalities, particularly in formerly barbarian Europe, was often modeled on that of Rome, with a *curia* corresponding to the Roman Senate, and magistrates similar to those of Rome. The municipal aldermen or councilmen were known as *decuriones*, and were drawn from men of property, known as *curiales*, in the community. In some cases this form of municipal government survived the barbarian invasions; in others it was revived with modifications during the High Middle Ages. Counties, however, continued to be basic political administrative units throughout the Middle Ages.

Rome gave to Europe the concept and practice of universal unity. The idea of world citizenship was fostered throughout the diverse peoples of the Roman Empire by a common Latin language, a single system of Roman law, and a progressive concession of Roman citizenship to all freemen (general by A.D. 212). It was ideologically reinforced by philosophical concepts, such as that of the Stoics concerning the universal fatherhood of God and brotherhood of man, as well as strengthened by religions, such as emperor-worship and in time even by Christianity. The after-image of the universal Roman Empire was effectively continued in the Middle Ages, with modifications, by the Catholic (Universal) Christian Church. Another concept bequeathed by the Romans was that of a *res publica*, a public concern or commonwealth, according to which the state with its government was a common enterprise of the citizenry for the common good. This ideal of commonwealth or public weal was repeatedly inculcated by Church writers during the Middle Ages.

A by-product of the Roman legacy was the image of a past Golden Age when general peace and prosperity, a higher form of civilization, and a more advanced culture prevailed. This partly imaginary vision gave medieval man a glorified model to emulate, and also helped to promote acceptance of Roman culture.

Roman law

One of the most significant and enduring contributions of Rome was Roman law: "a product of jurisprudence rather than legislation." At first each of the peoples in the Roman Empire was governed by its own traditional system of law. But as cases arose involving persons from various areas with different legal systems, they were heard and judged by special *praetores peregrini* or judges for travelers. In making their decisions, these judges used reason and equity, together with general principles of justice and laws common to various peoples, as well as a growing body of precedents. At the outset of their terms of office the *praetores peregrini* issued edicts stating principles by which they intended to be guided. They were also bound by edicts and responses of emperors and by decrees of the Senate. In doubtful cases they often requested the opinions of learned jurists or *jurisprudentes*, whose *responsa* were considered binding. The resultant law, known as the *Jus Gentium* or Law of the Peoples (as opposed to the Roman *Jus Civile* or Law of the City), gradually supplanted other legal systems in the Empire, and became the universal law. The Romans, having evolved an excellent system of law, organized it into a science, and made it the crowning study in advanced professional education, as well as a key to preferment in governmental service.

Roman law continued to be the law of the Byzantine Empire as well as theoretically that of a majority of the inhabitants of lands formerly in the Western Empire even after the latter's conquest by the barbarians. Although it was partly fused with Germanic law in medieval customary laws, Roman law was revived in greater fullness with the study and application of Justinian's *Code* in the High Middle Ages. Besides being the fundamental law of the states formed in the area of the old Roman Empire, Roman law was eventually received into Germanic and Slavic legal systems and strongly influenced English common law. Roman law also became a partial basis for the canon law of the Church, particularly with respect to general legal principles and procedures.

The Roman military system and governmental finance

The Roman army was a professional force of mercenary soldiers—well paid, privileged, and pensioned, excellently trained, equipped, and disciplined. Emphasis was on quality rather than on numbers. At first all soldiers were Roman citizens, but subsequently they came mainly from Italy, then from the provinces, and finally from among the barbarians. The Roman military machine was organized into armies, legions, cohorts, maniples, and centuries, together with auxiliaries such as engineers and medical personnel. Emphasis was placed on strategy and tactics, as well as economy of manpower. Security was stressed, and even overnight encampments or *castra* were carefully fortified and guarded. Permanent encampments, also known as *castra*, had stone walls with towers and gates and often became sites of new towns. The name for the medieval castle or *castellum* means "a small *castra*," which it imitated. Walls were erected by the Romans along critical frontiers where natural barriers were lacking, as in northern Britain and between the upper Rhine and the Danube. The medieval Byzantine army and fortifications continued Roman traditions, which inspired subsequent military reforms in the West.

Government and army were supported by numerous taxes. Levies were made on persons and property, as well as on occupations and articles of trade (such as customs duties and sales taxes). The government also imposed requisitions of goods (*annona*) and services. Roman methods of taxation were continued in the East by the Byzantines and adopted by the Moslems. But many of these taxes were allowed to lapse in the West in the Early Middle Ages. Some of them were revived in the High and Later Middle Ages. The Roman government also enjoyed subsoil rights, and derived revenues from the lease of such rights. This feature continued in former Roman lands and their colonies. Another important source of government income was the imperial fisc, consisting of extensive lands with attached laborers and equipment; the fisc became a leading source of income for early medieval kings.

The Roman Empire with its *Pax Romana*, general security, law and order, and common language, fostered economic prosperity. One evidence of this was the multiplication of towns. The Roman Empire has been characterized as a world of cities, and this was as true in recently barbarian Gaul, Britain, and Spain as it was in Italy, Greece, and the Near East. Many towns in the West were lesser imitations of Rome, with public basilicas, temples, theaters, amphitheaters, baths, townhouses, bridges, and aqueducts. Surviving remnants of Roman stone structures inspired medieval architects and engineers, as well as sculptors. Although the population of most Roman towns declined sharply in the Early Middle Ages, these towns generally recovered their size and surpassed it during the prosperous High Middle Ages. Most leading medieval cities in Europe within the boundaries of the old Roman Empire traced their origins back to Roman times.

The economy of the Roman Empire

Trade was active in the Roman Empire, profiting from the remarkable Roman roads which crisscrossed even the farthest provinces, as well as from the good order and security on the seas. The Mediterranean was a free thoroughfare of international commerce. The Black Sea was a lesser Mediterranean with which it connected, while the Red Sea was used for transit to the Indian Ocean and farther Orient. Many Roman trade routes in the West remained in operation even during the depressed Early Middle Ages, while many in the East continued in uninterrupted use in the Byzantine Empire. Practically the entire complex was revived and expanded in the High Middle Ages.

Although the older Eastern part of the Empire was industrially more advanced, there was considerable industrial development in the West. Most industry was on a small scale, and much of it was familial; but in a few instances industry was organized on a mass production basis, as in the case of pottery manufacture at Arretium, and of bronze ware at Capua, both towns in Italy. Mining was typically carried on in a capitalistic manner by means of slaves and captives, whose forced lot was often extremely miserable. A shortcoming of Roman industry was its failure to expand and develop labor-saving devices, partly because of cheap labor, and partly because of poor distribution of purchasing power. Following the emancipation of labor in the High Middle Ages, this condition began to be remedied. During the Early Middle Ages, ancient industries continued in the East, as well as in certain parts of the West, where they were subsequently revived in a widespread manner. The Romans developed a system of coinage which was based on a *libra* (pound) of silver as a money-of-account, and included the golden *aureus* or *solidius* (later shilling), and the silver *denarius* or *argenteus* (later penny) and *sestertius* (sesterce: one fourth of a denarius), and other silver pieces, together with lesser coins made of copper, bronze, or brass. The names of Roman coins and vestiges of their relative monetary values, as well as Roman financial practices and business contracts, were continued and revived in the Middle Ages, and passed on to the modern world.

The majority of the population were engaged in agriculture. The *latifundia* (large farm or estate) or villa system was widely diffused and tended to squeeze out small farmers, thus laying the groundwork for the early medieval manorial system. The two-field method of crop rotation prevailed in agriculture, with one half of the land being left fallow each year to recover its fertility. Roman agricultural methods generally continued into the Middle Ages, although with certain improvements. Thus the two-field system was modified and supplanted in many Transalpine areas by the more efficient and productive three-field system.

Roman society

Early Roman society stressed social virtues such as patriotism and piety (devotion both to parents and to the gods), obedience and courage, honesty and justice. Growing luxury and sensual indulgence among the upper classes and idleness and dependence among the masses gradually undermined the Roman character, but Roman ideals were still imbedded in customs and literature.

Roman society came to be structured in classes with a plutocratic aristocracy and bureaucracy at the top and propertyless slaves and proletariat at the bottom. At the apex was the very wealthy senatorial class, whose members had property of a million or more sesterces. Next came the *equites* or knights, whose property was worth 400,000 sesterces or more. Middle-class owners of a moderate amount of property were known as *curiales*, since they were eligible for seats on town councils (*curiae*). Below these came free persons possessing minimal amounts of property, such as small farmers; and below these the free but propertyless proletariat. A steadily growing number of free but economically dependant tenant-farmers or *coloni*—renting the property of others, especially as sharecroppers—were forerunners of the medieval serfs. At the very bottom were the slaves, who were usually captives of war or their descendants. Slaves were very numerous in the later Republic and early Empire, but their ranks were progressively thinned by manumission and marriage. The number of *coloni*, on the other hand, tended to increase steadily by an assimilation of both small farmers from above and slaves from below. A similar class structure survived with modifications in the Middle Ages, as in the case of knights and serfs.

A key Roman social institution was the family, which encompassed older children who lived at home as well as servants and dependents. The power of the *paterfamilias* or father of the family was great, and even extended over life and death in the earlier Republic. Many Roman customs concerning the family, including ascendance of the father, betrothals, and dowries, continued during the Middle Ages.

A certain hardness in the Romans' character was revealed by their fondness for violent and bloody forms of entertainment with great human and animal sufferings, as in gladiatorial combats, exposure of unarmed humans to wild animals, and beast-baitings by armed men. The lot of a comparatively few persons with great wealth, enervated by excessive luxury, contrasted severely with that of the needy masses, who often lost all ambition and became shiftless idlers. As many Romans gave themselves progressively to the unrestrained pursuit of sensual pleasures, marital infidelity, prostitution, and homosexuality became ever more common. These aspects of Roman society were partially eradicated in the Middle Ages with the fuller diffusion of Christianity and Christian mores.

For men of the Middle Ages the Roman Era was a Golden Age whose culture was to be cultivated and imitated, except insofar as it was disfigured by pagan polytheism and immorality. Latin, the common language of the Roman Empire, continued as the universal language of medieval Western Europe for government and law, diplomacy and religion, literature and learning. Itself enriched by many words and corresponding concepts derived from the Greek, Latin rendered a similar service for Teutonic, Slavic, and other languages, in addition to serving as the direct source of the Romance languages. Although well-educated persons in the earlier Roman Empire were usually bilingual with respect to classical Latin and Greek, Greek continued to be the favored language in the Eastern part, Latin in the Western part. By the outset of the Middle Ages, the study of Greek had largely lapsed in the West, as had that of Latin in the East, although revivals of such studies occurred in the High and Later Middle Ages.

Roman culture: Language and literature

The acknowledged prince among Latin poets was Vergil (d. 19 B.C.), and the chief work of Latin literature studied and imitated in both ancient Roman and medieval western and central European schools was his *Aeneid*, an epic which recounts the wanderings and trials of Aeneas, the reputed Trojan ancestor of the founder of Rome. The *Aeneid* foretells the coming of the Julian line and the greatness and virtues of Augustus, as well as a Golden Age which many medieval Christians identified with the Christian era. Dante refers to his "master" Vergil as "the fountain whence roll the streams of eloquence." Second only to Vergil in influence among the poets was Ovid (d. A.D. 18). His love elegies (*Amores*) and love letters (*Heroides*), with his *Art of Love* and *Remedy for Love*, became models and sources for the secular troubadours, minnesingers, and goliardic poets—and even for some mystics in the High Middle Ages. The urbane Horace (d. 8 B.C.), with his graceful *Odes* and praise of moderation and prudence, simplicity and rural life, and his *Art of Poetry* was often quoted and occasionally imitated. So also were Juvenal and Martial, with their poignant satire and pithy epigrams. The supreme model of Latin prose, both in antiquity and in the Middle Ages, was Cicero, who has been called the "founder of European prose," and who was imitated by such diverse figures as Sts. Ambrose and Gregory the Great, John of Salisbury, and Petrarch.

Classical Latin drama and historiography had limited influence during most of the Middle Ages until the Renaissance. Light and entertaining Roman drama, spiced with humor and drawing themes from ordinary life, was exemplified by the plays of Plautus and Terence which received little attention until the Renaissance. Although Roman historiography fared slightly better, only a fourth of Livy's long, laudatory, idealized, and partly legendary *History [of Rome] From the Founding of the City* (to A.D. 9) survived, as it was considered too long to be transcribed in its entirety. The more succinct *Histories* and *Annals* of Tacitus, which continued the history of Rome to A.D. 96, fared much better, while his *Germania*, concerning the early Germans, survived complete. Biographies included the interesting, anecdotal, gossipy *Lives of the Caesars*, written in Latin by Suetonius, and the *Parallel Lives of Famous Greeks and Romans*, written in Greek by Plutarch. Suetonius was imitated by Einhard in his ninth-century *Life of Charles the Great*.

Roman education and learning

The Romans took over the Greek system of general or liberal education and transmitted it to the Middle Ages. Classical general education was designed to civilize and humanize the student and to inculcate a common traditional culture. It aimed to enable the student to think accurately and express himself effectively in a universal language, in addition to giving him a basic fund of general information. Subjects studied consisted mainly of the encyclical disciplines (general studies) or liberal arts of grammar, logic, rhetoric, arithmetic, geometry, astronomy, and (theoretical) music. The core of the curriculum was intensive study and imitation of the classics, such as the works of Vergil, Cicero, Ovid, Terence, and Sallust. For some time the Greek language and Greek classics were taught along with the Latin. The study of literature was followed by intensive practical learning and application of rhetoric, a chief aim of which was facility of appropriate and effective verbal expression. Advanced education was professional, and included the study of medicine, architecture, and especially law. Influential treatises on education were written by Cicero and Quintilian, both of whom recommended a broad liberal arts curriculum. Much of Roman education was continued and revived with modifications in the Middle Ages.

Although the Romans took over the learning of the Greeks, they stressed practical and "applied," as opposed to theoretical and "pure," philosophy and science. The Romans preferred ethics or moral philosophy to metaphysics and theoretical philosophy. Stoic doctrines, such as

Geographical Milieu and Roman Heritage

the universal fatherhood of God and brotherhood of men, and a universal natural and Divine law, identifiable by reason, coincided with Roman ideals and actualities. As a result Stoicism was the favorite Roman philosophy, elaborated in the writings of such advocates as the freedman Epictetus, the philosopher Seneca (the Younger), and Emperor Marcus Aurelius. Many Romans, including Cicero and Horace, were avowed Eclectics, combining elements from various philosophies, while inclining to Stoicism, and sometimes to Scepticism or Cynicism. Roman Stoicism and idealistic Neoplatonism influenced many early Christian leaders whose influence, in turn, was felt during the Middle Ages.

Roman science descended in diluted form from the Greeks. The Romans were interested primarily in practical applications and were fond of epitomes and summaries. The limitations of Roman science are evident in Pliny the Elder's *Natural History*, an undigested, uncritical, encyclopedic presentation of ancient scientific information and misinformation, based on some two thousand books. Ancient medical knowledge was skimpily summarized in Latin in the shallow compendium of Celsus in the first century of the Christian era, but was more adequately presented in Greek in the *Techne* of Galen in the next century. The latter eventually became an important medieval medical text. *Practical sciences*

Knowledge of astronomy in the Roman Empire, as summarized in the second century by the Alexandrian Ptolemy, fell short of Greek astronomical speculation at its best. Ptolemy underestimated the earth's circumference, leading to the error of Columbus in believing that he had reached India when he had arrived at America. Ptolemy also postulated an earth-centered universe, in which the planets and sun revolved around the earth in epicycles or smaller circles, each revolving around a moving point on a larger earth-centered circle. The known world was admirably mapped and described in the Roman period by Ptolemy and Strabo, both of whom wrote in Greek. Ptolemaic astronomy and geography reigned supreme until the sixteenth century. Ancient Roman arithmetic was handicapped by the clumsy Roman numerals, although helped somewhat by the use of the abacus, a counting device with sliding balls on parallel rods.

Although deficient in interest in pure (speculative) science for its own sake, the Romans excelled in applied sciences. Treatises *On Aqueducts* by Frontinus, *On Agriculture* by Columella, and *On Architecture* (and engineering) by Vitruvius were resuscitated during the Middle Ages. Roman aqueducts brought water to towns from great distances, and Roman bridges spanned broad rivers. Excellent Roman roads, built with four layers of various types of stone, remained in use during the Middle Ages, and in some parts of Europe as late as the eighteenth century.

Medieval science and mathematics derived from the Romans. For some time men of the Middle Ages did not go beyond the practical, assimilative, encyclopedic Roman approach. Early medieval science actually fell below that of Rome. But in the High Middle Ages, scholars recovered and exceeded Roman science. During the Middle Ages general science leaned heavily on Pliny, medicine on Galen, astronomy and geography on Ptolemy, architecture on Vitruvius, and agriculture on Columella. Roman numbers and the abacus continued in use, but were eventually supplanted by Arabic numbers and the zero.

Roman architecture and art   Medieval arts grew directly out of the Roman. Roman architecture involved considerable use of arches, both as such and revolved into domes or prolonged into vaults. Favorite Roman building materials were stone and concrete, the latter apparently derived from the Etruscans. Roman architecture affected magnificent grandness as well as durability, and was inclined to be ornate. Homes of the well-to-do usually centered around a covered hall or *atrium* and featured a courtyard with a fountain. Roman architecture provided a point of departure for medieval Romanesque and Gothic architecture, as well as a point of return for Renaissance architecture.

At first Roman sculptors reproduced or imitated Greek models, but subsequently they developed a Roman form of realistic and personal sculpture, especially suited for portrayal of character. Miniature paintings were used to adorn and illustrate important and costly books. Walls and ceilings were often decorated with frescoes, made by painting on fresh plaster, and by mosaics, also used for floors. Fresco painting continued in the Middle Ages, and more costly mosaics survived for a time, while Roman miniatures were imitated in medieval Bibles and other religious books, and Roman sculpture provided models for High Medieval and Renaissance artists.

ROMAN DECLINE FOLLOWED BY INCOMPLETE RECOVERY.
Section 3.

(180–395)

> Behold the roads blocked by brigands, the seas choked by pirates, the bloodshed and horror of universal strife. The world drips with slaughter: murder, considered a crime when privately committed, is regarded as virtuous when publicly perpetrated. [From a letter of St. Cyprian of Carthage (third century of the Christian era).]

During the second to the fourth centuries (180–395), maladies and weaknesses of the Roman Empire became more obvious and virulent, and important changes set the scene for the Middle Ages. After a century of crisis, which brought it to the brink of disruption, the Empire achieved limited and ephemeral recovery—but only at the price of autocracy and totalitarianism. Meanwhile Christianity began to infuse new life into Roman civilization, which remained great and impressive, even in decline.

A century of crisis (180–284)   An "era of iron and rust," in the words of third-century historian Dio Cassius, succeeded the prosperous period of the Adoptive or Good Emperors. The previous system, whereby each Emperor (Augustus) adopted a competent Co-Emperor (Caesar) to assist and succeed him, lapsed when Marcus Aurelius, faced with an emergency, designated his inadequate son Commodus as Caesar. The Empire went rapidly downhill during the "century of crisis" (180–285) which followed the accession of Commodus. Corrosive forces, which would eventually bring about the dis-

Geographical Milieu and Roman Heritage

ruption of the Empire in the West, were gradually unleashed. The government came under the domination of the military, who repeatedly set up and overthrew emperors with callous irresponsibility. During this century thirty-four emperors obtained recognition in Rome (an average of one every three years), while twice as many unsuccessful imperial pretenders in the provinces brought the total to about one hundred. Most of these "Emperors" eventually met violent deaths. Civil wars were frequent, anarchy and bloodshed commonplace. As frontier defenses weakened, Germanic barbarians repeatedly invaded and pillaged as far as Italy and Asia Minor. Meanwhile, first the Parthians and then the related Persians overran the Empire's Asian provinces. Economic decline was hastened by instability and insecurity, and accompanied by a drop in population. The subjection of rural laborers to great landowners increased in the country, while depression and depopulation gripped the dwindling municipalities, particularly in the West. Increased taxes and oppressive burdens of supplies (*annona*) and services (*munera*) were levied upon the populace. Emperors increasingly resorted to autocratic methods and theocratic pretensions to bolster debilitated governmental authority. A by-product of the crisis was intensified persecution of the Christians as convenient scapegoats, accused of being subversive dissenters and regarded as objects of divine disfavor.

Commodus (180–193), who was irresponsible, cruel, and despotic, was eventually strangled, and civil war (193–197) ensued. The praetorians (imperial guard) elevated two successive candidates to the imperial office, while three contenders, each supported by his own army, arose in the provinces. Eventually Septimius (193–211) established a military despotism, disregarded the Senate, terrorized the aristocracy, and favored the army, which he recognized as the bulwark of his authority. His son Caracalla (211–217), a capricious despot, was soon assassinated. One notable act of Caracalla, however, was his extension of Roman citizenship to practically all freeborn provincials (A.D. 212), thus completing a long process. Caracalla even included his horse. The last two emperors of the house of the Severi (218–235) were weaklings under whom the government was for some time in the hands of women: the grandmother of the first, the mother of the second. Both emperors were eventually assassinated.

During the succeeding half century (235–284) known as the "Era of the Barracks Emperors," the military were generally in complete control. Emperors accepted in Rome were murdered at the rate of one every second year, and imperial claimants and usurpers multiplied in the provinces. One emperor, Gallienus, had to face eighteen contenders. Meanwhile, Germanic and Persian invasions reached their height. Shortly after the middle of the third century, a Roman general in the west, Postumus, established a Gallic empire, which controlled most of Western Europe outside of Italy. The kingdom of Palmyra under Queen Zenobia became similarly independent and dominant in much of the Near East. But when it seemed as if the Roman imperial structure was about to collapse, a strong man, Aurelian (270–275), called "Restorer of the Empire," re-

The absolute emperors (284–395): Diocletian

established Roman rule in both East and West. After both Aurelian and his able successor Proclus (276–282) were assassinated, chaos temporarily returned.

The dismal era of the Barracks Emperors came to an end in 284, with the advent of the so-called Absolute Emperors, who reorganized the Empire upon a frankly autocratic basis, revamped both central and local administrations, modernized the army, and used totalitarian measures and control to bolster the economy. The reforms of the Absolute Emperors (284–395), however, attacked the symptoms rather than the sources of the Empire's maladies and in the long run aggravated rather than solved most of the problems.

The first of the Absolute Emperors, Diocletian (284–305), an Illyrian-born general, issued a series of forthright military orders in an effort to correct what was wrong. Diocletian strongly insisted on the unlimited nature and divine origin of his power. He divided the Roman world roughly into two halves, each under an Augustus, and subdivided each of these into two parts with a Caesar over each. The Caesars were to have the right of succession on the death or resignation of the Augusti. Diocletian became Augustus in the East with his residence at Nicomedia, and Maximian became Augustus in the West with his residence at Milan. The Empire remained theoretically united and legislation was jointly issued.

Diocletian attempted to legislate the Empire back to health. Since the army had tended to dominate the government with unfortunate results, civil and military administrations were separated. To obviate uprisings as well as to improve local administration, the provinces were reduced in size and increased in number, although they were also grouped into Dioceses, such as that of Spain, and larger Prefectures, such as that of Gaul (which included Spain). The better to withstand both the barbarians and the Persians, the army was increased in size, and more troops were stationed along the frontiers. To combat spiraling inflation, an attempt was made to stabilize the coinage, while an edict in A.D. 301 fixed prices and wages. To replenish the straitened imperial treasury, taxation was reformed and standardized. To regain the favor of the gods, Christians were strenuously persecuted (A.D. 303ff.). To accomplish such measures, the bureaucracy was greatly increased. In A.D. 305, Diocletian retired after prevailing on his Western colleague Maximian to do likewise. Their Caesars now became Augusti: Galerius in the East, Constantius in the West.

But Diocletian's plan of peaceful succession was doomed to failure, as militarism was still in the saddle. Dissatisfaction was caused by the fact that Galerius Augustus dictated the choice of the new Caesars, whereas in the West both the former Augustus Maximian and the new Augustus Constantius wanted their own sons, Maxentius and Constantine, to succeed them. Civil war ensued. By A.D. 310 there were five competing "Augusti" in the Empire. In 311, the ailing Galerius was eliminated by death. In 312, Constantine became sole Emperor in the West with his defeat of Maxentius in the battle of the Milvian Bridge outside Rome.

Geographical Milieu and Roman Heritage

In the following year, 313, Constantine and his successful Eastern counterpart, Licinius, met at Milan, where they agreed on a policy of toleration for the Christians. Growing friction between the two culminated in Constantine's invasion of the East, where he thrice defeated Licinius and became sole Emperor in 324. Constantine continued and extended many of the "reforms" of Diocletian, with some modifications. He further increased the imperial autocracy, expanded the bureaucracy, stabilized the coinage and froze many occupations on a hereditary basis. At the same time Constantine established sole control of the whole Empire; made the succession hereditary in his own house; built a new capital known as "Constantinople" on the Bosporus; and eventually became a Christian *after* raising his sons as Christians.

Constantine and his family (312–363)

Constantine (d. 337) divided the Empire among his three sons and two nephews, but by 351 the sole survivor, Constantius, was in complete control (351–361). A determined supporter of Arianism, the strong Constantius forced orthodox Christian bishops into exile, and made his nephew Julian "Caesar" in the West. The latter, known as Julian "the Apostate" (361–363) made a futile attempt to restore paganism, but as he lay dying he is said to have exclaimed, "O Galilean, thou has conquered!"

All the successors of Julian were supporters of Christianity. After the brief reign of the orthodox Jovian (363–364), leading civil and military officials elected Valentinian I (364–375). The latter took up residence in the West, and, on the insistence of the army, appointed his brother Valens as co-emperor in the East. In the West, Valentinian I ably defended the frontiers, and suppressed rebellions. Gratian (375–383), his elder son and successor, showered favors on the Church, to which he transferred state support. Meanwhile Valens, pro-Arian emperor in the East (364–378), was decisively defeated by the Visigoths at Adrianople (378), where he lost his life. The Spanish-born general, Theodosius I, the Great (379–395), who was appointed by Gratian to succeed Valens, quieted the Visigoths. In addition to restoring imperial authority in the East, Theodosius brought about the convocation of the second Ecumenical Council of the Christian Church, which met at Constantinople in 381, condemned Arianism and other heresies, and did much to restore ecclesiastical unity and harmony. After Gratian was overthrown in the West in 383, Theodosius ousted the usurper (388) and restored legitimacy in the person of Gratian's brother, Valentinian II. When the Germanic general Arbogast overthrew Valentinian II (392), and installed a usurper, Theodosius again came West, defeated them, and reunited the Empire in 394. At his death the following year (395), Theodosius left the Empire divided between his two sons, Arcadius in the East, and Honorius in the West. This division proved permanent.

From Valentinian I to Theodosius the Great (364–395)

During the initial chaotic century of crisis (180–284), certain trends repeatedly asserted themselves. Included were absolutism, theocracy, bureaucracy, totalitarianism, heavy taxation, and military enfeeblement. Beginning with Diocletian, the government of the Empire became an

Growth of absolutism

autocracy of the oriental type, in which the Senate no longer had any real voice.

The Emperor became the sole source of authority. He sat on a throne wearing a gold diadem set with precious stones, holding a scepter, and surrounded by courtiers. He was approachable only by means of an elaborate ceremonial, which included prostrations. The theocratic nature of the imperial authority was emphasized. In the pre-Christian period, emperors had claimed either divinity or divine support. In the Christian period, they claimed the approbation and backing of the God of the Christians, who willed that men live in harmony and cooperation. The imperial majesty was spoken of as "divinity" or "divine"; the imperial palace was referred to as "sacred"; and the religion of the inhabitants of the Empire became a leading imperial concern.

The government of the Empire became quasi-totalitarian. Prices and wages were regulated in a clumsy manner but, even though the death penalty was prescribed for violation of controls, the attempt was never fully successful. Most occupations were frozen and made hereditary. The imperial bureaucracy became a swollen, often corrupt and inefficient, incubus, oppressing the heavily burdened populace. Because of the financial difficulties of municipal governments, emperors as early as Trajan had begun to appoint imperial curators (*curatores*) to assist and supervise the towns. At first limited in function, these curators eventually became the real rulers of the municipalities, which gradually lost their former self-government. Meanwhile the *curiales* or propertied class in the municipalities, who were eligible for positions on the town council or *curia*, became imperial lackeys responsible for the collection of taxes.

Despite a slump in the economy, taxes mounted and became more numerous, uniform, and inexorable. Both agricultural lands and those who worked them were subdivided into nominally equal economically productive units (*juga* and *capita*) and assessed accordingly. Taxes were often collected in kind. In addition to the old established taxes, there was an occupational tax, known as the *chrysargyrum*, levied even on prostitutes. The upper classes, and especially the large landowners of the sentorial class because of their power and influence, usually evaded their share of the tax burden. The government also greatly increased its burdensome exactions of supplies (*annona*) and services (*munera*).

Although instituted to save the Empire, absolutism and bureaucracy and their by-products were among the principal causes of its fall. Because they were impractical and untenable in the early medieval Germanic kingdoms, they actually contributed to the weakness of the latter and the eventual rise of feudalism.

Changes in the army

In general, the influence of the army in politics greatly increased. The army was increased in size until it came to number between 450,000 and 500,000 men. It was subdivided into about equal numbers of frontier troops or *limitanei*, and mobile field troops known as *comitatenses*. To cope with the horsemen of their adversaries, such as the Goths, the cavalry was eventually augmented, and changes were made in the equipment of the infantry. Thus a longer sword and lance replaced the former short sword and javelin. During the fourth century Germanic barbarians came to constitute a majority in the army. Germans were even sometimes recruited as entire tribes with the status of *foederati:* favored, subsidized allies settled on lands within the Empire. The army became less disciplined, less patriotic, and less reliable. New military titles such as those of *dux* (duke) and *comes* (count), which were to prevail during the Middle Ages, came into use.

In the century of crisis the economy of the Roman Empire suffered decline and dislocation from which it never fully recovered. Many formerly prosperous cities in the West shrank to as little as a fourth of their former size. Vast agricultural areas were no longer cultivated and became wastelands. Although the coinage, which had progressively depreciated, was partly stabilized by Diocletian and Constantine, it was still handicapped by a shortage of gold and silver. Many taxes were now paid in kind. In the country, large estates or *latifundia,* worked by dependent laborers or *coloni,* prevailed.

Economic decline and social stratification

One of the features of the Later Roman Empire was a greater stratification of society. Although transition from class to class was still possible, it was much less frequent. A widening gulf separated the upper classes or *honestiores* from the unprivileged masses or *humiliores.* The *honestiores* were immune from torture, penal servitude, and execution without imperial consent, and usually had their own courts. Members of the senatorial order utilized the economic depression to increase their great estates (*latifundia*) and the number of their dependents. Such large land owners were generally immune from the jurisdiction of local governments, and managed by various stratagems to evade their fair share of the tax burden. Imperial officials were a separate, privileged clique, and the military also constituted a special class, exempt from ordinary public burdens and responsibilities. In these privileged classes we may see forerunners of the feudal aristocracy of the Middle Ages.

Membership in the middle class of *curiales,* eligible to be members of town councils, hitherto esteemed an honor and a privilege, was shunned since the *curiales* were held responsible for the collection of taxes and other assessments imposed by the central government. As a result, the government made membership in the class obligatory and hereditary for all who possessed twenty-five or more *jugera* (fifteen or more acres) of land. Even the hitherto voluntary *collegia* or corporations of tradesmen and artisans in the towns became agencies of the imperial government, charged with rendering numerous compulsory services to the state.

Meanwhile in the country, more and more agricultural laborers became dependent *coloni.* Diocletian united lands and workers for tax purposes, and Constantine made the position of workers obligatory and hereditary. By extending a legal concept of *origo* already in long use in Egypt, many farmers were permanently attached to the land in the manner of medieval serfs, whose status they foreshadowed. Free small farmers increasingly sought the status of *coloni,* since they could thus secure relief from the immediate responsibility of paying taxes and obtain the protection of those who were more powerful (*potentiores*). Medieval serfdom was gradually coming into existence. (Originally *coloni* were simply farmers or settlers; subsequently they became renters or lessees; finally they were attached to the land.)

Cultural shift. Christian influences

While there was a marked decline in Roman secular culture, a new, creative Christian culture developed and adopted and revitalized many elements of the classical. Intellectual speculation came to be mainly concerned with religious questions. In philosophy a strongly religious, mystical, quasi-pantheistic Neo-Platonism conceived of all reality as emanating from the Divine "One" in progressive steps ("Intelligence," "World Soul," and so on), eventually returning to its original source by similar degrees, including asceticism and contemplation. There was also the beginning of a Christian theology which explained and defended Christian doctrines with the help of philosophical concepts and terms. This joint use of faith and reason was begun by the early Apologists and Catechists, and expanded by the great Greek and Latin Fathers, by whom, as Clement of Alexandria expressed it, Greek philosophy was often considered "propaedeutic" or introductory to Christianity, like a pedagogue leading his charge to the schoolmaster (Christ).

Whereas secular Latin and Greek literature produced little that was notable in this era, Christian intellectuals composed inspiring religious literature. The latter included sermons, letters, devotional poetry, hymns, Scriptural commentaries, and doctrinal treatises, which breathed a new spirit and were adorned and polished with love and devotion. Apologetic treatises were composed by Minucius Felix and Lactantius; hymns and devotional poetry by Ambrose of Milan and the Gregories; controversial tracts by Tertullian, Irenaeus, and Cyprian; inspiring sermons, homilies, letters, and scriptural commentaries by Basil, the Gregories, and Ambrose.

For some time education continued along previous lines, while the study of classical literature was cultivated with increased intensity in regions such as Gaul and Syria. After some initial hesitation, many Christian leaders endorsed the study of secular learning and classical literature as useful but subsidiary to religion. One of the most conscientious and objective of Roman historians, Ammianus Marcellinus, continued the history of Rome from 96 (where Tacitus left off) to A.D. 378. Eusebius of Caesarea, the "Father of Church History," composed a *History of the Christian Church* from its origins to his own fourth century, as well as a *Chronicle* which synopsized universal history. Eusebius included numerous references to personages who would otherwise be unknown and copious quotations from sources now lost. In the field of jurisprudence, the third century produced notable works on Roman law by authorities such as Papinian, Ulpian, and Paulus. Useful compilations were also made in other fields, such as the Greek medical encyclopaedia or *Techne* of Galen, and the Latin grammars (*Ars Major* and *Ars Minor*) of Donatus.

The most notable works of architecture and art were Christian. Following the recognition of Christianity, there was a boom in the construction and beautification of churches. At first the Christians utilized regular Roman basilicas transferred to them by the government or con-

Geographical Milieu and Roman Heritage

structed for their own use. The typical Roman basilica was a rectangular building of stone and cement, whose interior consisted of a high central nave, flanked by lower side aisles, and culminating in an apse. The Christians introduced many modifications tending to greater beauty and complexity. They adorned the interior with mosaics, frescoes, and sculpturing, as well as fine marble and graceful columns. They frequently enlarged the terminal apse, added a transept (cross section), and constructed stone vaulting over side aisles. Sometimes a dome covered the juncture of transept and nave. Fourth-century examples of Christian basilicas at Rome include Santa Maria in Trastevere and St. Paul's Outside the Walls.

Early Christian art was strongly affected by Near Eastern influences and was marked by strong feeling, extensive symbolism, and vivid narrative, as well as by a daring impressionistic quality which disregarded perspective and the third dimension. It thus broke with many classical traditions and was transitional to a new era in the history of art. Especially impressive were its rich and durable mosaics, which adorned walls, ceilings, and floors of churches.

In addition to the basic elements of a rich and sophisticated civilization, the Roman legacy to the Middle Ages included remarkable political institutions, a superb system of law, excellent Roman roads and public works, established patterns of commerce, and an advanced technology. Especially influential were Rome's cultural bequests: the Latin language and literature, classical education and learning, and Greco-Roman sciences and medicine, architecture and arts. Roman decline did not erase or substantially diminish this legacy; rather it opened the way for subsequent fuller, freer evolution. Meanwhile the Empire served as a beneficent matrix for the Christian Church, which eventually succeeded it. *The Roman legacy*

EUROPE'S physical geography and its human modifications are described at length in JEAN GOTTMANN, *Geography of Europe* (New York: Holt, 1950), and by GEORGE D. HUBBARD, *The Geography of Europe* (New York: Appleton, 1937). The Mediterranean world is included in NORMAN J. G. POUNDS, *Europe and the Mediterranean* (New York: McGraw-Hill, 1953). A correlation of certain geographical features and historical developments is essayed in DERWENT S. WHITTLESEY, *Environmental Foundations of European History* (New York: Appleton, 1949), and in NORMAN J. G. POUNDS, *An Historical and Political Geography of Europe* (London: Harrap, 1949). Useful atlases of European history include the old reliable *Hammond's Historical Atlas* (Maplewood, N.J.: Hammond, 1957); the relief-stressing EDWARD J. Fox, *Atlas of European History* (New York: Oxford U.P., 1957); and the text-accompanied ROBERT R. PALMER, *Rand McNally Atlas of European History* (New York: Rand McNally, 1957).

Convenient overviews of ancient Roman history and civilization are provided in a more comprehensive manner by CHARLES A. ROBINSON, *Ancient History*, 2nd ed., rev. (New York: Macmillan, 1967), and in more selective narrative fashion by CHARLES E. SMITH and PAUL G. MOREHEAD, *A Short History of the Ancient World* (New York: Appleton, 1939). Among several excellent histories of Rome, *References for Chapter 1*

ARTHUR E. R. BOAK, *A History of Rome to 565 A.D.*, rev. W. G. SINNIGEN, 5th ed. (New York: Macmillan, 1965), is concise and scholarly. The classic MIKHAIL I. ROSTOVTZEFF, *Social and Economic History of the Roman Empire*, ed. P. M. FRASER, 2 vols., 2nd rev. ed. (Oxford: Clarendon, 1957), is still valuable. The transformation of the Republic into the Principate is the subject of careful study by FRANK B. MARSH, *The Founding of the Roman Empire*, rev. (Oxford: Oxford U.P., 1927). Methuen and Macmillan have published, beginning in 1951, a series of volumes entitled *A History of the Roman World* . . . , in which HOWARD H. SCULLARD treats the period 753–146 B.C., FRANK B. MARSH 146–30 B.C., EDWARD T. SALMON 30 B.C.–A.D. 76, BERNARD W. HENDERSON A.D. 76–138, and HENRY M. PARKER A.D. 138–337, 2nd rev. ed. (London and New York). Even more exhaustive treatment is provided in volumes 7 to 12 of the authoritative, collaborative *Cambridge Ancient History*, 12 vols. (Cambridge: Cambridge U.P., 1923–1939). Readable origin sources are the *Histories* and *Annals* of Tacitus, 2 vols., tr. K. WELLESLEY and M. GRANT (Baltimore: Penguin, 1964–66) and 4 vols., tr. C. H. MOORE and J. JACKSON (Cambridge: Harvard U.P., 1937) for the first century of the Christian era, PLUTARCH's *Parallel Lives [of Famous Greeks and Romans]*, tr. B. PERRIN, 11 vols. (London: Heinemann, 1916–1926); Suetonius, *Works [Lives of the Twelve Caesars and Lives of Illustrious Men]*, 2 vols., tr. J. C. ROLFE (London: Heinemann, 1914–1920), and tr. R. GRAVES (Baltimore, Penguin, 1957); and the surviving books of AMMIANUS MARCELLINUS *Rerum Gestarum Libri*, tr. J. C. ROLFE, 3 vols. (London: Heinemann, 1935–1939) for the period A.D. 353–378. A good life of Constantine, which also treats of Diocletian and his colleagues, is that of LLOYD B. HOLSAPPLE, *Constantine the Great* (New York: Sheed, 1942). An authoritative discussion of Roman law, private and constitutional, is HERBERT F. JOLOWICZ (Cambridge: Cambridge U.P., 1952) and a readable, well-organized survey of the history and influence of Roman law by CHARLES P. SHERMAN, *Roman Law in the Modern World*, 3 vols., Vol. I: *History of Roman Law and Its Descent Into . . . Modern Law* (Boston: Boston Book Co., 1917).

Detailed studies of provincial and local government in the Roman world are provided by WILLIAM T. ARNOLD, *The Roman System of Provincial Administration* . . . , 3rd rev. ed. (Oxford: Blackwell, 1914); and JAMES S. REID, *The Municipalities of the Roman Empire* (Cambridge: Cambridge U.P., 1913). The provinces of the Empire and their organization and government are aptly described in VICTOR CHAPOT, *The Roman World* (New York: Knopf, 1928); while valuable treatments of Western European sections of the Empire are OLWEN BROGAN, *Roman Gaul* (Cambridge: Harvard U.P., 1953); ROBIN G. COLLINGWOOD and J. N. MYERS, *Roman Britain* (Oxford: Clarendon, 1937); SHEPPARD FRERE, *Britannia: A History of Roman Britain* (London: Routledge, 1967); and EDMUND S. BOUCHIER, *Spain under the Roman Empire* (Oxford: Oxford U.P., 1914). The Roman economy is the subject of MARTIN P. CHARLESWORTH, *Trade Routes and Commerce of the Roman Empire*, 2nd rev. ed. (Cambridge: Cambridge U.P., 1926).

Aspects of Roman civilization are treated in CYRIL BAILEY, ed., *The Legacy of Rome* (Oxford: Clarendon, 1923); MICHAEL GRANT in *The World of Rome* (Cleveland: World, 1960); RUSSEL M. GEER, *Rome*, in H. N. COUCH and R. H. GEER,

Classical Civilization (New York: Prentice-Hall, 1940); and, in especially comprehensive fashion, ALBERT A. TREVER, *A History of Ancient Civilization:* Vol. II, *The Roman World* (New York: Harcourt Brace, 1939); as well as by HAROLD MATTINGLY, *Roman Imperial Civilization* (New York: St. Martin's, 1957). The lives and writings of typical figures in the transitional fourth century are discussed by TERROT R. GLOVER, *Life and Letters in the Fourth Century,* reprint (New York: Stechert, 1924).

A classic study of Roman literature consists of the two volumes by JOHN W. DUFF, *A Literary History of Rome from the Origins to the Close of the Golden Age* (New York: Scribners, 1932) and *A Literary History of Rome in the Silver Age* . . . (New York: Scribners, 1927). A good treatment of Stoicism is provided by EDWARD V. ARNOLD, *Roman Stoicism* . . . (Cambridge: Cambridge U.P., 1911); of Neo-Platonism by THOMAS WHITTAKER, *The Neo-Platonists,* 2nd ed. (Cambridge: Cambridge U.P., 1928); and of education by AUBREY O. GWYNN, *Roman Education from Cicero to Quintilian* (Oxford: Clarendon, 1926). Roman architecture and art are surveyed by WILLIAM J. ANDERSON and R. P. SPIERS, *The Architecture of Ancient Rome,* rev. by T. ASHBY (London: Batsford, 1927); and HENRY B. WALTERS, *The Art of the Romans,* 2nd ed. (London: Metheun, 1928); and GEORGE M. HANFMAN, *Roman Art* (Greenwich, Conn.: New York Graphic Society, 1964).

THE CHRISTIAN FOUNDATION OF THE MIDDLE AGES
Chapter 2.

CHRISTIANITY originated in the Middle East as an offspring of the monotheistic, highly moral religion of Judaism. Despite almost three centuries of persecution, the Christian religion eventually became dominant in the Roman Empire. The Church, by the close of antiquity, had a well-established hierarchy and a well-developed body of teachings embodied in a copious religious literature. It had also successfully maintained its independence of the state, and was gradually succeeding the fading Roman Empire as the chief unifying, civilizing force in Europe.

CHRISTIANITY TRIUMPHS IN THE ROMAN WORLD.
Section 4.

Pagan gods honored by the nations [now] roost upon their lonely eves with horned owls and birds of the night. On military standards there is emblazoned the insignia of the Cross, which also adorns royal purple and flashing diadem. [ST. JEROME concerning the triumph of Christianity in a letter written in A.D. 403.]

THE HUMBLE origins, severe trials, dramatic growth, and eventual victory of Christianity in the Roman world, despite prolonged persecutions, make a stirring story. Its long ordeal was salutary for the Church,

Religion in the Roman world

which emerged purified and strengthened, with inspiring traditions and heroic examples. By the close of antiquity, Christianity was the established religion in the Roman world, a condition which continued in the states of Europe during the Middle Ages.

At the coming of Christianity, Rome had a powerful, prosperous, sophisticated Empire, but religious development lagged behind other progress. Existing pagan religions, including that of the Romans, were crude and primitive, encrusted with superstitions and inconsistencies, and peculiar to particular peoples and localities. A multitude of mythical gods and goddesses vied for attention, without providing the intellect and will with satisfying objects. Emperor-worship was generally regarded as little more than a political ceremony and symbol. Philosophies, such as Stoicism and Neo-Platonism, being too abstruse and debatable, failed to supply the human need for religion. Judaism, although an advanced religion, was too closely identified with the Jewish people and their customs.

The most successful and popular religions in the Roman world other than Christianity were the "mystery religions." These were usually simplified, "popularized" versions of advanced Eastern religions. Their name derives from the fact that their adherents practiced special secret rites known as "sacraments" or "mysteries" and that some of their doctrines could not be fully comprehended by reason. Popular examples of mystery religions included dualistic Mithraism, derived from Persian Zoroastrianism; the nature cult of Isis and Osiris, goddess and god of the earth and the Nile, from Egypt; and the worship of Magna Mater or the fertile Great Mother Earth from Asia Minor.

The mystery religions each taught a "myth" or story of human salvation, regarded by many as symbolic, such as that of the heroic adventures of the god Mithras and his slaying of the bull, whose blood begot various forms of life. Common rites included purificatory washing, expiatory sacrifice, fraternal communion, and the use of incense, processions, hymns, and public prayers in worship. Participation in prescribed ritual services satisfied religious instincts, promoted religious life, and engendered confidence in salvation. The mystery religions gained much currency, and shrines and temples to such deities as Mithras, popular with the military, were found as far away as Britain.

While in some ways Christianity resembled the mystery religions, in others it was different. Like the mystery religions, Christianity was the offspring of an old Near Eastern religion; had secret rites and doctrines reserved for the initiated, including "sacraments" or "mysteries" regarded as means of salvation; and contained some doctrines that were not fully comprehensible or demonstrable by natural reason. Unlike the mystery religions, however, Christianity had an actual, historic founder, who testified to his message by being willing to die for it. There were still alive believing eye-witnesses to the founder's life and teachings who were also willing to die for their faith. The doctrines of Christianity were more effective morally than those of the mystery religions, while its uplifting gospel of love had broad appeal.

The Christian Foundation

Rise of Christianity

The birthplace of Christianity was Palestine and its womb Judaism. In the first century, in this pious milieu, Jesus Christ taught a doctrine of love of God and fellowmen and a religion of the spirit as opposed to the letter of the law. Christ announced that he was the Messiah or Promised One, foretold by the Jewish Old Testament, who was to establish a spiritual "kingdom which would know no end." He said he was "the son of God," and "one with the Father." Christ was finally condemned and put to death for violating Jewish and Roman laws by refusing to retract his teachings concerning his divinity and kingship.

Christ's work was continued by his Apostles, chosen companions whom he had carefully instructed and commissioned to spread the "good news." At first the Apostles preached to the Jews in Palestine and then to those dispersed about the Eastern Mediterranean world, but soon they extended their gospel to the non-Jews or Gentiles. At the fore in Mediterranean missionary activities was the enthusiastic recent convert, St. Paul, "an Apostle born out of due time," who, preaching "to Jew and Gentile alike," organized Christian communities in several leading Mediterranean centers. Both "the Apostle of the Gentiles" St. Paul, and St. Peter, leader of the Apostles, were apparently put to death in Rome in the 60s, by which time there were Christian communities in Palestine, Syria, Asia Minor, Greece, Macedonia, Italy, and elsewhere.

The persecutions

Early Christianity was strengthened by over two and a half centuries of persecution by the imperial government. According to a Roman law (which may have been originally enacted under Nero) being a Christian made one liable to extreme penalties, including death. Christians were considered subversive radicals, whose refusal to sacrifice to the emperors was unpatriotic and insubordinate, and whose absention from the religious rites and festivities of the community showed that they were "enemies of mankind," and had incurred the wrath of the gods. They also proved convenient scapegoats. Tertullian observes that no matter what the catastrophe, "the cry goes up: 'The Christians to the lions.'" While there was apparently a standing law against being a Christian from the first century, the general policy of the Roman government was to look the other way. From time to time, however, the imperial government did make strenuous efforts to enforce the law.

The most severe persecutions began in the middle of the third century, by which time Christianity had a foothold in every part of the Roman world, and the Empire seemed to be losing its vitality and divine favor. As many considered that Christianity was responsible for the decline, Emperors Decius, Valerian, and Diocletian initiated severe general persecutions. The final and most extensive was ordered by a series of four decrees (303–304). Finally, in 311, Diocletian's successor, Galerius, dying of a painful disease, granted toleration to the Christians.

Successfully surmounted, the persecutions were actually benefical to the Christian Church. They excited public sympathy and admiration and won converts. The persecutions also fostered cohesion and unity within the Church to which they gave a glorious history and a galaxy of heroes known as martyrs, or witnesses. They firmly established the dis-

Expansion and triumph of Christianity

tinction between State and Church, and the latter's autonomy with respect to the former, notwithstanding the close cooperation that later developed beween the two.

Despite the persecutions, Christianity continued to expand. By the close of the third century Christians constituted an estimated 10 per cent of the population of the Empire and were particularly numerous in the cities. Property used for religious purposes was owned by Christians as corporate groups or *collegia*. In Rome alone there were already over forty Christian churches. The influence of Christians greatly exceeded their numbers.

The edict of toleration issued by the stricken Galerius was not accepted everywhere, and there was question as to whether the longstanding ban against Christianity had been really lifted. Accordingly when the new Western Emperor Constantine met with the new Eastern Emperor Licinius at Milan in 313, they jointly issued the explanatory rescript which has come to be known as the Edict of Milan. According to the Edict, "so that whatever godhead is enthroned in heaven may be favorable and propitious," the two emperors decided to "grant to the Christians and all men free right to practice whatever religion each desires." Henceforth, "All restrictions formerly imposed upon the Christians are to be set aside," and any "accustomed places of worship confiscated from Christians in accordance with previous instructions are to be restored."

Constantine and his pious mother, St. Helena, commenced the gradual imperial establishment of Christianity. They gave to the Church the Lateran Palace and constructed the first St. Peter's Cathedral in Rome. They also built several other churches and granted many more favors to Christians. Sunday was made a legal holiday, and the cross was widely used as a symbol. Church property was exempted from taxation. Extensive privileges were conferred on bishops and priests. Bishops were given the right to act as appellate judges whose decisions were final. The clergy were exempt from many public duties, including military service and various taxes. Bishops became intimate counsellors of the Emperor. Eventually Constantine declared publicly that he was a Christian and that he wished all his subjects to become Christians. He himself was baptized on his deathbed.

New difficulties were experienced by the Church under the first two successors of Constantine. His son, Constantius (337–367), who eventually emerged as sole Emperor, was a supporter of the minority creed of Arianism,[a] who banished orthodox bishops and replaced them with Arians. His successor, Julian the Apostate (361–363), unsuccessfully attempted to revive paganism. Julian recalled the orthodox bishops in the hope of inducing division in the Christian Church; but the people welcomed back the orthodox bishops and expelled the Arian usurpers.

Imperial encouragement of Christianity resumed after the early death of Julian. Emperors Jovian (363–364) and Valentinian I (364–375) lifted the restrictions that Julian had imposed on Christians. Gratian (375–383) transferred to the Christian Church the public financial support previously accorded to paganism. Gratian, Valentinian II, and Theo-

[a] Arianism, which gained many believers, asserted that Christ was divine by adoption, rather than by nature.

The Christian Foundation

dosius I jointly issued a decree in 380 directing that all should become orthodox Christians in communion with the Bishop of Rome, and that heretics and apostates should be punished. Theodosius I, the Great (379–395), convoked the Second Ecumenical Christian Council of I Constantinople (381), which denounced Arianism and other heresies. Theodosius also issued three decrees known as "the death knell of paganism" (391–392), in which he prohibited public acts of pagan worship and public profession of paganism, and forbade the people to enter pagan temples, which he ordered closed. Theodosius II and Valentinian III decreed the death penalty for offering pagan sacrifices in 435. The positions of paganism and Christianity in the Roman Empire had been virtually reversed. Most of the extensive privileges and prerogatives enjoyed by the Church and churchmen in the Middle Ages were established in the Roman Empire by the early fifth century.

Its adoption and endorsement by the Roman Empire had various effects on Christianity. The spread of the Christian religion was greatly accelerated. Many of the new converts, swept along by the general movement or impelled by secular considerations, were insincere, poorly instructed, or lukewarm. A considerable lowering of the average level of dedication and morality among members of the Church apparently resulted. The elimination of previous strains and dangers led to relaxation, and the fact that Christians now came to be honored and privileged attracted many for purely worldly reasons. As the number and variety of Christians increased, heresies arose, since converts often interpreted Christian doctrines according to their own preconceptions and predilections. As groups within the Church appealed to Emperors for their support, and as Emperors tended to assume with Christianity prerogatives they had previously enjoyed with paganism, "Caesaropapism" (efforts of rulers to control the Church) arose, and Church-vs-State friction developed. Meanwhile many who desired a more dedicated, sacrificial, demanding Christian life embraced monasticism.

Effects of imperial adoption of Christianity

The problem of Church and State relations existed for Christianity from the very beginning. The Jewish state persecuted Christ and, following his crucifixion, the Apostles. The Roman government persecuted Christianity for two and a half centuries. The distinction between Church and State was accordingly accentuated, and a tradition of separation firmly established. Still, even during the persecutions, the prevailing Christian attitude towards the State was one of submission in all things except sin. Political authority was regarded as coming from God, and injustices of rulers were accepted as the salutary hand of God, punishing and purifying. The Christian remembered the words of Christ, "Render to Caesar the things that are Caesar's. . . ," and those of St. Paul, "Let everyone submit himself to the ruling authorities, for there exists none that is not ordained by God. . . ."

Church and State

After Christianity came to be the established religion of the Roman Empire, the distinction between church and state continued, though it was in frequent danger of being violated. Both orthodox and heterodox sought imperial support for their views. Churchmen wanted to have

Christianity incorporated into imperial laws, and many emperors concurred. Emperors also cooperated in convoking and sponsoring Church councils. Constantine supported the side of orthodoxy against the Donatist and Arian heresies by convoking Church councils. His son Constantius took the opposite tack and supported the Arians against the orthodox; as did Valens, emperor in the East (364–378), who was also an Arian. Theodosius I, who was orthodox; took a very active part in Church affairs, opposing Arianism and other heresies (380ff.), and outlawing public paganism (391–392).

While imperial interference in Church matters declined in the West during the fifth century, it increased in the East. Emperor Theodosius II supported Monophysitism and managed to "pack" the so-called Robber Council of Ephesus (449) with Monophysite supporters; Emperor Zeno proposed a compromise formula of faith, the *Henoticon*, which satisfied neither side. At the close of the fifth century, another strong Monophysite was Emperor Anastasius I.

The Bishops of Rome defended orthodoxy, even in defiance of heretical Eastern Emperors. Despite the temporary setback of the Robber Council, Pope Leo I won out when his formula of faith was accepted two years later by the third ecumenical Council of Chalcedon (451). Pope Gelasius I, in a letter to the Monophysite Emperor Anastasius I in 494, formulated the doctrine of "the two swords": "There are two powers, O August Emperor, by which this world is chiefly governed: the sacred authority of the priests and the authority of the monarch. Of the two, the responsibility of the priests is greater, since they have to render an account to God even for the kings of men." The "two-swords" or two-authorities principle, with a slight "edge" in favor of the Church, remained the dominant theory of Church-State relations during the Middle Ages.

THE EARLY CHURCH.
Section 5.

> As it would be excessively long to enumerate in a work such as this the succession of all the bishops in all the churches, we shall limit ourselves to that of the greatest and oldest church, known to all, founded and established at Rome by the two glorious apostles Peter and Paul. . . . With this church, on account of its greater authority, every church—that is the faithful everywhere—must agree. . . . [St. Irenaeus of Lyons in *Against Heresies* (second century).]

THE SUCCESS of Christianity was partly due to its excellent organization. While to some extent this existed from the time of Christ and the Apostles, it also resulted from imitation of Roman governmental structure and practices.

Christ established a religious society, according to the New Testament. He spoke of his followers as a "church," a "kingdom," a "flock," a "body," and a "tree." In this society he appointed the Apostles to teach and rule in his name, and he established baptism with water as a rite of initiation. The Apostles regarded Christians as members of an organized society,

The Christian Foundation

which they spoke of as "the body" and "bride" of Christ, the "house" and "temple" of God, and the "church" and "kingdom" of believers. About A.D. 96, Bishop Clement of Rome, in a Letter to the Corinthians, characterized the Church as "a community," "a brotherhood," "a consecrated people," "a body," and "an army." Christians were persecuted and put to death by the Roman government for being members of this organization, but they could continue to enjoy life and liberty by severing connections with the Church.

A feature of this society from the beginning was unity. Christ prayed that his disciples might "remain one, as I and the father are one"; that there should be but "one flock and one shepherd"; and he warned that "the city or house divided against itself shall not stand." St. Paul insisted that there was only "one Lord, one faith, and one baptism;" and he condemned those who taught divergent doctrines and caused dissension as "wolves" and "corrupters" of God's word, who "shall not obtain the kingdom of God." St. Ignatius of Antioch early in the second century, spoke of the Church as a "community," a "choir," and a "symphony." St. Cyprian of Carthage in the third century, wrote: "God is one, Christ is one, and one is the Church of Christ." This belief in the necessity of Christian unity continued to be strong during the Middle Ages.

The episcopacy prior to the fourth century

The key unifying and directing agents in the early Church were the Apostles and, after them, the bishops. According to the New Testament, Christ commissioned the Apostles to preach, instruct, and minister in his name: "As the Father hath sent me, I also send you. Going therefore, teach ye all nations, baptizing them in the name of the Father, the Son, and the Holy Ghost." They were to teach with his authority: "He that heareth you, heareth me. . . "; impose obligations: "Whatsoever you shall bind on earth shall be bound also in heaven"; forgive sins: "Whose sins you shall forgive, they shall be forgiven them. . . "; and repeat the Last Supper: "Do this in commemoration of me."

In The Acts of the Apostles, St. Luke tells how they preached the Christian faith and ruled the Christian Church after Christ's crucifixion. The Apostles taught, legislated, judged and punished, and administered the sacraments, such as baptism. They also appointed coadjutors and successors. First, they named Matthias to take the place of Judas among the twelve, and later they added Paul to their number. They also appointed others to help, temporarily replace, and eventually succeed them in the ministry. Chance references show that St. Paul appointed Titus, Timothy, Dionysius, and Barnabas, as well as Luke, as such co-workers and lieutenants, and that John so appointed Polycarp. The Acts of the Apostles refer to these appointees as "bishops" (*episcopoi:* overseers).

At first groups of bishops and/or presbyters (elders, priests, or bishops) often shared authority in a given Christian community. But it is likely that one of their number, such as the eldest or the earliest converted or the most able, served as leader from the beginning; and very soon, to avoid friction and confusion, the practice developed of having only one bishop ruling each area: the so-called "monarchical bishop." For this organization, the Roman Empire served as a model. The territory under each bishop, which became known as his "diocese," generally corresponded to the local Roman *civitas* or county, ruled from its urban center. After the passing of the Apostles, the election of bishops was at first in the hands of the local Christian communities, both clergy and laity; later, it was frequently reserved to the clergy. Eventually, emperors and kings came to exercise considerable influence in ecclesiastical elections.

As Christ had insisted on his mission and authority, so the Apostles and bishops insisted on theirs. Bishop Clement of Rome in his Letter to the Corinthians (ca. A.D. 96) pointed out: "The Apostles appointed their first-fruits [earliest converts], after testing them by the Spirit, to be bishops and deacons for those who believe." A few years later, Bishop (St.) Ignatius of Antioch, in seven Letters written to various churches as he was awaiting martyrdom, urged: "One should look upon the bishops as upon the Lord himself"; and: "Submit to the bishop just as Jesus Christ in the flesh did to the Father." Sts. Irenaeus of Lyons in the second century and Cyprian of Carthage in the third century stressed union with the bishop as the best guarantee and assurance of correct belief and salvation. Thus, by the second and third centuries, the authority of the monarchical bishops was well established.

The episcopacy in the fourth and fifth centuries

Even as during earlier centuries the Roman government had made the Christian bishops the chief targets of its persecutions, so, after accepting Christianity, it made them leading objects of its solicitude and favors. During the distraught fourth and fifth centuries, bishops were empowered to carry on many functions of secular government. They were commissioned to act as judges; to protect the poor, the needy, and the oppressed, including slaves, orphans, and prisoners; to supervise or administer public relief funds; to see to the proper maintenance of public works; to report on the conduct of public officials; and to advise the latter on matters of government. This delegation of secular authority to bishops was especially common and extensive in the West, where imperial power was on the wane.

There was a hierarchy among the bishops. The bishops of leading cities in areas corresponding to Roman provinces came to be known as "archbishops" (chief bishops) or "metropolitans" (from *mater* and *polis*: mother city). Often the faith had been originally diffused from these more important centers. The bishops of key cities which had been seats of the Apostles came to be recognized as "Patriarchs," a title reserved for the Bishops of Rome, Antioch, and Alexandria by the Council of Nicaea in 325. The Bishop of Constantinople was added to the list by the Council of Constantinople in 381; and the Bishop of Jerusalem by the Council of Chalcedon in 451. At first the Bishops of Constantinople were content with being recognized as Patriarchs holding a position second only to that of the Bishop of Rome; but subsequently they sometimes claimed equality with Rome, as at Chalcedon in 451. This claim was, however, not accepted by the Bishop of Rome.

The Bishops of Rome

One of the controverted points concerning the early Church has been the position of the Bishop of Rome. Was he the head of the Church from the start, or did he gradually assume this position? Was he so as the successor of St. Peter and by virtue of Christ's commission to the latter, or merely as Christian bishop of the leading city of the Empire, and owing to the Christian desire and need to maintain tranquillity and unity in the Church? It must be noted that these questions cannot be completely and precisely answered on the basis of available historical sources. It can, however, be said that St. Peter, and after him the Bishops of Rome, exercised leadership in the early Church on various occasions, and that this greatly increased in the fourth and fifth centuries. In the beginning, when the Church was being persecuted and was seeking converts, precise definition of the full structure of ecclesiastical authority was not usually a major concern. Only occasionally did such a problem arise, and when it did it was usually solved on local levels by the bishops. But in some cases, when the scope of the problem precluded its solution at home, the authority of the Bishop of Rome was invoked.

The Petrine tradition

From an early date the Bishops of Rome occasionally exercised leadership in the Church, wherein they were accorded a certain primacy, although the title "Pope" (*Papa:* Father), originally more general, was not reserved for the Roman Bishop until the sixth century. Eventually the Bishops of Rome appealed to the New Testament on behalf of their claims to primacy. They pointed out that, according to the Gospels, Christ treated and designated Simon, whom he nicknamed "Peter" or "Rock," as the leader among the Apostles. Once, after a heartening confession of faith on Peter's part, Jesus said: *Thou are 'Peter'* [kephas: rock] *and on this rock* [kephas] *I will build my church, and the gates of hell shall not prevail against it. And to you I will give the keys to the kingdom of heaven; and whatsoever you shall bind on earth shall also be bound in heaven, and whatsoever you shall loose on earth shall also be loosed in heaven. . . .* (Matthew 16:18; Luke 9:18–21). While some regard this as conferring special leadership responsibilities and powers (or "primacy") on Peter, others interpret "the rock" on which Christ says he will build his church as the faith exemplified by Peter's immediately preceding declaration of his acceptance of the divinity of Christ. On another occasion Jesus, according to the Apostle John, repeatedly asked Peter: "Simon, son of John, do you love me more than these others do?" and when Peter answered in the affirmative each time, Christ directed him to care for his flock: "Feed my lambs. Shepherd my sheep. Feed my sheep." (John 21:15–17).

After Christ's execution, Peter several times acted as the leader of the Apostles. On Pentecost, after the descent of the Holy Spirit, Peter explained to the crowd that the preaching of the Apostles in diverse tongues was not due to their being drunk, since it was still early in the morning, but to the outpouring of the Spirit of God (Acts 2). Peter took the lead in rebuking Simon Magus for his attempt to purchase the gifts of the Holy Spirit (Acts 8:9–24); in chastising Ananias and Sapphira for withholding some of their goods from the Christian community (Acts 5:1–11); in deciding to teach the Christian religion to the Gentiles (Acts

10:24–48); and in releasing the latter from the disciplinary prescriptions of the Old Law (Acts 10:9–16; 15:1–21). Peter was several times both leader and spokesman for the Apostles, and was evidently recognized as such by the Jewish government, which singled him out for imprisonment (Acts 12:1–19). After being at Antioch for some time, Peter eventually went to Rome, where he was put to death by being crucified head downwards, according to tradition. St. Paul's life also apparently ended in martyrdom at Rome, so that Rome could advance a double claim to the title of "the Apostolic See."

The Bishops of Rome to 313

Very early in the history of the Church the Bishops of Rome acted as leaders among the bishops. This "primacy" was based partly on their claim to be successors of St. Peter and St. Paul, partly because of the distinguished record and many martyrs of the Roman Church, and partly because it was natural that the bishop of the imperial capital, who was also the sole Western Patriarch, should assume leadership. By common consent it was recognized that since the Church was one, it should have one head. Although we have only occasional records from the first three Christian centuries, references in surviving documents indicate that the Bishop of Rome sometimes exercised leadership in the Church even from early times. Bishop Clement of Rome, in a letter written to the Corinthian Christians about A.D. 96, assumed his authority to settle the disputed succession to the episcopal office at Corinth, and declared: "If any shall disobey the words spoken by God through us, let them know that they will be involved in no small transgression and danger." A few years afterward (ca. 107), St. Ignatius, Bishop of Antioch, who was about to be martyred, wrote a letter to the Church at Rome in which he said: *You are . . . a Church without blemish, which holds the primacy in the community of love. . . . Never have you had cause to envy anyone, since you have been others' teachers.* St. Irenaeus, Bishop of Lyons, in his treatise *Against Heresies*, written toward the close of the second century, said of the Roman Church: "It is necessary that every church should agree with this church on account of its preeminent authority." St. Irenaeus then traced the Apostolic succession in the Bishopric of Rome from Sts. Peter and Paul to his own day. The great Bishop, St. Cyprian of Carthage, in the middle of the third century, in a treatise *On the Unity of the Church*, characterized the Roman Bishopric as "the throne of St. Peter and the chief church whence priestly unity takes its sources."

Papal primacy in the fourth to fifth centuries

By the fourth to fifth centuries, the primacy of the Bishops of Rome was so frequently asserted and exercised that some suppose it originated in this period. At this time Rome was no longer the imperial capital even in the West, but the Roman Bishops could serve as implements for unity and order amidst the barbarian invasions. At the Council of Nicaea in 325, representatives of the Bishop of Rome apparently presided, and the decrees of the Council were referred to the Pope for his approval. Pope Julius I (337–352) restored Patriarch Athanasius to the see of Alexandria after he had been deposed by the Council of Tyre (335), declaring that bishops are to be judged by the Pope. In 343, the Council of Sardica (Sophia), held in present-day Bulgaria, recognized the right of appeal to

The Christian Foundation

Rome. Emperor Constantius strove unsuccessfully to obtain for Arianism the approval of Pope Liberius (352–366) "as a more weighty authority." The long-standing primacy of the Roman Bishop is attested to by the fact that the second Ecumenical Council of I Constantinople in 381 accorded the Bishop of Constantinople patriarchal status and a position of honor second only to that of the Bishop of Rome, "because Constantinople is the new Rome." The primacy of the Bishops of Rome in the Church was formally asserted by Emperors Gratian in 378, Theodosius I in 380, and Valentinian III in 445. Imperial support of Church centralization could, of course, be self-serving.

Papal primacy is clearly stated in the fifth century, when the Roman Empire in the West was collapsing. Innocent I (d. 417) repeatedly asserted Papal primacy in at least thirty-eight letters addressed to all parts of Christendom. He supported St. John Chrysostom against the Eastern Emperor Arcadius and the Empress Eudoxia and refused to accept the saint's "deposition" from the see of Constantinople. Referring to a decision by the Bishop of Rome, St. Augustine said: "Rome has spoken: the case is finished" [*Roma locuta est: causa finita est*]." And St. Jerome wrote to Pope Damasus: "I am joined in communion with your holiness, that is with the Chair of St. Peter. I know that the Church is built upon this Rock." Emperor Valentinian III asserted that "ancient usage" gave the Roman Bishops "a pre-eminence above all others to judge in matters of the faith" (445).

At a time when the collapsing Western Empire and Rome itself were threatened by the Huns and other barbarians, Pope Leo I successfully opposed Monophysitism, which had won the adherence of emperors and patriarchs in the East. Leo issued his doctrinal *Tome*, which came to be accepted as the authoritative statement of orthodox teaching. He condemned the pro-Monophysite "Robber Council" of Ephesus (449), as "sifted" and "packed" by the Emperor, and obtained its reversal by the Ecumenical Council of Chalcedon in 451, which endorsed his *Tome*. Leo clearly affirmed the primacy of the Pope as the successor of St. Peter, who had been given "the power of the keys." He declared: "We have the care of all the churches; and the Lord, who made Peter the prince of the Apostles, holds us responsible." Whatever may have been its origins, the concept of the primacy of the Bishop of Rome in the Church was firmly established by the close of antiquity.

Assisting the Apostles and, subsequently, the bishops, were various lesser officials. Priests or "presbyters" were often coadjutors of bishops in the care of souls and administration of the sacraments, exercising some but not all of the episcopal powers. The term presbyter as used in the Acts of the Apostles sometimes means elder, sometimes priest, sometimes bishop. These terms, presbyter and priest, seem often to have been used interchangeably; but very soon a clearer distinction becomes apparent.

Presbyters, deacons, and other officials

The head of the Church in each region or *civitas* came to be known as the "bishop," and his assistants, who shared some but not all of his powers, as "priests." The latter could consecrate the Eucharist and forgive sins, but could not ordain other priests.

As the Church expanded, a further division of functions was necessary. The office of deacon was established by the Apostles, who, finding themselves overburdened with duties, directed the Christian community to choose seven deacons to serve tables and take care of temporalities (Acts 6:1–6). The deacons were elected, and the office was conferred with prayers and imposition of hands. The deacons took care of finances, church property, and other necessities of life, maintained order in the church, and otherwise helped the bishops and priests. The office of deacon was continued in the medieval church. Various lesser orders were eventually established to handle other functions: subdeacons (lieutenant-deacons), acolytes (servers), exorcists (to cast out evil spirits), lectors (readers), and *ostiarii* or "porters" (doorkeepers). In A.D. 230 the Church of Rome had 46 presbyters, 7 deacons, 7 subdeacons, 42 acolytes, and 52 exorcists, lectors, and doorkeepers.

Church councils and early canon law

Leaders in the early Church held councils to settle disputed questions and determine courses of action. According to Acts, the Apostles gathered in Jerusalem to pray and consult, both when they chose Matthias to succeed Judas and later when the Holy Spirit descended upon them at Pentecost. About A.D. 51 they held a council at Jerusalem to decide whether or not converted gentiles should be made to conform to the disciplinary prescriptions of the Old Law. Regional councils of bishops were frequently held from the middle of the third century on, and bishops often consulted with their clergy in local synods. Examples of large interregional councils of bishops were those of Arles (314), Tyre (335), and Sardica (343).

Ecumenical or general councils of Church leaders assembled periodically following the tolerance of Christianity, primarily to deal with the great doctrinal controversies which rocked the Christian world in the fourth and fifth centuries.[b] The Council of Nicaea (325) condemned Arianism; that of I Constantinople (381) Arianism and other heresies; that of Ephesus (431) Nestorianism; and that of Chalcedon (451) Monophysitism. These early ecumenical councils were convoked by imperial summons, were held in the eastern part of the Empire, and attended mainly by eastern Bishops, although western Bishops were present, and the Bishop of Rome was regularly represented.

[b] Discussed in the following section.

The laws of the Church, collectively known as "canon law" (from *canon:* rule, ordinance), included enactments and interpretations by Church authorities, as well as obligations established by custom. Decrees of Church councils on various levels were a leading source of canon law, which often interpreted and applied the laws of the Old and New Testaments. Canon law borrowed much from the principles and procedures of Roman law. Various general collections of canon law, made prior to the fifth century, included the *Didache,* which was believed to have been the teachings of the Apostles, the *Didascalia,* which was based on the *Didache;* the *Apostolic Constitutions,* an expansion of the foregoing two collections; and the *Apostolic Canons* (eighty-five in number). The most important early compilation was the *Collection* made by the monk Dionysius Exiguus about A.D. 500, which included the decrees of general

The Christian Foundation

and regional councils, as well as fifty of the Apostolic Constitutions. Meanwhile, several regional collections of the law in given areas appeared in parts of the Greek East, Africa, Spain, and Gaul. Ancient collections of canon law became starting points for larger medieval collections, such as Gratian's (eleventh century).

Since Christians regarded their religion as a fulfilment of Judaism, they continued many of the latter's practices, such as observance of one day a week as holy (though this became Sunday rather than Saturday), meetings which included readings from the Bible and responsorial chant, periodic fasting, and pilgrimages.

Early Christian attitudes, practices, and standards

While rejecting pagan religions, the Church accepted some pagan practices. In deference to established social customs, Christian festivals were frequently made to coincide with previous pagan feasts, as in the case of December 25, formerly the Birthday of the Sun, which was observed as the Birthday of Christ; and January 1, the pagan New Year's Day, which was celebrated as the Feast of Christ's Circumcision. Pagan usages in worship, such as incense, candles, vestments, altar stones, holy water, and sacred oil, and genuflexions and processions, were also adopted. Even former pagan temples and sacred places were sometimes used by the Christians, as in the case of the Pantheon (Temple of All the Gods) at Rome, which became the Church of All Saints.

The Church adapted itself to most existing social institutions, but fought practices such as polygamy and infanticide that are forbidden in the Bible. It tolerated slavery but encouraged the emancipation of slaves; and discouraged warfare without completely condemning it under all circumstances. A distinction was accepted between religious society wherein, as St. Paul says: "there is neither bond nor free" (Galatians, 3:27–28) and secular society, wherein "slaves should not despise their masters because they are their brothers, but should serve them all the more faithfully." (I Timothy 6:2). At the same time the Church taught that masters should treat their slaves kindly, and observe their human dignity and rights, including the integrity of their families. The respectful attitude of Christianity toward the state has already been mentioned.

Church teaching relative to sex was strict and firm. Extramarital sexual relations were absolutely forbidden. Celibacy, or complete abstinence from sexual relations, practiced for religious motives, was deemed a more perfect state. The example given by Christ and early Christian leaders was powerful, and its rationale was explained by St. Paul: "He who is unmarried is concerned about the interests of the Lord and how he may please the Lord; whereas he who is married is concerned about worldly interests and how he may please his wife" (I Corinthians 7:32–34). Celibacy was a standard requirement for the monastic life and for the higher clergy. In the Western Church it came to be required also for the priesthood, at least in the fourth century. Matrimony was monogamous and a sacrament, dissolved only by the death of one of the contracting parties. The only exception was the "Pauline Privilege" in favor of a Christian convert whose unbaptized spouse refused either to be baptized or to allow the Christian to practice his or her religion unmolested.

Christian counsels on how to achieve a more perfect life were eventually distinguished from commandments whose observance was required of all believers. Some rigorists, such as the Montanists and Novatians, maintained that all the exhortations of Christ had to be observed under pain of sin, and that serious sin excluded one irrevocably from the society of the faithful. This would have reserved membership in the Church to a select few.

Special practices

Among special practices in the Church, the veneration of very holy persons (saints) was prominent. This custom may have originated in connection with reverence for Christian martyrs and their remains. There was apparently no real confusion between reverence of saints and worship of God. While some have asserted that the cult of saints was a substitute for polytheism, others have pointed out that it was a consequence of both natural respect for holiness and the doctrine of the community of Christian believers.

The "relics" (remnants) of the saints were considered to have a special efficacy. About A.D. 156, the Smyrneans wrote that, after their bishop Polycarp had been burned at the stake, "we took up his bones, which are more valuable than precious stones and purer than the finest gold." In the fourth century, St. Jerome explained: "We do not worship nor do we adore the relics of the martyrs, but we honor them in order the better to adore Him whose martyrs they are." Pilgrimages, consisting of visits to holy places, were regarded as having a salutary influence—a concept that no doubt descended from Jewish traditions.

Traveling to the Holy Land of Palestine was frequent among Christians by the fourth century. Such practices as the veneration of saints, reverence for holy relics, and pilgrimages continued to be popular during the Middle Ages. Following the example of Christ as well as Jewish precedents, fasting, especially during Lent, was practiced from early times, as also abstinence from meat on Friday in memory of Christ's crucifixion.

The Eucharist and other sacraments

The central act of Christian worship was the Eucharist: the "love feast," which fulfilled the instruction of Christ before His passion: "Take ye and eat. This is my body, . . . This is my blood . . . . Do this in memory of me" (Matthew 14:22–25). The consecration of the bread and wine in the Eucharist was reserved to the bishops and priests as (full and partial) successors of the Apostles. It was regarded as both a sacrifice and a sacrament: sacrifice inasmuch as it recalled and renewed the supreme sacrifice of Christ on the Cross; and sacrament because it included participation by the faithful in the Body and Blood of Christ.

Other Christian sacraments—external rites Christians regarded as having been instituted by Christ to give grace—included Baptism, by which persons were cleansed of sin and initiated into the Church; Penance, by which repentant Christians who confessed sins committed after Baptism to a priest were forgiven; Confirmation, wherein the Holy Spirit and special graces were imparted by anointing; Holy Orders, whereby the full or partial powers of the Apostles were conferred by imposition of hands; Extreme Unction or final anointing of those in danger of death;

The Christian Foundation 43

and Matrimony: the holy union of husband and wife. Use of the sacraments and the Sacrifice of the Mass, or Eucharist, continued to be basic and found their full expression in the medieval Church.

EARLY CHRISTIAN DOCTRINES.
Section 6.

> We believe in one God, the Father Almighty, Creator of heaven and earth, and of all things visible and invisible. And in one Lord, Jesus Christ, the only Son of God, begotten of the Father before all ages: light from light, true God from true God, begotten not made, of the same substance with the Father. . . And in the Holy Spirit. . . And in one holy, universal Church. . . . We acknowledge one baptism for the remission of sins, and we look for the resurrection of the dead and the life of the world to come. [From the *Nicene Creed* (325) of Christians, as modified by the Councils of Constantinople (381) and Chalcedon (451).]

JUST as the organization and practices of the early Church were well established by the end of antiquity, so were its essential doctrines. The evolution of Christian doctrine, which began as early as Apostolic times, continued with the help of respected and learned leaders known as Church Fathers. It was especially promoted in the process of dealing with novel interpretations of Church teaching.

From early times succinct summaries of essential Christian doctrines were made to provide prospective converts with statements of what they must accept in order to become Christians, as well as to clarify the tenets of the Church for all its members. These were known as "Creeds" (*credo*: I believe) or "Symbols." Earlier Creeds were ascribed to the Apostles. During the fourth century, after doctrinal disputes over the mysteries of the Trinity and the Incarnation, the orthodox majority stand was summarized in the Nicene Creed. Originally formulated by the Council of Nicaea in 325, this was subsequently added to by the Councils of Constantinople (381) and Chalcedon (451).

"Heresies"—doctrines contrary to those of the "orthodox" majority and accepted ecclesiastical authorities—began to arise in the Church as early as Apostolic times and stimulated the clarification and evolution of Church doctrines. A heresy (Gr. "school" or "sect") was a doctrine contrary to that generally accepted as traditional in the Church. Use of the term *heresy* does not necessarily involve a judgment as to validity. Heresies were much more numerous in the more speculative Greek-speaking eastern Mediterranean world than they were in the more practical West. A common source of divergent doctrines was the natural human tendency to interpret the new and unaccustomed in terms of the old and familiar. This often resulted in trying to mold Christianity to fit previous beliefs and personal preferences. Another source was the natural attempt to fathom and explain mysteries in Church doctrine. A third was the inclination of some to be excessively unbending and "literal" in disciplinary matters and Scriptural interpretation, so that they became "stricter than the Church." Fuel for heresy was provided by the pride

Heresies

and perseverance of spokesmen and leaders, adherence to personal commitments, and regional and racial loyalties and sensitivity. Numerous syncretic, disciplinary, and trinitarian heresies appeared in the early Church, among which it is possible to mention only a few principal examples.

Syncretic heresies consisted in combining Christianity with other religions and beliefs to the extent that it lost its own identity. While most heresies were syncretic to some extent, Gnosticism and Manichaeanism were especially so. *Gnosticism* was an eclectic type of religious philosophy, whose adherents held that leading religions such as Zoroastrianism, Judaism, and Christianity were identical in their ultimate essential meanings. It was the asserted prerogative of the Gnostics to pierce through the veils of external popular doctrines and attain the true mystical internal meaning or *gnosis*. Gnostic doctrines were current in the first, second, and early third centuries.

Manichaeanism was an adaptation of ancient Persian Zoroastrianism, originally preached by a Persian convert named Manes in the third century. Like dualistic Zoroastrianism, Manichaeanism taught the essential opposition and incompatibility between matter and spirit. There are two principles in the universe—good and bad, light and darkness, soul and body—in continual conflict. Certain physical things, such as eating meat, drinking wine, and having sexual intercourse, are essentially evil, and must be avoided by all who wish to be "perfect." Manichaeanism, a popular and persistent heresy, was revived in the High Middle Ages in the tenets of the Bogomiles in Bulgaria and those of the Albigensians in southern France.

Disciplinary heresies resulted from a refusal to accept certain practices and policies in the administration of the Church. *Montanism,* founded in the second century by Montanus, a former priest of Cybele, maintained that the age of prophecy had not ended and that prophets, such as himself, were to be preferred to priests. *The Novatians,* who originated in the third century with a priest named Novatian, held that *lapsi*—those who denied the faith during that time of persecution—could not be received back into the Church, even if they sincerely repented. *The Donatists,* so-called from their leader Donatus, who was uncanonically installed as Bishop of Carthage in the early fourth century, asserted that the validity of sacraments is dependent on whether or not the minister is in the state of grace and that therefore the consecration of his rival Caecilian was invalid because the consecrator was not in a state of grace.

Trinitarian heresies

The great heresies which rent the Christian world in the fourth to fifth centuries arose from divergent interpretations as to how Christ could be both human and divine, and how God could be both one and plural. The common effort of the heretics, conscious or unconscious, was to simplify the solution to the point where it was no longer a mystery. Similar heresies had already appeared. The Monarchists of the second century had held that the Father, Son, and Holy Ghost were merely different forms of the same God. The Sabellians of the third century similarly held that the Father, Son, and Holy Ghost are simply the same

God in different roles. The Adoptionists of the second century maintained that Christ is only the adopted son of God. The Apollinarists of the third century asserted that while Christ assumed a human form, he did not assume a human intellectual soul, as the divine soul took its place. Yet none of these earlier Christological heresies had won the adherence of whole peoples, including Patriarchs and Emperors.

Arianism

Arianism was originally taught in the fourth century by an Alexandrian priest named Arius, who had studied at Antioch. Arius stressed the human nature of Christ and maintained that Christ is not coequal and coeternal with the Father. According to Arius, Christ's divinity is of an adoptive or communicated type. The Son is of a similar substance (*homoiousios*) rather than of the same substance (*homousios*) as the Father.

Although Arius won many followers, his teachings were unequivocally condemned by Athanasius, Archbishop of Alexandria, who maintained that there are in Christ two natures, one human and the other divine, even though Christ is a single person. The Arians were able to drive Athanasius out of his patriarchal see several times, and their doctrine gained strong support in high places, as from Bishop Eusebius of Nicomedia, who eventually became Bishop of Constantinople. The first ecumenical Council of Nicaea (325), called by Emperor Constantine to deal with the problem, condemned Arianism and formulated the Nicene Creed, clearly stating the generally accepted beliefs of the Church.

But Arianism continued to spread. When Constantius became sole emperor, he drove the orthodox bishops of Constantinople and other sees into exile and replaced them with Arians, as has been noted. Several local councils were brought together to approve statements favorable to Arian doctrines.

Unwittingly Julian the Apostate helped the cause of orthodoxy by recalling the exiled bishops in the hope that the resulting conflict would weaken the Church. But the people generally welcomed back their orthodox bishops. Learned Church Fathers in both East and West eloquently explained and defended the traditional doctrines of the Church. Arianism rapidly lost ground and died out after being again condemned by the Second Ecumenical Council of I Constantinople in 381. Arianism, however, continued among the East Germans, by whom it was reintroduced into the Western Empire.

Nestorianism and Monophysitism

A product of the Christian school of Antioch and popular in its native Syria, Nestorianism attempted to solve the mystery of the Incarnation as well as to refute Arianism by saying that there are in Christ two persons, one human and the other divine. Nestorianism was condemned and largely eliminated by the Third Ecumenical Council held at Ephesus in 431. After being persecuted in the Empire, the remaining Nestorians were eventually driven to Persia, where the sect survives with a few adherents to the present day.

Partly the result of Alexandrian opposition to Nestorianism, Monophysitism stressed the oneness of Christ. The Monophysites maintained that there was only one nature in Christ—the divine—by which the human nature was absorbed. A leading early proponent was the Abbot Eutyches of Constantinople and this heresy is sometimes known as "Eutychianism." Monophysitism spread rapidly in the Near East, especially in its native Egypt. Several Patriarchs of Alexandria, and some of Antioch and Constantinople were Monophysites, as were also various Eastern emperors and empresses. A Council at Ephesus in 449, from which imperial soldiers excluded orthodox bishops, declared in favor of Monophysitism. But Pope Leo I as has been noted, stated the traditional doctrine in his *Tome,* and condemned this as a "Robber Council" (*Latrocinium*). The Fourth Ecumenical Council of Chalcedon accepted Leo's *Tome* in 451, condemned Monophysitism, and stated that Christ had "two natures, without confusion or transformation" which "subsist in one person."

Despite Chalcedon, Monophysitism persisted in the Near East. Efforts of Emperors Zeno, Justinian, and Heraclius to reconcile the Monophysites proved fruitless. Zeno tried to get around the problem by a vague formula of faith called the *Henoticon*, while Heraclius forbade further mention of "natures" and commanded that all be henceforth content with saying that there was only "one will" in Christ. But attempts at compromise satisfied neither the Monophysites nor the orthodox. In Egypt and Syria Monophysitism became identified with a nationalistic and racial protest against Greek imperialism and greatly weakened the early medieval Byzantine or Eastern Empire.

Although disruptive of religious concord, the heresies stimulated further elaboration and clarification of Church doctrines; made the hierarchy and clergy more desirous of unity; led to the calling of ecumenical councils; and contributed to improved ecclesiastical organization—all influences that continued into the Middle Ages.

The Fathers of the Church

Heresies also contributed to the rise of "Fathers of the Church": learned and saintly men who explained and defended in their writings what came to be accepted as orthodox teachings of the Church. The earlier Church Fathers included Apostolic Fathers, Apologists, Catechists, and Controversialists. Only a few of the writings of the Apostolic Fathers, some of whom lived in the time of the Apostles, have survived. Among these are letters written by St. Clement of Rome and St. Ignatius of Antioch. The Apologists explained and defended Christianity as harmonious with natural reason and philosophy. Early Apologists included Justin Martyr, Clement of Alexandria, and Origen in the East; and Minucius Felix, Tertullian, and Lactantius in the West. The Controversialists, such as St. Irenaeus and Cyprian in the third century, were primarily concerned with refuting current heresies, such as Gnosticism and Novatianism. The maturization of Church doctrines and the Patristic "Golden Age" came with the great Church Fathers of the fourth to sixth centuries. The great Eastern Fathers, who were generally earlier in point of time and who wrote in Greek included Sts. Athanasius, Basil of Caesarea, Gregory of Nazianzus, Gregory of Nyssa, and John Chrysostom. The great Western Fathers, who wrote in Latin, included

Sts. Hilary, Ambrose, Jerome, Augustine, and Gregory the Great. The writings of the Fathers were studied and invoked throughout the Middle Ages as authorities outranked only by the Bible and the pronouncements of Church councils.

The great Eastern Fathers

The great Eastern Fathers, who wrote in Greek, were mainly concerned with refuting the Christological Trinitarian heresies of the fourth to fifth centuries. St. Athanasius (d. 373), who was Archbishop of Alexandria for 45 years during the Arian controversy, perseveringly defended the divine nature of Christ although he was relentlessly persecuted by his enemies and repeatedly banished from his see. St. Basil, Bishop of Caesarea (d. 379), known as "the Great," composed the leading rule and guide for Eastern monks: the *Ascetica*. Basil has been called "the most influential of the Eastern Fathers" and was at the forefront in opposition to the leading heresies of his day. St. Gregory of Nazianzus (d. 389) cooperated with Basil in fighting Arianism. He became Archbishop of Constantinople, but as he was not suited to the trials of administration, he resigned to write and practice asceticism. He also obtained the title of Theologian for works such as his inimitable discourses on the Trinity. St. Gregory of Nyssa (d. 396) composed numerous theological works, many of which refuted current heresies. He also won fame as a preacher. His eloquent defense of orthodoxy brought temporary banishment under pro-Arian Emperor Valens. St. John Chrysostom (d. 407), who won his second name (golden-mouthed or golden-tongued) by his skill as an orator, has more surviving works than any other Eastern Father. Chrysostom was very effective in promoting Christian life, both as a priest at Antioch and as Archbishop of Constantinople. For his fearlessness, he incurred the opposition of lax clergy and brazen sinners among the laity, such as the Empress Eudoxia, with the result that he was deposed and twice banished, dying on the second arduous journey into exile.

The Western Fathers: Sts. Hilary and Ambrose

The Western Fathers of the Church, who wrote in Latin, were more practical than theoretical—with the exception of St. Augustine, the greatest of them all. The earliest of the great Western Fathers was St. Hilary of Poitiers (d. 368), who had spent some time in the East, where he imbibed the doctrines of the Eastern Fathers, which he transmitted to the West. With Pope Liberius, Hilary stoutly combated Arianism. He composed valuable theological works, including one *On the Trinity*, and expounded the Scriptures in a direct, literal manner. St. Ambrose, son of the Praetorian Prefect of Gaul, became, at an early age, Governor of Milan. During a tumultuous election in that strife-torn see, he was enthusiastically acclaimed archbishop by the congregation. In the latter capacity, Ambrose (d. 368) whose city had become the imperial residence in the West, became the leading spokesman of the Western Church. He asserted clerical authority, curbed incipient Caesaropapism, and sternly rebuked the moral transgressions of Emperor Theodosius the Great. The door of his study was ever open to members of his flock, and he helped to effect the conversion of St. Augustine. He composed beautiful hymns to attract the faithful who were being enticed away by the music of the Arians. Among his exegetical and moral works was one on *Offices,* modeled on that of Cicero, but written from a Christian viewpoint.

Sts. Jerome and Gregory the Great

After receiving an excellent education, which included thorough study of both Latin and Greek languages and literatures, St. Jerome (d. 240) withdrew to the Syrian desert, where he practiced extreme asceticism. On being ordained a priest, Jerome became secretary to Pope Damasus, who urged him to undertake a Latin translation of the Bible. Jerome first translated the New Testament from Greek, and then withdrew to Palestine, where he steeled himself to the task of further mastering Hebrew and translating the Old Testament. His excellent translation, which took twenty years, became the standard "common" version or *Vulgate* of the Western Church. Jerome is also noted for promotion of monasticism for women as well as men, for rebuttal of various heresies, and for his scathing criticism of abuses in the Church.

Besides further building up the organization of the Western Church, and promoting its expansion, Gregory I, the Great (d. 604), was the author of important practical religious writings. In his *Pastoral Care,* he provided a guide for those who were entrusted with the guidance of souls; in his *Dialogues,* he told interesting and edifying stories concerning the lives of the saints, one of which was his famous *Life of St. Benedict;* and in his *Moralia,* he inculcated Christian ethics and asceticism through a commentary on the Book of Job. All his works were very popular and influential during the Middle Ages.

St. Augustine

The most illustrious and doctrinally influential of the Western Fathers was St. Augustine of Hippo (d. 430). Medieval ecclesiastical libraries in the West were full of his books. After studies at Carthage and Rome, in the course of which he alternated between sensuous abandon and the quest for knowledge and enduring satisfaction, Augustine became a teacher of rhetoric at Milan. Meanwhile he kept a mistress by whom he had a son. He sought enlightenment, first in Manichaeanism and then in Neo-Platonism, but found satisfaction in neither. Eventually he was converted to the Christian way of life by the prayers of his mother, St. Monica, the influence of St. Ambrose of Milan, and the writings of St. Paul. After practicing a form of monasticism, Augustine became a priest and later Bishop of Hippo.

In refuting the various heresies that plagued North Africa in his day, St. Augustine developed explanations which became a primary source for Church doctrines on key problems such as grace, faith, and the Trinity, among others. Against the Manichaeans, Augustine taught that evil is only the absence of good. Against the Pelagians, he explained the effects of original sin, the necessity of divine grace, and the nature of Divine Providence. Against the Donatists, he demonstrated that the sacraments instituted by Christ confer grace by virtue of the acts performed, provided the recipient has the proper disposition, and independently of the state of the minister's soul. In refutation of Christological errors, Augustine explained that orthodox doctrines concerning the Trinity and Incarnation are reasonable, although still mysteries: not contrary to reason, but still unknowable without the aid of revelation. In his *City of God* Augustine explained that the true, eternal divine city is that of the good as opposed to that of the wicked. Secular catastrophes such as the sack of Rome do not affect the true city of God, which is spiritual. St. Augustine who explained Christianity in terms acceptable to reason, has always been the leading Patristic authority of the Western Church.

A problem that bothered many early Christians was that of the proper Christian attitude toward pagan literature and learning. Was not pagan literature filled with allusions to pagan deities and concepts contrary to Christian teachings? And was not pagan philosophy likewise corrupt with errors and devoid of supernatural vision? At very least, were they not both frivolous distractions from essential religious interests: the "vanity of vanities and universal vanity" condemned by the Book of Ecclesiastes (1:2)?

Early Christianity and pagan literature and learning

Since many passages in both Old and New Testaments may be interpreted as condemning concern with pagan learning and literature, a rigorist attitude was adopted by some of the early Christians. The outburst of Tertullian is famous: "What has Athens to do with Jerusalem? . . . Away with all attempts to produce a mottled Christianity, of Stoic, Platonic, and dialectical composition!" While Jerome was practicing great physical austerities in the desert, but continuing his affection for the classics, he had a dream in which Christ sorrowfully chided him, "Thou art a Ciceronian rather than a Christian. Where thy treasure is, there also is thy heart!" Pope Gregory I reproached Bishop Desiderius of Vienne for "holding conferences on ancient literature," admonishing him: "The same lips cannot sound the praises of Jupiter and those of Christ. How seriously improper is it for a bishop to sing what is ill-suited even for a religious layman. . . ."

But such was not the prevailing opinion. Nor was it the actual practice of the Fathers. Tertullian was mainly inveighing against the extreme syncretism that becomes heretical. Jerome continued to use and quote the classics, which he also taught. After all a dream is only a dream! Pope Gregory was mainly concerned with the precedence of weighty pastoral responsibilities, for in his estimation, the Bishop of Vienne had more important things to do than to teach the classics. While the Church Fathers maintained that classical literature and learning were to be approached only with caution and moderation, they also accepted such studies as normal and necessary. Indeed, the fact that they became Church Fathers was largely due to their mastery of pagan learning.

Joint employment of Christian revelation and pagan learning, in which St. Paul was a trail-blazer, was also seen in the works of early Apologists, such as Justin Martyr and Minucius Felix in the second century, and the Catechists such as Clement of Alexandria and Origen in the third century. Justin Martyr tried to show the essential agreement between the Greek philosophers and Christian teachings. Clement of Alexandria said that Greek learning was a "pedagogue" conducting man to Christ. Origen utilized Greek philosophy and learning in interpreting Christianity, and his student St. Gregory Thaumaturgus, who became a Father of the

Church, said: "No subject is forbidden to us." St. John Chrysostom urged that classical education be combined with Christian moral training and said: "Shall we raze the schools to the ground? That is not what I am saying, but neither should we destroy the dwelling place of virtue or bury the living soul."

St. Basil the Great endorsed pagan learning as a tool. In a letter to his former master, the pagan Libanius, he exclaimed: "O Muses, O learning, O Athens, what do you not give to those who love you!" St. Gregory Nazianzus said: "I hold nothing dearer on earth than learning, next to the joys of heaven and the hope of eternity."

In the West, as in the East, the Fathers of the Church were all men of considerable learning. St. Augustine, who had been a teacher of oratory and literature and a devotee of philosophy, said that the Christians should take what was good from the ancients and leave what was not, even as the Hebrews, in forsaking "the fleshpots of Egypt" had "despoiled the Egyptians."

Christianity on the eve of the Middle Ages

By the close of antiquity the Christian Church was ready for its key role in the Middle Ages. Despite two and a half centuries of persecution, Christianity had become the ascendant religion in the Roman Empire so that the terms "Roman" and "Christian" were virtually synonymous. Christianity was the official religion of the state, and the Christian clergy enjoyed extensive privileges. The organization of the Church was well developed. The Bishop of Rome (Pope) was recognized as having primacy in the Church, as were the Patriarchs in their respective regions, while the bishops were accepted as authoritative rulers of Christian communities. The doctrines of the Church were clearly defined, and all major divergent teachings except Monophysitism had been overcome. Solutions had been worked out for practical problems such as relations of church and state, warfare and slavery, sex and matrimony, traditional social and religious observances, and pagan literature and learning. Leaders in the Church had accepted classical culture and maintained both that the study of classical languages and literature was salutary and that the highest ideals of pagan philosophy were not contrary to the tenets of Christianity. The foundations for the Middle Ages as "the Era of the Church" were firmly established.

References for Chapter 2

GOOD general histories of the Church and Christianity include KARL BIHLMEYER and H. TÜCHLE, *Church History*, tr. V. MILLS and F. MULLER, 3 vols. (Westminster, Md.: Newman, 1958–66); PHILIP HUGHES, *History of the Church*, vol. I (New York: Sheed and Ward, 1934ff.); FERNAND MOURRET, A *History of the Catholic Church*, tr. NEWTON THOMPSON, vols. I and II (St. Louis: Herder, 1930ff.); PHILIP SCHAFF, *History of the Christian Church*, vols. I, II, and III (Grand Rapids: Erdmans, 1949–50); and THOMAS P. NEILL and RAYMOND H. SCHMANDT, *History of the Catholic Church* (Milwaukee: Bruce, 1957). Well-chosen collections of select historical documents are JEDIN HUBERT and J. DOLAN, eds., *Handbook of Church History* (to ca. A.D. 1500), 4 vols. (New York: Herder and Herder, 1965–70); HENRY BETTENSON, *Documents of the Christian Church* (Oxford: Oxford U.P., 1947); and COLMAN J. BARRY, ed., *Readings* in *Church History*, 3 vols. (Westminster, Md.: Newman, 1960–65).

Competing religions at the coming of Christianity are surveyed by SAMUEL ANGUS, *The Mystery Religions and Christianity* (New York: Scribners, 1925); TERROT R. GLOVER, *The Conflict of Religions in the Early Roman Empire* (London: Methuen, 1909); FRANZ CUMONT, *The Oriental Religious in Roman Paganism* (Chicago: Open Court, 1911); and FRANZ CUMONT, *The Mysteries of Mithra*, tr. T. J. McCORMACK (London: KEGAN PAUL, 1903).

Special works devoted to early Christianity include JULES LEBRETON and J. ZEILLER, *History of the Primitive Church*, tr. E. C. MESSENGER, 4 vols. (London: Burns 1946–48); LOUIS M. O. DUCHESNE, *Early History of the Christian Church*, tr. 3 vols. (New York: Longmans, 1909–1924); ERNEST W. BARNES, *The Rise of Christianity* (first two centuries) (London: Longmans, 1947); the well-written ROLAND A. BAINTON, *Early Christianity* (Princeton: Van Nostrand, 1960); the strongly rational HANS LIETZMANN, *History of the Early Church*, tr. B. L. WOLF, 4 vols. (London: Lutterworth, 1955); the clear and scholarly HENRY M. GWATKIN, *Early Church History* . . . , 2 vols. (London: Macmillan, 1909); the topical Oscar Cullmann, *The Early Church*, ed. A. J. B. HIGGINS (London: S. C. M. Press, 1956); the more specialized KENNETH SCOTT LATOURETTE, *History of the Expansion of Christianity*, vol. I: *The First Five Centuries* (New York: Harper, 1937); *The Pre-Nicene Church* . . . (London: Burns, 1935); and the excellent JEAN DANIELOU and H. M. MARROU, *The First Six Hundred Years* (New York: McGraw-Hill, 1964); together with HENRI DANIEL-ROPS, *The Church of Apostles and Martyrs* (New York: Dutton, ca. 1960).

The triumphs of Christianity and the Church in the fourth and fifth centuries are described by MAUDE A. HUTTMAN, *The Establishment of Christianity and the Proscription of Paganism* (New York: Columbia University, 1914); ANDREAS ALFOLDI, *The Conversion of Constantine* . . . (Oxford: Clarendon, 1949); ARTHUR H. M. JONES, *Constantine and the Conversion of Europe* (New York: Macmillan, 1949); JACOB BURCKHARDT, *The Age of Constantine the Great* (New York: Doubleday, 1956); the introductory ERWIN R. GOODENOUGH, *The Church in the Roman Empire* (New York: Holt, 1931); and the more detailed JEAN R. PALENQUE et al., *The Church in the Christian Roman Empire*, tr. E. MESSENGER, 2 vols. in one (New York: Macmillan, 1953). For Church and State in the later Roman Empire see the introductory part of SIDNEY Z. EHLER and JOHN B. MORRALL, *Church and State Through the Centuries* (Westminster, Md.: NEWMAN, 1954); and the final part of PALANQUE et al: as cited). A good biography of Constantine among several is that of LLOYD B. HOLSAPPLE, *Constantine the Great* (New York: Sheed and Ward, 1942).

The organization and institutions of the Early Church are the subject of EDWIN HATCH, *Organization of the Early Christian Churches* . . . (London: Longmans, 1907); JAMES A. CORBETT, *The Papacy* . . . (Princeton: Van Nostrand, 1956); JOHN CHAPMAN, *Studies on the Early Papacy* (London: Sheed and Ward, 1928) and FREDERICK J. FOAKES-JACKSON, *Peter, Prince of the Apostles: A Study in the History and Tradition of Christianity* (New York: Doran, ca. 1927); and CHARLES J. HEFELE, *A History of the Councils of the Church*, vols. I–III of 5 vols. (Edinburgh: Clark, 1896); as well as ROBERT V. SELLERS, *The Council of Chalcedon* (London: SPCK, 1953). Also useful is BERTHOLD ALTANER, *Patrology*, tr. H. C. GRAEF (New

York: Herder and Herder, ca. 1960).

Early monasticism is treated in the classic CHARLES F. MONTALEMBERT, *The Monks of the West* . . . , vol. I of 7 vols. (London: Blackwood, 1896); HERBERT B. WORKMAN, *Evolution of the Monastic Ideal* (London: Epworth, 1913 and Boston: Beacon, 1962); and HELEN J. WADDELL, *Vitae Patrum: The Desert Fathers: Translations* . . . (New York: Holt, 1936).

The doctrines and ideology of the early Church are treated by JOHN H. NEWMAN, *Essay on the Development of Christian Doctrine* (New York: Longmans, 1890); HENRY O. TAYLOR, *Ancient Ideals* . . . , vol. II (New York: Macmillan, 1930); FULBERT CAYRÉ, *Manual of Patrology and History of Theology*, vol. I (Paris: Desclée, 1936); and JOHANNES QUASTEN, *Patrology*, vols. I–III (Westminster, Md.: NEWMAN, 1950–1960). Particular Fathers are treated by the pithy, clear EUGENE DE FAYE, *Origen and His Work*, tr. F. ROTHWELL (New York: Columbia U.P., 1929); the concise PIERRE C. DE LABRIOLLE, *Life and Times of St. Ambrose*, tr. H. WILSON (St. Louis: Herder, 1928); the extended FREDERICK H. DUDDEN, *Life and Times of St. Ambrose*, 2 vols. Oxford: Clarendon, 1953); the readable VERNON J. BOURKE, *Augustine's Quest of Wisdon* . . . (Bruce: Milwaukee, 1945); the excellent PETER R. BROWN, *Augustine of Hippo* . . . (Berkeley: University of California, 1967); the evaluative HENRI I. MARROU, *Saint Augustine and His Influence* . . . (New York: Harper, 1957); the appreciative TREVOR JALLAND, *Life and Times of St. Leo the Great* (London: S.P.C.K., 1941); and the compact PIERRE BATIFFOL, *Saint Gregory the Great*, tr. J. L. STODDARD (London: Burns, 1929).

Relations of early Christianity and pagan classical culture are the subject of MAX L. W. LAISTNER, *Christianity and Pagan Culture in the Later Roman World* . . . (Ithaca: Cornell, 1951); the introductory Book I of GUSTAV SCHNÜRER, *Church and Culture in the Middle Ages*, tr. (Paterson, N. J.: St. Anthony Guild, 1956); PIERRE C. DE LABRIOLLE, *History and Literature of Christianity from Tertullian to Boethius*, tr. HERBERT WILSON (London: K. Paul, 1924); ARTHUR C. MCGIFFERT, *A History of Christian Thought* . . . , 2 vols. (New York: Scribners, 1932–33); and EDWARD K. RAND, *Founders of the Middle Ages* (Cambridge, Mass.: Harvard, 1929).

Among primary sources for early Christianity are *The New Testament* (available in several translations and editions); Eusebius of Caesarea, *Ecclesiastical History*, tr. KIRSOPP LAKE, 2 vols. (London: Heinemann, 1932), and tr. G. A. WILLIAMSON (New York: University, 1966); *The Ante-Nicene Fathers*, ed. ALEXANDER ROBERTS et al., new ed., 10 vols. (New York: Scribners 1911–1919); and PHILIP SCHAFF et al., *Select Library of the Nicene and Post-Nicene Fathers* (Series I), 14 vols. (New York: Christian Literature Co., 1886–1890), and Series II, 14 vols. (New York: Christian Literature Co., 1890–1900); and more recently, *The Fathers of the Church: A New Translation*, ed. L. SCHOOP et al., several vols. (New York: Cima, 1947ff.). This also includes *Early Christian Biographies*, ed. ROY J. DEFERRARI (Washington: Catholic University, 1952). Works of the particular Fathers such as St. Augustine are published in various translations and editions. An excellent one-volume collection of sources is DAVID AYERST and A. FISHER, eds., *Records of Christianity*, vol. I, *In the Roman Empire* (New York: Barnes and Noble, 1971).

The Barbarian Background

[THE BARBARIAN BACKGROUND   Chapter 3.

HE BARBARIANS, who were a third component of medieval Europe, deserve more attention and respect than they usually receive. Although, by the close of antiquity, they had not yet reached the stage known as "civilization," they had achieved considerable progress. The European barbarians were generally in a condition similar to that of people in the advanced New Stone Age, with domesticated animals, agriculture, textiles, and pottery, although they were already technologically in the more progressive Iron Age. Most of them were of the Caucasoid or White race and spoke Indo-European languages, as did their civilized European counterparts. From time to time Mongoloid barbarians from Asia invaded Europe through the Ural Gateway.

THE EUROPEAN BARBARIANS.
Section 7.

They have an abundance of cattle and grain . . . but . . . they live side by side in disunion. [Byzantine Emperor MAURICE referring to the Slavs (sixth century).]

AT THE close of antiquity, barbarians still occupied the two thirds of Europe beyond the Rhine and Danube. Among the barbarians, the tall, fair, long-headed Nordic type predominated in northwestern Europe, and the moderate-statured, medium-complexioned, round-headed Alpine type in central Europe. Most of the short, dark, long-headed Mediterranean type of people in southern Europe were already civilized. Miscellaneous variant and intermediate types were interspersed.

Europe's prevailing languages (then as now) seem to have been derived from a common Proto-Indo-European stem, possibly formed from pre-existing elements about 3500 to 3000 B.C. It is commonly supposed that an early homeland of the proto-Indo-European speakers was in the neighborhood of the Caucasus Mountains (cp. "Caucasoid"), whence they migrated southward into southwestern Asia and westward across Europe.   *The Indo-European languages*

The kinship of Indo-European languages can be seen in common words such as those for relatives, for parts of the body, and for numbers. Thus English "mother," "foot," and "three," are obviously related to the German "*Mutter,*" "*Fuss,*" and "*drei,*" as well as to the Latin "*mater,*" "*pes,*" and "*tres,*" and the Sanskrit "*mata,*" "*pat,*" and "*trayas.*" The relationship becomes more evident when one considers the interchangeability between the explosive consonants *f*, *p*, and *v*, as in English "*father,*" German "*Vater,*" and Latin "*pater,*" or English "*fish,*" German "*Fisch,*" and Latin "*piscis.*"

Among the Indo-European languages, the Asia groups include Indo-

Aryan, Median, Persian-Iranian, Armenian, Scythian, and Sarmatian. Among the European groups, the Greco-Latin includes classical Greek and Latin, together with the modern Romance languages of Italian, French, Spanish, Portuguese, Albanian, Rumanian, and (modern) Greek. The Celtic group includes Irish, Welsh, Highland Scotch, and Breton. In the Teutonic groups are German, Danish, Norwegian, Swedish, Dutch, Frisian, Flemish, English and Lowland Scotch. In the Slavic group are Russian, Ruthenian, Czech, Slovak, Serbian, Croatian, Slovene, Montenegrian and Polish. The Lettic (or Baltic) includes Lettish and Lithuanian.

The Indo-European speaking barbarians

From their original homeland, which may have been in southern Russia or western Turkestan in the vicinity of the Caucasus Mountains, Indo-European speaking peoples migrated westward across Europe and southeastward into southwest Asia, beginning about 2000 B.C. Their conquests were facilitated by hardy physiques and salutary social mores, as well as by the fact that they were pastoral and warlike, as opposed to the more sedentary and pacific agricultural peoples already occupying much of Europe. The Indo-Europeans early learned to use both iron and horses in warfare, which gave them tremendous military advantages.

Among the Indo-Europeans who fanned out to the west, the Greeks and the Latins moved into Mediterranean lands, where they became highly civilized. The Celtic-speaking peoples occupied northern Italy, the Iberian Peninsula, Gaul, and the British Isles, where many of them were civilized by the Romans in the interval from the second century B.C. to the first century of the Christian era. But the remaining Indo-Europeans of Europe were still barbarians, although in many cases well advanced. These Indo-European barbarians at the close of antiquity included the Germans, Balts, and Slavs, and a small independent Celtic fringe in the northwest.

Proto-Indo-European culture traits

Proto-Indo-European culture traits—those of the early Indo-Europeans prior to their dispersion—constituted a general least-common-denominator base for most of the peoples of Europe; some, such as the Balts, had not progressed far beyond this original condition. The Proto-Indo-Europeans were in the Neolithic (New Stone) Age of technological development, but on the brink of the Iron Age. Among the variegated tools of the proto-Indo-Europeans were handled and holed stone hatchets, axes, hammers, and stone knives, as well as wooden plows, harrows, and sickles. In addition to stone-headed hatchets and axes, their armory included stone and wooden daggers, swords, spears, lances, bows and arrows, and shields. They had pottery, but originally lacked the potter's wheel. They did weaving and sewing, made clothes and shoes, and used various personal ornaments, such as brooches and buckles.

The main economic activity of these early Indo-Europeans seems to have been pastoral. They kept various domesticated animals, such as sheep, oxen, goats, swine, dogs, and horses. That the horse held a very important place among them is indicated by the ritual of the horse sacrifice. At the same time, they also had agriculture and cultivated cereal grains such as barley and rye, as well as beans, lentils, and spelt, and flax and hemp. They were active and efficient hunters and fishers, using bows and arrows, spears, and traps in hunting, and harpoons, fishhooks, and nets in fishing. For transportation on land they used horses and carts with two wheels and a shaft. On rivers they employed rowboats; but they apparently had no word for the sea.

The early Indo-Europeans lived in walled or fortified villages, often located on eminences, with a strong place (like a citadel) for refuge in time of danger. They dwelt in huts or cabins of wicker, mud, or logs, sometimes partly excavated. Their simple dwellings, which lacked chimneys, had open fireplaces. They wore diverse articles of clothing, including coats, kilts, aprons, cloaks, and shoes. They wove both woolen and linen cloths, which they tailored and sewed. Their diet included ground grain, baked bread, cooked (e.g., grilled) meats, soups, salt, and an alcoholic drink (mead) from fermented honey. Their society, like that of other pastoral peoples among whom herding and fighting were prominent activities, was patrilinear—i.e., tracing descent in the male line. Their social common unit was a family-clan group consisting of at least three generations. They were evidently monogamous and had marriage ceremonies. They held private property and calculated wealth in terms of cattle.

Their political organization was tribal and quasi-democratic. Important decisions were made by councils of adult males. Justice was rendered by community judgments. They had recognized laws and moral standards and employed oaths and indemnities in the administration of justice. Their religion was a simple, polytheistic deification of natural forces. They worshiped nature-gods, among whom the sky god (*Jupiter, Zeus, Dyaus, Tiu*) was dominant. They had concepts of sin and retribution, made sacrifices and offerings to the deity, and maintained a holy hearth-fire. They calculated time by means of the solar year and lunar months, as well as by successive seasons, although they did not have a period corresponding to the week.

The Celts

Although the early Celts may have been proto-Nordic—tall, fair, and long-headed—they soon intermingled with the peoples they conquered and lost any such racial identity. As early as the second millenium B.C., the Celts seem to have been established in western Germany and the upper Danubian area. The Celts obtained the use of iron quite soon, and from about 1000 to 500 B.C. they were in the "Hallstatt" phase of iron culture (so-called from the finds in the vicinity of this Austrian town). A characteristic product of this age was the "great Hallstatt sword"—a large, heavy, double-edged iron weapon.

About 500 B.C., the Celts entered upon a new phase of more advanced culture and iron technology, known as "La Tene" from finds in Switzerland. Aided by improved arms and armor, as well as by other factors, the Celts now expanded over Gaul, northern Italy, the Iberian Peninsula, and the British Isles. In northern Italy they were known as Cisalpine Gauls. In Spain and Portugal the resultant intermixture came to be known as "Celtiberians." Successive waves of Celts also completed their occupation of the British Isles. The greatest period of Celtic expansion was from about 500 to about 250 B.C. In the period from the second century B.C. to the first century of the Christian era, the Romans conquered and subjected most of the Celts. Yet there still remained an independent Celtic fringe in Ireland, Wales, and Scotland.

Celtic culture traits

Despite their extraordinary expansion, the Celts never united politically and still consisted of numerous self-sufficient, sovereign tribes. Their identity was linguistic and cultural rather than political, although from time to time, they formed temporary, loose confederations. It is estimated that there were about sixty separate Celtic tribes or peoples in Gaul at the time of Caesar's conquest. The territory of each tribe was usually defined by boundary markers, such as stones, hedges, or posts, and each had its principal village or town. The latter was usually constructed on a natural or artificial hill for purposes of security, but sometimes on an island, as in the case of Paris, and sometimes even in the midst of marshes, as was Avaricum. The settlement was often surrounded by a wall and a ditch. In addition, there was a stronger fort or citadel for further refuge in time of danger. By the time the Romans subjected them, the Celts, like the Romans themselves, were dominated by a wealthy aristocracy, although their earlier condition was probably more equalitarian.

Both the Greeks and the Romans praised the Celts as brave, spirited, and freedom-loving. Their common military tactic was first to hurl their javelins and then to charge and engage their enemy in close combat with the sword. The Celts were skilled artisans. They made excellent iron swords, daggers, and helmets. From baser metals such as copper, as well as more precious ones such as gold, they fashioned numerous beautiful ornaments—brooches, torques, clasps, bracelets, and rings. They produced fine textiles and superior dyes. They made and wore trousers—the word *breeches* comes from Celtic. They were also expert leatherworkers, noted for their superb harness, and a special form of Celtic boot, called *caliga*, which became fashionable with the Romans. The notorious Emperor Caligula acquired his nickname as a boy from his little boots. The Celts produced numerous and varied, highly decorated, ingenious forms of pottery. They were famous for their manufacture of wheeled vehicles, such as chariots, wagons, two-wheeled gigs, four-wheeled carriages, and heavy traveling coaches. Some of these—the *cissum, carruca,* and *rheda*—were adopted, with their Celtic names, by the Romans. For water transportation they had both rowboats and sailboats.

By the time of Roman expansion, the Celts were settled agriculturalists. Private property in land was well established. Celtic society was stratified, and the local aristocracy, with whom the Romans cooperated, was usually ascendant. The Celts worshiped Gods connected with natural forces and objects, occasionally offering human sacrifices. Their citadels were often constructed atop hills (natural or artificial) where they had the tombs (*tumuli*) of their dead. They are described by their Greco-Roman contemporaries as lighthearted and voluble, idealistic and valorous. Honor was high on their list of virtues.

The Barbarian Background

Among the Celts a special class known as "druids" constituted an honored, international, learned fraternity. The druids were the acknowledged custodians of Celtic traditions and lore, secular and religious. They were declarers of the law, both human and divine, counselors and teachers concerning the visible and invisible worlds. To what extent (if any) they were judges and priests has been disputed. Ireland seems to have been a center par excellence for druidical education, especially after the druids were outlawed as subversive by the Romans. The druids have been described as "the cement of Celtic society."

The Celts also had bards, who were skilled in the composition of poetry accompanied by music. A characteristic Celtic musical instrument was the harp, and a characteristic poetic device the use of rhyme. They had epic poems and enjoyed dramatic representations. They at first measured time by the moon, but later coordinated this with solar time. In art, they were noted for their swirling, scroll-type linear decorations with frequent fantastic animal and human forms.

The Slavs

Beyond the Celts and the Germans—of whom more presently—were the Slavs, the least advanced of the major groups of Indo-European barbarians. The comparatively backward condition of the Slavs was partly due to their more remote, landlocked position, although Slavic deficiencies should not be exaggerated. Many, at least, of the early Slavs seem to have been proto-Nordic, i.e., tall and long-headed; but their features were soon modified by intermarriage with other peoples, so that their descendants were often more broad-headed and shorter. The early home of the Slavs seems to have been in the vicinity of the upper Vistula, Dniester, and Dnieper Rivers, in the neighborhood of the marshlands of the Pripet river. From this territory, which may have included the Vistula basin and much of that of the Oder, the Slavs eventually expanded in all directions.

In the process of their expansion the Slavs differentiated into three main groups: western, southern, and eastern. This diversification was partly due to geographic separation, partly to amalgamation with peoples found in particular areas, and partly to intruders such as the Avars and Magyars, who cut off one group from the other. A subsequent differentiating factor was the conversion of the western Slavs to the western form of Christianity, and that of the southern and eastern Slavs to the eastern form.

By the middle of the sixth century after Christ, the western Slavs were in the territory between the upper Dniester and the Elbe; the southern Slavs were already in the Danube Valley and the region of the Drave and Save Rivers and were beginning to invade the Balkans; and the east Slavs were located between the Dnieper and Don Rivers.

Culture traits of the early Slavs

While the early Slavs were still very close to the proto-Indo-Europeans in their way of life, they had progressed in various ways. For cultural radiations had gradually reached them from more advanced neighbors, such as the Scythians and Sarmatians to the south and the Germans to the west. Numerous words derived from the German indicate a great Slavic debt to their Teutonic neighbors.

Politically, the early Slavs were divided into numerous small, independent, tribal and municipal states. Tribes, in turn, were subdivided into clans and the latter into families. A typical economic unit was the semicommunal rural community. The early Slavic system of government and justice seems to have been semidemocratic, although their clans were ruled by chiefs (*zupans*), and their tribes by great chiefs (grand *zupans*). Kings did not begin to appear until the later fourth century when the word for this office and terms for justice, fines, and tolls seem to have derived from the German. They had a popular assembly or court known as a *duma*, and Byzantine writers in the sixth century stress their independent, democratic ways. Procopius says that they are "not ruled by a monarch, but have lived from the earliest times in 'democracy,' and so deliberate together concerning all their affairs. . . ." Maurice says that they are "kingless and hostile to one another."

Although Greek and Byzantine writers remark on the valor of the early Slavs and their love of freedom, some authors represent them as comparatively peaceful, mild, and easily managed. There is considerable evidence that this was not entirely so. They frequently raided their more advanced neighbors. Their tractability may have been due to their frequently helpless condition when confronted by more advanced adversaries. In military matters the Slavs lagged considerably behind the Germans, from whom they apparently derived words for "sword," "battle-axe," "helmet," and "armed band." For protection, they lived in moated villages, and their primitive fortresses were known as "*grads*."

The Slavs raised a wide variety of grains, fruits, and vegetables, and kept numerous domesticated animals. The fertile river valleys they inhabited were admirably adapted to agriculture, which was often practiced in a semicommunal manner. The same great rivers became arteries of trade with Greek settlements and outposts of the Roman Empire. The Slavs did much trapping and were skilled in the preparation of furs. They kept bees, from whose honey they produced mead. Prominent among their exports were beeswax and honey, as well as furs.

Their predominantly agricultural pursuits, the rigors of their climate, and their frequent subjection by more advanced neighbors gave many of the Slavs a certain stolidity and patience which made them particularly desirable as slaves. Because of their backwardness and political fragmentation, the early Slavs were easy prey for slavehunters. During the Middle Ages, Slavic lands became a leading source for slaves, so that their name became synonymous with this unfree condition.

Before marriage, the Slavs permitted considerable sexual freedom and even promiscuity, although after marriage they insisted on strict monogamy, at least on the part of their women. Wives sometimes committed suicide after the husband's death. In addition to being polytheistic, some of the Slavs had temples in which they worshipped idols, possibly imported from the Near East. Early writers describe the Slavs as lighthearted and pleasure-loving, hospitable and friendly, and great lovers of song and dance, with exceptional musical skills.

The Barbarian Background

Other Indo-European-speaking groups in Europe included the Balts, Scythians, Sarmatians, Thracians, Illyrians, and Ligurians. Of these, by the close of antiquity, only the Balts were unsubjected, the others having largely lost their independence and identity. The early Balts, whose name apparently means "white," occupied territory southeast of the Baltic Sea. They expanded and eventually included the Letts, the Lithuanians, and the Old Prussians. The Balts were similar in culture traits to the early southern Slavs, but probably less advanced. Their history has been largely a corollary to that of their more powerful German and Slavic neighbors, to whom they have often been subject.

Other barbarians in Europe

Scattered examples of Uralic- and Altaic-speaking barbarians, whose linguistic groups were originally associated with western and central Asia, existed alongside the prevailing Indo-European-speaking barbarians in Europe. The so-called Uralic languages derive their name from the Urals on the European-Asiatic frontier and are subdivided into Finnic and Ugric. Finnic-speaking peoples were more westerly and Caucasoid, Ugric-speaking more easterly and Mongoloid. The former often lived more by hunting and fishing, and the latter more by pastoral activities. The Ugric-speaking peoples included the ancestors of the Magyars and Bulgars, together with the Siberian Ostiaks and Voguls.

The Altaic-speaking barbarians, whose name derives from the Altai Mountains of Central Asia, were more definitely Mongoloid. Among Altaic speakers who successively invaded Europe during late antiquity were the Huns and the Volga Bolgars or Bulgars of eastern Russia (not to be confused with the Danubian Bulgars). Among Altaic speakers who invaded Europe during the Middle Ages were various Turks, the Petchenegs[a] and Cumans, the Mongols and Tatars (Tartars)—a combination of Turks and Mongols, and finally the Ottoman Turks.

[a] Or Pechenegs.

The Altaian invaders of Europe were generally warlike pastoral nomads, whose early homeland was on the great steppes of central Asia, where they herded their animals on horseback. They were inured to hardships and strife and were expert horsemen, highly proficient with the bow and lance. From time to time they erupted from the Asiatic steppes to plunder more civilized peoples.

THE EARLY GERMANS.
Section 8.

> Next after the Celtic tribes come the Germans, who inhabit the country to the east beyond the Rhine. The Germans differ but little from the Celtic race, save in their being fiercer, taller, and blonder. [STRABO concerning the early Germans in his *Geography* (first century of the Christian era).]

OF THE various Indo-European-speaking barbarians, the most important for medieval history were the Germanic (Teutonic) group. After the Romans completed their subjection of the Celts on the continent, the Germans were their immediate neighbors. The warlike Germans eventually overran most of the Roman Empire in Europe in addition to retaining much of the territory they already occupied beyond the Rhine and the Danube. As a result, the "new Europe" of the Early Middle Ages became primarily an amalgam of Germanic, Roman, and Christian elements.

Sources of information

Our principal sources concerning the early Germans are Roman writers. In the first century B.C., Julius Caesar in his *Gallic Wars* devoted some four to five pages (in modern English translation) to the Germanic barbarians. The most important written source concerning the early Germans, however, is Caius Cornelius Tacitus, whose succinct, informative *Germania* runs to thirty-seven pages of English translation and describes "The Geography, Manners, Customs, and Tribes of Germany." Although Tacitus evidently obtained much of his information at second hand, his account seems substantially correct, and much of what he says has been confirmed by subsequent research. It has been charged that Tacitus, who was critical of contemporary Roman political apathy and moral laxity, exaggerates contrasting German virtues. Yet what he says about their assemblies and voting, as well as their insistence on certain moral virtues, fits in with what we know about other later uncivilized Teutonic peoples. Furthermore, Tacitus does not conceal shortcomings of the Germans, such as their frequent unbridled drunkenness, gambling, and violence. Other Roman and Greek writers of the imperial period also make brief references to the Teutonic barbarians.

Conditions among the Anglo-Saxons and Scandinavians prior to their Christianization and civilization presumably reflected those of the early Germans. Important sources shedding light on the early Germanic barbarians are epics such as *Beowulf* and the *Sagas*. Much valuable information is also provided by archeological finds—weapons, implements, utensils, pottery, parts of boats and wagons, carving, and fabrics. Finally, we have the evidence of many deep-rooted Germanic customs, which survived in historic times, such as their ordeals, *wergelds*, sworn allegiance to a chief, and so on.

Identity of the early Germans

The name Germans was used in reference to these peoples by the Roman writers Caesar, Plutarch, and Tacitus. The terms *Teuton* and *Deutsch* did not enter common use until the eighth to ninth centuries of the Christian era, when the Latin word *theotiscus* or *teutiscus* and the German *deutsch* or *diutisk*, both probably deriving from a German root (*thiot, thiod, theoda*) meaning "people," came to be applied to the Germanic vernacular language and the people themselves.

The early Germans were of the White or Caucasoid race and the Indo-European linguistic family. As described by Roman authors they were obviously Nordic—tall, large-boned, and fair-complexioned, with blond or reddish hair, and blue eyes. The Germans of these early authors may have been direct descendants of proto-Indo-Europeans, influenced by a northern climate and as yet unmixed with other strains. But the expanding Germans soon became racially mixed by intermarriage with other peoples, and they also changed under the influence of new environments.

The Barbarian Background

Following the dispersion of the Indo-Europeans, the early home of the Germanic peoples seems to have been in the region west of the Baltic and east of the North Sea, which included southern Sweden, Denmark, northern Germany, and adjacent islands. Jordanes, writing of the Germanic Goths in the sixth center after Christ, obviously echoes an ancient tradition when he traces them back to *Scandza* (Scandinavia) as the *officina gentium*, the factory of the nations. It is possible that the early Germans established themselves in the northern area as early as 1000 B.C., bringing with them an Iron Age culture. Expanding from an early date, they spread northward into southern Norway and the Lake district of Sweden. To the southeast they occupied the area between the Oder and the Vistula.

Early German home and movements

After the great Celtic expansion, which slowed down by about 250 B.C., the Germans assumed the offensive, especially as the Celts seem to have been gradually assimilated by the peaceful, more agricultural, peoples they subjected. By the first century B.C., the Germans had occupied the extensive territory between the Rhine and the Vistula; and by the third century of the Christian era, they had also taken over the lands between the Danube and the Don. Meanwhile, any special racial characteristics they may have possessed probably began to change, owing partly to intermixture with indigenous peoples.

When the Romans first came into contact with them, the Germans were subdivided into numerous tribes. In the first century after Christ, Tacitus mentions about forty-five separate tribes, and in the following century Ptolemy estimates that there were about seventy different tribes. These tribes were very fluid in movement and of varying names. By the time of the great invasions comparatively few names remained, and these usually represented confederations or groupings, often referred to as "nations," such as the Alemanni, Franks, and Suevi.

Subdivisions of the early Germans

A convenient general subdivision lists the early Germans as East, West, and Far North Germans. The East Germans, who were in the Oder and Vistula valleys at an early date, included the Goths, Gepids, Vandals, Burgundians, Rugians, Lombards, and others. Having to traverse greater distances to establish themselves in the Empire during the great invasions, the East Germans eventually lost both their holdings in their old homeland and their identity in the Empire. The West Germans, who originally inhabited the area of the Elbe and Rhine valleys and the far south of the Danish peninsula, included the Franks, Alemanni, Thuringians, Bavarians, Hessians (Chatti), Angles, Saxons, and others. Since most of the West Germans retained their foothold in Germany while expanding into the Roman Empire, they were usually more permanently successful. The (Far) North Germans, or Scandinavians, remained in their early Germanic homeland and expanded still farther northward. Although they did not take part in the great invasions of the fifth century, they indulged in far-flung expansion about four centuries later at the time of the Vikings.

In addition to the basic culture traits of the proto-Indo-Europeans, the early Germans had many special characteristics of their own. Their cul-

Government

tural status was intermediate between that of the Celts and the Slavs. From the Celts, the Germans seem to have derived the use of such items as iron, carriages, and breeches. The early Germans first appeared on the European historical scene as seminomadic, semi-pastoral, semiagricultural hunters and warriors.

The tribe was the basic sovereign political unit among the early Germans, although tribes often formed alliances and sometimes joined in confederations. Supreme in tribal government was the assembly (*moot, gemot, Ding, Thing*) of full-fledged citizens or tribal warriors. Important issues such as the waging of war and the election of military leaders were decided in assemblies by popular vote. Despite the authority of the tribal assembly, the government still seems to have been partly aristocratic. Questions to be presented in the assemblies were apparently determined beforehand by the chiefs or leaders, and presented in a way that admitted of a Yes or No decision. No early Germanic institution has attracted wider attention than these tribal assemblies, as the asserted forerunners of medieval and modern congresses and parliaments. Tacitus says: *Concerning minor matters the chiefs deliberate, but about more important ones the whole tribe is consulted. Although the final decision rests with the people, the affair is always thoroughly discussed beforehand by the chiefs. These assemblies are held, except in cases of sudden emergency, on certain fixed days. . . . When the multitude thinks proper, they sit down, armed. Then the kings or chiefs address them, each being heard according to his age, noble blood, and reputation in warfare and eloquence. . . . If his sentiments displease them, they express their dissent with murmurs; if they approve they brandish their spears. The most complimentary form of assent is to express approbation with their weapons.* (Tacitus, *Germania*, xi.)

The form of government described by Tacitus seems to have been partly democratic, partly aristocratic, and partly monarchical. Whether Tacitus exaggerated the picture as a challenge to the Romans to reassert the power of the people and the senate cannot be determined. Tacitus tells us that the Germans had two forms of leaders. Their ordinary semihereditary chiefs, elected from a given family, ruled in peacetime, with limited power. This was probably also a partly religious office. In time of war, military leaders (*Herzogs* or Dukes), who were chosen for their ability, had temporary absolute power. Of the peacetime chiefs, Tacitus says explicitly: *Their kings do not have unlimited or arbitrary power* (*Germania*, vii). Of their wartime leaders, Julius Caesar says: *When a tribe is repelling invasion or attacking an outside people, magistrates are chosen to lead them in the war, and are given the power of life and death* (*Gallic Wars*. vi).

Local government was apparently organized along similar semidemocratic lines. Tribes were composed of clans. These clans (sibs or kin) were comprised of relatives, all descended unilaterally from a common male ancestor. Such clans had a corporate solidarity in the eyes of the law, so that they were considered responsible for their members. An offense committed against a member of one clan by a member of another clan made

The Barbarian Background

the second clan responsible to the first for retribution, so that the latter might collectively enforce its right.

When the Germans settled down and became less nomadic, geographical subdivisions such as hundreds and villages also appeared. A *hundred* was probably at first an area occupied by a hundred families or obliged to supply a hundred fighting men. Each of these subdivisions had its own assembly (*moot, gemot, Ding* or *Thing*) and local magistrates. In the administration of justice, the magistrate was regarded as the presiding officer of a popular court, and the decision was rendered by the people in assembly.

Much local administration seems to have been aristocratic, like that of lords over serfs. This condition may have been due both to the subjection of local agricultural peoples by conquering Germans, and to the growth of a distinction between professional warriors and ordinary farmers. Of peasant-serfs, Tacitus says: *Each has his own domicile and rules his own house. The master exacts a certain amount of grain or cloth or cattle as in the case of a tenant, and this is the extent of his servitude.* (*Germania*, xxv). And of the support of the military element by the agricultural element, he says: *It is customary for the several tribesmen to present voluntary offerings of cattle and grain to the chiefs. Though accepted as gifts of honour, these also supply the wants of the latter.* (*Germania*, xv.)

The laws of the Germanic barbarians consisted of social customs regarded as necessary and subject to penalty when violated. Although such laws varied in detail from tribe to tribe, they were generally similar. Their main purpose was to safeguard the welfare of the community, especially by maintaining internal peace and order. Early German laws were simple, direct, and unqualified. More serious offenses, such as treason or desertion, which jeopardized the security of the whole community, were punished in a way calculated to serve as a fearsome example to all, as by hanging from a tree. So too were vices which threatened to corrupt the entire community, such as marital infidelity on the part of women or homosexuality on the part of young men. According to Tacitus, such offenders were punished by being driven out of the village or left bound and weighted to expire in a morass.

Law and justice

Most offenses, however, were punished by fines, originally reckoned in cattle, later in money. Since fighting and violence were common among a rough and warlike people, physical injuries or death often resulted, frequently without premeditated intent. Such offenses were compensated for by means of payments (blood money or man money), carefully graded in terms of the injury inflicted and the person injured. Part of the fine went to the injured person or his survivors, part to the government. In the case of manslaughter or physical injury, the fine was known as *wergeld* or man money. This compensation obviated the perpetuation of enmities and feuds. Quarrels were also averted by having the inheritance of property governed by set rules so that it went to surviving relatives in a fixed manner.

Justice was usually administered by the community, meeting in assembly and presided over by its chief magistrate. Some Germanic groups had special persons known as "lawmen," who would declare the law. Ultimately the assembly would ascertain the facts, render judgment as to guilt or innocence, enunciate the traditional law, and assess the penalty. It was also recognized, as a result of long-standing custom, that the relatives of an individual had a right to demand and, if necessary, exact justice on his behalf from the guilty person or his relatives.

Usually, in a closely knit community, both the offense and the culprit were known. In cases where there was no doubt, justice was often summary and immediate. However, where the facts were difficult to ascertain various means were used to seek out the truth. Most of these had the common feature of invoking divine intervention to ascertain the truth. They also had a "lie-detector" aspect, in that they tested the psychological condition and reactions of the accused. In oaths and compurgation, the accused and those who believed in his innocence called upon God to witness and hence to punish them if they were lying. In ordeals the accused were subjected to tests in which God was given an opportunity to signify the person's innocence or guilt by influencing the outcome.

Warfare and the comitatus

The warlike habits of the early Germans are stressed in ancient sources. As is typical with many seminomadic, semipastoral peoples, warfare was endemic among the early Germans. Admission to warrior ranks was awarded in a formal ceremony in which a young man who had demonstrated his qualifications was presented with a spear and shield.

Their weapons included spears, javelins, battle-axes, swords, daggers, slings, and bows and arrows. Characteristic weapons were the short javelin or *framea* which could be thrown, and the *francisca* or battle-axe. Their ordinary armor was a large shield, but they sometimes wore helmets and leather jackets. Their large painted shields could also be used as sleds and surfboards. One of their favorite tactics was to hurl volleys of spears or javelins and then advance rapidly to close combat. They often used a wedge formation, with the point composed of selected young warriors. Early groups seem to have made very limited use of cavalry in warfare.

Two types of military organization are described by Tacitus. In the first, probably chiefly defensive, the Germans were organized into clans. In the second, probably used chiefly for offensive warfare, the military unit was the *comitatus*. In the *comitatus*, a prototype for medieval vassalage, warriors rallied around a chief to whom they bound themselves by oath. The moral bond thus created was regarded as most solemn, and a warrior who abandoned his chief on the battlefield was considered forever disgraced. The *comitatus* was very important in the rise of medieval feudalism.

Economy of the early Germans

The early Germans seem to have been in an economic state of development transitional between the pastoral and agricultural stages. Wealth was measured and fines were assessed in heads of cattle. Dairy products occupied a prominent place in their diet, and swine (pigs and hogs) were an important source of meat. They also kept poultry and bees, sheep and goats. They treasured their horses and sometimes attributed supernatural qualities to them. Hunting still provided part of their provender.

The Barbarian Background

At the same time the early Germans were steadily becoming more agricultural. Although probably at first mainly the work of women, children, and the aged, agriculture was also coming to be the regular occupation of able-bodied males—a peasant class, largely composed of serfs and slaves. Many of the early Germanic invasions were in large part quests for better agricultural lands. The early Germans seem often to have subjected earlier agricultural populations, who continued to till the land, with part of the ownership and part of the produce reserved to the masters, in a manner that resembled the medieval manorial system. Private property supplanted earlier semicommunal ownership and annual reassignment of lands. At first the Germans moved and made new clearings when the fertility of their land decreased, but in the course of time they learned to alternate the use of their fields, always leaving some fallow in order to recover their fertility. Grain was their chief agricultural product. Tribes closer to the Roman Empire, as in the Rhineland, were generally more settled and agricultural, those farther away more nomadic and pastoral.

Industrially, the Germans had the use of iron from sometime between 1000 and 500 B.C. Metalworkers were numerous and honored, and the name "Smith" was of common occurrence. Their artisans made excellent swords and implements, as well as pottery and textiles of wool and linen. The inhabitants of Frisia were noted for their weaving. The Germans were skilled in woodwork, woodcarving, and shipbuilding. Further German products included wagons, locks and keys, gold and silver ornaments, and soap which they exported to the Roman Empire.

The early Germans carried on trade by land and sea. Although, like the early Romans, they reckoned values in terms of cattle, they also knew and accepted coins as early as the first century of the Christian era. Among items of export were amber, furs, skins, honey, textiles, soap, and slaves. Imports included textiles, jewelry, weapons, wine, and iron. For overland travel and transport the Germans had horses and wagons. They made harness, bits, spurs, and stirrups for their horses, and often transported their families and belongings in covered wagons. On the sea they used longships equipped with numerous oars for rowers on both sides. In the fifth century after Christ, the barbarous Saxons were described as expert seamen who used sails as well as oars to propel their swift craft as they harassed the coasts with piratical raids.

Just as the economy of the early Germans was transitional between the pastoral and agricultural stages, so their society was partly democratic and partly aristocratic. The old notion that early German society was equalitarian and classless has been exploded, although it did contain elements of such a form of organization. Even by the first century there was a distinction between hereditary chiefs and subjects, aristocracy and ordinary freemen, warriors and farmers, free and unfree. The Germans had slaves, who included captives of war, insolvent debtors, and hapless gamblers. But the status of these slaves seems to have been more like that of medieval serfs, since each was allowed to have his own cottage, family life, and farmland, on condition that he render to his master a certain part of his produce. Eventually, the early Germans came to be dominated by a

Early Germanic society

landholding nobility of warriors, who also constituted the governing class.

Within tribes, marriage was endogamous, or limited to tribal members; but for clans it was exogamous, or restricted to persons outside of the closely related group. Wives were probably purchased or taken by force. Social organization was patrilinear, or reckoned in the male line. The father's power was almost unlimited over his children, whom he could reject or accept after birth; his power was somewhat less over his wife. Although subject to their husbands, women were held in high respect, and some were even considered to have the gift of prophecy. Widows were sometimes supposed to follow their husbands in death. Special ceremonies marked attainment of the principal stages of human life, such as reaching manhood, forming the matrimonial bond, and burial.

The early Germans lived in villages, which seem in certain instances to have become towns. While Tacitus tells us that the Germans did not have cities in the first century of the Christian era, Ptolemy lists fifty cities in Germany in the second century. This may, however, be merely a matter of terminology. Their villages, which often had walls or moats, contained rectangular or circular log houses constructed of wood, clay, and plaster, and surrounded by open spaces, rather than built up one against the other. Houses had steep, thatched roofs. Sometimes they were partly excavated or had basements for warmth in winter.

Men were fully dressed with tight-fitting, sleeveless undergarments of wool or linen, a tunic, trousers with belts and puttees, shoes or sandals made of leather, and a coarse woolen outer garment in the form of a cloak, often fastened together at the right shoulder with an ornamental brooch. In addition to similar items of clothing, women were wont to wrap themselves in garments of linen with decorative borders, leaving bare their arms, shoulders, and the upper part of their breasts.

The Germans consumed much milk, butter, and cheese, instead of the olive oil common in Mediterranean countries. Mead made from fermented honey, and beer from malted grain were favorite beverages. Theirs was a "realm of beer and butter." Hospitality was stressed as a sacred duty. Recreations of the German men included gambling, drinking, fighting, hunting, and competing in games and feats of physical prowess. They were fond of bathing, and many a battle was fought for the possession of warm springs.

EARLY GERMANIC CULTURE AND PROGRESS.
Section 9.

> They tell in ancient songs, the only kind of tradition and history they have, how Tiusto, a god sprung from the earth, and Mannus were founders of their race. [TACITUS, *Germania*, concerning the early Germans.]

ALTHOUGH they lacked writing, the early Germans had considerable culture, which was already notably increased by the time of the invasions through their contacts with the Romans.

The Barbarian Background

Religion of the Teutons

The naturalistic, polytheistic religions of the early Germans were complicated and confused by a proliferation and superimposition of gods, myths, and religious ideas. Thus the Germanic barbarians had two sets of divinities, male and female. By the first century the male deities were dominant, although they seem to have been superimposed on the female, who may have been dominant in the past. Among the male gods, Ziu (Twaz, Tiu, or Thiu), god of the sky and war, from whose name we get Tuesday, seems to have been originally the supreme and perhaps even the sole god. But Ziu (identifiable with Zeus, Jupiter, Dyaus-Pitar) the old Indo-European general sky god and father of the gods, was subsequently supplanted by more specific gods of the sky: Woden and Thor. Woden (or Odin), god of the wind, from whose name we get Wednesday (Woden's day), became the principal god in the south; while Thor (or Donar), god of thunder and lightning, from whose name we get Thursday, became the supreme god in the north. Similarly, there may have originally been but one supreme female goddess, the Earth Mother: Nerthus or Hertha, who was subsequently supplanted by partial counterparts such as Frigga, wife of Woden and guardian of the home and productivity; and Freya, goddess of the Spring and its fertile germination. It is either from Frigga or Freya that we get the name Friday. In addition there were Sunna, the sun goddess (Sunday); and Mani, the moon god (Monday).

The Germans also derived other gods from outside sources. Some were apparently worshipping the Egyptian earth goddess Isis at the time of Tacitus. When they came into contact with Roman mythology, the Germans were able to equate or approximate several of their gods and goddesses to those of the Greeks and Romans. The days of the week, which the North German Saxons took over from the Mediterranean world, were named according to their own deities with Thor as the supreme sky god, equivalent to Jove (Jupiter, Zeus).*

The Germans had sacred woods, groves, and trees. They also had a priestly class, although it does not seem to have been exceptionally powerful. They offered sacrifices, such as horses and cattle, to their gods, and

---

* THE WEEK

GERMAN DAY	GERMAN DEITY	LATIN DEITY	LATIN DAY
Sunday	Sunna (Sun)	Sun	*Dies Solis*
Monday	Mani (Moon)	Moon	*Dies Lunae*
Tuesday	Tiu (Sky god)	Mars	*Dies Martis*
Wednesday	Woden (Wind god)	Mercury	*Dies Mercurii*
Thursday	Thor (Thunder or Sky God)	Jove (Jupiter)	*Dies Jovis*
Friday	Freya or Frigga (Goddess of Spring)	Venus	*Dies Veneris*
Saturday	Seterne	Saturn	*Dies Saturni*

occasionally they even sacrificed human beings. For some time Christian churchmen regarded the eating of horsemeat as a sign of "unreconstructed" paganism. The Germans practiced augury and divination by such devices as interpreting the flights of birds and the neighing of horses. Sometimes disputes between tribes were settled by single combat between champions, the outcome being regarded as a divine verdict. The saved were to be admitted to the bliss of Valhalla in the sky. Their religion seems to have been a warrior's religion with a warrior's gods. Although not monotheistic, it was *henotheistic* with a tendency to stress the worship of a favorite god.

Morality among the Germans

The morality of the early Germans reflected both the healthy virtues and the raw vices of a simple semipastoral people living close to nature. Sexual continence was highly regarded and was possibly one of the secrets of their success. Premarital celibacy was required of the young, so that, according to Caesar, *To have had intercourse with a woman before twenty is considered a most disgraceful thing . . . (Gallic Wars,* vi). They were strictly monogamous, and adultery, at least on the part of a woman, was severely punished. Tacitus tells us: *Almost alone among the barbarians, they are content with only one wife. . . . They live in well-protected virtue. . . . Although their population is very numerous, adultery is very rare, its punishment being prompt and in the husband's power . . . (Germania,* xviii–xix). A husband could drive out or even put to death an adulterous wife. The Germans insisted on honor and courage. A man who broke his solemn oath was disgraced for life; a coward was weighted down and left to die in the mire; a deserter was hanged from a tree.

The early Germans also had their shortcomings. They were inclined to intoxication and physical violence. Especially in drunken sprees, they put little value on human life, and maimed or killed each other with reckless abandon. They could be cruel and vindictive. They had little control over their tempers, and often went berserk in private quarrels or public battles with a terrible *furor Teutonicus*. Fathers were often severe and cruel to their wives and children, as when a fallen wife was driven publicly from the house or an unwanted newborn infant was exposed outdoors to die. A similar fate awaited the very aged. In the old German poem *Wunderhorn*, a boy carries half of a large horse blanket to his aged grandfather, who has been put out to die, telling his father that he is saving the other half for him when he, too, becomes old. The Germanic barbarians could also be rapacious and perfidious. Whereas a wife was severely punished and put to death for adultery, there is no mention of any penalty except a stiff fine for her male counterpart. Various flimsy excuses were often conceived for violating promises or treaties. The Germans were also prone to reckless and excessive gambling. Some would go so far as to stake their wives and children and even their own freedom on the throw of the dice. When not fighting, warriors often lived in shameless sloth.

Miscellaneous culture traits

The early Germans had no system of writing. Occasional runes (from Gothic *run:* mystery) ascribed to them seem to have been nothing more than comparatively late partial adaptations of Mediterranean inscriptions.

The Barbarian Background

They did, however, have numerous traditional sayings, maxims, proverbs, and fables, handed down orally from generation to generation. They had poetry and music, also unwritten, which included epics concerning ancient heroes, didactic poems about their gods, ballads and chants to commemorate and inspire deeds of valor. Among their musical instruments was an S-shaped horn, fashioned from bronze, known as a *lurer* or *luder*. This long wind instrument (four to six feet in length) could produce twenty-two notes. Numerous examples have been unearthed. They reckoned time by solar years, lunar months, and nights, such as fortnights (fourteen nights). They did not at first have the week, which they adopted from Mediterranean peoples, changing the names of Greek deities into their own equivalents.

Prior to the Great Invasions of the fifth century, the Germans had numerous contacts with the Romans, both hostile and friendly. Warfare between the Germans and the Romans began as early as the second century B.C., towards the close of which (113–101 B.C.) the Cimbri and Teutones invaded the Empire. After defeating five Roman armies sent against them, and ravaging Gaul and Spain for over a decade, the Cimbri and Teutones were practically annihilated by the Roman general Marius. Julius Caesar derived his excuse for intervention in Transalpine Gaul (58–51 B.C.) from the fact that Germans had settled on the west bank of the Rhine, and were precipitating wild movements of other barbaric peoples against Roman territories, and attacking Roman allies such as the Aedui. Caesar not only foiled the purpose of the Germans to overrun Gaul but also drove them back across the Rhine.

Hostile contacts of Germans and Romans

Augustus endeavored to subject neighboring Germans and to extend Roman boundaries to the Danube and the Elbe. In the first enterprise he was successful, but in the second he failed. The Germans put up a stubborn resistance, and eventually trapped and annihilated three Roman legions in the battle of the Teutoberg Forest (A.D. 9). The debacle was such a severe shock to the aging Augustus that he decided to be content with the Rhine and the Danube as his borders.

In the beginning, the Romans had the advantage over their German adversaries. The Romans had better organization, training, and discipline, as well as superior equipment and supplies. Their excellent roads and flexible organization into independent legions gave them an effective mobility which the Germans could not match. The Romans also had the confidence and *esprit* born of past success. Whereas the Germans usually operated on a more haphazard basis, the Romans employed skillful planning, and followed their shrewd maxim, "Divide and conquer." But as time went on, the Roman Empire was weakening, while the Germans were learning and improving their military methods.

The second century was transitional. During its first half, the Germans were no serious threat; but in its second half they became more aggressive. Marcus Aurelius, last of the so-called Good or Adoptive Emperors, spent most of his reign fighting restive Germanic tribes along the middle Danube. During the confusion and misrule that followed his death, the situation rapidly deteriorated (180ff.). In the third century, when civil wars and anarchy were at their height in the Empire, the Germanic barbarians overran the Roman boundaries. One of the leading motives for Diocletian's reorganization of the Empire (ca. 284ff.) was to provide more effective defenses against the barbarians. Holding the Rhine and Danube frontiers against the Germans became a principal concern of fourth-century emperors.

Peaceful contacts

Meanwhile, friendly contacts between Germans and Romans were also numerous. As early as the first century after Christ, there was considerable trade between the Germans and the Romans, and this increased as time progressed. Christianity added a new encouragement to friendly German-Roman relations when missionaries began to carry the good tidings of Christ and Mediterranean civilization to the East Germans. Many Germans entered the Empire as household slaves, *coloni* (quasi serfs), laborers, settlers, soldiers, and *foederati* (allies). In the first century B.C., Julius Caesar was using German soldiers as auxiliaries, and by the fourth to fifth centuries of the Christian era, the majority of soldiers in the Roman armies were Germanic barbarians. Increasing numbers of Germans came to hold top military posts. Often whole tribes of Germans were brought into the Empire as *foederati* and settled in frontier provinces to protect the latter against their fellow barbarians. Such allies were allowed self-rule and usually received an annual subsidy. Frequently, young members of ruling families among barbarian allies were educated and trained in Rome or Constantinople. There were many intermarriages between Germans and Romans, and some of the Roman emperors had German blood in their veins.

Roman influences on the Germans

The Romans influenced the Germans in many ways. Compared with the Celts who had been the chief teachers of the Germans, the Romans were much more advanced dispensers of elements of progress. In imitation of the Romans and in order better to compete with them, the German tribes formed confederations, such as the Franks (free men) and the Alemanni (all men), eventually to be regarded as "nations": large groups of related people. The kings who ruled these groups became steadily more absolute and hereditary, as the Germans adopted principles from Roman constitutional law and were compelled to maintain a continuous wartime footing. The Roman concept of the monarchy was gradually assumed by the German kings in much the same way as Roman emperors had taken over Hellenistic and Near Eastern traditions. In the course of time the Germans also learned to imitate Roman military methods and techniques.

The economy and society of the early Germans were stimulated by Roman proximity. German-Roman trade constantly grew. The Germans were accepting Roman coins by the time of Tacitus, and were reckoning their *wergelds* and other fines in Roman money by the fourth century of the Christian era. The Germans steadily became more agricultural, so that the invasions were partly stimulated by a desire for better lands to cultivate. They also derived several household implements, such as plates, dishes, and glassware, from the Romans. They improved many of their technological processes, such as the grinding of grain and shipbuilding, by

The Barbarian Background

imitating the Romans. Medical practitioners appeared among the Germans. Housing was improved and great meeting halls were reared, although they were constructed of timber rather than of masonry. Social stratification increased, and there was a growing gap between German landowners and tenants, lords and serfs, warrior aristocracy and peasant farmers.

Moral, religious and cultural influences were also operative. For some time there was a considerable weakening of moral standards among the Germans, as usually happens when less advanced people come into contact with more advanced ones of differing *mores* and beliefs. The early Germans, whose religious concepts seem to have been both crude and fluid, applied many features from Roman mythology to their own somewhat parallel deities.

In the fourth century many of the eastern Germans were converted to Christianity as a result of the missionary work of Ulfilas, a grandson of Cappodocian Christians who had been captured and enslaved by the Goths. Ulfilas (Little Wolf), who grew up as a Goth, determined to labor for the conversion of his people. After clerical training Ulfilas was ordained a bishop by the Arian Archbishop Eusebius of Constantinople. To facilitate his work, Ulfilas adapted and expanded the Greek alphabet to meet Gothic requirements and translated the Bible and other religious works into Gothic. He omitted the warlike Books of Kings in the Old Testament because he felt that the Goths were already too bellicose.

From the Goths, Christianity spread to other eastern Germanic peoples such as the Vandals, Burgundians, and Lombards. But this Christianity was of the Arian variety, then ascendant in Constantinople, and their chance adoption of a Christian heresy later worked against the amalgamation of the East Germans with the orthodox Roman population after their invasion of the Empire. With Christianity came other features of Roman civilization, including fuller incorporation into the Mediterranean-centered Roman complex of civilized peoples, the alphabet and writing, and a certain amount of literature and learning.

Meanwhile, the Romans were also influenced by the Germans. The Roman army came to be made up mainly of Germanic barbarians, so that the terms *miles* (soldier) and *barbarus* (barbarian) were used interchangeably, as when a mother wrote that her recently enlisted son had "gone to join the barbarians." Eventually, the commanders of Roman armies were German. In the later fourth century, influenced by the Goths, the Romans modified their military tactics to put greater emphasis upon cavalry. It is probable that the Romans borrowed from the Germans the use of barrels, tubs, soap, and felt. A fad developed among the Romans for the imitation of things German. Roman women often had their hair dyed blond, and Roman men affected "gaily colored sleeveless garments, coats, wide trousers, and long hair in the barbarian fashion." It even became customary for newly elected Emperors to be raised on the shields of their bodyguard in the Germanic manner. *Influences of the Germans on the Romans*

The barbarians were an important component of medieval Europe. By the close of antiquity, considerable amalgamation of Germanic barbarian *Barbarian component* and civilized Roman elements was already under way, although much more of this remained to be accomplished in the Middle Ages. In the two thirds of Europe still barbarian at the close of antiquity, most initial medieval progress derived from a continuing infusion of more advanced Roman and Near Eastern elements of civilization. In the areas of the Empire that they invaded, the barbarians provided a new energizing force, as well as salutary elements from their own "unspoiled" Indo-European culture.

References for Chapter 3

READABLE surveys of the progress of the European barbarians are given by CARL W. BISHOP et al, *Man From the Farthest Past* (New York: Smithsonian, 1930), and MILES C. BURKITT, *Prehistory: A Study of Early Cultures in Europe and the Mediterranean Basin* . . . (Cambridge: Cambridge U. P., 1921), both of which carry man in Europe to the threshold of written history in one volume. GEORGE G. MACCURDY, *Human Origins: A Manual of Prehistory*, 2 vols. (New York: Appleton, 1924) does the same on a fuller scale in two volumes. Also valuable is the masterly ALFRED L. KROEBER, *Anthropology* . . . (New York: Harcourt, 1949).

Recommended for particular stages of the progress of the European barbarians are: HENRY F. OSBORN, *Men of the Old Stone Age* (New York: Scribners, 1915), fullest account of its subject in English; JOHN M. TYLER, *The New Stone Age in Northern Europe* (New York: Scribners, 1921) a semipopular work wherein Northern Europe means simply Europe beyond the Mediterranean; and VERE GORDON CHILDE, *The Dawn of European Civilization* (New York: Knopf, 1925) a scholarly discussion of the Neolithic, Copper, and Bronze Ages in Europe arranged according to geographical regions. Also treating this important transitional period is CHRISTOPHER DAWSON, *The Age of the Gods* . . . (London: Sheed, 1933) which attempts to survey with an emphasis on religion the cultural development of various groups in the Near East and Europe from the Upper Old Stone Age to the dawn of the Iron Age. Barbarian progress in England is told by JACQUETTA and CHRISTOPHER HAWKES, *Prehistoric Britain* (London: Chatto, 1948). Much broader than its title would suggest is the excellent CARLETON S. COON, *The Races of Europe* (New York: Macmillan, 1939).

Discussions concerning the Indo-European peoples in general are to be found in several of the aforesaid works, such as those by COON, DAWSON, and TYLER. A monumental classic of research concerning the early Celts is the two-volume work of HENRI HUBERT, *The Rise of the Celts*, tr. M. R. DOBIE (London: Kegan Paul, 1934), which takes their story to about 500 B.C., and *The Greatness and Decline of the Celts*, tr. M. R. DOBIE (London, Kegan Paul, 1934), which continues the account through the La Tene Period to the Roman, Germanic, and English conquests that ended Celtic independence. Works shedding light on the early Slavs include SAMUEL H. CROSS, *Slavic Civilization Through the Ages* (Cambridge: Harvard U. P., 1948), which has about fifty pages on the primitive Slavs and their migrations; OSCAR HALECKI, *Borderlands of Western Civilization* (New York: Roland, 1952), whose first two chapters discuss the early Slavs and their neighbors and movements; and J. PEISKER, "The Expansion of the Slavs," in *Cambridge Medieval History*, II, 418–458. The scholarly, information-packed monograph of Roman Smal-Stocki (or Stotskyi), *Slavs and Teutons: The Oldest Germanic*

The Barbarian Background

Slavic Relations (Milwaukee: Bruce, 1950) is an excellent survey of early Indo-European and Slavic culture traits, together with Germanic contributions to the Slavs, based on philological (linguistic) grounds. In GEORGE VERNADSKY'S monumental *History of Russia*, the first volume, entitled *Ancient Russia* (New Haven: Yale U. P., 1943), has four chapters on the early inhabitants of Russia to about A.D. 500, including the Slavs.

With regard to the Germanic barbarians before the invasions, our principal source of information is contemporary descriptions. A survey of the latter with summaries and extracts is provided by CARLTON H. HAYES, *An Introduction To the Sources Relating to the Germanic Invasions* (New York: Columbia U.P., 1909). A convenient collection of such contemporary sources is the fascicle entitled *The Early Germans*, ed. ARTHUR C. HOWLAND, in Pennsylvania University, Dept. of History, *Translations and Reprints*, VI, No. 3 (Philadelphia, U. of Pa., n.d.) which has pertinent passages from CAESAR, JOSEPHUS, and AMMIANUS MARCELLINUS in addition to the *Germania* of TACITUS. The latter, our principal source, is also available in *The Agricola and Germany of Tacitus and the Dialogue on Oratory*, tr. ALFRED J. CHURCH and WILLIAM J. BRODRIBB (London: Macmillan, 1911) as well as in other publications. A fascinating summary of information concerning the institutions and life of the early Germans skillfully drawn from a wide variety of written sources is FRANCIS B. GUMMERE, *Germanic Origins: A Study in Primitive Origins* (New York: Scribners, 1892), which reappeared later in revised form under the title *Founders of England* (New York: Stechert, 1930). The origins and movements of the early Germans and their relations with the Celts are emphasized by MARTIN BANG, "Expansion of the Teutons to A.D. 378," in *Cambridge Medieval History*, I, 183–217. Useful works on special aspects include GERALD B. BROWN, *Arts and Crafts of Our Teutonic Forefathers* . . . (London: Foulis, 1910); O. BROGAN, "Trade Between the Roman Empire and the Free Germans," in *Journal of Roman Studies*, XXVI, Pt. 2 (1936); and PIERRE D. CHANTEPIE DE LA SAUSSAYE, *The Religion of the Teutons*, tr. B. J. Vos (Boston: Ginn, 1902).

THE BARBARIANS AND THE EMPIRE IN THE AGE OF THE INVASIONS. Chapter 4.

GERMANIC barbarians overran the Empire in the West during the transitional fifth century. Until 455, the invaders sought favorable subordinate status within the Western Empire; but after 455, they dropped any serious pretext of obedience to the Western emperors, whom they soon discarded (476). The fall of the Roman Empire in the West was actually due to a variety of causes, internal as well as external, chief among which were the barbarian invasions.

a The four italicized Gothic words mean in succession "health!" and "make!" ("do" or "act") and "eat!" and "drink!" In the original, *jah* is used for "and."

THE BARBARIAN INVASIONS BEGIN.
Section 10.

Round me the Gothic *Hails* and *skapjam* and *matjam* and *drinkjam*a harshly resound. In such a din who could fit verses indite? [Anon. Latin epigram, evidently of the fifth century, referring to the disquieting presence of the Germanic barbarians.]

(ca. 378–455)

DURING the first half of the fifth century various Germanic barbarian invaders established themselves in several sections of the Western Empire. By the middle of the century the Visigoths were in control of southern Gaul, and the Vandals ruled in North Africa. Lesser groups also had footholds in the Empire. Although the Huns had begun the invasions, they did not establish a permanent state.

General causes and features of the invasions

For centuries the Germans had been periodically breaking across the frontiers of the Empire, attracted by prospects of wealth and leisure, abundance of food and drink, and a mild climate. The lands of the Empire were richly productive and well supplied with serflike *coloni* and others whose services the Germans could appropriate. The Germans were also fired by a love of adventure and a *Wanderlust* ingrained by centuries of seminomadic existence. Recent population growth coupled with poor agricultural methods spurred them to seek more *Lebensraum* (living space). In the centuries since Tacitus, the Germans, already warlike and formidable, had been gaining in strength and unity, organization and military capabilities, even as the native inhabitants of the Empire were becoming weaker and less capable of defending themselves.

The barbarian invasions, known to German historians as the *Völkerwanderung*, consisted of the migrations of whole peoples, in that their women and children and sometimes aged parents accompanied the warriors. All of the invaders were Germanic, except the Mongoloid Huns and the Iranian Alans, neither of whom established permanent homes on Roman soil. On the continent the Germans invaded as "nations" (from

The Barbarians and the Empire 75

nascor: to be born), confederations of theoretically related tribes under a common king. Such invading groups generally included recruits from various outside tribes and nations. Thus the Mongoloid Huns under Attila in the mid-fifth century included numerous Germanic Gepids, Heruli, Ostrogoths, and others. Among the Germanic invaders, the East Germans were initially the most successful; but the success of the West Germans was more lasting. Most of the invading East Germans were Arian Christians, whereas the West Germans were still pagan. The main invading Germanic nations, or confederations, are said to have numbered from about 100,000 to 200,000 persons, including noncombatants. Of this number only about 20 per cent, that is, about 20,000 to 40,000, were fighting men. In the territories they took over the Germans were usually greatly outnumbered by the native populations, sometimes an estimated 50 or 100 to 1.

The fifth-century invaders generally sought to "enjoy rather than destroy" the Empire. They sought and obtained the status of *foederati* (from *foedus:* treaty)—allies settled as privileged defenders in the areas they invaded. Their rulers were kings to their German followers, but imperial officials, such as consuls, to their Roman subjects. In many cases the barbarian occupation and the transition to complete German control were so gradual and quasi-legal that often the native Roman subjects hardly realized what was taking place. The majority of the population seem to have been apathetic although some, like St. Jerome, deplored the collapse that was in process. A few, such as Salvian and Orosius, considered the invasions a salutary warning sent by God and an opportunity to convert barbarians to Christianity.

The great invasions of the fifth century were triggered by the onslaught of the Huns in the later fourth century. Possibly descendants of the *Hiung-Nu* against whom the Chinese had constructed their Great Wall, the Huns were warlike, predatory nomads from the central steppes of Asia. In the 370s the Huns moved against the Ostrogoths who had a considerable empire to the north of the Black Sea. The resistance was soon crushed, and the Ostrogoths were subjected by the Huns. *The Huns*

Short, squat, round-headed, slant-eyed, and bronze-skinned, with straight black hair, the Huns were manifestly Mongoloid. They were uncommonly ugly from lacerations purposely inflicted on their faces, as well as from the scars of battle. As the poet Claudian says: "With horrid wounds they gash their brutal brows" (*In Rufinum*). The Huns habitually attacked and plundered their neighbors, from whom they also exacted tribute for the privilege of immunity.

Expert horsemen, the Huns had the reputation of eating, drinking, transacting business, and even sleeping on horseback. Their equestrian capabilities facilitated a sort of *Blitzkrieg* (lightning war). Large Hunnic armies would quickly traverse vast distances, strike rapidly before their victims were aware, and make off before they could retaliate. Expert archers, the Huns would rapidly maneuver about their enemies, discharging deadly arrows, then charging at the opportune moment, and as swiftly retreating, often only to turn upon a pursuing foe whom they caught off guard. The Roman poet Claudian writes of the Huns about 396:

> There is a race on Scythia's verge extreme
> Eastward, beyond the Tanais' frigid stream,[b]
> The Northern Bear looks down on no uglier crew:
> Base is their garb, their bodies foul to view;
> Their souls are ne'er subdued to sturdy toil
> Or Ceres' arts;[c] their sustenance is spoil.
> . . . .
> Not e'en the Centaur-offspring[d] of the cloud
> Were horsed more firmly than this savage crowd:
> Brisk, lithe, in loose array they first come on,
> Fly, turn, attack the foe who deems them gone."
> —From Claudian, *In Rufinum*

[b] The Don River.

[c] Agriculture.

[d] Mythological beings, half-horse and half-man.

The Hunnic whirlwind, gaining strength as it went, swept on into Pannonia (present-day Hungary) which they made the center of a sprawling empire. The Huns dominated many Germanic groups, such as the Ostrogoths, Gepids, Heruli, and Rugii, who, along with (non-Germanic) Sarmatians and Alans, swelled their armies. Hunnic rulers exacted tribute from the Eastern and Western Empires for refraining from attacks and for furnishing auxiliaries for Roman military operations.

The Goths

The Goths were related Germanic tribes whose earliest known home was in the Baltic area. They moved gradually southeastward to the area north of the Black Sea, where they were living early in the third century after Christ. Meanwhile they separated into the Visigoths (West Goths) and the Ostrogoths (East Goths), each under their own king. The Visigoths wrested Dacia from the Romans by the third quarter of the third century. Emperor Decius was slain fighting them in 251. The Visigoths occupied the fertile lands to the northwest of the Black Sea between the Danube and the Dniester, while the Ostrogoths held sway over the equally fertile, even more extensive territory north of the Black Sea between the Dniester and the Don.

Established in territories so proximate to the Roman Empire, the Goths made rapid strides towards civilization, as exemplified by their conversion to Christianity in the fourth century. As has been seen, Ulfilas (d. 381) carried the Arian brand of Christianity to them, devised a Gothic alphabet, and translated much of the Bible into Gothic.

The Visigoths in the Eastern Empire

After the Huns overran the Ostrogoths, the bulk of the Visigoths sought permission from the Eastern Emperor to cross the Danube into Roman territory. Valens admitted the Visigoths into Lower Moesia (present-day Bulgaria) in 376, and established them as *foederati* with allotments of land and support from Constantinople on condition that they help defend the frontiers of the Empire. A contemporary historian, Ammianus Marcellinus, describes the Visigothic entry: *They poured across the [Danube] river day and night without ceasing, . . . on board ships and rafts, as well as in canoes hollowed out of the trunks of trees.*

The Barbarians and the Empire

... A great many were drowned because, finding no room in the vessels, they tried to swim across. ... So numerous were the barbarians that one might as well have tried to count the waves of the African sea or the grains of sand driven by the wind.[e] Unfortunately, the Roman administrators appointed to provide for the needs of the Visigoths diverted much of the money allotted by the government for their provisions, as well as subjected them to various forms of extortion. In 387 the oppressed Visigoths revolted and began to ravage the countryside. Valens, without waiting for reinforcements, went out to meet them near Adrianople (378). During the hard-fought battle, the Gothic heavy cavalry suddenly appeared and turned the tide by its charge, which disrupted the Roman army and won the day. In the words of Ammianus Marcellinus: "Hardly a third of the Roman army escaped. Not since the battle of Cannae [crushing defeat of the Romans by Hannibal, 216 B.C.] has there been so destructive a slaughter in our history."[f] Adrianople marked the beginning of the ascendance of heavy cavalry in European warfare, as well as the commencement of the great barbarian invasions.

[e] Ammianus Marcellinus, Rerum Gestarum..., xxxi, ch. iv.

[f] Op. cit., xxxi, ch. 13.

Although the Goths in the Balkans were temporarily quieted by Theodosius I, the Great (379–395), their disturbances resumed under his weak son, Arcadius (395–408). Led by their ambitious chieftain Alaric (395ff.), the Visigoths again began to ravage the Balkan provinces. Even though they were twice on the point of being trapped by Roman armies, they were spared for political reasons. Mistrusting Stilicho, the Western Master of Soldiers, the advisers of Arcadius hit upon a plan designed both to rid the Eastern Empire of the Goths and to interpose a buffer against Western interference in Eastern affairs. Alaric was assigned as Master of Soldiers in Illyricum (in the northwest Balkans), where the Visigoths were given the status of *foederati* (397).

Once in Illyricum, Alaric, as had been expected, directed his attention to neighboring Italy. But his attempted invasions were parried by the competent Vandal general of the Roman army, Stilicho, who twice defeated the Visigoths, at Pollentia (402) and Verona (403). Stilicho similarly repulsed other German hordes who invaded Italy from beyond the Alps. However, Honorius, incited by his courtiers, became jealous, and foolishly had Stilicho put to death in 408, allowing Alaric to march into Italy virtually unopposed. Besides prolonged pillaging and plundering of northern Italy, Alaric eventually took and sacked Rome for three days in 410. Although they spared Christian churches, the Visigoths robbed and violated, killed and burnt with abandon. Their capture of the imperial capital shocked the civilized world. Inhabitants of the Empire sensed that the old world was tottering and that a new order was in the making. St. Augustine wrote his *City of God* to refute the accusation that Christian defection from the traditional Roman gods was responsible for the catastrophe.

The Visigoths in Italy

The Visigoths next proceeded to southern Italy with the object of crossing over to North Africa, the granary of Rome. But the ships intended to ferry them to Africa were destroyed in a storm. A further blow

Visigoths in Gaul and Spain

was the sudden death (410) of Alaric, who was clandestinely buried in the bed of the temporarily diverted Busento river. His brother Athaulf now led the Visigoths northward, taking along the Emperor's sister Placidia. Unable to come to terms with Emperor Honorius, Athaulf moved on to southwestern Gaul and married Placidia at Narbonne in 414. Still unable to obtain imperial sanction, in need of provisions, and hard pressed by the advancing Roman Master of Soldiers, Constantius, who was himself eager to marry Placidia, Athaulf crossed into Spain, where he was soon assassinated (415).

From the ensuing contest for control, the able Wallia (415–420) emerged the victor, and established a basis for negotiations by returning Placidia to her brother Honorius, from whom he now received a commission to recover Spain for the Empire. After decisively defeating the Siling Vandals and the Alans in Spain, Wallia and his Visigoths were assigned as *foederati* to southwestern Gaul. From their Kingdom of Toulouse, they conducted spasmodic operations against the Suevi and the Asding Vandals who still remained in the Iberian Peninsula. When the Vandals crossed over into North Africa in 429, Visigothic prospects in Spain brightened.

After the assassination of Valentinian III in 455, the Visigoths launched a full-scale occupation of the Iberian Peninsula. Under the strong Euric (466–485), they conquered most of the peninsula and expanded their holdings in southern Gaul from their capital at Toulouse. They became, for a while, the strongest barbarians in the West. Nevertheless, in a short time the rising Franks and Ostrogoths overshadowed them. They lost most of southwestern Gaul (Aquitaine) to the Franks (507) and all of southeastern Gaul (Provence) to the Ostrogoths (511). Of that country, the Visigoths retained only the Mediterranean coastline west of the Rhône (Septimania), so that henceforth their kingdom was practically confined to the Iberian peninsula, with its eventual capital at Toledo.

The Vandals take North Africa

The Vandals were warlike Germans whose early home was in northeastern Germany. By the first part of the fourth century the Siling Vandals were in southwestern Germany and the Asding Vandals in present-day Hungary. The Alans were apparently non-Germanic Indo-European-speaking Aryan nomads, who were earlier established in southern Russia, but were driven westward by the advancing Huns. The Suevi, who were originally located in the Elbe valley, were merely one of several Suevic peoples. After the weakening of the Empire's frontier defenses during Visigothic assaults on Italy, the Vandals, Alans, and Suevi broke across the Rhine into Gaul in the wintry night that divided 406 from 407. For almost three years (406–409), the Vandals, Alans, and Suevi ravaged and pillaged Gaul until "the whole of Gaul burnt like a torch" in the words of Bishop Orientius of Auch (fl. ca. 439).[g]

g In his *Commonitorium*, ii, 184.

In 409, the Vandals, Alans, and Suevi invaded and occupied the Iberian peninsula. Not long afterwards they were challenged by the Visigoths, who were commissioned by Rome to free the peninsula of bar-

The Barbarians and the Empire

barian intruders. The Siling Vandals and the Alans were practically exterminated by the Visigoths (416–418). But the apprehensive Roman government now called them off and settled them as *foederati* in southwestern Gaul (416ff.) Meanwhile, the Asding Vandals, joined by surviving Alans, moved southward into [V]Andalusia (southern Spain). In 429, taking advantage of a disagreement between the Roman commander in North Africa and the imperial government in Italy, an estimated 80,000 Vandals, including some 15,000 fighting men, moved southward across the Straits of Gibraltar into North Africa under Gaiseric or Genseric (428–477). Tardy resistance by Roman troops in North Africa was futile, and the Vandals took city after city. Carthage fell in 439, and the Roman government was forced to recognize the Vandals' independent rule in North Africa in 442.

The Huns, established in Pannonia (Hungary), dominated a loose empire in *Germania* and at the same time exacted tribute from their Roman neighbors. But about 444, a strong, ambitious Hunnic leader, Attila, came to sole supreme power, apparently by slaying his brother. Known to his followers as "The Little Father" and to the Romans as "The Scourge of God," Attila decided to seize at least a part of the Western Empire. Meanwhile, the discontented Princess Honoria, daughter of Valentinian III, on being forced to become betrothed to a man not of her own choosing, had sent Attila her ring with a plea that he come to her aid. Attila now claimed the hand of Princess Honoria and demanded half the Western Empire as her dowry, further asserting that he was invading the Empire in order to punish and repress the unruly Visigoths.

The Huns again

In 451, Attila invaded Gaul with a large force composed of Huns and German auxiliaries. Although Hunnic forces took and pillaged several towns in northern Gaul, they were met on the Catalaunian Plains by General Aetius at the head of a composite Roman army which included Visigothic, Frankish, and Burgundian *foederati*. The hard-fought bloody battle of Chalons (451) was counted a Roman victory since on the following morning it was found that the unsuccessful Huns had retreated.

After wintering in Pannonia, Attila and his army invaded Italy (452), where they took and pillaged several towns. But on their way to Rome they were met by a deputation headed by Pope Leo I, and Attila was prevailed on to change his plans. Whether Attila's decision to spare the Eternal City was due to the entreaties of Pope Leo, Attila's own superstitions, Roman gold and promises, or news of the approach of Aetius is uncertain. Attila and his horde now returned to Pannonia. In the year 453, on the morning after a wild celebration of his latest wedding, to a young Christian captive, the Hunnic leader was found dead in his bed. After Attila's death, dissension and factionalism arose among his sons and followers. Subject Germans, such as the Ostrogoths, Gepids, and Heruli, now revolted and overthrew their Hunnic overlords, who disappeared from history.

THE WESTERN EMPIRE SUCCUMBS.
Section 11.

> Each emperor who on Western soil is born
> Fails from the helm and perishes forlorn.
> [SIDONIUS APOLLINARIS, describing conditions during the supremacy of Ricimer.]

AMIDST the confusion of the barbarian invasions, the Western Empire disintegrated and succumbed in the fifth century, the victim of several maladies, assailants, and reverses.

The weakening of imperial authority in the West (395-455)

After the death of Theodosius I (395), the division of the Empire became definitive. Theodosius the Great assigned the Eastern half of the Empire to his elder son Arcadius, and the Western part to his younger son, Honorius. Each had a strong general of Teutonic descent as his chief minister. In the East, the Gothic Master of Soldiers, Gainas, became the dominant official, while in the West the strong Vandal Master of Soldiers, Stilicho, was even more influential. The rivalries of these ministers impeded cooperation between East and West, while the mounting internal problems peculiar to each area widened the gulf between them.

The weak Western emperors were forced to share control with their commanding generals, who were actually the chief directors of affairs. With the onslaught of the barbarians, the army became the sole bulwark between the Empire and extinction. The Roman armies were maintained on a continuous active wartime footing, and successful generals were honored as saviors. The timid Western emperors, who withdrew to the security of Ravenna, became ever more sheltered from public affairs, and more removed from the realities of life, as well as more jealous of their generals.

Honorius (395-423)

A boy of eleven at his accession, Honorius remained immature even in manhood, and the burden of protecting the Empire fell upon his father-in-law and chief general, the Vandal Stilicho. As long as he lived, Stilicho held the Visigoths off from Italy. Describing Stilicho's hardships as he moved with his troops through the mountains, the poet Claudian wrote:

> Through scenes like this in winter's thickest snow
> Upon his dauntless course pressed Stilicho.

and summarized the contribution of the vigorous Vandal:

> These sleepless toils, this ceaseless care
> Gave to the world a respite. . . .

But Stilicho was eventually arrested and put to death at the order of the jealous Honorius in 408, and the Visigoths were able to enter Italy without serious opposition. The Visigothic leader, Alaric, soon discarded the idea of negotiating with the slippery Honorius, a fact which led to the sack of Rome in 410. A contrast to the soft-spined, incompetent Emperor

The Barbarians and the Empire

was his intelligent sister, the beautiful Placidia. She had been first married (414) to the Visigothic King Athaulf, and subsequently (417) to the successful Master of Soldiers, Constantius, who became co-emperor in the West until his untimely death.

On the death of Honorius, the supporters of Placidia's son installed their candidate as Valentinian III (425–455). For some time the real conduct of affairs was in the hands of Queen Mother Placidia, but it was not long before she was compelled to share power with her chief military commander, Aetius, Master of Soldiers in the West. The competent Aetius, who has been called "the last of the Romans," had spent some time among the Huns, and was adept in dealing with the barbarians. Aetius reestablished imperial authority in Gaul, and repulsed the Huns at Chalons (451) with a combined force of Romans, Visigoths, Burgundians, Franks, and other German barbarians. But the Roman court party at Ravenna poisoned the mind of Valentinian III against his general, who was summoned, unarmed and unsuspecting, to court, where he was slain by the Emperor himself. One of Valentinian's courtiers remarked: "You have now cut off your right hand with your left." The following year (455) Valentinian was openly assassinated by former followers of Aetius.

Valentinian III (425–455)

The assassination of Valentinian III in 455 was a turning point. Henceforth, supreme power in the shrinking Western Empire rested in the hands of the Masters of Soldiers, who created and discarded puppet-emperors at will. This gave barbarian *foederati* in various parts of the West an excuse to renounce their previous obligations. Thus after 455 the Visigoths, Burgundians, and Franks expanded without restraint, and the barbarian soldiers in Italy began to demand the same prerogatives and emoluments obtained by Germans elsewhere. From 455 to 476 there were nine successive emperors in Italy, all of whom, except one, were forcibly deposed by the Masters of Soldiers. Meanwhile, imperial authority in the West outside of Italy virtually disappeared, being supplanted by the rule of barbarian kings in North Africa, Spain, most of Gaul, and Britain, and by that of Roman generals who became independent in northwestern Gaul and Dalmatia.

The disappearance of the Western Empire (455–493)

The Vandal King of North Africa, Gaiseric, posing as an avenger, seized upon the murder of Valentinian III as an excuse to attack and pillage Rome in 455. That same year, Maximus, an elderly Roman who was elected Emperor by the Senate, had only a few weeks of power before he was stoned and torn to pieces by a mob for failing to provide for the defense of Rome against the Vandals. His successor, the Gallo-Roman Avitus (455–456), who was elevated to the throne with Visigothic support, was soon overthrown by his Master of Soldiers, the Suevian count Ricimer.

Henceforth for sixteen years (456–472), Ricimer was the real master of Italy and what remained of the Western Empire. Being a German, however, Ricimer dared not personally assume the imperial purple, which he bestowed on four successive puppets.

Following the death of Ricimer, the Western Master of Soldiers, Orestes, a former lieutenant of Attila, proclaimed his own son, Romulus, nicknamed Augustulus, Emperor (475). But the following year the Germanic barbarian soldiery in Italy, mainly Rugii, Sciri, and Herculi, demanded for themselves a third of the lands of Italy, such as had been conceded elsewhere to barbarian *foederati*. When Orestes refused to make this concession, the German mercenaries, led by a young general, Odovacar, whom they had elected as their king, defeated and slew the Master of Soldiers. Odovacar, now in control of Italy, retired the young Romulus Augustulus to a villa on a substantial yearly pension (476), and brought the Roman senate to dispatch the imperial insignia to the Eastern Emperor Zeno, with the statement that one emperor would suffice. Odovacar, who obtained from Zeno the title of Patrician, henceforth ruled in Italy and some adjacent territories as King of the Rugians, Heruli, and Sciri, and Patrician of the Romans.

By the end of the fifth century the Roman Empire in the West had definitely fallen. Following the deposition of Romulus Augustulus (476), barbarian kings, first Odovacar and then the Ostrogothic Theodoric, ruled Italy as autonomous dictators, with little reference to imperial authorization, save the vague sanction of the distant Emperor of Constantinople. Meanwhile, the effective power of the central government was reduced to Italy itself and a few adjacent provinces. The imperial coronation in the West, discontinued in 476, was not resumed until the year 800.

Causes of the fall of the Western Empire

The question of the cause of the fall of the Roman Empire in the West has fascinated historians. The Empire fell because of the concurrence of a variety of causes. Collapse began in the chaotic century 180–284, was only temporarily and partly arrested in the century of recovery 284–395, and resumed its fatal course in the final century 395–476.

The main immediate cause of the fall of the Empire in the West was the barbarian invasions. These were in a sense twofold: external invasions from across the frontiers and internal subversion within the Roman army. During the three centuries since Tacitus, the Germanic barbarians had been steadily growing in strength, and were now organized into formidable "nations" of considerable size, on a more or less continuous wartime footing, increasingly conscious of their own military potentialities. It is unlikely that without the barbarian invasions the Empire would have fallen when it did. It is also probable that the Empire would not have been overthrown by the invasions had it retained its earlier vigor.

Maldistribution

Various general theories have been advanced as to the fundamental cause of the demise of the Western Empire. Some have attributed the fall to a cyclic law of history and life, whereby states and civilizations, even as living organisms, go through an inexorable pattern of birth, youth, maturity, old age, and death. Although this theory, held by ancient authors such as Polybius, and modern ones such as Spengler, is interesting, it cannot be demonstrated as a necessary law. Others have asserted that the fall of the Empire was providential and ordained by God as a step toward a better order: to make way for greater local self-determination on the one hand, and the increased influence of the Christian

The Barbarians and the Empire

Church on the other. Attractive as such an optimistic hypothesis may be, it is outside the scope of the science of history. Some authors say that since the benefits of the Roman Empire accrued to only a few and did not reach the masses, it failed to enlist the sympathies and support of the majority of the populace, and was doomed to eventual collapse. In other words, the Empire failed to assimilate and benefit its exploited urban proletariat and servile rural masses. This is in essence the view of Rostovstzeff and Toynbee, and it is, to some extent, a generalized statement of several of the more specific reasons we are about to consider. This diagnosis may be summarized as general "maldistribution"—political, military, fiscal, economic, social, and cultural.

Politically there was a maldistribution of governmental power, participation, and interest, as well as of the tax burden. The government of the later Roman Empire in the West was afflicted with certain serious maladies. The power of the later emperors was in theory autocratic, although autocracy was ill suited to both the temper and traditions of the West and to the weak character of the emperors who held the throne in this period. The sprawling, frontierlike West was an active germination area for revolts and independence movements throughout the history of the Empire. The two emperors Honorius and Valentinian III, who held the throne in the critical period from 395–455, were incompetent weaklings. The indeterminate manner of the imperial succession invited civil wars and made the army the decisive element, whose importance was enhanced by the fact that the Empire was being subjected to intense pressure from the barbarians.

Governmental maladies

Meanwhile, the imperial government had become oppressive. It sought to fix prices and wages, and made occupations both obligatory and hereditary. It extended its tenacles into the municipalities, where it exterminated remnants of effective self-government. It imposed ever-increasing burdens of services and supplies upon the people. Its demands were enforced by a swollen, grasping bureaucracy. The fifth-century historian Priscus tells us how a Greek explained his decision to flee the Empire and live among the Huns: "The laws and constitution of the Roman Empire are just, but the officials, not possessing the spirit of former times, are ruining the state." The fifth-century Salvian in his *Government of God* asks: "What else is the rule of certain men . . . but plundering?" Excessive and unfair taxation, aggravated by diminished ability to pay because of economic decline, bore heavily on the bulk of the population. One of the worst aspects of this taxation was its inequitable distribution. As Salvian summarized it: "The tributes due from the rich are extorted from the poor, and the weaker bear the burdens of the stronger." The government's device of making the middle class personally responsible for the collection of local taxes converted the *curiales* into grasping tax collectors, justifying Salvian's statement that "There are as many tyrants as there are *curiales*." At the same time the imposition of heavy financial liability upon the groaning local bourgeoisie caused a general attempt to evade this formerly esteemed classification.

Military ills

There was also a maldistribution of military power. As the military arm became more ascendant and apparently indispensable, it became less efficient and less reliable. One of the main causes of the fall of the Western Empire was that the army, which had come to be composed of and headed by barbarians, gained control of the government. The Roman element in the civil government was opposed to the barbarian element in the army, and within the army itself barbarian contingents and leaders fought each other for control. Internal tranquility was impossible in the presence of military rule. Eventually the Germanic warriors who were supposed to defend the Empire vied to share in its partition. Meanwhile, the practice of paying the soldiery by settling them upon lands along the frontiers tended to make them primarily farmers and only secondarily soldiers. There was a general breakdown in discipline and a lack of training in the mainly barbarian army of the Later Empire. Even more dangerous was the practice of admitting whole barbarian groups into the Empire as *foederati*. In Caesar's day the backward, poorly coordinated, ill-supplied Germans were regularly defeated by the tightly organized, well-disciplined Romans, with their superior equipment, commissariat, and leadership. But in the several intervening centuries, the Germans had learned much. Small tribes and loose tribal confederations had been superseded by more stable unions known as "nations," led by hereditary monarchs with broad powers. The Germans had acquired an appreciation of many practical principles of strategy and tactics. Some Germanic groups used cavalry with a skill that gave them a temporary advantage over the Romans. The heterogeneous Roman armies, composed largely of barbarians, were often unreliable. Whereas the Germanic invaders had definite objectives and unity, Roman forces were often divided by selfish personal ambitions and internal squabbles. Whereas most of the inhabitants of the Roman Empire had become unaccustomed to arms, practically every free adult German male was trained as a warrior. Thus, despite numerical inferiority in terms of population, the Germans usually had numerical superiority on any given field of battle. With their women and children exhorting them in the background, they also had superior psychological stimulation.

Economic retrogression and social stratification

Especially serious was economic maldistribution. As the "younger" West was more agrarian and less economically balanced and developed than the "older" East, the current economic recession hit the Western Empire much earlier and more severely than it did the East. A factor in the economic decline of the West was a drainage of gold to the more economically advanced East. An increased population shift from the towns to the countryside in the West aggravated the problem. Augmented concentration of agriculture on self-contained large estates, and reduction of more farm workers to the status of *coloni* or serfs reduced the market for goods and crippled commerce. The separation of the more agrarian Western Empire from the more industrial and commercial Eastern Empire eliminated the revenues that Western Emperors had formerly derived from the more opulent East. The Roman economy was no longer expanding as it had been in the days of the conquest and development of

The Barbarians and the Empire

new territories, or as it might have been through adoption of improved methods of production and greater regional specialization. The totalitarian legislation whereby the imperial government sought to revive the economy eventually worked to its deteriment. One of the most serious defects of the economy was the poor distribution of purchasing power, which was concentrated more and more in the hands of the great landowners who grew richer even as the majority of the population became poorer. Lack of purchasing power on the part of the masses crippled both commerce and industry.

With an increasingly stagnant agrarian economy, society took on an even more static, stratified aspect. Economic maldistribution was accompanied by unequal social advantages. The government contributed by freezing most workers and businessmen in their occupations, which were often made hereditary, thus setting up what was almost a caste system. Governmental officials, military personnel, the clergy, and especially the great and wealthy landed aristocracy were in a privileged class. Each of these groups had their special legal privileges, their own courts, and the means of ensuring their own well-being. The rest of the population in the Later Empire were unprivileged. Middle-class businessmen and free rural landowners, previously the most dynamic elements, were bound by law to the status of *curiales*, which entailed the obligation of collecting local taxes and exacting services imposed by the government. The "colleges"[h] of craftsmen and artisans were under the supervision of the central government, which required of them numerous burdensome services. The vast army of dependent *coloni* bound to the soil, were eking out a bare existence by laboring on the estates of the great landowners.

[h] *"collegia."* Cf. above.

Religious and moral factors probably contributed to the fall of the Empire in the West, though just how much is disputed. Pagan contemporaries loudly proclaimed that the catastrophes of their day, such as the sack of Rome by the Visigoths in 410, were due to widespread desertion of the pagan deities. It is true that Christianity challenged some of the things the Roman Empire stood for, such as subjugation, exploitation, and preoccupation with the physical aspects of life. The Church preached peace instead of war, patience instead of violence, and the spiritual instead of the material. In this sense, Christianity may have contributed something to the fall. On the other hand, by its high moral code and persevering purpose, Christianity strengthened the state, obedience to which it supported as a moral obligation, and the defense of which it eventually accepted as licit.

Religious transition and moral instability

Even after conversion, it took considerable time for people to become really Christian in outlook and habits. The West was still in a process of social and religious transition in which paganism had not yet been completely put away while Christianity had not yet established firm roots. Such a period is most trying for everyone, since neither the old nor the new is well entrenched. It takes much longer for a society and its customs to change than it does for individuals. Christianity became ascendant only in the eleventh hour. By the early part of the fourth century, only about one tenth of the people in the Empire were Christians.

Cultural change

There was also a maldistribution between secular and religious culture, as well as in their diffusion. The fifth century was one of recession and sterility in later Roman secular culture. Notable examples of architecture and art, as well as science and philosophy, are singularly lacking. In literature, the few pagan writers worthy of mention include the polished, shallow Symmachus, and the imaginative court poet Claudian, neither of whom outlived the first decade of the fifth century.

At the same time Western Christian culture displayed a burst of brilliance. As has been seen, the Patristic period in the West reached its apogee with St. Jerome (d. 420) and St. Augustine (d. 430). Excellent devotional poetry and hymns were produced early in the century by the Spanish-born Prudentius (d. 405) and by Paulinus of Nola (d. 431), a native of Gaul. Suggestive of the new spirit is the explanation of Paulinus to his old teacher Ausonius as to how a higher calling has led him to desert the service of literature for that of Christ: *Why bid the Muses . . . return to claim my devotion? . . . Now another force, a mightier God subdues my soul. He forbids me to surrender my time to the vanities of leisure or business and fictitious literature that I may obey His laws and see His light. . . .*

Some notion of the life of the old aristocracy in Gaul in the second half of the fifth century is given in the affected but gracious three volumes of letters by aristocratic Sidonius Apollinaris, who, after being prefect of Gaul, died as Bishop of Clermont. Meanwhile, classical education and intellectual culture was largely a sort of "hot house plant" kept alive artificially in schools and upper-class circles accessible only to a privileged few, except insofar as it was partially preserved by the clergy.

455ff.

THE BARBARIAN INVASIONS RUN THEIR COURSE.
Section 12.

The Roman Empire, having been gradually devastated, has been converted into a habitation of barbarians. . . . [Zosimus, *History*, iv, 59 (fifth century).]

THE YEAR 455, in addition to being a crucial turning point in the history of the Western Empire, was pivotal for the barbarian invasions. The assassination of the Western Emperor Valentinian III in 455 and the usurpation of supreme control in the West by Germanic generals constituted a signal and an excuse for the various barbarian *foederati* established in the Western Empire to become still more independent and to extend their holdings with ever less restraint. Further depositions and assassinations of shadow-emperors, who at best ruled over only a part of the Western Empire, served to confirm and deepen the conviction that the former territories of the Empire were "fair game" for those strong enough to seize them.

After 455, as has been seen, the Visigoths extended their control across southern Gaul as well as through the Iberian peninsula, becoming so powerful that their acquisitions and independence were recognized in 475 by the Western Emperor. Also after 455, as noted, the Vandals

The Barbarians and the Empire

brought under their rule the principal islands of the Western Mediterranean and built up an empire in North Africa that was recognized as independent by the Eastern emperors (476ff). At the same time, as we shall see, Italy, Gaul, and Britain came completely under barbarian control, so that by the close of the fifth century most of the former Roman Empire in the West was in barbarian hands.

The renown, wealth, and climate of Italy attracted the barbarians like a magnet. Practically all the major barbarian groups visited Italy during the Völkerwanderung. In the two decades from 455 to 476, although still supposedly ruled by puppet emperors, Italy was actually controlled by Germanic generals. During most of this time the Suevian kingmaker Ricimer was master (sc. from 456 until his death in 472). For one and a half decades following the deposition of Romulus Augustulus (sc. 476–ca. 490), Italy was ruled by General Odovacar, without the pretext of a Western Emperor, and with only vague reference to deputization by the Eastern Emperor. But Odovacar's rule in Italy was challenged in 489 by a large-scale invasion of Ostrogoths.

Italy in the age of invasions

The Ostrogoths were East Germans who had gradually moved southward from the Baltic region to the north of the Black Sea by the early third century. Here they had established control of the broad and fertile area between the Dniester and Don Rivers, and were converted to Arian Christianity in the fourth century. Despite strenuous resistance, during which two successive kings met death, the Ostogoths were overwhelmed and subjected by the advancing Huns in the early 370s. Henceforth Ostrogothic warriors participated in Hunnic military operations until, following the death of Attila in 453, they with other Germans revolted and regained their independence. The Ostrogoths were then accepted by the Eastern Emperors as *foederati*: first in Pannonia (present-day Hungary) in 454, and subsequently in Lower Moesia and Thrace.

The Gothic element became dominant in the Eastern Roman army and government during the ascendancy of Gothic kingmaker Aspar (ca. 450–471). Both the militant Marcian (450–457) and the resolute Leo I (457–474) were selected by Aspar. But Leo I eventually turned against the kingmaker and brought about his murder and that of his sons (471). Leo further checkmated the Goths by introducing into the army a large number of warlike Isaurians from mountainous southern Asia Minor. But under his successor, Zeno (474–491), the Ostrogoths became dissatisfied and demanded better lands than those assigned to them. Led by their able Amal chieftain, Theodoric, who had obtained a good education in Constantinople and had been Zeno's lieutenant, the Ostrogoths revolted and ravaged various Balkan provinces. Finally Zeno decided on a course which would at once divert the Ostrogothic menace and punish the unruly Odovacar for his audacity in seizing control of Italy.

Zeno sent Theodoric to Italy with a commission to replace Odovacar. Theodoric and his Ostrogoths entered the Italian peninsula in 489. After a series of victories, they forced Odovacar and his followers to take refuge in the almost impregnable fastness of Ravenna, approachable by land only over a single causeway surrounded by marshes. Unable to dislodge

Odovacar even after a two years' siege, Theodoric resorted to a ruse. Pretending a willingness to share the rule of Italy with Odovacar, he invited the latter and his leading officers to a banquet to celebrate the peace (493). In the midst of the festivities, Theodoric and his Ostrogoths suddenly attacked and slew Odovacar and his followers. The tricked Odovacar is said to have exclaimed, "Where is God?" To which Theodoric is reported to have cried, "Thus thou didst to my companions!" as he cut Odovacar through from shoulder to thigh with his sword. Henceforth Theodoric, although simulating submission to Constantinople, was known as "King of the Ostrogoths," "Patrician of the Romans," and "Governor of Italy." Under his enlightened rule (493–526), Italy prospered, and even the prejudiced Byzantine historian Procopius declared: *His manner of ruling . . . was worthy of a great Emperor. For he maintained justice, made good laws, protected his subjects from invasion, and demonstrated extraordinary prudence and valor.*

Byzantines and Lombards in Italy

After the death of Theodoric the Great in 526, dissensions soon broke out among the Ostrogoths. Taking advantage of their internal division, Justinian commenced the reconquest of the Italian peninsula in 535. It seemed that Belisarius had accomplished the subjection of Italy by 540, but the Ostrogoths soon resumed resistance which lasted for another fifteen years. By 554, however, the Byzantines controlled practically all of Italy.

The *Langobardi* or Lombards, so called from their long beards, were an East German Suevic people, located at an early date in the northern Elbe and Oder River valleys. The last of the German peoples to invade the Roman Empire, the Lombards were less respectful of Roman civilization than their predecessors. Accepted as *foederati* in Pannonia in the early sixth century, the Lombards gave some aid to Eastern Roman forces in the reconquest of Italy from the Ostrogoths. But their chief concern at this time was their bitter rivalry with their neighbors, the Gepids (also Germanic). Eventually, with the help of the Asiatic Avars, the Lombards decisively defeated the Gepids. The Lombard King, Alboin, converted the skull of the slain Gepid king into a drinking cup.

Following the death of Justinian, the bold Alboin led his Lombards into northern Italy (568). Here they rapidly conquered most of the Po valley, henceforth known as Langobardia or Lombardy. Making Pavia their capital, the Lombards also extended their conquests into north central and south central Italy. They came to be known to the native Italians as "Unspeakables." Their conquest was cruel and destructive, since they initially had no respect for either the Roman Empire or the Catholic Church. They made no pretext of becoming imperial *foederati* in Italy, lacked the restraint of previous invaders, and confiscated most of the land in territories they seized.

Lombard conquests in Italy were mainly limited to the interior of the peninsula. Urban-centered coastal regions such as those of Rome, Naples, Genoa, Ravenna, the Pentapolis, and Venice, together with far southern Italy and the island of Sicily, were retained by the Byzantines. The Lombards, who lacked a fleet, were unable to take strongly fortified coastal

The Barbarians and the Empire

cities which could be provisioned and reinforced by the Byzantine navy. Italy was now divided and remained so—a disunited "geographical expression"—until the middle of the nineteenth century.

Gaul in the age of invasions

Both the exposed position and the rich resources of Gaul invited barbarian incursions. As a result, East and West Germans alike invaded Gaul, which was soon divided between various groups. With the single exception of the Lombards, all the leading barbarian peoples who invaded continental Western Europe visited Gaul. Until the later fifth century, Roman rule persisted in the rich valley of the Seine under successive Roman Generals Aegidius and Syagrius. Both the Ostrogoths and Visigoths held sections of southern (southeastern and southwestern) Gaul as long as their kingdoms endured.

While the Visigoths and others kept the main Roman armies occupied with thrusts toward the heart of the Empire, the Vandals, Alans, and Suevi broke across the borders and ravaged Gaul (407–409) before they descended into Spain. In their wake came the Burgundians, Franks and Alemanni, who moved forward into Gaul (407), but were partly restrained by Roman prestige and Roman commanders, notably Aetius, until the assassination of Valentinian III in 455. Following the latter, the barbarians engaged in aggressive expansion. Thus the Visigoths added Septimania and Provence as well as the Iberian Peninsula to their Kingdom of Toulouse. The Hunnic invasion of Gaul under Attila in 451 was abruptly terminated by the victory of Aetius and his Germanic allies at Chalons in 451.

The Alemanni in Gaul

The *Alemanni*, as their name (all men) suggests, were a confederation of several Germanic peoples, formed by the close of the second century after Christ in the Rhineland to the south of the Main River, evidently as a result of the dual pressures from the Romans and neighboring Germans. In the third and fourth centuries the Alemanni repeatedly invaded the Empire. Although unable at this time to establish themselves permanently in the Empire proper, they did succeed in occupying the whole of the triangular salient between the upper Rhine and upper Danube which had previously been held by the Romans.

In the wake of the Vandalic invasion of Gaul in 407, many Alemanni crossed the Rhine and occupied Alsace and its vicinity, where they took such cities as Strasbourg, Speyer, and Worms. They also crossed the upper Danube into Rhaetia. Their advance into Gaul brought the Alemanni into competition with the Franks, who eventually defeated and subjected them.

The Burgundians in Gaul

The Burgundians were East Germans whose early home was between the middle Oder and Vistula Rivers. In the third century the Burgundians moved southwestward into the upper valley of the Main River, where for some time they were hemmed in by the more powerful Alemanni and Vandals. But during the westward movement of the latter in the early fifth century (406–407), the Burgundians crossed the Rhine in the vicinity of Mainz and Worms. When they sought later to move farther westward (about 435), they were met and severely defeated by an army of Huns in the employ of General Aetius, giving rise to the legend of the

Nibelungenlied. The depleted Burgundians were later (443) permitted by Aetius to settle as *foederati* in Savoy on the upper reaches of the Rhône. They fought on the Roman side in the battle at Chalons (451) and kept the *foedus* (treaty with Rome) until the assassination of Valentinian III. But from 455 on, the Burgundians expanded throughout most of the Rhône and Saône valleys. However, they were unable permanently to acquire the southernmost part of the Rhône valley, known as Provence.

The Franks to 481

The most permanently successful of the Germanic invaders were the Franks, whose name may mean "free" or "brave" or "wild." Their early home (Mainz) was on the right (east) bank of the Rhine, between the Main River and the North Sea. Like the Alemanni to their south, the Franks were a confederation of tribes formed, by the third century, for military cooperation and mutual security. By the fourth century the Franks were divided into two groups: Salian and Ripuarian, of whom the more progressive were the Salian Franks, located northward towards the sea in Holland. The name "Salian" seems to have been derived either from *sal*, salt, or from the Saale (Yssel or Ijssel) River located in this region. The Ripuarian Franks, whose name comes from *ripa*, bank, were located along the east bank of the Rhine in the (more southern) region opposite Cologne.

Like other Germanic barbarians established along the Roman frontiers, the Franks were anxious to secure lands in the Empire, which they invaded several times during the third and fourth centuries. Emperor Julian severely defeated the Salian Franks (358), but allowed them to remain as *foederati* in northern Gaul in the region between the Scheldt and Meuse Rivers. Two years later Julian also defeated the Ripuarian Franks, who had invaded the Empire and seized Cologne, and compelled them to retire across the Rhine.

In the early fifth century, the Salian Franks began to expand in northern Gaul, but they were checked by Aetius who defeated them in 431. Aetius, however, allowed the Salians to remain as *foederati* and to expand their holdings. Under Meroveus, the grandfather of Clovis, the Salian Franks fought on the Roman side in the battle of Chalons (451). The Ripuarian Franks advanced across the Rhine in the early fifth century, in the vicinity of Cologne and Treves, but their advance was slow and they were compelled to retake leading towns in the area several times.

After the assassination of Valentinian III (455), the Ripuarian Franks obtained control of the area between the Meuse and Moselle Rivers to the west of the Rhine, including such towns as Cologne, Treves, and Bonn. The Salian Franks, to their west, held the territory between the Meuse and the Somme, which included such towns as Charleroi, Namur, Tournai, and Cambrai in Belgium and far northwestern France. The Salian King, Childeric (d. 481), was apparently loyal to the Roman cause, which was represented by two successive Roman generals, Aegidius and Syagrius—father and son—who ruled in the valley of the Seine and in the extensive region between the Somme and the Loire Rivers. Childeric and his warriors helped the Romans ward off successive invasions by Visigoths, Saxons, and Alemanni. Further Frankish expansion at this

The Barbarians and the Empire

time was hampered, since they were divided into several small kingdoms, and hence were weak in comparison with their more unified neighbors. This deficiency, however, was remedied by Clovis, who succeeded his father Childeric as king of the Tournai Franks in 481, and expanded his control over the greater part of Gaul.

Conquered by successive waves of Celts in the course of the last five centuries before Christ, Britain (England) was added to the Roman Empire early in the Christian era. During the Roman occupation, which lasted for almost four centuries, Britain was partitioned into Roman estates, crisscrossed with Roman roads, dotted with Roman towns, and protected on the north by a stout Roman wall begun by Emperor Hadrian (ca. A.D. 120). It was defended by Roman legions and a Roman fleet. Britain also received Christianity during this period.

Britain in the age of invasions

When the Visigoths invaded Italy and other barbarians overran the continental frontiers of the Empire in the opening decade of the fifth century, Roman troops were withdrawn from Britain. The departure of the legions was a signal for neighboring barbarians to mount incursions on a large scale. The full story of the invasions of Britain is veiled in obscurity since contemporary historians have left us only fragmentary scraps of information. Venerable Bede, writing three centuries later, tells us that initially the adjacent Picts and the Scots to the north were the most troublesome. The Picts or *Picti* (literally "painted men"), so called from their habit of painting themselves before battle, were evidently fierce barbarians, probably Celtic in speech, who dwelt in the lowlands of Scotland. The Scots (*Scotti* in Scotland) seem to have been Celtic-speaking invaders who had migrated from Ireland to the Scottish highlands in the northern part of the island whence, given the occasion, they invaded Britain. There were also at this time seafaring Germanic invaders from the continent, often referred to indiscriminately as "Saxons."

Against these and other barbarians, the people of Roman Britain, who had apparently lost their military aptitude as a consequence of centuries of Roman rule, called in, according to Bede, Germanic barbarians from across the North Sea. The latter seem to have much resembled the later Vikings in their adventurous overseas travel in long, slim boats propelled by oars, and their alternation of peaceful trade with piracy and plunder. So troublesome, in fact, had these "Saxons" become that the Romans had been compelled to maintain a fleet in the Channel area to protect Gaul and Britain from their depredations. It is generally accepted that in the fifth and sixth centuries these Germanic newcomers were composed of closely related Saxons, Angles, and Jutes from northwestern Germany and the Danish peninsula across the North Sea.

Whether the Germanic barbarians who came to Britain in the fifth to sixth centuries did so at the invitation of the inhabitants and subsequently changed from protectors to conquerors, or whether they simply came as invaders, will probably never be known for certain. Perhaps they did so in both manners. Certainly they did not come in any single, organized, concerted expedition, but in a series of waves spread out over almost

Emergence of a new Western Europe

two centuries. Among various barbarians who made a bid for Britain, these seafaring Germanic invaders from the continent were most successful.

By the close of the fifth century a new Western Europe was emerging. Following the division of the Roman Empire into two states, the Western Empire disintegrated. Although its demise was partly traceable to internal reasons, the main cause was the incursion of Germanic barbarians. Initially playing the part of *foederati,* Teutonic groups occupied the various sections of the Western Empire. While their chieftains ruled their German subjects as kings, they initially ruled their Roman subjects as nominal delegates of the imperial government. The Germanic invasions resulted in a temporary retardation of almost every aspect of life in Western Europe. Yet despite their initial paralyzing effects, in the long run the invasions cleared the way for the rise of vigorous national states which would eventually gain world leadership.

References for Chapter 4

A BASIC work on this period, including its social, economic, political, military, and ecclesiastical institutions, is ARNOLD H. M. JONES, *The Later Roman Empire, 284–602,* 2 vols. (Norman: Oklahoma U.P., 1964). JONES also has a shorter survey entitled *The Decline of the Ancient World* (New York: Holt, 1966). The history of the Later Roman Empire in the West and the Barbarian Invasions is summarized, in condensed manner, by the reliable ARTHUR E. R. BOAK AND W. G. SINNEGEN, *A History of Rome to 565 A.D.,* 2nd ed. (New York: Macmillan, 1956); is given in fuller form by the source-based JOHN B. BURY, *A History of the Later Roman Empire . . . ,* vol. I, 2 vols. (London: Macmillan, 1889); and in still more extensive fashion by the collaborative *Cambridge Medieval History,* vol. I. This period is also the concern of FERDINAND LOT, *The End of the Ancient World and the Beginning of the Middle Ages* (New York: Knopf, 1931), which carries the subject from about A.D. 280 to 751; the brief, well-illustrated PETER BROWN, *The World of Late Antiquity, A.D. 150–750* (New York: Harcourt, 1971); and the concise, well-organized SOLOMON KATZ, *The Decline of Rome and the Rise of Mediaeval Europe* (Ithaca, N. Y.: Cornell, U.P., 1955) which runs from about A.D. 138 to 600 in synoptic fashion. The causes of the fall of the Western Empire are the preoccupation of the exceedingly short but well-written REGINALD F. ARRAGON, *The Transition from the Ancient to the Medieval World* (New York: Holt, 1936); as well as of FRANK W. WALBANK, *The Decline of the Roman Empire in the West* (New York: Schuman, 1953). The moralistic fifth-century priest SALVIAN (SALVIANUS), *On the Government of God . . . ,* tr. EVA M. SANFORD (New York: Columbia U.P., 1930) makes a vivid but exaggerated indictment of the vices of the Romans as the reason for their reverses. A penetrating analysis of factors in the decline is given by MIKHAIL I. ROSTOVSTZEFF, *The Social and Economic History of the Roman Empire* (Oxford: Clarendon, 1926). A general picture of civilization and life in the Empire from about 376 to 476, expertly based on the sources, is provided by SAMUEL DILL, *Roman Society in the Last Century of the Western Empire,* 2nd rev. ed. (New York: Macmillan, 1925). An elementary introduction to literature in the period is available in about 50 pages in FREDERICK A. WRIGHT and T. A. SINCLAIR, *A History of Later Latin Literature . . .* (New York: Macmillan, 1931); while painting and sculpture are ably treated by CHARLES R. MOREY, *Early Christian Art* (Princeton: Princeton U. P., 1942); and architecture is briefly treated by CECIL STEWART, *Early Christian, Byzantine, and Romanesque Architecture* (London: Longmans, 1954), pp. 9–46.

The most extensive account of the barbarian invasions available in English is the monumental classic by THOMAS HODGKIN, *Italy and Her Invaders*, 8 vols. in 9 (Oxford: Clarendon, 1885–1899). Since HODGKIN goes into detail on the history of all the barbarians who visited Italy: sc. the Visigoths, Huns, Vandals, Ostrogoths, Lombards, and Franks, and not merely those who settled there, his eminently readable work is practically a general history of the invasions. PASQUALE VILLARI's *The Barbarian Invasions of Italy*, tr. LINDA VILLARI, 2 vols. (London: Unwin, 1902) is much more limited in compass and secondary in nature but still useful. Convenient accounts of the various barbarian invasions are given in the already cited *Cambridge Medieval History*, vol. I. If available, JULIUS PFLUGK-HARTTUNG, *The Great Migrations* (Philadelphia: Lea, 1905), which is volume VI in his *History of All Nations* (tr.); and JOHN B. BURY, *The Invasions of Europe by the Barbarians* (New York: Macmillan, 1928) are also helpful. CARLTON J. H. HAYES, *An Introduction to the Sources Relating to the Germanic Invasions* (New York: Columbia U. P., 1909), one of the most valuable works on its subject, comprises short, pointed discussions of and extracts from Greek and Latin sources concerning the barbarian invaders down to the eighth century. The surviving books of *Ammianus Marcellinus* . . . , tr. J. O. ROLFE, 3 vols. (Cambridge: Harvard U. P., 1935–1939), which treat the period A.D. 353 to 378, are valuable for their description of the Huns and Visigoths at the outset of the invasions. More specialized works on the Huns are MARCEL BRION, *The Story of the Huns*, tr. F. H. MARTENS (New York: McBride, 1931) and E. A. THOMPSON, *A History of Attila and the Huns* (Oxford: Clarendon, 1948). Besides the occasionally credulous brief contemporary account of the Goths by the priest JORDANES in his *Gothic History*, tr. CHARLES C. MIEROW (Princeton: Princeton U. P., 1915), the history of the Visigoths and Ostrogoths is well treated by HENRY BRADLEY, *The Story of the Goths* . . . (New York: Putnam, 1888). In the eighth century the aristocratic Benedictine monk, PAUL THE DEACON (PAULUS DIACONUS), wrote a *History of the Lombards* which has been translated and annotated by W. D. FOULKE (New York: Longmans, 1907). For the Frankish invasion and conquest of Gaul, see our subsequent bibliography for The New West; and for the invasion and conquest of Britain by the Angles, Saxons, and Jutes, see our bibliography for Anglo-Saxon England.

(ca. 400–1050)

PART II. THE EARLY MIDDLE AGES.

HE EARLY MIDDLE AGES (ca. 400/500–1050) were a turbulent era of transformation, comparable to adolescence. A leading development was the difficult fusion of classical, Christian, and barbarian ingredients. After an initial period of incomplete combination and contrasting coexistence, coordination of these elements was improved in the Carolingian Age. The latter was transitional to the crude but workable compromise known as "feudalism," necessitated by new barbarian invasions. Meanwhile the Christian Church, the chief civilizing and cultural force in this troubled era, nurtured a gradual revival of culture, whose first harvest was the "Carolingian Renaissance." Actual leadership in most fields was enjoyed first by Byzantium and then by Islam, before it passed to the West during the High Middle Ages.

References for Part II

A GOOD introductory survey of general developments in the Early Middle Ages is ARCHIBALD R. LEWIS, *Emerging Medieval Europe*, A.D. 400–1000 (New York: Knopf, 1967). An excellent interpretative analysis and description of leading forces is CHRISTOPHER H. DAWSON, *The Making of Europe* (New York: Macmillan, 1932). A well-written, brief, interpretative history is JOHN M. WALLACE-HADRILL, *The Barbarian West, 400–1000* (London: Hutchinson's 1952). Another standard work is HENRY S. L. B. MOSS, *The Birth of the Middle Ages* (London: Oxford U. P., 1935). A brief introduction is provided by RICHARD E. SULLIVAN, *Heirs of the Roman Empire* (Ithaca, N. Y., Cornell U. P., 1960)(p.). Older, but still helpful, are CHARLES R. L. FLETCHER, *The Dark Ages, 300–1000 A.D.* (London: Murray, 1912); and JULIUS PFLUGK-HARTUNG, *The Early Middle Ages*, tr. J. H. WRIGHT (Philadelphia: Lee, 1905).

There are several good works which treat the period from about 395 or 400 to about A.D. 800 or 900, including CECIL DELISLE BURNS, *The First Europe . . . A.D. 400–800* (New York: Norton, 1948); MARGARET DEANESLY, *A History of Early Medieval Europe, 476 to 911* (London, Methuen, 1956); and FERDINAND LOT, *The End of the Ancient World and the Beginning of the Middle Ages*, tr. P. and M. LEON (New York: Knopf, 1931). For culture in the period, one may consult MAX L. W. LAISTNER, *Thought and Letters in Western Europe, A.D. 500 to 900* (New York: MacVeagh-Dial, 1931); and EDWARD K. RAND, *Founders of the Middle Ages* (Cambridge: Harvard U. P., 1928); as well as (for the sixth century) ELEANOR S. DUCKETT, *The Gateway to the Middle Ages* (New York: Macmillan, 1938).

(THE "NEW WEST": THE EARLY GERMANIC KING-
DOMS.   Chapter 5. (ca. 400–700)

HE "NEW WEST," which resulted from the barbarian partition of the Western Roman Empire, was characterized by multiplicity rather than unity, localism rather than centralization, internal warfare rather than tranquillity. Numerous lusty, immature Germanic states supplanted the Western Empire, and Europe's political center of gravity began to shift northward. The old Roman Empire, based on military power and having secular aims, was succeeded by the Christian Church, whose mission and appeal were mainly moral and spiritual. The Western economy became steadily more agrarian and society more stratified while culture was at low tide.

THE EARLY GERMANIC KINGDOMS ON ROMAN SOIL.
Section 13.

> In the third year after his entry into Italy . . . , Theodoric laid aside the garb of a private citizen and the dress of his race, and assumed apparel with a royal mantle. . . . He sent an embassy to Clovis and asked for his daughter [sister] Audefleda in marriage. Clovis freely and gladly gave her . . . believing that thus an alliance would be formed. . . . [An aspect of international relations in the "new West," related by Jordanes in his *History of the Goths* (sixth century).]

As THE Roman Empire in the West collapsed, several Germanic kingdoms took its place. Some of the latter were ephemeral, such as those of Odovacar in Italy and the Burgundians in southeastern Gaul. Others lasted somewhat longer, such as the rule of the Ostrogoths in Italy (about half a century) and that of the Vandals in North Africa (about a century). The kingdoms of the Visigoths in Spain and the Lombards in Italy endured for two to three centuries. Several lesser barbarian kingdoms coalesced or were absorbed by stronger states, as happened with the numerous early Frankish and Anglo-Saxon kingdoms. Only one state on the continent finally survived: that of the Franks.

After the deaths of their early leaders, the paths of these Germanic kingdoms became rough and difficult. In addition to international wars, the new states were afflicted by internal instability and violence, revolts and assassinations. Wars flared up frequently between the various kingdoms as they strove for ascendance over one another, claimed disputed territories, and interfered in each other's internal affairs. Within the several states violent rivalries developed between nobles and kings, and among the nobility, as well as between Romans and Germans, Catholics and Arians. Many rulers were assassinated or slain in battle, and most of their names have deservedly fallen into oblivion. One crippling weakness was a lack of adequate governmental machinery. The religious question was a leading cause for division, as most of the Germanic conquerors were Arians, whereas their subjects were Catholics.

The Vandal kingdom in North Africa

The Vandal kingdom in North Africa was for about a century the dominant power in the western Mediterranean. When the Vandals crossed over into North Africa in 429, they were led by their energetic, ambitious, statesmanlike King Gaiseric, whose successful reign lasted for half a century (428–477). Gaiseric extended Vandal control over northwestern Africa, where the Vandals were accepted by the imperial government as *foederati* in 435, and recognized as independent in 442.

Although never able to subdue the Berbers in the interior of North Africa completely, the Vandals assembled a strong fleet wherewith they secured possession of the main islands of the western Mediterranean. The Western Mediterranean Empire of the Vandals included Sicily, Sardinia, Corsica, and the Balearics, as well as present-day Morocco, Algeria, and Tunisia. Following the assassination of Valentinian III in 455, Gaiseric, posing as an avenger, sailed to Italy, took Rome, and thoroughly sacked the city. He carried off to Carthage the Emperor's widow and two daughters, one of whom became the bride of his son Hunneric. So formidable was the Vandals' naval strength at this time that they were able to defeat both a Western Roman fleet sent against them by Emperor Majorian in 460 and a large combined Eastern and Western fleet assembled by the Emperor Leo I in 464. The Eastern Emperor Zeno was constrained to recognize their conquests and conclude a "perpetual peace" with them in 476.

Vandal power declined under Gaiseric's successors. The Vandals seem to have been enervated by the mild North African climate and weakened by self-indulgence, luxury, and indolence. A main source of instability was the failure of the conquerors to intermarry with the local population. The fluctuating policy of the Arian rulers towards the Roman Catholic population was a thorny problem. Gaiseric's son, King Hunneric (477–484) at first showed toleration towards his Catholic subjects, but later persecuted them. The position of the Catholic Church improved under the next king, but deteriorated under the latter's successor. The aged Hilderic, who came to the throne in 523, was a Catholic. Unacceptable to the military and the Arians he was overthrown by the army and replaced by Gelimer (530–532). When Gelimer renewed earlier anti-Catholic, anti-Byzantine Vandal policies, he supplied a pretext for Byzantine intervention (532).

The Visigothic kingdom in Southwestern France and Spain

The Visigothic kingdom was one of the most advanced and powerful of the early Germanic states. Originally established in southwestern Gaul, it expanded to include Spain. After it lost most of its Gallic territory, the Iberian peninsula became its ultimate home. This story is typical of the early Germanic kingdoms, being marked by frequent assassinations and revolutions, and by the power of the nobility on the one hand and the influence of the Church on the other. The nobility succeeded in establishing the premise that the monarchy was elective. Spanish church councils meeting at Toledo periodically, and attended by lay leaders as well as ecclesiastical prelates, eventually became, in effect, national assemblies.

For almost two centuries the Visigoths remained Arian Christians, and hence heretics in the eyes of the orthodox population. Assassinations and depositions of monarchs were monotonously repetitious. Successive codifications of Visigothic and Roman law were made in King Euric's (466–485) *Statuta Legum* and Alaric II's (485–507) *Lex Romana Visigothorum* (or *Breviary* of Alaric), while a combined codification of both laws as evolved by custom was made by King Recesswinth in his *Forum Judicum* (*Fuero Juzco*) in 654. In 507 the Visigoths lost southwestern Gaul, except for a strip along the Mediterranean coast known as Septimania, to the Franks; but the intervention of the powerful Ostrogothic king of Italy, Theodoric the Great, saved them from further losses. After being invited to intervene in a civil war in Spain in the middle of the sixth century, the Byzantines held Baetica in the far south of the Iberian peninsula for about half a century. Following the conversion of King Recared to orthodox Christianity in 587, the frequent Church Councils of Toledo were political as well as ecclesiastical assemblies. They upheld simultaneously the elective nature of the monarchy and the fulness of monarchical power. But free election of kings by nobles and prelates contributed to political instability and numerous disputed successions and civil wars. The Arab menace from North Africa loomed large after 670 and culminated in an invasion from Morocco (711–718), resulting in the overthrow of the weakened Visigothic kingdom and the Moslem occupation of most of Spain for several centuries.

Italy was a magnet for most barbarian groups and a prize sought after by the Byzantines as well as by the Germans. Italy came under the indirect control of Germanic generals following the assassination of Valentinian III in 455, and under direct German control in 476, when General Odovacar (476–493), deposed the puppet emperor Romulus Augustulus and sent the imperial insignia to the Eastern Emperor Zeno (476). Odovacar ruled Italy as Zeno's nominal lieutenant, as well as elected king of the Germanic Rugii, Sciri, and Heruli. Meanwhile, the old Roman civilian government carried on much as before, though an estimated third of available Italian land was distributed among Odovacar and his followers. *Italy*

Odovacar was overthrown (488–493) by Theodoric the Great, King of the Ostrogoths, who controlled Italy, as well as Noricum, Rhaetia, and Pannonia to the north along the Danube, Provence in Southeastern Gaul, and the island of Sicily. Under Theodoric (d. 526), Italy enjoyed considerable peace and prosperity. Theodoric ruled as supposed representative of the Eastern Emperor and retained much of the old Roman government, including the Senate and other Roman officials. Order was restored, crime and brigandage suppressed, public works and improvements promoted. Land division on behalf of the Germans was made as painless as possible, and agriculture expanded. Although himself an Arian, Theodoric was friendly to the Catholic Church and pursued a policy of noninterference with the Papacy. His paternal international policy vis-à-vis the various barbarian kings of the West was partly implemented by royal intermarriages. After seeking unsuccessfully to preserve peace between the Franks and the Visigoths, he prevented the Franks from expanding beyond Aquitaine into Provence and Septimania. In his later years, *The Ostrogoths in Italy*

Theodoric became overly apprehensive and besmirched his reputation by a persecution of the Romans and Catholics.

Ostrogothic rule and power declined after Theodoric's death in 526. His daughter, Amalasuntha, served as regent for her young son for eight years. After her son's death she called to the throne her cousin Theodohad (534–536), who repaid her trust by having her murdered. When this gave the Byzantines an excuse to intervene, the Ostrogoths replaced Theodohad by Witigis (536–541), who stoutly resisted the invaders until he was captured and taken to Constantinople. Undaunted, the Ostrogoths again elected a new king, Totila (541), who continued resistance until he was slain in a skirmish in 552.

Byzantine Italy

After two decades of grueling warfare (534–554) the Byzantines subdued Italy, overthrowing the Ostrogoths and expelling the Franks. The Byzantines were helped by their command of the seas. Eventually they ruled Italy through a plenipotentiary exarch (Viceroy), located at the seaport and fastness of Ravenna, near the head of the Adriatic.

Within a decade after the death of Justinian, the Lombards invaded Italy and occupied much of the interior of the peninsula, especially the northern and central parts. Because of their maritime supremacy the Byzantines were able to retain control of territories around coastal strongholds, such as Venice, Ravenna, Genoa, Rome, and Naples, as well as southern Italy, and Sicily. The growing secular power of the Pope as the "Patrician" and "Duke" of the Roman Duchy was a feature of the period. Moslem conquests in the seventh to eighth centuries imperiled the Byzantine heartland and loosened the Byzantine hold on Italy. The Cesaropapist and heretical tendencies of the Byzantine emperors also served to alienate the West.

The Lombard kingdom in Italy

The Lombard kingdom was the latest as well as one of the most barbaric of the Germanic kingdoms established on former Roman soil. The Lombards, who had recently migrated from the farthest reaches of Germania, had little respect for Roman prestige, since the Empire had been so long defunct. They were fierce warriors and rugged individualists. They were also superstitious Arians, still half-pagan in the eyes of the local Roman and Catholic population, whom they oppressed.

Local Lombard dukes and counts enjoyed a large measure of autonomy. The Dukes of Spoleto and Benevento in the interior of Italy were, in fact, independent during most of Lombard history. The center of gravity of the Lombard kingdom lay in the Po Valley (Lombardy) in northern Italy, where their chief seat was Pavia.

The rough Lombard king, Alboin, who led their initial invasion and conquest of northern Italy (568ff.), was murdered in his bed (572) by his Gepid wife, whom he had forced to drink from her father's skull. His successor Cleph (572–574) was assassinated. The Lombard dukes then refused to elect a king for a decade, during which each ruled supreme in his own *civitas* or duchy. When the necessity of resisting Byzantine and Frankish pressures forced them to elect a king in 584, they chose Authari, who married a Bavarian Catholic princess, Theodelinda. On Authari's death in 590, his successor Agilulf married the attractive widow whose charm and piety helped obtain greater religious liberty and toleration for the Catholic population.

Succeeding Lombard administrations vacillated between pro-Roman, pro-Catholic policies and anti-Roman, anti-Catholic policies, until Catholicism was accepted as the official Lombard religion in the 670s. Religious peace and unity did not confer political tranquillity and stability, however, and periodic revolts and assassinations continued to characterize Lombard politics.

During the precipitous eighth century slump in Byzantine power in Italy, aggressive Lombard kings, Liutprand (712–744), Aistulf (749–756) and Desiderius (756–774) sought to conquer former Byzantine possessions in North Italy and unify the peninsula under their own rule. But their efforts were doomed by Papal opposition, ducal divisiveness, and Frankish intervention. The third Frankish invasion of Italy, led by Charlemagne (774), resulted in the overthrow of the Lombard kingdom and a substitution of Frankish control in former Lombard provinces.

One of the consequences of Frankish intervention in Italy was the establishment of the Papal States. From the time of Constantine's removal of his capital to the East, and Rome's replacement as imperial capital in the West, the Bishops of Rome had been entrusted with and had assumed increased political, judicial, military, and diplomatic responsibilities. Papal governmental responsibility continued under the Byzantines, and greatly increased as Byzantine power in the West declined. Eventually the inhabitants of the Roman Duchy and adjacent, nominally Byzantine territories looked to the Popes for temporal protection, as well as spiritual leadership. By the time of Pope Stephen (752–757), the Byzantine government recognized the Pope as a Patrician and Duke with a status similar to that of the Exarch of Ravenna.

The Papal States

Lombard ambitions to acquire Western holdings of the weakened and distracted Byzantine Empire included annexation of the Roman Duchy. After futile remonstrances to the aggressive Lombard kings, the Popes finally invoked Frankish aid in the eighth century. Although ineffective with Charles Martel, their pleas were favorably received by Pepin III and Charlemagne, who formally constituted the Papal States by their acts of 754, 756, and 774, as will be seen.

Conditions in England in the sixth and seventh centuries contrasted with those in other former Roman territories on the continent. In England, Anglo-Saxon Germanic political and social institutions, language, customs, and culture prevailed, although Roman influences, institutions, and culture soon began to intermingle. Our only written primary source of consequence concerning the early history of Anglo-Saxon England is Venerable Bede's *Ecclesiastical History of the English Nation,* written in the eighth century, and distinguished by Bede's objectivity and his "astonishing power of coordinating the fragments of information that came to him." Supplemental written sources include the sixth-century *Destruction of Britain* by Gildas and the ninth-century (ff.) *Anglo-Saxon Chronicle.*

Anglo-Saxon England (to about 700)

Germanic invaders entered Britain in successive waves. According to early tradition, the Angles, coming from the base of the Danish peninsula, occupied most of the North; and the Saxons, from the North Sea coast west of the Elbe, most of the South; while the Jutes, who may have come originally from the Danish peninsula of Jutland via the Rhineland, settled in a small southeastern projection of Britain. The Roman population and Roman civilization seem to have practically disappeared during the violent Germanic conquest. The native Celts were apparently either exterminated or enslaved or forced to flee into the hill country or to Wales, Brittany, or Ireland. Practically all traces of the Roman occupation of Britain except structural ruins disappeared. Germanic language and customs almost universally replaced the Roman and Celtic cultures. While elsewhere the Germanic conquerors were eventually assimilated by the Roman population, the reverse was true in Britain.

The Germanic invaders devoted themselves mainly to agriculture. Apparently accustomed to farming in the rich deep soil of alluvial plains, they seem to have kept to the lowlands, allowing the Celts to remain on the less desirable hills. The conquerors settled in nucleated villages, whence they went out to till the land, which they divided into fields and strips. To this day, traces of these are still sometimes discernible in aerial photographs. The Saxons, Angles, and Jutes seem to have shunned the towns which had grown up during the Roman occupation, except to pillage them. The political unity that had existed in Britain under Roman rule disappeared. Early Germanic political organization on the island was tribal and the land was at first divided into numerous petty kingdoms with what are now long-forgotten names such as Magonsaetan, Hwicce, Deira, Strathclyde, Manaw, Bernicia, Lindsay, Wreocensaetan, Pencersaetan, Toppingas, Feppingas, etc. But both geography and mutual interests, as well as foreign dangers and the ambitions of strong rulers, contributed to consolidation. By the middle of the seventh century seven larger kingdoms, known as the "Heptarchy," had been formed from the multiplicity of smaller states. In the south were traditionally Saxon Essex, Sussex, and Wessex; to the southeast purportedly Juttish Kent; and in the north assertedly Anglian Northumbria, Mercia, and East Anglia.

Christianization of England

Although Christianity was established in Britain in later Roman times, it was apparently mostly exterminated by the destructive Germanic conquest, except for Celtic Christian pockets which remained in the hill country and remote areas. Monk-missionaries from Ireland and Scotland soon revived the flame of Christianity in the more Celtic parts of Britain such as Northumbria, but they failed to organize the Church as a comprehensive, coordinated unit. Fuller organization of the English Church and the thorough conversion of England were promoted by missionaries from Rome. In 597, Pope Gregory I, "the Great," sent a mission led by St. Augustine, a monk of St. Andrew's, from Rome to Kent, whose Queen Bertha was a Catholic Frankish princess. King Ethelbert received the Roman monks favorably and allowed them to establish themselves at Canterbury ("the city of Kent"), which became England's primatial see. The Roman missionary movement was largely responsible for the con-

The "New West"

version of southern England, even as the Celtic movement was for northern England. The unification and progress of the English Church were promoted by the Council of Whitby (664) and by Papal appointment of the aged, but energetic and intelligent, Greek, Theodore of Tarsus, as Archbishop of Canterbury (669–690). The Council of Whitby, called by King Oswy of Northumbria to establish uniform ecclesiastical usages, decided to adopt Roman practices in such matters as the dating of Easter and the form of the clerical tonsure. With the aid of Abbot Hadrian in the South and Benedict Biscop in the North, Theodore both unified and vivified the English Church.

Trend to unity: the "Bretwaldas"

The concept of a single England was promoted by the Catholic Church which transcended political divisions. When Venerable Bede wrote his *Ecclesiastical History of the English People* in 731, he saw England as one from a religious point of view, despite its division into seven political kingdoms. Another unifying force was the tendency for the strongest king to dominate the others and to obtain leadership in the island, assuming the title of *Bretwalda* ("Broad-wielder" or "Ruler of Britain").

After the temporary ascendance of Kent under King Ethelbert (560–616), leadership shifted first to Northumbria (642–704) and then to Mercia (716–825). The early ascendance of the Angles prompted the name "England" which came to be applied to the country. Finally, about 825, the ascendance passed to Wessex, during the reign of King Egbert (802–839), who was grandfather of King Alfred the Great and ancestor of all subsequent English monarchs. By 850 there were only three to four truly independent kingdoms in England, with Wessex as the leader.

Anglo-Saxon institutions

Anglo-Saxon institutions differed from those on the continent in many ways. In England, institutions were more Germanic. Anglo-Saxon government has been characterized as a balance between three powers: king, aristocracy, and Church. The king was a limited monarch, and the kingship was regarded as partly hereditary, partly elective. The *Witan* or *Witangemot* (Wise Men or Meeting-of-the-Wisemen), an assembly of the leading great men of the kingdom, designated the successor to the throne, advised the king, declared the law, and acted as Supreme Court.

The "shires" ("shares" or "parts") of England, which corresponded to counties elsewhere, seem to have often been successors to earlier small tribal kingdoms. The "ealdorman" (elder-man) was at first the King's representative in the shire and headed the shire's moot or meeting as well as its military forces. Only later did he become identified with the "earl," who ruled several counties. The "sheriff" (or shire-reeve) was originally a lesser official, who was later promoted to the position previously held by the ealdorman, so that the sheriff then became the King's representative in the shire. The bishop was also an important local official, and with the ealdorman or earl and the sheriff, he presided over the shire court.

Judicial and deliberative assemblies (*gemots* or moots) were held on various levels, from the central court of the *Witangemot*, already mentioned, down through the shire-court, hundred-court, and village-court. The "hundred" may have originally been an area occupied by a hundred fighting men or a hundred families. The village or *tun* was a nucleated agricultural settlement whose members tilled the surrounding territory in a semicommunal manner.

The invaders had well-developed agriculture and metallurgy. Their economy was primarily agrarian, and their society seems to have included an aristocracy. The church in Anglo-Saxon England was originally organized on a semimonastic basis, whence the term *minster* (monastery) for cathedrals. For a while learning flowered with such scholars as Bede and Aldhelm, and English manuscript illumination led its field.

Barbarian kingdoms in Gaul

Gaul was initially divided among various barbarians. In the early fifth century, the Visigoths, as has been seen, established themselves in southwestern Gaul, with their capital at Toulouse. Thence they expanded to control all of southwestern Gaul, Septimania, and Provence. After their defeat by Clovis in 507, the Visigoths lost all their territory in Gaul save Septimania (along the Mediterranean, west of the Rhône). From the Kingdom in Italy, the Ostrogoths controlled Provence from 511 to 535, when it was ceded to the Franks as a price for their promised neutrality in the Ostrogothic struggle against the Byzantines. The Burgundians, who had been settled as *foederati* in the Savoy region in the early fifth century, expanded and occupied all of southeastern Gaul above Provence during the second half of the same century. The Burgundians were soon Romanized, as well as converted to Catholicism by c. 514, and King Gundobad (481–516) codified both Roman and Burgundian law for his subjects. Although the Burgundians successfully resisted the Frankish King Clovis, they were subjected by the latter's sons in 534. Burgundy had the status of a kingdom within Frankland from about 561 to 613. The Alemanni controlled the valley of the upper (southern) Rhine and adjacent territory until they were subjected by Clovis (496ff.). Fugitives from Britain settled in "Brittany" in the sixth century, and in the western districts of the peninsula the Celtic language prevailed. In far southwestern Gaul, the native Basques enjoyed considerable independence. Meanwhile, in the rich and expansive valley of the Seine, nominal Roman rule survived under the Roman Master of Soldiers Aegidius, and subsequently under his son Syagrius, who had their capital at Soissons. The Franks occupied the far north of Gaul.

RISE AND ASCENDANCE OF THE FRANKS.
Section 14.

The illustrious race of the Franks, established by God, courageous in war, faithful in peace, wise in their counsels . . . , converted to the Catholic faith and free from heresy . . . , this is the nation that shook off the galling yoke of the Romans in battle. [Prologue to the *Salic Law*.]

OF ALL the Germanic kingdoms, that of the Franks was the most successful. On the continent, the Frankish state expanded and endured until from it eventually emerged France and Germany and even Italy, as well as various smaller states. To some extent, institutionally and culturally, the Frankish state was also a parent of England and Spain as well as Portugal.

Several factors contributed to the success of the Franks. The land they occupied was centrally located in western Europe, and had rich natural resources, fertile soil, a temperate climate, adequate rainfall, and numerous river valleys. The Franks themselves had been long-time neighbors of the Roman Empire and were comparatively well advanced and adapted to Roman civilization. In contrast to most of the other barbarians, the Franks retained their homeland and even increased their holdings in Germany at the same time that they expanded in Gaul. They were converted to orthodox Christianity at an early date, thus obtaining the favor and support of the native Roman population and churchmen against their Arian and pagan German competitors. They also had greater security from attacks by strong naval powers, such as the Byzantines and Moslems, who controlled the Mediterranean Sea. An important factor was the able and energetic leadership of the early strong Merovingian kings and subsequent great Carolingian mayors and monarchs.

The early Franks were a confederation of several tribes in the lower and middle Rhineland who had come to regard themselves as closely related. Originally, the Salian Franks were situated northeast of the Rhine in the lower (northern) Rhineland, while the Ripuarian Franks were farther south along the Rhine's east bank (*ripa*) in the vicinity of Cologne. The Salian Franks were accepted as *foederati* in the Roman part of the Low Countries in the middle of the fourth century; during the fifth century both groups of Franks expanded their holdings in adjacent former Roman territories.

The founder of Frankish greatness was Clovis—the first "Louis," a grandson of that Merovech who had fought alongside the Romans against the Huns in 451. From Merovech comes the name "Merovingian." Clovis unified the Franks and extended his control over most of France and western Germany. He also consolidated his position by his conversion to orthodox Christianity. Clovis, who became King of the Tournai Franks in 481 at the age of 15, was strong, ambitious, hard, unscrupulous, and shrewd. Both his saintly wife, Clothilda, and the teachings of the Christian religion seem to have somewhat softened the roughness of his character, but Christianity only partly penetrated his barbarian soul. *Clovis (481–511) unifies the Franks*

During the course of his reign, Clovis unified the various tribes of the Franks, hitherto largely autonomous. He spurned no means, using force, intimidation, trickery, and downright duplicity to effect his purposes. On one occasion he persuaded an ambitious son to kill his father in order to gain the throne, and then occupied the kingdom "to punish the parricide." Another time he bribed sworn retainers (*leudes*) to betray their king, and when they later complained that they were being paid off with vessels of spurious gold (gilded copper), he declared: "This is the kind of gold deserved by anyone who intentionally lures his lord to his death," and added that they ought to be happy to have escaped execution. He deposed and tonsured one unlucky king along with his son, and when the son later remarked that his hair would grow back soon enough, he slew them both. Clovis systematically exterminated all who might possibly challenge his rule. Gregory of Tours tells us that when Clovis had eliminated all his known relatives, he complained: "Woe is me who live among strangers and have none of my kin to help me!" He did this, according to Gregory, not out of grief, but "craftily, to see if he could bring out of hiding some new relative to kill."

Expansion and conversion

Five years after his accession, Clovis, with the aid of the other Salian kings, challenged Syagrius, Roman ruler of the rich valley of the Seine in northwestern France. In the battle of Soissons (486), Clovis defeated Syagrius, who fled to Alaric II, king of the Visigoths. But Clovis threatened to attack Alaric unless he surrendered the Roman leader, so the Visigothic King turned over Syagrius, whom Clovis imprisoned and secretly slew. He thus removed any further danger to his recent acquisition of the strategic Seine valley.

As the Franks were expanding, the Alemanni were pushing westward. The Franks found it difficult to overcome their warlike fellow Germans, but Clovis persisted. During the hard-fought battle of Tolbiac (496), Clovis promised to become a Christian if his wife's God would give him victory. The Franks won and Clovis kept his promise. Eventually (by 507) the Alemanni were either subjected, displaced, or exterminated.

The early conversion of their King to Catholic Christianity was a factor in Frankish success. Clovis's wife, Clothilda, daughter of a former Burgundian King, together with Catholic bishops, such as Remi of Rheims, had been "working on" Clovis for some time in an attempt to bring about his baptism. But the Frankish victory over the Alemanni was a turning point. Following this success in battle, Clovis received instruction and was baptized with 3,000 of his followers at Rheims on Christmas Day in the year 496. The baptism was administered by Archbishop Remi, who is said to have told Clovis: "Meekly bow your head, O proud Sicambrian, and adore what you have destroyed, destroy what you have adored!" As a result of their conversion to orthodox Christianity, the Franks came to be accepted as the senior sons of the Catholic Church in the West, and henceforth enjoyed its special favor. The Franks now had the support of the Catholic bishops and the orthodox population in their contests with the other barbarians, who were either Arians or pagans. Conversion also opened the way to numerous beneficial and civilizing influences.

Explusion of the Visigoths from southwestern France

The political implications of the baptism of Clovis soon came into clearer relief. When Clovis set out to expel the Visigoths from Gaul, he used their Arianism as an excuse, saying piously, "It irketh me that these Arians hold part of Gaul. Let us go forth, with God's help, and bring this land under our own sway." In 507, Clovis, with a large army, marched into Aquitaine and met and defeated the Visigoths at Vouillé (Vougle) where King Alaric II was slain. The Franks now occupied all of southwestern Gaul except Visigothic Septimania, which they were prevented from acquiring by the intervention of Theodoric the Great. The attempts

The "New West"

of Clovis to acquire Burgundy were foiled by the craft of its capable King Gundobad, uncle of Clothilda.

Following his victory over the Visigoths, Clovis was recognized as Patrician and Consul by the Eastern Emperor, and thus became the nominal imperial representative in the lands he had conquered. He was clothed in purple, wore the chlamys in the Roman manner, and had a diadem placed on his head at his installation at Tours.

For a century and a quarter (511–639) after the death of Clovis, the Merovingians continued to be energetic and vigorous, if not always enlightened. A feature of this period was the establishment of "the fatal Frankish custom," whereby the Frankish realms were divided among the surviving legitimate sons of a deceased King. In theory, Frankland remained one, but in practice it was usually divided into smaller kingdoms. The customary components were Neustria, Austrasia, Aquitania, and Burgundy. The strongest of these and the main competitors for control were French-speaking Neustria, located in northwestern Gaul, the "new" territory of the Franks, and Germanic Austrasia, located in northeastern Frankland, the older "eastern" territory of the Franks. These subdivisions tended to coalesce periodically, as under Clothar I, Clothar II, and Dagobert, because of the continuing concept of Frankish unity, loyalty to the Merovingian line, external pressures, and the recurrence of strong kings.

The earlier Merovingians after the death of Clovis

The history of the Merovingian Franks was fraught with bloodshed and violence. Unrestrained passions and vindictiveness reached their height during the feud between the two queens, Brunhilda and Fredegunde.

The will of Clovis divided his realms among his four sons. Partly because most of the valuable crown lands were in northern Gaul, and partly because Frankland continued to be theoretically united, the four capitals were located not far from one another at Paris, Soissons, Rheims, and Orleans. The sons of Clovis continued the aggressive, warlike, unscrupulous policies of their father. On the death of King Clodimir, his brothers Clothar I and Childebert slew his children, and Clothar I married his widow, the more easily to secure his inheritance.

Profiting from internal dissension in Burgundy, the brothers now invaded that kingdom, where they defeated King Sigismund, and threw him, his wife, and children into a well (523). Finally in 534 they defeated Sigismund's successor and annexed the territory. Provence was acquired (536), as a price for promised Frankish neutrality during the Ostrogoths' fight for survival against the Byzantines. The Franks subsequently cooperated with the Byzantines, but their effort to hold northern Italy after the overthrow of the Ostrogoths was unsuccessful. In Germanic territory, Thuringia was conquered and subjected in a savage war (531). The intermarriage of the Merovingian house and the Bavarian Agilolfing line led to a loose association of Bavaria with Frankland. In his final years, the grasping Clothar I reunited all Frankland under his sole rule (558–561), but then proceeded to divide it among his four sons on his death.

Frede-gunde vs. Brunhilda

A leading feature of the ensuing period was a vicious feud between the Queens of Neustria and Austrasia, Fredegunde and Brunhilda. The eldest son of Clothar I soon died (567), leaving Frankland divided between King Chilperic of Neustria, King Sigebert of Austrasia, and King Guntram of Burgundy. King Sigebert of Austrasia had married the beautiful Visigothic princess Brunhilda, who came with an impressive train bearing rich treasures as her dowry. Apparently jealous of his brother, King Chilperic of Neustria married Brunhilda's sister, Galswintha, who also brought with her great treasure. But Galswintha became the victim of the deadly jealousy of Chilperic's unscrupulous mistress, Fredegunde, who had gotten rid of Chilperic's former wife by forcing her to retire to a nunnery, where Fredegunde had the queen murdered. The furious Fredegunde had her new rival, poor Galswintha, smothered in bed. After this, Fredegunde became the recognized wife of Chilperic.

Queen Brunhilda of Austrasia, who felt she could not let the murder of her sister go unavenged, encouraged her husband Sigebert to declare war on the Neustrian king. When the military successes of Sigebert's Austrasians brought the Neustrians to the verge of surrender, Fredegunde sent assassins with poisoned daggers to the court of Sigebert where, pretending to be negotiating terms, they killed the King. After Prince Meroveus, the son of Clothar I, fell in love with Brunhilda and married her at Rouen, Fredegunde had Meroveus pursued until in despair he had his own attendants kill him. At Fredegunde's command, Bishop Pretextatus, who had married Meroveus and Brunhilda, was deposed, tortured, and done to death. Fredegunde continued to have her enemies executed or murdered. She even attempted to smother her own daughter by shutting the lid of a chest on her head and she may have been implicated in the assassination of her husband (584). Her insatiable rivalry with Brunhilda lasted until her own death in 597; after which it was continued by her son Clothar II.

Queen Brunhilda, after the death of her husband and despite her foreign origin, managed to maintain herself in power in Austrasia, and even in Burgundy, as regent first for her sons, and later for her grandsons. But Brunhilda's autocratic methods and the tenacious persistence of her rule alienated the aristocracy. Discontent erupted into rebellion when she announced her intention to rule over Austrasia and Burgundy in the name of her great-grandson. Rebel Austrasian nobles joined forces with Clothar II of Neustria to overthrow Brunhilda in 613. The aged captive queen was tortured for three days and paraded around naked on a camel, after which she was tied by an arm, a foot, and her hair to the tail of a wild horse, and dashed to her death.

The last effective Merovingians (613–639)

Although Clothar II ruled a reunited Frankland (613–629), he was obliged to make Pepin of Landers, a leading Austrasian landowner, his "Mayor of the Palace" in Austrasia (613). He was also constrained to issue the so-called "Perpetual Constitution" of 614, which confirmed extensive privileges and immunities for the great nobles and churchmen. Counts were to be appointed from the districts they were to administer, making the office practically hereditary; and ecclesiastical elections were

The "New West"

to be free from royal interference. In deference to Austrasian pride, Clothar eventually appointed his young son Dagobert as King in Austrasia, with Mayor Pepin as the actual administrator. Clothar II also ruled Burgundy through a Mayor. Under Dagobert (629–639), the Merovingian line enjoyed a final flare of brilliance. One of his early acts was to declare his complete independence by deposing Mayor Pepin of Austrasia, who took refuge in Switzerland. After Dagobert, the Merovingians became "Do-Nothing Kings," with real power in the hands of the Mayors of the Palace in Neustria, Austrasia, and Burgundy.

CIVILIZATION IN THE EARLY GERMANIC KINGDOMS.
Section 15.

> Not without some great purpose has it been ordained that your Kings should share with the Roman Empire confession of the orthodox faith. [Pope Pelagius writing to the Bishop of Auxerre (c. 581) regarding the Frankish Kings.]

CIVILIZATION in the early Germanic Kingdoms consisted of Germanic and Roman elements. Part of the turbulence in these kingdoms resulted from the interplay of these strong contradictory ingredients which were in constant flux. A powerful catalyst was the Christianity of the Catholic (universal) Church. As a result of their early conversion to orthodox Christianity and their firm foothold in both Germanic and Roman territories, the Franks developed one of the best integrated, most enduring civilizations of all the Germanic peoples. Although our discussion focuses primarily on Frankland, much of it also applies to the other early Germanic kingdoms.

Political institutions

The coexistence of Roman and Germanic elements is nowhere better illustrated than in government. Whereas the Later Roman Empire stressed unity, conformity, and autocracy, the Germans were accustomed to more local self-determination, individual freedom, and limited monarchical power. Several regional Germanic kingdoms replaced the former universal Roman Empire in the West; and within these "national" kingdoms there were numerous semi-independent, partly autonomous local governments. There was also a renewed emphasis on the separation of Church and State, as political power was usually in the hands of pagans or heretics or only partly converted barbarians. An advantage was the fact that local government was liable to be better adapted to each place and people, and more responsive to the latter's needs. The very fragmentation and shortcomings of the government made possible greater political flexibility and more freedom, at least for the upper classes. Where before power had been concentrated, a balance of power now maintained, most frequently being shared by the king, the nobility, and the bishops.

The Monarchy

The central government in the early Germanic kingdoms was personal and loosely organized. Theoretically absolute, the monarchy was actually limited; supposedly powerful, it was in fact weak. It was repeatedly challenged and periodically changed by civil wars and assassinations. The office of the monarch was partly hereditary, partly elective. The aristocracy consistently strove to make the monarchy more subservient by insisting on the elective principle whenever possible. Civil strife was often engendered when they aligned themselves on opposite sides to support rival candidates. The aristocracy succeeded in firmly establishing the elective principle in Visigothic Spain with unfortunate results, although they did not have the same measure of success in Merovingian Frankland.

At first the Germanic monarchs had a dual position, since they were kings over their Germanic subjects but imperial representatives to their Roman subjects. In their royal capacity, their authority was often paradoxically more limited than in their vicarious office. Hence, kings strove to have the absolutistic Roman theory of government accepted, even as the aristocracy strove to retain the more limited Germanic concept. Eventually the two concepts blended, but in such a way that the result was unclear. The novel nature of the new government is underscored by the new title of "King" (*Rex* or *Rix*), which had been anathema to the Romans since the overthrow of Tarquin, but was actually a part of the names of early Germanic monarchs such as Alaric, Gaiseric, and Theodoric. According to the Germanic concept, the monarchy and its rule over the native population in occupied territories were personal possessions acquired by right of conquest and divine favor. An application of this concept was the disruptive Merovingian practice of dividing the realms among surviving legitimate sons in what has come to be known as "the fatal Frankish custom."

Political institutions

Political institutions in the central government of the early Germanic kingdoms were inadequate and indistinct. There was no organized bureaucracy for the continuing efficient conduct of governmental affairs. The definitions of an office and its attendant duties were often vague; too much depended directly on the monarch. Germanic kings, such as the Merovingians, customarily relied on the officials of their own personal household, such as the constable (count of the stable), seneschal (senior servant), and marshal (servant in charge of horses) in their administration. The mayor of the palace was originally in charge of the royal residences and estates. There was often no distinction between the accounts of the royal household and those of the government. Responsibilities often overlapped as in the case of the marshal and constable, and the seneschal and mayor of the palace.

On the other hand, admonitions of the clergy, as well as other influences, inculcated the concept of the divine source of royal authority and the monarch's responsibility to God. According to this concept, monarchical authority was contingent on services to the public welfare, and could be withdrawn if the ruler acted contrary to the common good.

The royal court of the Merovingians was migratory, moving from villa to villa. This was partly to make provisioning more direct and efficient, and partly because the Germanic monarchs preferred the open, healthful country and outdoor activities to the cramped, often unsanitary and unfriendly cities. At the same time, they referred to the current place

The "New West"

where their court was held as "the palace," in imitation of the Roman emperors.

The assemblies

The power of the old general assemblies declined as the new Germanic states expanded, partly because the Germanic "nations" now included several tribes, as well as occupied extensive territories, making assemblies more composite and difficult to convene and to handle. Among the Merovingian Franks the general assemblies were little more than military musters. The really effective meetings were the more select gatherings of the leaders of state and church—the assemblies of "notables" or "magnates." These meetings of "the great ones" were similar to the later feudal "Great Councils," from which upper legislative houses such as the English House of Lords have descended. The assemblies of the notables were the supreme court of the land, as well as an advisory body for the King, and they ordinarily certified or even determined the royal succession.

Local government

The early Germanic Kingdoms on Roman soil generally retained the old Roman territorial division into *civitates*, which usually came to be known as "counties." A similar system of subdivisions existed in Germanic territories, such as old Germania and Anglo-Saxon England, where the subdivisions seem generally to have corresponded to earlier tribal territories. In England such subdivisions were known as "shires" (shares, parts), in Germany as *Gaus* (districts, provinces) or *Grafschafts* (counties: from *Graf*: count). Such subdivisions were ruled over in the name of the king by officials known variously as "counts," *gastaldi, comites, ealdormen, Grafs*, sheriffs, and so on. These (actual or nominal) royal representatives exercised most of the powers of the king in their areas. They presided over local courts and administered justice; maintained law and order; collected taxes, fines, and other debts owed to the king; and mustered and led the county's forces in time of war.

The counts were often regarded by their subjects as petty tyrants. They frequently oppressed the local populace and harassed the local bishops, as we see in Gregory of Tours's *History of the Franks*. As time progressed, the power of such local rulers was often increased by "immunities" or special grants of freedom from the jurisdiction of royal courts, etc. Numerous immunities were granted by the Later Merovingians. The position of the counts eventually became hereditary and autonomous, as was recognized in Frankland by the Constitution of 614 issued by Clothar II. The power of the local nobility was a disruptive factor which promoted frequent civil war and eventually contributed to the rise of feudalism. Counts often had "viscounts" who assisted them and ruled over a part of their county.

Other common political subdivisions included duchies, hundreds, boroughs, and villages. Duchies usually included several counties, and their main original purpose was military. The dukes (*duces*: leaders) marshalled the forces of several counties in war. Such duchies were generally organized in areas that had been recently under alien rule or were more exposed to attack. Many Lombard dukes seem to have been equivalent to Frankish counts, while others, such as the Dukes of Spoleto and Benevento, were like petty kings. Hundreds were common subdivisions, both in Anglo-Saxon England and on the continent. While the exact origin of the term is obscure, the hundred seems to have been an area that originally provided a hundred fighting men or contained a hundred families. At the head of each was a "hundred-man" or *centenarius*. Towns or boroughs sometimes had a certain degree of self-government, often under and in conjunction with their bishop. Villages were ordinarily subject to the power of some local lord, but even they enjoyed a limited measure of self-government under their own officials.

Law in the early Germanic Kingdoms

Both law and justice in the early Germanic kingdoms exemplified the coexistence, and gradual fusion of Roman and Germanic elements. Since the Germans continued to be governed by their own laws after the invasions, for a while two systems of law and justice, Roman and Germanic, existed side by side, and were personal rather than territorial. From the beginning, the Germanic law of the conquerors was influenced by the Roman law of their subjects. Gradually, the two systems merged until there was a single combined system.

Germanic laws, originally unwritten, consisted of customs that were considered obligatory. Although similar, the exact provisions of Germanic laws varied from people to people. To instruct both their subjects and the courts, Germanic monarchs had summaries or "codes" of the leading laws of their people committed to writing. The laws contained in the Germanic codes consisted mainly of lists of penalties for specific types of offences, although they also contained various procedural, contractual, and hereditary provisions. They were usually committed to writing by clerics, who often inserted Roman and Christian ideas and prescriptions, as, for example, with respect to the royal authority and crimes of treason and their penalties.

After the Germanic conquest and occupation, Roman law also remained in effect as the customary law of the native population. For the convenience of their Roman subjects, and particularly for the use of judges, Germanic rulers also prepared simple summaries of certain provisions of Roman law. Such had been published in a partial and elementary form by the Eastern Emperor Theodosius II in 438 and had gained some currency in the West, being known as *The Theodosian Code*. For the convenience of his subjects and judges, the Visigothic King Alaric II had ordered a codification of Roman law which was called *The Roman Law of the Visigoths* (506) and was also known as *The Breviary (Short Summary) of Alaric* (506). This became the basic form of Roman law used in southwestern France and Spain and had a wide influence throughout Western Europe until the twelfth century. Among other Roman law codes used in the West were *The Roman Law of the Burgundians*, codified by King Gundobad in the early sixth century, and the so-called *Edict of Theodoric*, compiled for the great Ostrogothic King of Italy in the same period. The latter was mainly based on *The Theodosian Code* and the opinions of learned jurists.

In the course of time, as distinctions blurred and differences dissolved, elements of the Germanic and Roman law systems gradually fused by custom rather than by specific decrees and legislation. This fusion is exemplified in the *Book of Judgments* or *Forum of Judges* (*Fuero Juzgo*) of the Visigothic King Recceswinth (649–672), whose laws were applicable to Visigoths and Romans alike. This work was still quoted in Spanish courts as late as the nineteenth century. Similar customary fusion occurred in other countries, but was not usually codified in writing. Meanwhile Roman law continued to be ascendant in many of the strictly legal and more secular aspects of the Canon Law of the Church.

A similar evolution took place in justice. At first there were two kinds of secular courts—one for Romans and one for Germans. But this distinction gradually disappeared. The Roman law courts were often presided over by bishops, who also continued to administer the Canon Law of the Church even after the Roman system of courts had lapsed. Both for Germanic law and for the later combined German-Roman system of secular law, the customary method of judgment was initially by representatives of the community of one's peers (equals), instead of by professional judges, as had been the case with the Romans. Such courts consisted of a reasonable number of "good men" (*boni homines* or *rachimburgi*) who heard the case in the name of the community, under the presidency of the local administrative officer—usually the count or his representative. The county court known as the *mal, mall, mallus* or *placitum*, was the principal court, although there were also courts on other levels, such as those of the hundred and the vill, as well as that of the king. Each successive administrative level had its own court or moot.

Justice

Judgment of guilt or innocence and similar matters was usually a simple matter of eyewitness reports or common knowledge. But in serious cases where doubt existed, recourse was had to compurgation and ordeals, which called on God to witness and invited divine retribution in case of falsity. Compurgation was the corroboration of various coswearers, who asserted under oath the credibility of the person whom they supported. Ordeals were arduous physical tests or trials, whose outcome was ascribed to divine influence. Common forms of ordeals were those of fire and water; another test was judicial combat. Psychology played a part in ordeals, since confidence or lack of it could affect the outcome.

The ordeal of water might be with cold or hot water. In the ordeal of cold water, the accused person was bound and thrown into a body of water. If he sank, he was considered innocent; if he floated, he was adjudged guilty—the theory being that the pure water would receive the innocent but repel the guilty. In the ordeal of hot water, a part of the body of the person, such as a hand, was subjected to boiling water. Thus the hand might be plunged into a cauldron of boiling water to retrieve a piece of metal. If the flesh healed normally, the person was adjudged innocent; if not, he was deemed guilty. In the ordeal of fire, for instance, a person was required to hold a highly heated object, or walk over glowing coals, or run along a path enveloped in flames. Again, if the wounds healed normally, this was a sign of innocence; if not, the person was considered guilty. In the ordeal of the cross, a person had to stand with arms extended for a long period of time. In judicial combat, accused and accuser, or their representatives, fought each other on the assumption that God would vindicate the side that was right. After the conversion of the Germans, the clergy usually served as referees and supervised the administration of the "trial" and rendered a decision as to its outcome.

Penalties for various crimes were carefully assessed. The most common form was a fine. At first reckoned in cattle, fines came to be established in sums of money, with one to two *solidi* equal to one cow. Thus among the Salian Franks a convicted offender had to pay the following penalties:

3 *solidi* for assault and battery without bloodshed.
15 *solidi* for assault and battery resulting in bloodshed.
63 *solidi* for destroying the use of a hand, a foot, or an eye.
3 *solidi* for calling a man a coward ("rabbit") without justification.
15 *solidi* for calling a man a perjurer without justification.
43 *solidi* for falsely calling a woman a whore.
30 *solidi* for killing a slave or stealing a horse.
100 *solidi* for killing a free Gallo-Roman.
200 *solidi* for killing a free Frank.
600 *solidi* for killing one of the king's sworn bodyguard (*antrustiones*).
600 *solidi* for killing a priest.
600 *solidi* for killing a pregnant woman.
900 *solidi* for killing a bishop.

Some serious crimes, such as adultery or cowardice in battle were punishable by exile or death, occasionally with torture. Imprisonment was rare and was evidently considered an impractical bother.

Fiscal management and warfare

At first the Germanic kings tried to continue or revive the land-taxes and head-taxes collected by the Romans. But because of economic recession, popular resistance, and inadequate administrative machinery, they soon had to abandon this effort. The principal royal revenues came from the royal estates or "fisc" (whence our term "fiscal"). These royal estates had been acquired by various means, such as consignments during service as *foederati*; appropriations of former imperial public lands during the conquest; confiscations (as for rebellion); reversions (as at death without an heir); and outright purchase. Germanic courts such as the Frankish often moved from estate to estate, like locusts, consuming provender on each as long as it lasted. Other sources of royal revenue included booty from warfare, fines levied during the administration of justice, customs duties, and coinage. The Merovingians imitated the Roman money, even to the point of reproducing the images of the emperors on their own coins. A method sometimes used to increase royal revenues was debasement of the coinage.

Of the Franks, Sidonius Apollinaris says: "From their youth up, war is their passion," and the like may be said of other Germanic barbarians. Standing troops after the conquests were limited mainly to the royal bodyguard of the king, sworn to defend the royal person, and known as *antrustiones, housecarls*, or the like. Local magnates often had similar armed retainers or *leudes* (people) on a smaller scale. The main army consisted of the *ost* or muster of free, able-bodied Germanic warriors summoned by the royal *"heriban"* or call to arms. Typical weapons of

The "New West"

Frankish warriors included the *francisca* or throwing axe; the *scaramasax* or one-edged knife-dagger; the long two-edged sword; the *angon* or barbed iron javelin; and the *framea* or lance. Merovingian soldiery fought mainly on foot. Although at first reserved to Germans, the obligation of military service was later extended to other members of the population.

Economy and society in the early kingdoms

Although the economy of Western Europe generally declined to a near-subsistence level in the early Germanic kingdoms, international and Mediterranean trade continued on a diminished scale. Agriculture, already the chief economic activity in Western Europe, became even more important under the Germans. The large estates (*latifundia*, villas) farmed by dependent workers (*coloni*, serfs), continued and increased. As *foederati*, the Germans obtained a considerable part of the land and its appurtenances (buildings, serfs) for their support. This is usually stated as having been "a third," although exactly what it was a third of (imperial or public lands, private lands, lands of large landowners) is not clear. It is certain that there was no general and complete confiscation of lands from former owners and that the proportion of land taken by the Germans was greater in places originally settled than in areas later acquired.

Meanwhile, Western industry was hard hit. Many craftsmen moved from the towns to the villas of the powerful and affluent, and crafts became cruder. Most towns became shadows of their former selves, and many were ruled by their bishops as the natural leaders of the urban population. The coinage of money lapsed in many areas and was only slowly and partially revived.

Class differences, already well rooted in the Later Roman Empire, were deepened and increased. In addition to Later Roman distinctions, such as those between the privileged upper classes, ordinary freemen, hired workers, dependent *coloni* and slaves, a new category of serfs was inserted, and there was a new distinction between Germans and Romans. The Germans for some time constituted a class apart: a ruling class with their own *wergelds*, religion, and prohibitions against intermarriage with the native population. Some idea of the complex class system is seen in the varying wergelds listed above for the Salian Franks. The wergeld for killing a free Frank (200 solidi) was twice that for killing a free Gallo-Roman (100 solidi). Some say that this was because, according to Germanic law, the injured or his family had to be compensated with half of the fine levied, whereas there was no such provision in Roman law.

Religion and culture

At first most of the Germanic conquerors (mainly Eastern Germans) were Arians while the rest (Western Germans, such as the Franks and Anglo-Saxons) were pagans. For some time religious differences constituted a leading obstacle to assimilation. But within about a century and a half the pagans, and by the end of another century the Arians, were converted to orthodox (Catholic) Christianity.

The traditional separation of Church and State continued in the early Germanic kingdoms, although there was considerable mutual accommodation, and the Church supported the monarchy even as the monarchy supported the Church. This was especially true after the conversion of the

Germans to orthodox Christianity. The Germanic kings had claimed descent from the gods, and the Church recognized that their authority was divinely willed. But like the emperors in the Later Roman Empire, the Germanic monarchs began to intervene in Church affairs, such as the appointment of bishops, who had wide power and influence. If the monarchs tried to control the bishops, the bishops also tried to guide the monarchs, often with considerable success. Throughout the Germanic West the clergy enjoyed a privileged status, as is evidenced by their higher wergeld.

Monasticism spread rapidly and acquired great popularity. The monasteries were to a great extent a world apart from the violent, turbulent, secular world of warfare and bloodshed, and were often a place of refuge for sensitive, peace-loving, intellectual souls. Numerous monasteries were founded throughout the West. Although at first various rules were followed, the Benedictine form eventually prevailed.

The Germans who settled in the lands of the old Roman Empire were greatly outnumbered and soon adopted the popular local versions of Latin known as "Romance." In Germany itself there was a shift from the older Low German to the newer High German, although Low German continued to be spoken by the Dutch, Flemish, and Anglo-Saxons.

Culture was at a low ebb. Latin literature deserving of notice was rare; literature in the vernacular was practically nonexistent except for a little in the British Isles and Germany. Latin poetry was exemplified by the emotional Fortunatus; historiography by the credulous Gregory of Tours; didactic literature by the elemental Boethius, Cassiodorus, and Isidore of Seville. Minimal education and learning survived and were cultivated almost exclusively in Church schools. The form of architecture was ecclesiastical. Most churches were built of wood and on a small scale, while stone churches were tiny and plain. Sculpture reverted to a crude form reminiscent of primitive carving. Barbarian influences in manuscript illumination in the British Isles were constructive, however, and resulted in beautiful, intricately involved linear decorative patterns, as in the Book of Kells.

Conclusion   Elements of weakness in the early German kingdoms included the as yet unreconciled coexistence of Roman and Germanic elements; governmental instability; lack of international peace; decline of the economy, lapse of urban life, and a low level of culture. At the same time, collapse of the autocratic, fixed monopolistic order of the Late Roman Empire encouraged greater freedom and diversity, competition and progress, and helped to free men from the stranglehold of the past.

References for Chapter 5   GOOD histories of the Early Middle Ages which discuss the early Germanic kingdoms include CECIL D. BURNS, *The First Europe* . . . (New York: Norton, 1948), a stimulating study which singles out the main themes of the period from 400 to 800; MARGARET DEANESLY, *A History of Early Medieval Europe* . . . (2nd ed., London: Methuen, 1960), an excellent comprehensive coverage which goes into detail concerning various barbarian groups and early European states from 476 to

911; HENRY S. MOSS, *The Birth of the Middle Ages* ... (Oxford: Clarendon, 1935 and 1963), a logical, well-knit survey of the period 395 to 814; JOHN M. WALLACE-HADRILL, *The Barbarian West* ... (London: Hutchinson's, 1952); and FERDINAND LOT, *The End of the Ancient World and the Beginning of the Middle Ages* (New York: Barnes and Noble, 1953) and (New York: Harper, 1961), which treats the early Germanic kingdoms to 700 in Part III (237–407). ELEANOR SHIPLEY DUCKETT, *The Gateway to the Middle Ages* (New York: Macmillan, 1938) limits its discussion to the eventful sixth century. CHRISTOPHER H. DAWSON, *The Making of Europe* (New York: Macmillan, 1932) is a broad, illuminating interpretative study. The monumental contribution of THOMAS HODGKIN, *Italy and Her Invaders*, 8 vols. in 9 (Oxford: Clarendon, 1885–1899) treats at some length, and in gripping fashion, all the barbarian groups that went to Italy. Worthwhile, informative articles on the various barbarian groups and early kingdoms are to be found in *The Cambridge Medieval History*, Vols. I and II.

The Franks in particular are treated by LEWIS SERGEANT, *The Franks* ... (New York: Putnam, 1898), an old but good elementary survey; and also in Vol. I of the admirable CHARLES A. GUIGNEBERT, *Short History of the French People*, 2 vols. (New York: Macmillan, 1930), as well as in JACQUES C. FUNCK-BRENTANO, which though popular and superficial is rich in quotations and stories from original sources. Special aspects of Frankish history, including the evolution of the Frankish Kingship, are studied in JOHN M. WALLACE-HADRILL, *The Long-Haired Kings* ... (London: Methuen, 1962). A splendid study of life and institutions in Merovingian Gaul in the sixth century is SAMUEL DILL, *Roman Society in Gaul in the Merovingian Age* (London: Macmillan, 1926), which is based on surviving literature from the period. Equally useful is *Vol. I: Introduction* of O. M. DALTON's *Gregory of Tours, History of the Franks*, 2 vols. (Oxford-Clarendon, 1927), which covers much of the same ground in similarly superior fashion. Vol. II of Dalton's work is a fine, well-footnoted translation of Gregory's text, which goes to 591, and is our principal source for the period. GREGORY's *History of the Franks* is also well edited and translated by ERNEST BREHAUT (New York: Columbia U.P., 1916). The inferior but still useful continuation of GREGORY's *History*, known as ... *The Fourth Book of the Chronicle of Fredegar* has been translated by J. M. WALLACE-HADRILL (London: Nelson, 1960).

For the stories of the other early Germanic kingdoms, the best references in English are probably the various articles in the *Cambridge Medieval History*, Vols. I and II. A summary of the story of both the Visigoths and Ostrogoths from the earliest times to the overthrow of their kingdoms is HENRY BRADLEY, *The Story of the Goths* (New York: Putnam, 1888). The career of the greatest Ostrogothic leader is told by THOMAS HODGKIN, *Theodoric the Goth* (New York: Putnam, 1891). Something about the early Germanic kingdoms in the various countries is also to be found in their national histories, such as those of KURT F. REINHARDT and WOLFGANG MENZEL for Germany, LUIGI SALVATORELLI and HENRY B. COTTERILL for Italy; FRANK M. STENTON and ROBERT H. HODGKIN for Anglo-Saxon England; JACQUES FUNCK-BRENTANO and CHARLES GUIGNEBERT for France; and RAFAEL ALTAMIRA for Spain, as cited elsewhere. CHRISTIAN

PFISTER has good articles on "Germanic Laws," and "Salic Law and Other Frankish Laws" in the *Encyclopedia Britannica*, 13th edition. Besides Gregory of Tours and Fredegar (already mentioned), primary sources in translation include JORDANES, *Gothic History*, tr. Charles C. Mierow (Princeton: Princeton U.P., 1915); PAULUS DIACONUS, *History of the Langobards*, tr. W. D. Foulke . . . (New York: Longmans, 1907); *The Burgundian Code*, tr. K. Fischer (Philadelphia: Pennsylvania U.P., 1949); and VENERABLE BEDE, *Ecclesiastical History of the English Nation* (London: Dent, 1958).

⟮ BYZANTINE HISTORY AND CIVILIZATION.
Chapter 6.

AS THE Roman Empire in the West was succumbing to Germanic invaders, the Eastern Roman Empire was triumphing over its foes and gathering new vigor. For over another millennium the Byzantine Empire survived as a bastion of Europe and bulwark of Christianity. Meanwhile, the Eastern Empire was the converter and civilizer of Eastern Europe, an inspiration and model for Western Europe, and a faithful custodian and treasurer of man's cultural legacy from Greek antiquity. Although the Byzantine Empire gradually lost ground, its history was cyclic, with renaissances interspersed with recessions.

(284–610)

ORIGINS AND FIRST GOLDEN AGE OF THE BYZANTINE EMPIRE.
Section 16.

"The imperial majesty should be armed with laws as well as glorified with arms. . . ." [Justinian the Great in his *Institutes* (sixth century).]

DURING the period from 284 to 610 the Byzantine Empire emerged from the side of the Later Roman Empire, survived the fall of its less fortunate counterpart in the West, increasingly assumed a special character, and came to enjoy its "First Golden Age."

Origins of the Eastern Empire (284–395)

The beginnings of Byzantine history trace back to Diocletian's division of the Roman Empire into Eastern and Western halves (286). Diocletian (284–305) himself took up residence at Nicomedia in the Eastern part of the Empire. The division facilitated the defense of the Empire against its external enemies and recognized the divergent character of its parts. Although the Empire was thrice reunited under a single emperor in the fourth century, Diocletian's partition eventually prevailed. Diocletian also promoted the semioriental absolutism and highly regulatory bureaucracy that came to characterize Byzantium. He even tried to enforce religious uniformity, later a marked feature of the Eastern Christian Roman Empire.

Constantine the Great, who became sole Emperor in 324, transferred his capital to the east. Rejecting other possibilities such as ancient Troy

(Ilium) and Salonica (Thessalonica), Constantine chose the Greek colony of Byzantium as the site of his "New Rome." The capital on the Bosporus, which came to be known as "Constantinople" (Constantine's *polis* or city), was formally dedicated in 330. Constantine initiated a pro-Christian policy which was continued and expanded by his successors. Theodosius I, the Great, who tolled "the death-knell of paganism" with his edicts of 391–392, confirmed the close collaboration of Church and State which came to characterize the Byzantine Empire. He overcame the first "Gothic peril" to the Eastern Empire, which had resulted from the defeat of Emperor Valens by the Visigoths at Adrianople in 378. He took many Goths into his army, and pacified some Germans by concessions, others by forcible repression. He temporarily reunited the Empire, but definitively divided it between his two sons on his death (395).

There were several reasons for the survival of the Eastern Empire in the period following the death of Theodosius, which saw the extinction of the Empire in the West. The economy of the more populous and urbanized as well as agricultural Eastern Empire was more balanced, its commerce and industry more flourishing and stable. The great Eastern cities were more strongly fortified than those in the West. The Danubian frontier of the Eastern Empire was less extended and less exposed to the Germanic barbarians than the rambling Rhine-Danube frontier of the Western Empire. The broad lower Danube and its fortifications, and the rugged mountains of the Balkans stood between the Germanic barbarians and the heartland of the Eastern Empire. The chief enemies of the Byzantines were not migratory Germanic barbarians, but more settled and conventional Persians. Whereas the Germanic barbarians included several warlike peoples, operating on different fronts, and grimly determined to find lands where they and their families, whom they brought along, could settle, the Persian armies were less needy and less aggressive; they usually moved on more circumscribed and definite fronts with more limited objectives. The Byzantines could also afford to allow invaders to overrun much of their territory temporarily, provided they retained fortified strongholds from which they could recover their losses at opportune times. Since they had a dual heartland located in both the Balkans and in Asia Minor, the Byzantines could even temporarily lose the one so long as they retained the other. The Eastern Empire also had a larger number of free and self-reliant small farmers and middle-class merchants and artisans who were the economic and military backbone of the state. Finally, Eastern Emperors were quicker to detect and stamp out the threat of internal control by barbarians. *Survival of the Empire in the East (395–518)*

Prominent among reasons for the survival of the Eastern Empire was its capital, Constantinople, of which Napoleon declared that it "deserved an empire." Located on a hilly peninsula at the northeast corner of the Sea of Marmora at a crossroads of world trade, Constantinople was approachable by water only through the narrow, tortuous straits of the Bosporus from the Black Sea, and the Dardanelles from the Mediterranean. On its land side across the base of the peninsula, for a distance of five miles, it had two successive broad and lofty walls, rising behind a *Constantinople* wide moat. Each of the walls had some ninety-six towers and eleven gates, while the whole barrier was about 200 feet wide and 100 feet high. To the city's east was a seven-mile-long harbor known as the "Golden Horn," across whose entrance an effective barrier in the form of an iron chain was stretched in time of war. Protected by a moderately competent army and navy, Constantinople was virtually impregnable under conditions of ancient and medieval warfare. At its height, its population is said to have numbered from 500,000 to one million people, and its harbor was filled with ships from many foreign regions.

Surmounting the barbarian menace

Emperor Arcadius (395–408), who succeeded his father, Theodosius, in the East, on being threatened by renewed uprisings of the Visigoths, at first restrained them with the help of armies from the West. But, fearful of dominance by the Western Master of Soldiers, Stilicho, Arcadius and his ministers made the ambitious Visigothic leader Alaric "Master of Soldiers" in Illyricum (399), as a counterpoise to Stilicho. Located in the northwest corner of the Balkans, Illyricum was a natural point of departure for Italy. Stilicho held off the barbarians for some time, but after his execution by Honorius (408), the Visigoths invaded Italy, to the great relief of the Byzantines.

Nevertheless, the Gothic element was still strong in the Eastern Roman army, and the threat they posed became acute when the Ostrogoths were accepted as *foederati* in Lower Moesia and Thrace. The influence of the Goths in the mid-fifth century was so powerful that their leader Aspar became an "Emperor-maker," to whose favor both Marcian (450–457) and Leo I (457–474) owed their elevation to the throne. But after assuming the purple, Leo I refused to be a puppet of Aspar. To counterbalance the Goths, he brought into the army large numbers of warlike Isaurians from mountainous southwestern Asia Minor, and even married his daughter Ariadne to their leader, Zeno. Meanwhile, he had Aspar and his sons eliminated by assassination.

Zeno (474–491), who succeeded his father-in-law, was confronted successively by threats of Ostrogothic and Isaurian dominance. Zeno dealt with the Ostrogoths by using Odovacar's seizure of supreme power in Italy as an excuse to dispatch them westward. Quieting the hardy Isaurians took more time, but after several years Zeno was able to suppress a rebellion led by Isaurian chieftains, who wanted to control the government. Zeno's successor, Anastasius (491–518), eliminated the Isaurians' threat altogether by first expelling them from Constantinople and then defeating them in their homeland. With the transplantation of many Isaurians to other parts of the Eastern Empire, the threat of barbarian domination subsided.

Divisive heresies

Ultimately more serious for Byzantium than the political ambitions and pretensions of barbarian elements was the recurrent problem of divisive heresies aggravated by regionalism and racism. The Syrians and Egyptians bitterly resented being subject to "Greek" control, while their religious preconceptions conflicted with those that prevailed in the Byzantine capital. For some time Nestorianism was dominant in Syria, until it was overcome by the cumulative force of the orthodox Church, the Monophysites, and the Byzantine government. Meanwhile the Egyptians, partly as a reaction against Nestorianism, evolved their own heresy of Monophysitism, which maintained that Christ had only one nature, the divine.

The Egyptians and Syrians closed ranks around their own Patriarchs against the orthodox Byzantines. Attempts of Emperors and Patriarchs of Constantinople to restore ecclesiastical unity proved futile. Efforts to attain a middle ground usually provoked further controversies, as happened with the *Henoticon* of Zeno and the "Monotheletism" of Heraclius. Formulae meant to reconcile the Monophysites and the orthodox satisfied neither. Tension increased when the Monophysite Anastasius (491–518) became Emperor in the predominantly orthodox capital. Despite an economical administration which accumulated a large reserve in the treasury, Anastasius could never overcome the handicap of his Monophysitism, and his reign was marred by a series of revolts.

The Eastern Empire enjoyed its first "Golden Age" in the sixth century. During the so-called "Justinian Renaissance," much of the old Roman Empire in the West was recovered, Roman law was codified, extensive public works were completed, and a cultural renaissance occurred.

"First Golden Age" of the Byzantine Empire (518–610)

Justin I (518–527) was a soldier-emperor of peasant extraction. After becoming commander of the palace guard, Justin, who was childless, brought his young nephew and adopted heir Justinian to Constantinople. Justinian thus received a good education and an opportunity to learn the ways of the capital. He seems to have played an active part in the erratic election which raised his uncle to the throne. As Emperor, Justin's chief attributes were his orthodoxy in contrast to the Monophysitism of his predecessor; his mild, accommodating character; and his receptivity to the wise counsels of his nephew, who became his "Caesar."

Upon his uncle's death in 527, Justinian became sole emperor. He was inspired by two grand projects: to restore the Roman Empire around the Western Mediterranean, and to reestablish unity in the Christian Church. The first aim postulated the reconquest of the Mediterranean West; the second, the eradication of heresy in Egypt and Syria.

Justinian the Great

Justinian was fortunate in his selection of coadjutors. Among the latter was his wife Theodora. The gifted daughter of an animal-trainer, the attractive Theodora had been an actress and courtesan, and over the years had bestowed her favors on men of increasing importance. Aristocratic eyebrows were raised when the young Justinian defied public opinion and married this compromised commoner in preference to court beauties. But Theodora proved strong and competent, faithful and devoted, a moderating, realistic counterbalance to the intense ambition and idealism of her husband. Even her detractor Procopius was compelled to testify to her strength of character. Justinian's unscrupulous, grasping tax collector, John the Cappodocian, successfully contrived to provide his master with funds for the latter's ambitious projects. Justinian's leading general, the military genius Belisarius, won brilliant victories for his master, which were enthusiastically recounted by the general's secretary, Procopius. The loyal, efficient eunuch Narses, besides giving years of invaluable plodding service as a minister, successfully completed the previously dragging conquest of Italy, where he ended his days as imperial governor. The learned jurist Tribonian directed Justinian's monumental codification of Roman law. The skillful architects Anthemius of Thralles and Isidore of Miletus designed and superintended construction of Justinian's magnificent cathedral of Santa Sophia (Holy Wisdom).

Internal crisis: The Nike Riot (532)

Justinian's ambitious undertakings soon became unpopular, as the great costs and risks involved in his grand schemes became more apparent, and the autocratic methods used to implement them more distasteful. Growing opposition culminated in the furious Nike Riot of 532. The uprising, so called from the shouts of *Nike* (Victory) by the insurgents, was brought about by the extortions and the severity of John the Cappodocian and Tribonian. Beginning with demonstrations in the Hippodrome, where the rival sporting and political factions of the "Blues" and the "Greens" joined in common opposition to the Emperor, the disturbances spread to the streets and engulfed the city. Besieged in the imperial palace and disheartened by popular rejection, Justinian and his advisers were on the point of flight, when the dauntless Theodora made a brave speech recorded by Procopius: *If there were left to me no safety but in flight, I still would not depart. Those who have worn the crown should not survive its loss. Never will I live to see the day when I am not hailed as Empress. If you wish to fly, my Caesar, well and good. You have the funds, your ships are ready, the sea is clear. But as for me, I shall stay, since I accept the old saying: "The purple makes the best winding sheet."* Plans for flight were abandoned. While Narses negotiated to produce division among the rebel leaders, Belisarius with a small band of chosen soldiers trapped the insurgents in the Hippodrome. As the unarmed mob stampeded to the narrow gateways, the soldiers of Belisarius sternly slew them. The back of the revolt was broken and Justinian's government proceeded with its plans without further serious challenge.

Expansion in the West: North Africa

Justinian's title of "Great" rests partly on his reconquest of much of the former territory of the Roman Empire located around the Western Mediterranean. In this enterprise he was helped by the fact that the Western kingdoms of the Vandals, Visigoths, and Ostrogoths were involved in serious internal difficulties. The ruling Germans were still Arians, unacceptable to the native Catholic population, while the upper classes among the Germans themselves were split into competing factions. Their earlier military competence seems to have deteriorated. The various groups of Germans were also mutual rivals.

The first Western area which Justinian attacked was North Africa. Although the Vandals had the best navy in the Mediterranean, which had successfully intercepted an earlier expedition sent against them by Emperor Leo I (468), Vandal power was in decline, the Vandal aristocracy factionally spilt, and Vandal rule unpopular. Justinian intervened in opposition to a usurper, on the side of the "outs" versus the "ins," as well as on behalf of the persecuted orthodox population. For the invasion he assembled a fleet to transport an expedition of an estimated 18,000 men under the command of Belisarius. The danger of naval interception by the Vandals was reduced by staging via Sicily, conveniently made available for the purpose by the Ostrogoths. After landing in North Africa, Byzantine forces were quickly victorious. Decisively defeated in two major battles, the Vandal King Gelimer surrendered and was taken to Constantinople to adorn Belisarius' triumph. Although Vandal rule in North Africa was ended, the Byzantines were still faced with several revolts and dogged native resistance, especially in the interior. Not until 548 was Eastern Roman rule firmly established, and then mainly in coastal areas and the vicinity of key ports. Islands previously under Vandal control were also appropriated by the Byzantines.

Italy and Southern Spain

After overthrowing the Vandal kingdom, Justinian turned on Ostrogothic Italy (534ff.). Once more posing as a champion of legitimacy and orthodoxy, he sent two armies against the Ostrogoths, one under Belisarius via Sicily, and a second overland through Dalmatia. But the Ostrogoths proved a determined and formidable foe. Deposing their weak King, Theodahad, they elected the more warlike Witigis. Although the army of Belisarius was purposely kept small, because of Justinian's vague fear that his brilliant general might set himself up as an independent ruler, the Byzantines swiftly occupied Sicily, Naples, and Rome. After being besieged and hard-pressed in Rome, Belisarius again gained the initiative and marched victoriously across northern Italy to Ravenna, which opened its gates in 540. Belisarius brought back to Constantinople the captured Ostrogothic King Witigis as another trophy of victory.

After the departure of Belisarius, the Ostrogoths refused to accept defeat and elected a new and even more warlike King, Totila. They resumed their dogged struggle, which continued for fifteen more years. Various distractions, such as war with the Persians and ecclesiastical controversy, kept Justinian from dealing decisively with the Italian situation for some time. But eventually he sent westward his trusted lieutenant, Narses, provided with a large army and ample supplies. By virtue of increased resources and crafty diplomacy, Narses was able to overcome the Ostrogoths, evict the Franks who had designs on northern Italy, and reduce to submission the ravaged peninsula (554–562). Italy, Sicily, and Dalmatia were "restored" to the Empire, and Narses spent the remainder of his life as governor of Italy, which still suffered from the devastating effects of this destructive "Twenty Years' War."

The Byzantines were invited into Spain by a usurper who had recently seized control, but still faced serious opposition. Byzantine "helpers" established their own regime in the far southern part of the peninsula by 554. Justinian's expansionist efforts resulted in restoration of imperial dominion over most of the coasts and islands of the Western Mediterranean, which again became "a Roman Lake." Justinian could correctly call himself "Conqueror of the . . . Goths [Ostrogoths and Visigoths], Franks [in Italy], . . . Antes [Slavs and others in the vicinity of the Black Sea], Vandals, and Africans. . . ." (Proem. to his *Institutes*).

Troubles in the East

Prior to his campaigns in the West, in order to avoid having to fight on two fronts, Justinian purchased a "Perpetual Peace" from the Persians in 532 by agreeing to pay an annual subsidy. But it was not in the interests of the Persian Empire to allow Byzantium to become too strong, and during the Ostrogothic war, the Persian monarch, Chosroes I, anxious to obtain direct access to the Mediterranean and Black Seas, broke the peace (540). Several times in the ensuing two decades the Persians invaded Syria and adjoining areas as well as regions southeast of the Black Sea. But each time the day was saved by vigorous Byzantine counteraction, with Belisarius often cast in the role of savior. Finally, in 561 or 562, Chosroes I and Justinian agreed to a restoration of peace on the basis of mutual restitutions of territory, Persian withdrawal from the southern coast of the Black Sea, and resumed Byzantine payment of tribute.

Justinian's preoccupations elsewhere allowed the Bulgars, Slavs, and other barbarians north of the Danube to overrun much of the Balkans. Slavonization of the Balkans was begun as many Slavic intruders stayed on and settled down as agriculturalists and laborers.

The "Justinian Renaissance" and Code

Justinian carried out a vast program of public works, which included the construction of fortifications along the borders and the erection of numerous public buildings and churches. The most famous of the latter was his great cathedral of Constantinople, known as Santa Sophia, a huge, cruciform, modified basilica, surmounted by a large dome, and embellished with rich mosaics and multicolored marbles. On its completion, Justinian is said to have exclaimed: "O Solomon, I have surpassed thee!"

In other cultural fields the Justinian Age was likewise one of remarkable achievements. Whether one surveys the history of Byzantine literature, philosophy, mathematics, science, medicine, art, or music, he cannot but be impressed by the number of famous names in the sixth century. Outstanding among the internal achievements of Justinian, and his most enduring contribution was his law code. Justinian's codification of Roman laws, legal interpretations, and juristic principles (*Code, Digests,* and *Institutes*), known collectively as the *Corpus Juris Civilis,* made available a convenient, organized condensation of the vast body of laws, customs, decrees, edicts, precedents, opinions, and principles which constituted Roman law.

Imperial autocracy and "Cesaropapism"

In government the reign of Justinian marked a further step in the direction of autocracy, with the suppression of the Nike Riot (532) as an important milestone. Among evidences of monarchical absolutism were the formal declaration in the Justinian Code, the lavish expenses and heavy fiscal exactions involved in Justinian's ambitious projects, and his intervention in Church affairs. In the latter connection, Justinian is often referred to as the originator of Byzantine *Cesaropapism*. In pursuit of religious unity, Justinian first tried conciliatory persuasion. The "Affair of the Three Chapters" arose from his efforts to reconcile the Monophysites. By strenuous exertions, Justinian brought the Fifth Ecumenical Council of II Constantinople (553) to condemn selected passages from the writings of three semi-Nestorian ecclesiastics, who were otherwise in good repute, but unacceptable to the Monophysites. If Justinian thought this would silence the controversy, he was mistaken. His insistence on condemnation of the "Three Chapters" was too strict for many of the orthodox, and it did not satisfy the Monophysites. Eventually Justinian had to

Byzantine History and Civilization

abandon his policy of persuasion, but his final resort to force proved no more successful.

Justinian I won the title of "Great" for his many achievements. Of these, his reconquests in the West, although the most spectacular, were also the least enduring, while his codification of Roman law was the most influential. At his death, he bequeathed to his successors a host of troubles and an empty treasury.

The successors of Justinian (565–610)

In the half century (565–610) following Justinian's death the Empire rapidly deteriorated. It was still divided by religious dissension; barbarians continued to overrun the Balkans; and Byzantine holdings in the West were severely diminished. Almost immediately the Lombards invaded Italy (568), where they took possession of most of the Italian interior, leaving the Byzantines only coastal strongholds and the far south. By 624 the Visigoths had recovered southern Spain. In North Africa, the tenuous Byzantine hold, largely restricted to coastal areas, was repeatedly challenged by the native inhabitants.

In the East, the unstable Justin II (565–578) provoked war with the Persians by refusing to pay the tribute arranged by the peace of 562. The Persian war resulted in the loss of valuable territory in Upper Mesopotamia. Justin II broke under the strain, but fortunes temporarily improved under his adopted successor, Tiberius II (578–582), and subsequently the Byzantines even began to get the upper hand under the militant Maurice (582–602). But Maurice's strictness provoked a coup by the army, which set on the throne a crude centurion, Phocas (602–610). During the erratic reign of Phocas both external defenses and internal order collapsed. Posing as avengers for Maurice, the Persians overran Asia Minor and penetrated as far as Chalcedon (across from Constantinople). Meanwhile, Avars and Slavs swept across the Balkans.

BYZANTINE CRISES AND RECOVERY.
Section 17.

(610–1057)

> I alone command the seas. . . . [Boast of the Byzantine Emperor Nicephorus Phocas as reported by Liutprand of Cremona in his *Embassy* (tenth century).]

UNDER the Heraclian Emperors (610ff.), the Byzantines recovered and defeated the Persians, only to be confronted by a new and more powerful rival, Islam. To the latter the Byzantines lost over half their Empire, and were even in danger, for some time, of losing the whole. Recuperation, which began with the Isaurian accession (717), was arrested for over a century by the divisive Iconoclastic Controversy. Then for two centuries the Empire enjoyed progress and prosperity during the "Macedonian Renaissance" (867–1057), before it was confronted by a new "Time of Troubles."

The harassed Heraclian (continued)

Although the seventh century was one of Byzantium's darkest hours, this "Heraclian Era" (610–717) contained intervals when the sun broke through the clouds. Hope revived, for example, when the Persians were

Era (610–717) overcome by Heraclius and when the Moslems were halted by Constantine IV. Meanwhile, it became transparently clear that the old Roman Empire in the East had become different and definitely Byzantine. The use of Latin lapsed and was everywhere supplanted by Greek; the Eastern Empire was mainly restricted to the Balkans and Asia Minor; and its territories were reorganized along new lines.

Heraclius (610–641) overthrew the madman Phocas and initiated a new dynasty. With the government impotent, the provinces in confusion, the treasury empty, and the army disorganized, Heraclius could not at first repel the Persians. But he was assisted greatly by Sergius, Patriarch of Constantinople, who even contributed many precious vessels of the Church to raise necessary funds, and declared the resistance a religious crusade. The new government made grants of land in Asia Minor on condition of military service, and organized the provinces there into numerous "themes" with generals (*strategoi*) in complete control. Gradually, Heraclius assembled and trained a considerable army, while his new system of military governmental themes with resident soldiery eventually strengthened local defenses. In the interim, however, the Persians overran Syria, Palestine, and Egypt, and made numerous incursions into Asia Minor, while the Avars and Slavs, who became virtually supreme in the Balkans, besieged Constantinople.

Heraclius finally took action with boldness and skill. Leaving his threatened capital, he executed daring campaigns against the Persians in Asia Minor, Armenia, and Upper Mesopotamia during the years 622–628. In 626 he broke a combined Persian-Avar-Slavic siege of Constantinople. So thoroughly were the tables turned by his successes that in 628 Heraclius was able to capture the Persian capital of Ctesiphon and make Persia a virtual satellite. Heraclius henceforth added to his titles that of *Basileus* (Gr. "king"), formerly reserved for the Persian monarch.

But hardly had the Byzantines overcome the Persians, when they were confronted by a new, more formidable foe, Islam. After gathering momentum upon the deserts of Arabia, the Moslem whirlwind swept across Palestine, Syria, and Mesopotamia during the 630s. Fired by their new faith, the Arabs for some time carried all before them. Weakened by recent struggles, neither the Byzantine Empire nor Persia was able to cope with them. The Moslems eventually conquered all the Asian and African possessions of the Byzantine Empire except Asia Minor. Meanwhile the Slavic element was becoming dominant in the interior of the Balkan peninsula, henceforth often referred to as "*Sclavinia*."

As the new Moslem Caliphate grew into a powerful giant stretching from Spain to Northern India, several Caliphs made strenuous efforts to take Constantinople. Asia Minor was invaded almost yearly, and the Byzantine capital was subjected to three great sieges (669, 674–678, and 717–718). Emperor Constans II (Constantine III) (641–688), who had been decisively defeated on the sea in the "Battle of the Masts" (Dhu-al-Sawari) in 655, transferred his residence to the West. But strong Lombard resistance, Byzantine military reverses, and finally assassination foiled plans of Constans to conquer Italy. His militant son and successor,

Constantine IV, *Pogonatus* (the Bearded One), restored Byzantine morale by returning to Constantinople and withstanding fierce Moslem assaults on the capital during the so-called "Seven Years' Siege" (670–677). As a result of his successes, Constantine IV obtained a favorable treaty and a promise of annual tribute from the Caliph of Damascus.

With the accession of Constantine's unstable son, Justinian II, *Rhinometus* (Slit-Nose), in 695, the Byzantine Empire entered upon two decades of internal turbulence, one of whose by-products was a Caliphal decision to renew Moslem efforts to take Constantinople.

As the Moslems were making preparations for an assault on Constantinople, the Byzantines raised to the throne Leo III (717–741), a very able, experienced general of Isaurian or Syrian extraction. Leo skillfully organized the defences of Byzantine fortresses in Asia Minor, as well as those of Constantinople, and also assembled a modest fleet provided with "Greek fire," a chemical compound which would burn on contact. When the Moslems besieged Constantinople from 717 to 718, Byzantine seamanship, naval strategy, hydrographic knowledge, and use of "Greek fire" repelled their forces. Meanwhile, well-directed Byzantine sorties and the timely assistance of the warlike Bulgars, secured by adroit diplomacy, saved the capital from being taken by land.

The Isaurian Era (717–802)

Leo III and his son, Constantine V (741–755), followed up their new advantage with campaigns which expanded their frontiers until they included practically all of Asia Minor. The Isaurian Emperors expanded the theme system, and protected the military small-holdings which gave each region a ready supply of resident soldiery. In the Balkans the Bulgars were restrained, especially by Constantine V.

A serious internal quarrel, however, cast darkness over the reign of the Isaurians and that of their Amorian successors. This was the bitter Iconoclastic controversy, a religious and political struggle which lasted for a century and a quarter. All of the Isaurian emperors and most of the Amorians were supporters of Iconoclasm. Eventually branded by the Church as a heresy, Iconoclasm (*eikon*: image; *klao*: smash) consisted primarily in opposition to the use of holy images in religious worship. The Iconoclasts would do away with all representations of Christ, the Virgin, and the saints, and eliminate all veneration of such icons. To some extent Iconoclasm was a puritanical attempt to put Christianity on a more abstract, idealistic, and spiritual basis. But the movement also had political implications. The Iconoclasts wanted a more powerful imperial government and a stronger army. They were opposed to ecclesiastical privileges, immunities, and political influence; and they criticized the wealth, influence, and exemptions of the monks. They said that this weakened the economic basis of the Empire and lessened available military manpower. Primarily an Asian party whose support lay mainly in the Near Eastern part of the Empire, the Iconoclasts seem to have been influenced by Moslem and Semitic abhorrence of idols and biblical condemnations of idolatry.

The Iconoclastic controversy to 787

Just as they themselves were labeled "iconoclasts," so the "reformers" called their orthodox opponents "iconodules" (icon-worshipers). The latter, who were more moderate, traditional, and conservative, maintained that representations of Christ and the saints were licit and desirable, and in harmony with the externalism of both the Incarnation and the Sacraments. Prominent among defenders of icons were the ordinary clergy, the monks, women, and the European part of the population. Iconoclasm was condemned by the Papacy, and provoked uprisings in Byzantine Italy.

The Iconoclastic persecution was initiated by Emperor Leo III with an edict in 725 or 726. While Leo was a comparatively mild iconoclast, his son, Constantine V, nicknamed Copronymus (741–775), was a fanatical persecutor of iconodules. He mutilated and exiled many monks and suppressed several monasteries. Constantine's severe policy was continued by his son, Leo IV, the Khazar. Leo's Athenian widow, the Empress Irene, however, convoked and supported the Seventh Ecumenical Council of II Nicaea (787), which condemned the image-smashing movement, thus ending the first period of Iconoclasm.

Iconoclasm (815–843) and the Amorians

Iconoclasm was revived by Emperor Leo V, the Armenian (813–820), who convoked a Council (815), which renewed earlier decrees against icons. Although Iconoclasm was continued by the Amorians, Michael II (820–829) and Theophilus (829–842), it was neither so violent nor as effective in this second period as it had been in the first. Thus the indulgent Theophilus allowed his wife, Theodora, her "dolls," as he dubbed her icons. On her husband's death, Theodora became regent and straightway ended Iconoclasm by summoning a new iconodule council (843) which renewed the decrees of that convoked by Irene in 787.

During the Iconoclastic Era, the Moslems, aided by Byzantine distractions, secured naval control of the western Mediterranean, where they took over important islands and raided the coasts of Italy and southern France. The Lombards also took advantage of Byzantine division and increased their aggressions in Italy, where they appropriated Byzantine Ravenna with the Pentapolis to its south, and encroached on the Roman Duchy. Alienated by Isaurian Iconoclasm, and unable to obtain military assistance from Byzantium, the Papacy turned to the Frankish Carolingians. As a result, the Byzantines lost their remaining possessions in northern and central Italy, the independent Papal States were created, and the Papacy recognized a rival Empire in the West. Meanwhile, the Byzantine hold was loosened in southern Italy and Sicily. Further Byzantine difficulties included renewed Moslem aggressions in the Near East and Bulgarian pressures in the Balkans. Emperor Nicephorus I was killed in a disastrous expedition against the Bulgarians in 811, and his skull was converted into a drinking cup by Tsar Krum.

The prolonged Iconoclastic controversy split the Byzantine Empire at a time when it could otherwise have taken advantage of increasing Moslem weakness. It gave Bulgaria time to wax strong in the Balkans. It hastened the loss of remaining footholds in the West and precipitated the formation of a rival Western Roman Empire. And it delayed the advent of a general Byzantine Renaissance which might have occurred a century earlier.

Byzantine History and Civilization

The final condemnation of Iconoclasm by a Council held at Constantinople in 843 under the auspices of Empress Theodora opened a new era. Even though Emperor Michael III was a nonentity, since he came to the throne as a boy and was later reputed a drunkard, his reign from 842 to 867 was a period of progress and recovery, transitional to the Macedonian Age. The constructive nature of Michael's reign was due in large measure, first, to his competent mother, Theodora, and her shrewd minister, Theoctistus (842–856), and then to his able uncle, Caesar Bardas, who was the real ruler from 856 to 866. During the enterprising administration of Caesar Bardas, Byzantine armies seized the offensive against the Moslems; the conversion of the Slavs was initiated (c. 863); the Bulgarian king, Boris, was baptized in the Eastern Church (864); and a state-supported school of higher learning with endowed professorships was installed in the Magnaura Palace at Constantinople. *[Transition to the Macedonian Age (843–867)]*

Meanwhile, a Macedonian groom had been rising in the favor of Michael III. The Emperor's companion in drinking bouts and his accomplice in affairs of the heart, Basil the Macedonian gained increasing ascendance over his master. Eventually, Basil persuaded Michael to concur in the murder of Caesar Bardas and to agree to his own substitution as co-Emperor or Caesar (866). Within a year, when it appeared that his influence over the volatile Michael was slipping, the new Caesar had his benefactor assassinated and became sole Emperor.

The ensuing era of the Macedonian dynasty, which lasted for almost two centuries (867–1057), was a "Second Golden Age," when Byzantium reached its maturity. Byzantine autocracy, paternalism, bureaucracy, and military and naval efficiency were in full bloom, while Byzantine education, learning, art, and architecture flourished and produced new masterpieces. The Byzantines now seized the offensive and re-established their hegemony in the Eastern Mediterranean as well as throughout the Balkans, while Byzantine influence was revived in the West. *[The Macedonian "Golden Age" (867–1057)]*

Despite the violent manner of his accession, Basil I (867–886) proved an able ruler. He consolidated imperial power, promoted the theme system, championed the cause of small landowners, initiated a new law code, expanded military and naval operations, patronized scholarship and the arts, and constructed the beautiful *Nea* or "New Church" in Constantinople.

The gentle, scholarly Leo VI, the Wise (886–912), continued some of his father's projects, such as the completion of a new law code, known as the *Basilics* (Imperial Laws). But he pursued a mild foreign policy and lost territories in the Balkans to the Bulgarians, led by their powerful Tsar Simeon (893–927), to whom he was forced to pay tribute. Even more bookish was Leo's son, Constantine VII, Porphyrogenitus (913–957), "born in the porphry chamber" of the imperial palace, who patronized scholars and is credited with several learned treatises. Constantine VII preferred to leave to others the tedious direction of state affairs, in which field he fortunately had enterprising, efficient representatives.

The political indifference of Constantine VII proved beneficial inasmuch as it permitted his father-in-law, the able admiral Romanus *[Rule of relatives]*

Lecapenus, to take the reins of government. Romanus Lecapenus, who successively bore the titles of Father of the Emperor (*Basileopater*), Caesar, and Co-Emperor, was the real ruler from 919 to 944. Partly by diplomacy and partly by firmness, Lecapenus restrained the aggressive Bulgarians under their formidable leader Simeon. In Asia, Byzantine armies made progress against the Moslems in upper Mesopotamia and northern Syria. Eventually, Romanus Lecapenus was overthrown (944) by his own sons, who erroneously thought thus to hasten their accession, but who thereby actually accelerated their own downfall.

An ambitious beauty named Theophano, who had risen from humble circumstances to become the wife of the Emperor's son, dominated affairs during the declining years of her father-in-law, Constantine VII, as well as during the brief reign of her profligate husband, Romanus II (959–963). After the death of her wine-drenched spouse, Theophano married Nicephorus II, Phocas (963–969), a rugged, abstemious, eccentric general. Nicephorus recaptured the islands of Crete and Cyprus and pushed expansion against the Moslems in northern Mesopotamia and Syria. He also invited the Russians into the Balkans to restrain the Bulgars. Having tired of her strait-laced and inattentive husband, Theophano shamelessly cooperated in his assassination, which was accomplished by his handsome, dashing young nephew, General John Tzmisces, whom she intended to marry.

But ecclesiastical condemnation of the compromised Theophano was so insistent that John I, Tzmisces (969–976), was forced to dispatch her to a convent. As Emperor, Tzmisces continued the expansionist policies of Nicephorus Phocas. When the Russians, victorious over the Bulgarians, decided to stay on in the Balkans, Tzmisces, posing as a liberator, led north a Byzantine army (971), forced them to withdraw to their homeland, and neatly annexed eastern Bulgaria. In Asia, John continued the conquest of Syria and moved on into northern Palestine.

Final Macedonians (976–1056)

On the death of Tzmisces, young Basil II (976–1025), son of Romanus II and Theophano, succeeded to the throne and firmly grasped the reins. Perhaps disillusioned by his parents, Basil II never married, and his bachelorhood left him freer to concentrate on political and military affairs. After quelling several dangerous insurrections, he ruled in an autocratic manner. He was especially severe against the aristocracy, whose pretensions were inimical to the central government, and he strenuously opposed the growth of large estates at the expense of the small holdings of farmers and soldiers.

A soldier-emperor, Basil II pushed Byzantine expansion and earned the nickname of *Bulgaroctonus* or "Bulgar-slayer." Tsar Samuel of western Bulgaria had shrewdly profited from Basil's earlier preoccupations to expand his power over much of the Balkans. Despite initial reverses, Basil doggedly persevered and, after years of campaigning, eventually trapped Samuel's main army in mountain passes near Struma (1014). Bulgarian survivors, estimated at about 14,000, were blinded and sent back to their Tsar in pitiful bands of a hundred, each group led by a one-eyed comrade. Samuel suffered a stroke at the grisly spectacle, and died shortly thereafter. Bulgarian possessions were then incorporated into the Byzantine Empire, whose power once more extended throughout the Balkans.

Basil also continued expansion against the Moslems in the Near East, although at a decelerated tempo. He incorporated western Armenia into the Empire and obtained a right of inheritance to eastern Armenia. The conversion of the Russians was begun with the baptism of Basil's ally, Prince Vladimir of Kiev in 989.

When Basil II died in 1025, he was succeeded for one year (1025–1026) by his brother, the weak Constantine VIII. Following this, Byzantium was ruled for three decades (1028–1056) by the successive husbands of Constantine's daughters, the frivolous Zoe and the retiring Theodora. Under the uninhibited Zoe, who held the throne most of the time, the court became a stage for frivolity and a hotbed of intrigue. The civil aristocracy of the capital, who obtained control, neglected the military establishment, and weakened the fiscal and military foundations of the state by encouraging expansion of large estates at the expense of small landholdings. At the close of these three decades the Empire was distraught by civil war, at the same time being assailed by fierce Pechenegs (Patzinaks) from the North, Seljuk Turks from the East, and Normans from the West.

BYZANTINE CIVILIZATION.
Section 18.

> I am a Hellene by speech, yet . . . if anyone asked me what I am, I would answer: 'A Christian. . . .' [Gennadius, *Dispute (of a Byzantine) with a Jew* (fifteenth century).]

BYZANTINE civilization was a compound of Greek, Roman, Christian, and Oriental elements. The Greek element predominated in Byzantine language, literature, education, philosophy, and the sciences. The Roman aspect prevailed in Byzantine government, law, military, and social institutions. Christianity permeated Byzantine civilization, in which it was dynamic, inspiring, and all-pervasive. Finally, Oriental elements, mainly Near Eastern, were strong in such fields as religion, art, and architecture.

The heart of the Byzantine Empire was Constantinople, concerning which a twelfth-century Islamic traveler wrote: "Save for Bagdad, there is no city in the world to compare with it."[a] Until the development of gunpowder artillery, Constantinople was a virtually impregnable capital, as well as a cosmopolitan center of world trade: the heart of the Byzantine Empire and the epitome of its life.

Byzantine government was autocratic, bureaucratic, theocratic, and exceptionally efficient. That it was well adapted to its time and environment is demonstrated by its survival for over a thousand years. The source of all authority in the Byzantine state was the "God-given Emperor, who was supreme executive, legislator, judge, and commander-in-chief. Hailed as "Autocrator, Augustus, Basileus, and Glory of the Purple," the Em-

[a] Benjamin of Tudela, *Itinerary*, ed. and tr. A. Asher, 2 vols., Vol. I (London: A. Asher and Co., 1840).

Byzantine government

peror was ensconced in magnificent pomp and circumstance, and approached by an elaborate ceremonial which included multiple prostrations. He was elevated to the throne by being accepted by the army, aristocracy, Church, and people. But once he was installed, the Emperor's will was supreme and was regarded as the source of law, as is explicitly stated, for example, in the Justinian Code. At the same time, he was considered subject to divine law and was limited in practice by a traditionally accepted "divine right of revolution," which could depose an unacceptable or incompetent Emperor who had lost the support of his subjects or was unequal to a crisis such as foreign invasion.

The details of Byzantine government were carried on by an efficiently departmentalized bureaucracy, which contrasted with the poorly organized, informal governments of contemporary feudal states in the West. To cope with the constant pressure of foreign aggression, the Byzantine Empire was divided from the seventh century on into "themes," in each of which supreme military and civil authority were combined in a *strategos* or general, except where the burden of defense was chiefly naval, as in the Cibyrrhaoet (Cyprian) and Aegean themes, where the head was a *drungarius* or admiral.

The government was supported by numerous taxes, direct and indirect, and also had a monopoly of certain industries, such as silk production and mining. Byzantine government was extremely paternalistic, and carefully regulated numerous facets of its subjects' lives, including prices and wages, immigration and emigration, travel and employment, the purchasing of property and the charging of interest.

Byzantine law

An important Byzantine contribution was the codification of Roman law. Byzantine Emperors made three such codifications: the Justinian *Corpus Juris Civilis* (*Code of Civil Law*) in the sixth century, the Isaurian *Ecloga* (*Selections*) in the eighth century, and the Macedonian *Basilics* (*Imperial Laws*) in the ninth century. Inasmuch as the first code was in Latin, while the other two were in Greek, it was the former, Justinian's *Corpus Juris Civilis* or *Code*, which had the widest influence. This was composed of four parts: the actual *Code* of laws itself, the *Digest* of authoritative interpretations of the law by recognized legal authorities, and the *Institutes* or synopses of principles of law, supplemented by Justinian's *Novels* or new laws.

The Justinian codification, available in Latin, was extensively studied and widely adopted in Western Europe during both medieval and modern times. It has influenced all modern European and European-derived legal systems. The Byzantines also developed and organized commercial law in their *Maritime Code*, agrarian law in their *Farmer's Code*, and military law in their *Military Code*. *The Maritime Code*, also known as the Rhodian Sea Law, had a profound influence on the formation of Western mercantile and maritime law. An efficient system of justice functioned throughout the Empire.

Security

The security of the Empire was provided for by diplomacy, as well as by the army and the navy. When possible, the Byzantines preferred diplomacy. To this end, they sent magnificent embassies, made lavish gifts, paid generous bribes, rendered handsome tribute, exerted economic pressures, contracted foreign alliances, arranged matrimonial unions. Businessmen and missionaries, as well as professional statesmen, were Byzantine ambassadors; and the extension of imperial influence went hand in hand with the expansion of Byzantine commerce and the Eastern Church. The old Roman principle of "divide and conquer" was employed with barbarian neighbors, Moslem states, and Germanic and Slavic kingdoms.

The Byzantine army was a compact, efficient, carefully trained, well-equipped, ably commanded professional organization, which rarely numbered more than 120,000 men. For the Byzantines, warfare was a science, and their generals (*strategoi*) assiduously studied strategy and tactics, on which some Emperors wrote treatises. Military operations were adapted to the special character and weaknesses of their enemies. Deception and espionage were widely employed. Conservation of manpower was a cardinal principle, and a general who was victorious on the field but had lost too many men was deemed defeated. As has been observed, the Empire was eventually divided into themes, each with its own supreme commander or *strategos*, and its resident soldiery or *stratiotai*, who received grants of land on condition of military service. The holdings of the soldiery were zealously guarded by military-minded emperors, such as the Isaurians and Macedonians.

Although seapower was vital, the Byzantine navy had a varying history. This was partly due to interservice rivalries, the shortsightedness of certain emperors, the decline of the Byzantine merchant marine, and the high cost of naval maintenance. But the navy was expanded in the Macedonian period, so that Nicephorus Phocas could declare, "I alone command the sea!" Commanded by *drungarii* or admirals, the Byzantine navy included both heavier warships (*dromonds*) and lighter, faster craft (*pamphylians*). It was equipped with "Greek fire," a combustible compound of secret composition which would catch fire on contact and would burn even on water; it was tremendously effective against the wooden vessels of the day.

The Empire comprised some of the most flourishing commercial and industrial centers in the Mediterranean world, including Antioch, Ephesus, Thessalonica, and Constantinople. In the Golden Horn and other harbors of the Byzantine Empire could be found ships from every clime in the world. Byzantine merchants were middlemen for a great and profitable international commerce. Busy workshops in Byzantine cities produced all sorts of precious articles, especially costly luxuries and art objects—silks, tapestries, rugs, jewelry, cabinets, fine furniture.

The Byzantine economy

In the thirteenth century a Western observer, Robert of Clari, recorded his impression that "two-thirds of the world's wealth is concentrated in Constantinople." Until the mid-eleventh century, the Byzantine gold bezant was scrupulously maintained at full value and was widely preferred to all other coins, even, we are told, in far-off Ceylon.

In addition to imposing numerous taxes on business activities, the Byzantine government attempted to regulate the economy. Governmental intervention was usually beneficial, as in its provision of employment for the jobless, but was sometimes misdirected, as in the case of excessive limitation of interest from money loaned for maritime enterprises. Insufficient as compared to the risks, particularly after the rise of Moslem piracy, this controlled percentage caused capital to be diverted from the sea to land investments, and resulted in a progressive shrinkage of the Byzantine merchant marine, which was eventually displaced by enterprising north Italian carriers. Until the mid-eleventh century, small independent farmers were common, thanks to protective governmental policies, which helped to keep agricultural production high. But after the aristocracy obtained control of the government in the eleventh century, the great estates of the wealthy progressively swallowed up the small farms.

Byzantine society

Although often criticized by their less sophisticated Western contemporaries as effete and tricky, the Byzantines were, by and large, pious, orderly, moral, and industrious. Salutary influences included Christianity and Roman law, as well as a considerable middle class and a comparatively high degree of literacy. Yet Byzantine society had its weaknesses, such as the glaring contrast—common in that day—between the wealth of the upper classes and dire want of many rural peasants and urban poor. Many Byzantines had a tendency to excessive argumentation and factionalism. Court life was rife with intrigue and conspiracy. The aristocracy squabbled among themselves, as also with the imperial government. Business was prone to trickery and lawsuits. The populace was frequently volatile and easily incited to revolt. There was an urbane lack of scruples in business and politics which scandalized many Westerners.

The Eastern Church and Schism

A salient feature of the Byzantine Empire was the intense Christianity of its populace, whose loyalty was as much directed to their Church as to their State. The ambit of the Eastern Church was greater than that of the Eastern Empire, although the capital of both was Constantinople. Practically all of the southern and eastern Slavs, including the Bulgarians, Serbs, and Russians, were converted to Eastern Christianity in the ninth to tenth centuries; and their churches were initially organized under the Patriarch of Constantinople, who continued to enjoy a certain primacy even after the various Slavic peoples obtained their own Patriarchs. To facilitate and confirm the conversion of the Slavs, St. Cyril (Constantine) prepared a Slavonic alphabet and translated the Bible and liturgy into a Slavonic dialect (old Macedonian or Church Slavonic) in the ninth century.

The Eastern Church developed certain characteristics that distinguished it from the Western. After the division of the Empire, the two Churches moved farther apart. Political division was sealed and geographical separation accentuated by Germanic conquests in the West and by the Moslem "wedge" between East and West. A serious linguistic gulf and wall were added as knowledge of Latin died out in the East even as that of Greek did in the West. Differences in psychology and customs also contributed to divergence.

After Constantine moved his capital to the Bosporus, the Bishops of "new Rome" became rivals of the Bishops of "old Rome." The Second

Ecumenical Council held at Constantinople (381) declared that the Bishop of Constantinople was second only to the Roman Bishop in dignity "because Constantinople is the new Rome." In the following century, the Eastern Bishops in the Fourth Ecumenical Council at Chalcedon (451) put through a resolution recognizing the Bishop of Constantinople as a Patriarch equal to the Bishop of Rome, although Pope Leo I refused to accept and ratify this decree. In the sixth century, Patriarch John the Faster of Constantinople was reproved by Pope Gregory I for having assumed the title of "Ecumenical [Universal] Patriarch." Certain liturgical and doctrinal disparities, which multiplied in time, eventually become serious bones of contention. A fundamental difference was the Eastern concept of the Patriarchal, national organization of the Church, as opposed to Western emphasis on its Papal, ecumenical aspect.

Differences between the Eastern and Western Churches came to a head in the ninth to eleventh centuries because of rival claims of Popes and Patriarchs to direct Patriarchal jurisdiction over newly founded churches in Slavic areas; the extension of direct Papal administrative control in southern Italy and Sicily *pari passu* with the Norman conquest; and Cluniac-Gregorian insistence on Papal primacy, ecclesiastical uniformity, and clerical celibacy. Schism was narrowly averted in the later ninth century when Patriarch Photius denied the validity of Papal intervention in a dispute over the Byzantine Patriarchal succession. In 858, Caesar Bardas expelled Patriarch Ignatius of Constantinople from his see on a charge of treason and installed Photius, a learned layman, in his place. When the case was appealed to Rome, Pope Nicholas I decided in favor of Ignatius and denounced Photius as a usurper. Mutual excommunications ensued. To bolster their position, Photius and his supporters denied the authority of Rome to intervene. They also accused Rome of falling into heresy by including the *Filioque* in the Creed and using unleavened bread in the Mass. According to Easterners, the addition of the *Filioque* ("and from the Son") clause in the Creed was a violation of the decree of Council of Chalcedon (451), which had declared the final text of the Creed. They further maintained that the baked unleavened flour used in the Western Mass was not really bread. Although the Photian break was subsequently patched up, it was never completely repaired.

Relations between the Eastern and Western Churches again became strained in the mid-eleventh century as a result of extension of direct Papal jurisdiction in southern Italy, previously subject to Constantinople, and Cluniac-Gregorian insistence on Papal primacy and centralization. When Pope Leo IX sent intransigent legates headed by the fiery Cardinal Humbert to the haughty Patriarch Michael Cerularius in Constantinople, both sides ended by exchanging bitter recriminations and anathemas (1054). Thus began the great Eastern Schism, which has lasted to the present day. Despite repeated attempts to repair the breach, as in declarations of reunion at the Ecumenical Councils of Lyons in 1245 and Florence in 1439, the majority of the Byzantine clergy and populace refused to countenance obeisance to Rome, and the Schism continued.

The Early Middle Ages

Special features of the Eastern Church

Among special features of the Eastern Church was its more patriarchal, national nature which contrasted with the more centralized, international, ecclesiastical organization in the West. In imitation of the Byzantine Empire, with its Patriarch in Constantinople, other Eastern Orthodox states, such as Bulgaria, Serbia, and Russia, eventually obtained their own national Patriarchs. As the Byzantines used Greek in their liturgy, so the Slavic peoples employed Slavonic. The Eastern Churches recognized as binding only the decrees of the first seven Ecumenical Councils, beginning with I Nicaea in 325 and ending with II Nicaea in 787. Subsequent development of dogma, facilitated in the Western Church by further General Councils and continuous Papal authority, was impeded. The elaboration of faith by reason achieved by medieval Western theologians was not matched in the Eastern Church, whose doctrines and practices remained more static. Although monasticism was as strong in the Eastern Church as in the Western, it was more unchanging, conservative, and introspective. It did not perform such varied external services, nor did it organize into large congregations, or "evolve" into "active" religious orders with numerous charitable, educational, missionary, and other functions, as did Western monasticism. The mystical strain has also been stronger in the Eastern Church.

The question of Byzantine "Cesaropapism"

The Byzantine Church has often been accused of "Cesaropapism," or imperial domination in ecclesiastical affairs. To a certain extent there are grounds for this charge, but it is usually exaggerated. Although Eastern Emperors took a keen interest in religion, participated in religious disputes, legislated concerning ecclesiastical matters, appointed and deposed Patriarchs, and even on occasion composed theological tracts, this was more often as sons of the Church than as its masters. When Emperors such as Constantius, Valens, Theodosius II, and some of the Heraclians, Isaurians, and Amorians, supported sectarian doctrines, their efforts were doomed to failure and were eventually condemned as heretical by the Eastern as well as the Western Church. This was also true of the attempts of later Emperors to effect reunion with Rome, partly for political reasons. Such efforts were unsuccessful because they were opposed to the majority opinion in the Eastern Church.

Byzantine intellectual culture: Education

The intellectual culture of the Eastern Empire was fundamentally Greek, although with a Roman approach and Christian inspiration. It traced back primarily to Greek sources, and achieved its greatest successes in fields intimately associated with Christianity. Otherwise it maintained an imitative and reproductive, rather than a creative and progressive aspect. This was partly due to its own maturity, partly to its religious preoccupations, and partly to its extremely classical, traditional orientation. The level of Byzantine culture was, over a long period, much higher than that of the West.

Education was greatly esteemed, and learning was widely diffused among the upper and middle classes. On primary and secondary levels, education was mainly private and ecclesiastical, but on higher levels it was largely public. What is often referred to as the "University of Constantinople" actually consisted of loosely coordinated state-supported professorships of literature, rhetoric, philosophy, and law. Classical traditions prevailed in the curriculum. Attention in elementary and secondary education was concentrated on Greek grammar and rhetoric, with stress on the study of Greek classical literature. Philosophy and natural sciences were also cultivated to some extent. But law was the crowning secular study and qualified one for preferment in the civil service as well as for barrister and notary work.

Emphasis was placed on linguistic competence and literary learning. Greek classics were studied, and many Byzantines knew Homer by heart. Patriarch Photius memorized Homer at a very early age and Princess Anna Comnena quoted him sixty-six times in her historical poem, the *Alexiad*. Photius's *Myriobiblion* analyzed some two hundred and eighty works, the majority by classical authors. Numerous anthologies, epitomes, grammars, and works on rhetoric were composed.

At a time when advanced philosophy was dormant in Western Europe, the Byzantines continued to study and admire Plato, Aristotle, and other ancient philosophers. They passed their philosophical knowledge on to the Moslems and eventually contributed both indirectly and directly to the philosophical revival in the West during the High and Later Middle Ages. *Philosophy, theology, and sciences*

The Eastern Fathers blazed the way in the development of speculative and ascetic theology. The Iconoclastic Controversy stimulated theological speculation, as is exemplified by the works of St. John Damascene and Abbot Theodore of Studium in defence of the externals of religion. The same was true of later controversies concerning mystical illumination (Hesychism) and reunion with the West. Several laymen, including emperors, were authors of theological works. Yet the Byzantines never achieved the union of philosophical reason with religious faith which resulted in the harvest of Scholasticism and systematic theology in the West.

Greek science, mathematics, and medical lore were kept alive by the Byzantines, and some advances were registered. But the Byzantines, like the ancient Romans, were more adept in applied than in "pure" theoretical sciences. Their practical science was manifested in buildings such as Santa Sophia, fortifications such as those of Constantinople, mechanical clocks and animals, Greek fire, public sanitation, clinics, medicine, surgery, and "scientific" agriculture and animal husbandry.

The Byzantines achieved notable success in the writing of history in which they kept up the Greek tradition of composing more specialized accounts of circumscribed periods. They profited from the inspiration of a grand and ecumenical Roman and Christian theme. Examples from a long list of distinguished Byzantine historians include Procopius in the sixth century, Patriarch Nicephorus in the ninth century, Emperor Constantine VII, Porphyrogenitus in the tenth century, the polymath and statesman Michael Psellus in the eleventh century, Princess Anna Comnena and her husband Nicephorus Bryennius in the twelfth century, the *History writing and literature*

Grand Logothete Nicetas Choniates (Acominatus) in the thirteenth century, ex-Emperor John VI Cantacuzene in the fourteenth century, and courtier George Phrantzes in the fifteenth century.

Although Byzantine literature was polished, it was not particularly original. Poetry was handicapped by classical Greek forms and rules, although the current pronunciation of Greek was different from that in antiquity. In the field of religious poetry, such as hymns, ecclesiastical composers, led by Romanus the Melode (sixth century), broke away from classical models and used rhyme and accentual rhythm in the popular vernacular. Other famous early hymn-writers included the energetic Patriarch Sergius (seventh century) and the brilliant Church Father, St. John Damascene (eighth century). The Greek Fathers and subsequent writers also composed vibrant sermons and beautiful homilies as well as informative letters.

Byzantine architecture

Byzantine styles and structures occupy an important place in the history of architecture. During the Early Middle Ages, the leading Christian architects were Byzantines, whose forms became dominant throughout the Christian Near East and Eastern Europe. The Byzantines combined the modified Roman basilica and Christian innovations with Near Eastern domes and vaults in admirable fashion during the "Justinian Renaissance." The magnificent cathedral of Santa Sophia in Constantinople features a grand central dome (100 feet in diameter, and rising to a height of 180 feet), set on pendentives, which gracefully unite the base of the dome and the four supporting piers. The ground plan is that of a modified basilica, approaching a Greek cross in the almost equal length of nave and transepts (about 260 by 240 feet). A "halo" of forty windows about the base of the dome illuminates the lavish mosaics and rich marbles in the interior. A variation of the Justinian style was the rotunda-type church, exemplified by the domed octagonal chapel of San Vitale in Ravenna.

During the Macedonian Renaissance churches became more graceful, externally ornate, and airy. The exterior of churches was ornamented with designs in multicolored brick; the ground plan was in the form of an equal-armed Greek cross; the central dome, set on a drum, was surrounded by lesser domes over each of the arms; and the lightness and grace of the interior were enhanced by the use of columns instead of piers to support the domes. The widely imitated Macedonian Renaissance style was exemplified by the *"Nea"* or "New Church" of Basil I in Constantinople; St. Mark's Cathedral in Venice; various churches in Sicily and the Perigueux district of southern France; and especially by numerous churches throughout Byzantine lands and, with local modifications, in Bulgaria, Serbia, and Russia. In Russia, for example, bulbous domes replaced semicircular ones, partly to obviate large accumulations of snow and ice.

Byzantine art

The story of Byzantine art is to some extent an account of the fluctuating interplay of classical (Hellenic and Hellenistic) and Near Eastern (Syrian, Armenian, Anatolian, and Persian) elements. At the outset of the Middle Ages, Eastern realism and emotionalism were strong; during the austere Iconoclastic period a classical revival occurred; in the Macedonian Age both streams blended. Much Byzantine art was impressionistic.

The supreme form of Byzantine large-scale representation consisted in mosaics. These small cubes of glass and marble set in plaster had extraordinary durability and richness, as well as a subtle reflective quality wherein colors and moods varied in changing light. The Byzantines became the world's supreme masters of the mosaic form, exemplified in the Cathedral of Santa Sophia, as well as in churches at Ravenna and throughout the Byzantine world.

In the High and Later Middle Ages, frescoes generally replaced mosaics. Consisting of paint applied to and absorbed by fresh plaster, frescoes were, so to speak, "cheaper mosaics," which allowed greater freedom, naturalness, and realism, as well as more careful shadings of color. Enchanting frescoes are found in many smaller Byzantine churches in Greece and Macedonia.

Byzantine representational art on a smaller scale is represented by icons or sacred images, such as those of the Blessed Virgin and the Saints. Usually painted on panels of hardwood, these icons circulated widely in the West as well as in the East. They are exemplified by the still popular picture of Our Lady of Perpetual Help, said to have come from Crete. Such pictures are impressionistic and calculated more to elicit piety rather than strictly to represent natural reality. The Byzantines also excelled in other forms of art, such as bas-relief sculptures—in capitals of columns and carvings on thrones, doors, cabinets, and sarcophagi; exquisite metalwork; cloissoné enamels; and fine textiles, silks, tapestries, and rugs. Whatever their record in other fields, the Byzantines were certainly creative in architecture and art.

The Byzantine Empire was a bastion of defense for Christian Europe and a treasury of Greek classical culture. Byzantium Christianized and civilized the Slavs and contributed liberally to the civilization of Moslems. Byzantine influences on medieval Western Europe were also numerous. Byzantine examples encouraged ecclesiastical anointing of Western monarchs, resuscitation of the Western Empire, revival of Roman law, progressive centralization of political authority in the monarchy, and development of departmentalized government. Western commerce, industry, coinage, and finance were stimulated by contacts with Byzantium. The Byzantines transmitted works of Greek science, medicine, mathematics, and philosophy to Arab and Latin scholars. In theology, the Western Fathers drew their initial inspiration from the Eastern Fathers, and the Scholastics followed suit. The renewed study of the Greek language and literature during the Renaissance depended on Byzantine sources and assistance. It is estimated that 90 per cent of our copies of classical Greek literature have descended to us through Byzantium. Byzantine models also influenced the evolution of Western architecture and art.

Byzantine influences

References for Chapter 6

AMONG good general works on Byzantine history and civilization (listed alphabetically) are Norman H. BAYNES and H. St. L. B. Moss, eds., *Byzantium, An Introduction to East Roman Civilization* (Oxford: Clarendon, 1948), a collaborative series of essays; *The Cambridge Medieval History*, both the older Vol. IV and the more recent Vol. IV in two Parts (I and II), ed. J. M. HUSSEY (Cambridge: Cambridge U.P., 1966–1967), which contain specialized chapters by recognized experts; CHARLES DIEHL, *Byzantium: Greatness and Decline*, tr. Naomi Walford (New Brunswick, N.J., Rutgers U.P., 1957), primarily an analysis of factors; JOAN M. HUSSEY, *The Byzantine World* (London; Hutchison, 1957), a survey of high points, accentuating the ecclesiastical; GEORGE OSTROGORSKY, *History of the Byzantine State*, tr. Joan M. Hussey (Oxford: Blackwell, 1956), a scholarly political history, rich in bibliography and detail; STEVEN RUNCIMAN, *Byzantine Civilization* (New York: Meridian, 1956), a masterly, succinct treatment; and ALEXANDER A. VASILIEV, *History of the Byzantine Empire, 324–1453*, rev. (Madison, U. of Wis., 1952), the most comprehensive study by a single authority in English.

One of the earliest and still one of the best of more specialized historical accounts is JOHN B. BURY, *History of the Later Roman Empire from Arcadius to Irene, 395–800 A.D.*, 2 vols. (New York: Macmillan, 1889), a vivid narrative based on the sources, continued in his *History of the Eastern Roman Empire from the Fall of Irene to the Accession of Basil II (A.D. 802–867)* (London: Macmillan, 1912). Useful for the era of Justinian are ALEXANDER A. VASILIEV, *Justin the First* (Cambridge: Harvard U.P., 1950); JOHN A. BARKER, *Justinian and the Later Roman Empire* (Madison: U. of Wis., 1966); PERCY N. URE, *Justinian and His Age* (Harmondsworth, Eng.: Penguin, 1951); WILLIAM G. HOLMES, *The Age of Justinian and Theodora: A History of the Sixth Century A.D.*, 2 vols. (2nd. ed., London: Bell, 1912); and the well-informed PROCOPIUS of Caesarea, leading historian of the sixth century, *Procopius with an English Translation, History of the Wars. Gothic War. "Anecdota" or Secret History. Buildings*, tr. H. B. Dewing, 7 vols. (London: Heinemann, 1914–1940). On the Heraclian period (610–717), both Bury and appropriate articles in the *Cambridge Medieval History*, Vol. IV may be consulted; and on the Iconoclastic Era (717–867), in addition to Bury's works, EDWARD J. MARTIN, *A History of the Iconoclastic Controversy* (London, S.P.C.K., 1930). Cross-sections of the "Macedonian Renaissance" (867–1057) are provided by STEVEN RUNCIMAN, *The Emperor Romanus Lecapenus and His Reign: A Study of Tenth Century Byzantium* (Cambridge: Cambridge U.P., 1929), and the *Embassy* of the ninth-century Italian envoy of Otto I to Constantinople, BISHOP LIUTPRAND of Cremona, in his *Works* . . . , tr. F. A. Wright (New York: Dutton, 1930). For the eleventh century we have two works by gifted women: one by JOAN M. HUSSEY, *The Byzantine Empire in the Eleventh Century: Some Different Interpretations* in *Transactions of the Royal Historical Society*, 4th Series, Vol. XXXII (London: Royal Hist. Soc. 1950), and the other by Princess ANNA COMNENA, *The Alexiad* . . . tr. Elizabeth A. S. Dawes (London: Kegan Paul, 1926), a remarkable historical epic poem on her father, Alexius I. Comneus. Also available in translation is the eleventh-century *Chronographia* by the learned statesman, MICHAEL PSELLUS, tr. E. R. A. Sewter (London: Routledge, 1953; and Baltimore, Penguin, 1966). For the period of the Latin Empire (1204–1261), there is EDWIN PEARS, *The Fall of Constantinople, Being a Story of the Fourth Crusade* (London: Longmans, 1855); and ALICE GARDNER, *The Lascarids of Nicaea, the Story of an Empire in Exile* (London: Methuen, 1922); for that of the Paleologi (1260–1453), especially the fall, STEVEN RUNCIMAN, *The Fall of Constantinople, 1453* (Cambridge, Cambridge U.P., 1965); and EDWIN PEARS, *The Destruction of the Greek Empire and the Story of the Capture of Constantinople by the Turks* (London: Longmans, 1903).

With respect to Byzantine government, JOHN B. BURY is the author of various works, including *The Imperial Administrative System in the Ninth Century* . . . (London: Oxford, 1911). A key tenth-century source is the *De Administrando Imperio* of Emperor Constantine VII, Porphyrogenitus, ed. G. MORAVCSIK and tr. R. J. Jenkins (Budapest: Pázmany Péter Tutománpyegyetemi Görög Filologiai Intézet, 1949). Among partial translations of the *Corpus Juris Civilis* of Justinian are the *Digest*, tr. J. B. Moyle (Oxford: Clarendon, 1889). E. H. FRESHFIELD has made several translations of Byzantine law, including *The Ecloga, The Farmers' Law, The Rhodian Sea Law, The Procheiron*, and *The Book of the Prefect* in various *Manuals* . . . (Cambridge: Cambridge U.P., 1926, 1927, 1931, and 1938). Good treatments of the Byzantine economy are given by GEORGE OSTROGORSKY, "Agrarian Conditions in the Byzantine Empire . . . ," and STEVEN RUNCIMAN, "Byzantine Trade and Industry," in *The Cambridge Economic History of Europe*, I and II (Cambridge, Cambridge U.P., 1941–1942).

Representative works on the Byzantine Church include REGINALD M. FRENCH, *The Eastern Orthodox Church* (London: Hutchinson, 1951); ADRIAN FORTESQUE, *The Orthodox Eastern Church* (London: Catholic Truth Society, 1907); and GEORGE EVERY, *The Byzantine Patriarchate, 451–1204* (London: S.P.C.K., 1948). The relation of localism to heresy is brought out by ERNEST L. WOODWARD, *Christianity and Nationalism in the Later Roman Empire* (London: Longmans, 1916). The progressive breaking away from union with Rome is the subject of FRANTISEK DVORNIK, *The Photian Schism: History and Legend* (Cambridge: Cambridge U.P., 1948); STEVEN RUNCIMAN, *The Eastern Schism* . . . (Oxford: Clarendon, 1956); and SIDNEY H. SCOTT, *The Eastern Churches and the Papacy* (London: Sheed, 1928).

Good discussions of Byzantine culture are given in the already listed general works of NORMAN H. BAYNES and H. ST. L. B. MOSS, CHARLES DIEHL, JOAN M. HUSSEY, STEVEN RUNCIMAN, and ALEXANDER A. VASILIEV, as well as the *Cambridge Medieval History*, Vol. IV.

There are several good works on Byzantine art and architecture, including MANOLIS CHATZIDAKAS and A. GRABAR, *Byzantine and Early Medieval Painting* (New York: Viking, 1965); JOHN BECKWITH, *The Art of Constantinople* . . . (London: Phaidon, 1965); JOHN A. HAMILTON, *Byzantine Architecture and Decoration* (London: Batsford, 1933); DAVID T. RICE, *Byzantine Art* (London: Penguin, 1954); and ORMONDE M. DALTON, *Byzantine Art and Archeology* (Oxford: Clarendon, 1911). A good survey of Byzantine influence is CECIL STEWART, *Byzantine Legacy* (London: Allen and Unwin, 1947); a broader study is J. LINDSAY, *Byzantium into Europe* (London: Lane, 1952).

The Early Middle Ages

❮ THE MOSLEM CHALLENGE: RISE AND CIVILIZATION OF ISLAM.   Chapter 7.

ISLAM, latest of the world's great religions, originated in peripheral Arabia in the seventh century of the Christian era. During the lifetime of its Prophet, Mohammed,[a] the Islamic community became a state, which soon spread, under his Caliphal successors, through the Near East and North Africa. The Moslems also obtained temporary control of the Iberian Peninsula and Sicily and became permanently established in Iran, Northwestern India, and parts of South Central Asia. In the Islamic "Golden Age," the ninth to eleventh centuries, the Moslems enjoyed world leadership in many fields, and developed a flourishing civilization which contributed much to Western Europe. Later, much of the Islamic world, overrun by warlike peoples from inner Asia, lapsed into decline.

[a] The prophet's name is sometimes transliterated as Muhammed.

(to 632)

THE RISE OF ISLAM.
Section 19.

> There is no God but Allah, and Mohammed is his prophet. [The Creed of Islam.]

Arabia and the Arabs

PERIPHERAL Arabia lay in the twilight zone of history until an inspired, magnetic prophet arose in its arid confines in the seventh century after Christ. Preaching strict monotheism and a high code of morality, together with what was for the Arabs a new message of unity and brotherly love, Mohammed made many converts. He thus began the conversion and unification of the Arabian Peninsula, a work completed and extended by his devoted successors, the early Caliphs.

The world's largest peninsula, Arabia is four times the size of France. Like much of our southwestern United States, Arabia is mostly semidesert tableland. Here periodic rainfall and transient vegetation provide pasturage for the animals of the nomad population. Certain better-watered coastal areas, such as Yemen in the southwest and Uman in the southeast, are exceptions, as are occasional alluvial valleys and oases. A more typical Arabian area is the Hijaz, located in the western part of the peninsula, halfway up the coast of the Red Sea. In this semiarid, partly mountainous plateau, Mecca was a half-way point along the inland trade route that paralleled the seacoast. To the northeast of Mecca was Yathrib (later to be known as Medina) in the midst of a fertile oasis noted for its agricultural produce.

At the coming of Mohammed, Arabia was, as now, sparsely populated. Hardy, independence-loving, individualistic and combative, the Semitic Arabs were products of their desert environment. Of the bedouin Arabs, as of their reputed progenitor, Ishmael, it could be said: "His hand shall

The Moslem Challenge

be against every man, and every man's hand against him." Most of the Arabs were organized into separate independent tribes, each with its own council of elders (*majlis*) and its leader or *sheikh*. Among the more sedentary Arabs, the city-state was the successor to the tribe. Perennial rivalries between tribes led to recurrent *razzias* or raids, usually more dramatic than deadly.

The typical Arab was a nomadic pastoral bedouin, who lived off his camels, horses, sheep, and goats. The bedouins traded with more sedentary people for necessities and luxuries. There was a saying: "Every Arab is a tradesman, and sometimes a thief." Some Arabs, settled in cities such as Mecca, became full-time merchants who dealt in valuable products—some on a large scale, operating caravans of camels. A small proportion of the Arabs, located especially in the south, were farmers, raising grains, vegetables, and fruits, notably dates.

The Arab was proudly upright in many respects, unscrupulous in others. He was liable to indulge in promiscuity, drunkenness, gambling, and violence. Polygamy and infanticide were common. The Arabs were backward compared to their more civilized neighbors, and their original religion was polytheistic, superstitious, and primitive. It involved worship of natural objects, such as moon and stars, as well as springs and mountains. The Arabs were haunted by a fear of evil spirits such as desert-demons known as "*jinn.*" They had fetishes and idols, and their worship stressed ritual and forms to the neglect of morality. The Arabic alphabet was apparently derived from the Aramaic, Phoenician, or Sinaitic. The composition of the Koran by Mohammed came at the height of the heroic age of Arabic poetry, whose principal products were poetic *qasidahs* celebrating episodes in the perennial conflicts between Arabian tribes. Infiltration of outside culture into the Arabian peninsula in Mohammed's day was exemplified by the "Hanif" movement in religion, which propagated monotheism and greater spirituality and morality.

Islam's founder, Mohammed was born at Mecca in the 570s. Orphaned at an early age, he was reared first by his grandfather and then by his uncle. As a youth, Mohammed spent some time as a shepherd, which occupation was conducive to religious reflection. On reaching manhood, Mohammed entered the employment of a rich widow, Khadijah, who operated caravans on a large scale. Obtaining favor in the eyes of his employer, who was about fifteen years his senior, he was offered and he accepted her hand in marriage. Their married life was very happy. Of his good fortune, he says,

Mohammed the Prophet

> The Lord hath not forsaken thee, nor doth He despise thee:
> Did He not find thee an orphan and give thee a home?
> Did He not find thee wandering and direct thee?
> Did He not find thee destitute and enrich thee?
> (Koran, 93:5–8)

As a result of his marriage, Mohammed had leisure to devote to religious contemplation and prayer. He had come in contact with Jews and Christians as well as Hanifs, thus obtaining knowledge of more advanced religions. In the course of his meditations, he began to have visions, in which God revealed to him the Divine nature and will. Despite his reluctance to do so, Mohammed was directed to "recite" the heavenly "book" that was unveiled to him and to preach its message to his fellow Arabs:

> *Arise and preach*
> *And praise the Lord*
> *And cleanse thy garments*
> *And fly every abomination.* (Koran, 74:2–5)

When Mohammed began to disclose his revelations at Mecca, he was scorned, railed at, and even assaulted. However, he made some converts, beginning with his wife, Khadijah; his cousin, Ali; his merchant-kinsman, Abu Bakr; the strong and able Omar; and the slave, Zaid. Mohammed's revelations, as recorded in the Koran, intermingled solemn oaths and stern warnings with ecstatic descriptions of the beauty and goodness of God. Meanwhile the prophet also began to preach to pilgrims who came to Mecca.

The Hegira (622)

But the city fathers and businessmen of Mecca were alarmed by the preaching of this visionary, whose doctrines endangered traditional Meccan religious concepts and celebrations, which were economically profitable. Accordingly the Meccan *majlis* began to threaten and persecute Mohammed and his followers. Some of the neo-Moslems took refuge in Abyssinia, but the bulk of them, followed by Mohammed, gradually withdrew to Yathrib in the interior. This *Hegira* or Flight (622), which is regarded as the date of the definitive foundation of the new religion, came to be the beginning of the Moslem calendar (A.H.). In Yathrib, which came to be known as Medina (the City of the Prophet), Mohammed assumed the leadership of the Arab party. At first Mohammed was very friendly with the Jews, but when they began to argue that many of his allusions to their Scriptures were inaccurate, and otherwise opposed him, he changed his attitude and drove them from Medina.

Meanwhile, Mohammed's "companions" and their Medinese "helpers" began to engage in hostilities with the Meccans. The followers of Mohammed, fired by the new doctrine of the *jihad* or "holy war," eventually won out, and were allowed to return to Mecca on pilgrimages. Mohammed now purified the Meccan shrine or Kaaba of all its idols and fetishes save the "black stone," and made Mecca the sacred city of Islam. Many Arab tribes especially in the Hijaz, accepted Islam during the lifetime of Mohammed.

Islam was already becoming institutionalized, and several features of the Islamic constitution emerged during the lifetime of the Prophet. The principle of "Conversion or the sword" was applied to pagans, but "scriptuaries," who had a sacred book and a more advanced religion, such as Jews, Christians, and Zoroastrians, were allowed to keep their religion, although they had to pay tribute. The doctrine of the *jihad* or meritorious "holy war" to spread Islam also developed. Islam became a theocracy and a polity as well as a religion.

The Moslem Challenge

Mohammed, "the highly praised one," the kindly, devout, lovable, religious leader, took sick and died in 632. The pious, elderly Abu Bakr announced: "Whosoever worships Mohammed, let him know that Mohammed is dead; but whosoever worships God, let him know that God liveth and dieth not."

Islam: the religion of Mohammed

The religion preached by Mohammed in many ways resembled Judaism and Christianity, from which it was largely derived. The sacred Koran is replete with references to the Old and New Testaments. Abraham is mentioned about seventy times, Moses in thirty-four suras (chapters), and Mary and her Son, Jesus, on several occasions. Mohammed accepted the prophets of the Old Testament, and recognized Jesus as God's mouthpiece. But he considered Christ as simply a great prophet in a long line, of which he himself was the final voice or "seal."

Islam agreed with Judaism and Christianity in many ways, as in its doctrines concerning God and heaven and hell; its prescription of prayer, almsgiving, and fasting; and its possession of a treasured, sacred book. Like Judaism it prescribed pilgrimage to a holy city. In other ways it differed. It made Friday its weekly day of worship and rest, instead of Saturday or Sunday, and Mecca its sacred city, instead of Jerusalem. It established a stricter obligation of frequent, regular prayer (five times daily), yet it did not require ritual sacrifice or weekly attendance at worship, and it allowed greater sexual liberty. It had no definite organized priesthood or public sacrifice. And it rejected the Divinity of Christ.

The Koran

As Mohammed recited his revelations, they were written down in various ways on sundry materials: "scraps of parchment and leather, tablets of stone, ribs of palm branches, camels' shoulder-blades and ribs, pieces of board, and the breasts of men." Within two decades after the Prophet's death, his teachings were collected and organized into an authoritative canon. The Koran (Reading, Recitation, or Book) is regarded as the reproduction of a Divine exemplar unveiled by God. About two thirds as long as the New Testament, it consists of one hundred and fourteen suras or chapters, arranged in order of length, except for the first. The Koran has an exalted tone, and its prose poetry is reminiscent of the Psalms and ancient wisdom literature. The spirit of the Koran is reflected in the opening sura, which is the "Our Father" of Islam:

> *Praise be to Allah, Lord of all creation,*
> *The Beneficent and Merciful:*
> *Master of the Day of Judgment;*
> *Thee alone do we worship,*
> *Thee alone we ask for help;*
> *Show us the right path,*
> *The way of those you favor—*
> *Not the path of those who displease Thee,*
> *Nor of those who go astray.*

Key doctrines

One of the attractions of Islam is that its doctrines are simple, and similar to those of unrevealed natural religion. The cornerstone of faith, according to Mohammed, is acceptance of the pure oneness of Allah—a strict, uncompromising monotheism; while the greatest sin is *skirk:* the association of spurious gods with the one true God. God has ninety-nine excellent names, such as the All Knowing, the All Powerful, the Just, the Merciful, the Loving, the Sublime, the Tremendous, the Eternal. Mohammed taught the immortality of the human soul, the obligation of God's moral law, and divine retribution. Heaven is described, perhaps metaphorically, as a place of unblemished physical pleasures, having "gardens of delight," "cups from which derive no headaches or madness," "fruits," "flesh of fowls," and "fair ones with wide, lovely eyes," as well as "spreading shade and gushing water" (Koran, 56:10–31). Hell, on the other hand, is a fiery place of torment (Koran, 56:41–55).

Duties of Moslems

The basic religious obligation according to Mohammed is submission: acceptance of God's will. "Islam" and "Moslem" come from the same root as *"salaam,"* meaning to submit. Aside from general morality, the key obligations of Moslems are often referred to as "the five pillars of Islam." They include the creed, prayer, pilgrimage, fasting, and almsgiving. Every Moslem is required to accept the creed: "There is no God but Allah, and Mohammed is his prophet." This profession is recited often and is included in the muezzin's call to prayer. Moslems are to pray five times daily: at sunrise, noon, midafternoon, sunset, and early evening, facing toward Mecca. In Moslem cities, muezzins (criers) call the people to prayer from minarets (tall towers) at the appointed times. Another required manifestation of faith is pilgrimage. This old Semitic custom was already practiced by the Jews and Arabs. At first Mohammed accepted Jerusalem as his sacred city, but later he changed to Mecca. All Moslems must make at least one pilgrimage to Mecca, if at all possible. A series of ceremonies extending over several days is customary for pilgrims to Mecca. Fasting is prescribed during Ramadan, a lunar month whose place in the solar calendar varies. Moslem fasting consists in abstaining from all food and drink, as well as other physical pleasures, from sunrise to sunset. Legal almsgiving or *zakah* came to be fixed at about 2½ per cent of one's income, and was soon collected as a regular tax by the government. Civil rulers were supposed to apply the alms to good purposes.

Mohammed also prescribed the humane treatment of slaves and dumb animals, and the obligation of *jihad* or holy war, at least in the form of missionary activities, for the propagation of Islam. All Moslems must treat each other as brothers: "Know ye that every Moslem is a brother to every other Moslem, and that you are now one brotherhood." Polygamy was permitted, but restrained. Moslems were allowed only as many wives as they could properly care for, to a maximum of four. No limit was placed on the number of concubines. Infanticide was prohibited, as was the drinking of intoxicating beverages. Divorce was permitted for serious cause.

Islam opened up new vistas of faith, hope, and love for the Arabs, and was especially well adapted to the mode of life of nomadic peoples. But its lack of definite organization caused it to fragmentize easily, while its sexual liberality may have served to debilitate its ruling classes.

The Moslem Challenge

(632ff.)

THE CALIPHATE.
Section 20.

> The Arabs are like a rebellious camel, and the driver must direct them. By the Lord of the Kaaba, I will guide you in the way you should go. [Caliph Omar, speaking to his fellow Arabs at his accession (634).]

THE RELIGION and state founded by Mohammed survived and spread. One of the factors that enabled Islam to continue and succeed was the Caliphate. The "Caliphs" or "Successors" who followed Mohammed as heads of the Islamic community exercised much of his secular authority and some of his religious leadership. They governed the community of Islam, acted as supreme judges, directed Moslem armies, and led the Friday community religious services. Yet they did not inherit the prophetic office of Mohammed.

Mohammed failed to make any provision for the succession. His cousin and son-in-law, Ali, husband of his daughter Fatima, seemed to have the best hereditary claim, but the mild Ali did not make any serious bid for leadership. Directly after Mohammed's death, the old "companions" of the Prophet met and followed the Arab tribal custom of electing a new "sheikh." Their choice fell on the aged, devout Abu Bakr.

Thus began the era of the "Orthodox Caliphs." Each of the first four caliphs (632–661) was elected. All of them were early converts and close "companions" of the Prophet, giving them a special air of authenticity and orthodoxy similar to that of the Christian "Apostles." Under the Orthodox Caliphs the essential outlines of the Islamic constitution emerged and Islam set out upon the path of far-flung empire and universal religion. *The Orthodox Caliphs (632–661)*

The first Caliph, the venerable Abu Bakr, was an early convert and a leading lieutenant of his son-in-law, Mohammed. His election was willingly accepted by Ali. Immediately after his accession, he was confronted by a serious revolt of many of the Arab tribes that had become Moslem, but wished to secede. They felt that their covenant was only with Mohammed. They were tired of paying "tribute" to the Moslem central government, and wished to return to their old "self-determination." But Abu Bakr insisted that the Moslem community was permanent and indissoluble. In the ensuing *Riddah* or "Secessionist" Wars, Islamic soldiers, led by brilliant generals such as Khalid, "the sword of Islam," subdued the rebels. With their military momentum they proceeded to complete the conversion of most of the peninsula. The first Caliph also ordered an initial compilation of the Koran.

After Muhammad, the chief founder of the Islamic state was the second Caliph, Omar (632–644). The tall, strong, resolute Omar, who had been Abu Bakr's chief adviser, was a "man of steel": devout, austere, and frugal. He is said to have had only one shirt and one mantle, both much patched. As he showed the victorious Omar around the Temple of fallen Jerusalem, the sophisticated Byzantine Patriarch Sophronius reportedly remarked: "Verily this is the abomination of desolation[b] which was foretold by the Prophet as standing in the holy place!" Omar founded the Arab Empire and established the main lines of its political constitution. Unified by Islam, and forbidden to fight one another, the Arabs under Omar forsook their mutual *razzias* and turned to foreign conquest. Syria, Palestine, Iraq, Nearer Iran, and Egypt were conquered, while the annexations of Farther Iran and North Africa were initiated. During Omar's caliphate, constitutional precedents were established for the absolute theocratic power of the Caliph, the legal supremacy of the Koran, and the provincial system of Islamic government headed by Emirs.

[b] Cf. Matthew, 24:15; Mark, 13:14; Daniel, 8:13.

After a Christian Persian slave murdered Omar (644), an election commission chose as Caliph Othman, a pious octogenerian who was a member of the wealthy, influential Umayyad clan. Othman set up a commission which established the definitive text or "canon" of the Koran. Many Moslems, however, maintained an aversion to the Umayyads, their former persecutors, and this was increased by the nepotism of the somewhat senile Caliph. Among those opposed to Othman were Mohammed's young widow, Aisha, and his son-in-law, Ali. Eventually a band of insurgents, which included the son of Abu Bakr, assassinated Othman while he was reading the Koran.

Ali (656–661) and Civil War

Mohammed's son-in-law and cousin, Ali, was now elected Caliph. Ali, who was upright, honest, pious, and courageous, came to be regarded as a model of Arab chivalry. But he was somewhat naive, impractical, and indecisive. Since his support was chiefly in Mesopotamia, he moved the capital to Al-Kufah in Iraq. Partly due to his own indiscretions, Ali was soon confronted by opponents. The chief of these was Muawiyah, the powerful Umayyad governor of Syria, who called for vengeance for the murder of his uncle. He blamed the guileless Ali, since the new Caliph had failed to punish Othman's assassins. The opposing forces met in a hard-fought battle on the plain of Siffin near Kufah (657). Affixing pages of the Koran to their spears, Muawiyah's soldiers, who were losing, called for settlement of their dispute by the sacred text. The pious Ali, who had nothing to gain and everything to lose from arbitration, foolishly consented. The commission decided that both leaders should renounce their claims to the Caliphate. Since Muawiyah had no Caliphate to resign, but Ali was already the legitimately elected Caliph, the latter naturally refused to accept the unequal decision.

Ali lost some of his supporters as a result. Among them were the stern Kharijites, who denounced all compromise. Ali defeated them in a bloody battle at Nahrawan (659), but was soon assassinated by a Kharijite.

Expansion of Islam under the Orthodox Caliphs

The era of the Orthodox Caliphs was one of rapid expansion, which was initially accomplished largely by the sword, and was at first more political than religious. Some have considered this but another of several periodic eruptions from the Arabian peninsula. But this one dwarfed the others, since this was the first time the Arabs as a whole were united and ideologically inspired. Forbidden to fight each other as brother Moslems, and fired by the principle of the "holy war" for the propagation of Islam, the Arabs turned their warlike propensities on the outside world. They also

The Moslem Challenge

still had the armed forces, able generals, and military momentum that had subjugated Arabia. The two giants of the day, the neighboring Persian and Byzantine Empires, were exhausted by prolonged mutual conflict and debilitated by internal division.

The first step in the expansionist movement had been the suppression of the Secessionist movement and the completion of the subjection of Arabia, under Abu Bakr. A golden age of external conquests followed under the stern, efficient Omar. Arab armies were sent into Mesopotamia and Palestine-Syria. In the latter area, a three-pronged thrust netted several towns. As the weakened Byzantines were gathering their forces to expel the invaders, general Khalid made a brilliant march across the Syrian desert from Mesopotamia with reinforcements. A bloody Arab victory over a Byzantine army at Ajnadayn (634) laid open all of Palestine. Many Palestinian and Syrian towns, including Damascus, capitulated willingly or were betrayed into Arab hands by their Semitic inhabitants. A large Byzantine army of some 50,000 soldiers headed by the Emperor's brother was routed by "the sons of the desert" (636) on an intensely hot day at Yarmuk on the edge of the desert. The fate of Syria was sealed.

The Arabs then turned to the Persian Empire, where they had already established themselves at Hirah, on the edge of the Euphrates valley. When they met the forces of the Persian Shah at Qadisiyah (637), on the brink of the desert, the Arabian forces were again victorious and were able to overrun Iraq. Soon after taking Ctesiphon, the capital of western Iraq, the Arabs insured their conquest of eastern Iraq by a stunning victory at Jalula (637). Shah Yazdagird III now fled to the highlands of Iran, where Persian resistance stiffened. But still the Arabs could not be halted, and in 641 they defeated Yazdagird's army at Nihawand in central Persia. They took the Persian capital of Istakhr (Persepolis) in southern Persia in 649–650. Shortly afterwards the fleeing Shah, Yazdagird III, was slain for his treasure by one of his own subjects.

Egyptian and maritime successes

Meanwhile the Arabs were also expanding to the West. The conquest of Egypt was undertaken by the ambitious general, Amr, who, jealous of the successes of other Arab commanders, advanced into Egypt in 640 with only 3,500 soldiers. After taking the fortress of Pelusium in northwestern Egypt and receiving some reinforcements from Arabia, Amr moved against the key stronghold, Babylon, in the vicinity of present-day Cairo. As in Syria, the Arabs were assisted by the native population. After a protracted siege, Egyptian Babylon fell (641). The Arabs now moved on to rich and populous Alexandria, which, partly through the defection of its Patriarch-Prefect Cyrus, capitulated in 642. Temporarily reoccupied by the Byzantines in 645, Alexandria was again captured by the Arabs in 646. From Egypt, Amr's forces rolled westward into the Pentapolis and Tripoli.

Although the more conservative Caliphs were reluctant to commit their forces to the caprices of the sea, progressive Arab governors in Egypt and Syria built up fleets. A combined Egyptian and Syrian fleet defeated a great Byzantine armada of some 500 ships and almost captured the Byzantine Emperor himself in the battle of Phoenix or Dhu-al-Sawari

The Umayyad Caliphs (661–750)

(the Battle of the Masts) off the coast of southwestern Asia Minor in 655. Command of the eastern Mediterranean Sea now belonged to the Arabs.

Following the chance assassination of Ali, Muawiyah, the Umayyad governor of Syria, appropriated the Caliphate for his own house. Hereditary succession seemed the practical way to obtain stability in government. Semitheocratic kingship had long prevailed throughout the Near East. Pivotal Syria was an ideal base for Islamic power. In addition to having some claim as the nephew of the assassinated Caliph Othman, Muawiyah was an able, shrewd, persuasive leader, and was assisted by capable lieutenants.

With conciliatory tact, Muawiyah (661–80), while absolute, seemed to rule like a sheikh working with his council of elders. He explained: "I apply not my sword where my lash is enough, nor my lash where my tongue sufficeth." His gravest problem was how to deal with divisive, disaffected factions. Muawiyah did much for the cause of unity by giving Hasan, the pleasure-loving oldest son of Ali, a liberal pension. He also dispatched Amr to recover Egypt. And he employed Byzantine Syrians to build up an efficient bureaucracy. To insure dynastic continuity, he obtained the succession of his son Yazid.

After the brief reigns of the sickly Yazid (680–683), and his cousin Marwan (683–685), the able Abd-al-Malik (Father of Kings) (685–705) brought the rest of the Moslem world under control. In the East the Caliph's forceful agent Hajjaj, a former schoolmaster, was extraordinarily successful. Hajjaj's policy was stated in a sermon in the mosque of Al-Kufah in Iraq, where he announced: "O people of Al-Kufah, I see heads ripe for the harvest, and verily I am the man to reap them!" He is said to have put about 120,000 persons to death. Al-Husayn, Ali's second son, who had become the head of the Alid or Shiite (*shiah*: sect) party, which maintained that Caliphal succession should be hereditary through Ali, was intercepted and slain on his way from Arabia to Iraq with a small band, thus becoming a glorious martyr in Shiite eyes. Abdullah-ibn-al-Zubayr, who claimed the Caliphate and controlled Iraq and part of Arabia, was driven to take refuge in Mecca, where he was killed during a foray. Outlying Persian provinces were quieted, and the Moslem world was reunited and pacified.

Expansion under the Umayyads

Under Abd-al-Malik expansion resumed in East and West. In overcoming internal resistance, the Umayyads had built up an efficient military machine. Their more secular outlook led them to seek worldly aggrandizement, by expansion, which was also encouraged by the concept of *jihad*. Moslem armies soon pressed into Tunisia, where they took the key city of Carthage in 698. Thence they continued into Algeria and Morocco, converting the Berber tribesmen. Reinforced by many Berber recruits, the Moslems turned their eyes to Spain.

The Berber chieftain Tariq led a modest force of Moslems on a raid into southern Spain in 711 by way of Gibraltar (Jebal Tariq: the rock of Tariq). A large Visigothic army, collected by King Roderick, collapsed in the battle of Laguna de la Janda in Southern Spain (711). Tariq

The Moslem Challenge

pushed northward, occupying various cities, and finally established himself in the Visigothic capital of Toledo. Meanwhile Tariq's jealous superior, Emir Musa crossed into Spain with large reinforcements and took bypassed strongholds, such as Seville and Merida. On reaching Toledo, Musa put Tariq in chains for insubordination. After subjecting most of the peninsula, the triumphant Musa returned with his prisoner to the Caliphal court at Damascus, where, however, he was disgraced for attempting to deceive the Caliph. Besides Spain, the Moslems occupied Septimania, located in southern France along the Mediterranean coast west of the Rhone.

To the east, lieutenants of the harsh Hajjaj, after resubjecting Persia, pushed on across the Oxus River and conquered Transoxiana with its opulent cities, such as Bukhara and Samarkand, on crossroads of world trade between East and West, as well as Fargahnah, astride the Jaxartes. Arab armies penetrated Afghanistan and Chinese Turkestan and invaded populous northwestern India, where they conquered the rich valley of the lower Indus.

After securing command of the seas, the Moslems seized strategic islands of the eastern Mediterranean, including Rhodes and Crete. Taking Constantinople became their "grand project," to which they devoted all their available forces three times: in 669, 674–680, and 717–718, besieging it by land and sea without success.

Under the Umayyads, whose capital was Damascus in Syria, Islam became a "Byzantine successor-state," and the Caliphate was converted into something of a kingship (*mulk*.) The Umayyad government continued to use Byzantine administrative practices and even Byzantine Syrian officials. They kept Byzantine taxes and sought to take Constantinople. They also pushed expansion in the old Roman Mediterranean world.

On the other hand, a strict distinction continued to exist between the Arab aristocracy and non-Arab converts to Islam. The latter, who were known as *mawali* or "clients," were regarded as a sort of "second-class" Moslems. Gradually, Arab officials were substituted for Byzantine Syrians in the administration, and Arabic replaced Greek as the language of government. The life of the ruling classes became more luxurious and ostentatious. Magnificent caliphal palaces and villas were maintained for pleasure and recreation at the seaside and on the desert's edge; and beautiful mosques were constructed. Poetry and music were widely cultivated and enthusiastically admired.

Yet forces of unrest were growing. Many Moslems, particularly in Iraq and Iran, maintained that the Caliphate should be hereditary in the Hishamite clan rather than in the Umayyad house, since Mohammed was a Hishamite. Although the Hishamites were themselves divided into Abbasid supporters, holding for descent through al-Abbas, uncle of the Prophet, and Alids or Fatimites, supporting descent through Ali and Fatima, they were agreed on opposition to the Umayyads. Many believed that the Umayyads were too worldly, and neglectful of the religious aspects of their office. Non-Arabs also opposed the Arabian monopoly of

Decline and overthrow of the Umayyads

privilege and position under the Umayyads, while Persians opposed Syrian ascendance at Damascus. The Arabs themselves were divided into two great south and north Arab parties known respectively as Kalb and Qays. "Heretics" such as the Kharijites held that the Caliphate was elective rather than hereditary.

Opposition forces coalesced after an Abbasid uprising in "frontier" Khurasan. Led by capable generals, the revolutionaries seized stronghold after stronghold, and eventually overwhelmed the Caliph Marwan II on the banks of the Greater Zab River (750). They proceeded to exterminate all potential Umayyad rivals, and even the bodies of dead Umayyads were disinterred. Only the vigorous young Umayyad Abd-al-Rahman I managed to elude his pursuers by swimming the Tigris, and made his way to Spain, where he set up his rival dynasty.

The Abbasids at their height (750–847)

For some time victory-laden generals and opposing original claimants contended with each other for control. But the continuous strong leadership and shrewdness of the Abbasids won out over their rivals. The Abbasid reign was inaugurated in a deluge of blood, and its founder, Abu-al-Abbas (750–754) came to be known by the nickname of *al-Saffar*: the Blood-Shedder, from the policy he announced in the mosque at al-Kufah.

Al-Saffar's brother, *al-Mansur* or the Victorious (754–775) firmly established the dynasty on the throne. By statesmanship and duplicity, as well as by force, al-Mansur outwitted and exterminated both dangerous generals and Shiite rivals. He is considered "the fourth founder of the Caliphate" since he reorganized the government, doing so along Persian lines. He employed a *vizir* as a sort of prime minister, and moved his capital to Bagdad on the Middle Tigris. Located in the strategic vicinity of famous earlier capitals, Bagdad soon became one of the world's greatest cities with an estimated half a million to a million population.

The Abbasid Caliphate, a sort of Persian successor-state, attained its height in the days of Harùn-al-Raschìd and al-Mamun. The sophisticated Harùn-al-Raschìd (Aaron the Just) (786–809) uprooted the powerful Barmakid vizirs, who had come to rival the caliphs in wealth and display as well as in effective power, and became the hero of several tales in the *Arabian (Thousand and One) Nights*. The intellectual al-Manun (813–833), who became an adherent of the rationalist sect known as Mutazilites, liberally patronized learning, and established the famous Bayt-al-Hikmah or House of Learning in Bagdad. The apprehensive al-Mutasim (833–847) imported Turkish warriors as bodyguards and removed his capital sixty miles up the Tigris to Samarra.

The Abbasids contrasted with the Umayyads. They were based in Persia rather than Syria, so that the Persian element and Persian ways and culture became more prominent in Islam. Closely related to the Prophet, the Abbasids stressed the religious element in the Caliphal office, which tended to become politically weaker. They leaned more to the East than to the Mediterranean, so that Spain, Morocco, and Tunisia quickly slipped from their grasp, while no more all-out attempts were made to take Constantinople. Meanwhile Moslem civilization was becoming more cosmopolitan and cultured. Numerous translations were

The Moslem Challenge

made from Syriac, Greek, Persian, and Hindu. Higher education developed, and learning was eagerly pursued. Philosophy and theology were cultivated, while important progress was made in the sciences and medicine.

After al-Mutasim (d. 847), the political power of the Abbasids waned, and their office became mainly religious. The conduct of secular affairs slipped more and more from the Caliph's hands into those of secular counterparts. First the generals of the Turkish bodyguard established by al-Mutasim held power for about a century (847–945). Next, the Persian family of the Buwayhids overthrew and replaced the Turks (945–1055), and took the titles of *malik* (king), *shahanshah* (ruler of rulers), and *amir-al-umarra* (commander of the commanders). The Buwayhids were overthrown and replaced in 1055 by the Seljuk Turks, warriors from Turkestan so called from an early leader. The Seljuk leader Tughril Beg established himself alongside the Caliph as *al-sultan* (the one with secular authority).

Decline and disintegration of the Caliphate (847ff.)

Eventually, in 1194, the Abbasid Caliph Nasir (1180–1225) managed, with the help of the Khwarismians, to wrench himself free from the Seljuk yoke. But he soon found that he only had a new master: the powerful Khwarismian Shah. Caliph Nasir then enlisted Mongol aid to overthrow the Khwarismians (1216). But history repeated itself, and helpers again became masters when in 1258 the Mongols, led by Hulagu, took Bagdad and put the unlucky Caliph and most of his court to death.

As early as the second half of the eighth century the Abbasid Caliphate began to disintegrate. But the process did not attain full momentum until the ninth to tenth centuries, when various independent states emerged in several parts of the Moslem world, with more remote provinces taking the lead. Among disintegrative factors contributing to disintegration were regionalism and localism, racism and "nationalism," cultural diversities, traditional animosities, and the ambitions of local governors and victorious generals, as well as invasions of more warlike peoples. There were also the "running sores" of disagreement as to the caliphal succession and divisive "heresies," as well as the periodic rise of new "prophets" who claimed divine authorization. The autocratic nature of the Islamic state bred violence, while technological limitations militated against a universal caliphate.

Among new states which appeared in the Western part of the Moslem world were those of the Umayyads (756ff.) in Spain, the Idrisids (788ff.) in Morocco, the Aghlabids (800ff.) in Tunisia, and the Tulunids (868ff.) followed by the Fatimids (in the tenth century) in Egypt. New states in the East were those of the Tahirids (820ff.) in Khorasan, the Saffarids (867ff.) in Persia, the Samanids (874ff.) in Transoxiana, the Hamdanids (927ff.) in Northern Mesopotamia and Syria, and the Ghaznawids (962ff.) in Afghanistan.

The Caliphate held the Moslem world together as a political entity for over two centuries until Islam became firmly rooted as a religious and cultural entity. Eventually the Caliphate succumbed, but only after it had performed its historical function as a protective shell during a period of incubation.

The Early Middle Ages

The Moslem Challenge

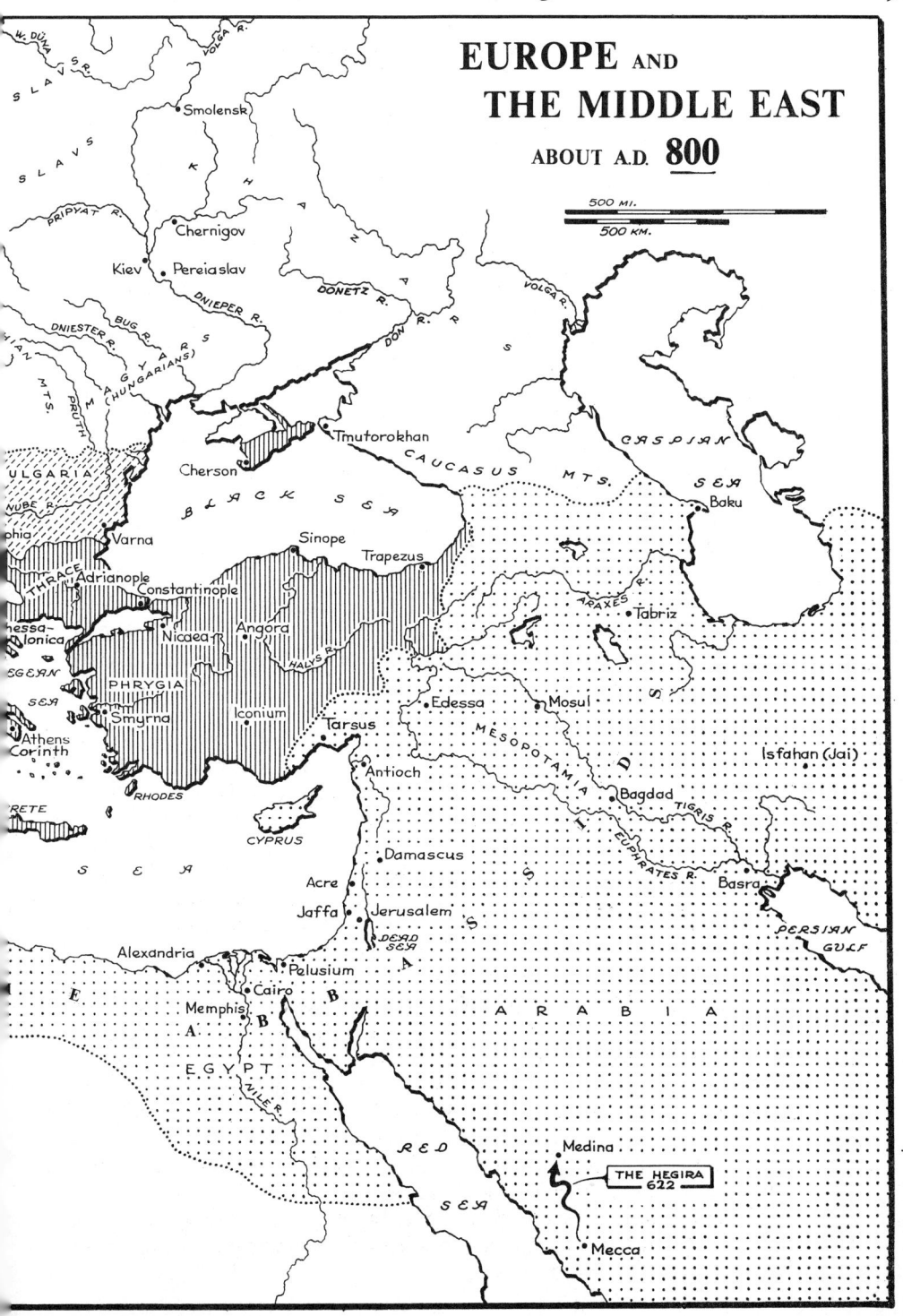

ISLAMIC CIVILIZATION.
Section 21.

> The Arabs . . . found the exercise of military and administrative command too engrossing to give them leisure for literary avocations. . . . As a result, they left such studies to the Persians and the mixed races which sprang from intermarriage of the conquering race with the conquered. On the other hand, they did not condemn men of learning, but recognized their value and appreciated their services. [The Arabic historian, Ibn Khaldun, in the "Prolegomena" to his . . . *History of the Arabs, Persians, and Berbers* (1385).]

AT ITS height, Islam begot a brilliant civilization which blended many diverse elements: Arabian and Byzantine, Greek and Roman, Hebrew and Christian, Persian and Indian, and others. Moslem civilization was dynamic and progressive from the ninth to the eleventh centuries, following which it tended to become static and backward. Factors contributing to this reversal included the disintegration of the Caliphate and breakdown of Moslem unity; the violent conquests and blighting rule of barbaric nomads such as the Turks; the restrictive effect of theocratic absolutism and the conservative views of influential theologians. Allowance of polygamy and concubinage also seems to have debilitated the ruling classes.

Moslem government

Government in the Moslem world was theocratic, autocratic, and bureaucratic. The Moslems regarded themselves as "the community of Allah," and a leading source of Islamic law was the Koran. Their head for some time was the Caliph or "Successor" of Mohammed. All powers were concentrated in the Caliphs, who for over two centuries (632–c. 847) ruled the Islamic world, first from Medina, then from Al-Kufah, next from Damascus, finally from Bagdad. The Caliphs exercised supreme political as well as religious authority until the mid-ninth century (c. 847), when the Abbasids lost political control to their Turkish bodyguard. In the tenth and eleventh centuries there were three Caliphal claimants, with the Fatimids of Cairo and Umayyads of Cordova each governing in their own region. Eventually most caliphal powers were actually assumed by local rulers, known variously as Emirs, Shahs, Sultans, Khans, etc. For practical reasons, the offices of rulers in the Moslem world soon became hereditary. Similarly, Moslem central government came to be organized into various departments (bureaus or *diwans*), each under a head or *vizir*. The powerful office of grand vizir developed and often eclipsed that of the nominal ruler. Departments of the Abbasid government included police, treasury, chancery, post office, etc. The postal department utilized relays of horses, mules, camels, and even carrier-pigeons.

Originally the various provinces were headed by *emirs* (or *amirs*) who operated as "vice-caliphs" in their areas, with a plenitude of delegated and assumed powers. But these emirs tended to become independent, and often set up their own local dynasties.

Moslem armies specialized in light, highly maneuverable cavalry and archers, and often had greater numbers than discipline. They enlisted

The Moslem Challenge

many peripheral, frontier-type peoples, such as Turks and Berbers. Their use of camels as "ships of the desert" to strike areas bordering on the deserts gave the Arabs the advantage of "desert power," or freedom of movement in hot, arid regions largely closed to their competitors. The results in territories bordering on deserts were comparable in many ways to those of sea power for coastal areas. By utilizing native shipwrights and sailors in conquered territories, such as Syria, Egypt, and Tunisia, the Moslems also built up fleets which won naval victories in the Mediterranean making it temporarily "a Moslem Lake."

Although the "sons of the desert" were unused to taxes save as a form of tribute, they soon adopted the fiscal systems of their conquered provinces, with modifications. The basic taxes of the ancient world, the land tax and the head tax (poll tax), were retained. The poll tax was regarded as a form of tribute and was imposed only upon unbelievers—a strong, continuing factor for conversions to Islam. The Moslems were required by the Quran to give alms or *sakah*, which was converted into a regular tax collected by the government and ordinarily ran to about 2½ per cent of one's income. Many indirect taxes, such as duties on imports and exports, and sales taxes were also continued.

A thriving Moslem commerce extended from the far East to the far West and included some of the world's most advanced economic areas. A common faith, language, and culture, and for some time a unified state, facilitated trade. Especially famous was the overland trade route known as "The Great Silk Way" or "Khurasan Highway," which linked the Moslem world of the Eastern Mediterranean with the Far East via such cities as Samarkand, Bukhara, and Mawr. The Indian Ocean and subsidiary seas were under Moslem control for some time, as also was the Mediterranean for a while. The wide scope of Islamic commerce is attested by the large numbers of medieval Arabic coins found in Russia, Finland, the Scandinavian countries, and Germany; and by the Arabic derivation of many of our commercial words such as risk, check, bazaar, traffic, tariff, caravan, and average. Our words for many industrial and agricultural products also come from Arabic. Moslem textiles, such as fine silks and cotton goods of many sorts, became famous. Many names of textiles derive from Moslem locations, such as "muslin" from Mosul, "damask" from Damascus, "gauze" from Gaza, "baldachin" from Bagdad, "taby" or "tabby" from the Attab quarter in Bagdad, "fustian" from al-Fustat (near Cairo), and "grenadine" from Granada. The words "satin" and "taffeta" also come from the Arabic. Other famous products with names of Moslem derivation include Toledo steel and Damascus blades, Cordovan and Moroccan leathers, colors such as lilac and crimson; and miscellaneous items such as divans, mattresses, and jars. Glassmaking was brought to Venice by Saracen artisans in the thirteenth century. The manufacture of paper was introduced from China via Khurasan and Moslem Spain to Europe. The word "ream" as a measure of paper comes from the Arabic. Among numerous agricultural plants that came to Western Europe through the Moslems, as is evidenced by

Economic prosperity in the Islamic world

their names, were cotton (*algodon*), rice (*arroz*), sugar (*sakkar*), spinach, oranges, lemons, apricots, artichokes, and various melons.

Moslem society

In Moslem society a fundamental distinction separated Moslems and non-Moslems in addition to the usual differentiations between aristocrats and commoners, rich and poor, free and slave. At first there was a sharp distinction between Arabs and non-Arabs, but this tended to lessen. Tolerated non-Moslems, such as Christians and Jews, were required to pay special taxes and were excluded from many offices. Christians were occasionally persecuted and were regularly required to wear distinguishing garb as well as forbidden to carry swords or ride horseback. Although the position of women in Arabia was improved, that of women in areas where monogamy had previously prevailed was generally depressed. The practices of secluding women in private quarters such as harems (*harem*: forbidden) and concealing their faces and figures by veils and drapery were evidently picked up in Persia.

Religious sects and Sufis

Various religious sects soon appeared in Islam. The orthodox majority were known as "Sunnites," because of their faith in traditions (*sunna*) as trustworthy standards in religious affairs. The Sunnites believe that Divine Providence guides and protects Islamic traditions. They accept the teachings of the "companions" of the Prophet as well as those of Muhammad. The Sunnites also believed that succession to the Caliphate might be either elective or hereditary or both.

The leading opponents of the Sunnites were the Shiites, who were partisans of the family of the Prophet. The Shiites rejected traditions coming from the mere "companions" of Mohammad, and accepted only those coming from members of his family. They believed in direct hereditary succession of the Caliphate in the family of the Prophet, through Ali and his lineal descendants. They attributed divine guidance and inspiration to hereditary successors of the Prophet, known as *Imams*. More moderate Shiites count descent from the Prophet down to Hasan and are therefore known as "Twelvers," while more radical ones stop with Ishmael and are accordingly known as "Seveners," or "Ishmaelites." The Ishmaelites included several extremist sects, such as the Druzes and Assassins. Many Shiites believe in a *Mahdi* or Messiah: a successor in the Prophet's family, who is at present in hiding, but will one day return.

The extreme rationalists known as "Mutazilites" originated in the eighth century. They denied the eternity of the Quran and were advocates of Greek philosophy. The Kharijites maintained that the Caliphal office was elective and deposable. The Qarmatians believed in a community of wives as well as of property. The Qadarites (*qadar*: power) emphasized free will as opposed to Islamic predestination.

Not exactly a sect, although often inclined to be separatist, were the *Sufis*. The Sufis are the dedicated professional mystics and ascetics of Islam, corresponding somewhat to Christian and Buddhist monks. Their name comes from their woolen habits (*suf*: wool). They originated in the eighth century and were organized into fraternities in the eleventh to twelfth centuries. The Sufis engaged in preaching and missionary activities and were important in the propagation of Islam. The Sufis stressed the intuitional approach in religion: direct mystical communion with God. Their viewpoint is expressed in these verses:

> *With my Beloved I alone have been*
> *When secrets tenderer than evening airs*
> *Passed, and the Vision Blest*
> *Was granted to my prayers.*

Moderate Sufism was reconciled with traditional Islam by the great theologian al-Ghazzali. Among more extreme, fanatical Sufis are the Dervishes and Rifs.

Moslem culture was a cosmopolitan composite, derived from many sources. About A.D. 850, the Golden Age of medieval Moslem culture began and lasted for two or three centuries. The galaxy of leaders of Islamic intellectual culture at its height was studded with brilliant stars, including translators Hunayn and Thabit, physicians Rhazes and Avicenna, astronomers al-Battani and al-Biruni, mathematicians and physicists Omar Khayyam and al-Haytham, theologians al-Ashari and al-Ghazzali, historians al-Tabari and al-Masudi, and philosophers Avicenna and Averroës. *Islamic culture: The Translators*

The main original impetus and content of Moslem intellectual culture came from translations. In the first phase (c. 750–850), most translations were made indirectly from the original, such as Greek, through a second language, such as Syriac. In the second phase (c. 850–950), translations were typically made directly from the original into Arabic. Among numerous translators, Hunayn and Thabit were outstanding. Hunayn ibn-Ishaq (d. 873), a Nestorian Christian, translated over a hundred Greek medical, scientific, and philosophical works into Syriac or Arabic and founded a school of translators at Bagdad. The Sabian (star-worshipping) Thabit (d. 901) established a similar school at Harran in Iraq, and members of his family to the fourth generation continued work as translators.

The Arabic language was rich, vigorous, colorful, and rhythmic. Persian and, to a lesser extent, Indian elements early gained an ascendance in Arabic literature. The latter was noted for its rhythmic accent, emotional appeal, and dramatic qualities. Arabic love poetry was inclined to be idealistic, allegorical, and rich in feeling and imagery. It featured a mystic glorification of woman and a sublimation of earthly love. An early form was the *nasad*, which was a reflective preface to the partly narrative, partly descriptive *qasidah* concerning the wars, exploits, and adventures of the nomadic Arabs. One such *nasad* begins: *Arabic literature*

> *Stay, let us weep, while memory strives to trace*
> *The long-lost fair one's sand-girt dwelling place;*
> *Though the rude winds have swept the sandy plain,*
> *Still some faint traces of that spot remain.*

By the ninth century, typical Arabic lyric poetry or *ghazals* such as the following developed:

> They called my love "a poor blind maid";
> "I love her more for that," I said,
> "I love her for she cannot see
> These grey hairs that disfigure me";
> She is a garden fair. . . ,
> Where though in beauty blooms the rose,
> Narcissuses the eyelids close.

A noted composer of *ghazals* was Abu-Nuwas (died c. 810), a boon companion of Caliph Harun al-Raschid.

In Spain, popular crossbred lyrics of a folk-song variety, known as *muwashashahs* and *zajals*, evolved by the eleventh century. Both were tender love poems in strophic form, of "grass-roots" origin, including recurrent refrains and evidently sung by groups. Many authorities believe that Moslem models in Spain inspired the original *chansons d'amour* of the troubadours in neighboring southern France.

Moslem literature is rich in religious poetry, including allegorical and mystical lyrics, known as *zhudiyat*, such as this:

> Though He be absent, yet every limb of mine beholds Him
> In all His charm and grace and loveliness:
> In music of the lute and flowing reed
> Mingled in consort with melodious airs,
> And in valleys green, where in cool of e'en'
> Gazelles roam browsing, and at rose-red dawn,
> And where the canopied clouds let fall their rain.

The Spanish-born mystic ibn-Arabi (d. 1240) made religious *muwashashahs* popular in the East. Here is an example:

> My heart is capable of every form:
> A cloister for the monk, a temple for idols,
> A pasture for gazelles, the pious one's Kaaba
> Or tables of the Torah or Quran;
> Love is my creed: wherever turn His camels
> Love is my creed, and love my faith.

Eastern mystics were fond of allegory. Ibn-Arabi in the thirteenth century wrote these lines:

> O Pearl Divine, white pearl that in a shell
> Of dark mortality art made to dwell!
> Alas, while common gems we prize and hoard,
> Thy worth incalculable is still ignored.

Various forms of Moslem literature evidently influenced Western literature. Spanish Moslem *muwashashas* and *zajals* seem to have influenced the development of the throbbing and beautiful medieval Spanish Christian religious hymns, as well as the southern French *chansons d' amour* of the troubadors. Dante's *Divine Comedy* may have been influenced by ibn-Arabi's early thirteenth century treatise concerning Mohammed's

The Moslem Challenge

reported "Nocturnal Journey to Heaven." Skeptical, sensuous, and ribald Arabic poems that were similar to the Goliardic poems of Westerners in the High Middle Ages were exemplified by numerous drinking songs, and by Omar Khayyam's *Rubaiyat* with its familiar praise of wine, women, and song. One such irreverent poem says: "They all err—Moslem, Christian, Jew and Magian." Imitating Near Eastern and Indian examples, the Moslems cultivated the art of storytelling. The famous *Thousand and One Nights* or *Arabian Nights*, a collection of stories in which the ninth-century Caliph Harun al-Raschid figures, seems to have been composed in the tenth century. Arabic short stories may have influenced later Western fictional collections such as Boccaccio's *Decameron* (*A Hundred Tales*) and Chaucer's *Canterbury Tales*.

Islamic philosophy and theology anticipated and stimulated the development of Western Scholasticism. Among the Moslems as with the Westerners, a key problem was the relation between faith and reason, revelation and philosophy. Another was the harmonization of mysticism and orthodoxy. Still another was attempted reconciliation of the two great Greek philosophers, Plato and Aristotle, since Moslem philosophy derived mainly from ancient Greek philosophy. *Islamic philosophy and theology*

Reputed to be the author of over two hundred and fifty books, the Arab al-Kindi (later ninth century) was an eclectic philosopher and a scientist who represented beginning attempts to reconcile Moslem faith and Greek philosophy. Early in the following tenth century, al-Ashari, regarded as "the founder of scholastic philosophy in Islam," was a convert from extreme rationalism to orthodoxy who employed Greek logic and philosophy to refute the radical rationalistic Mutazilites as well as to elucidate Moslem doctrines. Assimilation of Greek thought was continued in the same tenth century by al-Farabi, who combined Platonism, Aristotelianism, and mystic Sufism. Islamic Scholasticism reached new heights during the early eleventh century with the "sheikh of the learned," Ibn-Sina or Avicenna, who was also a medical writer, and who synopsized Aristotelian philosophy so that it might become conveniently available and palatable to the Moslems.

In the later eleventh century, al-Ghazzali (Algazel), reconciled the orthodoxy of the Sunnites with the mysticism of the Sufis and both of these with the wisdom of the ancients. He is known as "the Thomas Aquinas of the Moslems," and there are many similarities between "Algazel" and the "Angelic Doctor." Al-Ghazzali assailed extreme rationalism in his *Incoherence of the Philosophers*, and strove to put Islamic theology back on its feet in his *Revivification of the Sciences of Religion*.

The greatest of all Moslem Aristotelian philosophers was ibn-Rushd or Averroës (d. 1198). For a while most Aristotelian Western philosophers were known as "Averroists." Averroës, who lived in Spain and Morocco in the second half of the twelfth century and came to be known as "The Commentator" (upon Aristotle), believed in the harmony of faith and reason. But in cases of doubt he was inclined to follow reason more than faith, which eventually discredited him with both orthodox Moslems and Christians. On the basis of reason, Averroës subscribed to such beliefs as the eternity of the world and the oneness of a general "active intellect" apart from individual men, who have only a corporeal "passive intellect" and are not personally immortal. Such teachings were difficult to reconcile with Moslem and Christian doctrines. Averroës replied to al-Ghazzali's attack on rationalism with his *Incoherence of the Incoherent*.

Moslem mathematics and sciences

Drawing on Greek and other sources, the Moslems made progress in mathematics and the sciences. They adopted and developed the so-called "Arabic," really "Hindu" (Indian) number system, using nine numbers and the zero or "cipher" (from Arabian *sifr*: empty) with the decimal system. Algebra (Arabian *al jebr*: the binding) was developed by Moslem mathematicians such as al-Khwarizmi (ninth century) and Omar Khayyam (eleventh century). Analytical geometry was foreshadowed by the Moslems, who also founded trigonometry, whose key term "sine" comes from the Arabic.

In astronomy, the Moslems maintained several famous observatories and compiled catalogues of astronomical observations. Many of our astronomical terms, such as zenith, nadir, azimuth, and almanac, as well as our star names, such as Rigel, Betelgeuse, Altair, Aldebaran, and others come from Arabic. The Moslems developed and gave to the West various navigational instruments dependent on astronomy, such as the astrolabe, sextant, and quadrant. They also handed on such Greek hypotheses as the sphericity of the earth, its daily rotation on its axis, and its annual revolution around the sun.

In physics, besides translating and transmitting Greek works, Moslems made extraordinary advances, especially in optics, which was associated with the study of optical diseases, common among sons of the desert. Chemistry, originated by the Moslems, derives its name from the Arabic *al-chemi*, or alchemy, which was initially mainly concerned with attempts to transmute baser metals into gold and silver and efforts to discover an "elixir of life" capable of prolonging human terrestial existence.

The Moslems, who were great travelers, composed numerous atlases, geographies, and books of travel. One of these was a great summary of world geography compiled by the Hispano-Arab al-Idrisi for the Norman Sicilian King of Sicily, Roger II, in the twelfth century, and known as *Kitab Rujar (The Book of Roger)*.

Medicine

The Moslems also made great progress in medicine and pharmacopoeia. They translated Greek medical works, compiled and codified Greek medical knowledge, and further advanced medicine by original studies and clinical observations. Medical education in Western universities during the High and Later Middle Ages and in early modern times was largely based on Latin translations of Arabic medical works, such as those of al-Razi (Rhazes), Ibn-al-Abbas (Haly Abbas), Ibn-Sina (Avicenna), Abul Qasim (Abulcasis), and Ali-ibn-Isa (Jesu Haly), to mention only a few. Probably the best known Moslem medical writer was ibn-Sina or Avicenna (eleventh century), whose great *Canon of Medicine* summarized most existing Greek and Arabic as well as Persian and Hindu medical knowledge down to his own day. Avicenna's *Canon* was translated into Latin in the twelfth century and remained a medical text in

Western universities down to the seventeenth century. Hospitals and clinics, as well as medical schools and medical libraries, were maintained in the principal Moslem cities. Pharmacopoeia is especially indebted to the Moslems, who assiduously gleaned and recorded information concerning hundreds of valuable curative plants and drugs from their far-flung world. Western pharmacopoeia derives directly from the Moslems.

Moslem historiography is noted for its continuity, objectivity, breadth, and diversity, as well as its enthusiasm and detail. Among the most noted and authoritative of Moslem universal historians were al-Tabari and al-Masudi, both of whom lived in the ninth to tenth centuries, and were indefatigable researchers and travelers in the course of their investigations. Al-Masudi was also a noted geographer. Ibn-Khaldun in the fourteenth century produced what is regarded as the leading medieval philosophy of history. Al-Sahawi in the fifteenth century compiled a most outstanding treatise on historiography. *Historiography and jurisprudence*

Jurisprudence was considered a religious as well as a secular subject of utmost importance. While its principal source was the Koran, it also used tradition (*sunna*), common consent, analogy and reason. The various schools of orthodox Moslem jurisprudence are distinguished according to the degree of attention they allow each of these sources.

Education and learning were respected and cultivated for religious as well as for secular reasons. The three principal types of schools were mosque schools, *madrasahs*, and institutes of higher learning. From earliest times, *qurra* (Koran-readers) taught the recitation and reading of the Koran, along with related subjects, in the mosques, which thus became centers of elementary education. Many mosque schools or *kuttabs* came to teach a wide variety of additional subjects. *Madrasahs* were combinations of liberal arts colleges and seminaries. They were more advanced schools with a religious inspiration and orientation, which also taught liberal subjects such as literature, history, mathematics, sciences, and philosophy. An early *madrasah* was the so-called "Nizamiyah," founded at Bagdad by the powerful Persian vizir, Nizam al-Mulk, in the eleventh century. *Islamic education*

Among further educational institutions in the Moslem world were institutes of higher learning, dedicated primarily to the cultivation of science in a broad sense (i.e., all advanced organized knowledge), with their main emphasis on secular subjects. Such were the *Bayt al-Hikmah* or "House of Wisdom" founded at Bagdad by the rationalist Caliph al-Mamun in the ninth century, and the *Dar al-Ilm* or "Abode of Science" founded at Cairo by the Fatimid Caliph al-Hakim in the eleventh century.

Moslem architecture and art were complex, cosmopolitan, and diversified. Although derived from numerous sources, they had a certain common nature or unity. Moslem mosques, for example, tended to adopt regionally prevalent forms and thus present a pleasing variety, yet they also maintained a certain common identity. Among noted mosques were those of the holy cities of Mecca and Medina, and the so-called Mosque of Omar at Jerusalem, as well as the Abbasid Mosque at Samarra, the *Islamic architecture, art, and music*

Tulunid Mosque at Cairo, and the Great Mosque of Cordova. Partly modelled on the Kaaba at Mecca, mosques typically consisted of (unroofed or roofed) enclosures, surrounded by colonnades or arcades, with exterior minarets or tall slender towers whence muezzins could summon the people to prayer. Inside, the mosque had a *mihrab* or niche indicating the direction of Mecca, and a *minbar* or pulpit for the leader of the Friday services. Among representative secular structures were the Umayyad palace known as "The Green One" at Damascus, the Abbasid palaces at Bagdad, the Fatimid palaces at Cairo, the Alcazar at Seville, and the Alhambra or "Red One" at Granada.

Among characteristic features of Moslem architecture were delicate decorative effects, producing an aspect of airy lightness. Such included complex pointed, horseshoe, scalloped, or intersecting arches: stalactite or fretted vaulting; bulbous, ovoid, or stilted domes; spiral towers; pierced grills, lattices, and traceries of iron, wood, and stone; multicolored tiles, and enclosed courtyards and patios with plants and fountains of running water.

One reason for the distinctiveness of Moslem art is its avoidance of the depiction of human and animal forms. This stemmed from the Prophet's aversion to anything even remotely savoring of idolatry. Moslem art was mainly decorative rather than representational, and made liberal use of geometrical patterns, interlacing lines and curves, conventionalized plant and animal forms, and beautiful Arabic letters or calligraphy. Other crafts in which Moslems excelled were the making of exquisite ornate textiles, such as rich silks, tapestries and draperies, and fabulous oriental rugs; as well as the production of fascinating potteries, tiles, metalwork, leatherwork, carved ivory and crystal.

Among musical instruments of Arabic derivation are the lute (*al-ud*), guitar (*qitar*), and timbal (*al-tabal*), as well as the rebec (*rabar*), forerunner of the violin. From the same source have also come the tambourine (*bandair*) and cymbals (Spanish: *sonajas*), as well as the viol. The use of dancing girls as an adjunct of music was popular among the Moslems. It is probable that many Moslem tunes and verse forms entered the West through Spain, as well as through southern France, Sicily, and southern Italy.

Moslem influences

We have seen in passing many influences of the Moslems on the medieval West. Islam detached from Christianity most of the inhabitants of the Near East and North Africa, and blocked further expansion of Christianity and Western culture in Africa or Asia. The Moslems indirectly encouraged an increase in the religious and theocratic element in Western civilization. They were one of the factors contributing to the rise of feudalism, the predominance of cavalry, and the development of knighthood in the West, as well as eventual Western military hegemony. Moslem naval influences were equally potent, as is suggested by the Arabic origin of such terms as "admiral" and "sloop" and of nautical instruments such as the astrolabe and compass. Many of our commercial and business terms and devices, technological products and processes, and agricultural plants and techniques stem from the Moslems.

The Moslem Challenge

Western philosophy and theology and Western mysticism and hymnology are deeply indebted to the Moslems. Western progress in mathematics, the natural sciences, and medicine originally stemmed from translations from the Arabic. Western poetry and fiction, music and art owe much to the Moslems. To numerous sample terms already mentioned as derived from the Moslems may be added alcove, sofa, cable, atlas, shawl, azure, elixir, chess, checkmate, julep, syrup, soda, sherbet, and tennis. Although Arabic culture was not a main source of Western culture, it was an important contributor.

References for Chapter 7

THE BEST one-volume account of medieval Islam is PHILIP K. HITTI, *History of the Arabs* (New York: Macmillan, 1951), available also in condensed paperback. Less extensive on Islamic history till the Later Middle Ages, but better on the Ottomans is SYDNEY N. FISHER, *The Middle East* (New York: Knopf, 1966). One of the best short (paperback) introductions is BERNARD LEWIS, *The Arabs in History* (London: Hutchinson, 1950). Among other useful one-volume surveys, which include both history and civilization are MAULAVI S. AMIR ALI (or AMEER ALI SYED), *A Short History of the Saracens* (New York: Macmillan, 1900 and 1951) and HENRI MASSE, *Islam*, tr. H. Edib (New York: Putnam, 1938). Mainly straight history are EDWARD ATIYAH, *The Arabs* (Harmondsworth: Penguin, 1955) and CARL BROCKELMANN, *History of the Islamic Peoples*, tr. J. Carmichael and M. Perlman (New York: Putnam, 1947). Also useful are *The Cambridge Medieval History*, Vol. II, ff., which includes useful chapters on the Moslems; the *Dictionary of Islam* . . . , ed. THOMAS P. HUGHES, 2nd ed. (London: Allen, 1896); and *The Encyclopaedia of Islam*, ed. M. T. HOUTSMA and others, in four volumes (Leyden: Brill, 1913–1936), as well as a new edition of the latter by B. LEWIS, H. A. R. GIBB, and others (Leyden: Brill, 1960 ff.). Pre-Moslem Arabia and the outside influences which helped shape Islam are portrayed by DE LACY O'LEARY, *Arabia Before Mohammed* (London: Kegan Paul, 1927). Specifically Christian influences are highlighted by RICHARD BELL, *The Origin of Islam in Its Christian Environment* (London: Macmillan, 1926). Mohammad is the subject of numerous biographies, such as those of TOR ANDRAE, . . . *Mohammed* . . . , tr. T. Menzel (New York: Scribners, 1936), and EMILE DERMENGHEM, . . . *Mahomet* (New York: Dial, 1930); and FRANCESCO GABRIELI, *Mohammed and the Conquests of Islam* (London: World University, 1968); though probably still the best is that by WILLIAM MUIR, *The Life of Mahomet* . . . (London: Smith, Elder, 1878) which is based on extensive use of original sources. Also excellent is MUIR's *The Caliphate: Its Rise, Decline, and Fall* . . . , new ed. by T. H. WEIR (Edinburgh: Grant, 1915). Interesting readings from original sources are provided by WILLIAM H. MCNEILL and MARILYN R. WALMAN, *The Islamic World* (New York: Oxford U.P., 1973), and A. J. ARBERRY, *Aspects of Islamic Civilization* . . . (Ann Arbor: U. of Mich., 1967).

Among various lives of Harun al-Raschid are those by GABRIEL AUDISIO (New York: McBride, 1931), and HARRY S. PHILBY (London; Davies, 1933). Harun's mother and his wife are the subjects of NABIA ABBOTT's *Two Queens of Bagdad* (Chicago: U. of Chicago, 1946), likewise in popular style. The famous medieval Abbasid capital is described by GUY LE STRANGE,

Bagdad . . . (Oxford: Clarendon, 1900), also author of *The Lands of the Eastern Caliphate . . . to . . . Timur* (Cambridge: Cambridge U.P., 1905). A great Moslem leader during the Crusading period is discussed by STANLEY LANE POOLE, *Saladin and the Fall of the Kingdom of Jerusalem* (London: Putnam, 1926). POOLE's numerous works on Islam also include . . . *Egypt in the Middle Ages* (New York: Scribners, 1901), and *Medieval India* . . . (London: Unwin, 1903). Notable works on Moslem Spain are REINHART P. DOZY, *Spanish Islam* (London, Chatto, 1913), and BERNHARD and ELLEN WHISHAW, *Arabic Spain: Sidelights* . . . (London: Smith, 1912). HAMILTON A. R. GIBB, *The Arab Conquests in Central Asia* (London: Royal Asiatic Society, 1923), and A. B. HABIBULLAH, *The Foundation of Muslim Rule in India* (Lahore, India: Ashraf, 1945) are recommended for their subjects. A good survey of the Mongols who invaded the Moslem world is MICHAEL CHAROL (pseud. MICHAEL PRAWDIN), *The Mongol Empire: Its Rise and Legacy*, tr. E. and C. Paul (London: Allen, 1940), while the early Ottoman Turks are treated by HERBERT A. GIBBONS, *The Foundation of the Ottoman Empire* (Oxford: Oxford U.P., 1916).

Arabic civilization in general is treated in the collaborative *Legacy of Islam*, eds. Thomas W. Arnold and A. Guillaume (Oxford: Clarendon, 1931), as well as in *The Arab Heritage*, ed. Nahib A. Faris (Princeton: Princeton U.P., 1944). More limited to institutional descriptions are MAURICE GAUDEFROY-DENOMBYNES, *Muslim Institutions* . . . , tr. J. MacGregor (London: Allen, 1950); GUSTAVE E. VON GRUNEBAUM, *Medieval Islam* (Chicago: U. of Chicago, 1947); H. LAMMENS, *Islam: Belief and Institutions* (London: Methuen, 1929); REUBEN LEVY, *The Social Structure of Islam* (Cambridge: Cambridge U.P., 1957); and finally, THOMAS W. ARNOLD, *The Caliphate* (Oxford: Clarendon, 1924). Urban life in the Islamic World is the subject of *The Islamic City* . . . (Philadelphia: U. of Pa., 1970); and of ROBERT N. FRYE, *Bukhara* . . . (Norman: U. of Okla., 1965).

The key source for Islamic religion is the Quran or Koran, available in various English translations, such as those of E. H. Palmer (Oxford: Oxford U.P., 1933, etc.), G. Sale (Philadelphia: Lippincott, 1923, etc.), and M. Pickthall (New York: Knopf, 1930, also in paperback, New York: New American Library, 1953). A standard work on the development of Islamic beliefs is ARENT J. WENSINCK, *The Muslim Creed: Its Genesis and Historical Development* (Cambridge: Cambridge U.P., 1932); while another on the evolution of *hadith* is ALFRED G. GUILLAUME, *The Traditions of Islam* . . . (Oxford: Clarendon, 1924). A good explanation of the *Shiah* is DWIGHT M. DONALDSON, *The Shiite Religion* . . . (London: Luzac, 1955). Accounts of Islamic mysticism are REYNOLD A. NICHOLSON's *The Mystics of Islam* (London: Bell, 1914), and *Studies in Islamic Mysticism* (Cambridge: Cambridge U.P., 1921); and MARGARET SMITH's *Studies in Early Mysticism in the Near and Middle East* . . . (London: Sheldon, 1931), and *Readings from the Mystics of Islam* (London: Luzac, 1950). The propagation of Muhammad's religion is discussed by THOMAS W. ARNOLD, *The Preaching of Islam* . . . (New York: Constable, 1913).

A fascinating account of the evolution of Islamic learning is given by DE LACY O'LEARY, *How Greek Science Passed to the Arabs* (London: Routledge, 1948), also author of *Arabic Thought and Its Place in History* (London: Kegan Paul, 1939).

More specialized accounts are TJITZE J. DE BOER, *History of Philosophy in Islam*, tr. E. R. Jones (London: Luzac, 1933); EDWARD G. BROWNE, *Arabian Medicine* . . . (Cambridge: Cambridge U.P., 1921); and DONALD E. CAMPBELL, *Arabian Medicine and Its Influence on the Middle Ages*, 2 vols. (London: Kegan Paul, 1926). A standard history of Arabic literature is REYNOLD A. NICHOLSON, *A Literary History of the Arabs* (Cambridge: Cambridge U.P., 1941, etc.). Nicholson is also editor of *Translations of Eastern Poetry and Prose* (Cambridge: Cambridge U.P., 1922). A good short account is HAMILTON A. R. GIBB, *Arabic Literature* (London: Oxford, 1926). *The . . . Thousand and One Nights* or *Arabian Nights*, as translated v.g. by Edward W. Lane, are available in various editions, and so is the *Rubaiyat* of OMAR KHAYYAM. Muslim historical writing is the subject of FRANZ ROSENTHAL, *A History of Muslim Historiography* (Leiden: Brill, 1952); while Islamic historical theory is exemplified by IBN KHALDUN, *An Arab Philosophy of History: Selections from the Prolegomena*, tr. Charles P. Issawi (New York: Transatlantic, 1950); and Islamic geography by IBN BATTUTA, *Travels* . . . , tr. H. A. R. GIBB (London: Routledge, 1929). The key work on Islamic education is KHALIL A. TOTAH, *The Contribution of the Arabs to Education* (New York: Columbia U.P., 1926). For architecture there is KEPPEL A. CRESSWELL, *Early Muslim Architecture*, 2 vols. (Oxford: Clarendon, 1932–1940) and G. T. RIVOIRA, *Moslem Architecture*, tr. G. M. Rushford (London: Oxford, 1918); for art MAURICE S. DIMAND, *A Handbook of Muhammadan Art* (New York: Hartsdale, 1944), and EDGAR BLOCHET, *Musulman Painting: XIIth to XVIIIth Century* (London: Methuen, 1929); for music JULIAN RIBERA Y TARRAGO, *Music in Ancient Arabia and Spain* (Oxford: Oxford U.P., 1929).

❲ THE CAROLINGIAN EMPIRE AND RENAISSANCE. Chapter 8.

RIGINATING in Austrasia—the more Germanic part of Frankland—and displaying remarkable vitality, perceptivity, and moral fiber, the Carolingian line gradually supplanted the Merovingian. The Frankish state displayed new and vigorous life under the Carolingians, reviving from its earlier decadence, and reacting vigorously to external threats, notably that of the Arabs. The productive Carolingian era—an elevated plateau in early medieval history—had extensive influence on subsequent Western history.

FROM MAYORS TO MONARCHS: THE CAROLINGIANS TO 768.
Section 22.

The line of the Merovingians, from which the Franks were accustomed to choose their kings. . . . had long since lost all power, and no longer possessed anything of importance except the empty royal title. Both the wealth and power of the kingdom were in the hands of the Prefects of the Court, who were known as "Mayors of the Palace," and exercised full sovereignty. [Power of the Carolingian Mayors of the Palace as described by Einhard in his *Life of Charles the Great*.]

F OLLOWING the death of Dagobert (639), the Merovingians became "Do Nothing Kings" (*Rois fainéants*). Actual power in the various areas was exercised by the "Mayors of the Palace," who struggled among themselves for control of all Frankland, just as the Merovingians had done in the days of their personal rule. Out of the melee, the forceful Carolingians emerged as rulers of the whole of Frankland (687 ff.). Among the factors that promoted their rise—aside from the Merovingian decline—were their early appointment as Mayors of the Palace in Austrasia; their wealth and power as great landowners, augmented during their tenure of office; a Germanic habit of multiplying sworn retainers and soliciting the cooperation of their fellow nobles in assemblies; a reputation for piety and reasonably good morals; and enthusiasm for education and learning. The cooperation of the Carolingians with the Church in its missionary and reform efforts earned for them the support of eccleciastics and popes. The more warlike propensities, habits, and capabilities of the Austrasians, as compared with other peoples of Frankland, constituted another factor. Finally, the Moslem menace made the rest of Western Europe willing to accept strong leadership and direction.

The "Do Nothing" Merovingians (639–751)

When the Merovingians became mere figureheads and puppets following the death of Dagobert (639), supreme authority was exercised by their prime ministers: the "Mayors of the Palace." The Mayors of the Palace apparently encouraged—intentionally or otherwise—the deterioration or vitiation of their Merovingian overlords. The kings lived in indolence, dissipation, and without adequate training or education. They married early (at ages such as fourteen, fifteen, and sixteen) and died young (at ages such as twenty-three, twenty-four, and twenty-five) "worn out by precocious debauchery," as well as possible disease or foul play. They left weak, immature children to succeed them and repeat the vicious cycle. Each regency was administered by an energetic Mayor of the Palace, who dominated the monarch and public affairs until the feeble king followed his predecessor to an early grave. Charlemagne's biographer, Einhard, thus describes the situation by 751: *Both the wealth and power of the kingdom were in the hands of the Prefects of the Court, who were known as "Mayors of the Palace," and exercised full sovereignty. Content with the royal title alone, the King, with his long hair and flowing beard, used to sit upon the throne and play the part of ruler, receiving ambassadors, whencesoever they came, and giving them, on their departure, as though of his own power, answers which he had been instructed or commanded to transmit. But this was the only function that he performed* . . . (Einhard, *Life of Charles the Great*).

The Mayor of the Palace

The main original function of the Mayor of the Palace seems to have been the supervision and management of the royal properties. Just as there were mayors over individual royal estates, so there was a "mayor of mayors": the Mayor of the Palace. The Mayor of the Palace also had charge of the residence of the king, together with the royal retinue and servants. His office gave him control of the royal revenues, which came mainly from the estates he administered. He naturally became the right-hand man and chief adviser to the king, as well as the ordinary guardian and regent for a young king. He eventually supervised the administration of royal justice and controlled the army. He dispensed royal patronage, made appointments, and conducted foreign relations. He became in effect a sort of plenipotentiary, prime minister, and viceroy. As Merovingian authority declined, the power of their Mayors of the Palace expanded. Originally there were Mayors of the Palace for each of the component kingdoms in Frankland.

The Carolingian Mayors of the Palace played a three-fold role. First, they represented the great landed aristocracy of which they were members, and for whom they were leaders and spokesmen. Secondly, they represented the monarchy and the people at large. Finally, as heads of their own house, they promoted its interests and ambitions. The extent of Carolingian lands and the number of their retainers were already great at the outset, and their position as mayors gave them an opportunity to multiply both. The equating of their interests with those of the aristocracy and the Merovingian monarchy dissolved as their own dynastic prospects ascended.

From Pepin I to Grimoald (613–656)

The founder of the Carolingian mayoralty was Pepin I of Landen. In the two-pronged conflict against the imperious Brunhilda waged by Fredegunde's son King Clothaire II of Neustria and the disaffected Austrasian aristocracy, the Austrasians were led by two of their great landowners: Pepin and Bishop Arnulf of Metz. After the overthrow of Brunhilda, Pepin and Arnulf jointly ruled Austrasia in the name of Clotaire II (c. 613–626/7), until the pious Arnulf withdrew from both the mayoralty and the episcopate to seek sanctification as a hermit. Thereupon the aggressive Pepin became sole Mayor of the Palace in Austrasia, governing in the name of Clothaire II's young son Dagobert, who was appointed sub-king for Austrasia.

Dagobert evidently had his fill of the tutelage of Pepin, whom he promptly dismissed when he became king of all Frankland in 629. For a decade, Pepin was in exile. But the pre-eminent position of Pepin's house, was acknowledged by Dagobert in 632 or 634, when he appointed Ansegis or Ansegisel (Arnulf's son, who had married Begga, Pepin's daughter) as mayor in Austrasia. When Dagobert died in 639, Pepin promptly returned from his exile and resumed the mayoralty till his own death the following year (640).

In 643, Grimoald—son of Pepin I and brother of Begga, seized the mayoralty in Austrasia, where he ruled for the Merovingian Sigebert III, until the latter's death in 656. The powerful ambitious Grimoald had Sigebert's son shorn and sent to a monastery in Ireland, and tried to install his own son as king. But the Austrasian nobility revolted and sent both Grimoald and his son to Paris, to be imprisoned, tortured, and put to death by the Merovingian Clovis II. The Carolingian house was momentarily frustrated and its acquisition of the throne had to wait for another century.

The Early Middle Ages

Ebroin of Neustria (656–681) and his successors

Meanwhile the powerful energetic Ebroin became Mayor of the Palace in Neustria, and also succeeded in getting control of the mayoralties in Austrasia and Burgundy. A commoner by birth, Ebroin seems to have represented the Neustrian faction in favor of governmental centralization under a strong monarchy. In Austrasia, he had his puppet Willifoad installed as mayor, and in Burgundy he overcame the wily Bishop of Autun in a long drawn-out contest. A rebellion in Austrasia, led by the Carolingian Pepin II of Heristal, was also overcome (680). The following year, however, Ebroin was killed on his way to church by a landowner whom he had dispossessed. After the assassination of Ebroin, the mayoralty in Neustria—which had never attained the hereditary stability that it enjoyed in Austrasia—gyrated, and was held by four different individuals in seven years. Nevertheless, Austrasian forces led by Pepin II and Martin were again defeated by Mayor Warraton in 683.

Pepin II (678/687–714)

Pepin II of Heristal (the grandson of Pepin I) refused to give up hope. Finally, in the Battle of Tertry (687), he defeated and slew Berthar, Mayor of Neustria, who also controlled Burgundy. Pepin II now became overlord of most of Frankland. Only turbulent Aquitaine remained still independent.

An able ruler, Pepin II defeated the Alemanni, and established his family in the Dukedom of Bavaria. He recovered territory in the Low Countries that the warlike Frisians had occupied, and annexed part of Frisia itself. He supported the Church and encouraged Christian missionaries, such as St. Willibrord, who worked successfully among the Dutch. By the time that Pepin II died in 714, his two legitimate sons had predeceased him, and he left the mayoral office to be shared by his three young grandchildren under the regency of his wife, Queen Plectruda.

Charles Martel (717–41)

But many Austrasians refused to accept Plectruda as their ruler, and the Neustrians revolted and threw off the Carolingian yoke. Pepin had an illegitimate son named Charles, known in history as "Martel"—(the Hammer). Although imprisoned by Plectruda, Charles Martel managed to escape and assumed command of the Austrasian Frankish forces, which he led to victory over the Neustrians three times (716, 717, and 718). His successes induced even the most recalcitrant to accept his mayoralty. Martel subjected all Frankland, including the Alemanni, Burgundians, and Thuringians, as well as Bavaria and (eventually) Aquitaine. He also repulsed the Frisians, Saxons, and Arabs.

The narratives of Martel's subjection of Aquitaine and his repulse of the Arabs go hand in hand. Duke Eudes of (virtually autonomous) Aquitaine had contracted an alliance with a rebellious Spanish Moorish governor, he thereby incurred the wrath of the latter's overlord, Emir, Abd-al-Rahman ibn-Abdullah. The latter led an expedition into Aquitaine, where he defeated Duke Eudes, who then appealed to Charles Martel.

As Abd-al-Rahman and his troops, laden with booty, advanced north along the old Roman road from Poitiers to Tours (732), they were met by a large Frankish army led by Charles Martel. For a few days, the great armies confronted each other, sparring for an advantage. Finally the battle was joined. Against the furious charges of the Moslem horsemen, the

The Carolingian Empire and Renaissance

THE CAROLINGIANS
AS MAYORS AND MONARCHS
TO 870
DATES SHOWN ARE DATES OF RULE

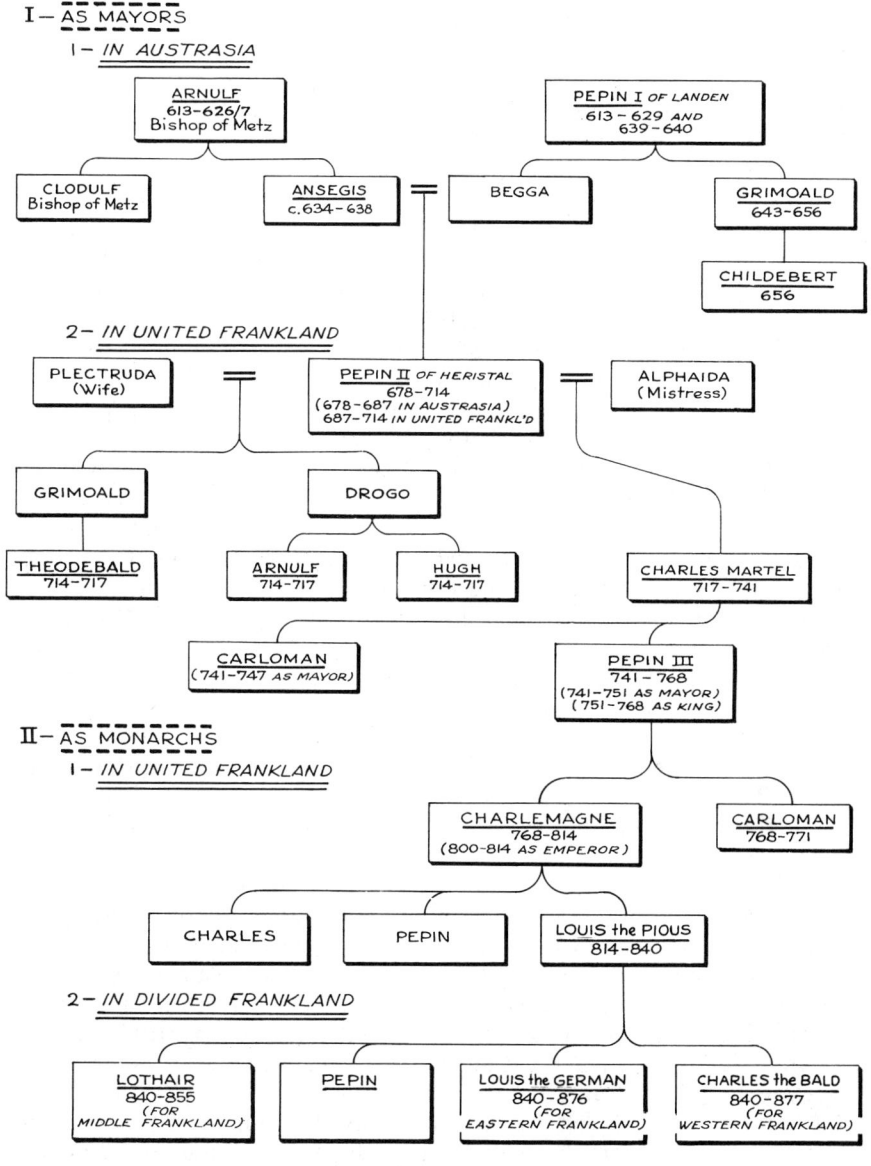

Franks, according to a chronicler "stood immovable as a wall, as if frozen in their place by the rigorous breath of winter. . . ." At a crucial point, the Frankish cavalry raided the Moslem camp, and many of the Arab horsemen withdrew to defend their possessions, throwing confusion into Moslem ranks. For the first time the Franks, who mainly fought on foot, had made effectual use of cavalry in a major battle: a milestone in history. Abd-al-Rahman perished in the fray, and the following morning the Franks found the Moslem camp deserted. The invaders had retreated, leaving behind most of their booty. Moslem expansion in the West had reached its high point; thereafter its hegemony in Western Europe was confined to the Iberian peninsula.

There has been a recent tendency to deny that the Battle of Tours (now often called "Tours-Poitiers" or just "Poitiers") was one of the decisive battles of history. It has been argued that this was primarily a plundering and punitive raid, and that the Moslems had already fully extended themselves. But how can we be fully sure of either of these assumptions? Even if the incursion had been only a raid might it not have led to a full-scale invasion had it been successful? Finally, the psychological impact of the victory was profound. This was the first time the Moslems had been decisively defeated in a major encounter in the West. And the fact that people looked on it as a turning point helped to make it so.

Martel and the church: military fiefs

Despite his victory over the Moslems, Charles Martel did not become a popular figure with churchmen. He rejected a Papal appeal for help against the encroachments of the Lombard King Liutprand, inasmuch as Liutprand had been his ally against the Moslems, although he did attempt to conciliate Liutprand and the Pope. In Frankland—on the pretext of grave public peril, and in order to obtain vassals and build up his cavalry to cope with the Moslems—Charles confiscated Church properties without compensation and distributed them as fiefs to followers who agreed to provide mounted military service. While the reform party among the clergy (led by St. Boniface) were acquiescent to this seizure, the majority of both the secular and religious clergy condemned the action.

Charles Martel contributed to the ultimate rise of feudalism by his liberal settlement of estates on the nobles with the precondition that they swear personal fealty to him, and promise to provide mounted military service. He took the title of "Prince" and ruled as an uncrowned king. Instead of making his children (as had his father) mayors of subordinate parts of Frankland, he ruled the whole directly as sole mayor. He became so strong in his later years that he even neglected to crown a Merovingian to serve as a figurehead king.

Pepin III, Mayor and King (741–751/68)

Martel was succeeded by his two sons, Carloman and Pepin the Short, between whom his will divided the mayoral responsibilities in Frankland—giving Carloman, generally speaking, the German part and Pepin the French part. For six years, Carloman and Pepin ruled amicably and cooperatively. In 747, Carloman withdrew to become a monk in Italy, and Pepin became sole mayor.

Pepin III was intelligent, competent, shrewd, and statesmanlike: a

The Carolingian Empire and Renaissance

worthy successor of Charles Martel and a fit forerunner of Charles the Great. He continued the enlightened policies of his predecessors, and added significant innovations—the most important of which was his acquisition of the royal title.

Pepin's assumption of the crown was planned cautiously and he skillfully avoided any re-occurrence of the Grimoald fiasco. First he sought Papal approval, seeing his opportunity in the difficulties of the Papacy. The Pope was nominally subject politically to the Eastern Emperor, but was in fact autonomous within his Duchy of Rome. Similarly, while the Merovingians possessed the royal title in Frankland, the Carolingians actually held all governing prerogatives. Pepin sent a delegation to Pope Zacharias, asking him whether he did not think it proper that he who ruled should also reign. Zacharias, replying in the affirmative, authorized the Carolingian succession and Merovingian deposition, and directed Bishop St. Boniface of Mainz to anoint Pepin as King. The last Merovingian, Childeric III, was retired to a monastery. Pepin then had himself elected and acclaimed King by an assembly of the Frankish magnates at Soissons. He was carried on the shoulders and shields of the aristocracy in the old Germanic fashion, after which he was anointed and consecrated as King by Boniface and his fellow bishops at Soissons (751).

Pepin's intervention in Italy and foundation of the Papal States

Papal approval of the Pepin's royal accession had been partly motivated by the Papacy's need of protection against the Lombards. The ambitious Lombard King Aistulf (v. 749–756) was renewing the Lombard drive to annex Byzantine and papal territories. Aistulf first took the districts of Ravenna and the Pentapolis (district including "five cities" to the south of Ravenna). He then indicated that he regarded the Papal States as subordinate to his overlordship, demanding that they pay taxes to him, while refusing to guarantee their independence.

Pope Stephen II—who had meanwhile succeeded Zacharias and to whom the citizens of these territories appealed—tried in vain to obtain positive assistance from the Byzantine emperor. When this was not forthcoming, he came to Aistulf's court and personally pleaded with the Lombard king. As the latter refused to desist, Stephen—seconded by a Frankish spokesman—requested to be allowed to visit Pepin III. Since to refuse would have been to provoke the Franks, Aistulf reluctantly gave his permission.

The Pope now crossed the Alps (753) into Frankish territory, where he was received with profound respect by the Frankish king and his court. Stephen reconsecrated Pepin III as King of the Franks, and decreed excommunication for anyone who would seek to overthrow the Carolingian line. He named Pepin and his sons, whom he likewise crowned, "Patricians of the Romans" with the connotation of authority in Italy and responsibility to protect Rome. Pepin, aided by papal entreaties, brought his Frankish noblemen to assent to intervention in Italy.

Despite remonstrances of Pepin III, Aistulf's acquisitiveness persisted. Pepin and his nobles, having determined on invasion, crossed the alps into Lombardy (754). At Susa, Pepin defeated a Lombard army which tried to impede his advance, and then moved on Pavia, the Lombard capital, which he besieged. The disheartened Aistulf submitted, and agreed to give up the towns and territories he had seized. Pepin now executed his so-called "First Donation" (of the Papal States—754) which transferred to the Pope the rule of the Ravenna and Pentapolis territories and the Roman Duchy and required the Lombard king to acknowledge Pepin as his overlord. But once Pepin had gone back across the Alps, Aistulf reneged on his promises. Not only did he refuse to turn over the stipulated territories, but he invaded the Roman Duchy and laid siege to Rome. The alarmed Pope urgently appealed to Pepin.

Once more, Pepin descended into Italy (756). This time he not only forced Aistulf to hand over the occupied territories previously ceded to the Pope, but he also obliged him to pay a large indemnity, together with annual tribute. Lavish bestowals on members of the Frankish court were also involved in the disposition. The so-called "Second Donation" of Pepin (756) was formally committed to writing and deposited in the papal archives. Byzantine demands to have their former territories restored were spurned. Instead these were turned over to the Pope, who was to rule them under Frankish protection. Papal territories were somewhat enlarged in the Second Donation, though not all of the ceded territory was actually transferred. The term "Patrician of the Romans" came to be regularly applied to Pepin.

Domestic rule of Pepin

Pepin's rule at home—like his intervention in Italy—was strong and successful. He maintained internal peace and order; suppressed separatist stirrings; and secured his realms against external enemies, such as the Saxons. He also fulfilled a Frankish project of long standing by taking Septimania, the territory along the Mediterranean west of the Rhône River (752–758), previously occupied by the Moslems.

Pepin wisely made peace with the Church in Frankland on the question of confiscated ecclesiastical properties. Lay beneficiaries were required to part of the revenues of the property as a sort of rent to the Church. Pepin himself confiscated and distributed Church properties as benefices with the same proviso. The organization of the Church in Frankland was improved. Mainz was made the primatial see, and St. Boniface became its first Archbishop. Each city of consequence obtained a bishop, and bishoprics were organized into provinces under archbishops. Church councils were held regularly, and Church reform was promoted. Clerical and monastic standards of education and exemplary life were raised. General acceptance of the Rule of St. Benedict was encouraged. Missionary activities were fostered. Standardization of the liturgy and of Church music was promoted. In numerous ways, the able Pepin III initiated and laid down guidelines for the constructive achievements of his celebrated son, Charlemagne.

CHARLEMAGNE ESTABLISHES AN EMPIRE.
Section 23.

By the wars that he waged in different parts of the world with utmost skill and success during the forty-seven years of his long reign, this mighty king

The Carolingian Empire and Renaissance

so nobly increased the Frankish kingdom that by his additions he almost doubled it. . . . [Einhard concerning the expansion of Frankland by Charlemagne, in his *Life of Charles the Great* (ninth century).]

THE SERIES of strong rulers of the Carolingian line culminated in Charlemagne. While his success was partly due to the achievements of his forebears, the number and magnitude of his own achievements and the enduring legacies of his reign set him apart as one of the most pre-eminent of European kings. Subsequent rulers of Germany, France, and Italy took pride in venerating Charlemagne as their predecessor. Subsidiary kingdoms also sprouted from the peripheries of the Carolingian state. Charlemagne, who regenerated the Roman Empire in the West, is revered by some in the Catholic Church as a saint; while pedagogues honor him as one of the most enlightened patrons of education. Institutions in the Carolingian state created precedents for many of the later institutions of Western Europe.

Charlemagne (*Carolus Magnus:* Charles the Great) is one of the few rulers in history on whom the appellation of "Great" (*Magnus*) is universally bestowed. Fortunately, much information concerning this dynamic leader and his reign is available in primary sources. Of these, by far the most valuable is the pithy information-packed *Life of Charles the Great* by his minister and secretary Einhard.

Charlemagne (768–814)

Einhard describes Charlemagne as a large man, reasonably good-looking, and kingly in appearance. He attests to Charlemagne's vigorous life and enjoyment of physical activities: *In accordance with the national custom, he took frequent exercise on horseback and in hunting, in which sports hardly any other nation on earth can equal the Franks. He enjoyed the vapors from natural hot water springs, and frequently practiced swimming, in which he was so proficient that no one could be regarded as his superior. Partly for this reason, he built his palace at Aachen [Aix-la-Chapelle], which is noted for its salubrious warm waters. . . .* Concerning Charles' interest in learning, Einhard states: *He was not content with knowing his native tongue: he also studied foreign languages. He became such a master of Latin that he could speak it as well as his own tongue; though he could understand Greek better than he could speak it . . . he cherished the liberal arts, and held those who taught them in great esteem, and conferred high honors upon them.*

Of Charlemagne's temperance and self-discipline relative to food and drink, Einhard says: *Charles was self-controlled in eating, and especially in drinking, for he abhorred drunkenness in anyone, and even more in himself and those of his household. . . . He rarely gave large banquets, and then only on great feast days, when he invited large numbers of guests. His meals ordinarily consisted of four courses, exclusive of the roasts, which his huntsmen were accustomed to bring in on the spit, and of which he was more fond than of any other dish. While at table, he listened to reading or music. The readings concerned the lives and deeds of men of olden times. He was fond, too, of Augustine's books, and especially of* The City of God. *He was so moderate in his use of wine that rarely allowed himself more than three cups in the course of a meal.*

Regarding Charles' respect for religion Einhard tells us: *He had the most devout and pious regard for the Christian religion, in which he had been reared from infancy. And therefore he built a large, extremely beautiful church at Aachen . . . as long as his health allowed, he would diligently attend church services, both in the morning and evening . . . he took the greatest care to have all the church services performed with the utmost dignity. He carefully reformed the manner of reading and singing [viz., the liturgy and church music] . . . he was [also] very active in relieving the poor and in the charitable donations that the Greeks call "almsgiving"* . . .

Nevertheless, Charles was neither an ascetic nor an angel. He was petulant when his physicians told him to eat boiled meat instead of roasts. He complained about fasting in Lent. He had several mistresses (Einhard lists four or five—although they may have been morganatic wives instead of mere mistresses), as well as a succession of legal wives (Einhard lists four). He is said to have had eighteen recognized children. He was so possessive of his daughters' attentions that he would not permit them to marry, despite the scandal that their inevitable interest in masculine gallantry aroused at court.

Charlemagne was a born leader, a superb executive, a successful general, and a great organizer. His reforms touched almost every aspect of Frankish life: political, judicial, military, naval, fiscal, monetary, commercial, agricultural, diplomatic, ecclesiastical, educational, architectural, and even musical. For three years (768–771) Charlemagne ruled jointly with his younger brother Carloman. Charlemagne ruled over the north and southwest, while Carloman ruled over the rest of the south of Frankland. On the death of Carloman (771) Charles annexed his portion and became sole ruler, while Carloman's family took refuge with the Lombard king.

Subjection of Northern Germany (Saxony)

Charlemagne, as Einhard notes, greatly expanded the kingdom of the Franks. The most difficult—and also the most significant and enduring—of Charlemagne's conquests was that of Saxony. This valuable territory, much greater in extent than modern Saxony, stretched across northern Germany from the Lippe and the vicinity of the Rhine to beyond the Elbe river. The Saxons, although somewhat advanced, were still in many respects in the condition of the early Germans as described by Tacitus in his *Germania*.[a] Saxony included numerous hardy, independence-loving, warlike tribes, which lacked any continuing cohesion or unity, although they cooperated periodically against their common enemy, the Franks. The Saxons were pagans, and they associated their hostility toward Christianity with their determination to remain free of Frankish domination. Their leaders were often restless and impulsive, and they frequently raided Frankish territories and violated peace agreements.

[a] See Chapter 3, Section 8.

Charlemagne's campaigns against the Saxons began in 772 and lasted for about thirty-two years, including a total of some twenty expeditions. At first, he may merely have meant to subdue the Saxons and make them tributary. If so, he soon concluded that the only way to pacify them was to incorporate Saxony into his realm. He and his advisers also wanted to

The Carolingian Empire and Renaissance

convert the Saxons to Christianity, both from spiritual and political motives. But a vicious circle tended to develop. Representatives of the Saxons would capitulate, but the tribes would overrule them and revolt, and the process would thus revolve. The Franks would conquer groups of Saxons in the spring and summer, leaving among them military garrisons and priests; but after the main Frankish armies had withdrawn, the Saxons would rise up and slaughter the Frankish soldiers and clerics. Leaders of the resistance, such as Widukind, would take temporary refuge on foreign soil, as among the Danes, only to return to rekindle their efforts.

Charlemagne's patience wore thin. After a particularly treacherous and bloody uprising, he beheaded some 4,500 Saxon captives at Werden by the River Aller (782). He also issued stern decrees designed to make the Saxons conform. The death penalty was instituted for robbing a church, participating in pagan worship, refusing to be baptized, and failing to abstain from meat during Lent—as well as for eating horsemeat and cremating the dead (regarded as pagan practices). Charlemagne had thousands of Saxons transported into other Frankish territories and supplanted with Franks.

Ultimately, the leader of the Saxon resistance, Widukind, conceding the futility of further resistance, surrendered on promise of amnesty (785) and was baptized, with Charlemagne as his sponsor. Even this did not end the struggle, although its intensity abated. In time, Charlemagne's persistence, and armed might—together with the proselytical zeal of Christian missionaries—prevailed.

Several other territories were also subjugated by Charlemagne. He concluded the conquest of the Frisians in the northern Netherlands and vicinity (parts of whose territory had previously been subjected by Pepin II and Charles Martel). The conquest of Bavaria was likewise accomplished. Although it had been nominally subjected by the Franks, this extensive duchy, which sprawled over southeastern Germany, had remained virtually independent. Duke Tassilo of Bavaria intrigued and allied with powers hostile to Frankland to maintain his autonomy. When, after an extorted oath of vassalage, Tassilo defied Charles and appealed to the Avars (while also seeking the support of Constantinople), Frankish armies invaded Bavaria from three sides. Charlemagne deposed Tassilo on a charge of treason and sent both the Duke and his family to monasteries.

Outlying areas and bordering peoples

Charlemagne also became involved in the complicated politics of Moslem Spain. Ostensibly espousing the cause of the "outs" against the "ins," he gradually occupied considerable territory in northeastern Spain to the north of the Ebro. This area came to be known as "the Spanish March" (Spanish Frontier Province), and later as the "County of Barcelona." Charlemagne's intervention and temporary foothold in Spain served to advance the Spanish Christian reconquest of the peninsula, and operated as an avenue for French influences in Spain. Charles also directed naval expeditions against the Balearics, Sardinia, and Corsica. He defeated the Danes, who had supported the Saxon resistance and had provided a haven for the Saxon leader Widukind. At the foot of the Danish Peninsula, he established a frontier county known as "the Danish March" (from which Denmark gets its name).

Warlike peoples along the eastern frontiers were made tributary. Among these were western Slavic peoples and the Avars. The Slavic peoples included the Sorbs, Wiltzes (Wiltzi), Obodrites, Bohemians, Slovenes, and Croats. Many of these were referred to as "Wends" or "Outlanders." Although defeated and made tributary, they were not incorporated.

Defeat of the Avars

For some time, the Avars—a predatory Asiatic people, whose western migrations had finally brought them to Hungary in the late sixth century—were the scourge of neighboring territories. Contemporaries referred to them as "Huns," since they so closely resembled the latter who had earlier occupied the same territory. The chief means of Avar support were plunder and extortion. Charlemagne was determined to end the Avar menace. With extensive forces, he penetrated the successive defences of their capital—known as "the Seven Rings of the Avars"—and seized their treasure, accumulated for centuries and stored in the innermost ring, the residence of the Khagan, or Khan of Khans. Einhard tells us that to carry off this great Avar treasure, fifteen wagons—each drawn by four oxen—were required, and that in no other war had the Franks ever been so enriched. The upper Danube was thus opened to the Germans, and Austria emerged as the East Mark of Bavaria in the western part of the territory previously occupied by the Avars. (Hence the German name for Austria: Öster Reich—Eastern Realm.)

Intervention in Italy

Charlemagne continued and carried to a logical conclusion his father's policy of intervention in Italy. Friction developed at the outset between Charlemagne and the Lombard King Desiderius, when the young Frankish monarch sent back his recently married wife Desideria to her royal Lombard father. Charlemagne's mother had arranged this ill-fated match, but the Pope condemned the Frankish alliance with "the stinking faithless race of the Lombards." (Charles seems to have been married previously—at least by common law—to Himiltrude, whom he appears to have preferred.) The second problem arose when the wife and children of Charlemagne's deceased brother, Carloman, took refuge with Desiderius. The final clash occurred when Desiderius resumed the traditional Lombard policy of seeking to expand into erstwhile Byzantine territories—including those that had been turned over to the papacy by the "Donation of Pepin."

After Pope Hadrian appealed to him for protection (773), Charlemagne first remonstrated with the Lombard king, and when this failed, he marched into Italy with a large army. While his army besieged Desiderius at Pavia, Charlemagne himself went to Rome, where he was again hailed by the Pope as "Patrician of the Romans." Charlemagne renewed, confirmed, and somewhat extended his father's Donation to the Pope (774). Pavia capitulated after a siege of eight months (773–774), and Charlemagne deposed Desiderius, sending him and his family to monasteries across the Alps. Charlemagne himself assumed the iron crown of the Lombards, which gave him the claim to be called "King of

The Carolingian Empire and Renaissance 177

Italy." He also subjected the Lombard Duchies of Spoleto and Benevento, and suppressed an uprising in the March of Friuli. In 780–781, the Pope crowned Charlemagne's son Pepin as King of Italy, and his son Louis as King of Aquitaine.

In 799, Pope Leo III, who had been elected Pope in 792 by a reform party, was brutally attacked and mutilated by his enemies, after having been accused of offences such as perjury and adultery. Unable to restore order, Leo appealed to Charles, who swiftly descended upon Rome, and assembled a council of dignitaries. After preliminary investigations, Charlemagne allowed Leo to purge himself voluntarily by oath and reinstated him, thereby salvaging the dignity of the Papal office (800). A few days later, as Charlemagne was kneeling in old St. Peter's Basilica attending Christmas Mass, the Pope suddenly approached him and placed a crown on his head, while members of the congregation proclaimed three times: "Hail to Charles, Augustus, crowned of God, great and peace-loving Emperor of the Romans!" Such was the celebrated restoration of the Western Empire and foundation of the medieval "Holy Roman Empire" in the year 800.

Charlemagne as Emperor (800ff.)

The question of Charlemagne's reaction has been raised by Einhard's observation: "At this time he [Charles] received the title of 'Emperor' and 'Augustus.' But at first he disliked this act so much that he declared that, had he anticipated the intention of the pontiff, he would not have entered the church on that day, even though it was a great festival."

There are several possible explanations. Charlemagne may have felt he should have been told beforehand. Or he may have been exhibiting a diffidence—whether real or feigned. He may have been trying to temper the opposition of some of his Frankish advisers and followers. Again, he may have been opposed to being crowned by Leo III so shortly after the Pope had been cleared of serious charges in his own court. He may even have had a presentiment of the subsequent Papal claim that the imperial office was a Papal benefaction, which could be withheld or withdrawn. Finally, Charlemagne may have felt that an imperial coronation at that time was disadvantageous to his relations with the Byzantines, who took umbrage at this arrogation of a title hitherto reserved to their emperor. Whatever his initial standpoint, Charlemagne soon began making use of his imperial title, and exerted every effort to get the Byzantines to accept it, which they eventually did.

Charlemagne carried on extensive relations with the Byzantines, and at least five embassies are known. For some time, a marital alliance was even suggested. Empress Irene (781 ff.) at first weighed the possibility of a marriage between her son and a daughter of Charlemagne. Next a marriage between Charlemagne and the Empress Irene herself was under consideration, but Irene was overthrown (802) before anything could come of the proposal. In 812, Emperor Michael accorded Charlemagne formal recognition as Emperor on condition that Charlemagne cede his claims to Venetia and Dalmatia.

Charlemagne's foreign relations

Embassies were also exchanged with the Abbasid Caliph of Bagdad, Harun-al-Raschid, who sought an alliance with the Frankish monarch in order to harass the rival Moslem Umayyad dynasty in Spain, as well as to further buttress his position in the East. Harun's gifts to Charlemagne included an elephant and a mechanical clock. Charlemagne was apparently authorized to act as Harun's agent in Umayyad Spain, and he seems to have been accorded a protectorate over Christians in the Holy Land.

In Western Europe, the "peace-loving Augustus" was tendered pre-eminence among Christian kings. King Alphonse of Galicia and Asturias in northwestern Spain called himself Charlemagne's "man" or vassal; and the powerful King Offa of Mercia, as well as other English kings, tenuously recognized Charlemagne as a sort of superking. Kings of the far-off "Scots" (Irish kinglets) hailed Charlemagne as "lord" and spoke of themselves as his "servants." Charlemagne also enjoyed an attenuated suzerainty over various Slavic peoples located to the East of Frankland.

As the aged Charlemagne grew weaker, anticipating his approaching death, he summoned his son, Louis the Pious from Aquitaine to Aachen, where he crowned him as his Co-Emperor and successor (813). Charlemagne's death came the following year at the age of 71, after he had contracted pleurisy while hunting. He had originally intended to divide his realms between his three sons: Charles, Pepin, and Louis; but only Louis survived him.

CAROLINGIAN CIVILIZATION AND RENAISSANCE.
Section 24.

> Charles was exceptionally anxious to find wise men and to provide for them in such a way that they might pursue philosophy [learning] in all comfort. Wherefore, with God's help, he rendered his kingdom, which was in darkness when it was committed to him by God, radiant with a blaze of fresh learning, hitherto unknown to our barbarism. [Walafrid Strabo, in his "Prologue" to Einhard's *Life of Charlemagne* (ninth century).]

AN EARLY blossoming of Western civilization in the Carolingian era resulted from a better blending of elements from various sources; mainly Roman, Germanic, and Christian, but also Byzantine, Celtic, and Jewish (Biblical).

Political institutions: central government

The amalgamation of diverse elements is well exemplified by Carolingian government. The Carolingian monarchy, originally elective, became hereditary; the kingship an emperorship. Although actually limited in power, the Carolingian monarchs claimed the full authority of Roman Emperors. And although the Frankish realms continued to be subdivided among legitimate male descendants, the theory of their unity persisted until the mid-ninth century. Biblical and Jewish rituals influenced the anointing and consecration of monarchs, and signified the latter's close alliance with the Church.

At his imperial coronation in 800, Charlemagne assumed the title of "Emperor." Coronation by the Pope—as well as the holding of some actual power in Italy—subsequently came to be accepted as necessary conditions for the imperial office. Although Charlemagne himself

The Carolingian Empire and Renaissance

crowned his son Louis the Pious Emperor at Aachen in 813, Louis later deemed it prudent to have himself crowned and anointed by the Pope, thus firmly establishing the latter tradition. The imperial office increased the theocratic aspect of the monarchy. The imperial position paralleled the Papal in stewardship of Christendom, and the condominium of Pope and Emperor was acknowledged.

While the Carolingians continued the governmental methods of the Merovingians to a considerable extent, they also instituted reforms. The office of Mayor of the Palace was dropped. The offices of Chancellor and Chaplain were combined, partly since clerics (whence "clerks") were used almost exclusively in the preparation and custody of official documents and records. Greater use was also made of ecclesiastics in other fields of the government.

A significant development—as seen in historical perspective—was the Carolingian revival of the Frankish assemblies. This action was motivated by the Carolingian need for widespread approval and cooperation during the "Carolingian Revolution" and for their many enterprises. There were both regional assemblies (as of the Austrasians or Neustrians), and fuller assemblies. The "Spring Assembly" was now held in May instead of March, and was called the "Mayfield." The Carolingians preferred May because the fodder necessary for horses was more commonly available then and the spring planting was also finished. The Spring Assembly, a distant precursor of the French National Assembly and the German Reichstag, was a general assembly. It promulgated legislation, administered justice, gave counsel, and supervised military mobilization. The "Fall Assembly" of the magnates (a forerunner of the French "Assembly of the Notables" and the German *Bundesrat*)—although smaller and less representative of the population at large—was more powerful. It was consulted on more fundamental questions—such as the royal succession— and it would often determine in advance what was to be proposed and enacted in the general assemblies.

Charlemagne instituted the *Missi dominici* (the Lord's emissaries): representatives of the monarchy who went through districts comprised of several counties, acting both as circuit judges and royal inspectors. The *missi* traveled in pairs, and usually consisted of a layman and a clergyman. They would try to make certain that everything was in order and conformed to royal wishes; and they would hear complaints, including those of the people against local officials.

Local government

The chief unit of local government was the county, and the chief local governmental official the count (*Graf*)—a continuation of the Merovingian system. The Carolingians extended and made more uniform the county system, as in Germany, northern Italy, and northeastern Spain. Each county was sufficiently large to constitute a meaningful, effective unit of government, but also sufficiently small so as not to constitute a threat to the monarch. Frontier counties known as "marches" or "marks" were increased in size and "beefed up" for military purposes. Their governors were known as "margraves" (*Markgrafs*: frontier counts) or "marquises."

Counts and margraves were fully authorized royal representatives in their areas. They presided over courts, administered justice, maintained law and order, collected taxes, mobilized troops, and led them to war. They were often assisted by viscounts or "lieutenant-counts," who might rule over a part of the county, and by *centenarii* (hundred-men) or *Gaumen* (district-men), who ruled smaller subdivisions. The office of "duke," as the military leader of several counties, was dropped by the Carolingians in favor of more centralization and less local autonomy. Thus Charles Martel suppressed the Duchy of Swabia, Pepin III and Carloman that of Thuringia, and Charlemagne those of Aquitaine and Bavaria.

The great Carolingians used such devices as oaths of fealty and conferral of lands as "benefices" or "fiefs" to strengthen their monarchical power and increase their military potential. In 789 and 792, Charlemagne charged his *missi* to exact general oaths of fealty from his subjects, and after he became Emperor required new oaths. However these institutions were eventually to work in the opposite direction to restrict and diminish monarchical power.

Law and justice

Charlemagne had the heretofore uncodified laws of further Germanic peoples, such as the Ripuarian Franks and the Bavarians, compiled. He also issued laws known as "capitularies"—from the fact that they were written down in little sections or chapters under headings (*capita:* heads). In such cases, Charlemagne usually invoked the cooperation of assemblies. His capitularies concerned a wide range of matters, such as conduct of the *missi dominici*, education of the clergy, operation of the royal estates, and subjugation of the Saxons. A large percentage concerned the Church and religion.

In order to improve the administration of justice, Charlemagne ordered the substitution of professional judges or *scabini* for the former courts composed of "good men and true" (*rachimburgi* or *boni homines*) representing the community. The burden of serving on the courts without recompense had become onerous, and justice frequently went awry because of a lack of adequate legal knowledge on the part of the ordinary citizenry. The *scabini* also restricted the power of the local courts. Charlemagne thus imitated the old Roman system instead of the Germanic system of justice, with a consequent augmentation of royal power.

Finance and warfare

As in Merovingian times, the primary source of royal income continued to be the royal estates. These were very numerous and comprised thousands upon thousands of acres, with the largest block of holdings in the northwest. The royal holdings included the old Merovingian crown-lands, as well as the family possessions of the Carolingians, and recurrent additions such as those obtained by confiscations and conquests. Several capitularies of Charlemagne were directed towards securing the more efficient and uniform operation of these estates. Supplemental sources of royal income included fines, tolls, tribute (as from the Slavs), booty (as from the Avars), a percentage of the income from certain lands of bishops and abbots, and gifts from subjects (as at assemblies), and from foreign governments (such as the Moslems).

The Carolingians increased the cavalry component in their armies until mounted horsemen became the principal military element. Both Charles Martel and Pepin III had confiscated church property and redistributed it as benefices on condition of vassalage and mounted military service. Charlemagne further increased the cavalry, but he also moderated the requirement of military service by providing that only one soldier need serve for each four "manses" (*mansi:* Hufen) of cultivated land (a considerable amount: about 120–480 acres).

Charlemagne also developed a sort of navy, and established forts along his coasts to ward off attacks of the Northmen.

Carolingian economy and society

Since the Carolingian economy was primarily agrarian, Charlemagne issued several capitularies designed to improve efficiency and increase production on the royal estates. He also regulated conditions of trade, as by forbidding trade at night and prohibiting purchase of crops before the harvest. He standardized weights and measures, as well as the coinage. He fixed the values and weights of various denominations of money, with 12 *denarii* or pennies to a *solidus* or shilling, and 20 *solidi* to a *libra* or pound. And he restricted the minting of money. During this period, the center of gravity of Western European commerce shifted northwestward toward the Low Countries, a fact probably associated with the rise of the Carolingians.

Meanwhile, the stratification of society increased, spurred on by the growing distinction between mounted warriors and manual laborers, the spread of manorialism and serfdom, and the more agrarian nature of life and work.

Church and State

The Church prospered under the Carolingians, who favored and encouraged it; but it also had to pay the price of greater lay influence in its administration. The Christian commonwealth was considered "one big family," with the Carolingian Emperor as "the father." This was partly based on Old Testament precedents, and Charlemagne was often addressed as "David" by members of his court. The ideal of organic Christian unity was promoted by metaphors used by Christ (for example, "vine" and "body"), and by *The City of God* of St. Augustine. Ecclesiastical advisers such as Alcuin encouraged Charles to regard his function as spiritual as well as secular. Thus Alcuin wrote: *Happy is a people who are exalted by a ruler and preacher of the faith, whose right hand brandishes a triumphal sword, and whose mouth makes the trumpet of the Catholic faith resound.* Charlemagne believed that he was simply looking out for the spiritual as well as the temporal interests of his "family."

The Carolingians were usually trying to promote the welfare of the Church. They were advised by churchmen and church councils, and were in continuous communication with their bishops and the Papacy. They promoted ecclesiastical reform, as well as expansion of the Church, along with the correction and standardization of the liturgy and the translated text of the Sacred Scriptures. They also legislated for the improvement of the education and qualifications of the clergy.

They supported Christian missionary projects. They summoned and participated in numerous Church Councils, such as those which condemned Adoptionism and added the *"Filioque"* to the Western Creed.

The Carolingian Empire and Renaissance

They incorporated church legislation and constructive suggestions by churchmen into their own laws. They ordered that improved education be made universally available in cathedral and monastic schools; prescribed higher standards for ordination; and directed observance of Roman forms in the liturgy and in church music. They condemned what they judged to be heresies, and sought to end ecclesiastical controversies.

A quite serious breach with the Eastern (Greek) Church occurred when a Frankish Council held at Aix in 808 decreed the addition of the "*Filioque*" to the Creed said in the Mass. The interpolation stated that the Holy Ghost proceeds "from the Son" as well as from the Father. This "tampering" with the original Nicean Creed—the final version of which had been determined at Chalcedon (451)—was vigorously rejected by the Byzantines. Although Pope Leo III was against this emendation for diplomatic reasons, he eventually accepted it.

Charlemagne regularly appointed bishops and often abbots. He was called by some "the Bishop of Bishops." Towards the Pope, he was very deferential, but he also seems to have regarded the Papal office as confined to purely spiritual functions and like that of a chief chaplain. In a letter to Pope Leo III (796), Charlemagne said: *It is our task, with Divine help, to shield everywhere with our arms the Holy Church of Christ from all her enemies abroad, whether these be the incursions of the heathen or the devastations of the infidel, and to fortify her from within by profession of the Catholic faith. It is your task, oh Holy Father, to assist the success of our arms with your hands raised in prayer to God like Moses, so that by your intervention, God willing and granting, the Christian people will always achieve victory. . . .*

Charlemagne favored and promoted observance of the Benedictine Rule among the monks, while his son Louis the Pious further promoted the reforms of St. Benedict of Aniane for Benedictines and the rule of St. Chrodegang of Metz for canons regular.

During the Carolingian period—often described as a "Renaissance" or "rebirth" of classical interests and learning—progress occurred in several fields of learning with the active support of Charlemagne and his successors. Charlemagne's interest in education is stressed by Einhard, who says *He paid the greatest attention to the liberal arts and bestowed high honors upon those who taught them.* Education was promoted in the palace school as well as in cathedral and monastic schools, by example as well as by legislation, and by the importation of foreign scholars as well as by insistence upon higher standards of learning among the clergy. A focal point of Carolingian education was the "palace school." The so-called "palace school" under Charlemagne's predecessors had been concerned mainly with non-academic training, but Charlemagne made it a real educational institution. He did this by importing foreign scholars, such as Alcuin from York, Theodulph from southern France, and Paul the Deacon from Italy. Eventually Irish scholars such as John Scotus Erigena (at the time of Charles the Bald) also found their way to the Frankish Court, which became celebrated for its patronage of learning.

The "Carolingian Renaissance": Education

The most famous headmaster of Charlemagne's Palace School was

Alcuin of York. Of noble Northumbrian birth, Alcuin had imbibed a love of learning from Elbert, a student of St. Venerable Bede. Alcuin inspired both his students and the Frankish court with his enthusiasm for learning. He became a chief adviser and mentor for Charlemagne's educational reforms. Alcuin's concern for his students was as great as his love for learning.

A subsequent master of the palace school was Theodulph, who had studied in southern France and Spain, and who eventually became Bishop of Orléans. Theodulph, who was an exceptionally gifted poet, gives us an intimate picture of the court circle, in which the kingly Charlemagne was called "David," the lyric Alcuin "Flaccus" (Horace), the epic poet Angilbert "Homer," the bulky Wibod "Vulcan," the industrious Einhard "Bezeleel" (builder of the Biblical Tabernacle), and the poetic Theodulph himself "Pindar."

More important in the long run were the cathedral and monastic schools. In a letter promulgating a capitulary of 787, Charlemagne says: *Be it known . . . that, in conjunction with our faithful advisers, we have judged it useful that in the bishoprics and monasteries committed . . . to our charge, care shall be taken that there be not only a regular manner of life conformable to holy religion, but also the study of letters. . . . Those who seek to please God by right living should not neglect to please him by correct speech. . . . We exhort you, therefore, not to neglect the study of letters, but rather to apply yourselves thereto with perseverance and humility. . . . There should be chosen for this work men who are both willing and able to learn, and likewise desirous of instructing others. . . .*

In a direction to his *missi* in 803, Charlemagne orders: *Priests are not to be ordained without an examination.*

Schools were also held in some parishes, especially in larger ones. When Theodulph became Bishop of Orléans, he ordered that this practice be universalized in his jurisdiction, and that instruction be free of charge. Subsequent legislation by Church Councils and by Emperors such as Lothar I continued and extended Charlemagne's laws concerning education, although with diminishing effect, owing to the growing weakness of the central government.

Copyists, script, and libraries

One of the most historically beneficial influences of the "Carolingian Renaissance" was widespread copying of ancient classical and early Christian manuscripts in the monasteries. It is said that 90 per cent of the Latin classical works which we now possess have survived due to the fact that they were transcribed during the Carolingian period. Numerous works of both classical pagan authors and Christian Church Fathers were copied and passed on to posterity. We are told that at the monastery of Fulda, no fewer than forty monks were occupied in copying manuscripts in the scriptorium.

During this time, copyists devised an exceptionally clear, attractive, highly readable cursive script for writing small letters, which is known as the "Carolingian minuscule." This new form of writing, which was early used at Corbie and Tours, may have been influenced by "insular" hands

The Carolingian Empire and Renaissance

used in the British Isles. It was selected and adopted for small letters by printers during the Renaissance, and remains our standard form of both writing and printing small letters.

Book-collecting and textual criticism became a fascinating activity for many scholars. One of these was Abbot Lupus of Ferrieres (ninth century), an avid bibliophile and painstaking scribe. Many libraries of considerable size were built up, particularly in monasteries such as Fleury, Corbie, Fulda, Reichenau, St. Gall, Bobbio, Lorsch, and St. Martin of Tours, as well as in urban centers such as Lyons, Cologne, Trier, and Metz.

Literary production and historiography

Surviving examples of Latin poetry from the Carolingian period fill four large volumes in the *Monumenta Germaniae historica*. Although much of this poetry is mediocre, some of it is eminent for its originality, intensity, and vivid expression, as in the case of certain poems of Alcuin, Theodulph, Sedulius Scotus, and Walafrid Strabo.

In addition, Einhard tells us that Charlemagne ordered a collection of ancient Germanic poetry; but the latter, if ever compiled, has not survived.

The Carolingian era was particularly productive in history-writing, to which various influences contributed. The great achievements of the Carolingians were an inspiring and appealing theme. The English practice of keeping annals in the monasteries was transported to the continent by monks such as St. Boniface and his associates. Italian and classical influences played a part, as in Einhard's *Life of Charles the Great*, which imitated Suetonius' *Lives of the Caesars*. Librarians and scholars at monasteries such as those of Lorsch, Fulda, and Reichenau, kept informative annals. Paul the Deacon, a noble Lombard monk, was encouraged to write a *History of the Lombards*, which he brought down to the eve of Frankish intervention. Subsequently, Count Nithard (an illegitimate son of Charlemagne's daughter Bertha and his poetic minister Angilbert) wrote a *History* of the reign of Louis the Pious (814–840) and the ensuing "War of the Three Brothers" (840–843).

Theological and philosophical speculation

The ascending level of culture and learning encouraged theological and philosophical speculation. Two monks of Corbie, Radbert and Ratramnus, took opposing views of the nature of Christ's presence in the Eucharist: the former holding for a real bodily presence, the latter for merely a spiritual presence. The Saxon monk Gottschalk taught predestination: that God has foreordained that individual men be damned or saved. The brilliant Irish monk, John Scotus Erigena, composed a treatise opposing this view, but drew much criticism because, in doing so, he upset the standard arguments against predestination. Erigena insisted on the unity of all God's attributes and the essentially negative nature of evil. When some Spanish Christians, including Bishop Felix of Urgel, held the theory of Adoptionism, or that Christ is merely the adopted son of God, he was opposed by Bishop Paulinus of Aquilea. The Carolingian theologians eventually took an intermediate position in the Iconoclastic Controversy, admitting the use of sacred images, but condemning excessive veneration of them. They also insisted on incorporation of the *"Filioque"* into the Creed (the statement that the Holy Ghost proceeds from the Father as well as from the Son) and Alcuin and Ratramnus of Corbie wrote treatises in support of this view.

John Scotus Erigena was a master of Greek as well as Latin. He has been characterized as "a brilliant comet" who prematurely flashed across the sky, a rationalist "born out of due time." He translated the *Celestial Hierarchies* of Pseudo-Dionysius the Areopagite from Greek to Latin. In his *Division of Nature,* John Scotus conceived of all being as proceeding from God by a series of emanations and returning to God by similar steps: the many both proceeding from and returning to the One. Scotus advocated a conception of the equivalence of religion and philosophy, and the oneness of God and nature. He even advanced the theory that reason is superior to authority.

In the field of political theory and social ethics, treatises for the guidance of monarchs were prepared by churchmen such as Archbishop Hincmar of Reims and Bishop Jonas of Orléans. Common to these was the concept of the ruler as having only limited authority entrusted to him by God, contingent on his proper use of it. Another concept was that of a semi-theocratic state in which the ruler followed the advice and counsel of his bishops.

The arts and music

Einhard records Charlemagne's construction of his famous church at Aachen, as well as splendid palaces at Ingelheim and Nimwegen, and even a great bridge across the Rhine near Mainz. The "Proto-Romanesque" style of architecture, with stone vaults, transepts, and towers, piers instead of columns, and smaller, easier-to-handle stones, made its debut in this period.

Carolingian manuscript illuminations and illustrations are noted for their narrative style, and their attempt to depict Scriptural allegory and events of Biblical history. Carolingian sculpture was crude, but with a strong primitive quality. The period saw the spread of Roman music and Gregorian plainchant at the expense of the earlier, less refined Gallic chant. Charlemagne sent Frankish ecclesiastics to study music in Rome, while Italian music-masters crossed the Alps to teach music in Frankland. The organ was introduced into Church services, probably from Constantinople.

Influence of Carolingian civilization

Carolingian precedents had a profound influence on subsequent European civilization. The modern states of France, Germany, and Italy emerged from the Carolingian Empire, to which Europe owes many of its monarchical traditions and governmental institutions. The medieval Western Empire was born with the coronation of Charlemagne in 800; and the diffusion in the West of the idea of sacred monarchy traces back to the Carolingian consecration. In this era, national assemblies developed, lawmaking was revived, and justice was reformed. Religious unity was promoted. The Benedictine Rule was extended throughout the West and monastic observance was improved. New impetus was given to education and learning. Latin literature was both preserved and renewed. Books were multiplied. Art took on new life, and certain features

The Carolingian Empire and Renaissance

of Romanesque architecture were anticipated. Seeds sown during the Carolingian Renaissance eventually produced an abundant harvest.

THERE are several excellent lives of Charlemagne which also treat his era, and discuss the preceding Carolingians. Among these are HENRY W. C. DAVIS, *Charlemagne* (London: Putnam, 1925); RICHARD WINSTON, *Charlemagne* . . . (Indianapolis: Bobbs, 1954); THOMAS HODGKIN, *Charles the Great* (London: Macmillan & Co., 1921); and JACOB MOMBERT, . . . *Charles the Great* (New York: Appleton, 1888); also the popularly written works of HAROLD LAMB, *Charlemagne* (New York: Doubleday, 1954) and CHARLES E. RUSSELL, *Charlemagne* . . . (Boston: Houghton, 1930). The main source for all of them continues to be the fine contemporary biography by Charlemagne's minister, Einhard, available in several editions, which is supplemented by half-legendary tales related a century later by the Monk of St. Gall to be found in *Early Lives of Charlemagne by Einhard and the Monk of St. Gall*, tr. and ed. A. J. Grant (London: Chatto, 1926). Good general works on the era of Charlemagne are CHARLES L. WELLS, *The Age of Charlemagne* (New York: Christian Literature, 1898); HANS PRUTZ, *The Age of Charlemagne* (Philadelphia: Lea, c. 1905); and STEWART C. EASTON and HELENE WIERUSZOWSKI, *The Era of Charlemagne* (Princeton: Van Nostrand, 1961).

Detailed articles or chapters on various subdivisions and special aspects of the period are to be found in *The Cambridge Medieval History*, Vol. II; and in MARGARET DEANSLEY, *A History of Medieval Europe from 476 to 911* (London: Methuen, 1960). Charlemagne and his period are, of course, treated in general works, such as LEWIS SERGEANT, *The Franks* (New York: Putnam, 1898). Viewing the era chiefly from the point of view of the Empire as an institution are HEINRICH FICHTENAU, *The Carolingian Empire*, tr. Peter Munz (Oxford: Blackwell, 1957); HERBERT A. FISHER, *The Medieval Empire*, 2 vols. (London: Macmillan & Co., 1898); and the paperback edited by RICHARD E. SULLIVAN, *The Coronation of Charlemagne: What Did it Signify?* (Boston: Heath, 1959). Selected legislation of Charlemagne is edited by DANA C. MUNRO as *The Laws of Charles the Great* in the U. of Pa. Dept. of History *Translations and Reprints* . . . , VI, No. 5 (Philadelphia: U. of Pennsylvania, n.d.). Two well-illustrated recent surveys are PETER MUNZ, *Life in the Age of Charlemagne* (London: Capricorn, 1969); and JACQUES BOUSSARD, *The Civilization of Charlemagne*, tr. (New York: McGraw-Hill, 1968).

The relations of Charlemagne with the Arabs are treated in the short work by FRANCIS W. BUCKLER, *Harùn al-Rashìd and Charles the Great* (Cambridge: Medieval Academy, 1931); while the general impact of Islam upon the early medieval West, especially in this period and in the economic and political fields, is the subject of HENRI PIRENNE, *Mohammed and Charlemagne* (New York: Norton, 1939). Pirenne's views on the subject are examined from several points of view and radically moderated by various authors quoted in ALFRED F. HAVIGHURST, ed., *The Pirenne Thesis: Analysis, Criticism, and Revision* (Boston: Heath, 1958).

The reorganization and expansion of the Frankish Church promoted by the great missionary-monk from

References for Chapter 8

England are seen in GODEFROID KURTH, *St. Boniface*, tr. Victor Day (Milwaukee: Bruce, 1935); while further details are found in the contemporary life of Boniface by WILLIBALD, *The Life of Saint Boniface*, tr. G. W. Robinson (Cambridge: Harvard U.P., 1916); additional light is shed in St. Boniface, *Letters*. . . , tr. E. EMERTON (New York: Columbia U.P., 1940). For further information on the Frankish Church, see books quoted for our chapter on the Early Medieval Church. A series of lifelike pen sketches of various persons prominent in the era, from Charles himself to Hincmar of Rheims, are provided in ELEANOR S. DUCKETT, *Carolingian Portraits* . . . (Ann Arbor: U. of Mich., 1962).

Carolingian intellectual and literary culture is well treated in MAX L. W. LAISTNER, *Thought and Letters in Western Europe, A.D. 500–900* (New York: MacVeagh-Dial, 1931). The best and earliest known work in English on Carolingian education is JAMES BASS MULLINGER, *The Schools of Charles the Great* . . . (Anastatic reprint: New York: Stechert, 1904). The English influence, particularly in culture, is treated in WILHELM LEVISON, *England and the Continent in the Eighth Century* (Oxford: Clarendon, 1946); and in SAMUEL J. CRAWFORD, *Anglo-Saxon Influence on Western Christendom, 600–800* (London: Oxford U.P., 1933).

An excellent work on early medieval education which stresses Alcuin is ANDREW F. WEST, *Alcuin and the Rise of Christian Schools* (New York: Scribners, 1892). Dependable lives of the great scholar and schoolmaster are: CHARLES J. B. GASKOIN, *Alcuin: His Life and Work* (London: Clay, 1904); and ETHEL MARY WILMOT-BUXTON, *Alcuin* (London: Marding, 1922); as well as the more specialized ELEANOR S. DUCKETT, *Alcuin, Friend of Charlemagne* . . . (New York: Macmillan, 1951). Excellent studies of Carolingian art and architecture are ROGER P. HINKS, *Carolingian Art* (London: Sidgwick, 1935); and KENNETH J. CONANT, *Carolingian and Romanesque Architecture, 800–1200*, in *The Pelican History of Art*, ed. N. Pevsner, vol. 13 (Baltimore: Penguin, 1959).

❨ DISINTEGRATION OF FRANKLAND AND THE ADVENT OF FEUDALISM.   Chapter 9.

OLLOWING Charlemagne's death, the Carolingian Empire disintegrated as a result of both internal stresses and external pressures. Prominent among the splintering forces were the attacks of Northmen, Moslems, and Magyars. By 888 the former Frankish Empire had broken up into several independent kingdoms, wherein still further disintegration led to feudalism.

FACTORS FOR DISINTEGRATION.
Section 25.

The cities are depopulated, the monasteries ruined and burnt, the countryside desolate. . . . The strong oppress the weak; the world is full of violence. . . . Men devour one another like fishes of the sea. . . . [Exemplary entries in ninth century sources.]

Disintegration and the Advent of Feudalism 189

THE PICTURE of Western Europe in the ninth century presented by contemporary monastic annals is indeed a dismal one. The *Annals of Xanten* in the Rhineland contain notations such as: (864) *According to their custom the Northmen plundered Eastern and Western Frisia and burned the town of Dordrecht, as well as two villages. . . . At the same time . . . the basilica of the Apostle Peter [in Rome] was taken and plundered by the Moors or Saracens, who had already occupied the region of Beneventum. The Saracens slaughtered all the Christians whom they found outside the walls of Rome . . . And they carried [many] men and women away as prisoners . . .* (850) *. . . The Northman Rorik . . . again took Dordrecht and did much evil treacherously to the Christians . . .* (851) *The Northmen inflicted much damage in Frisia and the Rhineland, and a mighty army of them gathered along the River Elbe against the Saxons . . .* (852) *The steel of the heathen glistened. . . .*

The *Annals of St. Vaast* in Northwestern Gaul include such entries as this: (882) *. . . The Northmen entrenched themselves at Condé and wrought terrible devastation in the [West Frankish] Kingdom of Carloman. They destroyed monasteries and razed monastic buildings and churches, and either killed the servants of holy religion by starvation or the sword or sold them beyond the seas. They slew the inhabitants; and none could resist them.* (883) *. . . The Northmen forced the Flemish to flee, and laid waste their land with fire and sword . . . The invaders went into winter quarters in the city of Amiens and devastated all the land to the Seine and on both sides of the Oise, and no man opposed them . . .* (884) *The Northmen ceased not taking captive and killing Christians, and destroying churches and houses, as well as burning villages. Through all the streets lay the bodies of the dead. . . . After long consultations and much goings to and fro, the leaders of the Northmen decided to impose a tribute of twelve thousand pounds of silver. . . . Still they raided in their customary manner beyond the Scheldt, and laid waste all things with fire and sword, and destroyed churches, monasteries, cities, and villages, and put the people to the sword.* (885) *The host of the Northmen forced their way to Reims. . . . The Franks followed them . . . and gave battle . . . but . . . retreated, and accomplished nothing. Thereupon the rage of the Northmen was let loose upon the land, and they thirsted for fire and blood. They killed numerous Christians and took others captive and destroyed churches. And none could resist them.*

Internal factors: Weakening of the central government

The Carolingian Empire was an extraordinary creation, built up and maintained by extraordinary persons, and promoted by extraordinary circumstances, especially the great Moslem menace. Such a coalition of conditions could not be expected to continue. If the economic and social liabilities of the sophisticated late (Western) Roman Empire subserved its collapse, how much more was this true for the simple agrarian economy and rural society of the Carolingian domain! If the advanced political, military, and fiscal institutions of the later Roman Empire were insufficient to ensure its perpetuation, how much truer was this for the poorly organized, backward Carolingian central government! The later

Carolingians were featherweights compared with their exalted progenitors. While the Carolingian state had been built up by indomitable men such as the able and stalwart Pepins, the ever-victorious Charles the Hammer, and the puissant Charles the Great, the later Carolingians incurred such cognomens as The Stammerer, the Fat, the Simple, and the Child.

A vulnerable spot in the heel of the Carolingian state was "the fatal Frankish custom" of subdividing the domains among surviving legitimate sons of each previous monarch. Partly a concession to regionalism and partly to military exigencies, this practice obtained the status of constitutional law. When Louis the Pious endeavored to jettison the custom, general opposition forced him to abandon his project. Lothair tried again after his father's death, without success. This convention promoted instability, and led eventually to permanent subdivision.

To obtain supporters and mounted warriors, as well as from piety and generosity, the later Carolingians continued to give away crown lands, thus dissipating their economic base and reducing their revenues. Meanwhile, the *missi dominici* (those special royal representatives who carried monarchical supervision and justice throughout the Carolingian realms) were allowed to lapse, thereby admitting greater local freedom from royal control.

Frankish central government continued to be loose and disorganized. The Carolingians did little to improve departmentalization in the central government. The structural reforms introduced by Charlemagne soon eroded after his death. The influence of churchmen in the government seems to have become excessive. One of the main weaknesses and mistakes of Louis the Pious was his extreme deference to ecclesiastical advisers. This was also true of Louis the Stammerer.

Growing autonomy of local governments

As the central government weakened, local governments became stronger and more independent. As commerce and industry declined, towns shrank, and subsistence agriculture became common. Political and economic relations became mainly local and self-contained, and centralized administration of large areas became financially unfeasible. Lack of upkeep of roads and bridges and the growing insecurity of travel cut down interregional intercourse, while widening disparity in languages and customs contributed to localism.

Hereditary tenure also fostered greater local autonomy. Originally appointive and deriving their authority from the arbitrary will of the monarch, the offices of counts, margraves, and dukes became hereditary, as it became the custom to accept eldest sons [of the previous occupants] as successors of their fathers. To allay the fears of his followers on the eve of their departure for a proposed expedition into Italy (from which some would not return), Charles the Bald went to the extent of formally guaranteeing the hereditability of their offices and benefices in his Capitulary of Quierzy (Kiersey—877).

Local officials and lords obtained from hard-pressed monarchs various immunities and privileges which extended their authority at the expense of the central government. Among such privileges were exemption from

Disintegration and the Advent of Feudalism

the operation of royal courts in their territories, dispensation from making feudal and other payments to the central government, and the right to coin money. Meanwhile since local rulers became responsible for local defenses, they tended to acquire supreme power in their own areas. Frequent raids and invasions—which occurred suddenly and at unexpected places—made it incumbent on each area to maintain its own defenses and to be prepared at all times. This put the main burden of defense upon local counts and lords, and encouraged the building of strongholds and forts; these could be used as easily against one's overlord as against outside invaders. In their "Capitulary of Mersen" (847)—issued jointly as a means of providing security against the Northmen—Lothair, Louis the German, and Charles the Bald declared: *We will, moreover, that each free man in our kingdom shall choose a lord, either one of us or one of our faithful: whomsoever he wishes. And we command, moreover, that no man shall leave his lord without just cause, nor should anyone receive him, except in such a way as was customary in the days of our predecessors.*

The foregoing led to the proliferation of feudal practices (discussed in the following chapter) which deprived the monarch of direct control over his nominal subjects and military forces outside of those of his own direct familial holdings. Interposed between the monarch and his subjects, including most of the fighting men, were the magnates, his vassals-in-chief—the counts, margraves, and dukes—who were the direct and governing rulers, according to the feudal principle: "My vassal's vassal is not my vassal."

While internal factors alone could have brought about the weakening of the Carolingian Empire and its subdivision into smaller kingdoms, it is doubtful whether they would have effected the degree of feudal disintegration that actually occurred. As in the Roman Empire in the West, it was foreign invasions that actually brought about the downfall of the imperial edifice. Bands of invaders struck at the Carolingian Empire from several directions: Scandinavian Vikings from the north, Slavs from the east, Magyars from the southeast, and African Moslems from the south. These onslaughts—sometimes called "the Second Barbarian Invasions" —were the immediate catalyst of disintegration.

External factors

In the Western Mediterranean, where they enjoyed naval supremacy, the Moslems harassed the Christians of southern France and Italy with repeated raids. Their chief targets were coastal towns, but they also penetrated the interior on their pillaging expeditions. Many of these raids were conducted as a form of private enterprise—a fact that made them the more difficult to repress. Most were undertaken by minor leaders with voluntary forces, rather than by sovereign governments. Some of the attacks, however, were instigated by the ambitious leaders of the smaller principalities into which the Caliphate was dividing: the Idrisids of Morocco, the Aghlabids of Tunisia, and the Tulunids and Ikshidids of Egypt. During this period, the principal islands of the western Mediterranean came under Moslem control, and became convenient bases for further expeditions against the Christian mainland. Sicily was conquered

Moslem attacks from the south

by expeditions from Tunisia; the Balearics were taken by Moslems from Spain and became a particularly obnoxious nest for pirates; while Moslem settlements were established on Corsica and Sardinia. Southern France suffered greatly from Moslem attacks upon its Mediterranean coasts. The Moslems established bases along the French Riviera at places such as Fréjus (Fraxinetun) between Marseilles and Nice. They raided and plundered French Mediterranean towns such as Marseilles (836) and Arles (842), and penetrated the Rhône valley as far north as Lyons. Peninsular Italy was even more exposed to Moslem attacks. Here, as in southern France, the Moslems established bases from which they raided other places. Typical of such was a fortified settlement on the Garigliano River between Rome and Naples, and another at Bari on the Adriatic. They attacked Naples (837), Venice (841), and Rome (846). At Rome they sacked old St. Peter's basilica and that of St. Paul-Outside-the Walls; the castle of Sant' Angelo was built as a place of refuge from their attacks. They pillaged Monte Cassino abbey in 852, and largely destroyed it in 881. Meanwhile, they obtained lasting control of certain points in southern Italy, such as Taranto.

Invaders from the east: Slavs and Magyars

The Eastern frontiers of civilized Europe were harassed by repeated raids of various barbarian peoples. Throughout the period, most of these were Slavic; but in the early tenth century, the Magyars (a people of central Asian origin) were a particularly grievous thorn pressing into the side of the Germans.

A more continuous threat were the Slavs, located beyond the Elbe and the mountains to its south, who included the Wends, Wiltzes, Sorbs, Bohemians, and Moravians. These tribes were a constant source of danger and harrassment. The Germans to their west bore the brunt of their attacks. Punitive expeditions only increased the likelihood of early reprisals by them—for revenge as well as booty. The Slavic Moravians built up a considerable empire in central Europe in the ninth century; their menace abated when they were converted to Christianity by missionaries from Constantinople later in the same century, and ceased when they were subjugated by the Magyars in the early tenth century.

The Magyars were nomads who had apparently migrated from the great basin between the Ural and the Altai Mountains; they spoke a Uralic language completely unrelated to any of the languages of Western Europe—or, for that matter, to those of the Slavs. They rode swift mounts, and used bows and arrows as their principal weapons. Since superficially they resembled the earlier Huns, contemporaries often referred to the Magyars by this name (whence "Hungarian"). They were described as "of short to medium stature . . . with small feet . . . waddling gait . . . large heads . . . broad faces . . . prominent cheekbones . . . broad, flat noses . . . and coarse, stiff hair."

After entering Europe through the Caspian sea area and tarrying for some time north of the Black Sea, the Magyars temporarily established themselves north of the lower Danube, whence they attacked and extorted tribute from the Byzantine Empire. Toward the close of the ninth century, they were forced to the west by combined Bulgarian and Pecheneg

Disintegration and the Advent of Feudalism

attacks. After being defeated by the Bulgarian King Simeon (895), the Magyars moved up the Danube into the great plain which became their final home and has ever since been known as Hungary.

In the succeeding decade, the Magyars overthrew the Moravian Empire (by 906), annexed its eastern territories, and resumed their old predatory activities. They ranged westward into Burgundy and southward into Italy, where they invaded Lombardy several times (899 ff.). They pushed as far west as Paris. They were especially active in attacking their immediate neighbors, the Germans. Beginning in 900, the Magyars repeatedly invaded Bavaria, Thuringia, Saxony, Franconia, and even Lorraine, and Burgundy. For some time—particularly during the reigns of Louis the Child (900–911) and Conrad of Franconia (911–918)— they seemed invincible. During this time the German dukedoms evolved as a defense measure, although the Magyars were not really held at bay until the Germans consolidated under the Saxon monarchs Henry I and Otto I. A weakness of the Magyars was that, owing to a lack of siege equipment and technical knowledge, they were unable to take strongly fortified places. Also they were at a disadvantage before direct frontal attacks of heavy cavalry. While the initial effect of the Magyars was to promote the division of Germany into duchies, their final effect was, paradoxically, to promote the unification of Germany. For they roved overland in large armies, and could most effectively be combated by large bodies of troops such as could be raised only by the King. After their defeat by Otto I in 955, the Magyars settled down in Hungary. In 1001, their ruler Stephen was converted to Catholic Christianity, and was recognized as King by the Pope.

THE NORTHMEN OR VIKINGS.
Section 26.

From the fury of the Northmen, oh Lord deliver us! [Invocation in the Christian litany during the ninth century.]
On all sides the Northmen devastated, raided, and massacred the Christians. [From the ninth century *Monuments of History of the Abbots of St. Philibert.*]

OF ALL the factors contributing to the disintegration of the Frankish Empire and the rise of feudalism, the chief was the incursion of the Northmen or "Vikings." Beginning in the later part of the eighth century, and becoming especially aggressive during the ninth and tenth centuries, far northern Teutonic peoples from Denmark, Norway, and Sweden raided Europe to their southwest, south, and southeast, as well as western lands of the North Atlantic. They established permanent settlements as far west as Greenland and as far east as Russia. The term "Vikings," often applied to them, may mean "sea-raiders," "creek men," or "men from the fjords."

These fierce Northmen were still pagan barbarians. They were generally of the "classic" Nordic type: tall, fair, blond, blue-eyed, long-headed, and large of bone and limb. They lacked urban life and regular writing; but had the use of iron and were skilled in both metalwork and

The "Men of the North"

woodworking. They farmed, despite geographical handicaps; and they were expert shipbuilders, skillful seamen, and accomplished traders. The Northmen had a considerable lore of myths, legends, stories, and poems, which they recited and revised to the accompaniment of music. Full of energy and zest for life, they were adventuresome, daring, and warlike. They conceived of their gods as warlike, and of their heavenly "Valhalla" as a happy warriors' festive hall. Aspects of Norse character were often paradoxical. They could be courageous yet superstitious, hospitable yet cruel, honorable yet treacherous, commercial yet piratical, efficient and energetic yet frequently drunk and indolent.

Since their land was mountainous and forested, it was only moderately and occasionally hospitable to agriculture, but it did provide furs and other articles desired by other peoples. Since their coasts were deeply indented by intrusions of the sea known as "fjords"—and also because adjacent waters were rich in fish—the Northmen were early attracted to the sea, and soon became great seafarers, fishermen, and traders. Among their articles of commerce were furs, fish such as dried cod, hemp, flax, tar, hides, falcons, and slaves. From spring to fall they carried on agriculture, fishing, trade, and piracy. Much of the winter they spent working on their boats, weapons, and ornaments, as well as feasting, drinking, and listening to exciting sagas related by their "skalds."

Causes and phases of Viking expansion

One of the causes of Viking expansion seems to have been population pressure due to limited natural resources. Another was the concurrent trend to stronger monarchical government in Scandinavia, which was distasteful to many freedom-loving souls, and especially to local lords accustomed to great autonomy. Another was the contemporary weakness and unpreparedness of Christian kingdoms. Still another was the facile transition from sharp trading to outright robbery, and the enticements of easy booty.

Viking expansion went through successive stages. In the first phase (to about 785), the Northmen were predominantly traders; in the second (about 785-850) they were mainly armed raiders operating in small contingents; in the third (about 850 ff.) they became invaders organized in good-sized armies, and exacting tribute for exemption from attack. In the fourth and final phase (about 875 ff.), some of the Northmen established themselves as the rulers in such territories as the "Danelaw" in northeastern England and "Normandy" (land of the Northmen) in northwestern France.

Each of the Viking peoples had their own "sphere of influence." Thus the Swedes had the Baltic area and Russia; the Danes the British Isles, Germany the Low Countries, and France; the Norwegians the islands of the North Atlantic—Iceland and Greenland—as well as the northeastern coast of North America and the southwestern coasts of Europe. The Danes controlled the so-called "Middle Passage," along with neighboring parts of Ireland, Scotland, and England, while the Norwegians controlled the so-called "Outer Passage" along with more remote parts of Scotland and Ireland together with Iceland and Greenland.

Disintegration and the Advent of Feudalism 195

Organized into *"hirds"* led by *"jarls,"* the Northmen ventured across the seas "through Northern mists" in swift, long, slim boats similar to racing craft. Measuring up to 80 feet or more in length, these boats were propelled by oars as well as by sails, and has as many as 70 or more rowers. Ships of the "Gokstad" class were about 78 feet in length with a beam of about 18 feet and a hull having less than 3 feet draft. They had double prows and were expertly constructed.[a] Their extraordinary mobility enabled Viking raiders to strike, plunder, and depart before their surprised victims could assemble forces to resist them. They could choose the point and time of attack as well as its duration; and once they were back on the water, there was little hope of overtaking them.

Viking techniques

[a] The actual Gokstad ship, whose hulk has been recovered, was 78 feet long with a beam of 16 feet and it had 32 oars. The gunwale was decorated with shields painted alternately black and gold, and the craft had a single sail.

The Vikings who raided in the ninth to tenth centuries were little better than professional pirates. They were hardy warriors and skillful seamen, accustomed to fighting and plundering. Their height and bulk —as well as their warlike habits and arduous life—gave them a marked advantage over their opponents. If wounded or frustrated, they often went "berserk" and furiously attacked without any regard for personal danger. Some of the Northmen were permanent "berserks:" special warriors of ill temper liable to furious seizures at any time. The fervent invocation "From the fury of the Northmen, Oh Lord, deliver us!" was included in the litany of the Western Church at this time.

The first Viking raids were modest in scope; but as their operations grew more ambitious, the Northmen assembled larger fleets until eventually they came to attack with hundreds of ships. The favorite objectives of the Northmen were monasteries and towns where they could easily find concentrated wealth and precious booty. At first they attacked isolated monasteries and settlements like those on Iona off western Scotland, Lindisfarne off northeastern England, Lambay off Dublin, and Noirmoutier off western France. They then raided coastal ports, whence they proceeded to inland points on rivers. At length, they would beach their boats and make their way across land, often with the help of commandeered horses. In such cases, they would usually establish a base for their operations in the region. For some time, they so used the island of Thanet in the Thames, Walchern Island at the mouth of the Scheldt in the Low Countries, and Noirmoutier. Next they adopted the "labor-saving device" of having potential victims pay tribute for exemption from attack. From this, it was only a step to take over the government of various areas; which they did in the Danelaw, Normandy, and parts of Ireland and Russia.

Early targets of Viking attacks were islands located to the west and southwest of Scandinavia, in and about the North Sea, such as the Shetlands, the Orkneys and the Hebrides, some of which the Northmen held for the duration of the Middle Ages. Some of their first recorded raids were made on the coasts of England. In 793 they plundered an destroyed the monastery on the holy island of Lindisfarne (off northeastern England) and massacred some of the monks. After several such raids, there was for a time a lapse in Norse onslaughts on England, evidently

The Northmen in islands northwest of Europe

owing to lucrative preoccupations elsewhere, as along the Frankish coasts. But in the 830s, Viking attacks in England were resumed. Large-scale Danish invasions of England occurred in the 850s, with the Danes wintering on the island of Thanet at the mouth of the Thames as early as 851. Most of northern and eastern England, including Northumbria, East Anglia, and Mercia, was overrun in the 870s, and the conquest of all England seemed imminent when Alfred the Great rose to "contain the Danes."

Scotland and Ireland were also early targets of the Vikings. The monastery founded by St. Columba on the Isle of Iona (off western Scotland) was raided by the Northmen in 795. Scandinavian sea-rovers obtained control of large sections in Scotland in the early ninth century and participated in the overthrow of the Picts.

The Northmen also won control of large parts of Ireland, where their first known raid was directed against a church situated on the isle of Lambay, just north of Dublin. Their chief and longest-held bases in Ireland were eastern ports such as Dublin, Waterford, and Wexford. The Norse kingdom of Dublin endured until the eleventh century. Much intermarriage of Scandinavians with the native Irish occurred.

France a favorite Viking target

France was particularly attractive to the Vikings because of its numerous wealthy monasteries and towns, and especially accessible because of its extensive coasts and several rivers. Charlemagne is said to have organized a fleet against Danish raiders about 800. Vikings sacked the monastery of Noirmoutier at the mouth of the Loire in the year of Charlemagne's death (814). The Northmen repeatedly returned to Noirmoutier and employed it for some time as a base.

Large-scale Viking operations in France began after the death of Louis the Pious (840). In the 840s, Paris and Rouen on the Seine were sacked, as were Nantes, Tours, and Orléans on the Loire. By 857, most leading French cities—including Bourdeaux, Poitiers, Angers, Beauvais, Quentovic, Chartres, Le Mans, Bourges, Blois, Paris, Rouen, Nantes, Tours, and Orléans had been sacked, often several times. The March of Paris or "Francia" was established against the Northmen by Charles the Bald and given to Robert the Strong; later it was raised to the status of a duchy by Charles the Fat. Paris successfully resisted severe Viking sieges in 861, 885–7, and 889. Besieged in 885–887 by a huge force of Vikings with numerous ships (one source says 40,000 Northmen and 700 boats), Paris was heroically defended by its count Eudes (or Odo). In recognition of this, the French magnates elected Eudes as their king (888) after the deposition of Charles the Fat. For some time, France suffered almost annually from destructive Viking raids, which lashed it almost to the limits of endurance. The *Chronicle of Amboise* informs us that *the country is laid waste as far as the Loire. Where prosperous towns once flourished, wild animals now roam; and where rich harvests formerly ripened on the plains, the thistle and the sharp-thorned briar now hold unchallenged sway.* A dozen "Danegelds" were paid by weak French kings to the increasingly brazen Vikings. In 911, Normandy was turned

Disintegration and the Advent of Feudalism

over by Charles the Simple to the Norse leader Rollo to act as a buffer. Rollo became a Christian and a nominal vassal of the French king.

In Germany and the Low countries

In the Germanies, the favorite marks of the Northmen were the Rhineland and the Netherlands. Early Viking raids on Frisia are said to have brought tears to the eyes of Charlemagne, although large-scale Viking attacks did not begin until the reign of Louis the Pious. The Northmen attacked and sacked numerous towns in the Low Countries, including Dorstad, Utrecht, Maastricht, Nimuegen, Liège, and Aachen. They established a base on the island of Walcheren at the mouth of the Scheldt, whence they raided and exacted tribute. For some time, they occupied much of Frisia and the northern Low Countries, with formal cessions by both Charles the Bald and Charles the Fat. A turning point came, however, when Arnulf decisively defeated them in a battle by the Dyle River in 891. Other parts of Germany were infrequent Viking targets, although Hamburg and Cologne were attacked.

In Mediterranean lands and eastern Europe

The Northmen ranged down the Atlantic coasts of Spain and Portugal, and passed through the Straits of Gibraltar. They sacked Seville in 844 or 845, and struck points along the Mediterranean coast of Spain from 859 to 862. In far southern France, they established a base on an island in the delta of the Rhône (c. 859–862), whence they struck and plundered cities as far north as Valence (150 miles up the river). They ravaged Nantes and Avignon; attacked Pisa (about 860); and raided Sicily and Morocco.

Adventuresome Swedes—known as "Varangians" and "Rus"—crossed the Baltic and penetrated Russia. Moving down the great Russian rivers, they first established a city-state at Novgorod, and later founded a principality at Kiev—from which modern Russia derives. Their ambition knew no bounds, and they even attacked Constantinople several times.

"Westward Ho" across the Atlantic

The Norwegians ventured across the northern Atlantic to Iceland and Greenland, and even to Newfoundland. They established a flourishing colony in Iceland, which came to be noted for conservative traditionalism and preservation of the pristine Norse language. They also established settlements in Greenland in the 980s. Sailing westward, Bjarni Herjolfsson apparently undershot Greenland and reached Newfoundland about 986, while Leif Ericsson reportedly duplicated Bjarni's voyage to North America about 1002. The points (in North America) where they put ashore were called—from their appearance—*Helluland* (flat-stone land), *Markland* (forest or wooded land), and *Vinland* (grape-vine land). There were probably subsequent Norse voyages to America, but no lasting settlements.

Lapse and results of the invasions

The Viking age came to a close in the tenth century. Viking expansion was obstructed by Alfred's victory at Ethandune (878), Eudes' successful defense of Paris (885–87), and Arnulf's defeat of the Danes on the Dyle (891). Factors included the gradual depletion of available Scandinavian manpower. which was being spread far and wide; the growth of political stability at home in Scandinavia; and the conversion of the Scandinavians to Christianity. Meanwhile Western Europeans were building castles and learning to defend themselves more effectively, while feudalism was providing improved military capabilities. Finally, some kings were beginning to "fight fire with fire" by acquiescing to Scandinavian settlements in frontier provinces.

The overall results of the invasions of the Northmen are disputed. Some writers affirm that Viking expansion gave new direction and drive to Western Europe by promoting commercial enterprises, stronger government, and political unification. They point to the stimulus given to the French monarchy by the strong Scandinavian government in Normandy and by the ensuing aggressive Norman monarchy in England. They cite the influence in England of Scandinavian institutions in the Danelaw and of Norman institutions following the Conquest (1066). They call attention to the strong Norman government in Sicily and the Swedish foundation of the Russian state. They stress the Norse genius for organization and enthusiasm for seafaring and commerce, as well as the Viking spirit of enterprise and love of adventure.

But there was also a dark and ugly side to the Norse invasions—piracy and pillage, bloodshed and slaughter, destructiveness and violence, and forcible subjugation of other peoples. The Northmen contributed to political disintegration and the rise of military feudalism in Western Europe, which hung on there for centuries. They retarded much promising culture in Ireland, England, and France, and brought to a partial halt the Carolingian Renaissance. And they probably set back the clock for Church reform as well as cultural rebirth.

In general, the "new barbarian invasions" of Northmen, Slavs, Magyars, and Moslems reduced Western Europe to its lowest medieval political, economic, and social level. Subdivision into lesser kingdoms was compounded by feudal fragmentation. Political and military localism were paralleled by an agrarian subsistence economy. The underprivileged masses of agrarian laborers were unfree, attached to the soil, and burdened with numerous oppressive dues. Widespread confusion, violence, and destruction contributed to religious, cultural, political, and economic decline.

(814–888)   COLLAPSE OF THE CAROLINGIAN EMPIRE.
Section 27.

> The three kings, coming together at Verdun in Gaul, divided the realm. Louis received the eastern part, and Charles the western. Lothair, who was older than his brothers, received the middle portion. [Contemporary report of the Treaty of Verdun (843) in *The Annals of Fulda*.]

During the ninth century, following the death of Charlemagne, the Frankish Empire disintegrated. Two and a half decades of monarchical vacillation and ebbing governmental authority (814–840), succeeded by three years of bitter civil war (840–843) resulted in the division of Frankland into three sovereign parts. But this was not the end. After four and a half more decades (843–888) of continued foreign in-

Disintegration and the Advent of Feudalism

vasions and occasional internal wars, dissolution had reached the point where there were six weak kingdoms in former Frankland, with feeble feudal ties being the main bond of internal cohesion within each.

Louis the Pious (814–840), who succeeded Charlemagne as Emperor, was learned, handsome, courageous, kind, and devout. But he was also weak, impressionable, vacillating, and unduly susceptible to the influence of stronger personalities—members of his own family and the higher clergy. His biographer Thegan observes: *He never laughed and nobody ever saw his white teeth. . . . He committed his affairs excessively to his councillors, owing to his extreme devotion to psalm-reading and singing.*

Louis the Pious (814–840)

Directly after his accession, Louis the Pious alienated many potential supporters by imprudent if forthright actions. He dismissed several of his father's trusted councillors, and brought in new ones, including somewhat impractical reform-minded clerics such as Benedict of Aniane. He banished from his presence many members of the court on charges of immorality—including the known lovers of his own unmarried sisters—and even prevailed on his sisters to withdraw from the court. During his reign, the Church acquired excessive influence in political affairs. Louis evinced his weakness by insisting on going to Rome to be crowned by the Pope (816), and refusing to be satisfied with his prior coronation by his father (813). And he allowed Pope Stephen IV to be elected without his consent and approval. His promotion of strict monastic and clerical reforms by his unqualified sponsorship of the Rule of St. Benedict of Aniane for monks and that of St. Chrodegang of Metz for the secular clergy also aroused considerable opposition from factions in both of these groups.

Louis the Pious stirred up his greatest hornet's nest by an attempt to regulate the succession in a way that would contravene the established Frankish custom of dividing the realms almost equally among surviving legitimate sons. In 817, Louis sought to introduce a new principle of succession and thus preserve the unity of the empire. According to this arrangement, his eldest son Lothair would receive the imperial office in its fullness, with the younger sons—as sub-kings—ruling lesser territories (Bavaria and Aquitaine) under Lothair's direction. It was a daring innovation which might have succeeded but for two factors: Louis kept vacillating, while the beautiful young Judith of Bavaria (whom he married [819] after the death of his first wife) schemed to secure a substantial independent portion for her young son Charles the Bald. Judith became the key figure in a "pressure group" which was determined to preserve the tradition of equal division.

The problem of the succession

Meanwhile Bernard of Italy, who had been governing that area as the son and successor of Louis' brother Pepin, revolted because the Act of 817 would have put him under Lothair. When Louis came to Italy, the uprising crumbled and the rebels surrendered. The leaders, including the young Bernard, were condemned to death, but Louis commuted their punishment to torture and blinding. After Bernard died from the shock, Louis felt remorse and did public penance at Attigny (822). This episode resulted in a loss of prestige.

Owing to the persistence of his wife Judith and the growing ascendance of her party at court, Louis made a revised disposition of his realms in 829, according to which Charles the Bald was to be given Suabia and adjacent territories. The other brothers and several dissatisfied magnates revolted. They were temporarily successful (830), and Lothair assumed the title of Co-Emperor. But a reaction set in, and Louis won his two younger rebellious sons over to his side by promising to extend their territories. At the end of the storm, Louis the Pious made a new disposition of his realms, increasing the portions of the two younger brothers and depriving Lothair of his position as Co-Emperor.

A fresh revolt of his sons in 833 forced Louis to abdicate and do humiliating public penance at Compiègne (833). Lothair again became Emperor and increased the shares of Louis the German and Pepin as a reward for their support. By the close of the year, however, a shift in favor of Louis the Pious restored him to power. Lothair's holdings were restricted to Italy. After a plot of Louis the German to initiate a new rebellion was disclosed, his father made a new disposition, greatly decreasing the portion alloted to Louis the German and proportionately increasing that of Charles the Bald (838). On the death of his son Pepin of Aquitaine in 838, Louis the Pious made yet another disposition, leaving only Bavaria to Louis the German, and dividing the remainder of Frankland between Charles and Lothair. Louis the German rose in revolt, and his father died while campaigning against him (840).

The War of the Three Brothers (840–843)

Following the death of Louis the Pious, Lothair tried to return to the arrangement of 817. He assumed supreme control and sought to relegate his brothers into subordinate positions. Much of Lothair's support came from the higher clergy and the magnates of the middle area. But his heavy-handed attempt served to weld his two younger brothers together into a mutual alliance. Most of their support came from the territories they already governed in eastern and western Frankland (Germany and France). The opposing armies met in a furious and bloody battle near Fontenay in central France (841). The outcome was indecisive. A contemporary poet, Angilbert mourned the unhappy fray:

> *Hell laughed at broken trust, brother from brother torn,*
> *And war cried out upon the fearful battle fray;*
> *And brother brother killed, and kindred slew their kin,*
> *And fathers to their sons no mercy dared to pay. . . .*
> *The peasants called it Fontenay, where fountains play,*
> *Fountains of blood that brought the ruin of the Franks,*
> *And on these fields and woods and marshlands horror stayed.*

Since the chief danger for Charles and Louis lay in the possibility that one of them might be lured from the alliance by liberal concessions from Lothair, the two, together with their followers, met in the following year at Strasbourg. In the famous Strasbourg Oaths (842), they vowed to make common cause against Lothair until their purposes were effected. In order that the followers of the brothers might understand the oath in

Disintegration and the Advent of Feudalism

each case, Louis the German swore in Old French and Charles the Bald in Old German. The oaths of the two brothers, in English translation read: *For the love of God and for the sake of our Christian peoples as well as ourselves, I promise that from this day forward, as God shall give me wisdom and strength, I will treat this my brother as a brother should be treated, provided that he does likewise with me. And I will not voluntarily enter into any dealings with Lothair which might injure this my brother.*

The Old French sworn by Louis the German read: *Pro Deo amur et pro christian poblo et nostro commun salvament, dist di in avant, in quant Deus savir et podir me dunat, si salvaraeio cist meon fradre Karlo et in adiudha et in cadhuna cosa, si cum om per dreit son fradra salvar dist, in o quid il mi altresi fazet; et ab Ludher nul plaid numquam prindrai, qui meon vol cist meon fradre Karle in damno sit.*

The Old German sworn by Charles the Bald read: *In Godes minna ind in this christianes folches ind unser bedhero gealtnissi, fon thesemo dage frammordes, so fram so mir Got gewizci indi mahd furgibit, so haldih tesan minan bruodher, soso man mit rehtu sinan bruodher scal, in thiu, thaz er mig sosoma duo, indi mit Ludheren in nohheiniu thing gegango the minan willon imo ce scadhen werhen.*

The followers of Charles and Louis then took, in their own respective languages, confirmatory oaths whereby they agreed to withdraw their support from their leader if the latter should fail to keep his solemn oath to his brother. The English translation of the oath taken in Old French by the followers of Charles reads: *If Louis shall observe the oath which he has sworn to his brother Charles, but Charles our lord, on his side, should be untrue to his oath, and we are unable to hold him to it, neither we nor any whom we can deter, shall give him any support.* The followers of Louis took a like oath in Old German.

The Treaty of Verdun (843) and the "System of Concord"

The Strasbourg Oaths held, and neither of the two younger brothers was lured from his alliance. As the combined armies of Louis and Charles advanced to meet the diminished forces of Lothair the following year, the elder brother realized that he had insufficient support for victory, and sent emissaries to make overtures for peace. After a preliminary truce, representatives of both sides agreed to terms of peace arranged at Verdun, which were then accepted by the three brothers. According to the famous Treaty of Verdun (843), Frankland was divided into three parts: central, western, and eastern. Each of the brothers was to be sovereign and independent in his own portion, but Lothair was to retain the title of Emperor with a certain pre-eminence. The Middle portion (which was Lothair's) included most of the Rhineland and Rhône-Saoneland, as well as Italy. It was roughly bounded on the west by the Scheldt, Rhône, and Saone Rivers; and on the east by the Aar and Rhine Rivers and the Alps, but it bulged eastward along the North Sea to include Frisia. The territory to the west (West Frankland or France) went to Charles the Bald; that to the east (East Frankland or Germany) went to Louis the German.

The Treaty of Verdun was a "continental divide" in history. It formally sanctioned the concept of multiple sovereignties and the existence of multiple independent states within the territories of the old Western Roman and Carolingian Empires. As Deacon Florus of Lyons summed it:

> *Earlier there was but one prince and one obedient people;*
> *Now both the name and the glory of empire have perished:*
> *What was a united kingdom has been shamefully divided:*
> *Instead of a king with a kingdom we have kinglets with*
> *fragments three.*

One consequence of the Treaty of Verdun was continuous rivalry between France and Germany over the Middle portion, which included the Rhineland, the Rhône-Saoneland, and Italy.

For some time after Verdun, the brothers tried a "System of Concord" whereby they met frequently and sought to decide upon common policies. They held conferences in 844, 847, 849, and 851; but the system soon broke down owing to their divergent interests and natural rivalries. After the death of Lothair in 855, Louis the German and Charles the Bald became bitter contestants for the middle portion and the imperial title. As early as 870, the Treaty of Verdun was modified by the Treaty of Mersen, which divided the northern part of the middle portion between them.

Middle Frankland after Verdun

As a result of the Treaty of Verdun, Lothair possessed the richer and slightly larger part, with the title of "Emperor." Included in his portion was a liberal share of the old Carolingian fisc (estates), whose earliest home and greatest holdings were in the Rhineland. But Lothair's share had a fateful flaw: it was precariously divided, geographically, ethnically, and linguistically; and it had strong, more homogenous neighbors on either side. It was segmented into at least three distinct parts by the Alpine mountain system and the Vosges, Ardennes, and associated mountains. Its population was composed of Mediterranean, Alpine, and Nordic peoples, and spoke various Latinic and Germanic languages.

At his death in 855—twelve years after the Treaty of Verdun—Lothair left his territory divided among his three sons, with Louis II as King of Italy, Charles, King of Burgundy in the Rhône-Saone Valley, and Lothair II, King of the Rhineland-Frisian section.

"Lotharingia"

The last-mentioned northern part of the middle portion—located in and adjacent to the Rhineland—came to be known as *Lotharingia* (the kingdom [*regnum*] of Lothair), from its first King, Lothair II (855–869). Present-day Lorraine (in German, Lothringen) is only a fragment of the old Lotharingia.

The paramount issue in the reign of Lothair II was the question of "The Divorce of Lothair." Although Lothair II had married the heiress Theutberga of French Switzerland in 855, he vastly preferred his mistress Waldrada. Theutberga failed to provide him with an heir, whereas Waldrada bore him several children. Lothair accordingly sought to have his marriage with Theutberga annulled so that he could legally marry Waldrada and secure the succession.

Besides having a weak case from the point of view of Church law,

Disintegration and the Advent of Feudalism

Lothair's efforts to obtain an annulment were strenuously opposed by his uncles, Charles the Bald and Louis the German—both of whom coveted the eventual annexation of his territories. His project was also opposed by bishops in the territories of Charles and Louis, such as the influential Archbishop Hinemar of Reims. Although a friendly council of his own Lotharingian bishops declared Lothair free to form a fresh union, Theutberga appealed to Pope Nicholas I, who reversed the verdict and compelled Lothair to take her back. While still trying to obtain his release, Lothair died in 869.

After the death of Lothair II without a legitimate heir, his uncle Charles the Bald occupied Lotharingia (869). The following year, Louis the German, who had been previously distracted, threatened Charles with war unless he gave him part of Lorraine. The resultant compromise is known as the Treaty of Mersen (870). The dividing line established by the latter roughly followed the course of the Meuse River and part of the upper Moselle to the head of the Saone valley. Most of modern Belgium went to Charles and most of modern Holland to Louis, while the rest of "Lothair's *regnum*" was divided between them. An attempt was made to divide the rich sources of revenue in the territory on an equal basis. Although the portions were of about equal value, that of Louis the German was somewhat larger.

Charles, who became King of Burgundy—the central section of the middle portion (in the Rhône-Saone Valley)—was sickly and unable to cope with the turbulence and anarchy of this troubled territory. Burgundy became a target of Moslem, Magyar, and Norse raids. In 879, the southern part of this territory was reconstituted as the separate "Kingdom of Provence" by Boso, who married a daughter of Louis II of Italy. The Kingdom of Provence included the counties of Lyons and Vienne, as well as present-day Provence. There was no lapse of the Kingdom under Charles the Fat, to whom Boso refused to submit. After Charles the Fat's deposition at Tribur (887), a separate kingdom was set up in the northern part of the Rhône-Saone valley by an adventurer named Rudolph. There were accordingly two kingdoms in the Rhône-Saone valley: that of Transjurane Burgundy (the northern part) and that of Provence-Arles (the southern part). The Kingdom of Burgundy was reunited by King Rudolph II in 933, and a few years later Otto I of Germany became its suzerain. *Burgundy and Provence*

Even more disturbed and turbulent was Italy, which was both a bone of contention between internal factions and a prey of external powers. The Italian scene was most complex. The Byzantines were entrenched in southern Italy, where they held Apulia and Calabria. In the same region there were independent city republics such as Amalfi and Gaeta, while the Moslems were in the process of trying to establish footholds in the area. The Papal States in central Italy were an autonomous factor in Italian affairs. Various dukedoms, counties, and marquisates were independent. External powers dabbling in Italian politics were numerous. The history of the Frankish kingdom in northern Italy is very involved. Lothair I, made King of Italy by his father in 817, ruled there for four *Italy* decades. He insisted on his right to approve Papal elections and on his lordship over the Papal States. Much of his attention was devoted to defending Italy against the Moslems. Louis II (855–875) succeeded his father as both King and Emperor, although his power was limited to Italy. Even here his authority was restricted, and much of his reign was devoted to fighting internal and external enemies, including the Moslems. After his death Italy became a bone of contention between rival Italian parties and powerful lords, such as the Dukes of Spoleto and Tuscany and the Marquises of Friuli and Ivrea. The neighboring kings of West Frankland, East Frankland, Transjurane Burgundy, and Provence intervened in Italian affairs, as did the Dukes of Suabia and Bavaria. The papacy likewise took part in the struggles. The mountainous terrain and segmented topography of Italy were conducive to the growing autonomy of local counts, dukes, marquises, bishops, and city-states. Charles the Bald invaded Italy in 875, and became Emperor until his death in 877. Charles the Fat was Emperor from 881 to 887. Thereafter, rival kings usually competed with each other in Italy, until German dominance began when Otto I of Germany obtained control in 951.

West Frankland or France after Verdun (to 884)

West Frankland or France was ruled for three and a half decades by Charles the Bald (840–877), an energetic, adaptable, well-educated king, who attracted several noted scholars such as John Scotus Erigena to his court.

Charles the Bald coveted Lotharingia, which he occupied on the death of Lothair II (869), but which he reluctantly shared with Louis the German by the Treaty of Mersen (870). Charles also aspired to the imperial crown, which he obtained after his invasion of Italy in 875. But he was unable to curb the growing incursions of the Northmen into France, and eventually paid tribute to them (845 ff.). As a means of fending off the Viking threat, Charles issued the Edict (Capitulary) of Mersen jointly with his brothers in 847. This called on every free man in the kingdom to choose a lord: either the King or some other lord. His Edict of Quiersy (or Kiersy), issued in 877 on the eve of his departure on a second expedition to Italy guaranteed that fiefs and offices should be hereditary in the families of those going on the expedition. Both edicts explicitly endorsed basic elements of feudalism. French possession of Italy and of the imperial crown was ephemeral, both being soon lost during the brief reigns of Charles' sons, Louis the Stammerer (877–879) and Carloman (877–884).

East Frankland or Germany and temporary reunification

The least developed and least populous—as well as the most exposed of the three portions of Frankland—was East Frankland, but it was this portion which was destined to be the first to become strong and united. The assertive, determined, ambitious Louis the German (843–876), who had repeatedly defied his father, invaded the kingdom of Charles the Bald in 858, while the latter was in Aquitaine fighting the Northmen. But he was forced to retreat on Charles' return. However, by threat of war he compelled Charles to relinquish over half of Lotharingia in the Treaty of Mersen (870). Louis' dream of empire in Italy was shattered by his illness and death. His will divided his realms among his three sons.

Disintegration and the Advent of Feudalism

Within six years, Charles the Fat (876–887), who had originally received Swabia, had succeeded to the portions of his two brothers.

Charles the Fat obtained Italy as well as the imperial crown (881), became sole ruler of Germany (882), and was accepted by the West Franks as their ruler (884). The unity of the Carolingian Empire was apparently restored. But the good luck of Charles—who had become corpulent, self-indulgent, dipsomaniac, and indecisive—soon ended. Despite attacks from all sides, Charles remained inactive. Eventually, he temporarily shook off his lethargy and brought an army to the vicinity of Paris, which was being besieged by thousands of Northmen. But instead of attacking the Northmen, he bought them off by paying them tribute and giving them permission to pillage Burgundy, which had refused to submit to his authority. This was too much for the magnates, who gathered at Tribur late in 887 and deposed the dissolute Charles. He died the following year (888).

Following the deposition of Charles the Fat (887), the magnates in each of the main sections of Frankland elected their own king. As the chronicler Regino of Prum says: *Then the kingdoms which had been under his sway broke off in fragments, and dissolved the bonds that had united them; and instead of acknowledging their lawful lord, each sought to create a king sprung from its own stock, which became a source of long wars.* . . . Six kingdoms emerged. The East Franks elected Arnulf, Duke of Carinthia, an illegitimate son of a brother of Charles the Fat. Arnulf (888–899), who was accorded a certain seniority by the other kings, enjoyed the dubious, ephemeral honor of being crowned Emperor toward the end of his life. The West Franks elected Duke Eudes (Odo) of Francia, the hero of the defense of Paris. In Italy, Berengar, Marquess of Friuli, and Hugh, Duke of Spoleto, vied for the crown. In the Kingdom of Arles (Provence), Louis of Provence, the son of Boso, continued to rule. Duke Rudolph was accepted as King of Transjurane, (Upper) Burgundy. Rudolph also unsuccessfully claimed the old kingdom of Lotharingia, which went, however, as a separate kingdom to Zwentibold, the son of Emperor Arnulf, in 895.

Definitive disintegration after 887

AMONG the best studies of the general history of the Later Carolingian period are accounts found in *The Cambridge Medieval History*, Vol. III, as well as sections in general works on the Early Middle Ages such as those by CHRISTOPHER DAWSON and MARGARET DEANSLEY. Special aspects of the disintegration of the Carolingian Empire are treated by JAMES W. THOMPSON in his *The Dissolution of the Carolingian Fisc* . . . (Berkeley: U. of Calif., 1935), and his *The Decline of the Missi Dominici in Frankish Gaul* (Chicago: U. of Chicago, 1903), as well as by CHARLES E. ODEGAARD, *Vassi and Fideles in the Carolingian Empire* (Cambridge: Harvard U.P., 1945).

While the Later Carolingian Empire has not attracted the attention of many historians, the contrary has been the case with the Vikings. Good general histories of the Vikings and their expansion are THOMAS D. KENDRICK, *History of the Vikings* (New York: Scribners, 1930); P. H. SAWYER, *The Age of the Vikings* (London: E. Arnold &

References for Chapter 9

Co., 1962); J. BRONDSTED, *The Vikings* (Baltimore, Md.: Penguin, 1970); and GABRIEL TURVILLE-PETRE, *The Heroic Age of Scandinavia* (London: Hutchinson, 1951). Fine studies of Viking civilization are MARY W. WILLIAMS, *Social Scandinavia in the Viking Age* (New York: Macmillan, 1920), and AXEL OLRIK, *Viking Civilization*, rev. (New York: Scribners, 1889). Also useful are the histories of particular Scandinavian countries, such as CARL HALLENDORFF and A. SCHUCK, *History of Sweden* (Stockholm: Fritze, 1929); KNUT GJERSET, *History of the Norwegian People*, 2 vols. (New York: Macmillan, 1915), Vol. I; and JOHN H. BIRCH, *Denmark in History* (London: Murray, 1938). For adventuresome and swashbuckling Scandinavian Eddas and Sagas, see BERTHA S. PHILLPOTTS, *Edda and Saga* (London: Butterworth, 1932); WILLIAM A. CRAIGIE, *The Icelandic Sagas* (Cambridge: Cambridge U.P. 1930); *The Prose Edda* and *The Poetic Edda*, tr. Henry A. Bellows (New York: American-Scandinavian Foundation, 1916 and 1923); as well as JOHN A. MCCULLOCH, *The Mythology of All Races . . .*, Vol. II. *Eddic* (Boston: MARSHALL JONES, 1930); and the particular Sagas such as the Njalas, Harolds, Eyils, Sturlagas, and Magnus Sagas, in various editions and translations. The history of the Northmen is further projected by CHARLES H. HASKINS, *The Normans in European History* (Boston: Houghton, 1915).

Little is available in English on the Magyars save CARLILE A. MACARTNEY, *The Magyars in the Ninth Century* (Cambridge: Cambridge U.P., 1930); and chapters in LOUIS P. LEGER, *A History of Austria Hungary*, tr. (New York: Putnam, 1889) and in ALEXANDER W. LEEPER, *A History of Medieval Austria* (New York: Oxford University, 1941).

❲ FEUDALISM: THE MEDIEVAL COMPROMISE.
Chapter 10.

EUDALISM prevailed in Western Europe following the break-up of the Carolingian Empire, and was at its zenith from the ninth to the thirteenth centuries. Feudalism was both long in gestation and slow in passing, and many of its incidental features persisted well into modern times. Since its main determinant was custom, both its precise form and its chronology varied from state to state; in Eastern Europe its coming and going were much later than in the West. In feudal states, governmental and military powers and responsibilities were intertwined with landholding, and the sovereignty today reserved to central governments was shared by local governments. The political and military superstructure of feudalism was sustained by an agrarian economic substructure of manorialism, with a sharp distinction between the landed aristocracy and the dependent agricultural serfs.

Feudalism: The Medieval Compromise

ORIGINS AND NATURE OF THE FEUDAL "SYSTEM."
Section 28

> Since the King has nothing left except his title and crown, and is incapable of defending his bishops and other subjects against threatening dangers, we see all of them committing themselves with joined hands to the service of the great. [A German prelate concerning the increase of vassalage in the Kingdom of Burgundy (about 1016).]

THE TERM *feudalism* refers to the system of conditional relationships and contingent ownership that prevailed during the Middle Ages. The word derives from *fieu* or *feu*, originally meaning cattle or wealth, and finally denoting real property. In feudal states, governmental and military responsibilities were associated with landholding by means of sworn contracts in a way disintegrative of monarchical sovereignty. While primarily political and military, feudalism had economic and social aspects. Feudalism with its vassalage must be distinguished from *manorialism* with its serfdom, since the former was on a higher plane and governed by a different set of rules than the latter. Feudalism was a compromise between Roman and Germanic political institutions. While feudal elements came and went gradually, feudalism as such existed only when *all* its essential elements were simultaneously present.

Although it differed in details from place to place, all feudalism did have certain essential features, including vassalage, fief-holding, military obligations, governmental responsibilities, and divided sovereignty.

1. Vassalage was a contractual relationship whereby a dependent (the *vassal*) swore to render to an overlord certain services that were considered "honorable" and were ordinarily military and governmental.

2. Fiefs were revenue-producing properties given to vassals to hold on condition of the faithful performance of feudal duties.

3. Military and governmental services were the main duties required of vassals as a condition for holding their fiefs.

4. Divided sovereignty resulted from the fact that many feudal vassals enjoyed certain privileges and prerogatives, such as the right of waging war, ordinarily reserved to sovereign governments.

Factors promoting feudalism

The components of feudalism gradually fell into place in the period from the Later Roman Empire on, until by the ninth century the full system prevailed in Western Europe, whence it spread to other parts of Europe. The system resulted from internal and external pressures which brought about transition to a more localized form of government and defense, without a complete loss of unity. Feudalism entailed a partial disintegration, without loss of the monarchical nucleus; many functions and powers previously reserved to the central government alone were now allocated to local administrations.

Causes of the weakening of the central government have been outlined in discussing the disintegration of the Carolingian Empire. They included the decline of the economy to a more agrarian subsistence level; the lapse of regular taxation and lack of adequate monetary income by the central government; use of land as the principal form of compensation for military and governmental services; and "modernization" of the army, which called for larger tracts of land to support mounted warriors. Further factors included a decline of monarchical power, owing to "a loss of Carolingian stamina; the "fatal Frankish custom" of dividing political legacies; and the progressive relinquishment of royal estates to obtain military and political supporters. Whereas with the earlier Carolingians, oaths, vassalage, and fiefs had been a means of strengthening the monarchy, these became elements of weakness under the later Carolingians.

Meanwhile the local aristocracy became more powerful and independent, not only because of the weakening of the monarchy, but also because their fiefs and offices became permanent and hereditary; their powers more extensive and uncontested; their immunities (legitimate and assumed) more numerous; their responsibilities for defense and government more extensive; their military strength more formidable; their appetite for power and territory more unrestrained. A leading factor promoting the rise of feudalism was the necessity of dealing with numerous scattered external unpredictable attacks, such as those of the Northmen, requiring the establishment of independent means of local defense. This need was met by the rise of local lords with their own strongholds or castles and bands of armed retainers or vassals. But a soldiery and strongholds sufficient to resist external foes could often defy overlords and monarchs as well, while added obligations and self-reliance expedited greater independence.

Origins of vassalage and dependent landholding

The term *vassal* derives from Celtic *gwas*—boy or dependent follower. At first, the term referred to a non-noble retainer, such as one owing menial services; but eventually it came to apply to upper-class aristocrats sworn to provide "honorable" military and/or governmental services. Other terms sometimes used for such persons included *fideles*—faithful ones; *homines*—men; *antrustiones*—trusted ones; *leudes*—people; and *gesiths* or *gasindi*—companions. The feudal vassal was thus a sworn supporter who owed "honorable" services to his lord. The *fief* (from *fieu* or *feu* property) was an income-producing grant, usually consisting of land, given to a vassal on condition that he provide certain services. The fief was the *quid pro quo* or compensation for military and other services in the feudal system.

The Germanic *comitatus* is recognized as the chief prototype of vassalage. Writing in the first century of the Christian era, Tacitus described the practice whereby Germanic warriors swore allegiance to a chief, thus creating a close bond of interdependence. Members of the *comitatus* had to be prepared to fight to the death alongside their chief. In the later Roman Empire, the influence of the *comitatus* penetrated the Roman army, whereof the Germans eventually became a leading component. On entering Roman military service, German soldiers often took oaths directly to their commanders, since this was for them a more familiar and binding relationship. Generals also often had special troops such as members of their bodyguard, who were sworn to uphold and protect them, and were known as *bucellarii* in that they received better

Feudalism: The Medieval Compromise

food, including a special type of biscuit (*bucella*). Another Roman prototype of vassalage was the relation between "patron" and "client," whereby great men or "patrons,"—like members of the senatorial class—had dependent followers or "clients," who often accompanied them and performed special services for them.

Among the early Germans, the practice of giving and holding extensive lands conditionally does not seem to have been widespread. On the other hand, it was quite common among the Romans to hold lands conditionally on all social levels. Such was the case with leaseholds and rentals, as well as with mortgages. Among the Romans, land held on condition of certain services was often known as a *precarium*, in that it had supposedly been granted in answer to prayers (*preces*). It was also known as a *beneficium*—a "gracious gift" or "benefit." Sometimes a weaker person turned over his property to a stronger one for purposes of security or to avoid taxes, and received it back in a form of conditional tenure (*precarium*).

In the Germanic Kingdoms, especially Frankland

In the early Germanic kingdoms, kings and overlords maintained bands of sworn retainers. In the case of the Merovingian kings, these were known as *antrustiones* or "trusted ones," and they constituted a royal bodyguard and enjoyed a triple *wergeld*. In the case of Frankish lords, they were known as *leudes* or "people" in the sense of followers. Among the Anglo-Saxons, they were known as *gesiths* or "companions," and in Italy as *gasindi*, a Latinized form of the German word.

Early Germanic kings like the Merovingians sometimes conferred lands in return for special services. Especially common were gifts of land known as "benefices" (*beneficia*) made to churches and monasteries to support their religious ministrations.

With the great Carolingians

The Carolingians, who rose to power with the help of their extensive estates and large bands of armed retainers, used their position and office to multiply both. Since they came from the more Germanic part of Frankland, they were more inclined to put great confidence in oaths as ensuring the support of their followers. Their sworn supporters were known as *vassi* and *fideles*. At first, the term *vassi* was used only for persons who were on the lower rungs of the social scale; but eventually it lost its stigma. That the position of vassal was no longer demeaning was shown when the Duke of Bavaria, Tassilo, became the vassal of Pepin III in 757.

In order to obtain mounted military supporters, the Carolingians—beginning with Charles Martel—confiscated and redistributed many Church holdings as *beneficia* or *precaria verbo regis*—benefices or conditional holdings on command of the king. Whereas Charles Martel did this without compensation to the Church, Pepin III required that the new holders of former Church lands pay a small rent to the Church, as well as render military and governmental services for the monarch. Useful ownership was enjoyed by the holder on condition of the fulfilment of these obligations. At first, such grants were known as *beneficia*; but later they were called ordinarily *fiefs*, and the term *benefice* came to be reserved for grants to the Church and churchmen.

Charles Martel greatly increased the number of his sworn supporters because he needed cavalry forces to more effectively attack and pursue mounted enemies such as the Moslems. Pepin III and Charlemagne continued this policy, while the latter also required that all men of consequence in his realms take an oath of fealty to himself.

Full feudalism (ninth century ff.)

Under the later Carolingians (c. 840 ff.), full feudalism finally evolved. Vassalage associated with fief-holding became widespread in much of Frankland, especially in the "feudal heartland" between the Rhine and the Loire rivers. The number of vassals and fiefs was greatly increased by the later Carolingians to obtain mounted supporters for their internal contests, and to defend their territories against foreign invaders. The Capitulary of Mersen (847) issued jointly by Charles the Bald and his two brothers declared: "We will that every free man in our kingdom choose a lord: either ourself or one of our *fideles*." A major part of the old Carolingian crown lands or "fisc" was given away as fiefs in order to provide support for a growing number of royal vassals.

Meanwhile "honors" or public offices came to be assimilated to "fiefs" or grants of property. Persons entering upon such offices assumed the position of vassals, rendered homage, and took oaths of fealty to the grantor. Holders of governmental and military offices were usually recompensed by concessions of landed estates, while large landowners usually had governmental powers and responsibilities, with oaths being required in each case. Eventually, too, fiefs and offices became hereditary and were regarded as part of the holder's family patrimony. The hereditability of offices and fiefs was recognized by Charles the Bald in his Capitulary of Kiersy (877), which provided that the holdings (fiefs or offices) of a participant who died on his forthcoming campaign to Italy would remain in the party's family. Actually, members of an incumbent's family were usually well-qualified by experience and training, as well as prestige, to succeed to his office; while a holder who had made improvements in a fief had some claim to have it regarded as a part of his patrimony.

The sovereignty of the central government was further eroded by grants of "immunities," whereby the central government was precluded from administering such functions as justice and taxation in many fiefs. At the same time, there were exceptions to fief-holding. Some nobles of the upper classes held territories as "allods" or "fiefs of the sun:"—family possessions free of feudal services. Some ordinary freeman held lands as direct "freeholds." Churches and monasteries often held lands in "frankalmoin" or free almsgiving, that is, as an outright gift with no "strings" or requirements attached. Rental or "socage" tenure, as in England, was nonfeudal, and exempt from feudal obligations.

Three stages of feudalism may be distinguished: (1) the "first feudal age" (c. 850–1050) when feudalism was young and still "open" and flexible; (2) the "second feudal age" (c. 1050–1250), when the system became more rigid, elaborate, and formal; and (3) the third and final feudal age (1250 ff.), when feudalism was fading from Western Europe.

Feudalism: The Medieval Compromise

A man became a vassal by rendering homage and swearing fealty. *Homage* (from *homo*—man)—was an external act wherby a person became the *man* (dependent supporter and retainer) of another. Homage was ordinarily rendered by a statement to the effect that "I become your man," accompanied by an *inmixtio manum* wherein the subject put his hands in those of the lord. This was often followed and sealed by a ceremonial kiss (*osculum*). *Fealty* (from Latin *fidelitas*—fidelity) was sworn by taking an oath, usually on some sacred object such as a Bible or altar or reliquary, that one would be faithful to his lord. One such formula was "I will be loyal and true to you, and will bear you allegiance for the lands I hold of you, and will loyally render to you the customs and services I owe you, so help me God." This was followed by investiture with the fief.

Vassalage and Fiefs

Although the right to hold a given fief as a vassal came to be hereditary, the relationship had to be initiated by external acts in each case. Thus a son who had a right to succeed his father had to render homage and be invested with the fief before he actually obtained his inheritance.

The fief normally consisted of land, the value and extent of which were roughly proportional to the number of knights required. But a fief or "fee" could also consist in any income-bearing right or "provision," such as a concession of urban rental property, or the lucrative position of protector or advocate of an abbey or church, or an engagement to pay a stipulated sum at given intervals. Thus, a *knight's fee* could consist in payment of money as well as in a concession of income-producing land or some other form of compensation. A fief was conferred by an external act such as the handing over of a symbolic rod, branch, stalk, or sheaf, accompanied by words such as "I concede to you the fief of _____;" or "I grant you in fee _____."

In the ideally "pyramidal" feudal system a monarch gave out large territories such as counties and dukedoms to his "vassals-in-chief," who were bound to supply him with large numbers of knights; these in turn gave out considerable lands to vassals who each supplied them with several knights; and so forth, until the process reached single knights with only one manor. There was thus, ideally, a progressive "parcelling out" of lands in diminishing parcels. As an alternative, lords could, and often did, maintain knights by equipping and supporting them at their own residence. But lords usually preferred to give knights manors and let them supply their own needs, an alternative more satisfying to the knight, especially if he wanted to marry and raise a family.

Subinfeudation and liege homage

In practice, the picture of feudal relations often became much more complicated. With the passage of time and the intervention of marriage, inheritance, and purchase, as well as new grants, many vassals held several fiefs, often from different overlords. Thus the powerful Counts of Champagne in the later twelfth century held some twenty-six fiefs from nine overlords, including the King of France and the Holy Roman (German) Emperor. The question arose: to whom did a vassal owe military and other services if his overlords were fighting one another? In partial solution of this question, there arose the concept of "liege" homage, whereby—among a vassal's overlords—one was his "liege lord," to whom he owed his services before all others. Ordinarily, this was the lord from whom he held most of his land. A declaration of liege homage was often included in an oath of fealty, although sometimes more than one overlord would require such an oath of the same vassal.

Dissolution of the feudal bond

The feudal relationship could be dissolved. It could be renounced by the vassal through a formal act known as *diffidatio* or defiance, whereby he formally and publicly withdrew his homage. In such a case, the verbal declaration of annulment might be accompanied by some external gesture such as the throwing back of a stalk or sheaf (*exfestucatio*). Normally such an act required a serious cause and involved relinquishment of the fief.

An overlord, for his part, could recover possession of a fief from a vassal judged guilty of infidelity (whence "felony"), which was punishable by forfeiture, although such a judgment was to be rendered by a vassal's "peers" (equals: fellow-vassals) and not merely by the lord.

Essential obligations of vassals

As long as he kept his fief and was not released from his promises, the vassal owed his overlord both essential and incidental obligations. Besides the general (and vague) respect and submission (Bracton's *subjectio et reverentia*) owed to their lords, the essential obligations of vassals to their lords ordinarily included military and governmental services. Also implicit in vassalage was the obligation to abstain from anything that might be harmful to one's lord.

The principal *raison d'être* of feudalism was to obtain military service and the fief was conceded as a means of support to a vassal who agreed to provide such. Fief-holders were obliged to appear for military service with their own equipment and supplies, and to maintain themselves in the field at their own expense. The obligation of defensive military service had no limitations: the vassal had to help defend his lord and the latter's property whenever and as long as an enemy chose to attack. This was reasonable, since whatever endangered the lord and his holdings usually also jeopardized the lord's vassal and his holdings. The obligation of offensive military service—as when one's lord attacked another lord—came to have certain limitations established by custom. Thus, the time for which a vassal was bound to serve in a year was ordinarily limited to forty days. After this period, a vassal could agree or disagree to an extension of the service, and he had a right to be compensated for the additional service. Ordinarily, too, vassals were not bound to extraterritorial military service, such as a crusade to the Holy Land, without their free assent. The same held true for English vassals of the Norman and Plantagenet kings with respect to overseas operations in France.

It was usually possible for vassals to obtain relief from military service by payment of *scutage* (shield-money) which compensated the lord for their absence and enabled him to hire mercenaries. Actually, commutation of military service to a money-payment came to be preferred by kings, and eventually it became a sort of tax and a leading source of royal revenue.

Feudalism: The Medieval Compromise

The governmental service owed by vassals to their lords included "suit at court" or periodic attendance at the lord's court in order (1) to participate in the administration of justice—as in cases concerning fellow-vassals; and (2) to give advice and counsel to the lord on problems such as military defense, proposed expeditions; and so forth.

Incidental obligations of vassals to their lords came to be customarily accepted in the feudal system. These included "reliefs" and "aids," as well as "hospitality." "Reliefs" were a sort of inheritance tax and expression of gratitude, to be paid on assumption of the fief. They also expedited an early conferral—which might otherwise be delayed, as the lord could profit from the revenues of the fief during a vacancy. The relief often consisted in a payment equivalent to the first year's estimated net revenue of the fief, or, in lieu of this, in something of considerable value, such as a war horse or arms.

Incidental obligations of vassals

"Aids" consisted in payments at times when it was generally considered that a loyal vassal should help his lord. They were the forebears of modern taxes. Aids were both "customary"—determined by custom; and "voluntary"—dependent upon a free decision by the vassals. Customary aids were generally due on three occasions: for the knighting of the lord's eldest son, for the marriage of the lord's eldest daughter, and for payment of ransom for the lord if he was taken prisoner. An occasional fourth customary aid that maintained in much of France, but not in Normandy and England, consisted of contributing to the lord's expenses when he went on a Crusade. In the aids for knighting and marriage, vassals obtained to some extent a *quid pro quo*, since they and their families could enjoy the festivities and entertainment connected with these events. In the ransom, a vassal could thereby obviate participation in warfare to obtain his lord's release; and he might also hold himself partly responsible for his lord's capture. For the Crusade, a contribution was again often a welcome substitute for arduous personal participation. "Voluntary aids," such as contributions towards overseas expeditions—were usually voted on by the vassals, with the majority prevailing.

The lord's right to "hospitality" from his vassal was known as the *droit de gite*. An overlord with a large retinue who stayed with a vassal for an extended period of time could literally "eat him out of house and home." Hospitality was often commuted to a modest annual payment —a welcome insurance.

The lord also had duties to his vassal. The main obligation of the lord was to provide the vassal with means of sustenance, usually in the form of a fief. This accomplished, the lord's obligations were minimal. He had to help his vassal defend his fief. Known as *mundeburium*, this defense (his *mund* or *munt*) was a sort of extension of the lord's protection of his own household.

Obligations and rights of the lord

The obligations of the lord are reflected in a Capitulary of 816, which states the reasons for which a vassal may be released from his duties to his lord: *If anyone shall wish to leave his lord and is able to prove against him one of the following crimes, to wit: that the lord has tried to reduce him to servitude . . . has plotted against his life . . . has committed adultery with his wife . . . has willfully attacked him with a drawn sword, or . . . has failed to protect him when able to do so, then the vassal is permitted to leave his lord.*

Since the lord retained ultimate ownership of the fief, he had the right to recover possession of it under certain circumstances. He also had the right to require its proper administration and the fulfilment of associated obligations. The lord could recover the fief by forfeiture and escheat and he could control its disposal and temporarily take it over by foremarriage and wardship.

Forfeiture of a fief could occur if a vassal seriously failed to fulfil his feudal obligations, as by refusing to provide his lord with military assistance when such was clearly due. Although it could be invoked in such cases, forfeiture was not always exacted, since the lord had to have enough force available to recover the property, and he also ordinarily had to obtain the assent of his other vassals. Violations whose penalty could be forfeiture were often overlooked for practical reasons.

Escheat was more common and usually easier to implement. Escheat could occur when there was no legitimate heir or heiress to the fief—as when a direct family line died out. In such a case, the lord had a right to reappropriate the fief, although he was normally expected to confer it on someone else, rather than keep it in his direct possession.

Foremarriage was the lord's right to approve or disapprove of the proposed marriage of a female heiress. This right was based on the fact that the woman's husband would be the one who would become the lord's vassal for the fief, and that he should therefore be someone who was acceptable to the lord and considered capable of performing the required military, governmental, and managerial services.

Wardship was the lord's right to take over the administration of a fief whose rightful successor was a minor or an unmarried female. In such instances, the lord could assume the administration of the fief and retain its net income after the payment of necessary expenses, until the heir became of age or the heiress married. In the case of ecclesiastical fiefs and benefices, the lord usually had a similar right during vacancies.

THE FEUDAL STATE.
Section 29.

Every man who holds a fief in the county of Clermont has a right to administer all justice in his fief, high and low, saving the rights of the count. . . . [From the *Customs of Beauvais* by Beaumanoir (thirteenth century).]

ALTHOUGH feudal government and feudal states would seem weak today, they were well adapted to existing conditions. In difficult times, they provided the minimal essentials of government, justice, and defense. Feudal government may be considered both in general—in its common essential elements; and in particular—as it existed with regional variations.

Feudal government was a compromise between Roman and German

Feudalism: The Medieval Compromise

institutions, between unity and localism, and between the ideal and the real. While retaining the institution of the monarchy and partial political unity on a larger scale—thus preserving the framework for modern "nation-states"—feudalism greatly increased the autonomy and scope of local aristocratic government. Feudal government was primarily geared to the provision of defense and the maintenance of internal order, and it was only secondarily if at all concerned with rendering other political services. It was adapted to operating in a time of great military peril, when the needs of defense were paramount, but economic resources and governmental revenues were minimal.

Contrary to a common misconception, feudal government was not incompatible with monarchy. In fact, feudalism was, in a sense, the preserver of monarchy, since one of its aspects was the perpetuation of monarchical states. Without the monarchy, there would have been, not feudalism, but only disintegration into numerous petty states. Despite its restricted jurisdiction, monarchy remained in the feudal system and retained some of its old prestige and authority. *Feudal monarchy and its limitations*

Yet the monarchy relinquished much of its power and property in order to obtain mounted military supporters. Its greatest sacrifice was the loss of direct control over most of its subjects. In feudalism, various strata of vassals intervened between the king and the populace at large, and the monarch ordinarily had direct control only over his immediate vassals—his tenants in chief. There was a saying: "My vassal's vassals are not my vassals."

The monarch did, however, have a more direct control over the inhabitants of his own family domains, as was, for instance, the case with the early Capetians in Ile de France. Monarchs also often had a measure of direct control over churches, churchmen, towns, and townspeople, to the extent that these were considered to be outside the feudal system.

Monarchs in the feudal system shared sovereignty with their vassals, and were *suzerains* rather than *sovereigns*. Many feudal vassals enjoyed certain prerogatives ordinarily reserved to sovereign governments. The right of conducting warfare is ordinarily reserved to sovereign governments. But in medieval feudalism, vassals could wage war on one another, and engage independently in foreign wars. The right of coinage—enjoyed today only by sovereign governments—was then possessed by many princes, lords, cities, and ecclesiastical establishments. Judicial immunities often exempted the territories of vassals from the jurisdiction of royal courts, giving vassals the right of final justice. Since justice was a source of revenue as well as power, such judicial immunities were especially prized by vassals. Finally, there were other forms of immunities enjoyed by many vassals, such as exemptions from new financial levies without their consent. Ordinarily, no involuntary new taxes could be imposed upon feudal vassals without their consent, and monarchs were excluded from collecting taxes from the subjects of their vassals.

Despite such limitations, feudal monarchs had substantial powers and prerogatives. They raised and led "national" armies and summoned and presided over "national" councils. They had a right to various feudal *Powers of feudal monarchs* services and dues from their vassals, such as governmental and military services, reliefs and aids, hospitality, and so forth. While weaker monarchs were often unable to exact fulfilment of these obligations from their greater vassals, stronger ones frequently secured them in due course. Feudal monarchs also had the right to recover direct possession of fiefs under certain circumstances, as in cases of forfeit and escheat. Feudal monarchs were the ultimate protectors of their realms as the accepted leaders for resistance to external enemies. Even at the lowest point of their fortunes, French kings successfully roused and led their vassals to repel German invasions. Feudal monarchs were the ultimate guardians of peace and order in their realms, with a recognized right to enforce the "king's peace." And they were the natural overlords and protectors of non-feudal elements in society, such as churches and monasteries, priests and monks, towns and townspeople, foreigners, and traders. Feudal monarchs continued to enjoy honor and prestige as heirs of proud Roman, Merovingian, and Carolingian monarchical traditions, and successors to Charlemagne, Clovis, and Caesar Augustus. Their persons were deemed sacred and their office divinely endorsed, since they were anointed and consecrated by the Church. They were also protected by solemn oaths sworn by their vassals.

Feudal monarchs had a large and indeterminate reserve of potential rights and powers that they could invoke. They could call into play various powers exercised (or presumed to have been exercised) by their Carolingian, Merovingian, and Roman predecessors. They could extend the concept of the "king's peace," and the "royal" or "national interest," to include an expanding variety of cases in the immediate jurisdiction of their courts. And they could exercise direct jurisdiction over inhabitants outside the feudal system proper. They could challenge doubtful exemptions, immunities, and special jurisdictions, and require that they be verified. Finally, they could employ feudal features and incidents to eventually establish a nonfeudal system. Thus they could convert feudal obligations into taxes, as did the Plantagenets; and they could retain confiscated fiefs in their direct possession, as did the Capetians. Once the balance of power began to tilt in favor of a feudal monarch, "all things were possible."

Feudal central government

Feudal central government was usually loosely organized. The very limited services of feudal government did not require a bureaucracy, while absence of taxation and lack of adequate income did not readily permit it. A common feature of fully feudal government was a lack of formal departments and of precisely delineated distinctions between the responsibilities of various officials. Also missing was a clear distinction between the familial and public aspects of royal government and finance. The excessive dependence on the person of the monarch in feudal government is exemplified by contrasts between the authority of successive kings, as in England. The extent of utilization of actual and potential royal powers depended chiefly upon the monarch.

Next to the monarch, the chief authority in feudal government was the Great Council, consisting of the direct vassals of the monarch: the great

Feudalism: The Medieval Compromise

lords, lay and ecclesiastical. The Great Council recognized new kings, deciding cases of doubtful or disputed succession; advised the king; and judged certain important cases, such as those involving magnates. Between meetings of the Great Council, a more compact body of select councillors and leading royal officials known as the smaller *Curia Regis* often carried on many of the ordinary functions of the Great Council such as those of *consilium* (advice) and *judicium* (judgment).

Feudal kings had various officials—usually with somewhat indefinite responsibilities and overlapping functions. A sort of substitute-king or prime minister—known variously as vicar, mayor, regent, or justiciar—was common. Not infrequently, the chancellor—who had charge of the drafting of important documents and the keeping of royal records—became the most powerful official. He was usually a cleric (whence "clerk"), since he had to know how to read and write, and must attend to the details of office work. A marshal or constable was often in charge of the royal army during the absence of the king, and second in command in the king's presence. There was also an official in charge of the royal finances who might be known as the chamberlain (i.e., keeper of the lord's chamber, where the royal treasure was often kept).

Feudal kings administered a limited amount of justice, both personally and through representatives. Often, certain royal officials who were better suited for this work would be deputized to act in the place of the king rendering justice, and would tend to become regular judges. Support of the royal government came mainly from royal domains (direct family political holdings) and estates, incidents of feudalism, commutation of feudal dues, and income associated with patronage of churches and monasteries.

Local government had numerous weighty responsibilities in the feudal system. The chief focal point of local government varied, being sometimes on the ducal or marquisate level, but more often on that of the county or shire. In addition to administrative duties, local officials such as counts had military, judicial, and police powers. They had their own vassals, and made war on one another, as well as sometimes against their monarch. Not infrequently, great lords became virtually independent, as did the Dukes of Normandy, Aquitaine, and Burgundy in France, and those of Saxony, Suabia, and Bavaria in Germany. Sometimes they even became kings, as did the Dukes of Bohemia and Francia (Ile de France), and the Counts of Castile, Aragon, and Oporto.

Local government: Law and justice

Local feudal law was a matter of custom, which varied from place to place, although it tended to have some common features. One typical feature was an emphasis upon long-continued possession or occupation in the determination of property rights; another was widespread use of fines as forms of punishment. During the High Middle Ages, and especially in the thirteenth century, some local forms of feudal law were gathered and codified into collections or "customaries," such as those of Normandy and Beauvais. Feudal justice was strongly influenced by Germanic customs. Thus, at least among the upper classes, an accused was judged by his fellows or *peers*, with an overlord such as the king presiding. Liberal

Feudal states

use was made of oaths and co-swearing and ordeals and duels, all of which invoked the "judgment of God."

Feudalism first developed in northern France and far western Germany, whence it spread to other parts of Europe and the Near East, with various local differences. France was the most feudal state in Europe. An early home of feudalism was the area between the Loire and the Rhine, where the Carolingians held their most extensive estates. Although feudalism soon spread over most of France, it remained stronger in the north. Up to the twelfth century, the kings of France rarely exercised their authority outside the royal domains except to a very limited extent. The independence of the great lords in feudal France is exemplified by the virtual autonomy of the Counts of Flanders and the Dukes of Normandy.

Although features of feudalism existed in Anglo-Saxon England prior to the Norman Conquest, full-fledged feudalism was not present until the Normans brought it from France. Norman feudalism as established by William I was a special centralized form, which contributed to the strength of the monarchy rather than detracted from it.

In the German empire, feudalism developed later than in France. During the Investiture contest and the Guelph–Hohenstaufen struggle in the High Middle Ages, German monarchs began to experiment with elements of feudalism. Thus Frederick I, Barbarossa, declared the dukedoms of Saxony and Bavaria of Henry the Lion forfeit, and agreed to redistribute them to his cooperating followers as fiefs of lesser extent. Frederick also contributed to the establishment of a feudal pyramid in Germany by recognizing his tenants-in-chief as *Reichsfürsten* or "Prince of the Reich," directly subject to himself, with extensive privileges and immunities. Although German feudalism came too late to save a monarchy distracted by the delusion of empire, it was extensively utilized by the princes, who eventually became the real power in medieval Germany.

Introduced into northern Italy by the later Carolingians, feudalism was continued there by subsequent German overlords, but was limited by the power of the Italian towns and the Church. Introduced into southern Italy and Sicily in the eleventh century by Norman conquerors, feudalism was used there, as in England, to strengthen the crown.

Governments in the emerging Christian states in the Iberian peninsula, and in the states of the Crusaders, were strongly influenced by French example. Many French knights participated in the Spanish "Reconquest," and many married into Spanish families. The original Portuguese royal house was partly French. In both Spain and Portugal, feudalism was calculated to strengthen the monarchy, and was moderated by the presence of many urban and other exceptions.

The early Crusaders in the Near East were mainly French knights with a strong conviction of their basic equality, especially in the crusading context, at a time when feudalism was at its height in France. Consequently, the Crusader states established in the Near East were intensely feudal. The supreme power in the Latin Kingdom of Jerusalem resided in the *Haute Cour* or High Court, a feudal Great Council composed of the great barons of the kingdom. The barons and other elements such as the

Feudalism: The Medieval Compromise

Military Orders retained extensive privileges and autonomy in their fiefs, while the principalities of Antioch, Edessa, and Tripoli were independent in all but name.

Feudalism in other states, such as those in Central Europe and the Balkans and Scandinavia, was usually only partial and modified. In some areas feudalism came late and lingered longer, without fulfilling all the conditions of classic feudalism, as was the case with Byzantine feudalism and Russian feudalism.

FEUDAL LIFE.
Section 30.

> A knight there was, and he a worthy man,
> Who from the moment that he first began
> To ride about the world, loved chivalry,
> Truth, honor, freedom, and all courtesy.
> [Chaucer's description of the "Knight" in his *Canterbury Tales*.]

THE FEUDAL aristocracy was essentially a military caste, living in fortifications, with an obligation to fight on horseback, and with even their recreations having a martial flavor. This select group of fighters traced its origins to neither a German nor a Roman aristocracy, and owed its position to neither birth nor wealth. It developed rather as a *de facto* class of mounted warriors, as its names in several languages—e.g., French *chevalier*, Spanish *caballero*, and German *Ritter*, all meaning "horseman"—indicate. Generally speaking, with few exceptions, only knights held fiefs and for these holdings their primary obligation was military. The known pedigrees of aristocratic feudal families are remarkably short. For a considerable time, the ranks of the feudal aristocracy were open to enterprising young men of whatever origin who were willing and able to assume mounted military obligations. It was not until the twelfth to thirteenth centuries that the knighting of persons of nonaristocratic birth came to be exceptional and was reserved to kings and great lords. Legislation to this effect was issued by Roger II of Sicily in 1140, Frederick I (Barbarossa) in 1152, and James I of Aragon in 1234.

The feudal aristocracy

At its height, the feudal aristocracy performed a necessary, honorable, difficult and dangerous function in society: that of armed defense, as well as government and management; and its recompense may not have been far out of line with its contribution.

There was a tendency for the feudal aristocracy to develop certain occupational characteristics. Among these were a roughness and readiness, a fortitude bordering on rashness and fatalism, a strong pride, and a proneness to anger and violence, as well as a wide contrast of moods. The feudal aristocracy also usually had a contempt for manual labor and business activities, other than the operation of landed property, frequently with a financial recklessness compounded by liberality.

Despite a theoretical parity among knights, there were marked gradations in aristocratic feudal society. At the top were the great lords or "mag-

Gradations in (continued)

feudal society

nates," such as dukes, earls, marquises, and counts; in between were lesser barons such as viscounts, castellans, and lords of several manors; while near the bottom were the lords of a single manor, and knights without fiefs, who were maintained in the household of their lord. *Sergeants* (Fr.) or *ministeriales* (L.) were a semiaristocratic, semiservile class. They owed, not military services, but the practice of their trades or crafts or professions, or the management of property, or governmental services. They came to be common in the civil service of monarchs, who often preferred them to members of the aristocracy.

Living conditions of the aristocracy

The living conditions of the feudal aristocracy, which were rough and crude at the beginning of the feudal period, improved and became more luxurious by the end of the era. Still, they would be regarded by most of us today as both difficult and hazardous. But the men of that day were a hardier sort who expected less, and the nobility were much better off than most of the peasants.

Most of the feudal aristocracy lived in the country in manor houses or castles. Their dwellings on their manors were usually simple, and even their castles were built of wood until stone came into increasing use in the High Middle Ages. The focal point in both manor-houses and castles was the great hall. Here the lord held court and carried on business; here meals were served, games were played, and the assembled company were entertained by song and story. Here, too, many or all of the inhabitants slept at night on rather makeshift bedding, and the lord and his lady might have a great bed on legs, enclosed by a canopy for warmth and privacy; or they might have a bower apart for themselves. The manor-house usually had an attic which could be used for sleeping and a cellar where food and beverages were stored, as well as a separate kitchen. Baking was usually done in a building apart to avoid fires. Larger manors and castles might have more rooms. At the outset of the period, windows were usually just that: openings to admit the winds, since they were small and unglazed, although they might have shutters. Originally, chimneys were usually absent so that smoke found its own way out through an aperture in the roof. Furniture was minimal, although some of it might be imposing, such as a wardrobe which served for a closet. Dwelling places were usually improved in the twelfth to thirteenth centuries, when rooms were multiplied, chimneys with fireplaces constructed, windows glazed, and furniture increased.

Food and drink were generally plentiful for the aristocracy. They usually had large quantities of meat of various sorts, such as beef, pork, fowl, and venison, in addition to the usual cereal (grain) foods, especially bread, which was the "staff of life." Fruit and green vegetables were seasonal afterthoughts. Salt was a basic condiment and honey was used for sweetening. Spices and other forms of flavoring were increasingly employed during the High Middle Ages. Alcoholic beverages were regularly consumed in large quantities, beer being common in the north and wine in the south. The impetuosity and fiery tempers of many of the aristocracy were probably partly due to an abundance of alcoholic drinks, although the limited alcoholic content was a saving grace. Prodigious amounts of food and drink were consumed to provide fuel for prolonged physical exertions and internal warmth as a substitute for external "central heating" as well as by way of insurance. Good appetite and large thirst were regarded as healthy. In the *Chanson de Guillaume,* the wife of the lord recognizes the young Girart by such signs and tells her husband:

> By God, fair sire, he's of your line indeed,
> Who thus devours a mighty haunch of boar,
> And drinks of wine a gallon at two gulps:
> Pity the man on whom he wages war!

Although much of the clothing of the aristocracy was homespun, they had a taste for finer cloths purveyed by peddlers from the east. The common male garb was a short tunic much like a loose elongated shirt, which was worn along with various types of hose, long and short. Outer garments such as the surcoat and mantle were worn as needed. Women preferred long flowing robes, sought finer materials whenever available, were fond of jewelry, and were much concerned with their headdress. Both men and women fixed and girded their garments with ornamental brooches and belts.

The life of the feudal aristocracy was ordinarily active. When not fighting or preparing for warfare, holders of fiefs were usually concerned with the management and government of their estates. Holders of delegated authority, such as stewards and bailiffs, had to be supervised and problems solved, court had to be held and abuses corrected, quarrels had to be composed, fines collected, discipline maintained, and punishments meted out. Horses had to be bought and reared, and the young knights trained. Part of a lord's time was spent riding about, inspecting his estates, and hunting both for recreation and for food. *Aristocratic occupations and recreations*

Milady supervised the management of the household, the work of the servants, and the early upbringing of boys, as well as the general training of girls. Much had to be done to keep the household going: water had to be drawn, wood cut, fires fed, meat cut and cured and stored, grain ground, bread baked, wine pressed, beer brewed, quarters cleaned, clothes washed, meals prepared and dishes washed, etc., in a never-ending cycle; and milady must see that it was not neglected.

Much time was also given to recreations, though not so much as is often imagined. The business of keeping alive in the absence of mechanization required a great deal of time. Physical recreations were common, especially among the men. Hunting was a favorite pastime, ordinarily conducted on horseback with various weapons, as well as falcons. Horse-racing was popular and a form of cross-country polo was played. Foot-races, jumping contests, wrestling, boxing, and fencing-matches were favored by the young. Other physical activities included fishing, swimming, riding, and rowing. Eating and drinking, singing and dancing, and listening to stories and songs and music were staple entertainments. More sedentary games, such as backgammon and chess, spiced by wagers, were also played.

A popular (though less frequent) form of entertainment was the tournament, in which knights—individually and in groups—competed with one another. Tournaments were large-scale armed contests, held at appointed times and places, usually under the aegis of some great lord or king. They were a form of simulated warfare, in which knights strove to unhorse or disable one another. The prize included general acclaim, as well as the horse or arms and armor of one's defeated adversary. Often knights were seriously wounded or even killed, since there was but a slight difference between tournaments and actual wars. Accordingly, combative tournaments were eventually banned by more sagacious kings. Tournaments were very popular in the twelfth and thirteenth centuries. Some knights, such as William Marshal in his younger days during the twelfth century, went from tournament to tournament gathering laurels and booty, much as our champion golfers do today. Roger of Hoveden in the same century wrote: *A knight cannot shine in war unless he has trained for this in tournaments. He must first see his own blood flow, have his teeth cracked, and be dashed headlong to earth....*

Marriage, the family, and women

Feudal marriages were often arranged by parents with a view to fiefs and material advantages. As a result, especially after the birth of a few children, the fancy of feudal nobles frequently strayed afield. Still, the family remained a paramount institution. Fiefs were generally conceived of as familial possessions, with the incumbent only a temporary administer or trustee. Older and younger members of the family, as well as unmarried females and unemployed sons, were customarily supported by the family fief. Family solidarity was strong.

Despite their inferior position, women in the feudal system had much more freedom and independence than their contemporaries in most Eastern societies. Monogamy was the strict law of both state and Church, and as long as his wife was alive, a man, whatever his rank, could not have another legal wife. Women could usually inherit fiefs, and they could serve as administrators even for kingdoms during the absence of their husbands or the minority of their sons. In addition to managing the feudal household, women supervised the education of young and female children. Despite their physical limitations, women were respected as having immortal souls and eternal destinies, with associated God-given rights. On the other hand, women could not ordinarily rule fiefs on their own; were subject to their husbands and parents, by whom they might be physically punished; and had no acknowledged part in the direction of public affairs. There was some improvement in the position of women in the High Middle Ages with the advent of chivalry, *chansons d'amour*, romances, more polite society, and growing devotion to Christ's Mother, so that women often came to be idealized.

Knighthood

The unit in the feudal system was the "knight," the individual full-fledged member of the feudal aristocracy, capable of fighting on horseback. The term *knight* (English) derives from Anglo-Saxon *cniht* (boy, man, or retainer), and is of more secondary origin, whereas the usual continental designation meaning "horseman" (Latin *eques*, French *chevalier*, Spanish *caballero*, German *Ritter*) was more primary and expressive.

The training of a knight usually occurred between the ages of seven

Feudalism: The Medieval Compromise

and twenty-one. It was considered better that the candidate be trained in some household other than that of his parents, and preferably at the court of some great lord or king. From about the age of seven to fourteen, the candidate served as a "page" or "valet" (diminutive of *vassal*) in a feudal household. During this time the youth was initiated into court life, learned how "to get along" with others, and performed various lesser services. He was taught a certain amount of good manners, respect, and obedience, the efficient fulfilment of assigned tasks, and how to participate in feudal recreations, including oftentimes how to play a musical instrument. During the High Middle Ages, the candidate might well be taught the elements of reading, writing, and arithmetic, especially if he was destined for an important position. Meanwhile, too, the page began to acquire some of the skills he must have as a squire, such as the ability to ride horseback. A medieval saying held that it was useless to try to train a person to be a good horseman if he had not learned the art by the age of twelve.

When he reached the age of about fourteen, the candidate was promoted to the rank of *squire* (*ecuyer*—shield-bearer), in which position he remained for about seven more years. The squire served as a knight's attendant, companion, disciple, and helper. He took care of the knight's equipment, including his horse; bore his extra armor such as his shield; accompanied the knight to battle; had custody of prisoners; and often participated in the fray, and came to the aid of the knight if the latter was wounded or unhorsed. Meanwhile, the squire gradually acquired the skills of a knight, as by charging the quintain, jousting on horseback, practicing with the use of the sword, lance, and battleaxe. He learned to hunt on horseback and participated in bull-baiting, bear-baiting, and so on. Finally when he had mastered the art of fighting on horseback and was judged to be sufficiently mature, e.g., at about the age of eighteen to twenty-one, the candidate was ready to be knighted.

While the ceremony of knighting eventually became quite complex, its essential features consisted in the *accolade* followed by the *adoubement*. The accolade was a stroke with a sword and the adoubement an investiture with arms, performed by a qualified person such as a knight, and accompanied by words such as "I hereby make you a knight." The investiture part of the knight's initiation seems to have been derived from the Germanic admission of a young man into the warrior class as described by Tacitus. While at first any knight could confer knighthood, this power by the thirteenth century was usually reserved to monarchs and great lords.

Initiation into knighthood

Initiation into knighthood was gradually elaborate. In a typical sequence the candidate took a bath and donned clean clothes (e.g., white garments), confessed his sins to a priest and obtained absolution, and kept an all-night vigil in a chapel. In the morning the candidate attended Mass and received Communion. Following this, he received the accolade, being dubbed a knight by a ceremonial blow, usually administered with the flat of the sword on the nape of the neck. He was then invested with arms (and armor) in the ceremony of adoubement. After being knighted,

The knight's equipment

[a] Introduced into Western Europe about the eighth century, possibly at the time of Charles Martel.

he demonstrated his prowess by such exercises as charging the quintain, jousting, or participating in a tournament.

The knight usually rode a great charger or *destrier*, a special breed of large horse developed for battle service, which seems to have been originally imported from Byzantium. He was securely seated on his great stallion by means of an oriental-type saddle, peaked in front and back, with attached stirrups,[a] which enabled him to remain in place despite the heavy shock of headlong charges. The total average weight of his arms and armor has been estimated to have been in the neighborhood of ninety pounds. His arms regularly included a lance with which he would attempt to unhorse or incapacitate his opponent; a two-edged sword, cross-hilted, and slung in a scabbard from a belt at his waist; and a dagger for fighting at close quarters and general utility; he often also had a mace or heavy club; a battle-axe; and even a bow and arrows.

The knight's armor included a metal helmet (which at first was conical) that might have a frontal extension over the nose or perhaps a visor. The helmet and visor were gradually extended downward so that they eventually protected the knight's whole head. The knight usually carried a round or oblong shield, with metal facing on a wooden base, that became kite-shaped by the twelfth century, and was decorated with a coat of arms by the thirteenth century. The knight's body armor evolved from a leather jacket (*broigne*) with pieces (scales) of metal sewn upon it, to a coat of mail or *hauberk* which consisted of steel links welded together to form a continuous fabric. This coat of mail ordinarily reached the knees and often had elbow-length sleeves and a hood. By the Later Middle Ages, well-fixed knights frequently wore outfits of intricately joined and jointed plates of steel which covered the entire body and made the knight a sort of armed tank. Unfortunately, however, this heavy armor greatly reduced the knight's mobility and effectiveness.

Partly because the increasing armor of knights made it more difficult to identify them, coats of arms or *escutcheons* (so-called because they were often inscribed on the knight's shield) were developed. The escutcheon of the Plantagenets included leopards, and that of the Capetians fleur de lis. Coats of arms were displayed on shields and banners, and sometimes on a knight's armor and the trappings of his horse.

Castles

A typical dwelling place of the feudal aristocracy was the castle, which was ordinarily of modest size, and constructed either of wood or stone. The castle (from *castellum*: diminutive of Roman *castra*—a military camp) was simply a fortified place: a local stronghold for security and refuge. Castles multiplied in France during the civil wars and the attacks of the Northmen from the ninth to eleventh centuries; as they also did in Norman England during the eleventh to thirteenth centuries as a protection for the new French rulers; and in the Germanies during the Investiture struggle and the Guelph vs. Hohenstaufen contest.

Early castles—such as those built in France against Viking attacks—were usually squarish or rectangular wooden (e.g., log) strongholds, surrounded by palisades and sometimes ditches, much like early American frontier forts. By the eleventh century, *motte and bailey* castles, such as

Feudalism: The Medieval Compromise

those constructed by the Normans in England, were common. These consisted of a *motte* (mound) surmounted by a tower (the *keep* or *donjon*), together with a more extensive *bailey* (courtyard). The bailey was surrounded by a wall and often also a ditch (*fosse*). The bailey might contain a well for water, as well as bake ovens, stables, quarters for servants, and so forth. It was also a place for recreation and physical exercise. While earlier *motte and bailey* castles were ordinarily constructed of wood, stone came into increasing use from the later eleventh century on. With stone as a building material, the contours of castles came to be more rounded, and easier to defend.

Castle-building became more sophisticated in the twelfth to thirteenth centuries, partly as a result of the Crusades and the opportunity to observe more advanced forms of fortification in the Near East. Features of high medieval castles included concentric construction with successive lines of defense; higher and thicker stone walls with projecting towers built at intervals for better defense and observation; and a water-filled moat with a narrow bridge (often a drawbridge), leading to heavy swinging gates or a single weighted gate dependent on gravity and mechanically raised. The outer walls were often provided with parapets (walled walkways) with crenellations (notches) to accommodate and protect defenders, as well as machicolations[b] allowing them to pour boiling oil or molten metal upon attackers. Splayed slits distributed about the walls and widening to the outside gave archers a wide range of targets; while corbels or projections from the face of the walls enhanced defense capabilities. Castles often made use of natural features, such as hills, cliffs, and rivers; and sometimes they were surrounded by the water of a lake, bay, or river. When fully developed in the High Middle Ages, castles gave an advantage to defenders which continued until the advent of gunpowder artillery.

[b] Openings between walls and parapets.

To penetrate castles, various siege techniques were employed. Thus castles were bombarded with projectiles calculated to breach the walls, wound or kill defenders, and set fire to buildings. Among projectile-hurling devices, *petrariae* could throw stones weighing up to about 500 pounds; *ballistae* could throw stones and bolts weighing up to about fifty-six pounds; and ordinary catapults propelled lighter missiles, such as arrows, darts, and firebrands. Walls were often approached behind and under mantles, screens, or "tortoises" formed by joining shields for cover. Contingents of soldiers using large battering rams sometimes broke through walls and gates, or scaled them with ladders or towers on wheels. Sometimes spikes were driven into crevices to allow what resembled mountain-climbing. Access to castles was also gained by means of tunnels and mines.

Feudal warfare

Warfare was endemic in feudalism. Feudal battles consisted primarily of charges and close combat of heavy cavalry. Since feudal armies were mainly made up of temporary heterogeneous levies, feudal warfare was usually poorly organized and poorly coordinated. The degree of cooperation was heavily dependent on the personal magnetism and forcefulness of the leader. Infantry was not entirely lacking. Foot soldiers carrying weapons such as bow and arrows, javelins, clubs, swords, and daggers frequently protected the flanks of the cavalry while on the march and in camp. They often initiated battles by shooting arrows at the enemy, and they helped to break cavalry charges with their volleys.

The aim in feudal warfare was not so much to annihilate as to rout or incapacitate the enemy and capture those who could fetch a ransom. Supply was poor, and feudal armies often lived mainly off the land. Peasants and townspeople were frequently considered fair game, and enemies sometimes rivalled one another in setting fire to each other's villages and towns. Plunder was regarded as a form of recompense.

The influence of warfare pervaded the knight's life. Many of his recreations—such as hunting, horse-racing, jousting, and tournaments, and even sedentary games such as chess—had a martial bent, while the lays of minstrels recounted military exploits. Strategy and tactics improved somewhat in the High Middle Ages, partly as a result of crusading in the Near East and growing sophistication. Meanwhile the importance of non-aristocratic elements in the army—such as engineers, infantry, and archers—increased.

Chivalry

The code of the knight (Fr. *chevalier*) is known as "chivalry." In earlier times, the concept of knightly virtues was limited and corresponded to simple qualities desirable in a military vassal—loyalty, fighting skill, and courage. In time, however—because of the influence of churchmen, poets, women, and those training young men for the knightly state—the catalogue of desirable knightly qualities was expanded and elaborated.

An ideal knight was to be reverent and pious, a protector of the Church and clerics, a foe of enemies of the Church, such as heretics, and willing, if necessary, to risk his life on Crusade. He was to be a friend and defender of the defenseless, such as widows and orphans, the aged and the poor, and generous and magnanimous even to his enemies. He should not attack the unarmed without warning. He must remain true to his plighted word at all costs. Knights were also expected to be gallant and gracious with the opposite sex, with, if possible, some skill in music and song. A knightly motto ran

> *My soul to God,*
> *My heart to the ladies,*
> *My life to the King,*
> *Honor for myself.*

The code of the gentleman today is partly descended from the knightly ideal. Chaucer described the knight in his company of Canterbury pilgrims as "a perfect, gentle knight" who "loved chivalry, truth and honor, freedom and courtesy."

Courtesy and courtly love

The "courtesy" of which Chaucer wrote was an observance of approved ways of court: the decorum and "good manners" that made life endurable and pleasant in the close company of a large body of people. It included tactful consideration and respect for ladies, gentility as opposed to rudeness, humility as opposed to pride, good manners at table, and consideration for the needs and feelings of others in all social intercourse. As applied to the opposite sex, courtesy was a compensation for the otherwise subordinate position of women, and was somewhat influenced by devotion to Mary, the mother of Christ.

Concepts of "courtly love" evolved partly as a result of the increased leisure and luxury of aristocratic life in the High Middle Ages, the fertile creative imaginations of troubadours and minstrels, and possible Arabic influences. Courtly love was usually tinged with sadness, induced by the fact that the object of one's affection was generally married, unresponsive, distant, or otherwise unattainable. Courtly love helped to elevate the position of women. It is attributed by some to the fact that ladies were often those who welcomed, fed, and showed various kindnesses to visiting minstrels. It was also an obvious product of the sex drive in feudal courts, where bachelor knights were common and men often outnumbered women. The language of courtly love was often permeated with feudal terminology, with the lover frequently in the role of a humble vassal. Sham "courts of love" for the solution of knotty problems of courtly love were sometimes held, as at the court of William IX of Aquitaine in the twelfth century. Andreas Capellanus (Andrew the Chaplain) in the same century compiled a guidebook *On the Art of Courtly Love*. Among the latter's dicta were these:

1. Marriage is no excuse for not loving. 5. That which a lover takes contrary to the will of his beloved is without relish. 14. Difficulties in wooing strengthen love. 23. A person in love eats and sleeps very little.

The Church influenced feudalism, and feudalism the Church. While some Church lands were held in *frankalmoin* (by free almsgiving) as freeholds, many were held as fiefs with feudal obligations. Feudal offices were often conjoined with ecclesiastical offices, and bishops and abbots frequently had governmental responsibilities for considerable territories. In fact, secular responsibilities often preempted much of their attention to the detriment of religious concerns. Feudal overlords usually preferred ecclesiastical vassals whose chief competence was secular. When overlords assumed the final right to name or confirm Church officials, they encouraged worldliness among the higher clergy, whose attitude also affected the rank and file. *The Church and feudalism*

Among examples of how the Church influenced feudalism, we have seen how the Church elaborated the conferral of knighthood to include religious elements and expanded the code of chivalry to embrace Christian virtues. The Church imposed important restraints upon feudal warfare by the "Peace of God" and the "Truce of God." The "Peace of God" and "Truce of God" originated at regional Church councils held in southern France in the late tenth and early eleventh centuries. The "Truce of God" forbade warfare during weekends (in honor of the passion, death, and resurrection of Christ), which eventually extended from Wednesday evening to Monday morning, as well as during holy seasons such as Lent, Eastertide, Advent, and Christmastide, and on holy days of obligation. The "Peace of God" outlawed attacks on noncombatants, such as peasants, townspeople, women, children, and the aged. Both the "Peace of God" and the "Truce of God" had a salutary effect, and the "Peace" influenced modern conventions concerning warfare. *The "peace" and "truce" of God*

The passing of feudalism

Feudalism receded gradually even as it had come. Its passing occurred during the High and Later Middle Ages, although some of its elements continued into modern times, and its timetable varied and lagged in Eastern Europe. Among factors contributing to the demise of feudalism were the cessation of the invasions of the Northmen; the expansion of commerce, industry, and prosperity; the growth of a money economy; the commutation of feudal dues; the partition of fiefs for purposes of inheritance or sale; the reversion of fiefs to direct monarchical control; and changes in warfare which reduced the importance of mounted warriors.

An evaluation of feudalism

While feudalism had serious shortcomings, it also rendered valuable services. On the negative side, it resulted in numerous small, semi-independent local governments, incapable of providing many needed public services. Usually roads and bridges were inadequately maintained, while excessive tolls and duties were collected, and brigands and pirates flourished. Excessive emphasis was placed upon personal relationships, to the neglect of concepts of the community and public welfare. The components of the body politic were too loosely bound together by oaths and customs, with a minimum of firm enforceable obligations. The central government was too dependent upon voluntary cooperation and moral responsibility. Obligations were often so indeterminate as to admit of easy evasion. Confusion frequently prevailed, private wars were common, and commerce was severely handicapped.

On the positive side, feudalism was a realistic adaptation to existing circumstances: a flexible workable compromise between Germanic and Roman elements. In a time of great insecurity, it provided local defense and government, without entirely sacrificing unity. It was just flexible enough, on the one hand, and just conservative enough on the other, to surmount contemporary challenges yet allow for future reunification. Those states, such as France and England, where feudalism prevailed in the early Middle Ages emerged strong and united at the close of the Middle Ages, whereas those such as Germany and Italy where mixed political patterns maintained, emerged weak and divided. Feudalism helped to give Western Europe a military proficiency which eventually enabled it to spread its colonies and civilization over the world. It encouraged the contract theory of government, according to which government is the result of a free agreement among the governed; and it contained the principle that all government is limited. Many favorable features of feudalism, first applied only to the upper classes, were progressively extended downward to benefit all the people. Feudal great councils eventually evolved into general representative assemblies, known as Parliaments, Cortes, Estates, Diets, etc. The principle of "No taxation without representation" or "No new taxes without popular consent" is traceable back to the feudal requirement of the imposition of other than customary aids upon the aristocracy. The modern "code of the gentleman," and many of our ideals of courtesy, good manners, and fair play also derive from feudalism.

Feudalism: The Medieval Compromise

Among general works, Marc Bloch, *Feudal Society* tr. L. A. Manyon (Chicago: U. of Chicago, 1961) is an excellent, comprehensive, scholarly treatment. The similarly authoritative François L. Ganshof, *Feudalism*, tr. P. Grierson (London: Longmans, 1952) is a briefer, more concise treatment that concentrates on political, legal, and military aspects. A good brief survey by a distinguished scholar is Carl Stephenson, *Medieval Feudalism* (Ithaca, N.Y.: Cornell U.P., 1942); while a concise summary followed by illustrative selections from primary sources is Joseph R. Strayer, *Feudalism* (Princeton, N.J.: Van Nostrand, 1965). Excellent selections from original sources are compiled in David Herlihy, ed. *The History of Feudalism* (New York: Harper, 1970). A good survey of the operation of feudalism in the government, economy, and society of medieval England is Marion Gibbs, *Feudal Order . . . English Feudal Society* (New York. Abelard-Schuman, 1953). Feudalism as a structure and form of society is the subject of Emma Lederer, *Feudalism . . .* (Budapest: Akademia Kiado, 1970). A collaborative study is Frederick L. Cheyette, ed., *Lordship and Community in Medieval Europe* (New York: Holt, 1968); another is Rushton Coulbourn, *Feudalism in History* (Princeton: Princeton U.P., 1956).

A stimulating and novel approach to the subject of medieval government is Frederic L. Cheyette, ed., *Lordship and Community in Medieval Europe* (New York: Holt, 1968), which consists of some two dozen essays. Miscellaneous aspects of the feudal system and feudal society are treated in some two dozen collected articles and addresses of Sidney Painter, *Feudalism and Liberty . . .*, ed. Fred A. Cazel, Jr. (Baltimore: Johns Hopkins U.P., 1961). Two chapters in Carl Stephenson, *Medieval Institutions* (Ithaca, N.Y.: Cornell U.P. 1952) concern feudalism. Over forty good selections from original sources are found in Edward P. Cheyney, ed., "Documents Illustrative of Feudalism," which is No. 3 in U. of Pa., Dept. of History, *Translations and Reprints from the Original Sources of European History*, Volume IV (Philadelphia: U. of Pa., n.d.).

The origins of feudalism are the subject of Robert S. Hoyt *Feudal Institutions: Cause or Consequence of Disintegration?* (New York: Holt, 1964), a collection of documents preceded by short introductions; as well as Charles E. Odergaard, *Vassi and Fideles in the Carolingian Empire* (Cambridge: Harvard U.P., 1945); and James W. Thompson, *The Dissolution of the Carolingian Fisc in the Ninth Century* (Berkeley: U. of California, 1935). Its passing is investigated by Bryce Lyon, *From Fief to Indenture . . .* (Cambridge: Harvard U.P., 1957).

Political and legal aspects of feudalism are treated in Edward Jenks, *Law and Politics in the Middle Ages . . .* (London: J. Murray, 1919); and Fritz Kern, *Kingship and Law . . .* (New York: Praeger, 1956). Feudal France and England are the subject of the more extensive Charles E. Petit-Dutaillis, *The Feudal Monarchy in France and England . . .* (London: Kegan Paul, 1936) and (New York: Barnes and Noble, 1964); as well as in the briefer Sidney Painter, *The Rise of the Feudal Monarchies* (Ithaca, N.Y.: Cornell U.P. 1951), which also includes Germany. More specialized studies of feudal states are Frank M. Stenton, *The First Century of English Feudalism, 1066–1166* (Oxford: Clarendon, 1932); James W. Thompson *Feudal Germany* (Chicago: U. of Chicago,

References for Chapter 10

1928); and Pasquale Villari, *Medieval Italy from Charlemagne to Henry VII*, tr. (New York: Scribners, 1910).

Among works on feudal society and life are the brief and readable SIDNEY PAINTER, *Medieval Society* (Ithaca, N.Y.: Cornell U.P., 1951); and the longer ACHILLE LUCHAIRE, *Social France in the Age of Philip Augustus*, tr. E. B. Krehbiel (New York: Ungar, 1957). Aspects of life on feudal estates are portrayed by WILLIAM S. DAVIS, *Life on a Mediaeval Barony* . . . (New York: Harper, 1923); MARGARET W. LABARGE, *A Baronial Household of the Thirteenth Century* (New York: Barnes and Noble, 1966); and SARRELL E. GLEASON, *An Ecclesiastical Barony of the Middle Ages* . . . (Cambridge: Harvard U.P. 1936).

Feudal warfare is discussed at length in CHARLES W. C. OMAN, *History of the Art of War: The Middle Ages*, 2 vols. (New York: Houghton, 1924), and more briefly sketched in his *The Art of War in the Middle Ages* . . . , ed. and rev. by J. H. BEELER (Ithaca, N.Y.: Cornell U.P., 1953). An excellent scholarly account is JOHN H. BEELER, *Warfare in England, 1066–1189* (Ithaca, N.Y.: Cornell U.P., 1966). Warfare is also the subject of ALEXANDER H. THOMPSON, "The Art of Warfare to 1400," in *Cambridge Medieval History*, VI, 785–798. Among good, well-illustrated works on medieval castles and fortifications are SIDNEY TOY, *A History of Fortification . . . to A.D. 1700* (New York: Macmillan, 1955); and ALEXANDER H. THOMPSON, "Military Architecture" in *Cambridge Medieval History*, VI, 773–784.

English castles are the subject of SIDNEY TOY, *The Castles of Great Britain* (London: Heinemann, 1953); and HUGH BRAUN, *The English Castle* (London: Batsford, 1936). Medieval military equipment is described and illustrated in CHARLES H. ASHDOWN, *Arms and Armour* (New York: Dodge, c. 1944); and in the famous Bayeux Tapestry, edited and explained by FRANK STENTON et al. in *The Bayeux Tapestry* . . . (London: Phaidon, 1957). Coats of arms and political and social history are correlated by NOËL DENHOLM-YOUNG, *History and Heraldry, 1254–1301* . . . (Oxford: Clarendon, 1965).

Still the most comprehensive treatment of medieval chivalry is the collaborative EDGAR PRESTAGE, ed., *Chivalry* . . . (London: Kegan Paul, 1928); while shorter discussions of the subject are provided by CHARLES T. WOOD, *The Age of Chivalry* . . . (New York: Universe Books, 1970); and SIDNEY PAINTER, *French Chivalry* . . . (Ithaca, N.Y.: Cornell U.P., 1940). Painter is also the author of the life of a champion feudal noble, *William Marshall* (Baltimore: Johns Hopkins U.P., 1933). Illustrative of feudal life and ideals are GEORGE B. FUNDENBURG, *Feudal France in the French Epic* . . . (Princeton, N.J.: Princeton U.P., 1918); *The Song of Roland*, available in various versions, including the poetic renderings by CHARLES K. SCOTT MONCRIEFF (Ann Arbor: U. of Mich., 1959) and D. SAYERS (Harmondsworth, Eng.: Penguin, 1957); and *Raoul de Cambrai: an Old French Epic*, tr. JESSIE CROSLAND (London: Chatto, 1926). Illustrative of later concepts of courtly love is ANDREAS CAPELLANUS (ANDRÉ THE CHAPLAIN) *The Art of Courtly Love*, tr. J. J. Perry (New York: Columbia U.P., 1941).

ECONOMIC RECESSION AND RURAL SOCIETY DURING THE EARLY MIDDLE AGES. Chapter 11.

THE EARLY MIDDLE AGES were, in general, a period of economic and social decline. But while the economy deteriorated in western and southern Europe, it expanded in northern and eastern Europe; and while commerce and industry languished, agriculture was healthy. Also, whereas the urban middle class dwindled to insignificance, the lot of many people in the countryside gradually improved. Signs of the beginning of an overall recovery appeared by the mid-tenth century.

THE DECLINE OF COMMERCE AND INDUSTRY.
Section 31.

> Towns have been depopulated and destroyed, and monasteries ruined and burnt; the whole countryside has been devastated and converted into a wasteland. [Archbishop Heriveus of Reims at the Council of Trosly in 909.]

EUROPEAN commerce and industry were constricted by a series of shocks and adversities during the Early Middle Ages. As a result, a semi-subsistence form of simple agrarian economy came to prevail. Among leading causes of prolonged economic decline were successive invasions by barbaric peoples; frequent warfare within as well as between the unstable new Germanic kingdoms; the breakdown of established economic processes and patterns; governmental inadequacy; general insecurity; and the severing or impairment of basic trade-routes by Moslem control of the Mediterranean.

Commercial depression

Western European commerce suffered a general slump from about A.D. 180–950, despite intervals of partial recovery. Deterioration actually began during the confusion and violence of the first century of Roman decline that included the "Barracks Emperors" (190–284). The rigid controls and artificial respiration administered by the "Absolute Emperors" (284–395) eventually aggravated the economic maladies of the Empire. The period of the Great Invasions (c. 395–500) was highly inauspicious. While the barbarians were not intentionally hostile to Roman civilization, the internal confusion and violence, insecurity and uncertainty they introduced hurt the economy. During the barbarian takeover there was notable "acceleration of the process of disintegration" owing to what has been called "the meeting of German immaturity and Roman decrepitude."

Although most of the invasions had spent themselves by about A.D. 500, conditions did not improve in the ensuing century (500–600). The internal weakness of the new Germanic kingdoms manifested itself in factionalism and civil wars, while there were numerous conflicts between states. Frankland was torn apart by continuing rivalry between Austrasia and Neustria. In Italy, the twenty destructive years of conquest by the

Byzantines were followed by the equally disruptive Lombard invasion. Conditions continued to deteriorate in the second ensuing century (600–718), with strife between ambitious mayors in Frankland, squabbles between opposing factions in Spain and Italy, and widening Moslem control of the Mediterranean. A temporary partial arrest of the decline occurred at the height of the Carolingian era (718–814), although this was offset by growing paralysis of Christian shipping in the Mediterranean.

Western European commerce probably sank to its lowest point during the early feudal period (814–950) due to political disintegration, fresh barbarian invasions (by Northmen and Magyars), the Moslem stranglehold on the Mediterranean, widespread brigandage and piracy, multiplication of tolls and duties, and neglect of public works, such as roads, bridges, and harbors. A notable decline probably came during the Norse invasions in the ninth to early tenth centuries; although some maintain that the Vikings helped to expand as much as to hinder commerce. Still, local trade did not entirely lapse, while some long-distance trade continued, especially in luxury items, accessories of religious worship, and common necessities such as salt, iron, fish.

About the middle of the tenth century, there was a rapid upsurge which was a prologue to the remarkable economic expansion of the High Middle Ages. An end of foreign invasions, growing political stability, waxing military strength, the expanding fleets and naval operations of the northern Italian towns, and the industry and enterprise of Western craftsmen and merchants, all contributed to an upswing of commerce and industry.

Although affected by conditions elsewhere, northern European commerce expanded during the Early Middle Ages. In the north, previously barbarian peoples were becoming civilized and trading more extensively with one another and with the civilized world to their south.

Conditions of commerce

Although early medieval maritime commerce continued to be principally located in the Mediterranean, it nevertheless declined sharply in this area. A secondary scene of maritime commerce was the North Atlantic, where the commerce of England, Scandinavia, northern Germany, the Low Countries, and Northwestern France was beginning to grow. Ships in the North Atlantic were usually "clinker-built" with overlapping riveted planks or plates; whereas ships in the Mediterranean area were usually "carvel-built" with flush fitted planks or plates, producing smooth sides. Ships in the north generally used square sails; those in the Mediterranean usually had "lateen" sails (triangular sails, called "lateen" from Latin). Western ships in this period were quite small and, as a rule, single-masted. Long-range overland commerce still used the old Roman roads, although most of these together with their bridges had fallen into disrepair. River transportation was utilized wherever possible because of its greater facility and economy and its comparative freedom from impediments and perils. Small-scale local trade continued to be carried on in towns and villages, at markets on market days, and at the shops of artisans and merchants, such as shoemakers, smiths, and bakers.

Enterprising merchants from the Near East—Greeks (Byzantines),

Economic Recession and Rural Society

Syrians, and Jews—were agents of long-distance commerce. Gradually, more and more North Italians ("Lombards") also participated. Traders usually dealt in more costly items of smaller bulk, which they transported overland on pack animals rather than in carts because of the deplorable condition of the roads. They frequently traveled in groups for protection against brigands and robbers. Items of early medieval commerce—besides such necessities as salt, iron, grain, and fish—included wines, honey, wax, arms and armor, flax, dyes, cloths, leather goods, and slaves, as well as aromatics, spices, silks and other fine textiles, sweet wines and dried fruits, jewels and jewelry, furs, and amber.

Commercial recession was accompanied by a decline of industry. Although most basic industries continued, they did so on a smaller, cruder scale. Focal centers of industry often shifted from the towns to the villas and manors of lords and monarchs, where craftsmen found more profitable employment. In general, industries now produced foods for local consumption, rather than for long-distance trade; and each villa and local area tended to become, as far as possible, self-sufficient. *Industrial decline*

Charlemagne's instructions to the stewards of his royal villas (*Capitularia de Villis*) direct that each of them is to see that in his district there are good "blacksmiths, goldsmiths, silversmiths, shoemakers, turners (lathe-operators), carpenters, swordmakers, fishermen, tinners, foilers (makers and workers of sheets of metal), soapmakers, brewers of beer, and makers of cider, berry wines, and various other beverages, bakers (to make pastry, etc.), netmakers, skilled in making nets for hunting, fishing, and fowling," and other craftsmen too numerous to mention. Some large estates had workshops where men and/or women cooperated in their respective specialties.

Generally speaking, craftsmanship declined, as the crude stonework and statuary in Carolingian churches attests. Some industries seem to have lapsed, as is evidenced by the abandonment of large-scale mines for such minerals as lead and tin. Still, there were exceptions. Many barbarians were skilled in metalworking and woodworking. Excellent textiles were made in the Low Countries from very early times, and Frisian cloths were already famous in Merovingian days. The Flemish were importing wool for cloth-making from England as early as the tenth century. Ordinarily, however, crude and inexpert "do-it-yourself" production (as in the making of homespun garments) prevailed.

Most towns dwindled to a fraction of their former size, and a few disappeared altogether during the Early Middle Ages. Rome—which had earlier counted 500,000–1,000,000 inhabitants—shrank to some 50,000 denizens by A.D. 600. By the tenth century, the *average* population of towns in Italy was an estimated 1,000–1,500. Meanwhile the *largest* towns in France and Germany had about 7,000–8,000 inhabitants. In the eleventh century, London—the largest town in England—had only about 8,000 people; while in 1086, a grand total of only about 40,000 people out of some 1,500,000 in England lived in towns. Many of the towns were largely ruins, and people took stones from antique structures to use in medieval building, and occupied only a part of the earlier town. The *Shrinkage of the towns*

Silver coinage

Germanic conquerors generally shunned the towns and preferred to live in villas, where the possibility of falling to an assassin was diminished and they were less vulnerable to the diseases endemic to the towns, wherein public health measures were poor. Meanwhile, bishops usually became the most important personages—and often the actual rulers—in the towns.

Although money was less available in the Early Middle Ages, its use did not cease. Even at the lowest point of economic activity in the ninth to tenth centuries, money was used for buying and selling and for the payment of fines. A bewildering variety of coins proliferated as feudal rulers on all levels, including lords and bishops, obtained or assumed the right to mint their own money. Lesser mints often imitated the better known and more valued Byzantine and Moslem coins, even to the point of putting Arabic inscriptions on their money. Debasement of the coinage was persistently practiced, until many coins came to have but a small percentage of their original value. Other abuses included "sweating" (melting), filing, and "clipping" coins to profit from the part of the precious metal thus purloined. *Denarii* (pennies)—silver at the time of Charlemagne—were progressively debased until they had become mainly copper (black *denarii*) by the thirteenth century.

Because of the low level of the economy and the growing shortage of gold in the West, Charlemagne abandoned gold coinage. He coined only silver *denarii* with a fixed value (seen in the following chart). The *solidi* (shillings), and *librae* (pounds) were not really coined, but were only "monies of account" used for calculation.

Carolingian Money and Equivalents

MONEY	denarius	solidus	libra
NATURE	coin; silver; 1/240 lb. of pure silver	money of account; formerly gold; 1/20 lb. of pure silver	money of account; formerly gold; 1 lb. of pure silver
VALUE	unit	12 *denarii* (12 d.)	20 solidi (240 d.)
SIGN	d	s	£
FRENCH EQUIVALENT	denier	sous	livre
ENGLISH EQUIVALENT	penny	shilling	pound
GERMAN EQUIVALENT	Pfennig	Mark	Pfund
BYZANTINE EQUIVALENT	dikerata	nomisma (bezant)	—
ARABIC EQUIVALENT	dirhem	dinar	—

From Carolingian times until the twelfth to thirteenth centuries, the *denarius* was the only one of the aforesaid coins actually minted in the West. The *obol* was worth half a penny. The only thing that remained constant about these monies was their names and relative values.

Means of credit and finance were deficient in the early medieval economy. The constricted nature of the mainly subsistence economy was one reason; but another was an ecclesiastical ban against the taking of interest from fellow Christians, largely based on Scriptural injunctions as in Exodus (22:25): *If you lend money to one of your poor neighbors among my people, you shall not act as an extortioner toward him by demanding interest from him*; and in Deuteronomy (23:20–21): *You shall not demand interest from your countrymen on a loan of money or of food or anything else.* . . . These prohibitions against taking interest obviously originated in the simple agricultural and pastoral economy and closely-knit society of the early Hebrews. They also reflected common conditions in the Early Middle Ages. In a simple rural society, the borrowing of money or goods is only necessary in times of dire need or emergency, as for survival during a famine or drought, or in case of illness or catastrophe. Thus, money is borrowed, not for investment, but for "consumption" of what it can purchase, and it is not productive of further money. Nor would it have been so if it had remained in the possession of the lender. The money was "sterile," as the saying went. Hence the requiring of interest from a neighbor was regarded as taking unfair advantage. Most lending activities were consequently carried on by Jews and "Syrians," who had no such inhibitions against taking interest on loans to (Western) Christians. Rates of interest were high, and pledges or "pawns" were usually demanded.

Financial eclipse

EARLY MEDIEVAL AGRICULTURE AND THE MANORIAL SYSTEM.
Section 32.

> I work very hard: I go out at dawn, driving the oxen to the field, where I yoke them to the plough. No matter how bad the weather is in winter, I dare not stay at home, out of fear of my lord. And when the oxen are yoked and the ploughshare and coulter attached to the plough, I must plough one whole field or more. [Answer of a Ploughman in an imaginary conversation between various workers (about A.D. 1000). Cited from Aelfric's *Colloquium* by Eileen Power in her *Medieval People*, p. 27]

AN ESTIMATED 95 per cent of the population of Western Europe lived in the country in the Early Middle Ages, and most of these were engaged in agriculture and related activities. Agriculture generally continued—without notable impairment—from classical antiquity, and in some respects it even made significant gains. The main form of agriculture was the cultivation of grains, such as wheat, rye, oats, and barley, which were the "staff of life." Where the climate was propitious, and even in many places where it was not, grape vines were grown for winemaking. Olives were an important agricultural staple in Mediterranean

Agriculture

lands. Fruits and vegetables of various sorts were subsidiary crops. Pastoral activities—such as the raising of cattle, sheep, goats, pigs, fowl, and horses—were practically universal. Wine and olive oil were produced in large quantities in southern Europe, beer and dairy products in more northern climes.

Extra-manorial land-holding

There were numerous kinds of landholding in the Early Middle Ages. On higher levels, the upper classes and the Church held land in large expanses in various forms of tenure. In the less usual case of outright *allodial holdings,* no regular dues to higher authorities were associated with the landholding. But in the more common case of *fiefs,* regular feudal obligations were owed to an overlord for the land. In some cases, the Church held land in *frankalmoin* as a "free alms" or outright gift, with only spiritual ministrations enjoined; but in other cases feudal dues were owed.

The fullest form of ordinary landholding by the rural population was *freeholding,* in which the freeman held land directly, without servile obligations being due for the land itself, although certain services and payments might be required to support local government and help provide defense. Many freeholders came to be partly or wholly assimilated to serfs, although some freeholding continued even in predominantly manorial areas. In some areas, particularly in less developed regions (as among some early Slavic peoples), communal ownership—whereby the members of communities or villages owned land in common—continued. In such cases, villagers were periodically assigned sections of land to cultivate according to their family needs. A possible remnant of this was the "commonage" or the villagers' rights to share in the use of pastures, woods, and "commons" in the manorial system. In some cases, the rental of agricultural lands continued in the Early Middle Ages. Sometimes the rent was paid in money, sometimes in kind. Whereas some renters had leaseholds, some were sharecroppers (*metayers*), who gave the overlord a certain percentage of their profit or produce.

There were also various small holdings, such as one to five acres, held on a temporary or permanent basis, by way of sufferance, convenience, or rental, whose occupants were known as "cotters," "borders," and "day-laborers." And simple "squatters" often occupied parts of uninhabited lands, such as forests, without obtaining any special deed or authorization. Hamlet-dwellers in less favored territories, such as coastal villages, usually owed only minimal services to lords.

The manorial system

The most prevalent and characteristic form of agriculture and rural landholding in the Early Middle Ages was the manorial system. Called *villa* in Latin, *ville* in French, *Hof* in German and *tun* in Anglo-Saxon, the "manor" or "manse" was the economic basis of feudalism. The manor was both seigneurial or designed to support the lord, and *communal* (with many aspects of joint ownership and cooperation. It also had a considerable private element in the personal holdings and rights of the manorial population. The interdependent cooperative aspect of the manor was strong: the lord governed and defended the rural populace, while the latter supported him by working, as well as farming their own

Economic Recession and Rural Society

holdings in a cooperative manner. The self-supporting, self-governing manor has been called the most efficient secular institution of the Early Middle Ages.

Evolution of the manorial system

The manorial system evolved from involuntary and voluntary subjection of the weaker to the stronger; because of a need for protection and security, and as an economic base to support mounted warriors, as well as by gradual assimilation of non-manorial farmers to manorial serfs.

The manorial system, which evolved gradually, both predated and outlived the feudal system. Cooperative agricultural villages of a semi-communal type seem to have been common in Europe prior to the Indo-European invasions, as well as in early Indo-European communities. But when invading Indo-Europeans such as the Celts and Germans subjected more sedentary agricultural peoples, these came to support the more aggressive, militaristic conquerors. This seems to have been the situation Caesar found among the Celts in Gaul, and that Tacitus describes as existing among the Germans of the first century of the Christian era.

While the very early Romans seem to have been mainly small independent farmers, the villa system soon developed even in Latium, as is exemplified by the rise of the patrician class. As the Roman *imperium* expanded, the Romans replaced many former landlords in more advanced areas, and spread the *latifundia* or *villa* system among less advanced peoples. The *villa* system, which was common in the provinces, spread in Italy under the Later Republic and Early Empire. Its rapid expansion was promoted in the Later Empire (180 ff.) by economic decline, political instability, recurrent violence, and foreign incursions.

Economic recession contributed to the spread of manorialism. Many small landholders, confronted by high taxes and diminishing markets as well as insecurity in the Later Roman Empire, sought the patronage and protection of the more powerful. Frequently, they voluntarily turned over their holdings to large landowners by *commendatio*, and received their land back as a *precarium* to be held in dependent tenure. Many small landowners were forced to sell their holdings in order to satisfy creditors, as well as by other pressures of various sorts, while some were gradually assimilated to their unfree neighbors in the course of time.

Manorialism also seems to have been common among the early Germans immediately prior to their entry into the empire. Manors with landlords and serfs were an established institution among the early Franks, Saxons, Alemanni, Frisians, and so on, by the time of the invasions.

Spread of manorialism

When the Germans established kingdoms on former Roman soil, they obtained both imperial properties and a part, such as a third, of the estates of large landed proprietors in the areas they occupied. Faced with increasing insecurity and deeper economic depression, large numbers of small landowners became affiliated with powerful German or Roman landlords.

Under the Carolingians, manorialism expanded due to the necessity of providing adaquate support for mounted warriors. Properties were distributed as fiefs to maintain military horsemen. The most feasible way of operating these properties so as to support their holders was as manors, which was the way many of them were already being operated. Manorialization reached its height during the renewed confusion and barbarian invasions which followed the death of Charlemagne (814). Prior incentives to manorialism were operative in full force, and manorialism also became the economic base for the emerging feudal system. By the middle of the tenth century, manorialism was prevalent in France, western and southern Germany, most of Italy, and northern Spain, and it soon also became strong elsewhere in Europe.

Physical aspects of the manor

Manors varied greatly in size and extent. A typical manor might have 750–1500 acres of arable land, with a resident complement of 15–30 families of serfs. The typical manor consisted of a nucleated village surrounded by cultivated fields, meadows, pastureland, wasteland, and forest. The village included the lord's manor house, miscellaneous buildings such as a church, and the dwellings of the peasants. The dwellings of the villagers were usually strung along one or two main streets, which ultimately led to neighboring population centers. The homes of the workers were located in proximity to one another rather than scattered in the fields—partly for mutual protection and security and partly to facilitate cooperative farming, as well as for easier socialization and because of custom. The huts or cottages of the peasants usually consisted of one or two rooms. They generally had sizable plots of land about them for vegetables and fruit trees, keeping animals, and the like. There was usually a village church with a parsonage and churchyard and graveyard in the vicinity. The lord's manor house had larger proportions and was better constructed. It might have several rooms or be limited to a large hall, with a bower (chamber for sleeping) and a cellar. There were also adjacent buildings for stabling horses, storing hay and grain, making wine, grinding grain, baking, forging metals, and so on. The ordinary manor did not have a castle, since it usually took several manors to support such. And the manor house was often occupied by the steward and his family, rather than by the lord himself, who might possess several manors, and visit a given one only occasionally. The manor house was usually adjacent to an enclosed area or "close" for the pasturage of the lord's horses and other animals, as well as a vegetable garden, a fruit orchard, and (perhaps) a flower garden.

Manorial land division and use

The main support of the people on the manor derived from its cultivated lands (*arable*). Peasant holdings of arable were scattered through two or three fields. In the older two-field system—which remained in force in the south—half of the arable was cultivated each year, while the other half was allowed to remain fallow. There might be only one yearly planting, or the half under cultivation might be divided into halves, with one planting in the fall and one in the spring.

In the three-field system—which came into wide use beyond the Alps from about the eighth century on—the arable was divided into three fields, and only a third of the land was left fallow each year. The other two-thirds were planted: one third in the fall and the other third in the spring. The "winter crop" was harvested in the late summer, the "spring crop" in the fall. The three-field system had several advantages. Production was increased by one sixth, whereas plowing was reduced by one-ninth, as fallow fields had to be plowed twice. The work was also distributed more evenly throughout the year, reducing the actual amount of work in any given season, and releasing time for further production or other activities. This permitted the further expansion of cultivated areas, as did also other improved agricultural methods and implements, such as the use of speedier horses and better plows. Another advantage was reduction of the risk of famine in case of a bad harvest.

The three-field system came to prevail in northern and western Europe, where rich soil was more common and rainfall more plentiful. In areas such as most of Mediterranean Europe, where rainfall was more limited and the soil less rich, the two-field system was retained, partly because the seasonal rainfall was not sufficient for a spring planting.

Holdings in the fields

The holdings of the peasants were distributed through the two or three "open" fields in several plots or strips of about one acre each. The acre was the amount of land that could be handily plowed in one working day, and was known as a *Morgen* (morning) in German or as a *journée* (*jour*, day) in French, since it represented a day's work. The total acreage held by a peasant depended both on what was originally deemed sufficient to support a man and his family in a given area and the amount of arable land actually available. This varied from place to place, a common total in England being a "virgate" of about 15–45 acres, or an average of about 30 acres. A common larger holding of a freeman—as distinguished from a serf—was a "hide" or *Hufe*, equivalent to about four virgates or a total extent of 60–180 acres (average about 120 acres).

The direct holdings of the lord—known as the *demesne*—often consisted of from one fourth to one third of the total arable. The demesne might be distributed through the open fields and intermingled with the holdings of the peasants; or it might be entirely apart in a separate area, enclosed by hedges or palisades and known as the *close*; or it might be partly intermingled and partly enclosed. The lord's demesne was worked for him by the villagers.

The holdings of the serfs were ordinarily distributed through the fields in a fairly equal manner, in long rectangular plots of about an acre (4,840 square yards). The acre measured four *rods* (22 yards) by one *furlong* (220 yards): a total of about 4,840 square yards. Acres themselves were frequently subdivided into (e.g. two to four) smaller strips. The furlong of 220 yards was the length of a furrow or the distance a team could ordinarily plow before needing rest; while the rod of five and a half yards (16½ feet) was the length of a goad which could reach and prod the farthest ox in a team of eight. The 220 yard dash was a furrow long, the 440 a round trip. It usually took about 72 furrows 220 yards long to plow an acre twenty-two yards wide. In the "open" fields, the separate strips of the peasants were not fenced, but were marked off by headstones and by *balks* (narrow raised ribbons or ridges of unplowed land).

Commons

Some lands on the manor were used in common by the inhabitants with certain restrictions. Among such were the pastures, meadows, forests, wastelands, and recreational and assemblage areas. Each tenant had a right to graze a fixed number of animals in the common pasture. To provide fodder for times when forage was not available in the pasture, the tenant also had the right to take a certain amount of hay from a part of the common meadow, which was often "lotted" off into strips marked by stones. If possible, the village was located near a stream, which was available to all for obtaining water, as well as for swimming and fishing (a favorite pastime). There might also be a pond for general use, such as watering animals. Each inhabitant had limited rights in the forest and untilled wasteland, although the sport of hunting wild animals often came to be reserved to the lords and their company. While trees could not be cut down without permission, peasants were allowed at intervals to fetch from the forest all the dead wood they could collect and carry. They would often pull down dead wood from trees with a long hook and carry their gleanings off in a "crook" (a large "V" set on a pole) —whence the expression "by hook and by crook." As agriculture expanded, homesteading rights were allowed to landless peasants who would clear or drain and settle on and cultivate unoccupied lands.

Operation of the manor

Operation of the manor was a cooperative activity, directed by officials representing the lord in conjunction with leaders elected by the peasants. Considerable planning and adjustments were necessary to coordinate tasks, times, work-animals, implements, and the like. Peasants typically combined their efforts and equipment. Thus they would unite their oxen—e.g., at the rate of about two apiece—to make up a team of eight oxen, while one peasant might provide a plow, another a harrow, another a cart, and so forth. Grain crops—which provided the main "staff of life"—included wheat, barley, oats, rye, millet, and so on. Legumes—such as peas and beans—were also cultivated, as were grapevines (wherever possible) as a source of wine. Vegetables—such as lentils and spinach—and various fruits were usually raised in home plots. The yield of grain in medieval agriculture was much smaller than in our own day. For wheat, it was typically 4 or 5–1—as compared with the quantity sowed—in contrast to present-day returns such as 25–1. Medieval shortcomings included sowing by hand rather than machine, using random rather than select seed, lack of fertilizer, and failure to use nitrogen crops in restoring soil fertility. The yield for other grains was somewhat better, such as a ratio of 10–1 for oats.

Agricultural advances during the Early Middle Ages

A spirit of enterprise and innovation in agriculture in the Early Middle Ages gave rise to various devices to increase production and reduce labor. The three-field system and its advantages have been seen. Use of a heavier-wheeled plow with an iron plowshare to cut into the earth and a moldboard to turn the sod became common and permitted deeper plowing with increased aeration of the earth and better drainage, as well as deep subsoil preservation of moisture. The heavy-wheeled plow enabled farmers to work more difficult ground, such as rocky or root-infested soil and moist, poorly drained bottom land. In Mediterranean Europe, where rainfall was much less plentiful, a lighter scratch plow was used, and the squarish fields were cross-plowed to conserve all possible subsurface moisture. The harrow—a square or rectangular frame with downward project-

Economic Recession and Rural Society

ing spikes—effectively broke up and pulverized larger clods of earth. A toothed sickle was employed to cut stalks more surely and evenly in harvesting. A fan separated the lighter chaff from the heavier grain in winnowing. Manure or animal-offing mixed with straw was often applied as a form of fertilizer to limited areas.

The number of oxen in a team was increased to eight and even twelve to permit deep plowing in stubborn and rocky soil. Eventually, faster horses were substituted for oxen, since horses could plow more rapidly, and could pull just as strongly, especially after the invention of the horse collar. This was a heavy padded oval device attached to the drawing traces, giving greater traction and enabling the horse to apply its full weight to the task. Tandem harness made it possible to use several horses in single file, with faster horses in the fore setting the pace. Iron horseshoes enabled horses to walk with comfort and safety over rougher places such as rocky soil. Water mills—already known in the Later Roman Empire—became widespread during the Early Middle Ages, and there were already over 5,000 water mills in England by 1086. Gears converted slow to rapid motion, and rotary to reciprocal (back and forth) motion. Other improvements whose use spread in the Early Middle Ages were stirrups, the crank, barrels and tubs, felt, soap, and trousers.

Serfs on manors owed their lords various services and dues in money or kind. Their main obligation was to spend about half their regular working hours in the service of their lord. They thus provided him, free of charge, with all the necessary labor for the upkeep of his land and properties, as well as for public works. The principal regular services of serfs were "week work," "boon days," and *corvees*. *Services and dues owed by the serfs*

In "week work," the serfs labored for the lord about half the workweek of six days, holidays excepted. "Boon days" referred to seasonal work, as during planting- and harvest-time, when it was necessary to work continually during each day until the job was completed. At such times the lord's lands had the priority. On "boon days," the lord usually provided food and drink, and festivities often resembled an early American harvest festival. *Corvées* were public works for the upkeep of roads, bridges, dams, ditches, fortifications, and the like, which could be required at any time, since the peasant was *corveable à merci*—subject to such levies at the arbitrary discretion of the lord. The aforesaid work was directed by the lord's officials aided by representatives of the peasants.

Serfs also owed their lord various payments in money or kind. It was a principle of feudal law that serfs were *taillable à merci*—taxable at the lord's discretion, though generally lords limited taxes to those established by custom. In addition to taxes for special purposes, the serfs ordinarily had to render tithes, first-fruits, *heriot*, *merchet*, a mortuary tax, and banalities.

The tithe was a percentage of the peasant's income (theoretically a tenth) which he might have to pay for the support of the Church. First fruits were a part of the natural multiplication of plants and animals. The *heriot* was a customary tribute rendered on succession to a serf's holding, and was often the estate's best animal. The *merchet* was a special tax on matrimony, particularly marriage outside the manor. The mortuary tax was a tribute, often the second best animal, rendered to the Church for funeral services, burial and upkeep of the church cemetery. Banalities were usually a part or percentage (such as a tenth) of grain ground, wine pressed, beer brewed, or bread baked in the lord's mill, wine-press, brewhouse, or ovens. In addition, serfs often owed the lord customary offerings at certain times, such as a certain number of eggs or chickens, a certain amount of honey, a load of wood, a calf, or a lamb, at Easter or Christmas. Sometimes peasants were required to pay an annual *chevage*, a head-tax (poll tax).

Another source of income for the lord consisted in charges and fines assessed in connection with the administration of justice.

Manorial specialists and pastoral activities

Each manor had its special artisans. Skilled craftsmen were more numerous on larger and royal and monastic manors. Included were smiths, millers, carpenters, cartrights, masons, bakers, brewers, coopers, shoemakers, and so on. Women often worked as spinners, weavers, dyers, tailors, and so forth.

Various kinds of animals were raised. Cattle were a source of dairy products, meat, leather, parchment, and other by-products. Each family ordinarily had a cow to provide it with milk, butter, and cheese. Goats served a similar purpose in mountainous areas. Sheep were a source of wool, food, sheepskin, and parchment. Oxen served as draft animals and beasts of burden, as well as for eventual food. Horses were used for travel, transportation, hauling, and plowing, as well as for recreational and military purposes. Pigs were a leading source of meat; they were kept in large numbers and allowed to feed and root in the woods. Cattle, sheep, and pigs were tended by herdsmen, often younger or older persons. In one district of England on the Devonshire coast, there were 1,168 swine-herds. Fowl—especially chicken and geese—were kept as sources of eggs and (occasional) meat. Bees were kept for their honey and wax, and to produce the ingredients for mead.

During the twelfth century, manorialism began to diminish in Western Europe, where it was virtually extinct by the close of the Middle Ages. As it ebbed in the West, it became more prevalent in central and Eastern Europe, where it survived in Russia until the mid-nineteenth century, and in Poland into the twentieth century.

Non-manorial agriculture

Much early medieval agriculture was non-manorial. Even after the introduction of Norman rule and continental customs into England, *Domesday Book* (1086) lists about 12 per cent of the population as freemen and 30 per cent as cottars or bordars, as against about 35 per cent who were villeins (serfs) and 9 per cent who were slaves. For some time manorialism was very limited in Saxony and along the eastern German frontiers, and was not common in Frisia and Scandinavia, exclusive of Denmark. Even in predominantly manorial areas—such as most of France, Germany, and England, together with much of Italy, Spain, and Denmark—certain areas (such as mountainous regions, small valleys, and seaside strips) were by nature unsuitable for the large-scale form of agriculture involved in manorialism.

Economic Recession and Rural Society

Much agricultural land was owned and operated by the Church. Among such lands were those of monasteries. Monastic lands were sometimes farmed by the monks themselves, sometimes by serfs. Not only did the Church take a lead in clearing, draining, and cultivating new land, but it also often provided an example of improved agricultural methods, practices, and implements. It inculcated—by word and example —the dignity and virtue of manual labor and industry. St. Benedict referred to idleness as "the enemy of the soul." And churchmen pointed out that, after the Fall, God commanded Adam and Eve: "Thou shalt earn thy bread by the sweat of thy brow."

The Church and the economy

Riches were regarded by the Church as a spiritual impediment, rather than an advantage. For had not the Bible said: "It is harder for a rich man to enter the Kingdom of Heaven than for a camel to pass through the eye of a needle." Loaning out money at interest to fellow Christians or greatly overcharging for goods or underpaying for labor were regarded as sinful.

EARLY MEDIEVAL SOCIETY OTHER THAN THE ARISTOCRACY.
Section 33.

> God hath shapen lives three:
> Boor^a and knight and priest they be. [Early Medieval saying.]

^a boor: peasant

THE VAST majority of the population of Western Europe during the Early Middle Ages lived in the country, where they were engaged in agricultural and pastoral activities. Rural life as a whole was simple and close to nature. With the decline of trade, the middle class had virtually disappeared, so that theorists were usually inclined to disregard it. Bishop Adalbert of Reims, about 1000, reflecting the prevailing attitude, divided society into *orantes, militantes,* and *laborantes,* and noted: "Although men think of God's household as one, it is really composed of three groups: some pray; others fight; while still others work with their hands."

Limited by both man-made and natural forces—including plagues, pestilence, sickness, warfare, medical ignorance, occasional famine, and economic stagnation—the population of Western Europe sank to such a low level during the Early Middle Ages that one authority characterizes the era as "the nadir of population (543–950)."

Population and its distribution

It has been estimated that the total population of Western Europe in the tenth century was about thirty million, with some nine million in France; one and three-quarter million in England; eight million in the Germanies; and four and a half million in Italy; with the remaining six and three-quarter million living in the Iberian peninsula and elsewhere. Proportionate loss of population in the towns was much greater than that in the countryside.

The concept of three main classes in society was not new with the Middle Ages. It was common in ancient societies, where the majority of the manual laborers were often slaves or semi-servile, and the fully free

The three classes of society

constituted a ruling minority. It is found in Plato's *Republic,* where society is composed of philosopher-rulers, warriors, and workers. A threefold class system seems to have been common among the Germanic peoples immediately prior to the Great Invasions. During the Early Middle Ages, the concept corresponded fairly well with reality. It has been remarked that there were three separate "worlds" in feudal society, each apart from the others: the world of the castle, the world of the cloister or rectory, and the world of the peasants in their villages.

At the top, in the two upper classes, were the spiritual and temporal leaders: the clergy and the aristocracy. The clergy, definitely a class apart, had the custody of religion and learning. They were not allowed to marry, nor did they ordinarily take part in wars. The feudal aristocracy were both the temporal rulers and physical defenders of the commonwealth. Because of their privileged position and their responsibilities, the feudal nobility did not have to participate in manual labor. Among the laity, the aristocracy were the only fully free class, which position they earned by fighting to protect the body politic. Constituting the broad base were the masses, whose principal concern was to provide the physical necessities of life for society at large. As John of Salisbury summarized society in the twelfth century: *The clergy are the eyes that see and point out the road to salvation; the nobles are the hands and arms that protect society, enforce justice, and defend the realm; while the lesser folk, like the lower parts of the body, support the upper parts.*

Actually, there was some fluidity in early medieval society. Peasants could rise into the aristocratic class or become members of the clergy. Men of daring and physical hardiness were often needed to fight off hostile barbarians and infidels, and to help repel bellicose neighbors. A man could often obtain a chance to move up into the warrior class by following the army in a humble capacity. Even ordinary lords could confer knighthood—and often did so in admiration or out of gratitude. Men of intelligence and spiritual perception, as well as human sympathy, were needed to serve in the clergy and minister to the religious needs of their fellows. Many men of lowly birth became ecclesiastical priors, abbots, bishops, and popes. One could fall as well as rise, and members of the aristocracy could lose their status and lands and privileges, as in punishment for an unsuccessful revolt. And persons of noble birth could move from the second to the first class by becoming monks or joining the secular clergy.

The clergy

Partly because they rationalized the system and were the learned class, concerned with eternal verities and values, the clergy were the first class, following precedents established by Plato for philosophers, and the Old Testament for priests. The clergy did not ordinarily marry, or take part in fighting, or engage in business; but rather lived apart from the secular world, in clerical and monastic residences and communities. There were, of course, exceptions: many of the clergy, both secular and regular, became involved to some extent in estate management and in aspects of secular government, while the upper clergy were lords temporal as well

Economic Recession and Rural Society

as lords spiritual. But such activities were always, in the common estimation, secondary to their clerical responsibilities.

To some extent and with some exceptions, the life of the clergy was comparatively tranquil, orderly, reflective, and spiritual, nor was it without compensations. If clerics were more restrained and restricted than lay persons, they were also better able to enjoy many of the better things of life for a longer time. If they were deprived of the amenity of a wife and the satisfaction of having children, they usually enjoyed the respect and even the love of their "flock," all of whom they considered as their spiritual "children." The clergy were also the chief scholars, authors, counselors, social workers and social planners of the day.

Clerics were classed as secular (ordinary) and regular (monastic) clergy, while the secular clergy were further subdivided into upper and lower clergy. The upper clergy were reckoned as members of the aristocracy, from which class they were often drawn. Bishops were on a par with the great lords and were members of feudal great councils, and they usually lived much as did other members of the higher aristocracy. The lower clergy usually lived on much the same level as members of the lower middle class. On the manor, the parish priest was usually supported by the parish land or "glebe" scattered among the strips of the peasants, by whom it was worked. The monks regularly lived in a world apart, in conformity with a monastic rule (*regula*)—whence the term "regular" clergy.

Rural laborers, serfs

Rural laborers, the majority of the population, usually had a dependent status, although there were numerous gradations among them. There were still some slaves in the Early Middle Ages, but their number was relatively small. Slavery was not as well adapted to a crude agrarian economy as serfdom, a step above it. The Church was unfavorable to slavery, although it did not absolutely condemn it, and it was especially adverse to enslavement of fellow Christians. Pagan captives were sometimes enslaved—as in the case of the Angles and Slavs—and a good slave and a good horse brought about the same price.

The typical medieval rural worker was a serf, with a position intermediate between that of slave and freeman. On the one hand, the serf was bound to the land, which he was not allowed to leave, even when it was transferred from one owner to the other. The serf owed the lord various services which occupied at least half of his working time, and he could be called upon to labor on "public works." He also owed his lord various payments, and could be taxed without his assent (was *taillable à merci*). Since over half of the serf's labors were directly or indirectly owed to the lord, he had limited time to support himself and his family, which he usually maintained at a bare subsistence level. The wills of English peasants list only a few effects of small value. The serf who was subject to his lord could not ordinarily sue the lord in civil cases or even appeal judgments of the lord's court. His status was hereditary and was transmitted to his children.

On the other hand, the serf had certain rights fixed by custom. While he could not leave his land, he also could not ordinarily be dispossessed. As long as he did his work and made his payments, he could operate his lands and profit from part of his labors. The demands his lord could make upon the serf were in practice limited by tradition and prudence, as well as by Christian teachings and personal conscience. The serf could theoretically accumulate money and property and buy his own freedom, although to save on a substantial scale was usually beyond his capacity. There were various ways besides purchase by which a serf, if he was ambitious, could obtain freedom. He could obtain permission from his lord to enter the clergy or military service, or he could become an artisan such as a smith or carpenter, and he could eventually escape to some town or frontier settlement, where greater freedom existed.

Small holders

Less well off than serfs, although freer, were the bordars, cotters, and crofters, who lived "on the fringes of the manorial system." According to *Domesday Book*, bordars and cotters composed about a third of the rural laborers in England in 1086. Peasants of this class had a small plot of land, such as one to five acres, together with a small cottage. They usually lived a marginal existence and supplemented their agricultural produce by working for wages. Although they had some servile obligations, these were not as great as for regular serfs. The bordars (borderers) were so called from the fact that they lived on the borders of the regular manor; the crofters from their tiny farms or "crofts" of a few acres; and the "cotters" (or cottagers) from their small cottages.

Hôtes (*hospites*; guests) were recent arrivals who were allowed to hold some land but were not a part of the manorial system. They were often initially in the same position as the bordars, crofters, and cotters. Eventually, often by dint of clearing, draining, and reclaiming new land, hôtes could become regular renters or serfs. Hôtes were particularly numerous in areas where new lands were being settled and developed.

Renters and freeholders

A step above the serfs were the rent-paying *villeins*. Although usually assimilated to the serfs in some respects, these renters—known as "socmen" in England and *censitaires* in France—were actually freemen. They did not have to render most of the services owed by the serfs, but instead paid a form of rent. They were not subject to the *chevage*, *merchet*, or *heriot* like the serfs, nor were they *taillable à merci* (viz., they were free from arbitrary taxation). They had personal freedom and could give up their holdings and leave the manor at will.

b Whereas previous percentages refer to the population at large; here they are confined to the farming class.

The highest status among the peasants was that of freeholders—free farmers who owned their holdings. In England, there was a further distinction between ordinary freeholds, which were free by custom, and those of which there was public record, whose owners were known as "copyholders" with "bookland." In England in 1086, according to *Domesday Book*, the farming class was composed approximately as follows: freeholders: about 15 per cent; serfs: 40 per cent; cotters and borders: 35 per cent; slaves: 10 per cent.[b]

The actual holdings of freeholders varied. Some held the traditional early German freeholder's "hide" (Eng.) or *Hufe* (Ger.), which consisted of about four virgates or possibly 120 acres. But some held more,

Economic Recession and Rural Society

and many less. Even freeholders were obliged to render some of the services owed by serfs, although to a much lesser extent. Of some 44,500 nonnoble freemen reported in *Domesday Book,* one fourth owed only military service, while three fourths owed only some of the lighter services owed by serfs.

Manorial government was partly cooperative. The peasants had a share in the government along with the lord, possibly as a carry-over from the semicommunal village. But the lord held the lion's share of power. Government of the manor on the lord's behalf was usually carried on by his officials, headed by the "steward" or "seneschal" (senior servant), who often supervised and administered several manors. The actual conduct of the local government of each manor was often in the hands of a bailiff, who frequently occupied the manor house (if it was not actually used by the lord or steward) and usually presided at the lord's manorial court. In some cases, the lord's court had "high" and "final" justice so that it could inflict the death penalty and its decisions could not be appealed to a higher court. Justice was regarded as an important source of income and there was a saying: "Justice is a great profit."

Government of the manors

The peasants on the manor usually had their own officials who represented them and handled many minor aspects of local government. Chief among these was the "reeve" or "provost," who was usually elected by the villagers and cooperated with the lord's bailiff in arranging schedules, supervising work, etc. The village might also have a constable, to serve as the "arm of the law." The peasants often had their own village court in addition to the lord's manorial court. The peasants usually acted as a sort of jury in both courts. Peasants owed service in their lord's court, just as present-day citizens owe jury duty. Other officials on manors included the beadle or crier; the cowherd, shepherd, and swineherd, in charge of watching over animals; the plowman to care for the lord's plows and the plowing of the lord's demesne; a dairymaid in charge of the dairy, etc.

The way of living of the peasants on the manors was very simple and elemental. While their living conditions would be considered almost unbearable by us today, they no doubt seemed quite natural to the peasants of that day. Even today we are accustomed to adjusting to a lack of conveniences when "camping out" or "in the service"; medieval peasants knew no other form of life. Being closer to nature, and out of doors much of the time, with plenty of fresh air and room, they were actually better off than many of our present-day slum-dwellers.

Living conditions of the peasants

The homes of the peasants were small. A typical hut might measure 15 by 30 feet, and consist of a wooden frame roofed with thatching or shingles and walled with wattle (interlaced rods, branches, and twigs), or wattle and mud. Windows, true to their name, were small unglazed vents. Generally the hut had only one or two rooms, and was very crowded. The floor was usually dirt and strewn with rushes or straw. A hole in the roof let in sunlight and let out the smoke from a fire on a hearthstone located, for example, in the middle of the floor. As a result, both the peasant and his abode were usually grimy and sooty. Piles or bags of straw, sometimes in a rough wooden box or frame, served for beds.

Fare

Furniture was usually minimal and crude. Domesticated animals were often under the same roof with humans.

The food and drink of the peasants were usually simple but abundant. Described as prodigious eaters and drinkers, the peasants needed plenty of "fuel" for their vigorous hardy life. The main "staff of life" consisted of grains and legumes in the form of black or brown (full-grained) bread, porridge or mush, accompanied by dairy products. Butter and beer prevailed in the north, and olive oil and wine in the south. Considerable amounts of milk, butter, cheese, and eggs were consumed. Meat and fish were eaten in quantities, often meager, that depended on their availability. Honey was widely used as a sweetener.

Pork products were a common form of meat, with fowl being reserved for special occasions. A problem with both meat and fish was the difficulty of preserving it. In season, vegetables—such as cabbage, beets, and lentils—together with fruits—such as apples, berries, and grapes—were eaten. During most of the year, the diet was poorly balanced and deficient in needed elements such as Vitamin C, provided by fresh fruits and vegetables. An interesting description of the diet and life of a "widow poor" who lived in "a small cottage" is given by Chaucer, who says in part:

> *She kept herself and her daughters twain;*
> *Three large sows had she and no more, 'tis plain,*
> *Three cows and a lone sheep that she called 'Moll.'*
> *Right sooty was her bedroom and her hall . . .*
>
> *Her board was mostly garnished, white and black,*
> *With milk and brown bread, whereof she'd no lack,*
> *Broiled bacon and sometimes an egg or two,*
> *For a small dairy business did she do.*[c]

[c] *The Canterbury Tales*, as translated by J. U. Nicolson.

Attire and aspect

Peasant clothing was usually made of wool or flax, homespun, coarse, loose-fitting and simple, sometimes supplemented by a leather jacket or woolen cape, and sometimes with leather breeches. Men regularly wore a loose-fitting tunic, belted at the waist, with hose and sometimes trousers; the women wore a long loose-fitting garment or dress frequently with some attempt at decoration. Fur was so rare as to be practically a sign of nobility. Peasants seldom had more than two changes of clothing, and they often wore the same clothing month in and month out, sleeping as well as working in it. Their shoes or boots were of the roughest, and were sometimes simply wooden clogs.

Peasants took few baths, often limited to dips in the stream or pond in summertime, or drenchings by seasonal rains. As a result they are described as being even smellier than most people. One writer remarked that *the devil did not want the peasants in hell because they smelled so badly.* They were usually bearded and often dentally defective. Many were maimed or deformed from some accident or misfortune. They were dirty and sooty from their labors and the fires in their cottages, as well as from a lack of bathing, at least in colder seasons. In *Aucassin and*

Economic Recession and Rural Society

Nicolette, a peasant is described as: *marvellously ugly and hideous. His huge head was black as charcoal and his eyes were set a handbreadth apart. He had big cheeks, a broad flat nose, thick lips redder than a collop, and ugly yellow teeth. He wore leggings and shoes of bull's hide, bound with cord of bark, and he was leaning on a big club.*

Contemporary writers sometimes described the peasants in such terms as these: *Nothing can penetrate their hard heads and stupid brains.—They have a shifty look.—They do not bear their need and poverty cheerfully, but are envious and backbiting, and proud. . . .*

Of a peasant, the chanson *Garin de Lorrain* says: *He had enormous hands and heavy limbs, . . . his shoulders were broad, his chest deep, his hair bristling, his face dark as coal. He went without bathing for six months, and none but rainwater ever touched his face.*

That derogatory descriptions are frequently exaggerated is suggested by the old German poem *Der arme Heinrich*, where it is said:

> The peasant, with God's help, hath spent
> A life both cleanly and content;
> He has muscles steeled by industry,
> And a wife of great activity.

Both the living conditions and way of life of the peasants improved with the growth of prosperity.

Man is a very adaptable creature who has had different standards and values at different periods in history, depending on circumstances. The life of the medieval peasant should not be judged by our standards and day, but by his. Like the lives of all men in all ages, the peasant's life had both its hardships and joys.

Hardships and consolations of peasants

The hardships of the medieval serf were mainly physical. Many peasant hardships are enumerated in the invocations of medieval litanies beginning with "From" and ending with "O Lord deliver us!" They included both natural and man-made disasters such as famine, drought and floods, plagues and pestilence, wars and raids of barbarians, such as the Northmen. Even without such tribulations, the peasant's life was a hard one. He began work as a boy, and worked every day except on Sundays and holydays from sunrise to sunset in all kinds of weather. His means were so limited that he was hard pressed by any kind of reverse.

Yet the life of the peasant also had its brighter side. The peasant usually had his health—his survival virtually necessitated that. He also had a form of "social security" in his place on the manor. He had the fascinating beauties of nature and the rounds of the seasons, the amenities of courtship and marriage, the joys of family life, and the satisfaction of accomplishing useful tasks. He ordinarily had adequate food and drink, made tastier by a strong appetite. With the poet he could have said:

> I said it in the meadow path,
> I said it on the mountain stairs—
> The best things any mortal hath
> Are those which every mortal shares.

Recreations

Medieval village life provided many opportunities for relaxation and pleasure. Since they lived in close proximity, peasants had considerable social intercourse. Holy days were holidays, free from regular work and celebrated with festivities. Important festivals, such as Christmas and Easter, were observed by a whole series of free days. In such seasons, as well as on occasions such as harvest time and boon days, there was a general spirit of good will, and plenteous food and drink. Practically all the villagers participated in some measure in the songs and dances common to such occasions. They even on occasion danced in the churches and graveyards. The younger and more vigorous participated in competitive physical events, such as foot races, the broad-jump and high-jump, wrestling, weight-lifting, throwing, and archery. Various sorts of games with elusive capricious balls—such as that of "passing the ball"—were popular.

Occasionally a great stir would be caused by the advent of some minstrel, musician, juggler, or "tumbler." Many entertainers combined several of these abilities. Fishing was an old and reliable plebian recreation. Poaching in the lord's hunting preserves or fishing pond often added spice to sport.

Advantages

Early medieval serfs were generally better off than the slaves who were so often the main labor source in ancient "more advanced" society. The serfs were free, except for the services and dues they owed their lord, and the restriction that they could not forsake the manor without their lord's permission. They had their own lands from which they could not be evicted and whose produce they enjoyed. Although they were attached to their land, their land was also attached to them, giving them "social security." Opportunities for further advancement were not absent, since early medieval society had considerable fluidity.

The Church and the peasants

One of the greatest consolations of the peasants was their religion, and one of their most helpful allies the Church. The Church ennobled and beautified the major events in the serf's life with its ceremonies and solicitude. It protected the serfs' morals and their households by its teachings, as well as preached a restraint of passions among equals and inculcated justice and charity among those of unequal status. The ordinary clergy lived close to the peasants as the "ministers" and "servants" of the "flock" committed to their care. The monks too were their exemplars, teachers, and counsellors. The clergy were in fact the chief social workers and counsellors of their day. Like chaplains in the army, they were also a leading liaison between the upper classes and the peasants.

Conclusion

If the economy and society of the Early Middle Ages were less advanced than in the Later Roman Empire, they were considerably freer with greater potential. While most commerce and industry were "hibernating," there were exceptions, as in the case of northern Europe; and agriculture was actually beginning to improve. More value was also being attached to individuals, whatever their status. It was generally recognized that, in addition to duties and obligations, the serf had an eternal destiny, dignity, and rights. The serf also had opportunities for self-improvement and advancement, as in military or ecclesiastical service and certain crafts.

Economic Recession and Rural Society

The rural semisubsistence type of economy prevalent in the Early Middle Ages influenced the structure of society, promoted feudalism, and simplified popular religion. Monasticism flourished in the prevailing rural environment, to which it was well adapted, and wherein the monks were agricultural and technological instructors as well as spiritual and religious teachers by example as well as by precept. Meanwhile, culture was largely left to the clergy, who attended the lamps of learning and art, and prevented them from being extinguished.

References for Chapter 11

GOOD general treatments of early medieval economy and society, with their limitations, are to be found in PROSPER BOISSONADE, *Life and Work in Medieval Europe* . . . , tr. Eileen Power (New York: Knopf, 1927), full of illustrative examples and Gallic exuberance; JAMES WESTFALL THOMPSON, *Economic and Social History of the Middle Ages (300–1300)* (New York: Century, 1928), a chronological and regional approach, rich in details; and HENRI PIRENNE, *Economic and Social History of Medieval Europe* (New York: Harcourt, 1937), a well-written general survey.

General economic histories providing introductions for this period are HERBERT HEATON, *Economic History of Europe* (New York: Harper, 1948); SHEPARD B. CLOUGH and CHARLES W. COLE, *Economic History of Europe* (Boston: Heath, 1941); and MELVIN KNIGHT, *Economic History of Europe to the End of the Middle Ages* (Boston: Houghton, 1926). The fullest study of medieval economic history available in English is the collaborative, authoritative *Cambridge Economic History of Europe*, ed. J. H. Clapham and E. Power, et al., (New York: Macmillan, 1941 ff., and rev. 1966), in which the first volume concerns *Agrarian Life in the Middle Ages;* the second *Trade and Industry, in the Middle Ages,* and the third *Economic Organization and Policies in the Middle Ages.* But even in this fine work, several key subjects are inadequately handled. A classic study for the economy and society of very early medieval Western Europe to the eighth century is ALFONS DOPSCH, *The Economic and Social Foundations of European Civilization* (London: Kegan Paul, 1937). Studies "of the first order" are ROBERT LATOUCHE, *The Birth of Western Economy: Economic Aspects of the Dark Ages* (New York: Barnes and Noble, 1956), which treats the fourth to the ninth centuries, and stresses France, Germany, and the Low Countries; and GEORGES DUBY, *Rural Economy and Country Life in the Medieval West,* tr. C. Postan (Columbia: U. of S.C., 1968). A careful, balanced compilation of illustrative primary materials is Roy C. Cave and H. H. Coulson, eds., *A Source Book for Medieval Economic History* (Milwaukee: Bruce, 1936). A standard and basic study of medieval English economic history is the first volume of EPHRAIM LIPSON, . . . *The Economic History of England,* 3 vols. (London: Black, 1915–1931).

For the history of commerce consult ARCHIBALD R. LEWIS, *Naval Power and Trade in the Mediterranean, A.D. 500–1100* (Princeton: Princeton U.P., 1951), and *The Northern Seas: Shipping and Commerce in Northern Europe, A.D. 300–1100* (Princeton: Princeton U.P., 1958). The much discussed and argued "Pirenne thesis," which maintains that there was a Moslem stranglehold which cut off Western trade in the Mediterranean during the Carolingian era and brought on the age of feudalism, is presented in HENRI PIRENNE'S *Mohammed and Charlemagne,* tr. B. Miall (London: G. Allen, 1945). Criticisms and evaluations of this thesis have been collected by Alfred F. Havighurst, ed., *The Pirenne Thesis: Analysis, Criticism, and Revision* (Boston: Heath, 1958).

Interesting special studies include DIRK JELLEMA, "Frisian Trade in the Dark Ages," in *Speculum*, XXX (1955), 15–36; JEAN LESTOCQUOY, "The Tenth Century," in *Economic History Review*, Vol. 17 (1947), 1–14, which stresses progressive aspects of this century; and ROBERT S. LOPEZ, "An Aristocracy of Money in the Early Middle Ages," in *Speculum*, XXVIII (1953), 1–43, which deals with moneyers and mints.

For agriculture in the Early Middle Ages, besides Vol. I of the *Cambridge Economic History* (already listed), a brief introduction is NELLIE NEILSON . . . . *Medieval Agrarian Economy* (New York: Holt, 1936), as well as the interesting, collaborative *Early Medieval Society*, ed. Sylvia Thrupp (New York: Appleton, 1967). Good accounts of manorial agriculture and organization are NATHANIEL J. HONE, *The Manor and Manorial Records* . . . (London: Methuen, 1906); PAUL VINOGRADOFF, *The Growth of the Manor* (London: G. Allen, 1905); and FRANÇOIS L. GANSHOF, *Manorial Organization in the Low Countries*, in Royal Historical Association, *Transactions*, 4th Series, XXXI, 29–59. Containing information on the economic and social aspects of the manorial system are articles by PAUL VINOGRADOFF in the *Cambridge Medieval History* entitled "Foundations of Society" (II, 631–655) and "Feudalism" (III, 458–484).

General works on medieval society include the short introduction by SIDNEY PAINTER, *Mediaeval Society* (Ithaca, N.Y.: Cornell U.P., 1951) and the more detailed study by PAUL VINOGRADOFF, *English Society in the Eleventh Century* (Oxford: Clarendon, 1908). An intensive investigation of the perplexing question of medieval populations is provided by JOSIAH C. RUSSELL, "Late Ancient and Medieval Population" in American Philosophical Society, *Transactions*, Vol. 48, part 3. (Philadelphia: American Philosophical Society, 1958).

Descriptions of agricultural operations and social life on English and French manors are provided by HENRY S. BENNETT, *Life on the English Manor*. . . . (Cambridge, Eng.: 1937), a colorful, detailed account; and WILLIAM STEARNS DAVIS, *Life on a Mediaeval Barony* . . . (New York: Harper, 1923), a readable, interesting picture. Life on ecclesiastical baronies is the subject of the briefer SARRELL E. GLEASON, *An Ecclesiastical Barony of the Middle Ages* . . . (Cambridge, Harvard U.P., 1936), and the longer EDWARD MILLER, *The Abbey and Bishopric of Ely: the Social History of an Ecclesiastical Estate* (Cambridge: Cambridge U.P., 1951). Village life is reflected in CLAIR H. BELL, *Peasant Life in Old German Epics* (New York: Columbia U.P., 1931; while a related work is RUTH MOHL, *The Three Estates in Medieval and Renaissance Literature* (New York: Columbia U.P., 1933). The life and rights and duties of medieval serfs are treated in a scholarly manner by PAUL VINOGRADOFF, *Villainage in England* . . . , (Oxford: Clarendon, 1927), and, with considerable material on pre-Norman times, by FREDERIC SEEBOHM, *The English Village Community*, 4th ed., (Cambridge: Cambridge U.P., 1940). Various aspects of village life as depicted in certain sources are presented by GEORGE G. COULTON, *The Medieval Village* (Cambridge: Cambridge U.P., 1926). The life of Bobo, an early medieval peasant, is among those depicted by EILEEN POWER in her *Medieval People* (New York,

Barnes and Noble, 1963). An interesting discussion of various types of medieval attire is provided by DOROTHY HARTLEY, *Mediaeval Costume and Life* (New York: Scribners, 1931). The Jews in this period are the subject of a specialized work by Solomon Katz, *The Jews in the Visigothic and Frankish Kingdoms of Spain and Gaul* (Cambridge, Mass.: Mediaeval Academy, 1937), and are included in the readings in JACOB R. MARCUS, ed., *The Jew in the Medieval World: a Source Book: 315–1791* (Cincinnati: Union, 1938).

❡ WESTERN EUROPE IN THE EARLY FEUDAL PERIOD. Chapter 12.

ESTERN EUROPE in the early feudal period (the ninth to eleventh centuries) was in an insecure and formative state. France—although the most feudal kingdom in Europe—was obtaining a degree of stability from the Capetians, and was developing an expanding sphere of influence, which extended to Spain and England. Most of Spain—the leading entryway of fructifying Islamic influences—was in Moslem hands; but an aggressive Christian "Reconquest" was mounting. Peripheral Anglo-Saxon England and Scotland were being increasingly Christianized and civilized by Irish and Continental influences, while at the same time hardy concepts of individual liberties and institutions of partial self-government were surviving.

FEUDAL FRANCE. (888–1106) Section 34.

> If we inquire into the matter, we find that the throne is not acquired by hereditary right . . . Let us then elect Duke Hugh, who is recommended by his conduct, his noble lineage, and his military following. [Speech of Archbishop Adalberon of Reims, nominating Hugh Capet to be King of France (987).]

FRANCE was the original home of feudalism, and conditions in France provide the basis for most descriptions of feudal institutions and practices. The French monarchy was considered to be partly elective and partly hereditary, and the French king was a suzerain rather than a sovereign: *primus inter pares* (first among equals): a leader of great lords like himself. Feudal warfare, knights, castles, and tournaments were a part of the everyday French scene; and in the bosom of *la belle France* were conceived chivalry, *chansons de geste* and *amour*, the Crusades, and the Peace and Truce of God.

Although nominally united and bound together by common ties of history, tradition, sentiment, and religion, the major component principalities of France were largely autonomous, save for a few responsibilities to the crown. Headed by the magnates or "peers of France," these principalities included duchies and important counties which achieved a status on a par with that of the duchies. The leading duchies were

Components of feudal France: Duchies

Francia, Normandy, and Aquitaine; while secondary in importance (as well as located on the periphery) were the duchies of Brittany, Gascony, and Burgundy.

The Duchy of Francia—known as the *Ile de France*—was the family domain of the Robertian and Capetian Kings of France. Strategically located in the rich middle valleys of the Seine and Loire rivers and including the important cities of Paris and Orléans, Francia was, however, neither the largest nor the richest of the French duchies. It was known as an *Ile* (island) from the fact that it was almost entirely surrounded by rivers, and as *Francia* because it was a remnant of the old western home or New Kingdom (*Neustria*) of the Franks.

The Duchy of Normandy, which occupied the western valley of the Seine and stretched along the coast of the English Channel, was probably the strongest of the French principalities. Scandinavian governmental genius contributed to the organization and administration of its effective political institutions. The duchy was created by Charles the Simple for the Norse military chieftain Rollo in 911. At his agreed-on baptism, Rollo (Hrolf) assumed the Christian name of Robert, which along with William became a favorite name with members of the ruling house. Although the "Normans" were rapidly Christianized and civilized by French influences, Norman policies were restless and expansionist. So strong was Normandy by the mid-eleventh century that its Dukes were able to take over and hold the throne of England. For some time there was a possibility that they would also do the same with all of France.

The Duchy of Aquitaine was the largest but also one of the most loosely governed of all the French duchies. Aquitaine—which included the fertile wine-producing valleys of the Garonne and Dordogne Rivers—had been reckoned as a kingdom occasionally in its history, and its dukes kept court in semi-regal splendor. Its strength did not match its size because it was highly feudalized, turbulent, and unruly. Morals were not as straitlaced in southern as in northern France. Duke William IX of Aquitaine was noted for his *chansons d'amour* and "courts of love," as well as for his unscrupulous politics. His capricious daughter Eleanor married and quarrelled with the kings of both France and England.

The Duchy of Brittany occupied the rugged out-jutting American peninsula in far northwestern France. Its original Celtic population had been reinforced by numerous refugees from Britain during the Anglo-Saxon invasion of that island. The inhabitants of Brittany were typically conservative, separatist, and independent, and they long clung to their Celtic speech and customs. Its Dukes were frequently a law unto themselves, allying themselves alternately with French and English kings.

The Duchy of Gascony in far southwestern France was partly Spanish as well as partly French, and its largely Basque population was presumably descended from the prehistoric indigenous inhabitants. Like the Bretons, the Gascons had their own treasured "provincial" customs, ways, and ideas, along with a strong jealous spirit of independence, and fighting and defiance of authority were common among them.

The Duchy of Burgundy, between the Loire and Saone rivers in mid-

The Early Feudal Period

eastern France, was likewise highly feudal and somewhat peripheral. Like the Bretons and Gascons, the Burgundians had a strong taste for independence and autonomy, which they indulged from time to time. The Duchy of Burgundy was to the northwest and west of the much larger Kingdoms of Provence (or Arles) and Upper Burgundy (or Burgundy)—located to the east of the Rhône and Saone rivers—with which it should not be confused, as the latter two kingdoms were in the Holy Roman (German) Empire rather than the Kingdom of France during most of the Middle Ages.

In addition to the great duchies, France had certain counties whose counts had expanded their holdings and had come to control several neighboring counties with the result that they had obtained a status similar to that of the dukes. Among such were the Counties of Flanders, Anjou, Toulouse, and Champagne-Blois.

The County of Flanders—located in the area of present-day Belgium and extreme northeastern France—was famous for its wealth. From early times, it had been noted as a textile-producing region as well as a natural crossroads of commerce. Its enterprising burghers were among the earliest in Europe to obtain charters conferring liberties and privileges of self-government. Its counts, many of whom were named Baldwin, frequently pursued independent policies.

Large counties

The County of Anjou—located on the Loire River in western France with Angers as its capital—was surrounded by aggressive neighbors. Its counts, many of whom were named Fulk, were noted for their violent warlike proclivities. The first Angevin (Plantagenet) King of England—Henry II—was a typical representative of this fighting brood.

The County of Toulouse—located in the sunny Midi (South of France) in Languedoc—had a Mediterranean climate and flourishing cities. Many of its pleasure-loving prosperous inhabitants were attracted to the more libertine aspects of Albigensian doctrines.[a] Languedoc—so-called from its southern French dialect (the *langue d'oc*)—was the early home of the art of the troubadours, with their love ditties, set to popular tunes. Many of the Counts of Toulouse were named Raymond.

[a] Explained in Chapter 22.

Champagne and Blois were two prosperous counties on either side of the *Ile de France*, and both were located in busy and fertile river valleys. For some time, the Counts of Champagne were also Counts of Blois. Champagne was especially noted during the High Middle Ages for its excellent wines and its highly successful fairs.

Frontier States with French affiliations—though not properly a part of feudal France—included the County of Barcelona (or Catalonia), the old Spanish March, which obtained its independence with the distintegration of the later Carolingian Empire; the partly Spanish, partly French Kingdom of Navarre in the western region of the Pyrenees; the Kingdoms of (Upper) Burgundy and Provence (Arles) in the Rhône-Saone valley; and the partly German, partly French Duchy (or Duchies) of Lorraine in the western part of the Rhine valley. The Kingdoms of Burgundy and Provence, along with the Duchy of Lorraine, were considered as parts of the Holy Roman Empire.

Frontier states

*Alter-
nating
Robertian
and Caro-
lingian
rulers
(888–
987)*

The rapid growth of feudalism and accompanying decline of monarchical power in France were promoted by the circumstances that France was both a prime target of Norse raids and the scene of prolonged civil war between rival dynasties for the French crown. For a century (888–987), the rival Robertian and Carolingian houses alternated in possession of the monarchical office without either obtaining secure and unchallenged possession of the throne. Civil conflict in France was encouraged by contemporary German monarchs with designs on the old Middle Kingdom, where their encroachments were assisted by French weakness. It was also in accordance with the interests and ambitions of the French aristocracy, since it kept monarchical contenders weak and dependent upon their cooperation.

Following the deposition of Charles the Fat, the West Frankish magnates met to designate a successor for France. Since the legitimate Carolingian heir, Charles the Simple was a child, and the Kingdom was still confronted by grave danger from the Northmen, the magnates chose as King Eudes or Odo (888–898), Duke of Francia, who had distinguished himself in the defense of Paris against Norse besiegers. Eudes was plagued during his reign by the continuing resistance of Carolingian supporters, and by further Norse incursions. In the hope of establishing internal peace and restoring a united front, Eudes nominated as his successor the Carolingian heir, Charles, who was now a grown man, and had meanwhile taken the field against him with the help of the German king. Charles the Simple (898–922) partly solved the Viking problem by granting to the Norse leader Rollo the Duchy of Normandy in northwestern France to be held as a fief on condition that he become a Christian and a royal vassal (911). Normandy, the gateway to France, became a buffer-state against other Scandinavians; but eventually it became a thorn pressing into the side of the French monarchy. Charles the Simple succeeded in occupying Lorraine; but his decision to take up residence there, and his appointment of Hagano of Lorraine as his prime minister—as well as other indications of German leanings—led to his deposition in 922.

The Robertian line was temporarily reinstated with Robert of Neustria (922–23) and his successor, Raoul (Ralph) of Burgundy (923–936). The next head of the Robertian house, Duke Hugh the Great of France—who had great power because of his extensive holdings, numerous vassals, and the support of Otto I of Germany—preferred to rule France indirectly, and cooperated in the recall of the Carolingian heir, Louis, from his exile in England. Louis d' Outremer (Louis From Across the Seas) (936–954), after obtaining the crown, divorced himself from Hugh's support and tutelage, precipitating renewed civil strife. The reign of Louis' son, Lothair (954–986) continued to be troubled by the plots of Robertian supporters. Louis V (986–987), the young son of Lothair, who succeeded his father, met sudden death within a year when he fell from a horse.

*Early
Capetians*

Since the direct Carolingian line in France ended with the premature death of Louis V, the magnates met to select a successor. There were two

The Early Feudal Period

leading candidates: the Robertian descendant, Hugh Capet, Duke of Francia, and a Carolingian claimant, Duke Charles of Lorraine, brother of the late French King Lothair. The sacred Carolingian tradition favored Charles; but national pride and the desire of the nobility to limit the monarchy by asserting the elective principle supported Hugh. The reported nomination speech of Archbishop Adalberon of Reims in favor of Hugh Capet was significant: *What shall we gain by making Charles king? He is neither honorable nor strong. Then, too, he has compromised himself deeply by becoming the dependent of a foreign king, and marrying a girl taken from among his own vassals. . . . Make a decision for the welfare rather than the ruin of our state. If you wish ill to our country, choose Charles; if you desire its prosperity choose Hugh . . . In him you will find a defender not only of the state, but also of your personal interests.* (*From Richer,* Four Books of Histories).

The direct Capetian line of French kings, descended from the Robertians and initiated by Hugh Capet, lasted in father-to-son succession until 1328. The early Capetians (987–1106) were weak feudal monarchs who exercised practically no direct authority outside their own domains, which were inferior in extent, resources, and income to those of some of their greater vassals. The latter rendered to their king little more than occasional military service and suit at court, and these at their own discretion. The early Capetians, who were not noted for aggressive ambition, did little to enhance their direct power or increase their domain. They were forced to participate in the shifting alliance among the great lords in order to retain their royal position and their own limited possessions.

On the other hand, these early Capetians were able to maintain themselves and their family in the royal office and thus make the crown hereditary. Their very inoffensiveness and moderation caused the great lords to be content to accept the Capetian succession, which each king insured by having his eldest son crowned during his own lifetime. The vigor and longevity of the Capetians provided male heirs for three and a half centuries. They never lost the support of the Church, which they enjoyed from the beginning, partly because of their moderate policies. Hugh Capet had received his name from his position as titular abbot of the monastery of St. Denis, for which he was entitled to wear a cope or cape; the Capetians derived considerable support and revenues from their role as advocates or secular representatives of various monasteries. They were indirectly strengthened by the threat of German invasion and the rivalry of English monarchs, who were their nominal vassals for holdings in western France.

Hugh Capet, Robert II, and Henry (987–1060)

The reigns of the first three Capetians were a matter of course. Hugh Capet (987–996), once elected, shrewdly maintained himself in power and foiled the efforts of Charles of Lorraine and the new pro-Carolingian Archbishop Arnulf of Reims to depose him. Hugh insured the succession of his son Robert by having him crowned co-king in 987, the very year of his own accession. Robert II (996–1031) is known as "the Pious," but his supposed piety seems to have existed largely in the imagination of his ecclesiastical biographer. For some time, Robert defied Papal opposition to his second marriage with his cousin Bertha, widow of the Count of Blois, in violation of impediments of both physical and spiritual consanguinity. In 1001, however, Robert was reconciled with the Pope when he put aside Bertha, and married Constance of Toulouse, who gave him several sons. Robert instituted a profitable policy of nibbling accessions for the royal domains. Acquisitions included Dreux, Melun, Troyes, and the Duchy of Burgundy. Henry I (1031–1060), Robert's second son, crowned during his father's lifetime, was faced at the outset by a revolt promoted by his own mother, the Regent Constance, who preferred her youngest son, Prince Robert. But Henry overcame Robert, whom he installed as Duke of Burgundy as a compromise. Henry also surmounted the successive opposition of the Counts of Blois and Anjou, and the Duke of Normandy.

Philip I (1060–1108)

Philip I (1060–1108) was transitional to the subsequent great Capetians, some of whose policies he anticipated. Without resorting to war, he made several minor but valuable additions to the royal domain, including the Gatinais, Vexin, Corbie, Bourges, and Gisors. Philip's main achievement was his success in resisting the attacks of the powerful new Norman kings of England, who—with greatly enhanced power—were attempting to use their Duchy of Normandy as a base for further expansion in France. Philip instituted the policy—which became standard with medieval French kings—of inciting and supporting Continental members of the English royal house against their English king. Thus, he successively supported Robert Curthose, the Duke of Normandy, both against his father, William the Conqueror, and against his brothers, William II and Henry I. Philip was also involved for several years in a quarrel with the Papacy over his illicit liaison with Bertrade de Montfort, the fourth wife of his friend, Count Fulk, the Brawler, of Anjou. Philip preferred Bertrade to his own wife, Bertha of Holland. Although Fulk was amenable and an obsequious French bishop married Philip and Bertrade, the Pope condemned the union. The chronicler relates that, as a result of a Papal interdict, it was the custom, at places where the King sojourned, for divine services to be stopped; but as soon as he was moving away all the bells would begin to peal. Whereupon, the King would laugh like one possessed, and say: "Do'st hear, my love, how they are ringing us out?'"

Eventually Philip was reconciled with the Pope by promising to put away Bertrade—which he did in public, while privately continuing his affair.

In the fertile bosom of early medieval France, feudalism developed, manorialism flourished, towns and trade gradually revived, education and learning spread, vernacular poetry blossomed, and Romanesque architecture began to dot the landscape with beautiful churches.

The Early Feudal Period

THE IBERIAN PENINSULA DURING MOSLEM DOMINANCE. (711–1086)
Section 35.

> O Commander of the Faithful, these are no common conquests! [Governor Musa of North Africa writing to Caliph al-Walìd concerning Moslem victories in Spain (eighth century).]

IN THE early eighth century, the Iberian peninsula came under Moslem Arab rule, except for small portions in the mountainous far north. During the ensuing era, there were really two Spains: the larger, more opulent, more advanced Moslem Spain; and the smaller, poorer, more backward, but expanding, Christian Spain. Gradually, the Christians won back section after section from the Moslems, until in 1086 over one third of the peninsula was again in Christian hands. Meanwhile, Spain was a meeting point between the East and West: a crucible for the mixing of diverse races and cultures: a Western entrepot for influences from the more advanced and cosmopolitan Moslem World.

The Spanish called the Moslem conquerors "Moors," since they came direct from Morocco. The Moslems often called their new state—particularly its more southerly part—"Andalusia" (Vandal-land), since it had previously been occupied by the Vandals. At first a part of the unified Umayyad Caliphate, Moslem Spain soon broke off under the Abbasids, and became independent, tending thereafter to break up into smaller states. Divisive tendencies—promoted by climatic, geographical, racial, and historical differences—affected both Moslem and Christian Spain.

Moslem Spain (711–1086)

After establishing themselves in Morocco, the Moslems looked covetously across the Straits to Spain. In 710, on the orders of Governor Musa of North Africa, a small force of about 500 Berbers made a reconnaissance in Spain. The following year, 711, Musa sent a Berber freedman, Tariq, with about 7,000 men—mostly Berbers—into southern Spain on a plundering raid. Tariq entered Spain via the stepping stone which now bears his name: Gibraltar (*Gebal Tariq*: the Rock of Tariq). At Laguna de la Janda in far southern Spain, Tariq's small contingent was met by a much larger force led by the Visigothic king, Roderick. But Tariq was completely victorious, owing largely to the treachery of the Visigothic king's political enemies; and Roderick disappeared. Encouraged by this success, Tariq converted his raid into a conquering expedition. Aided by the divided leaderless condition of the Visigoths and by defections of Spanish Jews, Tariq took several towns, by-passing stronger fortifications. By 713, he held the Visigothic capital of Toledo in central Spain.

Stung by the fact that his Berber lieutenant had exceeded his instructions and preempted the conquest, Governor Musa invaded Spain in 712, with some 10,000 troops largely composed of Syrians and Arabs. He reduced strongholds by-passed by Tariq, with whom he met up at Toledo in 713. He put Tariq in chains and took him along on a triumphal march to Damascus. Here the Umayyad caliph, al-Walìd, likewise humbled Musa for his own insubordination (715), so that he died an impoverished outcast.

After completing the conquest of most of the Iberian peninsula by 718, the Moslems seized Septimania (former Visigothic province along the Mediterranean west of the Rhône in southern France), whence they raided and harassed neighboring Frankish territories. But their effort to take Toulouse was repulsed in 721 by the forces of Duke Eudes of Aquitaine. And their plundering expedition into western France in 732 was shattered by the successful resistance of the Franks under Charles Martel in the battle of Tours-Poitiers.

The Moslem conquest of Spain had been the simultaneous work of Berbers, Arabs, and Syrians, who were frequently at odds with one another. This westernmost Emirate of the Umayyad Caliphs became a turbulent scene of bitter rivalries. From 732 to 755 there was a condition of civil war with 23 governors in as many years.

Umayyad Spain (756–1031)

A degree of peace and unity was established after the Umayyad heir Abd-al-Rahmàn I (756–788) arrived as a refugee from the East and took over the reins of government with the help of old adherents of his house, refusing to accept the Abbasid succession. Even under this strong and ruthless emir, local Moslem rulers such as those of Saragossa and Valencia were often in open defiance of the central government. Charlemagne's initial invasion of the peninsula in 778 was at the invitation of a confederation of rebel Arab chieftains of northern Spain. Carolingian intervention in Spain was also abetted by the new Abbasid Caliphate at Bagdad, anxious to smother the last flame of Umayyad resistance. The Frankish presence in northeastern Spain gave some aid and encouragement to the still free but feeble Christians of Asturias.

Although the Umayyad dynasty continued to rule in Spain for almost three centuries, its amount of control fluctuated. In 929, the strong Abd-al-Rahmàn III (912–961)—under whom the Moslem state in Spain reached its height—declared himself Caliph and converted the Emirate into the Caliphate of Cordova. In the latter part of the same tenth century, the brilliant aggressive Vizir al Mansur (977–1002), (the conqueror), made devastating incursions deep into Christian territory and threatened to turn the tide of the Christian Reconquest. When he died in 1002, a Christian chronicler wrote: "Al-Mansur died and was buried in hell." After this, however, Umayyad power swiftly crumbled. The last Umayyad Caliph—Hisham III—was confined with his family in a dark vault until he was deposed in 1031.

Taifas (1031 ff.)

In the "Era of the Taifas" (Petty States: 1031 ff.), Moslem Spain broke up into as many as twenty small kingdoms centered in leading cities such as Seville, Cordova, Granada, and Málaga. This fission invited a stepped-up Christian reconquest. Besides being able to pick off one petty state after another, the Christians could now play off their Moslem rivals one against another. Alarmed by the fall of Toledo in 1085, Moslem leaders invited in their coreligionists, the warlike Murabits (Almoravides) of Morocco (1086), who temporarily united Moslem Spain under a military dictatorship and stemmed the Christian Reconquest.

Civilization

The civilization of Moslem Spain was rich and brilliant, at least in the upper circles of society and in the prosperous towns. Industry and agriculture prospered. Many new processes—such as papermaking, and the production of silk and cotton textiles—were introduced. Spain was noted for superior products such as Toledan blades, Cordovan leathers, Grenadine gauze, and many forms of Moorish glazed tiles. Many new plants —including oranges, lemons, apricots, various melons, cotton, sugar cane, and rice—were introduced, and agricultural techniques were improved. Beautiful and populous cities such as Cordova, Granada, Seville, Malaga, Murcia, and Valencia graced the landscape. Cordova—the caliphal capital with an estimated half a million population—is said to have had 600–700 mosques, 700–900 public baths, 50–70 libraries, and 21 suburbs, and a total of about 200,000 homes and palaces.

Al-Andalus, westernmost outpost of Moslem civilization, was also one of its most progressive cultural areas. Schools associated with the Great Mosque of Cordova and the Mosque of Seville attained a status equivalent to that of universities. Education and learning were prized, and many persons built up impressive private libraries. Several rulers were generous patrons of culture. The caliphal library at Cordova is said to have had from 400,000–600,000 volumes, while in the city there were numerous book markets. An Arab writer declared: *Cordova is Andalusia's fair bride . . . Her gleaming crown consists in her long line of illustrious sultans, her lovely necklace is strung with pearls gleaned from the ocean of language by her poets; her dress is finely woven with the learning of her men of science; and her garments are embroidered by masters of all the arts and crafts.*

Much of the impulse to higher learning in philosophy, the sciences, mathematics, and medicine that characterized Western Europe in the High Middle Ages came from Latin translations of Arabic works made in Spain—e.g., at Toledo. Among great Spanish Moslem philosophers were Ibn-Bajjah (Avempace), Ibn-Tufayl, and Ibn-Rushd (Averroës). Ibn-Rushd was probably the greatest philosopher in the Moslem world, and was very instrumental in promoting Aristotelianism in Western Europe. The greatest medieval Jewish philosophers included Avicebron (Ibn Gabirol) and Maimonides, both of Spain. Several great philosophers were also great physicians—notably Averroës and Maimonides. Among other noted Hispano-Moslem medical authorities were Avenzoar (Ibn Zohr)-- one of Islam's greatest clinical physicians, and Abulcasis (Abu Khasim) —Islam's greatest surgeon. The acknowledged "Master" of Moslem mysticism was the Hispano-Arab, Ibn-Arabi.

Moslem Spain was notable for its lyric poetry and architecture. Arabic lyric poetry in Spain developed pleasing new forms, such as those of *zajals* and *muwashahshahs,* and had a special sensitivity to natural beauty and human love. Through Moslem Spain, many new musical forms and instruments—such as the lute and rebec (precursor of the violin)—came into Western Europe. The delicacy, grace, and lacelike beauty of Spanish-Moslem architecture were exemplified in the Alhambra or "Red One," the Nasrid castle at Granada; the graceful Giralda tower at Seville; and the intricate Great Mosque at Cordova, with its "forest" of over 1,200 delicate columns set amid "acres" of mosaics. It is estimated that in the pulpit of the Great Mosque there are about 36,000 separate panels of ivory and choice woods. A fairy-land palace called *Al-Zahra* was built at Cordova by Caliph Abd al-Rhaman III for his favorite wife.

Shortcomings of Moslem Spain

The ultimate downfall of the Moslems in Spain was due to their failure either to convert their Spanish subjects to Islam or to be themselves converted to Christianity. As a result, they failed to achieve a political, social, religious, and cultural unity in their state, which remained divided. Besides having to rule over a hostile alien population, the Moslems in Spain were sharply divided among themselves, largely along ethnic lines. Since the Moslems never succeeded in permanently solving their own differences or overcoming the geographical sectionalism in Spain, their state fragmentalized. The cleavage which continued to divide the Moslem ruling class from the Christian majority was aggravated by the Christian retention of their own laws and courts, and the proximity of sympathetic fellow-Christians in neighboring Christian states. The many Christians under Moslem rule who were partly Arabicized in speech and manners came to be known as "Mozarabs" or "quasi-Arabs." The minority of Christians who were converted to Islam, whether to escape the poll tax, to win preferment, or from conviction—came to be known as *renegados* or "renegades." Most Christians remained true to the faith of their fathers. Meanwhile, Arabic society on upper levels suffered from the complications induced by a plurality of wives and concubines.

The greatest asset of Moslem Spain was its nourishing contact with the civilization of the rest of the Moslem world, especially with that of the advanced Near East. Its greatest liability was the lack of amalgamation between its peoples, religions, and cultures, and the failure of the Moslems either to assimilate or to become assimilated to the Christian majority.

Christian Spain: Multiplication of small kingdoms

The historian Maqqari, reflecting on the Moslem conquest of Spain, wrote: *Would be to Allah that the Moslems had then extinguished the last sparks of a fire which was destined eventually to consume the entire holdings of Islam in these parts!* He referred to the small remnant of independent Christians in the northwestern part of the peninsula left unconquered by the Moslems. The free Christians remaining in the mountainous far north would in the following centuries gradually win back former Christian territories. This process, known as the *Reconquista*, had the character of a crusade. The Christians were helped by frequent division among the Moslems; the partly religious motivation of their endeavor; strong Church support; the sympathy and assistance of the Christian majority in Moslem territories; and reinforcement by volunteers from beyond the Pyrenees, especially from France. The common battlecry of the Spanish Christians, as they fought the Moslems was *Santiago!*—calling upon the Apostle St. James, whose body reputedly rested at Compostela (in far northwestern Spain). In the course of the Reconquest, several small Christian states developed.

Spanish tradition has it that after the death of King Roderick, a Visigothic noble, Pelayo, was elected to head the Christian resistance. Towards the close of the Moslem conquest of Spain a small band of Chris-

The Early Feudal Period

tians commanded by Pelayo were attacked by Moslem soldiers in a vale known as Covadonga, in the Cantabrian Mountains (718). Despite a deadly shower of stones and arrows, the Christians refused to surrender, and instead counterattacked and routed the Moslems. As a result of this victory, the small Christian kingdom of Asturias survived in the rugged vicinity of the "Peaks of Europe" in far northern Spain to the south of the Bay of Biscay. From this base, the Christians of Asturias subsequently took Galicia in the far northwest of the peninsula, which sometimes enjoyed the status of a separate kingdom.

In the latter part of the same eighth century, fellow-Christians from across the Pyrenees took the northeastern corner of Spain, and established there the "Spanish March" of the Franks. The kings of Asturias seem to have recognized a vague overlordship of Emperor Charlemagne. After the Carolingian Empire broke up, the Spanish March became independent and was known as the County of Barcelona, from its principal city.

In the ninth century, the kings of Asturias—who were moving their capital southward by stages (from Cangas de Onis to Pravia to Oviedo) as they gradually took more territories at Moslem expense—expanded across the Cantabrian Mountains and took the city of Leon, whither they moved their capital in the early tenth century. The kings of Leon also expanded to the southeast into north-central Spain in the vicinity of Burgos, which frontier area began to bristle with castles and hence acquired the name of Castile. To the doughty warrior Count Fernán González of Castile (mid-tenth century) is attributed the establishment of Castile's autonomy. Of him a popular poem declared:

> *By the name Fernando was the first count dight:*
> *Never in the world was there such another knight!*
> *Ever to the Moslems a source of mortal fright:*
> *They called him "Vulture Butcher" for his prowess in the fight!*

During the ninth century, the tiny kingdom of Navarre arose in the central part of the far North, straddling the Pyrenees. Navarre reached its height under King Sancho the Great (1000–1035), who expanded his realms and temporarily united much of Christian Spain. But on his death in 1035, Sancho the Great divided his sprawling possessions among his sons. García, the first-born, he made King of Navarre; another, Ferdinand, King of Castile; another, Ramiro, King of Aragon. Castile and Aragon thus obtained the status of kingdoms: they would subsequently become the most important states in Spain. Meanwhile, the Kingdom of Leon—which included the older kingdoms of Asturias and Galicia—remained independent, as also did the County of Barcelona.

Accelerated Reconquista and beginnings of consolidation

The *Reconquista* was greatly accelerated in the eleventh century, particularly in the period from 1031–1086 (which is sometimes known as the first period of the Spanish Crusade). Assuming the lead in the reconquest and initiating the process of consolidation were Castile and Leon. By 1037, the energetic Ferdinand I (1035–65) of Castile had overcome the King of Leon and united all of northwestern Spain under his sole rule. After a brief period of separation, Castile and Leon were again united under Alfonso VI of Leon (1065–1109). Increasing numbers of Moslem *taifas* were overcome and incorporated into the expanding kingdom. It looked as though all of Moslem Spain might be regained when Alfonso VI rode his horse into the sea at Tarifa in the extreme south of the peninsula. Alfonso made the Moslem Kingdom of Valencia tributary and took the County of Oporto, which would eventually expand and become the Kingdom of Portugal. He expanded his possessions to the Tagus River, where he took the centrally located former Visigothic capital of Toledo in 1085. This was the era of the famous frontier warrior Rodrigo Diaz de Bivar, hero of *The Poem of My Cid*. Alarmed, the Moslems now invited in their Berber correligionists, the Murabits—Almoravids—of Morocco (1086), to help them against the Christians. Led by their king Yusuf, the Almoravids decisively defeated the army of Alfonso VI at Zalaca (1086), and for some time the Reconquest was halted.

The civilization of Early Christian Spain (c. 718–1086)

The civilization of Early Christian Spain during the Moslem era (to about 1086) was composite and often paradoxical. On the one hand, the Christians had a hardy warlike type of society, inherited from the Visigoths and strongly influenced by feudal France. On the other hand, certain features of their civilization were more sophisticated, owing to Moslem influences. The monarchy in Spain, like that in France, was extremely limited. Feudalism spread, and the nobles—whose cooperation was so essential in defense and reconquest—enjoyed considerable autonomy. But even in this early period, the Spanish towns were important and had a large degree of self-government. Many obtained formal charters (*cartas*) granting them various privileges, including the right to have their own laws and courts (*fueros*). The towns were typically ruled by town councils (*concejos*) and assemblies (*juntas*). For some time, there were in Spanish society several distinct groups, each with its own laws and courts. Included were the recently conquered Moslems, known as *Mudejares*; Christians recently under Moslem rule, known as *Mozarabes* (semi-Arabs); Jews known as *Marranos* (pigs); foreigners known as "Franks"; and Spanish Christians who had been free for some time. Still another system of law—the canon law of the Church—governed those of clerical or monastic status.

The economy of reconquered regions usually continued much as it had been under the Moslems. The Moslems and Jews constituted the greater portion of the commercial, industrial, and financial classes; the Christians the majority of the landholding nobility on the one hand, and the dependent rural peasantry on the other. Members of the Spanish Christian upper classes were characteristically proud and aggressive, daring and adventurous, as well as accustomed to conquering, organizing, and administering new territories.

The chief source of strength and unity in Christian Spain was its common religion and common cause against the Moslems. The Christian clergy and monks enthusiastically promoted the Reconquest, and shared in the fruits of victory. A strong spirit of piety inspired liberal gifts to churches and monasteries. Located at a juncture of "two worlds," Spain was a fructifying funnel for Islamic influences.

The Early Feudal Period

ANGLO-SAXON ENGLAND
Section 36.

(c. 800–1066)

> At Edington, King Alfred fought with the whole force of the Danes, and put them to flight, and rode after them to their fortifications, and besieged them a fortnight. Then the Danes gave him hostages as security, and swore great oaths that they would leave his kingdom, and promised that their king should receive baptism. And they carried out their promises. . . . [Victory of Alfred the Great over the Danes at Edington (878), as narrated in the *Anglo-Saxon Chronicle*.]

IN THE period from 800–1066, England—which had previously been a composite of several small Germanic kingdoms—was fused into a single kingdom, largely through a common Christianity, the pressure of Scandinavian invasions, and the strong leadership of the kings of Wessex. The Danish conquest and rule of England in the first half of the eleventh century, and the Norman conquest and rule in the second half of the same century, contributed to strengthening the English monarchy. Although backward in some respects, Anglo-Saxon England was progressive in others.

Scandinavian incursions

England was one of the earliest and principal targets of Viking attacks. Its insularity and extended coasts made it particularly vulnerable, while its growing prosperity made it especially attractive. Monasteries were favorite early objectives, St. Cuthbert's Lindisfarne being attacked in 793, and Bede's Wearmouth and Jarrow in 794. Of the first recorded Viking raid, the *Anglo-Saxon Chronicle* states: *Heathen men savagely destroyed God's church on Lindisfarne with great plundering and bloodshed.* For a while Scandinavian attacks on England slackened, owing to preoccupations elsewhere; but from 835 on, their assaults became more frequent and severe. The assailants were called *Danes* by the English, but they also included Swedes and Norwegians. In 850, a large host of Danes with 350 ships wintered on the Isle of Thanet, opposite the mouth of the Thames. In 865, the Danes came with a "Great Army," bent on conquest and settlement. By 870, they had overrun most of England outside of Wessex.

Alfred the Great (871–899)

By the ninth century, Wessex had become the strongest of the Anglo-Saxon kingdoms. It came to the fore under Egbert (802–839), who became Bretwalda and is often reckoned as the first King of England. In 871, Alfred, who was a younger son, and who had been preceded on the throne by three of his elder brothers, became King of Wessex just as the Danes were beginning to overrun the kingdom. Resistance stiffened under Alfred (871–899), who is known in history as "the Great." The very year of Alfred's accession was his "year of battles," when he met the forces of the invading enemy eight times. From 872–876, Alfred bought temporary peace by paying annual tribute; and during this interval he built up his forces and defenses. When hostilities were renewed in 876, the fortunes of war oscillated until peace was agreed on. But in midwinter, 878, the Danes broke their agreement, attacked and surprised Alfred, who was forced to take refuge in the woodlands and marshes. In the spring, however, he emerged, rapidly gathered forces, and surprised and defeated the Danes at Edington or Ethandune (878). In the ensuing Treaty of Wedmore (878), the chastened Danes agreed to confine themselves to the Danelaw, which comprised eastern and northern England beyond the mouth of the Thames River, and their king, Guntrum, consented to embrace Christianity. England was divided between the Danes and the English. The Danelaw included most of the Northumbria, Mercia, and Essex. Anglo-Saxon southern and western England included Wessex, Sussex, and Kent, together with fringe portions of Mercia and Essex.

One of the results of the prolonged contest with the Scandinavians was to weld England into a single state under the leadership of the King of Wessex. Further large Scandinavian invasions were met and repulsed in 884–885 and 892–896 by Alfred, who somewhat enlarged his holdings. His sons completed the conquest of the Danelaw and the unification of England.

Reforms of Alfred

As means of defense against the Scandinavians, Alfred reorganized the Anglo-Saxon *fyrd*, constructed *burgs* which he provided with garrisons, and began a rudimentary English navy. The *fyrd*—the traditional militia of freemen—was weak because of incomplete representation of the population, lack of training, and the requirement that its members be allowed to return home to take care of their crops, flocks, and families. Alfred remedied these defects by extending the obligation to all able-bodied male citizens, but requiring only half of them to serve in the *fyrd* at a given time, in a rotating manner. Thus, while one half was training, the other half could take care of necessities at home. Alfred had fortifications (*burgs, burghs,* or boroughs) built at strategic places and manned by part of the men from the surrounding districts in a revolving manner. Shires were divided into sections or districts, with each district maintaining its own fortifications. Alfred is also regarded as "the Father of the English Navy" because he developed a sea force to fight off and pursue the Scandinavian raiders. According to Bishop Asser, *King Alfred commanded boats and long ships to be built throughout the kingdom in order to offer battle by sea to the enemy as they would approach.* (Asser, *Deeds of Alfred the Great*).

King Alfred did not win the title of "Great" simply by his military successes. He was also a superior ruler, administrator, and lawgiver, and one of history's famous promoters of education and learning. By Alfred's time, partly as a result of prolonged Viking incursions, the flame of the lamp of learning was low in England. In the preface to his translation of *The Pastoral Care* of Gregory I, sent to Bishop Werfurth, Alfred writes: *So general has the decay of learning become in our day that there are now very few on this side of the Humber* [outside of Northumbria] *who can translate and understand the Church services or render in English a Latin letter; and I believe that there are likewise few beyond the Humber who can do these things.* Alfred contrasts this with "the good old days" when "foreigners came to this land in search of wisdom and instruction." He concludes: *Therefore it seems better to me, if you agree, to translate some of the books which are most needful for all men to know into the language which we can all understand.* The learned Alfred trans-

The Early Feudal Period

lated or had translated into Anglo-Saxon Boethius: *Consolation of Philosophy*; Orosius: *History of the World*; Gregory I: *Pastoral Care*; Bede: *Ecclesiastical History of the English Nation*; and Augustine: *Soliloquies*. He also encouraged compilation in the vernacular of a running history of England known as *The Anglo-Saxon Chronicle*. He gathered around himself a circle of learned scholars to cooperate in the work of translation, to give him advice, and to constitute a palace school which would provide England with learned ecclesiastics.

Even before the death of Alfred, it became apparent that neither side would accept the Peace of Wedmore as a permanent solution. Danish raids into English territories soon resumed, and the English for their part sought repeatedly to recover the territories ceded to the Danes. Gradually, the alienated territories were brought under English rule, as Alfred's son Edward the Elder (899–925), and the latter's three sons, Ethelstan, Edmund, and Edred (925–955), won back, piece by piece, the Danelaw, including East Anglia, Mercia, and Northumbria. Under Edgar the Peaceful (959–975), Anglo-Saxon England—now a single kingdom—reached its height. Of Edgar's reign, the *Anglo-Saxon Chronicle* says *In his days there was prosperity, and God granted him that he dwelt in peace*. Meanwhile, a remarkable reform of English monasteries and the English Church was sparked by Archbishop St. Dunstan of Canterbury.

England under Alfred's successors (899–1016)

During the later tenth century and the early eleventh century, Danish incursions revived on a large scale. Ethelred the Redeless—the Counsel-less or Unready—(978–1016), was initially handicapped by coming to the throne at the age of eight. On reaching manhood, he was irresolute, imprudent, and cruel, and came to be hated and distrusted even by his own subjects. Instead of fighting off the invading Scandinavians, Ethelred adopted the policy of buying them off by tribute. Payments had to be steadily increased, and necessitated a general tax which came to be known as the *Danegeld* ("money for the Danes"). Another rash policy of Ethelred's was that of taking Danes into his own service. In 1002, angered over the apparent treachery of their leader, Ethelred indulged in a general massacre of these Danes and their families. Whereupon the tempo and ferocity of Danish attacks on England increased.

In 1013, enraged by the defection of one of his leaders, Sweyn (Swein) Forkbeard, King of Denmark, launched a large-scale invasion of England with the avowed objective of replacing Ethelred. When Sweyn died in 1014, he was succeeded by his son Canute (Knut). Lacking the support of his subjects, Ethelred was forced to flee to Normandy, and was succeeded by his son Edmund Ironsides, who came to the throne on Ethelred's death in 1016, but died later the same year.

Bereft of a leader and tired of warfare, the English accepted Canute as their king. Canute proved himself a wise and just ruler and won the appellation of "Great" in English history. He made England the headquarters of a large northern empire, which also included Denmark, Norway and Iceland, as well as an overlordship over Sweden. Canute, who was a Christian, married Emma, Ethelred's widow, and treated his English subjects with great consideration and discretion. He cooperated with

England as part of a Danish Empire (1017–1042)

the English bishops and favored the Church. His rule was beneficial to England for improved internal law and order and for increased foreign prestige and trade.

But Canute's sons, who were dissolute, incompetent, and cruel, enjoyed none of their father's popularity, forfeited English support, and both died early—Harold in 1040 and Harthacanute in 1042.

Edward the Confessor (1042–1066)

The Witangemot (Anglo-Saxon assembly of the magnates) took advantage of this opportunity to call back to England Edward, Ethelred's son, who had been in exile in Normandy. Known as "the Confessor" for his piety, Edward was at the time 40 years of age. A confirmed celibate, reared by monks, Edward was mild, weak, and indecisive. According to the chronicler, he had to be persuaded and reassured by the powerful Earl Godwin of Wessex and Bishop Lyfing of Crediton to assume the throne.

Friction gradually developed between the King and his Anglo-Saxon supporters. Earl Godwin for some time controlled the government, and Edward was obliged to pay for his support by making Godwin's two sons and one of his nephews earls. Edward also married Godwin's daughter Edith. On the other hand, Edward's personal tastes and inclinations were more Norman than English, largely owing to his upbringing. He brought many Normans to England and gave them high positions in State and Church. All of which, together with his lavish expenditures—such as those required for the construction of a magnificent new church for Westminster Abbey—aroused the opposition of the Anglo-Saxon nobility.

Eventually Edward broke with the domineering earl, and since public opinion was on the side of the King, Godwin was forced into exile (1051). But Edward's renewed and increased favoritism to his friends from the continent—and especially his appointment of Norman Robert of Jumièges to the powerful post of Archbishop of Canterbury—alienated English support, and Godwin was able to return and resume his ascendance (1052 ff.). The Witangemot now exiled several of Edward's Norman favorites, including Robert of Jumièges, who was replaced as Archbishop of Canterbury by a native Anglo-Saxon, Stigand. When Earl Godwin died in 1053, he was succeeded as leader of the Anglo-Saxon party by his eldest son, Harold.

The Norman Conquest (1066)

For some time, the question of the succession to the childless Edward had been uppermost. There were three leading competitors for the crown: Earl Harold Godwinson, King Harold Hardrada of Norway, and Duke William of Normandy. On the Confessor's death, the Witangemot elected Godwinson king. An Anglo-Saxon and the most powerful earl in England, Harold was also the brother-in-law of the King, and already for quite a while (about 1053–1066) had been the real head of the government. Harold appears to have been designated as successor by Edward on his deathbed. He was a born leader: able, prudent, brave, and decisive.

King Harold Hardrada of Norway, a famous and adventurous warrior, claimed the succession through the Danish line. Accompanied by Godwinson's disgruntled and jealous brother, Tostig, the displaced Earl of Northumbria, Hardrada landed in the north of England. With hastily

The Early Feudal Period

mustered forces, Harold Godwinson hurried north from London over a distance of about 200 miles to meet the invaders, who had taken York and were harrying the countryside. At Stamford Bridge, Godwinson's English army surprised and destroyed the Norwegian army, and both Hardrada and Tostig perished.

Duke William of Normandy also claimed the succession. Although of illegitimate birth, William had succeeded his father as duke. He was remotely related to Edward the Confessor, since the ruling houses of Normandy and England had intermarried. William claimed that his cousin, the Confessor, had promised him the succession during his visit to England in 1052; and that Harold Godwinson, shipwrecked on the Norman coast in 1064, had sworn to support his candidacy. William obtained the Papal blessing with a Papal banner for his projected invasion, since the Pope considered the English Church to be in a state of schism owing to the Anglo-Saxon deposition of the Archbishop Robert of Jumièges and his replacement by Stigand. William organized a large expedition to enforce his "rights." He gathered a large fleet and assembled an army estimated at from 10,000 to 15,000 men, including not only his own Norman vassals, but also volunteers from various parts of France. He also made an alliance with Tostig, whose thrust in the north enabled William to land unchallenged in southern England.

Harold decided to attack William before he could advance and take London. By forced marches he brought his fatigued and depleted Anglo-Saxon troops southward to the vicinity of Hastings, where they took up a favorable position on a hill along a road leading to London. Numerically, the two armies seem to have been about equal. On the English side, the *housecarls* (personal bodyguard of the king), *thegns* (knights), and *fyrd* (levies from the shires) were practically all infantry, whereas William's army was mainly composed of cavalry and archers. Closely packed with interlocking shields, the Anglo-Saxons stood firm against the attacks of William's cavalry. Eventually, however, elements of the *fyrd* were drawn out by feigned retreats and slaughtered. Still, the *housecarls* stood firm until William's archers began to shoot their arrows upward so that they fell almost perpendicularly into Anglo-Saxon ranks. As his troops began to waver, Harold himself was shot through the head (apparently through the eye) with an arrow. Bereft of their leader, the Anglo-Saxons melted away.

The victorious William moved on to London where he was accepted by the helpless Witangemot, and crowned at Westminster by the Archbishop of York. Completion of the Conquest took several years, as revolts against the Normans continued to break out. As the Conquest proceeded, the Normans erected castles to control the country. Resistance was especially strong in the north and west.

Anglo-Saxon civilization is of particular interest to us because of its carry-over in English and American institutions. In the period from 800 to 1066, Anglo-Saxon institutions and culture were affected by continental influences, but retained much of their own distinctive flavor. Although backward in some respects, Anglo-Saxon England was progressive in

Anglo-Saxon civilization

others, and far from benighted. A special feature of Anglo-Saxon institutions was their emphasis on the rights of individuals and their provision for popular participation in government.

Government

Anglo-Saxon government has been described as a balance between three elements: monarchy, nobility, and Church. Coronation services blended Roman and Christian with Germanic elements, and included such features as anointing, enthronement, and investiture, as well as royal oaths to protect the Church and people and to administer justice. The kings came to be recognized as protectors and servants of the people and the Church. The national Anglo-Saxon Witangemot or "meeting of the wise men," the leading men of the kingdom who were advisers to the king—was frequently called on to decide a disputed succession. Although the kingship was recognized as hereditary, a choice could be made among possible candidates as to the best qualified. The Witangemot was also called on to legitimize such important measures as promulgation of the laws of Ine and Alfred, and the exile of Earl Godwin. The nationwide direct tax or *Danegeld* established by Ethelred the Redeless to buy off the Danes was continued by both Canute and William the Conqueror, although for other reasons.

Trend to feudalism

There was a trend to feudalism in Anglo-Saxon England, although the full feudal system was not introduced until the Norman Conquest. As England was unified, former kingdoms tended to retain considerable autonomy, as also did the great earldoms and dukedoms which superseded them. The pressure of Danish incursions put a premium on professional military forces, as also did the weakness of certain English kings.

Lands known as *loanland*, or income, were often conceded by the king on condition of military service. Other lands known as *booklands* were granted by the king to lords or to the Church, exempt from all obligations save military service and the maintenance of fortifications and bridges. A new class of lesser landholding lords—known as *thegns* or "thanes," similar to landed vassals on the continent—appeared, as also did the *cnights* or knights, who were landless military retainers. Local jurisdiction such as *sac* and *soc* (cause and suit) was often granted to lords, providing immunities excluding their territories from the operations of royal justice.

Local government

The Anglo-Saxon balance of power between monarchy, nobles, and Church was manifest in local government. The shires (shares or counties) continued to be the chief governmental subdivisions. Shirecourts were presided over jointly by the earl, the sheriff, and the bishop. For purposes of defense, dukes were set over groups of shires by the successors of Alfred, and earls by the Danish rulers. The old term and position of *ealdorman* was now supplanted by that of *eorl* (Anglo-Saxon) or *jarl* (Danish)—terms which coalesced as *earl*,—denoting a military leader of several counties or shires. The power of the great earls is exemplified by that of Earl Godwin of Wessex.

As the old ealdorman had been replaced by the more powerful earl (set over several shires), the sheriff (shire-reeve) became the most powerful secular official in the shire. The king's representative in the shire, the sheriff collected taxes, raised and headed military levies, and saw to the administration of justice and implementation of the king's commands. The shire courts were jointly presided over by the sheriff, the earl, and the bishop. The bishops were important political as well as religious leaders, and participated in the Witangemot.

Hundreds or *wapentakes*—the Danish name—were political and military subdivisions of shires. Whether the hundred—a common subdivision among the Germans—originally designated a hundred fighting men, a hundred families, a hundred hides of land, or the like, is uncertain. The hundred had its own "reeve" or hundred-man, as well as its own "moot" or meeting and court.

Meanwhile, boroughs became distinct political and administrative units. The name derives from a root (*burg* or *burh*) meaning a fortified place. Alfred established fortifications (*burhs*) for defense against the Danes, and the Danes did likewise in their Danelaw. As town life grew during the revival of commerce in the tenth to eleventh centuries, these *burhs* acquired their own government, courts, and privileges, and each borough typically had its own reeve and moot.

Anglo-Saxon economy and society

The Angles, Saxons, and Jutes who settled in England were agricultural and pastoral peoples, as well as experienced maritime traders, and they continued these profitable activities. The manorial system of large estates, worked by dependent laborers, came to prevail in the fertile lowlands of England, although independent holdings were also present. There was much more trade and commerce in Anglo-Saxon England than is sometimes supposed, as is evidenced by the growth of towns.

Serfdom spread in England in this turbulent period, even as it did on the Continent. Various degrees of dependence developed among the peasantry. The old term *ceorl*—meaning freeman—now took on a new connotation of *churl*—villein or serf. There were numerous confusing degrees of dependence and freedom. The spread of serfdom was promoted by repeated foreign invasions, need for security, and increasing reservation of military service to a professional military class.

The term *thegn* (thane) came to designate members of the nobility. The *thegns* were the principal element in the army, the possessors of substantial estates, and the lords of other men. The *wergelds* (compensations for injuries) of *thegns* or nobles were three to six times those of ordinary freemen. *Cnights* (knights, from *knecht*—"servant" or "man") were armed household retainers of lords, and similar to landless knights on the Continent. Originally of lesser status, the *cnights* eventually came to hold a higher standing. Members of the bodyguard of the king, known as *housecarls*, had a special status and privileges, as well as a higher *wergeld*.

Anglo-Saxon Church and culture

The Church, a unifying uplifting force in Anglo-Saxon history, was also both wealthy and powerful. Bishops were reckoned as important political figures as well as religious officials, participated in the Witangemot, and presided alongside the earl and sheriff in the shire court. The Archbishop of Canterbury was recognized as the second highest personage in the kingdom. In the English Church—which had originally been organized along monastic lines—the election of bishops was often in the hands of monks, with cathedrals known as *ministers* (monasteries).

Rough and turbulent times led to a decline in clerical education and standards, as well as a deterioration of monastic training and observance. A temporary revival of education was promoted by Alfred the Great in the ninth century; and a general ecclesiastical reform movement by Archbishop St. Dunstan of Canterbury in the tenth century. Among features of Dunstan's reform were stricter observance of the law of celibacy among the clergy, as well as greater attention to learning among ecclesiastics in general. The cultural interests of Edward the Confessor in the eleventh century—as exemplified by his construction of Westminster Abbey Church—also had a favorable influence.

While simple and unsophisticated, the civilization of Anglo-Saxon England was hardy and vital. Its greatest virtue was probably its ingrained respect for the individual and his rights, together with its provisions for popular participation in government and in the administration of justice. England enjoyed the advantage of being on the frontier of European civilization, allowing for freer interplay of diverse influences, and fuller preservation of liberty and self-government.

References for Chapter 12

THE *Cambridge Medieval History*, Vol. III, continues to be one of the best sources of information on several aspects of this period, with articles on Early Feudal France (888–987 and 987–1106); Moslem and Early Christian Spain (The Western Caliphate": 718–1031); and Anglo-Saxon England (796–954 and 954–1066). The political evolution of the French and English states from the tenth to thirteenth centuries is the subject of a scholarly comparative study by CHARLES E. PETIT-DUTAILLIS, *The Feudal Monarchy in France and England . . .* (New York: Knopf, 1936; also paperback—New York: Harper, 1964).

The story of Early Feudal France is to be found in the chauvinistic, somewhat superficial, and popular, but also colorful accounts of JACQUES C. FUNCK-BRENTANO, *The Earliest Times* and *The Middle Ages*, tr. E. F. Buckley, (New York: Putnam, 1927 and 1923), and FRANCOIS P. GUIZOT, *A Popular History of France . . .*, tr. Robert Black, 6 vols. in four, Vol. I (New York: Bolles, 1872–1876), both especially useful for their anecdotes and quotations of sources.

More analytical is CHARLES A. GUIGNEBERT, *Short History of the French People*, tr. F. G. Richmond, 2 vols. (New York: Macmillan, 1930). French political history and institutions from 987 to 1328 are the subject of ROBERT FAWTIER, *The Capetian Kings of France*, tr. L. Butler and R. Adam (London: Macmillan, 1960). French civilization in the period is discussed by ALBERT L. GUERARD in *France* (Ann Arbor: U. of Mich., 1959).

The history of Spain in this period is told by RAFAEL ALTAMIRA Y CREVEA, *History of Spain . . .*, tr. Muna Lee (New York: Van Nostrand, 1949); GABRIEL JACKSON, *The Making of Medieval Spain* (New York: Harcourt, 1972); LOUIS BERTRAND and CHARLES PETRIE, *History of Spain* (New York: Appleton, 1934); ULICK R. BURKE, *A History of Spain . . . to the Death of Ferdinand . . .*, and CHARLES E. CHAPMAN, *History of Spain* (New York: Macmillan, 1927). The story of early Christian Spain is also surveyed in the introductory part of ROGER B. MERRIMAN, *Rise of the Spanish Empire . . .*, 4 vols., Vol. I (New

The Early Feudal Period

York: Macmillan, 1936), an excellent work. W. MONTGOMERY WATT, *A History of Islamic Spain* . . . (Edinburgh: Aldine, 1965) is a good introduction. Moslem Spain is also the topic of the detailed, largely anecdotal REINHART P. DOZY, *Spanish Islam* . . . , tr. F. G. Stokes (London: Chatto, 1918), as well as of the briefer, but more generalized and intelligible STANLEY LANE POOLE and ARTHUR GILMAN, *The Moors in Spain* (New York: Putnam, 1911), and the extensive SAMUEL P. SCOTT, *History of the Moorish Empire in Europe*, 3 vols. (Philadelphia: Lippincott, 1904). In the latter, Vols. I and II treat History, and Vol. III deals with Culture and Civilization. Moslem Spain is also surveyed by EDWYN HOLE, *Andalus: Spain Under the Muslims* (London: R. Hale, 1958); and is likewise the subject of Part IV (8 chapters) in the excellent PHILIP K. HITTI, *History of the Arabs* (New York: Macmillan, 1946).

Anglo-Saxon England is naturally a well-covered topic in books in the English language. Two reliable works in the Oxford *History of England* series are ROBIN G. COLLINGWOOD and J. N. MYRES, *Roman Britain and the English Settlements,* and (especially) FRANK M. STENTON, *Anglo-Saxon England* (Oxford: Clarendon, 1937 and 1947). A classic study is ROBERT N. HODGKIN, *History of the Anglo-Saxons*, 2 vols. (third ed., London: Oxford U.P., 1952); while DOUGLAS JERROLD, *Introduction to the History of England . . . to 1204* (London: Collins, 1949) is also useful. Select source readings are provided in R. W. CHAMBERS, *England Before the Norman Conquest* (London: Longmans, 1926). A good biography of King Alfred is CHARLES PLUMMER, *The Life and Times of Alfred the Great . . .* (Oxford: Clarendon, 1902); and another is LAURENCE M. LARSON, *Canute the Great . . .* (New York: Putnam, 1912). Our chief and practically sole narrative source for the early period to the eighth century is the highly respected Venerable Bede, *Ecclesiastical History of the English People,* available in various editions and translations, such as those of J. A. GILES, A. M. SELLAR, and L. SHERLEY-PRICE (the last published in paperback by Penguin, 1955ff.), and especially B. COLGROVE and R. MYNORS (Oxford: Clarendon, 1969). Other sources include ASSER, *Life of King Alfred,* tr. A. S. Cook (Boston: Ginn, 1906); *The Peterborough Anglo-Saxon Chronicle,* tr. H. A. Rositzke (New York: Columbia U.P., 1951); and *Six Old English Chronicles . . .* , tr. and ed. J. A. Giles (London: Bohn, 1848). Good brief general treatments of Anglo-Saxon England are available in general histories of England such as W. E. LUNT, *History of England* (New York: Harper, 1949) and BRYCE LYON, *A Constitutional and Legal History of Medieval England* (New York: Harper, 1960).

The Early Middle Ages

❲ THE WESTERN EMPIRE AND THE SLAVS IN THE EARLY MIDDLE AGES.   Chapter 13.

LTHOUGH initially the least developed, least populous, and least desirable of the states set up by the Treaty of Verdun (843), the German kingdom soon became the largest, strongest, most prosperous of the three. Within a century, the German monarchs won out over their French rivals, and annexed the old Middle Kingdom, originally assigned to Emperor Lothair I, which consisted of the Rhineland, Rhoneland, and Italy. With the acquisition of Italy, the German kings gained a claim to the imperial crown, which they obtained from the Papacy.

Meanwhile the Slavs expanded phenomenally, and by the close of the eleventh century they were Christianized, civilized, and organized into territorial states. Although the western Slavs were incorporated into the Latin Church and affiliated with the Western World, most of the southern and eastern Slavs were incorporated into the Greek Church and affiliated with Byzantium.

(888–973)   THE RISE OF THE MEDIEVAL GERMAN EMPIRE.
Section 37.

> King Otto came into Italy with a great multitude of followers of diverse nationalities, who filled the earth like locusts, and whose speech was unfamiliar. But the Romans, together with the Pontiff, went out to meet Otto and received him with honor . . . and they praised him and called him "Augustus." [*Chronicle of Benedict of St. Andrea*]

AFTER the end of the Carolingian line in Germany (911), the vigorous Saxon (Ottonian) line (918–1024) soon assumed leadership. The first two Saxon monarchs—Henry I and Otto I—dealt skillfully with external enemies such as the Magyars, and internal problems such as the dukes, and expanded Germany into an empire.

Located at a critical east-west juncture of the converging Great Plain of Europe, Germany was a "battleground of the races." The great rivers which might have served as natural boundaries in the area have generally been disregarded by both the Germans and their foes in favor of the edges of their fertile valleys which are often less definite and less defensible, but more economically desirable. The exposed nature of Germany disposed its inhabitants to become strong and militaristic, if only for survival. And the fact that central Europe is "a meeting place of the races" encouraged the imperial concept as a means of unifying and pacifying diverse peoples.

The German duchies   By the tenth century, the German state was divided into several major well-defined areas, the most powerful of which were the great stem- or tribal (*stammen:* tribes) duchies of Franconia, Suabia, Saxony, and Bavaria. Centrally located on the middle Rhine and lower Maine Rivers, the Duchy of Franconia was originally formed by the eastward expansion of the Austrasian Franks. The Duchy of Suabia, located to the south of Franconia in the Southwestern Highlands and Alpine Forelands region —the earlier seat of the Alemanni—controlled the central Alpine passes into Italy, and included Alsace, Switzerland, and Roman Rhaetia. To the north of Franconia, the great duchy of Saxony stretched across northern Germany; and following its incorporation by Charlemagne and its conversion to Christianity, rapidly became one of the most prosperous and progressive parts of Germany. Located in southeastern Germany, in the valley of the upper Danube, Bavaria was the southern counterpart of Saxony; and its freedom-loving inhabitants, like the Saxons, were inclined to be independent, rebellious, and insubordinate.

and marches

Besides the more powerful duchies, there were others of inferior strength. Despite its wealth and advanced civilization, the Duchy of Lorraine in the lower (northern) Rhineland was weak, and was soon feudalized and partitioned into numerous lordships, several of which were ecclesiastical. The Duchy of Thuringia, sandwiched in between eastern Saxony and eastern Franconia, was also weak and generally subordinate to Saxony. As Germany expanded, various "Marks" (marches, or border-counties) were established along the frontiers. Among such were the Ost Mark (Austria: the East Mark of Bavaria) and the Nordgau (the North Mark of Bavaria). There were also the (eastern) Saxon Marks known respectively as the North Mark, the Mark of Lausitz, and the Meissen Mark.

The medieval history of Germany and the Western Empire was conditioned by the counter-action of factors of strength and weakness. Among factors for strength and unity was the monarchical tradition—derived from the Carolingians, the Merovingians, and the Romans—which was reinforced and augmented by the Church, which supported and consecrated the monarch. Cooperation of the Church with the State was intimate in early Germany; and the Church was usually a leading pillar of the throne. A feeling of oneness was promoted by the fact that the Germans had a common language—mutually intelligible despite disparate dialects—as well as a comparatively homogeneous culture, with uniform customs and concepts. Cooperation was exacted by the fact that the Germans were threatened by common enemies: on the west by the French, on the north by the Scandinavians, and on the east by the Slavs and Magyars. The Magyars moved overland *en masse* and could be defeated only by large armies raised from Germany at large, which necessitated full-scale cooperation with their king. One of the greatest threats to the early German state thus eventually became one of the main causes of its strength. Some historians have maintained that the limited number of great duchies in Germany was also a factor of strength, since it cut down the potential sources of opposition to the monarch, and made it easier for the king (who was also a great duke) to secure ascendance by obtaining control of one or two additional duchies.

Factors of strength

Among factors of strength resulting from the empire were the cooperation elicited during successful external expansion and the rule of foreign territories. The Germans had a common interest in keeping their empire. The imperial concept also served to unify and pacify the diverse peoples of central Europe, and thus increased German security. The Emperor was conceived of as the political counterpart and protector of the universal Papacy and the secular head of the Christian commonwealth. The income from outlying provinces of the Empire—such as those in northern Italy—also contributed to the support of the German emperors.

Factors for weakness

For practically every strength in the German monarchy, there was a corresponding weakness; and under certain circumstances, it was possible for a factor of strength to become a source of weakness. Geographically, the German kingdom was vulnerable from its exposed position and indeterminate borders. Internally, its topography segmented it and precipitated regional differences. Racial differences, such as the fact that the Celtic strain was stronger in the south and west and the Slavic in the east; cultural differences, such as the fact that the west and the south were more Romanized; and historic differences, such as the fact that Bavaria and Saxony had long resisted Frankish domination, also weakened Germany.

The elective principle was another source of weakness, and the continued existence of allods still another. The German aristocracy insisted, with ultimate success, that the monarchy was elective and thus dependent. Allods (entirely private property) were, by tradition, free from the ordinary royal intervention, military obligations, judicial appeals, forfeit, etc. They were in fact considered, according to a contemporary expression, as "fiefs from the sun." Many of these allodial holdings enjoyed an uninterrupted history of virtual autonomy. During the Frankish conquest, numerous areas in Germany were not organized into the regular framework of monarchical control, and even during Carolingian times, many were never fully incorporated. As long as these independent holdings existed, there was a strong tendency for other holdings to become like them.

The extent of the Empire itself was an important source of weakness. The concerns and distractions connected with having possessions external to Germany dissipated monarchical attention and sapped monarchical energies. Especially burdensome was the possession of Italy, which necessitated "straddling the Alps." Most German monarchs had to shuttle back and forth repeatedly from Germany to Italy. Italian opposition to German rule increased as the weaknesses of the German emperors became more apparent, the Lombard communes more prosperous and powerful, the reforming Papacy more insistent on ecclesiastical independence. The ambitious pretensions of the Italian aristocracy and the proud memories of the Roman people added fuel to the flames. As soon as the emperors returned to Germany, the Italians would try to reassert their autonomy; while the imperial presence in Italy was regularly a signal for revolts in Germany.

Another serious problem was that of imperial relations with the Papacy. If popes and emperors were cooperating leaders of Christendom, who was

The Western Empire and the Slavs

ultimately superior? Since the popes were astride central Italy—as well as very influential throughout Europe—the emperors felt it was necessary to control Papal policies. On the other hand, the popes were eager to retain their autonomy and freedom of action, and hence fearful of any expansion of imperial power in Italy. Continual mutual distrust and friction resulted.

The transitional period of 888–918 in German history was one of partial disintegration engendered by foreign incursions and the rise of the dukes. Magyar raids into Germany became annual affairs about 900ff., and the tempo of their predatory activities was stepped up after their overthrow of the Moravian state. Neither Louis the Child (899–911) nor Conrad of Franconia (911–918) was able to cope with the Magyars. The ducal office was now revived, largely as a means of meeting the Magyar threat. The German dukedoms of the early tenth century were mainly regional assumption of leadership by local strong men.

Age of foreign incursions and rise of the dukes (888–918)

In each of the major areas, daring and ambitious heads of powerful families assumed the reins, becoming the military and political leaders (*duces*) of their peoples. In Saxony, the Liudolfinger family—originally defenders of the Eastern Saxon frontiers—came to rule, largely as a result of their victories over the Slavs and Danes. In Suabia, Duke Burchard's family were originally the defenders of the Alpine passes in Rhaetia (*duces Raetianorum*). In Franconia—where the old Frankish aristocracy held sway—the Conradiners eventually won out over the Babenbergers, who transferred their activities and leadership to the East Mark of Bavaria (Austria). In Bavaria, the Arnulfingers rose to power as military leaders of the Bohemian March. The new dukes made their offices hereditary and assumed increasing power. It became customary to choose German kings from the dukes, and most German kings were confronted during their reign with ducal rebellions.

The Duke of Carinthia, Arnulf (888–899)—an illegitimate son of Charles the Fat's brother—was elected king by the German assembly at Stuttgart following the deposition of Charles the Fat at Tribur (887). Arnulf defeated Scandinavian invaders in the battle of the Dyle river in 891, thus freeing the Low Countries from their menace; and successfully resisted the expanding Moravians with the aid of the Slovenes and the Magyars. After being accorded a certain seniority among the various successor kings, Arnulf intervened in Italy (894 and 896), where he was crowned Emperor by Pope Formosus (896). Arnulf's success in Italy was, however, limited and transitory. Having taken ill (poison was suspected), he returned to Germany, where he died in 899.

Arnulf was succeeded by a boy of six who died at the early age of 18, and is known to history as Louis the Child. The tempo of Magyar incursions mounted, and the dukes came to exercise supreme power in their various territories.

As the Carolingian line in the east had died out, the magnates now elected as king Conrad of Franconia (911–918), who was of Frankish descent, as well as duke of the old Frankish duchy. Although personally honorable and brave, Conrad was a weak king, unable to control the dukes or restrain the Magyars. He lost the German part of Lorraine to the French king, and incited the resistance of the dukes, whose principal leader was Henry of Saxony. On his deathbed, Conrad designated the redoubtable Henry as his successor.

The Saxon line: Henry the Fowler (919–936)

The acceptance of Henry of Saxony as king by "the leaders of the Frankish people" brought to power the Saxon (Ottonian) line, which ruled Germany from 918–1024. Henry I (919–936) is known as "the Fowler" from his fondness for hunting, in which sport he was engaged when the Franconian nobles brought him news of his election. That strong, self-reliant ruler is generally considered the real founder of the medieval German monarchy.

With regard to both the dukes and the Church, Henry the Fowler pursued a moderate yet firm policy. With the dukes, he followed the rule of "live and let live," allowing them considerable latitude within their own duchies, but requiring their cooperation in matters of general welfare. He insisted on control of the crown lands located in the various duchies; appointed a new Duke of Suabia loyal to himself (926); and made Thuringia a dependency of his Duchy of Saxony. He maintained an aloofness from the Church, and avoided any hint of dependence on the bishops, declining any ecclesiastical coronation at his accession.

Henry launched German expansion eastward into Slavic lands, and westward into the old Middle Kingdom of Lothair I. He occupied Lorraine during the civil struggles in France that followed the deposition and imprisonment of the hapless Charles the Simple, and forced the local Duke Gilbert to transfer his allegiance from the French to the German throne (925–928). Henry also set in motion the German *Drang nach Osten* (Drive to the East) by pushing German expansion into Slavic territory beyond the Elbe and the Saale. He founded the fortified settlement of Brandenburg on the old Slavic site of Brunabor, located between the Elbe and Oder. The Bohemians (Czechs) accepted German overlordship, and the old Carolingian Mark located to the south of Denmark was reconquered and reorganized.

Henry's most signal service, however, was his restraint of the formidable Magyars. After a Magyar chief fell into his hands, Henry—instead of accepting a ransom—insisted on a truce of nine years, during which he paid them tribute. Meanwhile he strengthened his defenses by promoting the construction of *Burgs* (fortifications, fortified towns) at strategic vantage points along the eastern frontiers of Saxony. The Saxons were induced to establish residence in or near the *Burgs*, which were provided with detachments of Henry's armed retainers. Besides this, Henry developed a local militia who were trained to fight on both foot and horse, and who took turns defending the *Burgs*. A percentage—such as a ninth—of the able men would remain at the fortification, guarding it, refurbishing its defenses, and training, while the rest went about their regular work. In addition, Henry built up a well-trained cavalry force for use against the mounted Magyars. Meanwhile, the mettle of his armed forces was tested and tempered in campaigns against the Slavic Wends. When the truce expired, and the Magyars came to demand their customary payoff, the

Germans defiantly threw a dead dog into their camp. The Germans and the Magyars clashed in battle by the Unstrutt River in the vicinity of Merseburg (933). The Germans came off victorious and the Magyar menace subsided for some twenty years.

If Henry I was the founder of the German monarchy, his son, Otto I —the Great—was the founder of the medieval German Empire. Although Henry I had been content to reign as a quasi-feudal king, Otto insisted on ruling as a sovereign monarch. Otto is important in German history, not only because of his accomplishments, but also for the precedents he established. The idealistic, high-minded, determined Otto—who had been chosen by his father in preference to his older half-brother, Thankmar—was duly elected during Henry's lifetime by an assembly of the princes. Following the old king's death, Otto's policies were indicated when he had himself solemnly acclaimed, anointed, and crowned at the old Carolingian capital Aix-la-Chapelle (Aachen), with full Germanic and ecclesiastical ceremonies. At the banquet which followed the coronation, the great dukes served as honorary officials of the royal household.

Otto I, the Great (936–973), and his defeat of the Magyars

As Otto's centralizing policies became more evident, he was challenged by four successive rebellions of increasing severity. Among his opponents were members of his own family, such as his younger brother Henry, his older half-brother Thankmar, and his son Liudolf. The final and most serious revolt (953–955) included a formidable coalition of the Dukes of Suabia, Bavaria, and Lorraine, as well as the Archbishop of Mainz and Otto's son Liudolf.

At a critical juncture in the German civil war, the Magyars intervened, possibly at the invitation of the rebel leaders. The country then rallied around the king, who assembled a large army, and went out to meet the invaders. In a decisive battle, fought at Lechfeld—a field by the Lech River in the vicinity of Augsburg (955)—the Germans completely routed the Magyars, who were never again a serious menace, nor was Otto's power ever again seriously challenged.

Otto I established Counts Palatine (Counts of the Palace) to look after royal interests in the duchies. On the death of Duke Eberhard (939), he obtained direct control of the Duchy of Franconia, whose possession came to be accepted as associated with the crown. Meanwhile, Otto entrusted the administration and defense of his own Saxon duchy more and more to his energetic lieutenants Herman Billung and Count Gero.

"Ecclesiastical policy" of Otto

As a means of controlling his realms, Otto I first tried a "family policy." Ducal offices, as they became vacant, were entrusted to members of his own family. His brother Henry was made Duke of Bavaria and his son Liudolf, Duke of Suabia. But blood ties were not as strong as personal ambitions and regional interests, and relatives proved no more reliable than other princes. Otto was soon disillusioned by the plots and rebellions of his brother and son, and abandoned his "family policy." He now adopted his famous "ecclesiastical policy," which became for some time a principal prop of the throne. This consisted in appointing Church prelates —rather than secular lords—to political offices, such as the administration of towns and counties. Since the clergy were forbidden to marry and ecclesiastical offices were not hereditary, bishops would not plot to extend their possessions and make them hereditary in their house. And since ecclesiastical offices were elective, the monarch could influence elections to bring about the appointment of men favorable to his cause. This "ecclesiastical policy" had been foreshadowed in some measure by the Carolingians. A related policy was that of granting immunities to monasteries, whereby the latter were exempted from the control of local rulers and made directly subject to the crown, with resultant profit for the latter.

Expansion and revival of the empire

Otto's reign, like that of his model Charlemagne, was marked by great expansion. To the east, Otto compelled the Duke of Bohemia to accept his overlordship, and he expanded German control beyond the Elbe-Saale line. In this Slavic territory, he established or reorganized several large border counties (*Marks*—marches) under "margraves" (counts of the marches). Included were Billungs Mark (with Hamburg and Lübeck), the North Mark (with Brandenburg) just south of the former, the Lusatian Mark (Mark of Lausitz), the Meissen Mark, and the Mark of the Nordgau (north district of Bavaria), established as a buffer against the Bohemians. In the extreme south was the old Ost Mark (Austria), and in the extreme north the old Danish (Schleswig) Mark. Points of departure for missionary activities and the extension of German influence, which proceeded simultaneously, included the bishoprics of Hamburg, Magdeburg, Prague, and Passau.

Otto I not only retained control of Lorraine, but also made Burgundy a vassal state (937), and kept its young king a virtual prisoner in his own entourage for some time. Following Otto's imperial coronation, Burgundy became a part of the empire.

For some time Italy had been the scene of warring factions, as rivalries persisted between the Dukes of Spoleto and Friuli and the Marquises of Ivrea and Tuscany. Papal involvement complicated the contests, while foreign intervention, such as that of the Kings of Burgundy and Arles (Provence) and the Dukes of Suabia and Bavaria kept the pot boiling. Italian kings were regularly opposed by anti-kings. King Hugh of Provence —who acquired the throne of Italy in 926—made his son Lothair co-king, and passed on the crown to him at his death (945). But Lothair never ruled, since Berengar II of Ivrea snatched control from his grasp.

Lothair's wealthy widow Adelaide complained to Otto I that she was being mistreated by Berengar, who had both appropriated her properties and tried to force her to marry his son. The decisive Otto I descended into Italy in 951, overcame Berengar II, assumed the crown of the Lombards, took Adelaide to wife, and left Berengar as his vicar (viceroy) in Italy. It was not long before complaints came to Otto from across the Alps. Italian refugees and Pope John XII charged that Berengar was an unjust tyrant and was encroaching on the Papal States. Otto I again descended into Italy, deposed Berengar (961), and went to Rome, where he was crowned Emperor by John XII (962). But Otto's Italian problems were not over, and he had to make further expeditions to Italy, where he spent most of the remaining twelve years of his life.

The Western Empire and the Slavs

Otto's Italian intervention soon embroiled him in conflict with the Papacy. As Emperor, Otto claimed the right to confirm Papal elections and to supervise the government of Rome. In the so-called "Privilege of Otto" (962), he brought the Romans to promise that they would not elect a Pope without imperial consent, and the Pope to agree that he would take an oath of fealty to the Emperor or his representative(s), and recognize an imperial representative (*missus*) as having the right to supervise the Roman government. Hardly had Otto left Rome when an Italian reaction occurred with Pope John at its head. Otto now returned to Rome, forced John to flee, and presided over a council composed of secular and religious leaders, who elected a new Pope, Leo VIII. Otto also exacted acceptance of a fuller "Ottonian Privilege" (963), which increased imperial supervision over the Roman government. But after Otto departed for Germany, John XII returned to Rome, and ruled until his death the following year (964). Although the schism was briefly perpetuated by John's elected successor, Benedict V, it ended after Otto forced Benedict to retire and the Romans accepted Otto's candidate, John XIII (965). When John XIII was run out of the city in 966, he was swiftly reinstated and the rebels were severely punished by the Emperor.

Otto's relations with the Papacy and Byzantium

Otto's Italian intervention also brought him into competition with the Byzantines, who still had territory in southern Italy. At first, Otto attempted to extend his rule over all of Italy, but his demands were summarily rejected by the Byzantine Emperor Nicephorus Phocas, who haughtily reminded the Emperor's envoy—Bishop Liutprand of Cremona—that the Byzantine navy commanded the seas. As a compromise measure, a marriage was later arranged between the Byzantine imperial princess Theophano and Otto's son, the later Otto II (972).

Otto's intervention in Italy has often been criticized for distracting the medieval German monarchy from what should have been its primary concern, and thus contributing to its ultimate failure to unify Germany. But the outcome could not have been forseen in Otto's day, nor was it a necessary consequence. If Otto I had not intervened in Italy, grave danger existed that the Duke of Suabia or the Duke of Bavaria or the King of Burgundy would do so—thus gaining an important advantage over their nominal sovereign. In addition to increased revenues, possession of Italy meant a right to imperial coronation with a legal title to the old Middle Kingdom of Lothair I, including the Rhineland and Rhôneland. Finally, the imperial office and concept could help German monarchs in their efforts to unify the diverse peoples of central Europe. Otto's "ecclesiastical policy" was similarly suited to its own time, although it would later become outdated and embarrassing. Otto's reign was generally beneficial. Contemporary with his political and military successes, a so-called *Ottonian Renaissance* in culture was encouraged by German political expansion and economic prosperity, as well as by fruitful contacts with Italy and Byzantium.

Evaluation of Otto's intervention in Italy

THE WESTERN EMPIRE ATTAINS AN EARLY APOGEE.
Section 38.

(973–1056)

> Even if Charles the Great had been alive and present, the rejoicing could not have been greater. [Wipo concerning the coronation of Conrad II at Mainz (1024).]

Following temporary setbacks under Otto the Great's two youthful and short-lived immediate successors, the Western Empire recovered and resumed its progress under the last representative of the Saxon house and the first two Franconian emperors. Whereas Otto II and Otto III were distracted by excessive concern with Italy and imperial dreams, Henry II, Conrad II, and Henry III again made Germany the principal basis of their power. At the same time, they retained an interest in Italy and renewed German eastward expansion. For a while, Germany was the leading power in Europe.

Otto II (973–983) and his Italian nemesis

Otto II—the son of Otto the Great and Adelaide, and the husband of Theophano—came to the throne at the age of eighteen. The new monarch shared the interest of his Italian mother and Greek wife in Italy. In Germany, Otto II put down three successive rebellions. In order to weaken the Duchy of Bavaria, which he entrusted to different hands, Otto detached its northern march (the Nordgau) from Bavarian overlordship, made Carinthia an independent duchy, and subjected the Church in Bavaria directly to the Emperor. Otto also repulsed French efforts to retake Lorraine.

Although relatively successful elsewhere, Otto II met disaster in Italy. From 980 on, he campaigned in Italy; but in 982 he suffered a crushing defeat in Calabria (southern Italy) at the hands of the Moslems and their Greek allies. In 983, he died at Rome while planning another expedition. A by-product of Otto's reverses in Italy was a great uprising of Slavic peoples beyond the Elbe and Saale in 983, whereby they regained their freedom from their German overlords.

Otto III (983–1002) and his disappointed dreams

Otto III, son of Otto II, was only three years old at his accession, and he died at the age of twenty-one. The regency was exercised first by his able mother, Theophano, and after her death by his grandmother, Adelaide, who shared her power with Archbishop Willigis of Mainz. Young Otto assumed personal power in 994 at the age of fourteen. During the ensuing decade, the direction of affairs was mainly in the hands of a cultured council of ecclesiastics. These included Bishop Bernward of Hildesheim, Abbot Odilo of Cluny, Archbishop Heribert of Cologne, and Otto's former tutor, Gerbert, who eventually became Pope Sylvester II. The policies of Otto III, largely conceived by his ecclesiastical advisers, have been variously estimated. While most have branded them as idealistic and impracticable, some have judged them reasonable and realistic. Otto's goal was expressed in the inscription on his seal: "Renewal of the Roman Empire." This actually involved two different plans: one for Italy, the other for the rest of the empire (outside of Germany).

Otto's policy concerning his eastern neighbors such as the Bohemians,

Poles, and Hungarians was to include them in a loose Christian confederation, presided over jointly by the Emperor and the Pope, leaving their internal government to their own rulers. Component peoples were to retain their identity and much of their autonomy, while being required to cooperate in such matters as foreign policy. Each was to have its own ruler, as well as its own church organization directly subject to Rome. Thus, Poland and Hungary were given their own primatial Archbishoprics and their rulers were recognized as kings, while Bohemia was conceded greater autonomy.

With regard to Italy, Otto insisted on strong direct control. Partly because a basic feature of his imperial concept was the close cooperation and partnership between Pope and Emperor, he increased the role of Rome and Italy. He constructed imperial palaces in Rome, and gave imperial officials high-sounding Byzantine and Roman titles. More control was exercised over both central and northern Italy, and particularly over lines of communication between Rome and Germany. Germans were appointed to the highest ecclesiastical offices in Italy, including the sees of Ravenna and Rome. Thus, Otto's cousin Bruno became Pope Gregory V (996–999), and Otto's former tutor, Gerbert, succeeded him as Pope Sylvester II (999–1002). *Failure of Italian policy*

The policies of Otto III were never effectively carried out since the sand in his hourglass was swiftly running out. Otto incurred much Roman and Italian criticism when he severely punished the principal instigators of an ephemeral Papal schism in 998 with great cruelty. In 1002, Otto was driven out of Rome by the rioting populace. A contemporary chronicler put on his lips the complaint: *You are my Romans. For you I left my country and kindred. For you I abandoned my Saxons and all the Germans . . . And now you have cast out your father, put my servants to a cruel death, and shut your gates against me!* Shortly afterwards, Otto III contracted smallpox and died, while still attempting to retake the city of the Caesars. His plan was soon abandoned by his successors.

When Otto III died without direct heir, the German princes elected his cousin Henry, Duke of Bavaria, who had strong ecclesiastical support. Henry II was energetic, efficient, upright, and well-educated, having been originally intended for an ecclesiastical career. He was a strong supporter of monastic reforms and a generous benefactor of religious causes; eventually, he was to be canonized. *Recovery under Henry II (1002–1024)*

Henry II made Germany and its immediate environs paramount in his policies. Although the barons were still turbulent at the outset of his reign, he overcame their initial resistance and obviated further serious opposition. He re-established security along the frontiers, where he restrained the powerful Polish king, Boleslaus the Mighty, recovered Bohemia, and purchased peace with the northern (Scandinavian) empire of Canute. Eastward expansion was gradually resumed, but although Henry II endeavored to establish a milder policy towards conquered Slavs—prohibiting their subjection to serfdom—he was unable to compel most of the Germans to comply. While Henry II relegated Italy to a secondary place in his planning, he devoted to it four campaigns, three of which he personally accompanied. He overcame his rival for the Italian kingship, Ardouin of Ivrea, who had momentarily been proclaimed King of the Lombards, and he opposed Byzantine expansion in the peninsula.

Both Henry II and his devout wife Queen Kunigunde endowed churches, monasteries, and convents with liberal munificence. Henry enthusiastically backed the missionary activities of the Church, and supported the reform movement which was associated with monasteries such as Gorze, Reichenau, and Hirschau. At the same time, he did not hesitate to utilize the German Church as an effective instrument for strengthening the monarchy. While he granted monasteries immunity from local control, he subjected them to royal supervision, controlled abbatial elections, and shared in the income from monastic properties. Similarly, while he renewed the Ottonian policy of conferring the administration of counties upon bishops—as in the case of Bamberg, Worms, Hildesheim, Cambrai, and Utrecht—he controlled the appointment of bishops and profited from his supervisory rights over the administration of their holdings. The men he chose for high Church offices were usually able and exemplary.

Height of the empire: the early Franconians (1024–1056)

Before his death, the childless Henry II had nominated as his successor Conrad of Franconia, who was duly elected as Conrad II, thus initiating the Franconian dynasty (1024–1125). Under the earlier Franconians—Conrad II and Henry III (1024–1056)—the "Holy Roman" German Empire enjoyed an early apogee. The German national concept as expressed by the term *Regnum Teutonicorum*—the Kingdom of the Germans—now definitely emerged. The German dukes were kept firmly in check, while the German Church—both episcopal and monastic—was an efficient instrument of royal policy. The frontiers were secure, and eastward expansion was under way. Bohemia was securely incorporated into the empire, and Poland and Hungary were dependent tributaries. The Rhineland and Rhôneland as well as Italy were securely held, and Papal appointments were made by the emperors. Meanwhile, the entire empire from the Tyrrhenian sea to the Baltic was enjoying an economic boom.

This prosperity and power were partly results of the groundwork laid by the Saxon house, and partly consequences of various devices employed by Conrad II and Henry III. These emperors used, as means of control, government through *ministeriales,* expansion of direct royal holdings, multiplication of royal castles, control of bishoprics and monasteries, support elicited from towns and the lesser nobility by the grants of royal charters and privileges, and an aggressive, successful foreign policy.

Conrad II lays the foundation (1024–1039)

Conrad II—a great-great-grandson of Otto I in the female line—was a strong, able realist, who was mainly responsible for the powerful position obtained by the early Franconian house. Towards the Church, Conrad II was cool and pragmatic. He stopped the lavish grants of royal lands and funds to churches and monasteries, manifested little interest in the ecclesiastical reform movement, and exploited to the utmost royal rights relative to bishoprics and abbacies. Conrad's primary effort was directed toward firm control of Germany. Early in his reign, he suppressed three

The Western Empire and the Slavs

serious ducal rebellions (1025, 1026–1027, and 1030), in all of which Duke Ernest of Suabia (his stepson) participated. The incorrigible Ernest eventually fled to the Black Forest, where he spent the rest of his life as a bandit and outlaw. As the duchies became vacant, Conrad turned them over to his son, Henry, who thus eventually held every duchy but Lorraine and Saxony. Conrad assiduously enforced royal rights over monasteries and bishoprics, and insisted on the *regalia* (royal rights) relative to markets. He kept strict control over royal estates, and sought to build up royal holdings in centrally located southern Saxony and Thuringia, a strategic gateway to the east, in the vicinity of rich mineral deposits.

As a means of restraining the great princes, Conrad II supported lesser lords or "rear-vassals" against greater lords or "vassals-in-chief," by recognizing the hereditability of fiefs. He made large-scale use of *ministeriales* (members of the servile class) instead of the nobility in offices of great responsibility, such as the charge of castles and the administration of counties. These *ministeriales* could not easily make their offices and holdings hereditary as did the aristocracy, who resented the preferment of non-nobles.

Conrad maintained control of Burgundy and Italy, and retained ascendance in east-central Europe. King Rudolph III of Burgundy, who was without direct heir, had designated Conrad as his successor (1025). Against the powerful French Count Odo of Blois and Champagne, who also aspired to succeed Rudolph, Conrad obtained the support of King Henry I of France, who regarded Count Odo as a dangerous rival. Conrad was thus able to occupy Burgundy on the death of Rudolph (1032), and its possession gave him control of western Alpine passes into the Italian peninsula. Although Conrad had considerable difficulty with the restless states of east-central Europe, he eventually compelled Bohemia and Poland to accept vassal status, and also settled the question of German boundaries with Hungary. Conrad made two expeditions to Italy (1026–1027 and 1036–1038), on the first of which he drastically punished Pavia for defying him. Conrad appointed Germans to high positions in Italy, and encouraged marriages between Germans and Italians. In Italy, as in Germany, he supported lesser vassals or *vavassores* against greater Italian nobles by declaring fiefs irrevocable except for proven guilt ascertained by judgment of ones' peers, as was customary in the feudal system.

The handsome, intelligent, cultured Henry III, who succeeded his father in 1039, was called "the most educated of kings." Although not "a man of steel" like his father, Henry profited from the latter's statesmanship, so that the German empire now reached "the meridian of its power." At his accession, Henry III held all the duchies of Germany—except Lorraine and Saxony—in his own hands. He was confronted however, by the recurrent rebellions of Duke Godfrey of Lower Lorraine, who had been alienated by the division of Lorraine on the death of his father (1043), and the appointment of his younger brother Gozelon as Duke of Upper Lorraine. The disgruntled Godfrey married Marchioness Beatrice of Tuscany, whose broad lands commanded the road to Rome, and he repeatedly conspired and revolted against the Emperor.

Apogee under Henry III (1039–1056)

Henry both continued and deviated from his father's policies. He kept on using *ministeriales* and building up the royal domains in Thuringia and southern Saxony, where he established his residence at Goslar, partly to control this strategic area, partly to win over the Saxons. But, unlike Conrad II, Henry III utilized and favored the Church in the manner of the Ottos and Henry II. He appointed bishops and abbots and even popes, used churchmen extensively as political officials, and depended partly on revenues derived from the Church. Although he utilized the Church, Henry also promoted its welfare. He supported Church reform and appointed able and exemplary men to religious offices. His appointment of his saintly uncle—Bishop Bruno of Toul—as Pope (Leo IX) in 1049 introduced the Cluniac-Gregorian reform into the Papacy. Henry III also induced Poland, Hungary, and Bohemia to accept his suzerainty, both by his prestige and by repeated campaigns (five into Hungary; two to Bohemia). But Duke Godfrey continued to be his implacable enemy, and the nobility resented many of his policies, including his use of *ministeriales*, liberality to the Church, and support of the ecclesiastical reform party.

Divided Italy (973–1056)

Although continuing to resent German overlordship, and revolting whenever a propitious occasion arose, the Italians profited by their connection with the transalpine empire. As the fleets of the Byzantines, Venetians, Genoese, and Pisans won control of the Mediterranean Sea from the declining Moslems, Christian trade in this area—in which Italy was pivotal—recovered and prospered.

Italy had come to be divided into three distinct political areas. Northern Italy—nominally under direct imperial control—was dominated by growing urban areas presided over by bishops, lords, and town councils, with interspersed rural areas ruled by counts, marquises, dukes, and other feudal lords. Central Italy was ruled by the Pope in a virtually autonomous manner, with only occasional imperial interference. Independent of Western imperial power, southern Italy and Sicily were an arena of competition between Byzantines, Moslems, and Lombards, as well as small city-state governments. Into this melee, a new element was injected in 1016, as Norman adventurers began to expand their control. In 1053, the Normans defeated a Papal army and took Pope Leo IX into honorable custody at Civitate. Later they obtained from the Pope formal recognition of their right to hold Apulia and other territories in southern Italy as papal vassals. During much of this period, German power in northern and north-central Italy along with German influence in central Italy was comparatively stable. German emperors attempted to control imperial Italy by appointment of Germans to high political and ecclesiastical offices, support of lesser vassals against their Italian overlords, and control of the elections of ecclesiastical prelates.

Conclusion

By the middle of the eleventh century, the German Empire was probably the strongest state in Europe, with the Byzantine Empire its only possible competitor. The German monarchy was vigorous and the hereditary principle seemed well established. The dukes were submissive to the monarchy, as were most German higher Church officials. The old Middle

The Western Empire and the Slavs

Kingdom—including Lorraine, Burgundy, and Italy—was securely in German hands along with the imperial title. But ominous clouds were appearing. Cluniac reformers, in control of the Papacy, were seeking to separate Church offices from imperial control. The German princes were jealous of the great royal power and the threat of its extension. And a weak regency for a boy king, headed by the naive Agnes of Poitou, followed the death of Henry III in 1056.

THE SLAVS AND THEIR STATES IN THE EARLY MIDDLE AGES.
Section 39.

The Chuds, the Slavs, the Krivichs, and other [Eastern Slavic] peoples spoke thus to the Varangian princes: "Our country is large and has everything in abundance, except that we lack order and justice: come, take possession, and govern us." [Appeal of various disunited East Slavic tribes to Scandinavian leaders as reported in the Russian *Chronicle of Nestor* (eleventh century).]

DURING the Early Middle Ages, the Slavs expanded and came into increasing beneficial contact with both Eastern and Western European civilization. In general, the western Slavs were drawn into the orbit of Western Europe and the Roman Catholic Church, the eastern and southern Slavs into that of Byzantium and the Greek Orthodox Church. Although comparatively backward and originally barbaric, the Slavs were energetic and industrious, as well as prolific. By the close of the Early Middle Ages, they were converted to Christianity and civilized. While drawing on more advanced civilizations to their west and south, they expanded into vast, sparsely settled, undeveloped areas to their east.

Christianity and civilization reached the Slavs in the ninth to tenth centuries. Sts. Constantine (Cyril) and Methodius—two Eastern Christian missionaries of the ninth century recognized as "the Apostles of the Slavs"—began the conversion of the Slavs, and translated various sacred writings into Old Slavonic (using the Cyrillic or Glagolitic alphabets). Most of the Slavs were incorporated into the Eastern Church, but the western Slavs (Poles and Czechs) and the Slovenes and Croats among the southern Slavs were organized under Rome.

While foreigners such as Bulgars, Northmen, and Franks provided the initial leadership which organized the Slavs into larger political entities, it was not long before they developed their own native leadership. The chief tutors of the eastern and southern Slavs were the Byzantines, while the Germans and Italians performed a similar service for the western Slavs.

During the Early Middle Ages, the Slavs expanded westward to the Elbe-Saale line, filling in the area vacated by the Germans during their invasions of the Roman Empire. They also expanded southward through the valleys of the Danube and Drave and Save Rivers to overrun and "Slavonize" the Balkans. And they expanded eastward and northward occupying most of the more fertile sections of the principal river valleys of Russia. Meanwhile, the Slavs organized into regional territorial states.

The early homeland of the Slavs seems to have been in the vicinity of the Pripet Marshes in the valleys of the Pripet, Bug, upper Dniester, and Vistula Rivers. Their expansion from this eastern Polish–western Russian homeland brought about their differentiation into three principal groups: western, southern, and eastern Slavs.

The western Slavs

The western Slavs soon occupied the central European area evacuated by Germanic westward expansion, including the territory between the Elbe-Saale River line and the farther reaches of the Vistula valley. In the process, they differentiated into Poles, Czechs, Moravians, Slovaks, Polabians, and Sorbs (Wends).

The far western Slavs—comprised of the Polabians and Sorbs (Wends) —were located between the Elbe-Saale line to the west and the Oder river to the east. They were eventually subjected by the Germans, by whom they were Teutonized, but the process took some time. They were made tributary by Charlemagne and were further subjugated by Henry I and Otto I, who incorporated them into the empire in marches strung along the eastern side of the Elbe and Saale Rivers. At the news of the defeat of Otto II in southern Italy, the far western Slavs rose in a general rebellion (983), and reestablished their independence.

Moravia

The first Slavic state of consequence was Moravia, located to the north of the upper middle Danube and along the Morava River. Moravia was unified by Moymir I, who died in 846; and Moymir's successor, Rostislav (846–870) initiated the conversion of the Slavs by requesting missionaries from Constantinople. The brothers Constantine (Cyril) and Methodius of Salonica and their companions who labored to convert the Slavs developed the Cyrillic or Glagolitic scripts (or both), and translated the liturgy and other sacred books into Old Slavonic. From Moravia, Christianity was carried to the Bohemians, Serbs, Croats, and Bulgarians. In the second half of the ninth century, the Moravian state built up a considerable Empire, which included the Czechs, Slovaks, Slovenes, Serbs, Silesians, and Galicians, as well as the Moravians, and reached its height under Svatopluk (870–894). But shortly after the latter's death, the Magyars moved across the Carpathians into Hungary and overthrew the Moravian state.

Bohemia

Situated on a plateau at the headwaters of the Elbe, and surrounded by mountains rich in minerals, Bohemia—"the land of the [Celtic] Boii"— was occupied successively by Germanic Marcomanni and Slavic Czechs. In the early seventh century (about 626 ff.), a Frankish adventurer named Samo unified the inhabitants of Bohemia and the neighboring Wends and Moravians against the Avars, but his state collapsed after his death (c. 661). For some time, the Bohemians were under Bavarian tutelage, and for a while they were tributary to Charlemagne. By the later ninth century, Bohemia was a part of the Moravian Empire, from which it received Christianity.

The Bohemians were for a while affiliated with the Eastern Church, although they were later incorporated into the Latin Church and gravitated back into the German-Bavarian orbit. A native dynasty—the

The Western Empire and the Slavs

Premyslids—ruled Bohemia from the ninth to fourteenth centuries. During these centuries they vacillated in their attitude to the Germans. In the early tenth century, King St. Wenceslaus' (Wenzel's) friendship with the Germans was resented by native zealots, and he was murdered by his brother, Boleslav I (929–967). The latter warred against the Germans and obtained for Bohemia both greater independence and additional territories. His son, Boleslav II (967–999), further extended Bohemian frontiers to build up an empire which included Moravia, Galicia, and Silesia. But his son, Boleslav III, lost his foreign possessions to Boleslaus the Great, King of Poland, and his throne to the latter's brother, Vladijov. This Polish prince, to strengthen his position in Bohemia, became a tributary vassal of the German Emperor, with the title of Duke. After Vladijov's death the native Premyslid dynasty was restored, but continued ducal subjection to the German Empire. Duke Bretislav I (1037–1055)—the "Restorer"—temporarily reconstituted a "Big Bohemia" by overrunning neighboring territories, but was resubjected by Emperor Henry III. His son Vratislav received the personal title of "King" for his lifetime from Henry IV in gratitude for his loyalty and military assistance; which title was made permanent and hereditary for the rulers of Bohemia by Emperor Frederick I, for similar reasons. Meanwhile, Bohemia remained part of the empire. German power seemed too immediate, the German alignment too well established, and Magyar and Polish threats too real for the Bohemians to do otherwise, though they often temporized and aspired to independence. Bohemia thus remained a part of the Empire, in which its ruler became one of the imperial electors.

Although the state of Hungary was founded by the Magyars in the tenth century, its population was mainly Slavic. Located in the fertile bowl of the Carpathians, Hungary was strategically situated in the middle Danube valley, at the crossroads of east-west and north-south routes. As a result, it became a temporary home for many invading barbaric and nomadic groups. The Magyars were a warlike predatory central Asian people, who—after being temporarily located to the north of the Black Sea in the ninth century—moved up the Danube and across the Carpathians into Pannonia (modern Hungary) in the 890s. Led by their ruler, Arpad, the Magyars overthrew the Moravian state by 906. Meanwhile, they began raiding, plundering, and exacting tribute in Italy, France, and especially Germany. Their annual raids became the terror of central Europe. Eventually, however, decisive German victories at the Unstrutt River (933) and the Lechfeld (955) so dispirited the Magyars that they settled down and adopted civilized pursuits. *Hungary and the Magyars*

Christianity was brought to the Magyars by German and Czech missionaries. Duke Geza (972–997) and his family accepted Christianity from the west at the time of Otto II (975), but at first the faith made little progress. St. Stephen (997–1038) was a constructive statesman. He actively promoted Christianity and embraced the federal "Christian Empire" concept of Otto III and Pope Sylvester II. The Hungarian Church was organized independently of the German Church under the

Archbishop of Gran, and Stephen received a royal crown from the Pope. Stephen encouraged the immigration of foreign craftsmen, artificers, and husbandmen, and Hungary became a "land of promise."

Since the conciliatory policies of Otto III were jettisoned by his successors, Hungarian ties with the German Empire were soon broken. The salutary reign of King Stephen was succeeded by four distraught decades of civil wars and foreign conflicts (1038–1077). In 1046, Hungary was overrun by the Pechenegs and in 1061 by the Cumans. Recovery came under Ladislas I (1077–1095), who restored order, annexed Bosnia and Croatia, subjugated the Pechenegs and Cumans (barbaric peoples of Asian origin), and made Hungary independent of both Pope and Emperor.

Poland in the Early Middle Ages

Located in the fertile valleys of the Vistula, Dwina, and upper Dniester Rivers, Poland is a pleasant and productive country. But—by reason of its very attractiveness as well as its exposed position—its history has been turbulent and troubled. Although threatened by the eastward expansion of the Germans, the Poles were saved by the rise of strong leaders, some measure of unification, and conversion to Christianity. The latter deprived the Germans of any religious excuse for expansion into Polish territory, threw a mantle of Papal protection over the Poles, and contributed to Polish unity and progress.

The divided tribes of Poland were united into one state by the Piast dynasty in the tenth century. For some time in the tenth and eleventh centuries, Polish rulers were at least nominal vassals of the German emperors. Under Mieszco I (c. 960–992)—the first to unite them—the Poles were converted to Christianity by Greek Orthodox and Bohemian missionaries. Boleslaus I, the Great (992–1025), the son of Mieszco I, raised the struggling Polish principality to the status of a great power and received formal recognition of his state from both Emperor and Pope about the year 1000, when Otto III crowned him as *patricius* and Pope Sylvester II raised Gnesen to the status of an independent archbishopric. Boleslaus, who finally took the royal title and crown in 1025, built up an empire which stretched from the Baltic to the Carpathians and from the Elbe to the Bug River, and included Pomerania, Silesia, Moravia, Lusatia, Bohemia, Slovakia, and Ruthenia, in addition to Poland. This Empire was, however, overthrown after the death of Boleslaus I, and Poland experienced alternating decline and recovery, subjection and independence in the ensuing eleventh and twelfth centuries.

The southern Slavs

The southern Slavs—who included the Serbs, Croats, Slovenes, Bosnians, Dalmatians, Bulgarians, and others—emerged by a two-pronged movement from both the western and eastern Slavs. In the fifth to seventh centuries, they moved into the Balkans via the lands of the upper middle Danube and lower Danube. The Slavs who had moved into the territories in the vicinity of the Black Sea and lower Danube accompanied Asian nomads on their raids into the northwestern Balkans during the sixth to seventh centuries, and many stayed on as agriculturalists and workers. In the northwestern Balkans, where Byzantine defenses were weak, the western Slavs moved in virtually without opposition. They were eventually cut off from the original western Slavs by the Magyar occupa-

The Western Empire and the Slavs

tion of Hungary. Their counterparts in the northeastern Balkans were similarly separated from the eastern Slavs by the various successive invaders who occupied the territories to the north of the Black Sea and lower Danube.

The southwestern Slavs: The Serbs and others

Detachments from the western Slavs migrated southward and southwestward into the central and western Balkans in the sixth to seventh centuries. In this area, they were accepted as vassal-allies by the Byzantine emperor Heraclius (early seventh century). Generally they were politically disunited, living in small districts (*zupas*), each with its own chief or *zupan*, although sometimes various districts came to be loosely united under a *Grand Zupan*. Political disunity among the southwestern Slavs was fostered by the mountainous topography of the Balkans, petty rivalries, the infrequency of serious threats to their autonomy, and diverse foreign alignments. After their conversion in the ninth century, religious divergences were an added factor, since some became associated with the Latin Church, although most were aligned with Constantinople.

When accepted as vassals and allies by Heraclius, the Serbs were established in the north-central Balkans in Upper (Inner) Moesia. The Serbs—who recognized Byzantine suzerainty most of the time from the seventh to twelfth centuries—received Christianity from Byzantium in the early 870s. From time to time, they temporarily renounced Byzantine overlordship. The Serbs were subjected by King Simeon of Bulgaria from about 924–931; and again briefly by King Samuel of Bulgaria in the later tenth century; but in each case they subsequently reverted to Byzantine overlordship. For a while in the eleventh century, the princes of Zeta became independent, incorporated Raska, and adopted the title of *Kral* (king); but their kingdom was ephemeral. The real unification and organization of the Serbs came under their Great Zupan, Stephen Nemanja, in the later twelfth century.

The Croats, Slovenes, Dalmatians, and Bosnians were located in and near the northwestern Balkans. The Croats were eventually subjected by Hungary, and the Slovenes by the Germans. The Dalmatians remained under Byzantine suzerainty during most of the Early Middle Ages, following which their territory became a bone of contention between Venice and Hungary. The Bosnians were alternately subject to the Byzantines, independent, and subject to the Croatians, Byzantines, and Hungarians. While the Croats and Slovenes were Western Christians, the inhabitants of Dalmatia and Bosnia were divided in their allegiance between the Roman Catholic and Eastern Orthodox Churches.

The Bulgarians

The Bulgarians were a predominantly Slavic people arising from the conquest and unification of various Slavic tribes by the Asian Bulgars, nomadic, warlike, equestrian Turko-Tartars, related to the Huns, Avars, and Pechenegs. Ruled by a khan or king, the Bulgars were north of the Black Sea as early as the fifth to sixth centuries, and figured in contemporary Byzantine history as both auxiliaries and invaders. After being dominated by the Avars from about 580 to 626, the Bulgars divided, some going to the region of the middle Volga basin—where they came to be known as *Volga Bulgars*; others known simply as Bulgars, moving westward to the region north of the lower Danube (c. 650 ff.). Contingents of eastern Slavs (Antes) had already infiltrated the northeastern Balkans and were on either side of the lower Danube at the coming of the Bulgars, who subjected them and occupied the territory known as the Dobrudja, just south of the Danube delta. The Byzantine Emperor Constantine IV undertook a campaign against the Bulgars at the mouth of the Danube in 679, but his forces were foiled by the terrain and demoralized by the Emperor's premature departure, so that the Bulgars were victorious.

The Bulgars, together with their Slavic followers, now (c. 680) occupied the territory to the south of the lower Danube known as Lower Moesia. Since the Bulgars were not numerous and the bulk of the new population was Slavic, they were rapidly Slavonized in physique, speech, culture, and customs. Originally, the Bulgars had worn turbans and baggy trousers, were polygamous, and practiced human sacrifice; but these customs were dropped, and the new amalgam was the predominately Slavic Bulgarians.

The peace made in 680 between Byzantines and Bulgars lasted for only about a decade. Reciprocal invasions and friendly relations alternated for the next two centuries (about 690–893). Khan Tergel (Tervel) helped the deposed Emperor Justinian II in 705, and also rendered valuable services to the Byzantines during the great Moslem siege of Constantinople (717–718). On the other hand, in 811 the formidable Khan Krum trapped and virtually annihilated a Byzantine army under Emperor Nicephorus I, whose skull he converted into a drinking cup. Although Krum took Adrianople, he was foiled by the defenses of Constantinople. Under Krum, Bulgaria temporarily extended its rule over much of the Balkans; but Bulgarian realms shrank rapidly after his death (about 813).

A turning point came with the conversion of the Bulgarians to Eastern Christianity at the time of Khan Boris (852–889). Hard-pressed by a Byzantine army and fleet, as well as by a famine, Boris agreed to receive Christianity from Constantinople. The Khan was baptized about the year 864, and his people followed suit. The Slavonic script and liturgy were introduced into Bulgaria by disciples of Constantine and Methodius, and the Bulgarians soon obtained an autocephalous church with their own archbishop.

First Bulgarian Empire (893–1016)

The century and a quarter following the death of Boris (893) was the period of the First Bulgarian Empire. Able, intelligent King Simeon (893–927)—who had been educated at Constantinople—built up an empire which stretched from the Black Sea to the Adriatic and from the Carpathians to Thessaly (northern Greece). Simeon—whose ambition was to take Constantinople and unite Byzantines and Bulgarians—assumed the title "Tsar [Caesar] and Autocrat of the Bulgarians and Greeks"; the Primate of Bulgaria was accorded Patriarchal status. The arts of civilized life were cultivated in Bulgaria.

Simeon's son Peter (927–969) subjected Serbia. The Russians—as allies of the Byzantines—overran eastern Bulgaria (967 ff.), which the ambitious Russian Prince Sviatoslav of Kiev then decided to occupy and

The Western Empire and the Slavs

annex. Whereupon the Byzantines ousted the Russians and took over eastern Bulgaria themselves (971). Meanwhile, western Bulgaria continued to remain independent. Samuel (976–1014), Tsar of western Bulgaria, brought about a considerable revival of Bulgarian power, and subjected much of the Balkans—including Macedonia and most of Thrace, as well as Epirus and Serbia. But Samuel was eventually defeated (1014) and humiliated by the determined Emperor Basil II, "the Bulgar-slayer." All of Bulgaria now became a Byzantine province, in which condition it remained for nearly two centuries (1018–1186).

Advantages of the eastern Slavs—eventually known as *Russians*—included their frontier position providing greater opportunities for expansion; their large northwestward and southeastward-flowing rivers, connecting them with both the Baltic and Black Seas; their resultant contacts with the Scandinavians and Byzantines; and the uplifting, unifying, civilizing influences of Eastern Christianity and Byzantine civilization. Smaller states to their west and southwest served as buffers against the Germans and Byzantines, while most of their neighbors were disunited or backward.

The eastern Slavs

At the beginning of the Middle Ages (in the fifth to sixth centuries), the eastern Slavs were located between the Dniester and the Don Rivers, with a salient projecting towards the Danube's mouth. What is today far northern Russia was then largely in the hands of Finno-Ugrian and Baltic[a] peoples, while present-day far-eastern Russia was occupied by peoples of both Caucasoid and Mongoloid stock. Far-southern Russia to the north of the Black Sea fluctuated in the possession of successive invaders, usually Asian nomads. The eastern Slavs were usually settled in autonomous self-governing communities with a preference for the edge of rivers. They were dedicated farmers, with agricultural and pastoral activities that were well developed. Urbanization and trade were also spreading along the rivers and in the direction of the Black Sea.

[a] Lithuanian, Latvian, Livonian, and Old Prussian peoples.

Throughout the Middle Ages, Asian invaders were generally ascendant in southern Russia. First the Huns replaced the Goths as masters of the area (370–454). Following the break-up of the Hunnic khanate, there was a period of division and independence (454–558), during which there was a widespread immigration of eastern Slavs (*Antes*). Generally speaking, the Antes predominated in southwestern Russia during this interval, and the Turanian Bulgars in south-central Russia. Next the Avars—a nomadic Asian people—became ascendant over much of southern Russia from about 558–626. Following this, the Bulgars under Kurt built up a short-lived Kaganate (Empire), which lasted from about 626–650. After the break-up of the latter, the Volga Bulgars went to far eastern Russia, while the Danubian Bulgars became dominant in far southwestern Russia. Throughout much of southern Russia, the Khazars —who were originally horsemen—established an enlightened progressive empire, which lasted until it was overthrown by Prince Sviatoslav of Kiev in the mid-tenth century. Other peoples such as the Magyars also had ephemeral states in the area. Prominent from the ninth to thirteenth centuries were the fierce Pechenegs and Cumans, nomadic hordes from

Far-southern Russia in the Early Middle Ages

The Early Middle Ages

Asia. The Pechenegs were eventually overthrown by the Comneni of Byzantium (in the eleventh to twelfth centuries), and were succeeded by the Cumans or Polovtsy (Polovtsi), who remained ascendant in southern Russia until the coming of the Tartars, by whom they were absorbed in the thirteenth century.

Rise of the Russian State

In the mid-ninth century (about 854), Rurik—a Viking leader from Sweden or Denmark—established control of Novgorod in northwestern Russia, where he built up a principality in the vicinity of Lakes Ilmen, Ladoga, and Beloe. The followers of Rurik seem to have been known as *Rus*, possibly from a name applied by the Finns to the Swedes in the Baltic area. Two of Rurik's followers—Askold and Dir—obtained control of strategic Kiev on the middle Dnieper in the late 850s. Rurik's successor, Prince Oleg (c. 878–912) subsequently took Kiev (sometime between 878 and 880) and established control of a region extending through much of northwestern and southwestern Russia. Some scholars identify Rurik as Danish; Askold and Dir as Swedish; Oleg as Norwegian. Oleg established his capital at Kiev, and this principality obtained control of much of Russia in the ensuing three centuries.

The principality of Kiev eventually extended north to the Baltic and the Lake Ladoga area, south to within 250 miles from the Black Sea, and east to the headquarters of the Volga. It competed with various Asian hordes that penetrated far southern Russia, and was alternately a friend and a foe of the Byzantine Empire. The princes of Kiev were expansionist, and even sought to take Constantinople from time to time in the tenth to eleventh centuries, but without success. Grand Duchess Olga —regent for her infant son, Sviatoslav (945–964)—was baptized as an Eastern Christian, but was unable to convert her aggressive son, who assumed personal rule in 964. Sviatoslav, who was compared by a chronicler to a leopard for the swiftness of his movements, overthrew the Khazar empire in southern Russia and defeated the Volga Bulgars. He was invited by the Byzantines to curb the Balkan Bulgarians (968), but after defeating the latter, he decided to annex Bulgaria. Whereupon Emperor John Tzmisces invaded Bulgaria, trapped two Russian armies, and forced Sviatoslav to retire to Kiev. On the way home, Sviatoslav was killed and his army was annihilated by the Pechenegs.

Conversion and civilization of Russia

St. Vladimir (972–1015) was a constructive statesman who made Christianity the state religion of Kiev. According to the Russian *Chronicle*, Vladimir considered various faiths before adopting Eastern Orthodox Christianity. He rejected Judaism because the Jews had been dispersed from their homeland, and Islam because it forbade intoxicating drinks, and he preferred Eastern to Western Christianity because the former had been the religion of his grandmother, and because of the splendors of Constantinople with its beautiful St. Sophia Cathedral. Vladimir—who had seized the valuable Byzantine city of Cherson in the Crimea—insisted on the hand of the Byzantine princess Anne in marriage, as a price for his restoration of Cherson to the Emperor. The mass baptism of the Kievans following Vladimir's conversion is vividly described by the *Chronicle* of Nestor (eleventh century): *Vladimir made known through-*

The Western Empire and the Slavs

out his villages: "Those, rich or poor, who do not appear on the bank of the river the day after will be considered rebels and traitors." On the appointed day, Vladimir, accompanied by priests from Cherson as well as priests of his empress, went down to the Dnieper River, where there was gathered an immense crowd. The people entered the water, some up to their neck, others only to their chest. The children stayed on the bank where water was poured over them. Some persons dove into the water and others swam about, while the priests read prayers. The spectacle was both curious and gratifying. At last, after all were baptized, they returned to their homes.

The Christianization of Russia and the subsequent close relationship with highly cultured Byzantium promoted Russian civilization. Yaroslav the Wise (1019/36–1054) promoted education, encouraged economic development, and codified Russian law (*Russkaya Pravda*), as well as beautified Kiev, and constructed the famous Kievan Cathedral of St. Sophia. He also defeated the formidable Pechenegs, and expanded westward. He arranged impressive marriage alliances between his house and several of the ruling houses of France, Poland, Hungary, Norway, Sweden, and Byzantium. But Yaroslav made a serious mistake by establishing a new "Rota System" plan of succession. According to this plan, each of the princes of the royal family was to receive a principality, with the eldest becoming "Grand Prince," and the succession proceeding by seniority rather than primogeniture. The ultimate result was that Russia became for two centuries a weak league of principalities, with repetitious struggles among its princes for territories and primacy.

References for Chapter 13

THE BEST survey in English for the constitutional evolution of the German state in the Middle Ages is provided by GEOFFREY BARRACLOUGH, *Origins of Modern Germany* (Oxford: Blackwell, 1957), whose *Medieval Germany, 911–1250. Essays . . .* 2 vols. (Oxford: Blackwell, 1938) also includes discussions both by Barraclough (Vol. I) and by recent German historians (Vol. II) concerning various moot and pivotal points of German medieval history. Although most general histories of Germany in English do not give adequate accounts of the medieval period, KURT F. REINHARDT, *Germany, 2,000 Years* is a praiseworthy exception; and VEIT VALENTIN, *The German Peoples: Their History and Civilization*, tr. Olga Marx (New York: Knopf, 1946) is fairly good on the subject. Informative articles are to be found in the *Cambridge Medieval History*, Vols. III and IV. A useful and informative, if over-interpretative, and for this reason criticized, work on the period is JAMES W. THOMPSON, *Feudal Germany* (Chicago: U. of Chicago, 1928). Incidental color may be gleaned from the old and popular, but superficial, translation of WOLFGANG MENZEL, *Germany From the Earliest Period*, 4 vols. (New York: Collier, 1899 and 1900), Vol. I; and WILHELM ZIMMERMAN's *Popular History of Germany*, 4 vols. (New York: Johnson, 1878), Vols. I and II.

A classic, scholarly, broad study of the Empire is HERBERT A. L. FISHER, *The Medieval Empire*, 2 vols. (London: Macmillan, 1898), while a more concise and chronological one is JAMES BRYCE, *The Holy Roman Empire*, rev. (New York: Macmillan, 1919). Worthwhile specialized studies include ERNEST RICHARD,

History of German Civilization (New York: Macmillan, 1911); FREDERICK HERTZ, *Development of the German Public Mind* (New York: Macmillan, 1957); and EDGAR N. JOHNSON, *. . . The Secular Activities of the German Episcopate* (Lincoln, Neb.: U. of N.P., 1932). Many sources for the history of medieval Germany and its Empire are given in OLIVER J. THATCHER and EDGAR H. MCNEAL, eds., *A Source Book for Mediaeval History* (New York: Scribners, 1905).

Probably the best account of Medieval Italy in English is LUIGI SALVATORELLI, *. . . A Concise History of Italy . . .*, tr. B. Miall (New York: Oxford U.P., c. 1940). Also useful are PASQUALE VILLARI, *Medieval Italy . . .*, tr. C. Hutton (New York: Scribners, 1910); and HENRY B. COTTERILL, *Medieval Italy . . . (305–1313)* (London: Harrap, 1915). For the Norman conquest of Southern Italy and Sicily, see JAMES VAN WYCK OSBORNE, *. . . The Greatest Norman Conquest* (New York: Dutton, 1937); and for Rome and Venice, FERDINAND A. GREGOROVIUS, *History of the City of Rome in the Middle Ages* (London: Bell, 1909); and WILLIAM C. HAZLITT, *The Venetian Republic*, 2 vols. (London: Black, 1915), Vol. I. An interesting original source in translation is LIUTPRAND OF CREMONA, *Works . . .*, tr. F. A. Wright (New York: Dutton, 1930), an account of pre-Ottoian tenth-century Italy, which includes his *Tit-For-Tat*, his brief *Deeds of Otto*, and his *Embassy to Constantinople*, made on behalf of Otto the Great.

Good introductions to the Early Medieval Slavs in general include the little work by SAMUEL H. CROSS, *Slavic Civilization Through the Ages* (Cambridge: Harvard U.P., 1948); the more comprehensive ALEXIS P. VLASTO, *The Entry of the Slavs into Western Christendom . . .* (New York: Cambridge U.P., 1970); the penetrating FRANCIS DVORNIK, *The Making of Central and Eastern Europe* (London: Polish Research Center, 1949), which, after background, concentrates on the various Slavic peoples and their relations with the Germans in the tenth and earlier eleventh centuries, as well as his broader *The Slavs and Their Early History and Civilization* (Boston: American Academy, 1956); and the sketchier yet reliable OSKAR HALECKI, *Borderlands of Western Civilization: A History of East Central Europe* (New York: Ronald, 1952), which concerns the area of Germany and Russia. Useful chapters on the Slavs and the various Slavic states in the period are to be found in the *Cambridge Medieval History*, II, 418–459; IV, 183–215, 215–230, 230–245; VI, 422–472; VII, 599–631. Excellent information on the relations of the southern and eastern Slavs with the Byzantines is available in ALEXANDER A. VASILIEV, *History of the Byzantine Empire* (Madison, Wis., U. of Wisc., 1952).

For Polish history in the period, see *The Cambridge History of Poland*, ed. W. F. Reddaway et al., I (Cambridge: Cambridge U.P., 1941), a standard introduction, or the briefer treatment in OSKAR HALECKI, *A History of Poland* (New York: Roy, 1956), as well as OLGIERD A. GORKA, *Outline of Polish History* (2nd ed., rev., London: Kolin, 1945). For Hungary there are C. A. MACARTNEY, *The Magyars in the Ninth Century* (Cambridge: Cambridge U.P., 1930); DOMOKOS G. KOSARY, *A History of Hungary* (Cleveland: B. Franklin, 1941); and OTTO ZAREK, *The History of Hungary* (London: Selwyn, 1939). For Bohemia see KAMIL KROFTA, *A Short History of Czechoslovakia* (New York: McBride, 1934) and FRANZ H. LÜTZOW, *Bohemia: an Historical Sketch*, rev. ed. (London; Dent, 1939). The southern Slavs are treated in WILLIAM MILLER, *The Balkans* (New York: Putnam, 1906); and FERDI-

NAND SCHEVILL, *History of the Balkan Peninsula from the Earliest Times* . . . (New York: Harcourt, 1922); as well as in Robert J. Kerner, ed., *Jugoslavia* (Berkeley, U. of Calif., 1949); and WILL S. MONROE, *Bulgaria* . . . (Boston: Page, 1914).

The best and most comprehensive account of Early Medieval Russia in English is provided by the first two volumes of GEORGE VERNADSKY, *A History of Russia* (Oxford: Oxford U.P., 1943 ff.), of which Vol. I., *Ancient Russia*, takes the story to 878, while Vol. II., *Kievan Russia*, carries it to 1237. VERNADSKY also has a short *History of Russia* (New Haven: Yale U.P., 1954). Among other good short accounts are BERNARD PARES, *History of Russia* (New York: Knopf, 1953) and BENEDICT H. SUMNER, *A Short History of Russia*, rev. ed. (New York: Harcourt, 1949), as well as FRANK NOWAK, *Medieval Slavdom and the Rise of Russia* (New York: Holt, 1930) in The Berkshire Series. Interesting special works include MIKHAIL GRUSHEVSKII, *History of the Ukraine* (New Haven: Yale U.P., 1941); NIKOLAI K. GUDZII, *History of Early Russian Literature* (New York: Macmillan, 1949); and DAVID R. BUXTON, *Russian Mediaeval Architecture* . . . (Cambridge, Cambridge U.P., 1934).

❦ THE CHURCH IN THE EARLY MIDDLE AGES.
Chapter 14.

IN ADDITION to its religious functions, the Church was the leading nucleus of unity and custodian and dispenser of civilization, learning, and the arts in Europe during the Early Middle Ages. The Church's central role was facilitated by its well-knit organization and educated, dedicated personnel, including its monks. The Church, although affected by its environment, did much to transform it.

PAPAL LEADERSHIP.
Section 40.

> The privileges of the Roman Church, conferred on St. Peter by the words of Christ . . . observed from of old, proclaimed by the holy ecumenical councils, and ever venerated by the entire Church, cannot by any means be diminished, violated, or altered. . . . [Pope Nicholas I in a letter to the Eastern Emperor Michael III (865).]

ALTHOUGH Papal primacy was only occasionally exercised in the Church during the Early Middle Ages, it was generally accepted when asserted. Meanwhile, the Papacy was confronted by multiple problems, including the threat of domination by secular governments, the rivalry of the Patriarchs of Constantinople, the difficulty of preserving the traditional doctrines and the spiritual vitality of the Church, the task of converting Arians and pagans, the obligation of providing pastoral care for an expanded, diversified flock, and the need to maintain ecclesiastical unity. By firmly resisting Caesaropapism, and by maintaining a delicate balance between competing secular powers, the Popes were able to foil successive efforts of Byzantine emperors, Lombard kings, Frankish monarchs, Roman nobles, Italian rulers, and German emperors to subject them to their policies. While various Eastern Patriarchs succumbed to divergent doctrines, such as Monophysitism, Monothelitism, and Iconoclasm, that were eventually rejected by the universal Church, the Papacy maintained an untarnished record as judged by ultimate Church acceptance. Despite the shortcomings of some Popes, the Papacy also continued to insist on its authority to render a final decision in ecclesiastical disputes as well as to provide unifying and enterprising leadership in the Church. The Popes supported monasticism, missionary activities, and Church organization in newly converted areas such as England and Germany. Considerable uniformity in liturgy, chant, Scriptural translation, and discipline was established in the Western Church under Papal guidance.

Papal leadership in the sixth century

The subjection of Italy to the Byzantine Empire by 554 increased the tendency of the Eastern emperors to try to dominate the Bishops of Rome. The outcome of an initial confrontation with the great Justinian was indeterminate. In an effort to conciliate the Monophysites, Justinian insisted upon ecclesiastical condemnation of the semi-Nestorian writings of three Eastern church leaders in the "Affair of the Three Chapters." To this end, he exiled the unsubmissive Pope Silverius, who refused to yield, and brought persistent pressure to bear upon his successor, Pope Vigilius, who eventually convoked the (fifth) Ecumenical Council of (II) Constantinople (553) to consider the question. The council's strong condemnation of the "Three Chapters" Vigilius initially resisted, but later, under imperial pressure, approved.

Meanwhile pretensions of the Patriarchs of Constantinople increased *pari passu* with Byzantine power. The Bishops of Constantinople first claimed Patriarchal status, confirmed by the (second) Ecumenical Council of (I) Constantinople (381), and accepted by the Papacy; and then claimed equality with Rome, asserted by the (third) Ecumenical Council of Chalcedon (451), but rejected by the Papacy. In the sixth century, the Patriarchs of Constantinople, as a result of the growing prestige of their capital contrasted with the declining fortunes of Rome, began to make a bid for supreme authority. But Pope Gregory I (d. 604) was quick to criticize this tendency, and rebuked John the Faster, Patriarch of Constantinople, for his presumption in assuming the title of "Ecumenical [Universal, Catholic] Patriarch," writing to him that "admitting this shameless title is nothing less than losing the faith."

Assisted by a decline of Byzantine power in Italy following the advent of the Lombards, the Bishops of Rome continued to insist on their primacy in the Church. Thus Pope Gregory I, in a letter to Bishop John of Syracuse, wrote: *With regard to the Church of Constantinople, who doubts that it is subject to the Apostolic See? . . . Is not the Apostolic See the head of all the churches?* Meanwhile the Papacy from time to time assumed increased active leadership in the Church. It also accepted growing responsibility for the temporal welfare of the people of Rome and adjacent territories, thrust upon it by the decline of Byzantine power. Popes worked to convert the pagan and Arian Germanic rulers of territories previously in the Roman Empire and sent missionaries to the barbarians beyond the former confines of the Empire. Byzantine emperors increased

The Church in the Early Middle Ages

the authority of the Popes in the Roman Duchy, where more and more duties were devolving upon the Bishop of Rome for want of anyone else able to fulfill them. Assisted by the revenues from their extensive properties, especially those in southern Italy and Sicily, the Popes assumed increasing secular burdens, such as provisioning Rome in time of need, buying off the Lombards, and paying the troops.

Gregory I, the Great (590–604)

The life of Gregory I (590–604) epitomized the numerous services rendered by the Papacy. Although he referred to himself as "the servant of the servants of God" and lived as such, St. Gregory has been called "the Great" and "the Founder of the Medieval Papacy." Born of a distinguished Roman family, Gregory obtained the rank of Prefect (chief civil official) of the city of Rome at the early age of 34. But he gave up this high post, founded seven monasteries with his wealth, and withdrew to one of them in Rome, where he permanently injured his health by his austerities. Against his personal desires, Gregory was called into the Papal service, was entrusted with delicate missions, including an embassy to Constantinople, and was eventually elected Pope by the clergy and people of Rome in 590.

Gregory's genius for organization and his patience with details so increased the revenues of the Papal States that he was able to devote large sums to charitable and humanitarian as well as religious projects. In the Papal States he gave great attention to the administration of justice, and promoted the welfare of his tenants and the citizens of Rome. On a broader scale, Gregory fostered the expansion of the Catholic Church by cooperating with Queen Theodelinda regarding the Arian Lombards in Italy, and with Bishop St. Leander of Toledo regarding the Arian Visigoths in Spain, as well as by sending missionaries to England. In the West he supervised the government of the Church, served as a final ecclesiastical court of appeal, and worked for the improvement of the clergy, composing his famous *Pastoral Rule* as a guide for those who had the care of souls. He also judged cases appealed from the Eastern Church, and restrained the ambitions of the Patriarchs of Constantinople. Gregory promoted observance of a uniform liturgy throughout the West, including use of the plain or "Gregorian" chant, which was cultivated in his reorganized "School for Singers" at Rome. He encouraged monasticism and fostered the spread of the Benedictine Rule, writing a much-read laudatory life of its originator, St. Benedict. The practical ethical nature of his numerous influential writings has already been noted.

Papal independence in the seventh and earlier eighth centuries

Although troublous times persisted in the following century and a half (ca. 604–751), the Papacy continued to uphold orthodoxy and in-increased its independence from the weakening Byzantine Empire. The Popes also promoted the conversion of both barbarians and Arians, and extended the episcopal organization of the Church. The Papacy was increasingly alienated from Constantinople by Byzantine sponsorship of heresies and adverse ecclesiastical policies in southern Italy and Sicily. Emperor Heraclius and his son Constans II strongly supported Monothelitism, holding for "one will" in Christ in the hope of reconciling the Monophysites (who held for "one nature"), despite the condemnation of this compromise doctrine by Rome. Monothelitism was firmly resisted by Pope Martin I, despite torture and exile, and was later condemned by the (sixth) Ecumenical Council of (III) Constantinople (680–681).

After the Byzantines lost Syria and Egypt to the Arabs in the seventh century, their concern about Monophysitism subsided, but was supplanted by Iconoclasm. Although this attack on the use of representations of sacred personages was vigorously conducted by most Byzantine Isaurian and Amorian emperors for a century and a quarter, it was firmly repudiated by the Papacy. Without renouncing Byzantine political authority, the Popes adroitly maintained their religious independence from the heretical Byzantines, as well as their political independence from the aggressive Lombards, profiting from the mutual confrontation of these two competing powers. Growing Papal discontent with Byzantine rule was, however, increased by Byzantine confiscation of extensive Papal properties in southern Italy and Sicily, and by Byzantine transferral of these areas from the direct Patriarchal administration of the Bishops of Rome to that of the Bishops of Constantinople. Popes sponsored and partly directed missionary activities in still pagan areas such as England, Frisia, and Germany, as well as the organization of the Church in these areas as they were converted.

Papal alliance with the Great Carolingians (751–814)

The Papacy allied with the Frankish monarchy during the Era of the Great Carolingians (751–814). This alignment resulted partly from progressive alienation from the Byzantines, and from Byzantine failure to protect the Roman Duchy from the Lombards. The Frankish alliance began when the Pope agreed to the coronation of Pepin III (751) and subsequently recrowned him (754); and when Pepin twice descended into Italy and constituted the Papal States (754 and 756). The alliance was renewed when Charlemagne answered the Papal plea for help by invading Italy, deposing the Lombard king and renewing his father's "Donation" (774). It was furthered by Charlemagne's intervention in Rome in favor of hard-pressed Pope Leo III and culminated in Leo's coronation of Charlemagne as Roman Emperor (800). The alliance meant that the Carolingian line and the Papacy should preside, side by side, over the Christian commonwealth, at least in the West, although questions regarding their exact relationship remained.

Aided by the powerful, cooperative Carolingians, the Papacy made progress toward establishing uniformity of Church practices, rites, and doctrinal interpretations in the Western Church. Both Pepin III and Charlemagne promoted standardization of the liturgy, the plain chant, the Latin version of the Scriptures (in the Vulgate form), and monastic regulations. For monks they favored the Benedictine Rule, and for the secular clergy that of St. Chrodegang of Metz.

Papal prestige in the era of the Later Carolin-

Whereas the Emperor was the stronger partner in the imperial-Papal alliance at the time of Charlemagne, the Papacy tended to become ascendant under the Later Carolingians (814–896). Louis the Pious felt it necessary to be recrowned Emperor by the Pope, although he had been previously crowned by his father; and both Lothair and Louis II were crowned by the Pope, solidly establishing the custom. Pope Nicholas I

The Church in the Early Middle Ages

prevented Lothair II of Lothairingia from divorcing his first wife and marrying his mistress, despite the consent of the King's local clergy. Efforts of Emperor Louis the Pious and his son Lothair to subject the Papal States more extensively to imperial authority were eventually unavailing. According to the "Constitution of Lothair" (824) two *missi*, one representing the Emperor and one the Pope, were to rule jointly over Rome, and an oath of allegiance to the Emperor, with a reservation of fidelity to the Pope, was to be required of the Romans; but these provisions soon fell into disuse. Nor were efforts of archbishops to restrict the power of the Pope more successful. Both Patriarch Photius of Constantinople and Archbishop Hincmar of Rheims challenged the authority of Pope Nicholas I (858–867) without success, although their actions portended the later Eastern Schism and Gallicanism. The pseudo-Isidorian "False Decretals" were apparently forged during this time by some French clerics to bolster Papal authority against the ambitious, domineering Hincmar.

gians (814–896)

The height of Papal prestige in this era came under forceful Pope Nicholas I (858–867). For Nicholas, Papal primacy in the universal Church was indisputable, as is emphasized by the extract from his letter to Emperor Michael I quoted at the head of this section. In further explanation of Papal primacy, Nicholas wrote: "The Pope holds the place of Jesus Christ in the universal Church. Divine Providence has placed him at the head of the universal Church, and has made his apostolate the cornerstone of the Church." In addition to quashing the attempted divorce and remarriage of Lothair II, Nicholas restored Bishop Rothade to the see of Soissons, overruling Archbishop Hincmar of Rheims, reprimanded and brought about the deposition of powerful Archbishop John of Ravenna, and effectively condemned the deposition of Patriarch Ignatius and the substitution of Photius in the see of Constantinople effected by Caesar Bardas. In a famous *Letter to the* (recently converted) *Bulgarians*, Nicholas answered various ecclesiastical questions advanced by King Boris and solved the King's doubts. Under the successors of Nicholas (867ff.), however, problems of the Papacy increased. A near-Schism resulted when Photius was restored to the see of Constantinople and accused the West of heresies. Another reverse occurred when the Bulgarians chose to be directly subject to the Patriarchate of Constantinople rather than to that of Rome in administrative matters.

During the early feudal period, in the so-called "Age of Iron," the naming of Popes first fell into the hands of Italian families: initially (896–904) the house of Spoleto and then (904–964) that of Theophylact. The house of Theophylact was eventually controlled by women: first Theophylact's wife, Theodora, and then her daughters, Marozia and Theodora the Younger. Marozia, who took up her abode in the Papal Castle of Saint Angelo, was called Madame Senatrix. She had an uncooperative Pope (John X) imprisoned and smothered. Both Marozia and Theodora were accused of having their lovers raised to the Papal throne. Marozia's son eventually became Pope John XI, and her grandson John XII. The reputation of the Papacy suffered during this period, as

The Papacy in the "Age of Iron" (896–1049)

some Popes were weak, venal, and licentious. Still, other Popes were energetic and led exemplary lives, and none of them deviated from orthodoxy or renounced the Papal claim to primacy.

An interval known as the Era of the German Imperial "Protectorate" of the Papacy (963–1003) followed. In 955 and again in 960–961, Otto I intervened in Italy in response to pleas from Pope John XII and others, and on the second occasion Pope John crowned Otto as Emperor (962). The following year, because of the treachery of Pope John, Otto brought a Roman synod to declare him deposed and elect an Antipope, Leo VIII. John regained the Papacy shortly after Otto's departure, but died the following year. Henceforth, Otto exercised control of Papal elections, as did his successors Otto II and Otto III. Popes named by these German Emperors were generally exemplary and effective, and religious progress included monastic reform movements such as that of the Cluniacs, and the conversion of Poland, Hungary, and Scandinavia. After the death of Emperor Otto III during a Roman uprising in 1003, Papal elections again fell under the control of Italian families until 1046. Emperors Henry II and Conrad II took limited interest in Italian affairs, and the houses of Tusculum and Crescentius obtained control of Papal elections. Some of the Popes in this interval were good, but others were a discredit to the Papacy. Finally, during an Italian squabble over a Papal election (1046), the reform-minded Emperor Henry III intervened and brought about the accession of his own candidate, Clement II. Henry III, who was an intimate friend of Abbot Odilo of Cluny and under his influence, appointed reform Popes. His third appointee, saintly Leo IX (1049), initiated a thoroughgoing reform of the Church.

Church and State in the Early Middle Ages

Relations between Church and State during the Early Middle Ages presented a continuous problem of maintaining a delicate balance. Prior to the conversion of the Germans to orthodox Christianity, relations between Church and State in the early barbarian kingdoms were strained. In the kingdoms ruled by Arian Germans, doctrinal and organizational differences were a continuing irritant; while in the kingdoms ruled by pagan Germans religious differences played a similar role, although relations were less hostile. During this time the Papacy played a difficult game of making accommodations first with Ostrogothic kings and then with Eastern emperors, and finally of playing off Byzantines versus Lombards.

Following the conversion of the barbarian invaders to orthodoxy, the Church came to have a strong position in states such as that of Visigothic Spain and the Anglo-Saxon kingdoms. In the case of the more calloused and skeptical Merovingian monarchs and Lombard kings, however, ecclesiastical considerations and strictures had less effect. The Church often suffered from the fact that the Germanic kings wanted to control the appointment of bishops. Furthermore it was diplomatic to seek monarchical confirmation of episcopal elections—which often contributed to monarchical control. Thus, for example, the Council of Orleans of (549) recognized the right of Frankish kings to approve the election of bishops before they were consecrated.

The Church in the Early Middle Ages

Whereas the relationship between Church and State under the Merovingian monarchs after Clovis was cool, it became warm and intimate under the Carolingians. Carolingian rule had a theocratic aspect, with close Church-State cooperation and intertwined roles. On the one hand, the Carolingians protected the Papacy against the Lombards, and gave the Popes the Papal States. On the other hand, the Papacy approved the Carolingian succession, anointed Carolingian monarchs, and conferred on them the imperial dignity. The Carolingians appointed bishops and utilized their services in their government, appropriated and feudalized much Church land to raise mounted warriors, and legislated for the Church as well as for the State. For a while, the working partnership between the Carolingians and the Papacy tended to be dominated by the power and personality of Charlemagne, who apparently came to regard the external administration of the Church in the Empire as primarily his own concern. But under the later Carolingians (814ff.) relations of Church and State adjusted in a fluctuating manner to a more equal condition.

In the period from 896 to 1054, the Church became partly "feudalized" and appointments to Church offices on all levels frequently fell under lay control. Italian families and German emperors often obtained control of the election of Popes, while monarchs frequently named and even invested bishops. Many local churches were proprietary, with lay feudal lords having the right to designate their holders. Meanwhile the growing reform movement, which spread from the monasteries to the secular clergy, sought to remedy this evil.

MONASTICISM TO THE ELEVENTH CENTURY.
Section 41.

You who are hastening to the heavenly fatherland, fulfil, with Christ's aid, this Rule, which has been written down as the least of beginnings. [From the Rule of St. Benedict of Nursia (sixth century).]

A LEADING pillar of the Church in the Early Middle Ages was monasticism. Although its primary purpose was the glorification of God and the sanctification of its members, monasticism performed many valuable auxiliary services for the Church and society.

Origins of monasticism

Christian monasticism is based on spiritual aspirations of human nature, Christian counsels of perfection, and the example of Christ and holy persons. Monasticism was not original with Christianity, since it was already practiced in other religions, such as Hinduism, Buddhism, and Judaism. Monasticism consisted in renunciation of the present world and its pleasures in order to achieve closer union with God and greater harmony with the Divine Will. Negative aspects of monasticism, such as withdrawal from worldly society and mortification of the flesh, were means calculated to achieve closer union with God. Christian monasticism was encouraged by counsels of Christ—such as "Sell all your goods and distribute them to the poor"; "give up your father and mother and all things for My sake"; and "take up your cross and follow me"—as well as by similar sayings of St. Paul.

Christian monasticism first arose in the southeastern corner of the Mediterranean world. During the third century many pious Christians, in search of greater perfection and to avoid the risk of denying the faith, withdrew to uninhabited places ("deserts"). As time progressed, increasing numbers of Christians sought monasticism as a road to higher perfection, or a form of penance, or a more secure means of keeping on the straight and narrow path of salvation, especially after imperial toleration led to a general Christian relaxation. Monasticism had increasingly wide appeal in the fourth and fifth centuries, as a state of life highly praised by the Church Fathers, an aid to asceticism, and a haven from the growing barbarism and violence of the extramonastic world.

Anchorites and semi-cenobites

The original Christian monks were hermits or "anchorites" who withdrew from society to practice austerities and to pray and contemplate divine things in solitude. Many of these anchorities had recourse to the dry deserts and other desolate areas of Egypt, Palestine, and Syria. Many of them practiced extreme forms of asceticism, as by totally abstaining from all but a meager vegetarian diet and spending long vigils in exhausting prayer. A few, known as "stylites," lived atop poles for years as a means of personal mortification and admonition to their fellows. Simon Stylite lived for thirty-two years on a tiny platform atop a pole, whose height he gradually increased to, it is said, about 60 feet. But strictly anchoritical monasticism had serious dangers, including possibilities of self-delusion and pride, as well as of mental instability, and an inclination to extreme forms of penance. And it lacked adequate opportunities for exercising the social virtues stressed by Christianity. Stimulated by man's need for cooperative social life, a compromise form of monasticism, intermediate between earlier solitary or anchoritical and the subsequent community or cenobitical types, developed as new anchorites sought the direction of experienced veterans. One of the earliest monastic leaders was St. Anthony (d. ca. 356) a monk for about seventy years, who obtained a great reputation for sanctity, wisdom, and miracles. As many who aspired to monastic life sought union with God under his guidance, a sort of half-anchoritical and half-cenobitical colony, headed by the venerable master, developed.

Cenobitical monasticism in the East

Meanwhile a truly cenobitical or community type of monasticism was established in the Nile Valley under the direction of St. Anthony's former disciple, St. Pachomius (d. 346). In the course of three decades (ca. 318–346), Pachomius founded eight or nine monasteries for men and two monasteries for women. A typical Pachomian monastery had thirty to forty buildings with about forty monks to a house. The monks were grouped and housed according to occupations, such as farming, cooking, shoemaking, weaving and ironworking. A basic amount of self-abnegation was required of all, beyond which individual austerities were allowed. The several Pachomian monasteries constituted a sort of congregation with a superior general and general chapter meetings.

About the middle of the fourth century, St. Basil of Caesarea (d. 379) founded a monastery of the Pachomian type, after first studying various types of monasticism then prevalent in the Near East. Basil's counsels and directions for the monastic life, gathered together under the title of *Ascetica*, came to be accepted as a basic Rule for monasticism in the Eastern Church. The Basilian Rule was prudent and judicious. It emphasized the social virtues, such as obedience, and prescribed many community activities, such as attendance at common prayers. Permission of superiors was required for austerities. Each monastery was autonomous under its own abbot, who had broad powers. Basilian monks also worked for the welfare of society, as by admitting outsiders into their schools and carrying on charitable activities. Eventually the Basilian Rule became ascendant in Eastern monasticism.

Western monasticism was originally inspired by Eastern example. Influential in bringing about the introduction of monasticism in the West were Sts. Athanasius, Jerome, and John Cassian, all in the fourth century. Exiled for his opposition to Arianism, St. Athanasius promoted monasticism in the West, where his *Life of St. Anthony* became very popular and influential. St. Jerome, who spent some time as a hermit and later became a monk living in community, enthusiastically praised and promoted monasticism for both men and women. St. John Cassian, after living for several years with monks in Egypt, established the Monastery of St. Victor's at Marseilles, with a Rule permeated with Eastern practices. Cassian also had a great influence through his *Conferences*, which discussed fundamentals of monastic life. Although inspired and influenced by Eastern monasticism, Western monasticism developed its own special characteristics and its own various forms. Among these were the Rules of Sts. Cassian, Honoratus of Lerins, Caesarius of Arles, and Columban.

Early monasticism in the West

In general, Western monasticism was inclined to be more socially conscious and more moderate and cautious in its austerities. This was partly due, no doubt, to the West's more rigorous climate, and the more practical bent of the Western mind. A partial exception was Celtic monasticism, which tended to be extremely austere. The Irish called monasticism "the white martyrdom," and Irish monks often practiced extraordinary mortifications, such as standing immersed in icy water for long periods. The rule of St. Columban has been characterized as "bristling with punishments." But Irish monks were also noted for scholarly interests and missionary activities. They carried the faith to Wales, Scotland, and northern Britain, where they established such monasteries as St. David's, Iona and Lindisfarne. Their houses abounded on the continental mainland: Luxeuil in France, St. Gall in Switzerland, and Bobbio in northern Italy being the most famous. But clannish Irish monasticism, with its poor organization and fierce asceticism, did not long endure off the emerald isle.

The monastic way of life was pursued by women as well as men. Prominent in the early history of feminine monasticism were St. Jerome's friend, St. Paula, and St. Benedict's sister, St. Scholastica. Double monasteries with houses of men and women in close proximity were occasionally established. Several such, controlled by their abbesses, dotted seventh-century England.

The Early Middle Ages

Benedictine monasticism: Its founder

Benedictine monasticism eventually prevailed in the Western Church. Its legislator, St. Benedict (ca. 480–ca. 545) was born of well-fixed parents in the little town of Nursia in northern Italy about 480. As a youth, Benedict went to Rome to study, where he was shocked by the licentiousness that he observed. He therefore withdrew to a mountainous wilderness about forty miles east of Rome. Here he lived as a hermit in a deserted villa of the Emperor Nero, known as Subiaco, devoting himself to prayer and mortification. Benedict gradually acquired a great reputation for sanctity and miracles. He reluctantly accepted the invitation of a group of neighboring monks to replace their abbot, who had died; but when he tried to enforce their Rule they sought to poison him. Benedict then returned to Subiaco, where he attracted numerous disciples. He eventually founded twelve monasteries based on his famous Rule. Having excited the jealousy of a local priest, Benedict left his monasteries each under its own superior, and withdrew to Monte Cassino, about half way between Rome and Naples, where he founded a new monastery.

Benedictine rule and life

St. Benedict's Rule is marked by moderation and practicality, as well as by Christian idealism and charity, and emphasizes social virtues. The moderation of St. Benedict's Rule put its observance within reach of all members of the monastic community. The Rule breathes both the prudent restraint of Roman law and the loving spirit of Christianity. Early in his Rule, Benedict explains: *We are founding a training school for the Lord's service in which we trust that nothing severe or burdensome shall be required.* Of drinking wine, he says: *In view of the weakness of the infirm, we believe that a pint of wine a day is enough for each. . . . Indeed we read that wine is not suitable for monks at all. But because, in our day, it is not possible to persuade the monks of this, let us agree at least that we should not drink until we are sated, but sparingly.* The Rule prescribes adequate clothing, sleep, food, and recreation. Its prescriptions are to be relaxed for the old, the young, and the infirm, as well as at the abbot's discretion. Benedict is very practical in his careful attention to certain details. Thus he provides that the younger brothers sleep dispersed among the older ones, so that the latter can keep a watch on the former and subdue their boisterous spirits. In the same vein, he forbids taking knives to bed, lest anyone have a bad dream and stab one of the brothers in his sleep.

There is a wise diversification of the monk's activities. Public prayer is interspersed with other activities throughout the day, and is to be "altogether brief." Intervals for private reading and meditation are provided. Manual labor allows the monks a healthful respite, while regular eating, drinking, recreation, and sleep are also prescribed. The amounts of time allotted for prayer, labor, and recuperation during the twenty-four hour period are comparable. Social virtues are enjoined and supernaturalized by the love of Christ. Preeminent is love: first the love of God with one's whole heart, and then love of one's neighbor as oneself. A key virtue is humility, whose steps or "degrees" are noted. Individualism is to be left at the door when one enters a Benedictine monastery.

One feature of the Benedictine Rule whose example helped to

The Church in the Early Middle Ages

strengthen and tranquilize society after the "Wandering of the Peoples" was the requirement of stability. A monk normally had to stay at the monastery where he originally became a member. St. Benedict severely criticized "gyratory monks" who wandered from place to place without a regular home or a fixed order of life.

The chief work of the monks, in Benedict's estimation, was to participate in public (cooperative) prayer: "the work of God" (*opus Dei*). Participation in common prayer was accordingly spread throughout the day (and night), with seven separate "hours" or "installments": Matins, Prime, Terce, Sext, None, Vespers, and Compline. The entire Psalter of 150 Psalms was to be recited during the course of each week.

Manual labor, amounting to about six to seven hours a day on the average, was required. Benedict says: "At fixed times the brothers should be occupied in manual labor." Later, intellectual labor was allowed as a substitute. Physical work was enjoined for various reasons: self-support, good example, Scriptural injunction, health of mind and body, and the fact that, as Benedict says, "Idleness is the enemy of the soul." The requirement that "At fixed times the brothers should be occupied in sacred reading" had important implications for the growth of learning, since it dictated that monasteries must have schools to give instruction in reading Latin. Letters thus became a sort of key to heaven, and literacy became standard among monks.

The Benedictine monasteries had elements of democracy, since all the monks were essentially equal and all participated in electing the abbot. On the other hand, the authority of the abbot, once elected, was to be accepted as coming from God. It should be noted that most of the monks were not priests.

Expansion

By St. Benedict's death (543), there were at least fourteen Benedictine monasteries and by the end of the sixth century his Rule prevailed in Italy; Benedictine monks were common in Sicily and in Gaul; and Benedictines had also apparently reached England. During the eighth century the Benedictine Rule was evidently brought to the Low Countries and Germany. The Benedictine Rule was promoted by both Popes and monarchs, and was so universal in Western Europe by 800 that Charlemagne could ask if there had ever been any other monastic rule. By 1300 there were thousands of Benedictine monasteries throughout Europe.

Reforms of Benedictine monasticism

In time, abuses and divergencies crept into many Benedictine monasteries so that reforms were needed. The occasional effect of the renewed barbarian invasions on monastic life is described by a Provincial Synod held at Rheims in 909: *Some monasteries have been destroyed by the heathen. . . . In surviving monasteries, the monastic rule is no longer observed and legitimate superiors are lacking, due to domination of lay abbots, with their wives and children, their soldiers and dogs.*

Reformers arose to meet the challenge. One of the earliest was St. Benedict of Aniane (d. 821), who was prominent in the councils of Emperor Louis the Pious (d. 840). The Emperor supported Aniane's proposed standardization of Benedictine observance. But Aniane's movement had limited success because of his early death, because he attempted to impose too many regulations in excessive detail, and because Carolingian power soon declined. However, St. Benedict of Aniane's ideas and efforts influenced subsequent reformers. In England Sts. Dunstan, Oswald, and Ethelwold (c. 970) promoted a vigorous reform movement which resulted in the so-called *Regularis Concordia* or "Agreement Concerning the Rule" being put into effect in Benedictine monasteries. German abbeys such as Gorze, Hirschau, and Reichenau, and French abbeys such as Corbie and Cluny developed similar movements for reform and standardization.

The Cluniac reform movement

The most important and influential of the early medieval Benedictine reform movements was associated with the monastery of Cluny in Burgundy. Founded in 910 by the Abbot Berno and endowed by Duke William the Pious of Burgundy, the monastery of Cluny was allowed freedom from lay control and was directly under the Papacy, which made it an object of special solicitude. Profiting from their freedom, the monks of Cluny elected a succession of competent abbots—Berno, Odo, Maieul, Odilo, Hugh the Great, and Peter the Venerable—who vigorously endeavored to return to the original spirit of St. Benedict. Aspects of the Cluniac reform were emphasis upon the devout recitation of the "Divine Office" in common as the most efficacious form of common prayer, recognition of the established liturgy of the Church as the highest form of public worship, freedom from lay control, and frequent commutation of monastic manual labor to intellectual and artistic work. Copying of manuscripts was deemed more meritorious than plowing.

As Cluny's reputation spread, the monastery attracted numerous aspirants and several daughter monasteries were founded. Each usually had its own prior, but was subject to the general surveillance of the Abbot of Cluny. Many older monasteries adopted the Cluniac reform and plan of organization. By the twelfth century there were an estimated 314 Cluniac houses. The spirit of the Cluniac reform not only affected Western monasticism in general but also spread to the secular clergy, as many Cluniacs were chosen to be bishops and eventually even Popes. In addition to fostering religious reform, the Cluniacs promoted education, Romanesque architecture and art, and military operations against the Moslems in the Spanish peninsula and the Near East.

The monks and monasticism made many contributions to both the Church and civilization in general. In the spiritual sphere, most monks faithfully pursued their primary objective—the worship of God and personal sanctification. The monastery was, as St. Benedict said, "a school for the service of God." By their example as well as by their verbal instruction, the monks also strengthened their fellow Christians. They felt that a like result followed from their prayers, in accordance with the belief that "More things are wrought by prayer than this world dreams of."

Contributions of monasticism

The monks were a pillar of the institutional Church. Monasteries conducted schools for the secular clergy as well as for monastic aspirants. They were a nursery for future bishops and Popes and other Church leaders. They supplied both missionaries for the conversion of infidels and preachers for the edification of the faithful. The monks composed works of piety, asceticism, and theology; and cultivated ecclesiastical arts, architecture, and music. They pioneered in the study of the Bible, the writings of the Fathers, and other religious works. Monasticism was also a germination ground for Church reform. It has been estimated that by 1300 Benedictine monasticism had provided the Church with some 15,000 bishops, 7,000 archbishops, 24 Popes, and 1,500 saints.

The secular contributions of the monks were numerous. They reclaimed wastelands, cleared forests, drained marshes, and made desolate places verdant. They improved agriculture and animal breeding, and they introduced advanced methods in industries such as winemaking and textile manufacturing. The monks were the chief schoolmasters of early medieval Europe, where they kept the flickering lamp of learning alight. They studied and composed works on philosophical, theological, historical, and even scientific subjects. They maintained libraries and *scriptoria* at a time when illiteracy was the rule even among the aristocracy. They built beautiful churches and other buildings of stone in a "world of wood," and filled them with art and music.

CHRISTIAN LIFE IN THE EARLY MIDDLE AGES.
Section 42.

> Among causes which have led astray priests and princes from the right path is the long-standing evil that the royal power interferes in church affairs, while priests . . . busy themselves with temporal and worldly matters. [Statement of the Council of Paris (828).]

EVEN though the Church claimed divine origin and guidance, none could deny that it was limited by the weakness and foibles of the humans who composed it, which were aggravated by the general confusion and retrogression of the period. And while, by and large, the Church was the chief source of enlightenment in the era, to each vista of light there corresponded a certain area of shadow. Nevertheless, if the clergy had certain shortcomings, they also rendered important services. And if many of the laity suffered serious spiritual and moral deficiencies, they often manifested great faith and admirable virtues.

Expansion of the Church

Second only to the expansion of the Church in Christian antiquity was its expansion during the Early Middle Ages. At the outset of the era, most of the country people in the old area of the Roman Empire were still unconverted, while most of the European barbarians were either pagans or Arians. But by the close of the Early Middle Ages, Christianity prevailed throughout most of Europe. The chief agents of Christian expansion during the Early Middle Ages were the monks, who were especially qualified for this difficult, demanding work by their spirituality, enthusiasm, and thirst for self-sacrifice. By their community life, the monks were able to help, comfort, and encourage one another, as well as to make up for each other's defects and survive temporary failures. By their corporate organization they were in a better position to initiate and sustain the work by conversion and to train native clergy.

But there were other agents as well: Popes such as Gregory I, monarchs such as Charlemagne, frontier bishops such as St. Ansgar of Hamburg-Bremen, and pious women such as Queen Theodelinda of the Lombards. One of the most effective means for the propagation of Christianity was the influence and proselytizing work of Christian wives with pagan husbands, as in the cases of Queen Clothilda with the Frankish King Clovis and Queen Bertha with King Ethelbert of Kent. Another means of conversion was the sword, although its use was less frequent and was discouraged by thoughtful ecclesiastics such as Alcuin, who criticized Charlemagne's forcible conversion of the Saxons. Treaties making certain concessions in return for baptism of the infidels were frequent, as in the case of King Guntrum of the Danes in England and that of Duke Rollo of the Northmen in France. Missionaries usually concentrated on the conversion of leaders, following which the conversion of whole peoples generally ensued. The good example, courage, and devotion of the missionary monks, for instance, Sts. Patrick, Boniface, and Ansgar, was a leading factor. A further attraction was the fact that Christianization was synonymous with progress and promoted acceptance into the community of more advanced European peoples.

Conversion of rural dwellers and Germanic invaders

At the close of classical antiquity, most of the rural population in the territory of the Roman Empire were still "pagan," which term (*pagani*) originally meant "country dweller." The devotion, zeal, and labors of clerics, particularly monks such as St. Martin of Tours, gradually effected the conversion of these *pagani*.

The Germanic barbarians who invaded the Roman Empire were either pagans or Arians, the work of Bishop Ulfilas (d. 381) and his fellow missionaries having brought about the conversion of most of the East Germans to the Arian form of Christianity then prevalent in Constantinople. The task of converting the Arian Germans to orthodox Christianity was actually more difficult than that of converting the pagan Germans and it usually took from one to two centuries. In some cases conversion was not effected until the Germans had ceased to be the ruling race in their area, as in the case of the Ostrogoths and Vandals. Arianism among the Germans soon became adulterated and encrusted with many barbarian superstitions. Their persistence in the heresy was largely caused by national and racial pride, a desire to preserve their own freedom and identity, and traditionalism. The conversion of the Arian Germans to the orthodox Christianity of the majority of the population was merely one aspect of their gradual assimilation, and it was greatly assisted by eventual intermarriage with the natives and with other Germans who were orthodox Christians. Catholic Christianity triumphed among the Arian Visigoths about two centuries after their entry into the Empire; and among the Arian Lombards and Burgundians about a century after their entry.

Unlike the Eastern Germans, the Western Germans were pagans at the time of the great invasions. The conversion of the pagan Franks to orthodox Christianity came about a century and a third after the admission of the Salian Franks into the Empire as *foederati* (361–363).

The Church

King Clovis was converted (496) through the influence of his Catholic wife, Clothilda, and that of Catholic bishops such as Remi of Rheims. Conversion of the rest of the Franks followed. The conversion of the Anglo-Saxons in England (ca. 596ff.) was really that of a pagan people in a pagan country, since the Roman and Christian population in this country had largely fled or been exterminated.

An early instance of conversion of a Western European barbarian people was that of the Irish. Previous efforts to convert the Irish had met with minimal success until the coming of St. Patrick (ca. 433). Patrick's sanctity, austerity, and intrepidity, as well as apparent divine favor, dispelled the initial hostility of the Irish chieftains, overcame the enmity of the pagan priests and druids, and won the confidence of the people. Ireland was rapidly converted, and the Church there was organized on a monastic basis. Learning was assiduously cultivated, and many Irish monks became avid scholars and zealous missionaries who labored to convert the Scots, Anglo-Saxons, Germans, Swiss, and others, and to revive the faith in Gaul and Italy. A notable missionary was St. Columba, who became the Apostle of Scotland; another was St. Columbanus, who made converts and founded monasteries in Gaul, Switzerland, and northern Italy. *Conversion of the Irish*

The Angles, Saxons, and Jutes, who invaded and conquered Britain in the fifth century, were converted to Christianity in the late sixth and early seventh centuries. Pope Gregory I sent a band of monks led by Augustine to undertake the conversion of the English (596). When Augustine and his companions faltered on the way, Gregory encouraged them to continue their mission, trusting in the Lord. The Italian monks went to Kent, where Queen Bertha, a Frankish princess from Paris, was a Catholic, interested in propagating the faith. They were allowed by the friendly King Ethelbert to settle at Canterbury, his capital, and to preach to the people. After various conferences and "signs" (marvelous occurrences), they converted the King (597). As his missionary labors proceeded, Augustine accumulated a number of perplexing questions, which he addressed to the Pope. One of these was what should be done with regard to pagan temples, holy places, and festivals; and Gregory's eventual answer, summarized, was "Christianize them." From Kent, missionary monks carried Christianity to the various other kingdoms of the Heptarchy, where despite several violent reactions and temporary reversions to paganism, the Angles, Saxons, and Jutes were converted. *Conversion of the English*

The conversion of the people of Scotland was largely the work of Irish missionaries and settlers. A leading base for the conversion of Scotland was the Island of Iona, off the southwestern coast of Scotland. Here a monastery was founded by St. Columba, who converted the king of the warlike Picts and established numerous churches. Irish missionaries were also active in Wales, where Christianity seems to have been continuous from Roman times. *Conversion of the Scots and the Dutch*

By the late seventh century, less than a century after the coming of St. Augustine to their own country, English missionaries were carrying the Gospel overseas to foreign countries. An initiator of this movement was the English monk St. Willibrord, who, together with eleven companion monks, preached the Gospel among the Dutch and Frisians (690ff.) with so much success that he came to be known as "the Apostle of the Dutch." The English monks established their headquarters at Utrecht, where relics of their missionary activities are still preserved.

Conversion of the Germans in Germany

Although Frankish and Irish missionaries had worked among the Germanic barbarians who remained in the Germanic motherland, an Englishman first organized the German Church and became recognized as "the Apostle of the Germans" in the first half of the eighth century. Winfrid, who subsequently obtained the name of "Boniface" (Doer of Good), was an English monk, who, after serving for three years as an assistant to Willibrod, obtained a commission from Pope Gregory II as missionary bishop east of the Rhine (722). With a safe conduct from the powerful Mayor Charles Martel, Boniface preached in Hesse and Thuringia, where he established many monasteries to serve as training centers and missionary bases. Among these his favorite was Fulda, which he strove to make a model monastery.

The Pope now made Boniface an archbishop, which gave great impetus to his work of organizing and expanding the Church in Germany. Boniface established bishoprics in Hesse, Thuringia, Bavaria, and eastern Franconia, and assumed leadership of a reform movement in the Frankish Church. Eventually Boniface returned as a missionary to Frisia, where he and some fifty of his companions were attacked and massacred by fanatical pagans (755). The conversion of the Germans was completed by Charlemagne when he conquered the Saxons. Several of his capitularies concerning the Saxons affirm their religious obligations and assess heavy penalties for failure to comply.

Conversion of the Scandinavians

The conversion of the Scandinavians was largely a result of German and English influences and missionary work. A leading Apostle of the Scandinavians was St. Ansgar (Anschar), originally a monk of Corvey, who preached in both Denmark and Sweden, and sent forth missionaries from his eventual see of Hamburg-Bremen. The Christianization of Scandinavia, which underwent many pagan reactions, began in the ninth century and was completed in the eleventh century. The work of conversion was slow in Scandinavia, because of the opposition of the conservative, predominantly rural populace. The conversion of Iceland and Greenland was undertaken from Norway about 1000ff.

Conversion of the western Slavs and Magyars

The conversion of the western Slavs was largely the work of missionaries from Germany, although Byzantine influences were also present. Many Moravians were converted to Christianity by Frankish missionaries during the reigns of Charlemagne and Louis the Pious. But since the Moravians feared Frankish domination, their king decided to turn to Constantinople for ecclesiastical organization. About 862, King Ratislav of Greater Moravia applied to Constantinople for missionaries, and the brothers Cyril (Constantine) and Methodius, who knew Slavic and were well educated and zealous, came and worked with considerable success among the western Slavs. They prepared a special Slavic alphabet (called Gagolithic), based on the Greek, with certain additions, and translated

The Church

the liturgy and the Bible into Old Slavonic. But the Papacy and the German Church considered this territory within the sphere of the Western Patriarchate, and Moravia and Bohemia were organized in the ninth century with the Latin liturgy and in direct administrative subjection to Rome.

Poland and Hungary were converted in the tenth to eleventh centuries. The effective Christianization of Poland began about a century later with the marriage of Duke Miezko of Poland to the Christian Bohemian princess Dubrowka and his attendant conversion (965–967).

German missionaries began to convert the Magyars of Hungary in the later tenth century during the reign of Duke Geisa or Géza, who was baptized along with his son Stephen, pursuant to a treaty with Otto II. The able, saintly Stephen, who married a German princess, spread the Church among his people and made Christianity the official Hungarian religion (997).

Conversion of the southern and eastern Slavs

The southern (Balkan) and eastern Slavs were almost entirely converted by Byzantine missionaries. A Bulgarian princess, who had been baptized while at Constantinople, helped to convert her brother, King Boris (Bogoris) of Bulgaria in 864. Boris requested missionaries from Constantinople, among whom may have been Methodius and his companions, recently expelled from Moravia and its dependencies. In 865, Bulgaria was temporarily organized under the Western Church, but by 870 Byzantine intrigues and pressures brought King Boris back to his earlier allegiance to the Eastern Church. The Serbs were converted at the time of Emperor Basil I (867–886) and were organized under the Eastern Church despite Papal opposition.

The conversion of the Principality of Kiev, forerunner of modern Russia, came in the tenth century. In 955, Grand Duchess Olga of Kiev was baptized at Constantinople. Her diplomatic grandson Vladimir was baptized about 988 in connection with his marriage to a Byzantine princess, and a mass baptism of the people of Kiev in the Dnieper River followed. Russian as well as most southern Slavic Christians used the Old Slavonic alphabet and liturgy developed by Sts. Cyril and Methodius.

Losses

The story of the Church in the Early Middle Ages was not exclusively one of expansion. Two serious setbacks were experienced. The first was the loss of many Christians in Near Eastern and African territories conquered by the Moslems. The second was the Great Eastern Schism, which separated most of the inhabitants of the Balkans, as well as Asia Minor and Syria, from the Western Church. These developments are seen in connection with the stories of Islam and Byzantium.

Church government: feudal involvements and lay patronage

Church government had both laudable features and defects in the Early Middle Ages. Among defects were feudal involvement and lay patronage. Ecclesiastical government was enmeshed in the feudal system; and just as feudalism militarized the aristocracy so it tended to secularize the clergy. In order to survive and carry on its many functions, the Church had to have a certain amount of income, which in this period was derived mainly from lands; but landholding involved the Church in the feudal system. In addition to being administrators of extensive landholdings, bishops were often the secular rulers of towns and adjacent territories. As vassals, they were subject to an overlord, usually the king, by whom they were often appointed, and to whom they did homage and swore fealty, as well as rendered feudal services. Abbots whose monasteries owned extensive estates also had feudal responsibilities, and were often named by lay overlords.

Many churches were "proprietary." Having been originally founded and endowed by a feudal overlord or monarch, they remained under the partial control and protection of the overlord and his successors. This mutually beneficial arrangement gave the lay "patron" the right to name candidates for the particular ecclesiastical position he had helped to create, to administer the church during a vacancy with resultant gain, and to serve as its "advocate" (representative and defender) with a certain percentage of its income. Many monasteries also were proprietary. Feudalization and lay patronage brought the Church a train of evils, such as secularization, lay appointments, simony, and nepotism, resulting in weakened spirituality, directly affecting the clergy and indirectly the laity.

Favorable features of Church government

The organization of the early medieval Church was much more advanced than that of most Western secular governments in the period. Most of the clergy, and especially the higher clergy, were well-educated men of superior abilities. On the Papal level, departmentalization of the Papal curia antedated that of most secular monarchies. Although the College of Cardinals was not formally established until the close of the period (1059), it was in embryo for some time. An element of democracy and representative government existed alongside more authoritarian features on most levels of church government. A frequent practice was the holding of church councils. Thus numerous national church councils were convoked in Merovingian Gaul in the sixth century (fifty from 506 to 595). After a lapse during the seventh century, they were resumed by the Carolingians in the eighth to ninth centuries. The national church councils held at Toledo in Visigothic Spain after the conversion of the Visigoths to orthodoxy included lay representatives along with members of the higher clergy, and legislated concerning both secular and religious affairs. Still more numerous councils, often known as synods, were held on archdiocesan and diocesan levels.

The Popes recognized certain bishops as "primates" in their countries, with special supervisory powers. The archbishops of Canterbury, Reims, and Mainz were Primates for England, France, and Germany. Archbishops supervised provinces, and bishops had dioceses. The diocese was the essential unit in the ecclesiastical structure. With their numerous responsibilities, bishops were usually very busy, although some were not as spiritual as others. Members of the bishop's court were often known as "canons." In the fourth to fifth centuries, as the Church spread in rural regions, parishes were established, and pastors, later known as rectors or curates, were given the care (*cura*) of souls and represented the bishops. The parochial system spread in the Early Middle Ages.

The clergy

While the clergy during the Early Middle Ages were children of their

The Church

times, they also did much to correct and improve the times. Many of the clergy were similar to the upper-class laity because of their political and economic as well as religious offices and responsibilities; and some became more secular politicians and executives than spiritual pastors and men of prayer. The fact that lay nominations to ecclesiastical offices were common frequently led to simony and nepotism, as well as to a more worldly, less single-minded, pious clergy. Many monarchs and lords used their customary right to appoint to ecclesiastical offices as a means to increase their power and income, so that the religious offices were often, in a sense, conferred for a price.

Appointments to religious offices because of blood relationship were common. It became a regular thing for royal and noble families to expect a younger son who had no other prospect to obtain a lucrative and important place in the service of the Church. Some clerics indulged in transient incontinence and some had regular mistresses or concubines, while in some areas, particularly in frontier states and more northern climes, clerical marriage was not unusual. Some clerics became addicted to sloth, gluttony, and drunkenness. While monks were not completely free from the shortcomings attributed to the secular clergy, they were much less susceptible to them. But many monasteries eventually relaxed their discipline and declined from their primitive enthusiasm and observance, so that they came to be in need of reform.

Despite their shortcomings, the clergy had many fine qualities and rendered many important services. They preached the doctrines of Christ, administered the Christian sacraments, and performed both spiritual and temporal works of mercy: hearing confessions, imposing penances, counseling those needing advice, visiting the sick, comforting the sorrowful, supplying the needs of the destitute, and burying the dead. They were the welfare workers of their day. Many of them became acknowledged saints. Even though there were gradations among them, both the secular and regular clergy gave an example of democracy. Their Christian view of life and realization of the basic equality of all persons contained elements of democracy. The principles of "one vote per person" and "the rule of the majority" prevailed in church meetings and elections. Archbishop Adalbero of Reims declared: *The divine law recognizes no distinction in nature between ministers of the Church, but confers equal status on all of them, however unequal they may be by rank or birth.* Reform movements helped to restore and preserve the religious health of the secular and regular clergy. Church councils repeatedly called attention to the need of reforms. And devoted churchmen, such as Sts. Theodore of Tarsus and Dunstan in England, and Boniface and Chrodegang of Metz in Frankland, and later the Cluniacs and Lorraine reformers assumed leadership in effecting reforms of the clergy, both regular and secular.

The Christianity of the laity in the Early Middle Ages likewise had shortcomings as well as positive features. Since most of the laity were unsophisticated and uneducated, their comprehension of Christianity was necessarily limited. Lack of a full understanding of Christianity often led to an exaggerated trust in such externals of religion as rites, relics,

The laity

and pilgrimages, as well as an excessive expectancy of special divine intervention, as by miracles and portents. Many survivals of paganism and remnants of barbarism took centuries to disappear. Among these were superstitions concerning certain places, dates, and circumstances, and beliefs in fetishes, omens, witchcraft, sorcery, ghosts, and fairies. The ingrained customs and practices of barbarism were not easily uprooted, as is evidenced by the cruelty and violence in Merovingian Frankland recounted by Gregory of Tours. The sanguinary Fulk Nerra of Anjou, in the early eleventh century, alternated between robbery, bloodshed, and penitential pilgrimages to Jerusalem (he made four).

The Christianity of the early Medieval laity also had many positive attributes. The previous virtues of the Romans and the barbarians continued and were strengthened by conversion to Christianity. The Church daily and weekly commemorated the bloody sacrifice of Christ in the Eucharist, and annually reenacted the inspiring life of Christ in the liturgy, as well as repeated his teachings by public reading of the Gospels and Epistles and by sermons. The externals of religion used by Christ and the Church to stimulate internal dispositions were psychologically sound and salutary. The Church consistently condemned moral and social aberrations such as adultery, polygamy, violence, infanticide, and unconcern for the weak. It sanctified the family and the home, and preached the unity of human society. Character was strengthened by Christian discipline, while penances and self-denial were required as means of self-control as well as religious worship. Restitutions and reparations for injuries were imposed as conditions for forgiveness, and extensive fasting and abstinence were required.

Although morality often fell short of the Christian ideal, society still accepted this ideal and strove to approximate it. Men might not always be just, honorable, honest, charitable, patient, and kind, but they recognized the desirability and necessity of such virtues. While it did not seek directly to overthrow most existing social institutions, the Church enunciated Christian ideals and the rules for such social institutions, as in the case of slavery and serfdom. It taught that all men are essentially equal; that slaves and serfs have certain inviolable rights; and that, while wives are administratively subject to their husbands, they are also their husbands' equals, to be treated with respect and love. While the Church recognized the right to private property, it taught that this right was a limited one that entailed corresponding obligations, and could lapse in certain instances. Among examples of the influences of Christianity on medieval society were the "Truce of God" and "Peace of God," and much of the code of chivalry.

Contributions of the Church

The Church was a dynamic, constructive force in early medieval Europe. In addition to its religious functions, it rendered many other services. Besides transmitting and propagating the religion of Christ, the Church gave Europe a certain amount of international unity. It was also a leading force for national unity within countries such as England, France, Germany, and Byzantium. It was a model of organization and efficiency for

The Church

the rising young states of Europe, as well as the leading and practically the sole charitable and social welfare institution of the day. And churchmen were both the chief patrons and the leading practitioners of the arts and music. Above all other secular services, the Church was the principal "educator of Europe." The clergy were the chief cultivators and transmitters of learning. As Frederick Artz has said: *In these backward and troubled times, the leaders of culture were a few enlightened monarchs . . . and the statesmen and scholars of the Roman Church. . . . In a brutal and poverty-stricken society, these struggling scholars kept learning alive. . . .*[a]

[a] *The Mind of the Middle Ages* (New York: Knopf, 1953), p. 222.

AMONG good histories of the Church in the Early Middle Ages are ALEXANDER C. FLICK, *The Rise of the Medieval Church* . . . (New York: Putnam, 1909); MARGARET DEANESLY, *A History of the Medieval Church* (London: Methuen, 1925); and HENRY DANIEL-ROPS, *The Church in the Dark Ages*, tr. A. Butler (London: Dent, 1959), and in 2 vols. (Garden City, N. Y.: Doubleday, 1962). Multivolume histories of the Church with good treatments of this period include PHILIP HUGHES, *History of the Church* [to about 1500], 3 vols., Vol. II (New York: Sheed, 1934–1947); FERNAND MOURRET, *History of the Catholic Church* [to about 1600], tr. Newton Thompson, 5 vols., Vols. III and IV (London: Herder 1941); and PHILIP SCHAFF, *History of the Christian Church*, 8 vols. (Grand Rapids: Eerdmans, 1949–1950). Good one-volume histories of the Church during the Middle Ages include ANDRÉ LAGARDE, *The Latin Church in the Middle Ages*, tr. A. Alexander (New York: Scribners, 1915); and the very brief MARSHALL W. BALDWIN, *The Medieval Church* (Ithaca, N.Y.: Cornell U.P., 1953); as well as LEONARD E. ELLIOTT-BINNS, *The Beginnings of Western Christendom* (London: Butterworth, 1948).

Concerning the Papacy in the period, see HORACE K. MANN, *Lives of the Popes in the Early Middle Ages*, 18 vols. (London: Kegan Paul, 1932); and the stimulating GEOFFREY BARRACLOUGH, *The Medieval Papacy* (New York: Harcourt, 1968). A good if very brief survey is given in JAMES A. CORBETT, *The Papacy: a Brief History* (Princeton, N.J.: Van Nostrand, 1956). Two good biographies of Pope Gregory the Great are FREDERICK H. DUDDEN, *Gregory the Great* . . . , 2 vols. (London: Longmans, 1905); and PIERRE BATIFFOL *Saint Gregory the Great*, tr. John L. Stoddard (New York: Benziger, 1929).

Valuable general works on monasticism include DAVID KNOWLES, *Christian Monasticism* (New York: McGraw-Hill, 1969); HERBERT B. WORKMAN, *Evolution of the Monastic Ideal* . . . (London: Kelly, 1913); LOWRIE J. DALY, *Benedictine Monasticism* (New York: Sheed, 1965); IAN C. HANNAH, *Christian Monasticism* . . . (New York: Macmillan, 1925); and JEAN DÉCARREAUX, *Monks and Civilization* . . . , tr. C. Haldane (New York: Doubleday, 1964)—the last of which treats in general terms the evolution and influence of monasticism from the barbarian invasions to the reign of Charlemagne. A mine of information is CHARLES F. R., COMTE DE MONTALAMBERT, *The Monks of the West*, 7 vols. (Boston: Noonan, 1861–1879). An excellent detailed reference is JOHN RYAN, *Irish Monasticism: Origins and Early Development* (London:

References for Chapter 14

Longmans, 1931); while for an early Irish monastic leader, see HELEN CONCANNON, *Life of St. Columban* . . . (St. Louis: Herder, 1915). A sound survey is CUTHBERT BUTLER, *Benedictine Monasticism* . . . (New York: Longmans, 1924); while good studies of the great Benedictine founder are JOHN CHAPMAN, *St. Benedict and the Sixth Century* (London: Sheed, 1929); JUSTIN MC-CANN, *St. Benedict* (New York: Sheed, 1937); and ILDEPHONSO SCHUSTER, *Saint Benedict and His Times* . . . , tr. J. Roettger (St. Louis: Herder, 1951).

The early Cluniac reform movement is portrayed by LUCY M. SMITH, *The Early History of the Monastery of Cluny* (London: Oxford U.P., 1920); and JOAN EVANS, *Monastic Life at Cluny 910–1157* (London: Oxford U.P., 1931). An excellent survey of its subject is LINA ECKENSTEIN, *Woman Under Monasticism* (New York: Russell and Russell, 1963).

Concerning the expansion of Christianity in the Early Middle Ages, see KENNETH S. LATOURETTE, *The Thousand Years of Uncertainty: A.D. 500–A.D. 1500*, Vol. II in his *History of the Expansion of Christianity*, 7 vols. (New York: Harper, 1937–1945). An interesting treatment of missionary activities is JAMES T. ADDISON, . . . *The Medieval Missionary: . . . The Conversion of Northern Europe, A.D. 500–1300* (New York: International Missionary Council, 1936).

For the conversion of the Celts and their missionary activities, see LOUIS GOUGAUD, *Christianity in Celtic Lands* . . . , tr. Maud Joynt (London: Sheed, 1932). In popular style, yet with a sound basis of scholarship, is LUDWIG BIELER, *Life and Legend of St. Patrick* (Dublin: Clonmore, 1949).

For the conversion of Anglo-Saxon England and the early history of the Church there, an extensive and careful coverage is JOHN GODFREY, *The Church in Anglo-Saxon England* (Cambridge: Cambridge U.P., 1962); while original sources are provided by ARTHUR J. MASON, ed., *The Mission of St. Augustine to England According to the Original Documents* (Cambridge: Cambridge U.P., 1897); and VENERABLE BEDE, *A History of the English Church and People*, tr. Leo Sherley-Price (Baltimore: Penguin, 1955), which is also available in other good versions. Original sources concerning the conversion of Germany are provided by C. H. TALBOT, ed. and tr., *The Anglo-Saxon Missionaries in Germany* (New York: Sheed, 1954); as well as BONIFACIUS (originally Winfred), *The Letters of Saint Boniface*, tr. E. Emerton (New York: Columbia U.P., 1940). For "the Apostles of the Slavs," see CYRIL J. POTOCEK, *Saints Cyril and Methodius* . . . (New York: Kenedy, 1941).

Among works dealing with special topics, those concerning the Eastern Schism or the split between the Eastern and Western Christian Churches include the authoritative and sympathetic STEVEN RUNCIMAN, *The Eastern Schism* . . . (Oxford: Clarendon, 1955); and the more general SIDNEY H. SCOTT, *The Eastern Churches and the Papacy* (London: Sheed, 1928); and ADRIAN FORTESQUE, *The Orthodox Eastern Church* (London: Catholic Truth Society, 1920). On distractions of bishops, see EDGAR N. JOHNSON, *Secular Activities of the German Episcopate, 919–1024* (Lincoln: U. of Neb., 1932); and on the contemporary liturgy, see LOUIS M. DUCHESNE, *Christian Worship* . . . , tr. M. L. McClure (London: Young, 1912). Cultural activities and contributions of Churchmen are described by GUSTAV SCHNÜRER, *Church and Culture in the Middle Ages*, tr. G. J. Undreiner, Vol. I (Patterson, N.J.: St. Anthony's Guild, 1956); and, on

Early Medieval Culture

a more limited scale, by JAMES M. CLARK, *The Abbey of St. Gall as a Centre of Literature and Art* (Cambridge: Cambridge U.P., 1926); and ELEANOR S. DUCKETT, *Anglo-Saxon Saints and Scholars* (New York: Macmillan, 1947). An interesting aspect is surveyed by BERYL SMALLEY, *The Study of the Bible in the Middle Ages* (Oxford: Clarendon, 1941).

([EARLY MEDIEVAL CULTURE IN THE WEST.
Chapter 15.

ARLY medieval culture in the West was more important for what it pioneered than for what it produced. If in many respects Western European education, learning, literature, and arts were in a state of decline in the Early Middle Ages, in others they were in a process of germination and were gradually beginning to break the shell of antiquity. The leading inspiration of this culture was Christianity, and its chief nurse and guardian the Church. Early medieval culture was stimulated and enriched by the cross-fertilization of diverse Greco-Roman, Germanic, Celtic, Near Eastern, and Christian elements.

To some extent, Western Europe in the Early Middle Ages was like a schoolboy, *"in statu pupillari"*: attempting to assimilate its cultural heritage from classical antiquity, while gradually learning to think for itself. The international character of early medieval Western culture is illustrated by the periodic shift of cultural leadership from one area to another: from sixth-century Italy to seventh-century Spain and Ireland, to eighth-century England, to ninth-century Frankland, to tenth-century Ottonian Germany, and finally to eleventh-century France. During this period both Byzantine and Moslem culture surpassed that of Western Europe in content, though not in spirit and promise.

EARLY MEDIEVAL EDUCATION AND LEARNING.
Section 43.

> There the Yorkish scholars felt the rule
> Of Master Aelbert teaching in the school:
> Their thirsty hearts to gladden well he knew
> With learning's stream and doctrine's heavenly dew.
> [Alcuin in his poem *On the Saints and Bishops of the Church of York* (eighth century).]

DURING the Early Middle Ages, education was institutionalized and fostered by the Church. The leading educational institutions were monastic and cathedral schools. The "seven liberal arts" were revered as the Biblical "seven pillars of Wisdom" and the "gateway to divine learning," a key to the mysteries of Sacred Scriptures and the way of salvation. Of Master Aelbert teaching youths in the Cathedral School of York, after saying that:

> Their thirsty hearts to gladden well he knew
> With learning's stream and doctrine's heavenly dew,

and describing Aelbert's instruction in both the seven liberal arts and divine learning, Alcuin goes on to say:

> And thus the double knowledge he conferred
> Of liberal studies and the Holy Word.

Schools: monastic

Education in early medieval Western Europe was mainly provided by the Church in schools connected with monasteries and cathedrals. Since monks needed to read, schools were established in monasteries at an early date. The monks were taught Latin grammar, along with reading, writing, and spelling, as well as some arithmetic. Some introduction to Latin literature, secular or ecclesiastical or both, was considered a part of grammar. Familiarization with literary and rhetorical devices as well as principles of Scriptural interpretation was often included. Not only the monastic Rule, but also the Scriptures, and the Fathers, as well as other Christian literature, were regularly studied. The monastic curriculum tended to expand because of the interrelation of the various branches of learning, plus the stimulated literary tastes and intellectual inclinations of the monks. Because of their manifest advantages and better facilities, monasteries became the leading centers of learning in the Early Middle Ages. Examples of famous monastic schools were those at Tours, Corbie, Ferrieres, Fleury, and Luxeuil in France; Fulda, Reichenau, Lorsch, and Hirschau in Germany; Malmesbury, Wearmouth, and Jarrow in England; Armagh and Kildaire in Ireland; St. Gall in Switzerland; Bobbio and Monte Cassino in Italy.

Cathedral schools

Besides the monastic schools, there were cathedral schools. One of the responsibilities of bishops was to provide clergymen to serve as replacements and coadjutors in their dioceses. This they normally did by maintaining a school connected with their cathedral and conducted by a representative known as the "scholastic" (*scholasticus*: schoolman). The Council of Toledo in 527 (or 531), for example, decreed that candidates for the priesthood "shall be instructed by a master, under the supervision of the Bishop, in a building belonging to the Church. When they reach the age of eighteen, the Bishop shall ask them whether they wish to marry. If they choose celibacy and vow its observance, they shall be dedicated to the sweet yoke of the Lord." The curriculum and procedures in the cathedral schools were similar to those in the monastic schools. Secular studies preceded and accompanied religious subjects; the curriculum tended to expand; and many "scholastics" eventually became bishops and further fostered learning. By the tenth to eleventh centuries, famous cathedral schools included those of Châtres, Orleans, Rheims, and Paris in France; Cologne, Metz, Salzburg, and Hildesheim in Germany; York, Durham, Worcester, and Canterbury in England; Liege and Utrecht in the Low Countries; Rome and Pavia in Italy; Toledo and Barcelona in Spain.

Other schools

There were other types of schools such as parish schools. Parish priests often gave instruction to young persons, including those who might serve or sing at ecclesiastical services, or who seemed promising ecclesiastical timber. Both churches and chapels frequently maintained "song schools" whose primary function was the preparation of singers (*cantores*) and readers (*lectores*) for church services. Chapels were often endowed on condition that the incumbent not only chant masses but also provide instruction in what came to be known as a "chantry school." In exceptional areas such as Italy, laymen continued to conduct schools and serve as tutors. An occasional type of school was the "court" or "palace" school, such as that of Charlemagne.

The curriculum of early medieval ecclesiastical schools included secular studies as well as religious learning. The secular studies inherited from classical antiquity were known as the "liberal arts" (from *ars*: a scientific body of knowledge concerning a subject; and from *liber*: free, freeing, or befitting a free man; or from *liberi*: children). Varro, in the first century before Christ, had listed nine such arts (including medicine and architecture); but the number came to be fixed at "seven" by the time of Martianus Capella in the fourth or fifth century. Cassiodorus refers specifically to "seven liberal arts" in his *Institutes of Divine and Secular Learning* in the sixth century, while Boethius in the same century divided the seven liberal arts into the "trivium" and "quadrivium." *The "Seven Liberal Arts"*

The "trivium" or "three-way" course of grammar, rhetoric, and logic was recognized as the foundation of learning. Grammar, which had a much broader scope than it has today, was respected as the key to all erudition, and hence received the most attention. For grammar provided the ability to read and understand Latin, the universal language of Western European literature and learning. Grammar included instruction in spelling and writing, and in correct composition and oral Latin, plus the study of Latin literature, both prose and poetry. In medieval practice, it also included much of ancient rhetoric. The study of grammar was greatly facilitated by excellent textbooks compiled in late antiquity. One was a compact synopsis, composed in the fourth century of the Christian era by Donatus, and known as the "Donat," which was still studied in early modern times. The other was a comprehensive scholarly survey composed about A.D. 500 by Priscian, which had more than 10,000 selected quotations from classical authors. *Trivium*

Rhetoric, which was often largely absorbed into grammar in the Middle Ages, consisted of advanced prose composition, together with auxiliary subjects. It was an accepted principle in classical antiquity that, while the elementary study of grammar made a man literate, rhetoric made him "eloquent" and polished. In its broader sense, ancient rhetoric, and sometimes medieval rhetoric, included additional subjects such as law, political theory, and history; but during the Middle Ages it was often reduced to the techniques of drawing up legal documents and composing formal letters.

Logic or dialectic was the art of correct thinking and valid argumentation. The study and practice of dialectics often moved on into the field of philosophy proper, and even into that of theology, by becoming involved in the actual discussion of questions as well as in analyzing techniques of discussing them. Neither logic nor rhetoric was very extensively studied in the Early Middle Ages: their day was yet to come.

Quadrivium

Studies of the mathematico-scientific quadrivium in the Early Middle Ages were elementary and largely limited to the practical. Some knowledge of arithmetic was of course necessary, and the subject was studied in brief treatments. Much attention was given to the mystical significance of numbers. Arithmetical computations were handicapped by the use of clumsy Roman numerals. Calculations were sometimes expedited by use of the "abacus," a Roman counting instrument composed of movable markers such as balls or beads set on bars or rods to represent ascending stages in the decimal system (units, tens, hundreds, etc.). Geometry was neglected, being often supplanted by geography. As late as the twelfth century, John of Salisbury said: "The study of geometry is little known among us, although it is better known in Spain and Africa" (i.e., among the Moslems). Astronomy was superficially studied, mainly to set the date of Easter and fix the ecclesiastical calendar, concerning which treatises were written by Bede, Alcuin, and Rabanus. Music was included in the quadrivium as a theoretical rather than a practical subject, although as time progressed the practical element was increased.

"Divine learning"

"Divine learning" was the culminating study in cathedral and monastic schools. Since the primary function of such schools was to train clerics and monks, religious studies were their "professional concern." "Divine learning" consisted in the study of Christianity, as found in the Old and New Testaments and commentaries thereon, as well as in the writings of the Fathers, such as St. Augustine, and the decrees of church councils and prelates. It also included liturgical works, and ascetic and devotional literature. Most ecclesiastical authors composed commentaries on some books of the Bible.

Expanding interests

Studies tended to broaden as time progressed. A certain amount of law and even some medicine were often part of the education of clerics. Literary learning, which included the study of classical literature, was often extensive, as is evidenced by lengthening lists of recommended works, actual library catalogues, and the manifest learning of scholars such as Alcuin, Lupus of Ferrières, and Gerbert. Lists of authors to be read were drawn up by intellectual leaders such as Cassiodorus (sixth century), Theodulph (ninth century), Walther von Speyer (tenth century), and Othlo of Emmeran (eleventh century), and there was a constant tendency for such lists to expand and to include more classical as well as ecclesiastical authors.

Remote beginnings of Scholasticism and its combination of faith and reason are discernible in the *Theological Tractates* of Boethius (sixth century) and John Scotus Erigena's *On the Divisions of Nature* (ninth century). Erigena, already noted in connection with the Carolingian Renaissance, was a brilliant Irish scholar who came to the court of Charles the Bald. Scotus translated the *Celestial Hierarchies* of Pseudo-Dionysius the Areopagite from Greek to Latin; and in his *Division of Nature* he combined Neo-Platonic ideas with Aristotelian views and Christian concepts to produce original doctrines. Stirring intellectual activity in the

Early Medieval Culture

ninth century was further evidenced by the controversy over Predestination aroused by the fatalistic doctrines of a young monk of Fulda named Gottschalk; and that over the presence of Christ in the Eucharist caused by Ratramnus of Corbie's opposition to the accepted doctrine of "transubstantiation," according to which the substances of the bread and wine are transformed into the substances of the body and blood of Christ at the Eucharistic consecration.

Although primarily for training monks and clergy, many monastic and cathedral schools also educated lay persons, such as the sons of kings and those of noblemen and the wealthy. Many persons who had been educated for the altar and cloister did not become monks and priests, but returned to the "world" with a good education as their consolation. Other lay persons were educated in parish, song, lay, and palace schools. Many early medieval monarchs were literate, as were Charlemagne, Louis the Pious, and Charles the Bald, Alfred of England, and the Ottos of Germany. Some members of the lay nobility, such as Count Nithard of Orleans, were also literate. Lay education by lay teachers never completely lapsed in Italy, while bardic schools continued in Ireland. *Lay literacy*

Books were very costly because they were copied and illustrated by hand on specially prepared parchment or vellum. By the close of antiquity the old roll or *volumen* form was replaced by the more convenient *codex* or rectangular bound form of book with leaves, such as is common today. Sacred books were often richly ornamented and illuminated. *Books, libraries, scriptoria, and scripts*

Most monasteries had a *scriptorium*—a special room or series of rooms set aside for the copying and illustrating of manuscripts, an occupation that was regarded as highly meritorious. Cassiodorus (sixth century) said that Satan received as many wounds as the monk inscribed words. The *scriptorium* was usually operated in connection with the library. It was common for monasteries to lend each other copies of works for copying and textual comparison. As Professor Sandys says: "It is primarily to the monasteries of the West that we are indebted for the survival of the Latin classics." Many early medieval monasteries had respectable libraries, which included classical as well as Christian works. Survivals of library catalogues, which may or may not be complete, show us that the abbey of St. Riquier had over 500 works, that of Reichenau at least 415 manuscripts, and that of Lorsch 590 titles in the ninth century.

Ancient classical writing consisted of formal, squarish "majuscules" or capital letters. But in the fourth to ninth centuries, these became more rounded "uncial" capital letters. The cursive (flowing) script of "minuscules" or small letters was developed by the monks in the sixth to seventh centuries, when various national hands—known as Insular, Beneventan, Visigothic, and Merovingian—appeared. In the eighth to ninth centuries, the script was both clarified and beautified in the new "Carolingian minuscule." The Carolingian soon displaced other book-hands, and eventually became the source of our modern Western writing and printing.

Early medieval intellectual leaders who worked against great handicaps to become educational trailblazers, usually combined a love of learning with a love of God. Early Italian leadership in learning was exemplified *Early medieval leaders* by Boethius and Cassiodorus. Boethius (d. 524), a Roman aristocrat with high connections, became a leading minister of King Theodoric the Great. Besides writing treatises on arithmetic, geometry, music, and probably also astronomy, Boethius translated (into Latin) and wrote commentaries on the basic logical treatises of Aristotle. While in prison, awaiting execution on false charges of treason, he wrote his *Consolation of Philosophy*, wherein "Philosophy" urges him to regard his fate in the light of truth and eternity. Another leading minister of Theodoric, Cassiodorus lived for almost a century and had two careers: one as a statesman until about 540, and the second as an abbot (ca. 540–583). Cassiodorus provided reading lists for the learning he deemed suitable for his monks in his *Institutes of Divine and Secular Readings* (or literature), and he encouraged the copying of manuscripts in his monastic *scriptorium*, establishing important precedents.

Isidore of Seville (d. 636) composed numerous works for the instruction of students in the episcopal school at Seville. He cites no less than 154 pagan and Christian writers in his *Etymologies*, a synopsis in twenty books of high points in leading fields of ancient learning, so called because of its references to real and imaginary roots of words.

One of the most attractive figures in early medieval education was the eighth-century Anglo-Saxon monk, St. Venerable Bede. Bede carried on the scholarly traditions of seventh century Archbishop Theodore of Tarsus and Abbot Hadrian, of whom he remarks that they "were well read in both sacred and secular literature" and "there daily flowed forth from them rivers of knowledge to water the hearts of their hearers." At the close of his universally praised *Ecclesiastical History of the English People*, Bede says: *I have spent my whole life in the same monastery . . . and I have ever taken delight in learning and teaching and writing.*

Alcuin and Charlemagne

Alcuin (d. 804), in the same tradition, was an ardent lover and disseminator of learning, who studied and taught at the cathedral school of York before becoming a leading figure in the Carolingian Renaissance. Besides teaching in the palace school, Alcuin seems to have inspired much of Charlemagne's legislation on education. In his poem *On the Saints and Bishops of the Church of York*, Alcuin describes the liberal arts as taught by his master at York:

> *To some he made the grammar understood*
> *And poured on others rhetoric's copious flood;*
> *The rules of jurisprudence some rehearse,*
> *While others recite in high Aonian verse,*
> *Or play Castalia's flute in cadence sweet*
> *And mount Parnassus on swift lyric feet.*
> *Anon the master turns his gaze on high*
> *To view the travelling moon, the sky*
> *In order turning with its planets seven*
> *And starry hosts that keep the law of heaven;*
> *The storms at sea, the earthquake's shock, the race*
> *Of men and beasts and flying fowl they trace,*

Early Medieval Culture

*Or to the law of numbers bend their mind
And search till Easter's date they find.
Then last and best he opened up to view
The depths of Holy Scripture, Old and New.*

The author of numerous works, Alcuin may be termed a poet laureat of learning, which he characterized as "bread," "honey," "milk," "wine," "flowers," "a garden," "fruit," an "orchard of pomegranates," "perfume," "fragrance," "gold," and "riches."

The sagacious Charlemagne promoted learning by emphasizing and building up his palace school, by bringing leading scholars to his court, and by issuing laws requiring abbots and bishops to maintain adequate schools and priests and monks to have a minimal education. That Charlemagne's capitularies were no "voice crying in the wilderness" is shown by the similar legislation of numerous church councils.

In the great monastery of Fulda there arose in the ninth century an educational leader who has been called "the Preceptor of Germany." This was Rabanus Maurus, who, after studies at the monasteries of Fulda and St. Martin of Tours, was successively *scholasticus* at Fulda, Abbot of Fulda, and Archbishop of Mainz. Rabanus was the author of numerous text books and commentaries, including an encyclopedic *De Universo*. In his work *On the Education of Clerics*, he advocated a generous course of studies, observing: *It is fitting that those who from an exalted station undertake the direction of the life of the Church should acquire a fullness of knowledge. . . . They should not be allowed to remain in ignorance about anything that appears beneficial for their own information or for the instruction of those entrusted to their care.* *Ninth century leaders*

The scholarly bibliophile, Abbot Lupus of Ferrieres (ninth century) was forever borrowing classical manuscripts in order to have copies made at his monastery and to use them for purposes of textual criticism. The learned and sensitive poet Walafrid Strabo, a product of Rabanus' school at Fulda, eventually became Abbot of Reichenau. Other ninth-century scholars of note included John Scotus Erigena, Bishop Haymo of Halberstadt, Abbot Liutpert of New Corbie and Hirschau, and Heiric of Auxerre. Among Heiric's pupils was Remigius (Remy) of Auxerre, who became a leading schoolmaster of the early tenth century, and taught first at Auxerre, then at Rheims, and finally at Paris. Another tenth-century leader was Abbot Odo of Cluny, a great friend of learning.

Meanwhile in ninth century England, King Alfred of Wessex, a lover of books and learning, maintained a palace school, encouraged education, and translated or had translated several key works from Latin into vernacular Anglo-Saxon.

Germany and the Empire enjoyed the so-called Ottonian Renaissance in the tenth century, whose blossoming was nourished by Italian and Byzantine as well as French influences. Bruno of Cologne (925–965), a younger brother of Otto I, was an indefatigable scholar who promoted learning as Archbishop of Cologne and ruler of the Duchy of Larraine. *Tenth century leaders*

Probably the greatest scholar of his age, Gerbert of Aurillac (d. 1003), beginning as a monk at Aurillac, eventually became Pope Sylvester II. Gerbert was a devotee of logic, literature, and mathematics, so skilled in natural sciences that popular superstition deemed him a magician. He is credited with introducing into Western arithmetic a new type of numbers and an improved abacus, as well as constructing an armillary sphere to demonstrate the sphericity of the earth and its relation to the heavenly bodies.

EARLY MEDIEVAL LITERATURE AND HISTORIOGRAPHY.
Section 44.

> No work of man's hand but the weary years
> Besiege and take it, comes its evil day;
> The written word alone flouts destiny,
> Revives the past, and spells the lie to death!
> [Rabanus Maurus, *In Praise of Literary Labor* (ninth century).]

Latin poetry in the Early Middle Ages

IN LITERATURE, as in other fields, the Early Middle Ages were a period of new departures. One of the most important of these was a break with the formalism, verbosity, artificiality, and ornateness of late classical literature.

Most literature of any consequence in early medieval Western Europe was written in Latin, which was at the time the universal language of government, law, the Church, and learning, as well as *belles lettres*, in the West. Aside from becoming more direct, simple, and "modern," plus adding some new terms and modifying the meaning of others, medieval Latin generally followed the rules of classical grammar, so that it was universally understandable.

Latin poetry served as a medium of expression for the feelings, appreciations, and idealism of early medieval clerics and monks. Coming more from the heart, early medieval Latin poetry often shed the rhetorical artificiality of later Roman poetry, and became more living and personal. It also evolved certain features which made it more popular, as well as better adapted to catchy music. These included *accentual rhythm*, in which repetitious patterns are based on the accent rather than the quantity of syllables; *rhyme*, in which terminal syllables are echoed at the end of verses, as in the case of "fame" and "came"; *assonance*, in which the repetition is found in vowels rather than entire syllables, as with "plain" and "dame"; and *alliteration*, in which letters such as the initial letters of words repeat themselves or are organized into otherwise recognizable patterns. The most outstanding extant examples of early medieval Latin religious poetry are hymns and sequences composed for singing at Mass. Several spontaneous and natural secular poems in Latin also survive.

In Latin poetry (as well as in other fields) the fourth to sixth centuries were transitional from classical antiquity to the Middle Ages. The Fathers of the Christian Church infused new life into both Latin and Greek poetry. In the West, St. Hilary of Poitiers (fourth century) was one of the earliest authors of Latin hymns (which were often set to existing popular tunes. The most noted fourth-century Latin Christian poet was St. Ambrose of Milan, who composed several beautiful hymns in which he popularized new poetic devices. Augustine tells that such hymns were originally used by the Arians to lure away the faithful, and by the orthodox to attract them back. Augustine says that the hymns of St. Ambrose stirred him first by their sensuous beauty and then by their spiritual meaning, and were thus instrumental in his conversion. An oft-quoted hymn of St. Ambrose is his picturesque *Hymn at Cockcrow*, which begins:

> *O Everlasting Architect,*
> *You alternate the day and night,*
> *And by the season's changes effect*
> *In sated hearts a fresh delight!*

The greatest Western Father of the Church, St. Augustine of Hippo (d. 430) was also himself the author of snatches of poetry such as

> *For the font of life eternal*
> *Panteth the enamoured soul;*
> *From its bonds the imprisoned spirit*
> *Seeketh freedom from control.*

In the fifth century, Christian poet St. Paulinus of Nola (d. 431), who gave up great possessions and high position to serve as bishop of the small town of Nola in southern Italy, protested against the criticism of his choice by his old master Ausonius:

> *In words of anger and love you reproach me . . .*
> *For choosing another part of the world . . . ,*
> *Forgetful of the life of refinement*
> *Spent with you in former days.*
> *Cease, I beg you, to wound your friend . . .*

The Spanish Prudentius (d. ca. 413), who had been called "the Horace and the Vergil of the Christians," was the author of numerous poems and hymns. In the course of his *Hymn for the Burial of the Dead*, Prudentius says:

> *Each sorrowful mourner keep silent!*
> *Fond mothers give over your weeping!*
> *None count these dear pledges as perished*
> *For is not death life's restoration?*

> *Though shrivelled, and lifeless, and buried,*
> *These seeds shall arise in bright beauty:*
> *Resurrected from the ground where we laid them*
> *Envisioning a new life eternal!*

> *Now take him, kind earth, for cherishing,*
> *And to thy tender breast receive him:*

> *The body of man I bring you,*
> *Still noble, even in decay!*

In the sixth century, the light-hearted Italian Fortunatus served for a while as a poet for the Frankish court. He later withdrew to Poitiers, where he became a priest and bishop, as well as father-confessor for the convent established by former Queen Radegunde. Fortunatus composed verses praising the hospitality of the convent and the virtues of its royal abbess as well as beautiful religious hymns. His *Vexilla Regis* (*The Banners of the King*) begins:

> *The royal banners forward go,*
> *The cross shines forth in mystic glow;*
> *Where He in flesh, our flesh who made,*
> *Our sentence bore, our ransom paid.*

Meanwhile, Irish monastic leaders and missionaries were writing inspirational poems in both Latin and Gaelic in the sixth century. Among poems attributed to St. Columbanus is the rolling "Boat Song," a stanza of which reads:

> *Heia!! fellows! Echo resounding sends back our "Heia!!"*
> *Placid is the clean-swept floor of the sea; the tempest,*
> *Stilled by the serene face of the ocean's arbiter, sleeps;*
> *Lulled by their own rocking motion the waves are quiet.*

Latin poetry of the Carolingian Renaissance

Following a lapse during the seventh and earlier eighth centuries, the Carolingian Renaissance produced a considerable harvest of Latin poetry in the eighth to ninth centuries. Among the sensitive poems of Alcuin is his touching *Lament for the Cuckoo*, wherein he mourns the absence of a gifted student and prays for his return:

> *Oh cuckoo that sang to us, and art fled:*
> *Where'er thou wanderest, on whatever shore*
> *Thou lingerest now, all men bewail thee dead:*
> *They say our cuckoo will return no more!*
>
> *Ah, let him come again: he must not die!*
> *Let him return with the recurrent Spring,*
> *And waken all the songs he used to sing!*
> *But will he come? I know not I.*

An even more talented poet was Theodulph of Orleans, whose barbed epitaph for the hard-hitting Archbishop Hincmar of Rheims was:

> *Here lies Hincmar; a thief by avarice fired:*
> *His only noble deed, that finally he expired?*

"The Teacher of Germany," Rabanus Maurus, probable author of the *Veni Creator Spiritus*, wrote in his "Poem to a Friend," addressed to Abbot Grimold of St. Gall:

> *Christ, who first gave thee for a friend to me,*
> *Christ keep thee well, wher'er thou art, for me.*
> ....
> *And may God, who brought us to this earth together,*
> *Reunite us in His holy house of Heaven.*

To the same Abbot Grimold, Walafrid Strabo, Abbot of Reichenau, who had been educated at St. Gall, wrote a poem *On Gardening*, including his recollection of his master in earlier days:

> *So you might sit in the small garden close,*
> *In the greenish darkness of the apple trees,*
> *Or where the peach tree cast its broken shade;*
> *And they would bring to you the shining fruit*
> *With the soft down upon it: all your boys,*
> *Your little laughing boys, your happy school,*
> *Carrying huge apples clasped in their tiny hands.*

Angilbert, who became Abbot of St. Riquier, was the author of a vivid poem describing the fratricidal *Battle of Fontenay* (841), quoted elsewhere.[a]

[a] In Chapter 9, section 27.

In the tenth century, Notker Babulus (the Stammerer), known as "the Monk of St. Gall," author of a partly legendary *Life of Charles the Great* pioneered the introduction of "sequences" into the liturgy. Sequences were hymns substituted for the prolongation of the final "a" of "Allelulias," as in Masses at Eastertide. Similar to sequences were the hymns known as "tropes," resulting from insertions between the words of the liturgy, as between the invocations of the *Kyrie eleison, Christe eleison, Kyrie eleison!* (Lord have mercy, Christ have mercy, Lord have mercy!). A typical tenth-century trope runs:

Latin poetry of the tenth century

> *Almighty Creator, both light and begetter of light,*
> *Who hast created all from nothing by a word of Thy command:*
> *Upon the human race, burdened with the weight of sin,*
> *O Lord have mercy!*
>
> *Sent from the citadel of heaven to this earth*
> *That thou might assume our flesh and be born of a pure virgin,*
> *That thou might wash away our sins by shedding thy own blood:*
> *O Christ, have mercy!*

Among poems in a mixed collection from the tenth century known as *The Cambridge Songs* is "The Nun's Complaint":

> *Spring emerges in wanton play,*
> *Dons his coat of colors gay,*
> *Strews the fields with flowery sheen,*
> *Decks the woods with foliage green.*
>
> *Beasts fit out their summer lair,*
> *Little birds their nests prepare:*
> *Singing welcome to the Spring*
> *'Neath their leafy covering.*

> All I hear and all I see
> Breathes enchantment; ah, but I:
> While the world is full of gladness,
> I o'er flow with tears and sadness,
> Sitting in my lonely cell . . . .

In *The Philologian and His Cat*, a studious tenth-century Irish monk compares himself to his cat;

> Pangur is proof the arts of cats
> And men are in alliance:
> His mind is set on catching rats,
> And mine on snaring science.

Vernacular literatures: Anglo-Saxon

During the Early Middle Ages some Western European vernacular literatures took halting first steps. Among the earliest was Anglo-Saxon (English) literature. We possess fragments of four early English narrative poems of which the most famous, most complete, is the story of *Beowulf*. Another is *The Battle of Brunanbarh* (ninth or tenth century), which begins:

> Athelstan King,
> Lord among Earls,
> Bracelet-bestower and
> Baron of barons,
> He, with his brother,
> Edmund Atheling,
> Gaining a lifelong
> Glory in battle,
> Slew with the sword-edge
> There by Brunanburh,
> Broke the shield-wall,
> Hewed the linden-wood,
> Hacked the battle-shield . . . .

Among early Anglo-Saxon religious poets, Caedmon (seventh century), an ex-cowherd who became a monastic scholar, rendered much of the Bible in Old English verse. In his hymn "The Master of the World," Caedmon says:

> Creator all holy: He hung the blue heaven
> A roof high uplifted, O'er the children of men;
> The King of mankind then created for mortals
> The world in its beauty, the earth spread beneath them.

Another noted early English poet, Cynewulf (eighth century), related stories of prophets and saints in verse. Anglo-Saxon prose also got an early start with King Alfred's translations and the *Anglo-Saxon Chronicle*.

Irish

Rivaling Anglo-Saxon literature was Irish or Gaelic literature. In Erin, bards and poets were honored and privileged, and predated Christianity as well as survived its establishment. Early Irish literature is characterized by romanticism and mysticism, extremes of joy and sorrow, flights of fancy, and fondness for the marvelous. Many early Irish narratives combine prose and poetry in tales of travel and adventure. *The Cuchulainn Cycle* is comprised of almost a hundred associated tales, of which "The Tragic Deaths of the Sons of Usnach" is an example. Early Irish literature contained a large body of lyric verse, including numerous short pieces with titles such as "The Deer's Cry," "The Hermit's Song," and "The Winter Song," the last of which tersely sketches its setting:

> *Take my tidings:*
> *Stags contend,*
> *Snows descend:*
> *Summer's end.*
>
> *A chill wind raging,*
> *The sun low keeping,*
> *Swift to set*
> *O'er seas high sweeping.*

German literature started with the translation of the Bible and other religious works into Old Gothic by Ulfilas and his missionary companions. That there were numerous early German poems we know from Tacitus, who refers to the "ancient songs" of the Germans, as well as from Einhard's reference to Charlemagne's order to have such collected and transcribed. All this old German poetry has been lost except a few fragments. Among these, the *Hildesbrandlied*, composed about A.D. 800, contains both pagan and Christian elements, and songs of war, love, and tragedy. Other vernaculars did not beget real literary works until the High Middle Ages.

German

Much early medieval prose consisted of letters, which constitute an integral part of the "works" of medieval writers such as Cassiodorus, Gregory, Alcuin, and Gerbert (Sylvester II). A common form of prose was didactic literature: treatises on such subjects as the liberal arts, the Scriptures, and asceticism. Sermons, "conferences," and colloquies fall in the same category.

Latin prose and drama

Drama evolved naturally from the antiphonal and responsorial dialogues in *tropes* (poetic insertions in the liturgy). In addition to taking part in conversational exchanges, participants began to act out the parts. Favorite early scenes included the Massacre of the Innocents, the Birth of Christ, the Resurrection, and the Coming of the Wise Men. Suggestive of considerable learning in convents was the composition in Latin of plays modeled on the comedies of Terence by a tenth-century German nun, Hrothswitha of Gandersheim.

History writing was common in the Early Middle Ages, and was done almost exclusively in Latin in the West. The shock of the breakup of the Roman Empire and its fall in the West at first inspired St. Augustine's interpretative *City of God* and Orosius' synoptic *History of the World*. Subsequent "national histories" or accounts of the early Germanic peoples and their "successor states" included Cassiodorus' volumi-

Early medieval historiography

nous *History of the Goths*, lost for lack of patient copyists; Jordanes' (sixth century) *History of the Goths*, a crude synopsis based on Cassiodorus' work; Isidore of Seville's loose *History of the Goths, Vandals, and Suevi*, who invaded Spain; Gregory of Tours' vivid *History of the Franks*, mainly about his own sixth century; "Fredegar's" inferior seventh-century continuation of the former; St. Venerable Bede's *Ecclesiastical History of the English People*, a model of scholarly investigation and moderation; Paul the Deacon's *History of the Lombards* (to 744), written at the request of Charlemagne; and Widukind of Corvey's (tenth century) *History of the Saxons*.

More specialized narratives appeared from time to time. Prominent among them were histories of bishops and their dioceses, such as Paul the Deacon's and Alpert's *History of the Bishops of Metz* (tenth to eleventh centuries); Heriger's *History of the Bishops of Liege* (eleventh century); and Richer's *History of the Bishops of Rheims* (eleventh century). Among other specialized works were Count Nithard's account of the civil wars following the death of Louis the Pious in his *Four Books of Histories*; and Bishop Liutprand of Cremona's *Antapodosis* or *Tit for Tat*, about the civil wars in Italy just before the intervention of Otto I in the mid-tenth century; as well as his story of his *Legation* (or *Embassy*) to the Court of Constantinople on Otto's behalf.

Besides occasional biographies of rulers, such as Einhard's *Life of Charles the Great* and Bishop Asser's *Life of Alfred* (the Great), clerical historians wrote numerous lives of the saints, their favorite "heroes." Such "hagiography" was often stylized, and aimed at moral edification as much as historical information. Examples are the *Life of St. Benedict* by Gregory I; the *Life of St. Sturm*, Abbot of Fulda, by Eigil: Anskar's *Life of St. Willehad*, Apostle of the Frisians; and Rimbert's *Life of St. Anskar*, Apostle of the Swedes.

A form of history writing known as "annals" evolved from the custom of making notations of events on previously prepared ecclesiastical calendars. Simple annals consisted of bare statements of events occurring each year (*annus*). From annals evolved "chronicles," which retained the "chronological" sequence, but told the story in a more connected fashion. Many more sophisticated better-organized chronicles are true histories; and the terms "chronicle" and "history" are often used interchangeably, as are the terms "annals" and "chronicles."

EARLY MEDIEVAL ARCHITECTURE, ART, AND MUSIC.
Section 45.

> Painting is to be admitted in churches so that the illiterate may learn from the pictures on the walls what they cannot read in books. [Letter of Pope Gregory I to the Bishop of Marseilles (sixth century).]

IN THE Early Middle Ages the visual and aural arts were comparatively advanced, partly because the recently converted barbarians had more to contribute, and partly because these arts, intimately involved in congregational religious ceremonies, were intensively cultivated.

Early Medieval Culture

Following toleration, the Christians, as has been noted, both adapted and imitated Roman public basilicas. The Roman basilica was a simple, impressive rectangular building, widely used for public functions and mercantile activities. It had a long, high central "nave," flanked by lower side aisles. Over the columns separating the aisles from the nave there rose "clerestory" walls pierced by windows. The wooden roof above the nave was of low pitch. Entrance to the basilica was often via a covered *narthex* (porch, portico, or lobby). At one end there was usually a terminal section (later "apse") where the praetor (or praetors) might sit surrounded by attendants and hold court.

Christian basilicas

When the Christians took over the basilican style, they progressively modified and elaborated it. The Christian basilica had in common with the Roman secular basilica that it was an assembly place; but it differed in that it was meant for the celebration of sacred mysteries and was a "*domus Dei*" or "house of God." It differed from the pagan temple in that it was a religious meeting place, whose principal beauty was internal rather than external. It has been said that the Christian church was "a temple turned outside in." The early Christian churches were in a sense both "beautified basilicas" and "enlarged temples."

In addition to liberal use of ornamentation, such as marbles, frescoes, mosaics, stonecarving, and gilding, the Christian basilicas had various structural innovations. An *atrium* or courtyard (like a cloister) preceded the *narthex*. The church was entered through rich and impressive doors. Aisles were sometimes multiplied, as in the Old St. Peter's at Rome, which had four of them. A definite "apse" or elevated terminal area appeared, and was enlarged and often rounded. The building was "oriented" from west to east, so that the congregation looked eastward, and faced the region of the rising sun, symbolic of Christ. Graceful marble columns were often surmounted by carved capitals. Frequently mosaics or frescoes decorated the walls, and galleries surmounted the aisles. As time progressed, a transept or cross-aisle was often constructed to transect the nave, just before the apse, giving the church the form of a Latin cross. A dome was occasionally erected over the junction of transept and nave; while a tower or towers might be included, to serve for bells and/or lookout purposes, as well as for esthetic effect.

One feature of the Christian basilica was an emphasis on voids (spaces), producing an ethereal impression. Another was an aspect of progression, whereby attention was drawn to the apse, as by a long line of pillars converging in perspective toward the altar.

An occasional style in early Christian churches was the "rotunda" or "central" type, in which a circular or polygonal building was constructed around a central dome-covered space, whose main axis was vertical rather than horizontal. Examples include the round tomb-church of Santa Constanza at Rome (fourth century); the circular-polygonal mausoleum of Theodoric the Great at Ravenna (fifth century): and the attractive octagonal Church of San Vitale at Ravenna (sixth century). The rotunda style was not so commonly used, because it was more difficult of execution and less adapted to focus attention on church services. Sometimes

Rotunda churches and Byzantine architecture

the basilican and rotunda styles were combined, as by building a dome over the intersection of nave and transept.

Combination of the cruciform basilica and domed rotunda was characteristic of Byzantine architecture in the Justinian Renaissance (sixth century), whose example *par excellence* is the great Cathedral of Sancta Sophia (Holy Wisdom) at Constantinople (Istanbul). In the subsequent style of the Macedonian Renaissance (ninth to eleventh centuries) the exterior of the church was decorated, and the construction was lighter and airier. Instead of only one dome there were now often several, and the drum for the central dome was made taller and was pierced with more windows. The ground plan was usually a Greek cross. The Macedonian Byzantine style was imitated in St. Mark's Cathedral at Venice as well as in some Sicilian and southern French churches, and many Balkan and Russian churches. In the Slavic churches the domes often became bulbous.

Early Germanic and Slavic churches

Churches in the early Germanic kingdoms beyond the Alps were of two kinds: stone and wood. Churches in stone were less common, as well as usually smaller and simpler, and most have disappeared. Since the early Germans and Slavs were much more proficient at working with wood than with stone, and had more good wood available, they commonly built wooden churches. These were tall and rectangular like "great halls," with steep, pointed roofs and squarish "block" pillars or circular "mast" columns of wood. These churches were often decorated with exquisite woodcarving, and frequently had towers, to serve as lookout posts and housing for bells. Most of these churches have likewise disappeared.

Proto-Romanesque

Preexisting forms were combined in the so-called Proto-Romanesque or Early Romanesque, which seems to have first appeared as a nascent style in Lombardy (northern Italy) in the seventh to eighth centuries, where it was executed by the so-called *Magistri Cominaci* (Master Masons of Como). It is exemplified in such early churches as Old St. Ambrose in Milan; and Old St. Michael's, Pavia; as well as in San Stefano, Verona. In the Lombard Proto-Romanesque, stone vaults spanned square sections, and criss-crossed ribbed arches of masonry carried the weight to clustered columns or bulky piers set at the four corners of each section. Such vaults were initially used over lesser parts of churches, such as the aisles and the apse, rather than over the nave.

During the Carolingian Renaissance, especially in the ninth century, features of this Proto-Romanesque, imported from Italy, appeared in Frankland, as in Charlemagne's Church at Aachen. In the Carolingian Proto-Romanesque style, stone vaulting spanned subordinate parts of the church, such as aisles, apse, and side-chapels, often in the form of ribbed vaulting. Carolingian Proto-Romanesque also had heavy piers instead of slender columns; splayed window openings; compound apses, side chapels, transepts, and towers, attached or separate. Building stones were usually small, windows minimal, and walls thick.

Art in the Early Middle Ages

After a temporary setback, most of the arts revived and launched forth upon new lines of development. Among stimulants were the cross-fertilization of diverse elements, such as Roman, Celtic, and Germanic components, the inspiration of Christianity, and the organized, dedicated

Early Medieval Culture

human resources of the Church and monasticism. Near Eastern influences were strong in early Christian art, with its emotionalism, expressionism, symbolism, abstractive transcendentalism, and fondness for gold and rich colors. Early Christian art did not glorify beauty, and often preferred signs of austerity in its subjects as indicative of spirituality. It also had a predilection for symbols, as if to stress the point that spiritual reality is ineffable. Thus Christ was frequently represented by a fish, whose Greek name *ichtus* corresponded to the initials of *"Iesous Christos, Theou Uios, Soter"* (Jesus Christ, God's Son, Savior). Another symbol for Christ was the vine. The four Evangelists were regularly represented in the Early Middle Ages by a man, a lion, an ox, and an eagle. The man stood for Matthew, who dwells on the human generation of Christ; the lion as king of beasts for Mark, who underlines the royal nature of Christ; the ox for Luke, who stresses the priesthood and sacrifice of the Savior; and the eagle for John, because of his soaring mystic flights. From earliest times, the Christians accepted the visual arts as "the Bible of the illiterate."

While the barbarian invasions and ensuing instability caused a temporary decline in art on the continent, Christian art flourished from an early date in the British Isles, where Celtic and Germanic influences were strong in arts such as manuscript illumination. The art of the Celtic and Germanic barbarians was mainly ornamental and linear, with a fondness for zig-zags, interlacing patterns, geometrical figures, and serpentine designs. The human figure was avoided, and animal forms were usually grotesque, marvelous, or composite. Designs tended to be imbalanced, giving an impression of movement, and the lines often carried the eye along in a seemingly endless manner.

Illumination of manuscripts

Utilization of barbarian art forms by Celtic and Anglo-Saxon manuscript illuminators is exemplified in eighth- to ninth-century copies of the Scriptures made at the monasteries of Lindisfarne and Kells. Early medieval monks lavished unstinting pains on the beautification and illustration of "the word of God." On the exquisite, superbly drafted "Cross Page" of the *Lindisfarne Gospels* (late eighth century), for example, the chalice-shaped arms of the cross are suggestive of the memorial of Calvary in the Eucharist. The stupendous "Monogram Page" of the *Book of Kells* (ca. eighth century) presents the initial Greek letters of the name of Christ: Chi (ch), Rho (r), and Iota (i), in a fascinating complex of intricately interrelated decorations.

In the Carolingian era and in the tenth century, book illumination took a turn in favor of more pictorial representation. The movement and imbalance of previous insular art are present, communicating to scenes an illusion of action. Illuminators not only illustrate events related in the sacred books, but also try to depict metaphorical and allegorical allusions. The dramatic action of the new style is exemplified by the naturalistic representation of St. Matthew in the act of writing in the *Lectionary of Karl the Great* (ca. 800) from the palace school; as well as in the nervous, electrified portrait of St. Mark in the process of receiving inspiration in the *Ebbo Gospels* (early ninth century) of the Rheims School. The extension of illustration to rhetorical and figurative expressions is seen in the fluttering, motion-filled sketches of the *Utrecht Psalter* (early ninth century) of the Rheims School, wherein the 150th Psalm, "Praise the Lord . . . ," is represented by numerous musicians playing various musical instruments, including an organ. In the style of the Ada School, the *Ada*, *Lorsch*, and *Soissons Gospels* picture soft, youthful faces with full nostrils and lips. Various other schools, such as those of Tours, Metz, and St. Gall, also attest the creative fecundity of the period.

The tenth-century Winchester School in England is exemplified by King Edgar's *Charter* to the New Minister (Monastery) of Winchester, which represents the King conferring the Charter; as well as by the *Benedictional* of St. Aethelwold, Bishop of Winchester, wherein the figures are very lifelike and are integrated with their frames. Meanwhile Carolingian artistic traditions of dramatic action and figurative representation continued to evolve in Germany during the Ottonian Renaissance, as in the case of the School of Reichenau.

Other forms of early medieval art

Other forms of early medieval art included woodcarving, metalwork, stonemasonry, and occasional murals. Ornamental woodcarving was highly developed, especially in northern areas. The Germanic peoples were also skilled in metalwork, an elaborate example of which is the sixteen-panelled bronze doors of the Cathedral of Hildesheim (ca. 1012), whose left door presents scenes from the Old Testament and whose right door depicts events from the New. Stonework from this period is rare and crude, since the stonemason's art fell into decline. Mural paintings, such as those in the palaces of Charlemagne and in some early churches, have all been lost.

Early medieval church music: "plain chant" and hymns

Assiduously cultivated for Christian worship, music made remarkable progress in the Early Middle Ages. Music, which appealed to the illiterate masses and barbaric breasts, as well as to persons of culture, was associated with Christian worship from earliest times as a carryover from Jewish worship. Among the early Christians, the ordinary method of singing was apparently, in accordance with the Jewish tradition, in a simple, solemn, prosaic "plain chant." But the early Christians also came to use, on occasion, more rhythmic, colorful, popular hymns similar to folk music.

Several regional types of liturgy with their own associated music gradually appeared, but the Roman liturgy and "plain chant" eventually superseded other forms throughout the West. The Roman or Gregorian "plain chant" or "plain song" was sung and cultivated by the Roman *Schola Cantorum*, which was given regular quarters and status by Pope Gregory I. The Roman plain song was a measured, unspectacular, monodic (unisonal) music, intended for congregational singing. It is described as "speech-song," since words are clearly enunciated, and the music is adapted to the words, rather than vice versa, so that the sense is stressed, rather than the melody. The plain chant scales are diatonic, using only regular tones and half tones, giving a sense of security, while the intervals between notes are limited. The effect is elevated and spiritual.

More chromatic (colorful), swinging, dramatic, rythmic melodies known as hymns also developed in connection with church services.

Early Medieval Culture

These tunes were often adapted versions of popular melodies. Augustine tells us that when the faithful were waiting in the Cathedral at Milan in fear of the Arian Empress they sang hymns to console themselves. In the eighth to tenth centuries the use of such melodies in church services was increased by the introduction of tropes and sequences into the liturgy of the Mass, as has been noted.

Polyphony and notation

Elementary polyphony in the form of *organum* developed by the tenth century. In *organum* the parts are parallel, at fixed intervals above or below the basic melody. In "strict" *organum* they are consistently parallel; while in "free" *organum* the prevailing parallel is broken from time to time, as when a note in one part is held while the other part continues. Both forms of *organum* probably arose naturally, as from chance singing at different pitches, for instance, when boys and men sang together.

One of the most significant musical development in the Early Middle Ages was musical notation. At first during the Early Middle Ages musical notes were represented by letters, as among the ancient Greeks and Romans. But soon they came to be represented by "neumes": strokes looking like accents, or combinations of such strokes. The next step was the conversion of the accentlike neumes into regular square notes representing both pitch and duration. A final step was the introduction of lines, whereby the tones on a scale could be more precisely indicated by placement of the notes on and between the lines of a staff. The particular pitch was indicated at the beginning of each set of lines.

Secular music

That there was much secular music in the Early Middle Ages we know from many sources. Churchmen repeatedly inveighed against some secular music as "voluptuous," "sinful," or "idiotic." That such songs were catchy is illustrated by a story told by Giraldus Cambrensis (eleventh to twelfth centuries) concerning a certain priest who, when turning to chant "Peace be with you" at Mass, inadvertently sang instead the refrain of a current popular song: "Sweet love the lover needs thine aid"! Besides love songs, drinking songs, and dancing music, there were swinging harvest tunes, pulsing boat songs, stirring ballads, soft lullabies, and rythmic folk music of all sorts.

Musical instruments and treatises

Although a variety of wind, string, and percussion instruments were in use in classical antiquity, the early Christians generally banned them from sacred services, partly because of their association with profane and pagan celebrations and entertainment. The ideal for church services was considered to be the human voice, without accompaniment (*a capella*). In the course of time, however, the organ, as an impressive and dignified instrument, came to be used in church services. The pipe organ, which appeared in Alexandria as early as the second century before Christ, is described by Cassiodorus (sixth century) as "built like a tower from diverse pipes out of which a very rich sound is produced by a blast from the bellows." The bellows for such organs were hand operated, as is exemplified by the *Utrecht Psalter's* illustration for the 150th Psalm. The hydraulic organ was in use by the ninth century, when Louis the Pious possessed one. In addition to the organ, the lyre, cithara, and psaltery were eventually accepted in Christian churches. In secular music, the range of musical instruments was much wider, and included such wind instruments as the flute, tuba, trumpet, and various horns; such string instruments as the harp, cithara, lyre, psaltery, and fiddle; and such percussive instruments as drums, bells, cymbals, and chimes.

In the ninth to tenth centuries, Remigius (Remi) of Auxerre, Hucbald of St. Amand, and Odo of Cluny wrote musical treatises still based mainly on the old *De Musica* of Boethius. But in the tenth to eleventh centuries, numerous treatises incorporated discussions of new developments, such as musical notation, harmony, and other practical points. In the tenth century, Bernelinus began to emancipate music in his *Cita et Vera Divisione Monochordi;* while full development of the new trend is found in the celebrated *Micrologus* of Guido of Arezzo (eleventh century).

References for Chapter 15

A GOOD general survey of most phases of medieval culture is FREDERICK B. ARTZ, *The Mind of the Middle Ages* (New York: Knopf, 1953). The part played by Christianity is discussed by CHRISTOPHER DAWSON, *Religion and the Rise of Western Culture* (New York: Sheed, 1950). Of broad coverage, though not including the arts and music, is the scholarly, comprehensive MAX L. W. LAISTNER, *Thought and Letters in Western Europe, A.D. 500–900* (London: Dial, 1931).

One of the best histories of medieval education is FREDERICK EBY and CHARLES F. ARROWOOD, *History and Philosophy of Education, Ancient and Medieval* (New York: Prentice-Hall, 1940). One of the finest treatments of early medieval education is ANDREW FLEMING WEST, *Alcuin and the Rise of Christian Schools* (New York: Scribners, 1892), which carries us through the early medieval period with repeated quotations of sources. Another splendid work which enlarges on the eighth to tenth centuries is JAMES B. MULLINGER, *The Schools of Charles the Great* (New York: Stechert, 1932). Useful readings are included in ELWOOD P. CUBBERLY, *Readings in the History of Education . . .* (Boston: Houghton, 1948). A superb general treatment is HENRY OSBORN TAYLOR, *The Medieval Mind,* 2 vols. (London: Macmillan, 1930).

Ireland's cultivation and transmission of learning are discussed in JOHN HEALY, *Insula Sanctorum et Doctorum: Ireland's Ancient Schools and Scholars* (Dublin: Sealy, 1912); and HUGH GRAHAM, *The Early Irish Monastic Schools* (Dublin: Talbot, 1923). The standard work on education in England is ARTHUR F. LEACH, *The Schools of Medieval England* (London: Methuen, 1915). English cultural contributions are treated by SAMUEL J. CRAWFORD, *Anglo-Saxon Influence on Western Christendom, 600–800* (London: Oxford U.P., 1933); and WILHELM LEVISON, *England and the Continent in the Eighth Century* (Oxford: Clarendon, 1946). A good study of curriculum and textbooks is PAUL ABLESON, *The Seven Liberal Arts* (New York: Columbia U.P., 1906).

Standard surveys of the history of medieval Latin literature are FREDERICK J. E. RABY's *History of Christian Latin Poetry from the Beginnings to the Close of the Middle Ages* (Oxford: Clarendon, 1927); and his *History of Secular Latin Poetry in the Middle Ages,* 2 vols. (Oxford: Clarendon, 1924). A brief but intelligent introduction is MAURICE HELIN, *History of Medieval Latin Literature,* tr. J. C. Snow (New York: Salloch, 1949). Anglo-Saxon literature is the subject of STOPFORD A. BROOKE, *English Literature from the Beginning to the Norman Con-*

Early Medieval Culture

quest; and CHARLES W. KENNEDY, *The Earliest English Poetry . . .* (London: Oxford U.P., 1943). Among useful collections of literary works with explanatory discussions are OTTO KUHNMUENCH, *Early Christian Latin Poets from the Fourth to the Sixth Century* (Chicago: Loyola U.P., 1929); PHILIP S. ALLEN, *Medieval Latin Lyrics* (Chicago: Chicago U.P., 1929); and HELEN WADDELL, *Medieval Latin Lyrics* (New York: Holt, 1948). General collections include LESLIE W. JONES, *Medieval Literature in Translation* (New York: Longmans, 1950); and JAMES B. ROSS, *Portable Medieval Reader* (New York: Viking, 1949); as well as the *Oxford Book of Medieval Latin Verse,* ed. S. GASELLE (Oxford: Oxford U.P., 1937). A good introduction to Anglo-Saxon vernacular literature is STANLEY B. GREENFIELD, *A Critical History of Old English Literature* (New York: New York U.P., 1965).

Both architecture and the arts are touched on in W. R. LETHABY and D. T. RICE, *Medieval Art . . . 312–1350* (New York: Philosophical Library, 1950); as well as in JOSEPH STRZYGOWSKI, *Early Church Art in Northern Europe . . .* (London: Batsford, 1928). A standard work is ARTHUR K. PORTER, *Medieval Architecture . . . ,* 2 vols. (New Haven: Yale U.P., 1912), whose Vol. I carries through the Romanesque. Other authoritative works are KENNETH J. CONANT, *Carolingian and Romanesque Architecture, 800 to 1200* (Baltimore: Penguin, 1959); THOMAS G. JACKSON, *Byzantine and Romanesque Architecture,* 2 vols. (Cambridge, Cambridge U.P., 1938); and the first volume of CHARLES A. CUMMINGS, *A History of Architecture in Italy,* 2 vols. (Boston: Houghton, 1927).

Reliable works on art include CHARLES R. MOREY, *Medieval Art* (New York: Norton, 1942); and JOSÉ OIJOAN Y SOTERAS, *Art in the Middle Ages . . .* (Chicago: University of Knowledge, 1940). Valuable, more specialized treatises are WALTER LOWRIE, *Art in the Early Church* (New York: Pantheon, 1947); FRANÇOISE HENRY, *Irish Art in the Early Christian Period* (London: Methuen, 1940); THOMAS D. KENDRICK, *Anglo-Saxon Art to A.D. 900* (London: Methuen, 1938); HAROLD PICTON, *Early German Art . . . to About 1050* (London: Batsford, 1939); THOMAS D. KENDRICK, *Late Saxon and Viking Art* (London: Methuen, 1949); ROGER HINKS, *Carolingian Art* (London: Sedgwick, 1935); and JOAN EVANS, *Cluniac Art of the Romanesque Period* (Cambridge, Cambridge U.P., 1950). Painting in the form of book illumination is specifically treated in ANDRÉ GRABAR and CARL NORDENFALK, *Early Medieval Painting . . .* (Paris: Skira, 1957); DAVID DIRINGER, *The Illuminated Book . . .* (New York: Philosophical Library, 1955); and JOHN A. HERBERT, *Illuminated Manuscripts* (London: Methuen, 1911).

Good general treatments of the history of medieval music, understandable by the laymen, are found in such works as THEODORE M. FINNEY, *A History of Music* (New York: Harcourt, 1947); CECIL GRAY, *History of Music* (London: Kegan Paul, 1947); and PAUL H. LONG, *Music in Western Civilization* (New York: Norton, 1941). More specialized treatises include the collaborative *New Oxford History of Music, Vol. II: Early Medieval Music up to 1300,* ed. ANSLEM HUGHES (London: Oxford U.P., 1954): the information-packed GUSTAVE REESE, *Music in the Middle Ages* (New York: Norton, 1940); and MARIE PIERIK, *The Song of the Church* (London: Longmans, 1947). On the development of musical notation, see CARL PARRISH, *The Notation of Medieval Music* (New York: Norton, 1957).

PART III. THE HIGH MIDDLE AGES

(ca. 1050–1300)

DURING the eleventh, twelfth, and thirteenth centuries medieval civilization gradually reached its zenith. France and England, and for a while Germany, became strong, well-organized states, while kingdoms such as Castile, Aragon, and Sicily, made similar progress. Individual rights and liberties were formally guaranteed by monarchs, and institutions of representative government developed. Law and jurisprudence were greatly improved and the jury system appeared. Overseas expansion began. The Commercial Revolution, with its application of capitalism and large-scale methods to international trade, was launched, and was assisted by several devices for the expansion of credit. Craft guilds contributed to the growing excellence and productiveness of industries, while the modern Industrial Revolution was foreshadowed by labor-saving devices and some large-scale production.

General progress accompanied economic development. Europe's population doubled. A dynamic middle class arose in the growing towns and organized into guilds and communes to obtain greater liberties and self-determination. Widespread emancipation of labor occurred. The influence of the Church reached an all-time high, with the Papacy temporarily ascendant in Europe, and Popes serving as international arbiters. Monasticism reformed itself, and vigorous new religious orders appeared. Christian theology attained maturity, as also did canon law. Christian ideals were socially accepted and respected, even though they were not always fully observed. The liberal arts were enthusiastically studied in cathedral and monastic schools, while a broadening spectrum of advanced learning was cultivated in universities. Christian humanism inspired increased study and appreciation of classical literature, while a zest for knowledge propelled pursuit of the sciences and philosophy. Vernacular literatures appeared and produced initial masterpieces. Impressive Romanesque and Gothic cathedrals, still the marvel of tourists, were constructed and adorned with forceful sculptures and unsurpassed stained glass. In many ways the High Middle Ages were a springtime of Western civilization.

References for Part III

SURVEYS of the history of the High Middle Ages are provided by ZACHARY N. BROOKS, *A History of Europe from 911 to 1198* (London: Methuen, 1938); CHARLES W. PREVITE-ORTON, *A History of Europe from 1198 to 1378* (London: Methuen, 1937); FRIEDRICH HEER, *The Medieval World: Europe 1100–1350* (London: Weidenfeld and Nicolson, 1967); GEORGES DUBY, *The Making of the Christian West, 980–1140* (Geneva: Skira, 1966), and *The Europe of the Cathedrals, 1140–1280* (Geneva: Skira, 1967), both tr. Stuart Gilbert; and the *Cambrige Medieval History*, vols. V and VI. Good source collections with introductory surveys are BRYCE D. LYON, ed., *The High Middle Ages, 1000–1300* (New York: Free Press, 1964) (p.), and CHARLES T. DAVIS ed., *Western Awakening: Sources . . . c. 1000–c. 1500* (New York: Appleton, 1967), (p.). Viewpoints on the question of a Renaissance in the twelfth century are presented in C. WARREN HOLLISTER, ed., *The Twelfth Century Renaissance* (New York: Wiley, 1969) (p.) in the "Major Issues in History" series. For features of the period from the late tenth to the early thirteenth centuries, see RICHARD W. SOUTHERN, *The Making of the Middle Ages* (New Haven: Yale U.P., 1953); and for aspects of the thirteenth century JAMES J. WALSH, *The Thirteenth, the Greatest of Centuries* (New York: Catholic Summer School, 1907). For intellectual and literary culture from about 1050 to 1250, one may consult CHARLES H. HASKINS, *The Renaissance of the Twelfth Century* (Cambridge, Mass.: Harvard U.P., 1927); and for political and social conditions MARC L. BLOCH, *Feudal Society*, tr. L. Manyon (Chicago: Chicago U.P., 1961).

❰ THE COMMERCIAL REVOLUTION: ECONOMIC AND SOCIAL PROGRESS IN THE HIGH MIDDLE AGES. Chapter 16.

DRAMATIC economic advances accompanied by revolutionary social changes helped to promote the general progress of Western Europe during the High Middle Ages and provided a foundation for far-reaching improvements in government, religion, and culture.

THE "COMMERCIAL REVOLUTION" AND INDUSTRIAL DEVELOPMENT. Section 46.

> He made handsome profits in all of his transactions, and accumulated great wealth by purchasing goods for a low price in certain places and selling them elsewhere for a high price. [Reginald of Durham, concerning the business life of St. Godric of Finchal before he became a monk (twelfth century).]

THE Commercial Revolution dawned in the High Middle Ages and brought about large-scale economic expansion. A prodigious growth of trade stimulated a boom in industrial production, which was accompanied by an expansion of coinage, credit, and financial devices. Agricultural and pastoral activities likewise expanded, as also did the extractive industries.

The Commercial Revolution consisted in widespread application of large-scale methods and capitalism to the purchasing and marketing of goods. The Commercial Revolution, which concerned the distribution of goods, is not to be confused with the later Industrial Revolution, which involved the production of goods. Western European commerce mounted rapidly during the High Middle Ages, and eventually surpassed its previous heights in the heyday of the Roman Empire. As the *Cambridge Economic History* says: *The startling surge of economic life in Europe in*

The Commercial Revolution

The High Middle Ages

the 'high' Middle Age is probably the greatest turning point in the history of our civilization.[a] The tide of commerce rose steadily in the period from about 950 to 1100, and reached its medieval peak from about 1100 to 1350. The *Cambridge Economic History* characterizes to the High Middle Ages as "the Golden Age" of southern European commerce and observes that *By the twelfth century Venice, Genoa, and other mercantile cities had surpassed in wealth the greatest business cities of the classic world.* In the late thirteenth and early fourteenth century, when the pinnacle was reached, the sphere of dirct or indirect influence of Western businessmen stretched as far as England, South Russia, the oases of the Sahara Desert, India, and China.[b] The same work labels this period "the Age of Expansion" of Northern European commerce,[c] and says: *Trade from the tenth century onwards . . . both in its changing volume and expanding geography . . . grew until some time in the fourteenth century. . . . During this period, northern economy was, so to speak, formed, for it was then that its separate regions, its trade routes, and its commercial connections composed themselves into a single trading area. In addition . . . the trading area gradually spread eastwards. . . .*[d]

Factors in the expansion of commerce

Among factors making it possible for commerce to expand in the High Middle Ages were Western European military and naval supremacy, increased security, greater political stability, growth of an enterprising spirit, cessation of Viking attacks, and Christian seizure of the offensive against the Moslems. The Crusades to the Near East provided valuable bases in Syria and Palestine for Asiatic trade. Increasing Byzantine dependence on Western shipping and naval protection enabled Westerners to obtain many special economic privileges in Byzantine territories.

Commercial expansion was self-accelerating, so that many results of expansion also became causes of further expansion. Thus the great population increase and growth of towns, the expansion of agriculture and enhanced industrial productivity, the increased availability of money and finance, and the emancipation of labor with its encouragement of individual initiative were causes as well as effects of the commercial revolution. An initial stimulus in many cases was the necessity of importing food into certain areas during temporary famines. A continuing cause was the excess of population with respect to food supply in commercial and industrial areas.

Routes and articles of commerce

Commerce was intercontinental, international, interregional, and local. Intercontinental commerce, which was mainly with Asia, but also throve with Africa, was both overland and maritime. Overland trade with the Far East moved via the Steppes and the Ural Gateway, and via the so-called Great Silk Way of Transoxiana and Armenia; that with Persia and India across the Syrian and Arabian deserts. Most intercontinental commerce was conducted part of the way by water, as on the Black Sea, the Red Sea, the Indian Ocean, and the Mediterranean. From Egypt, Syria, Palestine, Asia Minor, and Constantinople, most goods destined for the West were dispatched on ships to Italian, French, or Spanish ports. Inhabitants of the north Italian maritime cities of Venice, Genoa, and

[a] *Cambridge Economic History of Europe*, vol. II (New York: Cambridge U.P., 1952).
[b] Ibid., II, 289ff.
[c] Ibid., II, 155ff.

[d] Ibid., II, 159.

The Commercial Revolution

Pisa, were especially active in this Mediterranean trade; but French and Spanish merchants, operating from ports such as Marseilles and Barcelona, also competed for a share.

As they progressed westward, the crisscrossing routes of commerce became more numerous and complex. Favorite sea routes were coastwise or over short expanses of water, as in the Adriatic and Tyrrhenian Seas, the Bay of Biscay, the English Channel, the North Sea, and the Baltic. Much commerce moved on rivers and along old Roman roads. Local commerce simply expanded its former patterns. Leading focal centers of commerce included north Italian towns such as Venice, Genoa, Pisa, Florence, and Milan, and the towns of the Low Countries and adjacent northern France, such as Bruges, Dordrecht, and Amiens. Marseilles and Aigues Mortes in southern France and Barcelona and Valencia in Spain were also important commercial centers. In the Empire, Rhenish cities such as Cologne and Strassburg, and cities in southern Germany and Switzerland, such as Nuremberg and Basel, profited from their favorable position on trade routes. Towns along the German eastern and northern frontiers grew rapidly, as happened with Vienna, Prague, Magdeburg, Hamburg, Bremen, and Lübeck.

From Asia came less bulky, valuable articles that could bear the cost of long travel, such as fine textiles of silk, gauze, damask, and muslin, oriental rugs, sumptuous tapestries, spices, and condiments, perfumes and aromatics, precious gems and jewelry, drugs and medicines, dyestuffs, sweet wines, and dried fruits. From Southern Europe came woolen textiles, olive oil, wines, fruits, silver and gold—both worked and unworked, arms, armor, and cutlery; from Western Europe iron, timber, raw wool and textiles, hides and tallow, wines, grains, fish, and slaves; from Northern and Eastern Europe iron, copper, tin, and lead, as well as fish, honey, grains, timber, pitch, amber, beer, furs, and slaves.

From an early date, peddlers from the Near East, ("Syrians," "Greeks," and "Jews") were "traveling salesmen" in Western Europe. Westerners, such as North Italians ("Lombards"), Frenchmen, and Flemings, soon joined their number. As time progressed, many Westerners became full-time merchants or *negotiatores* (businessmen), on a growing scale. Some of these eventually employed agents or *factors* to handle their business. In 1292 at least sixteen Italian merchant houses had agencies and representatives in Paris.

Merchants

The rise of an enterprising young man from small beginnings to the position of a wealthy *negotiator* is illustrated by the career of St. Godric of Finchal prior to his conversion to the monastic life. His biographer says that as a boy Godric salvaged pieces of wreckage and drift cast up on the shore by the waves, and then tells us how he became a trader by *"retailing goods of small price . . . and peddling cheap wares across the countryside to the peasants. Then, little by little, he became associated with urban merchants. . . . Eventually, in company with other enterprising young men of similar mind, he began to launch upon bolder courses, and went by sea to the foreign lands that lie about us. . . ."*

Marketing and fairs

Local trade was mainly carried on at urban markets on set days of the week (market days). Artisans also sold their "manufactured" (made by hand) goods from their homes and shops. For large-scale wholesale trade there were "fairs" (from *feria*: holy day), described in Bracton's *Notebook* as glorified markets, held once a year, and lasting up to six weeks. Whereas markets were for retail goods, fairs were for wholesale transactions.

Especially famous were the fairs of Champagne in northeast France, held six times throughout the year for about six weeks in each case at four locations: Troyes (2), Provins (2), Lagny, and Bar-Sur-Aube. These Champagne fairs were almost constantly in progress at the times when fairs were possible. The Champagne fairs were the chief sites of international exchange in Western Europe, partly because of their favorable location on crisscrossing trade routes, partly because of their encouragement by the counts of Champagne. Merchants traveling to and from the Champagne fairs had special protection, while the fairs were well policed and efficiently controlled, and proceeded on schedule. After a preliminary period to permit the unpacking of goods, there were specified periods for various types of articles and transactions, such as ten days for the sale of textiles (drapes), ten days for that of animal skins, furs, and hides; a week for merchandise sold by weight (*avoir du poids*); and a final fifteen days for the settlement of accounts and financial transactions. The Champagne fairs incidentally became "the money market of Europe."

Factors favoring commerce

Contemporary technological advances included such navigational aids as the astrolabe, the mechanical clock, the magnetic compass, and the rudder. Obtained from the Arabs, the astrolabe enabled navigators to determine the precise elevation of the stars and thus ascertain their position with the help of astronomic tables. The mechanical clock made possible the precise determination of time under all weather conditions, and the magnetic compass expedited the exact setting of course at all times, while the rudder attached to the ship's keel served to keep the vessel on course. The Italians took the lead in the development and use of the pivotal compass, which is described by Alexander of Neckham in the twelfth century and Petrus Peregrinus in the thirteenth century.

Improved ships

Shipbuilding made considerable progress in the High Middle Ages, being spurred on by expanding trade and travel. Much larger ships were constructed—some having a capacity of 500 to 800 tons, and capable of carrying 800 to 1,000 persons. Masts and sails were multiplied, with fore and aft rigging, in the interests of speed and maneuverability. Enclosed "tops" reappeared on masts. Navigational rudders were attached to the sterns of ships for surer steering. The number of decks was increased, and forecastles and sterncastles were added.

Ships tended to differ according to regions. Ships in the Mediterranean were regularly "carvel-built" with flush planks and "lateen" (triangular) sails, which were much better for tacking. Many Venetian ships that transported Crusaders were about 84 feet long and 21 feet in beam and depth. At first the only "galleys"—long, slender craft propelled by oars as well as sails—were warships, but toward the close of the period larger

The Commercial Revolution

galleys were constructed as merchantmen to carry cargoes and passengers.

Ships in the north, as we have seen, were "clinker-built," with overlapping planks, and they used square sails. The Hansards developed large "cogs" with deep draught and straight ends, single masts, and huge carrying capacities. "Coasters" were smaller vessels, primarily designed for coastal travel and decked only over bow and stern, with reinforcing "through beams" projecting slightly at the edges.

Commercial law independent of local customs came into widespread use. Much of this "merchant law" traced back to the Byzantine code known as the Rhodian Sea Law. Among Western collections of commercial law were the Usages of Barcelona, the Statutes of Marseilles, the Laws of Oleron (an island off the coast of Aquitaine), and the Ordinances of Wisby (an island in the Baltic). This law was administered in special courts, such as those that operated at the fairs of Champagne, and the "piepowder" courts in England (from *pieds*: feet and *poudré*: dusty). *Other aids*

Further aids to commerce included commercial arithmetic, elementary education, guild and town schools (many of which appeared in the twelfth to thirteenth centuries), growing use of Arabic numbers, the production of paper as a more economical form of writing material, improved forms of commercial organization, and better financial devices.

The High Middle Ages were characterized by many forms of cooperative organization, an outstanding example being the guilds (gilds). The first guilds seem to have been undifferentiated unions of merchants of all sorts, but in the course of time the artisan-merchants organized their own "craft guilds." The guilds may have derived their name either from the money (*Geld*: gold) that the members paid into a common fund or from a word meaning a festive gathering. They were called *artes* in Italy and *gremios* in Spain. *Merchant guilds and hansas*

Guilds originated as early as the eleventh century when merchants began to congregate in large numbers in *faubourgs* (suburbs) and towns. In many cases the guilds seem to have been originally indistinguishable from the urban communes. The guilds admitted members for a fee (*geld*) and had their own government, organization, and regulations. Merchant guilds limited mercantile activities in their area to their members and authorized outsiders, regulated trade as to hours and conditions, worked for favorable laws and privileges for their members, and acted as political, social, fraternal, benevolent, and funereal institutions. They arranged recreational activities and assisted widows and orphans of deceased members. Many of the guilds eventually built their own guild halls, had their own chapels and chaplains, and even operated schools. In Italy guilds or groups of guilds were represented in town governments in a sort of syndicalism.

In some cases, as early as the twelfth to thirteenth centuries, and especially in the thirteenth, there arose leagues of towns or *hanses* (*hansa*: confederacy), which were primarily commercial but also had political and military features. One of their main purposes was to promote the common interests of their members when trading in foreign areas. Among early *hanses* were the Flemish Hanse of London, the Rhenish League,

The High Middle Ages

headed by Cologne, and the famous Hanseatic League of northern Germany, founded in the twelfth century.

Industrial expansion

Stimulated by commercial enterprise and increased markets, industry expanded. Industries tended to develop and thrive in commercial focal centers, such as those of northern Italy and the Low Countries. The leading industry of the age was the making of woolen textiles, although linen and silk cloths were also produced. Several northern Italian towns, as well as towns in the Low Countries and Artois, thrived on their manufacture of woolen cloths. "Flanders cloth" or "Frisian cloth" was in great demand, while the Florentines had a secret process for finishing cloth (the *Arte di Calimala*) that enabled them to import, improve, and sell at a profit even Flemish cloth. The cloth-producing industries of cities like Florence and Bruges were often organized on a capitalistic basis. By 1300 Florence had some two hundred *Arte de Lana* (craft of wool) workshops, while the *Arte di Calimala* had a street of its own.

The metal industries produced cutlery and tools, arms and armor, wrought iron, and other articles, including costly items made of precious metals. The leatherworking industries turned out footwear, harness, saddles, belts, purses, and the like. Shipbuilding was booming. The manufacture of both plate and blown glass, together with superb stained glass windows, became widespread, with Venice an early center for ordinary glass and France for stained glass windows. The papermaking industry was beginning in Italy and Spain. Carpenters and stonemasons were in great demand for the construction of churches, halls, and homes in towns and castles and manor houses in the country. Food industries, such as the milling of grain, baking of bread, salting of fish, and curing of meat, occupied many workers, as also did the making of wines and brewing of beer.

Extractive industries

A great expansion of extractive industries occurred in this "first great period of European mining." Iron and coal were mined in most countries, particularly in northern Spain, England, Germany, France, Belgium, Hungary, and Sweden; tin was mined in Cornwall and Bohemia; copper in Sweden, Bohemia, and Germany. Gold was mined from mountains in Germany, Bohemia, Hungary, greater Austria, and Spain, as well as panned from rivers such as the Rhine, the Rhone, and the Po. Silver and lead were mined in Spain, Italy, Germany, greater Austria, and Hungary. Timber was cut for export from the mountains of northern Italy, southern Germany, England, and Scandinavia. Salt was obtained by the evaporation of seawater, as at Venice, Pisa, and Marseilles, and from salt pans, as in France and Germany. Mercury was obtained from Spain, and alum and sulfur from Italy.

Industrial advances and conditions of labor

A trend to the use of labor-saving devices and some mechanization of industry, which was not present in classical antiquity because of the availability of abundant slave labor, developed in the High Middle Ages. The "kinematic chains"—the screw, wheel, cam, ratchet, pulley, crank, and connecting rod—were used increasingly, as were machines that utilized natural forces, particularly water and wind power. There were about five thousand water mills in England in the later eleventh century,

The Commercial Revolution

according to *Domesday Book*. Windmills were also introduced, apparently from Persia, in this period, and were constructed in areas where there was little available water power. There were one hundred and twenty windmills in the single banlieu of Ypres in the thirteenth century. Mechanical methods were utilized to some extent in the spinning and fulling of textiles, as well as for pumping out water, draining pits, operating lifts, and crushing ore in mining. Mechanical means converted rotary into reciprocal, and reciprocal into rotary motion, as well as rapid into slow, and slow into rapid motion. From the twelfth century *must be dated that increasing mechanization of life and industry . . . which characterizes modern civilization,* according to the *Cambridge Economic History.*

The conditions of labor were relatively humane. Although the average working day was about eleven to twelve hours, there were numerous holidays (holy days) that were free from work. Masters worked along with their journeymen and apprentices, most of whom could look forward to one day becoming masters themselves.

Most industry was conducted on a "domestic" or "quasi-domestic" basis. A full-fledged craftsman usually worked in his home or in its vicinity with the assistance of members of his family and sometimes with one or more journeymen and apprentices. But already examples of large-scale capitalistic industry operating on the "putting out" system or the "factory" system existed. In the "putting out" system extensively used in the textile industry, an entrepreneur bought up raw materials and successively allocated them to various artisans, such as spinners, combers, carders, weavers, fullers, and dyers. The entrepreneur paid the artisans at each step, usually on a quantitative ("piecework") basis, and marketed the finished product. In North Italian and Flemish cities, the "factory system" was often found, with numerous workers laboring together in large workshops, especially in the textile industry.

The organization of industry: craft guilds

Merchant guilds at first included artisans, but the artisans soon realized that their interests differed from those of full-time merchants so that they broke off and formed their own guilds as early as the eleventh century. In 1099 we find mention of a weavers' guild at Mainz. As fission continued, guilds of various types of artisans were instituted. By the later thirteenth century, there were about a hundred such guilds at Paris, fifty-eight at Venice, and thirty-three at Genoa. The average German town had twelve to fifteen guilds. Typical guilds were those of carpenters, blacksmiths, masons, tanners, shoemakers, harnessmakers, bakers, brewers, weavers, fullers, and dyers.

Craft guilds had several functions. They determined who could independently carry on crafts as certified masters; and who were sufficiently competent to become hired journeymen. They excluded the unqualified and uncertified from carrying on crafts. They fixed the terms and conditions for training apprentices; established standards for materials and workmanship; and regulated prices, hours of work, and times for sale of products.

In addition, craft guilds, like merchant guilds, served as fraternal, mutual benefit, and benevolent societies, and also as sponsors of religious, educational, and recreational activities.

There were three levels of workers in the craft guilds: apprentices, journeymen, and masters. On the lowest rung was the apprentice, who, often from about twelve years of age on, worked under the direction of a master for a specified time, ranging from about three to eight years, with seven years common. He usually received only his board and lodging, and there might even be a fee for his instruction.

After fulfilling the term of his apprenticeship, the trainee became a journeyman. The journeyman (from *journée:* day) could work for pay under the direction of a master, but he could not carry on business as an independent operator. In order to become a master the journeyman had to acquire enough skill to produce a "masterpiece" that would be accepted as a complete and adequate product of his craft. He also had to accumulate sufficient cash to pay the fee required by the guild, and be able to furnish his own tools and set up shop for himself. Finally, he had to be accepted into their select association by the other masters of the craft. Only the master was a fully qualified artisan, entitled to practice a craft on his own, and authorized to train apprentices and hire journeymen.

Many journeymen, however, remained at this level, as in the great industrial centers of northern Italy and the Low Countries, especially in the textile industry, which was frequently organized on a capitalistic basis. There were also numerous unskilled workers, such as wool carders, who were not organized into craft guilds. During the thirteenth century, discontented journeymen and other workers struck on several occasions. In the thirteenth-century Beaumanoir defined a strike as "an alliance against the common good, when any sort of people mutually pledge themselves not to work for so low a wage as before, and thus to force their wages to be increased, and agree among themselves not to work for less, and bring injuries and threats to bear on those of their comrades who will not join their alliance."

MONEY AND FINANCE, TOWN AND COUNTRY.
Section 47.

> Arras, a city replete with riches,
> Greedy for gain and rejoicing in usury.
> [From the "Philippide," a French satire by William the Breton (early thirteenth century).]

ACCOMPANYING commercial and industrial progress in the High Middle Ages there was an increase of coinage and the use of money, a multiplication of financial devices and an extension of credit, a growth of towns, and an expansion of agriculture.

Expanded coinage

Gold and silver mines were exploited in Bohemia, Hungary, greater Austria, Germany, Spain, and elsewhere. Coinage was greatly increased, and coins of greater worth were minted during the High Middle Ages.

The Commercial Revolution

From Carolingian times, only the *denarius* or penny had been coined in Western Christian Europe, while the *solidus* (nominally 12 d.) and *libra* (nominally 20 s.) were merely "monies of account." Originally a silver coin, the "penny" was progressively debased until it was mainly composed of copper and became, for example, the "black penny" or the *piccolo* (small penny). To remedy this, the Venetians late in the twelfth century (1192) began to coin a silver "great penny" or *grosso* (groat), nominally equivalent to the old silver *denarius* of Charlemagne and actually equal in worth to about twelve of the contemporary debased *denarii*. The coining of such groats spread rapidly. Henceforth there were two ways of calculating money values, depending on whether one was using the small penny or the great penny as a unit. In addition, there were many differences in values, depending on who had coined a given money.

In the thirteenth century, gold coinage was resumed in the West. Frederick II of Sicily began to coin gold *augustales* as early as 1231, but these never came into general use. In the mid-thirteenth century (1252), Florence began to issue gold coins known as "florins," which were somewhat similar to the old Roman *solidus*, the Byzantine *nomisma*, and the *dinar*. Other states soon imitated Florence with gold coins of similar value, such as *genoins* from Genoa (1254), *ducats* from Venice, *ambrosins* from Milan, and the sound *Louis d'or* coined by St. Louis IX of France. A new reckoning was now introduced, based on the gold coin (florin, ducat, etc.), which was supposed to be equal to twenty *solidi* or groats and to 240 (debased) *denarii*.

There was meanwhile a remarkable expansion of credit. Various forms of "paper" and promises to pay often substituted for hard cash. Credit facilitated the distribution of commodities for the mutual benefit of sellers, buyers, producers, and consumers, with a measure of gain for financiers. Credit was also eventually utilized to finance governmental operations and public projects. This evolution of credit and finance was partly prompted by a shortage of precious metals.

High medieval finance: exchange and banking

Exchange, or the changing of money from one form to another, was indispensable at the great international fairs. Since moneychangers exacted a fee for their services, they accumulated increasing wealth, which encouraged them to engage in further profitable financial transactions. As they sat at tables (*tavoli* or *banchi*), they came to be known as "bankers." They eventually accepted deposits of money at the start of fairs, sometimes paying a premium for the deposit, and lent out money at higher rates, such as 10 to 50 per cent, usually with some sort of collateral or security. They credited and debited accounts on the basis of orders put on paper, and formed a cooperative clearinghouse for accumulated debits and credits at the end of fairs. The bankers purchased at a discount promises to pay at a later date. Their transfers of funds on direction from depositors were often mere ledger transactions, crediting one account and debiting another. They facilitated the easy transfer of money on an international basis, since they often had branches in several cities.

Prominent among early medieval bankers were the Knights Templar, who acquired extensive wealth through pious donations to assist their work in the Holy Land. The Templars would accept "deposits" at their European "houses" or "temples," such as those in Paris and London, and give letters of credit and exchange that entitled the depositor to obtain cash from the order in the Near East. By the thirteenth century, the Templars were the leading bankers for the French and English kings.

The question of interest

A problem in the expansion of credit during the period was the Church prohibition against the exacting of interest, because credit was necessary for the developing Western European economy and would not be forthcoming unless interest were allowed. Fortunately Church prohibitions against usury were not so clear and firm when the Western European economy was beginning to expand, while as time went on various forms of evasion and compensation developed, such as withholding a part of the nominal loan, penalizing supposed late payment, and charging off the interest to some aspect of the transaction, such as a fee for exchange.

Church prohibitions against interest were gradually relaxed. Theologians such as St. Thomas Aquinas allowed the taking of reasonable interest on various grounds or "titles" such as these: (1) *periculum sortis:* the risk or chance that the borrower might be unable or unwilling to repay the debt; (2) *lucrum cessans:* the loss of actual or potential profit one might make if he did not loan the money; (3) *damnum emergens:* the damage, loss, or inconvenience that might be suffered by the lender, such as being unable to meet his own needs or those of his family, as a result of having loaned out the money; (4) *poena conventionalis:* an agreed-on penalty for late payment delayed beyond the accepted time; and (5) *donatio:* a free gift. Another concept according to which profit was allowed for a loan was that the lender was a sort of partner in a business enterprise and had an "interest" and hence a right to share in the profit. The partnership known as the *commenda* operated partly on this theory. Rates of interest were high, ranging from about 10 per cent to about 50 per cent. They varied according to location, purpose, person, and security. Thus they were less in Italy than in England, and less for mercantile ventures than for purely personal purposes.

Avoidance of loss in making loans was often made surer by requiring some form of security or "gage." This might be a "land-gage," in which land was put up as security. If it was a "live gage," the revenue of the security was applied to reduce the debt; but not if it was a "dead gage" (or mortgage). In the case of loans made for maritime commercial ventures, the security was often the ship or the cargo.

Forms of loans and "paper" transactions

Among forms of credit were promissory notes, letters-of-fair, and sea loans. Promissory notes were promises to pay at a future date, and might be formal and notarized or informal and unnotarized, as well as with or without witnesses. They might be a direction to a third party to pay in the same place or elsewhere at a future time, in the same currency or in a different form of money. Letters-of-fair were promises to pay at a later fair. Sea loans were money advanced for a maritime venture. If the venture was a success, the lender usually reaped a handsome profit, such as 20 to 30 per cent, but if it failed the lender might get back nothing or only a portion of what he had advanced.

The Commercial Revolution

Various "paper" transactions, wherein paper was used in place of money mainly for convenience, also amounted to forms of credit. Among such were checks, letters of credit, and bills of exchange. Checks were orders or directions to a third party to pay a specified person a certain amount on behalf of the issuer. In a letter of credit, a banker or agency could direct its own office or branch or representative or debtor to credit an account or pay the specified sum. In a bill of exchange, the addressee was directed to pay the bearer in a different coinage. The instrument was called a "bill" from the fact that it was an official document that might bear a seal (*bulla*), whereas "exchange" referred to the changing of currency involved. There was usually a charge for the exchange, but there might be a credit for the delay involved and the use of the money in the interval.

Partnerships: compagnia

To raise capital for large-scale mercantile ventures and to distribute risks, various forms of partnerships developed. A key legal principle was that of the unlimited financial responsibility of all parties in a true partnership, whereby each partner could be held fully responsible for the total indebtedness in case of default. The only true, continuing partnerships in this period were the "family" or "house" partnerships (*famiglias* or *case*) known as *compagnias* or companies (from *cum*: with, and *panis*: bread: sc. those who eat together). For only members of a common family and those intimately associated with them had enough common interest to bear the risk of unlimited responsibility. Originally the properties or "patrimonies" of closely knit families were conceived of as belonging to the family as a whole, although actually administered by the current head of the family. These *compagnias* were characterized by continuing duration, and by the unlimited liability of all partners. Persons who were not members of the family might be brought into the partnership by marriage or adoption. Examples of the many Italian family *compagnias* of the thirteenth century were the Bardi, Peruzzi, and Frescobaldi of Florence. By the close of the thirteenth century, the Bardi had fifteen partners, of whom five were not related members of the family, and all resided elsewhere than in Florence.

Commenda and societas

Temporary forms of quasi-partnerships for specific mercantile ventures were more common. Such partnerships avoided the burden of unlimited responsibility by assuming the guise of loans made to the shipper(s) or trader(s) who conducted the operation. Thus investors who did not personally participate were regarded merely as creditors by the law, and did not have any responsibility for debts contracted. Accounts were settled either at the end of a voyage or after a set period of time.

In the *commenda*, also known as an *accomodatio* or a *societas maris* (maritime association), an investor (or investors) entrusted his (or their) capital to a merchant (or merchants) for a specific venture. The investor normally received three fourths of the profit, with the active merchant or shipper receiving a fourth. The investor had to bear any loss of invested capital; but he was not bound by contracts made by the active merchant with other parties.

For land ventures there was a similar arrangement known as the *so-*

cietas terrae or land association. Here again there were both an investor and an active agent, with the investor receiving about three fourths of the profit or sustaining the loss, but not being bound by any indebtednesses incurred by the merchant. The *societas terrae* was ordinarily limited for a definite duration (v.g., one, two, or three years).

There were various modifications of the *commenda* and the *societas terrae*. There might be one or more investors and one or more agents. Several persons might buy shares or *loca* (places) in a *commenda* as co-investors. The merchant or shipper who was managing the enterprise might also be an investor, and would thus share in the profits both as the agent and as an investor.

The growth of capitalism

The beginnings of modern capitalism are found in the High Middle Ages. During this period, capital was accumulated in a variety of ways, such as by merchandizing activities (retail and wholesale), exchange services and other banking operations, advancing of credit, collection of taxes and tithes for a certain sum with a right to pocket the surplus, and investments in agriculture or urban properties, as well as by industrial production and mining. The eventual "big time" was in finance: "making money from money."

Capitalism was well developed in northern Italy by the thirteenth century, when Florence is said to have had some eighty important trading and banking houses, such as the Alfani, Bardi, Peruzzi, Pulci, Spigliati, and Spini; while lesser towns, such as Sienna and Lucca, boasted dozens of wealthy firms. As early as the twelfth century, there were capitalists beyond the Alps, such as William Cade of St. Omer, who loaned considerable sums to the English king and nobles. In the early thirteenth century, John Rynvisch and Simon Saphir of Ghent were creditors of King John of England, and Arras was noted for its capitalists such as the Louchards.

The Church and economic gain

The Church applied brakes to competition for economic gain. It reminded men of eventual death, and of a future life dependent on one's conduct on this earth. It forbade exorbitant interest and insisted on a "just price," although with regard to the latter its theory was precise enough only to condemn extremes. The Church also insisted on reasonable motives in the pursuit of gain, such as the support of one's family; and it especially condemned inordinate greed and lust for gain.

The growth of towns

Towns multiplied and expanded during the High Middle Ages, and it is estimated that over 2,000 new towns were established in Germany alone. The population of Paris and Venice is said to have reached about 150,000; that of Milan, Genoa, Naples, Florence, and Cordova about 100,000; that of Ypres, Bruges, Ghent, Cologne, and London, 40,000 to 60,000; and that of Nuremberg, Augsburg, Strassburg, Hamburg, Arras, Narbonne, and Brussels, 20,000 to 30,000.

Urban development was promoted by expanding commercial, industrial, and service activities, corporate unionization of the citizenry, privileges obtained from overlords, opportunities for gainful employment, and an influx of excess population from manors.

The sites of towns were usually determined by circumstances advantageous for trade, such as good harbors, as with Naples, Marseilles, and Barcelona; strategic, safer points a short distance inland on rivers, as with Bourdeaux, Rouen, London, and Antwerp; strategic locations still farther inland on rivers, as with Toledo, Tours, and Cologne; the confluence of rivers, as at Lyons and Mainz; bridges, as at Bruges and Cambridge; fords of rivers, as at Rome and Oxford; and crossroads of inland trade, as in the case of Milan, Nuremberg and Prague, Breslau, Vienna, Paris, and Amiens. Many towns grew up on the sites of old tribal settlements, as was the case with the greater part of the towns of Gaul, which were Celtic villages prior to the Roman occupation. Many had been established by the ancient Romans as administrative centers, trading posts, military strongholds, and colonization sites. Some were political capitals, others ecclesiastical centers. Many new towns on the frontiers arose as fortified settlements, a fact often revealed by the inclusion of *burg, burh, bourg,* or *borough* in their name, as in Magdeburg, Brandenburg, and Hamburg, or of "fort," as in Erfurt and Frankfort. Numerous towns began as settlements of merchants called *faubourgs* (*foris*: outside of; and *burgensis*: a fortified place) alongside rather than inside fortified places, partly because these were already crowded and partly also to avoid the fees that would otherwise be charged. In time, these settlements were themselves walled and rewalled as they expanded.

Expansion of agriculture and private landholding

Agriculture, the chief occupation of most of the people, expanded in the High Middle Ages. As the population of Western Europe doubled, and as living standards improved, the demand for food and drink and raw materials mounted. The growing towns provided ready markets for agricultural products, as also did rural districts, a result of increased specialization. Enterprising lords, peasants, and merchants cooperated in the lucrative expansion of agriculture. Within Europe, extensive additional lands were cleared, drained, or reclaimed, and brought under cultivation. In Flanders, by the close of the twelfth century, numerous lands along the Scheldt estuary and the North Sea coast were diked and reclaimed from the sea. In the thirteenth century, the Abbey of the Dunes had more diked than undiked land. In areas where the rainfall was inadequate, as in parts of Italy and Spain, dams, reservoirs, canals, and ditches were constructed to bring water to parched lands. Meanwhile, Western European agriculture also expanded externally with the conquest and occupation of new lands in the Baltic area, Central Europe, the Iberian peninsula, southern Italy and Sicily, and other Mediterranean islands.

Private rural landholding, as opposed to semicommunal, dependent manorial tenure, progressively increased. Land came to be regarded as primarily a means of obtaining money rather than as a source of supplies in kind. Services owed by serfs were often "commuted" into money payments, and the demesnes of lords were worked by hired "hands" or subdivided into small farms and "let out" or sold to peasant-farmers. Previous "commons" were often appropriated and rented out by lords, despite the resultant injustice to the peasants.

In many cases the lands now operated by peasants were held by leases, as in the case of "copyholders" in England and *censitaires* in

France. Sometimes the peasants were simple renters, as in the case of *fermiers* in France; and sometimes they were "sharecroppers" or *metayers*, who owed the landlord a certain percentage of their crop or profits. As time elapsed, some farmers became owners of their holdings. Private landholding encouraged increased industry, enterprise, and production.

Agricultural advances

Agriculture became more efficient. There was a wider diffusion of agricultural improvements that had begun to appear in the Early Middle Ages, such as the three-field system and use of horses, horsecollars and horseshoes, the heavy wheeled plow and the harrow, and water mills. Improved devices and practices such as crop rotation (often as a substitute for field rotation), better breeding and care of animals, and windmills were introduced. Crops became more specialized and better adapted to the regions where they were raised since they were intended for sale rather than consumption. Manure was often used as fertilizer. A treatise on the efficient conduct of agricultural and pastoral activities was composed in the thirteenth century by Walter of Henley, a former English gentleman who became a Cistercian monk. Henley's "Treatise on Husbandry" concerns estate management and regards the price of labor as a prime consideration.

Pastoral activities

General economic growth was accompanied by an expansion of pastoral activities. Almost every farm and manor had horses, cows, sheep, pigs, fowl, mules, asses, and bees. The full-time specialized raising of sheep, cattle, horses, and bees became very common. Breeds were sometimes crossed to produce stronger strains. Various kinds of horses were raised, such as great "chargers" for knightly warfare, lithe saddle horses for rapid transport, and heavy plow horses for plowing and hauling. The practice of "enclosing" lands for stock-raising was often found to be more profitable where the soil was poor, as in parts of England and Spain. Bees were regularly raised for their honey and wax. The Cistercians with their "granges" (convenient farming outposts) and "hôtes" (lay workers) became famous for sheep raising.

SOCIAL ADVANCES AND GENERAL PROGRESS.
Section 48.

> Whosoever shall dwell in the parish of Lorris for a year and a day, without any claim having pursued him there, and without having refused to present his case to us or to our provost, shall be permitted to dwell there freely, without molestation. [Privilege granted to the inhabitants of Lorris by King Louis VII of France (1155).]

IMPORTANT social changes attended high medieval economic expansion. New developments included a great population explosion, rapid growth of towns, general improvement of living conditions, the rise of a dynamic middle class, and widespread emancipation of labor.

Population explosion (continued)

Authorities estimate that the population of Western Europe doubled during the High Middle Ages. One assessment is that the number of inhabitants in Western Europe rose from about thirty million to about

The Commercial Revolution

sixty million. Estimates of late thirteenth-century populations are: France about seventeen million, Italy, a possible nine million, the Iberian peninsula, about nine million, England, about four million, and the Germanies, some seventeen million. The vast majority of people still lived in the countryside, but there was an increasing influx of people into the towns. Meanwhile there were important changes occurring in the structure of classes. *—and social changes*

Theorists now began to recognize the existence of a "middle class" between the aristocracy and the proletariat, not without the observation: "Rarely can the merchant be saved." Most of the middle class lived in towns and was composed of merchants, craftsmen, professional people, property owners, and the like. They conducted profitable businesses, providing employment for the laborers who came in from the countryside. Some of the bourgeoisie owned substantial properties in the country as well. The middle class in the towns usually lived in well-built homes, ate ample meals, and wore comfortable clothing. Largely by dint of their enterprise and cooperation the urban middle class soon became free, self-governing, and influential. There was also a rural middle class with larger holdings who lacked the status of "lords," but sometimes became assimilated to the lesser aristocracy, as was the case with the "knights" in England. *—The middle class*

One of the most effective instruments used by the middle class to advance its interests was unionization. We have seen how this class organized into merchant guilds and craft guilds, and even occasionally into *hanses*, or primarily economic leagues of towns. Another important form of organization was into communes. Whereas guilds were primarily economic, communes were primarily political. Communes sought to obtain political and juridical privileges for town dwellers. Their effectiveness is attested by the criticisms leveled at them by contemporary writers, who were often shocked by these revolutionary new institutions and their "pretensions." Thus Abbott Guibert of Nogent (twelfth century) wrote: *Commune is a new and reprehensible name for an arrangement whereby all the poorer classes pay their usual dues of service to their lord only once a year, and make good any breach of the laws by a payment that is fixed by law, and are entirely free from other exactions usually imposed on serfs.* *—Communes*

At first membership in the merchant guilds and communes was identical, as possibly were the institutions. But in time guilds and communes became distinct. Sometimes, as in some cities of Italy, the "priors" or heads of the principal guilds were members of the town councils.

The initial purpose of the sworn associations known as communes was to secure status and rights, privileges, and immunities, and a measure of independence and self-government. These privileges were eventually incorporated into charters obtained from overlords. Sometimes enlightened rulers voluntarily granted charters in order to attract settlers to new settlements or to increase the population of old ones. Sometimes the townspeople obtained their charters by purchase or contributions when the ruler was in need of money. Often charters were conceded after up- *—Town charters and urban government* risings by the townspeople, as was the case at Liege, Cologne, Speyer, Mainz, Beauvais, Tournai, and Cambrai. Monarchs granted charters to towns in order to withdraw them from the jurisdiction of local lords and subject them to their own control and protection, with a resultant increase in royal revenues and power. The privileges initially contained in the charters of some towns might simply be assumed by other towns by assimilation or usurpation that went unchallenged. In Italy the lesser nobles or *vavassores* dwelt in towns, engaged in business, and allied with the townspeople against the greater nobility and bishops. Often especially reluctant to grant freedom and self-government to townspeople were ecclesiastical authorities who ruled towns, because they thought more in terms of an established order, were less conscious of changing conditions, and were only temporary administrators.

Charters tended to become standardized. Thus the more conservative charter of Lorris granted by Louis VII to the little town of that name in the royal domain in 1155 became a model for many other early French charters, while the more liberal charter granted to Beauvais by Philip II became the like for many later ones. The charters (*fueros*) of Leon (1020) and Santiago in Spain became model charters in the Iberian peninsula. An early model charter in England was that granted by Henry I to London in the early twelfth century, while a later one was that of Henry II to Newcastle-on-Tyne. The charter of Freiburg (free city) was imitated in southern Germany; that of Louvain in the Low Countries.

Typical urban charters stipulated that anyone who lived without challenge in the town a year and a day was free. They also exempted townspeople from the servile dues and arbitrary taxation to which rural serfs were liable. Urban obligations were normally limited to a fixed rent or annual payment; and to anything beyond this the townspeople had to agree. Townspeople usually obtained the right to hold markets in perpetuity, and sometimes also that of holding annual fairs. They regularly won the right to carry on their own self-government, manage their own internal affairs, and decide cases in their own courts according to their own laws. Inhabitants of towns had the right to buy and sell real property, and to move about at will.

The actual government of towns tended to be dominated by the older and wealthier families. Besides the somewhat inchoate general town meeting, there was a more select "town council" consisting of councilmen, known variously as aldermen, *Rathsherren, boni homines, priores, echevins, jurées,* and consuls. Town governments usually established a curfew and prohibited trade outside of certain hours. Eventually they drew up building codes and provided police and fire protection.

The urban proletariat

Both by their charters and by custom, townspeople became free. Their only obligations of consequence were to pay a fixed annual sum and to cooperate in the defense of the homeland. Unchallenged residence in a town for a year and a day entitled one to share in the privileges of townspeople in accordance with the saying "Town air makes free."

As towns grew, the number of propertyless urban laborers who worked

The Commercial Revolution

for hire increased. The greatest advantages enjoyed by these workers were freedom and opportunity. There was a demand for their services in an expanding economy, and they had the prospect of improving their lot. Their greatest disadvantage was the want and suffering that could so quickly overtake them and their families in case of unemployment, illness, or some other misfortune.

The living conditions of most of the proletariat in the towns would be very unsatisfactory by our standards. Their quarters were usually cramped and dingy, sooty and smelly. Their furnishings were crude and meager; their diet was simple, monotonous, and defective. Sanitation was inadequate and health hazards were considerable. On the other hand, the urban proletariat did have abundant opportunity for social intercourse and exchange of information and ideas. A favorite resort of many was the neighborhood tavern.

Far outnumbering their urban counterparts were the rural proletariat, many of whom were freed from their former servile dependence during the High Middle Ages. Although encouraged by religious and humanitarian considerations, the emancipation of the serfs was mainly due to economic considerations. In the new economy, the final objective of rural landholding was monetary profit. For this, the direct payment of money by rural workers in return for their holdings was much more efficacious than the often perfunctory performance of manual services by serfs. If a tenant did not pay his rent, he could be evicted and a substitute obtained. If the lord needed laborers for a purpose such as working his demesne, he could hire them for the actual time they were needed. If they were lazy, he could fire them and hire someone else. Furthermore many lords now found it more profitable to subdivide their personal demesnes into rented holdings. Often lords needed—or thought they needed—considerable cash, and would sell part or all of their lands.

Rural society: The emancipation of serfs

Competition also encouraged the emancipation of rural labor. If workers could become free simply by going to a neighboring town or to some other lord's lands, their lord might have to free them to keep them working on his own property. Freedom was frequently offered as an enticement to obtain settlers on frontiers as well as at internal reclamation projects. The inhabitants of rural villages often organized and demanded charters similar to those enjoyed by their urban counterparts. Eventually the processes of assimilation and usurpation also came into play. With emancipation and the incentive of having their own holdings, whether owned or leased, in a milieu of economic opportunity, the majority of peasants improved their living conditions. However, there were some less strong, less fortunate peasants who barely survived or even lost their holdings by improvidence, prodigality, neglect, sickness, or accident. Meanwhile, continued inflation worked to the benefit of most rent-paying peasants, since rents were generally fixed, while prices kept rising. An English peasant could get twice as much for his produce in 1250 as his ancestor did in 1150, although his rent usually remained the same.

The feudal aristocracy reached the height of its power and influence in the eleventh to twelfth centuries. In France the feudal aristocracy was

The feudal aristocracy

The feudal aristocracy in the High Middle Ages ascendant at least until the time of Philip II, Augustus. In England it was definitely in the saddle during the reigns of Stephen and Henry III. In Spain its strength was exemplified by the actual career of El Cid Campeador, and by the rise of the counts of Castile and Oporto to the position of independent kings. In the Empire the aristocracy eventually won out over the Franconians and Hohenstaufen, while their privileges and power were explicitly recognized by such rulers as Henry V and Frederick I and II.

But the feudal aristocracy began to decline as it reached its apogee. This turn became particularly apparent in the thirteenth century. A basic factor was the growth of a money economy. Fiefs came to be looked upon more as a source of income than a source of knights and governmental officials. Mercenary soldiers often came to be preferred to landed knights for warfare, and commoners, such as lawyers, to nobles for the administration of government and justice. Feudal dues such as military service and hospitality were increasingly commuted to money payments. The lord gradually became more of a landlord, the vassal more of a tenant. Fiefs were often subdivided and rented out or sold. Sometimes the new holders owed only a part of what was previously due, such as "a twentieth of a knight's service," which meant an estimated value in money. Sometimes the dissolution of feudal relationships resulted from exceptions to the law of primogeniture, as when a lord would leave a part of his fief to a daughter or younger son. Contributing to the decline of the feudal aristocracy was the rising power of monarchs and the growth and prosperity of the middle class. The follies and foibles of the aristocracy itself played a part.

During this period, the aristocracy became more class conscious, formal, pretentious, and exclusive. In the thirteenth century, knighthood became hereditary. Meanwhile the class of knights expanded by natural multiplication, so that it is said that in the thirteenth century there were over twelve thousand knights in Aquitaine alone. It became more unusual to knight anyone not of noble birth, and the privilege of knighting such a person belonged only to kings and great lords. At the same time, the legal privileges of the aristocracy became more numerous and the gradations among the nobility more carefully defined. Distinctions were made between and within the classes of greater lords or "magnates" (such as dukes, marquises, and counts) and lesser lords (such as viscounts, castellans, barons, seigneurs, and knights with land). At the very bottom were the "bachelor" knights or "chevaliers" without land.

The training of knights was lengthened and made more complex. The ceremonial for entering upon the state of knighthood was elaborated; the role of the Church and religious rites and ideals was increased; and the code of the knight known as "chivalry" was expanded.

Recreations of the feudal aristocracy became more numerous, diversified, and sophisticated. Hunting with falcons became common, and the rules of the hunt became more elaborate. Tournaments became picturesque, complicated spectacles, sometimes involving whole groups pitted against each other. Chess playing was imported from the Near

East with the names of the figures changed to knights, castles, bishops, queens, and kings. In backgammon, the moves on a board were determined by dice throws. A popular pastime, particularly in southern France, was the flirtatious composition of love songs (*chansons d'amour*).

Although generally respected and loved, women were subject to men, and were largely restricted to the care and management of their household and children. If they inherited a fief, they had to find a suitable husband to manage it. The theory that women were the weaker sex was supported by the pastoral traditions of Indo-European and Semitic peoples, endorsed by the Bible, and accepted by churchmen. At the same time women never sank to the lowly position they held in many Eastern cultures. Monogamy was insisted on by the Church, which also condemned extramarital sex relations. The position of women was advanced in the High Middle Ages. Devotion to the Mother of Christ and the example of Christ were important influences, as also was the idealization involved in the *chansons d'amour* and chivalry.

The position of women

The Jews were generally looked down upon and segregated, and sometimes persecuted. In order to preserve their own religion and traditions, the Jews usually preferred to live apart from the rest of the populace, whose feasts and fasts they shunned, and they were consequently subject to misunderstandings and disadvantages. The Christian liturgy and the New Testament reminded Christians that many Jews had rejected Christ and contributed to his crucifixion. Eventually Jews were required to live in certain quarters or "ghettos," whether they wanted to or not, and they were often compelled to wear distinctive garb and badges. Since they were generally prohibited from owning land, they had to restrict themselves to such economic activities as trading and moneylending. Biblical prohibitions against usury did not forbid charging interest to other peoples, in this case Christians, which the courts allowed. But their position as creditors often made the Jews highly unpopular.

The Jews

Churchmen were generally more enlightened in their attitude to the Jews than were the general public, and usually opposed anti-Jewish pogroms. Rulers often accorded Jews special protection and utilized them as a source of money by way of loans. But when rulers were pinched for money or their debts became too great, they were often tempted to expel the Jews in order to acquire their property and become free from debts.

Economic expansion encouraged political consolidation and made available the means whereby it could be accomplished.

Monarchs used an increasing number of devices to raise their income and enhance their power. Among these were commutation of feudal dues to money payments; expansion of royal justice (also a source of income); and the establishment of profitable protectorates over towns and monasteries. Voluntary "aids" were wheedled out of representatives of the nobility, the clergy, and townspeople. Duties were levied on both exports and imports. Percentages of income or of property values were collected on the plea of some emergency such as the costs of a projected crusade. All dues were more efficiently collected.

Political developments

In the expansion of monarchical power, feudal prerogatives, such as forfeit, escheat, and foremarriage, were utilized. Earlier traditions, such as the Carolingian, also contributed, as did Church support and ecclesiastical consecration. The revival of Roman law and Greek political thought helped, since in late Roman law the will of the monarch was absolute, and according to Greek political theory the state was natural and necessary. More advanced governments, such as the Byzantine and Papal, served as models. There was a growing alliance between townspeople and monarchs in most countries. This was promoted by the fact that they had a mutual adversary, the aristocracy, and that the townspeople saw that strong central government would contribute to their prosperity. Monarchs conceded extensive privileges to towns (usually at no expense to themselves) and obtained in return annual payments, as well as voluntary "aids" in times of greater need.

Democratic gains

The High Middle Ages also saw increased representative government and recognition of individual rights. These occurred first on local levels, as in towns, then on regional levels, and finally on national scales, coming earlier in certain smaller kingdoms, later in some larger ones.

Representative government on national levels developed when representatives of the middle class were summoned to meet along with the king and the great lords in national assemblies. The first known assemblies of this type were the Spanish *Cortes* convoked in Leon (1188), Catalonia (1218), Castile (1250), and Aragon (1274). An incomplete English Parliament was called by Simon de Montfort in 1265, while more representative English Parliaments were brought together by Edward I, as in the case of his Parliaments of 1273, 1275, and 1295. The first Estates General in France was summoned by Philip IV in 1302, although several Provincial Estates were held before this time. Such broadly representative assemblies were usually summoned by kings to raise funds and troops to obtain popular backing in crises. Representatives bargained with their rulers for desired legislation and other favors as a condition for their consent. It eventually became a principle in English Parliaments that "Redress of grievances precedes grant of supplies."

Also obtained from monarchs in this period were formal charters, solemnly promising to observe the rights and privileges of their subjects. Examples were charters issued by English Kings Henry I, John, and Edward I, and Aragonese Kings Pedro III and Alfonso III.

Warfare

In warfare, infantry and archers became more important, and mercenary soldiers more common. Archers played an important part in the Norman victory at Hastings (1066), and North Italian townsmen in the victories over the Hohenstaufen at Legnano (1176), Parma (1248), and Bologna (1248). Urban militia figured in the battle of Bouvines (1214), while Swiss mountaineers foiled the German knights of the Hapsburgs, and Flemish burghers defeated the knights of Philip IV at Courtrai (1302). Sappers and engineers became increasingly important in sieges. Scaling towers were constructed to enable forces to surmount walls, and movable "cats" (covered shelters on wheels) were built to protect those burrowing below. Catapults and ballistas were used to shoot heavy projectiles. The crossbow and the longbow provided greater lethal power

The Commercial Revolution 361

for missile warfare. Defensive warfare made even more progress and castles were greatly improved.

Economic and social changes influenced religion and culture. Especially during the thirteenth century, there were indications of growing worldliness and skepticism. The idea of crusading lost its former attraction. Lust for gold became so prevalent that it was severely denounced by preachers. As the power of monarchs waxed, that of the Papacy waned. Ideas concerning the state and law derived from the Greeks and Romans provided an ideological basis for increasing monarchical power at the expense of that of the Church. Heresies sprouted and rationalistic trends increased.

Religious and cultural impact

Because of the growth of towns and the greater need for professional men, as well as the abundant knowledge made available by high medieval translations from Arabic and Greek, education expanded and universities arose. The content of instruction in cathedral and monastic schools increased, while municipal schools reappeared. Education of the laity resumed, and well-educated laymen, such as Beaumanoir, Glanville, and Dante, became more common. Vernacular literature catered to the lay tastes. Romanesque and Gothic architecture and sculpture expressed the civic pride and aesthetic inclinations as well as the religious faith of townspeople.

AN ENTHUSIASTIC general work, packed with interesting information, is PROSPER BOISSONADE, *Life and Work in Medieval Europe* (New York: Knopf, 1927) (p.). Other general works are the briefer, valuable, HENRI PIRENNE, *Economic and Social History of Medieval Europe* (New York: Harcourt, Brace, 1937) (p.); and the longer, older, but still useful JAMES W. THOMPSON, *Economic and Social History of the Middle Ages* (New York: Century, 1928), which runs to 1300.

Probably the most authoritative economic history of Europe is the *Cambridge Economic History of Europe*, a collaborative work by experts, whose initial vols. I–III (Cambridge: Cambridge U.P., 1942ff. and 1966) concern the economic history of the Middle Ages. Useful introductory surveys are given in such general economic histories as that of HERBERT HEATON, *Economic History of Europe* (New York: Harper, 1936); SHEPARD B. CLOUGH and CHARLES W. COLE, *Economic History of Europe* (Boston: Heath, 1941); and MELVIN KNIGHT, *Economic History of Europe to the End of the Middle Ages* (Boston: Houghton Mifflin, 1926). An excellent general overview, stressing developments in the High Middle Ages, is ROBERT-HENRI BAUTIER, *The Economic Development of Medieval Europe* (New York: Harcourt, 1971).

References for Chapter 16

A good general source collection is ROY C. CAVE and H. H. COULSON, *Source Book for Medieval Economic History* (Milwaukee: Bruce, 1936). Also recommended is WILLIAM CUNNINGHAM, *The Growth of English Industry and Commerce During the Early and Middle Ages* (Cambridge: Cambridge U.P., 1915).

A brief introduction is SUMMERFIELD BALDWIN, *Business in the Middle Ages* (New York: Holt, 1937) (p.). An excellent source book with valuable explanatory introductions is ROBERT S. LOPEZ and IRVING RAYMOND, *Medieval Trade in the Mediterranean World* (New York: Columbia U.P., 1955) (p.), which also includes various forms of finance and partnerships. Merchant guilds are well treated in the intensive study by CHARLES GROSS, *The*

Guild Merchant, 2 vols. (London: Oxford U.P., 1927), as well as in that of GEORGES RENARD, Guilds of the Middle Ages, tr. D. Terry (London: Bell, 1918), and GEORGES CLUNE, The Medieval Guild System (Dublin: Browne and Nolan, 1943). Specialized works include ELEANOR CARUS-WILSON, Medieval Merchant Ventures (London: Methuen, 1954); the original account of his Asian travels by MARCO POLO, The Travels of Marco Polo the Venetian, tr. William Marsden and rev. Manual Komroff (New York: Boni and Liveright, 1926); the interesting secondary account by HENRY H. HART, Venetian Adventurer . . . Marco Polo (Stanford: Stanford U.P., 1947), and Marco Polo: Venetian Adventurer (Norman: U. of Oklahoma, 1967); EUGENE BYRNE, Genoese Shipping in the XII to XIII Centuries (Cambridge, Mass.: Mediaeval Academy, 1930); and WILLIAM MITCHELL, An Essay on the Early History of the Law Merchant (Cambridge: Cambridge U.P., 1904). On the wool trade, see EILEEN E. POWER, The Wool Trade in English Medieval History (London: Oxford U.P., 1941). Some insight into medieval industries is given by LOUIS F. SALZMAN, English Industries in the Middle Ages (Oxford: Clarendon, 1923), and CHARLES J. SINGER et al., History of Technology, vol. II (Oxford: Clarendon, 1956ff.).

A brief survey of medieval agriculture is NELLIE NEILSON, Medieval Agrarian Economy (New York: Holt, 1936) (p.); another study is PAUL VINEGRADOFF, The Growth of the Manor (London: Allen, 1905). More limited in scope is EUGENII A. KOMINSKY, Studies in the Agrarian History of England (Oxford: Oxford U.P., 1956).

Concerning finance, one may consult vol. III of the Cambridge Economic History . . . , entitled Economic Organization and Policies in the Middle Ages, ed. M. M. POSTAN et al. (Cambridge: Cambridge U.P., 1963), as well as the above-cited work by LOPEZ and RAYMOND on Medieval Trade. . . . Good studies on banking are RAYMOND A. DE ROOVER, Money, Credit and Banking in Medieval Bruges (Cambridge, Mass.: Mediaeval Academy, 1948), and ABBOTT P. USHER, The Early History of Deposit Banking in Medieval Europe, vol. I (Cambridge, Mass.: Harvard U.P., 1943). On the rise of towns, see HOWARD SAALMAN, Medieval Cities (New York, G. Braziller, 1968); MAURICE BERESFORD, New Towns of the Middle Ages . . . in England, Wales, and Gascony (New York: Praeger, 1967); JOHN H. MUNDY and PETER RIESENBERG, The Medieval Town (Princeton, N.J.: Van Nostrand, 1958) (p.); HENRI PIRENNE, Medieval Cities (Princeton, N.J.: Princeton U.P., 1925) (p.); CARL STEPHENSON, Borough and Town . . . (Cambridge, Mass.: Mediaeval Academy, 1933); and GORDON C. HOME and E. FORD, Medieval London (London: Benn, 1927), as well as the article by ELEANOR C. LODGE on "The Communal Movement . . ." in Cambridge Medieval History, V, 624–657.

Introductions to medieval society are CHRISTOPHER BROOKE, The Structure of Medieval Society (New York: McGraw-Hill, 1971) (p.); and the brief SIDNEY PAINTER, Medieval Society (Ithaca, N.Y.: Cornell U.P., 1951) (p.); a random sampling is provided by EDWARD L. CUTTS, Scenes and Characters of the Middle Ages (London: Simpkin, 1925). For English society, see GEORGE G. COULTON, Medieval Panorama: The English Scene from Conquest to Reformation (New York: Macmillan, 1938) (p.); LOUIS F. SALZMAN, English Life in the Middle Ages (Oxford: Clarendon, 1931); and DORIS M. STANTON, English Society in the Early Middle Ages,

1066–1307 (Middlesex: Penguin, 1951). For French society, see ACHILLE LUCHAIRE, *Social France at the Time of Philip Augustus . . .*, tr. E. B. Krehbiel (New York: Holt, 1912). There are various good articles on aspects of high medieval society in the *Cambridge Medieval History*, vols. V, VI, and VII. For rural and feudal life, one may consult HENRY S. BENNETT, *Life on the English Manor . . . 1150–1400* (New York: Macmillan, 1938); GEORGE G. COULTON, *The Medieval Village* (Cambridge: Cambridge U.P., 1926); HERBERT THURSTON, *. . . Some Inexactitudes of Mr. G. G. Coulton . . .* (London: Sheed, 1927); GEORGE C. HOMANS, *English Villages of the Thirteenth Century* (Cambridge, Mass.: Harvard U.P., 1941); NATHANIEL J. HONE, *The Manor and Manorial Records . . .* (London: Methuen, 1906); WILLIAM STEARNS DAVIS, *Life on a Medieval Barony . . .* (New York: Harpers, 1923); SARRELL E. GLEASON, *An Ecclesiastical Barony in the Middle Ages . . .* (Cambridge, Mass.: Harvard U.P., 1934), MARGARET W. LA BARGE, *A Baronial Household of the Thirteenth Century* (New York: Barnes and Noble, 1965); and the very well-researched MICHAEL ALTSCHUL, *A Baronial Family in Medieval England: The Clares, 1217–1314* (Baltimore: Johns Hopkins, 1965). For further works on aristocratic life, warfare, and chivalry, see our chapter on feudalism.

Recommended works on miscellaneous special topics are ARTHUR P. NEWTON, *Travel and Travellers of the Middle Ages* (New York: Knopf, 1926); EILEEN E. POWER, *Medieval People* (Boston: Houghton, 1925); LOUIS F. SALZMAN, *Medieval Byways* (Boston: Houghton, 1913); RUTH MEHL, *The Three Estates in Medieval and Renaissance Literature* (New York: Columbia U.P., 1933); and the interesting collaborative melanges edited by SYLVIA L. THRUPP, *Change in Medieval Society . . .* (New York: Appleton, 1964).

⟨ EXPANSION AND CRUSADES IN THE HIGH MIDDLE AGES. Chapter 17.

ONE OF the most impressive aspects of the progress of Western Europe in the High Middle Ages was external expansion. This was the common work of traders and settlers, bishops and monks, lords and knights; and it had much the same inspiration as early modern European expansion: "Gospel, glory, and gold." The Crusades to the Near East were but one manifestation, albeit spectacular, of this general phenomenon.

TERRITORIAL EXPANSION OF CHRISTIAN WESTERN EUROPE.
Section 49.

As the land was in want of people, Adolph [of Holstein] sent messengers to all regions roundabout, even to Flanders, Holland, Utrecht, Westphalia, and Frisia, to proclaim that all who were in need of land should come and bring their families, and receive the very best soil. [Helmold, twelfth-century priest of Bosau, concerning Bishop Adolph of Holstein's recruitment of settlers for lands beyond the Elbe, in his *Chronicle of the Slavs*.]

The High Middle Ages

CHRISTIAN Western Europe expanded in almost every direction during the High Middle Ages. Contributing factors included improved political stability and military proficiency, rapid multiplication of the population, and increased demands for foodstuffs and other products. Rising standards of living and a need to provision rising towns as well as supply booming industries contributed to growing markets and expansion. A common propellant was the desire of princes, lords, bishops, merchants, entrepreneurs, and agriculturalists for more land and profit and power. Another was the missionary zeal of monks, priests, and prelates. A spirit of "do and dare" pervaded the age. The growing strength of Western Europe contrasted with the weakness prevalent in the areas of expansion.

Southwestward expansion in the Iberian peninsula

One of the earliest forms of Western Christian expansion was the *Reconquista* (Reconquest) of Moslem-held territories in the Iberian peninsula. This "liberation" movement, blessed by Popes, preached by clerics, and regarded as a holy endeavor, drew volunteers from various lands beyond the Pyrenees, especially France. Greatly assisted by the disintegration of the Umayyad Caliphate of Cordova into petty states, the Christian Reconquest speeded up in the eleventh century. A temporary high-water mark was reached when Alfonso VI of Leon took centrally located Toledo in 1085. The alarmed Moslems now called in warlike Berbers from Morocco, and for a century and a quarter (1086–1212) most Christian expansion in the peninsula was halted by Moroccan dynasties. In the early thirteenth century, an international Iberian Christian Crusade, backed by Pope Innocent III and led by Alfonso VIII of Castile, decisively defeated the Moroccan Almohades in the battle of Las Navas de Tolosa (1212). Reconquest of the rest of the peninsula was successfully pressed by King Ferdinand III of Castile and by King James I, the Conqueror, of Aragon, with the result that only the small kingdom of Granada remained Moslem by the later thirteenth century.

Expansion in the Mediterranean

As the Moslem offensive in the western Mediterranean subsided, the naval power of Genoa and Pisa grew. The Genoese and Pisans drove the Moslems from their bases in southern France and Italy as well as from the island of Corsica in the tenth century, and won control of the western Mediterranean during the eleventh century. Encouraged by Papal prompting and assistance, they jointly expelled the Moslems from Sardinia by mid-century. A joint Genoese–Pisan expedition of several hundred ships against Tunis (1087), a leading base of Moslem piratical activities, obliged the Emir of Tunis to release his Christian captives, pay a large indemnity, and exempt Genoese and Pisan merchants from import duties. Enterprising Genoa and Pisa also attacked other Moslem bases in the western Mediterranean, such as Sicily and the Balearics.

Eastward expansion of the Germans

In the Adriatic and Aegean Seas, Venice obtained similar control. By the early eleventh century, Venice had suppressed the Croatian pirates in the Adriatic and had become mistress of that sea as well as its northeastern coast. In the course of the eleventh century, Venice greatly expanded her commerce, and more and more Byzantine shipping was entrusted to Venetian bottoms. In return for vital naval aid against the

Expansion and Crusades

Normans, Venice obtained extensive trading privileges from the Empire (1082ff.). The Venetians extended their naval control through the Aegean and penetrated the Black Sea. But they were meanwhile challenged by the Genoese, who competed with them for maritime ascendance and Byzantine preference.

In the eleventh century, as has been seen, the Normans conquered southern Italy and Sicily, which were united by Roger II in the early twelfth century and recognized as a kingdom by Pope Anacletus in 1130.

German eastward expansion, which has been called "the great act of the German people in the Middle Ages," began in the tenth century, although most of the territories won beyond the Elbe were subsequently lost during the great Slavic uprising that followed the defeat of Otto II in southern Italy in 982. During the High Middle Ages, German eastward expansion was resumed. It was the collective work of princes, lords, bishops, missionaries, traders, farmers, and herdsmen, with little imperial participation. Motives were mixed, and included religious zeal, aggrandizement, land hunger, business enterprise, and monetary profit. Among great lay leaders in the twelfth century were Count Albert of Holstein, Duke Henry the Lion of Saxony, and Margrave Albert the Bear of Brandenburg. Among ecclesiastical leaders were the bishops of Hamburg-Bremen, Regensburg (Ratisbon), and Salzburg. German eastward expansion, which was much like the great westward movement in our own history, extended to the farther limits of the valley of the Oder, and embraced such valuable areas as Mechlenburg, Pomerania, and Brandenburg, as well as the eastern parts of Lusatia and Meissen. Many German settlements were named after a particular fortified stronghold (*burg*), and some after a hill (*berg*), a meadow (*au*), or a brook (*bach*). The crushing of a great Slavic revolt in 1163–1164 by a powerful German crusade helped to open up more remote Pomerania to settlement. Danzig fell into German hands and the whole region south of the Baltic as far as the Vistula came to be ruled by the Germans.

Whereas German expansion to the northeast proceeded mainly from Saxony, that to the southeast proceeded mainly from Bavaria. Its chief points of departure were the frontier sees of Salzburg, Regensburg (Ratisbon), and Passau. Initial expansion took place mainly in and from Austria, Moravia, and the Nordgau. Vienna, which had been a bone of contention between Germans and Magyars, was reoccupied by the Germans and became the capital of the *Ost Mark* in 1140. The territory of Austria proper was doubled by expansion down the Danube. Adjacent Carinthia, Carniola, and Styria were also occupied.

Although temporarily subjected to loose German suzerainty by the Carolingian and early Saxon monarchs, the Bohemians reasserted their independence in the tenth century at the time of Boleslav I and II. German overlordship was, however, firmly reestablished in the eleventh century, and Bohemia became a duchy and later a kingdom within the Empire. Silesia, to the northeast of Bohemia, was occupied by German settlers in the twelfth to thirteenth centuries, and became a German duchy in the thirteenth century. Moravia was incorporated into Bohemia in the eleventh century and raised to the dignity of a Margravure in the twelfth century.

Northward expansion of the Germans

The Germans expanded along the eastern coast of the Baltic in the thirteenth century as far north as the Gulf of Finland. Territory occupied included (from south to north) West Prussia and East Prussia (the latter is today north Poland), western Lithuania (Samogitia), Latvia (Courland), Livonia, and Estonia. Contemporary occupants of these areas were backward, barbaric, pagan Balts and Finns. Although the movement was initiated by bishops, missionaries, and traders, its difficulties were so great that its direction soon passed to military orders, notably the Teutonic Knights.

Early in the thirteenth century, enterprising Bishop Albert I led a group of German settlers to Riga, which he refounded, fortified, and made his episcopal see. To protect his settlement, as well as to subdue and eventually convert the fierce neighboring Finnish and Baltic tribes, Bishop Albert established a military order: the Knights of the Sword. The Knights of the Sword rapidly subdued the regions of Livonia and Estonia to their north, but suffered a severe defeat at the hands of the native tribes and Lithuanians when they attempted to expand their control into Courland to the south of the Gulf of Riga (1236).

The Teutonic Knights

In 1228 the Teutonic Knights accepted the invitation to come to the Baltic region extended by a Polish duke whose domains were being ravaged by incursions of Prussians. The Teutonic Knights, who were allowed to keep any lands they could conquer in the Prussian area, methodically subjected the population of Prussia and consolidated their hold by establishing several strongly fortified towns and castles. In 1235 they absorbed the local military order of Drobzin, which had been established by the Bishop of Kumerland; and in 1237 they merged with the Knights of the Sword and extended their activities into Livonia and Latvia. Although the Knights encountered strenuous resistance from the warlike Prussians and were challenged by repeated revolts, they completed the subjugation of Prussia by 1283. The Knights were equally successful along the Baltic coast to the north. They subjected the local population, constructed fortifications, repressed native uprisings, established towns, and encouraged German settlement. By the close of the thirteenth century, the Teutonic Knights controlled the entire Baltic coastline to the Gulf of Finland. Their efforts to expand into Russia were repulsed by its Tartar overlords in 1241 and by the Russian Prince Alexander Nevsky in 1242 in the so-called Battle of the Ice on frozen Lake Peipus. In the course of their expansion, the Teutonic Knights incurred the hostility and fear of the Poles and Lithuanians, whose access to the sea they blocked.

Expansion and Crusades

THE FIRST CRUSADE AND THE LATIN KINGDOM OF JERUSALEM.
Section 50.

God wills it! God wills it! [Response to Urban's appeal for a crusade to the Near East at the Council of Clermont in 1095, as reported by Robert the Monk.]

THE MOST dramatic example of Western European Christian expansion in the High Middle Ages was the Crusades: Church-sponsored armed expeditions to the Near East. The military operations of the Crusades were made at private expense with great sacrifices and risks, and were continued for two centuries. From one point of view the Crusades were "armed pilgrimages to make the world safe for pilgrimage"; from another they were the beginnings of Western European overseas expansion and colonialism. They marked Western Europe's transition from the defensive to the offensive. And they were a common European enterprise, although originally and primarily French.

General origins of the Crusades

The main general cause of the Crusades was the strong spirit of faith then prevalent in Western Europe. A second general source was the Judaeo-Christian tradition of pilgrimage, partly traceable to early nomadism, wherein formal religious worship was associated with certain holy places venerated as scenes of special divine manifestations. Pilgrimages were acts of penance and sacrifice, manifestations of piety, and opportunities for religious reflection and spiritual refreshment. Whenever contemporary conditions permitted, numerous Western Christians made their way as pilgrims to Palestinian places associated with the life of Jesus Christ.

Another source of the Crusades was Christian adoption of the "holy war" idea. This concept had promoted Moslem expansion, and had also been used by the Byzantines. The Western Christian "Reconquest" in Spain, as well as Pisan and Genoese naval operations against the Moslems in the western Mediterranean, were regarded as "holy wars" willed and blessed by God.

The Seljuk Turks

Turkish expansion over the Near East in the eleventh century upset the peaceful modus vivendi of Moslems and Christians. Emerging from the rough and nomadic highlands of Turkestan, a group of Turks known as Seljuks—from an early leader—entered the service of the Moslem Ghaznawid Khan of Afghanistan as mercenaries in the tenth century. After being converted to Islam, these Turks began to expand on their own in the eleventh century under a succession of aggressive leaders, Tughril Beg, Alp Arslan, and Malik Shah. They first appropriated the Persian domains of the Ghaznawids. By 1050 they had taken Isfahan, key to Persia, and in 1055 they acquired the Abbasid capital of Bagdad, where Tughril Beg established himself as secular ruler alongside the religious Caliph. As the expansion proceeded the Turks not only reached the Mediterranean in Palestine but also invaded Byzantine Syria, Armenia, and Asia Minor. When the Emperor Romanus Digenes went out to meet them with a large but composite army, he was defeated and captured by Alp Arslan at Manzikert near Lake Van in Armenia (1071). Having routed the Byzantine army, the Turks were able to occupy both Armenia and Asia Minor. The Turkish conquest resulted in the subjugation of many Eastern Christians to harsh, unenlightened rule, and frequent mistreatment of Western Christian pilgrims.

Meanwhile the Cluniac–Gregorian reform of the Church in the West stressed Papal leadership and precipitated a breakaway of the Eastern Church from union with the Western. Solicitous Popes came to regard military aid as a possible means of ending the Schism, while harassed Byzantine Emperors, concerned with saving their state, offered prospects of religious reunion as a lure to obtain Papal support. In 1073, the Emperor Michael Ducas made an appeal for aid to Pope Gregory VII, but the outbreak of the investiture struggle precluded compliance.

Immediate origins of the First Crusade

The launching of a Western expedition to the Near East had to wait for a partial lull in the investiture controversy during the pontificate of the able French Pope, Urban II. While Urban was conducting a reform council at Piacenza in northern Italy (1095), delegates from Emperor Alexius Comnenus came to ask for Western volunteers to help in the Byzantine counteroffensive against the Turks. Although Urban decided to raise an expedition that would help the Byzantines to fight the Moslems, he broadened the project into a movement to obtain Western Christian control of the Holy Land. At Clermont in southern France, where he held another reform council (1095), Urban publicly proclaimed the First Crusade. The Pope urged, among reasons for an expedition to the Near East, emancipation of the holy places from the infidels, the freeing of Eastern Christians from bondage, external diversion of the warlike propensities of Western Christians, and acquisition of worldly wealth and power in a land "flowing with milk and honey." In enthusiastic response to the Pope's appeal, the assembly took up the cry: "God wills it! God wills it!" Many joined on the spot, and affixed crosses of cloth to their garments. The Crusade was preached throughout Western Europe by bishops, priests, and monks. The bulk of the volunteers came from France and partly French lands, such as Lorraine and southern Italy and Sicily.

Motives of the Crusades

From the point of view of the Papacy, the Crusade gave promise of promoting the reunion of the Eastern and Western Churches as well as of increasing Papal prestige and helping to restore Western unity. That Urban II intended for the Crusader States to be in partial dependence upon the Papacy, as a sort of fief, is probable. The motives of the crusaders were mixed. Most of them seem to have been attracted by the idea of an armed pilgrimage to the holy places. Most apparently looked upon their expedition as an act of devotion and reverence, a penance for their sins, and a means of obtaining divine favor. The Papacy and preachers guaranteed plenary indulgences or full remission of temporal punishment due for sins to those who confessed and crusaded with the proper disposition.

Many crusaders looked for earthly gain in the form of booty, lands, income, and positions of honor. A person who had "crusaded" would enjoy somewhat enhanced stature even as does a modern war veteran. Crusading was also prompted by the restlessness of youth and middle age, desire for change and adventure, pressure of mob psychology, and concern for human respect. Crusading became a fad and "the thing to do." Attractions included a spirit of camaraderie and the thrill of a great gamble. Some no doubt went simply to get away from something: domestic problems, unruly subordinates, nagging debts, or a bad name.

The First Crusade was the only crusade that was fully successful. It was undertaken in the fresh enthusiasm of a new cause, and took by surprise a Moslem world unhinged by recent conquest and distraught by internal conflict. For since the death of Malik Shah (1092) the sprawling Seljuk conquests had disintegrated into numerous smaller warring sultanates.

The First Crusade: The Peasants' Crusade (1096)

The main First Crusade was prefaced by a tragedy. Relying on such concepts as "faith that moves mountains," preachers like the eloquent Peter the Hermit and leaders like the knight-errant Walter the Penniless enlisted large numbers of ordinary people, along with a few lesser knights and infantrymen, in the Peasants' or People's Crusade. The main body, led by Peter the Hermit, and possibly numbering 15,000 to 20,000 persons, set out from France in the spring of 1096 and picked up additional recruits at Cologne. As the disorderly mob proceeded across the Balkans, it had frequent clashes with the native populace. At Constantinople alarmed city officials quickly ferried the crusaders across the Bosphorus. After they began to plunder Turkish territory in Asia Minor, a punitive expedition was organized by the Sultan of Nicaea. No match for a real military force, the Westerners were slaughtered or enslaved, except for a small remnant who took refuge in an abandoned fort and were rescued by a Byzantine relief force. The bleached bones of the victims remained as a grim reminder to subsequent crusaders. Meanwhile in the Rhineland various contingents of volunteer crusaders, led by fanatics and adventurers, vented their spite on the Jews, whom they attacked and robbed in such cities as Worms, Mainz, and Cologne, as well as in Bohemia and Bavaria.

The Peasants' Crusade was a prelude to the main First Crusade, which it indirectly helped by causing the Turks to underestimate the military capabilities of the West. The Crusade of the Princes contained no crowned heads, since each of the leading European monarchs was involved in a dispute with the Papacy. It consisted of several virtually independent contingents, each led by a great lord. Among the princes were Raymond II, Count of Toulouse, one of the earliest and wealthiest volunteers; Robert Curthose, Duke of Normany, brother of King William II of England; Robert II, Count of Flanders, one of the most unselfish, efficient leaders; Count Hugh of Vermandois, brother of the excommunicated King Philip I of France; indecisive Count Stephen of Blois, husband of the strong-willed Adela, daughter of the Conqueror; and idealistic Godfrey of Bouillon, appointive Duke of Lower Lorraine, who was accompanied by two brothers: the realistic Baldwin, and another brother, the well-off Count Eustace III of Boulogne. From Norman Italy came the ambitious, unscrupulous Bohemund, Prince of Taranto, a son of the

Crusade of the Princes (1096–1099)

pioneer conqueror Robert Guiscard, together with his nephew Tancred. The Papal Legate, Bishop Adhemar of Le Puy, was a tactful, competent moderator, described as "skilled in doing all good things." The Crusade has been estimated as numbering from 5,000 to 10,000 knights, with some 25,000 to 50,000 additional soldiers, plus an equal number of noncombatants.

The Crusade of the Princes did not leave until the end of summer 1096, when the various contingents pursued their separate ways across the Balkans to Constantinople. As they arrived, the leaders were entertained and presented with gifts by Emperor Alexius Comnenus, who persuaded most of them to take oaths of vassalage for any territories they might conquer in former Byzantine lands in Asia, and then ferried the contingents across the Bosphorus to await their companions.

Nicaea and Dorylaeum (1097)

After the Crusade was assembled, it proceeded across Asia Minor. The first military action of the crusaders was to besiege Nicaea (about thirty miles inland), the capital of Turkish Anatolia or "Rum." The crusaders beat off a relief force organized by the Sultan, while the Byzantines transported ships overland and sealed the lake side of the city. One night the small garrison within the city surrendered to the Byzantines on favorable terms, and in the morning the surprised crusaders beheld Byzantine standards flying above the city walls. The angered leaders of the Crusade were conciliated by gifts.

The crusading army next split up into two groups to facilitate provisioning and foraging. Near Dorylaeum, about sixty miles southeast of Nicaea, the first contingent was attacked by a large Turkish force gathered by the Sultan of Rum. Bohemund formed the hard-pressed defenders into a compact group, which held out until the second contingent appeared on the scene and routed the outflanked Turks. Enriched by booty and stores, the crusaders resumed their way across Asia Minor, which was painful and difficult because of the "scorched earth" policy and guerrilla tactics of the Turks. The Turks destroyed crops and provisions, dried up or poisoned wells, and made surprise attacks. The route over the Taurus Mountains was particularly hazardous, and many men and animals plunged to death in the treacherous rain-drenched defiles.

Edessa

Meanwhile Baldwin and Tancred took a diversionary route via the south coast of Asia Minor. There Baldwin accepted the pleas of refugee Armenians, displaced by the Seljuks, and journeyed to Edessa in the interior, where he was welcomed as military commander and adoptive son by the Armenian ruler, Thoros. But soon an uprising, apparently "arranged," overthrew Thoros; whereupon Baldwin stepped into his place (1098) and the County of Edessa became a defensive outpost for the crusaders.

Antioch (1098)

After traversing the Taurus range, the fatigued and depleted crusaders arrived before Antioch, the leading metropolis of western Syria. Antioch was surrounded by some seven miles of strong walls with an estimated 400 towers and had its own water supply. Over seven months were spent in fruitless attempts to penetrate the formidable defenses, while the crusader army suffered greatly from the weather as well as from a shortage of supplies. The task seemed hopeless, especially when the crusaders heard that a large army under Kerbogha, Emir of Mosul, was approaching. Some, including Stephen of Blois, to the shame of his wife, Adela, gave up and returned home. But meanwhile the crafty Bohemund established contact with a disaffected enemy captain whom he bribed to allow the Normans to enter the city via his tower. After the Normans gained entrance to the city, they threw open the gates and a general massacre ensued. But hardly had the crusaders taken Antioch when they were besieged by the army of Kerbogha.

The crusaders were in a critical position—since they were low on supplies and weakened by the sicknesses that had broken out in the disrupted city. But a peasant named Peter Bartholomew reported that he had seen a vision revealing where he could find the holy lance that had pierced the side of Jesus. After digging for some time at a spot he designated, his companions unearthed a rusty object, which was hailed as the lance. Inspired with new confidence, the crusaders emerged from the city bearing the lance in a combined military formation and religious procession, which so surprised the Moslems that they were thrown into confusion and routed.

On to Jerusalem (1099)

After resting for a while, the main body of crusaders left Bohemund in command at Antioch and proceeded to Jerusalem. As they moved down the coast, they received the submission of lesser towns and bypassed stronger ones. On nearing Jerusalem, they were overjoyed at the spectacle of the holy city. After being temporarily frustrated by the towering walls of the ancient stronghold, they eventually obtained needed supplies, building materials, and technical assistance from a combined Genoese and English fleet, which had put into port at Jaffa (Joppa). Equipped with scaling towers and inspired by fasting and prayer, followed by a religious procession, the crusaders made fresh assaults that carried them across the walls and into the city. A terrible slaughter followed.

Hardly were they established in Jerusalem when the crusaders learned of a large army proceeding northward from Fatimid Egypt. Instead of waiting to be besieged, they decided to go out and meet the enemy. Proceeding down the coast they surprised the Egyptian encampment and routed the Fatimid army near Ascalon (1099).

The Kingdom of Jerusalem

After taking Jerusalem, the crusaders elected the conciliatory, modest Godfrey of Bouillon as their ruler. Godfrey declined to assume a crown in deference to the Kingship of Christ, took instead the title of Advocate (Protector) of the Holy Sepulchre. But Godfrey died the following year, and his brother, the bold Baldwin, came down from Edessa and assumed the royal crown. Energetic Baldwin I and his able immediate successors completed the conquest and occupation of Palestine and southwestern Syria. Bohemund and his successor Tancred similarly expanded the Principality of Antioch in northwestern Syria; while Raymond of Toulouse and his son did likewise in the intervening territory that became the County of Tripoli. The crusaders were greatly aided in their capture of

Expansion and Crusades

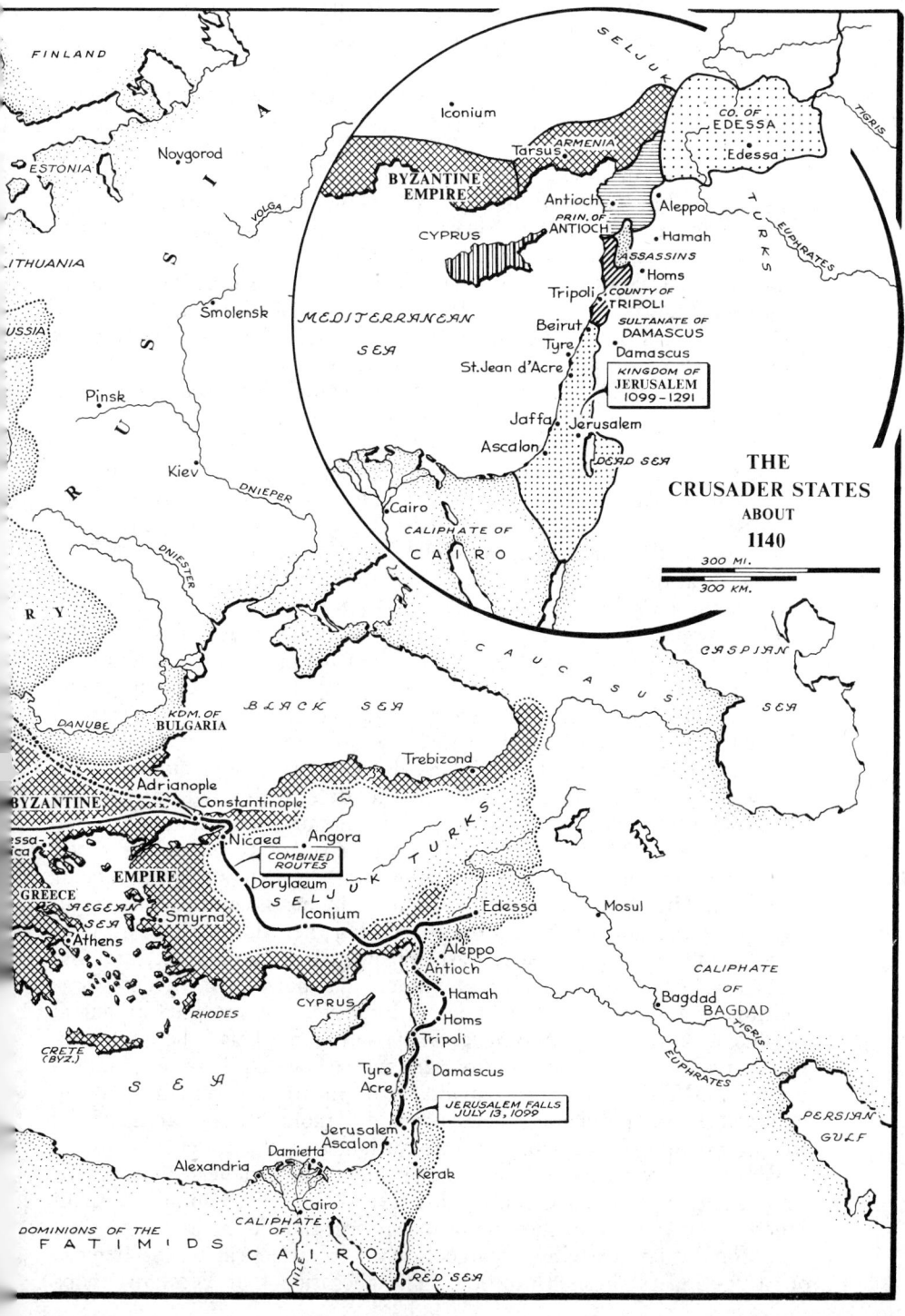

THE CRUSADER STATES ABOUT 1140

coastal strongholds by the fleets of the North Italian city-states, which obtained their own special "quarters" and trading privileges in the new acquisitions.

Government of the Crusader States

Although nominally one kingdom, the territory conquered by the crusaders in the Near East consisted of four autonomous states: the Kingdom of Jerusalem, the County of Tripoli, the Principality of Antioch, and the County of Edessa. The King of Jerusalem exercised no effective authority within the territories of his fellow princes. Although these states frequently cooperated, their own particular interests were paramount, and sometimes they openly competed.

The Crusader States were extremely feudal. Since most of the crusaders were from France and the Rhineland, they established in the Near East the kind of a political system with which they were familiar. The King of Jerusalem was a *primus inter pares* (first among equals) elected by and responsible to his fellows. Still, the crown tended to become hereditary at Jerusalem as elsewhere, and the king had a sacrosanct character as well as indefinite latent powers.

The supreme power in the Kingdom of Jerusalem rested in the Council of the Barons, known as the High Court (*Haute Cour*). Composed of the tenants-in-chief of the king, the High Court not only determined the succession to the throne and administered supreme justice but also decided critical questions, such as those of war and peace, and established laws for the kingdom.

The power of the central government was stringently limited by the privileged status of the great barons, the North Italians, the Church, and the Military Orders, as well as by the autonomy of the larger component states. The barons were often unruly. In various cities the North Italians enjoyed special exemptions, with their own quarters and courts amounting to extraterritoriality. The Church also had great independence. And finally the Military Orders were virtually states within a state, ruling their own castles and directing their own military operations.

Defense of the Crusader States

The Crusader States occupied a narrow strip of territory about 500 miles long, averaging about 40 miles in width, which was very difficult to defend. The Westerners were surrounded by hostile and jealous neighbors, while the bulk of their subjects resented their domination. Survival of these outposts in the Near East depended mainly on force, and the problem of maintaining sufficient military manpower and defenses was continuous and difficult. The basic military force was provided by feudal knights, who were supported by land-fiefs and money-fiefs. The latter consisted of allotments of income from designated sources. Transient knights from the West, who came individually or in armies, were usually unpredictable and unreliable. They often did more harm than good by stirring up the Moslems to renewed warfare and resentment.

Western armies in the Near East included foot soldiers and archers, who usually outnumbered the knights several times. The infantry's main function was to hold off the enemy and protect the knights until the time came for the latter's telling charge. They were also vital in the defense of castles and established positions. The allegation that Western troops were unorganized and undisciplined is exaggerated. And Western knights, with their heavy equipment, great chargers, and intensive training, were usually superior to Saracen soldiers.

The crusaders controlled the land by means of large castles, strategically sprinkled throughout frontier areas. The main object of the castles was not to prevent the enemy's entry but to command the countryside, hold the population in subjection, and withstand sieges, as well as threaten an invader's flanks and rear. Armies were not ordinarily maintained in the field during the cold and rainy season. Numerous imposing stone castles, such as Krak des Chevaliers, Kerak in Moab, Beaufort, Marqab, Sayhun, and Belvoir, were constructed with the most advanced features such as smooth stone walls (to prevent the enemy from gaining a foothold), double enceintes (successive concentric barriers), parapets, machicolations, projecting platforms, and tapering slits for archers.

A partial answer to the need for military manpower was provided by the military orders. These were genuine religious associations, devoted to the worship of God and the pursuit of perfection, living under a common Rule (modified Benedictine, Cistercian, or Augustinian), with vows of poverty, chastity, and obedience. Their main external activity was defense of the Holy Land against the infidels.

Military orders

The first military order was the Knights of the Temple or Templars, founded by a band of knights led by Hugh de Payens (or Payns) about 1118 to protect pilgrims on the way to Jerusalem. They were given quarters near the Temple by Baldwin II, provided with a Rule by St. Bernard, and sanctioned by the Council of Troyes (1128). The Templars ably held and defended several strategic castles such as those of Safed, Tortosa, and Athlit. Vowed to perpetual warfare against the Moslems, the Templars were described as "lions in battle" by the thirteenth-century author Jacques de Vitry, who says that *When the Templars are called to arms, they do not ask how numerous the enemy are, but where they are.* Eventually the Templars became famed as international bankers as well as intrepid warriors.

The Hospitallers or Knights of the Hospital of St. John of Jerusalem traced their origin back to a combined hospice and hospital for pilgrims founded at Jerusalem in the mid-eleventh century by merchants from Amalfi. Both their order and their work expanded after the founding of the Latin Kingdom of Jerusalem. During the 1120s their aggressive master, Raymond du Puy, expanded their services to include fighting the Moslems, and they became a military order like the Templars. Among great castles manned by the Hospitallers were Krak des Chevaliers and Margat in the County of Tripoli. They later transferred their activities to Cyprus, Rhodes, and Malta. Whereas the Templars wore a white habit with a red cross, the Hospitallers wore a black habit with a white cross.

The Teutonic Knights evolved from the Hospital of St. Mary of the Germans, which was founded at Jerusalem about 1127 and moved to Acre following the fall of Jerusalem in 1187. German knights who had come to Acre for the Crusade of Henry VI (which never eventuated) converted the institution into a military order for Germans in 1198. Finding their field of activity increasingly constricted in the Near East, the Teutonic Knights soon transferred their attention elsewhere: first to Hungary and then to the Baltic. A smaller order founded during the Third Crusade in 1191 to defend the holy places and bury the Christian dead was the English order of St. Thomas of Acre.

Conditions in the Crusader States

The Crusader States were important in expanding and developing Mediterranean trade with the West through the seaports of Palestine and Syria. The Western settlers in the Near East took on many of the ways and even some of the outlook of the local population.

At first the recently arrived Westerners had the edge over their Moslem neighbors. This period of "the Christian Offensive" extended to about 1131. Among Christian advantages were the initial division and rivalry among the Moslems, the momentum of expansion, reputation for military success, control of the sea, alliance with Byzantium, generous support from home, and strong early kings.

DECLINE AND FALL OF THE CRUSADER STATES.
Section 51.

> The question is asked . . . why our predecessors often withstood more numerous forces of the enemy, whereas our contemporaries are frequently defeated by smaller forces. . . . The former were religious men, who feared God, whereas a wicked generation has replaced them. . . . Also, those revered men who first came to the East were inured to military discipline . . . , whereas their successors have been ennervated by long continued peace. . . . Thirdly, while formerly each of the surrounding little states had its own ruler, today they have all been united under the power of one man: Saladin. [William of Tyre, *History of Deeds Across the Seas* (twelfth century).]

AMONG reasons for the decline of the Crusader States mentioned by William of Tyre above, the last-mentioned was probably the most important. In the twelfth century the Moslems gradually united, and the Christian advantage receded in proportion as the Moslems combined. There was a period of near equilibrium from about 1131 to 1174, when Christian monarchy was counterbalanced by Moslem monarchy. But from 1174 on, the advantage and offensive passed to the Moslems. One of the most unfortunate failures of the Westerners was their inability to maintain a stable and tranquil *modus vivendi* with their numerically superior Moslem neighbors, largely due to the recurrent arrival of fresh Saracen-hunting "crusaders." The flow of crusaders to the Near East in fulfillment of vows to "take the cross" was virtually continuous, as was also the reverse flow of those who had "satisfied" their pledges. In addition, there were periodic expeditions of some size: eight major Crusades and several smaller ones.

Moslem recovery begins (1127–1146)

A leading reason for the decline and fall of the Crusader States was the rise of strong, unifying Moslem powers in the Near East and their invocation of the old Islamic principle of the *jihad* or "holy war." The Moslem rally was started by Zenghi (or Zanghi), enterprising Atabeg (local prince) of Mosul on the upper Tigris. After subjecting his Moslem neighbors, Zanghi pushed westward, taking Aleppo in northern Syria in

1128. Following further acquisitions, Zenghi turned on the County of Edessa, whose capital he took during the absence of negligent Count Joscelin in 1144.

News of the loss of Edessa shocked Western Europe. Pope Eugenius III called for a Crusade and commissioned his ascetic friend, the fiery Bernard of Clairvaux, to preach it. Both King Louis VII of France and Emperor Conrad III of Germany were persuaded to take the cross, and raised large armies. The Germans made their way across the Balkans via Constantinople into Asia Minor (1147). But as they paused to refresh themselves at a little river near Dorylaeum the incautious Germans were surprised and massacred by a large Seljuk army. Conrad lost nine tenths of his army. The French likewise proceeded across the Balkans into Asia Minor, where they were relentlessly harassed by the Turks. After extensive losses, the survivors descended to the south central coast, whence the King and the cavalry proceeded by sea. Most of the infantry and pilgrims had to be left behind to make their way by land, and about half of them perished. Louis VII reached Antioch with only a fraction of his army. At Jerusalem, the joint council composed of leaders of both the native Christians and crusaders eventually decided to attack Damascus, the key city of inland Syria, although it was an ally of the Crusader States. The poorly managed operation was a fiasco, and resulted only in the defection of Damascus to Nurredin, who came to its aid. The Second Crusade both demonstrated that the Christians were not invincible and highlighted Moslem advantages.

The ill-fated Second Crusade (1147–1149)

Zenghi's successor, Nurredin (1146–1174), continued the expansionist policies of his father. The energetic Nurredin completed the conquest of the County of Edessa, seized most of the inland possessions of the Principality of Antioch, and extended Zenghid holdings through inland Syria, whose valuable capital, Damascus, he occupied in 1154. Despite their reverses, the Christians continued to put up strenuous resistance. They partially compensated for their losses to the north by expanding to the south, where they took Ascalon in 1153, whence they attempted to occupy Egypt.

Moslem expansion resumed by Nurredin (1146–1174)

As the enfeebled Fatimid Caliphate was at the point of expiring, successive Kings of Jerusalem vied with Nurredin for the possession of Egypt. For a while the wily Egyptian Vizir Shawar was able to play off one against the other. When Nurredin's forces invaded Egypt, Shawar would call in the Christians to counterbalance them. But eventually King Amaury of Jerusalem broke his treaty with Shawar and invaded Egypt on his own (1168), whereupon the Caliph called on Nurredin for help. Determined Egyptian resistance and a large army led by Nurredin's general Shirkuh, who was accompanied by his nephew Saladin, forced the Christians to withdraw. Shirkuh had Shawar decapitated and took over the vizirship; and when he died the following year Shirkuh's nephew Saladin succeeded him (1169). On the death of the Fatimid Caliph Al-Adid in 1171, the Sunnite Saladin declined to acknowledge a Fatimid successor, and recognized instead the overlordship of the Caliph of Bagdad.

The Moslems obtain the advantage under Saladin (1174 ff.)

After Nurredin's death in 1174, Saladin became the strongest leader of the Near Eastern Moslems. Meanwhile the Christians were divided following the accession of the childless leper, Baldwin IV. The Kingdom of Jerusalem became the scene of bitter rivalries between the baronial party, led by Count Raymond of Tripoli, and the court party, led by the King's sister Sibylla and her adventurer husband, Guy of Lusignan.

In the ensuing period (1174–1291) of "Moslem Monarchy Versus Christian Anarchy," the advantage passed to the Moslems. The delicate balance of power in the Near East was upset by a great Turkish victory over the Byzantines in the narrow defiles of Myriocephalon (1176). The "Latinophile" (West-admiring) Byzantine Emperor Manuel Comnenus had imprudently weakened his defenses in Asia Minor because of his excessive interest and involvement in Italian affairs. The calculating Sultan of Iconium invaded Byzantine territory in Asia Minor and then suddenly attacked, trapped, and massacred the incautious Byzantine army sent to expel him. Since Byzantine was no longer a serious threat to their flank, the Moslems could proceed against the Crusader States without restraint.

Following the death of Nurredin (1174), Saladin, already master of Egypt, took over Syria, Mosul, and Farther Transjordan from Nurredin's weak sons. Saladin allowed the Christians a respite while he consolidated his domains. But the smoldering fire of Moslem hostility was repeatedly stirred up by irresponsible raids and treaty violations. A capital offender was the rash Reginald of Chatillon, who was shielded by his friend, King Guy. The breaking point came when the irresponsible Raymond waylaid a large caravan in which Saladin's sister was a passenger.

Disaster: The Horns of Hattin (1187)

Saladin, at the end of his patience, organized a holy war against the Christians. He invaded Palestine with a large force in 1187, and besieged the fortress of Tiberias by the Sea of Galilee. The Christians set aside their disagreements and raised an army of an estimated 12,000 to 20,000 men.[a] Although his council decided to await Saladin by the well-watered springs of Sephoria, King Guy, egged on by Reginald and Grand Master Gerard of the Templars, changed the decision during the night, and set the unprepared army in motion toward Tiberias the following morning.

[a] About a third of which was cavalry.

As the Christian army, lacking sufficient water, toiled across the barren twenty miles in the July heat, it was attacked on its flanks by the Moslems. Parched with thirst, the Christians were obliged to camp for the night, during which the Moslems set fire to the surrounding brush. In the morning the Christians, half out of their minds with thirst, were slaughtered like cattle as they tried to force their way up the incline known as the Horns of Hattin (1187) to reach water. Most of the Christian army was slain or taken captive.

In the absence of any Christian force capable of opposing him, Saladin was able to occupy most of Palestine. City after city, castle after castle, fell like ripe fruit into his hands. Jerusalem was taken in 1187. By 1189 all that was left to the Christians were a few points along the coast: Antioch with its port of St. Symeon, the cities of Tripoli and Tyre, and a few castles.

Expansion and Crusades

Western Europe's answer to the loss of Jerusalem was the Third Crusade, the Crusade of the Kings. This formidable expedition, held by the German Emperor and the Kings of France and England, seemed sure of overwhelming success. But as the large German contingent, headed by Frederick I Barbarossa, journeyed overland the aged Emperor accidentally drowned in a stream in Asia Minor. Most of the Germans turned back to look after their interests at home. Meanwhile Kings Philip II Augustus of France and Richard I the Lionhearted of England sailed overseas. On the way, the adventurous Richard became involved in diversionary wars in Sicily and Cyprus. The crusaders converged on the key seaport of Acre, which was being besieged by survivors from the Kingdom of Jerusalem. After Richard's arrival, Acre was taken. Whereupon most of the non-English crusaders, including King Philip, returned to Western Europe. But by dint of great heroism and exertions Richard eventually won recognition of Christian possession of the seacoast from Jaffa to Tyre and freedom of access to the holy places for Christian pilgrims. As he made his way homeward in disguise in late 1192, Richard was taken prisoner in Austria and handed over to Henry VI, whose rival Tancred of Lecce Richard had recognized and assisted in Sicily. Henry eventually released Richard for a large ransom and his oath of vassalage (1194).

The Third Crusade (1189–1192)

During the thirteenth century there was a marked decline in the crusading spirit. The repeated failure of Crusades gave rise to a nagging feeling that "God does *not* will it!" The perversion of the movement by secular-minded participants, insincere monarchs, and Popes who used Crusades against political enemies in Europe undermined popular confidence. Domestic difficulties and intensified international rivalries preoccupied rulers and proscribed the "luxury" of crusading. In the Near East, the few remnants of the Crusader States were also perturbed by internal rivalries that seemed to intensify as their territory diminished.

Decline of the crusading spirit

The first major Crusade of the thirteenth century, the Fourth Crusade, demonstrated dramatically the secularization of the movement. The Crusade first attacked Western Christians, then turned on Eastern Christians; but it never engaged the Moslems. Like the First, the Fourth was a Crusade of barons; but it had an additional component: the Venetians, who were largely responsible for its subversion. The Crusade was set in motion by the enthusiasm of French lords such as Count Tibald of Champagne and Marquis Boniface of Montferrat, urged on by Pope Innocent III. Since the crusaders were short of funds to finance their voyage, they were persuaded by Doge Dandalo to reconquer Zara for the Venetians as part payment. Located across the Adriatic on the Dalmatian coast, this seaport was in Hungarian hands. Despite the fact that this meant attacking fellow Christians, the crusaders agreed, and Zara was taken for Venice, and subjected to a thorough sacking.

The Fourth Crusade (1202–1204)

The crusaders were next persuaded by young Prince Alexius Angelus to restore his blinded father Isaac to the throne of Constantinople. In return, Alexius promised to provide money, supplies, and ten thousand soldiers for the conquest of Egypt, as well as to promote a reunion of the Eastern Church with the Western Church. The crusaders agreed to this second diversion, which likewise succeeded. But after the restoration Alexius IV Angelus could not fulfill his terms, and he and his father were deposed by an internal, anti-Western revolution. The crusaders then took and sacked Constantinople, after which they elected Baldwin of Flanders Emperor, and the Venetians named a Latin Patriarch. The Emperor obtained one fourth of the city, and a right to a fourth of the Empire. The remaining three fourths of the city and the Empire were to be divided equally between the Venetians and the crusaders: three eighths to each. Various outlying parts of the Empire remained in Byzantine hands, while other parts became independent Latin states. The weak Latin Empire lasted only until 1261. The Fourth Crusade did much to discredit the movement.

The Children's Crusade

Shortly after the Fourth Crusade, a twelve-year-old shepherd boy, Stephen of Cloyes, preached a Children's Crusade in France, as did another lad, Nicholas of Cologne in Germany. Large numbers of young people of both sexes responded with enthusiasm. Several thousand French children went to Marseilles, where many were given free passage by unscrupulous entrepreneurs, who sold into slavery those who did not drown when one of the ships sank. Most of the German children never got beyond Italy; and great numbers never returned home.

The Fifth Crusade almost succeeds (1217–1221)

Pope Innocent III continued to press for a true Crusade, which finally came under his successor, Pope Honorius III. The Fifth Crusade (1217–1221) originally included Kings Andrew of Hungary, Hugh of Cyprus, and John (de Brienne) of Jerusalem (or Acre). But after the departure of Kings Andrew and Hugh, it fell under the control of the imperious Papal Legate, Cardinal Pelagius. The Crusade addressed itself to Egypt as the base of Moslem power in the Holy Land. After the crusaders obtained control of forts commanding the main entrance of the Nile River, Sultan al-Kamil offered the Westerners central Palestine, including Jerusalem and Galilee, in return for peace. King John and most of the barons favored acceptance, but Cardinal Pelagius, backed by Italian merchants and the military orders, and expecting the help of Frederick II, held out for more. Frederick II never arrived. Although the Christians succeeded in taking Damietta and Mansourah, their army was trapped when the Egyptians cut the sluices and opened the canals of the rising Nile, encompassing them with a lake. Cardinal Pelagius was obliged to surrender previous gains in order to obtain the release of the troops.

Crusade of the excommunicated Frederick II

During his candidacy for the imperial crown, Frederick II had made a vow to go on a Crusade; but he kept postponing its fulfillment. Finally losing his patience, Pope Gregory IX excommunicated the "Infidel Emperor" in 1227. Nevertheless Frederick, who had meanwhile married the heiress of Jerusalem, went on his "Crusade" in 1228. By skillful diplomatic negotiations, Frederick obtained possession of Jerusalem and the holy places, together with a narrow corridor of access, from the Sultan of Egypt. He crowned himself in Jerusalem with his own hands; but most of the Christians and clergy in the Near East refused to cooperate with him, and he soon returned to defend his lands in Italy against Papal troops.

The narrow corridor to Jerusalem was difficult to defend. Only a

Expansion and Crusades

decade and a half after Frederick's return to Italy, a combined army of Mameluks and Khwarizmian horsemen defeated the Christians at La Forbie (1244) and retook the Holy City.

St. Louis IX of France prepared a large Crusade, for which he built a special base of departure and supply on the Mediterranean, known as Aigues Mortes. The Crusade proceeded to Egypt, where it took Damietta at the mouth of the Nile. An offer of the Egyptian Sultan to trade Jerusalem for Damietta was rejected. At Mansourah, farther inland on the Nile, the Christian advance bogged down. Although the crusaders found a ford across the Nile that would allow them to attack the enemy, the King's younger brother, Robert of Artois, rashly led a charge of the flower of the French cavalry into an enemy trap in a town. The Moslems again took advantage of the rising Nile to trap the disheartened crusaders. Plagued by disease and disaster, as well as famine, Louis was forced to surrender. The King and his army were released for a huge ransom and the surrender of Damietta. Louis spent the years 1250 to 1254 in Palestine in efforts to strengthen Christian defenses and obtain allies.

The futile Crusades of St. Louis (1248–1250 and 1270)

The last major Crusade was the Second Crusade of St. Louis, made against the advice of his counselors. On the suggestion of the King's ambitious younger brother, Charles of Anjou, King of Sicily, the Crusade went to Tunis, which was represented as a crucial source of horses for Egypt and a fertile field for conversions to Christianity. After the crusaders reached Tunis during the heat of summer, they were frustrated by disease and fever, from which many died, including King Louis himself. The only positive result of the Crusade was a large indemnity paid to Charles of Anjou by the Emir of Tunis.

Various lesser Crusades in the thirteenth century, such as those of Count Tibald of Champagne (1239–1240), the *Infantes* (or Bastards) of Aragon (1269), and Prince Edward of England, failed to accomplish anything of importance. This was partly because the Crusader States were overshadowed by a gigantic struggle of two great powers: the Mongols and the Mameluks, on whose outcome their fate depended. Caught between them, the Western Christians in the Near East cast their lot with the more remote Mongols. But the Mameluks twice defeated the Mongols in Syria—at Ayn Jalut in 1260, and at Homs in 1280—and each victory was followed by anti-Christian Mameluk offensives. One by one, the last Christian strongholds in the Near East fell to the powerful Mameluks, who finally took Acre, the last possession of the crusaders on the Asiatic mainland, in 1291.

End of the Crusader States by 1291

Critics point out that the Crusades, continued for two centuries, represented a fearful waste of human lives, energies, time and resources. The Crusades failed to retain the holy places permanently, worsened the lot of pilgrims and Eastern Christians, stirred up religious intolerance and persecutions, and, instead of mending the Great Schism, aggravated it by increasing points of friction between East and West. The Crusades represented a mistaken appeal to force on behalf of things of the spirit; and the movement became more materialistic and secular as time progressed.

Evaluation of the Crusades

Defenders of the Crusades, on the other hand, argue that all human achievements are only temporary, that the physical and spiritual aspects of life are interrelated, and that force has often profoundly influenced the course of history. They regard the Crusades as a manifestations of idealism, faith, and heroism. They point out that the Crusades may have delayed the Moslem conquest of Constantinople and the Balkans, that they were a beginning of Christian overseas expansion, and that they promoted many forms of progress in the West.

Despite the overall negative evaluation that we must place on the Crusades, it is undeniable that they had some beneficial results. The Crusades to some degree promoted the political consolidation of Western Europe and helped kings to increase their power by diverting the warlike activities of many unruly barons. The Crusades established a precedent for the levying of direct taxes upon the nobility and clergy, as well as on the middle class. And they encouraged a spirit of fraternity and nationalism among participants of similar speech and culture. The Crusades stimulated Western Christian commerce in the Mediterranean. They provided new bases and ports for trade with the East. They encouraged the building of bigger and better ships. And they elicited new tastes for various items obtainable from the East, such as spices, condiments, perfumes, aromatics, and fine textiles. The Crusades fostered technological and financial advances, including large-scale international banking and the greater use of paper transactions and credit. They introduced Westerners to new industrial processes and products. They brought about improvements in the art of castle building and influenced other forms of architecture. The Crusades broadened Westerners by opening their eyes to viewpoints and and ways of life different from their own; and some had a certain leveling effect by putting all participants, noble and ordinary, in the common dangers. The Crusades also stimulated historiography and vernacular literature, and expansion of geographical knowledge and interests.

References for Chapter 17

AMONG narrative histories of the Crusades, the best in English is probably STEVEN RUNCIMAN's *History of the Crusades*, 3 vols. (New York: Cambridge U.P., 1951–1954), well written and based on the sources. More comprehensive coverage is provided, however, in the collaborative University of Pennsylvania *History of the Crusades*, ed. KENNETH M. SETTON (Philadelphia: U. of Pa., 1955ff.), planned to comprise five volumes. Convenient brief surveys are provided by ERNEST BARKER, *The Crusades* (London: Oxford U.P., 1925), and RICHARD A. NEWHALL, *The Crusades* (New York: Holt, 1927). Lighter popular accounts are provided by HAROLD LAMB, KONRAD BERCOVICI, and HILAIRE BELLOC in works each entitled *The Crusades* (1930, 1929, and 1937). A fine general history of the movement written by a contemporary in the later twelfth century is WILLIAM, ARCHBISHOP OF TYRE, *History of Deeds Done Beyond the Sea*, tr. E. A. Babcock and A. O. Krey, 2 vols., (New York: Columbia U.P., 1943). An excellently done account, consisting of some sixty readings from thirty primary sources interconnected by the editor's narrative, is JAMES A. BRUNDAGE, *The Crusades: A Documentary Survey* (Milwaukee: Marquette U.P., 1962). A handy bibliography is AZIS S. ATIYA, *The Crusade: Historiography and Bibliography* (Bloomington: Indiana U.P., 1962). A good work in paperback is HANS E. MAYER,

The Crusades, tr. John Gillingham (Oxford: Oxford U.P., 1972).

A good general account of the Crusades and the Crusader States is DANA C. MUNRO, *The Kingdom of the Crusaders* (New York: Appleton, 1935); a more detailed investigation is JOHN L. LA MONTE, *Feudal Monarchy in the Latin Kingdom of Jerusalem* (Cambridge, Mass.: Mediaeval Academy, 1932). The leading military orders are discussed in careful, detailed fashion by EDWIN J. KING, *The Knights Hospitallers* . . . (London: Methuen, 1931), and in a popular way by GEORGE A. CAMPBELL, *The Knights Templars* . . . (New York: McBride, 1937). Various aspects of Western military operations in the Near East are expertly presented by R. C. SMAIL, *Crusading Warfare (1097-1193)* (Cambridge: Cambridge U.P., 1956).

Among several contemporary accounts of the First Crusade, FULCHER (Fulcherius, Foucher) OF CHARTRES, *Chronicle of the First Crusade*, has been translated by M. E. McGinty (Philadelphia: U. of Pa., 1941), and extracts from various sources have been combined in a skillful mosaic by A. C. KREY, *The First Crusade: The Accounts of Eye-Witnesses and Participants* (Princeton, N. J.: Princeton U.P., 1921). The life of the first Western Prince of Antioch is told by RALPH B. YEWDALE, *Bohemund I, Prince of Antioch* (Princeton, N. J.: Princeton U.P., 1924); that of the first crusader to rule in Jerusalem by JOHN C. ANDRESSOHN, . . . *Godfrey of Bouillon* (Bloomington, Ind.: Principia, 1947). The viewpoint of a Byzantine is presented by ANNA COMNENA, *The Alexiad*, tr. A. S. Dawes (London: Paul Trench, 1928). Useful translated sources concerning the Second Crusade are ODO DE DEUIL, *De Profectione Ludovici VII in Orientem*, ed. and tr. V. G. BERRY (New York: Columbia U.P., 1948), and *De Expugnatione Lyxbonensi: The Conquest of Lisbon*, ed. and tr. C. W. DAVID (New York: Columbia U.P., 1936).

The critical interval between the Second and Third Crusades and the mounting Moslem power are the subject of MARSHALL W. BALDWIN, *Raymond III of Tripolis and the Fall of Jerusalem (1140–1187)* (Princeton, N. J.: Princeton U.P., 1936), and STANLEY LANE POOLE, *Saladin and the Fall of the Kingdom of Jerusalem* (New York: Putnam, 1906). Contemporary accounts concerning the Third Crusade have been translated and published in several English editions such as RICHARD OF DEVIZES and GEOFFREY DE VINSAUF (and JOINVILLE), *Chronicles of the Crusades* . . . (London: Bohn, 1848); *The Crusade of Richard I* . . . , ed. THOMAS A. ARCHER (New York: Putnam, 1889); *Three Old French Chronicles of the Crusades* . . . (Seattle: U. of Wash., 1939), which includes AMBROISE, ROBERT DE CLARI, and "The Chronicle of Rheims"; and AMBROISE, *The Crusade of Richard Lion-Heart*, tr. M. J. Hubert (New York: Columbia U.P., 1941). The Fourth Crusade has received much attention, as in translations of the contemporary accounts by an ordinary knight: ROBERT OF CLARI, *The Conquest of Constantinople* (New York: Columbia U.P., 1930), and by a great lord: VILLEHARDOUIN, *The Conquest of Constantinople* (London: Dent, Everyman's, 1915). An interesting scholarly account of a neglected subject is GEORGE Z. GRAY, *The Children's Crusade* (New York: William Morrow, 1972) (p.). Translated primary sources concerning subsequent Crusades are OLIVER, BISHOP OF PADERBORN, *The Capture of Damietta*, tr. J. J. Gavigan (Philadelphia: U. of Pa., 1948), for the Fifth Crusade; PHILIP DE NOVARA, *The Wars of Frederick III* . . . tr. J. M. Hubert (New York: Columbia U.P., 1936), about the Sixth Crusade; and JEAN, SIRE DE JOINVILLE, *The History of*

Saint Louis, tr. Joan Evans (London: Oxford U.P., 1938), concerning the Seventh and Eighth Crusades. Crusades and crusaders as seen by the Arabs are presented by selections in *Arab Historians of the Crusades,* ed. and tr. F. GABRIELI and E. COSTELLO (Berkeley: California U.P., 1969).

❡ THE WESTERN EMPIRE IN THE HIGH MIDDLE AGES. Chapter 18.

1056–1273

THE WESTERN EMPIRE, headed by German monarchs, was, with the possible exception of Byzantium, the strongest power in Europe at the outset of the High Middle Ages. Whereas the Byzantine Empire soon declined, the Western Empire increased in power, and enjoyed ascendance until the thirteenth century. But imperial power in the West was increasingly challenged by the German princes and the Papacy, joined in the twelfth century by the towns of northern Italy. Although the great, prolonged contest is often conceived of as simply a Church-State struggle between Emperors and Popes, it was actually much more complex. For the medieval contest between Empire and Papacy was only one aspect of a broader struggle between centralizing forces on one hand and decentralizing forces on the other. Anti-imperial forces favoring decentralization included German princes, North Italian communes, and free peasants (as in Saxony), as well as Popes; and secular opponents eventually did more to defeat the Emperors than did the Papacy.

THE LATER FRANCONIANS AND THE INVESTITURE STRUGGLE.
Section 52.

1056–1125

> Henry, King, not by usurpation, but by the holy ordination of God, to Hildebrand, who is not Pope, but only a false monk. [Opening of Henry IV's letter to Pope Gregory VII (January 24, 1076).]❘

DURING the era of the later Franconians (1056–1125), Papal resistance to monarchical control of Church appointments coincided with the continuing efforts of the German princes to make the monarchy more dependent upon their will. Since Papal victory would deprive the monarchy of one of its chief traditional supports and would tend to subject ecclesiastical nominations to aristocratic influence, the princes allied with the Papacy in its opposition to imperial appointments to bishoprics. As a result of civil wars and disorders there was a great growth of castle building and the maintenance of armed retainers, as well as feudal fief-holding and vassalage in Germany. Old sources of monarchical weakness, such as the power of the dukes, Italian opposition, the numerous allodial holdings and exemptions of the nobility, and the failure of successive rulers to adhere to a consistent policy, diminished the monarchy's power of resistance. Because of continuous need for military support in Italian

The Western Empire

campaigns, monarchs sided with the princes in their contest with the German towns, and thus failed to enlist the valuable cooperation of the towns.

Although both Henry IV and Henry V were shrewd and determined, they were also cold and selfish, and neither inspired great public confidence. The accession of the cynical, disillusioned young Henry IV, after a long minority, together with the fact that Church reform now moved into a more restrictive phase, combined to produce a crisis. Since Henry IV was only six years old at the death of his father (1056), the crown lost much ground during the ensuing decade because of the weakness and limitations of successive regencies. The ineffective first regent, Agnes of Poitou, the queen mother, was weak and unintelligent, "distinguished only for her piety" and "a cause of tears to Germany." Eventually both the young King and the regency were seized and controlled by Archbishop Anno of Cologne (1062–1064), who was succeeded by Archbishop Adalbert of Hamburg–Bremen (1064–1065). During the regencies, the German princes encroached on monarchical territories, assumed powers previously reserved to the crown, erected strong castles, and increased their private armies. Episcopal elections often evaded monarchical control, while the Cluniac reformers, by the famous electoral reform decree of 1059, excluded the Emperor from any part in naming or confirming Popes.

Henry IV (1056–1106)

When youthful Henry assumed personal rule in 1065, he set himself energetically to the task of recouping the powers of the monarchy. Only fifteen years of age, Henry was undisciplined, impetuous, skeptical, and unimpressed by religious authority. Although his academic education had been neglected, Henry was well supplied with native intelligence and was shrewd and resolute. Cold, calculating, and unscrupulous, Henry was determined to restore monarchical power. He proved an undaunted leader and a statesman who could hold out against seemingly overwhelming odds. Henry reasserted the royal right to lands lost and prerogatives eroded during the regency. He insisted on his right to appoint bishops and abbots. He invoked the royal ownership of forests and wastelands, many of which had been occupied by usurpers and squatters. He reestablished the royal residence at Goslar in southern Saxony, and resumed the Franconian project of building up a nucleus of royal domains in central Germany. He appointed servile *ministeriales*, usually from Suabia, to administer royal estates, domains, and castles. He multiplied royal castles in southern Saxony and Thuringia; and required services and payments from all from whom he could hope to obtain them.

The vigorous policies of the young Henry IV aroused angry opposition, particularly in Saxony. Henry's use of low-born *ministeriales* instead of local nobles as administrators was galling to the Saxon aristocracy. His assertion of royal rights over the rural population, obviously designed to enshackle them with obligations of serfdom, was opposed by the Saxon people. The first revolt (1070–1071) against Henry was led by the Saxon Otto of Nordheim, who had been made Duke of Bavaria by Agnes, and was supported by his friend, Magnus Billung, successor-apparent to the

Saxon revolts (1070–1075)

Dukedom of Saxony. The revolt was put down, and both Otto and Magnus were taken prisoner. The second revolt (1073-1074) resulted from Henry's apparent intention to withhold the Duchy of Saxony from Magnus after his father's death. Unable to arouse sufficient support, the King was finally obliged to come to terms with the rebellious Saxon nobility. The third Saxon revolt (1074-1075) originated from popular dissatisfaction with Henry's grasping acquisitive policy in Saxony and Thuringia. A number of Saxon peasants attacked and destroyed royal buildings and property at the Harzburg castle. The rioters desecrated chapels, altars, relics, and royal remains. Meanwhile the Saxon nobles also rose against the King. But the sacrileges and ferocity of the peasantry alarmed the other German dukes, so that Henry was able to raise a large army and decisively defeat the rebels at Langensalza (1075). The Saxon nobles and freemen were humiliated by being obliged to walk disarmed and barefooted before the King.

The investiture question

Meanwhile however, new trouble was brewing for Henry IV. The Cluniac–Gregorian reform party was preparing to launch a new phase of its campaign to purify the Church. An important part of Henry's program was renewed monarchical appointment of bishops. Whereas Henry III had used this power for the good and regeneration of the Church, wordly considerations, such as political control of appointees and exaction of financial contributions, were paramount with Henry IV. Supporters of Church reform had won control of the Papacy by 1049. A continuing dynamo of reform was Cardinal Hildebrand, later Pope Gregory VII. Whereas initial efforts of the reformers had been directed against clerical incontinence and simony, they now made lay appointments to clerical offices their target. In 1059 Pope Nicholas II attacked imperial control of Papal elections by a decree reserving the election entirely to the cardinals, the key ecclesiastical officials of the Roman Archdiocese. The next target was lay influence over episcopal elections. But elimination of such lay appointments met strenuous opposition, since bishops were civil as well as religious officials, whom monarchs regarded as important props of the throne. Monarchical control of episcopal appointments was especially important in the Empire, where both Ottonian and Franconian Emperors had entrusted the secular government of numerous towns and counties to bishops. Whereas the reformers wanted complete freedom of ecclesiastical elections, the German monarchs considered control of episcopal elections essential for their power.

Views of reformers

More throughgoing reformers such as Gregory VII felt that the spiritual responsibilities of bishops so far transcended their temporal concerns that episcopal appointments should be entirely controlled by the Church. In their view, Christians were essentially a spiritual family, with their primary purpose eternal salvation. The Pope, as head of this religious family, had the power, in case of necessity and *ratione peccati* (by reason of sin), to depose any monarch who obstinately and seriously endangered the spiritual interests of his subjects, as by opposing Church reform and appointing unworthy bishops. A more moderate group among the reformers, which included Cardinal Peter Damian, believed in a more

The Western Empire

patient, humble, spiritual approach. They would not use such extreme measures as deposition, which would invade the sphere of temporal power, but would rather rely on milder means such as persuasion, admonition, prayer, and, if necessary, excommunication. They would also respect traditional "constitutional" practices, such as the power of monarchs to have a voice in the selection of bishops. The moderates were in the minority, however, and the view of Hildebrand, which concurred with that of the more radical Cardinal Humbert of Moyenmoutier, prevailed.

German monarchs refused to accept the exclusively religious concept of episcopal appointments. Were not bishops also officers of the state? Had not their political offices been originally conferred upon them by German rulers, with Church approval? Was not the monarch's right to control their appointment constitutionally established by long-standing legal custom in both Church and State? Both sides in the investiture controversy looked upon society as one big family with common goals and interests. For the more secular-minded, the father of this family was the anointed and crowned lay monarch, who had religious as well as political power. For the more religious-minded, however, the father of the Christian family was the Pope. In their view, although the Pope's power was primarily religious, he had the right and obligation to intervene in the political sphere and remove lay officials when necessary to safeguard the spiritual interests of his flock. Gregory VII in particular had very exalted ideas of Papal power, and its transcendence over that of secular monarchs.

Monarchical insistence

While Henry IV was still entangled in the throes of the third Saxon rebellion (1074–1075), Gregory VII, at his Lenten synod in February 1075, excommunicated Henry's chief counselors and issued his famous Decree Against Lay Investiture. This declared that further conferral of ecclesiastical offices by lay persons was illegal and invalid, and that both lay persons presuming to confer church offices and clerics accepting such offices from lay persons were excommunicated. If strictly enforced, Gregory's prohibition would have deprived the German monarchy of a principal support of its power.

Papal prohibition of lay investiture

Not long after Gregory's issuance of the Decree Against Lay Investiture, Henry emerged completely victorious from his third struggle with the Saxons. Disregarding Gregory's prohibition and remonstrances, Henry continued to name and invest his own candidates for episcopal offices in Germany and Italy. Particularly challenging was his appointment of an Archbishop of Milan, passing over both the Papal-Patarin (popular) pro-reform candidate and the anti-reform candidate of the local clergy. Faced with a direct challenge in his "front yard," Gregory brought gradual pressure to bear in an effort to bring Henry to change his course. He wrote to the King in December 1075 urging him to dissociate himself from his counselors, and protesting Henry's appointments of bishops for Milan, Fermo, and Spoleto. He urged Henry to amend his ways, and offered to discuss modification of the decree; but he directed his legates to threaten Henry with excommunication and deposition if he continued his defiance.

Henry's defiance

Henry's reply was to throw down the gauntlet. He called his bishops together (January 1076) and they jointly condemned Gregory's action and called upon him to relinquish the tiara. Henry's letter to "Hildebrand" addressed the latter as "neither true Pope nor true monk," and went on to declare that Henry had received his kingly authority from God, who alone could take it from him. He concluded by demanding that Hildebrand resign: *Descend and relinquish the apostolic chair which you have usurped.* This charge of usurpation was made on the basis of alleged irregularities in the unanimous popular election of Gregory VII, as well as his failure to obtain imperial confirmation.

Gregory took his threatened action. In the name of St. Peter, he excommunicated Henry IV, and released Henry's subjects from obligations to him. Gregory thus took the unprecedented step of revoking the authority of a Christian king and gave Papal endorsement to the theory that the monarchy was elective and deposable. The Papal thunderbolt was succeeded by a general uprising of Henry's opponents and the advocates of princely power. Most of Henry's former supporters among the princes melted away, although several towns, indebted to Henry for his support and privileges, remained loyal. The princes met at Tribur (1076), declared Henry suspended from office as long as he was excommunicated, and summoned him to appear to be judged the following year at Worms. They invited Gregory VII to attend and participate in the judgment, and declared that unless Henry was absolved within a year he was to lose the throne.

Canossa (1077)

Henry shrewdly decided that he would go to Italy and obtain absolution from the Pope, and thus forestall the princes. In the depth of winter, with only a handful of followers, he made his way across the snow-covered Alps to the castle of Canossa, where Gregory VII had stopped to await a princely escort, which was to convey him to the meeting in Germany. Henry appeared as a humble penitent on three successive days in the courtyard of the castle before he was finally admitted to see the Pope. Although desiring to withhold judgment, Gregory VII was prevailed upon by the entreaties of his companions, as well as by his obligation as a minister of Christ to forgive a repentant sinner. Accepting Henry's protestations and his solemn promises to mend his ways, Gregory absolved the King and released him from his excommunication. The episode at Canossa was on the one hand a dramatic display of the moral power of the Papacy. But on the other hand it was a realistic victory for the deceptive diplomacy of Henry IV. At the price of external humility and temporary submission, Henry regained his throne, thwarted his opponents, and drove a deep wedge of distrust between the Pope and the German princes, who considered themselves bypassed and betrayed.

Henry's temporary recovery

Henry returned to Germany, reasserted his authority, and soon resumed his old ways. Many of the princes, however, refused to be swayed, and met at Forscheim (1077), where they elected Duke Rudolph of Suabia as anti-king. For some time, Gregory VII withheld his decision. Finally, as Rudolph's cause was slipping, and Henry obstinately continued his defiance, Gregory again excommunicated Henry (1080). But this time the

The Western Empire

Papal fulmination backfired, since most of the princes were apathetic, many German bishops declared Gregory deposed, and several Italian bishops elected an Anti-Pope (Guibert) as Clement III, who was supported by Henry. After Rudolph died as the result of a wound suffered in battle, the anti-Henrician party elected Count Herman of Salm, who never made notable progress and soon withdrew.

In 1081, Henry invaded Italy (1081–1084) and advanced upon Rome. After besieging the city three times, he finally gained entrance and forced Gregory to take refuge in the Castle of Sant'Angelo. Gregory called upon the Normans for help; and as Robert Guiscard with a large army advanced, Henry was obliged to withdraw. Once in the city, the Normans subjected Rome to a cruel sacking. Because of Roman wrath, Gregory was forced to accompany the Normans when they withdrew. Broken in health and spirit, he expired at Salerno (1085), saying with the psalmist: "I have loved justice and hated iniquity: therefore I die in exile."

With the field temporarily cleared, Henry IV was for a few years in the ascendance; but his victory was not final. Some of the German princes obstinately refused to submit, the Papacy continued resistance, the Countess Mathilda of Tuscany joined forces with the Welfs of Bavaria in support of the Papacy, and the King's own sons opposed him. *Henry IV overcome*

The diplomatic Urban II overcame the Anti-Pope and was universally recognized as Pope. As the opposition to Henry regained momentum, Henry's son Conrad was induced to become a candidate for the throne (1093ff.), and after his death (1104) the King's younger son, Henry V, joined the opposition (1104–1106). Henry V took his father prisoner by treachery, but the old king escaped. Finally Henry IV died at Liege in 1106, deserted by practically all his supporters save the Rhenish towns and the princes of Lorraine.

Although Henry IV died a seeming failure, his policies were soon resumed by his son. Unfortunately one of Henry IV's most "modern" and promising policies—his alliance with the towns—was abandoned by most of his successors.

The new king, Henry V, was cold and unscrupulous. To obtain English aid he married Mathilda, the daughter of Henry I of England. As a price for the support of the princes during his revolt against his father, Henry V recognized their partnership in the government of his realms. By accepting the throne from the princes prior to the death of his father, he implicitly agreed that the kingship was both elective and deposable. At the time, he acknowledged, apparently as a partial price, that *The removal of an individual from power can be repaired, even if he be head of state; but the overthrow of the princes would be the destruction of the kingdom.* For some time, all the important acts of the government, such as the appointment of bishops, were done "with the counsel of the princes." *Henry V (1106– 1125)*

Although Henry V initially laid claim to the throne with the support of Pope Paschal II, he soon resumed the old imperial policy of naming and investing bishops. He made several efforts to arrive at some suitable compromise with Paschal II, but without success. In 1108, Paschal reissued a general condemnation of lay investiture, excommunicating both the giver and the recipient.

Proposal of Paschal II

In 1110, Henry V descended into Italy with a large army for the double purpose of obtaining the imperial crown and obtaining a satisfactory solution to the investiture problem. Pope Paschal II now came up with an astounding offer: if Henry V would give up all ecclesiastical investiture, the Church would relinquish all the political offices and *regalia* (royal appurtenances) acquired since the time of Charlemagne and Louis the Pious. This offer was eagerly accepted by the King at Sutri (1111).

But when the Concordat of Sutri was announced in St. Peter's as a preliminary to the imperial coronation, such a tumult of protest, led by churchmen and nobles, ensued that a riot developed. The Emperor withdrew with the Pope and several Cardinals in his custody. Paschal II was held a prisoner for two months, and was prevailed upon to comply with the demands of the Emperor, which included imperial investiture of bishops with the ring and the staff prior to consecration. After the Emperor had returned to Germany, Paschal II, under pressure from all sides and disillusioned as to Henry's sincerity, renounced his concession of lay investiture on the grounds that Henry had exacted it by threat of force (1112). The Italian, German, and French bishops would not accept the Pope's simplistic solution.

In today's world, Paschal's original proposition would seem a reasonable solution. But in that day Paschal's radical solution, overturning long-established customs, and disrupting an existing order of society, was regarded as recklessly precipitous and dangerous. The Church would too suddenly lose its extensive properties and powers, while monarchical power would be excessively swollen by all that the Church surrendered. For this reason, the aristocracy and churchmen were strongly opposed. Furthermore there was no assurance that the unscrupulous Henry would keep his word.

Renewed conflict

In 1116 Countess Mathilda of Tuscany died, after having willed her personal possessions to the Papacy and the lands she held of the Empire to Henry V. When Henry V summarily occupied all Mathilda's lands without regard for Papal claims to a part of the inheritance, Paschal II, his frayed patience exhausted, excommunicated Henry (1116).

Just as the interests of the monarchy led Henry V to disagree with his former ally the Pope, so they finally brought him to break with his former comrades, the princes. After a period of cooperation with the princes (to about 1112), Henry began insisting on royal rights relative to courts, castles, monasteries, and churches, and resumed the Franconian use of *ministeriales* and exaction of servile dues. And just as these monarchical policies revived the investiture controversy, so they rearoused the princes to rebellion, resurrecting the alliance of the princes and the Papacy. There were three serious rebellions of the princes against Henry V: 1112–1113, 1114–1115, and 1118–1121. The Saxons and their Duke Lothar were a party to each; and Archbishop Adalbert of Mainz was also a prominent rebel. In general, the conflict was inconclusive.

The Western Empire

Meanwhile settlements of the investiture struggle had been arranged in France and England. These settlements were facilitated by the policy of Paschal II. While insisting on the abolition of lay investiture and maintenance of the formalities of canonical election, Paschal did not object to royal supervision, ratification, and indirect control of ecclesiastical elections, nor did he balk at episcopal oaths of fealty to secular monarchs. There was also a growing realization of the necessary distinction between the religious office of bishops, conferred by the Church, and their political offices and functions, conferred by the secular authority.

In France: Because of the weakness of the feudal monarchy as well as the more diversified and fragmented control of ecclesiastical appointments in France, the investiture controversy there never reached serious proportions. By 1104, when the excommunicated King Philip I made his peace with the Papacy, a *modus agendi* had been worked out without formal agreement. According to the practice accepted by both sides, a free canonical election was allowed, but secular influence was not rigidly excluded. Ratification of the election by the secular authority was usually required; and, following ecclesiastical consecration, the recipient took an oath of fealty to the king or prince.

In England: Although the contest in England was more drawn out and involved, a solution was attained by 1107. The invasion and subjection of England by William the Conqueror had been authorized by the Papacy to end what was regarded as a schism. Since William (1066–1087) was in the process of reorganizing and reforming the Church in England with the help of competent Archbishop Lanfranc, Gregory VII did not insist on English conformity to his decrees concerning lay investiture. He knew that William I was not disposed to obey, and recognized that the English Church was being restored to health. However, the Conqueror's brash son, William II, Rufus (1087–1100), contrary to the practice of his father, indulged in outright simony and appointed unworthy men to ecclesiastical offices, bringing the issue to a head. Since Anselm, the new Archbishop of Canterbury, was adamant in demanding compliance, and William was equally insistent in refusing it, Anselm was twice driven into exile.

When Henry I appropriated the English throne, following the sudden death of his brother (1100), he was in need of all the support he could get, and found it advisable to recall the Archbishop from exile. But since both Anselm and Paschal II were at first bent on a strict interpretation of the prohibitions against lay investiture, to the extent of excluding the oath of fealty to the king, Anselm was again forced into exile. As Henry I did not wish a permanent estrangement, and Paschal II was willing to make some concessions, a compromise settlement was finally achieved in the Concordat of London (1107). Although the election of high Church officials was to be canonical, it was to take place in the royal palace, so that the king could voice opposition to a candidate and propose the election of his own nominee. The election had to be ratified by the king, and the person elected was to take an oath of fealty

Compromise settlements in France and England

before consecration. Thus, although the king was to have no part in the ecclesiastical investiture, he could still effectively control appointments to bishoprics, at least in a negative manner.

The Concordat of Worms (1122)

Vacillating Paschal II was succeeded by resolute Callixtus II, who started off by excommunicating Henry V, and had the advantage of a concurrent revolt of the German princes led by Lothar of Saxony (1118–1121). Peace feelers and negotiations began almost immediately; but it was not until after much sparring that representatives from both sides, aided by the mediation of the princes, agreed on a settlement that was formally accepted by the Emperor and Papal representatives at Worms in 1122.

According to the Concordat of Worms officials were to be canonically elected, (i.e., elected according to Church law) in the Germanies (as was also the case in France and England); but the Emperor or his representative could be present and make his will manifest. Following the election, the investiture with the *temporalia* or insignia of secular office (such as the scepter) was to be first performed by the Emperor, *after* which the investiture with the *spiritualia* or symbols of religious office (such as the ring and staff) was to be made by churchmen. The Emperor would thus be able to control both election and investiture in the Germanies, although he could not directly elect or confer the ecclesiastical office.

In Burgundy and Italy both the election and the investiture were to be much more independent, with the interests of the Church and the Pope paramount. The election was to be completely canonical without any interference by the secular authority. And the initial investiture was to be made by the ecclesiastical authorities with the spiritual insignia, although the incumbent was to seek and obtain imperial investiture with the temporal insignia within six months.

Outcome

The investiture settlement in the Empire was a compromise. Imperial authority and interests were safeguarded while, at the same time, ecclesiastical conferral of Church offices was maintained. The part played by the Emperor was greater in Germany, less in Burgundy and Italy. As time progressed, imperial influences in ecclesiastical appointments even in Germany diminished, and the Church became more independent of the central government. An increase of princely power was one of the ultimate results of the investiture contest. The elective nature and conditional tenure of the monarchical office were affirmed. The castles and feudal armies of local princes multiplied across the land, numerous princely privileges were asserted or usurped, and monarchical authority was everywhere undermined.

1125–1197　FIRST PHASE OF THE GUELPH VERSUS HOHENSTAUFEN CONTEST AND PARTIAL IMPERIAL SUCCESS.
Section 53.

We hold our kingdom and empire, not as a fief of the Pope, but from God alone by virtue of our election by the princes. [Frederick I, Barbarossa, in his general *Letter* after the Diet at Besançon in 1157.]

The Western Empire

GERMAN imperial history from 1125 to 1268 is dominated by the long Guelph versus Hohenstaufen struggle. Originally a contest between two German princely houses for the throne, the conflict became a complex one involving several groups with various objectives. The Guelph (Welf) family was based in the duchies of Saxony and Bavaria, which were notorious for their separatist tendencies. "Welf" was a common name among the Bavarian rulers from whom the house descended on the male side. Largely because the Guelphs were not in power most of the time, they were pro-princely, pro-Papal, and proregional, that is, for "states' rights." The independence-loving North Italian townspeople generally belonged to this party, which had the support of the English Plantagenets. The Hohenstaufen (Ghibelline or Waibling) party was based in Suabia and Franconia, and received its name from the family's ancestral castle (Hohenstaufen), and the little village near it (Waiblingen), located in Suabia. The Hohenstaufen, who were in power most of the time, were pro-imperialist and anti-Papal, and favored centralization, or fuller subjection of the princes, the towns, and the Church to the imperial government. The Hohenstaufen had the occasional, half-hearted support of the French Capetians.

Beginnings of the struggle: Lothar II (1125–1137)

The roots of the Guelph versus Hohenstaufen struggle trace back to the election of 1125, which followed the death of Henry V. Henry had designated his nephew, Frederick, Duke of Suabia, as his successor. But, because of the opposition of the Church party and the desire of the princes to assert their right of election and reduce monarchical power, the electors chose instead Lothar of Supplingen, Duke of Saxony.

Lothar II (1125–1137) had been a consistent opponent of Henry V. The bypassed candidate, Frederick of Suabia, who was supported by his brother Conrad, Duke of Franconia, felt that he had been robbed of what was rightfully his, as both the closer relative and designated successor of Henry V. When Lothar tried to deprive the Hohenstaufen of many of their holdings as lands rightly belonging to the crown, they rebelled. Although at first the civil war went against Lothar, it subsequently veered in his favor. Lothar's position was greatly strengthened by an alliance with Bavaria, confirmed by the marriage of his daughter Gertrude to the powerful and wealthy Henry the Proud, Duke of Bavaria.

Before his death, Lothar designated Henry the Proud as successor to the throne, and turned over to him the Duchy of Saxony.

Resumption of the struggle under Conrad III (1138–1152)

The princes were, however, fearful of Henry's great power and wanted to reassert their right of election. Consequently they elected instead Henry's Hohenstaufen rival, Conrad of Franconia, brother of the previously designated Frederick. Although pleasant, handsome, and brave, "a Paris in appearance, a Hector in battle,"[a] Conrad III was weak, indecisive, and vacillating, which shortcomings became glaringly apparent during the ill-fated Second Crusade.

Conrad's greatest problem was the fierce opposition of the Guelphs, who refused to accept his election. Conrad sought to prevent Henry the Proud's inheritance of Saxony, maintaining that one person could not hold two duchies, and appointed Albert the Bear to the Saxon Dukedom.

[a] Godfrey of Viterbo.

When Henry the Proud refused to submit, Conrad decreed that his punishment should be the further loss of the Dukedom of Bavaria, to which he appointed Leopold of Austria. A prolonged and complicated civil war over the possession of Saxony and Bavaria ensued. Henry the Proud was succeeded in 1139 by his energetic son Henry the Lion, who was generally recognized in Saxony by 1142, and who also fought to recover Bavaria.

Frederick I, Barbarossa (1152–1190)

On Conrad's death, the princes again asserted their right of election by passing over his son in favor of his nephew, Duke Frederick of Suabia. This time, however, they acted on behalf of greater unity and tranquility. Since Frederick was popular, and had both Welf and Ghibelline blood in his veins, he was regarded as a compromise choice, capable of restoring order. Frederick, whose nickname Barbarossa means "Red Beard," was tall, handsome, and affable, as well as diplomatic, high-minded, and decisive. He could be pleasant even in refusing favors. Although inspired by great dreams, he could adapt his course to the facts of the moment. Frederick's general aim was to restore unity and royal and imperial power. He and his advisers felt strongly that his power came directly from God, in which opinion they were supported by principles of Roman law, whose study was being revived at this time. Frederick also felt that the imperial power belonged to him and his predecessors by the right of conquest, although he was realistic and trimmed his sails to suit the circumstances.

Frederick I and Germany: First phase (1152–1176)

Frederick's policies relative to both Germany and Italy may be divided into two general phases: (1) until the Battle of Legnano in 1176, and (2) following that battle. Until 1176, Frederick's main concern in Germany was to restore peace and concord, and obtain the cooperation of the princes, without, however, sacrificing the royal dignity and authority. In this project he was aided by a general reaction against the anarchy of the preceding period.

Frederick conciliated his Guelph relatives by allowing Henry the Lion to keep both Saxony and Bavaria, and by conceding lands in Tuscany and Spoleto to the elder branch of the family. He compensated Henry Jasomirgott for the loss of Bavaria by raising his margravate of Austria to ducal status, and conferring on it broad privileges. He also declared a *Landfrieden* ("land peace") through Germany, whereby breaches of the peace were to be punished severely. The death penalty was decreed for more serious crimes such as murder and grand larceny. Private warfare was forbidden, except under certain conditions. Frederick insisted on royal rights relative to episcopal elections and monasteries, and invoked his authority to appoint the Archbishop of Magdeburg after a disputed election. In the disputes of the princes with the towns, he supported the former largely because he needed their military cooperation in Italy.

Frederick and the rest of the Empire

Imperial power was extended on peripheries of the Empire. Burgundy was brought more directly under imperial control. In 1153, Frederick divorced his first wife, Adelaide, apparently for reasons of state, and in 1156 he married the beautiful and wealthy Beatrice, heiress to the

The Western Empire

County of Burgundy, thus acquiring a solid base from which to rule the Kingdom of Burgundy, which also included the Lyonnais, the Dauphiné, Savoy, and Provence. Shortly afterward, to put Burgundian affairs in order, he held his famous Diet at Besançon (1157). Bohemia was a docile vassal-state, which Frederick I recognized as a permanent kingdom; Hungary accepted German overlordship; and the King of Poland was forced to resume payment of tribute.

Italy occupied an important place in the plans of Barbarossa, who was resolved to restore and enhance imperial authority in northern Italy. as well as to exercise supervision over the Papal States, and, if possible, over the Papacy itself. Frederick, in short, aimed to be a real Emperor in Italy. These ambitions brought him into conflict with both the rising Italian communes and the Papacy, and necessitated six Italian expeditions. They also brought about a revival of the Guelf versus Hohenstaufen struggle.

Within two years after his accession, Frederick made his first expedition to Italy in order to assert imperial authority, restore peace and order, and obtain coronation as Emperor. As he proceeded through northern Italy, he encountered sullen resentment and open defiance. Finding himself unable to subdue hostile Milan, he destroyed various of its outlying castles, and razed its ally, Tortona, as a warning. On his way to Rome, Frederick was met by the English Pope, Adrian IV (1154-1159). But when Frederick declined to hold the Pope's bridle and help him to dismount in the usual manner, Adrian refused to give Frederick the kiss of peace. Negotiations continued for two days, until Frederick agreed to perform the customary service on being assured that the precedent had been set by Charlemagne. He and Adrian now proceeded to Rome. On being met by a magniloquent deputation from the Roman Senate, who insinuated that they could refuse to admit Frederick to Rome and prevent him from being crowned Emperor, Barbarossa refused to accept this theory. Frederick was crowned Emperor by Adrian, and meanwhile obtained the revolutionary leader, Arnold of Brescia, from a compliant baron and turned him over to the Papal government to be hanged. After a clash between his soldiers and the Romans, Frederick, whose troops were weakened by fever, returned to Germany. Following his withdrawal, Milan and her allies became more defiant, and the Emperor's relations with the Pope deteriorated.

First Italian expedition (1154–1155) and Adrian IV

In 1157, while Frederick was holding a reorganizational diet at Besançon in Burgundy, two cardinal-legates came from the Pope, protesting unpunished German mistreatment of the Archbishop of Lund during his return from Rome. At one point, the Papal letter spoke of the *beneficia* (benefices or benefits) the Pope had conferred on the Emperor. Since these were technical terms in the feudal system for the award of dependent fiefs, a tumult of protest arose from Frederick's court. One of the two Papal legates, Cardinal Roland, made matters worse by asking: "From whom does the Emperor hold the Empire, if not from the Pope?" Frederick saved Roland from being run through by the sword of the

The Besançon incident (1157)

indignant Otto of Wittelsbach by throwing the imperial cloak over the Cardinal. Frederick now circulated a public manifesto insisting that he derived his power directly from God alone: *The Divine power, from which comes all power in heaven and on earth, has committed to us, his anointed, the kingdom and empire to be ruled over* . . . . [and] *The kingdom, together with the empire, is ours by the election of the princes and from God alone.* . . . So great was the protest and so general the German opposition that Pope Adrian soon wrote (1158) to the Emperor that by *"beneficium"* he meant "not a fief" but a *"bonum factum"* or a "good deed" or "blessing" in the form of the imperial crown as a mark of the imperial dignity, which he had not "conferred" but "implaced" on Frederick, and Frederick accepted this explanation.

Second Italian expedition and Diet of Roncaglia

On his first expedition Frederick had learned what to expect in Italy. In 1158, he crossed the Alps into Lombardy with a great army, determined to assert his authority. Although many of the Italian communes were cowed into submission, Milan and her allies refused to bend. After taking lesser places, Frederick suddenly laid siege to Milan, and forced the city to capitulate within a month. His terms at this point were moderate though strict.

With Lombardy at his feet, Frederick held the Diet of Roncaglia (1158), which was attended by representatives from twenty-eight towns. Four jurists from Bologna, already noted for its revived study of Roman law, were also present. At the Emperor's request, the jurists outlined the *regalia* or prerogatives customarily reserved to the imperial government by Roman law, and the Council accepted the reservation of these sovereign rights to the Emperor. These rights, as recorded by Rahewin, included: *the right to appoint dukes, marquises, counts, and consuls* [in the towns]; *to coin money; to levy tolls; to collect the fodrum* [a tax in kind or money for the support of the imperial army when operating in Italy]; *to collect customs and harbor-dues; to provide safe-conducts; to control mills, fishponds, bridges, and water-ways; and to require a tax levied both on real property and on each person every year.* Frederick also asserted his intention to appoint superintendents known as *podestas* to supervise the government of the towns, and judges for districts. In addition, the jurists proclaimed the principle of late Roman law that *The prince's will has the force of law.*

Frederick was now at the height of his power in northern Italy. But the townspeople soon realized that many of the liberties and privileges they had labored so long to acquire had been lost. Friction rapidly developed between them and the *podestas* appointed by Frederick to oversee the towns, and the embers of resentment flared into open revolts.

Frederick, who was still in Italy, proceeded to suppress the revolts. Crema was ordered to destroy its walls, and when its citizens refused the town was leveled. Milan, was besieged for a year (1161–1162) until its starving inhabitants surrendered, after which the city was reduced to ashes and its populace forced to move to neighboring localities.

Pope Alexander III

After the death of Adrian IV in 1159, there were two parties among the Cardinals. The rigorists, who were in the majority, held for insistence on full Papal prerogatives and complete Church independence; whereas the moderates favored more conciliatory policies and compromise. The rigorists elected Cardinal Roland of Besançon fame, who took the name of Alexander III, and thus virtually waved a red flag before the Emperor. The compromisers and imperial supporters, who were in a minority among the Cardinals, withdrew and elected their own candidate, Cardinal Octavian, who took the name of Victor IV. Pretending impartiality, Frederick called a Council at Pavia (1160) to decide the issue. Alexander III refused to appear, saying that he had been duly elected and could not be judged or deposed by any human authority. But Victor IV appeared and defended himself, and the pro-Imperial Council of Pavia decided in his favor. Frederick supported the Anti-Pope, on whose behalf the courts of Europe were solicited, but eventually the Catholic world outside of Germany almost universally supported Alexander.

After Frederick again returned to Germany, the Italian towns renewed their resistance, rebuilt their walls, and girded themselves for conflict. They began to form leagues, such as the League of Verona (1164ff.), in order to put up a united front against the Emperor. Frederick's third Italian expedition (1162–1163) was too small to be effective. His large fourth Italian expedition (1166–1167) successfully took Rome and installed Anti-Pope Paschal III, who had been elected on the death of Victor IV in 1164, but Alexander III managed to escape. At the height of its military successes, however, the army of Frederick Barbarossa was seized by a deadly epidemic. So great were the casualties that Frederick withdrew, making his journey across northern Italy disguised as a peasant. *The Italian leagues and battle of Legnano (1176)*

It seemed that Frederick was being punished by God for his presumption, and Italian resistance revived. The Lombard League of northern Italian cities was formed in 1167, and soon joined forces with the League of Verona, coming to include most of the cities of Lombardy, Venetia, and the Piedmont. Pope Alexander III also joined the coalition, and a new, strongly fortified city named Alessandria, in honor of the Pope, was built astride the main route into Italy.

Frederick, bent on reestablishing his authority, descended into Italy with a large army in his fifth Italian expedition (1174–1178). After destroying Susa, Frederick besieged Alessandria, but abandoned the siege after six fruitless months. Since the allies had meanwhile gathered their forces, Frederick, feeling the need for further reinforcements, in a meeting at Chiavenna (1176) reportedly on bended knee implored Henry the Lion, who had refused to take part in this expedition, to come to his assistance. Henry refused, although he did send some reinforcements. In the decisive battle of Legnano later the same year (1176), at first the heavy cavalry of the Germans seemed to be winning. But the Italians held firm around their *carroccio*, a rallying point consisting of an ox-drawn wagon carrying a flag. After Frederick I was unhorsed, the Italians gained the advantage and won the day. The Milanese reported: *We have won a glorious victory over our enemies. The number of the slain and those drowned or taken prisoner is incomprehensible.*

The High Middle Ages

Frederick I and Italy after 1176

Following his defeat at Legnano, Frederick immediately set about adapting his policies to the new realities. First he resolved to establish peace on the most favorable terms possible, to do which he must separate the Pope from the communes. Patiently and cleverly he brought Alexander to conclude a separate peace at Venice (1177). As Frederick met the Pope at the entrance of St. Mark's Cathedral, he fell to his knees; but Alexander raised him up and embraced him. Frederick recognized Alexander III as the true Pope; and also accepted his independent right to appoint the Prefect of Rome.

A temporary truce was arranged with the Lombard communes, but a formal peace was not concluded until six years later. This permitted the advantage won by the towns at Legnano to dwindle, and their old mutual disagreements and enmities to resume. When peace was finally concluded at Constance (1183), Frederick was in a much more favorable position. The Emperor acknowledged the right of the towns to elect their own officials, follow their own laws, conduct courts, levy internal taxes, fortify themselves, and exercise their old *regalia* within their walls. On the other hand, the towns accepted the sovereignty of the Emperor, agreed to make contributions toward his campaigns in Italy (the *fodrum*), and recognized the right of appeal to the imperial courts as well as the Emperor's right to approve and invest the consuls they elected.

Compensation

Blocked from achieving his fuller purposes in northern Italy, Frederick now turned to Tuscany and the Romagna in north central Italy, as well as Ancona and Spoleto farther south. Here he sought to apply the plan that he had failed to accomplish in Lombardy. He organized the territory into districts and subdistricts, presided over by a hierarchy of imperial officials; and exacted a hearth tax as well as collected customs and tolls. He also acquired much of the Mathildine inheritance from the older branch of the Guelph family by purchase.

South of the Papal States, Frederick scored a dramatic victory. In 1177, he concluded a fifteen years' truce with his old rival, the childless King William II of Sicily, and obtained the hand of William's aunt and prospective heiress, Constance, for his son Henry VI, whom Frederick had already associated with himself in the government of Germany and Italy. Henry was married to Constance with great ceremony in 1186, and the German dream of dominating Italy seemed on the road to achievement.

Frederick and Germany after 1176: Humbling of Henry the Lion

After Legnano, Frederick's policy in Germany also changed. The crisis in northern Italy had disrupted the Emperor's friendship with Henry the Lion, and had brought into clear relief the latter's rivalry. Frederick felt that Henry was partly responsible for his humiliating defeat at Legnano. Meanwhile numerous complaints had been raised against the ambitious, grasping Henry, who was building up an ever-expanding, semi-independent state in northern Germany. Henry had pushed the conquest of the Slavs, the building of cities, the expansion of trade, and the development of agriculture beyond the Elbe. In his newly acquired territory, he appointed bishops without reference to any further authority, acted as an independent sovereign, and reportedly declared: *Here I am lord: and neither emperor nor archbishop has anything to say.* Besides conquering and subjecting the Slavs, destroying their strongholds, and building German fortresses, he brought in German, Frisian, and Flemish colonists, and settled them in the territory.

In his relentless drive for power, Henry became careless of the rights and interests of his subjects and neighbors as well as those of the Church, and numerous complaints were lodged against him. Much opposition also resulted from his support of the rising towns against the bishops and nobles.

Eventually Frederick's courts took up the charges brought by a Saxon bishop and a Saxon noble against the hard-riding Henry. But the haughty northern Duke refused to appear at Frederick's court, despite repeated summons. Whereupon his imperial fiefs were declared forfeit, and Frederick, who had taken the precaution of insuring the cooperation of the greater princes by preliminary concessions, proceeded against Henry. At first Henry the Lion held out successfully, and even won minor victories. But when the Emperor, with general support, brought the full weight of his forces against the Duke (1187), the latter's resistance crumbled, and his supporters melted away. Henry the Lion was deprived of his great duchies of Saxony and Bavaria, but was allowed to keep his ancestral possessions of Brunswick and Lüneburg. He was also obliged to go into three years of exile.

Previous to his confiscation of Henry's fiefs, Frederick had agreed to reallocate them. But in doing so he subdivided them so as diminish their threat to the crown. From the Duchy of Saxony he detached the western part (west of the Weser) or Westphalia, as well as various Church fiefs. Westphalia was given to the Archbishop of Cologne, and the diminished Saxony to the son of Albert the Bear. Similarly Styria was separated from the Duchy of Bavaria, which was given to Otto of Wittelsbach. *Concessions and feudalization*

Frederick also supported the princes in their contests with the towns, decreeing that those persons who dwelt in the environs or suburbs of the towns (*Pfahlburgers*) were not entitled to the same exemptions as those citizens who dwelt in the towns.

Barbarossa promoted the feudal articulation of Germany. The princes of the kingdom (*Reichsfürsten*) were singled out and accorded special privileges that set them above the lesser lords, while princely status was extended to many who had never before enjoyed it. At the apex of the theoretical pyramid was the monarch. Feudal practices were invoked and it was as a contumacious vassal that Henry the Lion was declared to have forfeited his fiefs.

Participating in the Third Crusade, Frederick was accidentally drowned in the Saleph River in Asia Minor.

Der alte Kaiser (the old Emperor), *Frederic Rotbard* (the Red-Bearded Frederick) became a favorite hero of German folk song and legend. According to one version, he was in a mountainous cave, whence he would one day return to reunite his people. Frederick had gone far towards reviving monarchical authority both in Germany and in Italy, but certain flaws marred his successes. He had relied excessively on the undependable support of the princes, in enhancing whose power he had *Evaluation*

Henry VI (1190–1197)

forfeited the support of the towns; and he had paid excessive attention to Italy, suggesting to his successors a similar policy, which was to be their undoing.

For a brief period the fruition of Frederick I's work seemed to come under his son Henry VI (1190–1197).

In Germany, Henry put down the new Guelph uprising stirred up by Henry the Lion that had broken out on Frederick's departure. Although revolt was renewed in more serious form in 1192 under the leadership of the Archbishop of Cologne, with the support of a broad spectrum of German princes, it was subdued by 1194, largely by diplomacy.

By concessions to the Pope, Henry obtained imperial coronation in 1191. But for some time he was unable to gain control of Sicily, where Tancred of Lecce, an illegitimate grandson of the former Norman ruler, Roger II, was crowned at Palermo in 1190. Tancred obtained the support of Richard I of England, who was on his way to the Holy Land, and effectively ruled Sicily until his death in 1194. But Richard I was taken prisoner in Germany in 1192 and turned over to Henry in 1193. The English King was compelled to raise a huge ransom and take an oath of vassalage with a pledge of nonresistance to Henry as the price of his release. With the ransom money and a large army, Henry was able to overthrow and take captive Tancred's weak son, William III, and secure the Sicilian throne. With his power well established, Henry planned his most ambitious project: a great Crusade. While the ostensible object of this Crusade was to reestablish Western control over Palestine and Syria, many felt that its primary objective was to be the Byzantine Empire, which was disrupted by internal dissension. But suddenly, at the height of his power, Henry VI—at only 33 years of age—fell sick and died.

1197–1273

FINAL PHASE OF THE GUELPH VERSUS HOHENSTAUFEN CONTEST AND FAILURE OF THE EMPIRE.
Section 54.

> This pestilential monarch had proclaimed . . . that the whole world has been duped by three deceivers: Jesus Christ, Moses, and Mohammed. [Pope Gregory IX concerning Emperor Frederick II.]

GERMANY suffered in the wake of the early death of Henry VI. Two decades of ruinous civil war (1197–1215) were followed by over three decades of disastrous misrule under absentee Frederick II (1215–1250), succeeded in turn by two and a half decades of anarchy (1250–1273). Frederick II sealed the disintegration of Germany by his prodigal disbursement of sovereign powers to the German princes, whose cooperation he sought for his ambitious Italian projects. When his Italian designs failed, his successors were left empty-handed. Hohenstaufen attempts to dominate Italy so alienated the Papacy that it determined to crush this "viperous brood," a purpose finally accomplished by 1268.

Civil war (1197–1215)

Since Henry's son and heir, Frederick, who was living in the Kingdom of Sicily, was only two years old at his father's death, Hohenstaufen supporters, including a majority of the princes, now elected the late King's younger brother, Philip of Suabia, to succeed him (1198). Philip, who accepted only after urging the rights of his nephew, was handsome and likable, mild and affable—perhaps too much so for his own good. The Guelph supporters, on the other hand, elected Otto of Brunswick, a younger son of Henry the Lion, as anti-king (1198). Although brave and warlike, Otto was dull, boorish, and bungling. A definite help, however, was the support of his uncle, Richard the Lionhearted of England.

Otto versus Philip

Civil war ensued. Since the Guelphs had English financial support and the Hohenstaufen that of the French, the struggle has been described as "the pound sterling versus the livre tournais." Fortune favored first one side and then the other. Innocent III delayed declaration of his choice until Otto seemed to be losing, and then his support for Otto was a temporarily effective shot in the arm to the latter's cause. But when Philip gained ground and seemed on the threshold of victory, Innocent began to negotiate, apparently with a view of recognizing him. Suddenly, however, Philip was assassinated by Otto of Wittelsbach because of a personal grudge (1208).

Otto of Brunswick was left alone in the field, victorious; but he soon lost Papal support as he began to break his pledges to Innocent and to assert control of the Church in Germany. One of his greatest offenses, in Innocent's eyes, was trespassing on Papal spheres of influence by invading Tuscany and southern Italy. Innocent III was determined that no emperor should encompass the Papal States by direct control of southern Italy and Sicily. Consequently, Innocent repudiated Otto IV and transferred his support to Frederick of Hohenstaufen (1210), after first obtaining from the latter pledges to relinquish direct rule of the Kingdom of Sicily, to go on a Crusade, and to respect the freedom of the Church. Innocent obtained the support of Philip II of France for Frederick, and arranged for Frederick's election by Hohenstaufen supporters in Germany (1211). Meanwhile Otto IV allied with John of England, who was attempting to recover his previous holdings in northern France from Philip II. Otto's defeat by Philip II at Bouvines (1214) was decisive. By the following year Otto's supporters melted away and Frederick II was supreme in Germany, being recrowned at Aachen in 1215. But the German monarchy had lost considerable ground during the two decades of civil war.

Otto opposed by Frederick II (1210–1215)

Frederick II, son of Henry VI and Constance of Sicily, and King of Sicily, had been made a ward of Pope Innocent III by his solicitous mother. Reared amid the intrigues of a long regency and civil war, Frederick had become wary and skeptical. Interested in science and learning, he wrote an extraordinary book *On Falconry*, a general study of several birds and their habits. He kept men of learning, such as Michael Scot, at his court, which also became famous as an Italian center for lyric poetry of the Provencal type. Partly as a result of his upbringing, and unrelenting Italian and Papal opposition to his designs, Frederick II became obstinate, cynical, and unscrupulous. His three successive wives suffered from his cruelty, as did his eldest son, Henry VII. Brought up in southern Italy and Sicily, Frederick was more Italian than German. He was also strongly

Frederick II (1215–1250)

influenced by Moslem and Byzantine customs. He kept a troop of dancing girls, regarded by many as his harem, and took along on his travels a menagerie of strange animals, including elephants and camels. Frederick was a strong believer in monarchical absolutism and was skeptical of Church doctrines.

Frederick concentrated on building up his power in Italy to the detriment of his power in Germany. He is said to have abhorred the cold, moist, overcast German climate, which contrasted with the warm and sunny climate of his native southern Italy and Sicily. He spent only ten years of his life in Germany, and was willing to make almost any concessions there to win German military support for his projects in Italy. Whereas he allowed the Germans maximum autonomy, he pursued absolute power in Italy. His Italian policy necessitated the subjection and control of both northern and southern Italy, with central Italy probably destined for the same fate. He was consequently opposed by the Papacy.

Frederick II and Germany: His concessions

In order to gain their support, Frederick II made extensive concessions to the German princes. Notwithstanding his pledges to the Papacy, he employed every wile to retain the crown of Sicily, along with the North Italian crown and the title of Emperor, for himself, with a son as co-King of Germany. To this end, Frederick finally persuaded the German princes to elect his son Henry VII King of Germany in 1220, partly by means of his "Concession in Favor of the Ecclesiastical Princes." Already in 1213, shortly after he became a candidate for the German throne, Frederick had solicited the favor of the ecclesiastical princes by his so-called Golden Bull of Eger, according to which the Church in Germany was almost entirely emancipated from imperial control, and enjoyed freedom of ecclesiastical elections.

By his Concession in Favor of the Ecclesiastical Princes (1220) and his Statute in Favor of the Lay Princes (1231-1232), Frederick II renounced the right to erect new castles, constitute new towns, grant urban charters, impose new tolls, or establish new mints in the territories of the princes without their consent. He also recognized existing mints, tolls, jurisdictions, and the like possessed by the ecclesiastical princes in their territories. The princes were referred to as "lords of the land" or "territorial lords," and the officials of the counties and hundreds were to be directly subject to them rather than to the Emperor. Towns were not to exercise jurisdiction over persons living in their suburbs (*Pfahlburgers*), nor harbor escaped serfs or other fugitives from princely authority. The lay and ecclesiastical princes in Germany thus became practically independent territorial sovereigns.

His father's interference in the government of Germany and prodigal alienation of the rights of the German crown, together with his own impetuosity, led young Henry VII to revolt against Frederick II in 1234-1235. However, Henry fatally miscalculated, because the interests of the German princes, both lay and ecclesiastical, were vested in a continuation of the indulgent policies of Frederick II. When Frederick came to Germany in 1235, he easily overthrew Henry VII, whom he replaced with a younger son, Conrad IV (1235ff.).

The Western Empire

Frederick II and the Papacy and Italy to 1227

The main concern of Frederick II was to obtain strong and effective control in Italy, to which end his other policies were subordinated. This adamant purpose brought Frederick into conflict with the Papacy. Frederick's offenses, in Papal eyes, included his refusal to observe his promise to give up the direct rule of the Kingdom of Sicily, his encroachments on territories claimed by the Papacy, and his prolonged failure to fulfill his vow to go on a Crusade. Added to these infractions were Frederick's refusal to allow freedom of ecclesiastical elections, his evident designs upon the Papal States, and his example of irreligion and immorality.

Innocent III, who might have kept his former ward in check, died within a year (1216) after Frederick's victory in Germany. Innocent's successor, the mild Honorius III, overlooked Frederick's unwillingness to give up the Sicilian throne and his postponements of his promised Crusade. Honorius' patience was sorely tried, however, when Frederick's failure to participate contributed to the failure of the Fifth Crusade (1217–1221), and when he had his son Henry proclaimed King of Germany by the German princes (1220). The Pope was somewhat mollified by Frederick's promises to surrender the Mathildine lands in Tuscany, respect Papal sovereignty in the States of the Church, exempt the German Church from imperial control, and go on a Crusade by 1227 under pain of excommunication. Frederick's attempt to bring the Lombard communes to heel failed, for they formed a second Lombard League and successfully resisted him (1226).

Frederick II and Gregory IX (1227–1241): Frederick's Crusade

The next Pope, Gregory IX, was a fiery, determined champion of Papal rights, whose first act was to insist that Frederick go on a Crusade that very year (1227) as promised. Frederick, who had meanwhile married Yolande, heiress to the Latin Kingdom of Jerusalem, seemed about to fulfill his vow. The Crusade was assembled, and Frederick set out. But his ship soon returned on the plea that the Emperor had taken ill and needed respite to recover. Although Frederick's excuse seemed genuine enough, Gregory IX declared him excommunicated (1228). Even though Frederick went on the Crusade the following year (1229), Gregory still refused to lift the excommunication. By diplomatic bargaining with Sultan al-Kamil of Egypt, Frederick obtained possession of Jerusalem and the holy places, together with a corridor of access. But Frederick soon alienated the local baronage and clergy, and he was crowned King of Jerusalem without enthusiasm, after which he soon sailed for Italy.

Reorganization of southern Italy

Frederick departed early from Jerusalem because of an invasion of southern Italy by Papal troops. On his return to Italy, Frederick speedily recovered occupied cities and alienated territories, and made the Treaty of San Germano (1230) with the Papacy on the basis of mutual concessions, including a lifting of Frederick's excommunication. Following this success, Frederick proceeded to regularize the administrative and legal system of his southern kingdom by means of the so-called Constitutions of Melfi (1231), which formalized a highly centralized, carefully organized, bureaucratic, "modern" type of state. Divine right absolutism was officially enunciated; a professional bureaucracy and professional judges were established; a standing mercenary army was constituted; and a regular system of courts with free justice for the needy was ordained. The Kingdom was divided into two vicariates: (1) southern Italy and (2) Sicily (with Calabria); and regulations were laid down for such things as the licensing of physicians. Frederick improved roads and bridges, encouraged industry and commerce, issued gold coins known as *augustales*, and promoted agriculture, as by introducing Eastern plants.

Temporary subjection of northern Italy and new break with the Papacy

Frederick next proceeded with his plans relative to northern Italy. He proclaimed that Italy was to "reenter the unity of the Empire," and that both Lombardy and Tuscany were to be truly subject to their Emperor. After marching across Papal territories without Papal permission, Frederick won a smashing victory over the Lombard towns at Cortenuova (1237). He then imposed upon northern Italy a centralized administrative system similar to that in his Kingdom of Sicily. The territory was divided into larger vicariates general under vicars general, and these were subdivided into vicariates whose vicars appointed judges for districts and captains for cities. The victorious Frederick apparently intended to extend a similar system through the Papal States. Without Papal permission, he installed his son Enzio as King of Sardinia, which the Pope considered a Papal fief. Frederick's presumption precipitated a new break with Pope Gregory IX, who excommunicated him a second time (1239). In an exchange of bitter denunciations, Gregory referred to Frederick as "a scorpion," "King of the Pestilence," and a "heretic" who denied both the virgin birth and the divinity of Christ; while Frederick denounced the Pope as a "madman," a "roaring lion," an "infidel," and "Anti-Christ." When Gregory IX attempted to summon an ecumenical council to meet in Rome, Frederick intercepted the Genoese vessels that were transporting many of the bishops, and effectively prevented the proposed meeting.

Frederick and Innocent IV (1243ff.): Final failure

Pope Gregory IX died in 1241. Following the seventeen-day Pontificate of Clestine IV, the Cardinals left the Papal throne vacant for nineteen months, while Frederick labored to obtain a candidate favorable to his interests. Eventually the Genoese Innocent IV was elected. Although at first Frederick thought the new Pope would be friendly, he subsequently observed that "no Pope can be a good Ghibelline!" Innocent IV was a wily diplomat and a persistent opponent. While feigning willingness to come to an understanding with Frederick, he escaped from Rome. Disguised as a soldier, he made his way to the port of Civitaveccia, whence he proceeded by sea to his native Genoa and thence to Lyons. Here, under French protection, Innocent IV held the First Ecumenical Council of Lyons (1245), and persuaded the assembled fathers to declare Frederick excommunicated and deposed. The Pope preached a "crusade" against Frederick, whose efforts to effect a reconciliation were fruitless. In Germany, the opposition party supported successive anti-kings against Frederick's son, Conrad IV. Although neither made much progress, they constituted a dangerous dagger held against the side of the Hohenstaufen dynasty.

Frederick's remaining years (1245–1250) were spent in continuing conflict with the Papacy and the North Italian towns. Innocent IV

The Western Empire

sternly refused to have any further negotiations with Frederick, who was badly defeated by the towns at Parma in 1248 and La Fossalta in 1249. As his military fortunes were beginning to improve, however, Frederick took sick, and he succumbed to dysentery in 1250.

Despite temporary successes, the career of the "amazing" Frederick ended in failure. As a result of the enmities he had aroused, Frederick dragged down with himself the rest of his dynasty. His son Enzio, captured in 1249, remained a prisoner of the Bolognese for the rest of his life. In Germany, the princes, at Papal urging, refused to acknowledge any further Frederick's son Conrad IV, whom Frederick had designated as his successor. Rejected in Germany, Conrad IV went to southern Italy in 1251 to help his illegitimate brother and viceroy, Manfred, overcome opposition. When Conrad died in southern Italy in 1254, the able Manfred continued to rule for twelve years as vicar for Conrad's young son, Conradin. Manfred succeeded in controlling most of southern Italy until the Papacy brought in Charles of Anjou, by whose superior forces he was defeated and slain at Benevento (1266). The young Conradin was persuaded to come to southern Italy and claim his inheritance. But the fifteen-year-old youth was defeated and captured by Charles of Anjou in the battle of Tagliocozzo (1268), after which he was publicly beheaded in the town square of Naples. *End of the Hohenstaufen (1250–1268)*

While extermination of the Hohenstaufen dynasty was being completed, Germany lapsed into general anarchy. During this Great Interregnum (1250/1256–1273) there were regularly two claimants to the imperial crown, neither of whom had effective control. After the death of Anti-King Henry Raspe in 1247, Count William of Holland succeeded him. But even when Conrad's cause in Germany became hopeless, the feeble William was unable to gain effective control. On William's death in 1256, four electoral princes, who had been liberally bribed, voted for the rich Richard of Cornwall, brother of Henry III of England; while four (Ottokar of Bohemia voted twice), similarly bribed, voted for King Alfonso X of Castile. Although Richard promenaded erratically about Germany, and "poured out money like water at the feet of princes," he never really ruled. Alfonso, whose candidacy was opposed in his own country as well as by the Papacy, did not even come to Germany. After the death of Richard of Cornwall (1272), the princes did not name a successor until they were brought to elect Rudolph of Hapsburg (1273) by the threat of Pope Gregory X that if they didn't elect an Emperor he would appoint one. "The Age of the Princes" in German history had arrived. *The Great Interregnum (1250/1256–1273)*

A GOOD constitutional history of medieval Germany is GEOFFREY BARRACLOUGH, *Origins of Modern Germany* (Oxford: Blackwell, 1957). German historians treat special topics in this field, after a general introduction, in BARRACLOUGH's *Mediaeval Germany, 911–1250 . . . ,* 2 vols. (Oxford: Blackwell, 1938). Articles in the *Cambridge Medieval History*, VI and VII, remain our best source of information for Germany in the High Middle Ages. Still informative is JAMES WESTFALL THOMPSON, *Feudal Germany* (Chicago: Chicago U.P., 1928), especially *References for Chapter 18* good for civil wars and German eastward expansion. FREDERICK C. HERTZ, *Development of the German Public Mind: The Middle Ages. The Reformation* (New York: Macmillan, 1957), gives a good summary of political highlights while tracing the evolution of German public consciousness.

General histories of Germany with good treatments of the Middle Ages include KURT F. REINHARDT, *Germany: 2,000 Years* (1 vol., hb., Milwaukee: Bruce, 1950) (2 vols., p., New York: Ungar, 1961; vol. I goes to about 1800); and VEIT VALENTIN, *... The German People: Their History and Civilization ...*, tr. O. Marx (New York: Knopf, 1946); as well as JOHANNES HALLER, *Epochs of German History*, tr. (London: Routledge, 1930). Multivolume earlier popular histories of Germany, of some value for their color, include WOLFGANG MENZEL, *Germany From the Earliest Period*, tr., 4 vols. (New York: Collier, 1900); and WILHELM ZIMMERMAN, *A Popular History of Germany*, tr., 4 vols. (New York: Johnson, 1878).

Of the various high medieval Emperors only Frederick II seems to have sufficiently aroused the interest of English biographers such as E. KANTOROWICZ, *Frederick the Second* (New York: Smith, 1931), and GEORGINA MASSON, *Frederick II of Hohenstaufen* (London: Stecher, 1957), for which the trail was blazed a century earlier by THOMAS L. KINGTON (T. L. K. Oliphant), *History of Frederick the Second ...*, 2 vols. (London: Macmillan, 1862). Two historical works by the noted twelfth-century Bishop OTTO OF FREISING have been translated as *The Two Cities: A Chronicle of Universal History to ... 1146 A.D.*, tr. C. C. Mierow (New York: Columbia U.P., 1928), and *The Deeds of Frederick Barbarossa*, tr. C. C. Mierow (New York: Columbia U.P., 1953). Classic older studies of the Empire are H. A. L. FISHER, *The Medieval Empire*, 2 vols. (London: Macmillan, 1898), and JAMES BRYCE, *The Holy Roman Empire* (New York: Macmillan, 1913).

For relations of the imperial government and the Papacy, see BRIAN TIERNEY, *The Crisis of Church and State, 1050–1300*, which has both text and documents; LUIGI STURZO, *Church and State* (New York: Longmans, 1939); SIDNEY Z. EHLER and JOHN B. MORRALL, *Church and State Through the Centuries ...* (Westminster: Newman, 1954), a collection of historical documents with commentaries; THOMAS F. TOUT, *The Empire and the Papacy, 918–1273* (London: Rivingtons, 1906); and GERD TELLENBACH, *Church, State, and Christian Society at the Time of the Investiture Contest*, tr. R. F. Bennet (New York: Macmillan, 1957).

⟨ THE MAKING OF ENGLAND AND FOUNDATIONS
1066–1307 OF THE ENGLISH CONSTITUTION.   Chapter 19.

ENGLAND, hitherto peripheral, became one of the leading states of Europe during the High Middle Ages. The conquest of England by the Normans, and their ties with France, opened up the island more fully to fructifying influences from the continent. The Normans made England the seat of an empire that included a good part of France, and was increased by the

The Making of England

Plantagenets. Because of their insular nature, frontier position, maritime trade, and Germanic traditions, the Anglo-Saxons were freer, more independent, and more democratic than most peoples on the continent. These traditions were not obliterated under the Normans and earlier Plantagenets, and they were reasserted and further developed under later Plantagenets. The English evolved institutions that have become part of the Western way of life, including the jury system, charters of human rights, and parliamentary government.

STRENGTHENING THE ENGLISH MONARCHY. Section 55. 1066–1199

> This King William . . . was kind to good men who loved God, but severe beyond measure to those who withstood his will. . . . Amongst other things, the beneficial order that William established . . . was such that any man, who was himself aught, might travel unmolested throughout the kingdom with a bosom full of gold; and no man durst kill another, however great the injury he might have received from him. [*Anglo-Saxon Chronicle*, concerning William I, the Conqueror.]

THE Norman Conquest (1066) led to a reorganization and strengthening of the English royal government. The Norman rulers and their Plantagenet successors utilized Anglo-Saxon and French institutions that contributed to their power and discarded those that weakened it. They also developed new institutions in order better to promote law and order, enhance royal revenues, and boost the strength and stability of their government. Among these measures were itinerant justices, common law, and certain taxes.

Advancing questionable claims to the English crown, with a Papal blessing and a large French following, energetic Duke William of Normandy defeated Harold Godwinson at Hastings, occupied London, and obtained recognition from the Witan together with the English crown (1066). Repeated Anglo-Saxon revolts gave William an excuse to confiscate the lands of defeated opponents all over England. These lands he redistributed as fiefs to his own followers. In doing so, however, William scattered the holdings of great lords, making them less dangerous to the crown, although on the frontiers he established somewhat larger earldoms for purposes of defense. The Normans built numerous motte and bailey castles to control territories as well as to ward off possible foreign attackers, such as the Scandinavians. *William I, the Conqueror (1066–1087)*

William introduced features of continental feudalism that tended to strengthen the English monarchy, while retaining Anglo-Saxon institutions that contributed to the same end. He introduced a modified, centralized form of feudalism, giving out lands in the form of fiefs, for which military service was required, and from which monetary income could be expected. He required the vassals of his vassals to swear fealty to him, commanding all landowners "that were worth aught" to make oaths "that they would be faithful to him against all other men," including even their *Strong monarchy* immediate overlords. William replaced the Witangemot with a feudal Great Council composed of his tenants-in-chief. Much of the royal business was handled by a petit *curia regis* (smaller court of the king).

Among features of the Anglo-Saxon monarchy that William retained were the "Danegeld," a direct tax originally established by Ethelred to buy off Danish attackers. William also utilized the *fyrd*, the native militia organized by Alfred, whereby all freemen were bound to provide military service when called upon by the king to defend the land. In the shires or counties, William retained and increased the power of the sheriffs, who were appointive royal representatives directly responsible to the king. Henceforth the sheriff or his lieutenant presided alone in local courts, since ecclesiastical courts, over which the bishops presided, were constituted separately, while the old earls and their functions were largely suppressed.

Further organization

During his absences on the continent, William left the government of England in the hands of a representative, the prototype for the later Justiciar, whose office came into clear relief under William II. For warfare, the Conqueror could theoretically rely on the services of about five thousand knights, owed from English fiefs, as well on that of the *fyrd*, which was comprised of most able-bodied freemen, and was a useful counterpoise against the former element. William enforced the Anglo-Saxon principle of "the King's Peace" whereby private warfare was outlawed. And he retained the Anglo-Saxon laws and courts, to which were added feudal and ecclesiastical courts, as well as the king's own court.

One of William's most "modern" measures was his famous *Domesday* survey (1086). Compiled by royal inquests, *Domesday Book* gave William comprehensive and detailed data concerning revenue-producing holdings throughout England, including lands, tenants, and livestock. The *Anglo-Saxon Chronicle* complained that "Not a single hide nor yard of land, nor indeed, though it seems a shame to relate what he felt no shame to do, a solitary ox nor cow nor pig was left out."

Relations with the Church and foreign powers

William replaced the Anglo-Saxon Archbishop of Canterbury, Stigand, who was considered an imposter by the Papacy, with Lanfranc, former Abbot of Bec in Normandy. The latter effected a reform and renovation of the Church in England. Better-trained Norman clerics gradually came to occupy most of the sees in England. Celibacy was enforced among the clergy. Monasteries multiplied and education was fostered. The Church had its own separate jurisdiction and court system. The building of Romanesque churches boomed. At the same time William declined to curb the royal authority in accordance with the wishes of the Church. He refused to become a vassal of the Pope, although he had conquered England with Papal backing. Despite Papal fulminations against lay investiture, he continued to appoint and install bishops in the old manner. And he required royal approval for clerical departures from England, for appeals from English courts to Rome, and for entry into England of Papal messengers.

William's foreign policy was aggressive. He marched into Scotland and compelled King Malcolm, who had been harboring English rebels, to render homage and promise to amend. He successfully parried the attacks and plots of King Philip I of France and the Count of Anjou on the continent. The Conqueror bequeathed the Duchy of Normandy and its dependencies to his prodigal eldest son, Robert "Curthose" (Short-stockings), and the Kingdom of England to his hard, impetuous second son, William Rufus (the Red). To his youngest son, the prudent Henry Beauclerc, he left a sum of money, £5,000, with the observation that one day all would be his.

Even the *Anglo-Saxon Chronicle*, which could not embrace the Conquest, could not help admiring the Conqueror. It noted that William was "very wise" and "great," and brought "good order" and peace to England. It observed that rich and poor alike "must will all the king willed if they would live or keep their lands or retain their goods." Of his severe forest laws, it quipped that *he loved the wild stags as if he were their father*. Finally, says the *Chronicle*, *The rich complained and the poor murmured, but he was so sturdy he recked naught of them*.

Results of the Norman Conquest

The Norman Conquest enriched English life and institutions with continental influences. English government was strengthened and reorganized along more efficient lines. The best of Anglo-Saxon and Norman institutions were utilized and the rest were allowed to lapse. The English economy was stimulated by increased contacts with the continent. On the other hand, serfdom and the aristocratic stratification of society increased. French became for over two centuries the language of English polite society, and many French terms entered the English language. Many English students were educated in the superior schools of France and improved methods and standards were introduced into English schools. Architecture surged forward, as the Normans were "great builders" who constructed numerous impressive castles and Romanesque churches.

The hard William II, Rufus, was in part a reflection of his father, whose policies of strong rule and centralization he continued. But unlike his father, Rufus was erratic, narrow, and selfish, fond of crude companions, impolitic, and imprudent. William II became an arbitrary despot, hated by nobles and commoners alike. A common cause of complaint was his extortions, partly occasioned by the need to pay the numerous foreign mercenaries who were the mainstay of his power. He was also hated for his severity and cruelty. He sequestered accustomed revenues of the Church, and quarreled with Archbishop Anselm of Canterbury over Church appointments, which he insisted on controlling despite the Gregorian reform movement. Eventually Anselm went into voluntary exile rather than submit to the young tyrant (1197). In 1100, while hunting in the forest, the red-haired despot was "accidentally" killed by an arrow shot through his back. No investigation was made and no punishment was meted out.

William II, Rufus (1087–1100)

Henry Beauclerc, the youngest, but the most intelligent and able of the Conqueror's three sons, seized the throne, disregarding the superior claim of his older brother, Robert Curthose of Normandy, who was still on Crusade.

Henry I, Beauclerc (1100–1135)

The High Middle Ages

Henry I (1100–1135) was known as "Beauclerc" ("Fine Cleric" or "Good Scholar"); he had originally been intended for the service of the Church and had received a good education. Henry was calculating, patient, and persistent, and preferred peaceful to violent means.

Conciliatory measures of Henry I

To solicit general favor, Henry issued a coronation charter, in which he promised to correct abuses and restore law and order. He also married the Scottish princess Edith, who was descended from the Anglo-Saxon royal house. When threatened by a rebellion and invasion led by his elder brother Robert in 1101, Henry bought him off by the promise of an annual pension of £2,000 (3,000 marks). But as he was determined to bring Normandy back into direct royal control, Henry intrigued and distributed bribes to form alliances with Robert's neighbors and to win over Robert's subjects. Finally Henry invaded Normandy, defeated Robert at Tinchebrai (1106), and subsequently kept him a prisoner in various castles until his death in 1134.

Shortly after his accession, Henry recalled Anselm from exile. When Anselm, imbued with the concepts of the continental reformation, refused to do homage for his holdings, the diplomatic Henry temporized. He agreed to allow the Archbishop his revenues while an embassy was sent to Rome to arbitrate the issue. The result was the compromise Concordat of London (1107), whereby the king agreed to forego investiture with the ring and the staff but was allowed to influence and confirm the election of bishops, as well as to require their homage before their investiture.

Governmental organization by Henry I

Henry I furthered the organization of the English government by his establishment of the Exchequer and by his institution of itinerant justices. The handling and supervision of the royal finances was at first one of several functions of the smaller (petit) *curia regis* (court of the king). Under Henry, however, the Exchequer, so called from the checkered cloth on which sheriffs rendered their accounts, went "out of court" and became a separate department. Henry's institution of itinerant royal justices ("justices in eyre") set up a rude system of circuit courts, and contributed much to the enhancement of royal income and power, as well as to the administration of justice.

Although Henry I had twenty-two children, only two of them, William Aetheling and Mathilda, were legitimate. After William Aetheling drowned during a shipwreck while en route from Normandy to England in 1120, the grief-stricken Henry decided to make his daughter, Mathilda, his successor. As a measure of security, Henry married Mathilda, widow of Emperor Henry V of Germany, to the strong Count Geoffrey the Handsome of Anjou, and persuaded the English barons to agree to her succession.

Anarchy under Stephen (1135–1154)

But the "imperious" Mathilda alienated many of the barons, and, following the death of Henry I, they collaborated in the accession of Stephen of Blois. Stephen was the son of the Conqueror's daughter Adela, who had married the Count of Blois. Stephen was easy-going, naive, and weak, although pleasant, chivalrous, and brave. He initially had the co-

The Making of England

operation of the Church, since his brother was Bishop of Winchester, and also won broad support by his concessions in two charters. But Mathilda pressed her claims and would not concede defeat. As a result, civil war raged throughout the distraught reign of vacillating Stephen, which is known as "the Anarchy." In general, Stephen prevailed by a narrow margin in England, while the Mathildine forces, led by Count Geoffrey, overran Norman territories on the continent. The results of Stephen's turbulent reign are ruefully described in the *Anglo-Saxon Chronicle: In this king's time all was discord and evil-doing and robbery. . . . For all the men of means built their castles, and held them against the king, and they greatly oppressed the wretched people. . . .*

In 1150 energetic Henry of Anjou, the son of Mathilda and Geoffrey, became Duke of Normandy and assumed his mother's claims. In 1151, on the death of his father, Henry also became Count of Anjou; and in 1152 he obtained southwestern France by marrying Eleanor, Duchess of Aquitaine. In 1153 he invaded England; and since King Stephen on the death of his son Eustace (1153) lost interest in the contest, a peace was arranged whereby Stephen would remain king until his death, whereupon Henry would succeed him. Stephen obligingly died the following year.

Henry II (1154–1189) of Anjou initiated the Angevin or Plantagenet line, which received the latter name from the sprig of yellow broom (*planta genesta*) that was an emblem of its adherents during the civil war. The short, stocky, reddish-haired Henry, so restless that he often paced up and down during Mass, was sharp and decisive, strong-willed, and quick to anger. Intelligent and well educated, a lover of good order, Henry ruled an "Empire" that stretched to the Pyrenees and included the western half of France. His policy was to restore monarchical power and make law and order prevail. Henry's first problem was to eliminate the anarchy that had prevailed during Stephen's reign. Unruly barons were suppressed. Unauthorized "adulterine" castles were either razed or garrisoned with royal soldiers. Malpractices by sheriffs and local lords were halted by judicial procedures such as the Inquest of Sheriffs (1170).

Henry II (1154–1189) establishes order and royal justice

Royal justice was extended throughout England by itinerant judges, royal writs, convocation of juries, and development of English common law. During Henry's reign the use of itinerant justices previously employed by Henry I to carry royal justice throughout the realms was revived. By the *Assize of Clarendon* (1166) and other ordinances, Henry II regularized the itinerant justices and determined their circuits. In 1179 there were four established circuits throughout the land and twenty-one itinerant justices. Henry also established (1178) a permanent royal court by ordering that five men were to sit continuously "to do justice" as a *curia regis* (court of the king), customarily at Westminster.

Earlier Norman monarchs had occasionally issued "writs" to bring cases before the royal court, but Henry II did so in a wholesale manner and for a moderate price. Following Stephen's reign, with its numerous usurpations by the use of force, one of the main questions was "To whom does such and such a property rightfully belong?" But such an investiga-

Royal writs and regional assizes

tion could be very long and tortuous. A more practical immediate question, more easily answered, was "who has the better claim to present (at least interim) possession?" To answer this, representative citizens from the neighborhood were summoned and sworn in to answer yes or no to a simple question, designed to settle this point, presented by a writ. Since the courts customarily used French at the time, the writs (which were also known as "assizes") had French names. (The term *assize* is capable of many meanings: it can mean a sitting or "session"; or an order or writ for such; or the resultant determination or decree.) In the writ of *Novel Disseisin* (Recent Dispossession) the question was asked: "Was the claimant recently dispossessed of the property?" In that of *Mort d'Ancestor* (Death of Forebear) the question was asked: "Was the property possessed at death by a forebear whom the claimant had the right to succeed?" In that of *Darrein Presentment* (Last Presentation) it was "Who made the last nomination or presentation to the benefice?" Another writ was that of *Utrum* (Whether), which directed the jurors to declare whether the property in question was a church benefice or a lay fief, and whether it was held in "frankalmoin" as church property free from secular obligations or in "lay fee" as a secular fief subject to feudal requirements. The first three of the foregoing were "possessory writs" or "petty assizes," capable of quick and easy answers, with prompt and ready "remedies."

More complicated, lengthy, and tedious, and consequently less commonly invoked, were the so-called proprietary writs or writs of right or grand assizes. These were designed to determine fundamental ownership or property rights rather than the simple right of immediate possession. They could become very involved and were susceptible to many delays. They also favored the possessor of the property since they exempted him from his earlier obligation to defend his right of ownership by duel or the ordeal of battle if challenged.

The jury system

Writs for the assignment of cases to the royal courts came into increasing demand because of the better and surer justice administered. This was owing partly to the superior qualifications of the royal justices; but even more to employment of the jury system in civil cases, instead of reliance on duels, ordeals, and compurgation.

The writs of Henry II called for the jury system since they ordered that the question at issue be settled by sworn inquests conducted among representative groups of local citizens. Sworn inquests had been used by the Carolingians and by the Norman monarchs of England for special matters, but they did not become a regular and ordinary part of the judicial system until the time of Henry II. The royal writ directed an official to summon a certain number of men (usually twelve) from the community to answer, under oath (hence the terms *jury* from jurare: to swear), the particular question addressed to them. Originally jurors were presumed to be familiar with the case, rather than the opposite, as today. The jurors were ordinarily summoned by the sheriff, and the sworn inquests were presided over and directed by the king's itinerant justices.

The Making of England

In criminal cases, for some time juries were employed only to serve the function of present-day grand juries: i.e., to decide what cases must be tried. The issue continued to be decided by traditional methods such as the so-called judgment of God or ordeal, whence our term *trial*. The "grand jury" or "jury of presentment" consisted of twenty-four persons: twelve from each hundred plus four from each of the three vills nearest to the scene of the alleged crimes, summoned to name, under oath, any persons in their community who were seriously suspected of major crimes but who had not yet been brought to trial. If deemed seriously suspect by a majority of jurors, a person would be turned over or "presented" to be tried according to established procedures, ordinarily by the ordeal of cold water. The jury of presentment obtained part of the power of a trial jury when Henry decreed in 1166 that even if an indicted man of bad repute was successful in an ordeal he must still abjure the realm, which in effect gave the grand jury the power of banishment.

Grand and petit juries

Although persons accused of serious crimes were sometimes allowed to have their cases decided by juries prior to the Fourth Lateran Council (1215), it was not until this council forbade clergy to participate in trials involving bloodshed that ordeals, in which the clergy had been moderators and referees, were abandoned in criminal trials. Compurgation and duels were not eliminated until later. Accused persons were sometimes forced to consent to trial by jury through the application of *peine forte et dure* (strong and severe pain) whereby successive weights were piled upon the prisoner until he agreed to such a trial. The smaller jury or *petit* jury used for criminal cases usually consisted of twelve persons.

The jury system spread rapidly. It came to be almost universally preferred, since it depended upon evidence and reason rather than upon psychological impact or supernatural intervention and thus led more surely to justice. The jury system was also calculated to give more protection to individual liberties, and it was based on a principle that contained germs of representative government.

One result of the spread of royal justice was the gradual evolution of English "common law," which like the Roman *jus gentium* was mainly the result of an accumulation of judicial precedents and the opinions of learned jurists. Among the latter was Ranulf Glanville, Henry's own justiciar, author of a *Treatise on the Laws and Customs of England*. Although primarily "case law," English common law drew liberally on Roman law and Church law, Anglo-Saxon and Danish customary law, and rational principles of equity.

Common law

In extending royal justice, Henry II came into conflict with the Church. The actual clash involved the opposition of two strong personalities: Henry II and Archbishop Thomas Becket. The son of bourgeois parents, Becket, who became a cleric, distinguished himself first in the service of Archbishop Theobald of Canterbury and then in that of Henry II, eventually becoming the latter's boon companion and trusted Chancellor. On Theobald's death, Henry, confident of the continued cooperation of Becket, made him Archbishop of Canterbury. But the previously light-

Henry II and the Church: Thomas Becket

hearted and worldly Thomas became a changed man given to prayer and penitence, and a zealous defender of the liberties of the Church.

When Henry II attempted to extend royal jurisdiction into the domain of the Church in the Constitutions of Clarendon (1164), Thomas refused to consent, despite the disposition of most of his fellow bishops to submit. Among provisions of the Constitutions were the restrictions that no prelates should leave England, there should be no judicial appeals beyond England, and there should be no imposition of excommunication or interdict in England without the king's approval. Revenues from vacant ecclesiastical prelacies were to accrue to the king, who was to nominate a successor and electors were to assemble in the royal chapel for the election. "Criminous clerks" or ecclesiastics accused of more serious crimes, such as murder, were first to be tried in ecclesiastical courts in the presence of a royal justice, and then, if condemned, were to be handed over to the royal courts for the application of penalties prescribed by secular law. Henry II argued for the Constitutions on the basis of old precedents; Becket took his stand on the dignity and rights of the Church.

Murder of the Archbishop

A widening rift between the King and his Archbishop ensued, and led to Becket's voluntary exile in France. Eventually the disagreement was partly patched up, but when Becket returned to England he suspended some of the bishops who had opposed him, including the Archbishop of York, who had crowned the young Henry. On learning of the punishment of his supporters, Henry II went into a paroxysm of rage and exclaimed repeatedly: "Will none of those who live off my bounty relieve me of this troublesome clerk?" Four of the King's knights took their master's words seriously, crossed the Channel, burst in upon the Archbishop in his own Cathedral, and slew him with their swords.

The reaction to the murder on all sides was one of horror and condemnation. Thomas, who had bravely presented himself to his brutal attackers and had apparently welcomed martyrdom, was popularly acclaimed a saint. To escape ecclesiastical censures and public reprobation, Henry disavowed responsibility and did public penance. He also abandoned further attempts to apply the stipulation of the Constitutions of Clarendon concerning criminous clerks, although he enforced other provisions.

Foreign and familial relations of Henry II

The conquest of the English-controlled portion of Ireland, which later came to be known as "the Pale" (a district, such as one set off by "pales": stakes), began during Henry's reign. The English Pope Adrian IV sent Henry an emerald ring as a token of his right to conquer the island, but the actual conquest was first undertaken (1169ff.) by Anglo-Norman barons along the Welsh frontiers. In 1171 Henry intervened and asserted his superior authority, and in 1177 he made his son John the lord of Ireland.

Henry also obtained homage from the princes of Wales. And he captured King Malcolm IV of Scotland, who invaded England as an ally of English rebels, and forced him to become his vassal in 1173.

Henry's chief external concern was about his holdings and claims in France. Henry spent twenty-one years of his thirty-four years as king on

The Making of England

the continent. Early in his reign, he asserted his wife's claim to the County of Toulouse, but desisted from his siege of its capital when King Louis VII, his overlord for his French holdings, gained entrance to the city (1159). He obtained possession of the valuable Vexin as a dowry for the prospective marriage of his five-year-old son Henry to the two-year-old Princess Margaret of France. Otherwise Henry's operations in France were mainly defensive, being directed at preserving control of his French territories against the efforts of his wife and sons on the one hand and the French monarchy on the other.

Henry's chief failure was with the members of his own family, most of whom eventually rebelled. This familial defection was mainly due to the domineering nature of Henry, which impelled him to keep all power in his own hands; the independent spirit of his neglected wife, Eleanor, who encouraged her sons to rise against their father; and French intrigues, notably those of Philip II. There were no less than four filial rebellions: in 1173–1174, 1181, 1186ff., and 1189. After the first, Eleanor was kept an honored prisoner. All of the King's sons—Young Henry, Geoffrey, Richard, and John—eventually revolted. After hearing of the participation of his favorite son John in the rebellion of 1189, the defeated and saddened King died.

Henry was succeeded by his eldest surviving son, Richard I, "the Lionhearted." Richard was strong and handsome, warlike and adventurous, a great military leader, chivalrous and popular. But he was selfish, impetuous, and impatient of the ways of diplomacy and statesmanship. And he was an "absentee monarch," since he spent most of his reign away from England in the Near East and in France. Richard bled England for his foreign enterprises and ransom, while his only enduring success was his recapture of English holdings in northwestern France from Philip II.

Absentee King— Richard I, the Lionhearted (1189–1199)

It is a tribute to the strong, well-organized government built up by Henry II and previous Norman rulers that the royal government functioned smoothly under the successive Justiciars (William Longchamps, Walter of Coutances, and Hubert Walter) who represented Richard during his absences. While Richard was away on the Third Crusade, John plotted to seize control, but Eleanor helped to defend Richard's rights and later effected a reconciliation. Eleanor also helped to arrange and raise a ransom for Richard when he was taken prisoner in Germany on his way home from the Third Crusade. On his return, Richard rapidly retook his French territories seized by Philip II during his absence, and he built a strong fortification known as Chateau Gaillard or "Saucy Castle" on a height overlooking the Seine, commanding the approach from the Ile de France into Normandy. Richard met an untimely death in France as the result of an infection from an arrow shot from the castle of one of his vassals which he was besieging.

LIMITING THE ENGLISH MONARCHY.
Section 56.

> No freeman shall be taken, imprisoned, dispossessed, exiled, or in any way destroyed, nor will we go upon him or send upon him, except by the lawful judgment of his peers or according to the law of the land. [Article 39 of Magna Carta, agreed to by King John at Runnymede (1215).]

EVEN as the Norman and early Plantagenet kings seemed on the verge of establishing something approaching royal absolutism, vigorous aristocratic and popular reaction arrested this trend in the thirteenth century. During the troubled, bungling reigns of the incompetent John and Henry III, English opposition to growing monarchical power limited the king, and obtained formal recognition of the basic rights of Englishmen, especially for members of the upper classes. The English also began to experiment with parliamentary representation of the people.

Among factors contributing to a limitation of the monarchy were a growing resistance to the rapid growth of royal power; abuse of the latter by erratic, despotic John and pliant, prodigal Henry III; and the overseas reverses of both inadequate rulers, despite heavy expenditures. Further factors contributing to a rise of representation in national government were the examples of the feudal Great Council, Church councils, and Anglo-Saxon moots; the experience of partial self-government in the towns; representative features in the English judicial system including juries and delegates from the juries to higher courts in cases of appeals; and the repetitious need for funds on the part of the royal government, due to French involvements, efforts to conquer Wales and Scotland, other expansionist and crusading projects, and inflation.

John (1199–1216) and his bungling

Although Arthur of Brittany, the young son of John's older brother Geoffrey, had perhaps a better claim, Richard designated his own brother John, a mature man, as his successor. John, who came to be known as "Lackland" and "Softsword," had already begun to acquire an unsavory reputation. Treacherous and selfish, John had betrayed both his doting, aged father and his genial crusader brother. He was cruel and unscrupulous, as well as prone to extreme contrasts of action and inaction, energy and languor: in short, he was probably psychotic. The erratic John soon aroused opposition on every hand. His marriage to already betrothed Isabelle of Angoulême, his probable murder of his nephew Arthur, his contest with Innocent III over an appointment to the Archbishopric of Canterbury, and his loss of valuable English possessions in northwestern France alienated support and excited animosities. His extortion of money by special, unprecedented scutages (payments in lieu of military service), forced loans, and abuse of feudal prerogatives, such as wardship, foremarriage, and royal rights relative to ecclesiastical benefices, had a like effect. John became even more hated when he used foreign mercenaries to enforce his arbitrary will.

In 1200, shortly after his accession, John obtained an annulment of his childless marriage with Isabel of Gloucester. Not long afterward, while traveling through southwestern France, he was attracted to the vivacious Isabelle of Angouleme. Despite the fact that Isabelle was already betrothed to one of his own vassals, Hugh of Lusignan, and that their match was strongly desired by the two families in order to unite their holdings, John violated feudal etiquette and married Isabelle without bothering to conciliate Hugh.

The outraged Hugh of Lusignan appealed to King Philip II, John's feudal overlord in France. Delighted, Philip summoned John to his court several times, and when John failed to appear the King and his curia declared John's holdings in France forfeit as those of a contumacious vassal (1202). Philip proceeded to occupy Normandy and its dependencies, while John temporarily lapsed into a strange lethargy.

John's loss of northwestern France

When John learned that an armed contingent under Arthur, whom Philip was supporting as the legitimate heir to the Angevin possessions, had trapped his mother Eleanor in the castle of Mirabeau in Poitou, he aroused himself temporarily, made a march of 80 miles in 48 hours with a relief force, and took Arthur and 200 of his supporters prisoners. Cruel vengeance was taken on many of the prisoners; and subsequently the young Prince Arthur mysteriously disappeared in one of the castles where John was keeping him.

The unsavory affair of Arthur, along with that of Hugh of Lusignan, and other blunders by John alienated many of the nobles of Maine, Anjou, and the Touraine, who went over to Philip II. The French King completed his conquest and occupation of Normandy and adjacent territories without serious opposition. Poitou for the most part resisted Philip, who desisted in order to consolidate his gains (1205).

In 1205 when a vacancy occurred in the Archbishopric of Canterbury, the monks, despite John's opposition, elected their sub-prior and sent him to Rome for the pallium. Whereupon the angered John compelled the monks to elect his own candidate, John de Gray. Faced with conflicting elections, Pope Innocent III quashed both, and appointed the learned and able Stephen Langton (1207). John refused to accept Stephen, and the heat of the quarrel intensified. Innocent III put England under an interdict (1207); John confiscated the properties of the Archbishopric of Canterbury (1208); and Innocent finally excommunicated John (1209). Both parties held fast to their positions until John, confronted with the dual threat of Papal deposition and a French invasion, accepted Stephen Langton in 1213. John also did homage to the Pope for England and Ireland, agreeing to pay an annual tribute of one thousand marks. John's nominal vassalage to the Pope, however, strengthened his position, since henceforth anyone who opposed him would also be opposing the Pope. It also left him freer to deal with Philip.

Contest with Innocent III followed by failure in France

Determined to recover northwestern France, John worked to encircle Philip with enemies. He formed alliances with princes in the Low Countries and the Rhineland, with lords in Normandy and Poitou, and with the Guelph Emperor, Otto IV of Germany. John and Otto planned to catch Philip in a vise: Otto advancing southward through Flanders, and John moving northward through Poitou. But while John dallied in the

The great revolt and Magna Carta (1215)

south and was delayed by a French diversionary force, Philip, with a large army, moved swiftly northward and intercepted Otto in Flanders. Here, before the allies could join forces, Philip defeated Otto in the battle of Bouvines (1214), decisive in the annals of three countries.

The discredited and bankrupt John then returned to England, where a movement to constrain him was already afoot among the barons. When John tried to impose a large scutage upon those who had not accompanied him on his campaign on the continent, most of the barons revolted (1215). They protested against his violations of legal, feudal, and ecclesiastical restrictions, his disregard for personal rights, his extortions and cruelties, and his use of large numbers of foreign mercenaries. The revolt was also a result of long-term grievances against the Norman and Angevin monarchs. Despite his crafty efforts, John was unable to separate either the churchmen or the Londoners from the barons. Finally, he agreed to terms arranged by a joint commission whose leaders were Archbishop Langton for the barons and William Marshal for the King. Capitulating, John met the barons on the field of Runnymede and affixed the Great Seal to the agreement known as Magna Carta (1215).

Although Magna Carta (the Great Charter) was primarily a feudal document, which set down in writing liberties commonly claimed by the barons and the Church in the feudal system, it had broader implications. It greatly limited the powers of the king and the royal government, and clearly established the principle that the king was subject to the law, and that in case he violated it his subjects had a right to compel him to conform. Most of the provisions of Magna Carta were specific promises by John to abandon previous abuses, such as the unjust exploitation of his feudal rights. It enumerated customary aids, stating that, apart from these, *No scutage or aid shall be imposed in our kingdom except with the common consent of our kingdom.* Most of the rights enumerated by Magna Carta were baronial. Ecclesiastical liberties, including the right of free ecclesiastical elections, were also affirmed in general terms. At the same time, some important provisions directly concerned commoners or freemen. The requirement of "common consent" for the levying of extraordinary scutages and aids was extended to apply to the city of London, and by implication other cities and towns. The customary rights and privileges of the towns were guaranteed by the statement that both London and "all other cities, boroughs, towns, and ports shall have all their liberties and free customs." The king promised not to sell or deny justice. Due process of law for all free persons was guaranteed: *No freeman shall be taken or imprisoned, dispossessed or exiled, or in any way destroyed, nor will we go upon him or send upon him, except by the lawful judgment of his peers or according to the law of the land.* Various other provisions also applied to free commoners as well as nobles. A commission of twenty-five, chosen by the barons, was to be established to see to the enforcement of Magna Carta. The chief contribution of Magna Carta was that it formally established the principle that the king was subject to the law, and that his subjects possessed certain inalienable rights, which they could, if necessary, force the royal government to observe. Largely

The Making of England

because of this, Magna Carta has stood as a beacon of Western liberties through the ages.

Neither the barons nor John observed the agreement for long. Many of the barons refused to accept the peace, and continued to raid and destroy John's properties. After observing the charter for two months, John abandoned any pretext of cooperation and appealed to Pope Innocent III for a release from his promises. Innocent declared the charter null since it was obtained by violence and lacked his own prior consent as John's feudal overlord. A minority of the barons supported John, who relied largely on foreign mercenaries. Most of the barons joined the rebels and invited in Prince Louis of France. The conflict was indecisive: at first fortune favored John, then Louis and the rebels. A crushing disappointment to John was the loss of his baggage train, including much of the royal treasure, in the quicksand of an estuary in the Fens. The distraught John died a few days later of a fever and dysentery, aggravated by "a surfeit of peaches and fresh cider."

The end of John (1215–1216)

The barons soon abandoned their French candidate in favor of John's nine-year-old son, Henry. Transition to normality was effected by the conciliatory but firm policy of able regents, first William Marshal (1216–1216), and then Hubert de Burgh (1221–1232). The latter remained in control for five years after Henry reached his majority, whereupon Henry III assumed personal control (1232). Henry was kindly, pious, generous, and artistic as well as a loving husband and father. But he had a weak will, lacked a realistic grasp of practical affairs, and was impetuous and vacillating, impractical and prodigal. A long score of baronial grievances against Henry III soon accumulated. A leading complaint was his excessive favoritism to foreign favorites, as the compliant Henry was "milked" by the Poitevan relatives of his former tutor Peter des Roches; by another Poitevan crowd brought in by his stepfather, Hugh of Lusignan (his mother's old love whom she now married); and finally by a swarm of Provencals and Savoyards who came with his own bride, Eleanor of Provence. In futile efforts to recover part of former English possessions on the continent, Henry engaged in costly, unsuccessful overseas campaigns in 1230–1231, 1234, and 1242. These served only to display his incapacity and further diminish his prestige. His failures exposed him to dispossession by the French king: but it was Henry's good fortune that the latter was the saintly and forgiving Louis IX. Another cause for discontent was Henry's subservience to the Papacy. The pious monarch made no opposition to increased Papal exactions, which included Papal taxation of the English clergy and an increase of Papal provisions (rights to appoint) for English benefices. The latter frequently resulted in the appointment of Italians, whom the English regarded as intruders.

Henry III arouses opposition (1216–1272)

Henry's "Sicilian Folly" finally brought baronial resistance to a head. Following the death of Emperor Frederick II, the Papacy cast about for a suitable candidate to overthrow Frederick's successors in southern Italy and Sicily. Henry III accepted in 1254 the designation of his second son Edmund to rule the Papal fief, although the Kingdom of Sicily lay over 2,000 miles away, and its retention by England would be neither per-

Sicilian venture

The High Middle Ages
THE ENGLISH MONARCHY
1216-1509

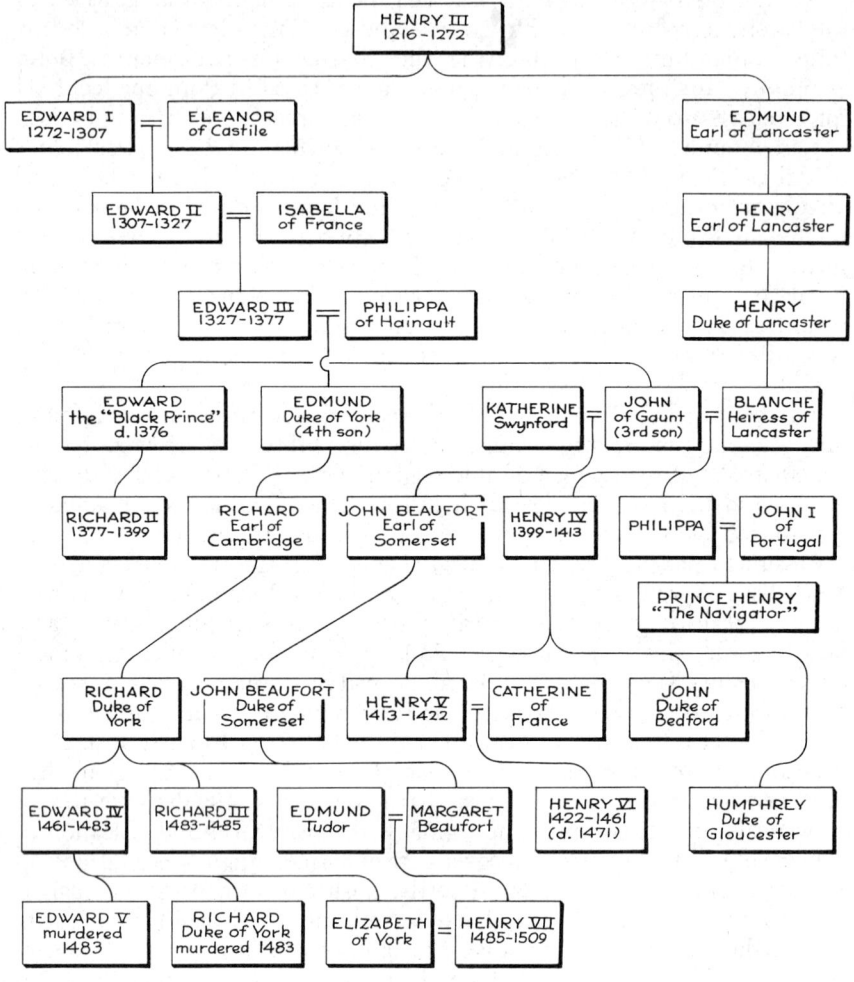

The Making of England

manent nor profitable. As a preliminary condition, Henry III agreed to pay, in installments, an immense debt of £90,000 (135,000 marks) previously incurred by the Papacy in the prosecution of the Sicilian War. When Henry was unable to meet the payment due in 1258, he was sharply reprimanded by the Pope, and appealed to his Great Council for financial help. A leading complaint against Henry III was his prodigal and lavish expenditures. Consequently the barons balked and demanded financial and other reforms as a price of their cooperation.

The Provisions of Oxford (1258) and the baronial commission

The condition laid down by the barons was that their bankrupt King accept participation of their representatives in his government. The hapless Henry could only accept. The resultant agreement, known as the Provisions of Oxford (1258), set up a baronial committee of fifteen, which was to supervise the royal government, with some of its members in constant attendance upon the King.

Although the rule by the baronial committee soon deteriorated, it did effect some reforms. It investigated and remedied certain abuses in local government by the sheriffs. And it concluded the Peace of Paris (1258), according to which, the English king was to possess, unmolested, augmented territories in Gascony and Guienne on condition that he take an oath of vassalage to the French king and abandon any further claims to French territories (e.g., Normandy and its dependencies).

Renewed civil war (1263—1265): Simon de Montfort

The unwieldy new government established by the Provisions soon caused the country to long for the good old days of royal government. Disagreement arose among the barons and many of them were won over to the royal party. The number of defections steadily increased. In 1261 the King obtained from the Pope a release from his promises to the barons; and by 1263 the two factions were at war.

The leader of the baronial party was Simon de Montfort, Earl of Leicester and husband of the king's sister, a younger son of the Simon de Montfort who was the leader of the French Albigensian Crusade.

In 1264, the baronial faction and the King submitted their dispute to the judgment of Louis IX of France. In the *Mise of Amiens* (1264) Louis declared the Provisions of Oxford invalid as an illegal invasion of royal rights and as a concession extorted by force. Whereupon the baronial party resumed the war. With inferior forces, Montfort brilliantly defeated the royal army at Lewes (1264), took the King prisoner, and dictated the terms. A reduced supervisory committee of the Provisions type dominated by Montfort, was restored to control of the government.

Montfort's parliament (1265) and his defeat

To broaden the base of his support, Montfort, in the name of the King, summoned the first English Parliament (1265). In addition to barons, Montfort called two knights from each shire (county), and two burgesses from each borough, but he limited his summons to those whom he might expect to be friendly. Although the meeting was only partly representative, it set an important precedent.

Montfort's appreciation of the potential contributions of the middle class was a factor in alienating many of his aristocratic supporters. Still more important was the dramatic escape from his hands of the King's son, "the Lord Edward," who now took command of the royal troops.

The royal cause was also helped by the defection of the Duke of Gloucester from the rebels and the support of the "Marcher Lords," the barons of the frontiers. With a growing army Edward marched on Montfort. At Evesham (1265), Simon's badly outnumbered supporters were overwhelmed and Montfort was brutally killed.

"Lord Edward" became the actual ruler of England during the final years of Henry III (1265-1272). By such measures as the Dictum of Kenilworth (1266), the royal power was reasserted and the laws and customs of the realm were reaffirmed. The former rebels were, however, allowed to repurchase their forfeited lands for up to a half of their actual value. The Statute of Marlborough (1267) confirmed several of the more constructive reforms accomplished during preceding years.

"THE EDWARDIAN COMPROMISE."
Section 57.

1272-1307

> Since we intend to consult and meet with the earls, barons, and other nobles of our kingdom with a view to providing remedies for the dangers which are presently confronting our kingdom, we strictly require you to cause two knights from the aforesaid shire, two citizens from each city in the same shire, and two burgesses from each borough, of those who are especially discreet and capable of working, to be elected without delay, and to come to us at the time and place aforesaid. [Typical summons issued by Edward I to a sheriff for the "Model Parliament" of 1295.]

EDWARD I (1272-1307) skillfully reconciled the opposing forces of centralization and strong monarchy on the one hand and local government and limited monarchy on the other. By the close of Edward's reign, many of the main lineaments of the English constitution were established as a result of "the Edwardian Compromise."

Edward I, "Longshanks" (1272-1307)

The first thoroughly English monarch since 1066, Edward I was tall (6 ft., 3 in.), whence his nickname, Longshanks, strong, brave, intelligent, and competent. He was a great statesman, legislator, and administrator, as well as a successful general. He had been well trained for his office during the later years of his father's reign, when he had been obliged to take the field in opposition to his old friend, Simon de Montfort, and had reestablished peace and order after Evesham.

One of the lessons Edward had learned during the reign of his father was the importance of winning the cooperation of his subjects. To this end, he used such devices as the calling of Parliament and the Confirmation of the Charters, and adopted the principle of the "community of the realm." Securing general cooperation was particularly necessary because of his grand projects. A further lesson Edward had learned was the need for strong, firm, just government. This he achieved by improving the organization of both the executive and judicial branches, by fuller exploitation of potential fiscal resources, by rounding out the English system of common law, and by further expanding the scope of royal justice. Although Edward was on a Crusade at his father's death, so well established was the royal government that he was immediately proclaimed king by the Great Council, and could take a leisurely two years in returning.

One of the great ambitions of Edward I was to unify all the island of Great Britain under the rule of the English crown. In this endeavor, he succeeded permanently with respect to mountainous Wales with its warlike and restless inhabitants, long a thorn in the side of more advanced England. Unification of most of Wales was achieved by Llewelyn ab Gruffydd, who had obtained formal English recognition as Prince of Wales in return for an act of homage to King Henry III. But at Edward's accession, Prince Llewelyn refused to renew his homage. Edward invaded Wales in 1277, 1284, and 1294. Part of Wales was incorporated into the English system after the fierce Welsh rebellion of 1282–1284; and the rest after that of 1294. The English shire system and royal itinerant justices as well as English law were introduced into Wales. Edward's infant son Edward was presented to a group of Welsh chieftains as their prince (1284) after they asked for a prince of their own, and henceforth it became customary for the heir presumptive to the English throne to be known as the Prince of Wales. *[margin: Foreign affairs: Conquest of Wales]*

Edward was only temporarily successful in his efforts to subject Scotland, despite persistent efforts that earned for him the title of "Hammer of the Scots." His opportunity for assertion of overlordship over Scotland came with the accidental death of King Alexander III (1286), followed by that of the latter's designated successor, his granddaughter Margaret, "the Maid of Norway," who was shipwrecked on her way to Scotland. Since the King of Scotland had been a nominal vassal of the King of England, Edward asserted his right as overlord to designate a successor, and accordingly appointed a commission that chose the compliant John Baliol (1292). The latter did homage to Edward for Scotland. *[margin: Efforts to subject Scotland]*

When Edward claimed that obligations assumed by the Scottish King in becoming his vassal included subjection to English courts and provision of soldiers for his French War (1294), the Scottish nobles abruptly called a halt. The Scots refused to supply troops, declared the Scottish estates of Englishmen confiscated, and invaded northern England (1295). Edward diverted troops assembled for a campaign in France to Scotland, where his forces temporarily prevailed. He left a commission of three to rule in his name. But daring William Wallace led a Scottish rebellion and defeated the English at Stirling Bridge (1297). Edward redressed the balance the following year with his Falkirk victory (1298). After eluding the frustrated English for some years, Wallace was finally captured and barbarously executed in 1305. But Robert Bruce, who had a good claim to the throne, assumed leadership of the resistance, murdered one of Edward's hated regents, and was crowned at Scone (1306). Although Edward continued the merciless fight until his death in 1307, he was unable to recover control.

The aggressive policies of Philip IV of France brought England into war with that country by 1294. Reasons for the Anglo-French conflict included French encroachments on English possessions and privileges in southwestern France and violent clashes between the English and French *[margin: Edward and France]*

And Philip IV

over fishing grounds. In one of these encounters the English fishermen and sailors won a great victory (1293), whereupon Philip demanded compensation. During negotiations, Edward surrendered part of Gascony to the French King as a pledge; but when the time was up Philip refused to restore the occupied territory. In the ensuing conflict (1294ff.), the Count of Flanders and Flemish middle-class townspeople allied with Edward, while the Scots allied with the French. The war was however, indecisive. In 1303, Philip, anxious to subject the Flemish burghers, and Edward, anxious to subject the Scots, concluded a peace, which did not, however, terminate reciprocal interference.

Taxation expanded

The extensive warlike enterprises of Edward I were very expensive, and necessitated increased taxation. Besides feudal reliefs and ordinary and extraordinary feudal aids, Edwardian direct taxes included scutage: a payment of money in lieu of military service; commutation of feudal dues such as hospitality; ordinary tallage: a fixed tax levied on towns and freemen; special tallage, such as taxes exacted from the Jews; the carucage: a tax on arable plowland; a poll tax graduated according to rank; and finally a personal property tax on movable goods. The most common and lucrative direct tax was that on movable goods, which could vary from one fifth to one thirtieth of their value, but usually ran in the neighborhood of a tenth. Values were assessed by "juries" or sworn groups of local citizens. This tax was often higher for city dwellers than for rural inhabitants. The tax on the personal property of the population at large was levied by Parliament; but in the case of the clergy it was negotiated with the English churchmen or with the Pope.

Indirect taxes developed into an important source of revenue. Export taxes included from one half mark to five marks on a sack of wool (300 hides or woolfells), and from one mark to ten marks on a last of leather (200 hides). A double export tax was levied on foreign merchants, for which they were allowed compensating privileges. Taxes on imports included two shillings on a "tun" (cask) of wine, and from one to over two shillings on a "piece" of cloth (a portion the size of a loom). Taxes on exports and imports had to be conceded by Parliament.

Parliament develops

Edward's perennial need of money was one of the principal reasons for the rise of Parliament. Originally the term *parliament* meant simply a meeting involving discussion (*parler*: to speak). Then it came to be applied to meetings of the Council of the King in a judicial capacity, which was usually the Great Council, generally held four times a year. These gatherings also transacted other business, such as answering petitions, advising policies, clarifying the law of the land, drawing up new legislation, and approving special "aids" or taxes requested by the king. Gradually under Edward I Parliaments came regularly to include representatives of the rural and urban middle classes, as well as members of the baronage and the Church. Even during the reigns of John and Henry, knights had on occasion been invited to attend meetings of the council.

Representation precedents

Well-established precedents existed for the application of the representative principle to Parliament. A similar representative principle was employed in the sworn testimony required at royal inquests, such as those for tax assessments. It was present in the jury system, both grand and petit, a form of inquest under oath used in criminal as well as civil investigations. When decisions of local cases were transferred to the central royal courts, as on appeals, representative delegations of four knights reported the local findings to Westminster. The representative principle was also used in local government.

Initially representatives of the people were added to the Great Council to deal with special crises. The first Parliament summoned by Simon de Montfort (1265) aimed to rally support from the middle class in the countryside and towns as well as from the barons for his waning cause. It set the pattern by summoning two knights from each shire and two burgesses from each borough, directing that such be locally elected. But it was not fully representative as Montfort addressed only those shires and boroughs that he considered friendly to his cause.

Parliaments of Edward I

Edward I assembled many Parliaments. Sometimes knights only were summoned along with the great lords, sometimes urban representatives only, sometimes both. Gradually the pattern of including both knights and burgesses prevailed. For his "Model Parliament" of 1295, called to deal with the peril occasioned by simultaneous revolts and attacks of the Welsh, Scots, and French, Edward directed the sheriffs to see that two knights from each shire and two burgesses from each borough and city were elected; and the bishops and abbots to see that representatives of the clergy were elected to attend the meeting. Edward's Model Parliament accordingly had four houses: (1) the great barons, lay and ecclesiastical (the old Great Council, later known as "Lords"); and representatives of each of the following—(2) lower clergy; (3) burgesses (townspeople); and (4) knights (rural middle class). Eventually, though not in the time of Edward I, the knights and the burgesses coalesced into what came to be known as "Commons," and the lower clergy dropped out, since they had their own annual convocations, leaving only two houses: "Lords" and "Commons."

The main purpose of Edward I in summoning Parliaments was to obtain support for his foreign wars by grants of special taxes. In addition to being much easier than dealing separately with the inhabitants of each rural area and town, this method enabled the king to invoke the principle of "the majority rules" whereby a simple majority could bind the whole. If he obtained approval of over half of those present, his cause was won. Each town and area authorized its representatives to deal in its name. Such assemblies also facilitated the promulgation of new legislation and the mustering of support for royal measures likely to arouse opposition, such as raising troops or limiting Papal power in England.

Bargaining for laws

Since attending Parliament meant inconvenience and expense, and granting the king's desires usually involved further sacrifices, representatives sought to obtain some compensation by petitioning the king to correct certain abuses, make certain laws, take or refrain from certain action. The members of Parliament were in a favorable bargaining position, since if the king did not grant them what they wanted they could refuse to grant him what he desired. It soon became an accepted parliamentary principle that "Redress of grievances precedes grant of supplies." Eventually, in the fourteenth century, petitioners would formulate their petitions or "bills" in the exact wording they wished enacted so that their purpose could not be subverted. While its exact form and full powers were not yet completely established, Parliament was an accepted English institution by the end of the reign of Edward I.

Confirmation of the charters (1297)

In order to solicit support, Edward I reaffirmed various rights and immunities of his subjects several times. Edward's Confirmation of the Charters (1297) was very significant since it contained a clause in which he agreed not to levy any new taxes without "the common consent of all the realm." While this limitation did not exactly mean that there was to be "no taxation without representation," it did obviously mean that some kind of general popular assent was to be obtained before new taxes were levied, and this was most easily secured through Parliament.

Legislation and improved governmental organization

Second only to his establishment of the parliamentary tradition was Edward's contribution to the English legal system. In his legislation, Edward employed Parliament as a cooperating agency. Edward's enactments rounded out English criminal and civil law, and much of the latter remained virtually intact from his time until the eighteenth century. Since most of Edward's legal contribution consisted in restating, clarifying, improving, and codifying previously established laws, he has been called "the English Justinian." Edward's *statutas* both "stated" and "established" the law, doing so in collaboration with Parliament.

Much of Edward's legislation was directed to improving the organization of the royal government. The *quo warranto* proceedings were instituted early in his reign to extend the jurisdiction of the royal courts by curtailing private and local jurisdictions. Edward also divided the central royal courts into three main branches: the Court of King's Bench, for cases involving the King, such as major crimes that were considered offenses against the King's peace; the Court of Common Pleas, for ordinary civil cases that were brought before the royal courts; and the Court of the Exchequer, for cases involving alleged debts to the crown.

Edward clarified the composition of the *curia regis* (royal council). In addition to the Great Council or Parliament (the full *curia regis*), there was a small continuous *curia regis* that included the king's close advisers and major department heads. A regular civil service with gradual promotions appeared, and improved methods were introduced in departments such as the Exchequer. The Chancery went "out of court" to become a separate department.

On local levels, Edward expanded "local government by royal command." Local officials, and especially ordinary citizens, were assigned a growing number of governmental functions, which they accomplished effectively under royal surveillance, as in the case of juries of various types, assigned to investigate criminal charges, declare property rights, assess taxes, and so on.

Military and eccle- (continued)

The army was greatly expanded and feudalism was further restrained by the prescription that all men having lands worth £20 or more a year must accept knighthood and provide for themselves the military equipment of mounted knights. Initiated during the reign of Henry III, this measure was implemented during that of Edward I. The extensive use of infantrymen, particularly longbow archers, along with cavalry, and the coordination of these two elements known as the "combined tactics," were evolved and perfected during the wars against the unconventional Welsh and Scots.

With regard to the Church, Edward was both firm and conciliatory. He taxed the clergy, restrained extension of clerical prerogatives, and forbade gifts of lands to religious houses without royal permission. He openly defied the *Clericis laicos* (1296) bull of Boniface VIII, which forbade the clergy to pay royal taxes without Papal consent. He declared that those clergy who refused to pay the fifth of the value of their movables that he demanded would be outlawed. On the other hand, Edward amicably shared with Boniface VIII a tax of a tenth on movables of the English clergy in 1301; and he allowed Clement V to levy an "annates" tax on English benefices in return for Papal permission to collect a "tenth" from the clergy for seven years.

siastical policies

During the High Middle Ages, England came to have a strong monarchy with a well-organized, departmentalized central government, while the English people began to play a more active, constructive part in the governance of the kingdom. Circuit courts employing the jury system and functioning in every corner of the land made royal justice both generally available and preferable. Royal charters repeatedly guaranteed the rights and liberties of Englishmen, as well as affirmed the limitations of the royal government. National representation in Parliament evolved from an extension of the representative principle. The concept of "the community of the realm" and the principles of "no taxation without representation" and "the will of the people is the source of the law" were foreshadowed. Taxation was expanded; and a "modernized" army was built up. Extensive liberties were conceded to towns, and local citizens participated more extensively in the conduct of rural as well as urban government.

English government in the High Middle Ages

EXCELLENT collaborative multi-volume histories of England include *The Oxford History of England*, ed. GEORGE N. CLARK (Oxford: Oxford U.P., 1934); CHARLES W. C. OMAN, *History of England* (London: Methuen, 1915–1955); and WILLIAM HUNT and REGINALD LANE POOLE, *Political History of England* (London: Longmans, 1905–1910). There are also good articles on English history in the *Cambridge Medieval History* (London: Cambridge U.P., 1911ff.; New York: Doubleday, 1949ff.), which has three volumes on the High Middle Ages.

An excellent recent, comprehensive one-volume treatment of its special subject is BRYCE LYON, *A Constitutional and Legal History of Medieval England* (New York: Harper, 1960), which includes excellent historical surveys; another is J. E. A. JOLLIFFE, *Constitutional History of England to 1485* (London: Black, 1948). FAITH THOMPSON is the author of a fine work on *Magna Carta* (Minneapolis: U. of Minn., 1950), as well as a good

References for Chapter 19

Short History of Parliament, 1265–1642 (U. of Minn., 1953). ARTHUR R. HOGUE treats *Origins of the Common Law* (Bloomington: Indiana U.P., 1966); and C. WARREN HOLLISTER, *The Military Organization of Norman England* (Oxford: Clarendon, 1965).

Works on special periods include G. W. S. BARROW, *Feudal Britain 1066–1314* (London: Arnold, 1956); H. R. LOYN, *The Norman Conquest* (London: Hutchinson, 1965); EDWARD A. FREEMAN, *The History of the Norman Conquest of England*, 6 vols. (Oxford: Clarendon, 1873 ff.); R. ALLEN BROWN, *The Normans and the Norman Conquest* (New York: Crowell, 1968); TIMOTHY BAKER, *The Normans* (New York: Collier, 1969); HENRY W. C. DAVIS, *England Under the Normans and Angevins (1066–1272)*, 13th rev. ed. (London: Methuen, 1949); FREDERIC W. MAITLAND, *Domesday Book and Beyond* (Cambridge: Cambridge U.P., 1897); AUSTIN LANE POOLE, *From Domesday Book to Magna Carta, 1087–1216* (Oxford: Clarendon, 1951); KATE NORGATE, *England Under the Angevin Kings*, 2 vols. (London: Macmillan, 1887); and FREDERICK M. POWICKE's *The Loss of Normandy, 1189–1204* (Manchester, Eng.: U. of Manchester, 1913), as well as his *The Thirteenth Century, 1216–1307* (Oxford: Clarendon, 1953).

Among numerous good biographies are DAVID C. DOUGLAS, *William the Conqueror* (Berkeley: University of California, 1907); FRANK BARLOW, *William I and the Norman Conquest* (London: English Universities, 1965); FRANK M. STENTON, *William the Conqueror* (London: Putnams, 1908); A. J. MACDONALD, *Lanfranc . . .* (London: Oxford U.P., 1926); EDWARD A. FREEMAN, *The Reign of William Rufus*, 2 vols. (Oxford: Clarendon, 1882); JOHN T. APPLEBY, *. . . King Stephen* (New York: Barnes and Noble, 1970), and *Henry II* (New York: Macmillan, 1962); H. A. CRONNE, *The Reign of Stephen . . .* (London: Weidenfeld and Nicolson, 1970); LOUIS F. SALZMAN, *Henry II* (Boston, Houghton Mifflin, 1914); RICHARD WINSTON, *Thomas Becket* (New York: Knopf, 1967); AMY R. KELLY, *Eleanor of Aquitaine and the Four Kings* (Cambridge, Mass.: Harvard U.P., 1950); JOHN T. APPLEBY, *John, King of England* (New York: Knopf, 1959); SIDNEY PAINTER, *The Reign of King John* (Baltimore: Johns Hopkins, 1949); KATE NORGATE, *John Lackland* (London: Macmillan, 1902); FREDERICK M. POWICKE, *Stephen Langdon* (Oxford: Clarendon, 1928); FREDERICK M. POWICKE, *King Henry III and the Lord Edward: The Community of the Realm . . .*, 2 vols. (Oxford: Clarendon, 1947); CHARLES BEMONT, *Simon de Montfort . . .*, tr. E. F. Jacob (Oxford: Clarendon, 1930); LOUIS F. SALZMAN, *Edward I* (New York: Praeger, 1968); THOMAS F. TOUT, *Edward the First* (London: Macmillan, 1893); and EDWARD JENKS, *Edward Plantagenet* (New York: Putnams, 1902).

England had several excellent historians during the High Middle Ages. Leading sources for successive segments of this era include WILLIAM OF MALMESBURY, *Chronicle of the Kings of England . . .*, tr. J. A. Giles (London: Bohn, 1847), for the period to about 1142; WILLIAM OF NEWBURGH, "History" in *Chronicles of the Reigns of Stephen, Henry II, and Richard I*, 4 vols. (London: Bohn, 1884–1889), which carries the account to 1198; ROGER OF HOVEDEN, *Annals*, tr. H. T. Riley, 2 vols. (London: Bohn, 1853), which runs to 1201; ROGER OF WENDOVER, *Flowers of History . . .*, tr. J. A. Giles, 2 vols. (London: Bohn, 1849), which goes to 1235; and MATTHEW PARIS, *English History . . . 1235 to 1273*, tr. J. A. Giles, 3 vols. (London:

Bohn, 1852–1854). Recommended collections of selections from various sources include EDWARD P. CHEYNEY, ed., *Readings in English History* . . . (New York: Ginn, 1922); R. TREVOR DAVIES, *Documents Illustrating the History of Civilization in Medieval England* (London: Methuen, 1927); MARGARET A. HENNINGS, ed., *England Under Henry III, Illustrated from Contemporary Sources* (London: Longmans, 1924); and GEORGE B. ADAMS and H. M. STEPHENS, eds., *Select Documents of English Constitutional History* (New York: Macmillan, 1924). An excellent, readable account of Ireland is A. J. OTWAY-RUTHVEN, *A History of Medieval Ireland* (London: E. Benn, 1968).

THE RISE OF FRANCE TO HEGEMONY IN EUROPE.
Chapter 20.

ALTHOUGH inferior in strength to both the Western Empire and England at the outset of the High Middle Ages, France became the leading state in Europe by the later thirteenth century. This was achieved mainly in two ways: by expansion of the royal domains (the direct holdings of the French monarchy) and by greatly improved organization and functioning of the royal government. A series of strong, energetic, intelligent, Capetian kings, blessed with good health and longevity, cooperated with the Church and the rising towns to increase their power. At the same time they prudently remained just and respectful in their dealings with the great nobles. French commerce, industry, agriculture, and towns grew apace. French prosperity had a solid basis in France's key geographical position, rich soils, copious rainfall, beneficent climate, and diversified resources. Meanwhile, competition with the English kings, who held extensive territories in France, forced the French monarchy to become strong or succumb.

GROWING POWER OF THE CAPETIAN MONARCHY.   1108–1223
Section 58.

> The Court of France met and decided that the King of England had forfeited all the land that he and his ancestors held from the King of France. . . . [Sentence of forfeiture imposed upon King John of England by King Philip II and his court as reported by Ralph of Coggeshall in his *English Chronicle* (thirteenth century).]

THE REMARKABLE Capetian kings who occupied the French throne from 1108 to 1314 were increasingly stimulated by intense and demanding rivalry with the Norman and Plantagenet kings of England. As a result of their success in this competition, the Capetians tripled their royal domains from 1108 to 1223. Meanwhile they also greatly improved and strengthened the royal government. As Capetian power grew within France, French prestige mounted in Europe.

Louis VI, the Fat, enhances royal power (1108–1137)

Louis VI who was as a youth tall and handsome and called the Battler, grew much more corpulent in later life, so that he eventually had to be hoisted onto his horse and was nicknamed the Fat. The chief contribution of this Iron-Clad Judge was to establish firm control throughout the royal domains of the Ile de France, where many castellans and lesser lords were oppressive tyrants and bold flaunters of royal authority. Louis, who eventually came to be recognized as the chief protector of the people and the Church, untiringly campaigned against insubordinate barons until he finally subjected them, often only after repeatedly defeating and pardoning them. Thus robber-baron Hugh of Crécy was in the end compelled to retire to a monastery; plunderer Hugh of le Puiset was forced to go on a Crusade on which he lost his life; and sadistic Thomas Marle was slain in battle. On being warned that it would be very difficult to subdue one of his barons who had a virtually impregnable castle, Louis scornfully declared: *What a disgrace it would be for the majesty of the crown if we were to hold back for fear of a bandit!*

Louis VI also began to extend royal authority outside the royal domains into the territories of his tenants-in-chief. When the uncle of the rightful heir to the lordship of Bourbon usurped that holding, Louis crossed Berry into Bourbon, took him captive, and forced him to disgorge his prize. When the Count of Auvergne replaced the rightful Bishop of Clermont-Ferrand, Louis VI compelled him to reinstate the prelate. After the Flemish Count Charles the Good was assassinated (1127), Louis marched in, conducted a judicial inquiry, and had his own candidate, William Clito, son of the dispossessed Robert Curthose of Normandy, elected Count. When the blundering policies of William Clito brought about a Flemish rebellion, however, Louis left him to his fate and accepted his replacement. When Duke William X of Aquitaine died on a pilgrimage to Compostella, leaving his daughter Eleanor as the King's ward, Louis promptly brought about a marriage between the heiress and his own son and heir, Prince Louis. To counteract the threat of the Anglo-Norman monarchy, Louis supported Duke Robert Curthose of Normandy against his brother, King Henry I. After Robert was taken prisoner, Louis supported Robert's son, William Clito, who claimed the Duchy of Normandy. And when Stephen of Blois seized the English throne on Henry's death, Louis supported the claims of Henry's daughter, Mathilda.

Civil service and urban charters

King Louis VI built up a French civil service by appointing lesser nobles and commoners to offices of power and trust. While their position was usually permanent, it was also dependent on the royal pleasure. The able Abbot Suger of St. Denis, Louis' prime minister, headed this service. This change was resisted by the powerful Garlande family, which had obtained possession of the chief offices in the kingdom. When Louis deposed from the office of seneschal Archdeacon Stephen Garlande, who also held the office of Chancellor, he had to face a rebellion that lasted for two years. Although he was not particularly sympathetic to the aspirations of the communes, Louis, for his own ends, granted some of them charters, one of which, that of Lorris, became a model for many sub-

The Rise of France

sequent charters. For this reason, though with only partial justification, Louis has been called "the Father of the Communes." Louis VI's policies, especially that of controlling obstreperous barons and halting their abuses, were very beneficial for the Ile de France. Abbot Suger, his admiring biographer, says that Louis "supported and protected the churches, the clergy, the laboring classes, and the needy."

Louis VII (1137–1180) is known in history as the Naive. During a dispute with young Louis, Pope Innocent II reportedly remarked: "The King of France is a child who must be educated." And Gervase of Canterbury wrote that Louis was "a very Christian King, but somewhat naive." Still Louis was not without character and courage. And most of his earlier mistakes were redeemed by his later conduct.

Louis VII, the Naive, (1137–1180)

Early in his reign, Louis VII unsuccessfully opposed both the Pope and the powerful Count of Champagne over an appointment to the Archbishopric of Bourges. He also foolishly supported a bigamous union of the Count of Vermandois with his (the King's) sister-in-law, despite the fact that the Count had repudiated his legal wife, who was still living and was the niece of the powerful Count of Champagne. On the poorly managed Second Crusade (1147–1150), Louis lost a large part of the French army in Asia Minor and engaged in a futile attack on Damascus.

Initial reverses

On his return from the Crusade, however, Louis began to evidence his backbone. With the advice of his counsellors, he had his marriage with Eleanor of Aquitaine annulled on grounds of consanguinity (1152). Eleanor had given bad example on the Crusade, had exposed herself to accusations of infidelity by her indiscretions, and especially had failed to give Louis a son. Renunciation of Eleanor meant the loss of Aquitaine, but chances of getting a son were improved, and turbulent Aquitaine was a dubious asset. Freed of the critical Eleanor, Louis married Adele of Champagne, who provided him with a gifted and able son, Philip II, and brought him the alliance of Champagne and Blois.

Louis VII eventually continued many of the policies of his strong father. In the royal domains, he kept on repressing unruly robber barons. He retained and expanded the civil service established by Louis VI. He also continued and increased the conferral of royal charters on communes; and he took a special interest in the liberation of serfs. He even increased royal intervention in various parts of France, particularly in defense of churchmen who appealed to him. Several times he intervened on behalf of bishops, monks, and other clerics in Burgundy, Champagne, Auvergne, and Languedoc. In promising the monks of Vezelay that he would bring to justice the Count of Nevers, Louis said: "You may rest assured that even if he possesses as much land as the King of England, I would not allow his violence to go unpunished!"

Subsequent achievements

Louis opposed further expansion by the powerful Henry II of England. When Henry besieged Toulouse with a large army, Count Raymond and the townsfolk appealed to Louis. The townspeople wrote: *After God we appeal to you as our good master, protector, and liberator.* Taking advantage of a feudal principle that forbade a vassal to attack his overlord, Louis came to Toulouse, gained entry, and then informed Henry II that he was unrightfully besieging his suzerain. Observing feudal law, upon which he, too, depended, Henry lifted the siege and withdrew.

Louis befriended and gave asylum to refugee churchmen from abroad. He both received and tried to intervene on behalf of Pope Alexander III when the latter was forced to flee by Emperor Frederick I, Barbarossa. He did the same with Archbishop Thomas Becket, who was forced into exile by Henry II. To the English King Louis wrote: *You speak of your "former Archbishop of Canterbury," while I do not dare to depose the humblest clerk in my kingdom.* After the death of Becket, when the latter's aide John of Salisbury fell under Henry's displeasure, Louis made John Bishop of Chartres.

Philip II, Augustus, (1180–1223)

During the final year of his reign, the old King was assisted in his government by his fourteen-year-old son, Philip II. After Louis' death, the spirited Philip soon made himself the master, disillusioning his mother's brothers, the Counts of Champagne and Blois, who expected to dominate the government. Philip II had a frail constitution, but a quick intelligence and a strong will. He almost died, apparently from sweating sickness, on the Third Crusade; and he became blind in one eye and corpulent as he grew older. But despite his physical limitations, Philip was a great monarch and, although he had no taste for war and preferred diplomacy, he was no coward, as he showed in the battle of Bouvines. Philip's great ambition was to increase the royal authority and unite France. At the same time he was both practical and cautious. He got good breaks as well as bad ones, but he took advantage of the former and surmounted the latter, to become "the founder of the French monarchy," known in history as "Augustus."

Northward expansion and victory

Shortly after his accession, and against the wishes of his mother and her brothers, the Counts of Champagne and Blois, the young King married the ten-year-old Isabella of Hainault, a niece of the Count of Flanders. He thus obtained the valuable County of Artois in northern France as a dowry, and later, on the death of his wife's childless sister, claims to her Counties of Vermandois and Amiens, which he successfully occupied. Meanwhile, Philip's disgruntled uncles, the Counts of Champagne, Blois, and Sancerre, organized a strong feudal alliance against the young King. The rebels were even joined by the Count of Flanders, who had been meanwhile rudely disillusioned in his own dream of controlling Philip. The greatest danger lay in the possibility that this coalition would be joined by the powerful Henry II of England. But Philip held a famous conference with the aging Henry at Gisors (1180), and persuaded him to remain neutral. Philip then successfully dealt with his rebel vassals individually, until the shaky coalition was dissolved.

Marital problems

Philip's first wife died at the age of nineteen (1190). To secure the assistance of the Danish fleet for a proposed invasion of England, Philip married Ingebourg, the sister of King Canute VI of Denmark. Despite Ingebourg's beauty, Philip developed a physical repulsion for her almost immediately, and persuaded a council of French bishops to dissolve the marriage on the plea that he and Ingebourg were related within a prohibited degree. He then proceeded, with their approval, to take a new wife, Agnes of Meran. But Ingebourg appealed to Pope Innocent III, who quashed the decision. For two decades Philip refused to give up Agnes and reinstate Ingebourg. In 1200, after France was put under an interdict by Innocent, Philip outwardly complied, although without real submission. Finally, in 1213, after the death of Agnes, and on the eve of his decisive conflict with John and Otto, Philip brought Ingebourg back to his court.

Relations with the Kings of England concerning English-held territories in France were a primary concern of Philip. Although Henry II of England had helped him by remaining neutral during his struggle with his rebellious barons, Philip II was undeterred by considerations of gratitude. One after another, he encouraged and supported Henry's rebellious sons—Henry the Young (d. 1185), Geoffrey of Brittany (d. 1186), Richard the Lionhearted, and finally John—against their father. *Philip II and Kings Henry II and Richard I of England*

At first King Richard and Philip, as recent allies, were seemingly "great friends," and even went on the Third Crusade together. But their friendship soon cooled, due partly to their different temperaments and partly to the prominence and successes of Richard on the Crusade. More fundamental, of course, were their conflicting royal interests. On returning home early from the third Crusade, Philip allied with John against the still-absent Richard. When Richard was taken prisoner and held for ransom in Germany, Philip bribed Richard's captors to keep him captive longer, and invaded and occupied part of Normandy (1192–1194). But when Richard was released early in 1194, he promptly turned the tables on Philip, whom he thoroughly defeated at Fréteval in 1194. Richard soon reoccupied Normandy, where he constructed the magnificent castle of Chateau Gaillard on a height overlooking the Seine at a gateway to the Ile de France.

A lucky break for Philip was the early succession of the erratic John to the English throne (1199). The new king soon played into Philip's hands, as well as alienated the support of many of his own barons by marrying Isabelle of Angoulême. When Isabelle's aggrieved fiancé, Hugh of Lusignan, appealed to the court of Philip II and John refused to answer the summons, Philip's court took the extreme step of declaring John's French holdings forfeit as those of a contumacious vassal, saying that "both he and his ancestors have long neglected to render all the services due for these lands . . ." (1202). Meanwhile Philip allied with Arthur of Brittany, son of John's deceased elder brother, with an agreement that Arthur was to have all of the English territories in northwestern France, except Normandy, which was to go to Philip. Philip promptly invaded Normandy. After being taken prisoner by John, the young Arthur (1202) was apparently murdered. The occupation of Normandy by Philip was completed by 1204, while that of Maine, Anjou, and the Touraine (1204–1205) became a virtual promenade, as many of the barons, disgusted by John, came over voluntarily to Philip. But southwestern France, including most of Poitou, together with Aquitaine and Saintonge, remained in English hands. *Philip and John*

Eventually John, after settling a long quarrel with Pope Innocent III, sought to recover his lost holdings. He allied with several of Philip's neighbors and some of Philip's nobles against the French King. Prominent among John's allies were Count Ferrand of Flanders and Emperor Otto IV of Germany. The plan to catch and crush Philip between Otto moving down through Flanders and John moving up from Aquitaine was frustrated when John dallied in the south and Philip moved rapidly northward and engaged the Germans in Flanders. In a bloody battle at Bouvines in 1214, the French troops, which included contingents from the communes, finally gained the advantage and seized the standard-bearing wagon of the Germans, who fled. Philip's decisive victory confirmed his recent acquisitions in northwestern France.

Projects of Prince Louis

When the English nobles revolted against John in 1216, and invited in Prince Louis of France, Philip II secretly assisted his son's costly expedition. But after most of the English nobles went over to young Henry III, following John's death (1216), and the French fleet was defeated in the English Channel by Eustace the Monk (1217), Louis was compelled to give up his claims in return for a promise of compensation for his expenses and pardons for his English followers (1217).

Philip did not take any active part in the Albigensian Crusade, although he permitted his subjects to participate and allowed his son Louis to do a short stint. Philip evidently chose this course partly because he was so involved elsewhere and partly because he didn't perceive any immediate gain for the crown. His decision relieved the monarchy of the obloquy and hatred connected with this bloody business, and put the crown in a better position later to reap the fruits of the Crusade.

Governmental progress

In addition to quadrupling the royal domains, Philip improved the royal government. The smaller *curia regis* (privy council of the king) became more distinct and professional. Collection of royal revenues was improved, and the income of the government was greatly increased. Additional revenues were obtained by a "decime" or "tenth," known as the "Saladin tithe," levied on the annual income and movables of those who did not participate in the Third Crusade; and by commutation of military services owed by lay and ecclesiastical lords and communes. Philip granted numerous charters to communes, further increasing royal influence and royal revenues. His appointment of *baillis* to supervise rural *prévôts* improved local government. Philip also walled and beautified Paris, straightened and paved its streets, and fostered the development of the University of Paris.

FURTHER PROGRESS OF FRENCH MONARCHICAL POWER.
Section 59.

1223–1314

> Be completely just and never deny justice to anyone on any account. If there is a dispute between a poor man and a rich one, uphold the former as against the latter until such a time as the truth of the matter is determined, and then do justice. [From the *Instructions* of Louis IX to his son Philip (III).]

The Rise of France

THE SUCCESSORS of Philip II during the following century continued the work of expanding royal control and strengthening the royal government. Like their immediate predecessors, they were remarkable, hard-working, dedicated rulers.

Despite the brevity of his reign, Louis VIII accomplished a great deal. Though of a feeble constitution, he was energetic and ambitious. It has been said that he "burnt himself out," as within three years he greatly expanded royal holdings in southern France. After the death of the strong Simon de Montfort the Elder (1218), who had won control of much of Languedoc during the Albigensian Crusade, his weak son Amaury was unable to maintain himself in power. Louis VIII accepted Amaury's offer of the distraught territory, and came to southern France, where his intervention was welcomed by both sides. The County of Toulouse and its dependencies were thus added to the Capetian domains on the principle that properties confiscated from heretics reverted to the crown. Meanwhile Louis took advantage of the weakness of the English government during the minority of Henry III, and the rebellious attitude of several southern French barons, to occupy Poitou and adjacent territories, such as Saintonge, Perigord, and the Limousin, and even the interior of Gascony. *Louis VIII (1223–1226)*

By his will, Louis VIII left to his sons other than Louis (IX), who was succeeding to the throne, several of his territories, which were given the status of "appanages," with special privileges and immunities. He left Artois and its dependencies to Robert; Anjou and Maine to Charles; and Poitou and its dependencies to Alphonse, who expanded his holdings by marrying the heiress of Toulouse. Louis IX faithfully carried out his father's will.

As Louis IX was only twelve at his father's death in 1226, the Kingdom was administered for some time by his mother, the pious, competent Blanche of Castile. Her aristocratic opponents were critical of the regent as a woman and a foreigner, and they called her "Dame Hirsent" (Madame Wolf) and accused her of keeping the young King "in bail." But Blanche successfully fulfilled the office of regent, and skillfully dealt with successive coalitions of rebellious barons. Her favorite device was to deal with the rebels separately, and detach various members of a coalition, while waiting for it to split into factions. She also took advantage of breaks such as Count Thibaud of Champagne's romantic attraction for her. On one occasion, while at the castle of Montlhery, the barons almost captured her and the young King, but they escaped with the help of the people of Paris, who lined the sides of the road as the royal party returned to the capital. Even after her son assumed personal power in 1234, Blanche continued to be most influential in the government, and was regent for Louis IX during his absence on his first Crusade (1248–1252). *Regency of Blanche of Castile (1226–1234)*

St. Louis IX was strongly influenced by his mother, who had declared that she would rather see her son contract leprosy than commit a mortal sin. Louis' great objective in life was to love and serve God and to enable *St. Louis IX (1226–1270)* others to do likewise. He felt that his leading responsibilities as king were to render justice and preserve peace. He admonished his son Philip: "Never deny justice to anyone on any account," and warned him: "Be loath to make war against your fellow Christians." He greatly expanded and improved royal justice in France and settled his differences with foreign countries by compromise agreements.

Louis IX was very charitable. He lived most simply and wore the plainest of clothes, to the chagrin of his wife. Louis had four hundred needy persons fed daily at the royal palace, and personally attended to the needs of lepers. He several times risked his life for his subjects while on Crusade, as when he refused to leave a ship carrying several hundred persons that was in danger of sinking, since he knew that it would be repaired more promptly if he remained on board. At the same time, Louis was complex and very human. He wore a hair shirt and mortified himself by mixing water with his wine, but he was pleasant and humorous. He was firm in his insistence on royal rights, and practical in his conduct of the royal government, yet he was extremely deferential to his mother. On the minus side, Louis was intolerant of Jews and Moslems, saying that the best way to argue with someone who insulted the faith was to put a sword through his belly. He put an excessive value on crusading, going on two great, costly, unsuccessful Crusades: the fatal second one against the advice of his counselors. And he was sometimes overconservative, as in his too static view of law and rights.

Conciliatory and honorable foreign relations

Louis sought peace in his dealings with other Christian monarchs, and made concessions to settle differences. With James I of Aragon, Louis concluded the Treaty of Corbeil (1258), whereby, in return for Aragonese recognition of Capetian acquisition of former holdings of Count Raymond of Toulouse, Louis recognized Aragonese acquisition of the lands of the County of Barcelona, the old "Spanish March" of the Franks.

Henry III of England had participated in at least two French rebellions (1234 and 1242) against Louis IX, both of which had collapsed; and his troubles at home as well as his weakness in southwestern France would have made his French territories easy prey. But Louis IX refused to take advantage of his "brother's" embarrassment. By the generous Peace of Paris (1259), in return for Henry's acknowledgment of vassalage for his holdings in southwestern France, and his renunciation of claims to territories in northwestern France, Louis recognized Henry's "rights" to Guienne and Gascony, and even returned to him certain adjacent territories.

Louis' reputation for justice and honesty was so widespread that he was invited on various occasions to act as an international arbitrator. He arbitrated a dispute between the King of Navarre and the Duke of Brittany, and another between the Count of Bar and his neighbors. He solved the question of succession in Flanders and Hainault. He was even called upon by both sides to judge the legitimacy of the Provisions of Oxford in the running dispute between King Henry III and his English barons.

The Rise of France

Although Louis was a loyal son of the Church, he was also a firm believer in the independence of secular government and in the dictum "Render to Caesar the things that are Caesar's . . ." While respectfully cooperative with Church authorities, he was not blindly obsequious. Louis rejected a request from the French bishops that a person excommunicated by the Church be automatically outlawed by the civil government, saying slyly that he would do this if the Church would allow the case to be tried in the royal courts.

Relations with the Church and the Empire

Louis refused to take sides in the struggle between the Papacy and Emperor Frederick II and tried instead to promote a peaceful solution. He opposed a papal offer of the imperial crown for his brother Robert of Artois, and declined to profit from Frederick's troubles by expansion into German territory beyond the Rhone or in the Rhineland, as he might easily have done. On the other hand, he insisted that Frederick release French prelates seized on their way to a general council called by Gregory IX. And he made known his intention to protect Pope Innocent IV's Council of Lyons when Frederick threatened to march on the latter.

Implementing Biblical injunctions, Louis took special care to promote a reign of justice. He is known as "the French Justinian" for his issuance of various laws or *ordonnances*, such as those defining the duties of royal officials, restricting private warfare, and forbidding judicial duels and ordeals. He built up the royal judiciary or *Parlement* and improved its effectiveness, encouraging greater professionalism in justice. Primarily to serve as judges who would redress violations of the rights of the people by royal officials, Louis set *enqueteurs* over the *baillis*. Because of his conservative respect for existing rights, Louis did not grant further charters to communes, with one exception: the new port of Aigues Mortes that he established for crusading purposes in southern France.

Internal policies and Crusades of Louis IX

Louis IX responded generously to Papal pleas for crusading to regain lost territories in the Holy Land. Louis' first Crusade (1248–1252), assembled at enormous expense, was directed to Egypt. After initial successes, the crusaders were defeated and most of them were captured. Louis and his companions were released only after the payment of large ransoms, following which the King spent a few years reorganizing and refurbishing the defenses of Western holdings in Palestine. His ill-conceived second Crusade (1270), which went to Tunis on the advice of Charles of Anjou, succumbed to disease. Victims included the King himself and other members of the royal family.

Philip III, who had participated with his father in the Crusade to Tunis, returned to France with the bodies of five of his relatives, including those of his father, Louis IX, and his own wife and child. Philip III is known as "the Audacious" or "the Bold" partly because of his unsuccessful intervention in the Spanish peninsula. He was strongly influenced by his uncle, Charles of Anjou, and his own wife, Marie of Brabant.

Philip III (1270–1285) and expansion to the south

Since his uncle, Alphonse of Poitiers, and the latter's wife, Joan of Toulouse, had both died childless on the Crusade to Tunis, Philip declared that their holdings had escheated to the crown, and promptly occupied their extensive fiefs in southern France, including Poitou, Toulouse, and Auvergne, together with adjacent territories. Philip also acquired both French Navarre and Champagne-Blois for his son Philip (IV), by arranging for the latter's marriage to Jeanne, heiress to these territories. Navarre was promptly occupied by a French army and put under a French administrator, but Champagne-Blois was administered by the English husband of Jeanne's mother until the mother's death in 1284, when it was taken over by the French crown.

Philip's reign is notable for an attempt to expand into the Spanish peninsula. After the refusal of Pedro III of Aragon to give up Sicily, which he had occupied following the "Sicilian Vespers," Philip III took up the cause of Charles of Anjou and the Pope. Philip also accepted the Papal offer of the throne of Aragon for his son Charles of Valois and invaded Aragon with a large army (1285). Although the French besieged and took Gerona, they were forced to retreat when their army was decimated by disease and their supporting fleet was defeated in the battle of Las Islas Formiguas (1285). Philip III himself died at Perpignan during the precipitous retreat.

Philip IV, the Fair (1285–1314)

Philip IV, the Fair (or the Handsome), was one of the great kings of French history, although the part Philip played, as well as the ultimate effects of his reign, has been variously evaluated. Philip was enigmatic to many of his contemporaries. Some have maintained that Philip IV was merely a figurehead and a passive instrument in the hands of his ministers. Bishop Saisset, who was put on trial by Philip, said: *The King is like the great horned owl. He only stares at one without uttering a word. He is . . . but a statue.* Such critics would argue that Philip's policies were due to his chief ministers such as Pierre Flotte and William de Nogaret, who had been trained in the absolutist concepts of Roman law in southern France.

But it would also seem that Philip IV had absolutist ideas himself, and that these influenced his choice of ministers. During Philip's long reign, royal policies to extend monarchical authority remained consistent, despite a succession of ministers. Also, Philip went out of his way to support such ministers as Nogaret when they became unpopular. That the more extreme claims and actions of some of his supporters may have exceeded the views of Philip IV is probable, but that Philip IV participated actively in the guidance of his own ship of state is practically certain. Philip's decisive character is indicated by his treatment of the wives of his three sons. Upon learning that the wives of two of his sons were carrying on illicit affairs with two knights, with the connivance of the third wife, Philip had them surprised during a secret tryst. The two knights were executed and the three wives were imprisoned. The first two wives were never allowed to return to their husbands: one died in prison, the other in a convent.

Expansion and policies

Expansion of the royal domains under Philip IV was piecemeal but totaled a considerable amount by the end of his reign. Besides Navarre and Champagne-Blois, acquired through his marriage to the heiress

The Rise of France

Jeanne, Philip profited by victories in Flanders and by the weakness of the Empire to acquire several small holdings. Among such were Lille, Douai, and Bethune in southern Flanders; Ostrevent, Toul, and Bar in the Rhineland; and Lyons, Viviers, and Valenciennes in the Rhoneland.

Philip IV wisely abandoned projects of French intervention in Spain and Italy. He dropped the defense of the claims of the Infantes de la Cerda in Castile, and he gave up the project of taking Aragon. He was satisfied with a partial compromise concerning Sicily, and abstained from supporting the Italian venture of his brother, Charles of Valois. Instead, he concentrated his military efforts on bringing into greater subjection the two great semiautonomous fiefs of Guienne-Gascony and Flanders.

Philip IV and Edward I of England

Guienne and Gascony were in the hands of the King of England, and were consequently independent of French royal control for all practical purposes. As clashes between French and English fishermen had recently led to English acts of piracy and violence, Philip summoned Edward to his court, and the latter sent his brother Edmund to represent him. At Philip's request, Edmund turned over border fortresses in Gascony to Philip for forty days as security; but at the end of the agreed-on time Philip did not surrender them.

In the war that ensued (1294–1303), Edward had Count Guy of Flanders as his ally. But the French won impressive victories and eventually took Guy prisoner. In 1297 Edward felt compelled to abandon the struggle and agreed to a truce on the basis of a restoration of the *status quo ante bellum* (situation before the war). Final peace was not arranged until 1303. As steps to peace, King Edward I married Philip's sister, Margaret, while his son Edward (II) married Philip's daughter, Isabella.

Philip and Flanders

French problems with Flanders eclipsed those in Guienne-Gascony. In 1294, Count Guy had incurred the wrath of Philip IV by marrying a daughter of Philip's enemy, Edward I, without Philip's consent. During the war between Edward and Philip, Guy was taken prisoner (1297) by the French, but the struggle in Flanders continued. Most of the Flemish upper bourgeoisie were friendly to the French King, for which reason they were known as "Leilarts" (a reference to the Capetian lilies); but most of the ordinary bourgeoisie and the Count were hostile to the French crown and friendly to the English. Much opposition to French rule stemmed from the heavy taxes imposed by Philip. Flemish discontent came to a head in the so-called Matins of Bruges (1302). At gray of dawn, the citizens of Bruges, who were soon imitated in other Flemish cities, suddenly massacred all discoverable Frenchmen, who were identified by their inability to pronounce correctly a certain Flemish phrase. The French army that was sent to punish the Flemish was severely defeated at Courtrai in 1302 by Flemish foot soldiers, who thrust the French cavalry back into a stream they had rashly crossed. Many of the embogged and unhorsed flower of French chivalry were massacred by Flemish commoners.

Eventually Philip obtained revenge at Mons-en-Pévèle (1304). Now it was the turn of Flemish burghers to be massacred by pitiless French knights. Peace was arranged with indemnities and securities for the French (1305); but the Flemish towns would not carry out the provisions. Eventually in 1312 a restive peace was secured by Count Robert (who had succeeded his father, Guy) by the surrender of Lille, Douai, and Bethune to Philip.

Philip IV and the Papacy

The story of the relations of Philip IV with the Papacy is told more fully in connection with that of the Church. Both Philip's struggle with Pope Boniface VIII in the years 1296–1297, over royal taxation of the French clergy without Papal consent, and his contest with Boniface in the years 1301–1303, over the trial of a French bishop in a royal court, resulted in victories for the King. After Boniface died from the shock of "the outrage of Anagni" (1303), Philip and his counselors were eventually exonerated by the compliant French Pope Clement V. In addition to getting Papal censures lifted, even for Nogaret, Philip was able to bring the Pope to agree to the suppression of the Templars. In 1311 Pope Clement V ordered deletion from the Papal registry of all matter that could be injurious to the King of France, and the bulls of Boniface VIII, *Unam sanctam*, *Salvator mundi*, and *Ausculta fili* were revoked.

Further organization of the French government

Philip and his ministers extended the organization of the royal government. Much of this development was spurred by Philip's continual need of funds. The treasury department, the *Chambre des Comptes*, was definitely constituted as a separate bureau of government. The royal judiciary or *Parlement* located at Paris came to be divided into three courts: the *Chambres* of Requests, Inquests, and Pleas. Meanwhile special royal commissions of high justice were set up in Normandy, Champagne, and Languedoc. Under Philip the *enqueteurs* were no longer primarily concerned with restraining encroachments by the royal government, but were instead leading extenders of royal power, one of whose primary functions was to increase royal revenues.

In his quest for greater revenues, Philip IV was undeterred by scruples or traditions. In addition to commutation of military services, regular and extraordinary feudal aids, and fixed and voluntary taillage from towns and villages, Philip levied sales taxes (*maltôtes*: evil levies) on essential commodities, as well as proportional taxes on income and property. He also taxed the clergy without Papal permission, exacted forced loans and "gifts," debased the coinage, suppressed the Knights Templars, and mercilessly milked the Jews and North Italians (Lombards).

The adverse public reaction to Philip's exactions is reflected by contemporary John of St. Victor, who wrote: *King Philip harassed and distressed the people of his realm with new exactions of every kind, including hundreths and fiftieths* [of the worth of properties], *imposing a yoke of unaccustomed servitude upon the necks of a once free people.*

The French Estates General, a national assembly representing commoners as well as the nobility and clergy, was first summoned during the reign of Philip IV, mainly for financial purposes. In 1302 the Estates General was convoked to obtain support for Philip's quarrel with

The Rise of France

Boniface VIII; in 1308 to endorse the suppression of the Templars, which would financially benefit the crown; and in 1314 to vote funds for Philip's prosecution of renewed war with Flanders.

EVOLUTION OF FRENCH GOVERNMENTAL INSTITUTIONS
Section 60.

> If any of our barons does not voluntarily accept this law, we will constrain him to do so; and our other barons shall be bound to help us with all their power, and in good faith. [Louis IX concerning enforcement of a royal law of 1230.]

During the High Middle Ages the French king came to be regarded as the leading monarch in Europe: "the greatest of mortal kings" according to Matthew of Paris. Contemporary commercial, industrial, and financial advances called for unity and cooperation over wider areas, and encouraged stronger, better organized, more efficient government. The growth of towns provided the monarchy with dependable allies, while its chief rival, the aristocracy, declined in comparative strength. The Crusades and other overseas enterprises (as in Sicily and England) diverted large numbers of French nobles from France. Many among the aristocracy sold land to finance overseas expeditions, or as a result of extravagance, fixed rents, divided inheritances, and so on. Many hard-pressed aristocrats entered the royal services to meet expenses.

Strengthening the royal government Strengthening the French royal government does not seem to have resulted from a carefully conceived, methodical royal policy, but rather from practical adaptations and taking advantage of opportunities. Generally, the Capetian monarchs were not extremely eager or over-hasty to expand their power, or unmindful of the rights of their barons. Instead they usually proceeded cautiously, in a legal manner, within the framework of existing feudal customs. Often their actions were more defensive than aggressive, being precipitated by the transgressions of their aristocratic subjects.

A principal means of extending royal power in France was enlargement of the royal domains. Here Philip II, Louis VIII, Philip III, and Philip IV were particularly active. By 1328 an estimated two thirds of France pertained to the royal domains. This expansion was mainly effected by feudal royal rights, such as forfeit, escheat, and foremarriage, as well as by purchase, *pariage*, and *sauvegarde*. Thus Philip IV purchased several fiefs.

In *pariage* (sharing), the monarch became a partner with the fief holder; in *sauvegarde* he became the latter's special patron and protector. In both cases, the prestige and power of the monarch so overshadowed the lesser holder that the monarch was the actual master.

As the French civil service and bureaucracy grew, royal officials became the chief promoters of an expansion of royal authority. The interests of these officials, who were drawn mainly from the clergy, the bourgeoisie, and the lesser aristocracy, were naturally with the monarch, from whom they derived their authority. In the course of time, more and more leading governmental officials were lawyers imbued with the absolutist principles of later Roman law. In cases of doubt such officials were prone to presume the existence of rights of the crown, but to scrutinize rights claimed by feudal lords in an adverse, often devastating manner.

Beginning in the twelfth century, Paris became the regular royal residence and the continuing seat of the developing departments of royal government. Beautified by Philip II, the French capital far outstripped all other Western European cities except Venice in population, and enhanced the prestige of the French monarchy.

During the High Middle Ages a mutually rewarding alliance developed between the French crown and the communes, facilitating the advance of royal power. Meanwhile the old alliance of the Church with the French continued; and the Papacy as well as the French bishops cooperated with the French monarchy, finding it a welcome counterpoise against less cooperative German and English monarchs.

The central government

In the course of the High Middle Ages, the power of the French King greatly increased. The king came to hold directly all major fiefs except Flanders, Brittany, Guienne-Gascony, and Burgundy. The royal right of intervention was, at least to some degree, accepted in most French territories. A long series of Capetian monarchs, made the royal succession unquestionably hereditary by primogeniture. The king was revered as God's representative, endorsed by the Church, and even believed by many to have a "divine touch," capable of healing certain diseases.

The Capetians built up a royal civil service and bureaucracy independent of the great nobility. Royal officials were drawn mainly from the bourgeoisie, the clergy, and the lesser nobility. Louis VI initiated the process by deposing the powerful Garlande family from control of the great offices of the state, and making Abbot Suger of St. Denis the head of his administration. This work was continued by Louis VII, Philip II, and their successors. By the time of Philip IV the crown was using civil lawyers extensively in its administration.

Gradually, the governmental *petit curia regis* (small royal council) became clearly distinct from the personal *hotel du roi* (the royal household), as well as a regular substitute for the feudal Great Council, most of whose functions it regularly performed. The personnel of the *curia regis* also came to be more clearly specified. At first, the same personnel handled all sorts of matters: deliberative, financial, and judicial; but in the course of time specialists versed in matters under consideration sat upon each type of case, thus contributing to the rise of separate departments of government.

The Parlement

The royal *curia* sitting as a court of justice came to be known as the *curia in parlemento* (*parler*: to speak or discuss). There was a natural tendency to have justice administered more and more by men learned in the law. At first legal specialists participated in the judicial sessions of the ordinary *curia regis*; but in time they administered justice apart from the *curia* by delegated authority. Louis IX expanded and improved the administration of royal justice. He appointed some thirty judicial officials to hear cases for the crown, thus formally establishing the royal *Parlement*. He personally supervised and reviewed the administration of justice from time to time, and issued special instructions for the guidance of his judges. Louis intended his *enqueteurs* primarily as sort of circuit judges charged to redress infractions committed by local royal officials, as well as irregularities. Part of the office of the *baillis* and seneschals was also judicial.

Although the royal *Parlement* came to be definitely located at Paris, Philip IV established temporary judicial commissions acting in the name of the king in various parts of the kingdom. Philip IV also subdivided the central royal judiciary or *Parlement* into three branches: the Chamber of Requests, which considered petitions that the royal court assume jurisdiction; the Chamber of Inquests, which conducted judicial investigations; and the Chamber of Pleas, which rendered actual judgment in cases presented to it.

Royal justice continually expanded because of the enlargement of the royal domains, the growing power of the king as compared to that of his great feudatories, the superior caliber of justice rendered in the royal courts, and an expansion of the concept of "royal" cases subject to the royal jurisdiction.   *Expansion of royal justice*

"Royal cases" (*cas royaux*) were cases over which the royal courts had direct jurisdiction, such as those concerning respect for the royal dignity and maintenance of the public peace (the King's Peace). So far was this indefinite concept expanded that Louis X in 1315 could vaguely declare that *the King's majesty has cognizance of pleas which, either by right or long standing custom, may and should belong to the sovereign prince and no one else*. The increased study and vogue of Roman law in the High Middle Ages greatly contributed to the expansion of royal jurisdiction, because of the practically unlimited jurisdiction of Roman imperial courts. Royal justice was readily available throughout France since part of the function of local royal officials, such as *baillis* and seneschals, was judicial. These officials usually conducted a continuous unrelenting war against feudal jurisdictions and "immunities." The right of appeal from the decisions of local courts to royal courts came to be generally recognized. The same was true with the royal "right of prevention" whereby the royal courts could summon persons in any cases whatever to appear, although such persons had the eventual right to be judged by those courts to which they were normally amenable.

According to the thirteenth-century French legal authority Beaumanoir, the feudal king had a right to issue "such laws for the common good as may please him." Before the time of Philip II, little use was made of this vague general power, but thenceforth it was increasingly invoked. Although the king was theoretically supposed to originate such laws in conjunction with his barons, he ordinarily issued them in his small *curia regis* and appealed to his barons to enforce them within their own jurisdictions. Failure to comply incurred the royal displeasure. To an *ordonnance* of 1230 dealing with the Jews, Louis IX added: *If any of our barons shall refuse to accept this* établissement, *we shall constrain him*   *Legislation* to do so. . . ." Louis IX issued several laws (*ordonnances* or *établissements*) defining the duties of royal officials, forbidding judicial duels, eliminating ordeals, and requiring a "cooling off" period of forty days (a "quarantine") between the declaration of war and commencement of hostilities in feudal warfare, and so on.

Financial evolution

During the High Middle Ages the French monarchy came to rely less on its income from royal estates and more on other sources. Most of the latter involved utilization of various incidents of feudalism. The royal income was greatly expanded, especially by the Philips. Philip II initiated a general fiscal reorganization that quadrupled the royal income; Philip III enhanced it by the extensive commutation of military service; and Philip IV employed an ingenious variety of means to increase his revenues.

By 1300, sources of royal revenues included income from royal estates; proceeds from the administration of justice, such as fees and fines; reliefs paid on succession to fiefs; annates paid on succession to some ecclesiastical benefices; ordinary feudal aids, such as payments at the knighting of the king's eldest son; extraordinary feudal aids, such as those voluntarily granted for royal Crusades; tallage (taxes) from towns and villages, both ordinary (customary) and extraordinary (voluntary); commutation of military services and of other feudal dues such as hospitality to money payments; income derived from the interim administration of fiefs and benefices during vacancies and wardships; fees as "advocates" or secular protectors of monasteries and churches; and special taxes on income (such as a fourth or a fifth) or on property value (such as a hundredth or a fiftieth), levied on both clergy and laity for such exigencies as Crusades and wars; as well as sales taxes (*maltôtes:* evil levies). Other less creditable sources of royal income included forced "gifts," "donations," or "loans"; debasement of the coinage; expulsion of creditors, such as the Lombards and Jews; and suppression of the wealthy Templars. Philip IV was an especially flagrant offender, and after his death in 1314 there was a general reaction against such abuses, resulting in the formation of anti-monarchical leagues.

The army and navy

With augmented royal revenues, the royal army came to include increased numbers of hired (mercenary) soldiers. Monarchs such as Philip II, Philip III, and Philip IV encouraged the commutation of miltary service to money payments. In *prisées* (evaluations) of 1194 and 1202–1203, Philip II set up rates for the commutation of military service due from communes and abbeys. An ordinance of Philip III, issued in 1274, established a scale of values for the commutation of feudal military service, and fines for failure to either appear or pay on time. This made it possible to demand a definite payment in lieu of personal services, and to collect an additional penalty for delay. It was a long step in the direction of modern taxation. In the early 1300s, Philip IV set rates of commutation at from one fifth to one half the annual revenue of a fief.

Primary reliance in warfare was placed upon heavy mounted cavalry. The towns often provided militia, usually infantry, whose function was

The Rise of France

auxiliary, as at Bouvines (1214). A principal function of the urban infantry was to protect the cavalry until such a time as the latter were committed to battle. The steel crossbow that shot an iron bolt was both popular and deadly. Genoese crossbowmen were hired by Philip IV. Construction engineers for the building of improved castles, and siege engineers for the sapping of fortifications, became increasingly important in the High Middle Ages.

During the Crusades the construction of French ships was improved and they became larger and more seaworthy. Philip II increased the French navy during his conquest of Normandy, and in connection with projects to invade England; as also did Philip III during his war with Aragon.

Royal administration of local government grew with the expansion of the royal domains and the removal of feudal intermediaries. From the eleventh century the Capetians set *prévôts* over districts smaller than the old counties. These *prévôts*, who have been described as primarily "farmers" and "businessmen," obtained their concessions by bidding and promising to pay periodically a certain amount for the right to govern the district and operate the royal estates therein for a profit. A type of official similar to the English sheriff was established when Philip II set *baillis* over groups of *prévôts*. These *baillis* were primarily governmental officials, rather than mainly property administrators as were the *prévôts*. The use of *baillis* seems to have resulted from use of similar officials on the continent by the English kings and found by Philip II in Normandy. In the south such officials were known as seneschals. The *baillis* were paid salaries and were removable at will. In the name of the king, they exercised full authority in the territories they administered. They held court for the administration of justice; they mobilized and assumed command of troops; and they saw to the collection of moneys owed to the king. Unlike the *prévôts*, they had a fixed salary and were strictly accountable for all they collected. *Local government*

Over the *baillis*, Louis IX set *enqueteurs*, *to receive in writing and to examine the grievances which may be brought against us or our ancestors, as also allegations of injustices of which our baillis, prévôts, foresters, sergeants, and their subordinates may have been guilty*. As special representatives of the royal authority, the *enqueteurs* gradually became general superintendents of the areas assigned to them, with eventual financial and administrative as well as judicial authority. Under Philip IV, one of their principal functions was to ferret out additional royal income.

Yet many serious limitations upon the royal authority still existed in France. Even where great vassals had been eliminated, as in Normandy, Maine, Anjou, Toulouse, feudalism was not extirpated, and lesser vassals remained with their own privileges, immunities, and local jurisdictions. Many towns, villages, churches, and abbeys had their own privileges, immunities, and jurisdictions. There still remained the great semi-autonomous fiefs of Flanders, Brittany, Guienne-Gascony, and Burgundy, as well as the specially privileged "appanages," such as Anjou and Artois, *Limitations on royal authority* held by members of the royal family as almost independent principalities.

In France, as in England, the king eventually found it more practical to obtain general support by dealing with leaders and representatives in joint assemblies.

The estates

A meeting of representatives of the various "states of life"—clerical, aristocratic, and bourgeois—was known as an "Estates." A more common form of such meetings consisted in provincial estates, whereas national or "general" estates were more difficult to assemble because of the greater distances and time and expense involved. Estates General were not held for France at large until the early fourteenth century, when they were summoned by Philip IV to give "aid" and "counsel" in times of crisis. Philip, who may have been influenced by the example of contemporary Parliaments in England and *Cortes* in Spanish states, summoned the Estates General in 1302, in 1308, and in 1314, as well as convoked several other similar meetings not fully qualifying to be called such. The three Estates included prelates and other representatives of the clergy, barons and other representatives of the nobility, and "procurators" or elected representatives of the towns. The Estates deliberated separately. They were considered to be representative of the country at large, and were convoked to obtain financial and other support for the monarch and his projects.

Crown and communes

An alliance of convenience developed between the French crown and the communes. The municipal political organizations in the rising towns frequently looked to the king for liberation from servile dues and for other privileges, and kings often issued charters granting townspeople both economic and political privileges and immunities. The towns profited since they obtained rights and privileges exempting them from baronial or episcopal control and giving them favorable legal status as well as various privileges. The king profited because whatever reduced the powers of his great vassals indirectly enhanced his own position, and because such charters usually provided for the payment of a fixed *taille* or tax to the crown as well as implied the possibility of additional voluntary extraordinary *tailles*.

Louis VI is known to have granted at least four charters to communes; Louis VII some twenty-five charters; and Philip II no less than seventy-eight charters. Earlier charters, such as that of Lorris, granted by Louis VI, of which there are over eighty examples, were more conservative. Later charters, such as that of Beaumont-en-Argonne, which was granted by the Archbishop of Reims in 1182, and of which there are over three hundred examples, were more liberal. Louis IX granted only one known charter to a town, and that was to the port of Aigues Mortes, which he established as a base for his crusading effort. Although he was reluctant to infringe upon what he considered the established rights of the local lords, Louis realized the value of the support of the communes as when he said in his *Instructions* to his son Philip (III): *Preserve the good towns and communes of your kingdom . . . with the charters that have been conceded to them by your predecessors. For if you have the support*

The Rise of France

of your towns, both your subjects and foreigners will be afraid to attack you.

As the twelfth century progressed the towns lost some of their municipal liberties. Because of increasing disputes between members of different classes, as between the upper bourgeoisie and the lower bourgeoisie and the working classes, the kings intervened more frequently in the affairs of the towns, many of which they came to dominate. Citizens of towns within the royal domains came to be known as *bourgeoisie du roi* (townspeople of the king). They enjoyed special royal protection wherever they went, even outside the royal domains proper. Many townspeople outside the royal domains sought and obtained this privilege in the thirteenth century.

Up to the time of Philip IV, the Church-State relations of the French kings with the Church, including royal relations with the Papacy, were amicable and mutually cooperative. The French Church was strong and healthy, and Frenchmen provided much of the leadership in the universal Church. The main schools of scholastic philosophy and theology developed in France, as did the leading university; while the beautiful new Gothic style of church architecture originated in France. Both the Cluniac and the Cistercian reforms originated in France, as did the Truce of God and the Peace of God. The Crusades to the Near East were initiated in France, whence came most of their volunteers. *State and Church in France*

There was no real investiture struggle in France, partly because of the comparative weakness of the French crown in the eleventh century. By about 1104, when Philip I was reconciled with the Papacy, a compromise solution had been worked out in practice whereby the election was free, but the king or other overlord had the right to ratify it. French kings often provided hospitality for refugee Popes as well as for other churchmen who were engaged in struggles with secular monarchs, as in the case of Thomas Becket and Alexander III. While dependable supporters of the Papacy, at the same time the Capetians firmly defended their own independence and prerogatives as monarchs. Thus Philip II refused to become directly involved in the Albigensian Crusade; Louis IX declined the Papal invitation to profit from the embarrassments of Frederick II; and Philip IV insisted on the royal right to tax and judge French clergymen without Papal permission.

During the High Middle Ages, France was a recognized leader in Europe in many fields. French governmental institutions provided models for those of other countries, and French knights were recognized as among the best—if not *the* best—in Europe. Frenchmen conquered England and southern Italy and Sicily, founded the Crusader States in the Near East, and were prominent in the Christian "Reconquest" of Spain and Portugal. French fairs were popular and prosperous. The Parisian "Book of Crafts" in 1291 listed 350 different trades. The population of France more than doubled, and Paris was eventually one of the largest cities in Europe. French townspeople and peasants obtained considerable freedom, while the French nobility developed ideals of chivalry and *noblesse* *French leadership in Europe oblige.* French cathedral schools begot the "Twelfth-Century Renaissance," with its humanism and revival of logic; and thirteenth century Scholasticism flowered especially at the University of Paris, the leading center of higher learning in Europe. French *chansons de geste, chansons d'amour*, and French "romances," were admired and imitated throughout Europe. Soaring Gothic architecture originated in France, as did beautiful stained glass windows, while French manuscript illumination and polyphonic music were recognized as the best in Europe.

References for Chapter 20

AMONG good general histories of France in English are CHARLES A. GUIGNEBERT, *A Short History of the French People*, vol. I: *Ancient Times and the Middle Ages* (New York: Macmillan, 1930), and ARTHUR A. TILLEY, *Medieval France* (New York: Hafner, 1964). Good articles are provided in the successive volumes of the *Cambridge Medieval History*; briefer, more generalized introductions are available in GEORGES DUBY and R. MANDROU, *A History of French Civilization*, tr. J. B. Atkinson (New York: Random House, 1967); ALBERT L. GUERARD, *French Civilization . . . to the Close of the Middle Ages* (Boston: Houghton Mifflin, 1921); ANDRÉ MAUROIS, *The Miracle of France*, tr. H. L. Binsse (New York: Harper, 1948); WILLIAM H. HUDSON, *France . . . And Its Development* (New York: Stokes, 1917); GUSTAVE MASSON, *. . . The Story of Mediaeval France . . .* (New York: Putnams, 1901); and VICTOR DURUY, *A History of France*, abridged and translated by Mrs. M. Carey (New York: Crowell, 1896). Chiefly useful for illustrative materials such as anecdotes and quotations from original sources are the old JACQUES C. FUNCK-BRENTANO, *The Middle Ages*, tr. E. O'Neill (New York: Putnams, 1923), and the still older FRANCIS P. G. GUIZOT, *The History of France . . .*, tr. R. Black, vols. I and II (New York: Dana Estes, n.d.).

A well-written account of the period from 987 to 1328 stressing political history is ROBERT FAWTIER, *The Capetian Kings of France*, tr. L. Butler and R. Allen (London: Macmillan, 1960); another, running to 1270 and also providing a parallel account of the development of the English monarchy is CH. PETIT-DUTAILLIS, *The Feudal Monarchy in France and England* (London: Routledge and Kegan Paul, 1949). A briefer more general version of the latter is SIDNEY PAINTER, *The Rise of the Feudal Monarchies* (Ithaca, N.Y.: Cornell U.P., 1950).

Accounts of particular figures and their activities include AMY KELLY, *Eleanor of Aquitaine and the Four Kings* (Cambridge, Mass.: Harvard U.P., 1950); WILLIAM H. HUTTON, *Philip Augustus* (London: Macmillan, 1896); WILLISTON WALKER, *On the Increase of Royal Power in France Under Philip Augustus* (Leipzig: Gressner and Schramm, 1888); JEAN, SIRE DE JOINVILLE, *Life of St. Louis*, of which there are various versions, such as those of R. Hague and N. De Wailly (New York: Sheed, 1955) and Joan Evans (London: Oxford U.P., 1938); FREDERICK PERRY, *Saint Louis . . .* (New York: Putnams, 1901); and FRANKLIN J. PEGUES, *The Lawyers of the Last Capetians* (Princeton, N.J: Princeton U.P., 1962).

Special subjects are treated by CHARLES H. HASKINS, *. . . Norman Institutions* (Cambridge, Mass.: Harvard U.P., 1918); FREDERICK M. POWICKE, *The Loss of Normandy (1189–1204)* (Manchester, Eng.: U. of Manchester, 1913); JOSEPH R. STRAYER, *The Administration of Normandy Under Saint Louis* (Cambridge, Mass.: Mediaeval Academy);

Joseph R. Strayer and Charles H. Haskins, *Studies in Early French Taxation* (Cambridge, Mass.: Harvard U.P., 1939); and Joseph R. Strayer, *The Royal Domain in the Baillage of Rouen* (Princeton, N.J.: Princeton U.P., 1936); J. C. L. Simonde de Sismonde, *History of the Crusades Against the Albigenses in the 13th Century* (Boston: Mussey, 1883); Winifred F. Knox, *The Court of a Saint* [Louis IX], (London: Methuen, 1909); John H. Mundy, *Liberty and Political Power in Toulouse, 1050–1230* (New York: Columbia U.P., 1954); Achille Luchaire, *Social France at the Time of Philip Augustus*, tr. E. B. Krehbiel (New York: Holt, 1912); and Joan Evans, *Life in Medieval France* (London: Oxford U.P., 1925)—well-documented surveys of French life; and Robert G. Anderson, *The City and the Cathedral* (New York: Longmans, 1948), consisting of popular vignettes.

(OTHER EUROPEAN STATES IN THE HIGH MIDDLE AGES. Chapter 21.

OTHER European states also rose to prominence during the High Middle Ages. In the Iberian, Italian, and Balkan peninsulas of southern Europe, where various small kingdoms jostled and competed with one another, Castile, Sicily, and Bulgaria became ascendant over their fellows. In east central and northern Europe, which were similarly divided, Hungary, Poland, and Denmark attained greater unity and strength. In Eastern Europe, Russia was strong until the mid-eleventh century, but was thereafter subdivided into rival principalities, which were subjected by Mongol invaders in the thirteenth century.

MEDITERRANEAN EUROPE: THE IBERIAN AND BALKAN PENINSULAS. Section 61.

> We, who are as good as you, promise to serve you, who are no better than we are, as long as you are faithful to your promises; but if not, not. [Reputed oath of fealty of the medieval Aragonese aristocracy to their king (apparently apocryphal, but reflecting a common attitude).]

THE Moslem Caliphate of Cordova and the Eastern Christian Byzantine Empire—formerly the leading states of the Iberian and Balkan peninsulas—both weakened seriously during the High Middle Ages. The Caliphate of Cordova broke up into several petty states, all of which, save one, were taken over by the growing states of Aragon, Castile, and Portugal. In the Balkans the Byzantine Empire lost most of its former holdings to the Bulgarians and Serbs, as well as (temporarily) to Western crusaders.

Dominated at the outset by the Caliphate of Cordova, most of the Iberian peninsula eventually came to be divided among three major Christian powers: Castile, Aragon, and Portugal. Following the dis-

The Iberian peninsula

The "Reconquest"

solution of the Caliphate of Cordova (1031) and its replacement by numerous petty states (*taifas*), the Christian Reconquest proceeded so rapidly that the divided Moslems were driven to call in from Morocco the militaristic Almoravides (Murabits) (1086), subsequently supplanted by the similar Almohades (Muwahhids) (c. 1147ff.). Although temporarily arrested, the Reconquest gradually resumed. After a great Christian victory at Las Navas de Tolosa in southern Spain (1213), the Reconquest was speeded up so that by 1300 only the small southern kingdom of Granada remained in Moslem hands as a tributary of Castile. Causes of Moslem decline included division among themselves, the inadequacy of short-lived dynasties ruling petty states, the fact that the majority of the populace remained Christian so that racial and cultural differences were accentuated by religious differences, the hardy qualities of the native Iberians, and French as well as ecclesiastical (including Papal) support for the Reconquest.

Elements of democracy and personal freedom

As a result of the continuing conflict with the Moslems a considerable degree of freedom and elements of democracy appeared at an early date in the Christian states of the Iberian peninsula. The distribution of power among the monarchy, the aristocracy, the Church, and the townspeople had a liberalizing effect. At the same time the Hispanic monarchs had considerable power, partly as a result of Moslem example and Roman traditions, but especially because of their position as necessary leaders in the wars against the Moslems. The aristocracy, too, was strong, as the main component of the fighting forces opposing the Moslems. The Church supplied an impelling religious motive for the resistance, as well as consolation for the hardships and sacrifices involved. As a result of long Moslem occupation, and high medieval prosperity, the towns in the Iberian peninsula were populous and expanding. But they were exposed to Moslem attacks, and their financial and military help was needed in the Reconquest. Consequently their inhabitants were accorded extensive privileges in royal charters (*fueros* or *cartas pueblas*) as early as the tenth century. Included in these grants were the rights to have considerable self-government, with their own elected officials and judges, their own courts, and freedom from additional taxation without their consent.

Cortes and charters

Popular parliaments or *Cortes*, with representatives of the urban middle class as well as of the nobility and clergy, appeared early in the Iberian peninsula. Fully constituted *Cortes* met in Leon in 1188, Catalonia in 1218, Castile in 1250, and Portugal in 1254, all well in advance of parliamentary assemblies elsewhere. Such *Cortes* voted additional financial subsidies for their monarchs, petitioned for desired laws and participated in their promulgation, decided questions of royal succession, and obtained formal recognition of the rights and privileges of their constituents. Interim committees known as *Diputationes* represented the *Cortes* between sessions. In Aragon there was a supreme *Justicia* who decided constitutional questions in a manner binding both nobles and monarch.

In Castile and Leon, where the Reconquest was on a larger scale, townspeople were accorded charters of liberties at early dates, while serfs were largely liberated during the High Middle Ages. In Aragon and Catalonia, where the privileges of the aristocracy were greater, the liberation of serfs and concessions of rights to commoners (outside of Saragossa and Barcelona) came more slowly because of stronger feudal traditions, resulting partly from closer ties with feudal France.

During this period, in connection with strenuous wars against the Moslems, military orders similar to those in the Holy Land developed in Spain and Portugal. Particularly important were the orders of Calatrava, Santiago, and Alcantara in Castile and Leon. These religious orders made war against the Moslems their principal external work. Their members took vows of chastity, poverty, and obedience, although "chastity" could mean abstinence from extraconjugal relations and "poverty" nonappropriation of funds of the order for personal use. Another development was the growth of *hermandades* (brotherhoods): associations of groups of towns for purposes of cooperation in matters of common interest, particularly defense against Moslems and brigands. Both the military orders and the *hermandades* wielded considerable power. *Military orders and hermandades*

While the Iberian Christian states derived much of their culture from Italy and France, they were also a principal gateway for the flow of elements of Moslem culture and learning into Western Europe. Particularly influential was the work of the translators of works of medicine, science, and philosophy from the Arabic carried on in Spain and encouraged, v.g., by Archbishop Roderick at Toledo in the twelfth and early thirteenth centuries. *Cultural influence*

The Kingdom of Castile, which emerged from the side of the Kingdom of Leon, eventually absorbed it to become the largest, most powerful state in the peninsula. Originally constituted as a separate kingdom for his son Ferdinand I by Sancho the Great of Navarre (1035), Castile was recurrently reunited with and separated from Leon until a permanent union was achieved under St. Ferdinand III in 1230. Notable among the Kings of Leon and Castile who promoted the Reconquest were Ferdinand I, who extended his realms south to the Mondego and Tagus Rivers; Alfonso VI, who took centrally located Toledo, the old Visigothic capital, in 1085; Alfonso VIII, who led combined Christian forces to victory over the Moslems at Las Navas de Tolosa (1213); and St. Ferdinand III (d. 1252), who took Cordova, Jaen, Murcia, and Seville, leaving only the Moslem Kingdom of Granada in the far south. *Castile and Leon*

Illustrative of the growing wealth and culture of Castile was Alfonso X (1252–1284), known as "the Wise," who obtained a claim to the German imperial crown by purchasing the votes of a majority of the electors. He compiled two important codes of law: one the *Fuero Real* (Royal Law), primarily customary; and the other, the *Siete Partidas* (Seven Parts), primarily Roman. Alfonso composed and promoted history writing in the Castilian vernacular in his extensive *Chronicle* and *General History*, and did the same for religious poetry in Galician in some four hundred *Cantigas de Santa Maria* (hymns in honor of the Blessed Virgin). He also advanced the science of astronomy by his so-called *Alfonsine* or *Toledan Tables*, comprising extensive astronomical data.

The High Middle Ages

Aragon and Catalonia

Aragon and Catalonia were united into a single kingdom in the mid-twelfth century, and made a good complementary combination. Aragon was mountainous and inland, with hardy, independence-loving fighters experienced in land warfare. Catalonia (the County of Barcelona) was maritime and commercial, with a cosmopolitan population skilled in naval warfare. The County of Aragon, like that of Castile, was constituted and left as a kingdom by Sancho the Great of Navarre for one of his sons, Ramiro I, in 1035. Both Aragon and Catalonia expanded rapidly and had a common Frankish background with a strong feudal aristocracy. On the death of childless Alfonso I, the Battler, in 1134, his brother Ramiro, a monk, was summoned to quiet the dissension. Within three years, the efficient Ramiro II made peace with Leon, married a Provencal heiress, begot a daughter named Petronilla, and betrothed the latter to Count Ramón Berenguer IV of Catalonia, who became her guardian, whereupon he retired to his monastery. The union of Aragon and Catalonia effected by the marriage of Petronilla and Ramón Berenguer became permanent on the accession of their son, Alfonso II, who also inherited considerable territories in southern France. Most of these territories were, however, lost by Pedro II, the Catholic, when he was defeated and killed by the forces of Simon de Montfort at Muret (1213).

The Aragonese-Catalonian part of the Reconquest was completed by James I, the Conqueror (1213-1276), who took and incorporated Valencia, as well as the Balearic Islands. James also conquered Murcia, which had revolted against Alfonso X of Castile, but turned back most of this to Alfonso. Boundaries between Aragon and Castile were amicably settled by the Treaty of Cazorla (1179) and ancillary treaties, while conflicting claims with France were compromised by the Treaty of Corbeil (1258). Aragonese energies and attention were increasingly turned to maritime expansion in the Mediterranean, including the occupation of Sicily by Pedro III (1283).

The requirements of their overseas operations constrained the Aragonese kings to extend extensive privileges to their subjects in the General Privilege of Pedro III (1283) and the Privilege of the Union of Alfonso III (1287). Among many rights guaranteed to nobles was that to renounce their allegiance to the king or even depose him if he failed to respect their rights and privileges.

Portugal in the High Middle Ages

Portugal emerged as a kingdom from the side of Leon in the twelfth century. Alfonso VI of Leon granted the County of Oporto (*Portus Cale*) by the mouth of the Duero River, together with the hand of his daughter Theresa in marriage, to Count Henry of Burgundy in 1095 for his services in the Reconquest. When her sister Urraca became Queen of Leon after the death of their father, Theresa also aspired to a royal status. She and her husband gained independence, and their son, Alfonso Enriquez, was recognized as a king by "Emperor" Afonso VII of Leon and the Papal legate in 1143. The Reconquest proceeded rapidly in Portugal. An English flotilla en route to the Holy Land aided in taking Lisbon at the mouth of the Tagus in 1147. By the mid-thirteenth century Portugal attained its present boundaries with the cession of the Algarve (in the far south) by Alfonso X of Castile (1263). The enterprising Portuguese turned to the sea for fishing and trade, developed their agriculture, and exploited their natural resources.

During the eleventh and twelfth centuries the Byzantine Empire controlled the greater part of the Balkans. But Byzantine rule weakened as time progressed, and in the later twelfth and early thirteenth centuries, following Byzantine reverses in Asia Minor, both Bulgaria and Serbia became independent. First the Bulgarians became ascendant through much of the Balkans (c. 1186–1258); and then the Serbs built up a large empire, which reached its height in the first half of the fourteenth century.

The Byzantine Empire: Reverses

The Byzantines lost most of their Asian empire to the Seljuk Turks in the eleventh century. Asian nomads, including the Pechenegs (Patzinaks), Cumans, and Uzes, periodically invaded the eastern Balkans, while ambitious Hungarians, Venetians, and Normans attacked the western Balkans. For half a century Constantinople and a great part of Byzantine Balkan holdings were in the hands of Western crusaders.

The Byzantine Empire declined under the aging Macedonian Empresses Zoe and Theodora (1025–1056), last of their line. The civil aristocrats of the capital, who were unconcerned with external defenses, became ascendant, a position they retained during the ensuing "Time of Troubles" (1057–1081). Meanwhile the Seljuk Turks overran the Asiatic provinces of the Empire, as the Pechenegs invaded the Balkans and the Normans conquered southern Italy. Byzantine sea power evaporated, superseded by that of the Venetians. In the same year, Byzantine loss of Armenia and most of Asia Minor was sealed by an overwhelming Turkish victory at Manzikert (1071). The loss of their holdings in southern Italy was completed by the fall of Bari in the same year.

Salvation for the faltering Empire came in the person of Alexius Comnenus (1081–1118), a member of the more militant rural aristocracy, which owned great estates in the provinces they wished to protect against invaders. Henceforth, until its fall, the Byzantine Empire was controlled by the sturdy rural landholding element, who organized defenses on a semifeudal basis. Military forces were now provided largely by land grants and holdings known as *pronoia*, whose possessors, the *pronoiars*, were responsible for providing a certain number of soldiers.

Partial recovery under the Comneni (1081–1176)

Alexius foiled the Norman thrust across the Balkans by enlisting Venetian aid to cut their supply lines, as well as by fostering a revolt against Norman rule in southern Italy. He practically annihilated the Pechenegs with the help of their former allies, the Cumans. Taking advantage of growing divisions among the Turks, he also began to reconquer parts of Seljuk-held territory in Asia Minor. Lacking sufficient troops to fulfill his projects, Alexius appealed to the Pope for volunteers from the West. In the wake of the ensuing Crusades, Alexius was able to recover Nicaea and other territories in northwestern and western Asia Minor.

John II, Comnenus (1118–1143), an exemplary "soldier-emperor," continued his father's policies and regained considerable territory in Asia Minor. He also compelled the Latin Prince of Antioch in Syria to recognize his suzerainty. In the Balkans, he completed the destruction of the Pechenegs. His successor, Manuel I, Comnenus (1143–1185), handsome and debonair, became excessively involved in Italian affairs and those of the Crusader States. Meanwhile the Seljuk Sultan of Iconium, Kilij Arslan II, was able to build up his strength to the point where he could challenge the Byzantines. When Manuel marched out with a large army to chastise the invading Turks, his troops were surprised and practically annihilated in a mountainous gorge at Myriocephalon (1176). This catastrophe reduced the Byzantine Empire to a second-rate power in the East, and removed a needed counterpoise against the Moslems for the Crusader States.

Byzantine decline (1176–1204)

Manuel's heir was his young son, Alexius II, whose Latin mother, Maria of Antioch, became regent. Jealousy and hatred of the Latins increased to such a point in the capital that many Westerners were massacred in a general uprising. An unscrupulous adventurer, Andronicus I, Comnenus, was able to take over the regency, and have Maria of Antioch and her son, the young Emperor either strangled or drowned. The unstable Andronicus I (1182/1183–1185) indulged in a reign of terror, which was terminated by a revolution led by Isaac II, Angelus (1185–1195), who initiated "the dynasty of the fratricidal Angeli." While the Angeli competed with one another for the throne, the Empire lost further extensive territories to the Turks in Asia Minor, and to the Bulgarians and Serbs in the Balkans. The founder of the line, Isaac II, was deposed and blinded by his ambitious brother, Alexius III, Angelus (1195–1203). Isaac's son Alexius, who escaped to the West, eventually succeeded in diverting the Fourth Crusade (1202–1204) to Byzantium with Venetian help, and came into fleeting power as Alexius IV (1203–1204).

Encouraged by great promises, the Fourth Crusade came to Constantinople, where it effected the overthrow of Alexius III and the accession of the young Alexius IV, along with the restoration of his blinded father, Isaac II (1203). But the wrath of the crusaders mounted as Alexius IV proved unable to fulfill his promises, and was overthrown by the populace. Alexius V, Mourtzouphlos (1204), elected in his stead, eliminated Alexius IV by strangling, but soon fled before the Westerners, who took over the capital.

The Latin Empire of Constantinople (1204–1260)

After thoroughly pillaging Constantinople for three days, the crusaders set up a government of their own. Baldwin, Count of Flanders, was elected Emperor, and a Venetian, Thomas Morisini, was named Patriarch. Like the Latin Kingdom of Jerusalem, the Latin Empire of Constantinople was extremely feudal, and the Emperors controlled only part of the Empire. Three eighths of the capital were in the hands of the Venetians, who enjoyed extraterritoriality and obtained several key seaports and numerous former islands of the Empire. Outlying territories went to those who could take and hold them. Boniface of Montferrat set up the Kingdom of Thessalonica to the north of the Aegean, while Attica was organized as the Duchy of Athens and the intensely feudal Principality of Achaia was set up in the Peloponnesus (southern Greece). Some

Other European States

territories remained in Byzantine hands, being administered by "governments in exile." Northwestern Asia Minor was ruled by the Byzantine Lascarids, whose capital was Nicaea; Epirus and eventually Thessalonica were ruled by the Angeli; and Trebizond (to the south of the Black Sea) was ruled by the Comneni—each of whom claimed to be the legitimate Byzantine Emperor.

Expansion of the Westerners was soon arrested. The "crusaders" were in the process of reducing the Byzantines of Nicaea when the powerful Bulgarian Tsar, Johannitza, challenged and decisively defeated their army at Adrianople in 1205. In 1222 Theodore Angelus of Epirus easily occupied the Latin Kingdom of Thessalonica, which was subsequently appropriated by the Lascarids of Nicaea, the strongest of the various competitors.

The enlightened Lascarids of Nicaea built up their state and developed its resources as well as strengthened their army. They repelled the Sultan of Iconium (1208–1209) and expanded their holdings in northwestern Asia Minor. They took over the Kingdom of Thessalonica from the Angeli in 1246, and made the Despotate of Epirus their satellite in 1254. In 1259 the strong, unscrupulous Michael Paleologus seized power as regent for the young John IV, whom he subsequently eliminated by deposition and blinding (1261). In the same year, with inside help, as well as Genoese assistance, the troops of Michael VIII took possession of Constantinople during the absence of the Latin army and the Venetian fleet, thus ending the Latin Empire.

The Latin conquest of Constantinople dealt the Eastern Empire a blow from which it never fully recovered. Several parts of the Empire were henceforth autonomous. Outlying parts of the Empire were never regained; and the Byzantine economy, already on the wane, suffered further decline.

Despite the shock of the Latin Empire, the Byzantine Empire survived for two more centuries, during which both its European and Asiatic territories were gradually appropriated by the Ottoman Turks. The Empire did, however, exhibit a fleeting interval of revival under Michael VIII, Paleologus (1261–1282). The greatest threat at this time came from the ambitious Charles of Anjou, who had recently (1261) taken over the Kingdom of Sicily (including southern Italy), and who dreamt of building up a great Mediterranean Empire that would include Constantinople. Charles, who obtained a foothold in the far western Balkans, was preparing a large expedition to the East when he was foiled by Byzantine intrigues. Byzantine agents stirred up Sicilian resentment against the French occupation of the island, and plotted with King Pedro III of Aragon, who regarded himself as heir of the displaced Hohenstaufen, since he had married Manfred's daughter. On March 31, 1282, on the pretext that a French soldier had insulted a Sicilian girl, an uprising, accompanied by a general massacre of Frenchmen, spread like wildfire over the island. Before Charles of Anjou could muster adequate troops and reestablish French authority, an Aragonese fleet, assisted by a Byzantine subsidy, landed troops and entrenched the Aragonese in control of the

Final epoch of the Paleologi (1261ff.)

island. Unsuccessful attempts to recover Sicily now absorbed the attention of Charles of Aragon; and the Byzantine Empire had again been saved.

Bulgaria as a Byzantine province (1018–1184)

Following the defeat of Tsar Samuel by Emperor Basil II, the Bulgar Slayer, in 1081, Bulgaria was subject to the Byzantine Empire for almost two centuries (1018–1186). But resentment smoldered among the Bulgarians as a result of Byzantine domination, taxation, and insistence on orthodoxy. Popular in Bulgaria was the "Bogomile" heresy, an extreme dualism apparently descended from Manichaeism. The disastrous defeat of Emperor Manuel I at Myriocephalon (1176) and subsequent Byzantine convulsions, followed by the accession of the incompetent Angeli, kindled the hope of Balkan peoples for independence. A Bulgarian uprising was triggered in 1186 by increased taxes demanded by Emperor Isaac II, Angelus. Leaders of the revolt, which was successful, were John Asen and his brother Peter Asen, who appear to have been Vlachs (Wallachians).

The second Bulgarian Empire (1186–1258)

The Asens established the so-called Second Bulgarian Empire, which lasted for three quarters of a century. The first ruler of newly independent Bulgaria, John Asen I (1186–1196), was able to organize and expand his state; but this did not save him from being assassinated by discontented *boyars* (nobles). The same fate was shortly accorded his able brother, Peter (1196–1197). But there was still another brother to carry on: *Johannitza* (Little John), also known as *Kalojan* (Handsome John). Energetic Johannitza (1197–1207) maintained Bulgarian independence and refused to submit to the sway of the Latin Empire, whose forces he decisively defeated in 1205. Because of his prowess against both Byzantines and Latins, Johannitza came to be known as "Slayer of the Romans." John Asen II (1218–1241),[a] the later successor of Kalojan, was the most attractive and successful of this remarkable family. Intelligent, moderate, and conciliatory, John Asen II was admired by the Byzantines as well as by the Bulgarians. He overcame his chief rival, Theodore Angelus, Emperor of Thessalonica and Despot of Epirus, at Klokonitza (1230) and expanded his Empire to include a large part of the Balkans. But his ambitions to unite Greeks, Bulgarians, and Latins under his rule and to make Constantinople his capital were repeatedly frustrated. His successors made the mistake of allying with the strong Byzantines of Nicaea against the weakening Latins of Constantinople. After 1258, Bulgaria rapidly declined and lost its empire. The country was pillaged and bled by Mongols and Tartars, its territories to the southeast were partly recovered by the Byzantines, and its territories to the northwest were partly appropriated by the Serbs and Hungarians.

[a] There was a confused interregnum from 1207 to 1218.

The emergence of Serbia

Partly because of its rugged mountainous terrain and its remoteness, Serbia did not emerge as an independent kingdom until the late twelfth century. By the close of the thirteenth century, however, Serbia was the leading competitor with Byzantium in the Balkans. The early Serbs were grouped politically into tribes or clans known as *zupas*, each under its own chief or *zupan*. During most of the Early and High Middle Ages until 1196, the Serbs were nominally subject to the Byzantine Empire.

Other European States

The area of the western Serbs was known as Zeta, that of the eastern Serbs as Raska (or Rascia). During the High Middle Ages the prosperity of Serbia greatly increased, and its mineral resources began to be exploited. During intervals of quasi-independence from the Byzantine Empire, the regions of Zeta and Raska were each ruled by Grand Zupans.

In the second half of the twelfth century, a strong leader named Stephen Nemanja emerged in Raska. Stephen was enabled by Serbian prosperity to employ mercenary soldiers, and become Grand Zupan of both Raska and Zeta (1186), and the practical independence of Serbia was secured. In 1196 he abdicated in favor of his son, Stephen II, and retired to a monastery.

Stephen II, Nemanjanid (1196–1228), completed and confirmed the independence of Serbia and became "the first crowned Kral (King) of all the Serbs" (1217). He eventually obtained autocephalous (self-governing) status for the Serbian Church in the Eastern Church.

The Nemanjanids promoted the spread of Christianity, constructed numerous churches and monasteries, encouraged education, and patronized the arts.

STATES OF EAST CENTRAL AND NORTHERN EUROPE.
Section 62.

> If one counts Hungary as part of Slavonia, then the extent of the Slavic world is so great as almost to beggar the imagination. [Helmold, Priest of Bosau, in his *Chronicle of the Slavs* (twelfth century).]

THE YOUNG kingdoms of east central and northern Europe grew in strength and prosperity during the High Middle Ages. Influenced by the example of their more advanced neighbors, their political and military institutions rapidly matured. There was an increasing profitable market for their agricultural and pastoral products, as well as for their diversified natural resources, which included minerals, timber, fish, and furs. Although comparatively small, these states were able to preserve their independence from their neighbors. Their history was marked by competition between monarchy and nobility, punctuated by wars of succession and the struggle to remain independent.

The states of east central Europe The states of east central Europe—Bohemia, Poland, and Hungary— were predominantly Slavic, and their histories during the High Middle Ages were similar. They were each Christianized and civilized along Latin lines, and they all had the common problem of resisting German domination, to which was added Tartar menace in the thirteenth century. Temporarily successful attempts of certain strong rulers to control several of these kingdoms at once soon collapsed. While some Emperors at the height of their power forced these states to accept vassalage, this was not permanent, except in the case of Bohemia. By a curious coincidence, each of these states was ruled by one continuous dynasty throughout the High Middle Ages: Bohemia by the Premyslids, Poland by the Piasts, Hungary by the Arpads.

Bohemia

Bohemia (Czechoslovakia) occupied a mountain-enclosed plateau in central Europe. Encompassed on three sides by German-dominated lands, Bohemia was already tributary to the Germans in Carolingian times. The Bohemians were forced to accept continued vassal status by the Ottonian and Franconian Emperors. But the Bohemian state had a special position in the Holy Roman Empire: one of considerable autonomy. Among reasons for the growing importance of Bohemia were its mineral wealth and its fertile soil. With temporary exceptions, the Bohemian rulers remained faithful vassals of the German Emperors, reaping rewards for their fidelity while increasing their autonomy. Meanwhile Moravia was permanently incorporated into Bohemia.

At first the native Premyslid rulers of Bohemia had only the status of dukes, but during the High Middle Ages they were elevated to the level of kings. In 1085 Duke Vratislav (1061–1092), who had supported Henry IV, received the personal title of king during his lifetime. In 1158, Vladislav II (1140–1172), who had assisted Frederick I, Barbarossa, with troops in Italy, obtained from Barbarossa the hereditary title of king for both himself and his successors. In 1212, by a so-called Golden Bull, Frederick II, who was seeking support for his imperial candidacy, both made the Bohemian kingship perpetual and granted further privileges to the Bohemians. Among these was a guarantee of free election of their own king and the right of the Bohemian monarch to invest Bohemian bishops. The obligation of providing military assistance on the part of the Bohemians was also limited, and could be commuted into a money payment.

Bohemian autonomy increased during the two decades of anarchical interregnum that followed the death of Frederick II (1250). The ambitious Ottokar II of Bohemia (1253–1278) claimed and seized the holdings of the extinct Babenbergers in Austria, Styria, Carinthia, and Carniola. But after Rudolph of Hapsburg was elected Emperor (1273), he challenged and defeated Ottokar, and appropriated these territories for his own house of Hapsburg.

Poland in the High Middle Ages

Centered in the fertile valley of the Vistula at the eastern extremity of the Great Plain of Europe, Poland managed to establish its complete independence of the German Empire during the High Middle Ages. But the German imperial "devil" was replaced during the thirteenth century by three others: the Teutonic Knights, the Tartars, and the Lithuanians.

Largely to resist German aggression the Polish tribes were united in the tenth century by Mieszco I (d. 965), who also, and partly for the same reason, accepted Christianity. Poland reached its greatest extent early under Boleslav I, the Great (992–1025), whose Empire included Pomerania, Silesia, Bohemia, Moravia, Lusatia, and Ruthenia. Boleslav was given a crown by Emperor Otto III in A.D. 1000 and eventually assumed the title of king, although he was forced to accept the suzerainty of Emperor Henry II. Meanwhile the Polish Church was organized directly under Rome.

Following the death of Boleslav I, the Polish monarchy experienced alternating reverses and recoveries, while generally accepting the loose

Other European States

suzerainty of the German Emperors. At the outset (1025–1038), Poland lost most of its external possessions, while a pagan reaction against Christianity also took place. Monarchical power and Polish unity were reestablished by Grand Duke Casimir I, the Restorer (1038–1055), who, however, accepted German suzerainty. The strong Boleslaus II, the Bold (1058–1079), resumed the title of king, as well as invaded Russia; but he was overthrown by a reaction that followed his execution of Bishop St. Stanislaus of Cracow. Decline resumed under Boleslaus's weak successor, who had participated in his overthrow and who dropped the title of king, which was not resumed for two hundred years. However, Boleslaus III, Wrymouth (1102–1138), restored order and recovered Pomerania.

Boleslaus Wrymouth made the mistake of establishing several large principalities for his younger sons, and willing that the Grand Ducal office should descend in his family by seniority rather than primogeniture. This "seniorate" had the same unfortunate results as the similar "rota system" had in Russian history, and Poland became a loose federation of virtually autonomous principalities under the Grand Duke of Cracow. The proposed plan of succession soon collapsed and bred contests and civil wars, nourished by rivalries between princes, struggles between princes and their magnates, sectionalism, German intrigues, and the menace of the Tartars and the Teutonic Knights, and eventually the Lithuanians. *Partitional period of Polish history (1138–1305)*

In 1226, Duke Casimir of Mazovia, which was being raided by the fierce, pagan Prussians, invited in the Teutonic Knights to overcome his harrassers. Shortly thereafter (1228–1230) the Knights settled in the regions of Thorn (Torun) and Kulm. Using castles as bases, they expanded their sway with remarkable success. Soon they became the leading rivals of the Poles, whom they shut off from the Baltic. In 1241 a Mongol-Tartar army ravaged Central Europe, including Poland, and burned the cities of Cracow and Sandomierz. Combined forces of the Polish princes were defeated by the invaders in the hard-fought battle of Lignica (Liegnitz) (1241). The stout resistance of the Poles, however, apparently helped to discourage the Tartars from attempting to take over Central Europe. A by-product of the expansion of the Teutonic Knights was the unification of the fierce tribes of the Lithuanians under Prince Mendovg (Mindovg) (d. 1265), so that Poland was confronted with another rival state. A compensation for the devastation wrought by the Tartars was large-scale German immigration into Poland, which contributed to the growth of Polish towns and agriculture. By the close of the thirteenth century a form of feudalism prevailed wherein the power of the Grand Duke was shared with several princes, and that of the princes was limited by the magnates, while lordships and serfdoms were multiplying. The achievement of complete independence from the German Empire was eventually more a result of German weakness than of Polish strength.

Located in the fertile valley to the north of the middle Danube, Hungary was dominated by a Magyar minority who ruled over a much larger composite Slavic population, to whom they became largely assimilated. Hungary was Christianized, civilized, and Westernized under the Arpad *Hungary in the High Middle Ages* kings, beginning with St. Stephen I (997–1038). An overriding Hungarian problem in the eleventh and twelfth centuries was to remain independent of the expanding German Empire; another was to remain independent of the Eastern Empire, whose possessions extended to its borders. Hungary suffered from the destructive thirteenth-century invasion of the Tartars, although this blight was partly effaced by subsequent German immigration. Because of its focal position, the population of Hungary was cosmopolitan and composed of Magyars, Slovaks, Serbo-Croats, Roumanians, and others, while Hungary was also a meeting place for Frenchmen, Germans, Italians, Moslems, Jews, Byzantines, and others. As a result, the Hungarians were inclined to racial and religious tolerance. Hungary's common speech was Magyar, and its learned language was Latin; but its customs and way of life were predominantly Slavic. In religion Hungary eventually affiliated with the Western rather than the Eastern Church. The Hungarian monarchy was more absolute than other monarchies in the West in the eleventh to twelfth centuries, but in the thirteenth century the power of the Hungarian aristocracy grew and that of the monarchy waned. Hungary's possessions included Croatia to the southwest and Transylvania to the east; and temporarily Dalmatia, Serbia (Rascia), and Galicia (Halich).

A "time of troubles" followed the progressive reign of St. Stephen I (d. 1038). In forty years (1038–1077), Hungary had six kings, three of whom died violent deaths. Meanwhile fierce Cumans and Pechenegs invaded the country. Hungary's fortunes improved under King Geza I (1074–1077), who became a vassal of Pope Gregory VII. St. Ladislas I (1077–1095) made Poland more independent, enforced law and order, and pacified the predatory Cumans and Pechenegs. Kolman (Colman) (1095–1114) improved the administration of the government, reformed taxation, incorporated Croatia, and expanded into Dalmatia.

The power of the Hungarian aristocracy increased at the expense of the monarchy in the thirteenth century. Weak King Andrew II (1203–1235) was forced to grant the Golden Bull of 1222, which limited the power of the monarch, guaranteed the right of trial before imprisonment for nobles, and provided for annual diets.

During the Tartar invasion at the time of King Bela III (1235–1270), the Hungarian army was almost annihilated in the battle of Mohi (1241). But King Bela managed to escape and did much to restore his country after the Tartar withdrawal. A policy that eventually worked to the disadvantage of the monarchy was the widespread building of castles, which, although originally constructed as a defense against the predatory Tartars, were later used to defy the monarch. Instability during the thirteenth century was further fostered by the pressure of the Cumans, inept Papal policies, and growing Hapsburg and Angevin intervention. During the final quarter of the thirteenth century, Hungary unwisely helped Rudolph of Hapsburg overthrow Ottokar II of Bohemia, thus contributing to the rise of Hapsburg power, which was later to destroy Hungarian independence. During the final decade of the thirteenth century, an Angevin claimant supported by the Pope competed for the throne with the last Arpad, Andrew III.

The peripheral Scandinavian states first emerged into clear historical light during the Viking invasions, which were partly due to unrest caused by the growing power of their kings. Originally there were numerous petty regional rulers in Scandinavia, but eventually unification into national kingdoms was achieved, mainly through use of force. Government on various levels included a *thing* (popular court or assembly) administering justice according to a common law. Christianity was introduced into Scandinavia in the tenth century by German missionaries. In the twelfth century each kingdom, in recognition of its separate political status, obtained its own Archbishopric. National consolidation was assisted by the development of *althings* (national assemblies) as well as by the spread of Christianity. The rise of saints such as St. Olaf in Norway, St. Canute in Denmark, and St. Eric in Sweden aided national unification. *[The Scandinavian states in the High Middle Ages]*

The three Scandinavian countries displayed a remarkable parallelism and interaction in their evolution. A strong tendency to expand manifested itself in each country, as is seen in temporary Danish rule of Norway and England, in Swedish expansion around the northern and northeastern Baltic, and in Norwegian overlordship over the so-called Western Isles, including Iceland. Scandinavian development was usually led by Denmark.

Monarchical power became strong in Scandinavia in the eleventh and early twelfth centuries. At first royal power rested primarily on a general, primarily naval conscription (the *leidang*) of rowers and warriors for coastal warfare; but in time royal armies were "modernized" to include horsemen or "knights" as in contemporary Western Europe. The resultant "feudalism" contributed to the Wars of the Pretenders between factions supporting rival candidates in each of the three countries from about 1130 on. These wars also became contests between opposing programs of monarchical centralization and aristocratic decentralization. The Wars of the Pretenders lasted for only a little over two decades (1035–1157) in Denmark, where they were, however, resumed spasmodically; but they endured for about a century in both Norway (ca. 1130–1227) and Sweden (ca. 1130–1210). After this, there was a reaction in favor of stronger monarchical power, which attained high plateaus in Denmark from 1157 to 1241, in Sweden from 1248 to 1290, and in Norway from 1227 to 1319. *[Royal power grows and then declines]*

Eventually feudalism, originally promoted by monarchs to increase their power by means of mounted warriors, boomeranged. Among features of feudalism in Scandinavia were landholding associated with governmental powers, an obligation of mounted military service, exemption from taxes, a dependent peasantry, and the fact that the assembly or *Parlementum* of the nobles and especially the council of the magnates played an increasingly prominent part in the government. By the beginning of the Later Middle Ages (about 1300) the nobility were ascendant in each of the Scandinavian countries. Meanwhile Scandinavia enjoyed great economic and social progress. Among leading economic pursuits were fishing, fur collecting, mining (as in Sweden), pastoral activities (mainly dairy type), and agriculture. Trade and industries, in which the Germans played an important role, began to flourish and a dramatic growth of towns occurred.

EASTERN EUROPE (RUSSIA) AND THE MONGOLS IN THE MIDDLE AGES.
Section 63.

> The Tartars took Kiev and sacked St. Sophia and all the monasteries . . . , and they slew all the inhabitants. [Russian *Chronicle* concerning the Mongol conquest (1240).]

WEAKENED by internal division during the "Age of the Princes" (1054–1237), Russia fell prey to the expanding Mongols, who ruled it for over two centuries (ca. 1237ff.).

The Age of the Princes in Russia (1054–1237)

The Principality of Kiev, forebear of modern Russia, declined after reaching its zenith during the reign of Yaroslav the Wise. At his death in 1054, Yaroslav established a "rota system" of succession, whereby supreme power was to descend to the eldest living member of the princely house, so that succession was based not on primogeniture but on seniority. Princely brothers were to rule over the leading cities of Russia. On the death of the Grand Prince, the eldest princely survivor was to succeed him and move to the capital of Kiev, with the other princes each moving up a step to a town of higher importance. The rota system did not work as it was too complicated, especially as the number of princes multiplied, and it did not take into account the natural desire of fathers to have their sons succeed them. Nor did it consider the growth of strong familial attachments to existing places of residence. It depended too much on abstract conceptions. And it made no provision for the fact that as time progressed the comparative importance of cities would change. The constant shifting of princes and their families from one city to another was conceivable only in a well-disciplined military organization or a highly centralized polity.

Even during the initial century of the Age of the Princes, troubles multiplied. On various occasions the authority of the Grand Prince was challenged; and the rota system was violated. At the very beginning (ca. 1054–1093) Russia was actually controlled by a triumvirate, which included the Princes of Chernigov and Perieslav in addition to the Prince of Kiev. Feuds between princes flared spasmodically into wars. After the troublesome Pechenegs (Patzinaks) in southern Russia were overcome by a certain amount of princely cooperation, they were succeeded by the similarly warlike and predatory Cumans (Polovtsy), whom Russian efforts failed to suppress. The rota rule of succession was upset when the people of Kiev insisted on having Vladimir Monomach, the Prince of Perieslav, as their ruler. Vladimir was an enlightened, progressive ruler, who promoted education and learning, and was especially solicitous for the disadvantaged. While Vladimir pursued the path of peace, he also restrained the ravages of the Cumans. Following Vladimir's death, a running feud developed between his heirs and the descendants of Oleg of Chernigov.

Following the death of Vladimir's second son and successor, Kievan ascendance ceased and Russia became a loose federation of virtually sovereign princes. Still a Grand Prince continued to be recognized, and a certain cooperation persisted. Kiev was eclipsed partly because the Cumans now impeded transit on the Dnieper waterway to the Black Sea and the Russian center of gravity was shifting to the developing northeast, and partly because it was taken and sacked by Prince Andrei of Suzdal in 1169, and by the Cumans in 1203. *Russia, a loose federation*

Ascendance now passed successively to the princes of Suzdal, Vladimir, and Smolensk, all in the northeast. Four keenly competing regions with divergent interests were then recognizable in Russia: Volynia-Galicia in the southwest, Novgorod in the north, the steppes in the far south usually dominated by Asians, and the rapidly growing northeast area of the so-called Russian Mesopotamia, between the upper Volga and Oka Rivers, which was rapidly becoming the heart of the "new Russia."

Although native Slavic elements remained strong in Russian institutions in the Age of the Princes, other influences, especially the Byzantine and Eastern Orthodox ones, were also important. As has been seen, Kievan Russia became a federation of largely autonomous principalities, under the presidency of a Grand Prince, whose power became more and more limited. Each prince had his own *drushina* or noble following, which included not only his personal bodyguard but also his boyars (nobles) and other officials. The boyars assisted the prince in his government, and owned, administered, and ruled various parts of his territory. The general council of the boyars had functions similar to those of the feudal councils of vassals in Western Europe. The capital of each prince was usually the leading city of his territory, and the *veche* (*vieche*) or town council of the capital generally had considerable influence on his government. In Novgorod the *veche* was dominant in the government, and appointed and deposed its princes. When Sviatopolk, Grand Prince of Kiev, sought to impose his son as a ruler upon the Novgorodians, they replied: "Send him—if he has a spare head!" Novgorod in fact was a republic, which called itself "Lord Novgorod the Great," and jealously guarded its independence. In the northeast, however, where several cities had recently been founded and organized by princes, as was the case with Vladimir and Moscow, the princes were more absolute. *Russian institutions in the Age of the Princes*

Much trade moved up and down the numerous Russian rivers, which generally ran to the northwest or southeast, and connected the Baltic and the Black Seas with easy intervening portages. Traffic, especially from east to west and vice versa, also moved overland in large quantity. As a result, Russia came to be more urbanized than most countries in Europe in the High Middle Ages, with perhaps 12 per cent of its population living in towns and cities by about A.D. 1200. Leading economic activities in Russia included hunting and trapping, especially for furs, agriculture, apiculture (the raising of bees), and pastoral activities on the open *Russian economy and society* steppes. Lumbering and iron mining were also carried on in various regions.

The population of Kievan Russia at its height is estimated to have been about eight million. Besides the Prince and his boyars and the bourgeoisie, other classes were the ordinary rural peasants or *smerds* and the so-called Church people, who included all persons whose main activity consisted in working for the Church. Slavery and serfdom increased notably in Russia in the High Middle Ages. The Russian Church enjoyed considerable autonomy, and was an important uplifting, moderating, and civilizing force.

The early Mongols

During the thirteenth century the Mongols obtained control of the greater part of Asia and Eastern Europe. The early Mongols were only one of several nomadic pastoral tribes, including the Naimans, Tartars (Tatars), Keraits, Merkits, Uighurs, and Kipchaks, who inhabited the eastern part of the Eurasian steppe zone, known as "Mongolia," although the term "Mongols" later obtained wider extension. In addition to carrying on migratory pastoral activities and fighting each other, these tribes sometimes raided the Chinese Empire to their southeast. Life in Mongolia was hard and precarious. In addition to the rigors imposed by far-ranging pastoral activities conducted on horseback amid extremes of heat and cold, tribe competed with tribe and man with man in a brutal struggle for possessions and dominance. Leadership was the prize of the strongest, shrewdest, and most popular, or most feared. Each tribe had its own khan or "king," while lesser units were headed by either hereditary chieftains or leaders with whom warriors chose to cast their lot.

The men of Mongolia used horses for their pastoral and military activities, and could remain on horseback for prolonged periods. In warfare, they were primarily horse-archers, whose chief weapon was the bow and arrow, in the use of which they were trained from boyhood. Their composite bow had a pulling weight of some 166 pounds, greater than that of the famous English longbow, and its lethal range was 200 to 300 yards. A favorite trick was to feign retreat and draw the enemy into the murderous crossfire of their arrows. The Mongols used widespread destruction and wholesale slaughter to punish those who refused to submit and to instill fear in those they sought to subject. Often they spared only those who could serve their interests, such as skilled artisans and comely females. The religion of the early Mongols was a combination of nature worship and shamanism (an effort to invoke divine forces by the activities of medicine men).

Chingiz Khan (1162–1227) builds an empire

The first to unite the peoples of Mongolia and coordinate their warlike potential was Chingiz Khan (Genghis Khan), whose original name was Temuchin. The propertyless young Temuchin became the leader of a band of adventurers. After becoming a coadjutor of the Khan of the Keraits, Temuchin eventually replaced his master. With a strong belief in a universal God, Chingiz sought to unite the several tribes of Mongolia. By diplomacy, force, careful planning, receptivity to new ideas, and persistent purpose, Temuchin succeeded in combining the several tribes of Mongolia into one confederation, by whose supreme assembly or

Other European States

kuriltay (*kuriltai*) he was recognized as "Chingiz Khan": "Most Powerful King" or "Supreme Emperor."

With a well-organized, expanded army Chingiz Khan turned to external conquest. One of his first and most difficult objectives was the powerful, populous Ch'in (Kin) Empire of northern China. The Mongols' strength lay in their swift, highly trained, well-coordinated cavalry, together with their devastating archery and confident, inventive leaders. Although at first baffled by strongly fortified cities, the Mongols overcame this problem by building walls around the city walls and by acquiring siege equipment. North China was subjected in successive stages (1211ff.), while a Mongol general invaded Korea. The powerful Kara-Khitans (Kara-Kitai) to the northeast of Turkestan were next overcome. When Chingiz sought to establish friendly relations with the Khwarizimian Shah Ala-al-Din, whose empire included Khwarizm, Transoxiana, Khurasan, Afghanistan, Persia, much of Iraq, and adjacent territories, he was contemptuously rebuffed. The Mongol envoys were insulted and even killed. With a force estimated at 100,000 horsemen plus supporting elements, Chingiz then (1219) invaded rich Khwarizm, whose teeming cities lay athwart the "Great Silk Way." Because of stubborn resistance or later rebellion, most of the key cities of Khwarizm and Transoxiana were taken and destroyed and their populations either slaughtered or enslaved. Shah Ala-al-Din sought refuge on an island in the Caspian, where he soon died, while his son Jalal-al-Din continued brave but futile resistance.

The first Mongol invasion of Russia (1223–1227)

After pursuing the Khwarizmian Shah to the foot of the Caspian Sea, with two divisions of 10,000 men each, the Mongol generals Jebe and Subutay obtained permission from Chingiz to reconnoiter "the Western Lands." When the Mongols attacked the seminomadic Cumans in southern Russia, the latter enlisted the aid of most of the leading Russian princes. Then a poorly coordinated Russian-Cuman army met the Mongols on the banks of the Kalka River in southern Russia (1223). The Mongols directed their main attack against the Cumans, who were the first to flee, thus disrupting the defense. The Mongols overcame stubborn Russian resistance by a perfidious promise of release on surrender, after which they crushed and smothered captive Russian princes under the platform on which Mongol officers held their victory banquet. The Mongol army next raided and pillaged towns and villages of southern Russia. But on receiving news of the death of Chingiz Khan (1227) Mongol forces withdrew and their leaders returned to Mongolia to attend the *kuriltay* that would elect his successor.

The successors of Chingiz Khan (1227ff.)

Chingiz allotted various spheres of influence to his four sons by his first wife. The first, Juchi (Juji) (who died before Chingiz but was succeeded by his four sons, including Batu), obtained the "western" (northwestern) lands; a second son, Jagatay (Chagatai), received the southwestern (south central) territory; a third son, Ugedey (Ogoday, Ogodai), received the eastern portion; and a fourth son, Tuluy (Tuli), held the north central part (the bulk of Mongolia) as a trustee for whoever might be elected. Chingiz had decreed that his third son, Ugedey, whom he considered the most able, should succeed him as Great Khan, and his will was carried out.

Ugedey (1229–1242) continued the work of his father. The subjection of the Ch'in (Kin) Empire of North China was completed as was that of Korea. Operations against the Sung Empire of South China were begun. The final defeat of Jalal-al-Din, the Khwarizmian Shah, was achieved. Syria was invaded by a Mongol army, but without success.

Second Mongol invasion

A great pan-Mongol army assembled from the various parts of the Empire invaded Europe under the command of Batu, a grandson of Chingiz. Batu's army included an estimated 50,000 Mongols and another 50,000 auxiliaries, mainly Turks. Its first victims were the Volga Bolgars, who were rapidly annihilated (1237). The initial attack on Russia was directed against northeastern Russia, which was rightly considered to be the main seat of Russian power. Meanwhile another Mongol army under Mongka (Mangu) dealt with the Cumans (Polovtsy) in southern Russia. The invasion took place in the winter of 1237–1238, so that the army could travel over the frozen rivers. Accustomed to the rigors of severe continental winters, the Mongols wore double sheepskin garments and wrapped the legs of their horses in protective skins. Riazan, Moscow, and Vladimir were taken during this campaign. The conquest of the Russian principalities was completed in 1240 with the taking of Perieslav, Chernigov, and Kiev. Since most of the Russian cities strenuously resisted, wholesale slaughter and destruction accompanied the Mongol advance.

From Russia, the Mongols invaded Poland and Silesia, and defeated a combined Polish and German army at Wahlstaat in 1241. Descending into Hungary via Bohemia and Moravia, they defeated a Hungarian army under King Bela at Mohi (near Pesth) (1241); and an advance force even approached the environs of Vienna. But when news was received of the death of the Great Khan Ugedey in December 1241, Batu and his fellow leaders returned to Karakorum to attend the *kuriltay*, while the army withdrew to southern Russia to be in a better position to influence events in Asia.

Mongka and Kubilay

Ugudey was succeeded briefly by his son Guyuk (1246–1248), whose early death may have been caused by poison. With the support of Batu, Mongka (Mangu), the son of Tuluy, was elected Great Khan. Under Mongka (1248–1259) the invasion of South China was pushed, as was also the conquest of southwestern Asia. Operations in southern China were under the command of the able Kubilay (Kublai), a brother of Mongka. Those in southwestern Asia were in the hands of Hulagu, another brother of Mongka. Hulagu first exterminated the Assassins, whose headquarters were at Alamut, south of the Caspian. He then proceeded to Bagdad, which he took after a long siege (1258). He executed the Abbasid Caliph and his ministers, along with most of the population. Hulagu established himself as Il-Khan or Regional Khan of Persia, Iraq, Khwarizm, and adjacent territories, where his Il-Khan dynasty lasted till 1335. But his efforts to take Syria were thwarted by the Mameluks of Egypt.

Other European States

The competent Kubilay Khan (1260–1294) completed the conquest of the Sung Empire of southern China, and spent most of his time building up and organizing an expanded Chinese Empire, which included the old Ch'in and Sung Empires of North China and eastern Siberia, with Korea and Burma as vassal states. The rulers of Indo-China also acknowledged his suzerainty. Kubilay, who founded the Yuan line of Emperors, made Peking his capital, sponsored public works such as the Great Canal, and promoted education and learning. Marco Polo dwelt at the court of Kubilay Khan and reported its wonders. Kubilay adopted the Chinese language and Chinese ways, including Buddhism. He gave up the project of conquering Western Europe, and endeavored instead to maintain friendly relations with Western rulers. He welcomed Western merchants such as the Polos, requested the Pope to send him Western scholars and technicians, and participated in a nominal alliance against the Mameluks of Egypt.

Under Kubilay's successors (1294–1307) the Mongol Empire was formally recognized as a federation with four practically autonomous states within the Mongol world: *Division of the Mongol world*

1. The Far Eastern Part, including China, Mongolia, and Eastern Siberia, ruled by the house of Kubilay.

2. The Central Part, including Transoxiana and adjacent territories, ruled by the descendants of Jagatay.

3. The Southwestern Part, including Iran, Iraq, and adjacent territories, ruled by the Il-Khans of Persia (the descendants of Hulagu).

4. The Northwestern ("Western") Part, including Russia, western Siberia, and Kazakhstan (north of the Aral Sea), ruled by the descendants of Juchi.

One of the most unstable, turbulent parts of the Mongol world was the Central Part. This soon broke up into Transoxiana and Turkestan, with subsequent further subdivisions. In the second half of the fourteenth century a strong, ambitious and hard young Mongol chieftain known as Tamerlane (Timur the Lame) (1336?–1405) surmounted numerous obstacles to rise to supreme power, and left death and destruction in his wake. By a long and ruthless career of conquest,[b] Tamerlane built up a huge empire that included Transoxiana, Khwarizm, western Turkestan, Khurasan, Afghanistan, Iran, Iraq, northwestern India, Syria, and Asia Minor. But after Tamerlane's death his loose empire soon broke up into fragments. The Great Moguls (Mongols) of India were established by a successor of Tamerlane. *Tamerlane*

[b] 1369–1405

Russia was the westernmost and only European part of the Mongol Empire. It constituted the most important part of the portion of Chingiz' son Juchi, which was inherited by the latter's son Batu, who led the horde of Mongols and Turks that effected its conquest (1237–1240). The Asiatic rulers of Russia were known as "the Golden Horde" and as "Tartars" or "Tatars." *Russia under the Mongols in the thirteenth century*

The Mongols preferred and dwelt in the far southern part of Russia, where their capital was at Sarai on the Lower Volga to the north of the Caspian Sea. They ruled Russia north of the steppes with Russian princes as their agents and tax collectors. Their main interest was to enforce respectful subservience, obtain recruits, and collect tribute, especially the latter. If the Russians failed in any of these respects, the Tartars would ride in and severely punish them; otherwise they allowed the Russians to rule themselves.

Among the Russian princes, the Mongols recognized one as Grand Prince, whose duty was to supervise and help keep in line the other princes and the people. Initially, each Grand Prince had to travel to Sarai and obtain his *yarlyk* or formal letter to act as a deputy of the Khan. Batu and his successors recognized the Princes of Vladimir as Grand Princes until 1341. The third Grand Prince of Vladimir, Alexander Nevsky, is famous. As Prince of Novgorod, prior to his accession as Grand Prince of Vladimir (ça. 1251), Alexander defeated in succession (1) the Swedes by the Neva River (1240), whence his nickname "Nevsky," (2) the Teutonic Knights on frozen Lake Peipus (1242) in the famous "Battle of the Ice," and (3) the Lithuanians (1245). Alexander also persuaded the Novgorodians to give up the hopeless project of resisting the Mongols, and to render nominal submission. Tartar rule in most of Russia persisted for over two centuries.

References for Chapter 21

USEFUL accounts of the history of Spain in the High Middle Ages are GABRIEL JACKSON, *The Making of Medieval Spain* (New York: Harcourt, 1972); RAFAEL ALTAMIRA, *A History of Spain* . . . , tr. Muna Lee (New York: Van Nostrand, 1949); LOUIS BERTRAND and CHARLES PETRIE, *The History of Spain* . . . (New York: Appleton, 1934); ULICK R. BURKE, *A History of Spain from the Earliest Times to the Death of Ferdinand the Catholic*, ed. Martin Hume, vol. I (London: Longmans, 1900); the *Cambridge Medieval History*, vols. VI and VII (articles by RAFAEL ALTAMIRA); and ROGER B. MERRIMAN, *The Rise of the Spanish Empire in the Old World and the New*, vol. I (New York: Macmillan, 1936). Works concerning special phases of Spanish history in the High Middle Ages include HENRY B. CLARKE, *The Cid Campeador and the Waning of the Crescent in the West* (New York: Putnams, 1902); RAMÓN MENÉNDEZ PIDAL, *The Cid and His Spain*, tr. H. Sunderland (London: Murray, 1934); EVELYN S. PROCTER, *Alfonso X of Castile, Patron of Literature and Learning* . . . (Oxford: Clarendon, 1951); JOHN E. KELLER, *Alfonso X, "el Sabio"* (New York: Twayne, 1967); JOHN B. TREND, *Alfonso the Sage and Other Spanish Essays* (London: Constable, 1926); CHARLES R. BEAZLEY, *James the First of Aragon* (Oxford: Blackwell, 1890); FRANCIS D. SWIFT, *Life and Times of James I, the Conqueror, King of Aragon, Valencia, and Majorca* (Oxford: Clarendon, 1894); and BERNARDO DESCLOT, *Chronicle of the Reign of King Pedro III of Aragon, A.D. 1276–1285*, tr. F. L. Critchlow (Princeton, N.J.: Princeton U.P., 1928).

Good treatments of Italy in the High Middle Ages are to be found in LUIGI SALVATORELLI, *A Concise History of Italy*, tr. Bernard Miall (New York: Oxford U.P., 1940), and JANET P. TREVELYAN, *A Short History of the Italian People* . . . , rev. ed. (London: Allen and Unwin, 1956). Recommended additional works include EVELYN M. JAMISON et al., *Italy: Mediaeval and Modern* . . . (Oxford: Clarendon, 1917), and HENRY D. SEDGWICK, *A Short History* of Italy (476–1900) (Boston: Houghton Mifflin, 1906). JEAN C. L. SIMONDE DE SISMONDI, A History of the Italian Republics in the Middle Ages (London: Dent, 1907) is also practically a general history of Italy. More limited in chronological span are HENRY B. COTTERILL, Medieval Italy . . . 305–1313 (London: G. G. Harrap, 1915), and HENRY D. SEDGWICK Italy in the Thirteenth Century, 2 vols. in 1 (Boston: Houghton Mifflin, 1933). Four good articles on Italy in this period are to be found in the Cambridge Medieval History, vols. V and VI.

The "Mediaeval Towns Series" (London: Dent, 1898ff.) includes several good histories of leading Italian towns, including Florence, Rome, Milan, Bologna, Naples, Sienna, Assisi, Verona, Lucca, Ravenna, and Perugia. The story of medieval Florence is well told by FERDINAND SCHEVILL, History of Florence . . . Through the Renaissance (New York: Harcourt, 1936), who also recounts that of Siena . . . a Mediaeval Commune (London: Chapman, 1909).

HORATIO R. F. BROWN is the author of several excellent historical treatises on Venice, including The Venetian Republic (London: Dent, 1902), and Studies in the History of Venice, 2 vols. (New York: Dutton, 1907). The story of medieval Venice is also told by WILLIAM C. HAZLITT, The Venetian Republic, 2 vols. (London: A. and C. Black, 1915).

WILLIAM F. BUTLER traces the development of republics of northern Italy to the early fourteenth century in his The Lombard Communes . . . (New York: Scribners, 1906), and DOROTHY MUIR specializes in thirteenth- to fifteenth-century Milan in her History of Milan Under the Visconti (London: Methuen, 1924). Rome and the Papal States are the subject of the classic FERDINAND GREGOROVIUS, History of the City of Rome in the Middle Ages, tr. A. Hamilton, 8 vols. in 13 (London: Bell, 1900–1906, etc.), and WILLIAM F. BARRY, The Papal Monarchy, 590–1303 (New York: Putnams, 1902). The founding and early story of the Norman kingdom in southern Italy and Sicily are ably recounted by JAMES V. OSBORNE, . . . The Greatest Norman Conquest (New York: Dutton, 1937), and EDMUND CURTIS, Roger of Sicily and the Normans in Lower Italy, 1016–1154 (London: Putnams, 1912). STEPHEN RUNCIMAN tells of the establishment and overthrow (1282) of Angevin rule in Sicily in his The Sicilian Vespers (Cambridge: Cambridge U.P., 1958).

For the Balkans in the Middle Ages, a sketchy but readable, well-organized introduction is WESLEY M. GEHWEHR, The History of the Balkan Peninsula, 2nd ed. (New York: Harcourt, 1933). Shorter overviews are provided by GEORGE E. MYLONAS, The Balkan States: An Introduction to Their History (St. Louis, Mo.: Eden, 1947), and CHARLES and BARBARA JELAVICH, The Balkans (Englewood Cliffs, N.J.: Prentice-Hall, 1965).

For the Byzantine Empire in the High Middle Ages, consult references for Chapter Seven. Excellent general works with fuller coverage are those of ALEXANDER A. VASILIEV and GEORGE OSTROGORSKY, as well as the new vol. IV on The Byzantine Empire (in two parts) in the Cambridge Medieval History (Cambridge: Cambridge U.P., 1966). Useful shorter surveys are those of STEVEN RUNCIMAN, CHARLES DIEHL, and JOAN HUSSEY. For the fall of Constantinople to the Latins in 1204, see EDWIN PEARS.

Helpful works on the various Balkan states are GEORGE C. LOGIO, Bulgaria: Past and Present (Manchester: Sherratt and Hughes, 1936); STEVEN RUNCIMAN, History of the First Bulgarian Empire (London: Bell, 1930); HAROLD W. TEMPERLEY, History of Serbia (London: Bell, 1917); STE-

PHEN CLISSOLD, ed., *A Short History of Jugoslavia* (Cambridge: Cambridge U.P., 1966); ROBERT W. SETON-WATSON, *A History of the Roumanians* (Cambridge: Cambridge U.P., 1934); and NICOLAE IORGA, *A History of Roumania*, tr. J. McCabe (London: Unwin, 1925).

The history of Bohemia (Czechoslovakia) in the High Middle Ages is authoritatively related by KAMIL KROFTA in his *Short History of Czechoslovakia* (New York: R. M. McBride, 1934), as well as in his article in the *Cambridge Medieval History*, VI, 422–447.

Concerning Poland in this period, we have the excellent *Cambridge History of Poland*, vol. I, a scholarly collaborative work edited by W. F. REDDAWAY et al. (Cambridge: Cambridge U.P., 1950). Less detailed although reliable are OSCAR HALECKI, *History of Poland* (New York: Rey, 1956), and ROMAN DYBESKI, *Outlines of Polish History* (London: Allen, 1925).

The story of Hungary in the High Middle Ages is well told by DENIS SINOR, *History of Hungary* (London: Allen and Unwin, 1959), and is also sketched by DOMOKOS G. KOSÁRY, *History of Hungary* (Cleveland: Benjamin Franklin, 1941).

Scandinavia in general is surveyed by HALVDAN KOHT, "The Scandinavian Kingdoms Until the End of the Thirteenth Century," in the *Cambridge Medieval History*, VI, 362–392; and there are various interesting, well-illustrated articles on the subject in the collaborative *Scandinavia: Past and Present: From the Viking Age to Absolute Monarchy*, eds. JORGEN BUKDAHL et al. (Denmark: Arnkrone, 1959). The history of Denmark is sketched by JOHN H. S. BIRCH, *Denmark in History* (London: J. Murray, 1938), as well as by JOHN DANSTRUP, *A History of Denmark*, tr. V. Lindbergh (Copenhagen: Wivel, 1948).

An excellent account of Sweden in the High Middle Ages is to be found in INGVAR ANDERSSON, *History of Sweden*, tr. C. Hannay (London: Weidenfeld and Nicholson, 1962); also useful is CARL HALLENDORFF and ADOLPH SCHNÜCK, *History of Sweden* (Stockholm: Fritze, 1929). Good works for the history of Norway are KAREN LARSEN, *A History of Norway* (Princeton, N.J.: Princeton U.P., 1948), and THOMAS K. DERRY, *A Short History of Norway* (London: Allen and Unwin, 1957).

The most comprehensive and authoritative treatment of Russia in the High Middle Ages in English is that of GEORGE VERNADSKY in his multivolume *History of Russia*, vol. II: *Kievan Russia* (London: Oxford U.P., 1948), and vol. III: *The Mongols and Russia* (Oxford: Oxford U.P., 1952). One-volume histories with from about 85 to 135 pages on the Middle Ages are SERGEI F. PLATONOV, *History of Russia*, tr. E. Aronsberg (Bloomington: Indiana U.P., 1964); MELVIN C. WREN, *The Course of Russian History* (New York: Macmillan, 3rd ed., 1968); BERNARD PARES, *History of Russia* (New York: Knopf, 1953); JESSE D. CLARKSON, *History of Russia* (New York: Random House, 1961); MICHAEL T. FLORINSKY, *Russia: A Short History* (New York: Macmillan, 1964); and IVAR SPECTOR, *An Introduction to Russian History and Culture* (New York: Van Nostrand, 1961). For the Mongols, consult MICHAEL PRAWDIN (pseud. for Michael Charol), *The Mongol Empire: Its Rise and Legacy* tr. Eden and C. Paul (New York: Free Press, 1961) (p.), originally published in German in 1937; and JEREMIAH CURTIN, *The Mongols in Russia* (Boston: Little, Brown, 1908); in addition to VERNADSKY.

APOGEE OF THE CHURCH DURING THE HIGH MIDDLE AGES. Chapter 22.

DURING the High Middle Ages the Church reached the apogee of its power and influence. Helping account for its ascendance were its universality, excellent organization and valued ministrations, together with the superior education of most of its ministers, the strong faith of many of its members, and the dedication, services, and example of its religious. Monarchs were not yet strong enough to challenge Church privileges and hegemony; while the hardships, perils, and uncertainties of contemporary life helped to promote ascendance of the spiritual over the temporal. During this period the administrative organization of the Church was completed, Popes led in Christian reform and were often "arbiters of Europe," religious orders multiplied and flourished, Christian doctrines matured and were coordinated with philosophy, the liturgy of the Church was fully formed, and Christian principles were firmly established in law and society.

THE ASCENDANCE OF THE PAPACY AND RELATIONS OF CHURCH AND STATE.
Section 64.

> Even as the moon, the lesser body, borrows all its light from the sun . . . so the royal power borrows all its dignity and splendor from the pontifical. [Innocent III after his election as Pope (1198).]

THE GREAT development of Church government during the High Middle Ages held especially true of the Papacy. Papal primacy was accepted throughout the Western Church, wherein the Pope was recognized as "the successor of St. Peter" and "the Vicar of Christ." The government of the Church became more centralized and the Papacy itself became a monarchy, both ecclesiastical with respect to the universal Church and political with respect to the Papal States. Popes claimed and exercised a "plentitude of power" within the Church, and even attempted to extend this in a supervisory manner to the secular governments of Christendom—although their efforts here were less successful. *Development of Papal government*

Papal power within the Church came to be virtually unrestricted, and the Pope became a sort of "universal ordinary" with direct local as well as general supervisory authority. Appointments to an increasing number of benefices throughout the Western Christian world came to be "reserved" to the Pope, as in the case of benefices of clerics who died in Rome as members of the Papal Curia—a means of providing for the support of a successor. The Papal practice of recommending clerics for benefices was often transformed into actual appointments or "provisions." As the number of Papal reservations and provisions multiplied, so did appeals to the Papal courts. Practically all ecclesiastical cases could be appealed to Rome, and the Papacy likewise also became a court of first instance in an increasing number of reserved cases, judicable only by the Holy See. So great did the judicial burdens of the Papal courts become that Innocent III had to impose limiting conditions for the acceptance of cases. To support its numerous projects, including crusades, the Papacy levied income taxes upon the clergy, beginning in 1199.

Papal Curia

To handle the growing volume of Papal business, Popes expanded the Papal government until it became a virtual bureaucracy, known as the Papal "Curia" or "Court," organized along the lines of the developing secular monarchical *curiae* or courts of Western Europe. The French Pope Urban II, who was active in this regard, apparently sought to imitate the royal *curia* in France. The Papal Curia shared with contemporary monarchical *curiae* the tendency to expand its jurisdiction and increase its power. The Papal writing office became a separate department known as the Chancery, which handled an enormous amount of correspondence and documents as well as records. To prevent forgery a special "chancery style," difficult to imitate, was adopted. Since a seal or *bulla* was attached to more important Papal documents, they were known as "bulls." A separate treasury department known as the *Camera Apostolica* (*camera*: room) was constituted. The Papal Chancellor and the *Camerarius* were frequently cardinals. To hear cases appealed to Rome, Popes frequently appointed special *auditores* (hearers, judges), who eventually constituted a continuing judiciary. At first the auditors simply reported their findings to the Pope, who made the decision, personally or in consistory; but subsequently they recommended decisions based on their findings, and finally they decided cases in the Pope's name.

Cardinals, legates, and general councils

Other institutions of the central government of the Church included cardinals, Papal legates, and ecumenical councils. The cardinals, who were the leading ecclesiastics of the Roman Archdiocese, were formally designated as the sole Papal electors and interim administrators of the Papal See by Nicholas II in 1059, and organized into a "college" or corporation in 1179. The cardinals also consulted with and advised the Pope in consistory, and came to constitute a sort of senate of the universal Church. Many of them came to hold key offices in the Papal Curia. Their number varied from about twenty to fifty. The Pope appointed legates or special representatives to investigate and deal with important matters in various parts of the Christian world. Besides ordinary legates, frequently known as *legati missi* (legates sent or delegated by the Pope), there were *legati a latere*, who were cardinal legates "from the side" of the Pope, empowered to handle matters of greater weight in his name. There were also *legati nati* (native legates) who were such *ex efficio*: i.e., by virtue of their office as head of the Church in their country, as was the case with the Archbishops of Canterbury and Toledo.

The holding of ecumenical (general) ecclesiastical councils was resumed during the twelfth century, and from 1123 to 1274 they were convened on the average of once every twenty-five years. Unlike the earlier ecumenical councils, they were held in the West, because of the Eastern Schism: the first four at Rome, the last two at Lyons.

Apogee of the Church

Canon law

Paralleling high medieval development of civil law, there was a considerable development of ecclesiastical or "canon" law (Gr. *canon*: rule, law). The latter's scope was much greater then than now, as to both persons (clerics, students, teachers, and church employees) and cases (all religion-connected cases, such as matrimony, sworn contracts, and wills). Sources of canon law included the Bible, the writings of the Fathers, the decrees of Church Councils and Popes, and the ordinary (general, traditional) teachings of the Church. Much canon law was regarded as a confirmation, clarification, or application of divine law as found in nature and revelation; while the rest consisted simply of ordinances of the Church, such as the laws of abstinence on Friday and fasting during Lent. Various compilations of canon laws were made from the fourteenth century on. More systematic collections, such as those of Bishops Anselm of Lucca, Burchard of Worms, and Ivo of Chartres, appeared in the eleventh century.

Epochal in the gradual systematization of canon law was *The Concordance of Discordant Canons* or *Decretum*, drawn up at Bologna about 1140 by a Camaldolese monk named Gratian. This was the first comprehensive organized compilation of canon laws and it was accompanied by a commentary. Gratian's excellent collection soon superseded others in the West and became a starting point for similar collections of subsequent legislation, which were made periodically. Official Papal collections of subsequent legislation were made by Gregory IX in 1235 and Boniface VIII in 1298. Gratian's collection placed special emphasis on the Pope's position as the supreme legislator and judge in the Church. Gratian, who used the dialectical method, first raised a question, then gave texts on both sides, and finally presented a solution. This begot several additional questions that were dealt with by subsequent commentators. The commentators from 1140 to 1234, such as Bandellini and Huguccio, are known as "Decretists," in that they started with the *Decretum* as a basis. In general they tried to explain the law and its applications, and answer questions deriving therefrom, as well as to harmonize discrepancies. From 1234 on the commentators are known as "Decretalists," in that they also used the *Decretals of Gregory VII*. The Decretalists, among whom were Innocent IV and Cardinal Hostiensis, went beyond particular laws to general legal principles. The canonists contributed to a growth of Papal authority as well as to an expansion of Church legislation.

Local Church government

In local Church government, bishops continued to be the principal pastors of their dioceses, with extensive temporal and political as well as religious responsibilities. The extension of Papal authority cut into episcopal authority, as in the acceptance of numerous appeals to Rome, and the exemption of many religious who were made directly subject to the Papacy. The clergy attached to the cathedral were often organized into communities of "canons," who followed a "Rule" to some extent. The chief official in the diocese under the bishop was usually a chancellor, vicar general, or archdeacon. Archdeacons, who were also usually priests, were often set over larger subdivisions of dioceses, with deans over smaller ones. Church councils or synods were held on diocesan,

Church discipline

provincial, and "national" levels, as well as from time to time on an international or "ecumenical" scale.

Conformity and order in the Church were maintained by canon law, ecclesiastical courts, and church-imposed penalties, including excommunication and interdict. Excommunication excluded a person from participation in the services and sacraments of the Church (except when in danger of death). An excommunicated person was regarded as an outcast who could expect eternal punishment if he died without absolution. If a person was declared *excommunicatus vitandus* his company was to be shunned under pain of sin. An "interdict" was sometimes used to bring recalcitrant rulers into compliance. Under an interdict, a territory such as a nation, a region, or a city, or any place where the ruler happened to be at a given time (as in the case of Philip I and Frederick II), was deprived of ordinary church services and sacraments. Usually celebration of the Mass and Communion and Matrimony were suspended, but conferral of Baptism, Penance, and Extreme Unction was allowed. Natural misfortunes suffered while under an interdict were often blamed on the person who was the cause of the interdict. An interdict imposed on France by Pope Innocent III in 1200 read in part: *Let all the churches be closed; let none be admitted to them except to baptize infants. . . . We permit Mass to be celebrated once a week, on Friday, early in the morning, to consecrate the host for the use of the sick; but only one cleric is to be admitted to see the priest.* Beginning with Gregory VII, Popes began to declare recalcitrant monarchs deposed and their subjects released from their oaths and obligations to them in more extreme cases. In the thirteenth century Pope Gregory IX established the Inquisition as a special tribunal to inquire into cases where persons were accused of heresy; and Innocent II proclaimed a crusade to stamp out the Albigensian heresy.

Reform of the Church under Papal leadership (ca. 1049, ff.): Leo IX

During the eleventh century (1049–1124) the Papacy assumed the lead in reform of the Church, a movement originally inspired by reforms in monasteries in Lorraine and Burgundy, including those of Brognes, Gorze, and Cluny, especially the last. So that ecclesiastical officials on all levels could be more fully dedicated to spiritual ideals and religious objectives, the reform endeavored to emancipate them from secular involvements. Means of liberation included abstension from sexual intercourse, whether in or out of matrimony, abolition of monetary considerations in appointments to Church offices, and withdrawal of power from laymen to name ecclesiastical officials. Inasmuch as the secular political aspects of this struggle are discussed in our treatment of the Western Empire, and the theory involved is included in our presentation of intellectual history, only a summary of developments and implications is given here. Papal-led reform of the Church was launched after Emperor Henry III of Germany appointed his reform-minded uncle, Bishop Bruno of Toul, to the Papal office in 1049. Bishop Bruno made his way as a pilgrim to Rome, where he was duly elected and took the name of Leo IX. Accompanying Bruno were other reformer-clerics such as the influential Humbert of Moyenmoutier and the devout Hildebrand. The latter

Apogee of the Church

eventually became the chief adviser and leading official in the Papal *Curia*. The energetic Leo IX (1049–1054) held numerous councils in Italy, France, and Germany, and, in conjunction with the last, issued stern decrees prohibiting and penalizing clerical incontinence and simony, as well as other clerical transgressions. Priests who kept concubines or attempted marriages were to be deprived of their offices or otherwise punished, as were clerics, including bishops, who purchased ecclesiastical preferments.

The Popes who followed Leo IX in the period from 1055 to 1073 continued the clerical reform movement. Consistency was provided by the continuing presence in the Papal entourage of reformers such as Peter Damian, Humbert of Moyenmoutier, and especially Hildebrand. A new phase of the reform movement, the elimination of lay control of appointments to ecclesiastical offices, was launched decisively by Pope Nicholas II (1059–1061) during the weak regency for Henry IV. In his famous Electoral Reform Decree of 1059, Nicholas II, who had himself been confronted by an Anti-Pope, reserved the election of Popes to the "cardinals," the principal clerics of the Roman Archdiocese: the cardinal-bishops of the seven Roman dioceses, the cardinal-priests of the principal churches of Rome, and the cardinal-deacons of the seven districts of Rome. Although confirmation of the election was still to be obtained from the Emperor, both he and the people of Rome were excluded from any role in the actual election. At first the nomination of candidates for the Papal office was reserved to the cardinal-bishops, but in 1179 roles were equalized and the cardinals were organized into a "college" or corporation. The "conclave" ("under key") system whereby the cardinals were to assemble within ten days after the death of a Pope, and remain behind locked doors until they elected a new Pope, was introduced in 1274.

Leo's successors (1055ff.)

In 1073, immediately after the death of Alexander II, the dynamic Hildebrand, long a leading force in the reform movement, was acclaimed Pope by the Roman clergy and people and accepted by the cardinals. Hildebrand, who took the name Gregory VII, notified but did not bother to obtain the assent of the Emperor. Gregory vigorously prosecuted Church reform, decreeing stern punishments for clerical incontinence and simony, and attempting to promote the installation of worthy clerics in ecclesiastical offices. Gregory supported the Patarin (popular reform) candidate for the key Archbishopric of Milan against the antireform clerical candidate, and invoked the historic Papal claim to appoint to a bishopric in the case of a disputed election. But Gregory was confronted by the counterclaims of Henry IV, and Henry's appointment of nonreform candidates to bishoprics. Recognizing that secular appointments to ecclesiastical offices for secular considerations were an almost insurmountable obstacle to reform, Gregory in his Lenten synod of 1075 solemnly forbade laymen to confer ecclesiastical offices, and clerics to accept such from laymen, under pain of excommunication for both parties. Conflicting with long-established customs that seemed to have force of constitutional law, the anti-investiture Papal edict, which

The investiture struggle (1075–1122) Gregory VII

Gregory insisted on implementing, was a virtual bombshell. The greatest, most immediate and vocal opposition came from the German monarch and his supporters.

After being openly defied and insulted by Henry IV, who appointed antireform candidates to the Italian bishoprics of Milan, Fermo, and Spoleto, and by the German bishops, who were opposed to any further extension of Papal power, Gregory took an extreme step. Having meanwhile allied with the discontented German princes, as well as with the anti-imperial Normans of southern Italy, Gregory declared Henry excommunicated and suspended (1076). The Papal claim to depose a Christian monarch from office was unprecedented. It was obviously used by Gregory as an ultimate resort to remove what he considered a serious obstacle to the spiritual interests of the faithful; but its implications were world-shaking, as it would ultimately subject the Emperor to the Pope and the State to the Church.

Henry's clever submission to Gregory at Canossa (1077), which lifted both the excommunication and his deposition from office, proved illusory, as Gregory obviously feared. It also broke the alliance between Pope and princes, as the former had acted alone and had imperiled the latter. Gregory's eventual support of the anti-imperial candidate elected by some of the princes, and his later renewed excommunication of Henry IV, had little practical effect except to provoke an invasion of Italy by Henry IV (1080ff.), who also supported an Anti-Pope, Clement III. After Henry attacked Rome (1085), Gregory had to call in the Normans and eventually died "in exile" (1085). Neither Gregory's condemnation of lay investiture nor his attempted deposition of a monarch had succeeded.

Gregory's successors

The so-called investiture struggle against lay appointments to ecclesiastical offices was continued by Gregory's successors. The diplomatic French Pope Urban II (1088–1099) overcame the Anti-Pope (Clement III) who had been set up by Henry IV, and continued to promote reform. Urban also launched the First Crusade, which greatly enhanced Papal prestige. Pope Paschal II clouded the issue by stressing the investiture or installation more than the actual naming or appointment of ecclesiastical officials. Paschal also vacillated in his policies. His offer to give up all political offices acquired by ecclesiastics since the time of Charlemagne (exclusive of the Papal States) if Henry would give up all lay investiture was vigorously resisted by both bishops and lay aristocracy. The bishops would lose regular revenues and powers upon which they had come to depend, while monarchical power would be vastly increased by direct control of important territories and towns and offices, which would further weaken the aristocracy. Because of a torrent of criticism and opposition, and the growing realization that he could not depend on Henry V to keep his part of the bargain, Paschal withdrew his concessions. Following the death of Paschal II, hopes improved for a settlement of the controversy with the election of the level-headed Calixtus II (1119–1124). Eventually both Emperor and Pope were so hard pressed by various problems that a compromise was possible. By the Concordat of

Apogee of the Church

Worms (1122), canonical election to ecclesiastical offices was safeguarded; but participation of the secular authority was allowed. Meanwhile in France and England similar compromise agreements were reached. Where previously there had been no established limitations on secular interference in ecclesiastical appointments, definite restrictions were imposed. Rulers still had a right to nominate Church officials and to veto elections, as well as to bring some pressure in favor of their preferred candidate. But they were formally excluded from directly electing or appointing persons to ecclesiastical offices, and the way was open for further diminution of their role in Church affairs.

Following its gains in the investiture struggle, the Papacy consolidated its control of the Church. Papal government continued to expand, and Papal political pretensions and involvements increased. As both the study and ambit of civil and canon law expanded, their respective representatives, the "legists" and "canonists" elaborated their theories. They disputed the question as to who had the ultimate authority in cases of conflict, the Papacy or the secular monarch. Ecclesiastical centralization, previously regarded as a means of reform, now obtained the status of an end. Exercise of Papal authority in the secular sphere, previously regarded as in extraordinary final resort in emergencies, now came to be considered an ordinary necessity.

First phase of the Papal struggle with the Hohenstaufen

The Guelph vs. Hohenstaufen contest, which began as a dispute between two princely families over the right to the German throne, expanded into a broader contest concerning the scope of imperial authority, which aligned the Papacy with the North Italian communes and the anti-imperial faction in Germany against the Hohenstaufen. Emperor Frederick Barbarossa (1152–1190) sought to establish effective imperial control in northern Italy and, as far as possible, in the Papal States. English Pope Adrian IV (1154–1159), on the other hand, strove to preserve and bolster Papal independence and authority. In the "stirrup" incident (1155), as has been seen, Adrian refused to confer with Frederick until the latter performed the customary service of helping the Pope dismount. In the *beneficia* incident, Adrian referred to the *beneficia* (benefices or benefits) he had "conferred" on Frederick; but was eventually constrained to write to the Emperor explaining that he used the word *beneficia* in the sense of "benefits" or "favors" rather than "benefices" or "fiefs." During a final conflict over Frederick's appointment of his chancellor, Rainald of Daissel, as Archbishop of Cologne, Adrian died (1159). The contest flared up again even more fiercely following the election of Pope Alexander III (1159–1181), who favored firmer opposition to Frederick's pretensions. Frederick supported an Anti-Pope, while Alexander allied with the Lombard League. The latter's victory at Legano (1176) led to Barbarossa's recognition of Alexander III in the Peace of Venice (1177).

Height of Papal power: Innocent III

The apogee of Papal prestige came during the pontificate of Innocent III. Contributing factors included the current weakness of the strife-torn Empire, the critical struggle between the English and French kings, and the strong will, keen intellect, and administrative genius of the dedicated, aristocratic Pope. Innocent, a vigorous 37 at his election, was trained in canon law and had a high sense of the powers and responsibilities of the Papal office. At his installation as Pope, he spoke of himself as "the viceroy of God," and "the judge of all," and said: *To me are the words of the prophet spoken: "I have this day set thee over nations and kingdoms, to uproot and demolish, to lay waste and destroy, as well as to build and to plant."* His concept of the "plenitude" of Papal power was so great that he believed he had both unlimited authority in the Church and almost unlimited authority to intervene in secular affairs.

Innocent III established peace, order, and strong government in Rome and in the Papal States. He also improved the organization of the central government of the Church, especially that of the Papal Chancery. The Papal registry of his Pontificate contains some 4,800 registered letters. To promote the interests of religion and morality, as he saw them, Innocent III became "the arbiter of Europe." He brought reluctant Philip II of France to take back his discarded lawful wife, Ingebourg of Denmark. He prevailed on recalcitrant King John of England to accept the Papal appointee to the contested Archbishopric of Canterbury. He annulled marriages of both the King of Leon and the heir to the throne of Portugal on grounds of consanguinity. During the disputed succession in the Empire (1197–1216), Innocent first deferred judgment, then chose Otto (IV) of Brunswick, and finally transferred his approval to his own ward, Frederick (II), and in each case his candidate was successful. To obtain the benefits of Papal protection, several kings were Papal vassals, including the kings of Aragon, Portugal, Sicily, and England.

Crusades

Innocent III was responsible for several Crusades. One of his major projects was to launch a Crusade to recover former Christian possessions in the Holy Land recently lost to Saladin. Although the Fourth Crusade (1202–1204), assembled as a result of Innocent's efforts, was diverted against his will to Zara and eventually to Constantinople, Innocent did not neglect the opportunity to set up a Latin Patriarchate at Constantinople. The Fifth Crusade (1217–1221) was also due to Innocent's efforts, although it occurred after his death. Innocent promoted a great Crusade against the Moroccan Almohades in Spain, which resulted in a decisive Christian victory at Las Navas de Tolosa (1212).

After gentler means failed to uproot Albigensianism in southern France, Innocent proclaimed the Albigensian Crusade to crush the heresy by force. He also wisely approved, on a provisional basis, the Dominicans and the Franciscans, by way of special exceptions to a policy against the creation of new religious orders. Finally he convoked the IV Lateran Council (1215). Attended by over four hundred bishops and more than eight hundred abbots and priors, this "great international congress" effected several important reforms. Provincial councils were to be held yearly. Cathedral schools were to provide free education. Bishops must provide sufficient preachers and confessors for the faithful. Priests were forbidden to officiate at ordeals, thus leading to their abandonment by secular courts. Relics were not to be sold. The clergy were forbidden to engage in trade; and clerical gambling and concubinage were strictly prohibited.

A renewed and aggravated struggle with the Hohenstaufen house followed Innocent's death. Whereas the aged, gentle Honorius III (1216–1227) patiently tried to persuade the new Emperor, Frederick II, to keep his promises to Innocent without result, succeeding Popes resorted to more forceful means. Gregory IX (1227–1241) eventually excommunicated Frederick II, and levied an interdict that applied to any place where Frederick might be at a given time. Innocent IV (1227–1241) withdrew stealthily to France, where he summoned the First General Council of Lyons (1245), which joined with him in declaring Frederick deposed. The prolonged efforts of Frederick II to obtain effective control of Italy were eventually foiled by the determined resistance of the Papacy and the North Italian communes. *Renewed Papal struggle with the Hohenstaufen*

During the second half of the thirteenth century, the Papacy became increasingly involved in secular political affairs, including the treacherous marshes of the so-called Sicilian question. In fact, the Papacy came more and more to act like an Italian secular power. Following the death of Frederick II (1250), the Papacy supported its own candidates for the Sicilian throne. After the project to enthrone the son of Henry III of England fell through, the French Pope Urban IV (1261–1264) offered the Sicilian crown to Charles of Anjou. With a strong French army and Papal support, Charles defeated and slew Frederick's illegitimate son, Manfred (1266), as well as defeated and executed Frederick's grandson, Conradin (1268). The French Pope Martin IV (1281–1285) gave full rein to Charles' ambitious projects to control the Mediterranean. But after Charles' great dream was shattered by the "Sicilian Vespers" (1282), followed by Aragonese occupation of the island, the Papacy became involved in a long but futile contest to oust the Aragonese from Sicily. The Sicilian War was detrimental to Papal prestige, not only because it failed but also because of increased invocation of religious sanctions for political purposes. Mounting French dominance in Papal councils was also becoming a growing cause of concern. *Era of the "Sicilian question"*

THE MULTIPLICATION OF RELIGIOUS ORDERS.
Section 65.

> 'Tis the rule and way of life of the lesser brothers [Friars Minor] to observe the Holy Gospel of our Lord Jesus Christ, living in obedience without personal possessions, in chastity. [Beginning of the Rule of St. Francis of Assisi.]

THE RELIGIOUS faith and enthusiasm of the High Middle Ages were manifested by the establishment of numerous new religious congregations and orders, as well as by a plentitude of candidates for the religious life. So great was this proliferation that the IV Lateran Council (1215) legislated that no additional religious orders should be authorized unless they adopted one of the existing older Rules.

Reformed Benedictines: Cluniacs and Cistercians

Benedictine monasticism continued to be the prevailing form of monasticism. Early medieval Benedictine reforms such as the Cluniac continued in the High Middle Ages. The Cluniac congregation flourished under able, long-lived Abbots Odilo (994–1048), Hugh the Great (1049–1109), and Peter the Venerable (1122–1157), and helped to promote a general reform in the Church. By the mid-twelfth century the Cluniacs had an estimated 314 houses with an estimated 110,000 monks. Meanwhile many other monasteries and monastic groups adopted Cluniac-inspired reforms without joining the Cluniac congregation, or continued independent reform movements such as those that originated at Brogne and Gorze in Lorraine. Even as the Cluniacs were monastic leaders in the tenth and eleventh centuries, the Cistercians assumed this role in the twelfth century. Both were "congregations" of reformed Benedictines, using as a basic guide the Benedictine Rule. But whereas the Cluniacs emphasized public prayer and work other than agricultural, the Cistercians stressed individual meditation and manual labor, together with austerity and simplicity of life. The Cistercians were founded by Abbot Robert of Molesmes, who soon returned to his original monastery. The "second founder" of the Cistercians was an Englishman named Stephen Harding, who became abbot and put the abbey on firmer ground by his strong leadership and by establishing regulations known as the Charter of Love (1119), which enjoined austerity, simplicity, and contemplation. In 1112, the struggling abbey received a further boost when a band of some thirsty aristocratic recruits led by the twenty-two-year-old Bernard, son of the Count of Fontaines, came seeking admission.

St. Bernard of Clairvaux

St. Bernard became the "third founder" of the Cistercian order and the most famous Cistercian in history. The enthusiastic Bernard persuaded numerous men and women to become Cistercians, including his own brothers and sister, and even his father. When only twenty-five, Bernard became the abbot of a new Cistercian foundation at Clairvaux. Under Bernard's leadership the Cistercians expanded rapidly, so that by his death in 1153 there were some 343 Cistercian abbeys scattered over Europe. By 1300 there were over seven hundred Cistercian monasteries. At first a devotee of chivalric ideals, Bernard became a knight and troubadour of Christ and His Mother Mary. His era is often referred to as "the Age of St. Bernard," since he was one of its most dominant figures, an influential confidant of Popes and bishops, kings and queens. Bernard inspired many of those with whom he came in contact with the flame of his devotion. Among his sayings were *The measure of love is to love without measure* and *On the path of holiness, we must either move forward or slip backward.*

Cistercian life and organization

The Cistercians were noted for their austerity. The Cistercian diet excluded meat, fish, and animal products, banning even milk, butter, and eggs. It was limited to such items as coarse bread, oil, vegetables, and fruit, together with salt and water. The Cistercian habit was made of undyed wool, from which they were known as "the white monks." They spoke only when necessary, and had practically no recreation in the ordinary sense of the word. Cistercian churches, unlike the Cluniac churches, were plain and practically without ornaments, but they were often graceful and beautiful with a "classic simplicity." The Cistercians took the Biblical injunction to earn one's bread by the sweat of one's brow literally, and spent about six hours a day in manual labor. Their persistent, religiously inspired labor resulted in great expansion of agriculture, especially since they sought out the most desolate places, which they often converted into verdant "paradises" by their toil. They had as associates lay brothers who helped till the lands. Returning to earlier Benedictine practice, the Cistercians cut down participation in public religious services to about six hours a day, and increased the time given to silent mental prayer and meditation. St. Bernard once said: *You will learn more in the forests than out of books.* Supreme authority in the order was vested in an annual General Chapter consisting of the abbots of the various houses. Each year the abbots of the four chief Cistercian houses visited and inspected the other abbeys. No one under fifteen was admitted to the order, in contrast to the admission and training of young children by other Benedictine houses.

The religious enthusiasm of the High Middle Ages also led to the establishment of exceedingly strict, austere, cloistered orders that went far beyond the original Benedictine Rule and ordinary Benedictine reforms in practices of self-abnegation and withdrawal from the world. Among such were the Camoldolese, Vallumbrosians, Grandmontines, and Carthusians, founded in the eleventh century, as well as the Carmelites, founded in the twelfth century. *Semi-anchoritical monks*

The Camoldolese monks, who originated at Camoldoli, Italy, added to the original Benedictine Rule austere practices such as fasting on bread and water. They let their beards grow long and wore a white or gray habit of undyed wool. Among noted Camoldolese monks were the greathearted reform Cardinal, St. Peter Damian, the renowned musicologist, Guido of Arezzo, and the famous canonist, Gratian. The Vallumbrosians, who received their name from their abbey, sought to restore what they believed to be the primitive austerity of the Rule of St. Benedict. The Grandmontines, also named from their chief abbey, lived a hermitical form of life and followed a Rule like that of the Camoldolese monks, but never found favor outside of France. The Carthusians, who obtained their name from their abbey in the western Alpine valley of La Chartreuse, became noted for their great austerity. They ate no meat and practiced almost perpetual silence, while dividing their time between prayer and work. The Carmelites, who were also very austere and essentially contemplative, were originally established on Mt. Carmel in Palestine by a crusader named Berthold in the mid-twelfth century, whence they spread to Western Europe in the thirteenth century.

At the other end of the spectrum were the "canons regular," secular priests living in community and following a rule, who were to some extent a compromise between secular priests and monks. The Augustinian Canons Regular or "Austin Canons" (to be distinguished from the Augustinian Hermits or "Austin Friars") developed during the High Middle Ages, when a large number of cathedral and collegiate chapters adopted *Canons Regular* the so-called Rule of St. Augustine, a collection of ascetical instructions attributed to St. Augustine. The Victorines, founded by William of Champeaux in 1113, were Augustinians, known as Canons Regular of St. Victor from their principal house at Paris. They flourished in the twelfth century, when they cultivated learning, theology, and mysticism, and included the famous scholar, educator, and theologian, Hugh of St. Victor; the noted mystic theologian, Richard of St. Victor; and the inspired mystical poet, Adam of St. Victor. The Premonstratensians were founded in 1120 by St. Norbert of Premontré, who was converted from a worldly life as a cleric living at the imperial court. He established an order of canons regular with a strict Rule half way between that of the Augustinian canons and that of the reformed Benedictines. The Premonstratensians became especially active in eastern Germany and Prussia.

Hospital and military orders. Pious lay associations

Several hospital orders were also founded in the High Middle Ages for the corporal works of mercy of caring for the sick and harboring those in need of shelter. Among such were the early Hospitallers of St. John, founded in Palestine by a merchant from Amalfi about 1050, and the Hospitallers of St. Anthony, founded in 1095 in the Dauphiné in southern France. Military orders combined fighting and if possible converting aggressive infidels with the religious life. Among military orders founded to supply needed military manpower for the Crusader States were the Knights Hospitaller of St. John, who now (about 1113) assumed military duties as well as performed hospital services;, the Knights Templar, founded in the early twelfth century (1118–1128) by two French Knights; and the Teutonic Knights, founded at Acre by German knights in the late twelfth century.

Several pious associations of devout laymen and laywomen also appeared. Among such were the Bridge-Building Brothers, founded in southern France in the eleventh to twelfth centuries, for the building and maintenance of bridges; the Humiliati of Lombardy, a pious association of workmen living in common; and various associations of "Poor Men," who stressed poverty, humility, and simplicity. The Poor Men of Lyons eventually became the heretical Waldensians. In the Low Countries and Germany, pious associations of women known as "Beguines" and of men known as "Beghards" lived in communities, pursuing good works. The great mendicant orders also established affiliated "Third Orders" for pious laymen and laywomen. While living in the world, they endeavored to pursue personal perfection as far as their state of life permitted.

Mendicant orders: The Franciscans

In the thirteenth century there arose a new type of religious known as "mendicants" or "beggars." Like the monks, the mendicants lived in communities and took vows of poverty, chastity, and obedience, but unlike monks, in imitation of Christ, they subsisted on alms and worked among the people. The mendicants rapidly became the most popular form of religious.

St. Francis of Assissi

One of the most universally beloved of all orders, that of the Friars Minor (O.F.M.: Franciscans) was founded in the early thirteenth century by St. Francis of Assisi. The son of a prosperous cloth merchant, Francis, who received this nickname from his fondness for things French, spent a typical, pleasure-seeking youth, distinguished by his high spirits and infectious enthusiasm. After temporary capture and imprisonment by Siennese forces, followed by illness, Francis decided to dedicate his life to God, and set about his mission, which he took from Christ's exhortation: "Go to the lost sheep of the house of Israel. Possess neither gold nor silver nor money nor scrip for your journey, nor two coats nor shoes nor a staff." Renouncing worldly possessions, Francis divested himself of his fine clothing and assumed the simple garb of an Appenine peasant: a gray robe girdled by a cincture. A basic point for Francis was absolute poverty in order to free his soul for the love of Christ and God's creatures. Among the latter he included not only his fellow men but also dumb animals and birds. A natural leader, Francis was soon joined by followers and eventually formed an "order" that was tentatively approved by Innocent III in 1209 after a dream that foretold their future services to the Church. Final Papal approval of the Rule came in 1221–1223.

In accordance with his great stress on poverty, Francis insisted that neither corporately nor individually were his followers to possess material goods. A second step in this freeing of the soul for the love of God was the renunciation of love of self by the virtue of humility, for which reason Francis called his group "the lesser brothers" (Friars Minor). The Franciscans sought to serve the needs, spiritual and corporal, of the lowly and neglected, the destitute, the sick, the afflicted, lepers, outcasts, and the like. Their main field of work was among the poor and unemployed in cities and towns.

The Franciscans spread so rapidly that by 1282 they had some 1583 houses. They eventually became the most numerous order in the Church. The order was headed by a minister general guided by policies established by periodic general chapters or meetings. The order was exempted from the jurisdiction of local bishops and was directly subject to the Pope. Provinces were headed by ministers known as "provincials." Very soon the Franciscans engaged in additional beneficial projects besides ministrations to the poor and the needy. Already in the thirteenth century they carried on missionary activities among the Moslems and Mongols, and Francis himself attempted to convert the Sultan of Egypt. They administered city parishes, especially in poorer districts, as well as preached in a migratory manner. They even became involved in education and scholarship as a result of the necessity of training priests for their own order. Among famous early Franciscan scholars were the theologians Alexander of Hales and St. Bonaventure and the scientists Roger Bacon and Adam Marsh. Among famous thirteenth-century Franciscan missionaries were John of Piano Carpini and William of Ruysbroeck, who ventured into the depths of Mongolia. *Franciscan expansion and work*

As the number of Franciscans multiplied, it became necessary to make adaptations in the originally stringent individual and collective rule of poverty. At first Francis and his followers had begged only enough for each successive meal and had slept in crudely improvised lean-tos. But when the order maintained students for the priesthood, requiring years in intensive studies, such makeshift devices were no longer practical. *Concessions*

Shortly before Francis' death the holding of property by trustees for use of the order was permitted, an arrangement reluctantly accepted by the saint. Under the generalship of the efficient but somewhat worldly Brother Elias, further concessions were made, and the protests of those who wished a stricter, more frugal way of life were silenced. As a result, a split arose in the order between the uncompromising minority known as "Spiritual Franciscans" or "Zealots" and the more flexible majority known as "Moderates." The Spiritual Franciscans, many of whom were original associates of St. Francis, wanted to return to the primitive life of itinerant preaching, migrant begging, and living in huts of branches, twigs, and bark. The dispute ran into the fourteenth century, when Pope John XXII decided in favor of the Moderates. Still many Spiritual Franciscans persisted and became out-and-out rebels, and some wrote tracts attacking the authority of the Pope. Eventually (ca. 1370) the orthodox Franciscans subdivided into the stricter "Observants," who believed in a "poor and scanty use" of worldly goods, and the "Conventuals," whose views on the subject were more flexible. Meanwhile an affiliated Second Order of Franciscans for females, known as "the Poor Clares," was formed; and a Third Order of "Tertiaries" for lay people appeared. Finally (1525) the very strict Capuchins were recognized as a distinct branch of the Franciscan order.

The Dominicans

Early in the thirteenth century (ca. 1205–1206), Dominic de Guzman, a pious Spanish canon regular, distressed by the religious havoc wrought by Albigensianism in southern France, established a company of preachers whose special purpose was to combat religious ignorance and error and inculcate solid faith by their learning, preaching, and personal holiness. Informally approved by Innocent III in 1209, Dominic's "Order of Preachers" was formally constituted as a mendicant religious order in 1216. In the pursuit of learning to combat heresy, the Dominicans were to be lifelong students, according to their rule that says: *Day and night, whether at home or traveling, let the brethren ever be occupied with reading or meditation.* The fathers were to live in houses of at least twelve preachers, with each house supervised by a prior and instructed by at least one doctor in residence. Dominican houses were often established in the vicinity of *studia generalia* or universities, and secular priests and clerics were admitted to the lectures of the Dominican professors. In pursuit of holiness, the Dominicans were to live an austere conventual common life in strict poverty, with perpetual abstinence from meat. The Dominican habit was of undyed white or gray wool. In formulating his Rule, Dominic drew on the ascetical counsels of St. Augustine and the statutes of St. Norbert of Premontré. Superiors were empowered to dispense from any part of the Rule to facilitate the work of preaching. Like the Franciscans, the Dominicans were mendicants, and had a minister general, regional provincials, and periodic general councils, as well as an affiliated female "Second Order" of nuns and an affiliated lay "Third Order" of lay persons.

In addition to their primary work of preaching, the Dominicans eventually became involved in many of the same external works as the

Apogee of the Church

Franciscans, including missionary, parochial, and educational activities. Some of their most important contributions were in the field of learning and in connection with the rising universities. Among noted Dominican savants were the scientist-philosopher-theologian, Albertus Magnus; the "prince" of medieval philosophers and theologians, Thomas Aquinas; and the great polymath and encyclopedist, Vincent of Beauvais. Because of their learning and their special campaign against heresy, the Dominicans were often assigned as inquisitors, whence they came to be nicknamed "hounds of the Lord" (*Domini canes*).

Of the two great mendicant orders, the Franciscans and Dominicans, Dante says:

> *The one all seraphic in fervency,*
> *The other shining with cherubic light*
> *For wisdom on earth.*

(Dante, *Paradiso*, Canto II, ll. 37–39)

Other mendicant orders developed, although they did not become so famous. The Augustinian Hermits or "Austin Friars" were formed by the union of various congregations of hermits following the Augustinian Rule into one mendicant order by Popes Innocent IV and Alexander IV in the mid-thirteenth century. The Mercedarians evolved from a pious association of laymen working for the redemption of captives (twelfth century) into a religious order of knights (thirteenth century) and eventually into a mendicant order (fourteenth century). The Servites, who originated in the thirteenth century as an association especially devoted to the sorrows of the Mother of Christ, eventually became a mendicant order in the fifteenth century.

Stimulated by the active participation of the new religious orders, preaching increased and improved. Most of the day's ecclesiastical heroes were religious order men who were forceful preachers, such as Sts. Bernard of Clairvaux, Norbert of Premontré, Dominic, and Anthony of Padua. Church expansion in the High Middle Ages consisted mainly in completing and consolidating the work of conversion begun in the Early Middle Ages. The Western Church was firmly established in the Scandinavian and west Slavic states, as well as in reconquered territories of the Iberian peninsula, southern Italy and Sicily, and on western Mediterranean islands. The Eastern Christian Church was similarly consolidated among the southern Slavs in the Balkans and the eastern Slavs and associated peoples of Russia. Although attempts to convert Asian Mongols and North African Moslems met with small success, the extent of the Western or Catholic Church in the High Middle Ages came to exceed that of the Roman Empire at its height.

Preaching and Church expansion

CHRISTIAN TEACHINGS AND LIFE IN THE HIGH MIDDLE AGES.
Section 66.

> Those things that establish in us the practice of religion and promote the worship of God . . . serve as a vivifying soul in the body of the commonwealth. [John of Salisbury in his *Statesman's Book* (*Policraticus*), (twelfth century).]

The High Middle Ages

CHURCHMEN elaborated, evolved, and correlated Christian doctrines more fully during the High Middle Ages with the help of logical thinking, scientific methods, philosophy, and broader learning. The intellectual activity of the period together with the changes that were occurring on all sides led to the rise of divergent doctrines contrary to the traditional teachings of the Church. Church authorities sought to eradicate these by every means at their disposal, including excommunication, interdict, and even use of force. Theologians more clearly defined and more fully explained the means of salvation, including the Christian sacraments and love and good works. Although neither clergy nor laity fully conformed to Christian ideals, they commonly accepted and frequently came near to achieving them.

Doctrinal development and increased humanization

Christian doctrines were further clarified and evolved as a result of the application of logic and philosophy to the doctrines of Christ and the Church and the great improvement of professional religious studies in cathedral and monastic schools and especially in the rising universities. Christian religious teachings were organized into an integrated body of knowledge known as theology, which was composed of three branches: dogmatic, moral, and ascetical.

Theological learning was perfected by a series of brilliant, dynamic scholars, including Anselm of Bec, Abelard, Peter Lombard, Alexander of Hales, St. Bonaventure, and St. Thomas Aquinas. Moral theology was emancipated from the formalism of the "penitential books," which like the old German law codes were mainly "a catalogue of punishments" for various types of offenses. More attention was now paid to securing avoidance of sin and the reform of the sinner, as well as to clarifying the nature of sin and conditions for both its commission and its eradication. An important contribution in this field was the *Summa Concerning Penance and Matrimony* by St. Raymond of Penafort (ca. 1235). Ascetical theology was promoted in both theory and practice by Cistercians such as St. Bernard of Clairvaux, Victorines such as Hugh and Richard of St. Victor, and Franciscans and Dominicans such as Sts. Bonaventure and Thomas Aquinas.

A significant development was greater humanization of the Christian religion through increased devotion to the human Christ and His Mother Mary, as well as increased emphasis upon the Christian doctrine of love. Greater attention was now paid to the human life of Christ and His consuming love for mankind, and to the imitation of Christ as the surest road to fuller perfection. Love for and imitation of Christ were fostered by meditation on the various events of His life, from His birth to His crucifixion. The manger scene at Christmastide and the stations of the Cross were introduced as aids to such meditation.

Another aspect of the same trend was increased devotion to Christ's Mother. Mary's intense love for her Son and her joys and sorrows with the various events of His life were subjects of meditation. Great trust came to be placed in Mary's love for mankind, and her position as a universal Mother and gracious intermediary with Christ. Events in Mary's life were meditated on in recitation of the fifteen decades of

Apogee of the Church

"Hail Marys" in the complete rosary, of which the present-day five-decade rosary is only a third. The full "Hail Mary" prayer was fixed at this time.

Lay piety and dissent

The intensified religious and mental activities of the High Middle Ages and more active lay involvement begot, as a by-product, divergencies from orthodoxy. Various forms of anticlericalism appeared, often as a reaction against the conservative policies and political meddling as well as the great wealth, pretensions, and dogmatism of many churchmen. In one of the most dramatic manifestations of anticlericalism, Arnold of Brescia, a liberal Augustinian canon who preached apostolic poverty and radical reform, led a communal revolt against the Bishop of Brescia. In 1139 Arnold was condemned and exiled by a Lateran synod. But in 1145 he returned to Italy and went to Rome, where he soon became the leader of a communal movement that sought to substitute popular government for Papal rule in Rome. Although initially supported and protected by the Roman senate, Arnold was eventually taken prisoner with the help of Frederick I and executed by the Prefect of Rome in 1155.

The Waldensians

Large-scale lay religious involvement led to occasional divergencies from generally accepted Church doctrines. Some of the revolutionary leaders and thinkers of the High Middle Ages became adjudged heretics when they held to their doctrines despite ecclesiastical condemnation, as happened in the case of the Waldensians and Albigensians. The Waldensians, who represented a reaction against growing worldliness and materialism, were founded in the 1170s by Peter Waldo, a wealthy merchant of Lyons, who gave up his riches and preached and practiced apostolic poverty and simplicity. Originally accepted by the Church, but subsequently forbidden to preach, the Waldensians eventually denied the whole existing hierarchial and sacramental system, declaring the Scriptures to be the sole rule of faith. The Waldensian heresy became particularly strong in southern France and northern Italy. Although condemned by Pope Lucius III about 1184, the Waldensians, often known as "Poor Men," survived until the fifteenth to sixteenth centuries, when they apparently merged with the Hussites and Calvinists.

The Albigensians

The strongest, most virulent heresy in the High Middle Ages was Albigensianism. So called from one of their chief strongholds, the town of Albi in Languedoc, the Albigensians were extreme dualists who believed in two powerful opposing principles, good and evil, and the absolute identification of all existing things with one of these forces. They were also known as *Cathari* (Pure Ones) and *Bulgari* (Bulgarians). The Albigensians became very strong in southern France and adjacent areas in the eleventh to thirteenth centuries. They had strong affinities with the ancient Manichaeans, who had been influenced by Persian Zoroastrian dualism, as well as with the medieval Bulgarian "Bogomiles" or "Paulicians."

Albigensians believed that all things of the flesh such as meat, sex, procreation, marriage, and even the human body were essentially evil. For them matrimony, which binds partners in perpetual cohabitation, was worse than transient sexual relationships, which might be broken off.

And death by voluntary starvation was one of the most meritorious of all possible acts. Strict adherence to Albigensian doctrines was impossible for most ordinary persons, who had to be content with mere acceptance of principles. Only a select few could actually follow the Albigensian *dicta,* and these, who were known as *Perfecti* (Perfect Ones), had to renounce, as far as possible, all things of the flesh, including meat, matrimony, and worldly possessions.

Albigensianism was several times condemned by the Church, and local rulers were called upon to repress it. The domains of Count Raymond of Toulouse were the chief Albigensian stronghold. Consequently Pope Innocent III excommunicated the Count and laid his lands under an interdict until he should uproot it. But when Innocent's legate was murdered by Raymond's men, Innocent called for a "Crusade" to exterminate the heresy. This "Albigensian Crusade" was mainly composed of knights from northern France, among whom Simon de Montfort emerged as the leader. The fighting, which dragged on for twenty bloody years (1209–1229), became progressively more desperate, cruel, and vindictive. Eventually the family of the Counts of Toulouse lost most of their lands and the heresy was largely exterminated.

Other heresies in the High Middle Ages

There were several other lesser heresies. The "Joachists" espoused and modified the teachings of the Cistercian Abbot Joachim of Flora, who had taught that the Church passed through three ages: the Age of the Father and the Old Testament; the Age of the Son and his Gospel; and the Age of the Holy Spirit, beginning in the thirteenth century (ca. 1260?). The final age was to be one of full liberty of spirit, and of prayer and song, when the whole world would become like a great, happy, monastery. The "Almaricians" espoused the teachings of Almaric of Bena, who taught that the period before Christ was the era of the Father, and that from Christ to his own time, the era of the Son, while the contemporary period was the era of the Holy Ghost, in which the Holy Spirit had become incarnate in every man, so that the law of the Gospel, and the sacraments had become obsolete. Both of these doctrines were condemned only after they were expanded following the death of their original founder.

Various pious associations of lay people lived in community and practiced personal poverty. Some of these eventually deviated from orthodoxy to the point where they were condemned as heretical. Among such were certain branches of the "Poor Men" or pious associations of workingmen in northern Italy and southern France, the "Apostolic Brethren," founded by Gerard of Parma in the thirteenth century, and the pantheistic, quietistic "Brothers and Sisters of the Free Spirit," who appeared in Germany and Italy in the thirteenth century and stressed emancipation.

The Inquisition

The Inquisition was formally established by Pope Gregory IX in 1229–1231 as a special ecclesiastical commission operating independently of local bishops and politics to investigate cases of alleged heresy in southern France, where Albigensianism and Waldensianism persisted. In the course of the thirteenth century, the Inquisition was extended to several other areas. The tribunal followed accepted procedures in Roman law for those accused of high treason, whereby torture was allowed to extract testimony and to prompt confessions. The rack and the *strappado* were common forms of torture. In the *strappado*, the prisoner was let fall from a height until jerked to a halt by ropes, which were often tied to his wrists behind his back. Sometimes the prisoner's feet were burned with hot coals to extract information from him. The accused was neither given notice as to the exact charges against him, nor told the names of his accusers, nor allowed to cross-question adverse witnesses.

The purpose of the inquisitors was both to convert the heretic, if at all possible, and to prevent the heresy from spreading. If the accused admitted and abjured his error, he was freed with a light penalty; but if he was obdurate or had relapsed into heresy as a second offender, stiffer punishment such as imprisonment or confiscation of his property was usually meted out. If, however, it was seen that there was no hope of retraction because of adamant refusal or further relapse, the accused might be formally condemned and turned over to the secular authority for the supreme penalty. If the convicted heretic was not executed within a year by the secular authority, the latter was liable to excommunication or deposition. The accepted mode of execution was burning at the stake.

Only a small proportion of those accused were actually executed. Out of 613 of the accused who were adjudged guilty by a typical inquisitor, only 45 persons were executed. Some inquisitors, however, were less moderate. Thus the Dominican inquisitor Robert de Bourge, who was himself a former heretic, caused the burning of 180 condemned persons on a single day in 1239; while the severity of the German inquisitor, Conrad of Marburg led to his murder in 1233 and the suspension of the Inquisition in his territory.

The liturgy and the sacraments

The "liturgy" or public services of the Church became further developed and standardized during the High Middle Ages. The language of the liturgy throughout the Western Church was Latin. The precise definition of the sacraments as seven external signs or visible helps instituted by Christ to give special divine assistance (grace) was established. The sacraments were distinguished from the sacramentals (such as holy water and the sign of the cross), which were of ecclesiastical institution. The sacraments served man at critical junctures of his life. Five were common to all Christians (Baptism, Confirmation, Penance, Holy Eucharist, and Extreme Unction); the remaining two were for special states of life (Matrimony and Holy Orders). Baptism, the sacrament of initiation into the Christian body, was performed by infusion (pouring of water) rather than immersion, and symbolized cleansing of the soul from the stain of original sin. Confirmation or "strengthening" was conceived as conferring special graces that enabled one to meet trials and temptations as a steadfast "Christian soldier." It was administered ordinarily by a bishop, by anointing with holy oil accompanied by a symbolic slap on the cheek. Reception of the sacrament of Penance, whereby the soul of a contrite Christian was cleansed of sins by sincere confession and the absolution of a priest (as Christ's representative), was prescribed at least once a year by the IV Lateran Council (1215).

The Holy Eucharist was considered to be a sacrament as well as a sacrifice, since it involved a communion or partaking as well as a consecrating and offering of Christ's body and blood under the appearance of bread and wine. The great love involved in the Eucharistic sacrifice and banquet came to be more fully appreciated during the High Middle Ages. At the close of life came the final anointing with holy oil known as Extreme Unction, to strengthen the soul, and perhaps even the body, in a time of crisis. Extreme Unction was usually preceded by Confession and Communion, which three sacraments were together known as the *Viaticum* or provision for the soul's journey to its Creator. Matrimony was the only sacrament administered by the recipients themselves. It consisted in the marriage contract between a Christian man and woman, expressly sanctified by Christ. The presence of a priest was not required as a condition for validity until the Later Middle Ages. Holy Orders, which conferred the priesthood in various degrees, were administered by anointing with holy oil and the imposition of hands, and were composed of four steps: the Subdeaconate, Deaconate, Priesthood, and Episcopate. The major orders were preceded by various minor orders of ecclesiastical institution.

Life of the clergy and laity

The High Middle Ages were an "age of faith," when people believed in the reality and paramount importance of a life hereafter. Accordingly, most persons strove to lead a Christian life, with varying degrees of completeness. One indication of the strong faith of this era was the large number of canonized saints from almost every walk of life: Popes and bishops, monks and nuns, mendicants and canons, scholars and preachers, laymen and lay women. Another evidence was the variety and popularity of religious congregations and pious associations, and still another the great number of magnificent churches built and adorned at great sacrifice.

There was, nevertheless, much human imperfection among both clergy and laity. Although most clerical vocations were probably embraced in a spirit of faith, love, and sacrifice, some were obviously inspired by baser motives such as ambition, fear, greed, or indolence. Some of the clergy became excessively worldly, and a few were virtual "wolves in lamb's clothing." Many bishops, priests, and monks were as much temporal administrators as they were spiritual shepherds, excessively absorbed in temporal concerns. Some of the clergy became involved in liaisons with women, while some gave scandal and neglected their duties by excessive drinking, sporting, gambling, or other selfish frivolities.

The life of the laity was mainly concerned with visible, secular everyday necessities. Many discounted the spiritual, religious, and eternal. Many were scantily instructed in Christianity or even were superstitious, although they usually seem to have grasped the essentials of the faith. And there was no lack of violence, cruelty, hatred, calumny, cheating, injustice, incontinence, and infidelity in society.

At the same time, most of the clergy seem to have given reasonably good example by celibate, restrained lives in the service of God and their fellow men. Most bishops and Popes were evidently dedicated, intelligent leaders, solicitous for the spiritual as well as the temporal welfare of their

Apogee of the Church

flock. Sometimes they had to appear lax and overlook shortcomings, hoping that time would cure them. The spirit of the practical bishop is seen in the statement of Bishop Ivo of Chartres during the investiture struggle: "When the salvation of people is at stake, we should moderate the strictness of the canons and use sincere charity for the cure of moral ailments." Local priests were usually close to the people and their problems, as well as to God and nature, with restricted means and limited temptations, so that many approached Chaucer's picture of the "Parson":

> There was a good man of religion, too:
> A country parson: poor, I warrant you;
> But rich he was in holy thought and work.
> He was a holy man and also a clerk,
> Who Christ's own gospel truly sought to preach:
> Devoutly his parishioners would he teach.
> Benign he was and wondrously diligent,
> Patient in adverse times and well content.
>
> . . . .
> Wide was his parish, houses far asunder,
> But never did he fail for rain or thunder,
> In sickness or in sin or any state,
> To visit to the farthest, small or great.

For all their shortcomings, the laity, too, were chastened and uplifted by the Christian religion. If the laity had faults and shortcomings, they were not condoned by the Church or contemporary society, or even by their own consciences. Most aspired at least eventually to "amend their lives." The integrity and health of the family were preserved in the vast majority of cases. Those guilty of violence and injustice were required to repent and make restitution. Examples of charity and religious generosity were seen on every hand. Many of the laity joined Third Orders and pious confraternities in pursuit of greater perfection.

Conclusion

The Church was reformed and partly emancipated during the High Middle Ages, although eventually the Papacy became excessively involved in politics. Christian ideals matured, and holy persons were revered as heroes. In addition to elevating minds and morals, the Church supported concepts of human dignity and inviolable rights, restrained warfare, promoted more enlightened administration of justice, elevated ideals of knighthood, kingship, womanhood, and labor, and restrained the businessman's lust for gain. It helped to improve the status of women and to eliminate slavery. Finally, the Church fostered culture. It supplied and maintained teachers and students, chartered and supported universities, cooperated in a revival of philosophy and the natural sciences, was a nursery for new drama and polyphonic music, and both inspired and financed magnificent architecture and art. A sober Protestant historian concludes: *But it can be safely asserted, when all debits and credits of baneful and beneficial are given just consideration, that the mighty Church at its height was the most powerful force in Europe for justice, for mercy, for charity, for peace among men, for honesty, for temperance,* for human rights, for social service, for culture, for domestic purity, for obedience to law and order, and for a noble, helpful Christian life, both for individuals and for states.[a]

[a] Alexander C. Flick, Rise of the Medieval Church (New York: Putnam's 1909), p. 602.

References for Chapter 22

AMONG several good surveys of Church history in the High Middle Ages are vols. II and III of PHILIP HUGHES, History of the Church (New York: Sheed, 1934–1947); ALEXANDER C. FLICK, Rise of the Medieval Church . . . to the Thirteenth Century (New York: Putnam's, 1909); HENRI DANIEL-ROPS, Cathedral and Crusade . . . , tr. John Warrington, 2 vols. (Garden City, N.Y.: Doubleday, 1963); the concise KARL BIHLMEYER and HERMANN TÜCHLE, Church History, vol. II: The Middle Ages (Westminster, Md.: Newman, 1963); and ANDRÉ LAGARDE, The Latin Church in the Middle Ages, tr. A. Alexander (New York: Scribners, 1915). Shorter summaries are given by MARSHALL W. BALDWIN, The Mediaeval Church (Ithaca, N.Y.: Cornell U.P., 1953), and MARGARET DEANESLY, A History of the Medieval Church, 590–1500 (London: Methuen, 1951). Useful for detail are FERNAND MOURRET, A History of the Catholic Church, tr. Newton Thompson, 5 vols. (to the Reformation) (London: Herder, 1941), and PHILIP SCHAFF, History of the Christian Church. 8 vols. (Grand Rapids: Erdmans, 1949–1950).

For the story of the Papacy in the Middle Ages, short surveys are the stimulating GEOFFREY BARRACLOUGH, The Medieval Papacy (New York: Harcourt, 1968); MARSHALL W. BALDWIN, The Medieval Papacy in Action (New York: Macmillan, 1940); and JAMES A. CORBETT, The Papacy: A Brief History (New York: Van Nostrand, 1956). A more extensive account is HORACE K. MANN, Lives of the Popes in the Early Middle Ages, 18 vols. (London: Kegan Paul, 1906–1929), which runs to 1304. The era of Gregory VII and the investiture struggle is treated in W. R. W. STEPHENS, Hildebrand and His Times (New York: Randolph, ca. 1888), and ALLAN J. MACDONALD, Hildebrand: A Life of Gregory VII (London: Methuen, 1932), as well as by SHAFER WILLIAMS, ed., The Gregorian Epoch: Reformation, Revolution, Reaction? (Boston: Heath, 1964). Also useful are JAMES P. WHITNEY, Hildebrandine Essays (Cambridge: Cambridge U.P., 1932); The Correspondence of Pope Gregory VII: Selected Letters, tr. Ephraim Emerton (New York: Columbia U.P., 1932); and H. E. J. COWDREY, The Cluniacs and the Gregorian Reform (Oxford: Clarendon, 1970). For the Papacy during the era of Guelph versus Hohenstaufen strife, see UGO BALZANI, The Popes and the Hohenstaufen (London: Randolph, 1901), and PAUL J. KNAPKE, Frederick Barbarossa's Conflict with the Papacy . . . (Washington, D.C.: Catholic University, 1939), together with GERD TELLENBACK, Church, State, and Christian Society at the Time of the Investiture Contest (Oxford: Blackwell, 1940). For the fulcral pontificate of Innocent III, see JOSEPH CLAYTON, Pope Innocent III and His Times (Milwaukee: Bruce, 1941); LEONARD E. BINNS, Innocent III (London: Methuen, 1931); and JAMES M. POWELL, ed., Innocent III: Vicar of Christ or Lord of the World? (Boston: Heath, 1963).

The growing centralization of Papal government in the Middle Ages and its theoretical basis are the subject of WALTER ULLMANN, The Growth of Papal Government in the Middle Ages (New York: Barnes and Noble, 1953); GEOFFREY BARRACLOUGH, Papal Provisions . . . (Oxford: Blackwell, 1935); and WALTER ULLMANN, Medieval Papalism: The Political Theories of the Medieval Canonists

(London: Methuen, 1949). The development of canon law in the High Middle Ages is surveyed in AMLETO G. CICOGNANI, *Canon Law*, tr. J. M. O'Hara (Westminster, Md.: Newman, 1934). Church-State relations and theories are the subject of EWART K. LEWIS, *Medieval Political Ideas*, vol. II (New York: Knopf, 1954), which contains both discussion and illustrative documents; CHARLES H. MCILWAIN, *The Growth of Political Thought in the West . . . to the End of the Middle Ages* (New York: Macmillan, 1932); and BRIAN TIERNEY, *The Crisis of Church and State, 1050–1300* (Englewood Cliffs, N.J.: Prentice-Hall, 1964).

Miscellaneous aspects of monasticism, including the Cluniac and Cistercian reform movements, are treated in WATKIN W. WILLIAMS, *Monastic Studies* (Manchester: U. of Manchester, 1938). The story of religious orders in England is well told by DAVID KNOWLES, *The Monastic Order in England 943 to 1216* (Cambridge: Cambridge U.P., 1940), and *The Religious Order in England (1216–1485)*, 2 vols. (Cambridge: Cambridge U.P., 1950–1955). Some of the practical realities of monastic life are portrayed in the contemporary *Chronicle of Jocelin de Brakelond . . .*, tr. and ed. L. C. Jane (London: Chatto, 1907). Much antimonastic material has been gathered in the tomes of GEORGE G. COULTON, *Five Centuries of Religion*, 4 vols. (New York: Cambridge U.P., 1950). Cluny in this period is treated by LUCY M. SMITH, *Cluny in the Eleventh and Twelfth Centuries* (London: P. Allan, 1930). For the Cistercians, see the *Compendium of the History of the Cistercian Order* by a Father of the Abbey of Gethsemani, Kentucky (Gethsemani, Ky.: Order of the Strict Observance, 1944); for their most famous saint, see WATKIN W. WILLIAMS, *Saint Bernard of Clairvaux* (Manchester: U. of Manchester, 1935), as well as JAMES A. MORISON, *Life and Times of Saint Bernard, Abbot of Clairvaux* (New York: Macmillan, 1907), and M. RAYMOND, *The Sage of Citeaux . . .* (New York: P. J. Kenedy, 1942). Among many works on the Franciscans are the scholarly RAPHAEL M. HUBER, *A Documented History of the Franciscan Order, 1182–1517* (Washington, D.C.: Catholic University, 1944), and the popular VIDA D. SCUDDER, *The Franciscan Adventure . . . The First Hundred Years* (London: Dutton, Dent, 1931); even more numerous are works on the order's saintly founder, such as OMER ENGLEBRECHT, *Saint Francis of Assisi*, tr. E. Hutton (New York: Longmans, 1050), as well as his more recent *St. Francis of Assisi: A Biography* (Chicago: Franciscan Herald, 1965); RAY C. PETRY, *Francis of Assisi . . .* (Durham, N.C.: Duke U.P., 1941); and JOHANNES JORGENSEN, *Saint Francis of Assisi*, tr. T. O'Conor Sloane (New York: Longmans, 1912). The female Franciscans are the subject of an anonymous *St. Clare and Her Order . . .* (London: Mills and Boon, 1912). For St. Dominic and the early Dominicans there are several good accounts such as BEDE JARRETT, *Life of St. Dominic* (Westminster, Md.: Newman, 1947); PIERRE MANDONNET, *St. Dominic and His Work*, tr. M. Larkin (St. Louis, Mo.: Herder, 1944); JEAN GUIRAUD, *Saint Dominic*, tr. K. de Mattos (London: Duckworth, 1901); AUGUSTA T. DRANE, *History of St. Dominic . . .* (New York: Longmans, 1891); and RALPH F. BENNETT, *The Early Dominicans* (Cambridge: Cambridge U.P., 1937).

Concerning dissent and the means the Church took to suppress it, see JEFFREY B. RUSSELL, *Dissent and Reform in the Early Middle Ages* (Berkeley: California U.P., 1968); STEVEN RUNCIMAN, *The Medieval Manichee . . .* (Cambridge: Cambridge U.P., 1947); JOSEPH R. STRAYER, *The Albigensian Crusade*

(New York: Dial, 1971); GEORGE W. GREENAWAY, *Arnold of Brescia* (Cambridge: Cambridge U.P., 1931); ALBERT C. SHANNON, *The Popes and Heresy in the Thirteenth Century* (Villanova, Pa.: Augustinian Press, 1949); and ARTHUR L. TURBERVILLE, *Medieval Heresy and the Inquisition* (London: Lockwood, 1920). There are several works on the early Inquisition, such as ELPHEGE VACANDARD, *The Inquisition*, tr. B. L. Conway (London: Longmans, 1928); JEAN GUIRARD, *The Mediaeval Inquisition*, tr. E. C. Messenger (New York: Benziger, 1930); and the early, well-researched classic study, HENRY C. LEA, *A History of the Inquisition of the Middle Ages*, 3 vols. (New York: Lea, 1887). Concerning the Church's influence on the economy, see JOHN T. GILCHRIST, *The Church and Economic Activity in the Middle Ages* (London: Melbourne, 1969).

⟨ HIGH TIDE OF MEDIEVAL CULTURE: THE RISE OF UNIVERSITIES AND SCHOLASTIC LEARNING. Ch. 23.

A PRODIGIOUS blossoming of culture occurred in the High Middle Ages. Various factors helped to promote this extraordinary cultural fecundity. The states of Western Europe had attained considerable stability and prosperity. A rich inheritance of classical Greek and Roman origins, preserved and augmented by Westerners, Byzantines, and Moslems, was available. Men of the period had a culturally "youthful" zest for knowledge and speculation, literature and the arts. The Christian faith and Church inspired and elevated culture, and patronized and propagated education, learning, literature, architecture, art, and music. The rising towns provided a congenial and stimulating habitat for the new culture.

HIGH MEDIEVAL EDUCATION AND THE RISE OF UNIVERSITIES.
Section 67.

[a] I.e., both civil and canon law.

They seek the laws[a] at Bologna, medicine at Salerno, philosophy at Paris, the black art [magic or science] at Toledo. [Medieval saying concerning leading centers of advanced learning.]

A GREAT expansion of education, which included the rise of universities, was a leading instrument of cultural progress in the High Middle Ages. In the twelfth century, John of Salisbury observed that "all are either teaching or learning the [liberal] arts." Economic progress and the rapid growth of towns caused a mounting demand and opportunity for learned professional people in such fields as law, government, medicine, and teaching. The zeal and vision of great scholars and schoolmasters, such as Fulbert and Bernard of Chartres, Hugh of St. Victor, Abelard, Peter Lombard, Albertus Magnus, and Vincent of Beauvais nourished the flame of learning. The continuing interest of the Church in education is exemplified by a decree of the III Lateran Council (1179): *Lest the opportunity for learning and education be denied to any poor children*

High Tide of Medieval Culture

due to the inadequate resources of their parents, let some sufficient benefice be set aside in each cathedral church to provide for a teacher who will instruct the clergy of that church and poor scholars gratis. . . . In other churches, too, and in monasteries, if in times past provision was made for such education, let it be reestablished.

The Church continued to maintain various types of schools, many of which expanded their student bodies and curricula, while numerous additional ones were founded. Cathedral schools located in the growing towns took the lead in promoting the new learning, and several became famous, as was the case with those of Paris, Chartres, Reims, Laon, and Orleans in France. Cathedrals often boasted three schools of ascending importance: one of music, one of liberal arts, and one of theology. At the same time monastic schools continued to be important homes of learning, as was the case with those of Bec, Fleury, Cluny, and St. Victor's in Paris. The basic curricula in the cathedral and monastic schools continued to be the "seven liberal arts," followed by "divine learning." But these studies were expanded, particularly by giving more attention to literature and logic and adding subjects such as law, medicine, natural sciences, and introductory philosophy.

The Church also maintained parish schools, chantry schools, and song schools. Besides reading, writing, and arithmetic, parish schools sometimes taught about the liberal arts and dispensed learning preparatory to ordination. Many parish priests spent some of their time teaching subjects such as reading, and most of them regularly trained youths to act as servers and singers for church services. Collegiate churches, staffed by canons living together, often maintained schools. Endowed "chantry" schools and "song schools" continued to provide some elementary education, such as reading.

In certain areas, particularly Italy, lay teachers frequently taught the young either on a tutorial basis or in small "schools." In Italy and the Germanies, including the Low Countries, municipalities often engaged teachers to conduct "public schools." In the Germanies, by the close of the thirteenth century, there were municipal schools in at least a dozen towns, including Lübeck, Hamburg, Breslau, and Munich. Advanced schools to prepare students for the learned professions also arose. Thus Bologna became famous for education in civil and canon law, and Salerno and Montpellier for instruction in medicine. Various church schools at Paris had high reputations for training in the liberal arts and theology. There was a notable increase in lay literacy, and most monarchs and members of royal families, as well as many members of the aristocracy and of the middle class, knew how to read and write.

The most important cultural development was the rise of universities. As C. H. Haskins says: *Universities, like cathedrals and parliaments, are a product of the Middle Ages.*[a] The term *universitas* (university) originally meaning a "totality" or "universitality," came, by the High Middle Ages, to denote a complete union or guild and was eventually reserved for an academic corporation or guild devoted to higher education. For some time the name for such an institution was *studium generale* (a general

Schools in the High Middle Ages

Rise of universities

[a] *Rise of Universities* (New York: Holt, 1923), p. 1.

place of study), since it accepted students from all areas and gave degrees everywhere recognized. Universities began to develop during the twelfth century, and they multiplied rapidly in the thirteenth and following centuries.

A factor in the rise of universities was the current trend to corporate organization for the effective achievement of desired ends. Another was the existence of a respected universal Church, which could grant a "license to teach anywhere." In this age of numerous jurisdictions, corporate organization was necessary in order to secure rights and privileges. Students and teachers involved in the pursuit of higher education and learning, especially those doing so in other than their own native cities, needed unionization. By unity they could bring joint pressures to bear to secure status and privileges, standarize requirements, and obtain acceptance of their conferral of the right to teach anywhere.

The first European universities developed at Bologna and Paris. They "evolved," instead of being "founded." They were at first unions composed sometimes of masters, sometimes of students. Their members grouped into "nations," according to their native regions and affinities, as well as according to professional fields of study; but eventually several such unions would coalesce into a common "university."

The University of Bologna

Bologna in northern Italy was already famous as a center of legal studies in the twelfth century, partly because of the prominence of famous masters such as Irnerius in civil law and Gratian in canon law. Students of law who had come to Bologna for their education and who felt the need to form unions first organized into "nations" according to the regions from which they came. Each nation was governed and represented by its own elected "proctor." These nations subsequently combined into two great "universities": the "Cismontane University" composed of students from "this" (Italian) side of the Alps, which included three nations; and the "Ultramontane University," composed of students from "beyond" the Alps, which had fourteen nations. Eventually the Cisalpine and Transalpine Universities combined into a single University of Bologna, which was at first presided over jointly by the two rectors and subsequently by a single rector. The proctors of the various nations constituted the governing board of the University.

Originally the students at Bologna hired and fired their masters, laid down conditions as to the number and length of lectures, and specified materials to be covered in classes. Masters were fined for infractions, such as regularly coming late to class or failing to cover required material. But the masters also organized and thus kept control of the granting of "degrees." Gradually the University came to include the masters as well as the students, and finally control passed into the hands of the masters, as the more permanent element. Meanwhile the three professional schools at Bologna—the municipal school for the study of civil law and rhetoric, the monastic school for the study of canon law, and the cathedral school for the study of the liberal arts and theology—formed a joint union, and all became parts of the one university. Eventually the University of

Bologna came to have all the four customary faculties of a medieval university: arts, medicine, theology, and law (civil and canon).

Rivaling the University of Bologna in age and soon surpassing it in fame was the University of Paris, which also came into being by the second half of the twelfth century. The University of Paris developed primarily as a union of masters, and its original *forte* was logic and philosophy (in "arts") and theology, rather than law or medicine. By the middle of the twelfth century, Paris was already famous as a center for the advanced education of clerics. Its masters and schools were all affiliated with the Cathedral School of Paris, and licenses recognized as qualifying the recipient to teach were conferred by the Chancellor of Paris in the name of the Archbishop of Paris. The fame of Paris grew as noted masters such as William of Champeaux, Abelard, Gilbert de la Porée, and Adam du Petit Pont congregated there, and students flocked thither from all points of the compass.

The University of Paris

In order to protect their rights and promote their common interests, the masters of arts at Paris organized into four general nations of masters of arts: French, Norman, Picard, and English. The "French" nation also included all of southern Europe, while the "English" nation also embraced northern and central Europe: sc. the Germans and Scandinavians. The four proctors of the nations of masters of arts at Paris elected a rector of their university. Most of the early evolution of the university at Paris thus occurred in the arts school. Subsequently separate faculties for other professional schools appeared and were incorporated into the general university.

One of the main original reasons for the evolution of the university at Paris was the determination of the masters to control the conferral of the license to teach. The Chancellor of the Archdiocese of Paris, who granted the license to teach, sometimes demanded a large fee and sometimes granted licenses on the basis of considerations other than academic qualifications. The masters sought to have the license to teach granted automatically and without charge to those students whom they certified as having fulfilled the requirements. Eventually the masters won out because they organized and presented a united front.

In 1200, as the snowballing result of a trivial incident, several students were killed by the townspeople of Paris, led by their provost. Philip II not only severely punished the provost and responsible burghers but also granted the University an extensive charter of privileges. In 1210 Pope Innocent III accorded the University of Paris the right to have a proctor at the Papal Court, and recognized it as a corporation with competence to sue in court. In 1215 the Papal legate, Robert de Courçon, gave a set of statutes to the University, which recognized its right to prescribe further statutes.

The evolution of the universities was similar to that of the economic guilds, but whereas the guilds evolved from unity to plurality, the universities evolved from plurality to unity. Both at Bologna and Paris the unionization seems to have occurred first in several nations within one professional school, which nations coalesced into a single general union or university. Other faculties, as they developed, were affiliated with and assimilated into the one organization.

The multi-plication of universities

National and urban rivalries and regional pride, as well as the growing demand for trained professional people, promoted a rapid multiplication of universities. By the end of the thirteenth century there were over twenty universities in Western Europe, and by the end of the Later Middle Ages over seventy-five. Most of these universities continued into modern times, though the existence of some was ephemeral.

The most rapid, early multiplication of universities occurred in Italy and France. Universities established in Italy by the end of the thirteenth century, besides Bologna (Europe's leading center for legal studies), were Padua (founded as the result of a migration from Bologna in 1222), Salerno (famous for medical studies), Vercelli (which resulted from a secession from Padua in 1228), Naples (which was founded by Frederick II in 1224, and absorbed Salerno), Arezzo, and Rome (established by Pope Innocent IV).

Early French universities, in addition to Paris (Europe's leading center for the study of philosophy and theology), included Montpellier (a rival of Salerno for medical studies), Orleans (famous for the study of law and rhetoric), and Toulouse (established by Pope Gregory IX as an antidote to the Albigensian heresy).

England's two great early universities arose as a result of migrations: Oxford from Paris, and Cambridge from Oxford. In 1167, Henry II, at war with the French, peremptorily ordered all English clerics studying at Paris to return to England within three months "as they loved their revenues." Cambridge seems to have risen to university status during a temporary *cessatio* or suspension of studies at Oxford. In Spain, the University of Salamanca, founded about 1220, became the leading university, since Palencia, established 1212–1214, lasted only to the middle of the century. The University of Valencia was established in 1245 by James I of Aragon; that of Seville in 1254 by Alfonso X of Castile. A Portuguese university was founded at Lisbon in 1288, though it was transferred to Coimbra early in the following century.

Privileges and organization of universities

The first universities evolved spontaneously, obtaining formal recognition and privileges only after they were already in existence. Subsequent universities, however, took the short route of obtaining authorization and privileges from Church and State at the time of their foundation. Some universities were first privileged by the secular authority, others by the Papacy. Authority to confer the right to teach anywhere (*jus ubique docendi*) was a fundamental privilege of universities. Another privilege was the right of students and teachers to be judged by university or ecclesiastical courts, since this made them less vulnerable to local favoritism and chicanery. Another was that of *cessatio* (strike), whereby members could suspend operations in order to enforce their demands. Universities also obtained the right to regulate the prices of books and board and lodgings and to have their own characteristic seal. A weapon used in extreme cases was that of *migratio*: transfer to a new site.

The organization of the University of Paris set the pattern for most European universities, although that of Bologna was favored in Italy. For some time the rector and the chancellor of the university were separate officials. At first the rector represented the students and/or teachers, whereas the chancellor represented the Church. Although the prestige of the chancellor was initially greater, the positions were soon reversed. Eventually the two offices were usually combined. The university governing board consisted of representatives of the various main components, usually known as procurators or proctors, and it was this council that elected the rector.

Most universities came to have several or all of the four fields of specialization: arts, theology, law, and medicine. Each faculty had its own organization and dean, and was represented on the university's governing council. Meanwhile professors developed their various specialities, thus promoting the advancement of learning. The most important faculty was that of "arts," whose courses were considered prerequisites for studies in other faculties as well as for teaching various non-professional branches of learning. *Faculties and colleges*

It became common for several students to rent a house and live together, somewhat in the manner of our present-day fraternities. Some form of organization necessarily evolved in such "colleges." Charitable persons of means occasionally made endowments for the maintenance of colleges for needy students. As time progressed, colleges came to include both rich and poor, and many provided instruction, so that they became pedagogical as well as residential. One of the best known colleges was that founded by Robert de Sorbon at the University of Paris in 1258 for poor students of theology, whence the famous "Sorbonne." Colleges were very popular in the English universities. Among early colleges at Oxford were Balliol (1261) and Merton (ca. 1263). At Cambridge the earliest college was Peterborough (1284).

Degrees or "steps" in the student's advance to mastery of his field included the bachelor's degree, the licentiate, and the master's degree. The bachelor's degree was conferred on students who were far enough along to be capable of instructing others under the supervision of a master. The bachelor in the academic world was thus similar to the journeyman in a craft or to a knight bachelor (*bas chevalier*) in the military. Studies for the bachelor's degree usually took three to four years. Reception of the degree was prefaced by a "determination": an examination to "determine" (ascertain) the individual's fitness for the degree. The licentiate was a license or official permission to teach, ordinarily bestowed by the ecclesiastical chancellor, and somewhat similar to our present-day teaching credential, though on a different level. The master's degree qualified one both to teach on one's own and to certify other masters. The masters who conferred this terminal degree welcomed the candidate into their number. It was comparable both to the master's grade in the craft guilds and to our present-day (academic) doctor's degree. One manifested fitness to receive a master's degree in arts by presenting and defending a "thesis" (proposition) or theses, on which he was questioned and chal- *Degrees* lenged by examining masters. Reception of the master's degree included the "inception" or "commencement," in which the candidate, invested with the cap and gown, commenced to teach, presenting and defending his thesis or theses, according to a salutary old Roman practice whereby one was regarded as having assumed an office only after he began to exercise its functions.

Instructional procedures

Lectures were the principal means of instruction. They elucidated subject matter, provided a gradual, systematic inculcation of knowledge, and brought the student into contact with intelligent informed minds. Originally the lecture was a form of reading, and the same Latin word (*lectio*: reading) was used for reading privately (studying), reading publicly (reading aloud), and elaborating on what was read (lecturing). Generally the greater part of the student's day (v.g., seven hours) was spent in attending lectures. Lectures on more important subjects, known as "Ordinary Lectures," were given in the morning; lectures on less essential topics, known as "Extraordinary Lectures," were given in the afternoon. Lectures usually consisted in reading aloud from some basic text and then explaining and commenting on it and related topics, as well as occasionally digressing.

The disputation (*disputatio*) was a scholastic exercise inherited from antiquity and described by Aristotle. It was a formal discussion of both sides of a question, consisting in the presentation of a thesis or proposed solution of a question by a proponent or "reasoner," and the counter-presentation of opposing arguments or challenging questions by an objector or "questioner." The disputation method, originally designed for philosophy, became so popular that it was applied to other fields of learning, not always with equally good results.

A requirement for advancement to degrees was "standing" for examination. Examinations were regularly oral and often public. In one form of examination, the candidate was presented with selected passages, given a few hours to study them, and then required to explain and defend them. The masters on the examining board questioned the candidate and voted as to his acceptability.

University life

The original universities were associations of teachers and students rather than buildings and campuses. Professors lectured in available halls and rooms, since the medieval university usually lacked a regular campus. Increasing numbers of students sought a university education. A leading authority estimates that there were 4,000 to 5,000 students at Paris and 2,000 to 3,000 at Oxford in the thirteenth century. Among students there were both the industrious and the lazy, the quiet and the obstreperous, the self-controlled and the dissolute, the frugal and the prodigal, the successful and the failures. Although most university students seem to have been serious, some plunged into a life of dissipation. One father wrote to his son at Orleans: "I have recently discovered that you live dissolutely, preferring play to work, and strumming a guitar while others are at their studies." The typical student was perennially short of funds. An Oxford student wrote home to his father: "I am studying at Oxford with the utmost diligence, but the matter of money stands greatly in the way of my success, as it is now two months since I spent the last of what you sent me."

A favorite recreation of students was to drink in taverns while indulging in noisy discussions, often leading to rumpuses, and sometimes culminating in clashes with local burghers, as in "town and gown" riots.

Chaucer pictures a conscientious Oxford student making the pilgrimage to Canterbury:

> *A clerk from Oxford was with us also,*
> *Who'd turned to getting knowledge long ago:*
> *As meager was his horse as is a rake,*
> *Nor he himself too fat, I'll undertake.*
>
> *. . . . .*
>
> *For he would rather have at his bed's head*
> *Some twenty books all bound in black and red*
> *Of Aristotle and his philosophy*
> *Than rich robes, fiddle, or gay psaltery.*

Many other students were not as serious, according to contemporary description:

> *Some are gaming, some are drinking,*
> *Some are living without thinking;*
> *Among those who make a racket,*
> *Some have lost their coat and jacket;*
> *Some have clothes of finest feather;*
> *Some are cleaned out altogether.*

Much education was effected by "on-the-job" apprenticeship training. Persons who desired to engage in legal and notarial work often prepared themselves by working with members of the profession, as also did surgeons, barbers, and dentists. Surgery was for some time a branch of barbering. The apprenticeship method was common in the crafts. One of the leading purposes of the guilds was to establish methods and standards of training candidates for membership. Architects and engineers were usually educated by on-the-job training, as also were artists.

"On-the-job training"

Following the tradition of the Old Testament and the Platonic school, as well as the cues of early medieval scholars, high medieval writers further evolved the concept of learning as a means of achieving a fuller, closer union with God. In their view, all reality is a great *epiphania* (showing forth) of God, eventually leading us to its Creator.

A strong impetus to intellectual progress was given by the enthusiasm of several stimulating teachers at Paris in the twelfth century. At the fore was the brilliant lecturer Peter Abelard, who became one of the founders of the new Scholastic movement. His approach was expressed in his motto *I doubt in order that I may understand* and his explanation thereof: *By doubting we are led to inquire, and by inquiry we come to perceive the truth.* William of Champeaux, a famous logician who taught Abelard, only to be challenged by him, subsequently founded the

Educational leadership and theory in the twelfth century

Parisian monastery of St. Victor's, whose monks became conspicuous for their learning and the cultivation of Platonic idealism and Augustinian mysticism. The most famous member of the Victorine school was the noted teacher Hugh of St. Victor. His *Didascalicon,* of which almost a hundred manuscript copies still survive, proposed a comprehensive plan of learning, including every sort of organized knowledge, divided into four main categories: theoretical, practical, mechanical, and logical. Hugh said: *The wise student gladly listens to all and reads all; he looks down on no writing, no person, no teaching. Despise no learning, because all learning is good.* . . . And again: *Philosophy* [general learning] *is the pursuit of wisdom . . . , which bestows on every kind of souls the benefit of its own divinity, and brings them back to the proper source and purity of their nature.*

A remarkable school, located about forty miles south of Paris, was that of Chartres, made famous earlier by its learned Bishops Fulbert and Ivo. John of Salisbury characterized the famous teacher Bernard of Chartres as "the most copious font of literary learning in Gaul in recent times"; and described Bernard's methods of teaching grammar: *In reading the authors he would point out what was simple and according to rule; . . . as well as explain the use of grammatical figures, rhetorical ornamentation, and sophistical quibbling. He would likewise indicate relationships with other studies. And since diction is lustrous either because its words are well chosen . . . or because of its metaphors . . . Bernard used to inculcate this. . . . Bernard would also bend every effort to bring his students to imitate what they were hearing. . . .* Bernard was succeeded as head of the cathedral school by his brother, Thierry of Chartres, who was one of the leading teachers of the scientific quadrivium and who prepared a voluminous compilation of extracts from previous works on the various seven liberal arts entitled the *Heptateuchon.*

An illustrious product of the schools in the twelfth century was John of Salisbury. In a work entitled the *Metalogicon,* John advocated a thorough study of grammar and logic. He pointed out that "*Just as eloquence, unenlightened by reason is groping and blind, so wisdom without the power of verbal expression is feeble and maimed.*" As a means of acquiring "eloquence," or facility of verbal expression, John advocated the study and imitation of classical models. For logic John recommended the study of Aristotle's complete *Organon,* consisting of seven books on the subject. John endorsed broad learning: *For the principles of all branches of learning are interwoven, and each requires the assistance of the others.* Another twelfth-century educational theorist was Conrad of Hirschau, a German monk and educator who composed a *Dialogue on the Authors or Didascalon,* in which he advocated a broad study of literature. Conrad says: *We should continually cultivate the philosophical disciplines . . . , for they engender scorn for the temporal and love for the eternal.*

Educational leaders and High medieval educational progress culminated in the thirteenth century with a galaxy of brilliant scholars, who emphasized broad general learning, then known as "philosophy." Robert Grosseteste, a versatile savant who became Bishop of Lincoln, promoted the scientific method at Oxford University. Roger Bacon, a daring, original thinker, besides urging a reform of ecclesiastical studies to include greater attention to foreign languages and the Sacred Scriptures, emphasized the value of pursuing the natural sciences and using the scientific method of direct observation. Albertus Magnus (Albert the Great) enthusiastically promoted study of the philosophical and scientific works of Aristotle, as well as made important contributions to such sciences as botany and mineralogy. St. Thomas Aquinas, "the Angelic Doctor," composed comprehensive *Summas*, which harmonized reason as found in Aristotelian philosophy and faith as found in the Christian religion. St. Bonaventure encouraged learning both by composing similar summaries of Christianity that combined philosophy and theology and by reconciling learning and mysticism. Bonaventure, a "Prince of Mystics," identified learning as the basic original step in the process of mystical perfection, and correlated it with religion, saying, *The wisdom of God lies hidden in every human cognition.* Thomas and Bonaventure were leading medieval thinkers: the former more analytic and Aristotelian, the latter more synthetic and Augustinian or Platonic.

Treatises advocating liberal education of the laity were written in the thirteenth century. Vincent of Beauvais, a learned Dominican who compiled four vast encyclopedic surveys or "Mirrors," entitled *The Mirror of Nature, The Mirror of Doctrines, The Mirror of Morality,* and *The Mirror of History,* wrote a treatise entitled *The Upbringing of Noble Children.* In the latter, Vincent advocated a broad, generous education of the lay upper classes, which would include the liberal arts and literature, history and the natural sciences, morality and religion. Explaining his encyclopedic interests, he exclaimed: *How great is the lowest form of beauty in this world, and how pleasing to the eye of reason!* Egidio Colonna (Aegidius of Colonna, Giles of Rome), outstanding Augustinian scholar, eventually head of his order, wrote a guidebook entitled *On the Governance of Rulers,* in which he included several chapters on the education of children of the upper classes. Egidio outlined a broad program of education, which included the seven liberal arts, the reading of classical as well as Christian literature, and the study of philosophy, political science, economics, and natural sciences. Youths were also to be trained in social ways and good manners. The academic education of women was likewise advocated.

THE RISE OF SCHOLASTIC PHILOSOPHY AND THEOLOGY.
Section 68.

> Human reason is related to the knowledge of the truth of faith . . . in such a way that it can glean certain likenesses of it, which are still not sufficient so that the truth of faith may be comprehended as being understood demonstrably or through itself. Yet it is useful for human reason to exercise itself in such proofs, however weak they may be, provided that there be present no presumption completely to comprehend or absolutely to demonstrate. [Thomas Aquinas, *Summa Contra Gentiles* (thirteenth century).]

The High Middle Ages

GIANT strides were made in learning in Western Europe during the High Middle Ages. Contributing factors, in addition to those already mentioned, included greater specialization, the advent of professional savants, the fructifying study of logic, and the work of translators.

The translators

The starting point for the great advances in learning in the High Middle Ages was the work of translators, who rendered in Latin the works of great Greek and Moslem scholars. Originally twice- or thrice-removed translations of Greek works were made from Arabic versions through intermediate languages such as Hebrew and Spanish. Often intermediate versions were faulty. Eventually Latin translations were made directly from the original Greek. Famous "schools" or gatherings of translators developed at Toledo in the twelfth century and at Palermo in the thirteenth century, and included industrious scholars from all climes.

In the general progress of secular learning during the High Middle Ages, there was a shift in emphasis in successive periods. During the eleventh century and the earlier twelfth century, grammar and literature were stressed; later in the twelfth century, logic; finally, in the thirteenth century, "philosophy" or general learning. Meanwhile religious learning or theology was continuously cultivated.

Humanism of the Twelfth-Century "Renaissance"

The first field of secular study to flourish in the High Middle Ages was literary learning, then included in the study of grammar. This resulted in what is known as the "first age of humanism," which reached its peak in the eleventh and early twelfth centuries. This humanism of the so-called Twelfth-Century Renaissance was a "Christian humanism," which was both more moderate than later medieval ("Renaissance") humanism and more subordinate to religion. Representative centers of this humanism were the cathedral schools of Orleans, Trèves, and Bamberg.

Scholars compiled numerous lists of recommended classical and Christian authors of ever-increasing length. These indicate growing interest in and familiarity with the writings of ancient classical authors. In the twelfth century, Conrad of Hirschau listed a total of twenty-three authors, including fourteen pagan authors. About the middle of the thirteenth century, Eberhard the German listed thirty-seven authors, about half classical and half Christian. In the later thirteenth century, Hugh of Trimberg, schoolmaster at Bamberg, listed eighty recommended authors, both classical and Christian, in his *Register of Many Authors*. Among twelfth-century writers evidencing great familiarity with and devotion to the classics were Hildebert of Lavardin and John of Salisbury. Hildebert, who became Bishop of LeMans and later Archbishop of Tours, was such an accomplished Latinist that some of his poems were long thought to be products of the classical period. John of Salisbury wrote a flawless Latin, liberally sprinkled with classical quotations.

Scholastic philosophy and theology: the eleventh century

The High Middle Ages witnessed the rebirth of speculative philosophy and the related accompanying evolution of theology as an organized science. The cooperative cultivation of philosophy and theology in this period is known as "Scholasticism," since it was a product of the medieval schools (*scholae*). The Scholastics took their cues from faith and accepted authorities, which included the Bible, the Church Fathers, and

Church Councils, as well as Greek and Arab philosophers, together with traditions of both civil and canon law. But they attempted to prove, explore, and evaluate the propositions of faith by reason. They used reason to test, weigh, interpret, and elaborate traditional beliefs, and assumed the latter as hypotheses for philosophical speculation. High medieval Scholasticism began during the eleventh century with the famous argument over the nature of "universals" or general ideas, which was encouraged by growing attention to dialectics (logic) in the liberal arts curriculum. Early Scholasticism was strongly influenced by the Augustinian-Platonic tradition emphasizing the reality of the spiritual and eternal as opposed to the material and temporal. Augustine's principle was "If you do not believe, you cannot understand."

Eleventh-century speculation was stimulated by challenging theses advanced by thinkers such as Berengar of Tours and Roscellin. Berengar of Tours denied the Church's doctrine of Eucharistic transubstantiation, according to which the substances of bread and wine are changed into the substances of the body and blood of Christ at the consecration in the Mass, despite the continuity of the "appearances" or "accidents" of the bread and wine. Berengar maintained that the substances of bread and wine persist since their accidents remain. Roscellin challenged the validity of universal ideas, maintaining that general concepts are mere "word-sounds" (*flatus vocis*) and that the only realities are individual, particular things. This position, known as "Nominalism" (from *nomina*: names), would apparently undermine the very foundations of philosophy and theology.

Question of universals

The Nominalism of Roscellin was opposed by St. Anselm of Bec and Canterbury, who taught the reality of universal ideas: i.e., that there are some kind of extramental realities corresponding to universal ideas. St. Anselm represents the common scholastic approach in the eleventh century, which was to begin with faith and then to prove, defend, and explain the doctrines of faith by natural reason. Anselm's motto, a rephrasing of Augustine's was *I believe so that I may understand*. At the same time, Anselm had great confidence in the power of reason. Most of Anselm's proofs suppose the reality of ideas or general concepts as a starting point. In the *Monologium* he essayed to demonstrate the existence of God by the ascending scale of being and perfection that should logically culminate in Absolute Good, Independent Existence, and Complete Perfection. In his *Proslogion*, Anselm attempted to prove God's existence by the so-called ontological argument, to the effect that the idea of God is that of a being "than which nothing greater can be conceived," but a being that has existence is greater than one which lacks existence, so the idea of God must include that of his existence. Obviously this argument projects from the realm of ideas to that of reality and is ultimately based on the Augustinian and Platonic concept of reality corresponding to our ideas. Although conservative, Anselm was an innovator in his extreme confidence in the ability of reason to demonstrate even deep doctrines of the faith, such as the Incarnation, as he attempted to do in his treatise *Why God Became Man*.

The High Middle Ages

The twelfth-century "strife over universals"

The discussion concerning the nature of universals continued in the twelfth century. Some scholars took an intermediate position between the Realism of William of Champeaux and the Nominalism of Roscellin. Abelard, who had been a student of both teachers, challenged the idealistic realism of William, and, according to his own version, drove his master into the religious life by defeating him in disputation. While Abelard's position has been variously interpreted, and some have asserted that he maintained that universals are only mental concepts (word concepts), his full and mature doctrine was apparently to the effect that universals are valid intellectual perceptions that represent realities: that is, objective conceptions produced by a mind making abstractions from real things. This solution, known as "Moderate Realism," and explained by John of Salisbury, Abelard's student, is a compromise position based on Aristotle. It holds that, while universals (general ideas) do not exist independently of particular things, they are valid in that they accurately represent similarities of real things.

Emergence of theology as a "science"

Though the beginnings of theology are traceable to the treatises of the great early Greek and Latin Church thinkers and Fathers, such as Origen and John Damascene and Augustine of Hippo, as well as to works of Boethius and Anselm, systematic theology as an organized "science" developed in the schools of the twelfth century with such writers as Abelard and Peter Lombard.

Besides being a logician, Abelard was something of a theologian. One source of his so-called "calamities"—troubles with his fellow ecclesiastics—was that he presumed to teach theology without a license and seemed to exaggerate the powers of reason. Although Abelard had no intention of becoming heretical, he did attribute extraordinary and seemingly excessive efficacy to human reason. In his *Dialogues*, reason presides as a judge over a debate between various religions. In his work *On the Trinity*, Abelard essayed to demonstrate and explain this profound mystery by reason, interpreting the three Divine Persons as the power, wisdom, and goodness of God. In his *Sic et Non* (*Yes and No*), Abelard partly anticipated the approach of Peter Lombard and the scholastic method by presenting opposing views of Church authorities on some 158 questions; but instead of solving or reconciling these conflicting opinions, he left this task to the reason of the reader. It was mainly for purporting to subject theology to the bar of reason that Abelard was attacked by St. Bernard of Clairvaux.

Abelard's most distinguished disciple was Peter Lombard, who finally became Archbishop of Paris. Peter Lombard composed *Four Books of Sentences* (opinions, propositions, theses), which ranged across the broad field of Christian beliefs in an ordered and reasoned manner. Taking a cue from both the *Sic et Non* and contemporary methods of teaching canon law, Lombard's *Sentences* presented what seemed to be opposing views and arguments on key religious questions but went beyond the *Sic et Non* by concluding in each case with an orthodox solution based on various proofs. Peter's *Sentences* were used as a basic textbook and outline for the study of theology until the sixteenth century. The great

Summas of the thirteenth century were extensive commentaries on or elaborations of the *Sentences*.

Scholastic philosophy and theology reached maturity in the thirteenth century. A great stimulus was provided by the fuller translation and study of the works of Aristotle and the Arabic philosophers. In addition to Aristotle's works on logic, which were already available, his *Physics, Metaphysics, Politics,* and *Ethics* and his works on various natural sciences were now translated, along with related works and commentaries by great Arabic scholars such as Avicenna and Averroes.

Maturation of scholasticism in the thirteenth century

Despite a general admiration of Aristotle as "the Philosopher," certain parts of his actual or supposed doctrines were unacceptable to orthodox theologians. This was especially true of the Aristotelian treatises and commentaries thereon available only in Arabic versions, since Moslem translators and commentators exaggerated and compounded antitheistic tendencies in Aristotle. Among such doctrines either found in or attributed to Aristotle by Avicenna and/or Averroes were the eternity of the world; the necessity of creation; the oneness of the active intellect, which would negate the independent existence and personal immorality of the human soul; the irreconcilability of faith and reason, which were supposed to be on dual tracks that would never meet, leading to the doctrine of the "double truth," which held that something could be true in religion yet false in philosophy; and "determinism," which denied the existence of free will.

Since acceptance of such doctrines would apparently undermine basic religious tenets, the inclusion of some of Aristotle's works, particularly his *Metaphysics* and his treatises on natural philosophy in the curriculum of the schools, was, for a while, occasionally forbidden by various Church authorities. Notwithstanding such prohibitions, these works of Aristotle continued to be utilized by many professors and scholars. Eventually, by the mid-thirteenth century, the prohibitions against works of Aristotle were lifted, especially as better translations directly from the Greek became available.

Meanwhile many theologians continued to study Aristotle and worked to understand, adapt, and utilize his doctrines. Among such scholars was William of Auvergne, who became Bishop of Paris in 1228. While using both Avicenna and Averroes, William "weeded out" such Aristotelian or pseudo-Aristotelian doctrines as universal determinism, double truths, the corporeality of the human soul, the oneness of the "active intellect," and the denial of individual human immortality.

Actually the first to correlate theology with philosophy on a broad scale were the Franciscans, who, while using Aristotle, did so in the Neo-Platonic Augustinian tradition. According to the Franciscan School, unreserved primacy is accorded to the "idea" or "revelation," and hence to "faith" and "will," which makes the act of faith accepting revelation. The first noted Franciscan to effect an extensive coordination of philosophy and theology was Alexander of Hales (d. 1245), a professor at the University of Paris. Alexander, with the help of collaborators, prepared a voluminous *Summa*, the first of its class which comprehensively covered

The Franciscan school and St. Bonaventure

the field of theology. This *Summa* followed the outline of the *Sentences*, the basic text, and was originally intended for the use of Franciscan students pursuing theological studies. In it Alexander used what became the standard scholastic method: first posing the question; next giving solutions and arguments contrary to the preferred answer; thirdly presenting the proposed solution and supporting arguments; and finally answering objections and disproving rejected propositions. In his arguments, based on natural reason as well as on the teachings of the Sacred Scriptures, Church councils, the Fathers, and theologians, Alexander employed pertinent selected parts from the Aristotelian *corpus*.

St. Bonaventure (d. 1274), a Tuscan (Italian) who studied under Alexander of Hales, taught at Paris, and eventually became the head of his order, was the greatest of the thirteenth-century Franciscan theologians. Bonaventure was an idealist in the Augustinian, semimystical tradition (or "realist" in the sense of one who attributes a reality to universal essences apart from individual beings). He accepted the extramental existence of realities corresponding to universal ideas. His philosophy and theology are found in his *Commentary on the Sentences*, his *Breviloquium (Short Summary)*, and *Journey of the Mind to God*. Bonaventure starts with faith and the love of God. Knowledge of God is innate, and ideas constitute our only real, abiding, final knowledge. Sensory experience is not an ultimate object of intellectual truth, nor does it have a key role in its attainment. In order to gain knowledge of first principles, our mind must be illumined by God, i.e., by divine ideas infused by God. Bonaventure used elements of Aristotle to explain and defend idealistic Augustinian theology.

The Franciscan school stressed "voluntarism" or will rather than "intellectualism" or natural reason. Their thought enhanced the roles of intuition and faith. They employed Aristotle and reason, but they did so as a convenient adjunct to and support for the Bible, the Fathers, and faith. They assigned the realm of the contingent and transitory to philosophy; that of the eternal and necessary to faith.

The Dominican school and St. Thomas Aquinas

The Dominican school differed from the more Augustinian and Platonic Franciscan school by utilizing Aristotle more fully and according a greater place to reason. They insisted that reason is a road and means to valid general knowledge, even as is faith. The senses are the ordinary avenues through which reason gets its data and obtains its primary knowledge. St. Thomas clearly distinguished between reason and faith at the same time that he defended both and exemplified their cooperation.

Albertus Magnus (d. 1280), a German Dominican who taught at Cologne and Paris, and eventually became Provincial of his order in Germany, defended and promoted the use of the complete works of Aristotle at a time when many of these were in disfavor. A "philosopher" in the broad (ancient and medieval) sense, Albertus was a polymath of universal interests, whose printed works fill twenty-three large folio volumes. As a scientist, he utilized the scientific works of Aristotle, and as a philosopher and theologian he also urged the use of Aristotle's other works.

High Tide of Medieval Culture

St. Thomas Aquinas (d. 1247), who came of a noble Neapolitan family and joined the Dominican order, wherein he studied under Albertus, brought Scholasticism to its height. His brilliant, superbly organized, eminently reasonable works still appeal to the intellect. Urged on by his master, Albertus, Aquinas devoted himself to the adaptation and reconciliation of Aristotle's philosophy to Christian beliefs and doctrines: the "Christianization of Aristotle." Aquinas was assisted in his work by a new, more accurate translation of Aristotle made directly from the Greek by his fellow friar, William of Moerbecke. Distinction between the proofs of faith and the proofs of reason helped Aquinas to discern two separable sciences: philosophy and theology.

In his apologetical *Summa Contra Gentiles* (*Summa Against the Pagans*), Thomas attempted to lead nonbelievers by the path of reason to the point of being able to make an act of faith. In his subsequent, longer *Summa Theologica* (*Summa of Theology*), Thomas essayed to cover the whole range of philosophy and theology. The *Summa Theologica* discusses in succession God and His Attributes, Creation and Creatures, Pure Spirits and Wholly Corporeal Beings, Man and the End of Man, Human Acts, Habits and Virtues, Vices and Sins, the Law and Grace, Theological and Cardinal Virtues, States of Life, Redemption and Salvation Through Christ, the Seven Sacraments, and Immortal Life. In treating various topics, Thomas uses the scholastic method and gives a prominent place throughout to reason. In proving the existence of God, for instance, Aquinas argues from the existence of motion to a Prime Mover, from secondary, intermediate causes to an original Uncaused Cause, from contingent, dependent beings to a self-existing, Necessary Being, from ascending graduations of perfection to an Infinitely Perfect Being; and from the order and design in the world to an Intelligent Planner.

Thomism did not become dominant in the thirteenth century. Because of its liberal Aristotelian content, it was still often confused with unacceptable Averroism. Many of the doctrines and approaches of Thomism were too novel and radical for more conservative theologians. But, despite criticism, the Dominican order by 1280 both accepted and required the study of the works of the Angelic Doctor. A similar course was soon followed by the Cistercians and Augustinians.

SOCIAL AND NATURAL SCIENCES IN THE HIGH MIDDLE AGES.
Section 69.

> The people do not exalt their ruler above themselves in order to make him free to exercise tyranny over them, but rather so that he may use the power they have given him to defend them against the tyranny and injustice of others. And when a ruler begins to foster evil and act tyrannically against the interests of his subjects . . . , is it not clear that he deservedly forfeits the dignity entrusted to him, and that the people are freed from his overlordship and their subjection to him since he has first broken the compact by reason of which he was appointed? [The contract theory of government as advanced by the monk Manegold of Lautenbach in a pamphlet about 1085.]

The High Middle Ages

IN THE Middle Ages, as in classical antiquity, the social and natural (physical) sciences were subdivisions of philosophy, which included all general knowledge of and quest for ultimate principles. The social sciences were included in moral philosophy, and the natural sciences in natural or physical philosophy; and both were cultivated for practical as well as intellectual reasons.

The social sciences: Political theory

The main concern of moral philosophy, which included the social sciences as well as ethics, was to provide principles for the guidance of humans, both as individuals and in society. Moral philosophy thus included economic theory and political science, as well as ethics. The social sciences grew in connection with current problems, such as those of the proper relations of Church and State, and of individual humans and the new money economy.

Recurrent debates concerning the proper relations of Church and State led eventually to a consideration of the nature of the State and its functions and powers. Most medieval political writers accepted certain basic assumptions, such as the dignity of man and the rights of individuals, the ascendancy of spiritual and eternal interests, the coexistence of Church and State as two autonomous institutions each with its own jurisdiction, the existence of a natural law stemming from the divine will and imbedded in the divinely constituted natures of things, and the ultimate derivation of all authority from God as well as its limitations in accordance with God's will. Current centralizing efforts of both Popes and monarchs challenged existing traditions and raised basic questions. Previous theory had generally recognized the reciprocal independence of Church and State and the supremacy of each in its own sphere. The question was now raised as to what were the limitations on the jurisdiction of each and which institution was to prevail in case of disagreement.

Theories of Church–State relations

The elaboration of more and more extreme theories of the respective powers of Church and State by pro-Papal lawyers or "canonists" on the one hand and promonarchical civil lawyers or "legists" on the other became a continuing feature of the High Middle Ages. As the Church–State controversy persisted and intensified, claims on either side became ever more extensive. The claims of the canonists rose from limited ecclesiastical independence to more complete ecclesiastical autonomy, to *limited indirect* Papal authority to intervene in secular affairs, to ever more *unlimited indirect* Papal power to intervene. Following this the canonists "leaped the gap" from indirect to *direct* Papal authority in secular affairs. At first the canonists claimed direct Papal power only on a very *restricted* scale but eventually they were claiming *broad direct* Papal power to supervise secular affairs. Meanwhile, the claims of the pro-monarchical legists were similarly expanded. The legists began by maintaining essential monarchical independence from the Church in the concerns of secular government, but then moved on to assertions of ever more complete independence, and eventually to total monarchical independence. From this they, too, "bridged the gap" and claimed increasing degrees of monarchical authority in ecclesiastical affairs, accompanied by a corresponding diminution of Papal authority. By the beginning of the fourteenth century, the Church was virtually reduced by some pro-monarchical theorists to a department of the State. By this time each side was claiming supremacy over the other.

The investiture controversy (1075–1122) begot about 115 known polemical tracts, of which about 65 were pro-Papal, and about 50 pro-monarchical. Encountering strenuous monarchical opposition to their contention that all ecclesiastical appointments should be exempt from lay intervention, the Cluniac-Gregorian reformers argued that the Pope had the right to intervene in temporal affairs and, if necessary, depose a monarch who blocked Church purification. Thus, while accepting the ordinary independence of State and Church, the reformers maintained the indirect right of Church authorities to intervene in political affairs in exceptional cases.

Theory during the investiture controversy (1075–1122)

An authoritative spokesman for the reform position was Pope Gregory VII. It is generally agreed that Gregory VII taught only that the Pope has an *indirect* right to intervene in political matters, a power whereby he can depose monarchs in extraordinary cases "by reason of sin" (*ratione peccati*), i.e., for grave moral reasons and to protect the salvation of souls. Most authorities held that Gregory did *not* maintain that the Pope had a direct right to rule nations or that monarchs ruled by delegated powers received from the Pope. But what are we to think of Gregory's *Dictatus Papae* (*Papal Dictate*) in which he makes many strong statements concerning rights reserved solely to the Pope, such as those of using the imperial insignia, having princes kiss his feet, deposing emperors, and releasing subjects from their fealty to rulers? Some hold that these propositions, which were committed to the Papal registry but never promulgated, constituted Gregory's compilation of various asserted rights of the Papacy to be used as bases for Papal propulsion of further reforms, which were certain to arouse strenuous opposition. Since Gregory was more a practical man of action than a political theorist, it is doubtful to what extent these were serious claims to rights. It may be argued that all of these prerogatives were either formalities honoring the Papal office or instances of exercise of an indirect power. Taken on face value, however, they would seem an attempt to set up a theocracy, making the Pope "the lord of the world," and, if seriously claimed, would represent an extreme digression from the gradual growth of Papal claims.

During the investiture controversy, a Papal supporter, Honorius of Augsburg (Augustodiensis) (early twelfth century), maintained that monarchs receive their power from God *through the Church*, to be retained only as long as they cooperate with the Church. Meanwhile Manegold of Lautenbach (d. 1085) advanced a rudimentary "contract theory" of government to justify withdrawal of popular support and allegiance from an offending monarch. Manegold alleged that the power of the secular ruler comes to him from God but *through the people*, who "elevate the ruler over themselves to prevent tyranny and wrongdoing." If the ruler himself becomes a tyrant, he violates this pact and loses his right to rule, so that the Pope's sentence deposing him is merely declaratory.

The theory of monarchical supporters during the investiture struggle was essentially defensive. Monarchical spokesmen stressed the independent nature of monarchical authority, and based their arguments chiefly on long-standing customs that had, they said, the force of constitutional law. They also invoked Christ's and St. Paul's teachings. They maintained that monarchical authority comes directly from God, and is responsible only to God. Henry IV spoke of himself as "king, not through usurpation, but through the holy ordination of God, with royal power conferred by God" and "subject to the judgment of God alone." The pro-monarchial *York Tractates* (*Anonymous of York*) composed about 1100, during the investiture struggle in England, went further and maintained the superiority of the monarchical power over the ecclesiastical, arguing that since Christ as King is God but as priest is man, so the royal power is divine and superior to the ecclesiastical, which is human.

Twelfth-century theory of Church and State

Theory concerning State and Church during the twelfth century was encouraged by further disputes. Pro-Papal champions came to maintain that the monarch receives his power from, or at least through, the Church, and that he is subject to ecclesiastical supervision. John of Salisbury (about 1159) wrote of the "sword" (power) of temporal authority: *The Prince receives "this sword" from the hand of the Church. . . . Although the Church possesses this sword, she wields it through the hand of the prince. . . .* And St. Bernard of Clairvaux likewise asserted: *Both swords, temporal and spiritual, belong to the Church. While the spiritual sword is drawn by the Church through the hand of the priest, the temporal sword is drawn for the Church through the hand of the warrior—at the behest of the priest and on the order of the emperor* [monarch].

During the twelfth century, the monarchical cause received support from the revived study of Roman law since, in the Justinian codification, the will of the emperor is the source of law and the civil ruler exercises considerable power over the Church. Monarchical proponents continued to maintain the complete independence of monarchical power. Thus Frederick I, Barbarossa, invoked Roman law in his dealings with the North Italian communes with respect to the *regalia*, and with the Papacy in regard to the Papal States and Papal elections. And he strenuously opposed any sign of a Papal pretense to restrict his authority, as in the "stirrup" and *beneficia* incidents.[c] In the latter case he declared: *The kingdom and the empire belong to us, having been granted to us by God alone, through our election by the princes.* Monarchical proponents also continued to insist on the constitutional force of long-established customs, as did Henry II of England in his Constitutions of Clarendon (1164) and his contest with Becket.

[c] See story of Western Empire in the High Middle Ages (Chapter 18).

Thirteenth-century theory of Church and State:

The apogee of pro-Papal claims came during the thirteenth century. Canonists stressed the position of the Pope as Vicar of Christ on earth, and concluded that either the Pope has sweeping indirect temporal powers or he has direct temporal power over political affairs. Authorities regard Pope Innocent III (d. 1216) as making a more restrained claim of indirect but far-reaching Papal power in temporal affairs. Innocent accepted the distinction and independence of two spheres of authority, but he also stressed the plentitude of spiritual power entrusted by Christ to His "Vicar," the Pope. This, he said, was "enough" to meet all exigencies. Writing to Philip II of France, Innocent asked: *Why should we wish to usurp the jurisdiction of others, when we cannot exhaust our own?* Still, the statements of Innocent III were often equivocal and sometimes suggest that he was claiming more. Thus Innocent compared Papal authority to "the sun" and monarchical authority to "the moon," which derives its light from the sun. *[Pro-Papal theory]*

As the thirteenth century progressed, many canonists came to assert a direct Papal power over temporal affairs. They stressed the unity of Christendom and the need for a hierarchy of powers. Involved in a desperate struggle with Emperor Frederick II, Popes Gregory IX and Innocent IV claimed direct power over temporal affairs. Gregory IX (1236) quoted the *Donation of Constantine* as an acknowledgment that *The Prince of the Apostles . . . should rule over material and corporeal things throughout the whole world.* And Pope Innocent IV asserted: *The Lord Jesus Christ has established in the Papal throne a monarchy that is not only pontifical but also regal.*

Subsequent thirteenth-century canonists further elaborated the theory of direct Papal authority over secular affairs. Cardinal Henricus of Ostia, known as Hostiensis (d. 1271), maintained that *"We should have but one head, lord of both spiritual and material things."* Of Christ's conferral of the power of the "keys" upon St. Peter, he said: *He did not say a 'key' but 'keys': one . . . spiritual, the other . . . temporal.* William Durant (d. 1295) declared of the Pope that *He is the successor of Peter and the Vicar of God Himself. Whence he rules all things and judges and disposes all things as he sees fit. . . .* Aegidius of Colonna (Giles of Rome), toward the close of the thirteenth century, based his theory upon the alleged principle of *dominium* (lordship, ownership, or dominion). According to Aegidius, since all human *dominium* is in the moral order, it is in a sphere headed by the Pope and subject to Papal control.

Theologians such as Thomas Aquinas were usually more restrained and moderate in their opinions, holding for cooperation but continued separation of State and Church. With Aristotle, Thomas held that the State is a natural institution, rooted in the very nature of man as a social animal, and hence prior to and independent of the Church. According to Thomas: *In those things that pertain to civil good, the secular power is to be obeyed rather than the spiritual, in conformity with the saying in Matthew: 'Render to Caesar the things that are Caesar's.'*

Meanwhile, the legists or civil lawyers, who upheld the monarchical cause, were helped by the current study of Aristotle's political works. According to Aristotle, man is a "political animal," since his nature demands life in society and this requires political authority capable of maintaining law and order. The political authority of the secular ruler is hence both prior to and independent of the ecclesiastical. Frederick II maintained not only that he was independent of churchmen in temporal mat- *[Pro-monarchical theory]* ters but also that churchmen were subject to him in many moral as well as temporal affairs. He argued that monarchs should confiscate the excess wealth of the clergy for the common good. The contest between Philip IV and Boniface VIII generated a considerable amount of promonarchical literature. The author of *A Dispute Between a Soldier and a Cleric* (1296) pointed out that only an authority that has the power to make laws in a given sphere has the power to render judgment concerning them. The author of *Antequam Essent Clerici* (*Before There Were Clerics*) (1296) asserted that the royal power existed before the ecclesiastical and that the clergy are members of the body politic, subject to its laws and taxes. The author of *Rex Pacificus* (*Peacemaking King*) (ca. 1301–1302) said that State and Church are separate and independent, and that just as Christ refused to exercise political power so the Pope should abstain from interfering in secular affairs.

Law   Thomas Aquinas defined law as *"an ordinance of right reason promulgated for the common good by him who has the care of the community."* He held that for a law to be a valid law, morally binding, it must be reasonable, promote the common welfare, and be properly promulgated (made knowable to the public). Law in general was divided into (1) "eternal law" or the plan of creation in the mind of God from all eternity; (2) "natural law" or the will of God as imbedded in the nature of created things and discernable by natural reason (such as the prohibition against murder); (3) divine positive law or the will of God as made manifest in revelation (as exemplified by the Biblical injunction regarding observance of the Sabbath); and finally (4) human (man-made) law, also ultimately deriving indirectly from the divine will, divided into (a) civil law or law promulgated for man's temporal good by the secular government (such as laws concerning the form of contracts) and (b) ecclesiastical law or law promulgated by the Church for man's spiritual welfare (such as laws concerning fasting and abstinence).

Roman law   A highly significant development in this period was the recovery and intensive study of Roman law as found in Justinian's *Corpus Juris Civilis*. The highly developed, prudent, rational Roman legal system was intensively studied in the medieval universities, and much of it was incorporated into existing legal systems and practices. The revival of Roman law is generally attributed to Irnerius (d. 1125), who taught civil law at Bologna in the early twelfth century and commented on the *Corpus Juris Civilis* as well as regularized legal training and casuistry. Irnerius and his successors until the mid-thirteenth century are known as "Glossators" in that they gave brief explanations of the laws in "glosses": short marginal and interlinear annotations. From the mid-thirteenth century on, the "Post-Glossators" or "Commentators" approached the law in a more philosophical, discursive "scholastic" manner, and endeavored to discuss general principles behind the laws as well as to adapt legal provisions to their own times and circumstances. They thus amalgamated Roman law and customary law, and applied the law in a reasonable, practical manner. The net result was usually a combination in various proportions of native customary law and Roman law, in practice as well as in theory. In Romance countries, such as Italy and Spain, the proportion of Roman law was greater; whereas in Teutonic countries, such as Germany and England, native laws played a larger part.

Customary law

Growing sophistication and Roman example encouraged the codification of native customary law and maritime commercial law. Saxon customary law was compiled in the *Sachsenspiegel* or *Saxon Mirror*, by a thirteenth-century Saxon judge, which came to be widely accepted in much of Germany. A similar codification of South German law, known as the *Schwabenspiegel* or *Suabian Mirror*, was, later in the same century, compiled for the first Hapsburg Emperor, Rudolph I. Among collections of feudal law in this period were *The Customs and Usages of Beauvais*, *The Customs and Usages of Vermandois*, and *The Usages of Artois*. Maritime commercial law was similarly codified in the *Consulado del Mar* (*Code of Barcelona*), the *Laws of Oleron* (an island off the west coast of France), and the *Laws of Wisby* (a Baltic island used by the Hanseatic League).

Canon law

Canon law, the law of the Church, also owed much to Roman law in its principles and procedures, although its main substantive sources were the Scriptures, the Fathers, and the decrees of Church councils and Popes. The first comprehensive codification of canon law was made in the twelfth century by a Camaldolese monk named Gratian, who taught at Bologna. In his *Concordance of Discordant Canons* or *Decretum* (ca. 1140), Gratian organized, commented on, and reconciled some 3,900 ecclesiastical laws on various topics. Gratian's *Concordance* became a standard text for the study of canon law. In the thirteenth century, the work was updated by supplemental collections made for Popes Gregory IX (in 1234) and Boniface VIII (in 1298).

Economic theory

Economic theory was considered a branch of moral philosophy and economic thinking was dominated by a concern for the general good, which was to be achieved mainly by observance of justice. A paramount consideration was the proper subordination of means to ends and the maintenance of a rational hierarchy of values.

According to medieval economic theory, the right to hold property is conceded by God to men as a means to effect their survival and promote their salvation and perfection. This right is conditional rather than absolute, since it is limited by the rights and needs of other human beings. The possession of property entails obligations as well as privileges, and wealth involves perils for the soul.

History writing in the High Middle Ages

History writing reflected the general progress and philosophical training of the period. Historical accounts became better organized, and their literary style improved, as they rose to meet the challenge of remarkable events.

The Crusades attracted the pens of numerous writers in Latin and the vernacular, including Fulcher of Chartres and Robert the Monk for the First Crusade, Odo of Deuil for the Second; Gui de Bazoche and Richard of London for the Third; Villehardouin and Robert of Clari for the

Fourth; and the Sire de Joinville for the two Crusades of Louis IX. A general history of the movement to his own time was composed by Archbishop William of Tyre in the later twelfth century.

English historiography took the lead in the High Middle Ages, as Anglo-Saxon historical traditions were cross-fertilized by Norman-French influences and inspired by the impressive Norman and Plantagenet Empire. Historiography was cultivated in monasteries such as those of St. Alban's, Canterbury, Malmesbury, Peterborough, and Durham. Among noted historians were William of Malmesbury, William of Newburgh, Roger of Hoveden, Henry of Huntingdon, Roger of Wendover, Matthew Paris, and Bartholomew Cotton.

An intelligent international *History* focusing on France and England was written by the twelfth-century Norman monk Odericus Vitalis. The main historians of the Crusades were French. Abbot Suger and the Monk Rigord wrote *Lives* of Louis VI and Philip II. A perspicacious French historian of the twelfth century, Abbot Guibert de Nogent, wrote an informative *Autobiography* vividly reflecting contemporary life, and *The Deeds of God Through the French* concerning the First Crusade. In the thirteenth century, the learned French Dominican, Vincent of Beauvais, compiled an encyclopedic *Mirror of History*.

In the Empire, an outstanding general historian was Otto of Friesing, an uncle of Frederick Barbarossa. Bishop Otto wrote a philosophic general history known as the *Chronicle of Two Cities*, in which he used the theme of the two "cities" or kingdoms, worldly and spiritual, developed by St. Augustine in his *City of God*. Otto also began a biography of his nephew, entitled *The Deeds of Frederick I*, later continued by the notary Rahewin. Popular among German and Italian historians were more limited and local stories of cities, bishoprics, and individuals, as well as general historical chronicles written in the vernacular, such as the *Rhymed Chronicle of Cologne*, the *Lieflander Chronik*, the *Chronicle of Holstein*, and the *Styrian Rhymed Chronicle*. Among informative Italian municipal annals and chronicles were those of Genoa, Pisa, Venice, Milan, and Bari, to mention a few. The perceptive Franciscan, Salimbene of Parma, was the author of an autobiographical *Chronicle* that depicts conditions in Italy during the reign of Frederick II. Meanwhile in Spain noteworthy histories were written in the vernacular under the aegis of Alphonso X, the Wise. Popular throughout Europe was the composition of biographies of bishops and saints. Lives of the saints were sometimes partly imaginative for purposes of edification, and often had fixed conventions, such as heavenly portents, miracles, and pious deathbed exhortations.

Natural sciences and mathematics

Despite the fact that most medieval scholars were churchmen, whose primary concern was usually theology and related philosophy, there was much interest in science. Many regarded the natural sciences as a "mirror" of God and a means of improving the lot of mankind; some saw them as a source of marvelous powers. Natural sciences and mathematics were included in the basic liberal arts course as well as in "natural philosophy," a part of the study of philosophy. Actually medieval scholars were more scientific-minded in an intellectual sense than were either the ancient Romans or Renaissance humanists. They had a broad, eclectic interest in general knowledge, independent of practical applications. Vincent of Beauvais wrote: *I am moved with spiritual sweetness towards the Creator and Ruler of the world when I behold the vastness, beauty, and permanence of His creation.*

A starting point for medieval scientific progress was the translation of scientific works of the Greeks and the Moslems into Latin in the twelfth to thirteenth centuries. Among representative translators were Adelard of Bath, Robert of Chester, John of Spain, Michael Scot, Robert of Grosseteste, and William of Moerbecke.

In the twelfth century, the Englishman Adelard of Bath stressed the necessity of going beyond one's own country and culture in quest of scientific knowledge, and William of Conches urged the direct observation of nature. In the thirteenth century, the Dominican Albertus Magnus observed that the knowledge of particular things can be attained only by experience. Robert Grosseteste, Bishop of Lincoln, who was skilled in Greek, urged the study of foreign languages and the use of mathematics and the experimental method. He explained that the scientific method was a search for causes, and showed how general principles could be established on the basis of observation and experimentation. And he distinguished absolute certitude, as arrived at in mathematics, from the probable certitude obtainable in the natural sciences.

The Oxford Franciscan Roger Bacon roundly criticized excessive confidence in the syllogistic method and disputations, and urged greater use of induction, observation, and experimentation, as well as the study of foreign languages. He predicted that experimental science would one day provide men with marvelous powers: *Navigational machines without rowers can be made so that the largest ships on rivers and seas can be moved with a single man in charge with greater velocity than if they were full of men. And wheeled vehicles can be made so that they can move with unbelievable rapidity . . . without being drawn by animals. Also flying machines. . . . And a small machine capable of raising and lowering enormous weights . . . and machines that can go to the bottom of seas and rivers without danger . . . , and bridges without piers or supports. . . .* Bacon was also one of the first to describe magnifying glasses, spectacles, and telescopes, as well as gunpowder. The great Franciscan philosopher-theologian Duns Scotus, at the close of the century, stated that the certainty of causal laws observed in experiments is guaranteed by the principle of the uniformity of nature.

The leading applied science was medicine. Out of some 30,000 *Medicine* medieval manuscripts from the Middle Ages surviving in England, it has been estimated that about 15,000 are on medicine. A very large proportion of the Arabic and Greek works translated into Latin in the twelfth and thirteenth centuries were medical treatises. An early trailblazer and translator of Greek and Arabic medical works from Arabic was Constantine the African, who influenced Salerno in the eleventh century. Among the medical counsels of "The Rules of Health of Salerno" were

Shun weighty cares; all anger deem profane;
From heavy suppers and much wine abstain;
Avoid idle noonday slumber, nor delay
The urgent calls of nature to obey.
At early dawn, when first from bed you rise,
Wash in cold water both your hands and eyes.

Medicine was one of the leading studies at medieval universities. Particularly noted for their medical studies were Salerno, Naples, Montpellier, and Padua. Surgery was "reborn" in the West in the thirteenth century. An important writer on surgery at this time was William of Salaceto, who taught at Bologna and urged a wider use of the surgical knife as a substitute for previously popular cautery; he also emphasized the importance of antiseptic healing. Another was his pupil, Lanfranchi of Milan, who brought advanced learning to Paris. Anesthetics were coming into use, as were mercury ointments and tinctures (alcoholic solutions of healing substances). Ophthalmology and optics were subjects of particular interest. Operations for cataracts are described. Spectacles, referred to as "discs for the eyes for reading," came into wide use in thirteenth-century Italy. Treatises were written on public sanitation and military hygiene. Hospitals multiplied, inspired largely by religious motives. There were 18 hospitals in England in 1123, and 170 more by 1215, while 240 new hospitals were founded there in the thirteenth century, bringing the total to 428. It is said that Holy Ghost hospitals were to be found in almost every town in Christendom.

References for Chapter 23

AMONG works treating high medieval culture in general are the broad survey by FREDERICK B. ARTZ, *The Mind of the Middle Ages* (New York: Knopf, 1954), and the brilliant interpretation by HENRY O. TAYLOR, *The Medieval Mind*, 2 vols. (London: Macmillan, 1930). CHARLES H. HASKINS, *Renaissance of the Twelfth Century* (Cambridge, Mass.: Harvard U.P., 1939), treats various aspects of thought, learning, and literature from about 1050 to 1250.

One of the best general treatments of education and learning in the period is FREDERICK EBY and C. F. ARROWOOD, *History and Philosophy of Education: Ancient and Medieval* (New York: Prentice-Hall, 1940). Also useful are ARTHUR F. LEACH, *The Schools of Medieval England* (London: Methuen, 1915), and ELWOOD P. CUBBERLY, *Readings in the History of Education . . .* (Boston: Houghton Mifflin, 1948). For the contribution of translators, see HASKINS, *Renaissance of the Twelfth Century*, as cited above, and DE LACY O'LEARY, *Arabic Thought and Its Place in History* (London: K. Paul, 1939).

The classic study of medieval universities is HASTINGS RASHDALL, *The Universities of Europe in the Middle Ages*, ed. F. M. Powicke and A. B. Emden, 3 vols. (Oxford: Clarendon, 1936). An excellent short account is GABRIEL COMPAYRÉ, *Abelard and the Rise of Universities* (New York: Scribners, 1897). A useful specialized work is LOWRIE J. DALY, *The Medieval University, 1200–1400* (New York: Sheed, 1961). A readable essay is CHARLES H. HASKINS, *The Rise of Universities* (New York: Holt, 1923). Interesting readings concerning life and work at medieval universities are provided by ARTHUR D. NORTON,

Readings in the History of Education: Medieval Universities (Cambridge, Mass.: Harvard U.P., 1909), and LYNN THORNDIKE, *University Records and Life in the Middle Ages* (New York: Columbia U.P., 1944). Good recent works include GORDON LEFF, *Paris and Oxford Universities in the Thirteenth and Fourteenth Centuries* . . . (New York: Wiley, 1968), and Joseph R. Jones and J. E. Keller, trs., *The Scholar's Guide* (Toronto: Pontifical Institute of Medieval Studies, 1969).

Probably the best study of educational theory in the period is to be found in EBY and ARROWOOD, already mentioned. Good for the monastic viewpoint is JEAN LECLERQ, *The Love of Letters and the Desire for God* . . . , tr. C. Misrahi (New York: Fordham U.P., 1961). Translated primary sources are HUGH OF ST. VICTOR, *Didascalicon: A Medieval Guide to the Arts*, tr. Jerome Taylor (New York: Columbia U.P., 1961), and JOHN OF SALISBURY, *The Metalogicon . . . A Twelfth Century Defence of the Verbal and Logical Arts of the Trivium*, tr. Daniel D. McGarry (Berkeley: California U.P., 1955). The instructional methods and influence of Peter Abelard are treated by D. E. LUSCOMBE, *The School of Peter Abelard* (Cambridge: Cambridge U.P., 1969).

General works on medieval philosophy include the comprehensive ETIENNE H. GILSON, *History of Christian Philosophy in the Middle Ages* (New York: Random House, 1955); the information-packed MAURICE DE WULF, *History of Medieval Philosophy*, tr. E. C. Messenger, 2 vols. (London: Longmans, 1925–1926); the brief, well-digested GORDON LEFF, *Medieval Thought* . . . (Baltimore: Penguin, 1958); and ARMAND A. MAURER, *Medieval Philosophy* (New York: Random House, 1962); as well as PAUL VIGNAUX, *Philosophy in the Middle Ages*, tr. E. C. Hall (New York: Meridian, 1959). A good general history of philosophy in this period is to be found in FREDERICK COPLESTON, *History of Philosophy*, vols. II and III (New York: Philosophical Library, 1952–1953). On Thomas Aquinas, see VERNON J. BOURKE, *Aquinas' Search for Wisdom* (Milwaukee: Bruce, 1965).

For the history of political theory in the Middle Ages, see CHARLES H. MCILWAIN, *The Growth of Political Thought in the West . . . to the End of the Middle Ages* (New York: Macmillan, 1933), a standard briefer treatment; and ROBERT W. CARLYLE and ALEXANDER J. CARLYLE, *A History of Mediaeval Political Theory in the West*, 6 vols. (Edinburgh: Blackwood, 1903–1936), a classic comprehensive coverage. An excellent work, which combines discussions with extracts from original sources, is Ewart K. Lewis, ed., *Medieval Political Ideas*, 2 vols. (New York: Knopf, 1955). Other good works on the subject are EDWARD JENKS, *Law and Politics in the Middle Ages* . . . (London: Murray, 1919); GEORGE H. SABINE, *History of Political Theory* (New York: Holt, 1937); FRITZ KERN, *Kingship and Law in the Middle Ages*, tr. S. B. Chrimes (Oxford: Blackwell, 1939); OTTO F. VON GIERKE, *Political Theories of the Middle Age*, tr. F. W. Maitland (Cambridge: Cambridge U.P., 1922); and JOHN B. MORRAL, *Political Thought in Medieval Times* (New York: Harper, 1958).

Roman law in medieval times is discussed by CHARLES P. SHERMAN, *Roman Law in the Modern World*, vol. I: *History of Roman Law* . . . (Boston: Boston Book Co., 1917); HERBERT F. JOLOWICZ, *Historical Introduction to the Study of Roman Law* (Cambridge: Cambridge U.P., 1952); and WILLIAM E. BRYNTESON, "Roman Law and Legislation in the Middle Ages," in *Speculum*, XLI (1966), 420–437. BEDE JARRETT has written on *Social Theories of the Middle Ages, 1200–1500* (London: Benn,

1926), and on *Mediaeval Socialism* (London: Burns, 1935).

A standard coverage of history writing is JAMES W. THOMPSON, *History of Historical Writing*, vol. I (New York: Macmillan, 1943). Another useful work is HARRY ELMER BARNES, *A History of Historical Writing* (New York: Dover, 1962), and a much briefer treatment is found in the collaborative *Development of Historiography*, ed. MATTHEW A. FITZSIMONS et al. (Harrisburg, Pa.: Stackpole, 1954).

A stellar contribution for the history of science is GEORGE SARTON, *Introduction to the History of Science*, vols. I and II (parts I and II) (Baltimore: Williams and Wilkins, 1927–1947); still valuable is the earlier trail-blazing LYNN THORNDIKE, *History of Magic and Experimental Science*, 8 vols. (New York: Macmillan, 1923–1958), complete to the seventeenth century. Brief introductions are ALISTAIR C. CROMBIE, *Medieval and Early Modern Science*, 2 vols. (New York: Doubleday, 1959), also entitled *From Augustine to Galileo* . . . ; and WILLIAM T. SEDGWICK and H. W. TYLER, *A Short History of Science*, rev. ed. (New York: Macmillan, 1939).

An excellent contribution to the history of applied science is CHARLES J. SINGER et al., *A History of Technology*, vol. II (New York: Oxford U.P., 1956). Another contribution is ABBOTT P. USHER, *A History of Mechanical Inventions*, rev. ed. (Cambridge, Mass.: Harvard U.P., 1954). Medicine is treated by LOREN C. MACKINNEY, *Early Medieval Medicine* (Baltimore: Johns Hopkins, 1937), and *Medical Illustrations in Medieval Manuscripts* (Berkeley: California U.P., 1965); JAMES J. WALSH, *Medieval Medicine* (London: Black, 1920); ARTURO CASTIGLIONI, *A History of Medicine* (New York: Knopf, 1947); and C. H. TALBOT, *Medicine in Medieval England* (London: Oldbourne, 1967). Geography is the province of CHARLES RAYMOND BEAZLEY, *The Dawn of Modern Geography*, vol. II (900–1260) and vol. III (1260–1420) (New York: Peter Smith, 1949), and GEORGE H. KIMBLE, *Geography in 1938*).

Leading scientists of the era are treated by THOMAS N. SCHWERTNER, *St. Albert the Great* (New York: Bruce, 1932); ALISTAIR C. CROMBIE, *Robert Grosseteste and the Origins of Experimental Science, 1100–1700* (Oxford: Clarendon, 1952); and ROBERT T. STEELE, *Roger Bacon and the State of Science in the Thirteenth Century* (Oxford: Clarendon, 1921).

❧ HIGH MEDIEVAL EXPRESSION: LITERATURE, THE ARTS, AND MUSIC.   Chapter 24.

REAT productivity in fields of creative expression characterized the High Medieval cultural springtime. Literary and artistic achievements paralleled and reflected intellectual and scientific advances. Gothic cathedrals mirrored scholastic philosophy and theology; realistic sculpturing attested to renewed scientific interest in nature; complex musical polyphony and lofty stone structures applied the "new" mathematics; literary works in the vernacular resulted from a spread of popular education and lay literacy. Freshness and vigor, religious inspiration and idealism, keen aesthetic appreciation that was also intellectual, and an untiring capacity for taking pains marked High Medieval literature, architecture, arts, and music.

High Medieval Expression

LATIN LITERATURE IN THE HIGH MIDDLE AGES
Section 70.

> Praise, oh Sion, thy salvation,
> Praise with hymns of exultation
> Christ thy King and Shepherd true!
> [Beginning of a religious hymn composed by Thomas Aquinas (thirteenth century) for the Feast of Corpus Christi.]

WESTERN European literature during the High Middle Ages was of two kinds: Latin and vernacular. Latin was the old, established, respected, universal medium of communication; the vernaculars were new, suspect, revolutionary, and regional.

Most literature in Western Europe during the High Middle Ages was written in Latin. Although medieval Latin used the basic classical Latin vocabulary, the meanings of old words were often modified and new words were added. And though medieval writers studied and followed the rules in the classical Latin grammars of Priscian and Donatus, their style and word order were more "modern" and direct. They tended to follow a simple, standard, lucid sequence of subject, verb, and predicate, with adjectives and adverbs in close proximity to the words they modified. *Latin literature*

Study and imitation of classical Latin literature increased in the twelfth century to such an extent that the era has been termed by some authorities the Twelfth-Century Renaissance. Some of the scholars of the period wrote in a style that was very close to that of the Latin Golden Age. Among such authors were Hildebert of Lavardin, Peter of Blois, and John of Salisbury.

The most prolific field of superior Latin literature was religious hymns. Breathing ardent love is the representative *Jesu Dulcis Memoria* of St. Bernard of Clairvaux (twelfth century), which commences *Latin religious poetry: Twelfth century*

> *Jesus the very thought of Thee*
> *With sweetness fills my breast:*
> *But sweeter far thy face to see,*
> *And in thy presence rest!*

The "sequence," a hymn inserted between the gradual and the gospel in the liturgy, was brought to perfection by Adam of St. Victor in the twelfth century. His "Sequence for Christmas" begins

> *Since a Savior is born for us*
> *With the angels in glad chorus*
> *Let our people join today:*
> *Sweetly sound our hymns uprising,*
> *Different voices harmonizing*
> *All our praises in one lay.*

During the thirteenth century, Latin hymn writing reached its height. The *Veni Sancte Spiritus* attributed to Stephen Langton, Archbishop of Canterbury, begins: *Thirteenth century hymns*

> Come Holy Ghost, send forth those beams
> Which gently flow in silent streams
> From Thy bright throne above.
> Come, thou father of the poor,
> And bounteous source of all our store,
> Come, fire our hearts with love.

The somber mood of the day of judgment imbues the awsome *Dies Irae* (*Day of Wrath*), used for Masses for the Dead, and ascribed to Thomas of Celano, which begins:

> Day of wrath and day of mourning!
> See fulfilled the prophet's warning:
> Heaven and earth in ashes burning!
>
> Oh what fear man's bosom rendeth,
> When from heaven the Judge descendeth
> On whose sentence all dependeth!

The sympathizing *Stabat Mater* (*Stood the Mother*) reflects the poignant sorrow of Christ's mother during the crucifixion of her son:

> Stood the mournful Mother, weeping,
> At the cross her station keeping,
> As He hung, her son and Lord:
> Where her soul, of joy bereaved,
> Crushed with sorrow, deeply grieved,
> Felt the sharp and piercing sword.

Hymns of Aquinas   Thomas Aquinas, one of the greatest medieval philosopher theologians, was also among leading hymn writers. Thomas composed several hymns for the Feast of Corpus Christi (Body of Christ). His *Verbum Supernum Prodiens*, for Lauds, begins:

> The Heavenly Word proceeding forth—
> Yet leaving not the Father's side,
> And going to his work on earth,
> Had reached at length life's eventide.
>
> By a false disciple to be given
> To foemen for his blood athirst;
> Himself, the living bread from heaven,
> He gave to his disciples first.

The *Lauda Sion Salvatorem*, sung at the Corpus Christi Mass, runs in part:

> What he did at supper seated
> Christ ordained to be repeated
> In His memory divine:
> Wherefore now, with adoration,
> Consecrate from bread and wine.
> Hear what holy Church maintaineth:

High Medieval Expression

> *That the bread its substance changeth*
> *Into Flesh, the wine to Blood.*

The *Pange Lingua*, sung at Vespers on the same feast, concludes with the *Tantum Ergo*:

> *Therefore we, before him bending,*
> *This great Sacrament revere;*
> *Types and shadows have their ending,*
> *For the newer rite is here;*
> *Faith, our outward sense befriending,*
> *Makes the inward vision clear.*

Latin secular poetry of a light and humorous, often sensuous, and ribald type, composed mainly for the recreation and entertainment of students and younger clerics, is called "Goliardic" from a mythical Bishop Golias, the supposed founder of the order. Goliardic poetry, although written in Latin, celebrated such things as wine, women, and song. It redounds with praise of Bacchus, Venus, Cupid, the Muses, springtime, wine, damsels, taverns, trysts, caresses and kisses, music, and fun. It liberally indulges in humor, satire, and parody, and seems bent on shocking by its nonconformity. Typical members of the Goliardic tribe are described in the *Song of the Open Road*: *"Goliardic" Latin poetry*

> *We in our wandering*
> *Blithesome and squandering,*
> *Tara, tantara, teino!*
>
> *Eat to satiety,*
> *Drink with propriety,*
> *Tara, tantara, teino!*
>
> *Laugh till our sides we split,*
> *Rags on our hides we fit,*
> *Tara, tantara, teino!*
>
> *Jesting eternally*
> *Quaffing infernally,*
> *Tara, tantara, teino!*

The familiar spirit of youth is reflected in *The Confession of Golias*:

> *To my mind all gravity*
> *Is a grave subjection;*
> *Sweeter far than honey are*
> *Jokes and free affection.*
> *All that Venus bids me do,*
> *Do I with direction,*
> *For she ne'er in heart of man*
> *Dwelt with dull dejection.*

Latin prose flourished in a variety of forms, including didactic and learned literature (such as treatises on philosophy and theology, re- *Latin prose and drama* ligious sermons and ascetical treatises, polemical tracts and political broadsides, letters and correspondence, and histories and biographies. Hagiography, the writing of lives of saints, flourished, and it developed a form of its own, part fact and part fiction, in which prodigies, miracles, and edifying incidents were often assumed or borrowed, and the author might freely use his imagination to point up a moral. A famous, very popular collection and rewrite of several saints' lives was the *Legenda aurea* (*Golden Readings*), compiled by Jacobus de Voragine (James of Varragio) about 1255.

Simple dramatic representations evolved from the narrative dialogues contained in tropes inserted in the Mass during the ninth to tenth centuries. These tropes were subsequently transferred from the sacramental Mass to nonsacramental Matins, where they could enjoy a much freer scope. Eventually they moved from the church to the churchyard, and even to the town square, so that still greater flexibility was encouraged. Touchs of comedy were introduced at an early date, as in scenes involving Noah, Balaam, and Herod. Thus Noah's wife became a nagging shrew, Herod a blustering bully, and Mary Magdalen, before her conversion, a flirting temptress.

Mystery plays

Various forms of religious dramatic representations in Latin appeared. "Mystery plays" were representations of events related in the Old and New Testaments, especially happenings connected with the life of Christ. One of the first of such was an Easter play known as *The Visitation of the Sepulchre* (*Whom Do You Seek?*) (tenth to eleventh centuries), of which there are no less than 480 extant texts. This concerns the coming of Mary Magdalen to Christ's sepulchre on Easter Sunday morning. In one typical, simple version, an angel seated at the sepulchre asks the three Marys, "Whom seek ye in this sepulchre?" To which they reply: "We seek Jesus of Nazareth, who was crucified." The angel tells them: "He is not here: He is risen, as He foretold. Go and announce his Resurrection." Whereupon the Marys turn to the choir and sing: "The Lord is risen."

Among popular representations associated with the life of Christ, *The Shepherds* (eleventh century) concerned the coming of the shepherds to see the newborn Christ in the stable at Bethlehem. *The Star* (eleventh century) represented the coming of the Wise Men from the East, guided by a marvelous star. Among further subjects dramatized in the twelfth century were the *Raising of Lazarus* from the dead; the parable of *The Bridegroom*; the *Massacre of the Holy Innocents* by Herod; and the conversation of the *Travellers* with the risen Christ on the way to Emmaus. During the thirteenth century the final *Suffering* (*Passion*) of Christ was dramatized, as were also the *Entrance* into Jerusalem on Palm Sunday, the *Entombment* on Good Friday, the prophecies of the various *Prophets* concerning the coming of Christ, the story of the prophet *Daniel* who was thrown into the den of lions, and so on.

Miracle plays

"Miracle plays" were dramatic representations concerning the lives of saints, which probably developed in connection with the celebration of feast days of various saints. A favorite topic was the Blessed Virgin, and many plays were written concerning her intervention on behalf of sinners. Another popular subject was the kind-hearted St. Nicholas, concerning whose generous acts of charity a legendary cycle of several episodes developed. In the "Three Daughters," good St. Nick dropped a bag of gold down the chimney to provide a dowry for three impoverished sisters who would otherwise have been unable to marry. In the "Three Clerics" episode, St. Nicholas intervened to save the lives of three students who would otherwise have been slain, cut to pieces, and put in a salting vat by a thieving, murderous innkeeper.

In the Later Middle Ages (fourteenth to fifteenth centuries) another type of religious play also developed: the allegorical "morality play," in which the characters represented general ideas, such as virtues and vices. Plays entirely divorced from religious themes also appeared.

VERNACULAR LITERATURES IN THE HIGH MIDDLE AGES.
Section 71.

> "Sir Oliver, and good Sir Roland bold—
> For God I pray, do not each other scold:
> No help it were for us the horn to blow,
> But nonetheless it may be better so."

[Archbishop Turpin to Roland during the fray at Roncesvalles in *The Song of Roland* (twelfth century).]

VERNACULAR literatures began to blossom and bear early fruit during the High Middle Ages. French literature took the lead and served as an initial model. The two leading dialects of French in this period were the *langue d'oeil* (language of "*oeil*" for "yes") of northern France and the *langue d'oc* (language of "*oc*" for "yes") of southern France. The *langue d'oeil* eventually won out, with the ever-growing ascendance of the North. *French vernacular literature*

Early in the High Middle Ages the so-called *chansons de geste* or "songs (poems) of [heroic] feats" began to be written down in the northern French vernacular. These epic poems seem to have often originated as profitable devices for the entertainment of French pilgrims en route to shrines such as those of St. James (Santiago de Compostela) in northwestern Spain and St. William of Toulouse in southern France. They had some slight historical foundation that was freely elaborated by successive minstrels. Many of these *chansons* were recounted orally as early as the ninth to tenth centuries, and were committed to writing in their present form in the twelfth to thirteenth centuries. Over eighty *chansons de geste* survive, and include related cycles such as the "Carolingian Cycle," the "Cycle of Doon de Mayence," and the "Cycle of Garin de Monglane." *French chansons de geste*

The leading cycle was the Carolingian Cycle, of which some thirty examples survive. Among these the most popular and finished story was the famous *Song of Roland*, which concerned the heroic resistance of Charlemagne's rearguard to a Saracen attack while returning from a campaign in Spain. The story apparently originated from a brief statement in Einhard's *Life of Charles the Great* to the effect that "Roland, *Song of Roland*

Prefect of the Breton March" was "killed along with many others" when Charlemagne's rearguard was ambushed by Basques during the withdrawal of his army from Spain through the Pass of Roncesvalles (778).

In the stirring story, Count Roland is commander of the Frankish rearguard treacherously set upon by an immense force of Saracens. Though his small force is many times outnumbered, Roland refuses to blow his oliphant (signaling horn) until all his companions are slain and he himself is dying. Meanwhile he and his comrades each slay numerous Moslems. The vivid, action-packed poem of 400 ten-line verses is replete with lofty, chivalric ideals and a strong Christian faith.

As the Saracens approach, "a hundred thousand strong," his comrade Oliver implores Roland to sound his horn for aid:

> Says Oliver: "Pagans in force abound,
> While of us Franks but few I count;
> Comrade Roland, your horn I pray you sound!
> If Charles hear, he'll turn his armies 'round."
> Answers Roland: "A fool I should be found!
> In Sweet France would perish my renown.
> With Durendal I'll lay on thick and stout,
> In blood the blade to its golden hilt I'll drown.
> Felon pagans to th' pass shall not come down;
> I pledge you now, to death they are all bound."

When battle is joined, the Franks fight "manfully" and "the paynims are slain by thousands." Deeds of valor abound. When Archbishop Turpin slays the Negro Prince Abisme, the Franks observe:

> That was a good deed of arms:
> Safe is the crosier in the hands of our Archbishop!

In spite of their valor, the Franks are gradually overwhelmed by the enemy's "mighty host," which has "full twenty battles" (divisions) and "seven thousand trumpets."

Only when his little force is practically exterminated does Roland reconsider:

> The count Roland great loss of his men sees,
> His comrade Oliver he calls and speaks:
> "Sir and comrade, in God's name that you keeps,
> Such good vassals you see lie here in heaps:
> For France the Sweet, fair country, may we weep,
> Of such vassals long desolate she'll be."

Finally the wounded and dying Roland sounds his horn. Despite the attempts of the traitor Ganelon to dissuade him, Charlemagne orders his army to retrace their steps. They are an impressive sight:

> That even-tide is light as was the day,
> Their armour shines beneath the sun's clear ray,
> Hauberks and helms throw off a dazzling flame

High Medieval Expression

> *And blazoned shields, flowered in bright array,*
> *Also their spears, with golden ensigns gay.*

Meanwhile the dying Roland weeps for his dead companions "as fits a gentle knight":

> *"Lords and barons, may God to you be kind,*
> *And all your souls redeem for Paradise,*
> *And let you there mid holy flowers lie!*
> *Better vassals than you never saw I!"*

As dying "beneath a pine he sits," Roland recalls:

> *The many lands where he went conquering,*
> *And France the Sweet, the heroes of his kin,*
> *And Charlemagne, his lord, who nourished him.*

Finally he prepares his soul for death:

> *He owns his faults and God's forgiveness bids:*
> *"Very Father, in Whom no falsehood is,*
> *Good Lazarus from death thou didst remit,*
> *And Daniel saved from the lion's pit:*
> *My soul in me preserve from all perils,*
> *And from the sins in life I did commit!"*

Other chansons de geste — Although the best known, *The Song of Roland* is only one among several *chansons* in the Carolingian Cycle. The Cycle of Doon de Mayence or the Feudal Cycle concerns rebellious vassals who are eventually overcome. The Cycle of Garin de Monglane or The Religious Knight Cycle was originally inspired by the life and shrine of the warrior-saint Count William of Toulouse, who in 804 withdrew first to the monastery of Aniane and then to his own monastery of Gellone.

In addition there are several miscellaneous *chansons de geste* of various sorts, as well as the Crusade Epics, such as the *Chanson of Antioch*, the *Chanson of Jerusalem*, and *The Swan Knight*. The *chansons de geste* reflect the chivalric ideals, feudal concepts, and contemporary life of the High Middle Ages when they were written.

French chansons d'amour — Lyric poems of various types, often referred to generically as *chansons d'amour* (love songs), also developed in France. These were originally composed in the *langue d'oc* of southern France by so-called troubadours (finders, inventors). The form soon spread throughout Western Europe. It has been conjectured that these love lyrics may have been originally inspired by similar forms among the Moslems.

A great fad for the composition of such lyrics developed in southern France in the twelfth century. Nearly 2,500 Provencal lyrics of the twelfth to thirteenth centuries are still extant, and we know the names of some four hundred southern French troubadours, as well as those of some two hundred of their northern French counterparts, the trouveres. Among early sponsors of the movement were Duke William IX of Aquitaine (d. 1127) and his daughter, Eleanor of Aquitaine, as well as his granddaughter, Marie of Champagne. Poetic contests often paralleled knightly tournaments at such courts.

Among such lyrics, the most important and prevalent form was the ordinary love song or *chanson d'amour* proper. This was usually addressed to some idealized and inaccessible female, such as the wedded wife or already promised daughter of a powerful lord. The simple *chanson d'amour* is exemplified by the following from a long *Canso* of Bernart de Ventadorn (twelfth century):

> *With love and with delight*
> *My heart is flooded quite:*
> *Winter seems like summer bright,*
> *Snowdrifts leafy bowers.*
>
> *Now though all around me freezes,*
> *I, in light attire,*
> *Can defy the bitter breezes,*
> *Warmed by true love's fire.*

Variations A variation of the love song was the *salut d'amour* or love letter. The dawn song and evening song were also popular. In the *alba* or dawn song, the lovers typically deplore the advent of a new day, which means that they must part, as in the following verses:

> *Ah, would to God that never night must end*
> *Nor this my lover far from me should wend,*
> *Ah God, ah God, the dawn it comes too soon!*

From the amorous *serena* or evening song comes the term "serenade."

Other forms included *planhs, tensos, sirventes,* and *reverdies.* The *planh* or lament is exemplified by the plaint of a girl whose lover has gone on a Crusade:

> *No time my sorrow can assuage*
> *Till I behold him once again;*
> *He roams in weary pilgrimage,*
> *And I await in ceaseless pain.*
> *And though my lineage urge me long*
> *With threats another's bride to be,*
> *In vain they seek to do him wrong—*
> *All idle seem their frowns to me.*

The *tenso* was in the form of a dialogue or debate. The *sirventes* were poems on other subjects than love, such as politics and religion. The *reverdie* was a rejoicing at the return of spring. The *chanson-a-toile* was a work song at the loom. In the *pastourelle* a knight meets and woos a maiden in a rural setting.

Romances A new genre of poetic fiction, the "romances," arose out of a mixed background of adventure stories and love songs, chivalric ideals and religious concepts, Celtic legends from the British Isles and classical traditions from the Mediterranean world. The romances were so called because they were originally composed in the Old French vernacular *roman* tongue derived from Latin. They were written in poetic verse, and were meant to be recited with musical accompaniment. They combined daring exploits and deeds of heroism with lovemaking and powerful human emotions and included in addition, much of the marvelous and miraculous. There were two main cycles of romances: the British and the Classical.

The most common and popular romances were those of the British or Arthurian Cycle, which included such stories as those of *King Arthur and the Knights of the Round Table, Sir Galahad and the Holy Grail, Perceval* or *The Romance of the Grail, Merlin the Magician, Tristan and Iseult, Aucassin and Nicolete, Sir Lancelot,* and *Eric and Yvain.* Much of this material seems to have been based on earlier Celtic traditions, legends, and popular tales. In addition to inclusion of a strong love theme and often stupendous adventures, they usually dealt with magic and various wonders, and frequently had an unhappy, tragic, or questionable ending.

Arthurian Cycle

In the early twelfth century, Geoffrey of Monmouth dedicated about a seventh of his largely legendary and fictitious *British History* to the supposed victories and power of the British King Arthur, who ruled an extensive kingdom with wisdom and justice. This theme was subsequently expanded and elaborated in verse, giving rise to a large number of stories concerning King Arthur and the Knights of his Round Table (where none had precedence), in many of which Arthur was little more than a background figure. Leading twelfth-century authors who contributed to elaborating and polishing the Arthurian tales in French were Wace, the Anglo-Norman composer of rhymed chronicles, with his *Roman de Brut* (Brut was the reputed ancestor of Arthur) (ca. 1155); the gifted French (Norman) poetess Marie de France (d. 1189), who gave literary form to the Arthurian stories recounted by minstrels in her *Lais;* and the productive, popular Chretien de Troyes (d. 1180) from Champagne, who related stories of the Arthurian Cycle in verse in his *Cliges, Lancelot, Eric and Enid, Yvain,* and *Perceval*. In the Grail (drinking bowl) story, the Grail was eventually identified with the holy chalice used by Christ at the Last Supper, preserved by Joseph of Aramithea, and finally brought to Britain. Robert de Boron (Robert of Born) about 1200 in his *History of the Holy Grail* Christianized the Grail story, and glorified the religious element in the adventures of knights such as Perceval and Sir Galahad, who embodied some of the religious ideals of the contemporary Christian military orders. With their growing currency and popularity, the stories of the Arthurian Cycle were adapted and further elaborated in the thirteenth century by great German poets such as Hartman von Aue, Wolfram von Eschenbach, and Gottfried von Strassburg.

Typical of the Arthurian romances was *Aucassin and Nicolete*. The son of the Count of Beauclaire, Aucassin falls in love with Nicolete, a former Moslem slave, purchased and brought up by an old crusading soldier of the neighborhood. Aucassin's "infatuation" is thus described:

Aucassin and Nicolete

> Aucassin was of Beaucaire,
> Of a goodly castle there,
> But from Nicolete the fair,
> None might win his heart away
> Though his father, many a day,
> And his mother said him nay.

To his parents who urge him to

> " 'Choose a maid of high degree
> Such an one is meet for thee.' "

Aucassin replies:

> "Nay, for these I have no care:
> Nicolete is debonaire,
> Her body sweet and face of her
> Take my heart as in a snare:
> Loyal love is but her share
> That is so sweet!"

Nor will he be dissuaded by the old crusader, who holds Nicolete a prisoner in her chamber and refuses to let Aucassin see her, saying: *If thou hadst word with her, and thy father knew it, he would burn in a fire both her and me.* To which Aucassin sorrowfully replies: *That is just what irketh me.*

But Aucassin will not be deterred from his love: neither by the persuasions and commands of his parents, nor by imprisonment, nor by all manner of hardships. He even rescues Nicolete from renewed captivity. When it is discovered ultimately that Nicolete is really the daughter of the King of Carthage, all are reconciled to the marriage. The vivid narrative is mainly in prose, with key descriptions and reflections in verse.

Classical cycle   The Classical Cycle of romances was inspired by known or supposed events of Greco-Roman (including Byzantine) history and legend, elaborated and ornamented with imaginative abandon. Although some of the Classical Romances actually appeared earlier than the Arthurian Romances, they were more restrained and restricted by the greater amount of historical data available concerning their subjects, as well as the more remote, less easily comprehensible nature of their setting. The Classical Romances are often subdivided into those concerning Ancient Rome, Ancient Greece, Alexander the Great, and the Byzantine Empire. They originated from the natural inclination to give poetic vernacular versions of stories included in such Latin works as the *Aeneid* of Vergil and the *Thebais* of Statius for popular entertainment.

Allegorical Romance   The romance also progressed into the realm of allegory, wherein figures and events become symbols for deeper meanings. The popular thirteenth-century *Romance of the Rose* had two authors. The composer of the first 4,200 verses was William de Lorris, who took the traditional approach of romantic love and chivalric ideals, and drew freely on Ovid and Andrew the Chaplain. In the poem William declares his infatuation with a

High Medieval Expression

beautiful rose on a gorgeous rosebush in a garden close. With his heart pierced by an arrow of the God of Love, he yearns to possess the rose and is favored by such characters as Gladness, Generosity, Hope, Nobility, and Courtesy, as well as Love itself. On the other hand he is opposed by such characters as Hatred, Wickedness, Avarice, Envy, Melancholy, Hypocrisy, Poverty, Slander, and Fear.

At the outset, William de Lorris describes his enchantment:

> *Beside the spring a while I stayed,*
> *Admiring how the crystals made*
> *Mirrors for all the lovely things*
> *That filled the garden . . .*
>
> . . . .
>
> *From all things mirrored there I chose*
> *A rose bush, charged with many a rose,*
> *Surrounded by a thick grown hedge,*
> *And doubt not if I held in pledge*
> *Paris and Pavia faithfully,*
> *My heart would surely then agree*
> *To render up the two, so I*
> *Might gaze on it unceasingly.*

Despite his ardor, the repeated efforts of the gentle and idealistic William, constantly deterred by new obstacles, end in failure and frustration.

Jean de Meun

The second part of the *Romance of the Rose* consists of some 18,000 lines composed by Jean de Meun. The second author had a more practical and realistic, even satirical approach, and indulged in several digressions displaying his sagacity and learning. In his account, Jean will not be balked, and calls in further down-to-earth forces such as Reason, Sweet-Speech, False-Appearance, Restraint, Genius, and Nature for his assault. By such unscrupulous stratagems, he gains possession of the rose—and then awakens.

Jean has been called "the Voltaire of the Middle Ages." His work is characterized by snatches of medieval learning and philosophical reflections. After describing various ways whereby men try to elude Death, Jean says:

> *And thus it is that all men try*
> *Vainly the grip of Death to fly.*
>
> . . . .
>
> *But he with fearful blackened face*
> *To all these fugitives gives chase.*
>
> . . . .
>
> *His foot will overtake at last,*
> *And though it seem as if he passed*
> *Some few, he turns himself again*
> *To strike them down. Futile and vain*
> *Is medicine at last; each one*
> *He catches when his course is run:*

The High Middle Ages

> *Even the great physicians he*
> *Seizes, however skilled they be.*

Yet it is not death, but life, aided by the resources of Nature, that will ultimately win out. Though individuals perish, life will continue with the aid of

> *Nature, who is the fond ally*
> *Of all live things beneath the sky.*

For fond Nature always manages to preserve the spark and seed of life:

> *All things Nature fashions so*
> *That never shall a species know*
> *The power of Death; but as one dies*
> *Immediately others rise*
> *To fill its place.*

Thus Death never really triumphs:

> *And still, no matter how he strives,*
> *All living things he never drives*
> *At once within his net, nor shapes*
> *His snares so well that none escapes.*

French stories (fabliaux) and drama

Fabliaux (stories) were versified fictional stories of an entertaining nature. Sometimes they were satirical or quasi-didactic; often they were simply amusing. Many high medieval *fabliaux* were based on folk tales or popular stories long current before they were written down, as was the case with *The Story of the Seven Sages*. Only some of the *fabliaux* concern animals, although the English term "fables" is often reserved for those *fabliaux* that endow animals with human characteristics. A leading example of such animal fables was the collection known as *Romance of Renard the Fox*, whose stock characters included the crafty and resourceful Renard the Fox, the timid Couart (Coward) the Hare, and the voluble Chanticleer the Cock.

The mystery and miracle plays that evolved from dramatic episodes in the liturgy of major feasts were originally composed in Latin. But it was not long before they were rendered in the French vernacular, since they were meant to entertain and edify the whole congregation. Among early mystery and miracle plays in French were *La Seinte Resurrection* (*The Holy Resurrection*) for Easter, which originated in England in the twelfth century; the *Mystere d'Adam* (*The Mystery of Adam*), written in Anglo-Norman French in the twelfth century, prefiguring the salvation of the world by the stories of Adam and Eve and Cain and Abel; the *Prophecies*, concerning the coming of Christ; and finally the very popular *Jeu de St. Nicolaus* (*Play of St. Nicholas*) by Jean Bodel. In the last, the Moslem King of Africa and his subjects, after defeating the Christians in battle, are converted to Christianity through the influence of good St. Nicholas. There were numerous plays known as *Les Miracles de Notre Dame* (*Miracles of Our Lady*) concerning incidents wherein the efficacious intercession of the Blessed Virgin saved sinners.

High Medieval Expression

Notable advances were made in German vernacular literature during the High Middle Ages, partly imitating French examples, but also expressing native German genius and vitality. In its eleventh- and early twelfth-century beginnings, German literature usually consisted of ecclesiastical and didactic poetry on such subjects as *Death, The Creed, Solomon, Judith,* and *Christ.* Signs of a new departure are seen in more worldly poems concerning *Archbishop Anno* and *King Rothari.* German versions of French *chansons de geste* such as the *Eneit* (concerning Aeneas) and the *Alexanderslied* and *Rolandslied* (*Lied*: song, poem) were made in the twelfth century, and already included much material that was native German.

German literature: The Minnesingers

German love lyrics or *Minnesang* (love songs), composed by the *Minnesingers* (love-singers), German counterparts of the French troubadours and trouveres, although influenced by French example, were still more original. German love lyrics soon developed their own characteristics, one of which was that they were generally more spiritual and idealized than the French *chansons d'amour.*

The art of the Minnesingers reached its height in the thirteenth century with Walther von der Vogelweide (Walter of the Birdmeadows), so called because he said that he had learned the art of composing songs from the birds, which are often featured in his poetry. A love song of Walther to his lady points out the beauties of May and then urges her:

Walther von der Vogelweide

> *Lady, part me from my sadness:*
> *Love me while 'tis May;*
> *Mine is but a borrowed gladness*
> *If thou frown alway.*

A "Day-dream" by Walther suggests his interest in birds:

> *'Twas summer,—through the opening grass*
> *The joyous flowers upsprang,*
> *The birds in all their diff'rnt tribes*
> *Loud in the woodlands sang.*

In a polemic against Pope Innocent III, Walther says:

> *A necromancer holds the Roman chair—*
> *In the black art Pope Gerbert's heir:*
> *But Gerbert gave none save himself to Hell—*
> *This one will give all Christendom as well!*

The leading medieval German heroic epic was the *Nibelungenlied,* often referred to as "the Iliad of the Germans," finished about 1200. Replete with bloodshed, intrigue, and tragedy, this long epic of over 11,000 lines was a composite of various legends. In it the daring Netherlandish prince Siegfried, who, by slaying two Nibelung kings has won a cloak whereby he can become invisible, and who gains bodily invulnerability (save for one fell spot) by overcoming a fierce dragon, woos the lovely Burgundian princess, Kriemhild. During his courtship, Siegfried

German epic poetry and romances

helps Kriemhild's brother, King Gunther of Burgundy, subdue and win the superhumanly strong Icelandic princess Brunhild by secretly replacing him in contests with Brunhild. On learning of the deception from the jealous Kriemhild, Brunhild is distressed, and confidants feel that her brother, King Gunther, is discredited. Whereupon Gunther's scheming minister Hagen decides to kill Siegfried, whom he treacherously murders during a hunt, utilizing information from Kriemhild about the hero's vulnerable spot. The hardened Kriemhild now relentlessly seeks revenge and marries Etzel (Attila), King of the Huns, whom she urges to war. Hatred, vengeance, bloodshed, and tragedy multiply. Finally the Burgundians are defeated and taken prisoner by a coalition that includes the Huns and Ostrogoths. Gunther is beheaded at Kriemhild's orders, and Hagen is slain by her own hand; whereupon the outraged, aged Ostrogothic hero Hildebrand cuts down Kriemhild. Two other German epics composed in the thirteenth century were the *Kudrum* (or *Gudrum*) with stories concerning the sea, and the *Heldenbuch* (or *Hero's Book*) with miscellaneous exciting adventure stories.

The German court epics were a further adaptation of the French romances of the Arthurian Cycle. Although the German poets of the thirteenth century used French themes and plots for their romances, they brought them to fuller development, with great sensitivity and idealism. Among leading German authors of works in this genre were Wolfram von Eschenbach with *Parzival*, Hartmann von Aue with *Iwein* (*Yvain*), and Gottfried von Strassburg with *Tristan*. An extract from the last is

> Love doth the loved one fairer make,
> And love a stronger life doth take;
> Love's eyes wax keener day by day,
> Else love would fade and pass away.

Early Italian literature

The rise of Italian vernacular literature in the thirteenth century was assisted by Franciscan and French influences. Early examples of lyric poetry in the Italian vernacular were the religious poems of Francis of Assisi and his associates. St. Francis saw God's love manifested in creation, as in his *Canticle of the Sun*:

> Praise be to Thee, my Lord, with all thy creatures,
> Especially to my wond'rous brother, the sun,
> Who lights up the day and brightness gives.
> . . . .
> Praised be my Lord for sister moon and the stars
> . . . .
> Praised be my Lord for brother wind
> And for the air and clouds
> And every form of weather.
> Praised by my Lord for sister water
> Who is so highly helpful,
> And humble and precious and pure.

High Medieval Expression

Sensitive mystical religious songs were composed by Francis' inspired disciple, Jacopone da Todi, one of whose poems was a possible prototype of Francis Thompson's *Hound of Heaven:*

> *Oh man, for thy soul's new birth.*
> *Who still wouldst fly from me,*
> *While I to save thee wait.*
> *Oh man, for thy soul's new birth.*

A religious impulse also stimulated the beginnings of Italian vernacular drama in the thirteenth century. Apparently inspired by French *chansons d'amour*, the *dolce still nuovo* (sweet new style) mentioned by Dante was cultivated by Italian poets such as Dante's master, Guido Cavalcanti, in the thirteenth century. Cavalcanti classes together:

> *Beauty in women, the high will's decree;*
> *Fair knighthood, arm'd for manly exercise;*
> *The pleasant song of birds; love's soft replies;*
> *The strength of rapid ships upon the sea;*
> *The serene air when light begins to be. . . .*

Although delayed by Moorish rule and the hardships of the Reconquest, as well as by a multiplicity of dialects, Spanish literature developed rapidly in the High Middle Ages, drawing on French and Moslem sources but displaying native vigor and flavor. One of the great classics of the Middle Ages, the swashbuckling *Poema de Mio Cid* was written about the middle of the twelfth century. The *Poem of My Cid* concerns the adventures and trials of an eleventh-century Castilian frontier hero, Rodrigo (Ruy) Diaz de Bivar, who is unjustly exiled by his King, Alfonso VI, but eventually obtains possession of the principality of Valencia by dint of shifting alliances and courageous leadership. The *Poem of the Cid* may be justly compared to *The Song of Roland*. The Cid's charge at Alcocer is thus narrated: *Spanish vernacular literature*

> *With bucklers braced before their breasts, with lances pointing low,*
> *With stooping crests, and heads bent down upon the saddle-bow,*
> *All firm of hand and high of heart, they roll upon the foe.*

Having slain in fair fight the father of his beloved, the Cid is nominated by the King to be her protector and accepts:

> *And now before the altar the bride and bridegroom stand,*
> *And when to fair Jimena the Cid stretched forth his hand,*
> *He spake in great confusion: "Thy father have I slain—*
> *Not treacherously, but face to face, my just revenge to gain*
> *For cruel wrong; a man I slew, a man I give to thee:*
> *In place of thy dead father a husband find in me!"*

Among other high medieval Spanish *cantares de gesta* were these concerning *King Roderick* of the Visigoths and Count *Fernan Gonzales* of Castile. In the thirteenth century King Alfonso X, the Wise of Castile, directed and helped prepare extensive vernacular histories known as the

Spanish History and the *General History*. Alfonso and his coworkers collected over 420 hymns in honor of the Virgin, known as the *Cantigas de Santa Maria*, one of whose typical lilting refrains are exemplified by

> Rose of all roses, fairest of flowers:
> Queen of all women, endowed with all powers.

Scandinavian literature

Early Scandinavian poetry, which was committed to writing from the tenth century on, has survived almost exclusively in Icelandic. It consisted mainly of *sagas*: stirring adventure stories about heroes and myths concerning the gods. Collections of sagas and other medieval Icelandic literature are known as *eddas*, a term also applied to their components. The *Older* (*Earlier*) or *Poetic Edda* is a collection of thirty-four poems written down between the tenth and twelfth centuries. The poems are almost entirely pagan in tone and spirit. The *Younger* (*Later*) or *Prose Edda* is a collection made by the great thirteenth-century Icelandic scholar and chieftain Snorri Sturluson. Intended mainly as a guidebook for poets, it contains legends, myths, histories, directions for poetic composition, and examples of earlier poetry.

THE ARTS AND MUSIC IN THE HIGH MIDDLE AGES.
Section 72.

> It was as though the world had bestirred herself, and, shaking off her old age, was clothing herself with a new white garment of churches. [Raoul Glaber (Monk of Cluny, d. 1044) concerning eleventh-century construction of Romanesque churches.]

THE High Middle Ages were a distinguished epoch in the history of architecture, art, and music. Products included magnificent Romanesque and Gothic cathedrals; imaginative and expressive as well as decorative sculptures; colorful storytelling stained glass windows, rich miniature painting in manuscripts; and complex harmonious polyphonic music. The chief subject matter and purpose were religious, but there was also progress in secular forms of the arts and music.

Romanesque architecture

The leading art in the High Middle Ages was architecture, which was mainly concerned with the construction of "the house of God" and "the meeting place of the Christian people." Earlier church architecture, as we have seen, employed Basilican, Byzantine, Germanic, and Proto-Romanesque styles. The full Romanesque style developed and prevailed in the eleventh century and the first half of the twelfth. Although Romanesque bore certain resemblances to classical Roman architecture, it was a new and different style. Romanesque utilized round, semicircular arches and had stone vaulting over the entire church, including the nave as well as the aisles. It was integrated, and emphasized spatial organization.

Romanesque stone vaulting

Full Romanesque was achieved when stone vaulting was used over the nave as well as over the aisles of churches. Stone vaulting had two main purposes: to cut down on the incidence of fires, which occurred frequently because of the means of lighting and heating in those days; and to give greater consistency and more balanced beauty to the interior of the church by use of stone throughout. Stone vaulting went through various steps in its evolution.

The initial and simplest form of stone vaulting was the so-called tunnel vault, produced by projecting the arch the entire length of the nave. The tunnel vault, however, had important shortcomings. Because of its unbroken continuity, it required meticulous perfection and absolute uniformity to avoid marring its appearance. It also had to be built in one continuous operation, and required a large and expensive amount of scaffolding. The tunnel vault demanded extra-heavy massive walls and allowed for very little window space. Finally, it produced a monotonous effect. Some relief was provided by segmenting the tunnel vault, whereby heavier protruding bands bearing a greater proportion of the weight crossed the vault at intervals.

More ingenious and pleasing was the groined vault. In this, the nave was divided into bays with weight-bearing piers at their four corners and two semicircular vaults intersecting each other at right angles in "groins" over each bay. Usually such bays were square with intersecting semicircular vaults of equal radius. The groins or intersections carried the main weight to the four supporting piers.

A further and important development was ribbed vaulting. In this, heavier intersecting arches were constructed laterally around as well as transversely across each bay (in the latter case along lines where intersecting groins would otherwise appear), giving a total of six weight-bearing arches for each bay. These arches carried the weight to four piers, with the rest of the vaulting being fill-in. An additional refinement of the ribbed vaulting system was to have one nave bay to each two aisle bays and to have a single arch crossing the nave bay from central pier to central pier (as in the churches of St. Stephen and The Trinity at Caen). In this case there were nine arches per nave bay: two on each side, one at each end, one across the middle, and two transverse arches.

The use of round arches helped to give Romanesque churches an air of solid containment and repose, which was accentuated by the fact that the walls had to be heavy and the windows small so as to support the great weight and outward thrust of the rounded stone vaulting. The window openings were often splayed outward in order to admit more light. Round "wheel windows" or "rose windows" appeared, although these were necessarily limited in their dimensions. Arches were often compounded, as along the aisles to convert larger arches into multiple smaller ones and provide a gallery above the lower aisle. Compound supports were also common, as in the "clustered piers" where each of the converging arches terminated in a protruding interlocked segment of the pier. The Romanesque is also noted for increased representational carving both inside and outside the church.

Other features of the Romanesque

The general plan of Romanesque churches was increasingly complex. Both the apse and the transept were elaborated, with radiating aisles or ambulatories and with side chapels and niches. Sometimes there were double transepts and sometimes even double apses, in which latter case entrances were at the sides of the church. Towers and occasional domes were also more frequent. Sometimes there was a tower over the entrance, or two towers might flank the entrance. Sometimes there was a tower or dome over the intersection of nave and transept. Occasionally towers and domes were multiplied.

Regional variations of Romanesque

Romanesque is characterized by regional variations. Its place of origin seems to have been Lombardy in northern Italy. Here a privileged order of stonemasons known as the *Comacini* or Master Stonemasons was already in existence as early as the seventh century. Here too we have the earliest known churches exemplifying the full Romanesque. The mid-eleventh-century Cathedral of Pisa is transitional with its wooden ceiling over the nave. The full Romanesque is seen in the Old St. Ambrose Church in Milan with its groined stone vaulting over both nave and aisles. Notable other early examples include the Church of San Michele at Lucca and Modena Cathedral. Special features of the Lombard and neighboring Tuscan styles of Romanesque architecture included detached towers apart from the church, as in the case of the "leaning tower" of Pisa, polygonal domes set over the intersection of nave and transepts, and blind arcades or rows of arches and pillars along the outside or inside walls of the church without any true arcade behind them.

There were numerous styles of Romanesque in France. Romanesque flourished in southern France, where it was especially cultivated by monasteries. The Provençal style was characterized by extensive representational stone carving of Biblical subjects in a manner reminiscent of the classical on the façade of the splendid western portal (the main entrance) of the church.

The Burgundian style was marked by a profusely carved, semicircular tymphanum or lunette over the entrance, as well as a large porch or narthex.

The Auvergnese style had a continuous tunnel vault over the nave and an octagonal tower over the intersection of nave and transept. The Aquitanian style featured multiple domes on pendentives and a stumpy, bossy tower reminiscent of a pinecone. In the Poitevan style, the side aisles were almost equal in height with the nave.

The Norman Romanesque style, which reached a high stage of development in Normandy, placed emphasis on vertical dimension and structural logic and had a minimum of decorations, together with an air of severity. The Normans developed advanced ribbed vaulting with sexpartite arches and even rudimentary flying buttresses.

The Norman style of Romanesque spread to England, where it was exemplified by Edward the Confessor's construction of Westminster, which was subsequently replaced. After the Conquest (1066) the building of Romanesque churches was promoted by the new Norman rulers for political as well as religious reasons. The English Romanesque is massive and squarish, with tall piers and numerous bays.

The Romanesque took strong roots in Germany, where it became a favorite style. The Germans went in for great complex churches with a multiplicity of structural elements, such as several towers, double transepts, double apses, and numerous side chapels.

The Romanesque also spread to Spain, where it was promoted by the Cluniacs and derived from southwestern France. Moslem influences were also apparent in such features as horseshoe and cusped arches, as well as the inclusion of fountains.

Gothic architecture evolved from the Romanesque in the twelfth century. The term "Gothic" was originally applied to the style as synonymous with "Germanic barbarian" by humanists and artists of the Italian Renaissance, who regarded it with contempt; but it is now recognized as one of the truly great achievements in architectural history.

Gothic architecture

Distinguishing elements of Gothic include pointed arches, flying buttresses, and large stained glass windows. Churches in this style were constructed as lofty integrated skeletons, whose framework of piers, ribs, and buttresses both reinforced each other and supported the intervening skinlike covering of glass and other lighter materials. Although each of these features had appeared in some degree in previous structures, they had never been completely integrated and carried to their full development.

Pointed arches allow for greater height and carry the eye upward as in prayer. Being pointed, they are not restrained in altitude by a fixed radius as are semicircular arches. Nor do they exert such a strong outward horizontal thrust since they concentrate more of it in a downward vertical direction. They allow greater flexibility and attention to practical and aesthetic considerations. Whereas round arches generally postulate limited heights, breadths, and lengths, conditioned by their fixed radii, pointed arches may be easily stilted for a variety of dimensions. Since the structure is a ribbed skeleton, it greatly cuts down the expense of construction per unit area because of the reduced amount of timber framework required during the building operation and the lesser amount of heavy stone for the final structure. The space between the ribs can be filled in with any appropriate weather-resistant material, such as glass or light stone. The flying buttresses contribute to the same general ends by reinforcing the ribs, absorbing the increased outward thrust resulting from augmented height, and carrying the latter from upper and inner areas to the lower and heavier external walls and piers. Made possible by the skeletal structure of interlocking pointed arches and flying buttresses, large stained glass windows along the walls beautified the church and bathed its interior in rich colored light.

As compared to previous styles, Gothic architecture has greater structural unity and articulation, as well as greater height and height impression. It also attains greater articulation of form and space, and greater vertical and lateral (west to east) movement. It is sprightly and airy for all of its mass, viewed both externally and in its light-flooded interior. Increased intricacy and complexity are counterbalanced by greater structural unity and logic. At the same time vastness of conception leaves room for greater freedom and variation, as in its broken skyline and differentiated towers. Gothic architecture has been described as "a symphony in stone" and "the architectural counterpart of the great theological *Summas*" that strove to coordinate every aspect of human experience. Fully to appreciate the Gothic achievement, it must be remembered that

Early Gothic

in these lofty churches stone and mortar were the basic structural materials on which the stability of the whole building was completely dependent, whereas today the supporting skeleton of large buildings is steel.

Gothic architecture is usually subdivided into Early, High, and Late Gothic. The new style originated in northwestern France in the second half of the twelfth century, in connection with efforts to achieve greater height and better articulation. The Early Gothic—of the twelfth century—is simpler and less sophisticated. Its initial example seems to have been the Abbey Church of St. Denis (about two miles north of Paris) as rebuilt (1140ff.) by Abbot Suger. The choir of the abbey church with its marvelous walls of stained glass surrounded by a circlet of chapels was described as a "lantern." The new style was soon adopted elsewhere and spread rapidly in the second half of the twelfth century, being exemplified in the cathedrals of Noyon (ca. 1150ff.), Sens, Senlis, and Laon.

High Gothic in France

In the thirteenth century, with High Gothic, the style reached maturity and attained its apogee of complexity, refinement, and integration. The fascinating unity and restrained grandeur of the exterior were surpassed only by the soaring upward movement and classic moderation of the complex, harmonious interior. France, the birthplace of Gothic, was also the scene of its greatest achievements. French High Gothic was characterized by impressive façades with rich stone carving; beautiful towers on either side of the western façade; a cruciform ground plan with a transept; successive levels of construction enhancing both the exterior and interior; abundant narrative sculpturing on outside and inside, subordinated to the general architecture; the impressive eastern aspect of the apse with its radial chapels, stained glass windows, and flying buttresses; and the jeweled radiance and mellow lighting of its superb stained glass windows. Southern French Gothic differed somewhat from northern French Gothic by having less glass and less sculpturing, as well as disguised buttresses.

Crowning examples of High Gothic are the great cathedrals of Paris, Chartres, Reims, and Amiens, each with its own special virtues. The Cathedral of Notre Dame, Paris, is noted for the charming flying buttresses around its apse, its humorous gargoyles, and the classic restraint of its western facade. It has double aisles (making a total of four aisles) around both its nave and choir. The Cathedral of Chartres, the simplest of the great Gothic cathedrals, is considered by many to be most beautiful. Its rich stained glass windows are unsurpassed. Its relatively simple, though beautiful western facade is rivaled by the richness of its north and south portals. Over ten thousand personages are represented in its windows and sculpturing; and it has some three hundred statues at its northern entrance alone. The two towers on either side of its front facade are unequal, being constructed at different times, but this does not diminish its beauty.

The Cathedral of Reims, noted for its magnificent, many-tiered western facade, replete with statues, has been characterized as "pompous." Altogether the imposing cathedral has some five thousand carved images. Its

High Medieval Expression

western façade has a great rose window above, a smaller one below. Its three portals are lined with series of statuary, and its twin towers are delicately ornamented. Stone window tracery made its debut at Reims. Most spacious of all the French High Gothic cathedrals, possessing the loftiest nave, and often characterized as the culmination of Gothic, is the Cathedral of Amiens (1220ff.). Amiens is 140 feet high at the apex of its nave, about 475 feet long, and 216 feet wide. The vast space it encloses is surpassed only by St. Peter's, Sancta Sophia, and Cologne Cathedral, the last being a slightly modified imitation. In France alone, some eighty cathedrals and over five hundred churches of cathedral proportions were constructed in the century from 1170 to 1270.

From France the new style soon spread to other countries. In most it was imported as High Gothic and soon became Late Gothic. Receptive to Gothic at an early date was England, where Henry III built Westminster Cathedral east of the nave, namely, the choir and transept, in the new style. English cathedrals are usually squarish or rectangular, with greater repose, and they generally stand in a park with landscaping that does much to beautify their appearance. The facade is often a sort of ornamental screen, bearing little structural relation to the body of the church, whose flying buttresses are often concealed. The crowning, best-integrated example of English Gothic was probably Salisbury Cathedral, built from 1220 to 1270, which featured double transepts, a high pointed tower over the juncture of the second transept and nave, and a squarish apse. *High Gothic elsewhere*

Spain, "an artistic province of France" in this period, also built numerous Gothic cathedrals, which often recall French cathedrals although they have a strong Spanish flavor.

Germany was not so receptive to Gothic, having already indulged strongly in Romanesque. The leading German example of the new style was Cologne Cathedral, which, despite its beauty, has been characterized as "a thin and dry amplification of the cathedral of Amiens, uninspired except for its twin towers, which rise five hundred feet in the air."

Gothic was even less popular in Italy, where Romanesque was more of a native form, and the thicker walls and small windows of Romanesque were better adapted to the sunny, warm climate. Still, Italian churches, such as the cathedrals of Siena and Orvieto, were built in the new style.

High medieval church architecture was constructed under the direction of master stonemasons, who were at once architects and sculptors, superintendents and craftsmen, entrepreneurs and contractors. Although they usually had preliminary general plans and sketches, much of their decision making and adaptation were done on the scene as the work progressed. Their training was mainly in the schools of practical apprenticeship and experience. *Master stonemasons*

There was also much secular building in stone during the High Middle Ages. Stone castles, which along with cathedrals came to dominate the landscape, were built with ever-increasing complexity and effectiveness. Many became virtually impregnable, with sturdy successive concentric walls, moats and drawbridges, portcullises and parapets, towers and tur- *Secular buildings* rets. Closely related to castles in form and function were the strong walls built around many towns in this period. Gates and towers both relieved the monotony and increased the efficacy of such walls, which were often approached on one or more sides by bridges. Most of the town halls and guild halls constructed in this period have unfortunately disappeared because they have been replaced by other structures.

Arts other than architecture

Arts in the High Middle Ages were characterized by unity amidst complexity, impressionism mixed with realism, intellectualism relieved by humor, and a strong religious spirit counterbalanced by an obvious appreciation of both natural and man-made beauty. High medieval art was deeply imbued with symbolism and allegory. A leading authority says: *The art of the Middle Ages is first and foremost a sacred writing of which every artist must learn the characters.*[a] Thus a nimbus behind the head signified saintliness, and a nimbus with a cross, divinity; horizontal undulating lines represented water, and concentric sinuous lines the sky; a hand emerging from a cloud symbolized divine providence and intervention. St. Matthew is represented as a man, because he dwells on the human generation of Christ; St. Mark as a lion, because he stresses Christ's lineage and dignity; St. Luke as an ox, because he elaborates on Christ's priestly sacrifice for mankind; and St. John as an eagle, because of his soaring mystic vision. Particular saints are identified by objects associated with their lives: St. Peter by a key, St. Nicholas by three golden balls, St. Barbara by a tower. Old Testament events are understood as prefiguring those of the New, so that the priest Melchisedeck offering bread and wine typifies Christ establishing the Eucharist, and Jonah in the belly of the whale foreshadows Christ's entombment prior to His Resurrection. High medieval art, like high medieval architecture, went through two phases: the simple, more direct, vigorous, but less developed Romanesque style; and the complex, better coordinated, technically superior, and more mature Gothic style.

[a] Emile Mâle, *Religious Art from the Twelfth to the Eighteenth Century* (New York: Pantheon, 1949), p. 1.

High medieval sculpture

The High Middle Ages were one of the great periods in the history of sculpture. Representational and decorative sculptures were an integral part of both Romanesque and Gothic cathedrals, whose sculptured figures frequently numbered in the thousands. High medieval sculpture was subordinated to architecture, but in such a way as to preserve its own vigor, originality, and naturalism. The figures of human beings represented in connection with Gothic cathedrals are usually elongated, yet the faces are those of real persons and their accoutrements have every semblance of reality. To a degree, the architecture reinforces the sculptures just as the latter beautify the former. The high medieval combination of impressionism with realism is particularly congenial to modern taste. Whereas Romanesque sculpture often has nervous movement, Gothic sculpture tends to breathe repose and completeness. One authority characterizes sculpturing in the French High Gothic cathedrals: *As statues in their own right, above criticism. As architectural decoration: unexcelled.* . . .[b]

[b] John I. Sewall, *A History of Western Art* (New York: Holt, 1953), p. 525.

High medieval sculpturing used bas-reliefs, figures emerging from a connected background as from pillars and capitals, and statues in the round. Favorite topics included figures and events from Biblical history,

High Medieval Expression

Church history, and lives of saints. All sorts of animals, real and imaginary, as well as plants and flowers were represented, along with various types of humans, including contemporary persons. Also depicted were activities of the workaday world, such as digging, sowing, harvesting, building with wood and stone, spinning, and weaving. General ideas were likewise represented, such as virtues and vices, bravery and cowardice, the seven liberal arts, and the zodiacal cycle of the year. To some extent, representations in medieval cathedrals were illustrated Scriptures for the laity, as well as summaries of both visible reality and faith in the invisible.

Painting: illumination of manuscripts

Painting existed principally in two forms: wall frescoes and illuminations in manuscripts. Fresco painting declined in the North because of the introduction of stained glass windows; elsewhere, as in Italy, its examples have usually been obliterated by time. Painting was for some time dominated by the formal, standardized "Byzantine manner," until the thirteenth century when the Italian painter Cimabue and after him the great Giotto, with his realistic frescoes of the lives of St. Francis and Christ, began to break away from it.

Anticipating many aspects of Renaissance painting were numerous excellent miniature pictures illustrating and adorning manuscripts. The chief producers of such illuminations were monks; their main themes sacred history; and their principal products illustrated religious books, including Bibles, Missals, and Lectionaries.

Romanesque illumination (to c. 1200) is inclined to be bold, dramatic, direct, and elemental. It often has luxuriant, free-running borders, sprinkled here and there with animals, birds, and human beings, extending around all or part of the text. It also employs large ornamental initial letters containing scenes illustrating the text. Gold backgrounds with lozenges, checkers, or other patterns are common.

Gothic illumination of the thirteenth century was more delicate, refined, harmonized with the text, and technically mature. Gothic illuminations were also smaller, owing partly to the fact that less clumsy, handier books now came to be preferred to the huge volumes of the Romanesque period.

Stained glass

The art of making stained glass windows attained the summit of its perfection in the High Middle Ages. This *ars Francigena*, born in northern France, utilized the large window spaces afforded by Gothic construction. The didactic and decorative function of previous wall murals was now performed by the large stained glass windows that replaced them. Illuminated by external light, the windows not only told their stories in a dramatic way but also bathed the church in a soft flood of rich and radiant colors.

The painstaking high medieval technique of making stained glass and composing pictures in this medium has never been equaled. Deep, rich colors were infused by adding pigments to molten glass, as well as by painting colored or clear glass with colored glass ground to powder and fusing this to the groundwork in a furnace. Various colors superimposed upon the same piece of glass were often separated by narrow strips of flat wire or thin metal (the *cloisonné* process). Glass windows representing various subjects and scenes were made by assembling numerous small pieces of glass (usually ranging from the size of a finger to that of a hand), setting them in ribs of lead reinforced and attached by strands of fine wire, and fitting these in sections of steel, all put within a framework of stone, giving them sufficient solidity to withstand the buffetings of the weather. Stained glass experts apparently worked in groups or "schools," moving to a new location when their work at a particular site was completed.

Other arts

Among arts that reached a high state of development was that of weaving representational tapestries. A superb example of a medieval tapestry having the simple vigor of the Romanesque era was the famous Bayeux Tapestry, celebrating the Norman Conquest of England (1066). This was made shortly after the Conquest, apparently by the ladies of Bayeux at the request of their bishop, brother of the Conqueror. This band of linen, 231 feet long and 20 inches wide, with 72 scenes depicting the story of the Conquest, includes some 1,512 objects, with over 600 humans and over 700 animals. Other arts displaying high competence were metalwork, carving in wood and ivory, and delicate embroidery.

Music in the High Middle Ages

The precocious trends in music already apparent in the tenth century reached full fruition in the High Middle Ages with a multiplication of musical compositions, the development of increasingly complex but better-harmonized forms of polyphonic music, the perfection of musical notation, and the rise of great musical composers and theorists, as well as the introduction of new musical instruments. Surviving musical compositions number several thousands.

Polyphony

Polyphonic music, composed of many parts, progressed rapidly in the High Middle Ages, when it passed through the stages of strict and free *organum* to those of the *conductus* and *motet* forms of counterpoint. In *organum*, while the old unmeasured tenor (from *tenere*: to hold) remained constant, simultaneous melodies at fixed intervals (such as a third or fourth) were added above or below it. In strict *organum* the additional parts paralleled the main melody of the tenor at fixed intervals. This form which originated in the Early Middle Ages, was much elaborated in the High Middle Ages. By the thirteenth century, free *organum* became common; in it the old tenor remained but the other melodies varied in other respects besides pitch and were not parallel. Free *organum* like strict *organum* was unmeasured. Among reasons for its origin was the fact that in strict *organum* occasions arose (such as the augmented fourth) when discord resulted if the strict parallelism was not broken. In free *organum* there was constructed above the old unmeasured tenor a melismatic series of notes that threw the original into the background. Double, triple, quadruple, etc., forms of both strict and free *organum*, depending on the number of melodies involved were composed.

Counterpoint

Full harmony or "counterpoint," in which all melodies were freely composed as well as measured, developed in the thirteenth century. Two forms of measured, freely composed counterpoint appeared: the *conductus* and the *motet*. In the *conductus* all the melodies (in addition to being measured) were freely composed and different, not excluding the tenor. In the *motet* (not to be confused with modern motets) the words used in the various parts as well as the melodies differed (*motet* derives its name from French *mot*, meaning "word"). The *motet* with multiple texts as well as multiple melodies was the most popular of thirteenth-century polyphonic forms. Besides using different texts in Latin, *motets* also frequently employed the vernacular; sometimes they paralleled the original words of the liturgy with secular songs or themes.

Meanwhile, partly in answer to the needs of evolving polyphony, musical notation was perfected. The line or staff of five or six lines came to be accepted; the "clef" or key was introduced to indicate pitch; and indications as to the duration of notes came into common use, thus establishing mensural music. Notes were distinguished as half (*minim*), full (*semi-breve*), double (*breve*), and quadruple (*maxima*) types. They were generally represented by triangles, diamonds, and squares, with and without stems.

Musical notation and music masters

Music masters who were geniuses appeared. In the early fore was Guido of Arezzo (eleventh century), an Italian monk who wrote an epochal *Great Treatise* (*Macrilogus*) *Concerning the Study of the Art of Music*, in which he explained such devices as staffs (lines), clefts (indication of key), and solmization, as well as *organum*. Masters Leonin and Perrotin, who were successively associated with the great choir of the Cathedral of Paris in the later twelfth and early thirteenth centuries, spearheaded new developments in complex free polyphony. In the thirteenth century, Franco of Cologne, a practical musician as well as a theorist, wrote a significant treatise entitled *The Art of Measured Music*, discussing counterpoint and notation.

DISCUSSIONS of literature, the arts, and music are included in FREDERICK B. ARTZ, *The Mind of the Middle Ages* (New York: Knopf, 1954). A good general survey of the various types of medieval literature is WALTER T. H. JACKSON, *The Literature of the Middle Ages* (New York: Columbia U.P., 1960). An early classic, now available in paperback, is WILLIAM P. KER, *Epic and Romance* (New York: Dover, 1957). Excellent collections with accompanying discussions are the fuller CHARLES W. JONES, *Medieval Literature in Translation* (New York: Longmans, 1950), and the earlier JAMES J. WALSH, *A Golden Treasury of Medieval Literature* (Boston: Stanford, 1930). Well-chosen examples are organized into five categories in JAMES B. Ross, ed., *The Portable Medieval Reader* (New York: Viking, 1949).

For Latin Literature in the High Middle Ages, see the general study by FREDERICK A. WRIGHT and T. A. SINCLAIR, *A History of the Later Latin Literature* . . . (New York: Macmillan, 1931); the briefer MAURICE HELIN, *A History of Medieval Latin Literature*, tr. J. C. Snow (New York: Salloch, 1949); and the profound, scholarly ERNST CURTIUS, *European Literature and the Latin Middle Ages*, tr. W. R. Trask (New York: Pantheon, 1953). Works on Latin poetry in the period include FREDERICK J. E. RABY's three volumes on *A History of Christian-Latin Poetry* . . . and *A History of Secular Latin Poetry in the Middle Ages*, 2 vols. (Oxford: Clarendon, 1927, 1934), and PHILIP S. ALLEN, *Medieval Latin Lyrics* (Chicago: Chicago U.P., 1931). A useful anthology is *The Oxford Book of Mediaeval Latin*

References for Chapter 24

Verse, ed. S. Gaselle (Oxford: Oxford U.P., 1937); more limited and specialized is Helen Waddell, Mediaeval Latin Lyrics (London: Constable, 1929). A superb collection of well-translated Latin hymns is Hortus Conclusus: A Series of Mediaeval Latin Hymns . . . (Washington, D. C.: Mt. St. Alban, 1936). Latin poetry of a secular nature is discussed and translated in John A. Symonds, Wine, Women, and Song (London: Chatto and Windus, 1886), and translated with brief introductions by George F. Whicher, The Goliard Poets (New York: New Directions, 1949).

Early French literature is surveyed in Urban T. Holmes, A History of Old French Literature . . . to 1300 (New York: Appleton, 1948), and discussed in Carl Voretzsch, Introduction to the Study of Old French Literature, tr. F. M. Du Mont (New York: Stechert, 1931). Among several translations of The Song of Roland are the versified renditions of C. K. Scott-Moncrieff (Ann Arbor: Mich. U.P., 1959), John O'Hagan (London, 1886), and Leonard Bacon (New Haven: Yale U.P., 1914). Good studies are John G. Robertson, History of German Literature, ed. Edna Purdie (Edinburgh: Blackwood, 1959) and George Ticknor, History of Spanish Literature, vol. I (New York: Harper, 1849). For early Italian literature, one may consult Karl Vossler, Mediaeval Culture: An Introduction to Dante and His Times, 2 vols. (New York: Harcourt, 1929). The story of The Cid has been translated into English verse by R. S. Rose and Leonard Bacon (Berkeley: California U.P., 1919). Otis H. Green, Spain and the Western Tradition: The Castilian Mind from El Cid to Calderon (Madison: Wis. U.P., 1964) has as its theme Spain's maturation in its literature. Scandinavian sagas and eddas are available in numerous translations.

Works on medieval drama include Karl Young, The Drama of the Medieval Church (Oxford: Clarendon, 1933); Edmund K. Chambers, The Medieval Stage, 2 vols. (Oxford: Clarendon, 1903); Fourteen Plays of the Church, tr. R. Schenkkan and K. Jurgensen (New Brunswick, N.J.: Rutgers U.P., 1948); and O. B. Hardison, Jr., Christian Rite and Christian Drama in the Middle Ages (Baltimore: Johns Hopkins, 1965).

One of the best general surveys of architecture and other arts in the High Middle Ages is to be found in John I. Sewall, A History of Western Art (New York: Holt, 1953); other good general treatments include Helen Gardner, Art Through the Ages (New York: Harcourt, 1936); and David M. Robb and J. J. Garrison, Art in the Western World, rev. (New York: Harper, 1942).

Still a classic in its field is Banister Fletcher's History of Architecture (New York: Scribners, 17th ed., 1961).

A well-illustrated, readable survey of the general story of architecture, with some 200 pages on the High Middle Ages, is Nikolaus Pevsner, Outline of European Architecture (Baltimore: Penguin, 1961). The standard monumental history of medieval architecture is Arthur K. Porter, Medieval Architecture . . . , 2 vols. (New Haven: Yale U.P., 1912). For castles and walls, see Sidney Toy, A History of Fortification, (London: Heinemann, 1955), and The Castles of Great Britain (London: Heinemann, 1953). An interesting study of processes of construction is Douglas Knoop and B. P. Jones, The Mediaeval Mason (Manchester, Eng.: U. of Manchester, 1933).

The ideology, significance, and symbolism of medieval art are discussed by Emile Mâle in his Religious Art from the Twelfth to the Eighteenth Century (New York: Pantheon, 1949), and his The Gothic Image: Religious Art in France in the Thirteenth Century (New York: Harper, 1958). ARTHUR GARDNER has composed authoritative works on *English Medieval Sculpture* . . . (Cambridge: Cambridge U.P., 1951), and *Medieval Sculpture in France* (Cambridge: Cambridge U.P., 1931).

Painting in general in the period is well handled and well illustrated by ANDRE GRABAR and CARL NORDENFALK, *Romanesque Painting* . . . , tr. Gilbert Stuart, ed. A. Skira (Geneva, N.Y.: Skira, 1958), and JACQUES DUPONT and C. GNUDI, *Gothic Painting*, tr. S. Gilbert, ed. A. Skira (Geneva, N.Y.: Skira, 1954). For high medieval illuminations in manuscripts, see DAVID DIRINGER, *The Illuminated Book* . . . (New York: Philosophical Library, 1955), and JOHN A. HERBERT, *Illuminated Manuscripts* (1911, republished, New York: Burt Franklin, 1958), both of which are extended, well-illustrated surveys. For stained glass, consult the delightful HUGH ARNOLD and LAWRENCE B. SAINT, *Stained Glass of the Middle Ages in England and France* (New York: Macmillan, 1955); the illustrative MARCEL AUBERT, *Stained Glass of the XIIth and XIIIth Centuries from French Cathedrals* (London: Batsford, 1937); and JAMES R. JOHNSON, *The Radiance of Chartres* . . . (New York: Random House, 1965).

The best, detailed scholarly histories of medieval music are the intensive and authoritative GUSTAVE REESE, *Music in the Middle Ages* (New York: Norton, 1940), and *The New Oxford History of Music*, vol. II: *Early Medieval Music to 1300*, ed. (Dom) ANSELM HUGHES (London: Oxford U.P., 1954).

ca. 1300–1500

(PART IV. THE LATER MIDDLE AGES: TRANSITION OR "RENAISSANCE"?

HE PERIOD from 1300 to 1500, known variously as the Later Middle Ages, the Age of the Renaissance, and the Era of Transition, was made turbulent by strong countercurrents. Whereas many have lauded the era as one of general renaissance or rebirth, many others have rejected this characterization, and some have maintained that it was a period of decline. Whereas all agree that there was a considerable revival of ancient classical studies and forms in literature and the arts during the Later Middle Ages, some have doubted whether this really represented progress, and many have rejected the idea of general revolutionary advances in most fields of human life.

The "Renaissance" thesis

The theory of a general renaissance originating in Italy during the Later Middle Ages was first fully formulated about a century ago. In 1860, a German Swiss historian, Jacob Burckhardt, published *The Civilization of the ... Renaissance in Italy* (written in German, but soon translated into other languages). Burckhardt maintained that "the birth of modern man" took place in Italy during the Later Middle Ages through an emancipation of the human spirit inspired by classical literature, history, and models. According to Burckhardt, the combination of the "special genius of the Italian people" and the classical inspiration produced revolutionary progress in most fields. Shortly afterwards (1875–1886) an English historian, John Addington Symonds, in his seven-volume *Renaissance in Italy*, elaborated the same thesis. The concept of a general renaissance was soon adopted by many historians, applied to various particular fields, and further developed, frequently with rhetorical abandon.

The "renaissance" thesis was, however, challenged almost as soon as it appeared. Some maintained that the Italian Renaissance was simply an Italian acceptance or adoption of a movement that had already appeared elsewhere in the High Middle Ages, especially in France. Others asserted that the Germanic spirit was at the root of Western success, and that modern individualism and progress resulted from a union of medieval Christianity and Teutonic realism. Some even put the advent of the Italian Renaissance earlier, making it a part of the High Medieval "Renaissance."

The revolt of the medievalists

Meanwhile many medieval historians pointed out that the fundamental assumption of the Burckhardt thesis—that the previous Middle Ages were "dark" and unprogressive—was erroneous, and arose from an ignorance of the Middle Ages, whose "darkness" was only in the mind of the beholder. They adduced evidence that in many fields the High Middle Ages were actually more creative and progressive than the Later Middle Ages. Professor Charles Homer Haskins wrote a scholarly book that he entitled *The Renaissance of the Twelfth Century*, Dr. William W. Walsh one that he named *The Thirteenth, The Greatest of Centuries,* and Johann Huizinga one picturing decline in the Later Middle Ages that he named *The Waning of the Middle Ages.*

Intermediate positions were eventually taken by several scholars, including Wallace K. Ferguson, John H. Randall, A. N. Whitehead, and George Sellery. According to such authorities, the Later Middle Ages were actually a period of contrasting developments. Continuity from the High Middle Ages was exemplified by the growth of representative government in the fourteenth and early fifteenth centuries, the further spread of capitalism, and the multiplication of universities. Instances of change included the eventual rise of strong nationalism accompanied by great growth of royal power in the later fifteenth century, the split of the middle class, and the development of the conciliar theory and nominalistic skepticism. Examples of decline included economic depression (1350–1450), violent class conflict, deterioration of Church prestige, and lessened philosophical productivity. Progress was exemplified by greatly expanded study and knowledge of classical literature and ancient history, important advances in painting and sculpture, cheaper mass production of books by printing, and augmented lay quest of greater perfection in religion. The Later Middle Ages were a kaleidoscopic period of contrasts and changes.

Intermediate compromise position

A BALANCED and authoritative one-volume history of the Later Middle Ages in English is WALLACE K. FERGUSON, *Europe in Transition, 1300–1500* (Boston: Houghton Mifflin 1962). A shorter, well-written work concerning the same period is ROBERT ERGANG, *The Renaissance* (Princeton, N.J.: Van Nostrand, 1967). Covering a broader span are HENRY S. LUCAS, *The Renaissance and Reformation* (New York: Harper, 1934), which stresses cultural developments, and S. HARRISON THOMSON, *Europe in Renaissance and Reformation* (New York: Harcourt, 1963). The first and classic presentation of the famous "renaissance" thesis is JACOB BURCKHARDT, *The Civilization of the . . . Renaissance in Italy,* tr. S. G. Middlemore (London: Phaidon, 1960), whose views are endorsed and elaborated by JOHN ADDINGTON SYMONDS, *Renaissance in Italy* (1887–1890), 3 vols. (Gloucester, Mass.: Peter Smith, 1967). Among presentations of the opposite view are GEORGE C. SELLERY, *The Renaissance* (Madison: U. Wis., 1950), and JOHANN HUIZINGA, *The Waning of the Middle Ages* (London: Arnold, 1924). The evolution and fluctuation of interpretations of the period are presented at length by WALLACE K. FERGUSON, *The Renaissance in Historical Thought . . .* (Boston: Houghton Mifflin, 1948). Shorter collections of selections presenting divergent views are by KARL H. DANNERFELDT, ed., *The Renaissance: Medieval or Modern?* (Lexington, Mass.: Heath, 1959) (p.), and DENYS HAY, ed., *The Renaissance Debate* (New York: Holt, 1965) (p.). Useful collections of original sources from the period include G. R. ELTON, ed., *Renaissance and Reformation, 1300–1648* (New York: Macmillan, 3rd ed., 1976) (p.); and DONALD WEINSTEIN, ed., *The Renaissance and Reformation, 1300–1600* (New York: Free Press, 1965) (p.). Specializing in the Italian scene are J. P. PLUMB, *The Italian Renaissance* (New York: Harper, 1961) (p.), "a concise survey of its history and culture"; and WERNER L. GUNDERSHEIMER, ed., *The Italian Renaissance* (Englewood Cliffs, N.J.: Prentice-Hall, 1965) (p.), a good collection of original sources.

References for Part IV

❮ RECESSION AND RECOVERY: LATE MEDIEVAL ECONOMIC AND SOCIAL CONDITIONS.   Chapter 25.

ECLINE and cross-currents adversely affected the economy and society during most of the Later Middle Ages. Prolonged commercial contraction and a general business recession depressed the economy. Internal division and strife, aggravated by economic distress, disturbed society. Toward the close of the period, however, the economy commenced to recover, and social strife began to subside. Corresponding changes, affected by economic and social conditions, meanwhile occurred in government, religion, and culture.

THE EBB AND FLOW OF COMMERCE AND INDUSTRY.
Section 73.

> A merchant wishing that his wealth be great
> Should always act according as is right;
> And he must be a man of long foresight
> Who never fails his promises to keep.
> Let him be pleasant, if he can, of looks,
> As fits the honored calling that he chose,
> Open when selling, but in buying close,
> Genial in greeting, and without complaints.
> He will be worthier if he goes to church,
> Gives for the glory of God, clinches his deals
> Without haggling, and wholly repeals
> Usury taking. Further he must write
> Accounts well kept and free from oversight.
> [Advice for success in commerce, from Dino Compagni's *Song on Worthy Conduct* (early fourteenth century, Florence).]

DESPITE a protracted period of economic depression during the Later Middle Ages, finance continued to evolve and capitalism grew. Further improvements were also made in commercial methods and industrial processes. Toward the close of the Middle Ages the economy revived and resumed its upward course.

"The great depression" (1350-1450)

Commerce began to level off in the period from 1300 to 1350, and economic expansion collapsed catastrophically from about 1350 to 1450. A great depression resulted, beginning somewhat earlier in some areas, later in others. Concerning the era, the *Cambridge Economic History* observes: *We are in the presence of an all-European depression.*[a]

a II, 338.

Various factors contributed to economic decline. The "Black Death," which struck in the mid-fourteenth century and periodically recurred, greatly reduced the population of Western and Central Europe, dislocating the economy and cutting down the demand for goods. The Hundred Years' War (1337-1453), which wasted resources and human lives on unproductive, devastating conflict, adversely affected not only the contestants, England and France, but also most of Europe. Recurrent civil wars in Western European countries had a similar effect.

Asian intruders, such as the Mongols and Ottoman Turks, blighted the areas they conquered. The dominance of warlike Mameluks and Ottomans in the Near East, as well as the revival of Moslem seapower, sharply reduced Christian trade in the Mediterranean. The breakup of the Mongol Empire increased the risks and costs and diminished the volume of overland transportation across Asia. Meanwhile the conversion of the Western Mongols to Islam put them in an opposing camp, hostile to Christians.

Still, there were regional and local variations and exceptions to the general picture. Partly because of a diversion of trade routes during the Hundred Years' War, the cities of Barcelona and Valencia in northeastern Spain enjoyed a period of commercial expansion. Towns of southern Germany such as Augsburg and Nuremburg also prospered from an increasing flow of trade. The Hanseatic towns of northern Germany reached the height of their prosperity in the fourteenth century, although they lost ground in the fifteenth century. East central and northern (Scandinavian) Europe began to share more extensively in the fruits of the Commercial Revolution in the fifteenth century. And, there were still increases in local and internal trade.

Recovery

From about 1450 on, a general economic revival restored Western European commerce to its former healthy condition. Factors included recovery from the Black Death, gradual restoration of population to its former levels, the end of the wasteful Hundred Years' War, and the rise of strong national monarchs who pacified their countries and adopted beneficial economic policies. Meanwhile new trade routes were developing, as in the Atlantic, and were beginning to supplant the old ones in some cases.

Changes in trade routes

Although previous patterns of commerce continued to a considerable extent, the volume of trade passing over old routes changed significantly, while new routes also developed. Overland trade across Central Asia and via the Black Sea and Constantinople was greatly reduced. A considerable amount of goods from the East continued to move across the Syrian Desert, although this trade had been adversely affected by the loss of the Crusader ports. Trade via the Red Sea and Egypt greatly increased. Most Eastern commerce was conducted through Moslem middlemen.

A revolutionary innovation, the operation of "Flanders Fleets" by North Italian cities, established direct overseas trading routes with Flanders and England. Genoa was the first to establish this direct overseas trade in 1300; Venice did likewise shortly afterward in 1314. Florence followed suit in the fifteenth century, after acquiring the harbor of Pisa. This shift of trade routes to the Atlantic helped to cause the ruination of the inland Champagne fairs. Meanwhile the economic development of northern and east central Europe contributed to a growth in the prosperity of the German towns.

Focal centers of trade

The focal centers of trade remained much as they were at the close of the High Middle Ages. Venice was "undoubtedly the first seaport of the world." The Venetians had an estimated 3,300 ships with some 36,000 sailors, and Venetian "convoys" operated over at least six routes or "lines" running to and from the Black Sea, Syria, Egypt, North Africa, Spain, and the North Sea. The Genoese were also famous for their commercial enterprise, and Genoa had 2,000 ships manned by about 25,000 sailors in the early fourteenth century. The towns of Flanders and Brabant were transfer points at the crossroads of trade from northern Italy via the "Flanders Fleets." Bruges was the financial and commercial center of northwestern Europe until its harbor silted up about the middle of the fifteenth century, when it was succeeded by Antwerp. It is said that a hundred ships sailed daily into the port of Bruges in 1435. In northern Europe the Hanseatic merchants of northern Germany were the principal carriers and traders. South German towns such as Augsburg, Nuremburg and Strasbourg grew rapidly in prosperity and population, especially in the fifteenth century.

Enterprising newcomers began to participate actively in large-scale commercial operations. Aided by the interest of Prince Henry the Navigator, the Portuguese sailed down the Atlantic coast of Africa, where they established bases and developed trade in items such as gold, ivory, and Negro slaves.

Before the close of the period, the Portuguese rounded the Cape of Good Hope and reached India by sea. Gradually the interest of Castilians was aroused, so that eventually Queen Isabella sponsored the voyage of Columbus that discovered the New World (1492). English merchants cut in on Hanseatic trade preserves in northern Europe, especially in the fifteenth century. At the same time, the commercial revolution was coming to such countries as Poland, Bohemia, and Hungary, while Catalonian merchants were enjoying unexampled prosperity.

Improved ships

Ships were greatly improved during the Later Middle Ages, and new types of seagoing vessels appeared. Ships were made more commodious for cargo and more comfortable for passengers, as well as more seaworthy, swifter, and better able to defend themselves. These developments were spurred by the growth of long-distance maritime trade. The number, size, and types of both masts and sails as well as the complexities of their rigging were increased. For more valuable goods, swift, long "galleys" propelled by both sails and oars were used. These commercial galleys, much larger than the fighting galleys used for naval warfare, were able to move rapidly under all kinds of conditions, in all kinds of weather. They were typically from 120 to 150 feet long, with a displacement of 100 to 300 tons, and a crew of 100 to 200 men. In addition to oarsmen, they carried archers and, by the fifteenth century, guns. The galleys had multiple decks as well as multiple sails, and often tiers of rowers.

In addition to commercial galleys, ships known as carracks and caravels appeared. For bulkier goods of lesser value, larger, faster, multimasted, multisailed carracks were built. Many of these carracks had multiple decks and even multiple "tops" on their masts. They also eventually had guns. Columbus' flagship, the *Santa Maria*, seems to have been a small carrack. Caravels were smaller, with a round bottom and shallower draft. They had less cargo capacity (e.g., 60 to 80 tons), but multiple sails and masts, and were designed to sail in all weather and rigged to tack against the wind. They were faster and more maneuverable, as well as safer in shallow and reefy waters. Such seem to have been the *Niña* and *Pinta*, which were preferred for exploration by Columbus after the larger *Santa Maria* went aground. In the north, large, roomy, broad-beamed, round-bottomed, straight-ended, square-sailed, single-masted "cogs" with a typical displacement of 100 to 500 tons continued to be used for carrying cargo of lesser value.

Portolani, detailed navigational charts of harbors and coasts, multiplied, and wide use was made of astronomical tables and navigational instruments such as the astrolabe, mechanical clocks, and magnetic compasses. Instruction and training for navigators were improved, as in the famous navigational school at Genoa, and in that of Prince Henry the Navigator at Sagres. Education of the children of merchants, at least in the "three R's" and sometimes in further studies, became more common. Hard times and sharper competition as well as the demands of large-scale operations spurred the introduction of more efficient business procedures and accounting methods: many towns, particularly in the Low Countries and Germany, maintained municipal schools, while private schools and tutors also taught commercial arithmetic and business correspondence. The accepted axiom that the merchant "must write accounts well kept and free from oversight" resulted in careful accounts of transactions by merchants and extensive records kept by cities. Accurate statistics were compiled. Thus the Florentine historian Villani gives us precise statistics concerning the population, occupations, production, and revenues of his city in the early fourteenth century. Double-entry bookkeeping was an important and useful innovation, in which every transaction was entered from two points of view, both as a debit and as a credit. A double check for accuracy was thus available, and the state of a business could be determined at a glance. The new system of bookkeeping, which developed at Genoa by the early fourteenth century, spread rapidly in Italy.

Further aids to commerce

Treatises on mercantile methods appeared. Some gave general advice (often sprinkled with moral admonitions) while others became very specific. Conspicuous among the latter was Francesco Pegolloti's *Practice of Commerce* (Florence, early fourteenth century), which included detailed information on such subjects as the several forms and sources of alum, the current selling prices of miscellaneous types of cloth at Ypres, and the exact costs of successive steps in cheese making in Apulia. An example of a treatise giving general advice on mercantile activities and investments was that of Benedetto Cotrugli in his *On Commerce and the Perfect Merchant* (Naples, 1458), in which he noted: *A very rich man must manage in one way, a rich man in another, and one who only has small capital in still another. A great merchant . . . should not keep all his money together, but should distribute it in various solid businesses. . . . Those who have a moderate amount of money, such as 4,000 ducats,*

Treatises

should manage in another way. They must not divide their capital, but must keep it firmly tied together, except that sometimes, though infrequently, they may make commenda *contracts [short-term investments] of 400 to 500 ducats, and [be sure to] get them back, and frequently check the accounting and clear the profits. . . . Those who have only a little money, such as 500 ducats, must personally get busy with this and not make* commenda *contracts or anything else. . . . Rather, they must help the money along with their own efforts. . . .*

Merchants Although Italian merchants and financiers continued to lead in the field of business in the Later Middle Ages, competition from a growing number of rivals among the Germans, French, Spanish, Flemish, and English increased. Boastful merchants such as the one described by Chaucer were apparently familiar figures in England in the late fourteenth century. When in foreign countries, mercantile agents or "factors" from given areas often lived together in places known as "factories" such as the Hanseatic "factory" (the "Steelyard") in London and the German *Fondaco dei Tedeschi* (Shop of the Teutons) in Venice.

As capitalism became more widespread, the great merchants came to be a class apart from ordinary merchants. In many cases the great merchants controlled the ordinary guilds; in other instances, they had their own special associations. London had its twelve great "Livery Companies," which had the exclusive right to have their own coats of arms; Paris its six "Corps de Marchands" or privileged merchant corporations; and Florence its powerful *Arti maggiori* (greater guilds).

The Hanseatic League The Hanseatic League, a large association of some fifty to eighty German towns for commercial purposes, reached the high point of its prosperity in the fourteenth century. It obtained a virtual monopoly on large-scale international commerce in the Baltic and North Sea areas. Hanseatic merchants enjoyed extensive privileges in the Scandinavian countries and England as well as in the Low Countries and Germany. Bulky Hanseatic "cogs" and "hulks" plied their persistent way between North Germany, Scandinavia, and Russia on the one hand and England and Flanders with their North Italian suppliers on the other. The League had four "quarters" (areas) with local capitals at Lübeck, Brunswick, Danzig, and Cologne, and agencies ("factories") at trading centers such as Bruges and London, and even Novgorod in Russia and Bergen in Norway. The aggressive Hansards obtained various monopolies, tariff reductions, exemptions, and privileges of extraterritoriality. But a shift of the customary spawning grounds of the herring southward from the Baltic to the North Sea, the expanding power of the German princes, disagreements among League members, and rising nationalism, together with growing resentment against Hanseatic privileges among native merchants in such countries as England, Poland, and Denmark brought about a decline of the League in the fifteenth century.

Marketing institutions Important changes in large-scale marketing occurred. Much of the international trade that had previously been carried on periodically at fairs was now conducted throughout the year in great commercial centers such as Venice, Florence, Genoa, Bruges, Antwerp, Paris, and London, by established "houses" with both "home offices" and "branches," as well as by "sedentary merchants" operating through "factors" and commission merchants. Exchanges and "bourses" for year-round buying and selling of wholesale goods and the conduct of financial operations also developed in several cities. The Rialto at Venice has been characterized as "a continuous fair."

Industry in the Later Middle Ages was subject to the great depression, but it also exhibited shifts and contrasts, together with important developments pregnant for the future. Continued specialization promoted industrial expansion, as did the further utilization of natural forces and application of labor-saving devices. *Industrial developments*

In the textile industry both the "factory" and "putting out" forms of capitalistic production were increasingly used. Waterpower became common in the fulling of cloths. Besides the great woolen industry, the silk industry, in which Venice is said to have employed three thousand workers, spread in northern Italy and was introduced into France by Louis XI in the later fifteenth century. The cotton textile industry also grew and new textiles were produced, such as combinations of silk and wool and silk and cotton.

Italy and the Low Countries continued to hold the lead in the manufacture of textiles. According to Villani, thirty thousand workers were employed in the woolen textile industry in Florence in 1338. But textile production began to decline in the Low Countries from about 1375 on, and in Italy during the fifteenth century. Both of these areas were plagued by numerous uprisings of workers, as well as decreasing ability to obtain good wool at reasonable prices.

Meanwhile the textile industry spread in Holland, Germany, France, and especially England. English exports of broadcloths rose from 3,040 in 1353 to 62,586 in 1482, by which date the total export of English cloths was 179,340. England produced abundant and excellent raw wool, guild regulations were less restrictive, and concerted violent unrest of workers was less frequent. Waterpower was also more plentiful in England. And the English government actively fostered a native textile industry.

Mining and metallurgy made important strides, especially in the second half of the fifteenth century. The Germans led in this field, and exploited the mineral resources of Germany, Bohemia, Greater Austria, and Hungary on a large scale. Mining was furthered by the construction of extensive vertical and horizontal shafts on successive levels, with reinforcing timbers and lifts. Horsepower and waterpower were utilized for pumping out water and the operation of lifts, as well as for rolling mills and huge hammers to crush the ore. Blast furnaces were constructed, and efficient water-driven bellows, capable of producing a continuous blast, were developed and used in making cast iron. Brass was made by combining zinc calamine with copper. And a new process for extraction of silver with the help of lead was invented.

New industrial developments were associated with warfare, waterpower, and printing. The production of arms and armor was stimulated by the Hundred Years' War. Gunpowder and gunpowder weapons were manufactured for use in warfare. Waterpower was also used in other industries besides mining and metallurgy, as in the fulling of cloth, the pulping of rags for paper, and woodworking. The new printing industry enjoyed phenomenally rapid growth in the second half of the fifteenth century. Introduced in the Rhineland in the middle of that century, printing with movable type spread rapidly, so that by 1500 there were thousands of presses in Europe. Printing naturally stimulated an expansion of the paper industry.

Transformation of the guilds and growth of capitalism in industry

The older craft guilds came under the control of the masters, who tended to make their own order a sort of closed corporation, reserved to their sons and relatives and other favored persons. Master's fees were hiked and the official standards for masterpieces were raised so that becoming a master was quite difficult. Ordinary artisans tended to remain journeymen or hired laborers. Often journeymen's guilds were formed both for mutual assistance and for common bargaining and representation. These, the true predecessors of our modern labor unions, were called *compagnonnages* in French and *Bruderschaften* in German. Among such were the Freemasons.

The guilds were often conservative, selfish, and narrow in outlook. They frequently impeded the improvement and modernization of industries, and were eventually bypassed. Their strength in the textile industries of Flanders and northern Italy had much to do with these industries' eventual decline.

Although most medieval industry remained small scale and "domestic," several industries were becoming more capitalistic. Large-scale capitalistic methods were particularly desirable in industries involving numerous successive operations or requiring the cooperation of numerous workers, or using costly machinery, as was the case with the textile, mining, and metallurgical industries. It has been estimated that while 30,000 workers were engaged in the woolen textile industry in Florence in 1338 there were only 200 textile firms in the city, which averages about one hundred and fifty workers per firm. In the fifteenth century, Amiens had factories with one hundred and twenty weavers. The capitalistic "putting out" system was used extensively in the textile industry in rural England.

Agriculture and pastoral activities in the Later Middle Ages

The story of agriculture generally followed the course of the rest of the economy. A leading factor in agricultural decline was a radical population drop resulting from the Black Death; another was the dislocation and devastation caused by prolonged warfare. In Western Europe, the elimination of manorialism and serfdom continued. So did the breakup of landed property and the multiplication of small landholders. Causes were much as in the High Middle Ages. Tenant farming was widespread, with formal or informal leaseholding the most common form. In 1500 it is estimated that five sixths of the land in France was held by *censitaires* and one third of the land in England by copyholders, both of whom were leaseholders. Sharecropping was common in some areas such as Tuscany. A certain amount of capitalism continued to infiltrate agriculture. Townspeople often invested part of their money in farmlands for security and status; while enterprising farmers frequently expanded their holdings.

Meanwhile in northern, east central, and eastern Europe, manorialism and serfdom increased, as also did large holdings.

Pastoral activities were expanded and often organized on a capitalistic basis, especially in England and Spain. Opportunities for profit were considerable, the number of laborers required was small, and much land was not too well suited for anything else in both countries. Many landowners kept flocks of from 4,000 to 25,000 sheep in England, where the Black Death stimulated pastoral activities since it made available considerable stretches of land and reduced the labor supply. Large holdings of livestock increased in Spain, where the *Mesta*, a privileged guild of sheep and cattle owners, owned one fourth of the sheep. It is said that Spain had about ten million sheep in the fifteenth century.

GROWTH OF CAPITALISM AND GOVERNMENTAL INVOLVEMENT.
Section 74.

A good rule in making exchange[b] is as follows: Beware of being in debt at a place and time when money can be expected to be dear, as during a fair. . . . Never be in a hurry to remit money where there is a shortage of it [and you have to buy it when it is high] or to withdraw it from a place where it is abundant [and you have to sell it when it is low]. . . . When you want money at a certain place, get it there by the quickest means possible, but without buying it at an excessive price. [Benedetto Cotrugli, *On Commerce* (Naples, 1458).]

[b] Exchange: changing one form of money into another; buying and selling money.

BOTH coinage of money and means of finance were expanded in the Later Middle Ages. Capitalists became prominent in several countries and loaned money at interest or otherwise provided credit in order to enhance their incomes. Rulers attempted to foster and regulate the economy of their countries in order to promote the prosperity of their citizens and increase governmental revenues.

Forms of money continued to multiply and become ever more numerous and confusing. Following the lead of the North Italians, governments coined not only large silver coins (*groats, grosses, Groschen*) but also gold money of varying weights and purities. Gold coins in particular varied widely in precious content and had various names—"florins," "ducats," and "genoins" in Italy; "florins," "nobles," and "crowns" in England; *ecus, couronnes, angels, francs,* and *cavaliers* in France; *Gulden* and florins, and so on, in the Empire. Changing the value of coins downward amounted to a royal pastime, especially with the French kings. Generally the florins and ducats of the north Italian city-states were preferred as most reliable, until they, too, came to be debased.

Money

Financial methods and devices continued to evolve in the Later Middle Ages. Banks and bankers multiplied, with the North Italians retaining a comfortable lead. Of Florence and its banking, Benedetto Dei, in a letter to a Venetian (1472), wrote: "The number of our banks is thirty-three," and pointed out that the number of their branch banks was still greater. Most banks and bankers also carried on other business operations. Thus

Finance: Banking and "paper"

the Peruzzi of Florence in the early fourteenth century collected taxes for the Papacy in England at a handsome profit. They then credited the accounts of the Papacy with ledger sums and purchased English wool with the money collected. The wool was taken to Italy, where it was made into expensive cloth, much of which was sold back to the English.

State banks for the handling of public funds and governmental financing appeared in the Later Middle Ages. Among such were the Bank of St. George in Genoa (1407ff.) and that of St. Mark in Venice, as well as state banks at Barcelona, Strasbourg, Nuremburg, Frankfort, Hamburg, and Augsburg. The Franciscans promoted cooperative banks known as *montes pietatis* (*monts de piété:* pious funds) for the less affluent. The *montes*, which were very similar to our present-day credit unions, and lent money to the poor and needy at moderate rates, spread, especially in Germany and Italy.

Permanent "bourses" or exchanges where investors dealt in commercial and financial paper as well as in commodities appeared. Greater security in financial transactions was provided by drafts, which were written orders of one bank to another to pay a third party, and by acceptances, which were formal written agreements on the part of a second bank to pay a third party as directed.

Credit and insurance

Economic life continued to be "permeated with credit." Profit was derived from both direct and indirect credit (the latter being exemplified by bills of exchange and the purchases of tax-collection rights). Many kings and princes made a regular practice of borrowing large sums to finance their governments and armies. Sometimes such loans were openly compulsory. A succeeding ruler might refuse to acknowledge his predecessor's debts. Rulers who borrowed were severely tempted to eliminate their creditors by banishing them or having their property confiscated on flimsy charges. Sometimes a ruler's debts became so great that he had to declare bankruptcy, as was the case with Edward III of England in 1340. Collateral for loans to monarchs was sometimes provided by custody of the royal jewels or the right to collect customs duties until the loan was repaid.

As borrowing became more common and its economic advantage more evident, ecclesiastical prejudice against allowing interest for loans evaporated. Even Popes and bishops became interest-paying borrowers. Thus Popes made it a common practice to grant Florentine capitalists the right to collect Papal taxes with an attractive profit in return for "cash in hand." A distinction was now made between legitimate, reasonable "interest" and excessive, immoral "usury." Many factors were to be taken into consideration in estimating the amount of allowable interest, which could even be as high as 50 per cent according to St. Antoninus.

With the Genoese in the lead, direct forms of true insurance were developed. For a liberal bonus, financiers would agree to assume or share the risk of shipwreck or piracy involved in a mercantile enterprise. At first such insurance was under the guise of a sale of goods to the insurer, payable to the insured in the event of loss.

Recession and Recovery

One of the most significant developments in the Later Middle Ages was a great expansion of capitalism. Capital continued to be accumulated by a variety of means, such as industry and commerce, mining and metallurgy, shipbuilding and shipping, banking and finance, exchange, minting of money (at a profit), rents, governmental concessions, and agricultural and pastoral activities. Such accumulations of capital became both greater and more common, while capitalism became prominent in many fields. Most large-scale commerce was—and had to be—capitalistic. The major industries in more advanced centers were often capitalistic, as in the "putting out" and "factory" systems. Besides being in banking and finance, capitalism infiltrated agriculture and pastoral activities and came to be associated with tax collecting, the conduct of government, and the waging of wars. *[Growth of capitalism]*

The North Italians continued as the principal capitalists in the Later Middle Ages, but they were challenged by increasing numbers of Transalpine entrepreneurs. Most North Italian capitalism was in the corporate hands of family associations or *compagnias*. Each of the major North Italian cities had numerous capitalistic families. An admittedly incomplete list of major Italian mercantile and banking companies in the Later Middle Ages includes 38 family companies for Florence, 34 for Pisa, 27 for Genoa, 21 for Lucca, 18 for Venice, 17 for Piacenza, 16 for Siena, 11 for Asti, 10 for Milan, and 7 for Pistoia. Among such were the Bardi and Peruzzi of Florence, the principal financiers of Edward III until his bankruptcy in 1340; the Medicis, whose huge income eventually helped them become dictators in Florence; the Arnolfini of Lucca, one of whose members had his portrait painted twice by Jan Van Eyck (once with his wife and once alone); Nicholas Bartholomew of Lucca, who became one of the bankers of Edward III; the Pazzi and Rucellai, whose *palazzi* are still showplaces in Florence, and Francesco Datini of Prato, who, beginning with nothing, became one of the richest men of his time, leaving some 500 ledgers and over 150,000 letters at his death. *[Capitalists]*

Among noted German capitalists were Tidemann of Limburg, the leading financial agent of Edward III after the fall of the Bardi and Peruzzi; William of Doovenvoorde, the counselor of Count William of Holland, with an estimated million dollars a year income; and Liutfried Muntprat of Constance, who left a fortune valued at millions of dollars. The Fuggers of Augsburg, who came into prominence in the fifteenth century, got their start with large-scale mining and metallurgy, and then branched out into various other business activities. A noted English capitalist was Richard Whittington of London, a great "merchant and mercer" who helped finance the early Lancastrians, and eventually became Lord Mayor of London.

Among a growing number of French financiers, one was Etienne Marcel, a leading Parisian merchant who headed the temporarily successful uprising of 1357–1358 against the royal government. Another was Jacques Coeur, who built up a large fleet of merchant vessels in the first half of the fifteenth century and arranged his own treaties with Eastern potentates, such as the sultans of Turkey and Egypt. Coeur, who became a leading counselor of Charles VII and financed the conquest of Normandy in 1449–1450, was eventually banished from France on flimsy charges.

Capitalistic organization

Although old forms of capitalistic organization continued from the High Middle Ages, new adaptations evolved. Thus the constitution of many of the old family *compagnias* was changed. Especially after the financial crash of the mid-1300s, it became a common practice to organize each branch separately, so as to establish a degree of limited liability and insure that a failure of one part might not endanger the whole. Increasing numbers of outsiders were also admitted into the companies so that their number sometimes exceeded that of true family members, as in the case of the Peruzzi.

The temporary *societates*, or partial partnerships, including the *societates maris* or *commenda* for maritime commerce, and the *societates terrae* for land trade, continued to have a measure of limited liability since only the active agent was responsible for debts contracted. These *societates* were now often extended over a period of years. Foreshadowing later limited liability, joint stock companies, *maone* (sing.: *maona*), which were privileged partnerships with limited liability, were chartered by the Genoese government to develop islands.

Government promotion of the economy

National governments began to attempt to regulate and promote the economy. Although town governments, especially in northern Italy, had long indulged in economic legislation, this was a new field for national governments. Spurred on by increasing needs for money, governments such as those of England and France now experimented with ways to improve their economies and increase their revenues. Amid much trial and error, fumbling and vacillation, a new "political economy" was born.

Promotion of the woolen textile industry by English kings and that of the silk textile industry by French monarchs were classic examples of governmental economic intervention. Thus Edward III of England encouraged the immigration of Flemish, Brabantine, and Dutch textile workers; and Louis XI of France imported silk workers from Italy. Some French kings attempted to break through the restrictive regulations of the guilds. Charles VI annulled rules of the Parisian corporations by allowing masters to take greater numbers of apprentices, shortened the term of apprenticeship, and lowered the barriers to the mastership.

English kings also fostered the woolen textile industry by restrictive legislation concerning exports and imports as well as by their fiscal policies. Edward III at one time forbade the export of English wool to Flanders and at another set a high tax of about 33 per cent on such exports. Since duties on the export of English cloth remained low (about 2 per cent) native entrepreneurs were thus encouraged to change the wool to cloth before exporting it. Edward III also forbade the purchase of foreign textiles. The government of Henry VI forbade the importation of silk cloths (1455) and that of Edward IV the importation of foreign-made woolen textiles (1464). The Burgundian Duke Philip the Good retaliated by forbidding importation of English wool into Flanders.

Recession and Recovery

Especially after the Black Death had caused a sharp increase in wages and prices, the English and French governments tried to control both, and the English government sought to freeze people in their occupations. In 1349 the English King and Council enacted an "Ordinance of Laborers," which was reenacted in the "Statute of Laborers" (1351). This legislation fixed the recompense of laborers, craftsmen, and artificers at pre-1349 levels. An English statute of 1416 established the wages of servants and laborers in both town and country. A basic concern of the French government was stabilization of the cost of living in Paris. The French government attempted to fix wages at times when they tended to rise precipitously, as in 1330 and 1332 after currency depreciations, and in 1351 after the Black Death. An ordinance of 1351 tried to keep wages from rising more than one third. Despite governmental efforts the wages of many artisans in England and France, as well as in Germany, doubled between 1300 and 1450. English labor laws of 1349 and 1351 also tried to prevent the movement of laborers from one position to another. According to an English law of 1388, anyone who had served in husbandry to the age of twelve had to continue to do so. In England, labor laws empowered local justices to fix local prices for victuals, and statutes established prices for poultry and candles. The French government repeatedly attempted to control the price of food in the capital. Both the English and French governments legislated to eliminate middlemen and prevent forestalling in order to ensure the direct and reasonably priced flow of foodstuffs from the countryside to the towns.

Governmental regulation and intervention

Wars and treaties had a strongly economic smack. The Hundred Years' War largely concerned economic interests. The wars between the North Italian city-states were mainly commercial. The war between the Hanseatic League and the King of Denmark in the 1360s ended with a commercial treaty (1370). England supported Portugal's successful resistance to incorporation into Castile and was rewarded with the commercial Treaty of Windsor (1386).

Initially governments fostered the expansion of their country's commerce by bestowing special favors on foreign merchants. Thus the Kings of England and Denmark for some time favored the Hansards, as did Louis XI. But eventually the protests of native merchants caused monarchs to privilege their own subjects over foreign competitors.

The concession of monopolies to native businessmen spread in the Later Middle Ages. Especially active in this regard were English monarchs. The government of Richard II, in the Navigation Act of 1381, forbade the shipment of certain types of goods in other than English bottoms. In the same century the English government limited the export of "staple" goods (wool, tin, and hides) to merchant-members of a privileged association known as "the Merchants of the Staple" and confined the traffic to certain "staple ports," domestic and foreign. In the fifteenth century, the English government also chartered the "Merchant Adventurers," who were given a monopoly on English trade with the Netherlands, Germany, Scandinavia, and Russia, in order to develop

Monopolies

direct trade with these northern European countries. Charles VII and Louis XI of France granted similar trading monopolies in the Mediterranean.

Overseas expansion

National governments began to take the lead in overseas exploration and colonization for purposes of trade, which had previously been left to private entrepreneurs. Early pioneers in this field were Portugal and Spain. The Portuguese ruling house of Aviz, stimulated by the interests of Prince Henry the Navigator, sponsored voyages down the west coast of Africa, where trading posts were established. Before the close of the fifteenth century, government-sponsored Bartholomew Diaz rounded the Cape of Good Hope (1488), and Vasco da Gama voyaged around Southern Africa to Calicut in India (1498). Funded by Queen Isabella, Christopher Columbus made his long-dreamed of voyage westward, which enabled Spain to stake out the first European claims in the "New World."

There were also miscellaneous other ways in which national governments began promoting and regulating the economy. The French royal government restricted seigneurial tolls, forbade the confiscation of agricultural plowshares, and tried to fix standard weights and measures; both the English and French kings repeatedly forbade the export of precious metals.

SOCIAL AND OTHER CONCOMITANTS OF ECONOMIC CHANGES.
Section 75.

> When Adam delved and Eve span
> Who was then the gentleman?
> [A slogan of the Wat Tyler Rebellion of 1381 in England.]

ECONOMIC stresses and hardships strained social bonds and divided society in the Later Middle Ages. Internal revolts and changes of government were frequent, while prolonged international warfare cast its shadow over much of Western Europe. Since parliamentarianism failed to resolve crises, and aristocratic factions resorted to warfare, strong monarchical governments arose to restore unity and order and were accepted by most of the people. Particularly penalized was the unpropertied proletariat.

Fluidity and division

Still the new conditions allowed greater social fluidity, while the intense competition bred greater imagination, drive, self-reliance, and individualism. A prosperous merchant might well be ruined and have to start all over again. Benedetto Cotrugli in his treatise *On Commerce* (Naples, 1458) says: *I have seen great men who, being impoverished, were not ashamed of renting horses to carters and of buying and selling on commission or of taking up innkeeping. . . . I have seen some of them become rich again in a very short time and have 10,000 ducats. . . .*

The corporate consciousness of the High Middle Ages was eroded as society became more fragmented and separatist. There were cleavages between the middle class and the proletariat and between the capitalistic

Recession and Recovery

upper bourgeoisie and the ordinary bourgeoisie, as well as between individuals. Some have lauded while others have deplored this increased individualism and splintering of society, which had two sides. On one side of the scale there were the dynamic enterprise and creative originality of numerous entrepreneurs, sea captains, explorers, *condottieri*, despots, authors, painters, sculptors, architects, etc. On the other side there were the narrow selfishness, merciless competition, crass worldliness, and disdain for tradition, religion, and morality of many members of "the new society."

Adversely affected by the Black Death, the persistence of warfare, and prolonged economic depression, the population of Western and central Europe declined by perhaps one third in the period from about 1348 to 1450, and only began to approach its former level by about 1500. Although population estimates vary greatly, the following figures seem probable as approximations.

Population changes

ESTIMATED POPULATIONS

COUNTRY	1300	1400	1500
France	17,500,000	11,500,000	15,000,000
England	3,700,000	2,300,000	3,500,000
Germanies	17,000,000	12,000,000	14,500,000
Italy	8,500,000	6,000,000	8,000,000
Iberian Peninsula	9,000,000	6,000,000	8,000,000

The dip in the population of towns seems to have been even greater than that among the population at large because of the highly contagious nature of the Black Death and may have run from 35 to 65 per cent. It is estimated that the population of most towns dropped on the average about 40 per cent by 1400, and that most had not wholly recovered their former strength by 1500.

The towns, which had enjoyed remarkable growth and prosperity in the High Middle Ages, were subjected to severe trials in the Later Middle Ages. In addition to the Black Death and the great economic depression, the towns experienced severe political crises. But even though the urban population was almost cut in half and volumes of production and trade were sharply reduced, town life continued to pulsate. In proportion to the reduced number of people, the reduced volume of trade was not catastrophic, and the towns soon recovered.

Conditions in the towns

The main focal centers of trade and production continued to be in the same areas as they had been in the High Middle Ages. Northern Italy has been described as "a quilt work of thriving city-states" and Flanders as "a continous city." Secular building on a more lavish scale continued in many towns, as is evidenced by numerous private homes, guild halls, and impressive public buildings that are still standing. Some towns even enjoyed a boom. Thus Barcelona and Valencia, Cologne and the towns of southern Germany, as well as the Hanseatic towns of northern Germany, increased in prosperity.

One of the greatest reverses suffered by many towns was a loss of much of the considerable independence they had enjoyed in the High Middle Ages. In the case of the English, French, and Spanish towns, the loss of independence and privileges was the result of the rising power of national monarchs, in that of German towns, to the rise of princely power, and in that of Italian towns to the rise of dictators and to renewed foreign intervention. The fact that the population at large in many towns lost its part in urban government was partly caused by the violent class struggles going on in most of them. The need for a strong hand to suppress strife and establish order was frequently satisfied by the rise of local dictators, known in Italy as "despots," or by royal intervention and appointment of supervisory officials, as occurred in France.

Split in the middle class in the Later Middle Ages

By the Later Middle Ages, the middle class was firmly established, but it had also split into competing groups. The upper middle class, known in Italy as the *popolo grasso* ("fat people"), was composed of the very wealthy, such as the great (wholesale) merchants, large-scale industrialists, and big-time financiers. The upper bourgeoisie sought political power in order to protect and enhance their wealth, and strove to control town governments, in which design they were successful more often than not. They frequently obtained aristocratic status by intermarriage with the aristocracy or by princely favor. They usually lived in luxury amid beautiful and pleasant surroundings, designed for display as well as for comfort. They also became interested in culture, both as a diversion and in order to improve their "public image." Besides impressive town houses, they often had extensive country estates.

The ordinary middle class in the towns, known in Italy as the *popolo minuto* (little people), included smaller property owners, ordinary shopkeepers, professional people, and the like—the bulk of the middle class. They usually occupied a secondary position in political affairs, as well as in business. Yet their way of life was generally comfortable and much superior to that of the proletariat. Their dwellings were usually attractive and snug, their food and drink abundant, and their clothes of good quality. An English queen complained that the wives of the burghers of Bruges were dressed in better clothing than she was. Most of the middle class lived a comfortable, fairly secure life, and though they were without the luxuries of the *haute bourgeoisie*, they were free from the risks of the great capitalists.

There was also a middle class in the country with larger than ordinary holdings. Many of the lesser aristocracy, such as the "knights" and "squires" in England, belonged to the middle class. In some cases, as in England, the rural middle class identified their interests with those of the urban middle class, to their mutual advantage; in others, as in France, they held themselves aloof. The mode of life of the rural middle class was usually both comfortable and prosaic.

The urban middle class continued to be organized in guilds and communes. But these associations often came to be dominated by the upper middle class. Sometimes journeymen's guilds were formed to counterbalance the ordinary craft guilds, which were controlled by capitalistic masters. Efforts of the ordinary bourgeoisie to compete with the great capitalists for control of urban governments were generally unsuccessful.

Later medieval society had a considerable degree of sophistication. Society in Renaissance Italy had a very modern aspect; and people in other areas were not far behind. Most of the lay pilgrims described in Chaucer's *Canterbury Tales* were from the ordinary middle class. Of this group, though essaying to rise higher, was the boastful merchant:

Middle class types

> There was a Merchant with a forked beard
> And motley dress; high on his horse he sat,
> Upon his head a Flemish beaver hat,
> And on his feet daintily buckled boots.
> He told of his opinions and pursuits
> In solemn tones, and how he never lost;
> The sea should be kept free at any cost
> (He thought) upon the Harwich-Holland ranges;
> He was an expert at dabbling in exchanges.

Surely of the ordinary urban middle class was the prudent lawyer:

> A Sergeant-at-the-law, who paid his calls,
> Wary and wise, for clients at St. Paul's
> There also was, of noted excellence.

Likewise the well-fixed artisans (evidently masters) who may have been rising from the ordinary to the upper middle class:

> A Haberdasher, a Dyer, a Carpenter,
> A Weaver, and a Carpet-Maker were
> Among our ranks, all in the livery
> Of one impressive guild-fraternity.

Typical of the rural middle class was the "franklin," a free rural landowner (freeholder) with larger than ordinary holdings, prosperous, pious, and a lover of good food:

> A landowner, a Franklin, had appeared;
> White as a daisy-petal was his beard.
> A sanguine man, high colored and benign,
> He loved a morning sop of cake in wine.

The proletariat in town and country bore the brunt of the current hard times. Their greatest assets were growing freedom and opportunity. Although in good times the urban proletariat enjoyed greater liberty and economic leeway than their rural counterparts, in hard times their position was correspondingly more difficult and precarious. The greatest peril confronting the urban proletariat was a lapse in their income due to unemployment or incapacity. The tavern was a resort for many, and the wolf was ever near the door. Urban workers usually lived in dark, cramped, poorly furnished tenements. Their diet was unbalanced, their food poor and simple, their garments limited and worn.

The proletariat

Yet we should not exaggerate the hardships of the urban proletariat. Many were better off than they might have been in the country, and they had greater opportunities. In times of depression, charity was usually available through the Church or guilds, and the possibility of better times loomed bright in the future. Many of the urban proletariat bettered their condition by industry, thrift, and resourcefulness.

There were likewise contrasts in the conditions of rural labor. The dissolution of the manorial system, which began in the High Middle Ages, was largely completed during the Later Middle Ages. Factors making for an elimination of serfdom included the great demands for labor following the Black Death as well as the continued spread of a money economy. Although they freed their serfs, landlords were often able to retain many of the incidental obligations of manorialism, such as tallage, *corvées*, *heriot*, and *merchet*. Still, many rural laborers profitted from the new conditions. While wages rose rapidly following the Black Death —increasing 50 per cent in England by 1400—rents generally remained fixed, to the renter's advantage. Many of the rural proletariat were able to save and purchase their own lands. Among Chaucer's pilgrims there was "a Plowman" who was a property owner, sufficiently solvent to pay his tithes readily and to give to the poor, as well as to spare the time and expense for a pilgrimage:

> . . . *an honest workman, good and true,*
> . . . *and he would help the poor*
> *For love of Christ, and never take a penny*
> *If he could help it, and, as prompt as any,*
> *He paid his tithes in full when they were due,*
> *On what he owned, and on his earnings too.*
> *He wore a tabard smock and rode a mare.*

Yet the lot of many other peasants worsened. Their security gone with the passing of manorialism, they lost their previous holdings through improvidence, laziness, or misfortune, and became hired laborers dependent on the "times" and seasons, and the number of competing hands, and the whims of the landlords. Still they had their freedom. While in the West labor was being emancipated, in Eastern Europe serfdom was being increasingly imposed upon the rural proletariat. This was partly because of the increased militarism of feudalism in the area, resulting from the necessity of fighting against aggressive Mongols (Tartars), Ottomans, and Slavs.

Beggars, migrants, and slaves

As a result of the the general economic depression and changing conditions, the number of paupers and beggars increased. These indigents were dependent upon the charities of individuals and religious institutions. We are told that in Florence alone there were some twenty-two thousand beggars. The number of migrant workers and tramps also increased. It is estimated that about twenty thousand workmen migrated into Brittany during the Hundred Years' War. Slavery also reappeared, as African "Blacks" and "Moors" were captured and sold by the Portuguese and others. The Portuguese explorations along the coasts of Africa, promoted by Henry the Navigator, were profitable in slaves as well as ivory, gold, and expanded geographical knowledge. There were an estimated twenty thousand slaves in Spanish-owned Majorca, and slavery also grew in Tuscany, Venetia, Istria, and Sicily.

Even as they were becoming less important, the feudal aristocracy became more pretentious, and made their strongest bids for power. During the wars of the fourteenth and early fifteenth centuries, the military services of the aristocracy were in great demand and they had a strong bargaining position. In the heyday of medieval parliamentarianism the lords were the dominant element in national assemblies. But the aristocrats helped to bring about their own downfall by their selfish arrogance, divisiveness, plots, violence, and disregard for the public welfare. They disrupted their countries by their prolonged civil wars, even as their military importance was being undermined by new tactics using archers, artillerymen, and pikemen, which restored the infantry to its ancient prominence in warfare.

The feudal aristocracy

With the enthronement of "Queen Money" the power of the great landholding aristocracy diminished in comparison with that of moneyed merchants, industrialists, and financiers. However, many of the aristocracy continued to live in the past and even increased their snobbishness. They stressed the importance of having the right blood and pedigree, and excluded others from knighthood. The code of chivalry became ever more involved. Castle building reached its apogee, and vast, imposing, complicated fortifications were constructed at a time when they were becoming obsolete due to gunpowder artillery. Armor became more elaborate and heavy, with complete suits of plate armor that made knights less maneuverable and often actually more vulnerable. Exclusive orders of chivalry such as the English Knights of the Garter and the Burgundian Knights of the Golden Fleece appeared.

In Italy, the aristocracy preferred to live in the towns and mixed with the upper bourgeoisie. They not only invested in businesses like the bourgeoisie did, but the two classes often intermarried. Beyond the Alps the aristocracy usually did not mingle with the middle class and shunned business and trade, preferring "a life of castle, camp, and court."

Pressures and strains brought about social unrest and uprisings. Among contributing causes were the want produced by the great depression, the ravages of the Black Death and prolonged warfare, the burden of increased taxes, and the oppressiveness of attempted government regulation. Increased individualism and intensified competition also played a part, while the fact that they were coming to be better off made the lower classes yearn for still greater benefits.

Social unrest and uprisings

Uprisings were more frequent in the towns, where the hardships produced by bad times were more severe. A common sequence in urban uprisings was initial cooperation of the ordinary middle class and the proletariat against the dominant upper middle class, temporary success, a growing split within the victorious combination, a winning over of the ordinary middle class by the upper middle class, temporary control of the government by the middle class at large, renewed division between the upper and ordinary middle classes, and finally a return to power by the upper middle class. A frequent variation was the interjection of a strong man or dictator at a certain point. Uprisings were numerous in northern Italy, the Low Countries, northern France, and western and southern Germany. Notable examples in Florence were the revolution of 1342, which followed the financial crash of the Bardi and Peruzzi, and that of 1378ff. known as the *Ciompi* (Confreres) revolt, which was headed by a wool carder.

Rural uprisings, although less frequent, were usually more violent and bloody. In addition to ordinary grievances, rural revolutionaries protested against the demanding of outmoded feudal dues and services. A general pattern in rural revolts was widespread rioting and looting, assemblage of a large force of peasants, a joint march on a seat of government, an interview with government authorities, a winning of supposed concessions, and a quick abandonment of governmental promises and execution of revolutionary leaders once the mobs were disbanded. Sometimes such revolts were directly suppressed by the slaughter of large numbers of poorly armed peasants by vindictive nobles. Among examples of peasant uprisings were the *Jacquerie* and *Tuchins* revolts in France, and the Wat Tyler and John Cade uprisings in England. The Wat Tyler Rebellion of 1381 in England was largely directed against the restrictive Ordinance of Laborers and a burdensome poll tax. It was jointly headed by Tyler and a clergyman named John Ball, and had as a slogan the couplet quoted at the head of this section. After the revolutionists were bought off by false promises and returned to their homes, their leaders were seized and executed. In Spain the serfs in Upper Catalonia revolted three times in the period from 1375 to 1471, and four times from 1351 to 1477.

Political concomitants of economic and social changes

Important political developments accompanied economic and social changes. A strong trend to representative government was fostered in the fourteenth century by the increased money and manpower needs of central governments and was assisted by a temporary working alliance between the middle class and the aristocracy. The Parliament in England, the Estates General in France, and the *Cortes* in the Iberian monarchies were all strong in the fourteenth and early fifteenth centuries. But in the second half of the fifteenth century the power of the monarchy was strengthened and parliamentarianism declined. Strong monarchs in this era included Henry VII in England, Louis XI in France, Ferdinand and Isabella in Spain, and Manoel I in Portugal. In similar manner the princes in Germany grew more powerful within their principalities, and despots ruled in the North Italian city-states. Even liberty-loving Florence came under the control of the Medici family. The aristocracy had so discredited themselves by their bitter factionalism and violence, resulting in destructive civil wars, that the middle class sought peace and order by supporting a strong monarchy. Changes in warfare such as the use of mercenary troops and gunpowder weapons that required greater capital outlays also tended to increase the monarch's power. Nationalism grew, personified in France by Joan of Arc and in Hungary by Jan Hunyadi. Expanding commerce and increased economic competition between areas also promoted unification. Town governments that had earlier been democratic tended to become plutocratic and oligarchical in the fourteenth century, and to be dominated by monarchical representatives or local dictators in the fifteenth century.

Strenuous competition between states led to improvements both in the techniques of international negotiation and in the conduct of warfare. The art of diplomacy took shape, with the Venetians in the lead. Permanent Venetian embassies were maintained in foreign capitals, and *The Reports of the Venetian Ambassadors* to their home government provided illuminating information concerning important contemporary personalities and conditions.

International relations: diplomacy and warfare

Warfare became more protracted and lethal, as in the case of the Hundred Years' War between England and France, the long duel between the Teutonic Knights and Poland, the continuing contest between Venice and Genoa for naval supremacy in the Mediterranean, the dogged resistance of the Bohemians to the Germans in the Hussite Wars, and the long struggle of the Swiss for independence from the Hapsburgs. Military developments both increased the effectiveness of warfare and decreased the role and importance of the feudal aristocracy. There was a growing use of missiles and projectiles. The arrows of English longbowmen defeated the French in several earlier battles of the Hundred Years' War, even as gunpowder artillery played a decisive part in its final phase. The fifteenth century saw an ever-increasing use of the *pot de fer*, the bombard, and the ribauld. The *pot de fer* was a short, squat, wide-mouthed "pot of iron," packed with lethal fragments projected by gunpowder. Bombards were large guns, which often used very heavy stone balls, highly effective for breaching walls. Ribaulds consisted of gun barrels clamped together or in ascending rows so arranged that they could be fired almost simultaneously against an enemy. The old cavalry charges of feudal warfare tended to give way to more closely coordinated "combined tactics," such as the English joint employment of longbowmen, infantry, and cavalry. More and more, too, warfare became as much a problem of financing as it was of military skill. Ships were staffed at first with archers, and later with guns (cannon) and artillerymen.

Economic and social developments also influenced religion. Competition for monetary income between lay rulers and Church leaders became intense. Monarchs tried to prevent reservations of the conferral of certain benefices to the Papacy, as well as unrestricted appeals of judicial cases to the courts of Rome, as is seen in the English *Statutes of Provisors* (1351) and *Premunire* (1353) and the French *Pragmatic Sanction of Bourges* (1438). The *Real Patronato* conceded by the Papacy to Ferdinand and Isabella gave them considerable control of the Spanish Church, first in Granada and then in America, and was subsequently extended to all Spain.

Related religious and cultural developments

The enhanced importance of the middle class also affected the Church. While some of the laity became more materialistic, others became more intensely religious. Many of the latter sought greater personal perfection by joining Third Orders or lay religious associations, or by pursuing mysticism. Some became involved in movements such as those of the Lollards and Hussites. Many of the pious as well as the materialistic agreed upon minimizing Church authority, rejecting tradition, and making individuals the ultimate formulators of their own beliefs and independent agents of their own salvation.

The laity also came to share more fully in culture, which came, in turn, to be more secular. Renaissance "humanism" stressed pagan classical literature, which became the core of the curriculum in the "new" education. The new curriculum was also expanded to include numerous subjects calculated to prepare the laity for various exigencies of secular life. The classical style of architecture, which was well adapted to secular edifices, private and public, was increasingly used for both ecclesiastical and secular structures. Neoclassical sculpture and painting likewise became more secular, natural, and realistic.

References for Chapter 25

GOOD treatments of economic and social conditions and related developments in the Later Middle Ages are to be found in WALLACE K. FERGUSON, *Europe in Transition, 1300–1500* (Boston: Houghton Mifflin, 1962), and EDWARD P. CHEYNEY, *The Dawn of a New Era, 1250–1453* (New York: Harper, 1936), as well as in PROSPER BOISSONADE, *Life and Work in Medieval Europe . . .* , tr. E. Power (New York: Knopf, 1927), and in JAMES W. THOMPSON, *Economic and Social History of the Later Middle Ages (1300–1530)* (New York: Century, 1931).

The best reference for late as well as earlier medieval economic history is the *Cambridge Economic History of Europe*, ed. J. CLAPHAM and E. POWER et al., vols. I–III (New York: Macmillan, 1941ff.). HARRY A. MISKIMIN, *The Economy of Early Renaissance Europe, 1300–1460* (Englewood Cliffs, N.J.: Prentice-Hall, 1969). Also useful are standard economic histories such as HERBERT HEATON, *Economic History of Europe* (New York: Harper, 1948), and MELVIN KNIGHT, *Economic History of Europe to the End of the Middle Ages* (Boston: Houghton Mifflin, 1926).

For commerce and finance, a very good reference is ROBERT S. LOPEZ and IRVING W. RAYMOND, *Medieval Trade in the Mediterranean World* (New York: Columbia U.P., 1955), which consists of selected documents preceded by excellent introductions. Another collection is that of GERTRUDE R. RICHARDS, *Florentine Merchants of the Age of the Medici* (Cambridge, Mass.: Harvard U.P., 1932), which consists of letters and other documents. FREDERIC C. LANE is author of two interesting, valuable studies: *Venetian Ships and Shipbuilders of the Renaissance* (Baltimore: Johns Hopkins, 1934) and *Andrea Barbarigo: Merchant of Venice (1418–1449)* (Baltimore: Johns Hopkins, 1944).

Popular introductions to the Hanseatic League are the brief HELEN ZIMMERN, *The Hansa Towns* (New York: Putnam's, 1907), and the more extensive, illustrated E. GEE NASH, *The Hansa: Its History and Romance* (London: Lane; New York: Dodd, 1929); a specialized study is JOHN A. GADE, *The Hanseatic Control of Norwegian Commerce During the Late Middle Ages* (Leiden: E. J. Brill, 1951). For the English wool trade, consult EILEEN POWER, *The Wool Trade in English Medieval History* (New York: Oxford U.P., 1941).

Concerning English trade and industry, see WILLIAM CUNNINGHAM, *The Growth of English Industry and Commerce During the Early and High Middle Ages* (Cambridge: Cambridge U.P., 1915), and the less comprehensive LOUIS F. SALZMAN, *English Industries of the Middle*

Ages . . . (Oxford: Clarendon, 1923).

Concerning banking, consult RAYMOND A. DE ROOVER, *The Rise and Decline of the Medici Bank* (Cambridge, Mass.: Harvard U.P., 1963), or his earlier, briefer *The Medici Bank: Its Organization, Management, Operation, and Decline* (New York: New York U.P., 1948) and his *Money, Credit, and Banking in Medieval Bruges* (Cambridge, Mass.: Harvard U.P., 1948); as well as RICHARD EHRENBERG, *Capital and Finance in the Age of the Renaissance: A Study of the Fuggers and Their Connections* (London: Cape, 1928), the first sixty-eight pages of which concern the Later Middle Ages; and ABBOTT P. USHER, *The Early History of Deposit Banking in Mediterranean Europe* (Cambridge, Mass.: Harvard U.P., 1943). Works concerning coinage include HEBERT E. IVES, *The Venetian Gold Ducat and Its Imitations*, ed. Philip Grierson (New York: American Numismatic Society, 1954), and ALBERT FEAVEARYEAR, *The Pound Sterling: A History of English Money* (Oxford: Oxford U.P., 1963).

Works on special topics include C. RAYMOND BEAZLEY, *The Dawn of Modern Geography*, 3 vols. (New York: Peter Smith, 1949); ARTHUR P. NEWTON, *Travel and Travellers of the Middle Ages* (New York: Knopf, 1926); and GEORGE O'BRIEN, *An Essay on Medieval Economic Teaching* (New York: Longmans, 1920).

The *Cambridge Medieval History*, 8 vols. and maps (Cambridge: Cambridge U.P., 1911–1936), has some good articles relating to late medieval society. Vol. VII has an article by CECIL ROTH on "The Jews in the Middle Ages," one by C. H. McIlwain on "Medieval Estates," and one by Eileen Power on "Peasant Life and Rural Conditions (c. 1100 to c. 1500)"; vol. VIII has an article by HAROLD J. LASKI on "Political Theory in the Later Middle Ages" and one by CHARLES OMAN on "The Art of War in the Fifteenth Century." A careful study of population at various times from the Later Roman Empire to the end of the Middle Ages has been made by JOSIAH C. RUSSELL, *Late Ancient and Medieval Population* (Philadelphia: American Philosophical Society, 1958; American Philosophical Society, *Transactions*, 48, pt. 3). The history of various European towns, with emphasis on the Later Middle Ages, is treated in several volumes of "The Medieval Towns Series" (London: Dent, 1898ff.). A general treatment of city-state governments is M. V. CLARKE, *The Medieval City State: An Essay on Tyranny and Federation in the Later Middle Ages* (London: Methuen, 1926); two excellent special studies are FERDINAND SCHEVILL, *History of Florence Through the Renaissance* (New York: Harcourt, 1936), and DAVID HERLIHY, *Pisa in the Early Renaissance: A Study of Urban Growth* (New Haven: Yale U.P., 1958).

The guild system and its decline in the Later Middle Ages are treated in GEORGE CLUNE, *The Medieval Gild System* (Dublin: Browns and Nolan, 1943); EDGCUMBE STALEY, *The Guilds of Florence* (London: Methuen, 1906); and CHARLES GROSS, *The Gild Merchant* . . . , 2 vols. (London: Oxford U.P., 1927). A well-documented study is that of SYLVIA L. THRUPP, *The Merchant Class of Medieval London (1300–1500)* (Chicago: Chicago U.P., 1948).

Snatches of life from every corner and level of society, although exaggerated in some respects, are extracted from source materials by GEORGE G. COULTON in his *Medieval Panorama: The English Scene from Conquest to Reformation* (New York: Macmillan, 1938). Four out of the six representative characters sketched by EILEEN E. POWER in her *Medieval People* (Boston: Houghton Mifflin, 1924; London: Methuen, 1950) (p.) are from the Later Middle Ages; whereas all of the six briefly presented by H. S. BENNETT in his *Six Medieval Men and Women* (New York: Atheneum, 1962) are from the same period. RAYMOND L. KILGOUR, *The Decline of Chivalry As Shown in French Literature of the Late Middle Ages* (Cambridge, Mass.: Harvard U.P., 1937), is an interesting study. A most comprehensive history of the Jews is SALO W. BARON, *A Social and Religious History of the Jews*, in 10 plus vols. (New York: Columbia U.P., 1952ff.), in which vol. 9 and 10 concern the Jews in the Later Middle Ages. A more specialized study is that of GUIDO KISCH, *The Jews in Medieval Germany: A Study of Their Legal and Social Status* (Chicago: Chicago U.P., 1949). A more succinct survey is provided by CECIL ROTH in the *Cambridge Medieval History*, VII, 632–664.

A general interpretation is essayed by ALFRED W. VON MARTIN in his *Sociology of the Renaissance* (New York: Oxford U.P., 1944); ideals prevalent among the cultured upper classes in Italy are reflected in BALDASSARE CASTIGLIONE, *The Book of the Courtier* (1520), tr. Thomas Hoby (New York: Dutton 1944), written at the beginning of the sixteenth century, and available in various translations and editions. Socioeconomic theories with a socialistic *tendence* are the special interest of BEDE JARRETT in his *Social Theories of the Middle Ages, 1200–1500* (London: Burns Oates, 1935), as well as in his briefer *Medieval Socialism* (London: Jack, 1935) and in his more specific *Saint Antonio and Medieval Economics* (St. Louis: Herder, 1914).

[ENGLAND AND FRANCE IN THE LATER MIDDLE AGES.   Chapter 26.

THE STORIES of England and France in the Later Middle Ages were closely intertwined, owing mainly to the continental holdings and claims of the English kings as opposed to the feudal rights and ambitions of the French monarchs. The complexities of this Gordian knot were severed by the sword of the Hundred Years' War. Partly as a result of the stress produced by prolonged warfare, external and internal, the monarchy was weakened in both countries during the fourteenth and early fifteenth centuries; but it grew stronger and more absolute in the later fifteenth century. Whereas a strong Parliamentary tradition of popular representation in government was established in England, the representative Estates General in France failed to root itself firmly in similar manner.

(1337-1453)   THE HUNDRED YEARS' WAR.
                                         Section 76.

> The English archers shot their arrows so skillfully and rapidly that it seemed as if it were snowing. [Froissart, concerning the Battle of Crécy in his *Chronicle*.]

THE Hundred Years' War between France and England (1337–1453) was really a series of armed conflicts, punctuated by truces and peace treaties. The Hundred Years' War finally settled the question of whether or not the English kings were to retain extensive and virtually independent possessions on the continent in territory nominally subject to the French kings. Besides profoundly affecting both England and France, the Hundred Years' War exercised an important influence on general European history.

Origins and outbreak of the war

The chief cause of the Hundred Years' War was the incongruous relationship whereby the English kings were nominal vassals of the French kings for Guienne and Gascony, yet refused to render most of their feudal duties for their fiefs. The indeterminate and fluctuating boundaries of these fiefs were another bone of contention. While the French kings were attempting to centralize their government, eliminate feudal intermediaries, and diminish limitations upon their authority, the English kings were endeavoring to secure greater independence and expand their French holdings. The fact that Guienne and Gascony brought the English a large income and cut off the French in the interior from the sea further aroused French jealousy and resentment.

Among other causes of conflict were English support of the Flemish against the French crown and French aid to the Scots against the English crown. While prosperous Flanders was a French fief, most of the Flemish resented French overlordship. On several occasions the Flemish revolted against their French count and French king. As the principal suppliers of wool for the Flemish textile industry, the English were natural allies of the Flemish middle and lower classes, with whom they had close business relations and whose resistance against the French they supported. Conversely the French were allies and supporters of the Scots. Since the days of Edward I, the English had claimed overlordship over Scotland, whereas the Scots had refused to submit, with the French lending encouragement and various types of assistance to the Scots.

The frequent clashes between French and English fishermen over fishing rights constituted another irritant. Meanwhile the dispossessed Robert of Artois, who had been banished from France on charges of forgery and attempted murder, urged Edward III to claim the French throne. Edward III was a grandson of Philip IV in the female line (as the son of Philip's daughter Isabella), and hence in the direct line of succession, whereas Philip VI was a descendant only in the collateral line. Edward's claim, however, had been voided both by precedent and by the French Assembly of Notables.

In 1336 the French fleet, which had assembled at Marseilles, was moved to the Norman coast, constituting an obvious threat against the English, who were fighting the Scots. Edward III straightway denounced Philip VI in Parliament and forbade the exportation of wool from England, while Philip VI, on his part, declared all the French holdings of Edward III forfeit (1337). Edward responded by sending a formal message of defiance to the French king. In the same year the English attacked the French island of Cadzand off the Flemish coast, thus beginning the war.

The Hundred Years' War lasted, on and off, for some 16 years, and was a seesaw struggle. In the first period the English were successful, in the second the French. In the third period there was a lull. The English won in the fourth period, but the French turned the tables in the final period. It has been aptly observed: *The English won the battles, but the French won the war.*

English advantages in the first period (1337–1360)

The initial advantage lay with the English. Even though France could boast a population several times that of England, French strength was more apparent than real. Much of France was held by quasi-independent vassals. The greatest loyalty of the populace was to their town or region or local lord. Great vassals, such as the Dukes of Brittany and Burgundy, were virtually autonomous, while collateral houses holding royal appanages, such as Anjou and Berry, enjoyed similar status. The inhabitants of southern France, the land of the *langue d'oc*, felt apart from and hostile to those of the northern land of the *langue d'oueil*. Similar aversion existed between the northern French and the German-speaking Flemish. The French kings placed their chief reliance on the clumsy old system of "hosting" vassals by summoning them to observe their feudal obligation of fighting for their king.

England, on the other hand, was stronger. The English king had a lucrative, dependable source of income in export taxes on wool, hides, and tin (known as "poundage") and an import tax on wines (known as "tonnage"); and Parliament was accustomed to granting further taxes, such as sales taxes and income taxes, for special purposes. The English kings had a regular army in the royal pay, a well-trained, coordinated, disciplined force built up during the Welsh and Scottish wars.

English leaders had been compelled to modify the old feudal tactics of direct cavalry charges in favor of the so-called combined tactics, in order to fight the unconventional Welshmen and Scots. In great battles such as Crécy, Poitiers, and Agincourt, the English took up a favorable position on an eminence approached over difficult terrain. The main body of the English dismounted and sought the protection of rocks, trees, hedges, and ramparts as well as constructed breastworks and implanted pointed stakes. As the enemy charged, English archers posted on the flanks and interspaced along the line mowed them down. The longbow, about the height of a man, had a maximum range of over three hundred yards and could pierce armor at a hundred yards. The English longbow could be shot three to six times as fast as the partly mechanical crossbows used by the Genoese archers who were regularly employed by the French. English archers had developed great accuracy with the longbow as a result of long practice, which was encouraged by the government. Unfortunately for the French, their sole tactic consisted in direct old-fashioned head-on charges, relying on their pluck and numbers together with their horsemanship and skill with lance and sword. When the enemy was sufficiently disrupted by the lethal arrows of the archers, the English foot soldiers would move onto the battlefield and finish off or capture the unhorsed French knights.

English victories

At the beginning of the war, although Edward III had obtained the alliance of various neighboring German princes, frequently by "gifts," and the Flemish had revolted against the French (1338), costly English expeditions in 1338 and 1340 were unable even to take Cambrai (1338) or Tournai (1340).

In 1340, however, the English obtained maritime ascendance with their crushing defeat of the French fleet, reinforced by Genoese elements off Flemish Sluys. The English outmaneuvered the French fleet by a rapid pivotal movement, which put the wind and sun at their backs, and used their longbowmen, whom they had stationed on their decks, with deadly effect. The French fleet was destroyed and thousands of French soldiers and sailors were lost. In Brittany, the English successfully intervened in 1341 on the side of John de Montfort, and thus secured a new ally and a new avenue of approach.

In 1346 Edward brought an estimated 15,000 men to Normandy and took Caen, whence he swung up the Seine Valley and through northwestern France on a pillaging raid. At Crécy, in far northwestern France, the English army of about 13,000 men was overtaken by a French force of an estimated 40,000 men that had been raised by Philip VI. Outnumbered three to one, the English took up a defensive position on a ridge at the edge of a woods, where they dismounted, dug pits to their front, and took advantage of natural cover. Squadrons of archers were stationed on the flanks of each of the three "battles" of men-at-arms. Although the French were exhausted by several days of forced marches, their leaders refused to wait. Wave after wave of French knights charged up the incline into the murderous range of the English longbows. As the wounded and unhorsed knights floundered in the muddy fields, the English moved to dispatch or capture them. French losses were estimated at 4,000 to 15,000 men; English casualties were negligible.

Crécy (1346) and Calais

Edward III now withdrew to the important seaport of Calais, which he besieged for almost a year. After a French army came to the neighborhood but failed to attempt a rescue, the famished burghers finally surrendered. Edward strongly fortified the city, which became a key English port and base. Froissart declared: *The English commons love Calais more than any other town, seeing that as long as they possess it, they carry the keys of France at their girdle.*

The war was now interrupted by the apocalyptic Black Death, which moved across Western Europe (1347–1350). When the contest was actively resumed in 1355, the Duke of Lancaster made a swift raid across northwestern France. The following year (1356), the Black Prince Edward with an army of an estimated five thousand to seven thousand men made another "grand cavalcade" northward from Bordeaux into the rich valley of the Loire. In the vicinity of Poitiers the Black Prince was overtaken by a large French army of an estimated fourteen thousand to twenty thousand men raised by King John the Good, and took up a defensive position on a slight elevation. Acting on the supposition that fighting on foot had won the day for the English at Crécy, King John had his men dismount. But as the French men-at-arms plodded up the incline toward the English, who were strung along a hedge and the edge of a wood, they were cut down like waddling ducks by the longbow

Poitiers (1356)

archers. As the final contingent, commanded by King John, engaged the hard-pressed English in hand-to-hand combat, the Black Prince sent a detachment of cavalry that had been held in reserve to assail the French from the rear. The English victory was even more complete than at Crécy. In addition to innumerable infantrymen, an estimated two thousand French knights were slain and two thousand taken prisoner. Among the latter was King John himself.

Treaty of Bretigny (1360)

The English now held a trump card in the person of the French king and the French were forced to negotiate. Eventually Edward settled for the Treaty of Bretigny (or Calais) (1360). The ransom of King John was set at the enormous sum of 3 million gold ecus, to be paid in installments. According to stipulations, Edward III was to obtain a much larger Aquitaine in full sovereignty, together with Ponthieu (the region of Crécy) and Calais; but he was to renounce his claim to the French throne. Edward's renunciation and the French transfer of sovereignty were to be delayed until the completion of other terms, which were never fulfilled.

French recovery (1360–1380)

A change of fortunes occurred in the second phase of the war owing to improved French leadership and new French strategy. The intelligent young French King Charles V had as ministers able Constable Bertrand Du Guesclin and capable Admiral Jean de Vienne, whereas the aging Edward III of England was becoming senile and an easy prey of favorites.

Using as an excuse an appeal from some of the Black Prince's discontented vassals in Aquitaine, and invoking the legal point that sovereignty there had not yet passed to the English, Charles intervened in southwestern France, renewing the war (1369). While the newly formed French fleet under de Vienne, reinforced by Castilian elements, won control of the sea, French armies, commanded by the redoubtable Du Guesclin, shunned pitched battles, yet took fortified place after fortified place from the English by surprise attacks and sieges as well as by arranging voluntary surrender. Popular songs compared Du Guesclin and his men to cats in their skill in scaling lofty walls and to sunlight in their ability to penetrate behind them.

One of Charles's steps was to obtain from the Estates General recognition of his right to levy a direct tax as well as a sales tax. With funds thus collected, he was able to build up a regular army, which made possible his military successes. By 1380, the English retained only coastal positions consisting of a strip from the vicinity of Bordeaux to that of Bayonne in the southwest, and the regions of the ports of Cherbourg, Brest, and Calais in the northwest.

Indecisive interval (1380–1415)

The third phase of the war (1380–1415) was a sort of breathing spell that saw only minor, desultory action. Both governments were preoccupied with serious internal troubles. In England, the last Plantagenet, Richard II, was enmeshed in quarrels with his barons that eventuated in his overthrow by 1399, while his successor, Henry IV (1399–1413), was mainly concerned with firmly establishing his new Lancastrian dynasty upon the throne. In France, the selfish regency of the uncles of the young Charles VI prevailed until 1388 and was renewed in 1392, when Charles manifested incurable insanity. The dominant fact in French politics now came to be a struggle for control between the houses of Orleans–Armagnac and Burgundy.

In the fourth phase of the war the English attained their greatest success.

English success in the fourth phase (1415–1429)

Whereas France, nominally ruled by the insane Charles VI, was divided by the violent struggle between the houses of Burgundy and Armagnac, new English enthusiasm was generated by the vigorous and ambitious young Lancastrian King, Henry V. The adventuresome Henry V promptly reasserted English claims, and, having secured a promise of neutrality from Burgundy, invaded France with an estimated 10,000 men (1415). After a month's siege, during which he used cannon to "bete dom the wallis," he took Harfleur by the mouth of the Seine. Leaving a sizable garrison at Harfleur, Henry moved northward through Normandy and Picardy toward Calais.

At Agincourt, the English now were overtaken by a French army of an estimated 12,000 to 24,000 men. In general, the battle of Agincourt (1415) was a repetition of Crécy and Poitiers. The English took up their position on a slight elevation at one end of a narrow corridor flanked by woods and implanted stakes to their front. The French were compelled to advance on a restricted front, over plowed fields recently soaked by driving rain. In the press and confusion they were mowed down by the lethal arrows of the English longbowmen, trampled by their own cavalry, slain or captured by the English infantry. At the close, the French had lost an estimated 6,000 to 10,000 men; the English only a few hundred.

After their smashing victory, the English occupied Normandy (1417–1419). As a result of the murder of Duke John the Fearless of Burgundy by the Dauphin's men in 1419, Duke Philip the Good of Burgundy allied with the English and obtained control of the French King and Queen. After further English successes, Duke Philip and King Henry negotiated the Treaty of Troyes (1420), according to which the Dauphin was disinherited, and Henry V was to marry the former's sister, Princess Catherine, with the right of succession to the French throne on the death of her father, Charles VI.

Treaty of Troyes (1420)

The Dauphin Charles and his supporters, including relatives ruling the appanages of Anjou, Berry, and Bourbon, refused to accept the Treaty of Troyes, and held out south of the Loire. Henry V of England died prematurely in 1422, and Charles VI of France later the same year. The rival claimants for the French throne were the infant Henry VI of England and the "disinherited" adult Dauphin, Charles. Young Henry VI was ably represented on the continent by his uncle, the Duke of Bedford, "a strenuous man, humane and just."

From 1422 to 1428 the war was at a standstill. The Duke of Bedford, regent in France, was handicapped by the initial confusion of government transition, the vagaries of his brother Humphrey of Gloucester, regent in England, the opposition there of the powerful Beauforts, the unreliability of the Burgundians, and the ingrained resentment of the French against foreign rulers. Meanwhile the Dauphin, Charles, was listless and inde-

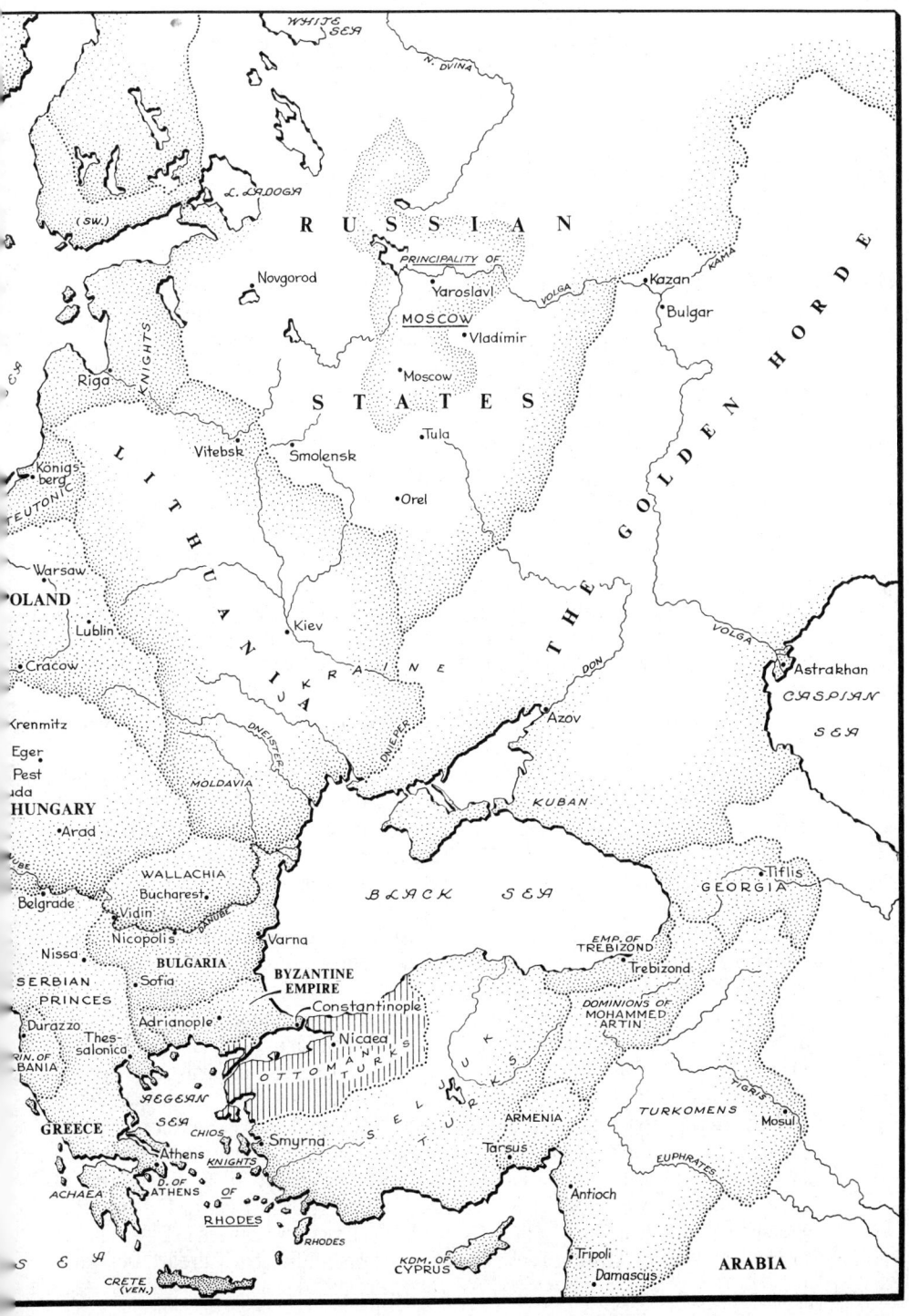

Final phase of the war (1429-1453): Joan of Arc

cisive, dominated by selfish favorites, given to the pleasures of the Loireland, and perennially short of funds. But in 1428 Bedford decided to act and besieged the key city of Orleans, at the gateway to the south. As no effective effort to relieve Orleans was made by the Dauphin, it seemed that final English victory was at hand.

At this point (1429) a young peasant girl of sixteen from the village of Domremy in northeastern France appeared at the court of Charles at Chinon and told of supernatural visions, which had instructed her to find and counsel the Dauphin. The coming of Joan of Arc marked the beginning of the fifth and final phase of the war. Several factors conspired to help the French cause, as the English weakness grew from day to day. In England strife between the Beauforts and Gloucester became more bitter until it resulted in the uneasy victory of the Beauforts. In English-occupied France the unpopularity of *les Goddams* increased. English alienation of the Burgundians and the essentially divergent interests of the two allies became ever more apparent. And capable English leadership would be lacking after the death of Bedford in 1435.

As the English weakened, the French grew stronger. The inspiration of Joan of Arc stirred French patriotism. Aggravated by the English occupation, the French became ever more conscious of their own nationality. Natural French advantages, including their superior numbers and resources, began to assert themselves. Able advisors and worthy ministers rallied to the Dauphin's service. The Estates General allowed the royal government to revive the taxes of Charles V. The government thus was able to maintain a regular army of an estimated 30,000 men containing roughly equal numbers of infantry and mounted men.

The appearance of "the Maid" at Chinon stirred the court of the Dauphin to unaccustomed activity. After extensive investigation, Joan was provided with a suit of armor and a horse, given a lesser command, and sent along with an army of about 4,000 to 6,000 men commanded to relieve beleaguered Orleans. The company of the Maid inspired the French soldiers, who overran the English positions and lifted the siege.

Since Joan insisted that the Dauphin be crowned at Reims, Charles was escorted by an army of 8,000 to 12,000 men to the traditional site of French coronations. After being established as an anointed ruler, Charles made a half-hearted feint at Paris. When the capital failed to surrender voluntarily, he withdrew south of the Loire.

Joan of Arc was henceforth permitted to engage only in small-scale activities. While attempting to relieve Compiègne, which was being besieged by the Burgundians, she was taken prisoner and turned over to the English (1430). Determined to demonstrate to the world that Joan lacked divine approbation, the English had her tried by a hand-picked ecclesiastical tribunal. Despite Joan's candor and consistency and her evident good faith and sincerity, she was convicted as a witch and a heretic and condemned to be burned at the stake (1431). During the execution, an English soldier is said to have exclaimed: "We have burned a saint!" Although the English had sought to discredit her and the French cause, the opposite occurred, and Joan became stronger in death than in life.

Encouraged by the example of the Maid, French patriots in the government launched upon reform and reorganization. The royal administration was purged. Burgundy was reconciled by concessions in the Treaty of Arras (1435). Recognition of the King's right to levy a direct tax, in addition to sales taxes, was obtained from the Estates General by 1439. The French army was reorganized. The *gens d'ordonnance* or regular mercenary soldiers consisted of about 10,000 to 15,000 infantrymen, known as *franc archers* or "Free Archers" (due to their exemption from taxation), and about 12,000 cavalrymen who were organized into companies composed of 100 lances, each of which comprised six men. The new army had gunpowder artillery, manned by technicians and helpers, many of whom were Scottish.

French victory: Results of the war

The French liberated the Ile de France and retook Paris in 1436. With the help of their "new weapon" of gunpowder artillery they gained speedy entrance into English-held fortified places without long sieges. Occasionally, as at Formigny (1450) in Normandy, and Castillon (1453) in Aquitaine, they used cannon effectively on the open battlefield. The effect of the cannon in battle was probably as much psychological as physical, since the blasting and shot frightened the horses and demoralized the men. The French took Normandy by 1450, Guienne and Gascony by 1453. When the war ended informally in 1453 all that remained to the English was Calais.

The Hundred Years' War decided that England was not to retain continental possessions of consequence. The English were thus left free to devote their attention to their own unification and democratization, industrial and commercial development, and eventual overseas colonial empire. The development of the English parliamentary tradition established precedents for modern representative government. France, for its part, was left free to proceed with its own unification so that it could eventually attain European leadership. The war encouraged French nationalism and left the French monarchy strong and on its way to early modern absolutism.

ENGLAND IN THE LATER MIDDLE AGES.
Section 77.

The King of England cannot arbitrarily change the laws or impose new taxes upon his subjects without their consent. [Sir John Fortescue in his *Praise of the Laws of England* (fifteenth century).]

THE English firmly established the tradition of limited monarchy and Parliamentary participation in their government during the Later Middle Ages, despite the fact that at the close of the period the monarchy was temporarily almost absolute. English territorial losses during the era were eventually largely offset by commercial expansion. Colorful charac-

The Later Middle Ages

ters and dramatic action enliven the narrative, illustrating the uneasiness of kingship and the disruptive influence of the feudal aristocracy.

The unhappy reign of Edward II (1307–1327)

Weak Edward II (1307–1327) was inordinately attached to selfish favorites, as well as apt to give uncontrolled vent to pent-up frustrations. After a crushing defeat by the Scots at Bannockburn (1314), Edward forsook his attempted conquest of Scotland. The great nobles and Parliament were soon emboldened to take matters into their own hands because of Edward's incompetence and his immoderate affection for Peter Gaveston, a Gascon adventurer. In 1310 they forced Edward II to accept a committee of twenty-one barons, the Lords Ordainers, to reform the government. The Ordinances of 1311 subjected the royal government to parliamentary supervision, and the following year baronial opponents captured and ruthlessly murdered Peter Gaveston.

For a while the deeply offended Edward seemed docile and cooperative. In 1322 an obeisant Parliament repealed the Ordinances of 1311, whereupon Edward embarked on a period of arbitrary, impolitic rule, vindictively striking back at his detractors and opponents with confiscations, imprisonments, and executions. Meanwhile rumor accused Edward of immoral relations with his inseparable companion and mentor, Hugh Despenser, and his unfaithful wife Isabella fled to France.

When Queen Isabella and her lover, Mortimer, returned to England with a small army in 1326, the barons and Parliament rallied to their side and Edward found himself virtually without supporters. The hapless King was taken prisoner, along with Hugh Despenser and his father, both of whom were tortured and hanged. Parliament declared Edward II deposed, and his young son Edward III king in his stead. His captors persuaded Edward II to abdicate, and then, moving him from castle to castle, apparently brutally murdered him.

Edward III (1327–1377)

Queen Isabella, who became regent for her young son, shared power with her "gentle Mortimer." A "Shameful Peace" was arranged with Scotland. But in 1330, Edward III, who had become seventeen, seized control, and promptly had Mortimer executed. Edward III was energetic, personable, and chivalric; a skillful general and statesman. But he was also vain, extravagant, and impractical. He committed England to the ultimately disastrous Hundred Years' War, which began as he was on the verge of subjecting the Scots. In the first phase of the war, the English won extraordinary victories over the French and obtained the advantageous Peace of Bretigny (1360); but these gains were canceled by their losses in the second phrase.

Because of Edward's chronic need of costly support for his bellicose foreign policy, Parliament was summoned forty-nine times in as many years, and made important gains. Edward and his Parliaments attempted to regulate the English economy in various ways. Growing English opposition to the French Papacy at Avignon found expression in the restrictive Statutes of *Provisors* (1351) and *Praemunire* (1353).

The unfortunate Richard II

The young son of the Black Prince, who became king as Richard II in 1377, was only ten years old at his accession. A long minority ensued. The new government inherited serious problems, including a losing war, an empty treasury, a demanding baronry, overbearing older relatives of the King, such as Duke John of Gaunt, and a discontented, overburdened populace. Popular unrest erupted in 1381 in the so-called Wat Tyler Rebellion, headed by a rough ex-soldier of that name and a socialistic priest named John Ball. The government and the young King at first pretended acceptance of peasant demands, such as the abolition of servile dues. But, after the rebels dispersed, governmental officials reneged on their promises and took vengeance on the rebel leaders.

(1377–1399)

In 1386, the barons forced the young King to appoint a reform council to supervise the royal government. Although pleasant, brave, and dramatic, Richard was easily led by favorites and erratic in his reactions. His laxity and extravagance bred opposition and lack of confidence, and he was imbued with autocratic ideas. In 1388, on the insistence of the so-called Lords Appellant, the "Merciless Parliament" insisted on the removal of five of the King's ministers and their execution or banishment on charges of treason.

For a decade the embittered Richard nursed his resentment. After the death of his beloved wife, Anne, he indulged in excesses of various sorts, and in 1397 he resorted to arbitrary rule. Richard forced Parliament to grant him the tax on wool for life, and vented his wrath upon his opponents, such as the Lords Appellant and his cousin, Duke Henry of Lancaster, by confiscations and executions.

In 1399, during Richard's absence in Ireland, the dispossessed Henry of Lancaster returned from exile, and England rallied to his side. Richard, who found himself virtually without supporters, was tricked into surrendering and forced to abdicate as "insufficient and useless." Parliament declared Richard deposed, and Henry of Lancaster king in his stead. Richard was kept for several months in harsh confinement in a dungeon without sufficient food or heat, where he died, apparently from starvation and cold.

With the accession of the Lancastrian dynasty, Parliament attained the height of power. Henry IV owed his throne to Parliament; Henry V required Parliament's support for his ambitious overseas operations; and Parliament was ascendant during the reign of Henry VI. For some time, Henry IV (1399–1413) had to devote most of his attention to suppressing recurrent rebellions. Because of his insecurity, and to consolidate his dynasty, the King acceded to the demands of Parliament, which began to audit royal accounts and supervise governmental expenditures. For similar reasons, Henry IV condoned a "bastard feudalism," consisting in local usurpation of royal powers; conciliated the Church by taking steps against the Lollards; and pursued a foreign policy of peace.

The Lancastrian dynasty (1415–1461): Henry IV, V, and VI

The ambitious, enterprising Henry V (1413–1422), discarding his father's caution, renewed the English claim to the French throne. Invading France with a large, well-equipped army, Henry V won control of northern France with Burgundian assistance, and obtained recognition of his right to succeed to the French throne. During his absences on the continent, his government in England was carried on by his brothers, Gloucester and Bedford. The unexpected early death of Henry V brought to the throne his young son, Henry VI (1422–1461), who, during a nominal reign of forty years, actually ruled very little. For two decades he was a minor, and after that a simple-minded, pious nonentity, periodically mad and unequal to kingship.

The Beauforts and Gloucester and York

In England there was a seesaw struggle to control the government between the Duke of Gloucester, who was regent there, and the Beauforts, a branch of the Lancastrians. During Henry's minority, which lasted until 1437, Gloucester usually held the edge; but after 1441 the Beauforts gained ascendance. The latter greatly strengthened their position by bringing strong-willed Margaret of Anjou from France to be Henry's queen. The Beaufort faction was initially headed by Cardinal Henry Beaufort, then by the Earl of Suffolk, and later by the Duke of Somerset. By 1447 the Earl of Suffolk was so strong that he could arrest the Duke of Gloucester, who died within five days under suspicious circumstances.

As the unpopularity of the Beauforts increased, Richard, Duke of York, a cousin of Henry VI and a prospective heir to the throne, became the leader of the opposition. From 1452 to 1455, York was in control of the government. In 1455, after being ousted by the Beaufort Duke of Somerset, with the aid of Margaret and the King, York appealed to force, thus beginning the Wars of the Roses.

Wars of the Roses (1455–1485)

The Wars of the Roses derive their name from the tradition that the Lancastrian emblem was a red rose and the symbol of York a white rose. The wars were mainly a contest between factions of the nobility, whom they eventually helped to discredit. The great lords had their own bands of armed retainers, and it was largely their unquenchable ambitions and proclivity to violence, vengeance, and anarchy that kept the conflict alive. In 1455, Richard of York defeated and slew Somerset, after which he was in control of the government until the following year, when he was ousted by the Queen's party. Although Richard of York returned to power after Warwick's victory at Northampton (1460), he was surprised, defeated, and slain at Wakefield later the same year. After a great victory of Richard's son, Edward of York, at Mortimer's Cross (1461), the Yorkists regained control, while Queen Margaret and her husband fled to Scotland whence Margaret continued the struggle.

Edward IV (1461–1483)

Although lazy and sensual, Edward IV, of York (1461–1483), was also clever and could be alternately charming and cruel. When Margaret of Anjou again put an army in the field, it was routed at Hexam (1464). The following year Henry VI was taken prisoner and confined to the Tower.

For some time, Edward IV was content to allow his dynamic cousin, the Earl of Warwick, to administer the government, while he enjoyed himself; but eventually this tutelage became unbearable. A definite break came with Edward's unexpected marriage to Elizabeth Woodville. When Warwick realized that his ascendance was being lost to the Woodvilles, he engineered a rebellion that temporarily put Edward in his power (1469–1470). After Edward recovered control, Warwick joined forces with the Lancastrians, and temporarily returned Henry VI to the throne.

England and France

Jealousies and defections in the Lancastrian party, however, weakened "the Kingmaker," whom Edward IV defeated and killed at Barnet in 1471. The final defeat of the Lancastrians came later the same year at Tewkesbury, where the royal couple were taken prisoner. Henry VI was later murdered in the Tower, Margaret was sent back to France, and Edward's slippery brother Clarence was reportedly drowned in a butt of his favorite wine.

Realizing the unreliability of parliamentary support, Edward IV ruled as an autocrat, and avoided calling Parliament as far as possible. He was able to dispense with solicitation of parliamentary grants because of his economies and the great wealth that he obtained by wholesale confiscations of the properties of the Lancastrians and their supporters. He obtained the grant of export-import duties from Parliament for life and called Parliament only six times in twenty-two years. But he was prevented from being a tyrant by his laxity. After the overthrow of Warwick, Edward's younger brother, Richard of Gloucester, controlled the administration.

Richard III (1483–1485)

Edward IV was succeeded by his son Edward V, a lad of twelve, with Richard of Gloucester as Protector. Rivalry for control ensued between Richard and the Woodvilles, with Richard claiming that Edward's children by Elizabeth were illegitimate, due to an earlier private marriage of Edward to Eleanor Talbot. After building up support, Gloucester had Parliament declare him King Richard III. Edward's two young sons were consigned to the Tower, where they disappeared. Richard's callous treatment of his rivals, and particularly the apparent murder of his brother's sons, made him a monster in the popular eye. Many of his former supporters deserted him. When Henry Tudor, Earl of Richmond, head of the Lancastrian faction, returned to England with an army lent by Anne of France, the country rallied to his cause. Richard's troops melted away and he was overwhelmed and slain on Bosworth Field (1485).

Tudor absolutism (1485ff.): Henry VII

At the accession of Henry VII, England was weary of strife and disorder. The war-sick country, particularly the middle class, was willing to support a strong but moderate government. "Tudor Absolutism" initiated by Henry VII consisted in ruling with a firm hand, yet using tact and moderation; in being absolute in practice though not in theory; and in persuading rather than commanding Parliament.

Henry VII was shrewd and thrifty, conciliatory yet firm. His main objectives were to restore order and to consolidate his dynasty. In order to conciliate the Yorkists, he married Princess Elizabeth of York, daughter of Edward IV. Despite numerous uprisings during the first twelve years of his reign, he avoided vindictive retaliations. Members of his first Parliament swore to observe his Statutes of Livery and Maintenance, which forbade keeping armed bands of uniformed retainers. To enforce the law against even the mightiest, he had his own council sit as an extraordinary Court of the Star Chamber. To solicit the favor of foreign powers, he married his children to members of other royal families: his eldest son Arthur and, after Arthur's early death, his second son Henry (later

Henry VIII) to Princess Catherine of Aragon; his daughter Margaret to King James IV of Scotland; and his daughter Mary to King Louis XII of France.

To avoid dependence on Parliament, Henry VII practiced strict economy. He augmented his royal revenues, as well as wooed the support of the middle class, by promoting the prosperity of the country. Parliament was summoned only once in the last twelve years of his reign.

Growth of the English Parliamentary tradition

The most important development in late medieval English history was the establishment of a tradition of popular participation in government through a representative Parliament with a limited monarchy. Among reasons for this, some of which have already been seen, were the previous experience of Englishmen with representative governmental institutions; the continuous and pressing financial needs of the English kings for military overseas operations, especially during the Hundred Years' War; the compactness of the kingdom and comparative ease of assembling a national legislature; the existence of a considerable middle class, composed of business men and landholders; and the cooperation between rural knights and urban burgesses, whose representatives combined into one effective house.

The two-house system (Commons and Lords) made the English Parliament effective. Originally Parliament had four houses—Lords (great lay barons and ecclesiastical prelates), Lower Clergy, Knights (rural landowners of consequence), and Burgesses (townspeople). The House of Lords was a continuation of the king's feudal Great Council, which was composed of his leading vassals and prelates, and continued to be the high court of the land. The lower clergy soon dropped out of Parliament, finding attendance burdensome, and being content to deal with the King in their annual "Convocations" and through the bishops. Gradually the Knights and Burgesses took to conferring together in order to confront the Lords with a united front, and combined into one "House of Commons," which greatly increased their bargaining power.

Rise and decline of Parliamentry power

The basic power of Parliament, recognized from the beginning, was that of levying taxes. This was based on the right of most of the constituents represented by Parliament members—townspeople and freemen, as well as the aristocracy and clergy—to be exempt from any additional levies except by their voluntary consent. The principle that new taxation must be approved by Parliament was foreshadowed as early as 1297, and clearly enunciated in the 1340s. The postulate of "no taxation without representation" thus traces back to the Middle Ages. Using this power to grant taxes as a lever, Parliament gradually obtained the recognized right of making laws in conjunction with the King. Early in the fourteenth century the parliamentary principle was established that "redress of grievances must precede grant of supply." Such laws were originally royal answers to Commons' "petitions," but in the course of time they became "statutes" or "bills," whose exact wording was formulated beforehand in Parliament, and were regarded as joint products of Parliament and king. Among other powers secured by Parliament were those of determining the royal succession, deposing kings, approving new royal lines, and impeaching royal ministers. Among privileges that came to be recognized as belonging to members of Parliament were those of freedom of speech in Parliament and freedom from arrest on their way to and from sessions.

In the mid-fifteenth century, Sir John Fortescue, in his *Praise of the Laws of England*, stressed the fact that England was a limited monarchy, in which taxation and legislation were products of the joint action of people and king, and were dependent on popular consent as well as on the royal will. He contrasted England to France, where the monarch was more absolute.

The advance of Parliamentary power was interrupted from the mid-fifteenth century, first by Yorkist and them by Tudor absolutism. In neither case, however, was the principle of monarchical absolutism enunciated; and in each absolutism was only partial and temporary, and more a matter of practice than of theory. Among factors contributing to the reaction were the abuse of Parliament by the Lords, and the consequent alliance of the middle class and the monarch in the interests of order, security, and "good business."

Governmental regulation of the economy developed in England during the Later Middle Ages. The government temporarily prohibited both the exportation of raw wool and the importation of woolen cloths during the reign of Edward III in order to build up a native textile industry. Edward encouraged Flemish artisans to migrate to England for this purpose. The Statutes of Laborers (1351ff.) attempted to fix the wages of laborers, and the Navigation Acts (1381ff.), passed during the reign of Richard II and after, required Englishmen to use English ships, or at least to give such their preference in carrying goods. Richard also forbade the exportation of "bullion" (uncoined gold or silver) by private persons. Privileges previously accorded to foreign merchants such as the Hansards were gradually withdrawn and granted to Englishmen. English merchants trading abroad were organized into government-backed monopolistic trading companies, such as the Merchant Adventurers and Merchants of the Staple. Henry VII encouraged an expansion of foreign commerce by obtaining favorable commercial treaties.

Governmental regulation of the economy

FRANCE IN THE LATER MIDDLE AGES.
Section 78.

> The Council of the King rides on his mule. [Contemporary saying concerning King Louis XI of France (1461–1483).]

BOTH France's constitution and geographical extent were pretty well determined by the close of the Later Middle Ages. From 1314 to 1429 the French monarchy was generally weak; but following the appearance of Joan of Arc in 1429 this trend reversed and the monarchy became more powerful. By 1500 most feudal intermediaries were eliminated, and

*France
under the
final
Capetians
(1314–
1328)*

*The first
Valois
(1328–
1364)*

*Charles
the Wise
as regent
and king
(1356–
1380)*

French monarchs directly controlled most of the Kingdom, and had both a direct tax and a standing army by unrestricted grants from the Estates General.

At the beginning of the Later Middle Ages, France was the most prosperous and populous state in Western Europe. Although the French economy was chiefly agricultural and French institutions were still basically feudal and conservative, France had numerous fine towns, and Paris was probably the largest city in Western Europe, with about two hundred thousand inhabitants. Although considerable progress toward unification had been made, much of France was still virtually independent of the King, as was the case with the great fiefs of Flanders, Brittany, Burgundy, and Guienne-Gascony, as well as the rich appanages of Anjou, Orleans, and Berry, together with their dependencies.

Philip IV was succeeded by his three sons: Louis X, Philip V, and Charles IV, one after the other, in rapid succession (1314–1328). None of them reigned long enough to make a lasting impression or left other than female children. The latter were passed over by the magnates, who alleged the principle of Salic law according to which landed property among the Salian Franks was inherited only by males.

When the last of the sons of Philip died in 1328, the magnates elected his nephew, Philip of Valois. Like many of the members of his house, Philip VI (1328–1350) was chivalric, courteous, and a patron of culture but extravagant, impractical, and wavering. Shortly after his accession, Philip VI was confronted by a Flemish uprising, which was sternly repressed after an overwhelming French victory at Cassel (1328). Philip failed to provide forceful leadership during the Hundred Years' War, and the power and prestige of the monarchy suffered from costly reverses at Sluys (1340), Crécy (1346), and Calais (1347).

Conditions became even worse under Philip's impractical son, John II, the Good (1350–1364), who was naive, dominated by chivalric ideals, and unable to distinguish the essential from the accidental. Defeated and taken prisoner at Poitiers (1356), John would have given England far more generous terms than were subsequently agreed on. He voluntarily returned to die in English captivity when his son, the Duke of Anjou, broke his parole in 1363. John also bequeathed serious problems to his descendents by turning over recently reverted Burgundy to his younger son Philip the Bold as an appanage.

After Poitiers (1356) the government of France was assumed by Prince Charles, the Wise, who was regent during the captivity of his father. Although frail and unfitted for the rigors of war, Charles was intelligent and studious as well as courageous and energetic. The young Prince was confronted by the demands and rebellion of the Estates General and the Parisians, led by merchant-prince Etienne Marcel and Bishop Le Coq of Laon. The Estates General, by a series of Ordonnances (1356–1357), attempted to subject the royal government to its supervision. Powerless to resist, the Dauphin submitted (1357–1358), and Marcel became temporary dictator. At one point Charles was compelled to witness the murder of two of his counselors in his own apartment. In 1358, on a pretext, he escaped to Compiégne and summoned a new Estates General.

Meanwhile, driven to extremes by plundering *routiers* and persistent tax collectors, many of the peasants of northern France rose in revolt in the Jacquerie (*jacques:* peasant) of 1358. Marcel was discredited when he made advances to the rebellious peasants and to the unscrupulous Charles the Bad of Navarre, as well as to the English. The nobility, joined even by Charles the Bad, made common cause to suppress the Jacquerie. Faced by disorder and insecurity, the Parisians reacted against the rebellion and put to death Marcel and some of his associates. The victorious Charles returned to the capital, proclaimed a general amnesty, and negotiated a less disastrous peace (1360).

Upon becoming King, Charles V, the Wise (1364–1380), had three main problems: to restore internal order, to strengthen the royal government, and to deal with the English. Eventually Charles the Wise defeated and dispossessed the malcontent Charles the Bad of Navarre and won over to his own side John de Montfort, successful claimant to the Dukedom of Brittany. Charles also dealt adroitly with the problem of the depredations and extortions practiced by unemployed bands of soldiers, known as *routiers* (wanderers), *ecorcheurs* (flayers), or "free companies." Some of these were enlisted in the new royal army; others were sent to Spain to fight for Henry of Trastamara in a Castilian civil war.

To support military operations against the English, Charles imposed new taxes with the consent of the Estates General. These included indirect taxes on the sale of merchandise, as well as on salt and on wine, and a direct tax. After obtaining these taxes, Charles continued to assess and levy them without further reference to the Estates General. With the help of his new income, he maintained a regular army, which under the command of Bertrand du Guesclin efficiently pursued limited objectives and avoided large-scale battles. Charles also built up a royal navy under the command of Jean de Vienne. As a way of forestalling the English and of neutralizing Flanders, the King arranged the marriage of his younger brother Philip the Bold of Burgundy to Margaret, heiress of Flanders, Artois, Nevers, Franche Comté, and adjacent territories. Helpful for a time, the growth of Burgundian territory posed a future problem as it provided a base for the later royal ambitions of the Dukes of Burgundy.

Since Charles VI was only twelve at his accession (1380), the regency was enjoyed for eight years by his selfish uncles, the Dukes of Anjou, Berry, Bourbon, and Burgundy. Ominous rebellions, largely over taxes, broke out in Paris, Flanders, and elsewhere, but were suppressed by force. In 1388, Charles VI assumed personal control and recalled his father's old counselors, derisively dubbed "the gargoyles" by their opponents. But only four years later, the King went raving mad during a strenuous expedition to Brittany, and never completely recovered. As a result, the King's irresponsible uncles, to whose council was added the King's imprudent younger brother, the Duke Louis of Orleans, ousted the "gargoyles" and assumed power.

Charles VI, the Mad (1380–1422), and Burgundy vs. Armagnac

The Later Middle Ages
THE FRENCH MONARCHY
1270 – 1515

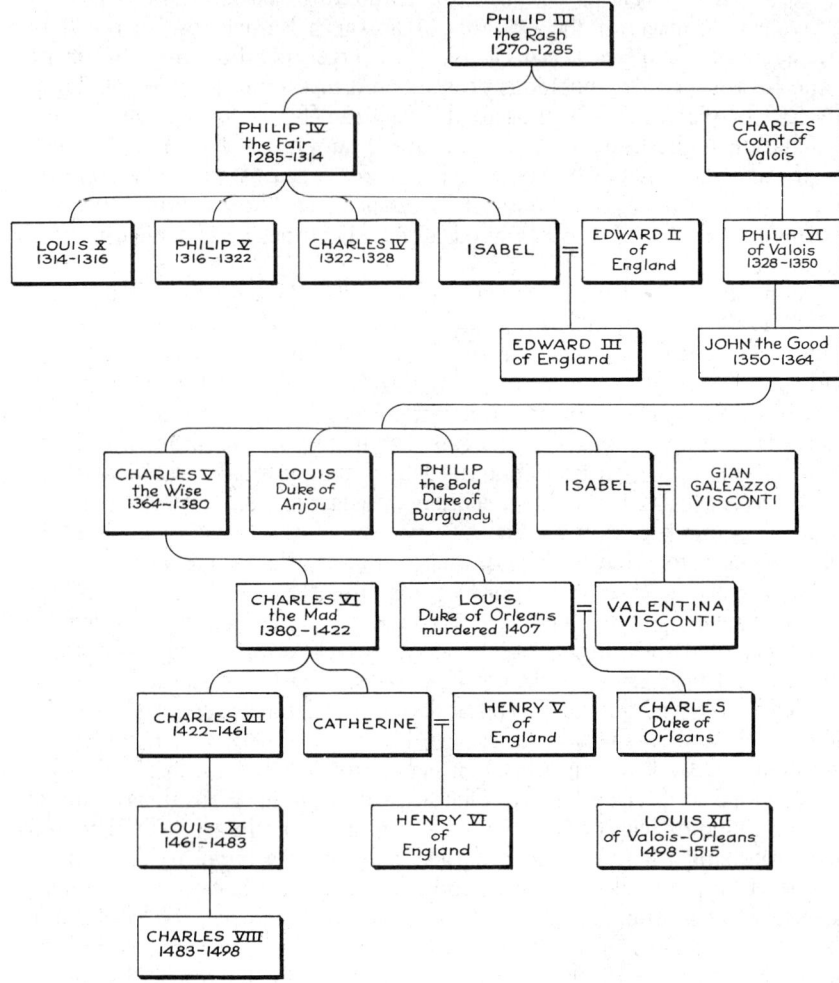

England and France

Duke Philip the Bold of Burgundy and Duke Louis of Orleans competed for control of the government. The contest reached new intensity when the bellicose John the Fearless succeeded his father, Philip, as Duke of Burgundy. One night in 1407, as the frivolous Louis of Orleans was returning from a visit to the apartment of his sister-in-law, the pleasure-loving Queen Isabella, assassins hired by John the Fearless murdered the Prince. The cause of Orleans was now taken up by the Duke's energetic father-in-law, the Count of Armagnac. Fortunes vacillated during the ensuing civil war. A Parisian uprising known as the Cabochienne and an attempt by the Estates General to reform the government failed. The Armagnacs were in ascendance from 1413 until 1418, when Burgundy returned to power with the cooperation of Queen Isabella, and a general massacre of Armagnacs in Paris followed.

The Duke of Burgundy, known as "the Grand Duke of the West," was one of the richest and most powerful rulers in Western Europe. In addition to the Duchy of Burgundy, he ruled the Franche Comté, Flanders, Nevers, and Artois. In his domains were some of the most prosperous industrial and commercial regions of Western Europe. Since Burgundian policy sought either to control France or (failing this) to build up an independent "Middle Kingdom," the Dukes of Burgundy dealt with both the French and the English during the Hundred Years' War, playing off one against the other. In 1419, Duke John the Fearless and the Dauphin Charles, in an attempt to effect a reconciliation, agreed to meet on a bridge at Montereau. During the interview, the Dauphin's followers, apparently excited and alarmed by the Duke's defiant attitude, attacked and slew him. The alienated Duke Philip the Good, who succeeded his father, obtained control of the King and Queen, cooperated with the English and arranged the Treaty of Troyes (1420), which disinherited the Dauphin in favor of Henry V of England.

Charles VII, known as "the Dauphin" until 1429, was at first weak, sickly, and apathetic, although he matured in later years. The Dauphin refused to accept the Treaty of Troyes (1420), and held out in southern France, where he had considerable support. But he remained the passive tool of successive favorites, until roused from his lethargy by Joan of Arc in 1429. Following the death of Joan of Arc (1432) and the overthrow of selfish La Tremoille (1433), abler royal advisers and ministers, such as Yolande of Anjou, Constable Richemont, General Dunois, and the financier Jaques Coeur, gained ascendance over Charles. The monarchy, greatly strengthened by concession of the right to levy a direct tax (*taille*) as well as indirect taxes on commodities (*aides*) by the Estates General, was able to maintain a well-equipped regular army and bring to a successful conclusion the Hundred Years' War (1453). Royal authority was also increased by the Pragmatic Sanction of Bourges (1438), which gave the French Church considerable independence from the Papacy, and enabled the King to control the appointment of prelates.

Charles VII, the Well-Served (1422/1429–1461)

The leader who extracted the Burgundian dagger from the royal side and removed many similar limitations from the French monarchy was

Louis XI, the (continued)

Spider King (1461-1483)

Louis XI. Although thin and unattractive, mean and superstitious, Louis was also shrewd, calculating, and hard-working: one of the most adroit and successful rulers in French history. Known as "the Spider King," Louis preferred diplomacy and duplicity to warfare, the distribution of gold to the use of force, and the subversion of his enemies singly, as well as indirectly and furtively, to open defiance.

Early in his reign, Louis was confronted by the so-called League of Common Weal formed by the great nobles to recover their alleged rights and to restrict monarchical power. The League forced the new King, who was neither popular nor prepossessing, to agree to the Peace of Conflans (1465), wherein he made various concessions, most of which he did not honor. Instead, Louis went to work quietly to divide and trick his opponents. His punishment of the leading culprits among his recreant vassals was terrible. Some were put to death after extreme tortures. The Count of Nevers and the Bishop of Verdun were confined for years on display in small cages without space to move around.

Defeat of Burgundy

Louis's chief opponent was his powerful cousin, Duke Charles the Bold of Burgundy, who was blunt, impetuous, and arrogant, as well as determined to consolidate Burgundian possessions into a recognized Middle Kingdom. Instead of fighting Charles directly, Louis incited Charles's subjects, such as the Liegeois, to rebel; and encouraged Charles's neighbors, such as the Swiss, to resist Burgundian expansion with armed force. His chief instruments were diplomacy and gold. When Edward IV of England invaded France with a large army in 1475 as Burgundy's ally, Louis bought him off by a liberal down payment and a promise of annual tribute. When Emperor Frederick III of Germany, who was about to negotiate conferral of a royal crown on Charles, suddenly withdrew, it was noted that agents of Louis XI had been active. Nevertheless, Charles kept multiplying his aggressive projects and his bitter enemies. Finally, after an unsuccessful attempt to take Nancy in Lorraine in the winter of 1477, the Duke's dead body was found stripped and naked in the snow.

Territorial gains

After the death of his archrival, Louis first attempted to get the Burgundian heiress, Mary, to marry his son, the Dauphin Charles. As Mary persistently refused, Louis next occupied the Burgundian holdings, except for Holland and Brabant. Mary then married Maximilian of Austria, the Hapsburg heir-apparent. After Mary's early death, Maximilian and Louis agreed (1482) to divide the inheritance. Louis got the Duchy of Burgundy, along with Picardy and the Somme towns, as well as a conditional right to Franche Comté and Artois as a dowry for the projected marriage of his son the Dauphin to Margaret of Austria. Maximilian obtained Flanders, Brabant, Hainault, the Dutch Low Countries, and Luxemburg, as well as rights in connection with the Franche Comté and Artois.

By purchase and reversion, as well as by marriage and by forceful occupation, Louis XI also recovered several former appanages for the monarchy. Included were Anjou, with its holdings of Maine, Bar, and Provence; Orleans, with its holdings of Poitou and Angoulême; Berry, with its dependencies; and Bourbon, with its holdings of La Marche and Auvergne. In addition, Roussillon and Cerdagne at the foot of the Pyrenees were occupied during a dynastic crisis in Aragon (1463).

While he mercilessly suppressed his rivals among the nobility, Louis XI solicited the support of the middle class. He purported to be a "bourgeois monarch" and even imitated the ways and dress of the middle class, as well as listened to their advice. He promoted French prosperity by encouraging industrial and commercial expansion. He introduced the silk industry, removed internal barriers to trade, encouraged fairs, and established a regular postal service.

Louis carefully avoided calling the Estates General, which might limit his power. He summoned it only once (1468) to have it declare Normandy inalienable from the crown. At the same time, he continued the careful assessment and collection of taxes, maintained a strong army, made the towns subject to royal control, and punished his opponents without going through the ordinary processes of justice.

Since the new King, Charles VIII, was only thirteen at his accession, his competent older sister, Anne of Beaujeau, exercised the regency on his behalf (1483–1492). Anne efficiently repressed the revolt of the nobility known as "the Mad War" and continued her father's work of unifying France. In 1488, the Duke of Brittany died, leaving his thirteen-year-old daughter Anne of Brittany as his heiress. Regent Anne of Beaujeau immediately sought to marry Anne of Brittany to her brother, the young King Charles. When Anne of Brittany strenuously refused, and instead married Maximilian of Austria by proxy (1490), Charles, at the direction of Anne of Beaujeau, marched forthwith into Brittany and compelled the young heiress (1491) to become his wife. *Charles VIII (1483–1498)*

Charles VIII, who assumed personal rule in 1492, was weak and impractical, yet grandiose and ambitious. His great dream was to obtain the Kingdom of Naples, which he considered a part of the royal inheritance from the house of Anjou. Encouraged to intervene in Italy by an appeal from the hard-pressed Ludovico Sforza, Regent of Milan, Charles made costly concessions to smooth the way for his expedition. He purchased the neutrality of Ferdinand of Aragon by returning Roussillon, that of Henry VII of England by giving him a pension, and that of Maximilian of Austria by retroceding French claims to Franche Comté and Artois (since he had married Anne of Brittany rather than Margaret of Austria). In 1494 Charles set out with an estimated 20,000 to 30,000 troops for Italy, and proceeded via Milan, Florence, and Rome to Naples, being welcomed everywhere with external deference. Naples surrendered peaceably to Charles VIII. But meanwhile a coalition known as the League of Venice was formed against him by King Ferdinand of Aragon, Emperor Maximilian, Venice, the Pope, and even Ludovico Sforza. The French were forced to withdraw from Italy, and by 1496 the old line was reestablished in Naples. A by-product of this expedition was an accelerated architectural and artistic Renaissance in France.

The most striking internal development in France in the Later Middle Ages was the growth of monarchical absolutism after an initial period of *Growth of French*

royal ab-solutism

royal weakness. Factors included the prestige acquired by victory in the Hundred Years' War, the territorial incorporation of most of France into the royal domain, the securing of direct as well as indirect royal taxes, and the establishment of a regular standing army, as well as the failure of the Estates General to impose effective limitations upon its concessions.

Why did not the Estates General establish precedents of representative government and limitations upon the monarch in France as Parliament did in England? Various factors help to account for this. Whereas England was small and compact, France was very large, and it was more difficult and expensive for French representatives to come together in one national assembly. And the French were also more provincial in their interests and loyalties and preferred to deal with the monarch in their regional assemblies (provincial estates). There was a much greater divergence between the countryside and the capital in France, so that the rural middle class failed to cooperate with the urban bourgeoisie as they did in England. The French Estates General also continued the unwieldy system of three houses or "estates," which made it difficult to obtain agreement. Finally the French had less experience with self-government and popular representative institutions on local levels than did the English.

Taxation and defense

The principal taxes supporting the French monarchy in the Later Middle Ages were the *aides*, the *gabelle*, and the *taille*. The first two were indirect taxes: the *aides* being sales taxes on merchandise, the *gabelle* an obligatory tax on salt. The *taille* (also known as the *fouage* or hearth tax) was a direct tax on property, whose glaring shortcoming was its exemption of the extensive properties of the nobility and Church. The Estates General recognized the right of the monarchy to levy and assess such taxes during the reigns of Charles V and Charles VII. But as no limitations were imposed, and no effective resistance to their continuation occurred, these taxes were subsequently levied without further reference to the representatives of the people.

The French eventually saw, during the Hundred Years' War, that a regular army and a royal navy would be necessary to repel the English, and for this purpose new taxes were established. The French army, which became a model of organization and discipline, consisted of infantry, cavalry, and artillery. The infantry was organized into companies of about 500 men, each commanded by a captain. The cavalry was composed of companies of about 600 men, each commanded by a captain and subdivided into 100 lances. The artillery, which had gunpowder weapons manned by special technicians and their helpers, consisted of heavy artillery or *bombardes* and lighter artillery or *coulevrines*.

"Gallican liberties"

The Church also bolstered French monarchical power. The Pragmatic Sanction of Bourges (1438) was a royal declaration of the so-called "Gallican liberties" of the French Church, according to which most appointments to benefices in the French Church were to be made in France and were hence subject to the French King, while most sources of Papal revenues from France were abolished.

England and France

EDOUARD PERROY, *The Hundred Years War*, tr. H. B. Wells (London: Eyre, 1951), skillfully interweaves the political history of both countries with that of the war itself. ALFRED H. BURNE concentrates on military history in his authoritative *The Crécy War . . . 1337 to . . . 1360* (New York: Oxford U.P., 1955) and *The Agincourt War* (Fair Lawn, N.J.: Essential, 1956). A fine older treatment is CHARLES W. C. OMAN's *History of the Art of War in the Middle Ages*, vol. II (Boston: Houghton Mifflin, 1924). The scholarly HENRY S. LUCAS writes about *The Low Countries and the Hundred Years War, 1326–1347* (Ann Arbor: U. of Mich., 1929). Noted original sources are JEAN FROISSART's *Chronicle*, tr. T. Johnes (New York: Colonial, 1901), which tells the story of the war to 1399, and its continuation by ENGUERRAND MONSTRELET, *Chronicles*, tr. T. Johnes (London: Bohn, 1849).

For England in the Later Middle Ages, useful surveys are the readable, well-documented KENNETH H. VICKERS, *England in the Later Middle Ages* (London: Methuen, 1921); VIVIAN H. GREEN, *The Later Plantagenets: A Survey of English History Between 1307 and 1485* (London: E. Arnold 1955); and CHARLES W. C. OMAN, *A History of England From the Accession of Richard II to the Death of Richard III (1377–1485)* (London: Longmans, 1920). The fifteenth century is well treated in the classic JAMES H. RAMSAY, *Lancaster and York . . . (1399–1485)*, 2 vols. (Oxford: Clarendon, 1892), as well as in the more recent ERNEST F. JACOB, *The Fifteenth Century* (Oxford: Oxford U.P., 1961). More specialized aspects are dealt with by THOMAS F. TOUT, *The Place of the Reign of Edward II in English History*, 2nd ed., rev. (Manchester, Eng.: U. of Manchester, 1936); CHARLES W. C. OMAN, *The Great Revolt of 1381* (Oxford: Clarendon, 1906); JOHN CAMMIDGE, *The Black Prince* . . . (London: Eyre, 1943); ROBERT B. MOWAT, *The Wars of the Roses, 1377–1471* (London: C. Lockwood, 1914); and JAMES GAIRDNER, *Henry the Seventh* (London: Macmillan, 1889).

Good treatments of constitutional developments in England in the period are provided by ALBERT B. WHITE, *The Making of the English Constitution, 449–1485* (New York: Putnam's, 1925); J. E. A. JOLIFFE, *The Constitutional History of England to 1485* (London: Black, 1948); G. L. HASKINS, *The Growth of English Representative Government* (Philadelphia: U. of Pa., 1948); and FAITH THOMPSON, *A Short History of Parliament, 1265–1642* (Minneapolis: U. of Minn., 1953).

Useful surveys of French history in this period include those in CHARLES A. H. GUIGNEBERT, *A Short History of the French People*, tr. F. G. Richmond, vol. II (New York: Macmillan, 1930); ALBERT L. GUERARD, *French Civilization . . . to the Close of the Middle Ages* (Boston: Houghton Mifflin, 1921); JACQUES C. FUNCK-BRETANO, *The Middle Ages*, tr. E. O'Neill (New York: Putnam's, 1923); and ARTHUR TILLEY, *Medieval France* (Cambridge: Cambridge U.P., 1922). Joan of Arc is the heroine of numerous biographies such as those of ANDREW LANG, *The Maid of France* . . . (London: Longmans, 1908); LUCIEN FABRE, *Joan of Arc*, tr. G. Hopkins (New York: McGraw, 1954); and V. M. SACKVILLE-WEST, *Joan of Arc* (London: L. and V. Woolf, 1947). Verbatim reports of the proceedings at her trial, including her own statements, are edited and translated under the title *The Trial of Joan of Arc* or *Jeanne d'Arc* by W. P. BARRETT (New York: Gotham, 1931) and by W. S. SCOTT (London: Folio Society, 1956). Charles V's colorful constable from Brittany is portrayed in ENOCH V. STODDARD, *Bertrand Du Guesclin . . .* (New York: Putnams, 1897), as is Charles

References for Chapter 26

VII's merchant-prince counselor in ALBERT B. KERR, *Jacques Coeur* . . . (New York: Scribners, 1927). The eccentric, shrewd Louis XI is a favorite subject of several accounts, including ANDREW C. HAGGARD, *Louis XI and Charles the Bold* . . . (London: St. Paul, 1913); DOMINIC B. LEWIS, *King Spider* (New York: Conrad-McCann, 1929); PIERRE H. CHAMPION, *Louis XI*, tr. W. S. Whale (London: Cassell, 1929); and PAUL MURRAY KENDALL, *Louis XI* (New York: Norton, 1971). The basic work on Charles the Bold is JOHN FOSTER KIRK, *History of Charles the Bold, Duke of Normandy*, 3 vols. (Philadelphia: Lippincott, 1863–8); shorter is RUTH PUTNAM, *Charles the Bold, Last Duke of Burgundy* (New York: Putnams, 1908). A key source for such works is the penetrating contemporary account by PHILIPPE DE COMINES, *Memoirs* . . . , tr. and ed. A. R. Scoble, 2 vols. (London: Bohn, 1855–6).

❰ CENTRAL AND EASTERN EUROPE IN THE LATER MIDDLE AGES. Chapter 27.

THE Later Middle Ages were a depressing period of shocks and adversities for Central and Eastern Europe. The previously strong German Empire disintegrated into a loose association of numerous practically autonomous states. Eastern Europe was dominated by unenlightened Tartars (Turks and Mongols), while the Balkans and Byzantium were subjected by militaristic Turks. Although Lithuania was temporarily united with Poland, and Sweden with Denmark (as well as Norway), neither union proved to be stable. Nevertheless, by the close of the period, strong powers were emerging in this area. The Hapsburgs of Austria were obtaining control of the German Empire and were forming matrimonial ties that would bring them the Low Countries, Spain, and extensive overseas possessions. The shrewd, hardy princes of Moscow were casting off the Tartar yoke and establishing a strong native government, thus beginning the unification of Russia. The Ottoman Turks were gradually building up a great Eastern Mediterranean Empire, whose capital was European Constantinople in the Balkans. In the north, Sweden was becoming strong and was about to establish its independence; while Poland and Lithuania obtained access to the Baltic and improved their prospects by decisive victories over the Teutonic Knights.

THE GERMAN EMPIRE IN THE LATER MIDDLE AGES.
Section 79.

Others seek gain by waging war, but Austria prospers by marriage [Matthias Corvinus of Hungary (fifteenth century) concerning the Hapsburgs of Austria.]

THE weakened German Empire suffered further losses of territories and strength during the Later Middle Ages. The German Emperors definitely lost Italy and overlordship over Poland, while in Bohemia they were confronted by fierce resistance. In the Baltic and North Sea areas, the Teutonic Knights were overcome and humbled by newly united Poland–Lithuania, and the Hanseatic League, after great initial prosperity, eventually lost its commercial domination. In the Rhineland and Rhoneland, French kings and dukes encroached upon imperial territories. Factors contributing to the weakness of the German Empire included the very limited power of the Emperors, the virtual autonomy of the princes, the Eastern interests and preoccupations of the Luxemburg and Hapsburg Emperors, the elective principle of imperial succession, and powerful Ottoman and French pressures.

Weakness of the Empire: "Age of the Princes"

The German Empire in this period, known as "the Age of the Princes," became a loose confederation of some two hundred to three hundred practically autonomous states, with an Emperor who had little effective power outside of his own familial domains. The Empire included two kingdoms, various duchies and margravates, and several counties, together with numerous prince-bishoprics, allodial lordships, and free cities. To make sure that the Emperors would not recover their previous powers, the German princes insisted on the electoral principle, and shifted the imperial office from one family to another, until their own power was firmly established. After the broad formal imperial recognition of their privileges by the Golden Bull (1356), the princes were content to keep in office the Luxemburg family, which issued it, until this line ran out. Then they accepted the related Hapsburgs, who remained in power partly because of growing pressures on the eastern frontiers, where they constituted a principal bastion.

Shorn of most of their power, the weakened German Emperors in the Later Middle Ages adopted a policy of *Hauspolitik*, whose primary objective was to increase the direct holdings of their family. This they could do by invoking and enforcing the imperial right to recover and dispose of territories vacated by escheat or forfeit, as well as by arranging advantageous marriages. In this way the Hapsburgs acquired Austria by forfeit and the Low Countries by marriage, while the Luxemburgers secured Bohemia by escheat.

Power in the Germanies shifted to the east during the Later Middle Ages, as is exemplified by the growing importance of Austria, Bohemia, and Brandenburg. Among reasons for this development were the continued economic evolution of these peripheral states, their larger size and tendency to expand at the expense of less advanced neighbors, and their need to be militarily strong to survive and withstand warlike powers on the frontiers. This military strength enabled them both to expand eastward at foreign expense and to dominate their more peaceful fellows. Along the western frontiers, the German states, which included numerous towns and prince-bishoprics, were much more minute and feudal, and their own inclinations as well as ecclesiastical interest and French intrigues conspired to keep them so.

Local polities

The powers and prerogatives of local rulers and governments within the Empire expanded during the Later Middle Ages. Originally acquired in various ways and increased as well as explicitly defined by Frederick

II's Concessions of 1220 and 1231–1232, they were further enhanced by privileges conceded by the Golden Bull (1356) of Charles IV.

At first many of the newly "independent" polities within the German Empire, bereft of the old supports of imperial backing and an established order, had some difficulty in maintaining stability and security. But gradually many principalities built up the machinery of government and the military forces necessary for their own defense, as well as eventually obtained the support of precedents established by continued custom. Many made effective use of the middle class in their councils and government.

The Diet

Among European representative assemblies, the German *Diet* (from Latin *dies*: day) or *Reichstag* (from German *Reich*: realm and *Tag*: day) was one of the latest to emerge. Representatives of the middle class were not summoned to imperial Diets until the time of Maximilian (1489ff.), when such meetings were composed of three houses, representing the electors, the prince, and the bourgeoisie. One of the reasons for this tardiness was the weakness of the imperial government and its inability to levy nationwide taxes (one of the chief reasons for the calling of parliaments). Another was the size of the Empire and the long distances that representatives would have to travel. Still another was the fact that the middle class and its interests were already represented in the local *Landtags* (territorial assemblies) of duchies, margravates, and so on in Germany from the fourteenth century on.

The revolving imperial office (1273–1347): Hapsburgs

Following the death of Frederick II (1250) and that of his weak son, Conrad IV (1254), the German electoral princes first chose as emperors rival foreign princes who, as was expected, failed to obtain effective control. Eventually prodded by the resultant anarchy and a Papal threat to appoint an Emperor, the princes elected a lesser count, Rudolph of Hapsburg (1273). The Hapsburgs, so called from their ancestral "Hawk's Castle" in southern Suabia, had acquired territories in Alsace and German Switzerland, as well as in Suabia, through imperial favor. Rudolph, a man of energy and decision, set about sternly enforcing the law. On one occasion he condemned and executed twenty-nine robbers at one time.

Although Rudolph of Hapsburg was accepted by most of the princes, his disappointed rival for the Imperial throne, Ottakar II of Bohemia, refused to acknowledge him. In 1274 the imperial Diet authorized Rudolph to recover imperial lands that had been alienated or usurped since the deposition of Frederick II by the Council of Lyons (1245). Rudolph defeated and captured Ottakar, whom one of his followers slew. The former holdings of the Duke of Austria, which had been appropriated by Ottakar, were declared to have escheated to the crown, and Rudolph obtained a rich cache that included Austria, Styria, Carinthia, and the Tyrol. The Bishop of Basel reportedly declared: *Sit firmly on your throne, O Lord, or the Count of Hapsburg will push you off!*

Alarmed by the swift rise of the Hapsburgs, the princes passed over Rudolph's son Albrecht and elected a lesser count, Adolph of Nassau (1292–1298). But Adolph alienated the princes by taking over Thuringia and Meissen, and was eventually defeated and slain in battle. He was succeeded by Albrecht of Austria (1298-1308), who is described by contemporaries as "hard as a diamond." To punish the Western German party that had opposed his election, Albrecht tried to suppress tolls in the Rhineland. Ten years after his accession he was murdered by a moody nephew.

Again the electors chose a lesser prince—Count Henry of Luxemburg, candidate of the Western party. Henry VII, who was half French in culture and outlook, and had high ambitions, greatly increased the holdings of his house by arranging the marriage of his son John to the heiress of Bohemia (1310). Dante saw in him a possible savior for distraught Italy, and called upon him to rescue the peninsula from factionalism. But when Henry made an expedition to Italy it was a dismal failure. *Henry of Luxemburg and Lewis of Bavaria*

The Eastern party elected Lewis (Louis) IV of Bavaria (1314-1346) on Henry's death. The handsome Lewis was a good soldier, but somewhat unstable, and his reign was turbulent. Hapsburg opposition to Bavarian Wittelsbach rule begot a civil war that lasted for eight years. Meanwhile Lewis became embroiled in a bitter contest with Pope John XXII, and the imperial court became a refuge for outspoken critics of the Papacy. Lewis, like Henry, made an expedition to Italy (1337-1340), but without lasting result. In the Declaration of Rense (1338), Lewis and the imperial electors formally asserted that the imperial office was independent of the Papacy.

Lewis greatly expanded the possessions of his house. He acquired the Tyrol by declaring the marriage of the estranged Margaret Maultasch to John Henry of Moravia invalid, and having his own son marry her. He also acquired Brandenburg for his son, and obtained much of the Dutch Netherlands by marrying its heiress. Eventually his opponents declared Lewis deposed, and elected in his stead Charles of Bohemia. Lewis died during the war of the succession.

The accession of Charles IV of Bohemia, grandson of Louis VII of Luxemburg, ushered in the occupation of the imperial throne by the house of Luxemburg for the ensuing hundred years, with the exception of a ten-year interval. Charles IV (1347-1378), a native Bohemian, born of a Bohemian princess, was well educated and capable. Charles promoted a "Czech Renaissance," during which Czech literature blossomed, and founded the University of Prague (1347). Through his influence, the Czech Church, under the Archbishop of Prague, became independent of the German Church. With the Hapsburgs Charles concluded the Treaty of Bruun (1364), which recognized their right to succeed to Luxemburger possessions, including the imperial throne, should his line die out, and vice versa. He entertained no pretensions with regard to Italy, which was comforting to the Papacy; and solicited the favor of the German princes by the liberal Golden Bull (1356). *The Luxemburg line: Charles IV of Bohemia (1347-1378)*

The Golden Bull (an imperial document bearing a golden seal) served as a constitution for the Empire from 1356 until 1806. Actually the Golden Bull for the most part stabilized the unwritten constitution of the Empire as it had come to exist, except that it further enhanced the *The Golden Bull (1356)* prerogatives of the princes and definitely excluded the Papacy from imperial elections. The imperial office was declared elective, reconciling the princes to making hereditary in fact what was elective in principle. Seven electoral princes, already indicated by custom, were designated: the prince bishops of Mainz, Trier (Treves), and Cologne; and four secular princes, one from each category: the King of Bohemia, the Duke of Saxony, the Margrave of Brandenburg, and the Count Palatine of the Rhineland. By omission of any specific provision, the Papacy was excluded from having a part in the election. So, too, were the free imperial towns, whose rights were limited, foreshadowing their subjection to the princes.

The electoral princes were allowed virtual sovereignty in their own domains. Their persons were held inviolate and they were to be accorded safe conducts when traveling through the realms. Their holdings were indivisible and were to descend intact to their heirs, as far as possible through primogeniture. Their territories were to be exempt from imperial officials and imperial courts; and the electors enjoyed the prerogatives of minting their own coins and exercising subsoil rights. These broad privileges and immunities guaranteed to the electoral princes were eventually assumed by their brother princes, the other dukes, counts, and margraves.

The last Luxemburg emperors (1378–1437): Sigismund

The next Luxemburg Emperor, Wenzel (Wenceslaus) (1378–1400), acquired the nickname of "the Drunkard." Given to alternating alcoholism, cruelty, tyranny, and inaction, in the face of grave crises, Wenzel was eventually deposed by the princes, who chose a lesser prince, the mild Count Ruprecht of the Rhenish Palatinate. Handicapped by the continued opposition of Luxemburger supporters, Ruprecht (1400–1410) cut a pathetic figure, and at one time had to pawn his crown to obtain needed funds.

The crown was then returned to the Luxemburgers in the person of Wenzel's brother, Sigismund, who was already King of Hungary. "A bonny fighter and keen sportsman," Sigismund (1410–1437) was handsome and brave, gallant and liberal, although prone to overextend himself. This circumstance was mainly due to his many offices and responsibilities as King of Hungary, King of Bohemia, Duke of Saxony, Margrave of Brandenburg, and German Emperor. Numerous perplexing problems confronted Sigismund, one of them being the expansion of the Ottoman Turks in southeastern Europe, which threatened his territories. He participated in the ill-fated Crusade of Nicopolis against the Ottomans (1396). Another problem concerned the Hussites in Bohemia. Partly in order to heal this rift, Sigismund helped to convoke and hold together the Council of Constance (1414–1418); but the Council's drastic action in burning John Hus and Jerome of Prague at the stake resulted in the prolonged Hussite Wars in Bohemia (1417–1436). Sigismund entrusted the Margravate of Brandenburg to Frederick of Hohenzollern, turned over an enlarged Saxony to the Wettins, and married his daughter to Duke Albert of Hapsburg, insuring the imperial succession of that house.

Hapsburgs (1438ff.):

Sigismund's son-in-law, Albert II of Austria, succeeded him, bringing to power the Hapsburg dynasty, destined to last for five centuries. Albert

Central and Eastern Europe

himself, however, was soon killed fighting the Ottoman Turks in Hungary, and his cousin, Frederick of Styria, the oldest living Hapsburg prince, succeeded him. Frederick III (1440–1493) spent much of his time studying the stars, in which he "read" the future greatness of Austria, and dabbling in acrostics such as "AEIOU," interpreted as meaning *Austriae est imperare orbi universali* ("It is Austria's lot to rule the entire world"), while his house suffered serious losses. Bohemia slipped from Hapsburg control when a native line (which lasted until 1526) was set up there under George Podiebrad (1458ff.); as also did Hungary, where native rule was established by Matthias Corvinus (1458). Frederick temporarily lost Vienna and a large part of Austria, Styria, and Carinthia (1485–1490); but these were later regained by Maximilian I. During Frederick's reign, the Dukes of Burgundy obtained the Low Countries, and the King of France acquired Provence, but part of these losses were also recouped after Maximilian I married Mary of Burgundy.

Frederick III

Frederick's son, energetic, handsome, intelligent Maximilian I, became the real ruler of Hapsburg holdings in 1486, when he was elected King with his father's consent. As Emperor (1493–1519), Maximilian I had grand designs. From his marriage (1477) to Mary of Burgundy, he eventually obtained the Low Countries and the Free County (*Franche Comté*) of Burgundy through a compromise agreement with Louis XI of France (1482). By a treaty of 1491, King Vladislav (Ladislas) of Bohemia and Hungary agreed that, should he die without male heir, his kingdoms would pass to the Hapsburgs. Maximilian I became involved in Italy when he joined the Pope and Venice in the League of Venice, and later in the "Holy League" (1513) against French aggression in Italy. The marriage of his son Philip the Handsome to Princess Joanna (*la Loca*) of Spain eventually resulted in Hapsburg preeminence in Europe at the time of their offspring, Emperor Charles V. The growing power of the Hapsburgs gave cause for alarm to the German princes.

Maximilian (1493–1511)

During the reign of Maximilian an attempt was made to revise the constitution of the Empire. Maximilian included representatives of the middle class in his Diets from 1493 on, in an effort to obtain broader support for resistance to both the French and the Ottoman Turks. These Diets sought to institute various political reforms. A *Reichsregiment* or Imperial Council with twenty members was established, along with a *Reichskammergericht* or Imperial Court with sixteen justices. The Empire was divided into six to ten *Kreise* (Circles) or administrative districts, each under a *Hauptman* (Head Man). And a general *Landfrieden* or universal peace between component states was declared. These attempted reforms failed, however, partly because Maximilian, fearful of encroachments on his powers, failed to cooperate fully; and partly because the imperial government itself lacked strength. Only the *Reichskammergericht* really functioned, but it soon fell hopelessly behind in hearing cases and it also lacked enforcement powers. Meanwhile the so-called Holy Vehm, a voluntary popular secret society intent on maintaining order, administered swift, sure, stern justice in its courts until its officials eventually became corrupt and venal.

The Later Middle Ages

The Swiss Confederation

The first democratic federal state in medieval Europe, the Swiss Confederation obtained its independence from the Empire in the Later Middle Ages. Cosmopolitan Switzerland was important because of its central location and control of vital routes to and from Italy. Although much of Switzerland was theoretically under the overlordship of the Hapsburgs, the hardy, freedom-loving Swiss stubbornly resisted efforts to subject them. To strengthen their resistance, the rural cantons (provinces, states) of Schwyz, Uri (independent since 1231), and Unterwalden formed a "Perpetual Pact" in 1291. This was the beginning of the Swiss confederation, which included all thirteen cantons by the close of the Middle Ages. The Swiss, who fought mainly on foot, skillfully used their rugged terrain and long pikes to defeat the horsemen of the Hapsburgs in the battles of Mortgarten (1315), Sempach (1386), and Nafels (1388), so that they were independent in practice by the end of the fourteenth century. Swiss independence was formally acknowledged by Emperor Frederick III in the "Perpetual Peace" (1474), and by Emperor Maximilian I in the Treaty of Basel (1499).

The Hanseatic League

The remarkable Hanseatic League, formed by towns in northern Germany in the thirteenth century, reached its fullest development in the fourteenth century. In the absence of an imperial government strong enough to protect them, maintain internal peace, and promote their interests abroad, the north German towns had banded together to do these things for themselves. At its height the Hanseatic League included seventy to eighty towns in four districts, with capitals at Lübeck, Danzig, Brunswick, and Cologne. The League had several "factories" (agencies) in the principal commercial cities of surrounding states, such as Bruges in Flanders, London in England, Bergen in Sweden, and Novgorod in Russia, as well as a base at Wisby on the island of Gotland in the Baltic. The League held periodic meetings, carried on diplomatic relations with foreign powers, and even waged war. In 1370 it defeated King Waldemar IV of Denmark and imposed upon him the humiliating Peace of Stralsund. But in the fifteenth century the League rapidly declined as a result of the rise of strong national monarchies in neighboring states, the growing subjection of member towns to German princes, and the migration of the herring, a staple article of their trade, from former spawning haunts in the Baltic to the vicinity of the Netherlands.

The Teutonic Knights in the Baltic

During the fourteenth century the Teutonic Knights completed their conquest, organization, and development of eastern Pomerania, Prussia, Samogitia, Livonia, Courland, and Estonia to the east of the Baltic, as far north as the Gulf of Finland. While German businessmen developed prosperous cities in this hitherto backward area, German landowners operated large rural estates with native serfs. *Ordenland* or "Land of the Order" was an independent principality headed by their Grand Master. Their aggressive stance with regard to Poland and Lithuania, and their acquisition of territories which cut both off from the sea, was a major cause in bringing about the union and cooperation of these two countries (1388ff.). Following this, the tide turned against the Teutonic Knights, who were severely defeated by the Poles and Lithuanians in the critical battle of Tannenberg (1410) and again in a war that lasted from 1454 to 1466. By the First Peace of Thorn (1411) the order was obliged to surrender Samogitia (to the north of Prussia). By the Second Peace of Thorn (1466) it was compelled to give up eastern Pomerania and western Prussia, and to hold eastern Prussia as a fief from the Polish king.

Despite political disunity, German civilization made considerable progress in the Later Middle Ages. In the mid-fifteenth century, the much-traveled Aeneas Sylvius Piccolomini (later Pius II) wrote: *Germany has never been richer or more prosperous. . . . No country in Europe has better and more beautiful cities.* The vigor of town life in Germany was exemplified by the activities of the Hanseatic League, numerous fine buildings, and many public municipal schools. The Christian humanism of the Renaissance was fostered in the schools of the Brethren of the Common Life and in the several universities founded in Germany during this period. Printing with movable type originated in the Empire, which was also a principal nursery of Late Gothic painting and sculpture.

Progress of German civilization

EAST CENTRAL AND NORTHERN EUROPE IN THE LATER MIDDLE AGES.
Section 81.

Nothing can be done in the world without the help of God and the King of Bohemia. [Contemporary saying concerning the quixotic King John of Bohemia (1310–1346).]

ALTHOUGH German pressures on East Central and Northern Europe continued during the Later Middle Ages, German interests in these regions were more dynastic (as in the case of the Hapsburgs and Luxemburgs), more politicoeconomic (as in that of the Hanseatic League), and more religiopolitical (as with the Teutonic Knights) than strictly imperial. In both East Central and Northern Europe, there was a tendency to unification, but resultant combinations were unstable and temporary. In these "borderland states" the power of the nobility vis-à-vis the monarchy grew and feudalism increased. The nobles often preferred to invite a foreign prince to be their king so that they could more effectively control him and keep the monarchy weak. These countries frequently intervened in each other's internal affairs, as also did their German neighbors. East Central Europe was constantly threatened and sometimes invaded by neighboring Tartars, Russians, and Ottoman Turks. The Church continued to have a position of great power in this area, but its authority was increasingly challenged, as in the case of the Bohemian Hussites.

Bohemia, with its fertile valleys surrounded by picturesque mountains rich in minerals, came into increasing prominence. It was the seat of Empire for almost a century, and the scene of a militant religious movement that presaged the great Protestant Revolt. The modern phenomenon of continuous Hapsburg rule of Bohemia was twice foreshadowed.

Bohemia in the Later Middle Ages

In 1310 the Bohemian nobles deposed Henry of Carinthia, who had ruled them for only three years, and offered the crown to John of Luxemburg, son of Emperor Henry of Luxemburg. John of Luxemburg (1310–

1346), an adventurous and daring knight errant, spent most of his time away from Bohemia, although he relied on it for his financing. As a result the Bohemian Estates, which included representatives of the towns and the lesser nobility as well as the greater lords, dominated the government. Despite his vagaries, John acquired the Egerland (Chebsko), Upper Lusatia, and Silesia for the Bohemian crown. From a sickness incurred while campaigning, John became blind in later life, but he died fighting for his friend the French king in the battle of Crécy (1346).

Charles IV of the Empire: Charles I of Bohemia.

Charles IV[a] (1346/7–1378), John's son by a Bohemian princess, has been called "the father of his country, but the stepfather of the Empire." Charles cherished his native land and successfully labored to promote its interests and progress, as well as a Czech Renaissance. He also acquired Lower Lusatia and Brandenburg for his son. The latter, Wenceslaus IV (1378–1419), the Drunkard, who was unbalanced by excessive drinking, alienated support by fits of cruelty, and became putty in the hands of stronger forces. During his reign the Bohemian Estates became powerful, and the Bohemians enjoyed considerable liberty. Growing interest in religious revival eventually led to the Hussite movement, which burst into a raging flame following the executions of John Hus and Jerome of Prague. When Wenceslaus began to try to repress the Hussites, an angered mob assaulted his anti-Hussite town council of Prague, threw the members from the windows of the council hall, and killed them on the spot. At news of the riot and "defenestration," Wenceslaus suffered a stroke, soon followed by another, from which he died.

The Hussites

When Emperor Sigismund, who was anti-Hussite, sought to succeed his brother as King of Bohemia, he met determined opposition. Six "Crusades" against the Hussites (1420–1431) failed to overcome the Bohemians, who were fighting for both religious freedom and political independence. The Hussites used carefully executed wagon formations and iron-tipped flails against the German cavalry, and were led by superb generals—Jan Zizka and "Holy" ("Bald") Prokop. The more moderate majority, who wished to retain their ties with the universal Church while obtaining limited concessions, eventually won out over the extremists, who rejected the Catholic hierarchy and the teaching authority of the Church. When the two groups came to blows, the moderates won out by severely defeating the extremists at Lipany (1434), and the way was clear for a compromise settlement on the basis of the "Compacts," worked out with the Council of Basel and confirmed in 1436. The Hussites won recognition of the right of the laity to receive holy communion under both species (bread and wine) and other concessions. Following peace with the moderate Hussites, Sigismund was accepted as their king by the Bohemians (1436–1437), following which Albert of Austria, his son-in-law, became king (1437–1439). After an interregnum, Albert was succeeded by his son, Ladislas I, Posthumus (1452–1457), who was also King of Hungary.

Weakened Monarchy

Able George Podebrad, a native Bohemian and a moderate Hussite, actually ruled from 1444 to 1471, and labored with success to restore unity and order in his country, despite Papal opposition. After the death of Ladislas, George was elected King (1457) and reigned until 1471. On Podebrad's death, his candidate, the Polish prince Vladislav,[b] was elected as their King Vladislav II (1471–1496) by the Bohemian Estates, but was opposed by Matthias Corvinus of Hungary, the Papal candidate. By the compromise Treaty of Olmutz (1478), Vladislav received Bohemia proper and Matthias Corvinus adjacent possessions. In 1490, when Matthias died, Vladislav both received back the separated provinces and was elected to the throne of Hungary by the Hungarian nobles, who wished to obtain a king they could control. Under Vladislav, a form of feudalism prevailed in Bohemia, with a weak monarch, a privileged, powerful nobility supported by serfs, and a subordinate townspeople.

[b] Vladislav is also spelled Wladislaus.

Poland and Lithuania in the Later Middle Ages

Both Poland and Lithuania became stronger in the fourteenth century. Since the encroachments of Teutonic Knights cut both states off from the Baltic Sea and further threatened their territories, Poland and Lithuania united in 1386. At first the union subordinated Lithuania to Poland, but soon it became a partnership. The union achieved its primary purpose of restraining the Teutonic Knights. At the same time, the power of this new political entity did not correspond to its size, both because of the loose nature of the union and because of the internal weakness of both countries.

Poland to 1386

The Polish "Partitional Period" (1138–1305) was brought to a close and the threat of foreign domination was alleviated by Vladislav I, the Short (1306/1320–1333), who established control of most of the Polish provinces and had himself crowned King of Poland in 1320. Polish willingness to restore the kingship was propelled by the growing menace of the Teutonic Knights, who seized Pomerania in 1307–1309, cutting off Poland's free access to the sea. Vladislav I, who obtained alliances with Lithuania, the Scandinavian countries, and Hungary, prevented the Knights from making further acquisitions.

Casimir III, "the Great" (1333–1370), purchased peace with the Knights and Bohemia by recognizing their acquisitions, and expanded to the southeast by taking Galicia from Lithuania. He improved and strengthened the organization of the royal government, codified Polish law, promoted economic development, and encouraged the immigration of foreigners, including Jews. Casimir also protected peasants and townspeople against the nobles. He promoted culture, and founded the Academy of Cracow (1364), which in 1400 became a university.

Louis the Great of Anjou–Hungary, the designated heir of the childless Casimir, ruled Poland (1370–1382) through his mother, Elizabeth, who was Casimir's sister. Louis had to make further concessions to the Polish nobles in his Compacts of Koszyce (1374). He was succeeded in Poland by his young daughter, Jadwiga of Anjou (1384ff.).

Lithuania to 1386

Unified in the mid-thirteenth century by Prince Mendovg (Mindovg) as a safeguard against conquest by the Teutonic Knights, Lithuania expanded considerably in western Russia in the fourteenth century. Meanwhile, however, Lithuania was attacked on its northern flank by the Teutonic Knights, and deprived of Samogitia, its outlet to the Baltic (1382). This led its Grand Prince Jagiello (1377ff.) to concentrate on patching up his differences with his powerful cousin, Prince Vitovt, and also to conceive the plan of marrying young Queen Jadwiga of Poland in order to unite the two countries against the Knights.

Poland–Lithuania (1386–1501)

The Polish nobles supported the union with Lithuania, and accordingly Jagiello married Jadwiga (1386). Jagiello was baptized a Roman Catholic, and was crowned King as Vladislav II (1386–1434). The attendant conversion of the Lithuanians from paganism incidentally deprived the Knights of their chief excuse for attempting to subject them. Since many Lithuanians, led by Prince Vitovt, opposed the subordination of Lithuania to Poland, Vladislav eventually accepted Vitovt as Grand Duke of Lithuania, which was to be autonomous except for its foreign policy and approval of the succession of its rulers by the Polish government.

In the hard-fought battle of Tannenberg (1410), the combined Polish and Lithuanian forces decisively defeated the great army of the Teutonic Knights. Gains of the victors in the First Peace of Thorn (1411) were limited, however, to the acquisition of Samogitia and an indemnity. The next Polish King Vladislav III (1434–1444), who was also King of Hungary, was an absentee monarch who lost his life on the ill-fated Crusade of Varna (1443–1444) against the Ottoman Turks.

Under Casimir IV (1447–1492), who was already Grand Duke of Lithuania, the government of the two countries was again united. Casimir completed the defeat of the Teutonic Knights and compelled them to accept the Second Peace of Thorn (1466) according to which eastern Pomerania and West Prussia were returned to Poland, and East Prussia was held by the Knights as a fief from the King of Poland. Casimir's eldest son became King Vladislav II of Bohemia (1471) and King of Hungary (1490); his second son, John Albert, became King of Poland (1492–1501); and another son, Alexander, became Grand Prince of Lithuania. Thus, by 1500, Jagiellonids were ruling in all four east central European countries. In each case, however, Jagiellonid rule meant a further weakening of the monarchy.

Hungary in the Later Middle Ages

During the Later Middle Ages Hungary was, for some time, the dominant power in Central Europe. Hungary's strength derived from its rich natural resources, both agricultural and mineral, its traditions of monarchical power, the governmental abilities of its Angevin and Hunyadi rulers, its close relations with Italy, and the pressure of the expanding Ottoman Turks. Hungary at its greatest extent in this period included the northern Balkan states. But, as with other East Central European countries, the blight of growing aristocratic power and feudal disintegration struck the Hungarian monarchy by the close of the fifteenth century.

The end of the Arpad line in Hungary was followed by eight years of civil war (1301–1308). The Angevin candidate, Charles Robert of Naples, won out and established his family upon the throne (1308–1382), ushering in a brilliant era. Both Charles I (1308/1310–1342) and his son Louis the Great (1342–1382) strengthened the Hungarian monarchy, making it more absolute. They greatly increased the income of the government, built up a strong army, fortified key Hungarian cities and towns, encouraged economic expansion and urban development, stimulated mining, and embraced the Italian Renaissance. Charles I built up a strong state, and at the same time expanded the Hungarian army. Louis I, the Great, expanded Hungarian possessions and satellites to include Dalmatia, Croatia, Bosnia, northern Serbia, and northern Bulgaria. Louis also became King of Poland, and twice intervened in the internal affairs of Naples. Besides constructing numerous fortifications, he founded the University of Pecs.

Louis the Great left two daughters: Jadwiga, who succeeded him in Poland; and Maria, who succeeded him in Hungary (1382ff.). During a struggle over the succession, Maria was saved by the intervention of her fiancé, Sigismund, who became King of Hungary (1387–1437) as well as Holy Roman Emperor (1410). Sigismund's chief concern was for Hungary, because of its great resources, its cooperative spirit, its greater peril, and the fact that it was his chief bastion against the Turks. Sigismund conducted numerous campaigns against the Turks, most of which failed; but his efforts helped both to arouse Europe and to deter the Turkish advance. An important contribution was the construction of elaborate fortifications, including the strategic first-class fortress of Belgrade.

Hungary's historic role was the defense of Western Christendom against the Turks. Her next two kings, Albert of Austria (1437–1439) and Vladislav I (1440–1444), who was also King (Vladislav III) of Poland, met early deaths in anti-Turkish campaigns which brought to power the leading hero of the Turkish wars, Janos Hunyadi, as Governor and Viceroy (1446–1456) for Ladislas (V) Posthumus (1444–1457), who was also King (Ladislas I) of Bohemia. Despite defeats in which he shared, such as Varna (1444) and Kossovo (1448), Hunyadi was usually victorious over the Turks, as at Semandria (1437) and Belgrade (1456). Unable to obtain the cooperation of the jealous magnates, Hunyadi built up his own personal estates to the point where they were capable of supporting a large part of his military establishments.

Hunyadi's mantle descended upon his second son, Matthias (Hunyadi) Corvinus (1458–1490), who was unanimously elected King by the Hungarian Estates. Matthias, known as "the Just," not only gave his country good government and promoted its prosperity but also fostered education and learning. He revived the University of Pecs, founded the University of Pressburg, and established the famous humanist Corvinian Library at Buda. Matthias Corvinus also turned his attention to the West, where he obtained temporary possession of half of Bohemia (Moravia, Silesia, and Lusatia), Lower Austria, and Styria.

Hungary declined following the death of Matthias (1490). The Hungarian nobles gained the upper hand and elected the weak Vladislav II, a Jagiellonid (already King of Bohemia), saying that they wanted "a king whose beard they could hold in their fist." Vladislav II (1490–1516), nicknamed "King All Right," who was also King of Bohemia, allowed complete feudal ascendance of the magnates and the subjugation of the peasants.

Scandinavia During the Later Middle Ages the nobility were ascendant in each of the three Scandinavian countries. The assembly of the nobles and/or the council of the magnates, particularly the latter, dominated the government, and elected and deposed kings at will, or replaced them by regents for extended intervals. The prevailing agrarian type of economy was congenial to feudalism and aristocratic rule.

A certain "denationalization" of the Scandinavian nobility resulted from their international marriages and a precedence of family interests over national concerns. This led to their willingness to elect foreigners as kings, including other Scandinavian monarchs, since foreign origin made a monarch more dependent on their good will, and the rule of more than one country divided his attention. The accession of foreign rulers was encouraged by intermarriages between ruling houses. The Black Death (1349–1350) also promoted the power and denationalization of the aristocracy by both encouraging international marriages, and increasing the size of their holdings, as well as by often necessitating the appointment of foreign clerics to ecclesiastical offices.

Native Scandinavian opposition to Hanseatic exploitation contributed to a growing willingness to unite. Partly to restrain the presumptuous Hansards, and partly to enhance their own power, the nobility of all three Scandinavian countries agreed to a union (1397). As it became evident that Danish interests were dominant in this Union, Sweden broke off by degrees.

Denmark

Aided by its favorable location and greater population density, Denmark was the strongest Scandinavian country in the fourteenth century. After a century-long decline of monarchical authority in Denmark (1241–1340), Waldemar IV (1340–1375) recouped royal power. Known as *Atterdag* (Another Day), Waldemar IV combatted feudalism and built up a national army, which included burghers and peasants as well as nobles. He allied with King Magnus of Sweden and Norway, and gave his able daughter Margaret as wife to the King of Norway.

Sweden

Sweden was dominated by its nobles after 1290. Partly to increase their own freedom of action, the Swedish aristocracy elected young King Magnus VII Ericsson of Norway as their king in 1319. The rule of Magnus Ericsson (1319–1365) was weak in Norway because of his prolonged absence, and in Sweden due to his foreign origin. Meanwhile the Swedish *Riksdag* came to include representatives of the towns. Eventually the Norwegians forced Magnus to relinquish the Norwegian throne to his son Haakon (1350), and he was overthrown in Sweden by a revolt of the nobles, who were irritated by his misrule.

Norway

In Norway, Haakon VI (1350–1380), who had married Margaret, the daughter of King Waldemar (*Atterdag*) of Denmark, was a good and popular ruler. But Haakon's efforts to improve Norway were hampered by the ravages of the Black Death and the commercial ascendance of the Hansards. Olaf, son of Haakon and Margaret, also had a claim to the throne of Sweden, and some prospect of succession to the throne of Denmark.

Scandinavia fol-

When King Waldemar IV of Denmark died in 1375, the Danish nobility elected his grandson, Prince Olaf of Norway, as their king. When his father Haakon died five years later, Olaf also became King of Norway, with his mother, Queen Margaret, as Regent. Hoping for a general union of Scandinavia, Margaret added to Olaf's titles that of King of Sweden, but her hopes seemed blasted when Olaf died prematurely in 1387.

lowing the Union of Calmar (1397ff.)

The extraordinary sequel was a tribute to the prudence, diplomacy, good reputation, and attractive personality of Margaret. Following her son's death, the Norwegians recognized Margaret as their "mighty lady and rightful ruler," while the Danish Council likewise accepted Margaret as their "rightful heir and ruler." The Swedish nobles, who had meanwhile become discontented with the rule of Albert of Mechlenborg, invited Margaret to dispossess him in 1388, and after her army defeated Albert, also accepted her as their "mighty lady and rightful ruler." To stabilize the Union, Margaret persuaded the Councils of each of the three kingdoms to accept her nephew, Eric of Pomerania, as her heir, and then called a great international Scandinavian assembly at Calmar (1397) to attend Eric's coronation and agree on formal union. The assembly was held and Eric was crowned, but the terms of the Union of Calmar were never fully and legally defined.

A shortcoming of the Union from the viewpoint of Sweden and Norway was the fact that the government was based in Copenhagen and that appointees to governmental position and ecclesiastical prelacies were usually Danish. Margaret, who ruled until her death in 1412, was more tactful and prudent in dealing with her subjects, but Eric, who assumed control in 1412, was openly absolutistic. As a result Eric was overthrown in Sweden by 1435, in Denmark by 1439, and in Norway by 1440.

The Union between Denmark and Norway continued, but Sweden soon became independent. Although Norway was practically eclipsed in this unequal combination with Denmark, the Norwegians did not defect, partly because the country was rough and sparsely settled. Following Eric's deposition, the Danes and Swedes accepted a foreigner, Christopher of Bavaria, as king in 1440, and the Norwegians followed suit in 1442. With the nobles entrenched in control, monarchical power sank to a low level. The improvident, free-spending Christopher, who was soon rejected by the Swedes, lost the Orkneys and Hebrides, and incurred great debts to the north German Hansards, who became his real masters. His successor, King Hans I (1481–1513) of Denmark, was recognized by the Swedes for only four years (1497–1501).

While Norway remained a relatively submissive partner in the Union, it was otherwise with Sweden, where mining, industry, and native trade as well as urbanization were more developed. The active middle-class burghers and independent farmers of Sweden inspired the lower nobility with their nationalistic fervor, with the result that repeated Swedish rebellions occurred. Although the upper aristocratic pro-Danish party in Sweden succeeded in restoring the Union three times between 1440 and 1520, for a total of about nineteen years out of eighty, the Swedes were ruled by their own king or (more frequently) regent for the remainder of the time.

RUSSIA IN THE LATER MIDDLE AGES.
Section 81.

> Two Romes have fallen; a third still stands; a fourth is not to be. [Filotheus, a monk of Pskov (early sixteenth century), concerning the succession of Moscow to Rome and Constantinople.]

AFTER reaching its height during the first half of the fourteenth century, Tartar power in Russia progressively declined. Russia came to be composed of four distinct areas: the steppes of southern Russia, ruled directly by the Tartars; western Russia, which was subject to Lithuania and under the influence of the West; northern Russia, where the democratic Republic of Novgorod was ascendant; and northeastern Russia, which was for some time under Tartar overlordship, but gradually became independent and eventually assumed the leadership in Russian liberation and unification. Here the princes of Moscow became successively Grand Dukes and chief representatives of the Tartar Khans of Sarai; independent rulers of an expanding native Russian state; and claimants of the right to rule all Russia and to be accepted as Tsars (Caesars): successors of the Eastern Christian Emperors.

Tartar rule During the thirteenth century Russia had come under the rule of the Mongols and associated Turkish peoples, jointly known as Tartars. The objective of the Tartars enunciated at the beginning of their occupation was to obtain "a tithe of everything." Accordingly they were content as long as they received their regular tribute of money and manpower. They allowed the Russian princes, who acted as their tax collectors, to continue ruling the native population as Tartar representatives. The Tartar capital was at Sarai on the lower Volga. By tradition the position of Khan was reserved for the descendants of Juchi, a son of Chingiz Khan, whose portion was the West. The power of the Khan was absolute. The Russian princes, including the "Grand Duke," whose office was retained, had to obtain a *yarlyk* (patent) from the Khan at their accession. Although the Tartars became Moslems, they allowed religious liberty to their Christian subjects, and granted extensive privileges to the orthodox Church and clergy. Still religious differences constituted a gulf between the Tartars and their Russian subjects. The Tartar economy in southern Russia has been described as a *symbiosis* or interdependent "living together" of pastoral nomads and settled populations. The destructiveness of the Mongol conquest initially set back the Russian economy, and the subsequent determination of Tamerlane to divert transasiatic trade routes was also very detrimental to southern Russia. Still, various parts of Russia enjoyed considerable economic progress.

Internal rivalries among Tartars Between members of the house of Juchi there was considerable rivalry, which increased as time progressed. Various strong men also seized power in part or all of the territory of the Golden Horde (which then included Siberia) and sometimes used Juchid Khans as their puppets. The first internal crisis came when a prince of Juchid descent named Nogay obtained control of the far western part of the territories of the Golden

Horde (1280) and challenged the authority of three successive legitimate Khans, until he was overthrown (1300). The Khanate of the Golden Horde reached the height of its power in the first half of the fourteenth century under Khan Uzbeg (1313-1341), who made Islam the official Tartar religion. More than two decades of civil wars, assassinations, and anarchy followed the death of Uzbeg's grandson (1359). A new usurper, Mamay, who was not of Juchid descent, then obtained supreme power in the far west. Meanwhile the Russian princes took advantage of Tartar division to increase their independence and withhold tribute, and when Mamay tried to force submission he was defeated by Prince Dmitri (Donskoi) of Moscow (1380). The following year (1381) Mamay was also defeated by Toktamysh, an energetic Juchid prince, who had become a lieutenant of Tamerlane. Toktamysh (1377–1381ff.) reestablished the unity of the Khanate of Sarai and brought the princes of northeastern Russia under his control. As he grew strong, Toktamysh became less and less subservient to Tamerlane, with whom he broke completely by 1386. But Toktamysh was decisively defeated by Tamerlane in 1395, and again, in alliance with Vitovt (Vitold) of Lithuania, by a lieutenant of Tamerlane named Egidey (1398), who then ruled supreme in Russia for over a decade (1398–1411) through puppet Khans.

In the fifteenth century the Tartars broke up into rival Khanates. The Khanate of the Golden Horde, with its capital at Sarai, then became only one of several rival Khanates that included in Europe the Khanate of the Crimea, the Khanate of Kazan astride the lower Volga, and the Khanate of the Nogay Horde to the north of the Caspian, and in Western Asia the Khanates of the Uzbeks and Kazakhs (Kirghiz).

While the Tartar impact is often overestimated, it was still considerable. It contributed to absolutism, and a lessening of the representative element in Russian government. Various other aspects of Russian life were also influenced, as was the case with court etiquette, diplomatic procedures, forms of taxation, manpower levies, penalties for offenses, and especially the military system. For some time Russians were required to serve with Tartar armies, while Tartars increasingly served in Russian armies, especially as the balance of power shifted from Sarai to Moscow. The Russians adopted Tartar military dress and equipment and Tartar military techniques, as in the case of the encirclement tactic and the maintenance of a concealed reserve in warfare. Meanwhile serfdom increased among rural workers, even as did the power of the nobles, known as *boyars*. In some ways Russian industry and commerce were adversely affected by the Tartar occupation; but in others they were promoted, as in the development of new trade routes, complexes, and relationships. Oriental influence increased in various incidental aspects of Russian life. The emergence of a class of hardy, independence-loving horsemen known as Cossacks on the southern frontiers was a by-product of the Tartar occupation.

Tartar influence

During the period of Tartar dominance, the various provinces of Russia were ruled by their hereditary princes, and the position of Grand Duke was continued by the Tartars. The so-called *rota* system of succession was

Russian principalities under (continued)

the Tartars

superseded by the appanage system wherein the princes each enjoyed considerable autonomy and stayed in their own principalities and passed on their office to one of their sons, usually the eldest, with junior sons receiving lesser territories, as available. This has also been called the "river valley" system, since principalities frequently corresponded to river valleys, as in the case of Moscow, located in the valley of the Moscva River.

The three main forms of government—oligarchical, democratic, and monarchical—were present in Russia in the Later Middle Ages. In western Russia the aristocracy dominated the government. In northern Russia considerable democracy prevailed in the city-state of Novgorod, later joined by its "daughter" Pskov. In the principalities of northeastern Russia and in the Tartar Khanates, the government was autocratic.

Western Russia and Lithuania

During the Later Middle Ages western Russia became independent of the Tartars and was taken over by Lithuania. Since the Lithuanians were converted to Roman Catholicism, and Lithuania and Poland were recurrently united from 1386 on, strong Western influences resulted. Lithuania was divided and weakened by its expansion because two thirds of the population were Russian and Orthodox as opposed to one third who were Lithuanian and Roman Catholic. Further weakness resulted from the multiplicity of Lithuanian involvements and rivalries, such as those with the Poles and Tartars as well as with Moscow.

Southwestern Russia, which included such fertile lands as the Ukraine, was favorably situated on east-west as well as north-south trade routes. The princes of this area, such as Daniel of Galich and Volynia, early achieved a measure of independence from the Tartars. But western Russia fell under the control of Lithuanian princes, who in the fourteenth century expanded into the Dnieper Basin and took over the whole of the Ukraine.

Lithuanian power reached its height under Grand Duke Vitovt (1392–1430). For a while it even seemed as though Lithuania might become dominant throughout Russia, as Vitovt took Smolensk, and the Russian Princes of Tver, Riazan, and Pronsk became his vassals, while Novgorod was his ally, as was also, at least nominally, the Prince of Moscow. But Vitovt's decision to intervene in Tartar affairs in favor of Toktamysh was a great mistake, as he suffered a severe defeat at the Vorskla River (1399), which forced him to give up his dream of conquering Russia and the Tartars. Following the rule of Vitovt, Lithuania declined. As the Lithuanian sun set in Russia, that of Moscow rose.

Northern Russia: Self-governing Novgorod

Ascendant in northern Russia was the quasi-democratic city-state of Novgorod, whose "empire" stretched from the Baltic Sea to the Ural Mountains and beyond. Novgorod was favorably located about 110 miles southeast of the Gulf of Finland on the Volkov River at a strategic crossroads of northern commerce. Supreme power in Novgorod resided in the hands of the *veche* (*vieche*), the popular assembly, and a town council composed of municipal leaders. The prince of Novgorod was elected by and answerable to the *veche*, by whom he could be "shown the road." The chief function of the prince was to provide military defense and security, and his residence was located outside the city. Eventually the

Novgorodians dispensed with the office of prince and substituted that of an elected mayor. Novgorod's form of government seems to have been influenced by Western examples, such as the self-government of the cities of the Hanseatic League.

Novgorod was the prosperous commercial center of northern Russia. Its main staple was furs, which its representatives gathered from the various provinces of its northern "empire." The Novgorodians referred to their city as "Lord (Sovereign: *Gospodar*) Novgorod the Great," and stoutly defended their independence against Swedes, Germans, and Russian princes. Aided by its remoteness and marshes, Novgorod escaped domination by the Tartars, who exacted from it only shadowy submission. But it eventually succumbed to Moscow in the second half of the fifteenth century. In the mid-fourteenth century the city of Pskov located on Lake Peipus (about 120 miles west of the Gulf of Riga) became independent of Novgorod. The government, policies, and the eventual fate of this "daughter of Novgorod" were similar to those of the mother city.

Growing ascendance of northeastern Russia

During the period of Tartar dominance, the heart and hope of Russia lay in northeastern Russia, the so called Great Russia or Russian Mesopotamia in and between the valleys of the upper Volga and Oka Rivers. In this favorable agricultural and commercial region were located several growing principalities, including Vladimir, Tver, Jareslavl, Suzdal, Riazan, and Moscow. Although outside the area of direct Tartar rule, northeastern Russia was under Tartar control and sufficiently adjacent to learn much from the Tartars. Its climate and soil were favorable for agriculture, and its position and rivers for commerce. It became a refuge for emigrants from southern Russia. And it was a frontier area whose inhabitants were hardy, self-reliant, and warlike.

While the princes of northeastern Russia were subject tributaries of the Tartars, they had considerable autonomy. As the representatives and tax collectors of the Tartars they shared in the Tartars' autocratic power; while as military collaborators they learned Tartar methods of warfare. As princely initiative had developed these states, their princes were ascendant and the *veche* or popular assembly was of secondary importance.

The Grand Ducal office and the rise of Moscow

The Tartars recognized Yaroslav I of Vladimir as Grand Duke (1242), and for a century the office of Grand Duke was associated with this city. In the first three decades of the fourteenth century there was fierce competition between the princes of Tver and Moscow for the Grand Ducal office, with the pendulum swinging first to the one side and then to the other. But from the time of Ivan Khalita (John Moneybags) of Moscow, who became Grand Duke in 1332, the office was associated with Moscow. In the mid-fourteenth century, the princes of Tver, Riazan, Suzdal, and Nizhni-Novogorod also obtained Grand Ducal status, with direct responsibility to Sarai, but the Grand Dukes of Moscow still retained precedence and some jurisdiction.

Moscow was well located for trade, being near the center of the complex of the leading riverways of the "Russian Mesopotamia." The vigor, strong character, and practical policies of a long line of able princes also contributed to the Muscovite success. The princes of Moscow curried the good graces of the Tartar Khans of Sarai as long as the latter held the upper hand, and then turned on them and withheld tribute. The Muscovite princes welcomed and utilized refugees and fugitives, both Russian and Tartar. They accumulated wealth and territories by every means possible. By persistent efforts and intrigues they obtained the Grand Ducal position, and they managed to bring to Moscow the Orthodox Metropolitan of Russia, thus giving their city great religious prestige. They did not scruple to join the Tartars, even against their fellow Russians, when this was to their advantage.

Moscow is first mentioned in surviving sources in the twelfth century. This little town on the Moscva River was given by Grand Duke Alexander Nevsky to his younger son Daniel in 1263. The original territory of Daniel, which was only about five hundred square miles, was increased some thirty times in the next hundred and fifty years. The ambitious Daniel (1263–1304) initiated an active policy of Muscovite expansion, and after his death in 1304 Moscow became a leading rival with Tver for the Grand Ducal office.

The Grand Duchy of Moscow (1332–1462)

In 1332 the clever Prince Ivan Khalita (John Moneybags) of Moscow won the favor of the Tartar Khan and obtained the title of Grand Duke, which he held until his death and managed to transmit to his son. Ivan was an excellent administrator, and the Orthodox Metropolitan of Russia, Peter, on the new Grand Duke's invitation, took up residence in Moscow. Ivan welcomed refugees from other parts of Russia and provided them with lands and tools. And he profited considerably from his position as tax collector for the Tartars.

While the reigns of Ivan's son and grandson were not particularly eventful, that of his great grandson, Dmitri Donskoi (1359–1398), was. Although opposed by the Princes of Suzdal, Tver, and Riazan, Dmitri overcame them all. His soubriquet came from his successful defiance and defeat of the Tartar ruler Mamay in the famous battle of the Kukilov Pole (Meadow) by the Don River (1380). Although the fruit of this victory was short-lived, Dmitri became a hero and a symbol for the Russian hope to overcome the Tartars.

Aided by Tartar weakness and division, Vasili (Basil) I (1389–1425) was able to withhold tribute from the Khan. He even obtained Suzdalia and Nizhni-Novgorod as a price for supporting Khan Toktamysh against Tamerlane.

Vasili II the Dark (1425–1462)

Vasili II (1425–1462), son of Vasili I, came to be known as the Dark, possibly because he was blinded by a rebellious prince; and his dealings with the Tartars brought about the accusation that he was their ally. In the first two decades of his rule (1425–1447) Vasili II was preoccupied with a series of contests with rivals, in one of which he was captured, deprived of his sight, and temporarily replaced (1446–1447). But a reaction occurred and Vasili II returned to power. His rival, Prince Shemiaka, was eventually poisoned by Muscovite agents in Novgorod (1453).

In the final fifteen years (1447–1462) of the rule of blinded Vasili II, Moscow became practically independent of Sarai and successfully resisted repeated Tartar sieges. The skillful defense of Moscow's stout walls was aided by the use of gunpowder artillery and firearms and liberal recruitment of Tartars. Several princely appanages, including the estates of rebels, were appropriated. Novgorod, which had befriended the rebels, was attacked (1454–1456) and forced to accept a treaty (1456) that gave the prince of Moscow various powers over the hitherto self-governing city. Muscovite colonists also expanded to the northeast.

Ivan III, known as the Great (1462–1505), completed the work of his predecessors and laid the foundation of modern Russia. Having witnessed the cruel results of disorders under his blinded father, Ivan determined to build up his princely power to the point where it would be secure from all challenges, internal and external. He continued Vasili's policies of refusing tribute to the Tartars and expanding Muscovite territories, being helped in his designs by the current weakness of the Golden Horde, Lithuanian preoccupation elsewhere, and the ambitious ideas of his wife, Sophia (Zoe) Paleologus, niece of the last Emperor of Byzantium. Muscovite armies frightened Tver and Viatka into submission, and the princes of Yaroslavl ceded their rights to Ivan. Ivan purchased the rights of the princes of Rostov, paved the way for annexation of Riazan by marrying his sister Anna to Riazan's prince, and gradually obtained the appanages of his brothers by escheat and confiscation. *Ivan III, the Great (1462–1505)*

The most difficult of Ivan's projects was subjection of the proud republic of Novgorod the Great. Frightened by Muscovite expansion, the Novgorodians acknowledged the suzerainty of Grand Duke Casimir of Lithuania, who was also King of Poland (1447–1492). But Casimir, who already had his hands full, failed to come to their aid. Taking advantage of division in Novgorod, Ivan began to interfere in their affairs. In 1477–1478 Ivan claimed sovereignty over Novgorod, besieged the city, and forced its citizens to capitulate. The following year, after sternly suppressing a revolt of the Novgorodian boyars, Ivan removed the great city bell, dissolved the municipal *veche* and town council, and eliminated the last vestiges of Novgorodian self-government. *Expansion*

Before the close of his reign Ivan III also won much western territory from Lithuania (1500–1503), and entirely discarded the Tartar yoke. As the declared champion of Eastern Orthodoxy against the Romanizing, Westernizing efforts of Polish-Lithuanian rulers, Ivan invaded Lithuania in 1500 and won a great victory at the Vedrosa River. Following further successes, a truce was arranged that allowed Moscow to occupy former Lithuanian possessions east of the Dnieper in the Chernigov-Severian area. When the Tartar Khan Ahmad came with a large army to demand tribute in 1480, Ivan gathered a large force and went to meet him. For several days the two armies faced each other across the Ugra River, after which both retreated. Ivan was accused of cowardice, but he had won his point, and the Tartars did not come again.

During the reign of Ivan, the princes of Moscow began to claim to be the heirs of Byzantium. As the overlord and protector of the only Eastern Orthodox Patriarch independent of foreign rule and as the husband of a descendant of the Byzantine imperial line, Ivan could be regarded as the *Heirs of Byzantium* successor of the Emperors of Constantinople. Ivan III assumed the title of "Tsar (Caesar) of All Russia" and adopted the Byzantine standard of the double eagle, as well as features of Byzantine court etiquette. Ivan centralized his government and issued a code of laws known as the *Sudebnik*. He imported Italian architects, built a stone "kremlin" (fortress) to replace the old wooden one, and constructed the Uspensky Cathedral of the Assumption in Moscow.

By the close of the Middle Ages, a dynamic new Russia centered in Moscow and organized along autocratic lines was emerging. Because of the less advanced condition of most of its neighbors, and the unifying, civilizing influence of its Eastern Orthodox Christianity, as well as the rich diversity of elements inherited from Byzantines, Tartars, Slavs, and others, the new Russia had a great future.

References for Chapter 27

GENERAL works concerning the German Empire with treatments of the Later Middle Ages include GEOFFREY BARRACLOUGH, *Origins of Modern Germany* (Oxford: Blackwell, 1957); HERBERT A. L. FISHER, *The Medieval Empire*, 2 vols. (London: Macmillan, 1898); KURT F. REINHARDT, *Germany: 2,000 Years*, Vol. I: *Rise and Fall of the "Holy Empire"* (New York: F. Ungar, 1961); VEIT VALENTIN, *The German People: Their History and Civilization*, tr. Olga Marx (New York: Knopf, 1946); and especially vols. VII and VIII of the *Cambridge Medieval History* (Cambridge: Cambridge U.P., 1936 and 1949). Excellent materials on this period are to be found in JOHANNES JANSSEN's classic *History of the German People at the Close of the Middle Ages*, vols. I and II. (London: 1896–1925), and in FREDERICK C. HERTZ, *The Development of the German Public Mind* (New York: Macmillan, 1957), whose treatment is broader than its title suggests. Works on German cities in the Later Middle Ages include ELIZABETH G. NASH, *The Hansa . . .* (London: J. Lane, 1929); HELEN ZIMMERN, *The Hansa Towns* (New York: Putnam's, 1889); MAUDE V. CLARKE, *The Medieval City-State . . .* (London: Methuen, 1926); and WILSON KING, *Chronicles of Three Free Cities: Hamburg, Bremen, Lübeck* (London: Dent, 1914). Concerning the Hussite movement and wars, consult MATTHEW SPINKA, *John Hus and the Czech Reform* (Chicago: Chicago U.P., 1941), and FREDERICK G. HEYMANN, *John Ziska and the Hussite Revolution* (Princeton, N.J.: Princeton U.P., 1955). Among biographies are BEDE JARRETT, *Emperor Charles IV* (New York: Smith, 1931), and MARIAN ANDREWS (pseudonym Christopher Hare), *Maximilian . . . Holy Roman Emperor* (London: S. Paul, 1914).

Brief, elemental information concerning the Slavic states in the Later Middle Ages with emphasis on Russia may be gleaned from SAMUEL H. CROSS, *Slavic Civilization Through the Ages* (Cambridge, Mass.: Harvard U.P., 1948), and FRANK NOWAK, *Medieval Slavdom and the Rise of Russia* (New York: Holt, 1930). The states of East Central Europe are treated on a larger, but still sketchy scale by OSCAR HALECKI, *Borderlands of Western Civilization* (New York: Ronald, 1952).

The story of Bohemia (Czechoslovakia) in the Later Middle Ages has attracted considerable attention, partly because of the Hussite heresy and wars. It is the subject of an authoritative work by KAMIL KROFTA, *A Short History of Czechoslovakia*

(New York: McBride, 1934), and of two detailed chapters by KROFTA in the *Cambridge Medieval History*, VII, 155–182, and VIII, 65–115. It is also briefly sketched by S. HARRISON THOMSON in his *Czechoslovakia in European History* (Hamden, Conn.: Archon, 1965) and more fully told by FRANZ H. LUETZOW, *Bohemia: An Historical Sketch*, rev. (London: Dent, 1939).

For Poland, the collaborative *Cambridge History of Poland*, vol. I, eds. W. F. REDDAWAY et al. (Cambridge: Cambridge U.P., 1950), is standard. Less detailed but similarly reliable works are OSKAR HALECKI, *History of Poland* (New York: Rey, 1956), and ROMAN DYBOSKI, *Outlines of Polish History* (London: Allen, 1925). Useful and informative is the article by ALEXANDER BRUCE-BOSWELL, "Poland and Lithuania in the Fourteenth and Fifteenth Centuries," in the *Cambridge Medieval History*, VIII, 556–586.

Hungary in the Later Middle Ages is treated by DENIS SINOR, *History of Hungary* (London: Allen and Unwin, 1959), in satisfying fashion; as well as by DOMOKOS G. KOSÁRY, *History of Hungary* (Cleveland: Benjamin Franklin, 1941); CARLILE A. MACARTNEY, *Hungary . . .* (Chicago: Aldine, 1962); OTTO ZAREK, *History of Hungary* (London: Selwyn and Blount, 1939); and FERENC ECKHART, *Short History of the Hungarian People* (London: G. Richards, 1931). Informative is the article by BALINE HÓMAN, "Hungary, 1301–1490," in the *Cambridge Medieval History*, VIII, 587–619.

A good survey of the history of Scandinavia is to be found in the chapter by HALVDAN KOHT, "The Scandinavian Kingdoms During the Fourteenth and Fifteenth Centuries," in the *Cambridge Medieval History*, VIII, 533–555; interesting facets are discussed in the collaborative *Scandinavia: Past and Present . . .* , eds. JORGEN BUKDAHL et al. (Denmark: Arnkrone, 1959). For the history of Denmark in the Later Middle Ages, see JOHN H. BIRCH, *Denmark in History* (London: J. Murray, 1938), and JOHN DANSTRUP, *History of Denmark* (Copenhagen: Wivel, 1948). For Sweden, see INGVAR ANDERSSON, *History of Sweden*, tr. C. Hannay (London: Weidenfeld and Nicolson, 1962), and CARL HELLENDORFF and ADOLPH SCHÜCK, *History of Sweden* (Stockholm: Fritze, 1929). For Norway, see KAREN LARSEN, *History of Norway* (Princeton, N. J.: Princeton U.P., 1948), and THOMAS K. DERRY, *A Short History of Norway* (London: Allen and Unwin, 1957).

The most comprehensive, authoritative treatment of Russia in the Later Middle Ages in English is that of GEORGE VERNADSKY in vol. III: *The Mongols and Russia* and vol. IV: *Russia at the Dawn of the Modern Age* of his *History of Russia* (London: Oxford U.P., 1952 and 1959). Useful one-volume histories with brief surveys of this period include SERGEI F. PLATONOV, *History of Russia*, tr. E. Aronsberg (Bloomington: Indiana U.P., 1964); BERNARD PARES, *History of Russia* (New York: Knopf, 1953); JESSE D. CLARKSON, *History of Russia* (New York: Random House, 1961); and MICHAEL T. FLORINSKY, *Russia: A Short History* (New York: Macmillan, 2nd ed., 1969). See also VASILI O. KLUICHEVSKII, *History of Russia*, tr. C. J. Hogarth, vol. I (London: Dent, 1911–1931), and ALFRED RAMBAUD, *History of Russia*, tr. L. B. Lang, ed. N. H. DOLE, vol. I (New York: Bolles 1879). An original source is *The Chronicle of Novgorod*, tr. R. Michell and N. Forbes (London: Camden Society, 1914), which runs to 1471. Concerning the Mongols in Russia, consult MICHAEL PRAWDIN (pseudonym for Michael Charol), *The Mongol Empire . . .* , tr. Eden and C. Paul (New York: Free Press, 1967) (p.), and JEREMIAH CURTIN, *The Mongols in Russia* (Boston: Little, Brown, 1908), in addition to Vernadsky. An interesting brief study is IAN GREY, *Ivan III and the Unification of Russia* (New York: Macmillan, 1967) (p.).

THE RISE OF SOUTHERN EUROPE IN THE LATER MIDDLE AGES. Chapter 28.

SOUTHERN Europe became increasingly important in the Late Middle Ages. The small, independent, enterprising Italian city-states were the scene of the most dynamic cultural movement of the day: the "Italian Renaissance." The several Christian states in the Iberian peninsula were eventually united to form two strong kingdoms, Spain and Portugal, which joined the number of leading European powers and took a lead in European overseas expansion. The Asiatic Ottoman Turks subjugated both Asia Minor and the Balkans and succeeded the Byzantine Empire in the eastern Mediterranean world.

THE STATES OF ITALY IN THE LATER MIDDLE AGES. Section 82.

> Since the fall of the Roman Empire, Italy had not known such great prosperity. . . . Subject to no dominion but her own, she abounded in population, merchandise, and wealth. [Contemporary Francesco Guicciardini, concerning Italy in the later fifteenth century in his *History of Italy*.]

Italian dynamism

THE late medieval period was a "golden age" for Italy, which was temporarily free from outside control. The fleets of the north Italian city-states became dominant in the Mediterranean, although politically Italy still remained a "geographical expression." In the far north of the peninsula were numerous city-states and petty lordships (*signorie*), in the center the Papal States, and in the far south the Kingdoms of Naples and Sicily. Practically all contemporary forms of government were represented in Italy: monarchy, theocracy, democracy, oligarchy, dictatorship, and lordships. Several North Italian states had many "modern" features, such as progressive income taxes, mercenary soldiers, and a regular diplomatic corps.

Intense rivalries—political, military, and economic—existed among the various Italian states. For some time, leading Italian states had employed foreign mercenary soldiers, headed by captains known as *condottieri*, who made contracts (*condotta*) with governments for their services and those of their troops. These mercenary armies were noted for their extensive use of strategy and tactics as well as their willingness to surrender promptly when they felt that they were outmaneuvered or outnumbered. They also made early use of gunpowder weapons. Wars between Italian states were frequent, and alliances were continually shift-

The Rise of Southern Europe

ing, until Cosimo de Medici of Florence managed by the Peace of Lodi (1454) to set up a temporary balance of power in the peninsula, with Florence, Milan, and Naples on one side, and Venice and the Papacy on the other. Cosimo's system lasted until the intervention of Charles VIII of France (1494).

Profiting from their favorable position, Italians carried on extensive maritime commerce in the Mediterranean and served as middlemen in trade with the East. Italian industries, such as the manufacture of textiles, cutlery, and glass, throve, and Italians were for some time the leading bankers and financiers of Europe. Italy was the original home and principal scene of the cultural "Renaissance" of the Later Middle Ages.

Leadership in Italian affairs was enjoyed by the North Italian city-states, which had many points in common with the Hellenic city states in the Golden Age of Greece (fifth century before Christ). During the Early Middle Ages the government of the towns of northern Italy was usually in the hands of bishops and feudal lords. At an early date *conjurationes* (sworn associations) were formed among the rural aristocracy and among the bourgeois and aristocratic inhabitants of the towns. The original purpose of such "unions" was to protect the rights and promote the common interests of their members, and obtain for them some share in the government of the towns. But as time progressed they successfully sought to obtain complete control of urban government as well as to extend their authority over the surrounding countryside (*contado*). Next the bourgeoisie fought with success to subdue the unruly nobles who lived in the towns and constructed small fortresses (towers or *torre*), indulged in violence, and considered themselves beyond the law. By the end of the twelfth century, semidemocratic urban communes were the rule in northern Italy. Meanwhile, aided by the difficulties and reverses of the German Emperors, these communes became more autonomous. Each reverse of the German Emperors during the investiture struggle and the Guelph versus Hohenstaufen contest meant further liberty for the North Italian communes, which were incidentally leading agents of the overthrow of imperial power in Italy.

The city-states of northern Italy

Independence and growing prosperity, however, brought new problems for the towns. Among these were their constant rivalries and frequent wars with one another and the internal competition between classes for control of the towns. The bourgeoisie in the towns eventually divided into the capitalistic upper bourgeoisie or *populo grasso* (fat people) and the ordinary middle class or *populo minuto* (small people), in addition to whom there were the proletariat or hired laborers. As the struggles between factions in the towns became more intense, strong men rose to supreme power, sometimes as the candidate of one or another faction, and sometimes as the result of a coup or a compromise. These "dictators" or "despots" were usually accepted eventually by the majority as an effective means of maintaining much needed order and security. At first such dictatorships were extraconstitutional and temporary; but in time many became permanent, and evolved into hereditary lordships or *signorie*. Finally *signori* (lords or "despots") ruled in practically all of

Rise of dictators (signori)

the Italian city-states, as seemingly the most practical, efficient, stable form of government then available. Florence, "the Athens of Renaissance Italy," clung to democratic institutions longer, but eventually succumbed to Medici dictatorship. Venice and Genoa were usually ruled by oligarchies.

Despots and condottieri

Typically the *signori* at first retained a front of republican forms, but subsequently discarded the mask. Eventually they sought to "legalize" their position by obtaining some sort of authorization from an Emperor or Pope. Many *signori* were benevolent rulers, whose policies included territorial expansion, construction of useful public works such as roads, bridges, harbor facilities, dams, drainage systems, and public buildings, as well as patronage of literature and the arts. Much of the power of the *signori* depended on their *condottieri*. Originally these men were chiefly foreigners, such as the Englishman John Hawkwood (Giovanni Acuti), the Frenchman Fra Moriale, and the German Werner of Uralingen. Many were made available by lulls in the Hundred Years' War. Eventually most of the *condottieri* came to be Italians, such as Barbiano, Colleoni, and Sforza. Among reasons for the use of the *condottieri* were their professionalism, the reluctance of well-off Italians to fight, and the fact that absolute governments could not rely on citizen soldiery. The armies of the *condottieri* were mainly horsemen ("men at arms"), and their warfare was highly technical and conventional.

Taxation

The North Italian city-states used numerous forms of taxation, some of which were quite "modern." One was the *catasto*, a property tax of about ½ per cent of value, also known as the *decima* (tenth). If property brought in 5 per cent profit a year, this would be 10 per cent of the income. Another was a progressive income tax, known as the *decima scalata* (scaled tenth) since the percentage collected was less for those with smaller incomes, greater for those with larger incomes. Sales taxes were also very common. One of the key political issues in the north Italian city-states concerned forms of taxation, since such could determine upon what classes the burden would mainly fall. Thus a sales tax would favor the rich, an income tax the poor.

Foreign relations

Clashes between the north Italian city-states were frequent. Many of their wars were partly commercial. Many arose from the fact that the stronger north Italian city-states such as Milan, Florence, and Venice were expanding their territories. The shifting of alliances was kaleidoscopic. Prolonged naval wars were fought between Genoa and Pisa for control of the western Mediterranean, until Genoa was finally the victor (1284); and between Venice and Genoa for ascendance in the Mediterranean and Black Seas with varying fortunes, until Venice won a decisive naval victory (1380). A by-product of the intense competition and intricate foreign relations of the north Italian city-states was the beginning of modern diplomacy with its maintenance of continuous embassies, accepted diplomatic practices, and submission of regular reports to the home government. The wily Venetians were at the fore in the development of diplomacy.

Milan

Located in the middle of the Po Valley, Milan (**Mediolanum**) was a

The Rise of Southern Europe

leading economic and political center in Italy from ancient times. During the Early Middle Ages the Archbishops of Milan were ascendant in its government; but during the High Middle Ages a vigorous communal government obtained control. The Milanese took the lead in resisting German attempts to dominate northern Italy. Bitter internal struggles between factions helped to promote the rise of dictators and eventually hereditary *signori* in Milan: first the Torriani (Della Torre) (ca. 1237–1277) and then the Visconti (ca. 1277–1447). The accession of the Visconti was the work of Archbishop Otto Visconti, who after defeating Napoleone della Torre imprisoned him in a wooden cage and dispensed to members of his own family the key offices of the government. Aided by ample revenues, the Visconti employed leading *condottieri* with large armies, by means of which they acquired control of the central Po Valley. Matteo Visconti obtained the title of imperial vicar from Emperor Henry VII (1311) and Giangaleazzo that of duke from Emperor Wenceslaus (1395). Giangaleazzo enjoyed an annual revenue of some 1.2 million florins, a fabulous sum in those days.

On the death of the hated Filippo Maria Visconti (1447), the Milanese set up the ephemeral "Ambrosian Republic," which lasted for only three years (1447–1450). Following this, Francesco Sforza, the former *condottiere* who had married Filippo Maria's daughter, returned and gained control. Francesco was a benevolent despot who gave the city good rule. Five of his family succeeded him until 1500, when the city fell under the control of France, followed successively by the Empire, Spain, and Austria.

During most of the Middle Ages, and until 1789, Venice was ruled by a merchant oligarchy in a continuous, stable manner. Although Venice was more interested in maritime commerce and overseas colonization than in the affairs of the Italian peninsula, still, in the Later Middle Ages, to obtain needed resources and for purposes of security the Venetians expanded their territory in northeastern Italy. At first the leading industry in Venice seems to have been salt-making through the evaporation of seawater in its shallow lagoons; but to this were later added various industries imported from the Near East, such as silk-making, glass production, and shipbuilding. The main forte of the Venetians was their maritime commerce; and in the fourteenth to fifteenth centuries Venice had over three thousand ships and thirty thousand sailors.

Venice

Originally founded by refugees from the barbarian invasions on islands in shallow lagoons on the northeast coast of Italy, Venice was nominally subject to the Byzantine Empire in the Early Middle Ages. At first Venice was ruled by a "doge" or duke, who theoretically represented the Byzantine Empire. For a while (sixth century ff.) the doge was very powerful, as the Emperor's representative. But with the decline of Byzantine power in Italy, Venice became more independent, and the Venetian bourgeoisie obtained more say in the government. The bourgeoisie initially first obtained a partnership with the doge, and then, in the eleventh to twelfth centuries, subjected him to their own control. The Venetian merchant oligarchy dominated the Great Council, which was, from the twelfth century, the supreme source of political authority in the state. With the so-called Closing of the Great Council (1297), its membership was reserved to descendants of some two hundred leading families, whose names were eventually listed in the "Golden Book" (1315ff.). In addition to the Great Council, the Venetian government had a Senate and a Cabinet, to which was added in 1310 the Council of the Ten presided over by the doge, which became the supreme political agency in the State.

During the era of the Latin Empire of Constantinople (1204–1261) the Venetians obtained several islands and ports that had formerly belonged to the Empire. Venice expanded its holdings in Italy in the fourteenth to fifteenth centuries by acquiring several small neighboring states, including Padua, Verona, Vicenza, Brescia, and Bergamo. This brought Venice into competition with powers such as Milan and the Papacy. Meanwhile Venice engaged with Genoa in a long struggle for maritime ascendance that ended with a decisive Venetian naval victory in the "War of the Chioggia" (1378–1380). The growth of Ottoman Turkish power in the Near East, including the Balkans, brought an end to Venetian commercial supremacy and the loss of most Venetian bases in the eastern Mediterranean and Black Seas. Disastrous wars with the Turks (1464–1479 and 1499ff.) as well as Portuguese establishment of an all-water route to the Far East around the Cape of Good Hope contributed to Venetian decline.

Florence, a republic

"The Athens of Italy," Florence was the chief home of the Italian Renaissance and the leading citadel of contemporary democracy. Florence was also a leader in the woolen textile industry and one of the foremost financial centers of Europe. The Florentines established a self-governing commune and obtained a large measure of autonomy from their overlords, the Marquisses of Tuscany, by the early twelfth century. During the Guelph versus Ghibelline struggle, Florentine branches of the two parties vied for supremacy in the city. The victorious Guelph party established the Ordinances of Justice in 1293, which restrained the turbulent aristocracy and forced them to demolish their towers and desist from violence. The Ordinances put governmental power firmly in the hands of the middle-class priors (presidents of the guilds), who constituted Florence's governing board or *Signoria*. By the early fourteenth century, the main theme of Florentine history was a running struggle between the great capitalists and the ordinary citizens. Each party from time to time invoked strong men. Following the financial crash of 1339ff., which included the bankruptcy of leading Florentine financial houses, the adventurer Walter de Brienne was made "Captain of the People" by the upper middle class (1342), but became distasteful even to his sponsors, and was run out of the city the following year. Although the ordinary middle class came into power for a while, the upper middle class soon regained ascendance (by ca. 1347).

Unrest in Florence

As a result of long-standing grievances, the Florentine proletariat, who were known as *ciompi* (confrères, pals), allied with the ordinary middle class, who had been without a voice in the government and rose up in revolt in 1378. For a while (1378–1382) Florence was controlled by the

The Rise of Southern Europe

revolutionists, who were headed by an unskilled wool carder named Michele di Lando. But eventually the upper middle class wooed the ordinary middle class away from their alliance with the proletariat. The upper middle class and ordinary middle class shared control, although soon the *populo grasso* regained their supremacy. At the head of the upper middle class at the time were the Albizzi, who employed the *condottiere* John Hawkwood (ca. 1387ff.). The chief champions of the lower classes were the Medici, who were also generous patrons of the Renaissance. Meanwhile Florence expanded its control in Tuscany, and obtained direct access to the sea by forcibly taking Pisa (1402) and purchasing Livorno or Leghorn (1421).

The popularity of the Medici with the majority of the populace, as well as their power in the government, steadily increased. Salvestro de Medici had supported Michele di Lando during the *ciompi* rebellion, and Giovanni de Medici, who was *Gonfalonier de Justicia* (Standard-bearer of Justice: chief executive) for a while (1421ff.), temporarily established a graduated income tax (the *decima scalata*), which bore less heavily on the lower classes. In 1433 Cosimo de Medici, current head of the family, was exiled as a result of the failure of an expedition against Lucca; but the following year he was recalled by popular demand. From 1434 until 1737, with brief exceptions, the Medici ruled Florence. At first they controlled Florence indirectly as political "bosses" from behind the scenes. The canny Cosimo de Medici (1434–1464) ruled his native city by remote control, and established both a progressive income tax in Florence and a balance of power system in Italy.

Medici rule

Eventually Medici rule in Florence became open and direct. In 1478 the Pazzi family and other conspirators attempted to overthrow the Medici by assassinating both Giuliano de Medici and his brother Lorenzo while they were attending church services. The plotters succeeded in murdering Giuliano, but not Lorenzo, and they were soon slaughtered by a mob. As a result of the failure of the Pazzi conspiracy, the Medicis emerged stronger than ever. A lapse in Medici control occurred when the weak Piero de Medici (1492–1494) lost Florentine support by excessive concessions to Charles VIII of France, so that the angry Florentines reestablished their Republic (1494–1512). The eloquent and fiery Dominican Girolamo Savonarola obtained an ascendance from about 1494 to 1498, but his attempts to reform and purify the Florentines soon tired them, while his denunciations of the worldliness of the clergy as well as his refusal to submit to Church authority aroused ecclesiastical condemnation, bringing about his downfall. The Medici returned to power in Florence in 1512, and, except for a brief restoration of the Republic (1527–1531), ruled as Dukes of Florence and Tuscany until 1737.

The Papal States, stretching across central Italy, were turbulent during most of the Later Middle Ages. Papal secular government was usually weak because of the ecclesiastical preoccupations and responsibilities of the Popes and their generally advanced age. The mountainous, geographically subdivided nature of the Papal States encouraged the defection of local lords. The intense rivalries of the great Roman and Italian

The Papal States

families were often directed against those who wore the Papal tiara. Communal aspirations led to urban attempts such as that of the Romans under Cola di Rienzi (1347–1354) to obtain self-government. The expansionist policies of powerful neighbors, such as Milan, Venice, Florence, and Naples, constantly threatened and often absorbed outlying parts of the Papal States.

During the seven-decade absence of the French Popes at Avignon (1309–1377), virtual anarchy came to prevail in the Papal States. Eventually the Papacy sent the able Cardinal Gil Albornoz, who had already acquired military and administrative experience in the service of the Spanish crown, to regain control of the Papal States. Albornoz expertly restored order (1353–1367), issued the Aegidian Constitutions (1357) as a governmental blueprint, and made it possible for the Papacy to return to Rome. But during the Great Western Schism (1378–1417), Papal power became once more feeble and insecure and Papal control over outlying areas of the Papal States weakened. Nor did the end of the Schism mean a full restoration of Papal power, since many areas and persons retained their former stance, and conciliarism continued to harass the Popes until about the middle of the fifteenth century.

Among leading concerns of the "Renaissance Popes" (1417ff.) were the reestablishment of effective government in the Papal States and the recovery of lost outlying territories. These aims, as well as maintenance of the integrity of the existing Papal States, necessitated involvement in international alliances and occupied much of the attention and energies of Popes such as Sixtus IV, Innocent VIII, Alexander VI (Borgia), and Julius II. Alexander VI made his unscrupulous illegitimate son, Cesare Borgia, his Captain General of the Papal States; and fiery old Julius II personally led Papal armies against political enemies.

"The Two Sicilies": the kingdoms of Sicily and Naples

At the outset of the eleventh century, southern Italy was divided into numerous petty states and dependencies, including Byzantine holdings, while the island of Sicily was controlled by the Moslems. In 1016 a band of Norman pilgrims, stopping off at Salerno, helped a local prince fight his foes. Since they found this military service both profitable and successful, growing numbers of Normans came to southern Italy to fight for local lords. In time they were rewarded with fiefs, and won independent territories of their own.

Several sons of a Norman seigneur named de Hauteville thus came to southern Italy (ca. 1034ff.). By 1046, William de Hauteville ruled Apulia, a former Byzantine holding in far southeastern Italy. His brothers Drogo and Humphrey succeeded him; and finally a younger brother named Robert, known as "Guiscard" (the Fox), an unscrupulous "ruddy giant," became the "leader of the wolf pack." Guiscard conquered Calabria and eventually became the ruler of far southern Italy. Meanwhile, answering the pleas of southern Italians, Pope Leo IX gathered an army in 1053 and sought to halt the expansion of the intruders. But Leo was defeated and taken prisoner by the Normans, to whom he made concessions. By 1059 Guiscard was recognized as "Duke of Apulia and Calabria, and future Lord of Sicily," by Pope Nicholas II. In 1084 the Normans were

The Rise of Southern Europe

called in by Gregory VII to save Rome from falling to the Germans.

By 1098 the Normans had completed the conquest of both southern Italy and Sicily, and in 1130 Duke Roger II of Sicily, who had managed to unite the peninsular and insular Norman holdings, was recognized as "King of Sicily" by Pope Anacletus II, who needed his support against an Anti-Pope. The able Roger II contributed to the further organization of a strong state with centralized government and built up Sicilian naval power. Meanwhile, beginning with Guiscard, the Normans made several attempts to expand into the Balkans at Byzantine expense but were repeatedly foiled by Byzantine craft, Venetian intervention, and bad luck.

Following the death of William II (1189), the Kingdom of Sicily came into Hohenstaufen possession. A native of the southern kingdom, Frederick II further strengthened and centralized its government by the Constitutions of Melfi (1231). Following Frederick's death, the Papacy, which claimed overlordship over the kingdom, refused to accept continued Hohenstaufen rule, and called in Duke Charles of Anjou. The latter defeated first Manfred and then the final Hohenstaufen, Conradin, who was beheaded at Naples (1268).

The grand projects of the ambitious Charles of Anjou, who ruled the Kingdom of Sicily from 1266 on, were forever doomed by the "Sicilian Vespers" (1282), a native uprising, following which the house of Aragon seized Sicily. All the efforts of the Angevins and the Papacy and the Kings of France to regain the island for the house of Anjou were unsuccessful, largely owing to Aragonese successes on the sea. *Angevin–Anogonese rivalries*

During the Later Middle Ages, the two Kingdoms of Sicily and Naples, each known as "the Kingdom of Sicily," were singularly backward and unprogressive, because of their rule by foreign dynasties, their excessively feudal condition, the exploitation of the populace by foreign overlords, and the maldistribution of wealth and purchasing power. A further disturbing element in the history of Naples was the development of competing foreign claims to the throne which was recurrently disputed among Angevins, Hungarians, Aragonese, and others, especially during the reign of the dissolute Joanna II, until it was finally obtained by Alfonso V of Aragon (1443).

The kingdoms of Naples and Sicily together with that of Aragon were now united under Alfonso V, the Magnanimous, who took up residence at Naples and was a generous patron of the Renaissance. On his death (1458), Alfonso bequeathed Sicily and Aragon to his brother John, but Naples to his illegitimate son Ferrante (Ferdinand) I. Because of Ferrante's misrule the Neapolitans welcomed the intervention of Charles VIII of France (1494); but on the hasty return of Charles to France the Neapolitan throne was again disputed. In 1500, King Ferdinand of Aragon and King Louis XII of France agreed to a joint occupation of the Kingdom of Naples; but in 1502–1503 the wily Ferdinand seized and occupied the whole of southern Italy.

SPAIN AND PORTUGAL IN THE LATER MIDDLE AGES.
Section 83.

> From the union of the scepters of the two kingdoms [Castile and Aragon] there have resulted so many and such marvelous benefits . . . that we . . . may well apply to ourselves the words of our blessed Redeemer: "Blessed are the eyes that see the things that you see!" [The contemporary chronicler Andrés Bernáldez concerning the reign of Isabella and Ferdinand in his *History of the Catholic Monarchs*.]

THE constitutional history of the states in the Iberian peninsula corresponded to the general European pattern during the Later Middle Ages. During most of the period, for one and three quarters centuries (ca. 1300–1474), most Spanish monarchs were weak, contentious *Cortes* (parliaments) strong, and the aristocracy typically proud, unruly, and addicted to civil wars. The final quarter century (1474ff.), however, saw growing political unification, consolidation, and strength. The last trend occurred even earlier in Portugal. Meanwhile Portugal and Spain began to assume the lead in a burst of overseas expansion that was to revolutionize world history.

Castile in the Later Middle Ages (to 1474)

Until the 1470s Castile and Aragon were frequently distraught by revolts of the aristocracy, growing demands of the representative *Cortes*, and intrigues and intervention of outside countries. In Castile, Kings John II and Henry IV were incompetent; several monarchs were minors at the outset of their reigns (as in the cases of Ferdinand IV, Alfonso XI, Henry III, and John II); and some had illicit sexual relations that gave rise to disputed successions as well as resulted in civil wars and foreign intervention. Attempts to resume Castilian expansion during the Later Middle Ages did not meet with success until the time of Ferdinand and Isabella. Castile's repeated efforts to recover Portugal failed, partly because of English support of the Portuguese cause and partly because of the determined resistance of Portuguese patriots. Occasional Castilian attempts to expand into North Africa were also unsuccessful.

The tone of the period was set during the reign of Alfonso X, the Wise (1252–1284), whose foreign and domestic mistakes precipitated civil wars. Conflict over the succession continued during the reign of Sancho IV (1284–1295), who became king contrary to his father's will and maintained himself mainly by "murder and massacre." The long regency for Sancho's son Ferdinand IV (1295–1312) was even more turbulent. Don Alfonso de la Cerda, who claimed the throne, was supported by many nobles and towns, as well as by the Kings of Granada and Aragon. Only the wisdom and courage of Alfonso's mother, Maria de Molina, and the loyalty and military ability of Guzman "El Bueno" (the Good) saved the throne. Another long minority ensued during the reign of Alfonso XI (1312–1350), who was only one year old at his succession. When he came of age, Alfonso XI spent much of his reign fighting the Moors of Granada and North Africa, over whom he won notable victories such as Rio Salado (1340) and Rio Palmones (1343). Alfonso captured Algeciras, but died of the Black Death while besieging Gibralter. Alfonso had an acknowledged mistress, the beautiful Doña Leanor (Eleanor) de Guzman, who gave him several illegitimate children. Alfonso's legitimate son, Pedro I (1350–1369), known as "the Cruel," soon stirred up opposition by his excessive harshness. Leanor de Guzman's sons were alienated when she was imprisoned and murdered; and public opinion was further alienated when Pedro deserted (and imprisoned) his wife, Blanche of Bourbon, for his mistress, Maria de Padilla.

In league with the King of Aragon, Leanor de Guzman's son, Henry of Trastamara, claimed the throne and headed a revolt against Pedro. The French and Aragonese supported Trastamara, while the English supported Pedro I until they were alienated by his excessive cruelties. The Trastamara protagonists finally won the great victory of Montiel (1369), and Henry of Trastamara personally killed Pedro I. Henry II of Trastamara (1369–1379), who won the title of "the Gift Giver" by his liberal distribution of lands and titles, successfully resisted the claim of the English Duke, John of Gaunt, to the Castilian throne. But Henry also alienated many by his cruelties, such as his imprisonment of the daughters of Pedro I, and he became involved in wars with the Kings of Aragon, Portugal, Navarre, and Granada, as well as England.

House of Trastamara (1369–1504)

Although John I (1379–1388) married the heiress to the throne of Portugal, his attempt to take over that kingdom on the death of his father-in-law failed because of stout Portuguese resistance, supported by English aid. Another long regency (eleven years) followed the accession of John's young son, Henry III (1388–1406), and a still longer one that of John II (1406–1454), who was only two at his accession. After John II assumed personal rule, his favorite, the Constable Alvaro de Luna, gave Castile reasonably good government until the mind of the King was poisoned against him and he was executed (1452); whereupon the lawless nobility came to power.

A state of virtual anarchy ensued under weak Henry IV (1454–1474), who was physically deformed and psychologically abnormal. Henry was so dominated by his favorite, Beltran de la Cueva, that the latter was reputed to be the real father of Henry's supposed daughter Juana, who came to be known as "la Beltraneja." Eventually many of the nobles revolted, and offered the crown to the King's sister Isabella. She worked out a compromise with her brother whereby he was to remain king but was to recognize her as his successor. However, Henry later revoked this promise and recognized Juana as his daughter and successor.

The kingdom of Aragon in the Later Middle Ages comprised several states—Aragon, Catalonia, Valencia, and the Balearics—under a common sovereign, with each retaining its own institutions. Gradually, however, the lines of separation dissolved, and common institutions developed. Partly because of continuous overseas involvements, necessitating their support, the *Cortes* of the component states and the general *Cortes* of Aragon wielded considerable power. The so-called Liberties of Aragon,

Aragon in and Later Middle Ages (to 1479)

consisting of rights and privileges enjoyed by the aristocracy and the middle class, continued to be extensive. Meanwhile Aragonese involvement with Castile became closer, largely by marital ties.

Mediterranean expansion became a dominant theme in Aragonese history during the Later Middle Ages. In 1282, Pedro III occupied the island of Sicily and entangled Aragon in prolonged struggles over this island. Generally the Sicilian crown was held by a relative of the Aragonese king. The right to conquer and rule Sardinia and Corsica was ceded to the Aragonese king by the Pope (1295), and the conquest of Sardinia was partly accomplished (1323–1324). The Aragonese crown temporarily gained territories in the very heart of Greece when the independent Catalan Duchy of Athens was offered to and accepted by King Pedro IV of Aragon in 1381.

Sicilian War

Pedro III (1276–1285) committed Aragon to Mediterranean expansion by intervening in Sicily (1282), to which he had a claim through his wife, Constance, although the Papacy had assigned the island to Charles of Anjou. Pedro III prepared a great expedition, ostensibly against North Africa. After the violent uprising against the French (1282) known as the "Sicilian Vespers," a deputation of Sicilians offered the crown of Sicily to Pedro, who diverted his expedition and quickly occupied the island. Angevin attempts to dislodge him were unsuccessful, largely because of maritime victories of the Aragonese navy under the skillful Genoese Admiral Roger Loria. The Angevins, the Papacy, and the French king Philip III formed a formidable coalition against Pedro. But when Philip III led a great French invasion into Aragon in 1285, an Aragonese naval victory off the Islas Hormisdas cut off French supplies by sea, and an epidemic seriously crippled the French army, which was forced to retreat beyond the Pyrenees, suffering great losses. During the Sicilian War, Pedro III was forced to grant to the Aragonese nobles and townspeople[a] the so-called General Privilege (1283) with concessions that included such provisions as the right of all nobles to leave the service of the King without prejudice and a royal promise to convoke annual *Cortes*. During the reign of Alfonso III (1285–1291), Sicily became a separate kingdom under his brother James. Exigencies of the Sicilian War also forced Alfonso to grant the nobles and bourgeoisie the Privilege of the Union (1287), which included the acknowledged right to depose the king if he failed to observe their privileges. In return for Papal recognition of his right to conquer Sardinia and Corsica, James II of Aragon and Sicily (1291–1327), eventually agreed both to relinquish the throne of Sicily and to help evict his brother Frederick from its government (1295). In 1302, however, Charles of Anjou recognized Frederick in return for certain concessions.

[a] Joined in the "Union"

Pedro IV, known as "the Ceremonious" (1336–1387), was hard and cruel. At an opportune moment, Pedro threw down the gauntlet to the Union and overcame its forces in the decisive battle of Epila (1348). He then forced the Union to dissolve, and inflicted terrible punishments on its leaders. In Valencia, they were compelled to drink the molten metal of the bells that had called them to their meetings. Pedro IV gained the

Balearics by defeating and slaying his brother and accepted the offer of the Catalan Duchy of Athens made by a Catalan deputation (1381). He also supported the successful candidacy of Henry of Trastamara in Castile.

During the reign of Martin I (1395–1410), Sicily reverted to the Aragonese crown. After Martin died without direct heir, the ensuing question of the succession to the Aragonese throne was settled peaceably by the Compromise of Caspe (1412), arbitrated by a commission which adjudged the throne to the capable Castilian prince, Ferdinand de Antequera (1412–1416). Alfonso V, the Magnanimous (1416–1458), who inherited Aragon, Valencia, Catalonia, Majorca, and Sicily, also took over the direct rule of Naples (1443) on the death of its Queen Joanna II. Alfonso V is chiefly famous for his lavish patronage of the Renaissance in Naples, where he lived for the final fifteen years of his life. John II (1458–1479), who succeeded to all of Alfonso's domains except Naples, was a strong, shrewd ruler. Although unsuccessful in his attempt to take over Navarre, the kingdom of his first wife, John II skillfully arranged the marriage of his son, Ferdinand, to Isabella of Castile, celebrated in 1469.

When King Henry IV of Castile died in 1474, many Castilian nobles and churchmen supported the candidacy of Isabella. But Prince Ferdinand was only able to bring a small army to his wife's assistance, whereas King Afonso V, the African, of Portugal with a large army came to the aid of the Princess Juana, who also had strong support in southern Spain. Although Afonso V of Portugal came promptly to Juana's assistance, he delayed closing with Isabella and Ferdinand, allowing them time to gather support so that they were able to build up their forces and defeat him at Toro in 1476. They then rapidly consolidated their position, so that when Afonso again invaded in 1479 they were easily able to defeat him at Albuera. In that same year Ferdinand succeeded his father as king in Aragon.

The unification of Spain under Ferdinand and Isabella (1474–1516)

Isabella and Ferdinand were intelligent and ambitious, devoted to the business of ruling, and anxious to make Spain strong and great. But Isabella was pious and scrupulously just whereas Ferdinand was more pragmatic and deceitful. Ferdinand was a hero to Machiavelli, who compared him to a fox and said to him: *A certain Prince of our day is always preaching peace and good faith, although he is the mortal enemy of both.*

Although the union of Castile and Aragon under Isabella and Ferdinand was only "personal," and the two countries retained their own separate institutions, "the Catholic Monarchs" labored energetically to make their position and power identical in each—especially in Castile. Public documents had the signatures of both; coins bore both of their images; and they presided jointly over meetings of the Royal Councils, saying *Tanto monta, monta tanto Isabel como Fernando*: "Isabella and Ferdinand have the very same power."

Isabella and Ferdinand also labored skillfully to centralize political power. Isabella managed to have the masterships of the three great military orders in Spain (Santiago, Alcantara, and Calatrava) assigned to her husband. The presidency of the powerful *Hermandad* or league of towns

Royal power

was likewise brought under royal control by making its president appointable by the monarchs and one of its main functions the defense of royal authority. *Corregidores* (literally "correctors") were sent as royal representatives into the towns.

Ferdinand and Isabella avoided, as far as possible, calling the *Cortes* of Castile, which they recognized as potentially restrictive of royal power. There were no meetings of the *Cortes* from 1483 to 1498. They restrained the aristocracy by revoking special grants and privileges conceded in previous reigns, appointing many of them to high-sounding but powerless positions with pensions at court, and increasing their number so as to make their position more commonplace. The Royal Council (*Consejo Real*) was regularized and reorganized. It met every morning, except on Sundays and holy days, for three to four hours. Ferdinand and Isabella regularly attended the meetings, which began in the warmer months at 6 A.M. and in the colder ones at 9 A.M. The Catholic Monarchs obtained from the Pope (1482) the *Real Patronato* (Royal Patronage), whereby they had special rights relative to the Spanish Church, including the right to nominate candidates for ecclesiastical offices in Granada, subsequently extended to Spanish America, and eventually to all of Spain.

Persecution of Jews and Moslems

The reign of Ferdinand and Isabella was marred by religious persecution. An especially powerful and questionable instrument in the hands of the Catholic Monarchs was the Inquisition. Introduced into Spain by a Papal bull of 1478, the Spanish Inquisition was under royal control and became an instrument to enforce political uniformity as well as religious orthodoxy. It used the Roman procedure of extracting evidence by torture. It often concealed the names of accusers and the nature of the accusation, thus crippling the defense. It could inflict the supreme penalty of death by fire, although it also used other punishments. Intended to "purify" and "unite" the country, the expulsion of the Jews (1492ff.) and Moors (1502) proved a serious blow to the Spanish economy as well as an ugly blot upon the Spanish record. The decrees called for expulsion or conversion, but acceptance of the first alternative meant virtual impoverishment, because of the shortness of time allowed for compliance (four months for the Jews and two and a half months for the Moslems) and the further prohibition against the export of gold and silver. In order to save their property, many Jews and Moors became nominal Christians.

Expansion and foreign relations of "the Catholic monarchs"

Ferdinand and Isabella greatly expanded their realms. They ended Moorish political power in the peninsula by conquering Granada, which had long resisted reduction because of its mountainous terrain, formidable fortresses, and rich resources. They raised a large army, fostered a crusading spirit, and used the new weapon of cannon against Granada's fortifications, while they took advantage of and further fostered division among the Moslems. After ten years of effort they finally entered the city of Granada in triumph in 1492. Terms of surrender included a guarantee of religious liberty for the Moslems, although this promise was afterward broken. Toward the end of his life, Ferdinand realized the Aragonese ambition of taking Navarre (1512). First he made a treaty

The Rise of Southern Europe

of alliance with the rulers of Navarre, and then, on learning that they had made a secret treaty with the French king, demanded permission for his troops to cross Navarre. When this was denied, he brought his army into Navarre and took over the country.

The Catholic Monarchs were encouraged by their success in completing the Reconquest to finance Columbus's attempt to find a direct water route to the Far East by sailing westward. Accordingly Columbus made his famous voyage (1492), which resulted in the surprising discovery of an unknown land, the American "New World," where Spain became the first and leading colonizer. Ferdinand also fulfilled the longstanding Aragonese ambition to take the Kingdom of Naples. He first cooperated piously with the Papacy in preventing French occupation of Naples, then agreed with the French on a joint conquest and occupation, and finally took advantage of a disagreement and his more strategic position to oust the French.

Advantageous marriages of the children of Ferdinand and Isabella that enhanced Spain's position included that marriage of Princess Juana to Archduke Philip of Austria, whose offspring was Emperor Charles V; that of Princess Isabella to Don Afonso of Portugal and then, on his death, to King Manoel I, the Fortunate; and that of Princess Catherine, first to Prince Arthur of England and then to his brother, the future Henry VIII.

Enterprising little Portugal emerged from the side of Leon during the twelfth century. The Portuguese Reconquest, completed by 1249, set the pace for the rest of the peninsula. Once independent, the Portuguese jealously guarded their freedom, being frequently helped by England, with which country they developed a close and enduring alliance. From the fourteenth century on, the Portuguese took the lead in overseas exploration and expansion.

The rise of Portugal (to 1279)

Confronted by the warlike Almoravides from Morocco (1086ff.), King Alfonso VI of Leon invoked the assistance of French knights. He married his legitimate daughter Urraca to one of these, Raymond of Burgundy, and his illegitimate daughter Teresa to another—Raymond's relative, Henry of Burgundy, whom he made Count of Portuscale (whence "Portugal") on the Douro River. When Alfonso left the throne of Leon and Castile to his daughter Urraca, with Henry and Teresa in vassal status, the latter were highly dissatisfied. As Portugal continued to expand and became ever more independent, Teresa eventually took the title of queen in defiance of her half-sister.

Afonso I Enriquez (1128–1285), the son of Teresa and Henry, obtained recognition of royal status from "Emperor" Alfonso VII of Leon and Castile, as well as from Pope Alexander III. Afonso Enriquez also expanded southward, taking Beja, Merida, and Santarem, and finally, with English assistance, the key port of Lisbon. This work was continued by subsequent Portuguese kings, among whom Sancho I (1185–1211) is known as *Povoador* for his repopulation of depopulated areas. Afonso III (1246–1279) completed the Portuguese Reconquest by occupying the Algarve in the extreme south (1249).

The consolidation of Portugal (1279–1385)

The consolidation of Portugal during the next hundred years began with King Diniz (1279–1325), the Farmer King. The practical and enlightened Diniz promoted agriculture and independent farming; and established Portugal's first commercial treaty with England. He also founded the University of Coimbra, first located at Lisbon (1290ff.); and expanded Portuguese law as well as improved the administration of justice.

Afonso IV (1325–1357) sent an expedition to explore and claim the Canary Islands. Pedro I (1357–1367) devoted himself so zealously to the administration of justice that he came to be known as *O Justiciero*. Ferdinand I (1367–1383), last of the Burgundian line, claimed the throne of Castile, for which he fought three unsuccessful wars. On the death of King Ferdinand, the nobles, who resented the prospect of Castilian dominance, rebelled against his widow. With English assistance, the liberty-loving Portuguese, led by João, Grand Master of the Order of Aviz, defeated the Castilians at Aljubarotta in 1385, thus preserving their independence.

The Portuguese Age of Exploration (1385–1481)

The Portuguese *Cortes* declared the monarchy elective and chose João of Aviz, whose energetic house soon raised Portugal to prominence among European powers. The century 1385–1481 is known in Portuguese history as "the Age of Exploration." João I (1385–1433) made a close political and commercial alliance with England known as the Treaty of Windsor (1386), and took Ceuta in 1415, thus obtaining an important base in North Africa. The most remarkable of João's five sons, Prince Henry the Navigator, launched Portugal upon a course of overseas exploration and expansion. Prince Henry, who remained unmarried in order to concentrate on his combined geographical, commercial, and religious interests, established his residence at Sagres, in far southwestern Portugal, where he maintained an informal academy for sea captains. One of Henry's ideas was to effect a juncture with a reported Christian African prince known as Prester John (apparently the King of Abyssinia) and thus outflank the Moslems.

Ships sent out by Prince Henry rediscovered the Madeiras, Azores, and Cape Verde Islands, and sailed down the Coast of Africa, reaching, in succession, Cape Bojador (1434), Rio de Ouro (1436), Cape Branco (1441), and Cape Verde (1445). Meanwhile the Portuguese began a profitable trade of captive Negroes, gold, and ivory obtained in Africa.

Afonso V (1438–1481), known as "the African," made numerous expeditions to Africa, where he captured several bases, including Arzila and Tangier. The Guinea coast was explored and Portuguese posts were established along the west coast of Africa. Afonso's reign was transitional to the Age of Empire.

The Portuguese Age of Empire (1481–1580)

During their "Age of Empire" (1481–1580) the Portuguese monopolized direct overseas trade with the Far East, while royal absolutism grew at home. João II, the Perfect (1481–1495), first king of the new era, broke the power of the nobility. Confronted by plots to overthrow him, João waited until the last moment so that the guilt of the chief conspirators could be clearly established, and then executed over eighty

The Rise of Southern Europe

leading nobles, after which peace and order ensued. João was an enthusiastic patron of exploration. During his reign Bartolomeo Diaz rounded the Cape of Good Hope (1487). João arranged the Treaty of Tordesillas (1494), wherein Portugal received a right to Brazil in the New World. Meanwhile the crown grew immensely wealthy from the confiscated property of treasonable nobles, as well as from the profits of the slave trade and the gold brought back from Africa.

Under Manoel I (1495–1521), known as "the Fortunate," the wealth of the Far East began to pour into Portugal. A direct sea route to India around southern Africa was opened up by the voyage of Vasco da Gama (1498). The Portuguese won command of the Indian Ocean in the Far East, with bases at Goa, Malacca, Canton, and Ormuz, under the leadership of successive competent Viceroys Almeida and Albuquerque. The Portuguese also established bases along the east coast of Africa, and gained control of much of the coastline of Morocco.

THE BALKANS AND THE OTTOMAN TURKS.
Section 84.

> Having received permission to loot, the soldiers eagerly thronged into the City [Constantinople] ... and acted in accordance with the saying: "Slaughter their aged and take captive their young." [Account of the Ottoman occupation of Constantinople (1453) by the Moslem historian Sa'ad ed-Din.]

THE overshadowing event in eastern Mediterranean history in the Later Middle Ages was Ottoman Turkish conquest of the Balkan peninsula, accompanied by the subjection of Bulgaria and Serbia, and attended by the demise of the Byzantine Empire. European Constantinople became the capital of a Turkish Empire that included the Balkans and Asia Minor and soon expanded over most of the Near East.

Following the death of Michael VIII, Paleologus (1282), the Byzantine Empire resumed its downward spiral. Although the Paleologi dynasty founded by Michael VIII held the throne for two centuries (1260–1453), the Empire was weakened internally by various maladies and eventually overwhelmed by the Ottoman Turks. The Empire of the Paleologi was a shadow of its former self. The capital had suffered greatly as a result of its occupation by the Latins. The Emperor controlled only the far northwestern corner of Asia Minor, along with much of Thrace and Macedonia, and other scattered holdings. The Latins still held most of Greece, and many of the Aegean islands were still in Latin hands. The Despotates of Epirus and Morea were largely autonomous, although satellites, while the "Empire of Trebizond" was entirely independent. The shrinkage of the Empire entailed decreased manpower and resources.

Factors in the fading of the Byzantine Empire (1282–1453)

The Empire became partly feudal. Large tracts of lands or *pronoias* were taken over by feudal overlords known as *pronoiars*, who agreed to provide a number of fighting men proportionate to the size and value of their holdings. This semifeudal landholding aristocracy figured prominently in the destructive civil wars that marred Byzantine history in the fourteenth century. A key weakness of the restored Empire was its faltering economy. North Italian carriers skimmed off most of the profits of Byzantine international commerce. So impoverished did the Empire become that Emperor John V, while traveling in the West in 1369, was taken prisoner by the Venetians and held as a debtor until redeemed by his son Manuel II.

Division

A series of civil wars undermined the weakened Byzantine Empire and encouraged foreign intervention, especially by the Serbs and Ottoman Turks, who were enabled to expand at the expense of the Empire.

A further source of internal division was religious disagreement, especially concerning the question of reunion with the Western Church. Most Byzantines opposed reunion because it would mean submission to the Roman Pope and Latin domination. But several Emperors and some Byzantine ecclesiastics supported reconciliation, largely, it appears, to obtain Western assistance against the mounting Ottoman advance. East and West agreed on temporary reunion at the Council of Ferrara–Florence (1437–1439); but this was frustrated when the majority of the Byzantines refused to cooperate, apparently favoring the slogan: "Better the turban than the tiara!"

Failure to halt the Ottomans

Two major Western attempts to halt the Ottoman advances were unsuccessful. The international "Crusade of Sigismund" or "Crusade of Nicopolis" (1396), led by King Sigismund of Hungary, later Emperor, was overwhelmed by the Turks at Nicopolis on the southern Danube. The similar "Crusade of Ladislas" or "Crusade of Varna" (1443–1444), led by Vladislav III of Poland and the Hungarian hero John Hunyadi, was also crushed by the Turks at Varna by the Black Sea in 1444.

The Byzantine merchant marine, and with it the Byzantine navy, continued to shrink, largely as a result of excessively restrictive governmental policies concerning allowable interest from maritime commercial investments, until Byzantium became dependent on North Italian naval protection. When John VI, Cantacuzene, began to build up a small navy, the Genoese forced him to desist. The North Italians retained command of the seas and continued to obtain a lion's share of Byzantine maritime commercial profits.

The final Byzantine Emperors (1282–1453)

The weak Andronicus II (1282–1328) engaged Aragonese mercenaries known as the Catalan Grand Company to help recover territories in northwestern Asia Minor. But the Catalans later revolted, and established themselves as autonomous rulers of the so-called Duchy of Athens and Thebes. Andronicus II also lost territories to Venetians, Bulgarians, Serbs, and Turks. Eventually his son deposed him, and established himself as Andronicus III (1328–1341). After the death of Andronicus III, his minister, John Cantacuzene, had himself crowned as John VI (1341–1354), disregarding the claim of Andronicus's son, who was crowned as John V. Cantacuzene obtained the assistance of the Ottoman sultan, while John V obtained Serbian help. John VI's popularity declined and his power collapsed (1354), partly because of his unsavory allies, who obtained a foothold in the Balkans. John V, who ruled most of the time from 1354 to 1391, faced four more civil wars: three led by his son, Andronicus IV, and one by his grandson, John VII. For a while (1376–

The Rise of Southern Europe

1379) John V was ousted from power but he later recovered control, this time with Turkish assistance. Meanwhile, the Ottomans expanded rapidly in the Balkans, and forced John V to become their vassal in about 1373.

Handsome, brave Manuel II (1391–1425) spent much of his time endeavoring to obtain assistance from the West. During the early years of his reign, Constantinople, surrounded on all sides by Ottoman holdings, was in a virtual state of continuing siege by the Ottoman Turks, led by aggressive Sultan Bayazid. But eventually Bayazid had to lift the siege in order to defend his Asiatic possessions against the terrible Tamerlane. John VIII (1425–1448), like his predecessors, sought aid from the West. A large Byzantine delegation headed by both Emperor and Patriarch attended the Ecumenical Council of Ferrara–Florence (1437–1439), where they agreed to reunion on Western terms. A sequel to the Council, the Crusade of Varna (1443–1444), although initially promising, ended in disaster.

The last Byzantine Emperor, Constantine XI (1448–1453), died fighting at a breach in the walls as Constantinople fell to the Ottoman Turks in 1453. The long-lived Byzantine Empire was finally ended, and the proud "Queen of the Bosphorus" became a Moslem capital. Within a decade the Ottoman Turks completed their conquest of remaining fragments of the Eastern Empire.

After being united into one kingdom in the late twelfth and thirteenth centuries, Serbia enjoyed a fleeting Empire in the first half of the fourteenth century. Stephen Uros II (1268–1321) and mild but firm Stephen Uros III (1321–1331) expanded at Byzantine expense in Macedonia and overcame a Bulgarian–Byzantine coalition by decisively defeating the Bulgarians at Velbuzd (Kjustendil) in Bulgaria (1330). Serbia reached its medieval zenith under Tsar Stephen Dushan (1331–1355). Supported by the Serbian nobility, Stephen deposed his father, who was not considered sufficiently aggressive. The dynamic Dushan built up a Serbian Empire that included Macedonia, Epirus, Albania, Thessaly, western Bulgaria, and adjacent territories. Stephen Dushan conferred the title of Patriarch on the Serbian Archbishop and was crowned as Tsar (Emperor) at the Serbian capital of Skoplje. He was planning to take Constantinople when death overtook him (1355), so that the poet mourned:

Evanescent Serbian greatness and Bulgarian eclipse

> *Even as the imperial city was nigh*
> *The Day of Doom overtook Dushan.*

After Dushan died, his Empire disintegrated. Although the Serbs stoutly resisted the Ottoman colossus, and Prince Lazar finally assembled a coalition that included Bosnians, Macedonians, and Wallachians, they were overcome by the Turks in the hard-fought battle of Kossovo I (1389), known as "the Field of Blackbirds." Following the death of Lazar's son, Stephen Lazarevic (1427), the Ottomans devoured Serbia piece by piece until they finally took its last major stronghold of Smederevo in 1459.

Following the demise of John Asen in 1241, previously strong Bulgaria rapidly declined. The Bulgarians never recovered from their crushing defeat by the Serbs at Velbuzd (1330), and weakened Bulgaria soon fell to the Ottoman Turks. It became a tributary vassal state to the Ottomans in 1366, and was incorporated directly into their growing Empire following the Ottoman occupation of the Bulgarian capital of Trovno in 1393.

Beginnings of Rumania

Rumania, as a unified state, did not emerge until modern times, but its beginnings trace back to the two principalities of Wallachia (to the south) and Moldavia (to the north) during the Later Middle Ages. Since the Rumanian language is derived from Latin, the Rumanians claim to be descendants of Roman provincials. Threatened by the expansion of the Tartars on the one hand and Ottoman Turks on the other, the chief problem of the Rumanians was to retain their independence. Mirchtea the Great of Wallachia (1386–1418) aroused Ottoman ire by joining the Christian resistance to Turkish advances at Kossovo (1389) and Nicopolis (1396), and then by defeating the Turkish troops that invaded Wallachia to punish him. Although Sultan Mohammed I temporarily forced Wallachia to accept tributary status (1417), a fierce Wallachian ruler, Vlad the Impaler (1455–1462 and 1476–1477), who owed his nickname to his favorite mode of execution, refused to acknowledge Ottoman suzerainty. Ottoman influence contrived to get Vlad temporarily dethroned (1462) and eventually assassinated (1477). But meanwhile Stephen IV, the Great, of Moldavia (1457–1504) repelled powerful Mohammed II, the Conqueror, as well as exercised a vague suzerainty over Wallachia. In 1512, however, the Rumanians became tributary to the Ottoman Turks, although they still retained considerable self-government.

The Ottoman Turks: Thirteenth century

The Empire of the Ottoman Turks succeeded the Byzantine Empire in the Balkans and eventually dominated the Eastern Mediterranean world. Following Seljuk defeat of the Byzantines at Myriocephalon (1176), remaining Byzantine territories in Asia Minor were gradually won by the Turks. Many of the Turkish warriors were *ghazis*: volunteers who sought to carry on the *jihad* (holy war) for the Moslem faith.

Among petty Turkish Moslem states that arose in Asia Minor, following the disintegration of the Seljuk Sultanate of Rum in the thirteenth century, one was ruled by Osman or Otman, whose followers came to be known as "Ottomans." The Ottoman state was originally located in and about the small town of Sugut in far northwestern Asia Minor, about 45 miles south of Nicaea. Being on the immediate frontier of Byzantium, the Ottoman state had to keep on a warlike footing and had opportunities for expansion at Byzantine expense. Its leaders such as Osman became *ghazis*, fired by religious motives as well as by hope of material gain. Their adoption of the "holy war" concept made the Ottoman state a rallying point for religious warriors who came from various parts of Islam. Because of Ottoman tolerance and possibilities of gain, many of their Christian subjects cooperated with them and growing numbers even became Moslems.

Fourteenth century

Osman (1289–1326), a wise, judicious ruler, expanded his holdings by taking neighboring Byzantine territories in northwestern Asia Minor. His army eventually seized the important walled city of Brusa (1326), which

The Rise of Southern Europe

opened the way to the Sea of Marmora to the north. Osman's conciliatory policies won the approval and support of many of his non-Moslem subjects. Orkan (1326–1359), who succeeded his father Osman, improved the organization of the Ottoman army and government, and completed the Ottoman occupation of northwestern Asia Minor by taking the pivotal cities of Nicaea (1331) and Nicomedia (1337) and advancing to the Straits. Orkan was also able to obtain a foothold in the Balkans because he supported the Byzantine usurper, John VI, Cantacuzene, against the legitimate emperor John V in a Byzantine civil war, following which he remained on the Byzantine side of the Dardenelles despite Byzantine remonstrances. After an earthquake had damaged its defenses, he occupied the fortress of Gallipoli (1354).

Murad I (1359–1389) obtained control of a large part of the Balkans. Whereas his father had been officially only a *beg* (*bey*) or prince, Murad I was recognized as a *sultan* with full and sovereign authority. He took Adrianople, about 130 miles inland from Constantinople (1365) and made it his capital. In 1371 he overcame a strenuous attempt of the Balkan Christians to arrest his advance in the second battle of the Maritza River. Bulgaria now became a vassal state of the Ottomans, as did the Byzantine Empire. The Ottomans advanced into the heart of Serbia, taking Albania, Nish, and Sofia (1384–1385). Although Prince Lazar rallied the Serbs and other Balkan Christians for an all-out stand against the Ottomans, their composite forces were decisively defeated at Kossovo (1389). During the battle, a Serbian noble, pretending to be a defector, slew Sultan Murad in his tent. But Murad's strong son Bayazid took command, won the day, and had Prince Lazar, who was taken prisoner, executed after the battle. Serbia, too, became a vassal state of the Ottomans.

Bayazid I (1389–1402), a proud, choleric warlord, defeated a large body of Western crusaders under Emperor Sigismund at Nicopolis in 1396. He subjected many of his fellow Moslem princes in Asia Minor, thus precipitating intervention by the Tartar conqueror Tamerlane (Timur the Lame), to whom the displaced Turkish lords appealed. At Angora (Ankara) in 1402, Bayazid was decisively defeated and taken prisoner by Tamerlane, by whom he was borne about as a trophy and used as a footstool, until he died, apparently by his own hand.

Fifteenth century

Although Tamerlane confiscated the recently acquired possessions of Bayazid in Asia Minor, he did not disturb Ottoman holdings in the Balkans. After a decade of civil war (1402–1413) between the sons of Bayazid, the youngest, Mohammed, who seems to have been the ablest, emerged as the victor. Mohammed I (1413–1421), known as "the Gentleman," pursued a peaceful, conciliatory policy in order to rebuild and consolidate Ottoman power. But his son Murad II (1421–1451) fought several successful wars against both Balkan peoples and Moslem emirs. Murad's siege of Constantinople in 1422 had to be lifted because of difficulties at home. But in 1430 he took the key port of Thessalonica; and at Varna in 1444 he defeated a large body of crusaders from the West. Murad also restored Ottoman hegemony in Asia Minor, and introduced several administrative reforms, including the *devshirme*, a levy of the ablest youths from the Christian population.

Mohammed II, the Conqueror

Mohammed II, the Conqueror (1451–1481), besieged Constantinople in 1453 with some 150,000–175,000 soldiers (about ten times the number of the city's defenders) and an estimated three or four hundred ships. His army was equipped with numerous heavy cannon, operated by foreign technicians, which pounded the great walls with huge stone balls. The Turks evaded the great chain stretched across the mouth of the city's harbor, the "Golden Horn," by transporting ships overland. After fifty-four days, the Turks poured into the city through breaches in the walls made by their cannon, and subjected it to three days' sack. After taking Constantinople, Mohammed completed the conquest of the Balkans. Serbia was incorporated into the Ottoman Empire by 1459; Bosnia by 1462; and Albania by 1467; while Wallachia and Moldavia (modern Rumania) became tributary by 1512. Venice was driven from its Balkan bases and forced to pay tribute in 1479. Mohammed II also took Azov and the Crimea in southern Russia, as well as Armenia in Asia. By the mid-sixteenth century, the Ottomans had defeated Persia and had taken both Mesopotamia and eastern Syria; had humbled the Mameluks and taken their former possessions in Egypt, western Syria, and Palestine. They had also subjected the "Barbary States" of North Africa (Algeria, Tunisia, and Tripoli); and had conquered and occupied most of Hungary.

Ottoman institutions

The Ottomans had a certain genius for governmental and military organization that enabled their empire to hold together much longer than that of the Seljuk Turks. Yet the fact that their state was essentially militaristic eventually contributed to its decline and disintegration. A key weakness of the Ottomans in the Balkans was the barrier that existed between them and most of their subjects because of their failure either to convert their subjects to Islam or to be converted to the Christian religion of their subjects. This condition was accentuated by the "millet" system (*millah*: religion or nationality), whereby subject peoples were grouped and governed according to their religions under their own religious leaders. Provincial governors and supervisors representing the sultan were known as *begs* (*beys*) or *pashas*. A special head tax was required of non-Moslems. Even more unwelcome was the so-called *devshirme* or child-tribute. Periodically, such as every four or five years, Ottoman officials required from their Christian subjects a certain proportion of intelligent, healthy youths of a certain age (such as one out of every four or five boys ten to fifteen years of age). These boys would then be intensively trained as Turks and Moslems and prepared for various services to the state. Some would be designated for governmental work, others for military service. Although legally slaves and thus the property of the sultan, they had extensive privileges and preferment and often great power. Some became grand viziers and leading generals.

The Ottoman army at its height used the most up-to-date types of equipment, such as the latest and largest forms of cannon. They were already equipped with handguns by 1500. The *devshirme* levy was the source of the famous elite troops known as the Janissaries (*Yeni Cheri*:

The Rise of Southern Europe

New Troops). These fanatically dedicated, highly trained crack troops constituted a sort of Ottoman Praetorian Guard: a select corps attached to the person of the sultan. Although always limited in number, there were about twelve thousand Janissaries in the early sixteenth century. During the Later Middle Ages, the Janissaries were not permitted to marry and had to live in barracks as long as they wished to retain their status. Besides the Janissaries, the Ottoman army had both cavalry and infantry: feudal, regular, and auxiliary.

References for Chapter 28

ACCOUNTS of the history of Italy in the Later Middle Ages are to be found in general histories of Italy by LUIGI SALVATORELLI, *A Concise History of Italy*, tr. Bernard Miall (New York: Oxford U.P., 1940); JANET P. TREVELYAN, *A Short History of the Italian People* . . . , rev. (London: Allen and Unwin, 1956); and EVELYN M. JAMISON et al., *Italy, Mediaeval and Modern* . . . (Oxford: Clarendon, 1917); and JEAN C. L. SIMONDE DE SISMONDI, *A History of the Italian Republics in the Middle Ages* (London: Dent, 1907). The political and social history of Renaissance Italy is described by JOHN ADDINGTON SYMONDS, *The Age of the Despots* (1887) (New York: Putnam's, 1960), and by HENRY B. COTTERILL, *Italy from Dante to Tasso, 1300–1600* (New York: F. A. Stokes, 1919). Shorter but authoritative summaries are to be found in sections of WALLACE K. FERGUSON, *Europe in Transition, 1300–1520* (New York: Houghton Mifflin, 1962); four good articles on Italy in this period are included in the *Cambridge Medieval History*, vols. VII and VIII. Also useful is JOHN GAGE, *Life in Italy at the Time of the Medici* (New York: Capricorn, 1968) (p.). Several leading Italian towns are the subject of good accounts in the "Mediaeval Towns Series" (London: Dent, 1898ff.). Florence and Siena have attracted the able pen of FERDINAND SCHEVILL in his *History of Florence . . . Through the Renaissance* (New York: Harcourt, 1936) and his *Siena: The Story of a Mediaeval Commune* (London: Chapman, 1909). Venice, too, has been a favorite, as in the works of HORATIO R. F. BROWN, *Venice . . .* (New York: Putnam's, 1893), *The Venetian Republic* (London: Dent, 1902), and *Studies in the History of Venice*, 2 vols. (New York: Dutton, 1907). Brown has also translated POMPEO G. MOLMENTI, *Venice . . .* , 6 vols. (London and Chicago: J. Murray, 1906–1908). Other works on Venice include WILLIAM C. HAZLITT, *The Venetian Republic*, 2 vols. (London: A. and C. Black, 1915); F. C. HODGSON, *Venice in the Thirteenth and Fourteenth Centuries* (London: G. Allen, 1910), and FREDERICK C. LANE, *Venice: A Maritime Republic* (Baltimore: Johns Hopkins, 1957).

Various rulers of Italian states and their principalities are treated by DOROTHY MUIR in her *History of Milan Under the Visconti* (London: Methuen, 1924); CECILIA M. ADY, *History of Milan Under the Sforzas*, ed. E. Armstrong (London: Methuen, 1907), *The Bentivoglio of Bologna: A Study in Despotism* (London: Oxford U.P., 1937), and *Lorenzo de Medici . . .* (London: English Universities, 1960); as well as by FERDINAND SCHEVILL, *The Medici* (London: Gollancz, 1950); GEORGE F. YOUNG, *The Medici* (New York: Modern Library, 1933); and EDWARD ARMSTRONG, *Lorenzo de Medici* (New York: Putnam's, 1896). A classic history of Rome is FERDINAND GREGOROVIUS, *History of the City of Rome in the Middle Ages*, tr. A. Hamilton, 8 vols. in 13 (London: Bell, 1900–1906). Conditions in contemporary Italy are reflected in *The Ves-*

pasiano Memoirs, tr. W. George and E. Waters (New York: Lincoln Mac Veigh, 1926), by a contemporary Florentine bookseller; and in NICCOLÓ MACHIAVELLI's *The Prince,* rev., tr. L. Ricci (London: Oxford U.P., 1935); as well as in BALDASSARE DE CASTIGLIONE's *Courtier,* tr. L. E. Opdycke (New York: Liveright, 1929). Contemporary histories include NICCOLÓ MACHIAVELLI, *History of Florence and the Affairs of Italy . . . ,* tr. C. W. Colby (New York: Colonial, 1901), and FRANCESCO GUICCIARDINI, *The History of Italy,* tr. A. P. Goddard, 10 vols. (London: Z. Stuart, 1763).

For the Iberian peninsula in the Later Middle Ages, one may consult general histories such as RAFAEL ALTAMIRA Y CREVEA, *History of Spain,* tr. Muna Lee (New York: Van Nostrand, 1949), and ULICK R. BURKE, *History of Spain,* ed. MARTIN A. S. HUME, 2 vols. (London: Longmans, 1900). There are articles by RAFAEL ALTAMIRA in the *Cambridge Medieval History,* VII and VIII. There is also an article by EDGAR PRESTAGE on "Portugal . . ." in the *Cambridge Medieval History,* VIII. Ferdinand and Isabella are treated by HENRY B. CLARKE in the *Cambridge Modern History,* I; and by J. M. BATISTA I ROCA, in the *New Cambridge Modern History,* I, which likewise includes accounts of Portuguese and Spanish expansion in the New World by H. V. LIVERMORE and J. H. PERRY. Good general discussions of Spanish civilization are given by RAMÓN MENÉNDEZ PIDAL, *The Spaniards in Their History,* tr. W. Starkie (London: Hollis and Carter, 1950); JOHN B. TREND, *The Civilization of Spain* (Oxford: Oxford U.P., 1944); and JOAQUIM P. DE OLIVEIRA MARTINS, *A History of Iberian Civilization,* tr. A. F. Bell (Oxford: Oxford U.P., 1930). Essays and extracts from Spanish historians are provided by ROGER HIGHFIELD, ed., *Spain in the Fifteenth Century, 1369–1516,* tr. F. M. Lopez Morillas (New York: Harper, 1972) (p.).

For the period of Ferdinand and Isabella there are numerous works. MARTIN A. S. HUME is author of *Queens of Old Spain* (New York: McClure, 1906), and *Spain: Its Greatness and Decay: 1479–1788* (Cambridge: Cambridge U.P., 1913). The classic masterpiece by WILLIAM H. PRESCOTT, *History of the Reign of Ferdinand and Isabella,* 3 vols. (Philadelphia: Lippincott, 1893), has stood the test of time. A recent treatment is JEAN H. MARIEJOL, *The Spain of Ferdinand and Isabella* (New Brunswick, N.J.: Rutgers U.P., 1961). Queen Isabella is the heroine of WILLIAM T. WALSH, *Isabella of Spain . . .* (New York: McBride, 1930), and IRENE A. PLUNKET, *Isabel of Castile . . .* (New York: Putnam's, 1915). Pacification and unification under Ferdinand and Isabella are described in MARVIN LUNENFELD, *The Council of the Santa Hermandad. . . .* (Coral Gables: U. of Miami, 1970).

The Spanish Inquisition is the subject of several works including CECIL ROTH, *The Spanish Inquisition* (London: Hale, 1937); ARTHUR S. TURBERVILLE, *The Spanish Inquisition* (London: Oxford U.P., 1949); and the earlier classic of HENRY C. LEA, *A History of the Inquisition of Spain,* 4 vols. (New York: Macmillan, 1906–1907). Related works include HENRY C. LEA, *The Moriscos of Spain: Their Conversion and Expulsion* (Philadelphia: Lea, 1901); CECIL ROTH, *A History of the Marranos* (Philadelphia: Jewish Publication Society, 1932); and VALERIU MARCU, *The Expulsion of the Jews from Spain,* tr. (New York: Viking, 1935).

Good general histories of Portugal include HAROLD V. LIVERMORE, *History of Portugal* (Cambridge: Cambridge U.P., 1947); CHARLES E. NOWELL, *History of Portugal* (New York: Van Nostrand, 1952); and GEORGE YOUNG, *Portugal: Old*

The Rise of Southern Europe

and New . . . (Oxford: Clarendon, 1917). The taking of Lisbon in 1147 with English assistance is described in the *De Expugnatione Lyxbonensi: The Conquest of Lisbon*, ed. and tr. C. W. David (New York: Columbia U.P., 1936). The early movement of Portuguese exploration and expansion is treated by EDGAR PRESTAGE, *The Portuguese Pioneers* (London: Black, 1933); CHARLES R. BEAZLEY, *Prince Henry the Navigator* (New York: Putnam's, 1895); JOAQUIM P. DE OLIVIERA MARTINS, *Golden Age of Prince Henry the Navigator*, tr. J. J. Abraham and W. E. Reynolds (London: Chapman, 1914); and ELAINE SANCEAU, *Henry the Navigator* . . . (New York: Norton, 1947).

For general works on the Balkans in the Middle Ages, consult listings in our Chapter 21, including works of FERDINAND SCHEVILL and WESLEY GERWEHR, GEORGE E. MYLONAS, CHARLES and BARBARA JELAVICH, and WILLIAM MILLER for the Balkans in general; and ALEXANDER A. VASILIEV, GEORGE OSTROGORSKY, CHARLES DIEHL, STEVEN RUNCIMAN, JOAN HUSSEY, NORMAN BAYNES, and H. ST. L. B. Moss for the Byzantine Empire. See also DONALD M. NICOL, *The Last Centuries of Byzantium* (New York: St. Martin's, 1972); EDWIN PEARS, *The Destruction of the Greek Empire and the Capture of Constantinople by the Turks* (London: Longmans, 1903); STEVEN RUNCIMAN, *The Fall of Constantinople . . . 1453* (Cambridge: Cambridge U.P., 1965); and especially the *Cambridge Medieval History*, vol. IV, parts I and II (rev.), for the Byzantine Empire; GEORGE C. LOGIO for Bulgaria; HAROLD W. TEMPERLY and STEVEN CLISSOLD for Serbia; and ROBERT W. SETON-WATSON and NICOLAE IORGA for Rumania.

For the emergence of Ottoman power and the Ottoman state, good works are the briefer PAUL WITTEK, *The Rise of the Ottoman Empire* (London: Royal Asiatic Society, 1938), and the more extensive HERBERT A. GIBBONS, *The Foundation of the Ottoman Empire . . . (1300–1403)* (Oxford: Oxford U.P., 1916). Another good treatment is that of F. TAESCHER, "The Ottoman Turks to 1453" in the *Cambridge Medieval History*, vol. IV, part 1 (rev.). An interesting general overview, although somewhat superficial, is GEORGE J. EVERSLEY, *The Turkish Empire: Its Growth and Decay* (New York: Dodd and Mead, 1917); another, even more sketchy, is STANLEY LANE POOLE, *The Story of Turkey* (New York: Putnam's, 1888). Concerning vain attempts to arrest Turkish expansion in the Balkans, see AZIZ S. ATIYA, *The Crusade of Nicopolis (1396)* (London: Methuen, 1964), and OSKAR HALECKI, *The Crusade of Varna . . . [1444]* (New York: Polish Institute, 1943). An excellent account of the final fall of the Byzantine capital to the Turks is that of STEPHEN RUNCIMAN, *The Fall of Constantinople, 1453* (Cambridge: Cambridge U.P., 1965). An excellent interpretive survey is PAUL COLES, *The Ottoman Impact on Europe* (London: Coles et al., 1968).

DECLINE OF THE CHURCH IN THE LATER MIDDLE AGES. Chapter 29.

CONFLICTING currents and decline also afflicted the Church during the Later Middle Ages. The Papacy was debilitated by its Avignon residence, the Great Western Schism, and the Conciliar Movement, as well as by growing secularism and lack of moral leadership. The authority of the Church was undermined by humanism, mysticism, monarchism, nationalism, and revolutionary theories and movements while its spiritual energy was sapped by the religious lassitude and moral deficiencies of many of its ministers. Yet all was not darkness: There were bright spots among the shadows on the religious scene. Many of the laity and clergy sought to be genuine Christians, participated in pious movements, and worked for ecclesiastical reform.

1294–1378

ERA OF FRENCH ASCENDANCE IN THE CHURCH. Section 85.

In garb of shepherds rapacious wolves are seen from here o'er all the pastures!
[Dante Alighieri in his *Commedia*.]

DURING the period from about 1294 to 1378, French influence became ascendant in the central government of the Church, adversely affecting its international position and prestige. Philip IV of France led a successful monarchical attack upon ecclesiastical privileges and Papal authority by challenging clerical immunities from taxation without Papal consent and from the jurisdiction of secular courts. He also successfully exerted influence to bring about the election of a French Pope, who was favorable to his interests and took up residence in French Avignon. (While culturally and geographically French, Avignon was not at the time politically French.) Successive French Popes appointed and maintained a majority of French Cardinals, who elected French Popes and continued residence at Avignon under the shadow of the French monarchy for seven decades.

External factors promoting Church decline

Various factors, both external and internal, promoted Church decline in the Later Middle Ages. Among factors external to the Church as an institution were nationalism, monarchism, parliamentarianism, intensified economic competition, growth of the middle class, humanism, and new philosophies. Nationalism emerged as a potent force in the Later Middle Ages. Its effect on the Church was exemplified by French efforts to control the Papacy during the Avignon residence and the Great Western Schism; the English Statutes of *Provisors* (1351) and *Praemunire* (1353); the German Golden Bull (1356) and Concordat of Vienna (1448); the Hussite movement in Bohemia; and the voting by nations at the Council of Constance (1414–1418), as well as by the concordats arranged by the Papacy with various countries. Monarchism, or the growth of monarchical

Decline of the Church

power and claims, brought monarchs into growing competition with the Church over such questions as clerical exemption from taxation and immunity from the jurisdiction of royal courts. Its workings were especially manifest during the reigns of strong monarchs such as Philip IV of France, Edward III of England, and Ferdinand and Isabella of Spain. The growing competition for money between ecclesiastical and secular governments generated mounting frictions, intensified by economic depression, monetary inflation, and expanding needs. This rivalry came into clear relief during Papal contests with monarchs such as Philip IV and Edward III.

The contemporary trend to "parliamentarianism" or popular representation in national government was applied by some to the Church in the form of "conciliarism." The conciliar theory tended to undermine the authority of the Papacy since it supposed the final authority in the Church to be a sort of general consensus, flowing upward from the faithful at large. Elaborated with varying degrees of completeness in the works of theorists such as Marsiglio of Padua, Conrad of Gelnhausen, and John Gerson, this revolutionary theory concerning the constitution of the Church threatened to disrupt existing ecclesiastical government.

Late medieval social and cultural developments also challenged ecclesiastical authority. The growing middle class was inclined to be hardheaded, skeptical, worldly, individualistic, and opinionated, as well as jealous of any threat to its money, power, or values. Although many among the middle class sought greater religious realization, the contemporary Church was not immediately prepared to take adequate care of their needs, being primarily geared to a different type of society. The middle class was conversely disposed to be critical of churchmen and Church practices. Renaissance humanism tended to diminish the supernatural and otherworldly interests of its admirers, and detracted from ecclesiastical prestige and authority by its emphasis upon the classical, pagan, and natural. New philosophies were no longer concerned with cooperating closely with religion. Ockhamism, with its nominalism and skepticism, contradicted scholastic theology, while revived Platonism and Aristotelianism pursued their own independent, rationalistic, secular courses.

Factors within the Church as a religious institution that contributed to its decline included the prolonged vicissitudes of the Papacy and the personal shortcomings of many Popes, the excessive centralization of Church government, the worldly lives and distracting secular involvements of many churchmen, the frequent weakening of religious orders, cumbersome, often corrupting administrative practices, the ultraconservatism of many ecclesiastics, and revolutionary new religious theories and movements. *Internal factors for decline*

The Christian world was scandalized and confidence in the Papacy was undermined by the violent quarrel between Boniface VIII and Philip IV; seven decades of exclusively French Popes during the Papal residence at Avignon; the confusing Great Western Schism, with first two and finally three competing Papal claimants; the disruptive Conciliar Movement;

and finally the worldly preoccupations of the Renaissance Popes. Several Popes lived in such an extravagant and sensual way that they seemed more concerned with this life than with the world to come, while some were noted more as patrons of the Renaissance than as religious leaders. Many cardinals lived like secular princes. There were many deficiencies in the conduct of both secular and religious clergy on all levels. Many administrative practices that were understandable in their origin but subsequently noxious had crept into the fabric of the Church. Among such were required payments of money for Church offices and ministrations, "provisions" or the reservation of many ecclesiastical appointments to Rome, "pluralism" or the holding of multiple benefices each calling for religious ministrations, "absenteeism" or absence from one's parish or bishopric, "nepotism" or conferral of Church benefices on relatives, undue aristocratic and monarchical influence in the naming of Church officials, and "appeals" or excessive transfer of judicial cases to the higher court of Rome.

Excessive centralization and secular concerns

Many writers hold that the government of the Church had become excessively centralized, and that the ill effects were now being fully felt. This centralization which had already progressed far in the High Middle Ages, was further increased in the Later Middle Ages. The Pope was conceived of as having "a plentitude" of unlimited power throughout the Church, with universal direct jurisdiction. By the early fourteenth century appointments to all major ecclesiastical benefices, such as bishoprics, and to many minor benefices as well, were theoretically reserved to the Pope. What had been useful earlier for the promotion of Church reforms now worked in an opposite direction. The Popes and their Roman coadjutors became overwhelmed with Church business, which they were often unable to handle properly, and which also undermined and discouraged local episcopal responsibility, as well as led to other evils.

Concern for the secular government of the Papal States also involved the Papacy in international politics, alliances, and even warfare, all of which tended to obscure the spiritual vision of the Papacy as well as to diminish public respect. A further abuse was the growing use of ecclesiastical penalties to implement secular policies. Timidity, conservatism, and lassitude led many Church officials to disregard the need for reforms. Many Popes were paralyzed by their fear of conciliarism, while many churchmen enjoyed their comfortable way of life and were apprehensive of any change. Criticism of the foibles of clerics and various ecclesiastical abuses was common in contemporary literature. Among revolutionary theories and movements, some, such as conciliarism, would radically change the government of the Church; others, such as extreme mysticism, would bypass priestly ministrations and the ecclesiastical hierarchy; still others, such as Lollardism, would substitute an entirely new form of Church.

Philip IV versus Boniface VIII:

A violent quarrel between Pope Boniface VIII and King Philip IV of France introduced the decline of Papal prestige in the Later Middle Ages. Boniface VIII, an accomplished canonist, had helped persuade the naive ex-hermit Celestine V to resign (1294), after which he was himself

Decline of the Church

elected Pope. Boniface was fearless, undiplomatic, and pedantic, needlessly "flaunting red flags at the Gallican bull." The government of Philip IV, dedicated to royal absolutism and imbued with concepts of Roman law, was in the hands of unscrupulous lawyers who were undeterred by ecclesiastical threats and censures, and determined to expand royal power. Boniface VIII was handicapped in his struggle with Philip IV by the compromising circumstances of his accession, as well as by the bitter hostility of the Colonna faction, inflamed by the Pope's favoritism to members of his own family.

Taxation (1296–1300)

The initial tussle with Philip IV resulted when both the French king and the English king taxed the clergy without Papal consent to help pay for war against each other. Although Boniface issued the bull *Clericis laicos* (1296), which began, "Laymen have always been hostile to the clergy," and forbade taxation of the clergy without Papal permission under penalty of excommunication, both Philip IV and Edward I of England refused to submit. To force compliance, Philip IV forbade the export of precious metals, precious stones, and negotiable currency from his country, thus cutting off Papal revenues from this source; whereas Edward I declared that any cleric who refused to pay the stipulated taxes in England would be outlawed and lose royal protection.

Meanwhile Boniface VIII was faced with a serious revolt of the Colonna faction in the Papal States. There was also a possibility that the French king might join with the Colonna cardinals in demanding a general council to consider Boniface's deposition. Accordingly, in a series of bulls (including *Ineffabilis amor*, 1296; *Romana mater*, 1297; and *Etsi de statu*, 1297) Boniface gradually allowed that in cases of necessity, determinable by their king, clergy could be taxed without first obtaining Papal consent. Subsequently reassured by his victory in the Papal States and by the great success of his Papal Jubilee of 1300, in which tens of thousands of pilgrims came to Rome, Boniface issued a bull, *Recordare rex inclytae* (1300), admonishing Philip to reform his ways.

The second phase of the contest began in 1301, after Philip IV had the French Bishop Saisset of Pamiers arrested and held for trial in a royal court. Saisset, appointed by Boniface VIII as a Papal legate in southern France, was accused of blasphemy, heresy, and treason in the royal court, which adjudged him guilty and condemned him to prison. Boniface immediately protested against this procedure as contrary to the traditional "privilege of the clergy," whereby ecclesiastics were judged only by ecclesiastical courts. He also sent a fatherly letter to Philip in 1301, beginning *Ausculta fili* (Listen my son), in which he called upon the king to submit to the Pope as the Vicar of Christ. Meanwhile the Pope summoned the French bishops to a council in Rome.

Philip IV versus Boniface VIII: jurisdiction (1301–1303)

To rally support against Boniface, Philip called the first French Estates General (1302), in which his Chief Minister, Pierre Flotte, presented a garbled version of the Papal letter. Each of the three Estates then directed separate letters of protest to Rome.

After Philip's army was defeated by the Flemish burghers at Courtrai (1302) and Pierre Flotte was killed in what seemed to be divine retribution, Boniface VIII issued his famous bull *Unam sanctam* (1302). Beginning with the assertion that God has established one holy Church, to which He wills that all men belong, Boniface affirmed that the Lord has willed that all men be subject to the Pope, as the head of this Church. In behalf of the Papal claim of temporal power, Boniface invoked the argument that God has entrusted to the Church and hence to the Pope two swords of authority: one spiritual and one temporal. The spiritual is superior to the temporal, which the Pope entrusts to the secular monarch, to be used for the Church and subject to its direction, since subsidiary inferior things are subjected to superior ones. The bull concluded: *It is altogether necessary for salvation that every human creature be subject to the Roman Pontiff.*

Anagni assault

As Boniface was preparing to take more drastic action, Philip allowed his new Chief Minister, William of Nogaret, to journey to Italy, where Nogaret was joined by Sciarra Colonna, a bitter opponent of the Pope. At the head of several hundred mercenaries Nogaret and Colonna burst in upon and seized the Pope at the small town of Anagni (1303). Boniface, who was insulted and struck by Colonna, apparently suffered a paralyzing stroke. Nogaret intended to hold the Pope for trial by a general council, but the inhabitants of the district rose against the intruders and forced them to flee. The badly shaken Boniface died within a few weeks; and a contemporary said of him: *He came in like a fox; ruled like a lion, and died like a dog.*

Completion of the French victory: Clement V

Philip sought to complete his victory by obtaining Papal exoneration for himself and his ministers together with formal Papal denunciation of Boniface VIII. The first Pope following Boniface was the Italian Benedict XI (1303–1304), able former master of the Dominicans. Benedict was conciliatory with the French monarch, and forgave most of the former opponents of Boniface, except seventeen persons, including Sciarra Colonna and William of Nogaret, whom he summoned to trial. But before the date set for trial, he died. French influence next secured the election of the French Bertrand de Got, Archbishop of Bordeaux, who became Pope Clement V—a partial compromise, since Bordeaux was under English rule. The new Pope (in office 1305–1314), who was weak, ailing from cancer, and vacillating, sought to hold the line to some extent, but he was forced to give in to Philip on most matters. Clement formally absolved Philip IV and his associates from responsibility for the attack on Boniface, and even declared that they had been motivated by good and pure motives, except for Nogaret, whom he nevertheless absolved. At the same time, Clement carefully abstained from condemning Boniface VIII, as Philip kept insisting.

Clement likewise reluctantly gave in to Philip regarding the Templars. Philip continuously demanded the suppression of the wealthy Knights Templar since they no longer performed important services. The suppression of the Templars would benefit the French crown, since its large debts to the Templars would be extinguished, and the government also stood to profit (directly or indirectly) from confiscation of their considerable properties. Philip wrung admissions of guilt from many Templars

Decline of the Church

by threats and tortures, and put several of them to death after they retracted their "confessions." Eventually the Pope and the Council of Vienne declared the Templars suppressed (1311). During the suppression, Philip IV cruelly executed numerous Templars under various pretexts.

One of Clement V's most consequential and controversial actions was his residence at Avignon (1309ff.), which initiated seven decades of Papal residence within the French sphere of influence, followed by four decades of Schism. Although nominally in the Empire, Avignon was socially and culturally French as well as overshadowed by French power. Clement and most of his successors apparently did not intend to make Avignon a permanent residence, but it became such for seven decades under as many Popes.

The Avignon residence of the Papacy (1309–1378)

Clement seems to have originally established a temporary residence at Avignon so that he might better judge the case of the Knights Templar. During the Avignon residence all the Popes and the vast majority of cardinals created (111 out of 134) were Frenchmen, who felt more secure and relaxed in congenial Avignon with its delightful climate. Meanwhile the inhabitants of Rome and the Papal States were in rebellion. In trying to arbitrate the differences between the French and English kings that erupted into the Hundred Years' War, the Popes found Avignon convenient. Clement V resided in a part of the convent of the Dominicans at Avignon, but as time progressed the Avignon Popes found it necessary to construct additional buildings for their government and retinue. They also purchased Avignon in order to ensure themselves greater liberty. During the Middle Ages it was not unusual for the Popes to be absent from Rome for extended periods; but there was no previous parallel for the continuous Avignon residence.

Among old established sources of Papal income that declined in the Avignon period were these:

Papal revenues at Avignon

Revenues from the Papal States: Normally a major source of income, these were greatly diminished during the Avignon residence.

Tribute (Census): Feudal dues from states held as Papal fiefs, as in the case of Naples, Sicily, Sardinia, and so on.

Court Fees: Fees charged by the Papal courts, as on acceptance of appeals and in cases of the first instances.

Tithes: Levies of a certain percentage (such as a tenth) of the value of movables or annual income, occasionally imposed upon members of the clergy.

"Peter's Pence": An annual payment made by several northern countries, such as the Scandinavian countries and England.

Owing to diminution of traditional sources of Papal revenues, the Avignon Popes had to devise new taxes. Most of the newly exploited sources of income had some precedent in the past, but they were regularized, universalized, and enforced in the Avignon period. Included were the following:

Services (Servicia): Fees for Papal appointment to higher ecclesiastical offices, often very large.

Annates: Similar fees for appointments to lesser ecclesiastical offices, often amounting to a year's revenue.

Expectancies: Fees for Papal promises to make appointments to certain benefices when they should become vacant.

Vacancy Income (Medii fructus): The right to the income from a benefice during a vacancy.

Spoils (Spolia): The right to take over the personal property of intestate benefice holders who died in or near Rome without legal heir.

Reservations and Provisions: Papal income was greatly increased by a multiplication of reservations and provisions, terms sometimes used interchangeably. A "reservation" consisted in making the holder of a given benefice regularly appointable by the Pope, whereas a "provision" consisted in Papal intervention to "provide" an incumbent for a benefice in certain instances, as when a local election was quashed.

Procurations: Fees for the support of the Pope or his representatives and attendants during a period of actual or possible visitation.

In addition to the aforesaid, there were various miscellaneous fees. "Minute services" (*servicia minutae*) were fees added to "ordinary services" (*servicia ordinaria*) for administrative steps involved in Papal appointments to important benefices. A host of miscellaneous fees were connected with various Papal dispensations, absolutions, indulgences, concessions, and favors. Income was further derived from fines levied as punishment, charges for bulls, and the sale of honorary offices in the Papal court.

Demand for Papal return to Rome

As the Avignon residence continued, popular demand for Papal return to Rome grew. Clamor rose from all parts of the Church, but it was particularly insistent from leading churchmen, theologians, pious lay persons, and saints. St. Catherine of Siena and St. Bridget of Sweden repeatedly implored Avignon Popes to return to Rome. Many inhabitants of Rome and the Papal States also besought the return of the Pope in order to restore peace, order, and prosperity to their area. Arguments for Papal return included the fact that Papal primacy in the Church derived from the Pope's position as Bishop of Rome and that a bishop should occupy his see and minister to the needs of his flock. The Pope was the rightful political ruler of the Papal States, and should see to their proper administration. Sovereignty in the Papal States gave the Pope the necessary independence for free, impartial policies and action. The Papal residence at Avignon was a source of great scandal and division in the Church, since it gave the impression that the Papacy was subject to the French monarchy. Other reasons for return to Rome were the fact that the Papal States were normally a main source of Papal revenues, and that so-called free companies of soldiers, released during lapses in the Hundred Years' War, were harassing and demanding tribute from the Avignon Papacy.

The Avignon Popes (1309–

Following Clement V (1309–1314), who initiated the Avignon residence, the second Avignon Pope, efficient, aggressive John XXII (1316–1334), insisted vigorously on Papal authority and independence, as in his dealings with the Spiritual Franciscans (whose extreme concepts of

Decline of the Church

poverty he condemned) and with Emperor Lewis IV of Bavaria. (The Emperor and Pope attempted to dominate one another.) His strong policies aroused opposition in both the Church and the Empire. Although seventy-two at his accession, the vigorous John devised and exploited many new sources of Papal income. Benedict XII (1334–1342), an austere Cistercian, promoted reform in religious orders. Clement VI (1342–1352), a Benedictine who was noted for his lavish prodigality, as well as for his learning, purchased Avignon from the Queen of Naples (1348). Innocent VI (1352–1362), a competent administrator, sent Cardinal Albornoz to reestablish order in the Papal States (1353). The efficient, firm Albornoz succeeded so well that he has been called "the second founder of the Papal States." Urban V (1362–1370), a former Benedictine abbot, returned to Rome, but Italian uprisings and the renewal of the Hundred Years' War soon caused him to go back to Avignon. Gregory XI (1370–1378), despite his worldliness, was persuaded by Sts. Catherine of Siena and Bridget of Sweden to return to Rome, where he died within a year.

1377) and Avignon influence

Although French by birth and friendly to the French Kings, the Avignon Popes were not subservient to the French crown. They were on the whole able, devoted churchmen. While they found Avignon more to their liking than Rome, most of then were apparently persuaded to stay there on a temporary basis, for what seemed good reasons. Still, despite its excuses, the Avignon Residence was detrimental to the Papacy. It exposed the Papacy to widespread criticism, incited divisive nationalistic feelings in the Church, and undermined the loyalty of many of the faithful. It also led to an increase in Papal taxation and pretensions, in order to make up for Roman losses. It encouraged the French monarchy and other powers to become overbearing and excessively demanding with the Papacy. During the Avignon residence, several rulers, including the Kings of Hungary, England, Portugal, and Bohemia, obtained control of episcopal appointments as well as reduced their dependence on the Papacy.

THE GREAT WESTERN SCHISM, CONCILIARISM, AND THE RENAISSANCE POPES. (1378–1500)
Section 86.

> In Rome itself we have a Pope
> In Avignon another;
> And each one claims to be alone
> The true and lawful ruler.
> [From a contemporary poem by Peter Suchenwirt concerning the Great Western Schism.]

INSTEAD of ending with the Papal return to Rome, the ill effects of the Avignon residence actually worsened. Roman pressures helped to bring French cardinals to elect an Italian Pope, but since he did not measure up to their expectations they repudiated him and elected a Frenchman. The French claimant returned to Avignon while the Italian claimant remained in Rome, producing the impasse of two Popes and creating the Great Western Schism. Splitting the Church into two camps and greatly weakening it, the Schism also begot the Conciliar Movement, which directly challenged the existing and traditional Papal constitution of the Western Church. After the Schism was ended by a General Council, the "Renaissance Popes" were threatened by conciliarism and confronted with serious problems to be solved and damage to be undone in the Papal States and Rome. As a result, they and their advisors were distracted from their primary religious responsibilities to the point that they temporarily seemed to become more secular statesmen and administrators than spiritual leaders.

The Great Western Schism (1378–1417)

The immediate sequel—and legacy—of the Avignon residence of the Papacy was the Great Western Schism (1378–1415). For four decades rival claimants contended for the Papal office, with Christendom divided into opposing camps. The early death of Gregory XI (1378), following his return to Rome, precipitated a crisis. The majority of the cardinals (eleven out of sixteen) were French, and many preferred Avignon to Rome. Would the cardinals again elect a French Pope, and return to Avignon? While the cardinals met in conclave, rioting crowds of Romans angrily shouted: *We want a Roman, or at least an Italian!* At one point a deputation met with the cardinals and declared that they could not vouch for their safety unless they complied with the popular demands. Eventually the cardinals compromised by electing an Italian whose see was in French-controlled territory: Archbishop Prignani of Bari in the Kingdom of Naples. To make sure that the crowd would be mollified, some of the cardinals bedecked the old Cardinal of St. Peters, who was a Roman, with Papal insignia and presented him to the crowd, leaving disclosure of the real choice until the next day when tempers had cooled.

The cardinals afterward acknowledged and enthroned the new Pope, Urban VI, attended his court, and petitioned him for favors. As Vice-Chancellor of the Roman Church, prior to his election, Prignani had been mild, cooperative, and ingratiating with the cardinals. But as Urban VI his character seemed to change, so that he became harsh and imperious, and berated the cardinals, severely criticizing their way of life and threatening penalties unless they reformed. The cardinals began to feel that they had made a serious mistake. They were also upset by Urban's adamant refusal to consider returning to Avignon.

Eventually all the cardinals, except the aged Cardinal of St. Peter's, withdrew, one by one, so that they would not excite suspicion, to Anagni. Here they invoked the legal principle that duress can invalidate an election, and asserted that in electing Urban they were constrained by undue threat of violence. Declaring the previous election invalid, they called upon Urban V to relinquish the Papal throne and proceeded to elect a new Pope. Their choice was French Cardinal Robert of Geneva, who had been a leader of the opposition, and who took the name of Clement VII. But Urban VI refused to give up the Papal throne, declared the rebellious cardinals excommunicated, and appointed new cardinals in their places. The rebellious cardinals and the new claimant, who had meanwhile obtained the support of the French King and Queen Joanna

Decline of the Church

of Naples, sought to take Rome with Neapolitan support. On failing to do so, they repaired to congenial Avignon.

Rival "obediences" and prolongation of the Schism

The groups supporting the rival Popes were known as their respective "obediences." The main pillar of the Avignon Popes was France. Allies of France, such as Scotland, Aragon, Castile, and, in a vacillating way, Naples, recognized the Avignon line. Rivals of France, and their satellites, such as England, Flanders, and Portugal, plus most Germans and Italians, Bohemians, Poles, and Hungarians, and Danes, Swedes, and Norwegians, supported the Roman Popes. The Great Western Schism was prolonged because both sides honestly felt they were right, because both Popes claimed unqualified final jurisdiction that they felt bound to uphold, and especially because rival nationalities found it advantageous to support their own candidates. According to the traditional view of the constitution of the Church, the Pope had unlimited jurisdiction, independent of General Councils, whereas General Councils required Papal convocation and confirmation. The oligarchical inclinations of the cardinals, who wanted to control the Popes whom they elected, contributed to the outbreak and the perpetuation of the Schism. To some extent, the Schism was a reaction against growing Papal centralization of Church government.

The two lines

The burden of proof weighed mainly upon the Avignon line, which was also handicapped by the fact that it was overshadowed by the French monarchy, upon which it depended so much for its continuation. French support became ever more difficult to retain, and the terms for its continuation, which culminated in an assertion of extensive "Gallican liberties" by the French government in 1408, became even more distasteful to the Avignon Popes. Clement VII (1379–1394) soon lost the support of the King of Naples. He also had trouble with the University of Paris as well as with his own College of Cardinals, leaders of both of which wanted to end the Schism. Benedict XIII (1394–1422), the second Pope of the Avignon line, had been one of the original electors at Anagni. The aged Benedict was obstinate and wily, pretending to consider plans to end the Schism, but always managing to evade them. He finally lost French backing and was forced to take refuge in his family's ancestral castle at Perpignan in Aragon, where he died, almost without supporters, in 1422.

The Roman line of Popes fared better than the Avignon line. Its origin was prior, its base the traditional seat of Papal government, and its support broader and more disinterested. Even so, it too, in the end, lost most of its supporters. Urban VI (1378–1389) became progressively more tyrannical. When six of the cardinals whom he had appointed plotted to overthrow him, he imprisoned, tortured, and executed them, apparently having five of them thrown into the sea. The final Roman Pope of the period, Gregory XII (1406–1415), was an austere Venetian, seventy years old, who was expected to end the Schism by way of cession, but who infuriated the cardinals by his reluctance to resign.

Efforts to heal the Schism

Energetic efforts to end the Schism were soon under way, with leadership in the discussion initially assumed by the University of Paris, and the cause of reunion actively supported by scholars. Several rulers who sought

The Conciliar Movement

to heal the breach included Richard II and Henry IV of England, Charles VI of France, and Emperors Wenzel and Sigismund of Germany. Three possible ways to end the Schism were suggested in a letter from the University of Paris to the King of France in 1394: the way of cession, the way of arbitration, and the way of a General Council. In the way of cession, each Pope would resign and the cardinals would then elect a new Pope. The problem was to obtain the resignations. In the way of arbitration, the question of legitimacy would be submitted to a neutral and impartial board of judges. The difficulty lay in determining the membership of the panel of judges and ensuring its impartiality. The final suggestion, the convocation of a General Council, was the most appealing. It was a traditional expedient for Church crises, and could enlist general support. There were two possible ways in which the Council could proceed. One was to obtain approval and pledges of cooperation from the rival Popes; the other was to meet and proceed without the collaboration of the claimants.

The Conciliar Theory was elaborated during this period by various writers as a means of terminating the Schism. Proponents of this theory maintained that the General Council of Church prelates is superior to the Pope, whom it can, if necessary, depose. In support of this thesis, Conrad of Gelnhausen maintained that the Church is the body of all believers and that they are represented in a General Council, which is supreme and infallible. Christ is the only real head of the Church, of which the Pope is merely the chief magistrate. The General Council can even abolish the Papal office. According to Henry of Langenstein, although Christ established the Church, He did not determine exactly how it was to be governed, but left this to the decision of the Church itself.

Councils of Pisa (1409) and Constance (1414–1418)

Acting on the more extreme Conciliar Theory, the majority (twenty-two) of the cardinals, with the cooperation of most of the monarchs of Western Christendom, but without that of the two existing Papal claimants held a General Council at Pisa (1409), attended by a large number of prelates and proxies from all parts of the Church. Unable to obtain the support of either Papal claimant, the Council of Pisa declared them both deposed, and commissioned the cardinals to choose a new Pope. The cardinals elected the aged Franciscan Archbishop of Milan, who took the name of Alexander V, but he survived for only a few months (1409–1410). He was succeeded by John XXIII (1410–1415)—a worldly prelate of lax ways, described by contemporaries as "shrewd and astute, but poorly suited for the religious life." The Council of Pisa had merely added a third Pope, since neither of the other Popes would resign. Still it indirectly promoted an earlier end to the Schism, as it weakened both of the other Popes and made them more amenable to negotiation.

Strenuous efforts were now made by many persons to bring the Schism to an end. With the energetic help of the German Emperor Sigismund, a General Council was convoked to meet at Constance, in Switzerland. The new council was attended at its height by three patriarchs, twenty-nine cardinals, thirty-three archbishops, a hundred and fifty bishops, and more than a hundred abbots, as well as by numerous proxies. It also attracted over three hundred doctors, and eleven ruling monarchs, plus ambassadors from twelve other Christian princes. The Council had three objectives—to end the Schism, to adjudge the doctrines of Wyclif and Hus, and to promote reform in the Church—with their relative importance generally rated in that order. Since the percentage of bishops from certain areas such as Italy was much greater than that of bishops from elsewhere, members of the Council decided to vote by "nations." There were five nations: Italian, French, German, Spanish, and English—each with a single vote. Lesser nationalities were included in similar or neighboring nations. Thus all the peoples in the British Isles were included in the English nation, and all those of Northern and Eastern Europe in the German nation.

Learning its lesson from Pisa, the Council of Constance took pains first to obtain the approval and resignation of existing Papal claimants. The shrewd Pisan Pope, John XXIII, came to the Council in the hope that it would support his claim, and when he saw that this was not to be the case he fled; but he was apprehended with Emperor Sigismund's help and brought back to the Council. Confronted with the threat of prosecution on various charges, John resigned. After extensive negotiations, the Roman Pope, Gregory XII, finally agreed to approve the Council and resign, provided that the Fathers would at least implicitly recognize his legitimacy, which they did. Only the aged Avignon Pope, the stubborn Benedict XIII, absolutely refused to resign, although he had lost most of his following and had been forced to retire to his ancestral castle on the rocky Aragonese coast. Eventually the Council of Constance decided to disregard Benedict, and representatives of the nations, together with the cardinals, elected Cardinal Odo (Oddone) Colonna, who became Martin V (1417ff.). After the death of Benedict XIII in 1422, his successor recognized the Roman Pope. Most authorities regard the Roman Popes as probably the legitimate line during the Schism. The Council of Constance and the Popes of both the Pisan and Avignon lines also eventually recognized the Roman Pope. So have subsequent Popes, some of whom have taken the names of Avignon and Pisan Popes.

End of the Schism

One of the most important results of the Great Western Schism was the Conciliar Theory and Movement, which opened up the question of the constitution of the Church and the bases and extent of Papal primacy. The Council of Constance passed two decrees that supported the Conciliar Theory. The first, *Sacrosancta* (1415), affirmed that the "sacred and holy" General Council "represents the Catholic Church, and has immediate power from Christ, which anyone, of whatever status and condition, even if holding the Papal dignity, must obey in matters pertaining to the faith, the extinction of the Schism, and the form of the Church." The second decree, *Frequens* (1417), called for the regular and "frequent" convocation of General Councils every ten years, although the first two councils were to be held sooner, at intervals of five and seven years. Pope Martin V, however, avoided endorsing these decrees by approving what the Council had done *concilialiter* but not what it had done *nationaliter*. "*Nationaliter*" had reference to meeting and voting

Conciliarism at Constance and after

separately, "by nations," whereas *"concilialiter"* had reference to doing so as a body, or General Council. According to the traditional ecclesiastical theory, Papal concurrence was necessary for a valid General Council and its legislation.

While the Council of Constance did not attempt radical general reform, it did effect some minor reforms. The failure to effect general reform was largely due to the multiplicity of problems the Council had to face, the difficulties of the enterprise, the opposition of vested interests, and a prevailing desire for greater local autonomy. Separate concordats were meanwhile established with the German Empire, England, France, Spain, and Italy, as well as with the Scandinavian and Central European countries (which were included in the German Concordat).

The Council considered the Wyclifite and Hussite doctrines. The latter presented a pressing problem in Bohemia, where the Hussite movement and political revolution had combined in an explosive mixture. The Council condemned the teachings of Wyclif and Hus, and despite their safe conducts, executed two leading Bohemian proponents—John Hus and Jerome of Prague. It thus precipitated the Hussite Wars between Bohemians and Germans, which raged from 1419 to 1436 and beyond.

Early "Renaissance" Popes" (1417–1447)

The Popes from 1417 to 1535 are often referred to as "the Popes of the Renaissance." The earlier Popes in this period were transitional to subsequent full-fledged Renaissance Popes, and had many "medieval" as well as "Renaissance" qualities. Under the transitional Popes (1417–1771), when the Renaissance movement first began to influence the Papacy, two overriding problems still took precedence—the Conciliar Movement and the Moslem menace. At the same time, Papal "reception" of the Renaissance, the physical restoration of Rome, and full recovery of the Papal States were definitely launched. The first, immediate problem the Early Renaissance Popes had to face was conciliarism. They recognized the Conciliar Movement as a serious threat to their position and power, and accordingly sought to evade and thwart it.

Elected at Constance, Martin V (1417–1431) was cautious and conciliatory, but he also sought to restore the fullness of the Papal prerogative. He sidestepped the more revolutionary acts of the Council of Constance by refraining from approving them. In accordance with the decree *Frequens*, Martin summoned first the Council of Pavia–Siena (1423ff.) and then the Council of Basel (1431ff.) The first Council (1423–1424) was very poorly attended by only about twenty-five bishops and a few other prelates. It adjourned after denouncing heresy and schism and agreeing to reconvene at Basel in 1431. Meanwhile Martin V initiated the Renaissance in Rome by employing Renaissance architects, painters, and sculptors.

Eugenius IV (1431–1447) was a pious, observant Augustinian who had a troubled, eventful Pontificate. Because of the insecurity of his position, the Pope suffered in silence the Pragmatic Sanction of Bourges, which limited Papal powers in France; and made various concessions to the Empire in the Concordat of Vienna (1448), formally concluded after his death. Leading developments in his reign are associated with the Council of Basel–Ferrara–Florence.

Council of Basel–Ferrara–Florence (1431–1449)

The conciliar question came to a head at the General Council of Basel, promised and convoked by Martin V, which met in Switzerland in 1431 under the sponsorship of Eugenius IV. It was very poorly attended at first by only fourteen to twenty bishops, although attendance at Basel grew somewhat until it temporarily reached some seven cardinals, five archbishops, and forty-three bishops. For a brief period the Council enjoyed the support of the French, English, Castilian, and German governments. Attendance at the Council fluctuated, never being impressive.

The main initial concern of the Council at Basel was the question of the Hussites. The fathers present, including the able Papal Legate Cesarini, dealt patiently with the Bohemian representatives, sometimes listening to speeches that lasted for two to three days. At one point Cesarini replied to an old Bohemian bishop who asked whether he was to be given a fair hearing: *Yes, but pause occasionally to let us clear our throats.* After encouraging a growing split among the Bohemians, the Council agreed to a compromise settlement with the more moderate majority party, contained in Compacts of Prague (1433), which included permission for the laity to receive communion under both species (bread and wine). After the extremists or "Taborites" were defeated by the moderates and Emperor Sigismund (1434), the general rebellion against Church and Empire subsided.

Split

Although a small but continuing nucleus of Council members at Basel were concerned with enforcing the extreme Conciliar Theory relative to Church government, they were handicapped by the limited number of bishops in attendance, the protracted duration of the Council, "distractions" such as conciliation of the Hussites and "reunion" with the "Greeks," Papal diplomacy, and the skill of the presiding Papal legate, Cesarini. Cesarini managed to delay the extremists and win over some of the more important leaders present, such as Nicholas of Cusa and Aeneas Sylvius Piccolomini (later Pope Pius II), to the Papal position. Meanwhile, the Pope negotiated with various governments to ensure their support. Finally, aided by Byzantine interest in a reunion of the Eastern and Western Churches, the Pope was able to transfer the Council to Ferrara in northeastern Italy, as a site much more convenient for the "Greeks" (1437). Still a number of diehard fathers (some twenty-five bishops and seventeen abbots) refused to accept the transfer to Ferrara, and continued to meet at Basel. This small "Rump Council of Basel" (1437–1449) asserted the absolute supremacy of the General Council, pronounced Eugenius deposed, and elected Anti-Pope Felix V (1439ff.). But Felix was brought to abdicate in 1443, and the Conciliarists were defeated, losing both governmental and popular support. Shortly after the death of Eugenius IV, the Council of Basel made peace with his successor, Nicholas V, and was formally dissolved (1449). Skilful Papal diplomacy had avoided conciliar domination and preserved the fullness of Papal authority, but at the cost of sacrificing needed reforms.

The Later Middle Ages

Attempted reunion

Meanwhile several prelates from the Council of Basel, together with many new members, reconvened at Ferrara to discuss reunion with representatives of the Eastern Church. Some seven hundred Byzantines came west and were maintained at Papal expense during the meeting. Included were the Byzantine Emperor, the Patriarch of Constantinople, the Bishops of Nicaea and Kiev, twenty other bishops, and several other high dignitaries of the Eastern Church and Empire. Discussions continued at Ferrara from 1437 to 1439, but eventually an outbreak of the plague and faltering finances caused the Pope to transfer the Council to Florence, where an apparent "reunion" of the two churches was effected (1439–1442). The Eastern representatives accepted both the primacy of the Pope and the essential doctrines of the Western Church. On his part the Pope promised to secure naval assistance for the Eastern Christians, currently hard-pressed by the Moslems. But the Eastern Christian Church and populace refused to accept the reunion, which soon collapsed.

The Renaissance Papacy from 1447 to 1471

Subsequent Popes became more closely identified with the cultural Renaissance. Although serious and devout, Nicholas V (1447–1455) is chiefly noted for his intelligent patronage of the Renaissance, including his refounding of the Vatican Library. Desirous of making Rome the cultural as well as the religious capital of the West, Nicholas collected some 5,000 volumes of precious classical manuscripts in Latin and Greek; employed numerous humanists, copyists, and translators; and undertook a restoration of Rome on a grand scale.

Pius II (1458–1464) was a noted humanist and prolific author (Aeneas Sylvius Piccolomini) who had been somewhat lax in his earlier years but reformed as he matured. Pius II worked desperately to organize a Crusade against the Moslems, even to the extent of planning to accompany the crusaders personally despite an illness from which he died prior to the proposed departure. Pius clearly condemned the extreme Conciliar Theory in his bull *Execrabilis* (1460). Although the next Pope, Paul II (1464–1471), a "splendor-loving Venetian," spent lavishly for display, he was personally upright and devout. He dissolved the "Roman Academy" of the humanists because of its apparent pagan tendencies.

Popes of the High Renaissance (1471ff.)

With two fleeting exceptions (Pius III and Adrian VI) for less than two years, the Popes for the next six decades were "typical" Renaissance Popes, largely immersed in worldly affairs, such as recovering the territorial integrity of the Papal States and patronizing the cultural Renaissance. They frequently encouraged a loss of respect for the Papacy by unexemplary lives, lack of scruples, vindictiveness, nepotism, and family ambitions. Sixtus IV (1471–1484) of the della Rovere family sought to make the Papacy a strong secular power, and waged wars against Florence, Naples, and Venice. He named at least six of his relatives cardinals, and used them as princes in his Papal monarchy. He also patronized the arts of the Renaissance, including building the Sistine Chapel. Innocent VIII (1484–1492) used his illegitimate children, begotten while he was still a layman, as instruments of his policy.

Alexander VI (1492–1503), the former Cardinal Rodrigo Borgia, was

Decline of the Church

the most notorious of the Renaissance Popes. He won his election over his della Rovere rival by promises and bribery. As a cardinal, Alexander kept a mistress, whom he continued to support as Pope. Like Innocent before him, Alexander used his children to strengthen the Papal States in ways that also promoted their own interests. Romans accused his daughter Lucretia of poisoning her first husband, and Machiavelli recommended the Pope's son Cesare, who became Captain-General of the Papal States, as a model of political unscrupulosity. Cesare Borgia was guilty of several murders, including those of his sister's second husband and several of his captains whom he suspected of disloyalty. He used every means, fair and foul, in order to consolidate and expand the Papal States, with considerable success, until his father, the Pope, suddenly sickened and died, while he himself became seriously ill for several days. During this interval Cardinal Giuliano della Rovere managed to have the pious Francesco Piccolomini, a nephew of Pius II, elected Pope Pius III, foiling the prostrate Cesare. Subsequent Renaissance Popes (1503–1534) belong to modern rather than medieval history.

Alarmed by the possibility of the Conciliar Movement, Renaissance Popes steered their course between and away from General Councils. In doing this, they sacrificed the possibility of thorough reform and were compelled to accord secular monarchs and governments extensive powers over the churches in their countries, as in the English Concordat of 1418, the French Pragmatic Sanction of Bourges (1438), the Concordat of Vienna (1448) with the Hapsburg Emperors, concessions to German princes and Italian city-states, and the *Patronato* privileges of Ferdinand and Isabella of Spain.

TRENDS, THEORIES, AND LIFE IN THE LATE MEDIEVAL CHURCH.
Section 87.

You are Christians in name only, for you act like heathens. Cursing, lying, murder, theft, and adultery are common among you, and there is no shame in crime. [Aeneas Sylvius Piccolomini (later Pope Pius II) writing in 1453.]

VARIOUS contemporary theories and movements undermined the authority of the late medieval Church and attracted many of its members and ministers. Many mystics emphasized the internal and individual aspects of religious life to the depreciation of its external and social side; some theorists such as Marsiglio of Padua assailed the hierarchical constitution of the Church without challenging its doctrines; still others, such as Wyclif and Hus, became full-fledged dissenters by rejecting traditional teachings of the Church and by refusing to accept the authority of its officers. Some movements such as mysticism were ambivalent, strengthening the Church in some respects, weakening it in others. The ferment and skepticism of the age adversely affected the religious convictions and life of many of its members; and some sought solace in secular movements such as humanism. At the same time, there were many devout faithful in all states of life.

Ambivalent influences: Mysticism

A strong mystical movement that sought a more direct, perceptible union with God through prayer and contemplation as well as austerity and good works existed in the late medieval Church, and affected the laity as well as the clergy. Inasmuch as it increased devotion and holiness, mysticism served to strengthen the Church; but insofar as it stressed direct individual rapport with the divinity apart from organized religion it weakened the Church. Traditionally, there were three main steps in mysticism: purgation, illumination, and union, although medieval writers often distinguished additional finer gradations, frequently totaling seven. Purgation involved asceticism and renunciation of physical pleasures and self-will, the better to be free for spiritual illumination and union with God. Union with God was an act of the affection and will as well as the intellect.

Lay associations

Especially from the later thirteenth century on, increasing numbers of the laity sought to practice mysticism. Prominent among promoters of the movement were Dominican and Franciscan preachers. Dominicans, such as Meister Johann Eckhart (d. 1327) and his disciples Johann Tauler and Heinrich Suso, zealously propagated mysticism in Rhenish Germany, obtaining numerous converts in centers such as Strasbourg and Cologne. An early German society of orthodox mystics, the Friends of God, combined mysticism with great reverence for the sacraments and Church authority. Meanwhile mysticism obtained wide currency among Third Orders composed of Franciscan and Dominican lay affiliates, and among the Beghards and Beguines, pious associations of lay persons living a religious life in common.

Although most individual mystics and pious lay associations remained orthodox and united with the institutional Church, others, such as the Brethren of the Free Spirit and some of the Beguines, Beghards, Fraticelli, and Flagellants, were eventually condemned by Church authorities. Not a few combined emphasis on austerity, good works, and the interior life with growing criticism of the clergy, denial of the authority of the ecclesiastical hierarchy, and minimization of the role of the sacraments and Mass in obtaining salvation.

Undermining influences: Humanism and new philosophies

Among new theories that were not essentially revolutionary, yet served to undermine the influence of the Church, were humanism and Ockhamism. In their enthusiasm for the classics, the humanists sought not only to revive the study and imitation of classical works and forms but also to recapture the spirit of the classical authors. Although many of the humanists lauded and retained Christian ideals along with humanistic values, as in the case of Vittorino da Feltre, Aeneas Sylvius (Pius II), Cardinal Jiménez, and Erasmus, others became entirely absorbed by the naturalism, sensism, and rationalism of the ancient pagan authors, and some even adopted pagan attitudes and ways.

In philosophy there was, on the one hand, a natural reaction against the ascendance of scholasticism, but, on the other hand, a tendency to over-

Decline of the Church

elaborate scholasticism. Whereas some, such as Ockham, in frustration attacked the basic assumptions of scholasticism, others, such as Duns Scotus, spun such fine webs of scholastic distinctions and qualifications that they lost contact with reality. Prominent among philosophers whose theories tended to undermine the whole edifice was William of Ockham. His insistence on the sole reality of individual entities, except as verbalized concepts (terminism), attacked the very foundations of philosophy and theology, and fostered skepticism and materialism.

In accordance with the contemporary humanistic movement, some philosophers sought to revive the direct study and acceptance of the ancient philosophers, without the mediation of Christianity. Many preferred Plato, partly because of his more literary style and imaginative presentation, and many of these, such as Plethon, preferred the semi-mystical interpretations of the Neo-Platonists. Others such as Ficino sought a "purer, original Plato." Still other philosophers, such as Achillini and Pomponnazi, preferred a dechristianized Aristotle rather than the Aristotle of Thomas Aquinas, and interpreted the great Stagirite in a materialistic or pantheistic sense.

Particularly during Church-State struggles, the heavy artillery of revolutionary theories concerning the constitution of the Church was wheeled into place and directed against the Papacy. Authors of such theories included Pierre Dubois, Marsiglio of Padua, and the conciliarists, all of whom had proposed radical views concerning the Church. Pierre Dubois (d. 1312), in his tract *Concerning the Recovery of the Holy Land*, maintained that the powerful French king was the true successor of Charlemagne and the rightful head of a sort of United States of Europe. All Church property should be turned over to the French king to be used to promote peace, progress, and a united effort to recover the Holy Land. While the Pope is the successor of St. Peter and the head of the Church, his authority is exclusively spiritual. William Durand (d. 1328), while accepting Papal primacy, accused the Pope of overstepping his authority and violating the rights of bishops and synods by intervening excessively on local levels. Marsiglio of Padua (d. 1334) advanced the most extreme revolutionary theory concerning both Church and State. In his *Defender of the Peace* (ca. 1325), Marsiglio declared that the people are the source of authority in both State and Church. The primary human society is the State, in which the ruler is the supreme representative of the people, and the law the people's sovereign will. Within the State the Church is a secondary society in which the Pope serves as an administrative head for the people. The supreme authority in the Church is the General Council, which best represents the people at large.

Revolutionary theories: Dubois, Durand, Marsiglio, and Conciliarism

The Conciliar Theory, as has been seen, simply maintained that the General Council of Church prelates is superior to the Pope, whose authorization it does not require and whom it may depose. The Conciliar Theory was especially prevalent during the Great Western Schism, when it was espoused by numerous authors as well as by the Councils of Pisa and Constance. Although revived later at the Council of Basel, it was formally condemned by Pope Pius II in 1460.

660 The Later Middle Ages

The teachings of Wyclif and Hus

Although there were many subversive trends in the Church in the Later Middle Ages, there were only two serious formal heresies—those of John Wyclif and John Hus. Most of the doctrines of the latter trace back to those of the former. John Wyclif, an English priest and professor at Oxford in the fourteenth century, has been called "the morning star of the Reformation." Wyclif first entered the public arena as a defender of the English monarchy against Papal claims to annual tribute and Papal appointments to English beneficies. Eventually he broadened his argument to a denial of the whole hierarchical constitution and teaching authority of the Church. In its place, he urged private study and interpretation of the Bible as the rule of faith, to which end he translated the Bible into English. Wyclif rejected both transubstantiation in the Eucharist and the necessity of confessing one's sins to a priest. He severely criticized the wealth and worldly lives of the clergy, and urged that the state take over and administer Church properties. Wyclif also condemned religious orders and their founders, as well as universities and their degrees. Although his doctrines were condemned by English ecclesiastical authorities, Wyclif escaped punishment, largely because of his protection by powerful John of Gaunt, Duke of Lancaster, and others in high places. He attracted many followers, known as Lollards, and trained lay disciples, known as Poor Priests, who spread his doctrines through the countryside. Eventually the English government persecuted the Lollards until the movement went underground.

Wyclif's doctrines spread to Bohemia, where they became part of a revolution against both the orthodox Church and German overlordship. Transmission of Wyclif's revolutionary doctrines was facilitated by close relations between Bohemia and England, while their tenacity and intensity in Bohemia were increased by fusion with nationalistic opposition to German overlordship. A leading Bohemian exponent of Wyclif's teachings was John Hus, a professor of theology who became rector of the University of Prague. Although the Hussites did not follow Wyclif in all of his doctrines, they accepted several of them and added the necessity of communion under both kinds (wine as well as bread), whence they are often known as "Utraquists" (*utraque*: both) or "Calixtines" (*calix*: chalice). Hussite doctrines included denial of the authority of the Pope and of the need for mediation between Christ and the individual.

Hussite Wars

John Hus, as has been noted, came to the Council of Constance in 1414 with a safe conduct from the Emperor, but the Council condemned his teachings and burned him as a heretic (1415). Jerome of Prague, a Bohemian nobleman who had come to support Hus, suffered the same fate the following year. Shocked by the executions, the Bohemians spurned Sigismund's attempted conciliation and broke into open rebellion. The bloody Hussite Wars lasted from 1419 to 1435. Under brilliant military leaders such as Ziska and Prokop, the Bohemians won victory after victory over the Germans, using such tactics as wagon fortifications. Eventually the Hussites split into two parties: the "Utraquists," the more moderate majority who were willing to compromise; and the

"Taborites," a more extreme minority who were not. The Council of Basel conciliated the moderate majority by minor concessions, and peace was secured after the moderates won a great victory over the Taborites in 1434. The Hussite heresy, however, persisted among the so-called Moravian Brethren, and merged into the Protestant movement of the sixteenth century.

Church and State in the Later Middle Ages

Just as the balance of Church-State relations favored the Church in the High Middle Ages, so it favored the State in the Later Middle Ages. The dependence and weakness of the Papacy during the Avignon residence and the Great Western Schism, followed by the spiritual irresponsibility of the Renaissance Popes, caused a loss of respect for the Papacy. There was no longer any real possibility of the Papacy dominating or deposing secular monarchs. Instead, it was put on the defensive, and its main problem came to be the maintenance of its own independence and authority. For a while in the early fourteenth century the old question of Papal superiority over secular monarchs was still discussed. Dante and the French legists at the time of Philip IV insisted on the full independence of the secular authority; and the French legists further insisted that the clergy was subject to the monarch in secular affairs. But then Papal opponents seized the offensive. Marsiglio of Padua would have reduced the Church to a department of the State, which he regarded as the all-embracing social institution of the people, who were sovereign in both.

Meanwhile, monarchs were less influenced by the Papacy, and obtained various privileges concerning the administration of the Church in their own countries. The English monarchy prohibited both Papal appointments to English benefices (Provisors, 1351) and appeals to the Pope in cases cognizable in the king's court (Premunire, 1353). The French monarchy established wide exemptions from Papal control and substituted extensive royal control of the French Church with the Pragmatic Sanction of Bourges (1438). The German monarchy excluded the Pope from any part in imperial elections in the Golden Bull of 1356, and obtained various exemptions for the German Church in the Concordat of Vienna (1448). And the Spanish monarchy obtained wide privileges concerning the Church in Spanish realms through the *Real Patronato* (Royal Patronage) initially conceded by Alexander VI.

Christian life in the Later Middle Ages

The exact condition of Christian life in the Later Middle Ages is difficult to assess. The very fact of extensive contemporary criticism may be a sign of increased spiritual sensibility, and criticism is liable to hyperbole. Still, shortcomings among both clergy and laity seem to have increased in this period. A consciousness of need for reform was evidenced at Church Councils, although corrective action was regularly postponed, due to preoccupations, fears, and vested interests. Among leading causes for this inertia was Papal apprehension of General Councils.

The clergy

Contemporary writers frequently criticized the clergy in the Later Middle Ages, accusing many of them of worldliness and greed, loose living and unchastity. Some of the clergy received appointments for secular reasons, such as monetary contributions, family influence, or political expedience. On the other hand, it is evident that many "unsung" clergymen led holy lives, and it is safe to say that the majority of the clergy fulfilled their basic duties. Several Popes in the period were excessively concerned with worldly affairs, such as building and politics, although this concern was partly due to their positions as rulers of the Papal States as well as Popes. Nevertheless, scandalous Popes were the exception, and the majority of late medieval Popes were reasonably good men. Even the much criticized Avignon Popes led good personal lives, as also did most of the Popes of the troubled Conciliar Era (1418–1471). The Renaissance Popes (from 1471 on) were the least exemplary, although their main fault was not that they were irreligious but that they were not religious enough. Even Popes who had earlier led less exemplary lives reformed after their accession to the Papacy, as did Pius II.

Prelates

Their high office and considerable income, combined with a lack of weighty continuing responsibility, helped to make some of the cardinals the worst offenders. Most of the cardinals had multiple benefices that brought them large revenues without the burden of any immediate care of souls. Some of the cardinals lived in magnificent palaces, giving and attending rich banquets, with considerable drinking, and sometimes lascivious entertainment. Some kept mistresses. Other cardinals, however, were holy, hard-working churchmen, as were Cardinals Nicholas of Cusa, Pierre d'Ailly, and Jiménez de Cisneros.

Many bishops and abbots were worldly administrators, appointed mainly for secular reasons, whose way of life resembled that of secular princes. Still, most bishops were men of sound character, who lived in the public spotlight and bore heavy secular and religious responsibilities, which gave them little spare time for sin. Many of them were, in the words of the otherwise critical Wimpheling (1450–1528): "Of unblemished reputation, with abundant piety, generosity, and humility." Many priests, both in remote country districts and at the courts of the mighty, were negligent or lukewarm in their "care of souls," and some indulged in drunkenness, gluttony, and concubinage. Many were poorly educated in things religious, and some were primarily interested in personal comfort and pleasure. Yet the majority of priests apparently acquitted themselves well, helped by the responsibilities of their position and the trust and respect of their flock. Chaucer praises the "parson," of whom he says in part:

> *There was a good man of religion, too,*
> *A country parson, poor, I warrant you,*
> *But rich he was in holy thought and work.*

And even Wimpheling asserts that there are "countless true priests . . . , richly equipped with knowledge, and blameless in life and morals."

Religious orders

Religious orders were adversely affected in the Later Middle Ages by diminution of their earlier fervor, decimation by the Black Death, and a decline in vocations, accompanied by a growth of surplus income. Many abbots led luxurious lives, and laxity was common among religious. Yet the very fact that they entered and persevered in houses of religion meant that most at least tried to live in a holy manner. It is probably safe to say that most religious pursued their vocation in a reasonably satisfactory manner. Many attained formal or informal sanctity, as did Sts. Vincent Ferrer, Bernardino of Siena, Cajetan, Peter of Alcantara, Thomas Villaneuve, John Capistrano, Antonius, and Bridget of Sweden, to mention only a few.

Life of the laity: Elements of weakness and strength

The laity were adversely affected by catastrophes such as the Black Death, the Hundred Years' War, and the great depression, and shocking spectacles such as contests between rival Popes, which shook their faith. Some became pessimistic; others put excessive confidence in religious externals; and still others became discontented with their limited involvement in the Church, as active participation was mainly reserved for the clergy. Drunkenness and sexual immorality were common, although probably less so than today because of less means and an associated social stigma. Houses of prostitution were licensed and regulated by the government in Germanic lands on the theory that it was better to recognize and restrict illicit sexual intercourse. Hardness and cynicism were often induced among city dwellers by unscrupulous business dealings and "dog eat dog" competition.

On the other hand, there were several evidences of growing spirituality. Many of the laity consciously and effectively pursued an ascetic life, whether on an individual basis or in organizations. Orthodox lay religious organizations included the Brethren of the Common Life and the Friends of God. Some of the laity, in pursuit of perfection, went beyond the bounds of orthodoxy, as in the case of the Lollards and Hussites and the Brethren of the Free Spirit, and many of the Fraticelli and Flagellants. There were many highly religious lay persons, among them the uncanonized Jan Ruysbroeck, Gerhard Groot, and John Gerson, and the canonized Sts. Catherine of Siena and Joan of Arc. Several translators rendered the Bible in the various vernaculars for lay use. At least nineteen editions of German translations of the Bible appeared prior to Luther's revolt. Printing with movable type promoted lay spirituality, since it made possible the inexpensive reproduction of religious works. The Bible was by far the most popular product of the early printing press.

The Brethren of the Common Life and the Devotio Moderna

A leading early orthodox Flemish mystic, John (Jan) Ruysbroeck (d. 1381), had among his disciples Gerhard Groot (d. 1384), who in conjunction with his own disciple Florent Radewyns founded the Brethren of the Common Life. Their good works at first consisted in preaching and copying and distributing religious literature; but the Brethren eventually entered the field of education in order to instill habits of piety in the young. The Brethren practiced and promoted a form of intense personal piety known as the New Devotion (*Devotio Moderna*). Their excellent schools spread in the Rhineland, where they had many famous disciples, including Thomas à Kempis, reputed author of *The Imitation of Christ*, and Nicholas of Cusa, brilliant theorist and dedicated leader of reform in Germany, as well Erasmus, "the prince of Northern humanists."

During the Later Middle Ages new forces challenged the Church. Although religion was strengthened by the stimulation of popular movements for piety and demands for reform, the forces that were to bring about the sixteenth century Reformation and Counterreformation were already apparent in the late medieval Church.

References for Chapter 29

A WELL-ORGANIZED treatment of the Church in the Later Middle Ages from a Protestant viewpoint is ALEXANDER C. FLICK, *The Decline of the Medieval Church*, 2 vols. (New York: Knopf, 1930). Other Protestant treatments include HERBERT BRUCE, *The Age of Schism . . . the Church . . . A.D. 1304 to A.D. 1503 . . .* (New York: Macmillan, 1907), and LEONARD ELLIOTT-BINNS, *The History of the Decline and Fall of the Medieval Papacy* (London: Methuen, 1934). Informative general treatments from the Catholic viewpoint are FERNAND MOURRET, *A History of the Catholic Church*, tr. N. Thompson, vol. V (London: Herder, 1941), and PHILIP HUGHES, *A History of the Church* vol. III (New York: Sheed, 1934–1947). Also valuable is the succinct KARL BIHLMEYER and HERMAN TÜCHLE, *Church History*, vol. II: *The Middle Ages* (Westminster, Md.: Newman, 1963). A good introductory overview is the one-volume THOMAS P. NEILL and RAYMOND H. SCHMANDT, *History of the Catholic Church* (Milwaukee: Bruce, 1957); still briefer is MARGARET DEANESLY, *History of the Medieval Church 590–1500*, 7th ed. (London: Methuen, 1951). Informative articles on Church history in this period are found in the *Cambridge Medieval History*, Vol. VII and Vol. VIII.

Church-State relations in the Later Middle Ages are sketched by LUIGI STURZO, *Church and State* (New York: Longmans, 1937), and pertinent historical documents are cited with comments by SIDNEY Z. EHLER and JOHN B. MORRALL, *Church and State Through the Centuries* (Westminster, Md.: Newman, 1954). Theories concerning Church and State and their proper mutual relations are well presented with selections from leading primary sources by EWART K. LEWIS, *Medieval Political Ideas*, 2 vols. (New York: Knopf, 1954), especially in vol. II, and are discussed in R. W. and ALEXANDER J. CARLYLE, *Medieval Political Theory in the West*, vols. V and VI (Edinburgh: Blackwood, 1903–1928), and JOHN N. FIGGIS, *Studies of Political Thought from Gerson to Grotius, 1414–1625* (Cambridge: Cambridge U.P., 1907).

Contemporary opinions concerning the transitional struggle between King Philip IV and Pope Boniface VIII are presented in CHARLES T. WOOD, ed., *Philip the Fair and Boniface VIII* (New York: Holt, 1967). Pope Boniface is sympathetically treated by THOMAS S. R. BOASE, . . . *Boniface VIII* (London: Constable, 1933), as well as by LUIGI TOSTI, *History of Pope Boniface VIII and His Times*, tr. E. J. Donnelly (New York: Christian Press, 1911). A one-volume general story of the Avignon residence of the Papacy is not available in English, although the era is covered in more general works previously cited. The scholarly MANDELL CREIGHTON, *A History of the Papacy from the Great Schism to the Sack of Rome*, 6 vols., rev. (London: Longmans, 1919), begins at 1378 after a prefatory sketch of the period of Boniface VIII (1294–1303) and the Avignon residence (1305–1378). The story is taken up in 1447, after a preliminary one-volume résumé of the period from 1305 to 1447, by LUDWIG PASTOR, *The History of the Popes from the Close of the Middle Ages*, 40 vols., tr. and ed. F. I. Antrobus *et al.* (London: J. Hodges, 1891–1953). wherein vols. II–VI have a wealth of information concerning the period from 1447 to 1503.

A good work concerning the Great

Western Schism is LOUIS SALEMBIER, *The Great Schism of the West*, tr. M. D. (London: Kegan Paul, 1907). The period is also surveyed in a popular manner in connection with the life of BALDASSARE COSSA (Pope John XXIII) in the interesting consecutive two volumes by Eustace Kitts, *In the Days of the Councils* . . . (London: Constable, 1908) and *Pope John XXIII and Master John Hus* . . . (London: Constable, 1910). The development of the Conciliar Theory from Gratian to the Great Schism is surveyed by BRIAN TIERNEY, *Foundations of the Conciliar Theory* . . . (Cambridge: Cambridge U.P., 1955); the sources and outbreak of the Western Schism are related by WALTER ULLMANN, *The Origins of the Great Schism* . . . (London: Burns, Oates, 1948). The earlier part of the Council of Constance is the subject of JAMES H. WYLIE, *The Council of Constance to the Death of John Hus* (London: Longmans, Green, 1900).

Pope Alexander VI and his family have been the subject of numerous studies including ORESTES FERRARA, *The Borgia Pope* . . . (New York: Sheed, 1940); JOHANNES BURCHARDUS, *Pope Alexander VI and His Court: Extracts from the Latin Diary of Burchardus* (New York: Brown, 1921); and RAFAEL SABATINI, *The Life of Cesare Borgia* . . . (London: Stanley Paul, 1912). *The Commentaries of Pius II* have been translated by Florence A. Graff (Northampton, Mass.: Smith College, 1947). The expansion of Papal revenues during the Later Middle Ages is surveyed and exemplified from original sources by WILLIAM E. LUNT, *Papal Revenues in the Middle Ages*, 2 vols. (New York: Columbia U.P., 1935).

Piety, mysticism, and asceticism in the Later Middle Ages are studied by PIERRE POURRAT, *Christian Spirituality*, tr. W. Mitchell and S. Jacques, vol. II (New York: Kenedy, 1922ff.); EVELYN UNDERHILL, *Mysticism*, 14th ed. (London: Methuen, 1944); and ALBERT HYMA, *The Christian Renaissance: A History of the "Devotio Moderna"* (New York: Century, 1924), also published as *"Devotio Moderna"* . . . . Special aspects of the subject are surveyed by J. M. CLARKE, *The Great German Mystics: Eckhart, Tauler, and Suso* (Oxford: Oxford U.P., 1949); WILLIAM R. INGE, ed., *Light, Life, and Love: Selections from the German Mystics*, 3rd ed. (London: Methuen, 1935), R. M. INGE, *The Flowering of Mysticism: The Friends of God* (New York: Macmillan, 1939); and ALBERT HYMA, *The Brethren of the Common Life* (Grand Rapids: Erdmans, 1950). *The Imitation of Christ*, which has been ascribed to THOMAS À KEMPIS, has seen various translations and editions including that of Richard Whytford ed. by R. Hudleston (London: Burns Oates, 1925).

Leading reformers and mystics in the Later Middle Ages are treated by JAMES L. CONNOLLY, *John Gerson* . . . (Louvain: Librarie Universitaire, 1928); SAMUEL KETTLEWELL, *Thomas à Kempis* . . . (New York: Putnam's, 1882); HENRY BETT, *Nicholas of Cusa* (London: Methuen, 1932); ALICE CURTAYNE, *Saint Catherine of Siena* (London: Sheed, 1934); JOHANNES JORGENSEN, *Saint Bridget of Sweden*, 2 vols. (London: Longmans, Green, 1954); and HEIKO H. OBERMAN, *Forerunners of the Reformation* (New York: Holt, 1966). Wyclif and Hus and their movements have been the subject of various studies, including HERBERT B. WORKMAN, *John Wyclif* . . . , 2 vols. (Oxford: Clarendon, 1926); JOHN STACEY, *John Wyclif and Reform* (Philadelphia: Westminster, 1964); MARGARET DEANESLY, *The Lollard Bible* (Cambridge: Cambridge U.P., 1920); MATTHEW SPINKA, *John Hus and the Czech Reform* (Chicago: Chicago U.P., 1941,), and *John Hus: A Biography* (Princeton, N.J.: Princeton U.P., 1968); F. H. VON LUTZOW, *The Life and*

Times of Master John Hus (London: Dent, 1909); and HOWARD KAMINSKY, A History of the Hussite Revolution (Berkeley: California U.P., 1967). Selections from various pertinent original sources are edited by MATTHEW SPINKA in Advocates of Reform from Wyclif to Erasmus (Philadelphia: Westminster, 1953). The Inquisition in this era is treated by various works earlier cited for the High Middle Ages as well as by WILLIAM T. WALSH, Characters of the Inquisition (New York: Kenedy, 1940), and WALTER F. STARKIE, Grand Inquisitor . . . Cardinal Ximénez . . . (London: Herder, 1940). Information concerning religious orders in the Later Middle Ages is provided by DAVID KNOWLES, The Religious Orders in England (1216–1485), 2 vols. (Cambridge: Cambridge U.P., 1950–1955).

⁅ RENAISSANCE AND LATE GOTHIC CULTURE.
Chapter 30.

COUNTERCURRENTS competed in late medieval culture, as in other fields. Late Gothic culture continued and elaborated that of the High Middle Ages, often in an excessively involved manner. Renaissance culture, on the other hand, drew its inspiration from that of classical antiquity and attempted to revive classical forms, standards, and spirit, especially in literature and the arts. Renaissance culture originated in Italy, where it was enthusiastically adopted. It came to be known in literature as humanism, in the arts as classicism. For some time Transalpine culture was mainly Late Gothic; but gradually native forces together with Italian influences led to an acceptance of Italian Renaissance culture beyond the Alps, where it was often combined with Late Gothic elements into a new fusion.

ITALIAN RENAISSANCE LEARNING AND LITERATURE.
Section 88.

> Petrarch restored Helicon's font, which had been covered with mud and rushes, to its pristine clarity; he reopened the Castilian cave, whose entrance was overgrown with tangled weeds, and reinstated Apollo in his ancient temple; he brought back the Muses, who had become sullied by rusticity, to shine with their former luster. [Giovanni Boccaccio concerning Francesco Petrarca (Petrarch) in a letter to Jacob Pizzinghe (ca. 1370).]

THE Italians became the cultural leaders of Europe during the Later Middle Ages, with a civilization which drew inspiration from the classical. Factors contributing to Italian cultural hegemony included the current difficulties and preoccupations of other European peoples, the temporary freedom of Italy from foreign interference and control, Italian wealth, and the stimulating city-state form of government prevalent in northern Italy. The spirit of enterprise as well as the capital produced by Italian business activities encouraged cultural interests and creativity. Italian patriotism and pride, conscious of a glorious past and a rich heritage, stimulated cultivation of classical culture. Italy's potential, according to many Italians, had too long been eclipsed by a dark "Gothic night."

Humanism was the dominant intellectual spirit and force in Italian Renaissance culture. The term *humanism* derives from Cicero's praise of *litterae humaniores* or "especially human learning," which, according to him, comprises those studies that develop the higher human faculties and feelings that distinguish men from beasts. Central in humanistic studies was that of classical literature, whose cultivation could make men "eloquent" (able to communicate with facility and effectiveness) as well as "learned" (lettered). According to the humanists, "eloquence" and "learning" were best acquired by the study and imitation of the Latin language and classical literature, which alone were sufficiently universal, well developed, and opulent to serve as fit instruments of general communication and enlightenment. In addition, men of culture should also study Greek and classical Greek literature. Subsidiary humanistic studies included history, geography, the liberal arts, archeology, mythology, and paleography. According to the humanists, one should seek to acquire the spirit of the classics. The ideal humanist was to have keen appreciation of this life and nature, be ambitious for worldly success and fame as well as eternal salvation, respect manly *virtú* and patriotism, and cultivate the social graces.

Humanism

Late medieval Italy was congenial to humanism. Italian commercial and industrial development had promoted a great expansion of the Italian middle class and had encouraged education. For the education, refinement, and intellectual entertainment of literate lay persons, a considerable body of secular literature was desirable. But the only substantial body of good lay literature available in the West at the time was that of classical Latin, as the vernaculars were still in their infancy. Classical Latin literature was the old, honored, native literature of Italy, and its mastery was not difficult for educated Italians. Its study would furthermore encourage the idea of a united, independent Italy, according to the humanists. Humanism was also encouraged by a reaction against the excessive subtlety of late medieval scholasticism, as well as by the skepticism and obscurantism of new philosophies, such as Ockhamism.

Typical activities of the Italian humanists included the study of Latin grammar and rhetoric; the reading, interpretation, and analysis of classical Latin literature; the imitative composition of Latin prose and poetry; and, ideally, study of classical Greek and its literature, often concluded by translation of some classic Greek work into Latin. Supplementary humanistic activities were the reading and interpretation of the Scriptures and the Fathers (as far as possible in the original texts); the study of history and other related subjects; and the collection and collation of ancient manuscripts. Works in imitation or explanation of the classics were usually composed in Latin, but sometimes also in the vernacular.

The great Dante Alighieri (1265–1321) was transitional to the Renaissance. On the one hand, Dante sympathized with as well as synthesized the ultimate tendencies of high medieval culture. On the other hand, he

Transitional Dante

was intimately familiar with the classics, which he deeply admired and frequently quoted. In his *Divine Comedy*, which is partly a mosaic of medieval concepts, Dante quotes Vergil about two hundred times and Ovid about one hundred times. On his meeting with Vergil, his guide through Hell and Purgatory, Dante exclaims:

> *Art thou Vergil, then—the fountain*
> *Whence roll the streams of eloquence along?*
> *Oh light and glory of the sons of song!*
> *So favor me as I thy page have sought*
> *With unremitting zeal and study long:*
> *Thou art the master of my thought!*

Dante wrote in both Latin and the vernacular. Although his concepts about life and reality were medieval, his appreciation of the classics and his use of the vernacular were Renaissance and modern.

Petrarch: Father of Renaissance humanism

Francesco Petrarch (1304–1374) is recognized as the father of Renaissance humanism. Petrarch, who was ecstatic in his admiration of classical literature, spent most of his life studying and imitating classical works, as well as promoting humanism. Petrarch was born in Florentine territory, but his father was exiled because of his political affiliations, and the family moved to Avignon. From an early date Petrarch was attracted by classical literature, and although he was educated in law he vastly preferred literary pursuits. Petrarch became a cleric, supported himself from his benefices, and spent much of his time at a sylvan retreat known as Vaucluse (the Valley Enclosed).

Petrarch had a passionate devotion to classical authors, to many of whom he wrote intimate letters. Among his numerous works in classical style, he produced a great unfinished epic poem entitled *Africa* concerning Scipio Africanus and his subjection of Carthage, which ushered in Rome's overseas Empire. The high point in Petrarch's career came when he was crowned poet laureate by the Roman Senate in 1341. He collected a considerable personal library of classical works, including a copy of Homer, which he treasured although he was unable to read Greek.

In his later years, Petrarch moved from one Italian capital to another, enjoying the hospitality and patronage of various rulers, and engaging in an apostolate on behalf of humanism, without forsaking his classical studies. Of the latter, he wrote: *My tireless spirit pores over the pages [of the classics] until it has exhausted both fingers and eyes. Yet I feel neither hunger nor cold, and only seem to be reclining on the softest down.* When Boccaccio, one of his most famous disciples, urged the aging Petrarch to relax his classical studies (1373), Petrarch replied: *I desire that when death comes it find me reading and writing.* His wish was fulfilled the following year. A contemporary reported: *He closed his days in the library, where he was found leaning over a book as if sleeping.*

Boccaccio and Salutati

The humanistic seed sown by Petrarch rapidly took root in receptive Italy. Among Petrarch's early converts to humanism was the noted author Giovanni Boccaccio (1313–1375), who switched from the composition

Renaissance and Late Gothic Culture

of masterpieces in the vernacular to Latin and classical studies in 1350. Instead of vivid realistic works such as the *Decameron*, written in Italian, Boccaccio now composed rather colorless Latin treatises on *The Genealogy of the Gods, The Fortunes of Great Men, Famous Women,* and classical geography. Boccaccio was even persuaded to study Greek and to attempt a translation of Homer, but the latter reflected his own linguistic deficiencies as well as those of his teachers.

Another pillar of early humanism was Coluccio Salutati (1330–1406), a distinguished scholar and statesman, who held the important post of Chancellor of Florence (Secretary to the *Signoria*) for thirty years, despite a succession of administrations. Gian Galeazzo Visconti, despot of Milan, declared that one of Salutati's superb Latin letters was more potent than "a thousand Florentine horsemen." It was in the circle of Salutati that the humanistic (neo-Carolingian) book hand was developed.

Humanistic leaders realized that Greek classical authors were the masters and models of the Latin classical authors. Initial attempts to master Greek were hampered by a lack of qualified teachers. Eventually, however, the learned Byzantine scholar Manuel Chrysoloras, who visited Italy as an emissary of his Emperor (1393), consented to instruct in Greek at the University of Florence (1395ff.). Chrysoloras had many humanists as his eager students. Greek learning was similarly promoted by Georgios Gemisthos Plethon (d. ca. 1450) and Archbishop Bessarion of Nicaea (d. ca. 1475), who stayed on in the West and was made a cardinal by Nicholas V. It became customary for an accomplished humanist to be skilled in Greek as well as Latin, and to essay the translation of one or more Greek works into Latin. Greek manuscripts were avidly hunted; and Hellenic academies were established. Classics of Greek literature were being printed by the later fifteenth century.

Greek studies

Italian humanism attained maturity in the so-called *Quatrocento* (fifteenth century). The new generation of Italian Renaissance scholars included Bruni, Poggio, Guarino, Aurispa, Alberti, Poliziano, Valla, and Piccolomini. Leonardo Bruni (1370–1444), Apostolic Secretary to four Popes and then Chancellor of Florence for two decades, was a humanist of wide interests. Bruni translated Plutarch's *Lives*, Demosthenes' *Orations*, Plato's *Republic*, and Aristotle's *State* from Greek to Latin, and wrote a number of histories and biographies, an essay on educational theory, and ten volumes of letters. Poggio Bracciolini (1380–1459) was an indefatigable collector of manuscripts as well as a prolific author, recovered numerous valuable classical manuscripts by ransacking old monastic libraries, and was noted for his literary duels and biting satire. Poggio's most significant accomplishment, however, was the invention of the humanistic book hand, from which Roman type later developed. Guarino da Verona (d. 1460) brought fifty-four Greek manuscripts from Constantinople; and Giovanni Aurispa (d. 1450) brought no less than 238 Greek codices from the Byzantine capital. Pope Nicholas V (1447–1455) purchased numerous Greek manuscripts for the Vatican Library and commissioned a metrical translation of Homer into Latin for ten thousand gulden.

Italian humanism at its height

Alberti, Poliziano and Valla

Leon Battista Alberti (d. 1472), a wealthy aristocrat, approximated the Renaissance ideal of the *uomo universale* (universal man). Besides being an expert architect, painter, and musician, Alberti composed treatises on architecture, painting, and sculpture, and was a philosopher, mathematician, poet, dramatist, historian, and archeologist, as well as something of an economist and sociologist. A protégé of the Medici was learned Angelo Poliziano (Politian) (d. 1494), professor of classical languages at the University of Florence, who became famous for his translation of Homer as well as his excellent poetry in the vernacular.

The work of Lorenzo Valla (d. 1457) was an example of both the expert textual criticism and the pagan propensities of the Later Renaissance. Valla attacked the authenticity of the Donation of Constantine and the Apostles' Creed on philological grounds, demonstrating that they could not have been composed in the periods to which they were ascribed. In a book *On Pleasure* Valla manifested sympathy for the doctrines of Epicurus, but his views did not prevent him from remaining in the employ of Pope Nicholas V.

Patrons of humanism

Thomas Parentucelli and Aeneas Sylvius Piccolomini were noted humanists who became Popes Nicholas V (1447–1455) and Pius II (1468–1464). Nicholas V built up the Vatican library by acquiring thousands of precious manuscripts, and hired a corps of translators to render Greek works into Latin. Pius II, prior to becoming Pope, was a copious author of autobiography, history, geography, poetry, and fiction.

Italian humanism was nurtured by the generosity of enlightened patrons, among whom princely families and rulers, such as the Gonzagas of Mantua, the D'Estes of Ferrara, and the Medicis of Florence, were prominent. Wealthy individuals such as Niccolò Niccoli and Palla Strozzi of Florence also patronized humanism.

Following its heyday in the fifteenth and early sixteenth centuries, Italian humanism often tended to degenerate into what has been called "Ciceronianism": an emphasis on style as opposed to content.

Humanistic education in Italy

Among numerous humanistic treatises on educational theory, Piero Paolo Vergerio composed one of the earliest and best, entitled *On the Training of the Freeborn* (about 1400). Similar works were written by Leonardo Bruni, Aeneas Sylvius Piccolomini, Battista Guarino, Maffeo Vegio, and Leon Battista Alberti. These treatises drew on the theories of Cicero and Quintilian, as well as on previous medieval theory and practice. Italian Renaissance educational theorists agreed on making classical languages and literatures the continuing "core" study. At the same time, they advocated a broad, diversified curriculum, including such subjects as grammar, rhetoric, literature, history, geography, philosophy, mathematics, and natural sciences. They also prescribed training in drawing, painting, and music, as well as horseback riding, swimming, and dancing, without omitting military training and self-defense. Finally all stressed the necessity of religious instruction and moral training.

The earliest humanistic schools were organized by Vittorino da Feltre and Guarino da Verona (the Elder) in the fifteenth century. Vittorino conducted a school known as *La Giacosa* (the Joyous House) at Mantua, primarily for the princely family of the Gonzagas, while the Guarinos did likewise for the D'Estes at Ferrara. These schools were eminently successful and attracted students from various parts of Italy as well as from Transalpine countries.

The most notable development in philosophy in Renaissance Italy was a revival of Platonism. Italian humanists were in general cold toward the technicalities of Aristotelianism but attracted by the poetic imagination and literary style of Plato. A by-product of Greek studies in Italy was the study of Plato, particularly Plato as interpreted by the ancient Neo-Platonists, whose philosophy was strongly tinged with mysticism.

Philosophy in Renaissance Italy

The Byzantine scholar Georgios Gemisthos Pletho or Plethon (d. 1450) persuaded Cosimo de Medici to found a Platonic Academy at Florence and stayed there after the Council of Ferrara–Florence (1437–1439) to teach Platonic and Neo-Platonic philosophy. Plethon's leading pupil, Marsilio Ficino (1433–1499), also patronized by the Medicis, translated Plato's works into Latin and propagated a Platonism strongly flavored with Neo-Platonism.

The precocious young Count Giovanni Pico della Mirandola (1463–1494), who became a leading Renaissance philosopher, sought to reconcile Plato and Aristotle, as well as Jewish, Moslem, and Christian thought. In his *Oration on the Dignity of Man*, Mirandola conceived of man as a microcosm reflecting the macrocosm of the universe.

Italian humanists took an active interest in politics, and many of them nourished a dream of unifying Italy. Dante Alighieri urged in his *De Monarchia* subjection to the authority of the Emperor as a means of stilling internal conflict in Italy. Dante also advocated exclusion of the Church and the Papacy from politics. Early in the fourteenth century, Marsiglio of Padua, a former rector of the University of Paris who withdrew to the anti-Papal court of Lewis the Bavarian, composed *The Defender of the Peace* (1324), in which he traced authority in both Church and State to the will of the people, whose sovereignty he maintained. Marsiglio held that the Emperor or civil ruler was the general head of the community, whereas the Pope was in charge of only one aspect of human life, as a sort of chief of a department within the state. Marsiglio taught that all human authority is derived from the consent of "the whole body of the citizenry or its prevailing (*valentior*) part." Marsiglio may have composed his treatise in collaboration with Jean of Jandun.

Political theory in Renaissance Italy

Shortly after 1500 the ideology of practical politics in Renaissance Italy was expressed by Niccolo Machiavelli in *The Prince* (1513). Machiavelli urged that a ruler should not be bound by the ordinary rules of morality but should be free to use deception, injustice, and oppression to secure his objectives.

History was highly esteemed by the humanists, even as it had been by Cicero. Various humanists composed histories in Latin, modeled on works of classical historians. Among these were Leonardo Bruni's *History of Florence*, which he carried down to 1404; Poggio Bracciolini's *History of the People of Florence*, for the century from 1352 to 1455; and Flavio Biondo's *Decades of History . . .* , which treated the period from

Renaissance historiography in Italy

412 to 1440 and was mainly a thinly connected collection of extracts from cited sources.

More informative and direct because more natural and less structured were histories written in the vernacular. In the fourteenth century, Giovanni Villani, a merchant, composed a Florentine *Chronicle* to 1348 written in Italian and notable among other things for the inclusion of economic and social statistics. Giovanni's *Chronicle* was continued to 1364 first by his brother Matteo and then by his nephew Filippo. The task of recording Florentine history in the vernacular was ably resumed a century later by Niccolo Machiavelli in his *History of Florence,* which brought the story to 1492. Humanist interest in biography was exemplified by Petrarch's *Illustrious Men* and Boccaccio's *Illustrious Women* and *Life of Dante,* as well as by the autobiography of Petrarch in his *Letter to Posterity,* and that of Aeneas Sylvius Piccolomini in his *Commentaries,* all in Latin.

Vernacular literature in Renaissance Italy: Dante

Despite the insistence of the humanists upon the virtues of Latin, the best literature in the Later Middle Ages was written in the vernacular; and Italian literature in particular made great strides. Dante, Petrarch, and Boccaccio were the masters of early Italian vernacular literature.

Dante Alighieri (d. 1321), the greatest author in Italian literature, came at its very outset. Although an admirer of classical Latin literature, Dante composed most of his works in the language of his native Tuscany. Passing glimpses of a beautiful girl in church inspired the lovely sonnets to Beatrice found in his *New Life.* His *Banquet* presented a philosophical feast for those who understood only the vernacular. But Dante's masterpiece is his panoramic and profound *Divine Comedy,* in which he visits Hell, Purgatory, and Heaven. As he progresses, Dante beholds various virtues and vices personified, and comments on the various types of persons with whom he had become familiar in actual life. Beatrice moralizes:

> *Never did you see, in art or nature,*
> *Anything so sweet, as were my limbs and beauteous form,*
> *That now are dust;*
> *If this sweetest thing thus failed thee with my death,*
> *What other mortal thing should tempt you?*
> *When first you felt the dart of perishable things*
> *In my departing for better realms,*
> *Thou shouldst have pruned thy wing to follow me,*
> *And never stooped again.*[a]

a(*Paradiso,* Canto XXXI)

Fourteenth century

Although ordinarily disdainful of the vernacular, Petrarch made a fortunate exception in the case of his wistful sonnets to his beloved Laura. Giovanni Boccaccio, after a heart-breaking disappointment in a love affair with a proud, high-placed Neapolitan beauty, turned to writing. His most famous work is his *Decameron,* which includes a hundred realistic, often risqué and satirical tales told by a group of ten young women on ten successive nights at a villa whither they had fled during the

Black Death. These stories were an important landmark in introducing prose fiction as a form of Western literature.

After a lapse of three quarters of a century, the circle of Lorenzo the Magnificent effectively revived Italian vernacular literature at Florence in the mid-fifteenth century. Lorenzo and some of his associates, such as Poliziano and Pulci, composed poems, pageants, and plays in the vernacular, partly for the entertainment of the populace. In one of his carnival songs, Lorenzo says:

Fifteenth century

> Listen well to what we're saying:
> For tomorrow have no care!
> Young and old together playing,
> Boys and girls be blithe as air!
> Every joyless thought beswear!

The Roland theme became prominent in Italian literature in the later fifteenth century, but with much changed interpretations. Thus Luigi Pulci (1432–1484) made Roland's squire, the giant Morgante, and the latter's companion, the stunted giant Margutte, the principal characters in a quasi-comedy. Matteo Boiardo (1441–1494), in his *Orlando Innamorado*, cast Roland in the unfamiliar role of a great lover. Lodovico Ariosto (1474–1533) went a step further in his *Orlando Furioso*, wherein Roland becomes crazy with frustration when his beloved falls in love with the wrong man as the result of a confusion of love potions.

TRANSALPINE LEARNING AND LITERATURE IN THE LATER MIDDLE AGES.
Section 89.

> Eternal God, in his unfathomable wisdom, has brought into existence the laudable art whereby men now print books and multiply them so greatly that every man may either read for himself or hear read the way of salvation. This valuable art was invented in Germany . . . [in the period] from about 1440 to 1450. [*Chronicle of Cologne* (1499).]

TRANSALPINE EUROPE was an arena for the interplay of Late Gothic and Renaissance cultural elements. Although the old cultural stream, the Late Gothic, which was more religious and otherworldly, had passed its prime, it continued to prevail and was still capable of remarkable productions. The new culture of the Transalpine Renaissance, which was more secular and natural, was better adapted to the interests and needs of an educated laity. Transalpine Renaissance culture was composed of two streams which combined and reinforced each other: one a spontaneous native adaptation to lay needs in the contemporary world, the other emanating from Italy.

The humanistic enthusiasm of the Italian Renaissance gradually spread beyond the Alps. Western Europe was a cultural community united by a universal Church, a common Latin language of learning and diplomacy, and well-established patterns of interregional intercourse. Conditions and needs in Transalpine countries were becoming similar to those in Italy.

Humanism takes root beyond the Alps

With the growth of a prosperous, ambitious middle class beyond the Alps it was natural to turn to the rich literary legacy inherited from classical antiquity as the Italians had done.

Among early transmitters of Italian Renaissance ideas, churchmen, scholars, and artists from Italy and persons from Transalpine countries who had studied or traveled in Italy were prominent. Other means of transmission included correspondence, books, and art objects. Although somewhat delayed by the Hundred Years' War and the Black Death, Italian influences came into clear relief in most Transalpine countries during the fifteenth century.

While sharing many of the essential features of Italian humanism, Transalpine humanism also developed special aspects. Humanism beyond the Alps was inclined to be more serious and practical, as well as more religious and moralistic. Many Transalpine humanists were very interested in studying and translating the written records of early Christianity—the New Testament and the works of the Eastern Fathers. In general, they were more interested in the Greek language and literature than were most Italian humanists. They were also critical of existing religious errors and social follies, and urged reforms of various sorts. It would almost seem that, on crossing the Alps, humanism changed its color to suit the more somber Transalpine climate and outlook.

Early humanism in the Germanies and Netherlands

Universities with chairs of philosophy and theology were not established in the Germanies until the Later Middle Ages, and when constituted they were more susceptible to contemporary humanistic influences. Meanwhile nonuniversity German schools continued to follow a more "literary" curriculum, wherein grammar and the classics, both pagan and Christian, were still leading objects of study.

Trailblazers of Renaissance humanism in the Germanies included Agricola, Hegius, and the Brethren of the Common Life. An early pioneer of humanism in the Germanies was Rudolf Agricola (or Huysman) (1444—1485), who became a professor at the University of Heidelberg after studying for about ten years at Pavia and Ferrara. Agricola promoted classical studies at the Heidelberg court as well as in the University, so that Erasmus says of him that he was "the first to bring us the breath of higher culture out of Italy."

Another pioneer was Alexander Hegius (d. 1498), headmaster of the school of the Brethren of the Common Life at Deventer, who successfully developed and cultivated a combined classical and Christian curriculum.

The Brethren of the Common Life, founded in the fourteenth century by Gerhard Groot to develop the interior life and foster religious devotion, at first undertook the copying and distributing of pious books, and subsequently conducted schools for the young. They combined extensive classical studies and intensive religious training at their schools in the Netherlands and Germany such as those at Deventer, Windesheim, and Zwolle. Many leading Northern humanists were trained by the Brethren. The University of Heidelberg was especially hospitable to the "new learning," but humanistic chairs were also established in other universities, such as those of Erfurt, Ingolstadt, and Wittenberg.

Johann Reuchlin (1455–1522), a learned classical scholar at the University of Heidelberg, skilled in both Latin and Greek, also took up and defended the study of Hebrew. The poet Conrad Celtes (1459–1508), who studied under Agricola at Heidelberg, became a sort of knight errant of humanism, going about singing its praises and founding literary societies.

The generally recognized "Prince of Northern Humanists" was, however, Desiderius Erasmus of Rotterdam (ca. 1466–1536), who became an accepted humanistic leader beyond the Alps, even as Petrarch had been in Italy. The illegitimate son of a priest, Erasmus studied at Deventer and entered the Augustinian Order. But later he obtained a release from the monastic life and gradually devoted himself entirely to humanistic studies and writing. Among the works of Erasmus were a critical edition and a Latin translation of the Greek New Testament; a collection of several hundred *Adages* (sayings, proverbs) from classical authors; *In Praise of Folly*, criticizing many of the foibles and failings of his day; and seventy-two *Familiar Colloquies* wherein he discusses in easy, intimate fashion a wide spectrum of topics. Although an advocate of reforms, Erasmus later refused to join the Protestants. Among his patrons were Thomas More and Henry VIII in England.

Erasmus

Humanism entered England through many avenues in the fifteenth century. Among these were the visits of Italian humanists such as Piero del Monte and Poggio Bracciolini in search of English employment and the travels of Englishmen to Italy as students and sightseers. Among prominent fifteenth-century English promoters of humanism were the wealthy Bishop William Grey of Ely, Earl Tiptopf of Worcester, the powerful Duke Humphrey of Gloucester, and Archbishop Neville of York (younger brother of "Kingmaker" Warwick). Among Oxford savants who taught Greek and translated Greek works were the scholarly William Grocyn and the physician Thomas Linacre. The clergyman John Colet, who reorganized the School of St. Paul's along humanistic lines, and Chancellor Thomas More, who befriended Erasmus and promoted humanism at Oxford, stood out among friends of humanism at the beginning of the sixteenth century.

Early humanism in England, France, and Spain

Simultaneously, Italian humanism was winning supporters in France and Spain. As early as the fourteenth century, members of the house of Valois, who held the throne of France and ruled important French duchies, were lovers of books and patrons of culture. Valois bibliophiles and benefactors included King Charles V, the Wise, Duke John of Berry, Duke Louis of Orleans, and Duke Philip the Good of Burgundy. In the fifteenth century, Louis XI promoted the Renaissance by encouraging Italian immigration into France. The invasion of Italy by Charles VIII was an additional stimulus to the French Renaissance. Meanwhile Italian and Greek humanists were invited to teach at the University of Paris.

Among prominent fifteenth-century French humanists were Gaguin, d'Etaples, and Badius of Asche. Robert Gaguin (d. 1501), a former professor of rhetoric at the University of Paris who became head of the Trinitarian Order, promoted humanistic studies and collected classical books, as well as became the leader of a humanistic circle. Lefevre d'Etaples, or "Stapulensis," a profound scholar who had studied in Italy, stressed Christian humanism. In addition to numerous erudite works, editions, and translations, d'Etaples advocated that general education begin with classical languages and literatures, move on to philosophy, continue with the Scriptures, and culminate in mysticism. The Parisian publishing house of Asche, founded by the scholarly Josse Badius Ascensius, was famous for the publication of numerous classics and the works of the early Christian writers.

Among fostering centers of fifteenth-century humanism in Spain were the old University of Salamanca and the new University of Alcalá. Cardinal Jiménez de Cisneros, a learned Franciscan who became Primate of the Church in Spain, founded the University of Alcalá in 1499 with chairs of Greek and Oriental languages as well as Latin. Jiménez also masterminded compilation of the famous Complutensian Polyglot Bible, a scholarly edition of the Sacred Scriptures in four parallel texts (Hebrew, Aramaic, Greek, and Latin). Other noted teachers of Greek in fifteenth-century Spain were Arias Barbosa, a Portuguese who taught at the University of Salamanca for two decades; Antonio De Nebrixa (or Nebrija), a Spanish nobleman who taught at the Universities of Seville, Salamanca, and Alcalá; and Fernando Nuñez, who taught at Alcalá and Salamanca.

Transalpine education in the Later Middle Ages

Education made important gains beyond the Alps during the Later Middle Ages. Transalpine universities continued to multiply, and universities were established in countries where they had not previously existed. The first university in the German Empire, that of Prague, was founded in 1348; and by 1500 there were fourteen universities in the Empire. Universities also arose for the first time in Denmark, Sweden, Poland, Hungary, Scotland, Belgium, and Switzerland. Many of the new universities were more "modern" and flexible in their attitudes toward new movements such as humanism.

Meanwhile general education came to be increasingly provided for the Transalpine laity in schools such as those of the Brethren of the Common Life in the Low Countries and Germany and the new public grammar schools or "colleges" in England. These schools usually inculcated a "Christian humanism," which combined religious and moral training with the study of the classical languages and literatures.

Printing

One of the most pregnant developments in the period was the invention of printing with movable type. Block printing had already existed for centuries in the Orient, whence it seems to have been introduced into the West. The new system of printing with movable metal type, whereby letters were cast individually, set in formats that could be changed, and used over and over, was invented in the Rhineland about 1440 by Johann Gutenberg of Mainz and his associates. Thanks to Germanic mechanical aptitude and the increased availability of paper, produced increasingly in the West from the twelfth century on, books could be printed rapidly and cheaply, thus facilitating both communications and a great expansion of education and learning. After spreading with rapidity in the Rhineland, printing soon came to France, Italy, England, and other countries. Among noted early printers were Johann Heynlin and William Fichet of the Sorbonne Press, Josse Badius Ascensius in Paris, Aldus Manutius in Venice, and William Caxton in London.

After its brilliant productions in the thirteenth century, philosophy declined. Following Duns Scotus, scholasticism tended to become excessively subtle, pedantic, and presumptuous. Besides discouraging constructive philosophic thought by his numerous distinctions and meticulous hair-splitting, Scotus negatively encouraged Ockhamism by his insistence on the reality of universals and positively encouraged mysticism by his emphasis on the will as opposed to the intellect.

Philosophy and political theory

Ockhamism, developed by William of Ockham (d. ca. 1349), an Oxford Franciscan who eventually took refuge at the anti-Papal court of Lewis of Bavaria, became popular among thinkers throughout Western Europe. According to Ockham, only particular individual things are real, whereas generalizations, although convenient as tools, are merely arbitrary mental signs. Ockham thus not only rejected the extreme realism of his fellow Franciscan Duns Scotus but also challenged the ultimate validity of philosophic and theological speculation. His principle, known as "Ockham's razor," advocated economy in thought, to the effect that "entities are not to be multiplied without necessity." According to Ockham, it is preferable to speak of individual beings and cases themselves, instead of complicating matters by discoursing on abstract *species* and *genera*, principles and generalizations. Ockham's approach, which obtained wide vogue, tended to undermine scholasticism and discourage philosophical speculation, while promoting scientific observation.

Novel political theories were advanced in the Later Middle Ages. In the fourteenth century the French Aristotelian, Jean (John) of Jandun, apparently collaborated with the former rector of the University of Paris, Marsiglio of Padua, in composing the *Defensor Pacis* (1324), which argued for popular sovereignty in both State and Church, as well as the primacy of the secular government. The French lawyer Pierre Dubois, in his work *On the Recovery of the Holy Land*, advocated control of Church properties and revenues as well as of the Church's external administration by the king of France, seen as a means of financing a great invincible Crusade against the Moslems.

Novel political theories

In the fifteenth century, an Englishman, Sir John Fortesque, in his *Praise of the Laws of England*, lauded the superiority of the English system of government over the French. Whereas the French, according to Fortesque, had a "regal government"—a despotism without popular participation—the English had a "political government"—a limited monarchy, in which the people participated through Parliament. In his *Memoirs*, the French statesman Philippe de Commines presented the unscrupulous, unchivalric practices of Louis XI as models of statecraft, anticipating the "end justifies the means" political doctrine advanced shortly thereafter by Machiavelli. At the same time, Commines praised the English parliamentary system, and said that subjects should not be taxed without some kind of popular consent.

Natural sciences, inventions, and historiography

This period was comparatively sterile in the natural sciences, with certain exceptions. The particularism of Ockhamism, which called for an empirical study of individual entities, paved the way for the great scientific advances of succeeding centuries. Progress was made in the theory of motion. Whereas Aristotle had assumed that rest is the natural state of material bodies and motion a transitory quality communicated by external forces, John Buridan (d. ca. 1358) and Nicholas Oresme (d. 1382) maintained that motion is as natural a state as is rest, thus anticipating the theory of inertia. They explained the fall of an arrow in flight by the dual forces of air resistance and the earth's attraction. Oresme compared the universe to a clock that God has set in motion and allowed to run on its own. Nicholas of Cusa (fifteenth century) held with Oresme that the earth revolves on its axis. He maintained that the universe is boundless, that the earth cannot be its center, and that each star is the center of its own system with its own force of gravity.

As a result of navigational explorations such as those of Columbus, Cabral, and Cabot and more scientific methods such as those promoted by the school of Prince Henry the Navigator, maps were improved and geographical knowledge was greatly expanded.

Among important inventions of this era, besides printing with movable type, were the use of gunpowder in warfare, the mechanical clock, the process of distillation, and spectacles for reading.

Late Gothic historiography, concentrating on the aristocratic and chivalric aspects of history, was exemplified in the fourteenth century by Jean Froissart's *Chronicle* concerning the Hundred Years' War to 1399, for the first part of which he used the *Chronicle* of Jehan le Bel. Froissart's account was later continued to 1444 by Enguerrand de Monstrelet. Realistic, analytic historiography was exemplified in the later fifteenth century by the *Memoirs* of Philippe de Commines concerning the rule of Louis XI. Shortly thereafter the Italian humanist Polydore Vergil was commissioned by Henry VII to write a *History of England*, which he did with painstaking objectivity.

Transalpine vernacular literatures

The Later Middle Ages were relatively sterile for the Transalpine vernaculars, with the exception of English. The most notable works portrayed contemporary conditions of life. In English literature, *The Vision of Piers Plowman*, apparently by William Langland (d. ca. 1400), was an alliterative allegorical poem stressing the need for social reform. One of the earliest and greatest masterpieces of English literature, the *Canterbury Tales* of Geoffrey Chaucer (d. 1400), presented vivid, penetrating, entertaining pictures of various types of persons to be met in fourteenth-century England. The *Tales* consist of a series of twenty-four short stories related by English pilgrims on their way to the shrine of St. Thomas Becket. Priceless are Chaucer's sketches of the Merchant, the Knight, the Squire, the Prioress, the Clerk, the Monk, the Yeoman, the Housewife, the Plowman, the Miller, and so on, including the following:

Renaissance and Late Gothic Culture

> *A knight there was, a worthy man,*
> *Who from the moment he first began*
> *To ride about the world loved chivalry.*
> *With him there was his son, a youthful squire,*
> *A lover and a lusty bachelor,*
> *With locks well curled as if they'd lain in press.*
> *There was also a nun, a prioress,*
> *Who, in her smiling, modest was and coy:*
> *Her greatest oath was but "By St. Eloy!"*

The greatest French writer of the period was an unconventional ex-cleric who devolved into a frequenter of taverns and an associate of lawbreakers. François Villon (d. ca. 1463) wrote numerous pulsating poems concerning everyday life among the lower classes in Paris, as was the case with his "Great Testament" and "Little Testament" and his "Ballad of the Women of Paris" and "Ballad of the Hanged." The latter, composed by Villon while awaiting an execution that he and his fellows narrowly escaped, realistically described their anticipated pitiable condition after the hanging:

> *The rain out of heaven has washed us clean,*
> *The sun has scorched us black and bare,*
> *Ravens and rooks have pecked out our eyne,*
> *And feathered their nests with our beards and hair.*

There were no noteworthy productions in late medieval German literature to compare with those of preceding and succeeding periods. Of note in Spanish were the love-adventures of the Archpriest of Hita; the plays of Juan del Encina, "the father of Spanish comedy"; and the *Amadis de Gaula*, a collection of chivalric romances in prose.

RENAISSANCE AND LATE GOTHIC ARTS AND MUSIC.
Section 90.

> Painting is the child of nature, or more correctly the grandchild of nature. For all visible things are children of nature, and these have given birth to painting. [Leonardo da Vinci in his *Treatise on Painting*.]

THE contrast between the Italian Renaissance and Late Gothic cultural currents was particularly obvious in late medieval art and architecture. In Italy, Renaissance art and architecture imitated classical models, utilized classical forms, developed classical themes, and were guided by classical principles and feeling. In countries beyond the Alps, Late Gothic art and architecture continued to evolve the techniques, styles, and subjects developed in the High Middle Ages. In some instances, as in painting, both streams borrowed elements from each other, so that a blending and fusion of Late Gothic and Italian Renaissance components occurred, although the latter eventually prevailed.

Italy was the birthplace of a classical revival in the arts as well as of one in literature and literary learning. Italian Renaissance art shared the *Italian Renais-* (*continued*) *sance art: general features*

general features of Italian Renaissance culture, including classicism, naturalism, realism, and secularism. It also displayed great originality and individualism, a drive for technical perfection and keen esthetic appreciation.

Classicism: Italian Renaissance arts were originally inspired, at least in part, by antique classical models. The influence was more direct in sculpture and architecture, less so in painting. Renaissance artists and architects depicted classical as well as Christian subjects, traditions, and history, employed classical elements and norms, and were strongly influenced by the classical spirit. Nevertheless, the classical aspects of Italian Renaissance arts should not be exaggerated. They were not slavishly imitative; and classical influences were often minimal, sometimes only ideological. Renaissance arts developed along independent lines as time progressed.

Naturalism and Realism: Renaissance artists strove to attain closer conformity to nature and sought to represent things as they actually appeared to the human eye and mind. They studied anatomy and the laws of perspective and accurately depicted such aspects of scenes as light and shadow, and the distant dimming of outlines and dulling of colors. They used living human models and depicted actual objects of nature, such as trees, flowers, and shrubs. And they brought their colors into closer conformity with the various hues found in nature.

Secularism and Laicism: Partly as a result of the foregoing, as well as a more secular outlook and increasing lay patronage, art became more worldly and human in its subject matter, presentation, and spirit. Representation of contemporary and historical events and portraits and landscapes of an entirely secular nature increased. Even sacred and religious figures were presented in the form of existing personages amid contemporary surroundings. Nudes and semi-nudes, both male and female, were increasingly represented.

Originality and Individualism: Art specialists today can determine the authorship and origin of Renaissance paintings and sculptures by their distinctive features. Renaissance artists took a pride in developing their own individual method and style in quest of reputation and fame as well as out of a love of art.

Perfectionism and Art for the Sake of Art: A final feature of Renaissance art was its consuming drive for technical perfection and intense esthetic spirit, which often looked no further than the production of a beautiful art object, in the spirit of *Ars gratia artis:* "Art for the sake of art."

Productivity and schools

During the Renaissance there was a phenomenal production of works of art in Italy—partly as a consequence of the leadership of great masters, partly to satisfy keen Italian artistic appreciation, and partly as a contemporary fad or fashion. Numerous paintings and works of sculpture were produced, as several "schools" developed in different localities. Special styles were cultivated by certain masters and were continued and elaborated by their disciples, as in the case of the Florentine, Pisan, Sienese, Umbrian, and Venetian schools. These schools influenced one another, as also did the various arts, especially since the same artists were often skilled in several fields.

Particularly in painting the Renaissance was "the Age of the Masters" in art history. Italian painting exemplified with special fullness the general characteristics of Renaissance art, such as greater secularism, interest in man in the present world, individualism, and originality. Although few examples of ancient painting survived, classical influences were exerted upon painting through sculpture, classical literature, and observance of classical norms, such as restraint, harmony, and suavity. Italian Renaissance painting achieved greatly enhanced naturalism and realism through improved mastery of spatial representation, perspective, *chiaroscuro* (light and shadow), dimming of color in the distance, subtle shades of color, and anatomy. It also developed or utilized improved materials, such as pigments, solvents for colors (such as oils), and forms of supporting surfaces (such as canvases). Much of our knowledge about Italian artists comes from their masterpieces; much also from their *Lives* as related by Giorgio Vasari in the mid-sixteenth century.

Italian painting

Prior to the fourteenth century, Italian art, according to Vasari, was dominated by the "Byzantine manner," which was formal, conventional, and symbolic rather than free, natural, and realistic. In the later thirteenth century, however, Cavallini, Duccio, and Cimabue began to display classical qualities and depart from the Byzantine manner by making their pictures more naturalistic, suave, and appealing. Cimabue's gifted pupil Giotto di Bondone (d. 1336) made a distinct break with the Byzantine way of painting. Of him Vasari says: *The gratitude which painters owe to Nature, which is ever their best model, is due to Florence's painter Giotto, seeing that he alone succeeded in resuscitating art and restoring it to that path which alone can be called the true one.* Giotto made great progress in naturalistic representation, dramatic storytelling, and balanced composition. He depicted human emotions and provided his scenes with a natural background. At the same time his paintings have an extraordinary attractiveness and beauty. His masterpieces include famous frescoes depicting the *Life of St. Francis* in the Basilica of St. Francis at Assisi and the *Life of Christ Together with His Mother Mary* in the Arena Chapel at Padua.

A new phase of Renaissance painting was initiated a century later by Masaccio (d. 1428). His real name was Guidi, but he was known as "Masaccio" or "Lubbery Tom" because of his careless or sloppy personal habits. "Tom" had a very brief career—he apparently died at the age of twenty-six or twenty-seven after having fled from Florence to Rome, possibly because of his debts. Masaccio greatly advanced naturalism and realism by his much improved perspective, anatomy, psychology, groupings, and narrative genius. Among his remarkable works that became models for his successors were *The Expulsion of Adam and Eve from the Garden*, wherein Eve appears crushed by shame, and *The Tribute Money*, in which Christ is shown paying the required tax to the collectors.

The Dominican Fra Angelico (d. 1455) is famous for his delicate, devout religious paintings, such as his *Annunciations*, his *Assumption of* the Virgin, and his Deposition from the Cross. The paintings of Fra Angelico, whose favorite subject was the Virgin Mary, have been characterized as having "spirit without perspective." Those of his contemporary, Paolo Ucello (d. 1475), the "bird man," who delighted in secular subjects, have been characterized as having "perspective without spirit." Ucello's works are well exemplified by his *Battle Scenes*.

Sandro Botticelli (d. 1510) combined classical and naturalistic trends in painting to achieve a delicate idealization of nature. Although Botticelli depicts many female nudes, these have a gentle dignity and artistic detachment that disarms sensuality, as in his *Birth of Venus*, wherein the unclothed goddess is emerging from a seashell on the shore of the sea. Similarly devoid of lewdness and crudity is his *Primavera (Spring)*: a complex picture including five unattired females, a nude cupid, and two partly attired males, in addition to over thirty species of plant life.

The earliest masters of an emerging rich and colorful Venetian style were the Bellinis: Jacobo (d. 1470) and his sons Gentile (d. 1507) and Giovanni (d. 1516). In addition to numerous Madonnas, the Bellinis painted scenes from the story of Venice and several noted portraits, such as those of the Turkish *Sultan Mahomet* II by Gentile and the Venetian *Doge Loredano* by Giovanni.

Leonardo da Vinci (1452–1519) ushered in the so-called High Renaissance with its Grand Manner, characterized by idealism, intellectualism, and technical perfection. Among the geniuses of the High Renaissance, Leonardo da Vinci was one of the most versatile: an engineer and scientist, inventor and artist. Although his paintings are limited in number, they are of the highest order and conspicuous for their mastery of anatomy and psychology, composition, and technical competence. They include his famous *Last Supper*, depicting Christ foretelling his betrayal, the contrast-filled *Virgin of the Rocks*, and the enigmatic *Mona Lisa*. In his *Treatise on Painting*, Leonardo urges attention to nature and observes that it is the work of the artist to express inward spirit as well as outward form. Subsequent masters of the High Renaissance in painting, such as Raphael and Michelangelo, belong to the sixteenth century.

Italian Renaissance sculpture

Italian sculpture predated painting in its "release from the medieval manner." Among initiators of the Italian Renaissance in sculpture were a school of Pisan sculptors of the late thirteenth and early fourteenth centuries known as "Pisanos." The main works of the Pisanos were bas-reliefs for pulpits, altar fronts, doors, tombs, and the like.

Niccola Pisano (d. 1278) first imitated the figures of classical sarcophagi in his marble pulpits for the Baptistry of Pisa and the Cathedral of Siena, and in his coffin for St. Dominic. His son, Giovanni Pisano (d. ca. 1317), further developed the same style in a modified manner influenced by Gothic sculpturing in his pulpits for the Cathedral of Pisa and St. Andrea at Pistoia. Giovanni's pupil Andrea Pisano (d. 1348) made his sculptured scenes more lifelike by grouping his figures naturally, instead of crowding them together.

The new movement gained full expression with Lorenzo Ghiberti

(d. 1455), who rivaled the naturalism, realism, and narrative power of contemporary painting in his exquisite bronze bas-reliefs. In the competition to determine who was to sculpt the panels of a pair of doors for the Baptistry of the Cathedral of Florence, Ghiberti won with his design for *The Sacrifice of Isaac*. After Ghiberti spent two decades executing the first pair of doors, for which he sculpted a total of twenty-eight panels representing scenes from sacred history, the syndics of Florence commissioned him to execute a second set of doors with a total of ten larger panels, on which he spent a quarter of a century. So superb were the bas-reliefs that Michaelangelo declared that they "would grace the portals of Paradise."

Donatello ("little Donato") (d. 1466) brought Renaissance sculpture to maturity and emancipated it from architecture. After having worked as a goldsmith and served briefly under Ghiberti, Donatello studied ancient sculptures in Rome. He then proceeded to carve several excellent free-standing sculptures in the round, such as his (young) *David, St. George, St. Mark, St. Peter, St. John the Baptist,* and *Il Zuccone* ("Pumpkinhead": old David). His masterpiece was a large, free-standing bronze equestrian statue of the Florentine condottiere *Gattamelata,* which was the first of its kind since antiquity.

Another great fifteenth century sculptor was the versatile Andrea del Verrocchio (d. 1488), who was also a painter and goldsmith. Among Verrocchio's famous works were his *Boy and Dolphin,* representing a trotting boy with a dolphin wriggling in his arms, for the fountain of the Palazzo Vecchio (Old City Hall) at Florence, and his imposing bronze equestrian statue of the fierce *Bartolomeo Colleoni,* forceful *condottiere* of Venice.

Italian Renaissance sculpture reached its culmination in the sixteenth century with the great Michelangelo, whose overshadowing genius was exemplified by his calmly sorrowful *Pieta* (*Lamentation of Christ*), his daring youthful *David,* and his stormy, wrathful *Moses.*

Italian Renaissance architecture closely imitated the forms of classical architecture—its columns, capitals, and entablatures—as well as studied its principles and strove to conform to its proportions. At the same time, it retained much originality, if only because many of its buildings, such as Christian churches and Renaissance town houses, lacked classical models. Filippo Brunelleschi (d. 1446) assiduously studied the remnants and plans of ancient structures at Rome and ushered in Italian Renaissance architecture. On his return to Florence, Brunelleschi entered the competition to design and construct a dome for the unfinished Cathedral of Florence. After some hesitation, the Florentine syndics finally accepted his daring plan for a lofty dome rising from a polygonal base 150 feet wide to a total height of 305 feet above the ground. In addition to this dome, other works by Brunelleschi at Florence, were his Pitti Palace, Pazzi Chapel, and Foundling Hospital façade, all showing a strong classical influence. Born of aristocratic and wealthy parents, Leon Battista Alberti (d. 1472) was a universal genius. Among his notable structures were the Palazzo Strozzi (or Rucellai Palace) and the façade of the Church of

Architecture of the Italian Renaissance

Santa Maria Novella at Florence. Alberti wrote treatises on *Painting*, on *Sculpture*, and on *Architecture*. Donato Bramante (d. 1514), an enthusiastic student of classical architecture, is chiefly noted as the original architect of the great new cathedral of St. Peter's in Rome.

Transalpine arts in the Later Middle Ages

The predominant Transalpine art style in the Later Middle Ages was Late Gothic. Only toward the close of the period did the influence of the Italian Renaissance style begin to make itself clearly and fully felt beyond the Alps. Late Gothic art was inclined to be elaborate, detailed, and dramatic, as well as executed with a high degree of craftsmanship. It was often more secular in its approach, models, and themes than was high medieval art. Its inspiration was medieval French Gothic rather than ancient Roman classical art, and it had more Germanic and Christian elements than did Italian Renaissance art.

As in the case of Italian Renaissance painting and sculpture, there was an increase of naturalism, realism, and secularism in late medieval Transalpine art. The main difference was that whereas the Italian movement was influenced more directly by classical models and conceptions, with the result that it had a more universal and secular aspect; Transalpine art was more detailed, particular, and religious. Eventually in the lands beyond the Alps the two styles blended.

Late Gothic painting: The Van Eycks and others

Within Late Gothic itself there were two trends: "mannerism" and "realism." Late Gothic mannerism, also known as the "international style," tended to suppress the ugly, harsh, and painful, and to emphasize the sweet, beautiful, and pleasing. Its tone was sometimes that of an idealized chivalry, and sometimes one of religious rapture. Late Gothic mannerism, which first developed in connection with miniature painting, was popular to about 1450. It is exemplified by the so-called *Très Riches Heures* (Very Rich Hours) of the Duke of Berry, painted by the Brothers Limbourg to illustrate a *Book of Hours* containing the Divine Office (fifteenth century). These exquisite miniature pictures portray idealized scenes, as in the illustration for "August," wherein richly clad, elongated aristocratic figures ride noble steeds across an idyllic field, with a magnificent castle crowning the background. Gothic mannerism was also exemplified by the sweet and appealing Madonnas of Stephen Lochner of Cologne.

About 1450 Late Gothic mannerism was superseded by Late Gothic realism, which attempted to include every possible detail: the harsh and grotesque along with the lovely and attractive. Late Gothic realism cooperated in establishing the "representative convention," whereby it became an accepted principle that works of art were to be "true to life" and "mirror nature." The great initiators and leaders in the new style for both miniature and large-scale paintings were the Van Eyck brothers, Hubert (d. 1426) and Jan (d 1440). The Van Eyck miniatures known as the *Très Belles Heures* (the *Very Beautiful Hours*), which were eventually scattered to various points such as Milan and Turin, are filled with realistic perspectives and numerous details from everyday life, such as those depicting *The Landing of Duke William of Bavaria* at Vere on a windswept Dutch estuary and the *Baptism of Christ* in the Rhineland

Renaissance and Late Gothic Culture

amid local scenery. The acknowledged masterpiece of the Van Eycks was their *Adoration of the Lamb,* painted for the altarpiece of the Church of St. John's (now St. Bavon's) at Ghent. A triptych, it actually contains some twenty subjects. Its main theme is the mystic Adoration of Christ, whose sacrificial blood saves mankind. The Van Eycks are credited with developing or perfecting oil painting. Their paintings have often been described as "photographic" in their detail, but they have qualities of perception and intuition that transcend photography. Among noted pictures by Jan Van Eyck are his portraits of the merchant *Jan Arnolfini and His Wife* in their bedroom and of *Chancellor Rolin Adoring the Christ-Child Held by the Virgin* in a beautiful room overlooking a river.

The so-called Master of Flemalle carried on the Van Eyck tradition as did Roger Van der Weyden, Hugo Van der Goes, and Hans Memling. The work of the Master of Flemalle, coworker of the Van Eycks, is represented by his *Portrait of a Gentleman.* *Successors of the Van Eycks*

The Flemish Roger Van der Weyden (d. 1464), whose strong piety was imbued with the *Devotio Moderna,* painted realistic pictures full of movement and representing emotional elements of the Christian religion, such as *The Descent from the Cross, The Entombment of Christ,* and *The Last Judgment.*

The Adoration of the Shepherds by Hugo Van der Goes (d. 1482) was shipped to Florence, where it became the Portinari Altarpiece and influenced Italian Renaissance art.

Hans Memling (d. 1494), a Hollander who carried imitation of the Van Eycks to a high degree of technical perfection, also showed influences of Italian Renaissance art in such religious paintings as his serene *Marriage of St. Catherine.*

The first independent genius after the Van Eycks was Albrecht Dürer (d. 1528), a many-sided artist who became "the Leonardo da Vinci of Northern art." Dürer, who had visited Italy and was influenced by Italian Renaissance art, introduced features of the latter into Northern art, which became more idealized, epic in concept, and "serene" or "smoothed out." Besides producing excellent paintings, such as his *Jerome Hochschuler* and *Portrait of a Man,* Dürer is particularly famous for his fascinating, spiritually profound etchings, such as *St. Jerome in His Study, St. Anthony Before Nuremberg,* and *Melancholia.*

The somewhat excessive sweetness of Late Gothic mannerism in sculpture is exemplified by the statue of the Virgin known as "Notre Dame de Paris" in the Cathedral of that name, as well as by numerous exquisite little statuettes in gold, silver, and ivory. *Late Gothic sculpture and architecture*

Late Gothic realism in sculpture, on the other hand, is exemplified by the remarkable masterpieces executed by Claus Sluter (d. 1406) at the Carthusian Monastery of Champmol near Dijon, the burial place of the Dukes of Burgundy. The most remarkable of these is the *Well of Moses,* so-called from its most impressive figure. Six extraordinary, realistically carved prophets surround the hexagonal well-head, with overhanging angels at the corners. The anatomy as well as the appearance of the aged Moses is very accurate and true to life.

Late Gothic architecture, which was a continued elaboration of High Gothic architecture, was increasingly used for secular as well as religious edifices. Its various techniques are known as Perpendicular, Rayonnant, Decorated, and Flamboyant. Late Gothic Church architecture strove for dramatic effect as well as originality. An impression of tremendous height was given by concentrated emphasis on vertical lines in the Perpendicular style; dazzling radiance was suggested by numerous emanating lines in the Rayonnant style; and richness and profusion were stressed in the complexities of Decorated Gothic. In England, the Perpendicular, Rayonnant, and Decorative styles, often combined, are exemplified in the late medieval Cathedrals of Bristol, Ely, Lincoln, Exeter, Wells, and Gloucester, as well as in the Chapels of Eton College and King's College, Cambridge.

The intricately elaborated Flamboyant style of Late Gothic architecture in secular buildings is seen in town halls, guild halls, and marketing halls, as well as in occasional private residences in Flanders, northwestern France, and Germany. Among examples are the town halls of Bruges, Brussels, Louvain, Ghent, Middleburg, and Siena, the great Cloth Hall of Ypres, and the guild houses and halls of many Hanseatic towns of northern Germany.

Music in the Later Middle Ages

Music in the Later Middle Ages was dominated by two themes: the further evolution of polyphony toward greater complexity and harmony, and the copious production of complex and variegated forms of popular and secular music. The polyphonic trend was Late Gothic, whereas the popular and secular tendency partook of the nature of the Renaissance. The art of lay composers addressed popular as well as religious music, and lay and secular elements and themes became more prominent in musical production.

In the fourteenth century, polyphonic music developed greater freedom and complexity. Music was composed for a larger number of parts (v.g., four to nine; and even as many as thirty-six parts), time values were shortened, rhythmic patterns became more complicated, and dramatic effects increased.

A form of church music that reached a zenith at this time was the "motet," in which several voices with disconnected movements occur simultaneously.

There was also a notable increase in the composition of secular polyphonic music. Popular music composed in many parts included dance tunes such as "rounds" (rondels, *rondeaux, rondos*) in which the main theme was repeated by several voices after each successive incident or part, and *virelais* and *ballades* (*ballatas*), in which one or two other strains were interpolated between the repetitions. Hunting songs (*chases* or *caccias*) had several parts, successively introduced, which took up and repeated the same melody. Madrigals were polyphonic pastoral lyrics. Certain Italian dance forms, whose nature is suggested by their names, such as *estampitas, trottos,* and *saltarellos,* used human voices in various parts accompanied by musical instruments. Music was immensely popular among all classes of society.

Renaissance and Late Gothic Culture

In the fifteenth century Flemish, Netherlandish, and Burgundian composers rejuvenated polyphonic religious music with fresh inventive vigor and made great strides towards greater harmony by abandoning mechanical and theoretical counterpoint and by composing the various parts together, rather than in succession, giving all a somewhat equal weight. They also abandoned overdramatic contrasts and strove for greater simplicity and unity. Meanwhile secular musical compositions continued to multiply. Folk songs of all sorts spread throughout Europe, and there was considerable interchange of melodies from country to country. Important new musical instruments included the violin (from the old rebec) and the spinet (from the old clavichord).

Culture in the Later Middle Ages was marked by a growing secular content and lay spirit. The more religious, clerical-inspired, God-centered, universal, integrated culture of the High Middle Ages gradually gave way to the more secular, lay-minded, man-centered, diversified, disjunctive culture of modern times. European culture, which had previously drawn its chief inspiration from the supernatural Christian faith as found in the Bible, the Fathers, and Church doctrines, came to be increasingly based on the world of experience as found in nature, classical literature and art, and personal feelings.

Conclusion

EXCELLENT general information on late medieval culture is given by WALLACE K. FERGUSON, *Europe in Transition, 1300–1500* (Boston: Houghton Mifflin, 1962), and by HENRY S. LUCAS, *Renaissance and Reformation*, 2nd ed., (New York: Harper, 1960). Also useful are EUGENIO GARIN, *Italian Humanism: Philosophy and Civic Life in the Renaissance*, tr. Peter Munz (New York: Harper, 1965); GIUSEPPE TOFFANIN, *History of Humanism*, tr. (New York: Las Americas, 1954); and HANS BARON, *The Crisis of the Italian Renaissance* (Princeton, N.J.: Princeton U.P., 1966). Counterbalance is provided by JOHAN HUIZINGA, *The Waning of the Middle Ages* (London: Arnold, 1924), and GEORGE C. SELLERY, *The Renaissance* (Madison: U. of Wis., 1950). Varying estimates of the Renaissance in successive eras are presented by WALLACE K. FERGUSON, *The Renaissance in Historical Thought* (Boston: Houghton Mifflin, 1948).

Concerning humanism in Renaissance Italy, good general treatments include those by JOHN ADDINGTON SYMONDS, *Renaissance in Italy* (1887–1890), 3 vols. (Gloucester, Mass.: Peter Smith, 1967); ROBERTO WEISS, *The Dawn of Humanism in Italy* (New York: Haskell House, 1970); JOHN E. SANDYS, *A History of Classical Scholarship*, 3 vols. (Cambridge: Cambridge U.P., 1903–1908); and PAUL O. KRISTELLER, *The Classics and Renaissance Thought* (Cambridge, Mass.: Harvard U.P., 1955). A good introduction is JOHN H. WHITFIELD, *Petrarch and the Renaissance* (Oxford: Oxford U.P., 1943). A useful collection is MERRICK WHITCOMB, *A Literary Source Book of the Italian Renaissance* (Philadelphia: U. of Pa., 1903). Concerning archeological activities, see ROBERTO WEISS, *The Renaissance Discovery of Classical Antiquity* (New York: Humanities, 1969). Transitional Dante Alighieri is the subject of many works, including JEFFERSON B. FLETCHER, *Dante* (New York: Holt, 1916); EDMUND G. GARDNER, *Dante* (New York: Dutton, ca. 1923); and THOMAS G. BERGIN, *Dante* (Boston: Houghton, 1969). Petrarch is the subject of EDWARD H. TATHAM's *Fran-*

References for Chapter 30

cesco Petrarca (London: Macmillan, 2 vols., 1925, 1926); selections from his correspondence are edited by JAMES H. ROBINSON and H. W. ROLFE in Petrarch, the First Modern Scholar and Man of Letters . . . (New York: Putnam's, 1914). On Coluccio Salutati see BERTHOLD L. ULLMAN, The Humanism of Coluccio Salutati (Padua: Editrice Antenore, 1963), and on Poggio Bracciolini, the Rev. WILLIAM SHEPHERD, The Life of Poggio Bracciolini (London: Longman, 1837) and BERTHOLD L. ULLMAN, The Origin and Development of Humanistic Script (Roma: Edizioni di Storia e Letteratura, 1960). The Medici rulers of Florence and patrons of the Renaissance are treated in FERDINAND SCHEVILL, The Medicis (New York: Harcourt, 1949), and SELWYN BRINTON, The Golden Age of the Medici . . . 1434–1494 (Boston: Small, Maynard, 1925). Italian education and educational theory are surveyed, with translated readings of leading treatises, by WILLIAM H. WOODWARD, Vittorino da Feltre and Other Humanist Educators (Cambridge: Cambridge U.P., 1905). BALDASSARE CASTIGLIONE's Courtier (1520), available in various translations, reflects educational ideals of the Renaissance. Good histories of Italian vernacular literature are FRANCESCO DE SANCTIS, History of Italian Literature, tr., 2 vols. (New York: Harcourt, 1931), and ERNEST H. WILKINS, History of Italian Literature (Cambridge, Mass.: Harvard U.P., 1954).

Transalpine humanism and literature are treated in MARGARET M. PHILLIPS, Erasmus and the Northern Renaissance (New York: Macmillan, 1950); ROBERTO WEISS, The Spread of Italian Humanism (London: Hutchinson, 1964); PERCY S. ALLEN, The Age of Erasmus (Oxford: Oxford U.P., 1914); and GIUSEPPE TOFFANIN, History of Humanism, tr. (New York: Las Americas, 1954). Selections are presented by HAROLD H. BLANCHARD, ed., Prose and Poetry Translation . . . (New York: Longmans, 1949), and MERRICK WHITCOMB, A Literary Source Book of the Continental Renaissance in Renaissance (Philadelphia: U. of Pa., 1903). Specialized aspects are surveyed by ALBERT HYMA, The Christian Renaissance . . . (Grand Rapids: Reformed Press, 1924), and WILLIAM H. WOODWARD, Studies in Education During the Age of the Renaissance (Cambridge: Cambridge U.P., 1906).

The coming of the Renaissance to England is the subject of LEWIS EINSTEIN, The Italian Renaissance in England (New York: Columbia U.P., 1913); LEONARD ELLIOTT-BINNS, England and the New Learning (London: Religious Tract, 1937); and ROBERTO WEISS, Humanism in England During the Fifteenth Century (Oxford: Blackwell, 1941). The advent of the Renaissance in France is the subject of ARTHUR A. TILLEY, The Dawn of the French Renaissance (Cambridge: Cambridge U.P., 1918), and The French Renaissance (New York: Macmillan, 1919). Burgundian culture is touched on in A. CARTELLIERI, The Court of Burgundy, tr. (New York: Knopf, 1929).

For Renaissance art, in addition to already listed general histories of art, a principal source is still GIORGIO VASARI, Lives of the Most Eminent Painters, Sculptors, and Architects, written in the sixteenth century and available in many editions. Italian art is treated by HEINRICH WÖLFFLIN, Classic Art: An Introduction to the Italian Renaissance, tr. P. and L. Murray (London: Phaidon, 1959); Transalpine art by OTTO BENESCH, The Art of the Renaissance in Northern Europe . . . (Cambridge, Mass.: Harvard U.P., 1945).

For painting, a good general work is PADRIAC GREGORY, When Painting Was in Glory, 1280–1580 (Milwaukee: Bruce, 1941). On Italian painting, BERNHARD BERENSON's authoritative *Italian Painters of the Renaissance* (Oxford: Clarendon, rev. ed., 1930) is the sequel to his works on Florentine, Venetian, northern Italian, and central Italian painters of the Renaissance (published 1900–1907). A good earlier work is FRANK J. MATHER, *A History of Italian Painting* (New York: Holt, 1923); two more recent ones are LIONELLO VENTURI and R. SKIRA-VENTURI, *Italian Painting: The Creators of the Renaissance*, ed. A. SKIRA (Geneva: A. Skira, 1950), and *Painting: The Renaissance* (Geneva: A. Skira, 1951). Transalpine painting is treated by ERWIN PANOVSKY, *Early Netherlandish Painting: Its Origin and Character*, 2 vols. (Cambridge, Mass.: Harvard U.P., 1953); ALFRED STANGE, *German Painting: XIV–XVI Centuries*, ed. A. GLOECKNER (New York: Macmillan, 1950); and FRANK J. MATHER, *Western European Painting of the Renaissance* (New York: Holt, 1939).

In the field of sculpture and architecture, good works on Italian sculpture are ERIC R. D. MACLAGAN, *Italian Sculpture of the Renaissance* (Cambridge, Mass.: Harvard U.P., 1935); JAMES POPE-HENNESSEY, *Italian Renaissance Sculpture* (New York: Phaidon, 1958); and DAVID A. CRAWFORD (D. A. Balcarres), *Evolution of Italian Sculpture* (London: J. Murray, 1909). Good works on Renaissance architecture are WILLIAM J. ANDERSON, *The Architecture of the Renaissance in Italy*, 5th ed. (New York: Scribners, 1927); CHARLES H. MOORE, *Character of Renaissance Architecture* (New York: Macmillan, 1905); and RUDOLF WITTKOWER, *Architectural Principles in the Age of Humanism*, 2nd ed. (London: A. Tiranti, 1952).

For Renaissance music, in addition to general works already cited, consult HARRY E. WOOLRIDGE, *The Polyphonic Period . . . 1300–1600*, 2 vols. (Oxford: Clarendon, 1901–1905); GUSTAVE REESE, *Music in the Renaissance* (New York: Norton, 1954); and *The New Oxford History of Music*, vol. III: *Ars Nova and the Renaissance* (Oxford: Oxford U.P., 1954–1960).

Late medieval philosophy is treated in general works such as those of FREDERICK C. COPLESTON, MAURICE DE WULF, ETIENNE GILSON, and PAUL VIGNAUX. More specialized treatments are ERNST CASSIRER *et al.*, *Renaissance Philosophy of Man* (Chicago: Chicago U.P., 1948); NESCA A. ROBB, *Neoplatonism of the Italian Renaissance* (London: Allen and Unwin, 1935); and PAUL O. KRISTELLER, *The Philosophy of Marsilio Ficino* (New York: Columbia U.P., 1934), and *Eight Philosophers of the Italian Renaissance* (Stanford: Stanford U.P., 1964).

Works on political theory include JOHN N. FIGGIS, *Studies in Political Thought from Gerson to Grotius, 1414–1625*, 2nd ed. (Cambridge: Cambridge U.P., 1935); FOSSEY J. HEARNSHAW, *The Social and Political Ideas of Some Great Thinkers of the Renaissance and the Reformation* (New York: Barnes, 1949); and PAUL E. SIGMUND, *Nicholas of Cusa* (Cambridge, Mass.: Harvard U.P., 1963).

For the history of science, in addition to already cited general histories by GEORGE SARTON and LYNN THORNDIKE, see HERBERT BUTTERFIELD, *The Origins of Modern Science: 1300–1800* (New York: Macmillan, 1951), and ALISTAIR C. CROMBIE, *Augustine to Galileo: The History of Science, 400–1650* (London: Falcon, 1952). For geography, see CHARLES R. BEAZLEY, *The Dawn of Modern Geography*, 3 vols. (New York: Smith, 1949).

Of the enormous literature on the invention of printing, only one nineteenth-century work remains of any value, THEODORE L. DE VINNE's seminal *The Invention of Printing* (New York: Hart, 1876). The significant modern literature in English consists of the following works: OTTO W. FUHRMANN, "The Invention of

Printing," in *A History of the Printed Book* (*The Dolphin*, No. 3), ed. LAWRENCE C. WROTH (New York: The Limited Editions Club, 1938) and his *Gutenberg and the Strasbourg Documents of 1439* (New York: Press of the Woolly Whale, 1940); DOUGLAS C. MCMURTRIE, *The Gutenberg Documents* (New York, 1941); HELLMUT LEHMANN-HAUPT, *Peter Schoeffer of Gernsheim and Mainz* (Rochester, N.Y.: Leo Hart, 1950); VICTOR SCHOLDERER, *Johann Gutenberg, The Inventor of Printing* (London: British Museum, 1963); and ALLAN STEVENSON, *The Problem of the Missale speciale* (London: The Bibliographical Society, 1967).

EPILOGUE.

HE MIDDLE AGES were a dynamic, formative era in Western history. The vigorous national states of Europe arose in this period, which saw the development of Western political institutions and traditions. From the Middle Ages come the concepts that government is limited by the will of the people as well as by that of God, and that a divinely instituted natural law bestows on all persons certain inalienable rights. From the Middle Ages also derive detailed specific charters of human liberties that have been reiterated and refined in modern bills of rights.

The Middle Ages begot representative national assemblies (Parliaments, Estates, Diets, *Cortes*), which participated in legislation and in the formulation of national policies and were forerunners of modern democratic legislatures. National systems of law and justice, liberally imbued with conclusions of natural reason as well as with principles of Roman law, evolved in this period. The administration of justice was improved by requirements of due process and by the right of appeal, as well as by the use of sworn juries of fellow citizens.

Meanwhile there was an extraordinary development of Western military and naval proficiency. Europe's overseas expansion began with the Crusades and the occupation of various islands and coastal bases in the Mediterranean and Black Seas, followed by settlements on islands in the adjacent Atlantic and along the western coast of Africa. Before the close of the Middle Ages, European navigators had sailed around the southern tip of Africa to India, and across the Atlantic to America.

The Commercial Revolution began in the Middle Ages with a great expansion of large-scale international trade, accompanied by rapid growth of capitalism and credit. Beginnings of the later Industrial Revolution may be discerned in large-scale capitalistic production in some industries, often employing labor-saving mechanisms, including water-, wind-, and animal-propelled machinery. Extensive new areas of Europe were subjected to cultivation, and agricultural techniques were improved. Modern urbanization was foreshadowed by a prolific growth and expansion of towns. A dynamic middle class unionized in communes and hanses as well as merchant and craft guilds to enhance its effectiveness. Widespread emancipation of the working classes anticipated modern democratic free-

Renaissance and Late Gothic Culture

dom and equality. Medieval chivalry foreshadowed the modern code of the gentleman.

The Catholic Church attained maturity in its organization and doctrines. The Papacy exercised leadership in the Western Church, which was also guided by highly developed systems of dogmatic and moral theology and regulated by complex compilations of canon law. Vigorous religious orders promoted piety, and the institutions and ideals of European society were more fully Christianized. New religious theories and movements anticipated both the Protestant Reformation and the Catholic Counter-Reformation of the sixteenth century. Meanwhile the Greek or Eastern Orthodox Church, which converted and incorporated, uplifted and civilized the southern and eastern Slavs, broke off from the Western Church. And Islam became a great religious and cultural as well as a partly political and economic community, which won many former Christian territories in the Near East and North Africa.

Important gains were made in culture. Education was promoted by close institutional association with the Church, which sponsored learning and conducted many monastic and cathedral schools, as well as contributed patronage and personnel to new institutions of higher learning. Universities arose as corporate unions to emancipate, improve, and standardize training for the learned professions and promote advanced knowledge, as well as obtain privileges for professors and students. Philosophy and natural sciences were revived and coordinated with religious faith. The classical literatures of Greece and Rome were copied, treasured, studied, and imitated, while the various national vernacular literatures arose and begot their first classics. Masterpieces of Romanesque, Gothic, and Renaissance architecture and art that still excite admiration and wonder were produced. The progress of music was promoted by the development of musical notation, a proliferation of musical instruments, and composition of complex polyphonic works. ❡ Much of the essential foundation and framework of Western civilization was established during the formative Middle Ages.

APPENDIX. MEDIEVAL POPES AND RULERS OF MAJOR STATES.

I. MEDIEVAL POPES

(Antipopes are shown in italics. Names followed by an asterisk are those of popes of the Avignon line after the Great Schism of 1378.)

314–335	Sylvester I	684–685	Benedict II
336	Mark	685–686	John V
337–352	Julius I	686–687	Conon
352–366	Liberius	687–710	Sergius I
355–365	*Felix II*	701–705	John VI
366–384	Damasus I	705–707	John VII
384–399	Siricius	708	Sisinnius
399–401	Anastasius I	708–715	Constantine
401–417	Innocent I	715–731	Gregory II
417–418	Zosimus	731–741	Gregory III
418–422	Boniface I	741–752	Zacharias
422–432	Celestine I	752–757	Stephen II
432–440	Sixtus III	757–767	Paul I
440–461	Leo I the Great	767–768	*Constantine*
461–468	Hilary	768	*Philip*
468–483	Simplicius	768–772	Stephen III
483–492	Felix III	772–795	Adrian I
492–496	Gelasius I	795–816	Leo III
496–498	Anastasius II	816–817	Stephen IV
498–514	Symmachus	817–824	Paschal I
514–523	Hormisdas	824–827	Eugenius II
523–526	John I	827	Valentine
526–530	Felix IV	827–844	Gregory IV
530–532	Boniface II	844	*John VIII*
533–535	John II	844–847	Sergius II
535–536	Agapitus I	847–855	Leo IV
536–537	Silverius	855–858	Benedict III
537–555	Vigilius	858–867	Nicholas I the Great
555–561	Pelagius I		
561–574	John III	867–872	Adrian II
575–579	Benedict I	872–882	John VIII
579–590	Pelagius II	882–884	Marinus I
590–604	Gregory I the Great	884–885	Adrian III
604–606	Sabinianus	885–891	Stephen V
607	Boniface III	891–896	Formosus
608–615	Boniface IV	896	Boniface VI
615–618	Deusdedit	896–897	Stephen VI
619–625	Boniface V	897	Romanus, Theodore II
625–638	Honorius I		
640	Severinus	898–900	John IX
640–642	John IV	900–903	Benedict IV
642–649	Theodore I	903	Leo V
649–655	Martin I	903–904	*Christopher*
654–657	Eugenius I	904–911	Sergius III
657–672	Vitalian	911–913	Anastasius III
672–676	Adeodatus	913–914	Lando
676–678	Donus	914–928	John X
678–681	Agatho	928	Leo VI
682–683	Leo II	928–931	Stephen VII

Appendix

931–935	John XI	1154–1159	Adrian IV
936–939	Leo VII	1159–1181	Alexander III
939–942	Stephen VIII	1159–1164	*Victor IV*
942–946	Marinus II	1164–1168	*Paschal III*
946–955	Agapitus II	1168–1178	*Calixtus III*
955–964	John XII	1179–1180	*Innocent III*
963–965	Leo VIII	1181–1185	Lucius III
964–966	Benedict V	1185–1187	Urban III
965–972	John XIII	1187	Gregory VIII
973–974	Benedict VI	1187–1191	Clement III
974	*Boniface VII*	1191–1198	Celestine III
974–983	Benedict VII	1198–1216	Innocent III
983–984	John XIV	1216–1227	Honorius III
984–985	*Boniface VII*	1227–1241	Gregory IX
985–996	John XV	1241	Celestine IV
996–999	Gregory V	1243–1254	Innocent IV
997–998	*John XVI*	1254–1261	Alexander IV
999–1003	Sylvester II	1261–1264	Urban IV
1003	John XVII	1265–1268	Clement IV
1004–1009	John XVIII	1271–1276	Gregory X
1009–1012	Sergius IV	1276	Innocent V
1012–1024	Benedict VIII	1276	Adrian V
1012	*Gregory VI*	1276–1277	John XXI
1024–1032	John XIX	1277–1280	Nicholas III
1032–1044	Benedict IX (resigned)	1281–1285	Martin IV
		1285–1287	Honorius IV
1045	Sylvester III	1288–1292	Nicholas IV
1045	Benedict IX (deposed)	1294	Celestine V
		1294–1303	Boniface VIII
1045–1046	Gregory VI	1303–1304	Benedict XI
1046–1047	Clement II	1305–1314	Clement V
1047–1048	Benedict IX	1316–1334	John XXII
1048	Damasus II	1328–1330	*Nicholas V*
1049–1054	Leo IX	1334–1342	Benedict XII
1055–1057	Victor II	1342–1352	Clement VI
1057–1058	Stephen IX	1352–1362	Innocent VI
1058–1059	*Benedict X*	1362–1370	Urban V
1059–1061	Nicholas II	1370–1378	Gregory XI
1061–1073	Alexander II	1378–1389	Urban VI
1061–1064	*Honorius II*	1378–1394	Clement VII*
1073–1085	Gregory VII	1389–1404	Boniface IX
1080–1100	*Clement III*	1394–1423	Benedict XIII*
1086–1087	Victor III	1404–1406	Innocent VII
1088–1099	Urban II	1406–1415	Gregory XII
1099–1118	Paschal II	1409–1410	*Alexander V*
1100	*Theodoric*	1410–1415	*John XXIII*
1102	*Albert*	1417–1431	Martin V
1105–1111	*Sylvester IV*	1423–1429	*Clement VIII**
1118–1119	Gelasius II	1425–1430	*Benedict XIV**
1118–1121	*Gregory VIII*	1431–1447	Eugenius IV
1119–1124	Calixtus II	1439–1449	*Felix V*
1124–1130	Honorius II	1447–1455	Nicholas V
1130–1143	Innocent II	1455–1458	Calixtus III
1130–1138	*Anacletus II*	1458–1464	Pius II
1143–1144	Celestine II	1464–1471	Paul II
1144–1145	Lucius II	1471–1484	Sixtus IV
1145–1153	Eugenius III	1484–1492	Innocent VIII
1153–1154	Anastasius IV	1492–1503	Alexander VI

Appendix

II. RULERS OF FRANKLAND
(613–987)

The Carolingians (613/687–911/987)

As Mayors of the Palace

Pepin I of Landen (613–629)
Ansegis (Ansegisel) (632–638)
Pepin I of Landen (639–640)
Grimoald (643–656)
Pepin II of Heristal (678/687–714)
Charles Martel (717–741)
Pepin III, the Short (741/747–751)
 (King 751–768)

As Monarchs

Pepin I, King of the Franks (751–768)
 (Formerly Mayor Pepin III)
Charlemagne and Carloman (768–771)
Charlemagne alone (771–814; Emperor 800–814).
Louis I, the Pious (Emperor 814–840)

WEST FRANKLAND (France)

Charles I, the Bald* (840–877)
Louis II (877–879)
Louis III (879–882) and
Carloman (879–884)
Charles II, the Fat (884–887)
[Odo (Eudes) (888–898)] (A Robertian)
Charles III, the Simple (898–922)
[Robert of Neustria (922–923)] (A Robertian)
[Ralph of Burgundy (923–936)] (A Robertian)
Louis IV (936–954)
Lothair (954–986)
Louis V (986–987)
 Last Carolingian king of West Frankland; succeeded by Hugh Capet

MIDDLE KINGDOM (Italy, Burgundy, Lotharingia)

Lothair* (840–855)
Burgundy
Charles (855–863)
Lotharingia
Lothair II (855–869)
Italy
Louis II* (855–875)
Charles the Bald* (875–877)
Charles the Fat* (877–887)

*Crowned Emperor

EAST FRANKLAND (Germany)

Louis II, the German (840–876)
Carlmann (876–880) and
Louis (876–880) and
Charles II, the Fat* (876/880–882/884–887), who reunited the Empire (884–887)
Arnulf* (887–899)
Louis the Child (899–911)
 Last Carolingian king of East Frankland; succeeded by Conrad of Franconia
Conrad of Franconia (911–918)

Appendix

III. WESTERN KINGS AND EMPERORS OF GERMANY (919–1519)

Saxon Kings of East Frankland (919–973)
Henry I, the Fowler (919–936)
Otto I, the Great (936–973)

Saxon Emperors (968–1024)
Otto I, the Great (962–973)
  (Formerly merely King 936–962)
Otto II (973–983)
Otto III (983–1002)
Henry II, the Saint (1002–1024)

Franconian Emperors (1024–1125)
Conrad II, the Salian (1024–1039)
Henry III, the Black (1039–1056)
Henry IV (1056–1106)
Henry V (1106–1125)

Saxon Emperor (1125–1137)
Lothair II (III) (1125–1137)

Hohenstaufen Emperors (1138–1254)
Conrad III (1138–1152)
Frederick I, Barbarossa (1152–1190)
Henry VI (1190–1197)
Philip of Suabia–Hohenstaufen (1198–1208; not crowned) } Rivals
Otto IV, of Brunswick–Welf (1198–1215)
Frederick II (1211/1215–1250)
  Rival of Otto IV, 1211–1215; also King of Sicily 1197–1250
Conrad IV (1250–1254; not crowned)

The Great Interregnum in Germany (1254–1273)

Hapsburg, Luxemburg, and Other Emperors (1273–1519)
Rudolph I, of Hapsburg (1273–1291; not crowned)
Adolph I, of Nassau (1292–1298; not crowned)
Albert I, of Austria (Hapsburg) (1298–1308; not crowned)
Henry VII, of Luxemburg (1308–1313)
Louis IV, of Bavaria (1314–1347)
Charles IV, of Luxemburg-Bohemia (1347–1378)
Wenceslaus of Luxemburg (1378–1400; not crowned)
Rupert of Bavaria (1400–1410; not crowned)
Sigismund of Luxemburg (1410–1437)
Albert II, of Austria (Hapsburg) (1438–1439; not crowned)
Frederick III, of Styria (Hapsburg) (1440–1493)
  Last Emperor crowned at Rome.
Maximilian I, of Hapsburg (1493–1519)

IV. RULERS OF ENGLAND
(802–1509)

Anglo-Saxon Rulers (802–1066)

Egbert (802–839)
Ethelwulf (839–858)
Ethelbald (858–860)
Ethelbert (860–866)
Ethelred (866–871)
Alfred the Great (871–899)
Edward the Elder (899–925)
Athelstan (925–939)
Edmund I (939–946)
Edred (946–955)
Edwy (955–959)
Edgar the Peaceful (959–975)
Edward the Martyr (975–979)
Ethelred the Unready (979–1016)
Canute (1016–1035)
  of the Danish House
Harold I (1035–1040)
Hardicanute (1040–1042)
Edward the Confessor (1042–1066)
  of the House of the West Saxons
Harold II (1066)

Anglo-Norman Kings (1066–1154)

William I, the Conqueror (1066–1087)
William II, Rufus (1087–1100)
Henry I (1100–1135)
Stephen (1135–1154)

Angevin Kings (1154–1399)

Henry II (1154–1189)
Richard I (1189–1199)
John (1199–1216)
Henry III (1216–1272)
Edward I (1272–1307)
Edward II (1307–1327)
Edward III (1327–1377)
Richard II (1377–1399)

Lancastrian Kings (1399–1461)

Henry IV (1399–1413)
Henry V (1413–1422)
Henry VI (1422–1461)

Yorkist Kings (1461–1485)

Edward IV (1461–1485)
Edward V (1483)
Richard III (1483–1485)

Tudor Kings (1485–1603)

Henry VII (1485–1509)

V. KINGS OF FRANCE
(987–1515)

Capetian House (987–1328)

Hugh Capet (987–996)
Robert the Pious (996–1031)
Henry I (1031–1060)
Philip I (1060–1108)
Louis VI (1108–1137)
Louis VII (1137–1180)
Philip II, Augustus (1180–1223)
Louis VIII (1223–1226)
Louis IX (1226–1270)
Philip III (1270–1285)
Philip IV (1285–1314)
Louis X (1314–1316)
Philip V (1316–1322)
Charles IV (1322–1328)

House of Valois (1328–1515)

Philip VI (1328–1350)
John (1350–1364)
Charles V (1364–1380)
Charles VI (1380–1422)
Charles VII (1422–1461)
Louis XI (1461–1483)
Charles VIII (1483–1498)
Louis XII (1498–1515)

Appendix

VI. BYZANTINE EMPERORS

Zeno (474–491)
Anastasius I (491–518)
Justin I (518–527)
Justinian I, the Great (527–565)
Justin II (565–578)
Tiberius (578–582)
Maurice (582–602)
Phocas I (602–610)
Heraclius I (610–641)
Constantine III (641)
Heracleon (641)
Constans II (641–668)
Constantine IV (668–685)
Justinian II (685–695)
Leontius II (695–698)
Tiberius III (698–705)
Justinian II (again) (705–711)
Philippicus (711–713)
Anastasius II (713–715)
Theodosium III (715–717)
Leo III (717–741)
Constantine V (741–775)
Leo IV (775–780)
Constantine VI (780–797)
Empress Irene (797–802)
Nicephorus I (802–811)
Stauracius (811)
Michael I (811–813)
Leo V (813–820)
Michael II (820–829)
Theophilus I (829–842)
Michael III (842–867)
Bardas (842–866)
Theophilus II (867)
Basil I (867–886)
Leo VI (886–912)

Alexander III (912–913)
Constantine VII (913–959)
Romanus I (919–944)
Romanus II (959–963)
Basil II (963–1025)
Nicephorus II (963–969)
John I (969–976)
Constantine VIII (1025–1028)
Empress Zoë (1028–1050)
Romanus III (1028–1034)
Michael IV (1034–1041)
Michael V (1041–1042)
Constantine IX (1042–1054)
Empress Theodora (1054–1056)
Michael VI (1056–1057)
Isaac I (1057–1059)
Constantine X (1059–1067)
Andronicus (1067)
Romanus IV (1067–1071)
Michael VII (1071–1078)
Nicephorus III (1078–1081)
Alexius I (1081–1118)
John II (1118–1143)
Manuel I (1143–1180)
Alexius II (1180–1183)
Andronicus I (1182–1185)
Isaac II (1185–1195)
Alexius III (1195–1203)
Isaac II (again) (1203–1204)
Alexius IV (1203–1204)
Alexius V (1204)

Latin Emperors

Baldwin I (1204–1205)
Henry (1205–1216)
Peter de Courtenay (1216–1217)
Robert de Courtenay (1218–1228)
Baldwin II (1228–1261)

Nicaean Emperors

Theodore I (1206–1222)
John Dukas (1222–1254)
Theodore II (1254–1259)
John IV (1258–1261)
Michael VIII Paleologus (1259–1282)

The Paleologi

Andronicus II (1282–1328)
Michael IX (1295–1320)
Andronicus III (1328–1341)
John V (1341–1347)
John VI (1347–1354)
John V (restored) (1335–1376)
Andronicus IV (1376–1379)
John V (restored) (1379–1391)
John VII (1390)
Manuel II (1391–1425)
John VIII (1425–1448)
Constantine XI (1448–1453)

❰ INDEX

A

Aachen (Aix la Chapelle)	173. 174. 279.
Council (808)	183.
Abacus	19–20. 322.
Abbas, -al	149.
Abbasid Caliphs	150–151. 154. 260.
Abbey of the Dunes	353.
Abd-al-Malik	148.
Abd-al-Rahman I	150. 260.
Abd-al-Rahman III	260. 262.
Abd-al-Rahman ibn-Abdullah	168. 170.
Abelard, Peter	486. 494. 497. 501. 506.
Absolute Emperors, Roman	22–24.
Abu al-Abbas	150.
Abu Bakr, caliph	142. 143.
Abulcasis	261.
Abu-Nuwas	158.
Abyssinia	632.
Accolade	223.
Accounting and bookkeeping	553.
Achaia, Principality of	454.
Acre	375. 379.
(1291)	381.
Acre (measure)	239.
Acts of Apostles	35. 39.
Ada School of illumination	336.
Adalberon of Reims, archbishop	257.
Adalbert of Hamburg-Bremen, archbishop	385.
Adalbert of Mainz, archbishop	390.
Adalbert of Reims, archbishop	243.
Adam du Petit Pont	497.
Adam of St. Victor	482. 521.
Adelaide, queen and empress	280. 282.
Adelard of Bath	517.
Adele of Champagne	431.
Adhemar of le Puy, bishop	370.
Adid, al-, caliph	377.
Adolph of Nassau, emperor	598.
Adoptionists	45.
Adoptive (Good) Emperors	12. 20.
Adoration of the Lamb	685.
Adoubement	223.
Adrian IV, Pope	395. 396. 414. 477.
Adrianople (378)	23. 77.
(1205)	455.
(1365)	637.
Advocate	211.
Aegidian Constitutions (1357)	624.
Aegidius, Master of Soldiers	89. 90. 102.
Aegidius of Colonna	513.
see also Egidio.	
Aelbert of York	319.
Aelfric	235.
Aeneid	17.
Aetius	81. 89.
Afghanistan	151. 367. 465. 467.
Afonso I, Enriquez, of Portugal	452. 631.
Afonso III of Portugal	631.
Afonso IV of Portugal	632.
Afonso V of Portugal	629. 632.
Africa	668.
north	96. 120. 123. 146–148. 638.
Portuguese and	632–633.
west	562.
Aghlabids	191.
Agilulf, King of Lombards	98–99.
Agincourt (1415)	574. 577.
Agnes of Meran	433.
Agnes of Poitou, empress	287. 385.
Agricola, Rudolph	674.
Agriculture	
advances	241.
in Anglo-Saxon England	100.
in early Germanic kingdoms	113.
in Early Middle Ages	235–243.
in High Middle Ages	353–354.
in Later Middle Ages	556.
Roman	16.
three-field	238–239. 354.
two-field	16. 238–239.
see also various countries and peoples.	
Ahmad, khan	615.
Aides	591. 594.
Aids, feudal	213. 424.
voluntary	359.
see also Aides.	
Aigues Mortes	381. 437. 446.
Aisha	146.
Aistulf, King of Lombards	99. 171.
Ajnadayn (636)	147.
Ala-al-Din of Khwarizm	465.
Alamut	466.
Alans	78. 89.
Alaric I, King of Visigoths	77. 80. 118.
Alaric II, King of Visigoths	97. 104. 110.
Albania	635. 638.
Albert I (Albrecht) of Austria, emperor	599.
Albert II of Austria, emperor	600. 604. 607.
Albert of Holstein	365.
Albert of Mechlenborg	609.
Albert I of Riga, bishop	366.
Albert the Bear	365. 393. 399.
Alberti, Leon Battista	670. 683.

Index

Albertus Magnus 485. 494. 503. 508–509. 517.
Albigensians 44. 255. 478. 484. 487–488.
  crusade against 434. 435. 478.
Albizzi family 623.
Alboin, King of Lombards 88. 98.
Albornoz, Gil, cardinal 624. 649.
Albuera (1479) 629.
Albuquerque, viceroy 633.
Alcalá, university 676.
Alcantara, military order 451.
Alchemy 159.
Alcuin 182. 183. 185. 310. 319. 322. 324. 325. 328. 331.
Alemanni 89. 104.
Alessandria 397.
Alexander II, Pope 475.
Alexander III, Pope 397–398. 432. 447. 477. 631.
Alexander V, Pope 652.
Alexander VI, Pope 624. 656–657. 661.
Alexander III of Scotland 423.
Alexander of Hales 483. 486. 507.
Alexander Nevsky 366. 468. 614.
Alexander of Neckham 344.
Alexandria (642 and 646) 147.
Alexiad 135.
Alexius I, Comnenus, emperor 368. 370. 453.
Alexius II, emperor 454.
Alexius III, Angelus, emperor 454.
Alexius IV, Angelus, emperor 379–380. 454.
Alexius V, emperor 454.
Alfonso I of Aragon 452.
Alfonso II of Aragon 452.
Alfonso III of Aragon 360. 628.
Alfonso V of Aragon 625.
Alfonso VI of Leon 264. 364. 451. 631.
Alfonso VII of Leon 452. 631.
Alfonso VIII of Castile 364.
Alfonso X of Castile 405. 451. 453. 498. 516. 535. 626.
Alfonso V, the Magnanimous, of Naples 625. 629.
Alfonso de la Cerda, Don 626.
Alfred the Great 101. 196. 265–267. 272. 323. 325. 330.
Algebra 160.
Algeciras 627.
Algeria 638.
Ali, caliph 142. 145. 146. 148.
Alids 148.
Aljubarotta (1385) 632.
Allah 143–144.
Allods 210. 236. 276.
Almaric of Bena 488.
Almaricians 488.
Almeida, viceroy 633.
Almohades (Muwahhids) 450. 478.
Almoravides (Murabits) 264. 450. 631.
Alp Arslan 367.
Alpert 332.
Alphabet, Cyrillic (Glagolitic) 287–288.
Alphonse of Poitiers 435. 437.
Alphonso (Spanish), see Alfonso;
  (Portuguese), see Afonso.
Alps and Alpides 6.
Alsace 275. 598.
Altaic 59.
Alvaro de Luna, constable 627.
Amadis de Gaula 679.
Amalasuntha 98.
Amaury of Jerusalem, king 377.
Amaury of Toulouse 435.
Ambrose of Milan, St. 46–47. 327.
Ambrosian Republic, Milan 621.
Ambrosins 349.
America ("New World") 562. 631.
  Northmen 197.
Amiens 343. 556.
  Cathedral 541.
Ammianus Marcellinus 26. 76.
Amr, general 147.
Anacletus II, Pope 625.
Anagni 650.
  outrage of 1303 440. 646.
Anastasius I, emperor 34. 118–119.
Andalusia (*al-Andalus*) 79. 259. 261.
Andreas Capellanus 227.
Andrei of Suzdal 463.
Andrew II of Hungary 380. 460.
Andrew III of Hungary 461.
Andronicus I, Comnenus 454.
Andronicus II, emperor 634.
Andronicus III, emperor 634.
Andronicus IV, emperor 634.
Angeli 454.
Angelico, Fra 681.
Angevins 411–427. 460. 606–607.
Angilbert of St. Riquier, abbot 184–185. 200. 329.
Angles 91. 100. 271.
Anglia, East 100.
Anglo-Saxon Chronicle 99. 265. 267. 330. 409. 411.
Anglo-Saxon England, see Anglo-Saxons; England.
Anglo-Saxons 95. 99–102.
  see also England.
Angon 113.
Angora (1402) 637.
Angouleme 592.
Anjou, county of 255. 258. 433. 435. 445. 574. 588–589. 592.
Anna Comnena 135.

Index

Annals of Fulda	198.	Architecture	691.
Annals of St. Vaast	189.	Byzantine	122. 136.
Annals of Xanten	189.	Carolingian	186. 334.
Annates	648.	Crusades	382.
Anne of Beaujeau	593.	early Christian	26–27.
Anne of Brittany	593.	in Early Middle Ages	114. 332–334.
Anno of Cologne, archbishop	385.	in England	686.
Annona	15. 21. 24.	in Germanic kingdoms	334.
Ansegis, mayor of palace	167.	Gothic	539–543. 679. 686.
Anselm of Canterbury, St., archbishop, (Anselm of Bec)	391. 409–410. 486. 505–506.	in High Middle Ages	536–542.
		Islamic	161–162.
		Italian Renaissance	679. 683–684.
Anselm of Lucca	473.	Late Gothic	679. 686.
Ansgar (Anschar, Anskar), St.	310. 312. 332.	Proto-Romanesque	334.
		rotunda	333–335.
Antes	293.	Roman	20.
Anthemius of Thralles	120.	Roman basilican	333.
Anthony of Egypt, St.	304–305.	Romanesque	408. 536–539.
Anticlericalism	487.	Slavic	334.
Antioch	370–371. 374. 377. 453–454.	Spanish-Islamic	261.
Antoninus, St.	558. 663.	Archpriest of Hita	679.
Antrustiones	112. 208–209.	Ardouin of Ivrea	284.
Antwerp	552. 554.	Arezzo, university	498.
Apollinarists	45.	Arians and Arianism	23. 32–34. 40. 45. 76. 96–98. 113. 299. 302. 310.
Apologists	46. 49.		
Apostles	31. 34–40.	Ariosto, Lodovico	673.
Apostolic Canons	40.	Aristocracy	208.
Apostolic Constitutions	40–41.	decline	358.
Appeals, in Church justice	644.	in Early Middle Ages	219–229. 238. 244.
Apprentices	348.		
Apse	333.	gradations	219–220.
Apulia	203.	in High Middle Ages	357–359.
Aquitaine	105. 168. 178. 181. 254. 433.	in Italy	567.
Arabia and Arabs	124. 140. 147.	in Later Middle Ages	567. 569.
Arabian (Thousand and One) Nights	150. 159.	living conditions	220–221. 238.
		recreations	358–359.
Arabic		Aristotelianism	643.
alphabet	141.	Aristotle	135. 502–503. 506–507. 659. 677–678.
calligraphy	162.		
language	141. 149.	Arithmetic	18–20. 322.
literature	157.	Arius	45.
numbers	160.	Arles, kingdom	205. 255.
translations to	157.	Armagnac	577. 591.
Aragon		Vs. Burgundy	589–591.
expansion	628.	Armenia	129. 342. 367. 453.
in High Middle Ages	438. 449. 451–452.	Arms and armor	555. 567.
		Army	
in Later Middle Ages	593. 626–631.	feudal	207. 212. 215.
Liberties of	627–628.	French	444. 581. 594.
Sicily	625. 628. 631.	Later Roman	21.
Aramaic	141.	Roman	14–15.
Arcadius, emperor	23. 77. 80.	Arnold of Brescia	395. 487.
Archbishops	36.	Arnolfini of Lucca	559.
Archdeacons	473.	Arnulf of Carinthia, emperor	197. 205. 277.
Arches	537–539.	Arnulf of Metz	167.
pointed	539.	Arnulf of Reims, archbishop	257.
		Arnulfingers of Bavaria	277.

Index

Arpad, Hungarian leader 289.
   line 457. 459–461. 606.
Arras 352.
Arte de Lana 346.
Arte di Calimala 346.
Arthur, King 529.
Arthur of Brittany 416–417. 433.
Arthur Tudor, prince 585.
Arti maggiori 554.
Artillery, gunpowder 594. 630.
Artisans, Chaucer's 565.
Artois 435. 445. 589. 592–593.
Arts 691.
   allegory 542.
   Byzantine 136–137.
   French Gothic 684.
   Early Christian 26–27.
   in Early Middle Ages 335–336.
   in High Middle Ages 340. 520. 536–544.
      Italian Renaissance 679–680.
      Late Gothic 679. 684–686.
   liberal, *see* Liberal arts.
   "schools" in Renaissance 680.
   symbolism 542.
Artz, Frederick 317.
Arzila 632.
Ascalon (1099) 371.
   (1153) 377.
Ascensius, *see* Badius Ascensius.
Asche, publishing house 676.
Asen family 456.
   Johannitza (Kalojan) 456.
   John I 456.
   John II 456.
   Peter 456.
Ashari, -al 159.
Asia Minor 368. 370. 453. 467.
Askold 294.
Aspar 87. 118.
Assassins 466.
Assemblies 180.
   Frankish 180.
   national 690.
   of notables 180.
Asser, bishop 266. 332.
Assize of Clarendon (1166) 411.
Assizes 411–412.
Astrolabe 160. 344. 553.
Astronomy 18–19. 160. 322.
   Roman 19.
Asturias 263.
Asu 5.
Athanasius of Alexandria, St., archbishop 38. 45–47. 305.
Athaulf 78.
Athens, Duchy of 454. 628–629. 634.
Atrium 333.

Attila 79. 89.
Aucassin and Nicolette 249. 529–530.
Auditores, Papal 472.
Augsburg 352. 552.
Augustales 349.
Augustine of Canterbury, St. 100. 311.
Augustine of Hippo, St. 39. 46–48. 50. 77. 86. 182. 267. 322. 327. 331. 506, 516.
   rule 482.
Augustinian Canons 481–482.
Augustinian Hermits 485.
Augustus Caesar 69.
Aurelian, emperor 21–22.
Aurispa, Giovanni 669.
Ausculta fili (1301) 440. 645.
Austin Canons, *see* Augustinian Canons.
Austin Friars, *see* Augustinian Hermits.
Austrasia 105–107. 165–168.
Austria 176, 275. 280. 365. 394. 596–598. 601. 607.
Authari, King of Lombards 98.
Autocrator 129.
Auvergne 438. 593.
Avars 88. 123–124. 175–176. 293.
Avempace 261.
Avenzoar 261.
Averroes 159–160. 261. 507.
Averroism 509.
Aviçebron 261.
Avicenna 157. 159. 507.
Avignon, Papacy 624. 642. 647–649. 651–653.
Aviz, House of 562.
Ayn Jalut (1260) 381.
Azores 632.

B

Babylon (Egypt) (641) 147.
Bachelor
   academic 499.
   knight 499.
Backgammon 359.
Bacon, Roger 483. 503. 517.
Badius Ascensius 676–677.
Baetica 97.
Bagdad 150. 154. 367. 466.
Bailiffs 221. 247.
Baillis 434. 437. 443. 445.
Baldwin I of Flanders, emperor 380. 454.
Baldwin I of Jerusalem, king 369–371.
Baldwin IV of Jerusalem 378.
Balearics (islands) 192. 364. 452.
Balkans 124. 126–127. 449. 453–457. 596.
   feudalism 219.
   in High Middle Ages 453–457.
   in Later Middle Ages 618. 633–638.
   Slavonization 122. 287. 290.

Ball, John	568. 583.	Becket, Thomas	413–414. 432. 447.
Balliol, college	499.	Bede, Venerable, St.	91. 99. 102. 184.
Ballistae	225. 360.		267. 322. 324. 332.
Baltic Sea	554.	Bedford, Duke of	577. 580. 583.
Balts	59. 366.	*Before There Were Clerics* (1296)	514.
Bamberg	504.	Begga	167.
Banalities	242.	Beggars	566.
Banks and banking	349–350. 557.	Beghards	482. 658.
state	558.	Beguines	482. 658.
Bannockburn (1314)	582.	Bela III of Hungary	460. 466.
Baptism	42. 489.	Belgium	255.
Bar	592.	Belgrade	607.
count of	436.	Belisarius	119–120.
Barbarians	21. 53–73.	Bellini, Gentile	682.
Germanic	25. 59–73. 117. 234.	Bellini, Giovanni	682.
invasions	74–93. 193–198. 244.	Bellini, Jacobo	682.
see also particular groups.		Benedict V, Pope	281.
Barbary States	638.	Benedict XI, Pope	646.
Barbiano	620.	Benedict XII, Pope	649.
Barbosa, Arias	676.	Benedict XIII, Pope	651. 653.
Barcelona	175. 255. 263. 343. 436. 452.	Benedict of Aniane, St.	183. 199. 307–308.
	563.	rule	199.
Usages of	345.	Benedict of Nursia, St.	243. 299.
Bardas, Caesar	133.		305–307. 332.
Bardi	351. 559. 568.	rule	183. 299. 306–307. 481.
Bari (1071)	453.	Benedictine Rule, see Benedict of Nursia.	
Barnet (1471)	585.	Benedictines	480–481.
Barracks Emperors, Roman	21. 22.	see also Brogne; Cistercians; Cluny;	
Bartholomew, Nicholas, of Lucca	559.	Gorze; Monasticism.	
Basel-Ferrara-Florence, see Councils,		*Benedictional* of St. Aethelwold	336.
ecumenical.		Benefices (*beneficia*)	181. 209.
Basil I, the Macedonian, emperor	127.	Beneventum (*Benevento*)	98. 177. 189.
	136. 313.	(1266)	405.
Basil II, emperor	128–129. 293. 456.	dukes	109–110.
Basil of Caesarea, St.	47.	*Beowulf*	60. 330.
rule	47. 50. 304–305.	Berbers	96. 147. 154. 364.
Basileus	129–130.	Berengar I of Friuli, King of Italy	205.
Basilicas		Berengar II of Ivrea, King of Italy	280.
Christian	333–334.	Berengar of Tours	505.
Roman	26–27. 333.	Bergamo	622.
Basilics	130.	Bergen	554. 602.
Bathing, peasant	248.	Bernard of Chartres	494. 502.
Battle of Brunanbarh	330.	Bernard of Clairvaux, St.	377. 480–481.
Battle of the Masts (Dhu al-Sawari)			486. 512. 521.
(655)	124.	Bernard of Italy, king	199.
Batu	465–467.	Bernardino of Siena, St.	663.
Bavaria	168. 175. 181. 275–277. 282.	Bernart de Ventadorn	528.
	365. 399.	Bernelinus	338.
Bayazid I, sultan	635. 637.	Berno, abbot	308.
Bayeux Tapestry	544.	Bernward of Hildesheim, bishop	282–283.
Bayt al-Hikmah, Bagdad	150. 161.	Berry	574. 588–589. 592–593.
Beatrice of Burgundy	394–395.	Berserks	195.
Beatrice of Tuscany	285.	Bertha, daughter of Charlemagne	185.
Beaufort, Cardinal Henry	584.	Bertha of Blois	258.
Beaufort family	577. 584.	Bertha of Holland	258.
Beaumanoir	361. 443.	Bertha of Kent, queen	100. 310–311.
Beauvais, Customary of	217.	Berthar, Mayor of Neustria	168.
Bec	495.	Berthold	481.

Index

Bertrade 258.
Besançon, Diet of (1157) 395.
Bessarion of Nicaea, archbishop 669.
Bezant 131. 234.
Bible 504. 660. 667.
    Complutensian Polyglot 676.
    in Later Middle Ages 663.
    New Testament 674.
    see also Scriptures, Sacred.
Bills of exchange 351. 558.
Billung, Herman 279.
Billung, Magnus 385.
Billungs, Mark 280.
Biondo, Flavio 671.
Bishops 32. 34–36. 45. 50. 112. 234. 473. 490. 662.
    in Germany 279–280. 284.
    of Rome 133.
    see also Papacy.
Black Death 550. 561. 563. 566–567. 575. 608. 662–663.
Black Sea 15. 551.
Blacks 566.
Blanche of Castile, queen of France 435.
Blois 255. 258. 432. 438–439.
"Blues and Greens," parties 120.
Bobbio, monastery 305.
Boccaccio, Giovanni 666. 668–669. 672.
Boethius 114. 267. 321–323. 506.
Bogomiles 456. 487.
Bohemia 278. 280. 283–286. 288–289. 313. 365. 395. 457–458. 552. 596–597. 599–600. 603–605. 607. 654. 660.
    Church in 649.
    government 605.
Bohemund of Taranto 369–371.
Boiardo, Matteo 673.
Boleslaus I, the Great, of Poland 289–290.
Boleslaus II of Poland 459.
Boleslaus III, Wrymouth, of Poland 459.
Boleslav I of Bohemia 289. 365.
Boleslav II of Bohemia 289. 365.
Boleslav III of Bohemia 289.
Boleslav (Boleslaus) I of Poland 289–290. 458.
Bolgars, Volga 466.
Bologna 396. 495–496. 518.
    university 496–498.
Bombards (*bombardes*) 569. 594.
Bonaventure, St. 483. 486. 503. 508.
Bondone, Giotto de 681.
Boniface VIII, Pope 427. 440. 441. 473. 514–515. 643–646.
Boniface, St. 170–171. 310. 312. 315.
Boniface of Montferrat 379. 454.
Book of Judgments 111.
Book of Kells 114. 335.
Book of Roger (*Kitab Rujar*) 160.
Bookland 246. 270.
Books 323.
Boon days 241.
Bordars 236. 242. 246.
Borgia, Alexander VI, Pope 624. 656–657. 661.
Borgia, Cesare 624. 657.
Borgia, Lucretia 657.
Borgia, Rodrigo 656.
    see also Alexander VI, Pope.
Boris of Bulgaria, khan 127. 292. 301. 313.
Boroughs (*burgs, bourgs, burghs*) 266. 271. 353.
Bosnia and Bosnians 291. 607. 638.
Boso of Provence 203. 205.
Bosporus 117.
Bosworth Field (1485) 585.
Botany 503.
Botticelli, Sandro 682.
Bourbon 589. 593.
Bourgeoisie 355.
    du roi 447.
    see also Middle class.
Bourges 258.
    see also Pragmatic Sanction.
Bouvines (1214) 401. 418. 434.
Boyars 463.
Brabant 592.
Bracton 344.
Brandenburg 278. 365. 597. 599–600. 604.
Bremen 312. 343.
Brescia 622.
Breslau 495.
Brethren of the Common Life 603. 663. 674. 676.
Brethren of the Free Spirit 658. 663.
Bretigny, Treaty (1360) 576. 582.
Bretislav I of Bohemia 289.
Breviary of Alaric (II) 97. 110.
Bridge Building Brothers 482.
Bridget of Sweden, St. 648–649. 663.
Brienne, Walter de 622.
Britain
    barbarian invasions 91–92. 99–100.
    Germanic kingdoms 100–102.
    see also England.
Brittany 102. 254. 442. 445. 566. 574–575. 588–589. 593.
Brittany, Duke of 436.
Brogne, monastery 474. 480.
Brothers and Sisters of the Free Spirit 488.
Bruges 343. 352. 552. 554. 564. 602.
Brunelleschi, Filippo 683.
Brunhilda, queen 106. 167.
Bruni, Leonardo 669–671.
Bruno of Cologne 325.

704 Index

Bruno of Toul, bishop 286. 474.
  see also Leo IX, Pope.
Brunswick 399. 554. 602.
Brusa (1326) 636.
Brussels 352.
Bruun, Treaty of (1364) 599.
Bryennius, Nicephorus 135.
Bucellarii 208–209.
Buddhism 467.
Bukhara 149. 155.
Bulgaria and Bulgarians 127. 128. 449. 487.
  Byzantine province 456.
  Church 313–314.
  decline 456.
  in Early Middle Ages 291. 294.
  First Empire 292–293.
  in High Middle Ages 453. 455–456.
  in Later Middle Ages 607. 635–636.
  Second Empire 456.
Bulgars 122. 291–293.
  Turanian 293.
  Volga 291. 293–294.
Bundesrat 180.
Burchard of Suabia, duke 277.
Burchard of Worms 473.
Burckhardt, Jacob 548.
Burgesses 586.
Burgh, Hubert de 419.
Burgos 263.
Burgs (*bourgs, burghs, burhs*) 266. 271. 278. 353.
Burgundian Gate 6.
Burgundians 89–90. 102.
Burgundy 105–106. 168. 205. 280. 285. 287. 392. 442. 445. 574. 588. 591–592.
  county 395.
  duchy 254. 258.
  dukes 258. 577. 589.
  Free County (*Franche Comté*) 601.
  Kingdom 203. 205. 255. 395.
  Upper Kingdom 255.
  Vs. Armagnac 589–590.
Buridan, John 678.
Burma 467.
Buwayhids 151.
Byzantine Empire 12. 15. 46. 116–139. 370. 449. 596.
  Amorian era 125–127.
  Angeli 454–456.
  architecture 333–334.
  army 131.
  art 136–137.
  and Bulgaria 292.
  and Charlemagne 177.
  Church 132–134.
  Church and State 134.
  civilization 116. 123. 129–137.

Byzantine Empire [cont.]
  Comneni 453–455.
  and Crusades 368.
  culture 134–137.
  despotates 633.
  in Early Middle Ages 118–119. 302.
  economy 131. 231.
  and Germanic barbarians 87. 118.
  Golden Ages 119–123. 127–129.
  government 129–130. 132.
  Heraclian era 123–125.
  in High Middle Ages 453–456.
  Iconoclastic era 125–127.
  influence 137. 149.
  Isaurians 118. 125–127.
  and Italy 88–89. 98. 203. 281. 286.
  Justinian Renaissance 119–123. 136.
  landholding 453.
  in Later Middle Ages 618. 633–635.
  Latin Empire of Constantinople 380. 454.
  law 130.
  Macedonian era 127–129. 136. 453.
  navy 131. 634.
  Paleologi 455–456.
  and Russia 615–616.
  and Slavs 287. 291–292.
  and Spain 97.
  survival 117–119.
  "Time of Troubles" 453.
Byzantium 117. 596.

C

Caballero 219. 222.
Cabochienne 591.
Cade, William 352.
Cadzand 573.
Caedmon 330.
Caen
  churches 537.
  (1346) 575.
Caesar, Julius 237.
Caesar Bardas 127. 301.
Caesarius of Arles, St. 305.
Caesaropapism 33–34. 123. 134. 297.
  Byzantine 134.
Cajetan, St. 663.
Calabria 203. 282. 624.
Calais 576. 581.
  (1346–47) 575.
Calatrava, military order 451.
Caliphs and Caliphate 124. 140. 145–151. 153–154.
Calixtus II, Pope 392. 476.
Calligraphy, Arabic 162.
Cambrai (1338) 575.

Index

Cambridge Economic History 341–342. 347. 550.
Cambridge Songs 329.
Cambridge University 498. 499.
Camera Apostolica 472.
Camoldolese monks 481.
Canary Islands 632.
Canonists 477. 510. 512–513.
Canon law, *see* Law, canon.
Canons
    clergy 473.
    regular 481–482.
Canossa (1077) 388. 476.
Cantares de gesta 535.
Canterbury 311.
Canterbury Tales 159. 678.
Cantigas de Santa Maria 451. 536.
Canton 633.
Canute the Great, king 267. 268. 270.
Canute VI of Denmark 432.
Canute of Denmark, St. 461.
Cape Bojador 632.
Cape Branco 632.
Cape of Good Hope 633.
Cape Verde Islands 632.
Capetians 216. 429–449.
    early 257–258.
Capistrano, John, St. 663.
Capitalism and capitalists 352. 559–560. 690.
    in agriculture 556.
    industrial 347. 556.
    in Late Middle Ages 557–560.
Capitularies 181.
Capuchins 484.
Caracalla 21.
Cardinals 314. 472. 475. 642. 644. 662.
    French 649.
Carinthia 277. 282. 598. 601.
Carloman, King of France 204.
Carloman, King of Franks, brother of Charlemagne 174.
Carloman, brother of Pepin III 170.
Carmelites 481.
Carolingian Franks 94. 165–188.
    architecture 186.
    army 182.
    arts 186.
    Charlemagne 172–178.
    church 182–183. 280. 303.
    civilization 178–188.
    disintegration 188–206.
    economy 182.
    Empire 165. 172–178. 201–202.
    enemies 189–198.
    finance 181.
    government 178–182. 189–191.
    history-writing 185.

Carolingian Franks [cont.]
    influence 186.
    later 190–191. 207–208.
    law 181.
    Mayors of Palace 165–171.
    money 235.
    and Northmen 198.
    painting 186.
    poetry 185.
    society 182.
Carolingian Renaissance 178. 322. 324.
Carolingians 165–188. 198–206. 256.
    chart 169.
Carthage 12. 79. 96.
    (698) 148.
Carthusians 481.
Carving 544.
Casimir I of Poland 459.
Casimir III of Poland, the Great 605.
Casimir IV of Poland-Lithuania 606. 615.
Casimir of Mazovia, duke 459.
Caspian Sea 465.
Cassel (1328) 588.
Cassian, John, St. 305.
Cassiodorus 114. 321–324. 331–332.
Castile 263. 358. 449. 450. 451. 452. 552. 561. 589.
    in Later Middle Ages 626–631.
Castillon (1453) 581.
Castles 224–225. 361. 375. 384. 407. 411. 445. 459. 541–542. 567.
    concentric 225.
    motte and bailey 224–225.
Castra 14–15.
Catalan Grand Company 634.
Catalonia 451–452. 568.
Catapults 360.
Cathari 487.
Catherine of Aragon, Queen of England 586. 631.
Catherine of France, Queen of England 577.
Catherine of Siena, St. 648. 649. 663.
Caucasus Mountains 53.
Cavalry 444–445.
Caxton, William 677.
Cazorla, Treaty of (1179) 452.
Celestine V, Pope 644.
Celibacy 41.
Celtes, Conrad 675.
Celtiberians 56.
Celts 54–57. 61. 91. 276.
    and Romans 56.
    "Celtic Fringe" 56.
    in Britain 100.
    "La Tene" culture 55–56.
Censitaires 353. 556.
Centenarii 110. 181.

Cerdagne	593.
Cesarini, Papal legate	655.
Cessatio (strike)	498.
Ceuta (1415)	632.
Chalcedon, *see* Councils, Ecumenical.	
Chalons (451)	79. 81. 89.
Chambre des Comptes	440.
Champagne	255. 431–432. 438–439.
fairs	344. 551.
Chancellor, academic	499.
episcopal	473.
Chansons d'amour	158. 359. 527–528.
Chansons de geste	525–527.
Carolingian cycle	525–527.
Chanson of Antioch	527.
Chanson de Guillaume	221.
Chanson of Jerusalem	527.
Doon de Mayence cycle	527.
Garin de Monglane cycle	527.
The Swan Knight	527.
Chant, plain	299–300. 336.
Charlemagne	99. 171. 173–186. 196. 197. 210. 263. 288. 300. 310. 321. 323–325. 331. 526.
expansion	174–177.
foreign relations	177–178.
and religion	174.
and succession	178.
Charles III, the Fat, emperor	203. 256. 271.
Charles IV, emperor	599. 604.
Charles V, emperor	601. 631.
Charles I of Bohemia, king	604.
Charles II of France, the Bald	190. 197. 199–204. 210. 323.
Charles III of France, the Simple	197. 256. 278.
Charles IV of France	588.
Charles V of France	576. 589. 675.
as regent	588.
Charles VI of France	576–577. 589–590.
Charles VII of France	560. 562. 591.
as Dauphin	577. 580. 591.
Charles VIII of France	593. 619. 623. 625. 675.
Charles I of Hungary	606–607.
Charles Martel	99. 168. 170–171. 182. 209–210. 260.
Charles of Anjou, King of Sicily	381. 405. 437. 455. 479. 625. 628.
Charles of Burgundy	202. 203.
Charles of Lorraine	257.
Charles of Valois	438.
Charles the Bad of Navarre	589.
Charles the Bold of Burgundy	592.
Charles the Good of Flanders	430.

Charters	
Beauvais	356.
Freiburg	356.
Leon	356.
London	356.
Lorris	356. 430. 446.
Louvain	356.
Magna Carta	418–419.
Newcastle-on-Tyne	356.
of rights	360. 450–451.
urban	355–356. 430. 431. 446. 450.
Chartres	495. 502.
cathedral	540.
Chateau Gaillard	415. 433.
Chaucer, Geoffrey	226. 248. 491. 501. 554. 565. 566. 662. 678.
Checks	351.
Chernigov	462.
Chernigov-Severia	615.
Cherson	294.
Chess	358–359.
Chevage	242. 246.
Chevalier	219. 222. 226.
Chiavenna (1176)	397.
Childebert, Frankish king	105.
Childeric, Frankish king	90.
Childeric III, Frankish king	171.
Chilperic of Neustria, king	106.
China	342. 464–467.
Chin Empire	465–466.
Sung Empire	466–467.
Chingiz Khan	464–465.
Chivalry	226–227. 316. 358. 567.
Choniates, Nicetas	136.
Chosroes I	121–122.
Chretien de Troyes	529.
Christ, Jesus	34–39. 44–46. 303. 359. 524.
Christianity	2. 4. 13. 17. 20. 23. 26. 29–52.
Byzantine	132–134.
and culture	26–27. 86.
early doctrines	43–50.
early expansion	32. 71.
and early Germans	71.
early practices	41–43.
evolution of dogma	486.
persecutions	31–32.
in Roman Empire	32–33. 82. 85–86.
and State	33–34.
see also Church.	
Christopher of Bavaria	609.
Chrodegang of Metz, St.	183. 199. 315.
Chronicles and annals, municipal	516.
Chronicle of Amboise	196.
Chronicle of Holstein	516.
Chrysargyrum	24.

Index

Chrysoloras, Manuel 669.
Church 2. 13. 29–52. 95. 111. 661–664. 691.
  abuses 643–645.
  in Anglo-Saxon England 100–101. 268. 271–272. 302.
  in Bohemia 599. 604.
  in Bulgaria 292.
  clergy 490–491. 661–662.
  Conciliarism 642. 644.
  contributions 316–317.
  councils, *see* Councils, church.
  and culture 491–492. 494–496.
  decline 642–656.
  dissent 487–488. 660–661.
  doctrines 486–487.
  early 35–43.
  in Early Middle Ages 94. 244–245. 297–318.
  Eastern 117. 127. 132. 133. 173. 287–295. 305. 313. 368. 691.
  and economy 234–235. 243. 352.
  expansion 100. 309–313. 485.
  and feudalism 226. 227. 303. 313–314.
  in France 447. 594. 644–647.
  in Frankland 104. 168–172. 182. 302–303.
  French ascendance 642–649.
  in Germanic kingdoms 113–114. 302.
  in Germany 284. 310.
  government 34–40. 313–314. 471–479. 643–644. 647–648. 652–653. 655. 657.
  Great Western Schism 642. 649–653.
  in High Middle Ages 471–494.
  in Hungary 290. 313.
  in Iberian Peninsula 450.
  investiture struggle 475–477.
  in Ireland 311.
  laity 314. 491. 663.
  in Later Middle Ages 569–570. 642–666.
  in Low Countries 312.
  reform 368. 386–392. 474–475. 480–481. 491. 511.
  religious orders 662–663.
  in Russia 294–295.
  in Scandinavia 197. 312. 461.
  in Serbia 313.
  and Slavs 287–292.
  in Spain 302. 569. 630.
  taxation 645. 647–648.
  see also Christianity; *particular countries and peoples*.
Church and State 31–34. 113–114. 183. 302–303. 384–406. 454. 471. 474–479. 510. 512–514. 644–647. 661.
  in England 408. 419. 421. 427.

Church and State [cont.]
  in France 257. 431. 433. 437–438. 440–441. 447.
  in Germany 275–277. 278–284. 286.
  in Spain 630.
  theories 510–514.
  in Western Empire 275–277. 284. 286.
Cicero 18. 19. 667. 670.
Ciceronianism 670.
Cid, el 264. 358.
Cimabue 543. 681.
Cimbri and Teutones 69.
Ciompi 568.
  revolt of (1378) 622–623.
Cistercians 480–481. 486.
City of God 49. 77. 331.
Civitates 109.
Clarence of York 585.
Classicism in art 666. 680. 683.
Claudian 75–76. 80.
Clement I, Pope 35–36. 38. 46.
Clement V, Pope 427. 440. 646–647.
Clement VI, Pope 649.
Clement VII, Pope 302. 651.
Clement III, Anti-pope 389. 476.
Clement of Alexandria, St. 46. 49.
Cleph, King of Lombards 98.
Clergy 244–245. 644.
  in Early Middle Ages 314–315.
  in High Middle Ages 490.
  in Later Middle Ages 661–663.
  regular 245.
  secular 245.
Clericis Laicos (1296) 427. 645.
Clermont, Council (1095) 367. 368.
Clients 209.
Clocks 344. 553.
Clodimir, King of Franks 105.
Clotaire II, King of Franks 167.
Clothar I, King of Franks 105–106.
Clothar II, King of Franks 109. 106.
Clothilda, queen 104. 105. 310–311.
Clothing 221.
  peasant 248.
Clovis, King of Franks 91. 102–105. 311.
Clovis II, King of Franks 167.
Cluniacs, *see* Cluny
Cluny 315. 495.
  congregation 480.
  monastery 474.
  reform 308. 474.
Coats of arms 224.
Coeur, Jacques 559. 560. 591.
Coimbra University 632.
Coinage
  feudal 215.
  in early German kingdoms 112.
  in High Middle Ages 348–349.

Later Roman 25.
see also Money.
Colleges 499.
Collegia of craftsmen 25. 32. 85.
Colet, John 675.
Colleoni, Bartolomeo 620.
Cologne 103. 343. 353. 399. 554. 563. 602.
   cathedral 541.
Coloni 16–17. 25. 74. 84–85. 113.
Colonna
   faction 645.
   family 645.
   Odo (Oddone) 653.
   Sciarra 646.
Columba, St. 196. 311.
Columban, St. 305.
Columbanus, St. 311. 328.
Columbus, Christopher 552–553. 562. 631.
Columella 19.
"Combined tactics" 427.
Comitatus 64. 208.
Comites 109.
Commencement, university 500.
Commenda 350. 351–352. 560.
Commendatio 237.
Commerce
   agents 343.
   aids 553.
   articles 343.
   in Early Middle Ages 231–233.
   expansion 342–346.
   in High Middle Ages 341–346.
   in Later Middle Ages 550–555.
   markets and fairs 344.
   Roman 15. 231.
   routes 342–343.
   treatises 553.
Commercial Revolution 2. 340–346. 690.
Commines, Philippe de 677–678.
Commodus, emperor 21.
Common Pleas, Court of 426.
Commons 353.
   House of 586.
   manorial 239–240.
Communes 355. 446–447.
see also *Conjurationes*.
Community of the realm 422.
Commutation, feudal 359. 444.
Compacts of Koszyce (1374) 605.
Compacts of Prague (1433) 655.
Compagnias 351. 560.
Compass, magnetic 344. 553.
Compiègne (1430) 580.
Compromise of Caspe (1412) 629.
Compurgation 64. 111.
Concessions in Favor of Princes 402.

Conciliar movement in Church 643–644. 649–650. 652–657. 659.
Concordats 454. 654.
   London (1107) 391. 410.
   Sutri (1111) 390.
   Vienna (1448) 642. 654. 657. 661.
   Worms (1122) 392. 476–477.
Condottieri 563. 618. 620–621.
   equestrian statutes 683.
Conductus 544.
Confession of Golias 523.
Confirmation 42. 489.
Confirmation of the Charters (1297) 426.
Conflans, Peace of (1465) 592.
Conjurationes 619.
Conrad II of Franconia, emperor 284–285. 302.
Conrad III, emperor 377. 393–394.
Conrad IV, emperor 598.
Conrad I of Franconia, King of Germany 193. 277.
Conrad IV, King of Germany 404. 405. 598.
Conrad of Gelnhausen 643. 652.
Conrad of Hirschau 502. 504.
Conrad of Marburg 489.
Conrad, son of Emperor Henry IV 389.
Conradin 479. 625.
Consejo Real 630.
Constable 108. 247.
Constance, Peace of (1183) 398.
see also Councils, Ecumenical.
Constance of Sicily 398.
Constance of Toulouse 258.
Constans II, emperor 124. 299.
Constantine (Cyril) and Methodius, Sts. 292.
Constantine I, the Great 22–23. 32. 116–117.
Constantine IV, emperor 124–125. 292.
Constantine V, emperor 125–126.
Constantine VII, emperor 127. 128. 135.
Constantine VIII, emperor 129.
Constantine XI, emperor 635.
Constantine the African 517.
Constantinople 23. 116. 117–118. 120. 129. 131–132. 135. 294. 380. 434. 453. 551. 635.
   bishop of 130.
   conquest 633. 635. 638.
   Latin Empire 380. 454. 622.
   Latin Patriarchate 478.
Constantius, emperor 22. 32. 134.
Constantius, general 78. 81.
Constitution of Lothair (824) 301.
Constitutions of Clarendon (1164) 512.
Constitutions of Melfi (1231) 403. 625.
Consulado del Mar 515.

Index

Controversialists 46.
"Convocations" 586.
Copenhagen 609.
Copyholders 246. 353. 556.
Copying manuscripts, Carolingian 184.
Corbeil, Treaty of (1258) 436. 452.
Corbie, monastery 258. 308.
Cordova 261–262. 352. 451.
    Caliphate 260. 364.
Corps de Marchands 554.
Corpus Juris Civilis 122. 130. 514.
Corregidores 630.
Corsica 192. 364. 628.
Cortenuova (1237) 404.
Cortes 360. 446. 450. 568. 626–627. 630.
Corvées 241.
Corvinian Library 607.
Corvinus, Matthias (Hunyadi), of Hungary 607.
Cossacks 611.
Cotrugli, Benedetto 553. 557. 562.
Cotters 236. 242. 246.
Cotton, Bartholomew 516.
Coulevrines 594.
Councils, feudal "national" 215.
Councils, Church 32–34. 40. 43. 314. 475. 478. 505. 508.
    Carolingian 182–183.
    of Toledo 97.
Councils
    Ecumenical 472. 651.
    Basel-Ferrara-Florence (1431–1439/1449) 634–635. 654–656. 661. 671.
    Chalcedon (451) 34. 36. 39–40. 43. 133.
    Constance (1414–1418) 600. 642. 652–654.
    I Constantinople (381) 33. 39–40. 43. 45. 298.
    II Constantinople (553) 122. 298.
    III Constantinople (680–681) 300.
    Ephesus (431) 40. 45.
    Florence (*see* Basel-Ferrara-Florence).
    III Lateran (1179) 494–495.
    IV Lateran (1215) 413. 478. 479. 489.
    I Lyons (1245) 133. 404. 437. 479. 598.
    I Nicaea (325) 37. 38. 40. 43. 45. 134.
    II Nicaea (787) 126.
    Pavia-Siena (1423) 651.
    Pisa (1409) 652.
Counterpoint 544–545.
Counts and counties 13. 25. 109. 180.
    Frankish 109.
    Palatine 279.
Courland 366. 602.
Court of the Star Chamber 585.
Courtesy 226–227.

Courtrai (1302) 439. 645.
Courts
    "piepowder" 345.
    shire 271.
Courts of love 227.
Covadonga 263.
Cracow 459.
Crécy (1346) 574. 575. 604.
Credit 349–351. 558. 690.
Creeds
    Apostle's 670.
    Christian 43.
    Nicene 43. 183.
Crescentius 302.
Crete 128.
Crimea 294.
    Khanate 611.
Croatia 291. 460. 607.
Crofters 246.
Crossbow 361–362. 445.
Crusader States 374–382.
    conditions 376.
    decline 376.
    defense 374–375.
    fall 381.
    feudalism 218.
    government 374.
    Kingdom of Jerusalem 371–381. 403.
    weaknesses 374.
Crusades 361. 363–384. 515–516.
    Albigensian 478. 488.
    Children's 380.
    decline 379.
    Edward I 381.
    evaluation 381–382.
    Fifth 380. 403. 478.
    First 367–371. 476.
    Florence (1439) 133.
    Fourth 379–380. 478.
    against Frederick II 404.
    of Frederick II 380.
    Henry VI's project 400.
    Infantes of Aragon 381.
    influences 342. 381–382.
    Kings' 379.
    Louis IX 381. 516.
    Moslem counter-offensive 377–379.
    motives 368.
    Nicopolis (1369) 600. 634.
    origins 367–369.
    Peasants' 369.
    Princes' 369–370.
    Second 377. 431
    Sixth 403.
    Spanish 478.
    Third 399. 432–433.
    Tibald 381.
    Varna (1443–1444) 606. 634–635.

Index

Ctesiphon 124. 147.
Cuchulainn Cycle 331.
Culture
  in early Germanic Kingdoms
    67–68. 71. 114.
  in Early Middle Ages 319–339.
  in France 447–448.
  in High Middle Ages 494–547.
  Italian Renaissance 666–673. 679–684.
  Late Gothic 666. 673–679. 684–687.
  in Late Middle Ages 570. 666–690.
  Late Roman 26–27.
  Roman 17–20.
  Transalpine Late Medieval 666.
    673–679. 684–689.
Cumans 453. 460. 462. 463. 465. 466.
Curatores 24.
Curia Regis 217.
  France 434. 442
Curiales 13. 16. 25. 83. 85.
Customs of Beauvais 515.
Customs of Vermandois 515.
Cynewulf 330.
Cyprian of Carthage, St. 35–36. 38.
Cyprus 128.
Cyril (Constantine) and Methodius, Sts.
  132. 287. 288. 292. 312–313.
Cyrus, patriarch-prefect 147.
"Czech Renaissance" 599.
Czechoslovakia and Czechs 288. 599.

D

Dacia 76.
Dagobert, King of Franks 107–108.
  166–167.
Dalmatia 291. 460. 607.
Damascus 147. 154. 377.
Damietta 380–381.
Dandalo, Doge of Venice 379.
Danegeld 196. 267. 270. 408.
Danelaw 194. 266–267.
Daniel of Galich 612.
Daniel of Moscow 614.
Dante Alighieri 158–159. 361. 485. 599.
  661. 667–668. 671–672.
Danube River 7. 61. 69. 76–77.
Danzig 365. 554. 602.
Dar-al-Ilm 161.
Dardanelles 117.
Datini, Francesco, of Prato 559.
Deacons 39–40. 490.
Decameron 159. 669. 672–673.
Decimal system 160.
Decius, emperor 76.
Declaration of Rense (1338) 599.
Decretalists 473.

Decretals of Gregory VII 473.
Decretists 473.
Decretum (of Gratian) 473. 515.
Decuriones 13.
Defender of the Peace 659. 671. 677.
Degrees, academic 499–500.
Dei, Benedetto 557.
Della Rovere, Giuliano, cardinal 657.
Della Rovere family 656.
Demesne of lord 239.
Denarius 16. 234–235. 349.
Denis, St., monastery 257.
Denmark 175–176. 278. 449. 461. 561.
  596. 608.
  Danish March (*Mark*) 278. 280.
Der Arme Heinrich 249.
Desert power 154–155.
Desideria 176.
Desiderius, King of Lombards 99. 176.
Despenser, Hugh 582.
Despots, *see* Dictators.
D'Estes 670.
Destrier 224.
Deutsch 60.
Deventer, school 674.
Devotio Moderna (New Devotion) 663.
Devshirme (child-tribute) 638.
Dialectics, *see* Logic.
Diáz, Bartholomew (Bartolomeo)
  562. 633.
Dictators 619–620.
Dictatus Papae 511.
Didache or Teachings of Apostles 40.
Didascalia 40.
Dies Irae 522.
Diets, German 598. 601.
Diffidatio 212.
Dinar 234. 349.
Dinarides 6.
Diniz of Portugal, king 632.
Dio Cassius 20.
Dioceses, Roman 22.
Diocletian, emperor 22. 31. 70. 116.
Dionysius Exiguus 40–41.
Dionysius the Areopagite, Pseudo- 322.
Diplomacy
  Byzantine 130–132.
  Italian 620.
  in Later Middle Ages 569.
Dir 294.
Dirhem 234.
Disputations, academic 500.
Dispute Between a Soldier and a Cleric
  514.
Divination, early German 68.
Divine Comedy 672.
Divine learning 320. 322. 495.
Divine Office (*Opus Dei*) 307.

Index

Diwans 154.
Dmitri Donskoi 611. 614.
Dobrudja 292.
Doctor (degree) 499.
Domesday Book (1086) 242. 246–247. 347. 408.
Dominic de Guzman, St. 484.
Dominicans 478. 484–485.
  Second Order 484.
  Third Order 484.
Donatello 683.
Donation of Charlemagne to Papacy (774) 176.
Donation of Constantine 513. 670.
Donatists 34. 44. 48.
Donatus 26. 321. 521.
Dordrecht 189.
Dorylaeum (1907) 370.
Drama 18. 331. 524.
Drobzin, military order 366.
Droit de gite 213.
Druids 57.
Drungarii 130–131.
Drushina 463.
Dubois, Pierre 659. 677.
Ducats 349. 557.
Duchies and dukes 25. 62. 109–110. 181. 217. 275.
Duma 58.
Dunois, general 591.
Duns Scotus 517. 659. 677.
Dunstan, St. 267. 272. 308. 315.
Durand, William 659.
Durant, William 513.
Dürer, Albrecht 685.
Dyle River (891) 197. 277.

E

Ealdorman 101. 109. 270.
Earl 270.
Earth Mother 67.
Ebbo Gospels 335.
Eberhard of Franconia, duke 279.
Eberhard the German 504.
Ebroin, mayor in Neustria 168.
Eckhart, Johann, Meister 658.
Eclectics 19.
Ecloga 130.
Economy
  in Anglo-Saxon England 271.
  Byzantine 131–132.
  Church teachings on 352.
  early German 64–65.
  early Indo-European 54–55.
  in Early Middle Ages 231–243. 250–251.
  in England 587.

Economy [cont.]
  focal centers 563.
  in France 588.
  in Frankland 207. 231–232.
  and government 557. 560–562. 587.
  in High Middle Ages 340–354.
  Islamic 155.
  in Later Middle Ages 550–562. 642.
  Roman 15–16. 21. 25. 231.
  Russian 463.
  in Scandinavia 193–194. 461–462. 609.
  Spanish 264.
  tenth century 232.
  in Venice 621.
Ecumenical Councils, *see* Councils, Ecumenical.
Eddas 536.
Edessa, county 370. 374. 377.
Edgar the Peaceful, King of England 267.
Edict (Rescript) of Milan (313) 32.
Edington (878) 265–266.
Edith, daughter of Godwin 268.
Edmund Ironsides 267.
Edmund, son of Henry III 419.
Education 691.
  in Anglo-Saxon England 272.
  apprenticeship 501.
  Byzantine 135.
  early Christian 26. 49–50.
  in Early Middle Ages 114. 319–326.
  in High Middle Ages 361. 494–503.
  Islamic 161.
  of laity 503.
  in Renaissance Italy 670–671.
  Roman 18–19.
  theory 501–503. 670.
  of women 503.
Edward the Confessor, King of England 268. 272.
Edward I of England, king 360–361. 381. 421–427. 439. 573. 645.
  "Edwardian Compromise" 422–427.
Edward II of England 423. 582.
Edward III of England 559–560. 573. 576. 582. 643.
Edward IV of England 584–585.
Edward of York 584.
Edward the Elder 267.
Egbert of Wessex, king 101. 265.
Egerland (Chebsko) 604.
Egidey 611.
Egidio Colonna (Aegidius of Colonna) 503.
Egypt 147. 381. 437. 551. 638.
  Fatamid 151. 371. 377.
Egyptians 118–119.
Einhard 18. 165–166. 173. 177. 183–186. 332. 525.

Index

Eleanor of Aquitaine 254. 411. 415. 417. 430–431. 527.
Electoral princes, Western Empire 600–601.
Electoral Reform Decree (1059) 475.
Elias, Brother 484.
Elizabeth of York, queen 585.
Emirs 154.
Emma, queen of England 267.
Empire, Byzantine, *see* Byzantine Empire.
Empire, Eastern Roman, *see* Byzantine Empire.
Empire, Roman, *see* Roman Empire.
Empire, Western 278–284. 286.
  Age of Princes 597–603.
  civil war 401.
  in Early Middle Ages 274–287.
  factors of strength and weakness 275–277.
  feudalism in 218.
  Franconian Emperors 284–287. 384–392.
  government 276. 597–598. 601.
  Great Interregnum 405.
  Guelph vs. Hohenstaufen Contest 392–406.
  Hapsburgs 598–601.
  in High Middle Ages 384–406.
  Hohenstaufen era 393–405.
  Investiture Controversy 384–393.
  in Later Middle Ages 596–603.
  Luxemburgers 599–600.
  and Papacy 384–406.
  Saxon (Ottonian) Emperors 274–284.
  see also Germany; Holy Roman Empire.
Encina, Juan del 679.
England 13. 551. 561.
  Angevin 411–427.
  Anglo-Saxon 99–102. 218. 265–273.
  aristocracy 358.
  army 426.
  Church 649. 651.
  Church and State 427.
  classes 246.
  common law 413.
  culture 266. 272.
  economy 271. 555–556. 560. 587.
  education 266. 272.
  government 101–102. 270. 407–416. 418–419. 421–422. 424–427. 581–582. 586–587.
  in High Middle Ages 407–428.
  justice 411–414. 426.
  in Later Middle Ages 572–587.
  laws 413. 426.
  Norman 268–269. 407–411.
  Northmen 195. 198. 265–266.
  Parliament 424. 581–583. 585–587.
England [cont.]
  population 355.
  taxation 424–425. 586.
Enqueteurs 437. 440. 443. 445.
Enzio of Sardinia 404–405.
Ephesus, Robber Council of (449) 34. 39. 46.
Epictetus 18–19.
Epila (1348) 628.
Epirus 455. 633. 635.
Equites 16.
Erasmus, Desiderius 658. 663. 675.
Eric of Pomerania, King of Denmark, Norway, and Sweden 609.
Eric of Sweden, St. 461.
Ernest of Suabia 285.
Escheat 214. 216.
Essex 100. 266.
Estates General 360. 440–441. 446. 568. 572. 576. 580–581. 588–591. 594. 645.
Estates Provincial 360. 446.
Estonia 366. 602.
Étaples, Lefevre d' 676.
Ethandune (878) 197.
Ethelbert of Kent 310–311.
Ethelred the Redeless 267. 270. 408.
Ethelwold, St. 308.
Ethics 510.
Etruscans 12.
Eucharist, Holy 42. 490.
Eudes of Aquitaine 168. 260.
Eudes (Odo) of France, king 196. 205. 256.
Eudoxia 47.
Eugenius III, Pope 377.
Eugenius IV, Pope 654–655.
Euric 78.
Europe
  climate 7–8.
  central 8–9. 596–603.
  east central 457–462. 603–607.
  Eastern 9. 462–468. 596. 610–616.
  gateways 6.
  geography 4–9.
  "New West" 92. 95–116.
  northern 457. 461–462. 603. 607–609.
  preliterary 53–73.
  southern 449–457. 618–641.
  Western 8. 92–116.
Eusebius of Caesarea 26.
Eusebius of Nicomedia 45.
Eustace III of Boulogne 369.
Eustace the Monk 434.
Eutychianism, *see* Monophysites.
Evesham (1265) 422.
Exchange and exchanges 555. 557–558.
Exchequer 410.
  Court of 424.

Index

Excommunication 474.
Execrabilis (1460) 656.
Exfestucatio 212.
Expansion of Christian Europe 363. 690.
   overseas 562.
Expectancies 648.
Expression, in High Middle Ages 547.
Exploration, Portuguese 632–633.
Extreme Unction 43. 490.

F

Factories, commercial 554.
Factory system, early 555.
Faculties, university 497.
Faiblaux 532.
Fairs 344.
   of Champagne 345.
Falcons and falconry 358. 401.
Falkirk (1298) 423.
False Decretals 301.
Family, Roman 17.
Farabi, -al 159.
Fargohnah 149.
Fathers
   Apostolic 46.
   Church 43. 46–50. 504. 508. 667.
   Eastern 46–47. 674.
   Western 46–48.
Fatima 145.
Fatimids 154.
Faubourgs 353.
Fealty, oath of 211.
Fee, knight's 211.
Felix V, Anti-Pope 655.
Felix of Urgel, bishop 185.
Felony 212.
Ferdinand I de Antequera, King of Aragon 629.
Ferdinand II of Aragon, king, *see* Ferdinand of Spain.
Ferdinand I of Castile 263. 451.
Ferdinand III of Castile 364. 451.
Ferdinand IV of Castile 626.
Ferdinand I of Portugal 632.
Ferdinand of Spain (II of Aragon) 568–569. 593. 625. 629. 643. 657.
Ferguson, Wallace K. 549.
Fermiers 354.
Fernán González of Castile, count 263.
Ferrante (Ferdinand) I of Naples 625.
Ferrara 655. 656.
Ferrer, Vincent, St. 663.
Feudalism 206–230.
   in Anglo-Saxon England 218. 270.
   aristocracy 219–229.
   Carolingians and 170–172. 181–182.
   castles 224–225.
   chivalry 226–227.

Feudalism [cont.]
   Church and 227.
   commutation 212.
   courtesy 226.
   evaluation 228.
   factors 207–208.
   in France 253–255.
   in Germany 218.
   government 214. 216–217.
   in Italy 218.
   knights 223.
   law 217.
   liege homage 211.
   life 219.
   marriage and family 222.
   military service 212.
   monarchy 215.
   in Norman England 407–408.
   obligations of lords 213.
   obligations of vassals 212–213.
   origins 170. 188–210.
   passing 228. 358.
   in Scandinavia 461–462.
   society 219–229.
   states 214. 228. 253.
   warfare 225–226.
   women 222.
Ficino, Marsilio 659.
Fideles 208–210.
Fiefs 181. 207–208. 211–212. 219. 236. 358.
Fieu or *feu* 207–208.
Filioque (in Creed) 133. 183.
Filotheus, Monk 610.
Finance 348–352. 557–560.
   in early Germanic kingdoms 112.
   early medieval 235.
   high medieval 348–352.
   late medieval 557–560.
Finland and Finns 366.
Fisc 15. 112. 181–182. 210.
Flagellants 658. 663.
Flanders 424. 432. 442. 445. 551–552. 573. 588–589. 592.
   county of 255.
   economy 560.
   Flemish 189.
   'Fleets" 551–552.
Fleury 495.
Florence 343. 352. 551. 554–556. 559. 566. 568. 619–620. 622–623. 668.
   cathedral 683.
   government 622–623.
   in Later Middle Ages 622–623.
   Medici dictatorship 623.
   Republic 622–623.
   University of 669.
Florins 557.

Florus of Lyons	202.
Flotte, Pierre	438. 645.
Fodrum	398.
Foederati	25. 70. 75. 78–79. 81. 86–87. 90. 102–103. 112–113. 118. 310.
Fontenay (841)	200. 329.
Food and drink	
aristocratic	220–221.
middle class	354.
peasant	248.
Foremarriage	214.
Forefeiture	214. 216.
Formigny (1450)	581.
Formosus, Pope	277.
Forscheim (1077)	388.
Fortescue, John	581. 587. 677.
Fortunatus	114. 328.
Forum of Judges (Fuero Juzco)	97. 111.
Framea	64.
Franc archers	581.
France	13.
aristocracy	356.
army	444. 581. 594.
Capetians	257. 429–447. 588.
Carolingians	204–205. 256–257.
Church	594. 651.
counties	255.
culture	447–448.
duchies	253–255.
in Early Middle Ages	191–192. 253–259.
economy	555. 588. 593.
feudal	218. 253–259.
frontier states	255.
government	431. 434. 440–447. 593–594.
in High Middle Ages	406–448.
justice	437. 443.
in Later Middle Ages	572–581. 587–594. 631.
law	437. 443–444.
manorialism	238.
and Naples	631.
and Navarre	630–631.
navy	445.
Northmen	196–198.
origins	102. 186. 201–202.
population	355.
taxation	440. 444. 446. 534. 589. 591. 594.
Valois	588–592.
Franche Comté	589. 591–593.
Francia, duchy	254.
Francis of Assisi, St.	482–483. 534.
Francisca	64. 113.
Franciscans	478. 482–485.
Observant	484.
Second Order	484.
Franciscans [cont.]	
Spiritual	484. 648–649.
Third Order	484.
Franco of Cologne	545.
Franconia and Franconians	275. 277. 284–287. 358. 393.
Frankalmoin	210. 236.
"Franklins" (freeholders)	565.
Franks	89–91. 95. 97. 99. 102–107.
advantages	103.
Carolingian Era	165–193. 198–206.
Church	310.
civilization	107–116.
Clovis	103–105.
Constitution of	614. 106. 109.
counts	109.
disintegration of empire	188–206.
expansion	90–91. 104–105.
'fatal custom"	105. 190. 208.
in Italy	98. 121.
influence	102–103.
Merovingian Era	102–116. 165–166.
origins	103.
Ripuarian	90. 103.
Salian	90. 103. 588.
unification	104–105.
warfare	112.
see also Carolingian Franks, Carolingians, Merovingian Franks.	
Fraticelli	658. 663.
Fredegar	332.
Fredegunde, Queen of Neustria	106.
Frederick I, Barbarossa, emperor	218. 289. 379. 394–400. 432. 458. 477. 512.
Frederick II, emperor	380. 400–405. 437. 478–479. 513. 625.
concessions	598.
Frederick III, emperor	592. 601.
Frederick of Hohenzollern, margrave	600.
Frederick of Sicily, king	628.
Frederick of Suabia	393.
Freeholders	236. 246–247.
Frejus	192.
French, Old	201.
Frequens (1417)	653–654.
Frescobaldi	351.
Frescoes	137.
Freya	67.
Friars Minor (O.F.M.), see Franciscans	
Friends of God	658. 663.
Frigga	67.
Frisia and Frisians	168. 175. 197. 312.
Friuli	177. 204. 280.
Froissart, Jean	678.
Frontinus	20.
Fuero Juzgo	111.
Fuero Real	451.
Fuggers, bankers, of Augsburg	559.

Index

Fulbert of Chartres 494. 502.
Fulcher of Chartres 515.
Fulk Nerra of Anjou 316.
Fulk "the Brawler" of Anjou 258.
Furlong 239.
Fyrd 266. 269. 408.

G

Gabelle 594.
Gaguin, Robert 676.
Gainas 80.
Gaiseric (Genseric) 79. 81. 96.
Galen 19. 26.
Galerius, emperor 22. 31–32.
Galicia 263. 460.
Gallic Wars (of Julius Caesar) 60. 68–69.
"Gallican liberties" 594. 651.
Gallienus 21.
Gallipoli (1354) 637.
Galswintha, queen 106.
Gama, Vasco da 562. 633.
García of Navarre 263.
Garigliano River 192.
Garin de Lorrain 249.
Garlande, Stephen 430.
Garlande family 430. 442.
Gascony 254. 435–436. 439. 573. 581.
Gasindi 208.
Gastaldi 109.
Gatinais 258.
Gaul 12. 69. 74. 95.
    age of invasions 89–91.
    Celtic 55–57.
    Germanic kingdoms 102.
    Visigoths 78. 96–97.
Gaus 109.
Gaveston, Peter 582.
Gelasius, Pope 34.
Gelimer, King of Vandals 121.
Gemot 62–63. 101.
General Privilege of Pedro III of Aragon (1283) 452. 628.
Genghis Khan (Chingiz Khan) 464–465.
Genoa and Genoese 342–343. 347. 352–353. 364. 445. 551–554. 559. 574. 620. 634.
Genoins 349.
Gens d'ordonnance 581.
Genseric, see Gaiseric.
Geoffrey of Anjou 410–411.
Geoffrey of Brittany 415. 433.
Geoffrey of Monmouth 529.
Geography, European 4–9.
    Germany 274–275.
Geometry 18–19. 322.
    analytical 160.
Gepids 88.
Gerard, Grand Master, Templars 378.

Gerard of Parma 488.
Gerbert of Aurillac 282. 322. 325. 331.
    see also Sylvester II, Pope.
German barbarians, see Germans, early; Germanic barbarians.
German Empire, medieval, see Empire Western.
German language, old 200.
Germania (of Tacitus) 18. 60–72.
Germanic barbarians 25. 59–73. 117.
Germanic kingdoms
    architecture 334.
    aristocracy 108.
    assemblies 109.
    Church and religion 113–114.
    civilization 107–116.
    counties 109.
    education 114.
    finance 112.
    government 107–109.
    justice 111–112.
    law 110–111.
    warfare 112–113.
Germanies 495.
    population 355.
    see also Germany.
Germans
    Arian Christianity 71.
    barbarian invasions 69–70. 74–93.
    culture 66–71.
    early 59–73.
    east 75.
    economy 64–65. 70–71.
    expansion 61.
    government 62–63.
    justice 63–64.
    law 63.
    living conditions 66. 70–71.
    military advances 84.
    morality 68.
    recreations 60.
    religion 67.
    and Romans 69–71.
    shortcomings 68.
    society 65–66.
    subdivisions 61.
    technology 65.
    west 75.
    see also Germanic barbarians, Germanic kingdoms.
Germany 69. 459. 561.
    Church 310. 312.
    civilization 603.
    duchies and dukes 193.
    in Early Middle Ages 192. 274–287.
    economy 555.
    expansion 278. 280–281. 365–366.
    feudalism 218–219.

Index

Germany [cont.]
  geography   274–275.
  and Italy   274–287.
  later Carolingian   204–205.
  in Later Middle Ages   596–603. 654.
  literature   533–534.
  manorialism   238.
  marks   275.
  Northmen   197.
  origins   102. 201–202.
  see also Empire, Western.
Gerona   438.
Gerson, John   643. 663.
Gervase of Canterbury   431.
Gesiths   209.
Geza I of Hungary, king   460.
Geza of Hungary, duke   289.
Ghazals   157–158.
Ghazis   636.
Ghazzali, -al   157. 159–160.
Ghent   352.
Ghettos   359.
Ghibellines, in Florence   622.
  see also Hohenstaufen.
Ghiberti, Lorenzo   682–683.
Gibraltar   148. 259.
Gilbert de la Porée   497.
Gilbert of Lorraine, duke   278.
Gildas   99.
Giotto   543. 681.
Giraldus Cambrensis   337.
Gisors   258.
  (1180)   432.
Glanville, Ranulf   361. 413.
Glass, stained, see Stained glass windows.
Glass industry   346.
Glebe   245.
Glossators   514.
Gloucester, Duke of   583–584.
Gnesen   290.
Gnosticism and *gnosis*   44.
Goa   633.
Godfrey of Bouillon   369. 371.
Godfrey of Lower Lorraine, duke 285–286.
Godric of Finchal, St.   341. 343.
Godwin of Wessex   268. 270.
Gokstad ship   195.
"Golden Age," concept of   14.
  Roman   17.
Golden Bull (1356)   597. 599–600. 642. 661.
Golden Bull of Andrew II (1222)   460.
Golden Bull of Eger (1213)   402.
Golden Bull of Frederick II for Bohemia
  (1212)   458.
Golden Horde, Khanate   610–611.
Golden Horn (harbor)   118. 638.
Gonzagas   670.

Gorze, monastery   284. 308. 474. 480.
Goslar   286. 385.
Got, Bertrand de, archbishop   646.
Goths   24–25. 71. 76. 121. 332.
  see also Ostrogoths; Visigoths.
Gothic style   3.
  architecture   539–543.
  in England   541.
  in France   540.
  in Germany   541.
  in Italy   541.
  Late   541.
  painting   543.
  sculpture   542.
  in Spain   541.
Gottfried von Strassburg   529. 534.
Gottschalk (of Fulda)   185. 323.
Government and economy   557. 560–562.
  Anglo-Saxon   270.
  Byzantine   129–130. 132.
  Carolingian   178–182.
  Church   471–479. 643–644. 647–648. 652–653. 655. 657.
  in Christian Spain   264.
  in Crusader States   374.
  early German   62–63.
  in England   407–416. 418–419. 421–422. 424–427.
  feudal   207–208. 216–217.
  in Florence   622–623.
  in France   431. 434. 440–447. 593–594.
  in Germanic kingdoms   107–109.
  in High Middle Ages   340. 359–360.
  in Iberian Peninsula   450–451.
  Indo-European   55.
  later Carolingian   207.
  in Later Middle Ages   568–569. 586–587.
  manorial   247.
  Milanese   621.
  monarchism   568.
  of Mongols in Russia   468.
  of Ottoman Turks   638.
  representative   360. 568.
  Roman   23–25.
  Russian   462–463. 612.
  in Sicily   403.
  urban   356.
  Venice   621–622.
  Western Empire   597–598.
  see also various states and peoples.
Grafs   109. 180.
Grafschafts   109.
Grail, holy   529.
Grammar, Latin   18. 26. 135. 321. 667.
Granada   450–451. 630.
Grandmontines   481.

Index

Gratian, emperor 32. 39. 473. 481. 496. 515.
Great Council, feudal 216–217. 228. 425. 586.
Great Moguls of India 467.
Great Plain of Europe 6.
"Great Silk Way" 155. 342. 465.
Greater Zab River (750) 150.
"Greek fire" 125. 131.
Greek language 17. 132. 667. 674.
    literature in 135. 667. 674. 691.
    studies in 669. 671. 674.
Greenland 197.
Gregory I, Pope 46. 48–49. 100. 133–134. 267. 298–299. 311. 331–332. 336.
    Pastoral Care 266.
Gregory II, Pope 312.
Gregory V, Pope 283.
Gregory VII, Pope 368. 386–389. 473–476. 511. 625.
Gregory IX, Pope 380. 400. 403–404. 437. 473–474. 479. 488. 498. 513. 515.
Gregory X, Pope 405.
Gregory XI, Pope 649–650.
Gregory XII, Pope 651. 653.
Gregory of Nazianzus, St. 46–47. 50.
Gregory of Nyssa, St. 46–47.
Gregory Thaumaturgus, St. 49–50.
Gregory of Tours, bishop 104. 109. 114. 316. 332.
Grey, William, of Ely 675.
Groats (*grossos*) 349. 557.
Grimoald, mayor of palace 167.
Groats (*grossos*) 349. 557.
Grocyn, William 675.
Groot, Gerhard 663. 674.
Guarino, Battista 670.
Guarino da Verona 669–670.
Guelphs 389. 393–405.
    in Florence 622.
    vs. Hohenstaufen 477–479.
    in Italy 619. 622.
Guesclin, Bertrand du, constable 576. 589.
Gui de Bazoche 515.
Guibert of Nogent, abbot 355. 516.
Guicciardini, Francesco 618.
Guido of Arezzo 338. 481. 545.
Guido Cavalcanti 535.
Guienne 436. 439. 573. 581.
Guienne-Gascony 442. 445. 588.
Guilds 564.
    craft 347–348. 355. 556.
    functions 347–348.
    halls 345. 542.
    journeymen's 556. 564.
    merchant 345. 347. 355.

Guilds [cont.]
    priors 355.
    schools 245.
Guinea coast 632.
Gundobad of Burgundy, king 102.
Gunpowder artillery 569. 581. 594.
    weapons 555. 594.
Guntrum, King of Danes 266. 310.
Gutenberg, Johann 676.
Guy of Flanders 439.
Guy of Lusignan 378.
Guyuk 466.
Guzman "*el Bueno*" 626.
Gwas 208.

H

Haakon VI of Norway 608.
Hadrian, abbot 101. 324.
Hadrian, Pope 176.
Hagano of Lorraine 256.
Hail Mary (prayer) 487.
Hainault 592.
Hajjaj 148.
Hakim, al- 161.
Hallstatt, culture 55.
Hamburg 343. 352. 365. 495.
    missionary base 312.
Hamburg-Bremen, bishops 365.
Hanifs 141–142.
Hans I of Denmark 609.
Hanseatic League 345–346. 551. 554. 561. 597. 602.
    factories (agencies) 602.
    towns 563.
Hanses 345. 355.
Hapsburgs 596. 598–601.
Harfleur (1415) 577.
Harold Godwinson, earl and king 268–269. 407.
Harold Hardrada of Norway 268.
Hartmann von Aue 529. 534.
Harun al-Raschid, caliph 150. 177–178.
Hasan (son of Ali) 148.
Haskins, Charles H. 495. 548.
Hastings (1066) 269. 407.
Hattin (1187) 378.
Hauberk 224.
Hauptman 601.
Hauspolitik 597.
Haute bourgeoisie 564.
Haute Cour 374.
Hauteville
    Drogo de 624.
    Humphrey de 624.
    Robert de, Guiscard 624.
    William de 624.
Hauteville family 624–625.

Hawkwood, John	620. 623.	Heresies	44–48.
Hebrides	609.	Christological	44–46.
Hegira (622)	142.	disciplinary	44.
Hegius, Alexander	674.	in Eastern Roman Empire	118–119.
Heidelberg University	674–675.	syncretic	44.
Helena, St.	32.	Trinitarian	44–46.
Helmold of Bosau	457.	*Heriban*	122.
Henoticon	34. 46. 119.	Heribert of Cologne, archbishop	282.
Henricus of Ostia (Hostiensis)	513.	Heriger	332.
Henry II, emperor	283–284. 302. 458.	*Heriot*	241. 246.
Henry III, emperor	284–287. 289. 302. 386.	Herman of Salm	389.
		Hermandades	
Henry IV, emperor	384–389. 475–476.	brotherhoods	451.
Henry V, emperor	389–393.	leagues of towns	629–630.
Henry VI, emperor	375. 379. 398. 400–401.	Heruli	97.
		Hesychism	135–136.
Henry VII of Luxemburg, emperor	401–403. 599. 621.	Hexam (1464)	584.
		Hide (of land)	239. 246.
Henry II of Castile (Trastamara)	589. 627. 629.	Hijaz, al-	140. 142.
		Hilary of Poitiers, St.	46–47. 326.
Henry III of Castile	627.	Hildebert of Lavardin	504. 521.
Henry IV of Castile	626–629.	Hildebrand	484.
Henry I of England	256. 356. 360. 391. 409–415.	*see also* Gregory VII.	
		Hildesbrandlied	331.
Henry II of England	356. 431–433. 512.	Hildesheim Cathedral	336.
Henry III of England	416. 419–423. 427. 434–435.	Himiltrude	176.
		Hincmar of Reims, archbishop	203. 301. 328.
Henry IV of England (Lancaster)	576–577. 583–585.	Hippodrome	120.
Henry V of England	591.	Hirah, al-	147.
Henry VII of England	568. 585. 593.	Hirschau, monastery	284. 308.
Henry VIII of England	585–586. 631. 675.	Hisham III	260.
		Hishamite (clan)	149.
Henry I of France	258. 285.	History writing	515–516. 671. 678.
Henry I of Germany, the Fowler	193. 274–278.	annals and chronicles	332.
		Carolingian	185.
Henry of Bavaria, duke	279.	in Early Middle Ages	331–332.
Henry of Burgundy and Portugal	452. 631.	English	516.
Henry of Carinthia	603.	in High Middle Ages	515–516.
Henry of Huntingdon	516.	Islamic	161.
Henry Jasomirgott of Austria	394.	in Later Middle Ages	671–672. 678.
Henry of Lancaster	583.	Roman	18.
Henry of Langenstein	652.	*Hiung-Nu*	75.
Henry the Lion of Saxony	218. 365. 394. 397. 398–399. 400–401.	Hohenstaufen	358. 392–405. 477–479. 625.
Henry the Navigator	552. 562. 566. 632. 678.	Holland, economy	555.
		"Holy League"	601.
Henry the Proud of Bavaria, duke	393.	Holy orders	490.
Henry Raspe, anti-king	465.	*Holy Resurrection*	532.
Henry of Trastamara, *see* Henry II of Castile.		Holy Roman (German) Empire	255.
		see also Empire, Western.	
Henry Tudor	585.	Holy Vehm	601.
see also Henry VII.		Homage	211.
Henry the Young	415. 433.	Homer	135. 668–669.
Heptarchy	100. 311.	*Homines*	208.
Heraclian Emperors	123–125.	Homs (1280)	381.
Heraclius, emperor	46. 124–125. 291. 299.	*Honestiores*	25.
Hercynian Mts.	6. 9.	Honoratus of Lerins, St.	305.

Index

Honoria, princess 79.
Honorius, emperor 23. 77. 80. 83. 118.
Honorius III, Pope 380. 403. 479.
Honorius of Augsburg 511.
Honors (public offices) 210.
Horace 18. 184.
Horses 241–242. 354.
Hospital orders, of knights 482.
Hospitality, feudal 213.
Hospitallers of St. Anthony 482.
Hospitallers of St. John 482.
Hospitals 518.
   Holy Ghost 518.
Hostiensis, Cardinal 473.
Hôtes 246.
Housecarls 112. 269. 271.
Housing, peasant 247–248.
Hrothswitha, of Gandersheim 331.
Hucbald of St. Amand 338.
Hufe 246–247.
Hugh Capet of France, king 257.
Hugh de Payens (Payns) 375.
Hugh of Crécy 430.
Hugh of Cyprus, king 380.
Hugh of le Puiset 430.
Hugh of Lusiguan 417. 433.
Hugh of Spoleto, duke 205.
Hugh of Trimberg 504.
Hugh of Vermandois, count 369.
Hugh of St. Victor 482. 486. 494. 502.
Hugh the Great, Abbot 308.
Hugh the Great, duke 256.
Huizinga, Johann 549.
Hulagu, il-khan 151. 466–467.
Humanism 322. 340. 642–643. 658. 667.
   in England 675.
   in France 675.
   in Germanies 674.
   Italian Renaissance 667–671.
   in Low Countries 674–675.
   patrons 670.
   in Spain 675.
   Transalpine Renaissance 672–676.
   twelfth-century 504.
Humbert of Moyenmoutier, cardinal 133. 387. 474–475.
Humiliati of Lombardy 482.
Humiliores 25.
Humphrey of Gloucester 577. 675.
Hunayn ibn-Ishaq 157.
"Hundred" 63. 101–102. 110. 271.
Hundred Years' War 550–551. 561. 572–581. 582–584. 588–591. 663.
   courses and phases 573–581.
   origins 573.
   results 581.

Hungary and Hungarians 76. 395. 449. 453. 552. 600–601.
   Angevins 460–461.
   Church 313. 649.
   in Early Middle Ages 283–286. 289–290.
   in High Middle Ages 457. 459–461.
   in Later Middle Ages 606–607.
   Ottoman conquest 638.
Hunneric 96.
Huns 74–76. 79. 83. 293.
Hunyadi, John (Janos) 607. 634.
Hus, John 600. 653–654. 657. 660.
Husayn, -al 148.
Hussites 569. 600. 603. 654. 660. 663.
   Taborites 661.
   Utraquists 660.
   wars 600. 654. 660.
Hygiene 518.
Hymns 326–329. 336–337. 521–523.

I

Iberian Peninsula 96–97.
   culture 451.
   in Early Middle Ages 259–264.
   feudalism in 218.
   governments 450–451.
   in High Middle Ages 449–453.
   in Later Middle Ages 618. 626–633.
   Moslems in 259–264. 449–451.
   population 355.
   representative government in 450.
Ibn' Arabi 158–159.
Ibn-Rushd, *see* Averroes.
Ibn Sina, *see* Avicenna.
Iceland 197.
Iconium 454–455.
Iconoclasm 123–127. 135. 298. 300.
   persecution 126.
Iconodules 127.
Icons 137.
Idrisi, -al 160.
Idrisids 191.
Ignatius, patriarch 133. 301.
Ignatius of Antioch, St. 35–36. 38. 46.
Ikshidids 191.
Ile de France 254.
Il-Khans of Persia 466.
Illumination of manuscripts 114.
Illyricum 118.
Immunities, feudal 210. 215–216.
India 342. 467. 562. 633.
Indian Ocean 155. 633.
Indo-China 467.
Indo-Europeans
   early culture traits 54–55.
   economic life 54–55.

719

Index

Indo Europeans [cont.]
  government   55.
  languages   53–54.
  Proto-   54–55.
Industries
  capitalistic   347. 555–556. 559.
  domestic   347.
  in Early Middle Ages   231. 233.
  extractive   346.
  in High Middle Ages   346–348.
  in Later Middle Ages   555–556.
  mechanization   690.
  organization   347.
  Roman   15–16.
  silk   593.
  textile   233. 346. 555. 560. 587.
  training   348.
Infantes de la Cerda   439.
Infanticide, and early Christianity   41.
Infantry   360. 444.
Inflation   357.
Ingebourg of Denmark, Queen of France   432–433. 478.
Innocent I, Pope   39.
Innocent III, Pope   379–380. 401. 403. 416. 417. 419. 433. 474. 477–479. 484. 512–513.
  Crusades   478. 533.
Innocent IV, Pope   404–405. 473. 479. 513.
Innocent VI, Pope   649.
Innocent VIII, Pope   656.
Inquest of Sheriffs (1170)   411.
Inquisition   488–489.
  in Spain   630.
Insurance   558.
Interdict   474.
Interest   34. 235. 243. 558.
  titles to   350.
Investiture   211.
  Investiture Struggle   384–393. 475–477. 511–512.
    in England   391.
    in France   391. 447.
Iona   195–196.
Iran   467.
Iraq   465. 467.
Ireland   100.
  and Church   311.
  English in   414.
  Northmen in   196.
Irenaeus of Lyons, St.   36. 38.
Irene, empress   177.
Irnerius   496. 514.
Iron Gate   6.
Isaac II, Angelus, emperor   454.
Isabella of England, queen   439. 582.
Isabella of France, queen   591.
Isabella of Hainault   432.
Isabella of Spain (Castile), queen   552. 562. 568. 569. 627. 629. 643. 657.
Isabella of Portugal, queen   631.
Isabelle of Angoulême   416–417. 433.
Isfahan   367.
Isis and Osiris   30.
Islam   124. 140–165. 177–178. 294. 313. 485. 630. 654. 691.
  Abbasid caliphs   150–151.
  art   161–162.
  and Byzantium   123–129.
  civilization   154–163.
  and Crusader States   376–381.
  and Crusades   369–382.
  disintegration   151.
  doctrines   143–144.
  economy   155.
  education   161.
  finance   155.
  government   154.
  influence   162–163.
  literature   157–159.
  music   162.
  mysticism   156.
  natural sciences   160.
  navigation and navy   162.
  origins   140–144.
  Orthodox Caliphs   145–148.
  philosophy   155–156. 159.
  religion   143–144.
  society   156.
  in Spain   259.
  theology   159.
  Umayyad Caliphs   148–150.
  warfare   154–155.
Islas Formiguas, Las (1285)   438.
Islas Hormisdas   628.
Isaurians   118.
Isidore of Miletus   120.
Isidore of Seville, archbishop   114. 324. 332.
Istakhr (Persepolis) (649–65)   147.
Italy   13. 81. 102. 105. 123. 176. 203–205. 276–287. 299. 353. 458. 476. 495. 555. 567. 620.
  barbarian invasions   82. 87–89.
  Byzantine   98. 121. 454.
  Carolingian   201. 203–205.
  Central   623.
  city states   619–623.
  in Early Middle Ages   82. 87–89. 97–99. 280. 282–283. 286–287.
  economy   231. 348.
  feudalism in   218.
  government   404. 618–620.
  in High Middle Ages   365. 384–405. 449.

Index

Italy [cont.]
  Investiture settlement 392.
  in Later Middle Ages 599. 618–625.
  literature 535.
  Lombard Kingdom 98–99.
  manoralism 238.
  Normans in 286.
  northern 619–623.
  population 355.
  Renaissance 619. 667. 679–684.
  southern 133. 624–625.
  Visigoths 118.
  see also Empire, Western.
Itinerant Justices 410. 423.
Ivan Khalita of Moscow 613–614.
Ivan III "the Great" of Russia 615.
Ivo of Chartress, bishop 473. 491. 502.
Ivrea, March and Marquis 204. 280.

J

Jacobus de Voragine 524.
Jacopone da Todi 535.
Jacquerie (1358) 568. 589.
Jadwiga of Poland, queen 605–606. 607.
Jaffa (Joppa) 371. 379.
Jagatay 465.
Jagiello of Lithuania 605–606.
Jagiellonids 606. 607.
Jalal-al-Din of Khwarizm 465. 466.
Jalula (637) 147.
James I of Aragon 219. 364. 452.
James II of Aragon and Sicily 628.
James IV of Scotland 586.
Janissaries (*Yeni cheri*) 638–639.
Jarrow 265.
Jean de Meun 531–532.
Jean of Jandun 671. 677.
Jebe 465.
Jehan le Bel 678.
Jerome, St. 39. 46. 48–49. 75. 86. 305.
Jerome of Prague 600. 654.
Jerusalem 144.
  Kingdom 367. 371–381. 403.
  see also Crusader States.
Jesu dulcis memoria 521.
Jesus Christ, see Christ, Jesus.
Jews 235. 359. 369.
  clergy and 359.
  in Spain 630.
Jihad 142. 376. 377. 636.
Jiménez de Cisneros, cardinal 658. 662.
Joachim of Flora, abbot 488.
Joachists 488.
Joan of Arc, St. 580–581. 587. 591. 663.
Joanna I of Naples 625. 629. 650–651.
João I of Portugal 632.
João II of Portugal 632.

Johannitza of Bulgaria 455.
John X, Pope 301.
John XI, Pope 301.
John XII, Pope 280–281. 301–302.
John XIII, Pope 281.
John XXII, Pope 484. 648.
John XXIII, Pisan Pope 599. 652–653.
John I, Tzmisces, emperor 127–128.
John II, Comnenus, emperor 453.
John IV, Lascaris, emperor 455.
John V, Cantacuzene, emperor 634–635. 637.
John VI, emperor 634. 637.
John II of Aragon 625. 629.
John Asen of Bulgaria 635.
John I of Castile 627.
John II of Castile 626–627.
John I of England, king 360. 401. 415. 419. 433. 478.
John II of France 576. 588.
John Baliol 423.
John Chrysostom 39. 46. 47. 50.
John Damascene, St. 135–136. 506.
John de Brienne, king of Jerusalem 380.
John de Gray 417.
John of Berry 675.
John of Bohemia, king 603–604.
John of Gaunt 583. 627. 660.
John of Luxemburg 603.
John of Piano Carpini 483.
John of St. Victor 440.
John of Salisbury 244. 322. 432. 485. 494. 502. 504. 506. 512. 517. 521.
John of Syracuse, Bishop 298.
John Scotus Erigena 183. 185–186. 322. 325.
John the Cappadocian 119.
John the Faster, patriarch 133. 298.
John the Fearless of Burgundy 577. 591.
Joinville, Sire de 516.
Jordanes 61. 332.
Joscelin of Edessa, count 377.
Journeymen 348.
  guilds 564.
Jovian, emperor 23. 32.
Juana, la Beltraneja 627. 629.
Juana (Joanna), la Loca of Spain 601. 631.
Juchi 465. 610.
  house of 610.
Judism 44. 294.
  and Christianity 41.
Judith of Bavaria, empress 199.
Julian the Apostate, emperor 23. 32. 45.
Julius I, Pope 38.
Julius II, Pope 624.
Julius Caesar 12. 60. 68–69. 84.
Juries 412–413. 424. 425.
Jurisprudentes 14.

Index

Jus Civile 14.
Jus Gentium 14.
Justicia, in Aragon 450.
Justiciar 408. 415.
Justice 690.
  Carolingian 181.
  in England 411–414. 426.
  in France 437. 443.
  early German 63–64.
  in Germanic kingdoms 111–112.
  manorial 247.
  Papal 472.
Justin I, emperor 119.
Justin II, emperor 123.
Justin Martyr 49.
Justinian I, emperor 46. 88. 119–123. 298.
  Code 14. 130.
Justinian II, emperor 125. 292.
Justinian Renaissance 119–123. 334.
Jutes 91. 100. 271.
Juvenal 18.

K

Kaaba 142.
Kalb party 150.
Kalka River (1223) 465.
Kamil, al-, sultan 380. 403.
Kara-Khitans (Kara Kitai) 465.
Karakorum 466.
Kazan, Khanate 611.
Keller, Christopher 2.
Kenilworth, Dictum of (1266) 422.
Kent 100. 266. 310.
Kerak 375.
Kerbogha of Mosul, emir 371.
Khadijah 142.
Khalid, general 145. 147.
Khanates, Tartar, in Russia 611.
Kharijites 146. 150. 156.
Khazars 294.
Khurasan, 150. 465. 467.
  Highway 155.
Khwarizm and Khwarizmians 38. 151. 465.
Khwarizmi, -al 160.
Kiersey, see Quiersy.
Kiev 462. 466.
Kiev, Principality 197. 294. 313. 462.
Kilij Arslan, sultan 454.
Kindi, -al 159.
King Edgar's Charter 336.
King's Bench, Court of 426.
King's Peace 216. 408. 443.
Klokonitza (1230) 456.
Knights 222. 271. 355. 358. 564. 586.
  equipment 224.
  initiation 223–224. 244.

Knights [cont.]
  Roman 16.
  training 223. 358.
Knights Hospitaller of St. John 375. 482.
Knights of the Round Table 529.
Knights of the Sword 266.
Knights Templar 349–350. 375. 440–441. 482. 646–647.
Koran 142–143. 145. 154.
Korea 465. 467.
Kossovo I (1389) 635. 636. 637.
  II (1448) 607.
Krak des Chevaliers 375.
Kreise 601.
Kremlin 616.
Krum, Khan of Bulgaria 292.
Kubilay Khan 466–467.
Kufah, al- 146. 148. 154.
Kukilov Pole (1380) 614.
Kulm 459.
Kunigunde, queen and empress 284.
Kuriltay (kuriltai) 465. 466.
Kurt, Khan of Bulgaria 293.
Kuttabs (mosque schools) 161.

L

Laborers
  conditions of 238. 247–250. 357. 565.
  emancipation 354.
  in Early Middle Ages 235. 242. 245–250.
  in High Middle Ages 346–348. 354–357.
  in Later Middle Ages 565–566.
  migrant 566.
  rural 238. 245–251. 347. 354. 357. 568.
  urban 357. 565.
Ladislas I of Bohemia, and V of Hungary 604. 607.
La Forbie (1244) 381.
La Fossalta (1249) 405.
La Giacosa 670.
Laguna de la Janda (711) 148. 259.
Laity
  education 503.
  in Early Middle Ages 315–316.
  in High Middle Ages 490.
  in Later Middle Ages 663.
La Marche 593.
Lake Peipus (1242) 366. 468.
Lament for the Cuckoo 328.
Lancastrians 583–585.
Lancelot 529.
Landholding 207. 246.
  Anglo-Saxon England 270.
  in Early Middle Ages 236.

Index

Landholding [cont.]
  in Germanic Kingdoms   237.
  in High Middle Ages   353.
  manorial   238–239.
Lando, Michele di   623.
Lanfranc of Canterbury, archbishop   391. 408.
Lanfranchi of Milan   518.
Langensalza (1075)   386.
Langland, William   678.
Languages, Indo-European   52–54.
Langue d'oc   525. 527. 574.
Languedoc   255. 435.
Langue d'oueil   525. 574.
Laon   495.
Lascarids   455.
Las Navas de Tolosa (1212)   364. 450.
Lateran Councils, *see* Councils, Ecumenical.
Latifundia   16. 25. 113. 237.
Latin language   13. 17. 132. 321. 489. 521. 667.
  medieval   521.
Latin literature, *see* Literature.
La Tremoille   591.
Latvia   366.
Lauda Sion Salvatorem   522.
Lausitz Mark   275.
  see also Lusatia.
Law   340. 495. 499. 514–515. 690.
  Byzantine   130–131.
  canon   40. 473. 496. 514. 515.
  Carolingian   181.
  Church, *see* canon.
  civil   496. 514.
  codes   97. 110–111. 122. 515.
  commercial (merchant)   345.
  common   412. 413. 514.
  Divine   18. 473. 514.
  English   412–413. 426.
  feudal   217.
  France   437. 443–444.
  Germanic   63. 110–111.
  Islamic   161.
  Justinian Code   122.
  natural   18. 510. 514. 690.
  Roman   14. 97. 110–111. 130. 360. 443. 512. 514. 690.
  Russian   295. 616.
  Salic   588.
  Visigothic codifications   97.
Lawmen   64.
Laws of Ine and Alfred   270.
Lazar of Serbia, prince   635. 637.
League of Common Weal   592.
League of Venice   593. 601.
League of Verona   397.
Leander, Bishop of Toledo, St.   299.

Learning
  in Early Middle Ages   319–332.
  in High Middle Ages   494. 503–518.
  theory of   501–503.
Le Coq, bishop   588.
Lechfeld (955)   279.
Lectionary of Karl the Great   335.
Legati, Papal   472.
Legenda aurea   524.
Legists   477. 510. 512–514.
Legnano (1176)   394. 397. 398. 477.
Leidang   461.
Leilarts   439.
Leo I, Pope   34. 39. 46. 79. 133.
Leo III, Pope   177. 183. 300.
Leo VIII, Anti-Pope   302.
Leo IX, Pope   286. 302. 474–475. 624.
Leo I, emperor   87. 96. 118. 120.
Leo III, emperor   125–126.
Leo IV, emperor   126.
Leo V, emperor   126.
Leo VI, emperor   127.
Leon   263. 450–451.
Leonardo da Vinci   682.
Leonin, Master   545.
Leopold of Austria, duke   394.
Letters of credit   350. 351.
Letters-of-fair   350.
Leudes   112. 209.
Lewes (1264)   421.
Lewis IV of Bavaria, emperor   599. 649. 671. 677.
Lex Roman Visigothorum   97.
Liberal arts   18–19. 319. 321. 340. 495. 499.
Liberius, Pope   39. 47.
Libra   16. 234. 349.
Libraries   185. 323. 669.
  Vatican   669.
License to teach   496. 497. 498.
Licinius, emperor   23. 32.
Lieflander Chronik   516.
Liegeois   592.
Lignica (1241)   459.
Lille   439.
Limbourg brothers   684.
Linacre, Thomas   675.
Lindisfarne   195. 265.
  Gospels   335.
Lipany (1434)   604.
Lisbon   632.
  University of   498.
Literacy, of laity   323. 361. 495.
Literature
  Anglo-Saxon   330.
  Byzantine   136.
  early Christian   26. 86.
  in Early Middle Ages   326–332.

Literature [cont.]
 English   330. 678–679.
 French   525–532. 679.
 German   331. 533–534.
 Greek   18. 134–136. 669. 674–676.
 in High Middle Ages   520–536.
 Irish   330–331.
 Islamic   157–159.
 Islamic in Spain   261.
 Italian   534–535.
 in Late Middle Ages   667–670. 672–673. 678–679.
 Latin   17–18. 185. 321. 323. 326–330. 521–525. 666–670. 674–676. 691.
 in Roman Empire   17–18. 86.
 Scandinavian   536.
 Spanish   535–536.
 vernacular   330–331. 361. 516. 525.
Lithuania   366. 596. 602. 605–606. 612. 615.
Lithuanians   458. 459. 468.
Liturgy   489.
 Slavonic   134.
Liudolf of Suabia, duke   279.
Liudolfingers   277.
Liutprand, King of Lombards   99. 170.
Liutprand of Cremona, bishop   281. 332.
Livery and Maintenance, Statutes of   585.
Livery companies   554.
Livonia   366. 602.
Livorno (Leghorn)   623.
Livy   18.
Llewelyn ab Gruffydd   423.
Loanland   270.
Lodi, Peace of (1454)   619.
Logic   18. 321. 486. 505. 507.
Lollards   569. 644. 660. 663.
Lombard League   397. 403. 477.
Lombards   88–89. 95. 98–99. 123. 126. 170–172. 176–177. 185. 233. 284. 299. 302. 332. 397.
London   233. 352. 554. 602.
Longbow   361–362. 574.
Lords, feudal   214. 217.
Lords, House of   586.
Lords Appellant   583.
Lords Ordainers   582.
Loria, Roger   628.
Lorraine   202–203. 255. 256. 275. 278. 280. 282.
 reformers   315.
 see also Lotharingia.
Lorris   354.
Lothair I, emperor   191. 200–204. 274. 278. 301.
Lothair of France, king   256.
Lothair II of Lotharingia   202–203. 301.
 divorce question   202–203.
Lothair of Provence and Italy   280.
Lothar II, emperor   390. 392. 393.
Lotharingia   202–203. 204–205.
 see also Lorraine.
Louchards   352.
Louis d'or   349.
Louis d'Outremer, King of France   256.
Louis the Pious, emperor   177. 178. 180. 183. 185. 190. 196. 199. 307. 323.
Louis the Stammerer, King of France   190.
Louis V of France   256.
Louis VI of France   430. 442. 446. 516.
Louis VII of France   354. 377. 430–432. 442. 446.
Louis VIII of France   419. 434. 435. 441.
Louis IX of France, St.   381. 419. 421. 435–437. 441. 442–447. 443.
 Instructions to son   446–447. 560–562. 568. 587. 588. 591–593. 675. 677.
Louis XII of France   586. 625.
Louis the Child, of Germany, king   193. 277.
Louis the German, of Germany, king   191. 200–204.
Louis I, the Great, of Hungary   605–607.
Louis II of Italy   202–203.
Louis of Orleans   589. 591. 675.
Low Countries   277. 555. 561. 592. 596. 601. 674.
 Church in   312.
 Dutch   599.
 economy   348.
Lübeck   343. 495. 554. 602.
Lucius III, Pope   487.
Luke, St., apostle   35.
Luneburg   399.
Lupus of Ferrieres, abbot   185. 322. 325.
Lusatia   280. 365. 458.
 Lower   604.
 Upper   604.
 see also Lausitz.
Luxemburg   592.
 Emperors   597. 599–600.
Luxeuil, monastery   305.
Lyons   439.
 Councils, see Councils, Ecumenical.

M

Macedonia   635.
Macedonian Renaissance   136. 334.
Machiavelli, Niccolo   629. 657. 671. 672.
Madeiras   632.
Madrasahs   161.
Magdeburg, archbishop of   394.
Magistri Cominaci   334.
Magna Carta (1215)   418.

Index

Magna Mater 30.
Magnus VII Ericsson of Norway and Sweden 608.
Magnus Billing 385.
Magyars 188. 191–193. 275. 277. 278–279. 288. 289. 313. 459–460.
Mahdi 156.
Maimonides 261.
Maine 433. 435. 592.
Majlis 141.
Majorca, slavery 567.
Majorian, emperor 96.
Mal (mall, mallus) 111.
Malacca 633.
Malcolm IV of Scotland, king 414.
Malik Shah 367. 369.
Maltôtes 440. 444.
Mamay 611. 614.
Mameluks 381. 467. 638.
Mamun, al- caliph 150. 161.
Manegold of Lautenbach 509. 511.
Manfred of Sicily 405. 479. 625.
Manichaeanism 44. 47–48. 456.
Mannerism in art 684–685.
Manoel I of Portugal 568. 631. 633.
Manor 238–240.
  church 242–243.
  house 220. 238.
Manorial system 207. 235–243.
  in Carolingian Era 237.
  church 243.
  in Early Middle Ages 237–238.
  evolution 237–239.
  government 247.
  justice 247.
  see also Manor.
Mansourah 380.
Mansur, al- 150. 260.
Manuel I, Comnenus, emperor 378. 454. 456.
Manuel II, emperor 635.
Manuscript illumination 335. 543.
  see also Painting.
Manutius, Aldus 677.
Manzikert (1071) 453.
Maone 560.
Maqqari 262.
Marcel, Etienne 559.
Marcian, emperor 118.
Marco Polo, *see* Polo.
Marcus Aurelius, emperor 19. 20. 69. 87.
Margaret Maultasch 599.
Margaret of Anjou 584.
Margaret of Austria 592.
Margaret of Denmark 609.
Margaret of Flanders 589.
Margaret of France 415.
Margaret of Scotland, "Maid of Norway" 423.
Margaret Tudor 586.
Margat Castle 375.
Margraves 180. 280–281.
Maria de Molina 626.
Maria of Antioch 454.
Maria of Hungary 607.
Marie de France 529.
Marie of Brabant 437.
Marie of Champagne 528.
Maritza River, II (1371)
Mark (money) 234.
Markets and marketing 554.
Marks (marches) 275. 280–281.
Marlborough, Statute of (1267) 422.
Marozia 301.
Marranos 264.
Marriage and family, monogamy 359.
Marseilles 343. 380. 573.
  Statutes of 345.
Marsh, Adam 483.
Marshal, William 222. 418. 419.
Marsiglio of Padua 643. 657. 659. 661. 671. 677.
Martin IV, Pope 479.
Martin V, Pope 653–655.
Martin I of Aragon 629.
Marwan I, caliph 148.
Marwan II, caliph 150.
Mary, mother of Christ 359. 486–487.
Mary of Burgundy 592. 601.
Mary Tudor 586.
Masaccio, Guidi 681.
Master of Flemalle 685.
Masters
  in guilds 348.
  in universities 496–497. 499–500.
Masters of Soldiers 80.
Mathematics 135. 322. 516.
Mathilda of England 389. 410–411. 430.
Mathilda of Tuscany 389. 390.
Matins of Bruges (1302) 439.
Matrimony 41–43. 222.
  Albigensians and 487.
Matthew of Paris 441. 516.
Matthias Corvinus of Hungary 605.
Maurice, emperor 123.
Mawali 149.
Mawr 155.
Maxentius, emperor 22.
Maximian, emperor 22.
Maximilian I, emperor 592–593. 598. 601.
Maximus, emperor 81.
Mayors of Palace, Frankish 165–171.
Mecca 140–144.
Mechanization 346.
Mechlenburg 365.

Medicis
- Cosimo de — 619. 623. 671.
- family — 559. 568. 623. 670.
- Giovanni de — 623.
- Giuliano de — 623.
- Lorenzo de — 623. 673.
- Piero de — 623.
- Salvestro de — 623.

Medicine — 495. 499. 517. 518.
- Byzantine — 135.
- Islamic — 160–161. 261.
- surgery — 518.

Medina — 140. 154.
Mediterranean Sea — 7–8. 15. 155.
Meissen — 275. 280. 365. 599.
Memling, Hans — 585.
Mendicant orders — 482–485.
Mendovg (Mindovg) of Lithuania — 459. 605.
Mercedarians — 485.
Merchant, Chaucer's — 565.
Merchant Adventurers — 561–562.
Merchants of the Staple — 561. 587.
Merchet — 241–242. 246.
Mercia — 100.
Meroveus (Merovech) — 90. 103. 106.
Merovingian Franks — 90–91. 103.
- civilization of — 107–114.
- Do-Nothing Kings — 107. 166–170.
- royal line — 112. 165–166.

Mersen, Capitulary of (847) — 204. 210.
- Treaty of (870) — 202–204.

Merton College — 499.
Meseta — 7.
Mesopotamia — 147. 151. 638.
Mesta — 557.
Metayers — 236. 354.
Metallurgy — 555.
Michael I, emperor — 177.
Michael II, emperor — 126.
Michael III, emperor — 127.
Michael VII, emperor — 127. 368.
Michael VIII, Paleologus, emperor — 455. 633.
Michael Cerularius, patriarch — 133.
Michael Scot — 401. 517.
Michelangelo — 683.
Michele di Lando — 623.
Middle Ages — 2. 690.
- Early — 94–339.
- foundations — 4–93.
- High — 340–547.
- Later — 548–691.

Middle class — 243. 690.
- ordinary — 562–563. 564.
- upper — 562–564.
- urban — 564.
- rural — 564.

Middle Kingdom — 274. 286–287. 591–592.
Mieszco (Miezko) I of Poland — 290. 313. 458.
Migratio (transfer) — 498.
Mihrab — 162.
Milan — 343. 352–353. 395. 559. 619–621.
- Archbishopric — 387. 475.
- government — 621.
- Visconti — 621.

Military, *see* Army.
Military orders — 482.
Militia — 360. 445.
Millet system — 638.
Milvian Bridge (312) — 22.
Minbar — 162.
Mineralogy — 503.
Mining
- in Late Middle Ages — 555.
- Roman — 16.
- in High Middle Ages — 346.

Ministeriales — 220. 285–286. 385. 390.
Minnesingers — 533.
Mirabeau, castle — 417.
Miracle plays — 524–525.
- vernacular — 532.

Mirandola, Giovanni Pico della — 671.
Mirchtea of Wallachia — 636.
Mirrors of Vincent of Beauvais — 503.
Mise of Amiens (1264) — 421.
Missi dominici — 180. 190.
Mithraism — 30.
Moesia — 76. 87. 118. 292.
Mohammed (Prophet) — 140–145. 154.
Mohammed I, sultan — 636–637.
Mohammed II, sultan — 634. 638.
Mohammedanism, *see* Islam.
Mohi (1241) — 460. 466.
Moldavia — 636.
Monarchism — 44.
Monarchy — 360–361. 642–643.
- feudal — 215–217.

Monasticism — 183.
- anchorites — 304.
- Benedictine — 306.
- Celtic — 305.
- cenobitical — 304–309.
- contributions — 308–309.
- in early German kingdoms — 114.
- in Early Middle Ages — 251. 303–309.
- Eastern — 304–305.
- in High Middle Ages — 340.
- origins — 303.
- reforms — 307–308. 480–481.
- semi-anchoritical — 481.
- Western — 305–309.

see also Benedictines; *various forms.*

Index

Money
  in Early Middle Ages   121. 234–235.
  in High Middle Ages   348–349.
  in Later Middle Ages   557.
  Roman   16. 22.
  see also Coinage.
Mongolia   464–465. 467. 483.
Mongols   151. 381. 449. 459. 462. 464–468. 485. 551. 566. 610.
  in Russia   464. 468.
  see also Tartars.
Mongka   466.
Monica, St.   47.
Monophysites   34. 40. 45–46. 119. 122. 298–300.
Monopolies   561.
Monotheletism   119. 298. 299–300.
Mons-en-Pévèle (1304)   440.
Monstrelet, Enguerrand de   678.
Montanists   42. 44.
Monte, Piero del   675.
Monte Cassino   192.
Montereau, bridge   591.
Montes pietatis   558.
Montfort, John de   575. 589.
Montiel (1369)   627.
Montpellier   495. 518.
  university   498.
Moors   259. 566. 630.
Moots   62–63. 101. 271.
Morality, sexual   359.
Moravia   192. 277. 288–289. 312–313. 366. 458.
Moravian Brethren   661.
More, Thomas   675.
Morea, despotate   633.
Moriale, Fra   620.
Morisini, Thomas, Patriarch   454.
Morocco   96. 97. 259. 364. 633.
  Aghlabids   151.
Mortgarten (1315)   602.
Mortimer, Lord   582.
Mortimer's Cross (1461)   584.
Mosaics, Byzantine   137.
Moscow   463. 610. 613. 466.
  princes   613–616.
Moslems; *see* Islam.
Mosques   162.
Motet   545.
Moymir I, of Moravia   288.
Mozarabs   262. 264.
Muawiyah, caliph   146. 148.
Mudejares   264.
Muezzins   144.
Mundeburium   213.
Munera   21. 24.
Munich   495.
Muntprat, Liutfried   559.

Murabits   260. 264.
Murad I, sultan   637.
Murad II, sultan   637.
Murcia   451. 452.
Muret (1213)   452.
Musa, emir   149. 259.
Music   18.
  Byzantine   136.
  early German   69.
  in Early Middle Ages   336–338.
  forms   686.
  harmony   687.
  in High Middle Ages   520. 544–545.
  instruments   337–338. 687.
  in Later Middle Ages   679. 686–687.
  notation   337. 545.
  polyphony   544–545. 686–687.
  treatises   338.
Mutasim, al-   150–151.
Mutazilites   150. 156.
Muwashashahs   158.
Myriobibilion   135.
Myriocephalon (1176)   378. 454–456. 636.
Mystery of Adam   532.
Mystery plays   524.
  vernacular   532.
Mystery religions   30.
Mysticism   657.

N

Nafels (1388)   602.
Nahrawan (659)   146.
Naimans   464.
Nancy (France)   592.
Naples   192. 352–353. 518. 593. 607. 619. 625. 650.
  Angevin   625.
  Kingdom   618. 624–625. 631.
Narbonne   352.
Narses   119–121.
Narthex   333.
Nasad   157.
Nasir, caliph   151.
Nationalism
  in Church   653.
  in Later Middle Ages   642.
  see also Nations.
Nations   70. 74–75.
  at Council of Constance   653.
  in universities   496–497.
  states   690.
Natural History (of Pliny)   19.
Navarre   255. 263. 436. 438–439. 452. 629–631.
Navas de Tolosa, Las (1212)   478.

Index

Navigation Acts, English (1381 ff.) 561. 587.
Navy, Byzantine 131.
  English 266.
  French 445.
Nea (New Church) of Basil I 136.
Nebrixa, Antonio de 676.
Neo-Platonism 19. 26. 30. 47. 671.
Nepotism, in Church 644.
Nero, emperor 31.
Nestorianism 40. 45. 119.
Netherlands, see Low Countries.
Neustria 105–107. 168.
Neva River (1240) 468.
Nevers 589.
  count of 592.
Neville of York, archbishop 675.
Nibelungenlied 89–90. 533.
Nicaea 453. 455. 637.
  (1097) 370.
  sultanate 369.
Niccoli, Niccolò de 670.
Nicephorus I, emperor 126. 292.
Nicephorus II, emperor 128. 281.
Nicephorus, patriarch 135.
Nicephorus Bryennius, see Bryennius.
Nicholas I, Pope 133. 203–204. 300–301.
Nicholas II, Pope 386. 472. 475. 625.
Nicholas V, Pope 655. 656. 669. 670.
Nicholas, St. (Santa Claus) 525.
  Play of 532.
Nicholas of Cologne 380.
Nicholas of Cusa, cardinal 655. 662. 663. 678.
Nicomedia 22.
Nicopolis, Crusade (1396) 600. 634. 636.
Nihawand (641) 147.
Nike Riot (532) 120.
Nithard, count 185. 323. 332.
Nizam al-Mulk 161.
Nizamiyah 161.
Nizhni-Novgorod 614.
Nogaret, William de 438. 440.
Nogay, prince 610.
  and Golden Horde 611.
Noirmoutier 195. 196.
Nominalism 505–506.
Nomisma 349.
Norbert of Premontré, St. 482. 484.
Nordgau (mark) 275. 280. 282.
Nordic 53.
Normandy 194. 196–197. 254. 256. 409–410. 417. 433. 575. 577. 581. 593.
  Customary of 217.
  Dukes of 258.
Normans 453.
  in Italy and Sicily 365. 476. 624–625.
North Mark, see Nordgau.

North Sea 554.
Northmen (Vikings) 61. 188–189. 191. 193–198. 205. 224. 256.
  economy and society 193–194.
  and England 265–269.
  influences 197–198.
  and Ireland 196.
  and Low Countries 197.
  settlements 195–197.
  warfare 194.
Northumbria 100. 266.
Norway and Norwegians 461. 596. 608–609.
Notker Babulus 329.
Novatians 42. 44.
Novgorod 197. 294. 463. 468. 554. 602. 612–613. 615.
  Republic 610. 612.
Numbers
  Arabic 20. 160.
  Roman 19–20.
Nuñez, Fernando 676.
Nun's Complaint 329–330.
Nuremberg 343. 352. 552.
Nurredin 377–378.

O

Oaths 64.
  of fealty 181.
Obol 235.
Ockham, William of 659.
Ockhamism 643. 667. 677–678.
Odericus Vitalis 516.
Odilo of Cluny, abbot 282. 302. 308.
Odo of Blois and Champagne 285.
Odo of Cluny, abbot 308. 325. 338.
Odo of Deuil 515.
Odovacar, king 82. 87. 95. 97. 118.
Olaf of Norway, St., king 461.
Olaf of Norway and Denmark, king 608.
Oleg of Chernigov 463.
Oleg of Kiev, prince 294.
Oleron, Laws of 345.
Olga of Kiev, grand-duchess 294. 313.
Olmutz, Treaty of (1478) 615.
Omar, caliph 145–146. 159.
Omar Khayyam 160.
Ophthamology 518.
Oporto 264. 452.
Optics 518.
Ordeals 111–112.
Order of Preachers (O.P.), see Dominicans.
Orders, holy 479–485.
Ordinance of Laborers (1349) 561.
Ordinances of Justice (1293) 622.

Index

Ordinances of 1311   582.
Ordinances of Wisby   345.
Ordonnances of Louis IX   444.
Oresme, Nicholas   678.
Orestes (emperor)   81–82.
Organum (music)   337. 544.
Origen   46. 49. 506.
Origo   25.
Orkan (Orkhan), *bey(beg)*   637.
Orkney Islands   195. 609.
Orleans   495. 504. 580. 588. 592.
   university   498.
Ormuz   633.
Orosius   75. 267. 331.
Orvieto, cathedral   541.
Osman   636.
Ost Mark (Austria)   280. 363.
Ostrogoths   76. 79. 82. 87. 95. 97–98. 118. 121–122. 302.
Oswald, St.   308.
Oswy of Northumbria   101.
Othlo of Emmeran   322.
Othman, caliph   146.
Otto I, emperor   193. 203. 256. 274. 279–280. 323.
   ecclesiastical policy of   279–280.
Otto II, emperor   281–282. 302. 313. 323. 365.
Otto III, emperor   282–283. 289–290. 302. 323. 458.
Otto IV, emperor   401. 417. 434. 478.
Otto of Brunswick, *see* Otto IV.
Otto of Friesing, bishop   516.
Otto of Nordheim   385.
Otto of Wittelsbach   396. 399. 401.
Ottokar II of Bohemia, king   405. 458. 460. 598.
Ottonian Emperors   274. 278–284.
   Renaissance   281. 325. 336.
Ovid   17–18.
Oviedo   263.
Oxen   241. 242.
Oxford University   498. 501. 503. 675.

P

Pachomius, St.   304.
Padua   518. 622.
Pagans (*pagani*)   310.
Pages   223.
Painting
   "Byzantine Manner"   543. 681.
   Carolingian   186.
   in Early Middle Ages   334–336.
   fresco   137. 543.
   in High Middle Ages   536. 543.

Painting [cont.]
   Italian Renaissance   681–682.
   in Later Middle Ages   681–682. 684–685.
   manuscript illumination   186. 543. 684.
   Transalpine Gothic   684–685.
Pale, in Ireland   414.
Palencia, University of   498.
Paleologi   455–456. 633.
Palestine   31. 42. 638.
Palmyra   21.
Pange Lingua   523.
Pannonia   79. 87.
Pantheon   39.
Papa   37.
Papacy   50. 97. 99. 133. 491. 510. 558. 593. 599. 631. 691.
   in Age of Iron   301–302.
   Avignon   642. 643. 647–649. 661. 662.
   Avignon during Schism   650–653.
   and Bohemia   604.
   and Byzantium   300.
   and Carolingians   168–172. 176–178. 300.
   in Carolingian era   300–301.
   Curia   471. 472. 478.
   in Early Middle Ages   297–303. 314.
   and England   419.
   finance   647.
   and France   440–441.
   and Germany   281–302.
   in High Middle Ages   340. 361. 384–406. 471–479.
   justice   472.
   in Late Middle Ages   600. 601. 642–656.
   primacy   36–39. 297. 298. 301. 471.
   reform of Church   474–475. 480–481.
   Renaissance   624. 644. 649–650. 654–657. 662.
   and Spain   450. 630.
   and Western Empire   276–277. 384–405. 477–479.
   see also Church and State; Papal States.
Papal States   99. 171–172. 176. 203. 299. 471. 476. 618. 623–624. 647. 657. 662.
   origin   171–172. 176.
Paper   155. 261.
   financial   351.
   industry   346.
Papinian   26.
Pariage   441.
Paris   197. 347. 352. 353. 442. 482. 495. 497. 554. 588.
   (1436)   581.
   (Francia), March of   196.
   Peace of (1259)   436.
   university   496–498. 676.
Parlement   437. 440. 442–443.

Index

Parliament   360–361. 424–427. 446. 568. 572. 574. 581–583. 585–587. 642–643.
   "Model" (1295)   425.
   Montfort's (1265)   421.
Parma (1248)   405.
Paschal II, Pope   389–392. 476.
Paschal III, Anti-Pope   397.
Pastoral activities   242. 354. 557.
Passau   365.
Patarin   475.
Patriarchs   36–37. 45–46. 132. 134.
   Bulgarian   134. 292.
   of Constantinople   132–133. 297. 325.
   Russian   134. 615.
   Serbian   635.
Patrick (St)   310. 311.
Patrons   209.
Paul, St., apostle   31. 35. 38. 41.
Paul the Deacon   183. 185. 332.
Paula, St.   305.
Paulinus of Nola   86. 327.
Pavia   171–172.
   (774)   176.
   Council (1160)   397.
Pax Romana   12. 15.
Pazzi Conspiracy   623.
Peace of God   227. 316.
Peace of Paris (1258)   421.
Peasants   247–250.
   living conditions   238–240. 247–250.
   religion   250.
   see also Laborers, rural; Serfs.
Pechenegs   129. 192–193. 290. 291. 293–294. 453. 460. 462.
Pecs, University of   607.
Pedro II of Aragon   452.
Pedro III of Aragon   360. 438. 455. 628.
Pedro IV of Aragon   628–629.
Pedro I of Castile, the Cruel   627.
Pedro I of Portugal   632.
Pegolloti, Francesco   553.
Peine forte et dure   413.
Peking   467.
Pelagians   48.
Pelagius, cardinal   380.
Pelayo   262.
Pelusium   147.
Penance   42. 489.
Penitential books   486.
Pentapolis   120. 147.
Pepin of Aquitaine   200.
Pepin of Italy   177. 199.
Pepin I, of Landen   107. 167. 168.
Pepin II, of Heristal   168.
Pepin III, the Short   99. 170–172. 182. 209. 210. 300.
   Donations to Papacy   171–172.
Perfecti, Albigensian   488.

Perigeux district   136.
"Perpetual Pact," Swiss (1291)   602.
Perieslav   462.
Perrotin, Master   545.
Persia and Persians   117. 121–122. 124. 147. 150. 151. 465. 638.
   Samanids   151.
Persian Empire   121–122. 147.
Peruzzi   351. 558. 559. 568.
Peter, Metropolitan of Russia   614.
Peter, St., apostle   30. 31. 37–39.
Peter Bartholomew   371.
Peter Damian, St.   386–387. 475. 481. 494.
Peter des Roches   419.
Peter Lombard   486. 506.
Peter of Alcantara, St.   663.
Peter of Blois   521.
Peter of Bulgaria, Tsar   292.
Peter the Hermit   369.
Peter the Venerable, abbot   308.
Peter Waldo of Lyons   487.
Peterborough College   499.
Peter's Pence   647.
Petrariae   225.
Petrarch (Petrarca), Francesco   666. 668. 672. 675.
Petronilla of Aragon   452.
Petrus Peregrinus   349.
Pfahlburgers   399. 402.
Pharmacopoeia   161.
Philip I of France   258. 391. 409. 447.
Philip II of France   356. 379. 401. 417. 432–435. 441–447. 445. 478. 497. 513. 516.
Philip III of France   437–438. 441. 444.
Philip IV of France   423. 438–441. 443–447. 514. 588. 643–647. 661.
   Vs. Boniface VIII   644–647.
Philip V of France   588.
Philip VI of France   573. 588.
Philip of Austria   631.
Philip the Bold of Burgundy   589. 591.
Philip of Suabia, imperial claimant   401.
Philip the Good of Burgundy   560. 577. 675.
Philip the Handsome of Hapsburg   601.
Philologian and His Cat, The   330.
Philosophy   135. 486. 495. 502. 510.
   Arab   505.
   see also Islam
   Byzantine   137.
   Carolingian   185.
   Christian   50.
   Greek   505.
   Islamic   156. 159. 261.
   in Later Middle Ages   659–660. 677.
   moral   510.
   natural (physical)   510.

Philosophy [cont.]
   in Renaissance Italy 671.
   Roman 18–19.
   Scholastic 503–509.
   see also Scholasticism.
Phocas, emperor 123–124.
Phoenicians 141.
Phoenix (Battle of the Masts) (651) 148.
Photius, patriarch 133. 135–136. 301.
Phantzes, George 136.
Physics 160.
Piacenza, Council of (1095) 368.
Piasts 457–459.
Piccolomini, Aeneas Sylvius 603. 657–658. 670. 672.
   see also Pius II, Pope.
Piccolomini, Francesco 657.
   see also Pius III, Pope.
Picts 91.
Piedmont 397.
Pierre d' Ailly 662.
Pilgrimages 42.
Pious associations 490.
Pisa 343. 364. 551. 559. 620. 623.
   Council (1409) 652.
   old Cathedral 538.
Pisanos 682.
   Andrea 682.
   Giovanni 682.
   Niccola 682.
Pius II, Pope 603. 655. 656. 658. 659. 670.
Pius III, Pope 657.
Placidia, princess and empress 78. 80–81.
Plantagenets 216. 411–427.
Plato 135.
   Republic 244.
Platonic Academy, Florence 671.
Platonism 643. 671.
   see also Neo-Platonism.
Plectruda, queen 168.
Plethon, Georgios Gremisthos 659. 669. 671.
Pliny the Elder 19.
Plows 354.
Pluralism (of benefices) 644.
Plutarch 18.
Plutocracy, Roman 16.
Podestas 396.
Podiebrad, George, of Bohemia 601. 604–605.
Poem of the Cid 535.
Poetry
   Carolingian 185.
   Celtic 57.
   early German 69.
   Goliardic 523.
   Islamic Spanish 261.
   Latin 114. 326–330. 523.

Poggio Bracciolini 669. 671.
Poitiers (1356) 574. 575. 588.
Poitevan Gateway 6.
Poitou 417. 433. 435. 438. 592.
Polabians 288.
Poland 395. 466. 449. 552. 596. 602. 607. 612.
   in Early Middle Ages 283–286. 289.
   in High Middle Ages 457–459. 605.
   in Later Middle Ages 605–606.
   Lithuania 606.
   manorialism in 242.
   Partitional Period 605.
Political theory
   contract concept 509.
   in High Middle Ages 510–514.
   in Late Middle Ages 677–678.
   in Renaissance Italy 671.
Poliziano, Angelo 670. 673.
Pollentia (402) 77.
Polo, Marco 467.
Polovtsy 294.
Polygamy, early Christianity and 41.
   Islamic 144.
Polyphony, see Music.
Pomerania 365. 458. 602. 605. 606.
Ponthieu 576.
Poor Clares 484.
Poor Men 482. 488.
   Waldensians 487.
Poor Priests 660.
Popolo grasso 564. 619.
Popolo minuto 564. 619.
Population
   in Early Middle Ages 243.
   in High Middle Ages 340. 352–355.
   in Late Middle Ages 563.
   rural 235. 243.
   Russian 463–464.
   urban 352.
Portolani 553.
Portugal and Portuguese 264. 449. 452–453. 552. 561. 566. 622.
   Age of Empire 632–633.
   Age of Exploration 632.
   Church 649.
   consolidation 632–633.
   expansion overseas 562. 626. 632–633.
   feudalism 218.
   in High Middle Ages 631.
   in Later Middle Ages 618. 626. 631–633.
   see also Iberian Peninsula.
Post-Glossators 514.
Postumus, general 21.
Pot de fer 569.

Potentiores	25.
Poundage	574.
Poverty, as religious ideal	482–483.
Praemunire, Statute of (1353)	569. 582. 642.
Praetores peregrini	14.
Pragmatic Sanction of Bourges (1438)	569. 591. 594. 654. 657. 661.
Prague, University of	599. 676.
Praise of Folly	675.
Preaching	485.
Precarium	209. 237.
Premonstratensians	482.
Premyslids of Bohemia	289. 457–458.
Presbyters	35. 39.
Pressburg, University of	607.
Prester John	632.
Pretextatus, bishop	106.
Prévôts	434. 445.
Priests	490.
see also Presbyters.	
Prignani of Bari, archbishop	650.
Primates, ecclesiastical	314.
Prince, The	671.
Printing	555–556. 676.
Pripet Marshes	288.
Priscian	321. 521.
Privilege of Otto (962 and 963)	281.
Privilege of the Union, Aragonese (1287)	452. 628.
Procopius	88. 119–120. 135.
Proctors, university	499.
Procurations (of benefices)	648.
Prokop, "Holy" (Bald)	604. 660.
Proletariat	563.
in Later Middle Ages	565–566.
see also Laborers.	
Promissory notes	350.
Pronoias and *pronoiars*	453. 633.
Pronsk	612.
Proto-Romanesque, see Architecture.	
Provence	97. 102. 105. 592.
Kingdom	203. 205. 255.
Provisions of Oxford (1258)	421. 436.
Provisions, Papal	471. 644. 648.
Provisors, Statute of (1351)	569. 582. 642. 661.
Provost, manorial	247.
Prudentius	86. 327.
Prussia	366. 602. 606.
Psellus, Michael	136.
Pskov	612. 613.
Ptolemy	19.
Pulci, Luigi	673.
Putting out system	555.

Q

Qadarites	156.
Qadisiyah (637)	147.
Qarmatians	156.
Qasidahs	141. 157.
Qays party	150.
Quadrant	160.
Quadrivium	322.
Quiersy, Capitulary (877)	190. 204. 210.
Quintilian	18. 670.
Quo warranto	426.
Qurra (Koran-readers)	161.

R

Rabanus Maurus	322. 325. 326. 328.
Rachimburgi	111. 181.
Radbert of Corbie	185.
Radegunde, queen	328.
Radewyns, Florent	663.
Rainald of Dassel	477.
Raising of Lazarus	524.
Ramadan	144.
Ramiro I of Aragon	263. 452.
Ramiro II of Aragon	452.
Ramón Berenguer IV of Barcelona	452.
Raoul Glaber	536.
Raoul (Ralph) of Burgundy	256.
Raska (Rascia)	291. 457.
Ratislav of Moravia	312.
Ratramnus of Corbie	185–186. 323.
Ravenna	80. 87. 98. 126.
Raymond du Puy	375.
Raymond of Burgundy	631.
Raymond of Penafort, St.	486.
Raymond of Toulouse, count	371.
Raymond of Tripoli	378.
Razzias	141. 146.
Real Patronato	569. 630. 657. 661.
Realism	
artistic	684. 685.
philosophical	505–506.
Reccared of Spain, king	97.
Reclamation	353.
Reconquista (Reconquest), Iberian Christian	262–264. 364. 450–452. 630–631.
Recordare rex inclytae (1300)	645.
Recovery of the Holy Land	659.
Recreations	221. 250.
Red Sea	551.
Reeve	247.
Reform, ecclestical, see Church; monastic, see Monasticism.	
Reformation	2. 664. 691.
Regalia	285. 396. 398.
Regensburg (Ratisbon)	365.

Index

Reginald of Chatillon 378.
Reginald of Durham 341.
Regino of Prum 205.
Regularis Concordia 308.
Reichenau, monastery 284. 308. 323.
Reichsfürsten 218. 399.
Reichsregiment 601.
Reichskammergericht 601.
Reichstag, German 598.
Reims 189. 495.
    Cathedral 540–541.
Relics, veneration of 42.
Reliefs, feudal 213. 424.
Religion, in Roman Empire 30.
    see also Christianity, Church, Judaism.
Religious orders 479. 490.
    Dominicans 484–485.
    Franciscans 482–485.
    hospital 482.
    in Later Middle Ages 661–663.
    mendicant 482–485.
    military 482.
    Third 482. 658.
    of early Germans 67.
Remi, Archbishop of Reims 104. 311.
Remigius (Remi) of Auxerre 325. 338.
Renard the Fox 532.
Renaissance 2. 3. 666–684.
    Czech 599.
    French 593.
    Italian 548–549. 619. 666–673. 679–684.
    in Later Middle Ages 619. 666–671. 673–677. 679–684.
    Papacy and 654–657.
    thesis of 548–549.
    Transalpine 673–677.
    twelfth century 504. 521. 548.
    see also Carolingian, Justinian, Macedonian, Ottonian, twelfth-century Renaissance(s).
Raymond II (IV) of Toulouse 369. 431. 436.
Raymond VI of Toulouse, count 488.
Renegados 762.
Reservations (of benefices) 471. 648.
Reuchlin, Johann 675.
Rhaetia 275. 277.
Rhetoric 18. 135. 321. 667.
Rhine River 7. 61. 103.
Rhodian Sea Law 345.
Rhymed Chronicle of Cologne 516.
Rialto 555.
Riazan 466. 612–615.
Ribaulds 569.
Richard I of England 379. 400–401. 415. 433. 576. 582–583. 587.
Richard II of England 652.

Richard III of England 585.
Richard of Cornwall 405.
Richard of Gloucester 585.
Richard of London 515.
Richard of St. Victor 482. 486.
Richard of York 584.
Richemont, constable 591.
Richer 332.
Ricimer 81. 87.
Rienzi, Cola di 624.
Riga 366.
Rigord, monk 516.
Riksdag of Sweden 608.
Rimbert 332.
Rio de Ouro 632.
Rio Palmones (1343) 627.
Rio Salado (1340) 627.
Ritter 219. 222.
Robert I, Bruce, of Scotland, king 423.
Robert II, the Pious, of France 257–258.
Robert Curthose of Normandy 254. 258. 369. 409. 410. 430.
Robert de Boron 529.
Robert de Bourge 489.
Robert de Courçon 497.
Robert de Sorbon 499.
Robert Grosseteste 502. 517.
Robert Guiscard 370. 589. 624. 625.
Robert of Artois 381. 573.
Robert of Chester 517.
Robert of Clari 131. 515.
Robert II of Flanders, count 369.
Robert III of Flanders, count 440.
Robert of Jumièges, archbishop 268.
Robert of Molesmes, abbot 480.
Robert of Neustria 256.
Robert the Monk 367. 515.
Robert the Strong of Francia 196.
Robertians in France 256.
Rod (measure) 239.
Roderick, Archbishop of Toledo 451.
Roderick of Spain, king 259. 262.
Rodrigo Diaz de Bivar 264.
Roger II of Sicily 219. 400. 625.
Roger Bacon 483. 503. 517.
Roger of Hoveden 516.
Roger of Wendover 516.
Roland, cardinal 395–397.
    see also Alexander III, Pope.
Roland, prefect 525–527. 673.
Rollo of Normandy 197. 254. 256. 310.
Roman Academy 656.
Roman Empire 4. 8–27. 95.
    Absolute Emperors 231.
    army 14–15. 21. 69–71. 84. 90.
    Barracks Emperors 231.
    and Christianity 31–34. 50. 84.
    culture 26–27.

Roman Empire [cont.]
  decline   20–27. 69–70. 80–93. 95.
  economy   15–16. 21. 24. 82–85.
  and early Germans   71. 103. 231.
  government   12–14. 22–25. 83.
  influence   9–27. 107.
  law   14. 360.
  society   15. 25.
  taxation   15. 25. 83.
Romance languages   54. 114.
Romance of the Rose   530–532.
Romances   528–532.
  Arthurian Cycle   529–530.
  Classical Cycle   530.
Romanesque style
  in architecture   536–539.
  in painting   543.
  in sculpture   542.
Romanus I, Lecapenus, emperor   128.
Romanus II, emperor   128.
Romanus IV, Digenes, emperor   367.
Romanus the Melode   136.
Rome   12. 32. 36–39. 77. 79. 98–99. 126.
       192. 233. 281. 283. 299. 487. 648.
  University of   498.
Romulus Augustulus, emperor   81. 82.
                                 87. 97.
Roncaglia, Diet of (1158)   396.
Roncesvalles (778)   526.
Rorik   189.
Roscellin   505.
Rostislav of Moravia   288.
Rostov   615.
Rotunda churches   333.
Roussillon   593.
Rudder   344.
Rudolph I of Burgundy   203. 205. 285.
Rudolph I of Hapsburg, emperor   405.
                       458. 460. 515. 598.
Rudolph of Suabia, duke   388.
Rugii   97.
Rules of Health of Salerno   517.
Rum, sultanate   370. 636.
Rumania   636.
  language   636.
Runnymede   418.
Ruprecht of the Rhenish Palatinate,
  count   600.
Rurik   294.
Rus   197. 294.
Russia and Russians   9. 128. 293. 313.
                  463. 561. 603. 612–613.
  Age of Princes   462–464.
  army   615.
  and Byzantium   615–616.
  Church   294–295. 464. 614.
  civilization   295.
  in Early Middle Ages   293–295.

Russia and Russians [cont.]
  economy   242. 463. 610. 611. 613.
  expansion   615.
  government   462–463. 610–613.
                                 615–616.
  in High Middle Ages   366. 462–468.
  in Later Middle Ages   610–616.
  law   295. 616.
  Mongols   464. 467.
  see also Tartars.
  Northmen   197–198.
  population   463–464.
  principalities   611–615.
  society   463–464.
  Tartar rule and influence   610–615.
Ruthenia   458.
Ruysebroeck, Jan   663.
Rynvisch, John   352.

S

Sa'ad ed-Din   633.
Sabellians   44.
Sac and *soc*   270.
Sachsenspiegel   515.
Sacraments   30. 42–43. 315. 489–490.
Sacrosancta (1415)   653.
Saffar al-   150.
Sagas   60. 536.
Sagres   553. 632.
Sahara Desert   342.
Sails   344.
St. Denis Abbey, church   540.
St. Gall, monastery   305.
St. Mark's Cathedral, Venice   136.
St. Paul's Outside the Walls   27.
St. Paul's School, London   675.
St. Riquier, monastery   323.
St. Sophia, Kiev   462.
St. Thomas of Acre, Order   376.
St. Victor's, monastery   495. 501.
Saintonge   433.
Saints   42. 490.
Saisset of Pamiers, bishop   438. 645.
Saladin   377–378.
  tithe   434.
Salamanca, University of   498. 676.
Salerno   495. 517–518.
  University of   498.
Salimbene of Parma   516.
Salisbury, cathedral   54.
Salsburg   365.
Salutati, Coluccio   669.
Salvator mundi, bull   441.
Salvian   75.
Samarra   150.
Samarkand   149. 155.
Samo the Frank   288.
Samogitia   602. 605.

Index

Samuel of Bulgaria, Tsar 128. 291. 293. 456.
San Germano, Treaty of (1230) 403.
San Vitale, Ravenna 136. 333.
Sancho IV of Castile 626.
Sancho I of Portugal 631.
Sancho the Great, of Navarre 263. 451–452.
Sandys, John Edmis 323.
Sanitation 357. 518.
Sant' Angelo Castle, Rome 389.
Santa Claus; see Nicholas, St.
Santa Maria in Trastavere 27.
Santa Sophia, Constantinople 120. 122. 136. 334.
Santiago, military order of 451.
Santiago de Compostela 262.
Saragossa 260.
Sarai, Khanate 467. 610. 614.
Sardica, Council of (343) 38–39.
Sardinia 192. 364. 628.
Sauvegarde 441.
Savonarola, Girolamo 623.
Savoy 90.
Saxon Emperors 274–284.
Saxons 91. 271. 174–175. 385–386.
   in England 100.
Saxony 174–175. 275. 276. 277. 278. 285. 365. 385–386. 390. 393. 394. 600.
Scabini 181.
Scandinavia 61. 275. 485. 551. 561.
   Church in 197–198. 312.
   feudalism 219.
   in High Middle Ages 461–462.
   literature 536.
   Union of Calmar (1397) 609.
Scaramasax 113.
Schism, Eastern 133. 472. 656.
   Great Western 624. 649–653. 661.
Schola Cantorum, Rome 336.
Scholastic (*scholasticus*) 320.
Scholastica, St. 305.
Scholasticism 3. 322. 501. 503–509.
   Dominican School 508–509.
   Franciscan School 507–508.
   late medieval 667.
Schools
   cathedral 320. 322. 495.
   chantry 321. 495.
   collegiate 495.
   monastic 320. 322. 495.
   municipal 361. 495. 553.
   navigational 553.
   palace 321.
   parish 320. 495.
   professional 495. 496.
   public grammar 676.
   song 321. 495.

Schwabenspiegel 515.
Schwyz 602.
Sciences
   natural 135. 137. 495. 509. 516–518. 678.
   Roman 19.
   social 509–516.
Scipio Africanus 668.
Sciri 97.
Sclavinia 124.
Scone 423.
Scotland 100.
   Church in 311.
   in Early Middle Ages 196.
   in High Middle Ages 409–410. 414. 423.
   in Later Middle Ages 573. 582.
Scots 91. 178.
Scotus, Duns 517. 659. 677.
Script
   Beneventan 323.
   Carolingian minuscule 184–186. 323.
   Insular 323.
   Merovingian 323.
   Visigothic 323.
Scriptorium 323.
Scriptures, Sacred (Bible) 320.
   see also Bible.
Sculpture
   in early Germanic kingdoms 114.
   in Early Middle Ages 336.
   in High Middle Ages 536. 542–543.
   Italian Renaissance 682–684.
   Late Gothic 685.
   Roman 20.
Scutage 212.
Scythia 76.
Sea Loans 350.
Sea of Marmora 117.
Sedulius Scotus 185.
Seljuk Turks; see Turks.
Semandria (1437) 607.
Sempach (1386) 602.
Senatorial class, Roman 16.
Seneca, the Younger 19.
Seneschals 247. 443.
Sentences, of Peter Lombard 506–507.
Septimania 78. 97. 102. 104–105. 172. 260.
Septimius Severus 21.
Sequences 326. 328. 521.
Serbia and Serbs 291–293. 460. 607. 634. 638.
   Church 313.
   Empire 635.
   in High Middle Ages 453. 456–457.
   in Later Middle Ages 635.

Index

Serfs 16–17. 63. 65. 113. 241. 242. 245. 249. 271. 353.
   dues 245.
   emancipation 357.
   rights 246.
Sergeants, feudal 220.
Sergius, Patriarch 124. 136.
Services (*servicia*) 647. 648.
Servites 485.
Seven Sages 532.
Severi 21.
Seville 45.
   University of 498.
Sex, Christian teaching 41–42.
Sextant 160.
Sforza, Francesco 620. 621.
Sforza, Ludovico 593.
Sharecropping 236. 556.
Shawar, Vizir of Egypt 377.
Sheikh 141.
Shemiaka, prince 614.
Shepherds, The 524.
Sheriffs 101. 271. 408.
Shiites 148. 156.
Ships and shipbuilding 232. 344–345. 346. 445.
   caravels 552–553.
   carracks 532–533.
   cogs 345. 553.
   dromonds 131.
   galleys 552.
   of Northmen 195.
Shires 270. 423.
Shirkuk 377.
Siberia 467.
Sibylla 378.
Sic et Non 506.
Sicilian Vespers (1282) 438. 479. 628.
Sicilies 624.
Sicily 96–98. 133. 191–192. 198. 286. 299. 364. 365. 400. 401. 403–405. 419. 421. 438. 449. 479. 567. 618. 624–625.
   Angevin 455. 625.
   Aragonese 455–456. 625.
   Byzantine 120–121.
   government 404.
   in Later Middle Ages 624–625. 628–630.
   question 479.
   "Vespers" uprising (1282) 438. 479. 628.
Sidonius Apollinaris 80. 86. 112.
Siena, Cathedral 541.
Siete Partidas (*Seven Parts*) 451.
Sigebert of Austrasia 106.
Sigebert III of Austrasia 167.

Sigismund, emperor 600. 607. 634. 652. 655.
   Crusade of (1396) 634.
Sigismund of Burgundy, king 105.
Signori 619–620.
Signoria, Florentine 622.
Silesia 365. 466. 604.
Silverius, Pope 298.
Simeon of Bulgaria, tsar 127–128. 193. 291–292.
Simeon Stylite 304.
Simon de Montfort, the Elder 421. 435. 452. 488.
Simon de Montfort, the Younger 360. 421–422. 425.
Simon Magus 37.
Simon Saphir 352.
Sistine Chapel 656.
Sixtus IV, Pope 656.
Slaves and slavery 16. 41. 58. 65. 113. 242. 245. 316. 566–567.
   Christianity and 41.
Slavonic
   liturgy 292.
   Old (language) 132. 287–288. 313.
   script 292.
Slavs 57–58. 132. 176. 276. 278. 282–283. 287–297. 398. 485. 566. 691.
   and Church 127. 287–292. 294–295. 312. 313.
   early home 288.
   in Early Middle Ages 191–192. 274. 287–297.
   eastern 293–295.
   expansion 287–288.
   in High Middle Ages 365. 457–461.
   southeastern 124. 291.
   southern 290–293.
   southwestern 291.
   western 288–291. 312.
Slovenes 277. 291.
Sluter, Claus 685.
Sluys (1340) 575.
Smerds 464.
Smolensk 463. 612.
Societates, maris 351. 560.
   terrae 351–352. 560.
Society
   Byzantine 131–132.
   Carolingian 182.
   classes 246.
   early German 65.
   feudal 219–229.
   fluidity 244.
   in early Germanic kingdoms 113.
   in Early Middle Ages 243–252.
   in High Middle Ages 354–359.
   in Later Middle Ages 550. 562–572.

Index

Society [cont.]
  in Renaissance Italy 565.
  in Russia 463.
  Later Roman 85.
  of Northmen 193–194.
  in Spain 264.
Soissons 102.
  (486) 104.
Solidus 16. 112. 234. 349.
Somerset, Duke of 584.
Song of Roland 525–527. 535.
Song of the Open Road 523.
Sophia (Zoe) Paleologus 615.
Sophronius, Patriarch 145–146.
Sorbonne 499.
Sorbs 288.
Spain 13. 69. 96–97. 178. 186. 264. 596. 630.
  in age of invasions 89.
  aristocracy 358.
  Byzantines in 121.
  Charlemagne and 175.
  Church 630.
  early medieval Christian 259. 262–264.
  early medieval Moslem 259–262.
  expansion 562. 630–631.
  feudalism 218.
  government 629–630.
  in High Middle Ages 367. 449–453.
  in Later Middle Ages 618. 626–631.
  literature 535–536.
  manorialism 238.
  Moslem 148–149. 260–263.
  Northmen 197.
  overseas 626. 630–631.
  reclamation 353.
  society 264.
  Umayyad 151. 260–262.
  unification 629–631.
  Vandals 78–79. 96.
  Visigoths 78. 96–97. 108. 148–149. 259.
  see also Iberian Peninsula.
Spanish March 175. 255. 263.
Spoils (*spolia*) 648.
Spoleto 301.
  duchy and dukes 98. 109–110. 177. 204. 280.
Squires 223–224. 564.
Stabat Mater 522.
Stanislaus of Cracow, bishop, St. 459
Stained glass windows 536. 539. 543–544.
Stamford Bridge (1066) 269.
Staple goods 561.
The Star 524.
State and Church; *see* Church and State.

Statuta legum 97.
Statutes in Favor of the Princes (1220 and 1231–1232) 402.
Statutes of Laborers (1351 ff.) 561. 587.
Stephen II, Pope 99. 171.
Stephen IV, Pope 199.
Stephen of Blois, King of England 410–411. 430.
Stephen I of Hungary, St. 289–290. 313. 460.
Stephen I Nemanja of Serbia 457.
Stephen II Nemanjid of Serbia 457.
Stephen III (Uros II) of Serbia 635.
Stephen VI (Uros III) of Serbia 635.
Stephen VII Dushan of Serbia 635.
Stephen Harding, abbot 480.
Stephen Langton, archbishop 417. 521.
Stephen Lazarevic of Serbia, king 635.
Stephen of Blois, count 369. 371.
Stephen of Cloyes 380.
Stephen IV of Moldavia 636.
Stewards 221. 247.
Stigand, Archbishop of Canterbury 268. 408.
Stilicho 77. 80. 118.
Stirling Bridge (1297) 423.
Stoicism 13. 18–19. 30.
Stone vaulting
  Gothic 539.
  Romanesque 536–537.
Strabo 19.
Stralsund, Peace of (1370) 602.
Strappado 489.
Strasbourg 343. 352. 552.
  Oaths (842) 200–201.
Strategoi 124. 131.
Stratiotai 131.
Strozzi, Palla 670.
Struma (1014) 128.
Studia generalia 484. 495–496.
Sturluson, Snorri 536.
Sturm, St. 332.
Stylites 304.
Styria 598. 601. 607.
Styrian Rhymed Chronicle 516.
Suabia 18. 200. 275. 277. 278. 393. 598.
Subdeacons 490.
Subiaco 306.
Subinfeudation 211.
Subsoil rights 15.
Subutay 465.
Sudebnik (law code) 616.
Suetonius 18. 185.
Suevi 78. 89.
Suffolk, Earl of 584.
Sufis 156–157.
Suger, Abbot 430. 443. 516. 540.
Sugut 636.

Sultans 151. 154.
Summa Contra Gentiles 509.
Summa Theologica 509.
Summas 507.
  in stone 539.
Sung Empire 467.
Sunna 161.
Sunnites 156.
Suso, Heinrich 658.
Sussex 100. 266.
Sutri, Concordat of (1111) 390.
Suzdal and Suzdalia 463. 614.
Svatopluk of Moravia 288.
Sviatopolk of Kiev 463.
Sviatoslav of Kiev 292–294.
Sweden 461. 594. 608–610.
  economy 609.
Sweyn Forkbeard 267.
Switzerland and Swiss Confederation 592. 598. 602.
Syagrius, general 89. 90. 102.
Sylvester II, Pope 282. 289–290. 325–326.
  see also Gerbert of Aurillac.
Symonds, John A. 548.
Syria and Syrians 118–119. 128. 147. 151. 235. 466–467. 638.
Syriac, language 157.

T

Taborites 655.
Tacitus 18. 60–72. 174. 208. 223. 237.
Tactics, military, changes in 569. 574.
Tagliocozzo (1268) 405.
Tagus River 264.
Taifas 260.
Taille (tallage) 241. 245. 246. 444. 446. 591. 594.
Tamerlane 467. 610. 635. 637.
Tancred of Antioch 370. 371.
Tancred of Lecce 379. 400.
Tangier 632.
Tannenberg (1410) 603. 606.
Tapestries 544.
Tariq 148. 259.
Tartars 294. 366. 458. 459. 460. 462. 464. 467–468. 596. 603. 610.
  influence of 611.
  in Russia 610–615.
  see also Mongols.
Tassilo of Bavaria 175. 209.
Tauler, Johann 658.
Taxation 228. 242. 245.
  capita 24.
  Church 645. 647–648.
  Crusades and 382.
  decima scalata 620.

Taxation [cont.]
  in Early Middle Ages 241.
  in England 424. 425. 574. 586.
  feudal 215.
  in France 434. 440. 444. 446. 589. 591. 594.
  in High Middle Ages 359.
  in Italy 620.
  juga 24.
  progressive income 620. 623.
  Roman 15. 24.
Technology, advances 344.
Templars, *see* Knights Templar.
Temuchin 464.
  see also Chingiz Khan.
Terence 331.
Tergel (Tervel), Khan of Bulgaria 292.
Tertullian 31. 46. 48.
Terty (687) 168.
Teutoberg Forest (A.D. 9) 69.
Teuton 60.
Teutonic Knights 366. 375. 458. 459. 596. 597. 602. 603. 605.
Thabit 157.
Thanet, Isle of 196.
Thankmar 279.
Thegan 199.
Thegns (Thanes) 269–271.
Themes 124.
  Aegean 130.
  Cyprian (Cibyrrhaoet) 130.
Theoctistus, minister 127.
Theodahad, King of Ostrogoths 98. 121.
Theodelinda, queen 98. 299. 310.
Theodora, empress (6th century) 119–120.
Theodora, empress (9th century) 126–127.
Theodora, empress (11th century) 129. 453.
Theodore Angelus 456.
Theodore of Studium, abbot 135.
Theodore of Tarsus, archbishop 101. 315. 324.
Theodoric the Great, King of Ostrogoths and Italy 82. 87–88. 97. 105. 324.
Theodosian Code 110.
Theodosius I (Emperor) 23. 32–34. 39. 47. 77. 80. 117.
Theodosius II, emperor 33. 134.
Theodulph of Orleans, bishop 183. 185. 322. 328.
Theology and theologians 486. 499. 506. 513.
  Byzantine 137.
  Carolingian 185.
  Islamic 159.

Index

Theology and theologians [cont.]
  Scholastic   503–509.
  see also Scholasticism.
Theophano, Byzantine empress   128.
Theophano, Western empress   281–282.
Theophilus, emperor   126.
Theophylact, house of   301.
Theresa of Portugal   452. 631.
Thessalonica   637.
  Kingdom   454–455.
Thessaly   635.
Theutberga   202–203.
Thibaud of Champagne   435.
Thierry of Chartres   502.
Things   62. 63. 461.
  Althings   461.
Third Crusade   379.
Third orders, *see* Religious orders.
Thomas à Kempis   663.
Thomas Aquinas, St.   350. 485. 486. 503. 509. 513–514. 521–523.
Thomas Becket, *see* Becket, Thomas.
Thomas of Celano   522.
Thomism   509.
Thor   67.
Thorn   459.
  First Peace (1411)   602. 606.
  Second Peace (1466)   603. 606.
Thoros of Edessa   370.
Thrace   118.
Three Chapters   122.
Thuringia   105. 275. 278. 285. 598.
Tiberius II, emperor   123.
Tidemann of Limburg   559.
Tinchebrai (1106)   410.
Tiptopf of Worcester, earl   675.
Tithes   241. 647.
Toktamysh   611.
Toledan Tables   451.
Toledo   149. 259. 264. 504. 260. 364. 451.
  (1085)
  Council (527 or 531)   320.
  Councils   97.
Tome of Leo I   39. 46.
Tonnage   574.
Tordesillas, Treaty of (1494)   633.
Toro (1476)   629.
Torriani (Della Torres)   621.
Tortona   395.
Tostig   268–269.
Totila, King of Ostrogoths   121.
Toulouse   78. 102. 431. 438.
  County of   255. 415. 435.
  University of   498.
Touraine   433.
Tournai   103.
  (1340)   575.
Tournaments   222. 358.

Tours (Tours-Poitiers, 732)   168. 170. 260.
Towns   352. 441. 494. 690.
  conditions   563.
  in Early Middle Ages   233–234.
  government   356.
  halls   542.
  Hanseatic   551.
  in High Middle Ages   352–353.
  in Iberian Peninsula   450.
  in Later Middle Ages   563–564.
  population   352.
  in Roman Empire   15.
  sites   353.
  of southern Germany   551.
Translators and translations   504. 517.
Transoxiana   149. 342. 465. 467.
  Hamdanids   151.
Trastamara, house of   627.
Trebizond   455.
Très Belles Heures   684.
Très Riches Heures   684.
Trèves   504.
Tribur (887)   203. 205. 277.
  (1076)   388.
Trigonometry   160.
Tripoli   147. 378. 638.
  County of   371. 374.
Trivium   321–322.
Tropes   329. 331. 524.
Troubadours   227.
Trovno   636.
Troyes   344.
  Council (1128)   375.
  Treaty (1420)   577. 591.
Truce of God   227. 316.
Tuchins   568.
Tudor absolutism   585–587.
Tughril Beg   367.
Tulunids   151. 191.
Tuluy   465.
Tunis   364. 381. 437.
Tunisia   638.
  Tulunids   151.
Turkestan   467.
Turks   150–151. 154.
  government   638.
  in High Middle Ages   636.
  in Later Middle Ages   618. 633. 636–639.
  Ottoman   551. 566. 596. 600. 603. 607. 634–636.
  Seljuk   129. 151. 367–369. 453.
Tuscany   280. 401. 622. 623.
  Dukes of   204.
Tusculum, house of   302.
Tutors   495.
Tver   612–615.

Twelfth-century Renaissance	521.
Tyler, Wat, Rebellion of 1381	562. 583.
Tyre	378. 379.
Tyrol	598.

U

Ucello, Paolo	682.
Ugedey, khan	465–466.
Ukraine	9.
Ulfilas, bishop	71. 76. 310. 331.
Uman	140.
Umayyads	140. 148–150.
of Cordova	154.
Unam Sanctam (1302)	440. 646.
Union, Aragonese	628.
Union of Calmar (1397)	608–609.
Universals, controversy over	505.
Universities	494–503. 676. 691.
Alcalá	676.
Bologna	496–498.
charters	498.
Coimbra	632.
Constantinople	135.
degrees	499–500.
in England	498–499.
faculties	497.
Florence	669.
in France	498.
in Germanies	674.
in High Middle Ages	495–503.
instruction	500.
in Italy	498.
in Later Middle Ages	676.
life	500–501.
nations	497.
organization	499.
Paris	496–498.
Pecs	607.
Prague	599. 651–652.
Pressburg	607.
privileges	498.
Salamanca	676.
Unstrutt River (933)	279.
Uomo Universale (ideal)	670.
Ural Mountains	5–6. 9.
Gateway	342.
Urban II, Pope	368. 389. 472. 476.
Urban IV, Pope	479.
Urban V, Pope	649.
Urban VI, Pope	650. 651.
Uralic languages	59.
speakers	192.
Uri	602.
Urraca of Leon, queen	452. 631.
Usages of Artois	515.
Usury	350.
laws	235.
Utraquists	660.
Utrecht Psalter	337.
Uzbeg, khan	611.
Uzes	453.

V

Valencia	260. 264. 452. 563. 628.
University of	498.
Valens, emperor	23. 34. 47. 77. 134.
Valentinian I, emperor	23. 32.
Valentinian II	23. 32–33.
Valentinian III	33. 39. 78–79. 81. 83. 86. 89. 97.
Valet	223.
Valhalla	68.
Valla, Lorenzo	670.
Vallumbrosians	481.
Valois, house	588–592. 675.
Vandals	74. 78–79. 80–81. 86. 89. 95. 96. 120.
Empire of	96.
navy of	96. 120.
Van der Goes, Hugo	685.
Van der Weyden, Roger	685.
Van Eyck	
Hubert	684–685.
Jan	559. 684–685.
Varangians	287.
Varna (1444)	607.
Crusade (1443–44)	634. 637.
Varro	321.
Vasari, Giorgio	681.
Vassals and Vassalage	207. 208. 211. 215.
dissolution	212.
obligations	212–213.
Vasili I of Moscow	614.
Vasili II of Moscow	614.
Vassi	209.
Vatican Library	656. 669.
Vavassores	285.
Veche (*vieche*)	463. 612.
Vegio, Maffeo	670.
Velbuzd (1330)	635. 636.
Venetia and Venetians	397. 453. 569.
Venice	177. 192. 342. 343. 347. 352. 353. 364. 365. 379–380. 551. 552. 554–555. 559. 601. 619. 620–622. 634. 638.
"doge"	621.
economy	621.
government	621–622.
Golden Book	622.
Great Council	621.
League of	593.
Peace of (1177)	398. 477.
Veni Sancte Spiritus	521.
Verbum Supernum Prodiens	522.

Index

Vercelli University 498.
Verdun, Treaty of (843) 197. 201–202. 274.
Vergerio, Piero Paolo 670.
Vergil 17. 668.
Vergil, Polydore 678.
Verona (403) 77. 622.
Verrocchio, Andrea de 683.
Vexilla Regis 328.
Vexin 258. 415.
Viaticum 490.
Vicenza 622.
Victorines 482. 486.
Victor IV, Anti-Pope 379.
Vienna 365.
Vienne, Council of (1311) 647.
Vienne, Jean de, Admiral 576. 589.
Vigilius, Pope 298.
Vikings, *see* Northmen.
Villaneuve, Thomas, St. 663.
Villani, Filippo 672.
Villani, Giovanni 553. 555. 672.
Villas 236. 237.
Villehardouin 515.
Villeins 242. 246.
Villon, François 679.
Vincent of Beauvais 485. 494. 503. 516. 517.
Virgate 239.
Visconti
  family 621.
  Filippo Maria 621.
  Giangaleazzo 621. 669.
  Matteo 621.
  Otto 621.
Viscounts 109.
Visigoths 74. 76–78. 85–86. 89–90. 95. 102. 104. 299.
  in Gaul and Spain 96.
  in Italy 77.
  in Spain 120.
Vision of Piers Plowman 678.
Vitamin C 248.
Vitovt (Vitold) of Lithuania 606. 611. 612.
Vitruvius 19.
Vittorino da Feltre 658. 670.
Vizir 150. 154.
Vlad the Impaler 636.
Vladimir, city 463. 466. 468. 613.
Vladimir Monomach of Russia 462.
Vladimir of Kiev, St., prince 129. 294–295. 313.
Vladislav II of Bohemia 458. 601. 605.
Vladislav I of Hungary 607.
Vladislav II of Hungary 607.
Vladislav I of Poland 605.
Vladislav II of Poland-Lithuania 605–606.
Vladislav III of Poland 607.
  Crusade 634.
Volynia-Galicia 463.
Vorskla River (1399) 612.
Vouillé (507) 104.
Vratislav of Bohemia 289. 458.

W

Wace 529.
Wahlstaat (1241) 466.
Walafrid Strabo, abbot 185. 325. 329.
Walchern Island 195. 197.
Waldemar IV of Denmark 602. 608.
Waldensians 487. 488.
Waldrada 202–203.
Wales 423.
Walid, al-, caliph 259.
Wallace, William 423.
Wallachia 636. 638.
Walsh, William W. 548–549.
Walter of Henley 354.
Walter the Penniless 369.
Walther von der Vogelweide 532. 533.
Walther von Speyer 322.
Wapentakes 271.
War of the Chioggia 622.
War of Three Brothers 185. 200.
Wardship 214.
Warfare
  Celtic 56.
  Christianity and 41. 367.
  feudal 215. 225–226.
  Hunnic 76–77.
  in High Middle Ages 358. 360.
  in Later Middle Ages 569.
  Later Roman 84.
  naval 569.
  sieges 225–226.
  Slavic 58.
  see also Army, Hundred Years War, Hussites, *and various countries.*
Wars of the Roses 584–585.
Warwick, Earl of 584.
Wat Tyler Rebellion (1381) 568. 583.
Water mills 241. 346.
Waterpower 555. 556.
  see also Water mills.
Weapons, Frankish 112–113.
  gunpowder 555.
  of knights 223–224.
Wearmouth and Jarrow 265.
Wedmore, treaty of (878) 266. 267.
Week, days of 67.
  work 240.
Welfs, *see* Guelphs.
Well of Moses, Dijon 685.
Wenceslaus (Wenzel), emperor 600. 621.

Wenceslaus of Bohemia, St. 289.
Wenceslaus IV of Bohemia 604.
Wends 278. 288.
Werden (782) 175.
Wergelds 63. 70. 112–114. 271.
Werner of Uralingen 620.
Western Empire, *see* Empire, Western.
Westminster Abbey 268. 272.
Westphalia 399.
Wessex 100. 265–266.
Whitby, Council of (664) 101.
Whittington, Richard 559.
Wibod 184.
Widukind of Corvey 332.
Widukind of the Saxons 175–176.
Willehad, St. 332.
William I of England 258. 270. 407–409.
William II of England 258. 369. 391. 409.
William II of Sicily 398. 625.
William III of Sicily 400.
William Aetheling 410.
William Clito 430.
William de Lorris 530–531.
William de Nogaret, *see* Nogaret, William de.
William Marshal, *see* Marshal, William.
William IX of Aquitaine 254. 527.
William X of Aquitaine 430.
William of Auvergne 507.
William of Champeaux 482. 497. 501.
William of Conches 517.
William of Doovenvoorde 559.
William of Holland, anti-king 405.
William of Mainz, archbishop 282.
William of Malmesbury 516.
William of Moerbecke 509. 517.
William of Newburgh 516.
William of Nogaret 646.
William of Normandy 268. 269.
 see also William I of England.
William of Ockham 677.
William of Ruysbroeck 483.
William of Salaceto 518.
William of Toulouse, St., count 525. 527.
William of Tyre, archbishop 376. 516.
William the Pious of Burgundy 308.
Willibrord, St. 168. 312.
Wimpheling 662.
Winchester School 336.
Windsor, Treaty of (1386) 561. 632.
Wisby 602.
Witangemot 101. 268. 270. 407.
Witigis, King of Ostrogoths 98. 121.
Wolfram von Eschenbach 529. 534.
Women 222. 226–227. 359.
Woodville
 Elizabeth 584.
 family 584.
Worms, *see* Concordat of Worms.
Writs, royal 411–412.
Wunderhorn 68.
Wyclif, John 653–654. 657. 660.
 see also Lollards.

X

Ximénez de Cisneros (Jiménez de Cisneros), cardinal 658. 662.

Y

Yarlyk 610.
Yarmuk (636) 147.
Yaroslav the Wise of Kiev 295.
Yaroslav the Wise of Russia 462.
Yaroslav II of Vladimir 613.
Yazdagird III, shah 142.
Yazid 148.
Yemen 140.
Yolande of Anjou 591.
Yolande of Jerusalem 403.
York, house of 584.
York, school 324.
York Tractates 512.
Ypres 347. 352.
Yuan Emperors 467.
Yusuf, king of Almoravides 264.

Z

Zacharias, Pope 171.
Zahra, Al- 262.
Zaid 142.
Zajals 158.
Zakah (alms) 144.
Zalaca (1086) 264.
Zara 379.
Zenghi (Zanghi) of Mosul, *atabeg* 376. 377.
Zeno, emperor 34. 46. 82. 87. 96. 97. 118.
Zenobia, Queen 21.
Zero 160.
Zeta 291. 456.
Zhudiyat 158.
Ziu 67.
Zizka, Jan 604. 660.
Zoe, empress 129. 453.
Zoroastrians 44. 142.
Zupas and zupans 58. 291. 456–457.
Zuzdal 613.
Zwentibold of Lotharingia 205.

D
117
M23
25679

DATE DUE			
02/27/94			
5-13-02			

D 117 M23 25679
McGarry, Daniel D.
Medieval History and
Civilization.

D 117 M23 25679
McGarry, Daniel D.
Medieval History and
Civilization.

DISCARDED

Immaculate Conception Sem
LIBRARY
Huntington, New York